SERGEY PROKOFIEV
DIARIES 1907–1914
PRODIGIOUS YOUTH

In the field of music administration and management, Anthony Phillips worked with leading Soviet-era musicians, orchestras, opera and ballet ensembles, becoming General Manager of London's Royal Festival Hall concert hall complex, a position cut short by the dissolution of the halls' then owners, the GLC, in 1986. Since then he has worked as International Operations Director of an opera and ballet touring management company in the USA and Europe, continuing to develop, in the immediate post-Soviet environment, his relationships with Russian musicians and organisations. More recently he has concentrated on translations and annotations of memoirs and letters by Russian writers and composers, including *Story of a Friendship*: Shostakovich's letters to his friend Isaak Glikman (Faber, 2000), *Anton Chekhov: A Life in Letters* (with Rosamund Bartlett) (Penguin Classics, 2004), the *Diaries* of Sergey Prokofiev in three volumes (Faber, 2006, 2008, 2012) and *Svetik: A Family Portrait of Sviatoslav Richter* (Toccata Press, 2015).

Further praise for this volume:

'[Phillip's] translation captures the full exuberance of a youth who can already declare, in 1914, "I am in no doubt that given time my classic status will be beyond contention."' David Nice, *BBC Music Magazine*

'Anthony Phillips . . . is to be congratulated on his fluent and lively translation, erudite annotations and penetrating introduction.' Andrew Thomson, *Musical Times*

'The first volume of Prokofiev's diaries, beautifully translated by Anthony Phillips . . . shows an unaffectedly free, truly conversational style. It tells, often wittily, an eloquent tale of a hyperactive, funny if often selfish personality growing up in pre-revolutionary St Petersburg, one who observes events, personalities and himself with unusual sharpness.' Stephen Pettitt, *Sunday Times*

'A fascinating record for posterity . . . The reader gains a vivid insight into life in pre-revolutionary St Petersburg, seen through the eyes of a rapidly maturing Music Conservatory student . . . Prokofiev was anything but dull, and his legendary quick wit leaps off the page.' Fergus Johnston, *Irish Times*

by the same author

SERGEY PROKOFIEV DIARIES 1915–1923
Behind the Mask
Translated and Annotated by Anthony Phillips

SERGEY PROKOFIEV DIARIES 1924–1933
Prodigal Son
Translated and Annotated by Anthony Phillips

STORY OF A FRIENDSHIP
The Letters of Dmitry Shostakovich to Isaak Glikman
with a commentary by Isaak Glikman
Translated by Anthony Phillips

Sergey Prokofiev
Diaries

1907–1914
PRODIGIOUS YOUTH

TRANSLATED AND ANNOTATED BY
Anthony Phillips

faber

First published in 2006
by Faber & Faber Limited
Bloomsbury House
74–77 Great Russell Street
London WC1B 3DA

This paperback edition first published in 2022

Typeset by Agnesi Text, Hadleigh
Printed and bound by CPI Group (UK) Ltd, Croydon, CR0 4YY

All rights reserved
© The Sergey Prokofiev Estate, 2002
This translation © Anthony Phillips, 2006

The right of Anthony Phillips to be identified as translator
of this work has been asserted in accordance with
Section 77 of the Copyright, Design and Patents Act 1988

*This book is sold subject to the condition that it shall not, by way of
trade or otherwise, be lent, resold, hired out or otherwise circulated
without the publisher's prior consent in any form of binding or cover
other than that in which it is published and without a similar condition
including this condition being imposed on the subsequent purchaser*

A CIP record for this book
is available from the British Library

ISBN 978–0–571–38091–6

Printed and bound in the UK on FSC paper in line with our continuing
commitment to ethical business practices, sustainability and the environment.
For further information see faber.co.uk/environmental-policy

2 4 6 8 10 9 7 5 3 1

For Karine
who knows, loves and plays the music

Contents

Plates, ix

Foreword by Svyatoslav Prokofiev, xi

Introduction, xvii

Acknowledgements, xxiv

A Note on Text, Transliteration, Dates, Forms of Address and Other Conventions, xxvi

THE DIARIES

1907, 1

1908, 31

1909, 75

1910, 135

1911, 197

1912, 231

1913, 283

1914, 577

Index, 799

Plates

1 Maria Grigorievna Prokofieva
  © *The Serge Prokofiev Estate, Paris*
2 Sergey Alexeyevich Prokofiev
  © *The Serge Prokofiev Estate, Paris*
3 Glazunov and Yesipova
  © *Library of the St Petersburg Conservatoire*
4 Prokofiev in 1910
  © *The Serge Prokofiev Estate, Paris*
5 Lyadov's Composition Class
  © *The Serge Prokofiev Estate, Paris*
6 Rimsky-Korsakov and Glazunov
  © *Lebrecht Music and Arts*
7 The General Studies Class of the St Petersburg Conservatoire, 1907
  © *The Serge Prokofiev Estate, Paris*
8 The Great Hall of the Conservatoire
  © *Library of the St Petersburg Conservatoire*
9 The Small Hall of the Conservatoire
  © *Library of the St Petersburg Conservatoire*
10 The St Petersburg Conservatoire
  © *Library of the St Petersburg Conservatoire*
11 Nevsky Prospect
  © *The Serge Prokofiev Estate, Paris*
12 Terioki Railway Station
  © *Russian National Library, St Petersburg, seen on http://terijoki.spb.ru, a website devoted to the history of Terioki/Zelenogorsk*
13 Anna Yesipova
  from Solntse Rossii, *No. 150 (December 1912), issue devoted to the St Petersburg Conservatoire*
14 Prokofiev in 1913
  © *The Serge Prokofiev Estate, Paris*
15 The Zakharov dacha
  from Terijoki Album, *Finnish Community of Terioki, 1976, seen on http://terijoki.spb.ru, with thanks to Alexander Bravo*
16 Sergey Diaghilev
  © *Sasha, courtesy of Serge Prokofiev Estate, Paris*

17 Boris Bashkirov
    © *Serge Prokofiev Estate, Paris*
18 Nikolay Tcherepnin
    © *RIA Novosti*
19 Nikolay Myaskovsky
    © *Lebrecht Music and Arts*
20 The Conservatoire Ball, 1908
    © *RIA Novosti*
21 Svyatoslav Prokofiev
    © *The Serge Prokofiev Estate, Paris*
22 With Zakharov and the Karneyev Sisters
    © *The Serge Prokofiev Estate, Paris*
23 Playing to Morolyov, 1910
    © *The Serge Prokofiev Estate, Paris*
24 With Zakharov at Terioki
    © *The Serge Prokofiev Estate, Paris*
25 Arrival at Morolyov's house, 1913
    © *The Serge Prokofiev Estate, Paris*
26 The 1914 St Petersburg World Chess Championship
    © *ChessBase (www.chessbase.com) with thanks to Bill Wall*

Foreword to the Russian edition

SVYATOSLAV PROKOFIEV

From early childhood I have always had a tendency to write things down.
          Sergey Prokofiev, *Autobiography*

Had I not been a composer, I would probably have become a writer or a poet.
          Sergey Prokofiev, *Diaries*, 23 November 1922

Many people write diaries. Ordinary people and extraordinary, the interesting and the commonplace, the poetic and the prosaic, rough diamonds and persons of refined sensibilities. Diaries are the great leveller, for they share a universal objective: to record the thoughts, observations and feelings that the author is reluctant to entrust to another human being. A diary is the reflection of the person who wrote it. It is his alter ego, his closest and most trusted companion, to whom everything, without exception, may be confided.

What diaries contain can be as various as those who write them. One may be a dry account of the times and the course of events, transcribed with methodical accuracy. Another may consist of occasional jottings that represent *cris de coeur* at moments of exaltation or despair. Still another may be a finished literary production peopled with a large cast of characters, conversations and lyrical outpourings.

Prokofiev's Diaries are a unique artistic endeavour, fully deserving their own opus number in the catalogue of his works. He lived in an era rich in events of great significance for the history of Russia and the world, a time of explosive cultural development and events that in time would come to be seen as milestones. From his earliest childhood, individuals with whom his destiny was intertwined would themselves prove to be far from ordinary, and would leave their own mark in the world.

He began writing a diary at a very young age. At first he devoted much attention to childhood interests, but soon there began to appear penetrating, not always flattering, descriptions of people he encountered, minutely detailed critical analyses of what was going on around him, invariably from a highly idiosyncratic point of view. This relationship to the outside world is maintained throughout the Diaries, the only difference being that as time goes by more and more attention is paid to music, Prokofiev's closest companion at the centre of his life whom he never, whatever the circumstances, abandoned so long as he lived.

Prokofiev wrote his Diaries in notebooks. He wrote with reasonable regularity, sometimes several pages in a single day. Long gaps could occur when he was travelling or on concert tours, when he would either write nothing at all or content himself with scribbled jottings in notebooks or on pieces of paper, aggregations of vowel-less words that would later serve as aides-memoires to events that had occurred or ideas that had come to him. Unfortunately, he did not always subsequently transcribe these 'nuclear ideas' in full, and it is no longer possible to interpret them. But whenever Prokofiev did manage to complete them, one reads the jubilant phrase: 'Caught up with the Diary.'

It was a miracle that the Diaries from the Conservatoire days and soon thereafter survived at all. Maria Grigorievna, the composer's mother, preserved some of them and despite all the hazards involved in her departure from Russia across the Black Sea and the internment to which all Russian émigrés were subjected in the Prince's Islands off the coast of Turkey, brought them with her to France. Another tranche was removed by friends, among them Boris Asafyev, from the family's flat in Petrograd wrecked during the years of the Revolution, and later given to Sergey Koussevitzky. Koussevitzky in turn passed them to Nikolay Myaskovsky, ever a loyal friend to Prokofiev, who returned them to him in 1927 during the composer's first return to the USSR after he left it in 1918.

Prokofiev was a talented story-teller with an undoubted literary gift, as the Diaries themselves bear witness, not to mention short stories, letters, verse translations and his own opera libretti. He was also a bully, a *Wunderkind*, a composer and pianist of genius, not at all a dry stick but rather a young man of extremely romantic temperament. All these qualities are much in evidence throughout the 'Conservatoire' section of the Diaries. On 29 November 1909 Prokofiev wrote, 'My life is rich in impressions and events, and I eagerly introduce them into my Diary. But it is much easier and more agreeable to write about romantic adventures than about other, more arid matters . . . this is why my young ladies occupy so much space.'

It should be noted, however, that such an apparently inconsequential attitude did not prevent the young composer from creating at the time such masterpieces as the First and Second Piano Concertos, *The Ugly Duckling*, the First Violin Concerto, the *Scythian Suite*, the *Classical Symphony*, the opera *The Gambler*, and so on, as well as graduating brilliantly from St Petersburg Conservatoire and taking First Prize in the Conservatoire's piano competition.

Recalling the impressions he recorded in his Diary of this prize-winning performance in the Piano Competition, he writes on 28 February 1928: 'Every competition represents a heightened manifestation of egotism, a compulsion to succeed over the corpses of one's rivals, and hence a meanness of spirit which must be resisted. And yet I am unable to read this passage in my Diaries without thrilling to the fire and precision with which it is written, and the irresistible way in which the reader is drawn into the atmosphere of that time.'

The Diaries are a truly authentic document in which it is possible to trace the gradual transformation of the romantic, impassioned youth into the mature, dispassionate, seasoned composer and virtuoso pianist, precisely aware of his own worth and of what he wanted to achieve. In the midst of the terrors and dangers of the Civil War he displayed all the courage and resolve needed to risk crossing war-torn Siberia en route to the US, where having no friends to welcome him he was prepared to rely solely on his own resources. These pages of the Diaries describe the tribulations of his journey through Siberia, Japan, Hawaii and finally to the US, followed by his first days in a new land, the joy of unexpected meetings, new friends and contacts in the world of music. Here also will be found an account of how he met his future wife and the mother of his two sons: Lina Prokofieva.

As Prokofiev found, the world outside Russia was not waiting to welcome him with open arms; far from it. Only through his talent, his utter dedication to music, his energy, his extraordinary capacity for hard work and his unconquerable optimism did he succeed in establishing his undisputed status as the outstanding composer and virtuoso performer that he was.

In the pages of his Diaries Prokofiev gives detailed accounts of his meetings with a huge range of celebrated figures. Here are Stravinsky, Diaghilev, Koussevitzky, Benois, Asafyev, Meyerhold, Capablanca, Rachmaninov, Scriabin, Borovsky, Suvchinsky, Lunarcharsky, Kerensky, Balmont, Tcherepnin – a complete list would fill more than a page. We meet them sketched in colourful and illuminating contexts, with different casts of actors, invariably with penetrating observations and a mercilessly objective critique of their failings – a critique, however, that is always ready to give way to a generous assessment whenever the subject merits it. Prokofiev often uses direct speech as a device to delineate personality more sharply. His descriptions of a newly encountered city or the background to events are always full of exhaustive detail, at times incorporating lyrical digressions. From childhood he had always loved nature and walking, and in the Diaries seldom passes up the chance to tell us about the countryside he is observing. This is a regular feature of the period of his life he spent in Europe.

Mention must be made of the fact that Prokofiev liked including in the Diaries his views on professional matters. We often find him setting down his ideas for new compositions, analysing his performances in one concert or another, just as he does those of other musicians, or presenting succinct descriptions of compositions by his contemporaries. There are revealing passages dealing with his well-known (but imperfectly understood) ability to write out scores quickly and economically: thus he notes on 14 January 1926, 'I estimate the total number of bars a page of manuscript paper will contain, then note down the orchestration and what instruments are to be employed, that is to say how many lines will be needed for that particular page of the score. In this way when the time comes to write out the score, it is a matter of purely mechanical work, almost of transcribing.'

Prokofiev devotes a considerable amount of space to philosophical reflections. While still a young man he developed an interest in figures such as Kant and Schopenhauer, whose writings he discussed extensively with his friend Max Schmidthof. Later, in America, he became attracted to Christian Science – less for its religious than its philosophical aspect. He found in Christian Science a basis for the self-analysis and self-control that is indispensable to an artist, indeed to any man. Some propositions of Christian Science, however, did not escape his typically critical inspection.

Prokofiev's first return visit to the USSR after his departure in 1918, a visit in which he was accompanied by his wife Lina, produced such a strong impression on him that with his wife's help he prepared the diary entries of his stay there specifically for the press. But for various reasons it was not published, and this material, complete with Prokofiev's annotations, was preserved by Lina and later published separately by my brother Oleg to mark the centenary of the composer's birth.[1] In the interests of maintaining an uninterrupted narrative flow for the complete Diaries it will be included in future volumes of the present edition.

Many people have asked themselves what was it that made Prokofiev and his family finally return to Russia in 1936 and have attempted to find the answer in purely economic terms. Reading the Diaries makes it clear how Prokofiev himself would have accounted for his decision. He missed Russia desperately, the country in which he had spent the happy years of his childhood and youth, surrounded by his friends, the Russian language, and nature. On 19 December 1928 he writes, 'Walking home I thought of Russia and my terrible longing to be there. And in fact, I ask myself what the devil am I doing here rather than there, where I am wanted and where I myself find everything much more interesting? . . . It has taken me some time to realize how strongly I am drawn there and how firmly I have in fact made up my mind to return!'

[1] *Sovietskii Zhurnal* (Syntaxis, Paris, 1990); *Soviet Journal 1927 and Other Writings*, translated and edited by Oleg Prokofiev with Christopher Palmer (Faber and Faber, London, 1992).

Yet doubts continued to assail him. Many years had passed, the country had changed greatly, as had its people. On 31 May 1929: '. . . went to the cinema and saw a film in Russian. Much pleasure and the feeling of being at home, especially stirred by the image of a field of rye. To go to Russia, or not to go?' In the end, despite everything, particularly misgivings about the repressive nature of the Soviet machine, Prokofiev and his family finally returned to their homeland in 1936.

Prokofiev did not take his Diaries with him. Indeed, he ceased to write them altogether – a circumstance we can but regret today. The manuscripts we have do contain some pencilled annotations in his hand, the latest of which is dated 1936. He obviously appreciated the seriousness of what he had written, and did not want it to fall into the hands of the authorities. After all, how many names the Diaries contained, how many events, and how freely everything was described! Myaskovsky, who lived in the USSR until his death, destroyed his own diaries in the last years of his life, keeping only a handful of individual extracts from them. (O. P. Lamm writes of this in her book *Myaskovsky: Pages from a Creative Life* (Moscow, 1989)).

Prokofiev left the whole of his Diary and a portion of his correspondence in a safe in the US, a fact that we his family learned only after his death. In 1955 the archive was transferred to the Board of Foreign Jurisprudence of the USSR. A subsequent meeting of the S. S. Prokofiev Estate Committee determined where the archive should be deposited, but neither I nor my brother Oleg, still less our mother Lina Prokofieva, was invited to this meeting. The Committee decreed that the documents should be placed in the State Archive (TSGALI),[1] and on 26 April 1955 an Act was passed to which we were invited to subscribe our names *post factum*. The Act laid down that the documents would be held in the TSGALI, with access denied for fifty years except to the composer's heirs, M. A. Prokofieva,[2] Oleg and Sviatoslav Prokofiev.

Inasmuch as the moral right to publish Sergey Prokofiev's Diaries belongs to the members of his family (his heirs), we decided that the changed times had made it our duty to publish this priceless document. Preparing the text for publication was no easy task: it was not merely a matter of editing but of actual deciphering. I use this term because from 7 June 1914 onwards, to save time when 'scribbling notes on the run', as he put it (7 July 1914), Prokofiev started to employ a system of writing down words with the vowels eliminated. This became a typical and permanent manner for documentation for him. Thus, for example, 'chmd' for 'chemodan' (suitcase); 'snchl' for 'snachala' (at first); 'rstrn' for 'restaurant'; 'udrl' either for 'udral' (did a

---

1 Tsentral'nyi Gosudarstvennyi Arkhiv Literaturnogo Isskustva (Central State Archive of LIterary Art), now RGALI (Russian State Archive of Literary Art).
2 Mira Alexandrovna (Mendelson) Prokofieva, the composer's second wife.

bunk) or 'udaril' (hit) and so on. As may be seen, some words do not give up their meaning immediately and can be interpreted only according to context. Sometimes words were written out in full, or almost so, usually in the case of specific words or proper names or phrases in a foreign language, and so on. Naturally in such cases we have retained the original spelling. Our most difficult task was to decipher unfamiliar names, and this often entailed exhaustive researches.

Our primary aim has been to unravel and publish this exceptional document, which will answer many questions and help ultimately to shed light on Prokofiev's life and art from his time as a student of St Petersburg Conservatoire until his return to Russia. A reading of the Diaries yields a comprehensive portrait of Prokofiev as an amazingly hardworking, intelligent, perceptive, kind, but demanding, person. There were times when he could be acerbic and harsh, but overall the Prokofiev character was a fully integrated one.

We have kept references and comments to the minimum since we were reluctant to turn this first edition into a musicological tome loaded with long and detailed commentaries and a comprehensive index of names, biographical details and so on. These alone would occupy several books, and I am sure that specialists will in due course fill this need.

In conclusion I should like to express my gratitude to all the members of my family who have contributed to the work of preparing my father's Diaries for publication, in particular the invaluable assistance of my son Sergey, without whom there would have been no possibility of this work seeing the light of day.

I also gratefully acknowledge the collaboration of colleagues at RGALI, who supported the idea of the present publication.

Paris, January 2002

Introduction

For most of his life, Prokofiev wrote copiously about his experiences, his composing activities, his hopes, plans, fears, achievements and disappointments. In the intellectually and culturally limited environment of the isolated village in rural Ukraine where he grew up, the notion that both the exterior and interior circumstances of his life were worthy of record took root early on and became part of his mental furniture. 'Sergushechka,' said his mother, presenting him with a thick, handsomely bound notebook when he was twelve, 'write down in this everything that comes into your head. Don't leave anything out.' For the next thirty years, by and large, he complied, until he came to contemplate and finally consummate his permanent return to the Russia that had in the meantime become the Soviet Union. At this point the caution that progressively imposed itself on even his outspoken temperament reduced to a trickle the flow of here-and-now notes, thoughts and comments he was so accustomed to committing to paper.

The uniqueness of the *Diaries* Prokofiev wrote between 1909 and 1933 lies not in any single attribute, but in a combination of them. The first is what Svyatoslav Prokofiev, the composer's elder son and together with *his* son the dedicated decipherer, transcriber, interpreter and editor of the collection of manuscript notebooks, rightly describes as miraculous in his Foreword to the Russian edition of the *Diaries*, reproduced at the start of this volume: the circumstances in which the pre-Revolutionary-period *Diaries*, left behind with almost all Prokofiev's other papers, manuscript scores and possessions in Petrograd in 1918, were preserved. Determined and courageous friends and family – his mother Maria Grigorievna Prokofieva, Boris Asafyev, Nikolay Myaskovsky, Serge Koussevitzky – kept them safe all through the turmoil of revolution, emigration, civil war and the convulsive chaos of the Bolshevik state during the 1920s, allowing Myaskovsky to restore those papers still in Russia to their owner on his first visit to the Soviet Union in 1927. Secondly, it lies in the vast range and scope of the personalities, experiences and events encountered in their pages, along with the idiosyncratic wit and intelligence with which the writer records them. The result is a crystalline and truthful picture of the times, crammed with all manner of cultural, personal, social and practical insights, all the better for sometimes seeming inconsequential. How much we owe to Maria Grigorievna for urging her son to put it all in.

The third quality is the uninhibited freedom with which the reader is admitted into the interior landscape of a supremely talented, imaginative and penetrating mind, to watch it grow in stature from the brash personal and professional self-confidence of precocious youth to the objective, balanced understanding of the mature artist. Held up before us, in its exceptional emotional candour, is a warts-and-all portrait of the artist as a young man, a portrait purged of sanitizing make-overs or attempts to justify attitudes and conduct that he knew would present him in a less than favourable light. Sometimes, so ruthlessly is the lid removed that one is tempted to wonder whether anyone concerned to protect his interests would have approved Prokofiev as 'authorized biographer'. It is fascinating, and moving, to witness the vulnerable young man with his desperate need for true love and ideal friendship coexisting uncomfortably with the pushy, self-confident genius who grabs every available opportunity to shine, even when he is perfectly well aware that show-offs and provocative iconoclasts do not usually win popularity competitions among peers or teachers.

Fourthly, one can only marvel at the author's fabulous powers of recall that allow him time and time again to reproduce incidents and conversations whose startling detail makes them leap off the page. The *Diaries* form a priceless new primary source for scholars to establish dates, facts and attitudes that have hitherto been misperceived and misrepresented to a far greater extent than with most artists of Prokofiev's stature, a consequence both of his fragmented, peripatetic life and of his later years spent under a Soviet regime generally reluctant to allow objective scrutiny of contemporary history and influences. Lastly, there is the limpid prose that flows so naturally from his pen, the graceful alighting on the *mot juste*, the narrative skill and masterful use of irony and dialogue, the descriptive set-pieces of the landscapes and cityscapes he loved so much, the juxtaposition of comedy and tragedy, the virtuoso command of tone and nuance – all constant reminders that, as he said himself, Prokofiev felt himself to be as much a writer as he was a composer.

All through the period of the *Diaries* Prokofiev collected material, made notes, preserved correspondence (both ways, keeping drafts of letters he wrote as well as the letters he received) which he sent annually to the binders to be collated in chronological order, meticulously building up an ordered history of his creative life. What led him to devote so much time and energy, and so consistently in the midst of a relentlessly busy and far from secure career as composer and performer, to this archival predilection and to the immense canvas of his *Diaries*? There are clues in something that happened nearly thirty years after he started writing them, when on 1 June 1937 the composer sat down at his desk in his newly allocated Moscow apartment not, as we have seen, to continue a lifetime's habit of recording on paper the immediate circumstances of his life and thoughts, but to make a start on writing his autobiography. Dealing with the past, this would presumably be a less risky enterprise. Still savouring what he doubtless felt to be the deep calm of the Motherland's bosom after the hurly-burly of fifteen *Wanderjahre* through America and Europe, his mind was overflowing with projects, especially the ambition to get on with developing the 'new simplicity' of a musical language that would – as he had recently explained in a newspaper article entitled 'Paths for Soviet Music',[1] fulfil the needs of society and the epoch by combining 'seriousness with an element of lightness, or lightness with an element of seriousness . . . while avoiding the trivial and the stereotyped'. But alongside these urgent tasks it was time to take stock and get down to the long-considered 'biography of himself'.

The delightful account that resulted[2] opens with a characteristically clear-eyed 'Apologetic Introduction'. Of course it is not apologetic at all, and in fact Prokofiev's choice of adjective, *izvinitelnoye*, carries in context a rich semantic cargo suggesting not just penitence but explanation, excuse and propitiation (a good example of the colour and precision of Prokofiev the master wordsmith). It is a concise, pithy statement of intent, and casts an illuminating retrospective light on the genesis of the *Diaries* and their author's desire to expose to a wider audience the inner workings of the creative mind.

> Is it worth writing one's own biography, particularly a long one? Of course not. The trouble is if I don't write it others will, and they are bound to get it wrong. They will get it wrong from the most conscientious motives; in fact, if I may so express it, they will misrepresent conscientiously, that is, not from any ill intent but from lack of information and founded on the most logical of premises.
>
> Well, let them. It will not be such a tragedy, and my music will be none the worse for it. But there is another side to the question: I have amassed quite a quantity of material – diaries, letters, notebooks. And I very much do not want this material to moulder away to dust. If I am the one to sort it out I have at least this advantage: I am in a position to read between the lines much that even the most amiably disposed biographer will not be able to perceive. Thus, on occasions when something has not been successful, I shall have made a note in the diary: 'Didn't come off. No matter', when the truth is that the cat was tearing at my soul with its claws. Or perhaps I may have jotted down a conversation, and when I later read my notes a whole series of circumstances will rise up in my mind that are actually a lot more interesting than the conversation itself.

---

1 S. S. Prokof'ev, 'Puti sovetskoy muzyki', *Izvestiya* No. 267, 16 November 1934; quoted in V. Varunts (ed.), *Prokof'ev o Prokof'eve: stati i interv'iu* (Sovetskiy Kompozitor, Moscow, 1991).
2 S. S. Prokof'ev: *Avtobiografiya*, edited by M. Kozlova (Sovetskiy Kompozitor, Moscow, 1973; rev. edn, 1982); hereafter *Autobiography*.

The Apologetic Introduction continues:

> Overhearing someone say in my presence: 'I would make it obligatory for all famous people to write their autobiography,' I thought to myself: 'Well, I've already got the material, so the only thing I have to do now is become famous.' And mentally I resolved that by the time I was forty I would have composed enough to want to take a break, and that could be the time to settle down to my biography. But when I came round to nearing forty the boastfulness of youth had subsided, my view of life had matured, and the question presented itself, whether there was any justification for speaking so much and at such length about myself? It was at this point that my interest in maintaining a diary waned, and the idea of writing my autobiography faded away of itself.
>
> But what was to be done with all the material? Should I just leave it? Throw it away? The true greatness of Gogol may have consisted in this, that he burned his manuscripts! That he dared to do so! More precisely: might it not be a precondition of creating a masterpiece that one must be prepared, without batting an eyelid, to destroy one's work should the reason for that work's existence not be absolutely clear to its creator? I hesitated.
>
> In the end two arguments prevailed: there have been achievements in my life, and therefore some may find my autobiography valuable. And secondly, I have met a good many remarkable people, and my accounts of them may be interesting.

Two years after launching into the *Autobiography* he introduced in this disarming manner, Prokofiev abandoned it, having got no further than eighteen years of age in July 1909, thus depriving us of a lot more potentially delightful reading matter (even as it is it runs to 200,000 words). But after another two years he acceded to a request from the journal *Sovetskaya Muzyka* (*Soviet Music*) to write a more succinct account of his life, and did so, this time getting as far as the year 1936 – that is covering his childhood, his years of study at the Conservatoire and the whole of his time abroad. But it too breaks off almost in mid-phrase, just after the Prodigal Son's return to the Motherland. (This second autobiographical essay is known as the *Short Autobiography*,[1] to distinguish it from the much longer in words albeit shorter in compass *Autobiography*, the one with the Apologetic Introduction excerpts from which I have quoted above.)

Happily the *Diaries* (which as we are told Prokofiev prudently did not

---

1 S. S. Prokof'ev: *Kratkaya avtobiografiya*, in S. Shlifshteyn (ed.), *S. S. Prokof'ev, Materialy, dokumenty, vospominaniya* (Gosudarstvennoye Musykal'noye Izdatel'stvo, Moscow, 1956 and 1961). An English translation by Oleg Prokofiev and Christopher Palmer is included in *Soviet Journal and Other Writings*, op. cit.

take back with him to the Soviet Union) fill a large part of the gap left by the uncompleted autobiographies, long and short. Volume I of the *Diaries* is mostly taken up with St Petersburg and its Conservatoire. Prokofiev loved them both deeply, the larger world of the city and the confined, hothouse world of the Conservatoire; they so entered his bloodstream that the pages are filled with atmospheric accounts of activities, meetings, confrontations, numberless walks, passions and enjoyments of various kinds. Prokofiev loved the Conservatoire and he loved its traditions, but the love stopped short of reverence for what he perceived as its hidebound academicism. It is hard at this distance not to have some sympathy for Glazunov and his professorial colleagues, faced with the impossible task of reconciling a teaching institution's *raison d'être* of turning out impeccably schooled students, with the unquenchable ambition of a precocious genius – particularly one as little interested in taking prisoners as was the adolescent Prokofiev. Even the jaundiced eyes of the author of the *Diaries* cannot altogether obscure either Glazunov's essential generosity of spirit, or that at least he recognized his unruly charge's special gifts. (More, evidently, than can be said for Lyadov.) The notorious incident of Glazunov's discomfort at being obliged, as Director, to announce to a waiting world the award of the Rubinstein Prize for a performance of a work[1] with which he so cordially disagreed, may be forgiven when it is remembered that the prize was supposed to be for playing the piano, not for innovative composition. After all, the prizewinner himself admits that choosing a new work in an unfamiliar idiom was a tactic intended to give him an advantage over possibly better equipped classical instrumentalists. But all's fair in love and war and music competitions; at least Glazunov and his colleagues let him play the piece and thus make history, as well as giving the diarist material for a great cliffhanger narrative.

If the piano competition story has a companion piece – and it has, because at great cost to Prokofiev's nerves the two events were going on almost simultaneously – it must be the detailed account of the 1914 International Chess Tournament held in St Petersburg. For years Prokofiev had been poring over every detail of the eleven participants' personalities and exploits, but they were still remote heroes of almost mythical stature; now suddenly they were in shoulder-rubbing proximity, engaged in life-and-death struggles a few feet away from him in the smoke-filled rooms of the St Petersburg Chess Club. Aside from their phenomenal intellectual feats these were genuinely larger-than-life characters, and the delight with which Prokofiev sketches pen portraits of this extraordinary collection of people, their dangerous feats of triumph and disaster, is Balzacian in its colour and insight.

---

1 Prokofiev's graduation performance of his own First Piano Concerto, Op. 10.

St Petersburg, the gilded capital of an Empire and a society teetering, apparently unwittingly, on the brink of upheaval and extinction, is the constant backdrop against which the *Diaries* evoke Prokofiev's emerging consciousness of himself as an artist, the heady arena in which he began to flex his creative muscles. Musically it was moving at a dizzying rate from the complacent afterglow of the Belyayev circle establishment represented by the Russian Symphony Concerts and eminences such as Rimsky-Korsakov, Glazunov and Lyadov along with lesser figures like Wihtol and Lyapunov, through the progressive and cosmopolitan but derivative Tcherepnin, to cutting-edge new milieus such as the 'Stray Dog' café, where the Acmeists Osip Mandelstam and Anna Akhmatova and the Futurist Artur Lourié recited their poetry and played their compositions to an audience of initiates. Then there were the Evenings of Contemporary Music started by the 'Nevsky Pickwickians' Nouvel and Nurok, that gave Prokofiev his first public platform, and the ever loyal sounding-board, support and fellow modernist that was Myaskovsky. Finally, towards the end of this first volume can be glimpsed emerging from the Korsakovian undergrowth the most explosive iconoclast of them all, Igor Stravinsky.

Writing in 1913 to Myaskovsky a week after seeing *Petrushka* in the Ballets Russes Paris season, Prokofiev delivered himself of a not quite off-the-cuff but still spontaneous critique of the unprecedented success being enjoyed abroad by the composer who was for the foreseeable future to be his rival for the affections of the music-loving public of the West. The letter offers a revealing insight into Prokofiev's reaction to his maverick compatriot's new concepts of rhythm, harmony and texture. After sincere and generous appreciation of the score's wit, its entertaining and brilliantly orchestrated illustration of the balletic action on stage, Prokofiev goes on to express scepticism about the score's true musical worth, and concludes:

> Even if one concedes that Stravinsky is breaking through a new door, he is doing so with the small, sharp knife of passing fashion, not with the mighty axe that would truly earn him the right to be called a Titan.[1]

As Stephen Walsh has perceptively remarked,[2] to a Conservatoire-trained musician like Prokofiev or Myaskovsky, unlike audiences in Paris or London, it would have been extraordinarily difficult at first blush to see past the initial impression that all Stravinsky had done was raid the store-cupboard of tunes Russians imbibe with their mother's milk, and dress them up in modish harmonies and aural tricks.

1 M. G. Kozlova and N. R. Yatsenko (eds.), *S. S. Prokof'ev i N. Ya. Myaskovsky, Perepiska* (Sovetskiy Kompozitor, Moscow, 1977).
2 S. Walsh, *Igor Stravinsky, A Creative Spring, Russia and France 1882–1934* (Jonathan Cape, London, 2000).

These were by no means to be Prokofiev's last thoughts on *Petrushka* or Stravinsky, but they were one great artist's initial reaction to the singular work of another. How is it possible to know what goes on in the mind of such creators? The great American biologist Edward O. Wilson, making in *Consilience, The Unity of Knowledge* a powerful assault on entrenched but artificial barriers that persists between science, the humanities and the arts, argues that all true human creativity, in whatever sphere, is of a kind:

> To put it in a nutshell: knowledge, obsession, daring. The creative process is an opaque mix. Perhaps only confessional memoirs, still rare to nonexistent, might disclose how scientists actually find their way to a publishable conclusion. In one sense scientific articles are deliberately misleading. Just as a novel is better than the novelist, a scientific report is better than the scientist, having been stripped of all the confusions and ignoble thought that led to its composition. Yet such voluminous and incomprehensible chaff, soon to be forgotten, contains most of the secrets of scientific success.[1]

What is true of the scientist and the novelist and their works is equally so of the artist and the composer. In their kaleidoscopic diversity, Prokofiev's *Diaries* open a treasure trove of entertainment and information, and while the author's lucid style and penetrating eye do very well at keeping incomprehensible chaff, confusions and ignoble thought at bay, I believe their greatest value of all lies, as Wilson suggests, in their sidelong illumination of at least some of the secrets of his life-enhancing art. Prokofiev wrote his *Diaries* because he thought one day they would be interesting to people. He was right.

ANTHONY PHILLIPS
Argyll, June 2006

---

1   Edward O. Wilson, *Consilience, The Unity of Knowledge* (Little, Brown & Co., London, 1998).

Acknowledgements

Prokofiev's *Diaries* would never have become available to the general reader in an intelligible form without the years of selfless labour lavished on them by the composer's elder son Svyatoslav, his son Serge Prokofiev Jr and Serge's wife Irina. Nor in particular would this version for English-speaking readers have come about without their tremendous moral, practical and financial support and that of the Serge Prokofiev Foundation. I should like them to know how much I appreciate not only their personal encouragement but also the friendly patience with which they tirelessly provided advice, help, and prompt replies to innumerable queries that, in many cases, only members of the composer's family could possibly know. I am also deeply grateful to Noëlle Mann, Curator of the extraordinarily comprehensive resource that is the Serge Prokofiev Archive at Goldsmiths College in London, and editor of the Foundation's journal *Three Oranges*. This publication, for its combination of enthusiasm and scholarship, is quite rightly regarded as in a completely different league from even the most enlightened fanzine; long may it flourish.

Mstislav Rostropovich – catalyst, champion and friend to Prokofiev as to so many composers – enthusiastically supported the idea of bringing the *Diaries* to an English-speaking readership and wrote a characteristically generous endorsement which he kindly allowed the publishers to cite.

On matters both musical and Russian I have greatly valued help from two pianists who have extensive knowledge of Prokofiev's music: Dmitry Alexeyev (who lent me his copy of the *Diaries* and made me read them soon after they first appeared) and Irina Anastasieva at the Gnessin Russian Academy of Music in Moscow. Errors of fact, interpretation and judgement are, however, mine.

Yelena Goncharova, Deputy Director of the Library of the St Petersburg Conservatoire. was a source of sympathetic and practical advice about pictures preserved in the Conservatoire's archive; Alexander Bravo, whose private initiative it was to establish and maintain a fascinating website about Terioki/Zelenogorsk, went out of his way to provide the photograph of the old Terioki Railway Station; Bill Wall and ChessBase kindly provided the photograph of those involved in the 1914 St Petersburg International Chess Tournament.

Belinda Matthews, Lesley Felce and Elizabeth Tyerman at Faber and Faber and Jill Burrows, my irreproachable copy editor, have supported and helped much more than they probably realize, for which I am very grateful now and hope to continue to be through the long road ahead of Volumes II and III.

A. P.

A Note on Text, Transliteration, Dates, Forms of Address and Other Conventions

The manuscript of Prokofiev's *Diaries* is contained in a series of notebooks, now preserved in the Russian State Archive of Literature and Art in Moscow (RGALI). They are not merely handwritten, but mostly composed in a vowel-free shorthand of the author's own devising, a parallel version of the shorthand he developed for the laborious process of writing out orchestral scores. The Herculean task of deciphering, transcribing and editing considerably more than three-quarters of a million words was carried out by the composer's son and grandson, and the text I have translated is that published by them under the sprkfv imprint.

Russian orthography can be transliterated into Latin script in a bewildering variety of ways. My aim in rendering the hundreds of Russian names and proper nouns that appear in the text has been to make them as accessible and phonetically plausible as possible to the English-speaking reader, largely consistent with the system adopted by the *New Grove Dictionary of Music and Musicians* (London: Macmillan, 1980) but with modifications intended to make the results look less alarming than a strict adherence would often make them. Names of people and places already familiar to English readers have been kept in their forms of common usage even when they depart from the system, hence Alexander, Tchaikovsky, Rachmaninov, Diaghilev, Koussevitzky, Schlüsselberg. (Strictly, Prokofiev's own name ought to be Prokof'yev). However, in bibliographical references I have adhered to the *Grove* system.

In place of the standard Russian formal way of referring to a person – the first name followed by the patronymic (Alexander Konstantinovich), roughly corresponding to the English Mr, Mrs, Miss followed by the surname – I have generally resorted to the English custom of first name followed by surname (Alexander Glazunov) when the reference is simply to an individual appearing in the narrative, but I have preserved the Russian style when the author is either directly addressing an interlocutor or enjoys a long-running or a close personal relationship with the person concerned. Where it seems appropriate, but not invariably, I have followed the Russian custom of attaching feminine endings to women's surnames.

Prokofiev's *Diaries* cover a period of time when the instability of Russia and Eastern Europe caused frequent changes to geographical names – streets, districts, towns, whole regions – no doubt to confusion at the time and even more so almost a century later. Street names in St Petersburg/ Petrograd/Leningrad/St Petersburg have undergone many changes, while the resort towns Prokofiev so much enjoyed visiting in the north-west of what was until the First World War the Karelian Isthmus of the Autonomous Grand Duchy of Finland had at that time Finnish names: Terioki, Yukki, Kuokkala. From 1917 to 1939 the area remained in independent Finland but changed hands several times during the Winter War and the Second World War. Only with the Peace of Paris in 1947 was the border finally settled, with the consequence that places in the Leningrad Oblast of Russia now have Russian names (Terioki is today Zelenogorsk; Kuokkala is Repino). As a general rule I have preserved in the text the names Prokofiev used.

During the whole period covered by this first volume of the *Diaries*, indeed until 1 February 1918, Russia continued to use the Julian calendar (the Russian Orthodox Church still does); therefore the date in Russia was thirteen days behind the same date in Europe and America. While in Russia, Prokofiev naturally dates his diary entries according to the local custom, but he also continued to do so when making his first trips abroad in 1913 and 1914.Thus the date on which he records attending a performance of *Khovanshchina* in the Théâtre des Champs-Elysées appears in the *Diaries* as 3 June 1913, while in Paris it was actually 16 June. Where there is any risk of confusion I have noted whether the date in question is OS (Old Style, i.e. Russian Julian) or NS (New Style, Western Gregorian).

A. P.

1907

3 September

I begin this record – a diary, if you will. I had already decided in the spring that I would begin it in the autumn, when I got to St Petersburg. Today I went to sit my first academic exam (to move up from the fifth to the sixth form) in Physics. They made me wait from 1 o'clock until 4 o'clock, at which point Rusinov, the Head of the Academic Studies (who teaches Physics) suddenly informed me that I would be taking all my General Subjects Finals next spring, including History and Physics in their entirety! 'I advise you to sign up for all the appropriate academic courses this year, so that you will be able to take your Finals next spring with everyone else at the end of the course.'

Now I must decide what to do. At first I was very downcast: academic classes, my God! But there is a positive side to it: the prospect of a summer off is a bonus. Also, there are not more than two hours of lessons a day, that's not so bad, and there is no homework. I'll get to know all the girls in the sixth form too: so far, after three years at the Conservatoire I don't know a single one nor have I wanted to: this year I've been thinking, well, if I meet any that's fine, and if I don't, that's fine too. Today there was one girl (evidently from the fifth class) taking the exam, and she had a boy with her who looked as though he had only just left school. When she emerged from her exam they rushed up to one another and disappeared into a dark corner to talk about how she had got on. Ye gods! For one moment I felt a pang of real envy! The strange thing was, it was the boy I felt particularly drawn to, so much so that for a moment I wanted to get to know him.

Today I went to see Myaskovsky for the first time; he is still ill, so I did not spend more than half an hour with him. We didn't talk about anything that we had not already discussed in our letters. I told him again that his last sonata (the one in E minor with the fugue) is his best, and he thinks so too. He has written a good deal over the summer: two sonatas, more than ten songs, a lot of smaller piano pieces, and he has just finished a quartet.[1] I said, 'I'm not going to write a quartet.'

'Never mind, some time you will,' he replied.

Oh, if only I could have a free summer, I would compose so much!

---

1 Piano Sonata in D minor (two movements); Sonata in C minor (one movement); 12 Miniatures for Piano *Flofion* (Fourth Book); 7 Songs on texts by Baratynsky; String Quartet in F.

6 September

My exams are finished. I got a 4 in German, but that is the only one in which I missed getting a 5.[1] This made a dramatic impression, the Conservatoire teachers are very pleased. Better than last year: then out of seven subjects I got three 5s (French, Arithmetic and History) and four 4s (German, Geography, Religious Knowledge, Russian). But everything in general seems to be going my way! Aunt Tanya and Mama said so the other day, and I sensed it even before that: fate frequently meets my wishes halfway, and I have good luck in everything. There was a good example today: my examiners in Russian and the History of the Church were supposed to be the two Petrovs, both lay brothers and both of them about eighty years old, both martinets in marking and never known to give more than a 4. And what happens? Neither of them turned up! So my examiners were another priest and another Russian teacher (from the Junior classes) and they both gave me 5. Splendid!

Yesterday I saw Zakharov[2] in the Conservatoire. 'So,' I said, 'you're still alive? Not been hanged yet?'

'What are you talking about?'

'I saw in the paper that someone called Zakharov had been condemned to death.'

He cannot be as serious about music as he was: all he has written during the summer are a few songs and piano pieces.

'That's terrible,' I say. 'Saminsky[3] and Elkan are both writing fugues.'

'What of it? Good for Saminsky.'

'Well, Saminsky, all right, but Elkashka, for heaven's sake!'

I bought *The Twilight of the Gods* and am playing it with enormous pleasure. Myaskovsky lent me his E minor Sonata (No. 1 perhaps, or No. 2, anyhow one of his earliest). It is so much weaker than his Sixth, the one in D minor with the fugue; he has obviously made great strides in the past two years. There is a young pianist called Akhron[4] in Yesipova's[5] class, a real

---

1 The Russian marking system goes from 1 (weakest) to 5 (strongest).
2 Boris Zakharov (1887–1942), pianist, fellow student and (with interruptions) close friend of Prokofiev. Zakharov later had some success as a pianist in Russia and Europe, but was eclipsed by the international fame of his violinist wife Cecilia Hansen.
3 Lazar Saminsky (1882–1959), composer, conductor (mainly choral) and musicologist, notably on Jewish music. Emigrated to America in 1920.
4 Isidor Akhron (1892–1948), pianist and composer, who emigrated to the US in 1922 and had a successful career, notably partnering Jascha Heifetz. His elder brother Iosif (1886–1943) was a pupil of Leopold Auer and also had a successful post-Revolution career abroad, both as a violinist and composer, first in Berlin and later in the US.
5 Anna Yesipova (1851–1914), one of the most brilliant pianists of her generation, admired by Liszt and Tchaikovsky. Like Prokofiev's other teacher, Alexander Winkler, she studied with Theodor Leschetitsky in Vienna, but unlike Winkler she married her teacher. After enjoying an acclaimed virtuoso career in Europe and America she returned to St Petersburg in 1893 to take up a professorship at the St Petersburg Conservatoire.

comedian. 'What's the use of all this theory?' he says, 'you should see my brother, now he's a real composer!' He goes on for a quarter of an hour about this brother and what a great composer he is. From a long speech I learned only that the brother graduated from the Conservatoire as a violinist and has had four pieces (small ones) published, so he must be a genius!! By the way, about that couple I mentioned earlier: apparently after the exam yesterday they had a row and have now split up, how do you like that!? She was taking her Geography exam at the same time as mine in History (she is a class below me but my History teacher had not turned up and so I was being examined by the Geography man). She was doing fine until suddenly: 'What does the Volga flow into?' 'I don't know . . .' Afterwards I told her if it had been me I wouldn't have given her more than a 1. She took this rather amiss.

The Karlsbad chess tournament has finished, the First Prize going to Rubinstein. He is now therefore a champion, and next summer will take part in the Champions' Tournament, where I believe he will be very successful. A few years down the line he'll be playing Lasker . . . Yanovsky's and Chigorin's stars are fading. It seems clear that Rubinstein is set to end up champion of Russia, as in practice he already is.

10 September

Conservatoire classes[1] started today. As a matter of fact they didn't really start, but everyone assembled and chatted with one another, and that was nice. Lyadov put up a notice requesting all gentlemen studying Theory to come in a week's time, on the 17th, and Rimsky is said not to be starting until the 20th. No one expressed surprise at this; it's par for the course with these teachers. Winkler[2] however is horribly punctual and appeared today: I thought I'd better make myself scarce.

I must learn Beethoven's C minor Concerto and the Bach fugue that he gave me over the summer. As for the academic classes, they kept fobbing us off, the time dragged on and on, as always happens at the Conservatoire, until finally it was announced that there would be no classes today. Well, all right, but there will be tomorrow. There are no lessons in my subjects on Saturdays, but I have two hours on Tuesdays, Wednesdays and Fridays, and three hours on Mondays and Thursdays. Saw hordes of Theory students (everyone except Asafyev[3] and Kankarovich[4]).

1 Specifically Music disciplines rather than the academic classes in General Subjects.
2 Alexander Winkler (1865–1935), Prokofiev's first piano teacher at the St Petersburg Conservatoire. Winkler, a student of Theodore Leschetitsky, also wrote music criticism for the *St Petersburg Gazette*. He emigrated from the Soviet Union in 1925.
3 Boris Asafyev (1884–1949), who as well as being a prolific composer wrote musical criticism under the pseudonym Igor Glebov, became one of the earliest and staunchest propagandists for Prokofiev's music. Three of his twenty-eight ballets (*The Fountains of Bakhchisarai, The*

Myaskovsky did not like my C minor Sonatina at all: 'God knows what this is supposed to be! Operetta music, and the cheapest kind at that!' I was obviously right not to submit it, even though personally I am rather fond of the first movement; the only thing that met with Myaskovsky's approval was the last movement with the leaps in it. In turn I comprehensively demolished his C minor Sonata (No. 1) and asked him to let me have a look at his No. 4 ('Pittoresque'). I agree with him that one-movement sonatas are feasible, in fact I am even beginning to think this may be the right way to do it. Nevertheless, my next sonata will be in three movements; the point is that the movements will be short and the form compressed. In any case I'm not going to take a huge amount of trouble with this sonata (No. 4), the important thing is just to get it done. No. 2 was a different matter.[1] Myaskovsky thinks there should be more counterpoint in the development. I expect he's right.

Zakharov gave me his song to look at: I haven't done so yet, but it is probably all right by his standards. Myaskovsky is warming to Asafyev's children's opera[2] (his second): he says the development of the leitmotivs is correct and well done. I must ask to see it. I really wanted to go to *Kitezh*[3] with Myaskovsky today, but there were no tickets ... By the way, Morolyov[4] very much liked the Sonatina I wrote in the summer, and has even asked if he can copy it!

13 September

What's new? Time flies so quickly, but there is nothing much to write about. For the time being my days are spent between the Conservatoire and home. There's not much urgency to start the classes, very much *à la* Conservatoire, anyhow there haven't been any for three days now. Apparently they will start on Monday. I'm going to the General Subject lessons; so far they are pretty boring and I occupy myself covering my exercise book with beautiful landscapes. The History teacher is a comedian who enjoys teasing his students,

---

Flames of Paris, The Stone Guest) are still in the repertory, and after the Revoluton he concentrated mainly on the relatively safe area of music for children. He never moved away from his city and survived the 900 days of the Leningrad blockade from September 1941 to January 1944.
4   [See p. 5.] Anatoly Kankarovich (1885–1956), composer of operas and ballets, with later career as an opera conductor in Moscow and Petrograd. 'A thin, dark-haired youth with a pale face and a sloping forehead that made him look as though part of his skull had been sliced off.' (*Autobiography*.)
1   These are, of course, sonatas of the composer's juvenilia, not the numbered sonatas given opus numbers. The first movement of this early Sonata No. 2 was, however, subsequently reworked to appear as the single-movement official Sonata No. 1 in F minor, Op. 1.
2   *The Snow Queen*.
3   *The Legend of the Invisible City of Kitezh and the Maiden Fevronia*, opera by Rimsky-Korsakov, composed in 1904 but not produced until 1907.
4   Vasily Morolyov (1880–1949), music-loving, chess-playing veterinary surgeon in Sontsovka to whom the composer dedicated his first published opus, the Sonata No. 1 in F minor, Op. 1.

especially the girls (the male students describe him as a 'rotter'!). He made the following announcement to the class: 'Gentlemen, you will recall that last year our Conservatoire was the subject of a liberation movement,[1] in consequence of which our History studies have fallen seriously behind... Gentlemen, we are now half a year behind, and so have only got as far as Humanism.' But I have already covered everything I need for the exam, even the Seven Years War, so now I shall have the pleasure of doing it all over again.

The class has an odd configuration: seventeen girls and three boys! Apparently there may be three more in time. There are only two desks for the boys; I'm sitting at the second, next to a half-Russian half-German with a surname something like Wallenstein, Vansheyev, something like that, a nice enough fellow if he weren't so deadly serious. He is six months older than me. As for the girl students (all seventeen of the poor things are squashed on to four desks) I haven't yet struck up an acquaintance with any of them. I look at it like this: there's plenty of time. I'm in no hurry, I always manage to get things done. I may give the impression of not wanting to make friends, but I don't think I'm the loser by it.

17 September

Lyadov's group of theory students met together at the Conservatoire at eleven o'clock today. Lyadov himself appeared, and all of us Fugue students went into the room. As soon as he saw us: 'Ah, here come the fuguists! Well, gentlemen, Wednesdays and Saturdays at one o'clock. Good day to you.' And out we went again. What a waste of time!

Asafyev promised to let me look at his new opera in due course, and Myaskovsky gave me his 'Pittoresque'. Although he still thinks the *Finale* of my Sonatina is rubbish, he said he was beginning to warm to the first movement. About time! On his recommendation I bought Medtner's *Fairy Tales*, Op. 8. Today, 17 September, is the name-day of half the women in St Petersburg – Vera, Nadezhda, Lyubov, Sofia. As it happens, however, we don't know many. The Pavskys[2] have not called on us yet, so we confined ourselves to a telegram today. I sent Vera Reberg[3] my congratulations yesterday. By the way, I keep on thinking about Leskov's[4] *At Daggers Drawn*, I like it so much. He

---

1 The consequences of the 1905 strikes and resignations by students and faculty, effects of which continued into the 1906–7 academic year.
2 The Pavsky family were friends of the Rayevskys (Prokofiev's uncle, aunt and cousins) and the son, Vanya, became a particular friend of the young Prokofiev although three years younger, Prokofiev approving very much of Vanya's enthusiasm for chess and the battleships of the Russian Navy.
3 Vera, Zinaida and Nina Reberg were the daughters of Dr Alfred Reberg, the Prokofievs' family doctor in Sontsovka. The photograph reproduced on the dust-jacket of the present edition was taken on a visit to the Rebergs in the summer of 1908.
4 Nikolay Leskov (1831–1895), writer of novels, novellas and short stories, best known in the West

has such amazing characters; on one side gangsters, criminals, terrible people but so wonderfully sharp and clever; on the other good, honest folk whose wits are no match for the first, and it is impossible to say where one's sympathies lie. The ending is most disagreeable. Leskov's descriptions of events are so quick and economical that everything comes out so marvellously graphic and vivid! His style is excellent, and the unfailing wit is far better than in his *Cathedral Folk*.

20 September

Went to the dentist to have two teeth filled.

Today there were nine people in the General Subjects class: Dobrzhenets, Piastro, Shurtsman, Schmidt, Vanscheidt: all fine Russian names, reminding one of islands in the Pacific! There were three others, goodness knows what their names are. Ilyusha Gvirtsman[1] is a Jew, tall, rather good-looking, quite lively, not that bright but all right. Mishka Piastro[2] is also Jewish, short and stout, a peaceable sort of chap; I'm told he is a good chess player. To talk to he seems pretty knowledgeable. I must play with him soon; we've already talked about it several times. Dobrzhenets is a Pole, red-haired, doesn't give the impression of being particularly clever although apparently he came out near the top last year. All these three are violinists, and then there are two horn players. Schmidt is a pugnacious German. Konstantin Vanscheidt, whom I have already mentioned, is probably the best of the bunch, the most reliable at least and the best-looking. As for the girls, the most striking are Anisimova, Esche, Fliege and Bessonova. The last named is a bold, lively girl, a dizzy scatterbrain and a bit of a show-off, a child trying to present herself as a grown-up young lady, which doesn't make for a very pleasant impression. Fliege is somewhat the same, only more restrained. Esche is a much more modest character, and spends most of the time in the class drawing. I noticed her last spring and worked out that her rather unusual name consists of E–C–H–E, all the letters representing notes.[3] I tried them out on the

---

for the novella *Lady Macbeth of the Mtsensk District*, on account of Shostakovich's eponymous opera. *At Daggers Drawn* (1870) is a novel highly critical of the movement known as radical nihilism and earned Leskov the reputation of being ultra-conservative. *Cathedral Folk* (1872) satirizes the clergy in a cathedral town, the central figure being based on Avvakum, the seventeenth-century leader of the Old Believers.

1   Ilya Gvirtsman (1893–?), violinist, fellow student of Prokofiev at the St Petersburg Conservatoire.
2   Mikhail Piastro, violinist and fellow student of Prokofiev at the St Petersburg Conservatoire – 'a stout, round-headed youth whose silhouette reminded me of a pawn' (*Autobiography*).
3   In English notation this would be E–C–B–E, based on Prokofiev's transliteration of the name into French. The theme (marked *semplice e dolce*) survived as the second subject of the first movement of the Sonata No. 3, Op. 28, itself a reworking of the sonata Prokofiev originally composed in 1907. Prokofiev also made a theme out of the German lettering of the name

piano, turned them this way and that, and got quite a decent theme which I used as a secondary subject in my Third Piano Sonata that I was writing at the time. When Myaskovsky looked through the sonata he found this theme 'super-fresh' and marvellously beautiful.

But the girl who most interests me (in so far as any of them do at all) is Anisimova. I put her down as no more than fifteen, perhaps less, and I think I am probably right about this. Is she beautiful? I suppose she is, although her features are not particularly regular, but she is full of life, health and gaiety. (I still remember her from four years ago, in my first year, when I was in an academic class with her for ten days.) Last spring I was performing in my public piano exam as one of Winkler's pupils, and after us it was the turn of Paletik's students, among them Anisimova.[1] We were all together in the artists' room, so we exchanged a few words and I could have pursued the relationship then as she seemed quite amenable to the idea, but I was lazy and let it slip. Anisimova did not interest me much then. She has got much prettier over the summer.

25 September

Today is my name-day, so I had to be home for dinner. But it was not a particularly festive occasion because Papa's everlasting duties with his job prevented him from coming and he will not be here until early next month. The only guests were the Rayevskys[2] and E. M. Petrova. I used to regard this day as something special and always looked forward to it, perhaps because I knew I would be getting presents. I got some today too, quite a lot in fact. Aunt Tanya,[3] Mama and Papa gave me a chessboard, a very good and expensive one. Papa also gave me an opera that I wanted and some chocolate. From Mlle Roblin I got a tiny little Finnish knife and two French books, from Mme Petrova a gold pencil box, and from Aunt Katya[4] 3 roubles. I expect my godfather will also give me something. Altogether a good haul, and I'm happy.

Tomorrow morning at the Conservatoire I have my first conducting class with Tcherepnin. I took the day off today and missed academic classes. Mlle

---

E–S–C–H–E, i.e. E–E flat–C–B–E, for a short piano piece written in 1910, the autograph of which survives. The Esche sisters were Yelizaveta (this one, the elder), and Sofia.

1 'Anisimova was small, very wholesome, with a dimple on her chin and always showing her irregular teeth.' [Subsequent note by author.]
2 Yekaterina Zhitkova, Prokofiev's mother's elder sister (Aunt Katya), was married to Alexander Rayevsky (Uncle Sasha), a prominent and well-connected civil servant in St Petersburg. Their children, the composer's cousins, were Andrey (Andryusha), Alexander (Shurik) and Yekaterina (Katya).
3 Tatyana Zhitkova, Prokofiev's maternal aunt (d. 1912).
4 Rayevskaya.

Louise Roblin is staying with us at the moment. When I was seven she came more or less straight from Paris to Sontsovka as my governess. She was at that time a seventeen-year-old girl and stayed almost two years. Then she left, and then when I was twelve she came back and stayed another year. She now lives in Pskov, where she has a lot of pupils, but she hasn't forgotten us because she loves Mama very much, and sometimes comes to stay for a few days, as now. When she was first at Sontsovka I had just learned to play chess, and I taught her to play as well. Since then she has had quite a bit of practice. We played 8 games and the result was 6–1–1.

The last time I saw Zakharov, he said to me, 'Come over some time; I have a friend of the same age, and we can play chess!' 'Thank you.' 'So you'll come?' 'Yes, of course, I'd like to.' While I should very much welcome a closer friendship with him, I naturally won't go the first time I'm asked. If he repeats the invitation, and then once again, and makes it specific for a definite time, then I'd like to go very much.

28 September

Everything is jogging along fine. Conservatoire classes are warming up a bit too, and I'm getting more used to them. I've started conducting classes with Tcherepnin.[1] There were three of us supposed to be studying conducting this year, but all sorts of extra people turned up and it has all become rather a muddle. Tcherepnin put up a notice inviting us to present ourselves on such-and-such a day, but remembering what had happened with Lyadov, I did not respond to the call. When he asked where I was and someone told him that I was probably in a General Subjects class, our respected senior instructor pronounced, 'Obviously he prefers academic work to art! . . .' A professorial witticism worthy of our former Director Bernhardt.[2]

Everything is much the same as it was in my cattle-stall, as I call the academic classroom. I am not especially fond of my male fellow students and tend to keep out of their way. The female of the species excites peculiar

---

1   Nikolay Tcherepnin (1873–1945), composer and conductor, among the first to recognize and promote Prokofiev's genius as a composer and, after initial doubts, support him as a conductor. An exceptionally skilful and accomplished, if derivative, composer Tcherepnin was virtually a house provider of scores (notably *Le Pavillon d'Armide*, *Narcisse*, *The Enchanted Kingdom*) for Diaghilev's initial Paris ballet seasons of the Ballets Russes.
2   August Bernhardt (1852–1908) was Director of the St Petersburg Conservatoire from 1898 to 1905, adopting in 1905 a firmly reactionary position in the face of the widespread student and faculty protests led by Rimsky-Korsakov, Glazunov, Lyadov and others, and supported *inter alia* by Prokofiev. The eventual result, the closing of the Conservatoire in autumn 1905, ended Bernhardt's reign (in fact he had already resigned in the spring) and when the Conservatoire reopened as an autonomous higher-education establishment in spring 1906 Glazunov was appointed Director. See also p. 188, n. 1.

feelings in me, a mixture of tension and boredom that changes minute by minute. I have decided I don't like Anisimova, and in any case she is the youngest member of the class. There's no brooking the stupidity of some of the people in this class; it's quite incredible.

Myaskovsky is suffering from inflammation of the blind gut. This is quite a common condition and these days is easily cured, but I think it takes at least five to six weeks to get over. Poor fellow! I've written to him, I hope I'll find time somehow to go and see him, but he lives quite a long way away, at least seven versts.[1]

1 October

I have just returned from Ozerki[2] where I went with Aunt Tanya for a couple of days: we left yesterday morning and this evening we're already back again. Aunt Tanya's friends the Ponofidins live there, a husband and wife with no children. They own three dachas and have plenty of money, high-class people, very well educated and hospitable, extremely generous and cultivated. This is the first time I have been to their house. Some people called Borkovsky live in one of their dachas, they are very old friends, especially of Aunt Tanya. True aristocrats. Not long ago they had 40,000 a year, but now they've run through all of it and live in poverty, hoping to be rescued by an inheritance of some kind. A nephew, Kolya Akafyev, was there for the two days of the holiday. I've known him for a long time, but don't see much of him. He is fourteen and a half, a cadet at military school, and a gifted painter. If all goes well he will be a great artist. He is quite intelligent, but desperately spoiled.

Also in the party was Nikolay Viktorov, an extremely nice man and a singer who gets the odd engagement here and there, an excellent baritone and a most amusing and witty man. We played piano duets and sang together, played croquet and lotto, went for walks and bike rides, and he made us laugh all the time. Altogether I had a very good time and they seem to have liked me, as I did them. Sergey Ponofidin was not there; he is said to be a good chess player with a gift for analysing games. I was pressed to come and stay again.

Conservatoire work continues: Tcherepnin is in love with the idea of natural horns and keeps repeating, 'In my new piece I am thinking of including natural horns; I think it will sound really fresh and new . . .' I thought of saying, 'Pull the other one, I'll believe it when I hear it', but decided to hold my tongue. I played a ten-game chess match with Mlle Roblin, and the result was 8–1–1. She left yesterday.

1 A verst is slightly more than a kilometre.
2 Seaside resort on the Gulf of Finland.

3 October

Papa arrived this morning. He had hoped to be here in time for my name-day, but the constant demands of his work have only now released him. He has been travelling since 27 September, staying in Kharkov and with Sontsov.[1]

Yesterday Balayev, our Russian teacher (I call him 'Balalayev' because he chatters on like a balalaika) made us choose roles in *Woe from Wit*[2] to read in class (practically the whole of Act III) and is now suggesting that we learn our parts by heart. I am Anton Antonovich Zagoretsky. I love *Woe from Wit*, and Zagoretsky is a good part, so I shall enjoy learning it. I lost my History textbook, and missed preparing two of the lessons while looking for it. But I took some comfort from the fact that no one in the class today had done their prep either. When the teacher started calling people up, most of them declined, so they were given a 2. Suddenly: 'Prokofiev!' Naturally I was not going to refuse and be condemned to a 2, so I boldly went up to be questioned. To my joy (I am always so incredibly lucky!) he asked me old stuff, about Luther and the Italian Humanists. My answers were very full and I probably got a 5, or maybe 4.5. Amazing! But now I'll have to go and buy another copy of the book. I wrote a whole heap of thank-you letters for my name-day. Papa thinks my handwriting is dreadful. I did get a present from my godfather – 10 roubles.

6 October

This evening is the first concert in Ziloti's series. I have not taken out a subscription this year because it is too expensive, but I went to the rehearsal yesterday. This is what has happened with rehearsal passes: Tcherepnin promised to get them for us, but there are thirteen conducting students and Ziloti sent Tcherepnin only ten. Our respected senior instructor left out of his largesse Orlov, whom he does not like much, one other student, and me. Why me? Perhaps I am another one he does not much care for, or perhaps

---

1 Dmitry Sontsov, a wealthy former fellow student of Prokofiev's father, Sergey Alexeyevich, at the Agricultural Academy, was the owner of the estate at Sontsovka in the Ukraine and employed him as manager.
2 Play in verse by Alexander Griboyedov (1795–1829), originally banned by the censor and one of the most famously subversive of Russian satires. The main protagonist, Chatsky, is the emblematic 'superfluous man', too clever and idealistical to be remotely effective, and as such a character type central to Russian literary imagination from the moment of his first appearance. Griboyedov was also a distinguished diplomat and in 1828 was responsible for negotiating Russia's peace treaty with Persia. Subsequently appointed Russian Minister to Tehran, he and his staff were murdered inside the embassy there by fanatical Islamic rioters.

because I am the youngest and the least likely to make a fuss. Seeing me coming into the class, he cried, 'I suppose you're offended!'

'???'

'By not getting a rehearsal pass.'

I embarked on a long speech, laying stress on the fact that Saminsky, who had scraped into the conducting course on a 3, which he should not really have been allowed to do, had been given a pass whereas I, who was there fully legally, had not.

'How do you know? Saminsky might turn out to be a much better conductor than you. After all, I can't make thirteen tickets out of ten, can I?'

'No doubt, but what am I supposed to do?'

'Well, whatever you please. Shoot me if you like!'

'No, I don't want to do that, all I want to know is how to get hold of a pass.'

'Try to get in as a Theory student.'

I turned to go.

'But look here, what about the lesson?'

'I want to get my rehearsal pass first.' And I went out.

He was very offended by this. I did get a ticket as a Theory student (for only one concert though), and then went back to the class. He paid no attention to me: when it was my turn to play he asked others to do so, and when I questioned him again about tickets, he cut me off sharply: 'What do you think I am, some sort of expert on box offices? Did you bring a symphony with you?' and so on.

I sat there for a little longer, but as it was obvious I was going to have to wait for ever to get my turn, and as I was hungry, I slipped quietly out. Some students told me later that what I did was regarded in the nature of a demonstration. But although I have no desire whatever to fall out with him, what can I do if I have respect for all the teachers except Tcherepnin, who fails so signally to deserve any.[1]

---

[1] In the *Autobiography*, after describing this encounter, Prokofiev writes: 'I went home angrily muttering under my breath, "I respect all my teachers except Tcherepnin, for whom I have no respect at all." But I was wrong: of all my teachers Tcherepnin was musically the liveliest and most interesting, although a person composed of great paradoxes. He always had stimulating and informative things to say about conducting, but when he stood on the platform the orchestra would fall apart in his hands. He was no less interesting on the future of music, taking for example an E major chord and jabbing B flat major triads on top of it. "It will end by people writing all the black notes and all the black notes together," covering all the white notes on the keyboard with his left arm up to the elbow and the black notes with his right arm "and then they will see there is nowhere to go". I don't know how correct he was, because the development of music does not depend alone on the succession in which notes are written, but at the time he appeared to me such an innovator that he made my head spin.' (op. cit.)

10 October

In the break between classes today I heard my name being called by Nodelman,[1] one of the girl students. 'What it is, we're planning a ball, and we decided to ask you to be master of ceremonies.'

'You must excuse me, but I don't know anyone and I've no idea how to set about that sort of thing. I'd be terrified!'

'I realize it's a responsible job, but we have to choose two female students and one male, and we chose you, or rather you weren't actually chosen, but you did get the most votes.'

I thanked her, saying that of course I was moved to tears ('Moved to tears, even!' she said) but I still must decline. After a few more words we parted. I had been in the Conservatoire since early morning and was extremely tired, and could not think straight. But later it occurred to me that perhaps my refusal had been a mistake. To begin with, it might not be as difficult and nerve-racking a job as I imagined, and it was certainly flattering and a great honour to be asked. Secondly, I had spent no more than a month in the class, but girls whom I had made no effort to cultivate at all were now doing me the honour of voting for me to act as master of ceremonies, and was it not rather arrogant to have turned it down so brusquely? I set off to find Nodelman, whom I found downstairs with another girl, Fliege. I questioned her about exactly what would be entailed, and established the following details: first, the ball was to take place at Christmas, in other words there was plenty of time; Glazunov had apparently provided funds for the ball and there were other sources of finance as well, in fact there was plenty of money; then they wanted to incorporate some sort of preliminary entertainment and based on my reading of Zagoretsky I seemed to be a good speaker so they definitely wanted me to participate in that as well. When I started havering, she said, 'Well, we don't want to ask Dobrzhenets anyhow!' The upshot was that I didn't say yes and I didn't say no, and we parted amicably. I'll just wait for more details to emerge – there's plenty of time!

Today Tcherepnin brought in a wad of rehearsal passes for the Shreder concerts.[2]

'Whom did I disappoint last time?' he asked.

'Me!'

'We'll start with you this time then.' This was just for show, however, as there were plenty of tickets for everyone, and even some left over. 'I'm not going to give you any conducting to do for some time yet, though.'

With Lyadov we are writing triple fugues. The best so far are Zakharov's,

---

1 Ida Nodelman, piano student at the St Petersburg Conservatoire.
2 Concert series organized by Ivan Shreder, owner of the Shreder piano factory and showrooms in St Petersburg.

Elkan's and mine. Asafyev doesn't attend, Myaskovsky is ill, Kankarovich's and Saminsky's are not so good. Last time I played for him, Winkler was full of praise for my Bach G minor Fugue. He didn't stop me once, and kept saying, 'Good, very good', all the way through, which I have never in my life heard from him before.

14 October

It's amazing how punctilious Lyadov has become. He has given four classes in a row, all of them starting at one o'clock sharp. Apparently this is due to Saminsky: for some time he has been talking about sending Lyadov a letter, and has been asking which of us would be prepared to sign it. But the letter never got written, so apparently Saminsky went direct to Glazunov on his own account. This suited us fine, but it meant that Saminsky took all the consequences on his own head. Yesterday the Director came himself to the class. Saminsky's work book was immediately gone through with a fine toothcomb, and maliciously found to be full of mistakes. It was a deeply uncomfortable situation and terrible to see. Glazunov fixed his eyes on him and never let them drop for an instant. He also looked at one of my exercises (which had actually been done not badly at all): 'That's good style . . .' Incredible luck: I'm always being told I have no style; in comes Glazunov – and suddenly my work is good style! If Lyadov ever complains to Glazunov that Prokofiev's work lacks style, well now I've got direct proof of the contrary.

In the General Subjects cattle-stall yesterday I had to write an essay on 'Helen in Tauride'; I was late and had to rush, but it seems to have turned out all right, except I think I may have mixed up the goddesses Artemis and Aphrodite. But maybe I didn't.

I had a letter from Morolyov in which he says the reason for such a long delay in writing was the autumn round of inoculations. Well, fine. For no particular reason he now addresses me in the intimate form. That's all right too. I've already replied. I wrote the letter in the form of a circle, the lines spiralling in towards the centre, then through the centre and out again the other side, like the grooves on a gramophone record. I thought up the idea of writing like this some time ago but this is the first time I've tried it out; it's interesting and original, but an awful fiddle to write.

18 October

I definitely want to join a chess club before long. I know of two: at 44 Nevsky and 55 Nevsky. What I must do is find out the days on which they meet. I already know 55 Nevsky, but not the other one, which I would prefer because apparently Malyutin goes there, and he is the only one of the chess 'greats'

I know and have played against. It's always better when there are people you know.

Mama is going to Moscow tomorrow. My godfather is ill; he has not been well for about three years, has now suffered a stroke and is paralysed in the extremities on his left side. We don't know what the outcome will be, but it does not look very good. I'm very sorry for him, the poor man. And he is on his own; there are four nieces, it is true, but they are not the same as your own family.

I have been thinking about the fourth-year girls and my relationship with them. I've been in the same class with them for six weeks now, and have not got to know a single one of them. Whichever way you look at it, this is a strange situation, and I don't think anyone else in my position would behave as I do. What should I do now? Thus far matters have just taken their course without any intervention, but what is it leading to and how will it end? On reflection I came to the somewhat unexpected conclusion that for the time being I should wait until the girls themselves make a move to approach me. And oddly enough this makes sense, because in a month's time there will be activity around the preparations for the famous ball and entertainment. There were signs of this beginning to happen when Nodelman called me over a few days ago.

When I examine my feelings, I realize that sitting at home I think pleasurable thoughts about the girls, and sometimes go so far as to regret that I don't know any of them yet: some of them are very nice, especially Glagoleva,[1] Esche and Meingard. When I go into the Conservatoire I also find them very nice and would welcome any of them starting a conversation with me, but it never occurs to me to make the first move. But once it happens I shall be very glad.

The conclusion I draw from all this is that if necessary it will be up to me to initiate the relationship. What pretext can I use? One interesting idea would be to miss a lesson and then the next day enquire what had happened in my absence. If by Wednesday no progress has been made, that is what I will do, particularly as in any case I shall miss the first lesson, Physics, because of Lyadov's Fugue class, and the second class is History, for which I already have two 5s and so would be no sacrifice. Also, I could go and see Myaskovsky on his sick bed. I was there the other day; he is getting better and convalescence is under way. I told him I had finished my Fourth Sonata, so he said, 'Well, bring it over and let me have a look at it.'

---

1 Leonida Glagoleva, pianist, fellow student of Prokofiev at the St Petersburg Conservatoire.

20 October

Lyadov did not appear today. Kicking my heels in the corridors while I was waiting, I bumped into Nodelman and Co. bustling up in my direction. 'We were looking for you!' I was tempted to say that I was looking for them too, but refrained. They were taking advantage of a cancelled lesson to get together and choose a comedy to read through for the Christmas show. It was all done very properly: one of the administrators came in to supervise; she sat quietly and tactfully on the side. The ensuing din was so terrible that after a while I got a headache and went home to bed.

The meeting was a complete waste of time. I suggested a committee of four people should be in charge of running the whole thing, but for some reason this did not meet with approval. Balayev had apparently proposed a play called *The Old Wives' Summer* but nobody, not even Balayev, knew who had written it. Eventually, after more hellish noise, it was announced that classes would be resuming in a quarter of an hour's time. Sensibly, it was decided that two people should stay behind to wait for one of the teachers from the opera class who had some theatrical experience, and ask him to recommend a play. But when were we all to meet again? Tomorrow, in the Conservatoire, at one o'clock.

I decided I would go to this meeting. Of the girls, the one I like best is Glagoleva. Not to mention that she is beautiful, she has a reputation for being talented, and she has an attractive speaking voice. She has interested me for quite some time.

24 October

Yesterday we read through something else for the famous entertainment, but in my opinion it too was absolute rubbish. Even so, most people decided that it was better than previous suggestions and unless we could find anything better it would have to do. But this is not every interesting. More fascinating were the elections. What happened was that our female students had now hit on the idea of electing a committee of four people to oversee everything, exactly as I had suggested a few days earlier, except that I had had in mind three girls and one boy, but they decided to have two of each. The names of the candidates were all put up on a board, and when the votes were counted, the results were: Gvirtsman 18 (unanimous), Nodelman 15, Abramycheva[1] 14, myself 12, Piastro 6, Esche 4, Glagoleva 3. It follows that I had six votes against, and I believe that five of these were from the male

---

1 Olga Abramycheva (1890–1965), pianist and fellow student of Prokofiev at the St Petersburg Conservatoire.

students. Gvirtsman did brilliantly, and rightly so, since of all the men he most deserves to be on the committee, and will be more use than any of the others. It is obvious that I was the girls' choice, but why? Looking dispassionately at myself, I am clear that I shall be not merely a useless but a positively harmful member of the committee. I pointed out that, as our history teacher is fond of saying, I am like the cardinal who, serving God, does not believe in Him; thus I shall be on the organizing committee and closely involved with the organization of a show that I don't believe will ever happen. Not only that, but I am extremely busy, and there is worrying talk of the committee having a tremendous amount of work to do.

In the first place, chess. I've been meaning definitely to go to the Chess Club. It has been announced in the newspapers that the establishment at 55 Nevsky is organizing a tournament of the strongest players, Malyutin among them. Clearly I must go and watch; play is on Tuesdays and Fridays, and I missed the first day, which was yesterday, because of going to *Tannhäuser*, so I must be there on Friday. Then there is the matter of the rehearsal passes for the Ziloti concerts in which, as explained, Tcherepnin had 'disappointed' me. Suddenly Ziloti himself took it into his head to substitute yellow passes for the green ones he had previously issued. He sent Tcherepnin ten yellow passes with a note saying that the green ones were no longer valid, and our respected senior instructor gave them to Kankorovich asking him to give them out to all those who were already in possession of green ones. This was news to me, when suddenly I was approached by Kankorovich (with whom, by the way, I had had a slight tiff). Kankorovich said to me, 'Mr Prokofiev, have you got a green rehearsal pass?'

'What if I do?'

He explained.

'Well, do let me have one now.'

We resolved our quarrel.

A pleasantly witty variant by Zakharov today of the well-known proverb: 'Better late than never – as the man said, arriving five minutes after the train left.'

27 October

It's appalling how busy I am these days, like a squirrel on the treadmill! So many times I've sat down meaning to write my diary, and only now am I settling down to do it. I'll start with Thursday. At the end of the lesson there was a cry of 'Nobody leave!' and we started to read a new play, *A Local Shakespeare*,[1] in which they insisted that I took one of the parts. At first I dug

---

1 Play by Ilya Gurlyand, a lawyer and writer born in 1868 whose prose stories were at one time

my heels in, but later graciously relented. I really wanted to go home because I was very tired and still had Winkler's class in the evening, but then I noticed Glagoleva sitting on the front bench, and I'd like to know what she thinks of all this, so I stayed.

In the middle of reading the play, when there was a pause, those listening declared that it was a boring lot of rubbish, so we decided to abandon that one and go on to Shchepkina-Kupernik's[1] *Portrait of a Summer*, which we had read before and some people liked, but I did not. I said I did not want to read because my throat was tired, and I proposed that Glagoleva should read instead, which she agreed to without demur, and in fact read very well. The majority decided, against my protests, that this was the play to do, so *Portrait of a Summer* was decided upon and I was unanimously chosen for the role of Yury.

Although I had made a bit of a fuss, actually they were right, and eventually I came round to the idea. The plot concerns a young girl of seventeen called Shurochka, whom everyone thinks of as just a child, calling her 'Kroshka' ('Crumbs'), while her own view of herself is that she is quite grown up. She has fallen in love with an older family friend, Yury Petrovich, more like an uncle, thirty-eight years old, who always laughs at her and teases her. Nevertheless, with every hour that passes he finds in her more and more to attract him. Guests arrive, and there is a game of forfeits. Yury's forfeit is to tell a story. In it he reveals his growing feelings for Kroshka, whose forfeit, when it is her turn, is to kiss someone. She kisses Yury and then runs away. General confusion. Everyone then goes to drink tea, except Shura, who appears only when Yury calls for her to come in. Finally, declaration of love and marriage.

I was immediately cast as Yury, the leading male. But the part of Kroshka caused a huge row. As soon as the reading was over, Glagoleva announced that she wanted to play Shurochka, but was immediately attacked by Nodelman and the rest of the group, who told her 'as a friend' that 'you're very good, but a bit too tall for Kroshka, and Sadovskaya or Alpers would be better'. Glagoleva insisted, refusing the offer of other parts. The argument went on for ages. I proposed a competition. Glagoleva seized on this, and since none of her opponents could find a reason to argue against it, it was settled that the contestants would read before Ridal (the theatrical expert) and ask him to pick the winner. Five people put their names down:

---

admired by Chekhov. Despite his Jewish roots, Gurlyand seems to have turned against his co-religionists and had some association with the notorious 'Black Hundreds', the extreme right-wing, monarchist, anti-Semitic and anti-Revolutionary groups who promoted pogroms and acts of terrorism in the early years of the twentieth century. Gurlyand fled to France immediately after the 1917 February Revolution.

1 Tatyana Shchepkina-Kupernik (1874–1952), poet, dramatist, friend of Tchaikovsky and Chekhov, probably best known as a translator (Shakespeare, Rostand).

Glagoleva, Sadovskaya, Alpers, Anisimova and Abramycheva. Glagoleva looked triumphantly about with a supercilious air of modesty, sure of success in the competition. Justifiably: she had everything going for her and barring dirty tricks – which, be it said, was in the circumstances quite an important point – her victory should have been in no doubt. The remaining roles were assigned to Esche, Bessonova, Osipova, Gvirtsman and Piastro. Nodelman nobly declined to take part.

The meeting, which was appallingly badly and noisily handled, lasted about two hours, most of which I spent talking to Glagoleva. It is amazing how things turn out: I had long been thinking about her from a distance, and now here was I possibly about to partner her on stage and even kiss her! I shall have to get hold of a copy of the play, no easy task, and learn my lines as Yury, even more of a problem.

Yesterday I made my first visit to the Chess Club, home of the Chess Society (55 Nevsky). Aunt Tanya was firmly opposed to it and did not want me to go. The club makes a very favourable impression: a long, softly lit room; two long tables covered with a heavy, grey felt cloth, with eighteen to twenty chessboards set out, flanked on either side by time-clocks. Some people were sitting down and playing while others walked around and watched. Famous front-rank players simply wander in, chat to one another and share a joke, then play a game. It is an extraordinarily pleasant environment. I followed the play for two-and-a-half hours, mostly a Lebedev–Freyman match and an Alapin–Rosenkrantz match. How enjoyable it was to see face to face players whom I had long known from their matches, or from their pictures, or from their tournament league tables, and how fascinating to watch them locked in struggle with one another across the board, knowing that both were forces to reckon with, and that a single move could decide the outcome of the game!

Now for the second match. Lebedev was lucky to win the first game against Rosenkrantz, but now with a confident and supremely arrogant expression he already has Freyman's pieces in a vice-like grip. A minute into the game he saw victory within his grasp. I did not see how this game developed, but I know that in fact Lebedev lost. Alapin arrived, a chic forty minutes late, his clock having long ago been started. He played quickly, always trying to simplify the game by exchanging pieces. By the endgame of an evenly matched game he had only a slight advantage, but Rosenkrantz made a small error and lost.

About eleven o'clock I was challenged to a game by a student. He had previously won several games in a row against some distinguished gentleman or other. Not knowing his calibre I started off playing for a draw, and indeed the game very nearly was a draw, but then he blundered, lost a rook, and conceded. The second game also seemed to be heading for a draw; I was after a win but made some tactical errors and had to settle for a draw. By the third game I was tired, and after losing a piece, lost the game. All the games were quick ones – so-called *Schnellpartien*. When we had finished he invited me to his home, told me his name was Vasily Vasilievich Struve, and said he thought it would be more enjoyable if we were to play at his home rather than at the Club. I accepted happily, and we walked home together friends. Next week, on Saturday, I will visit him.

Mama returned from Moscow this morning. My godfather has survived the crisis but will be ill for a long time and may very well not recover the use of his left arm and left leg. Poor, poor man! My mother and my aunt gave me a bit of a row for my disobedience in going to the Chess Club, but harmony has now been restored.

Dancing lessons have started again, as last year and the year before in the Pototskys'[1] apartment. So far it is rather a boring group: three gentlemen – Vanya Pavsky, Kostya Skalon and I, and three ladies – all little girls no more than eight years old. Last year it was better, there was Lyolya Skalon, in whom I became very interested, although I must admit I had got bored with her by the spring. All the same, it was quite jolly and pleasant company. However, we are now additionally promised an exceptionally tall law student of seventeen, Lyolya Skalon again and one other girl, and if they don't come then the Frolova sisters will.

2 November

Have just returned from *Lohengrin*. A good opera, very good, but I place it below *Tannhäuser* and even *The Flying Dutchman*. The other day I visited a now-convalescent Myaskovsky and met there another officer who is also a musician. I have just met him again and had a talk with him. I said that there is much more material in *Tannhäuser*; he said that this is because *Tannhäuser* is a finished work of art while *Lohengrin* is, so to say, a sketch for the Grail, and it is very possible that Wagner put a great deal more into the first than he did into the second. Rimsky-Korsakov has come up with a new concept for his course on theory of composition: four years for the less talented instead of six. The only effect this might have on me is that I might be able to get my diploma and qualify as a Free Artist[2] next spring.

---

1 The Pototskys, like their friends the Pavskys, formed part of the elite Rayevsky circle. Stepan Pototsky, a fashionable surgeon, was chief medical officer at the Obukhov Hospital. The salon of their Government-provided apartment was large enough for balls and dancing lessons.
2 'Professional Freelance Artist'. In pre-Revolutionary Russia musicians who completed their training and graduated from recognized institutions, and who were not employees of institutions, were known as 'Free Artists'.

5 November

On Saturday the first thing I did was visit Struve to play chess. His father lives in quite a spacious government apartment, but exactly who he is I have no idea, except that the family is of Russified German origin. I proposed that we should play seriously, for example a match of the first to win five games; he agreed, and we decided on the best of ten games. I won the first game; in the second he had me tightly boxed in but for a long time could not press his advantage, so that the game stood even until I exposed my knight and lost. He is not quite as strong a player as I am, and I am sure I shall end up the winner. He is glad to have me to play with and says what we should do is practise more and then join the Society. The arrangement suits me down to the ground, although it would be better still if he were a just a little stronger than me.

I have just taken out the score of Strauss's *Salome* but I don't think I shall study it. Try as I may, I just cannot accept this music. It will be interesting to see what Myaskovsky thinks of it when I talk to him. I am finishing my Sonata No. 4 and thinking of dedicating it to him; it has quite a lot of 'invention' ('Oh, you're such an inventor!' he always says in such circumstances).

Well, as for the famous show, it is now going to be directed by Feona, an actor from the Komissarzhevskaya Theatre,[1] and the first rehearsal is next Saturday. In the meantime we all got together and rehearsed: the result was pretty much of a mess. Some thought it was not too bad, it could have been much worse, and in time would turn out all right. But my own view, which I did not hide, was that it was nothing of the kind. Up to a point they may have been right: some of them had no experience of the stage, and this was true of myself: I could have everything perfectly off by heart at home, but once on the stage, worse than useless. My part, although I liked it a lot while I was learning it, eventually became a real trial to me, mainly because I was never off the stage from start to finish. So far, the people who know their lines best are Glagoleva and Bessonova. The latter's role of a very affected young lady is so tailor-made for her that she is very successful in it. Alpers plays Shura, the longest, hardest and stupidest role; this is all very fine, but God knows, she is not up to the task! As for Glagoleva, I myself now agree that she would have been too tall.

9 November

This whole business of the Christmas show is becoming a bore, and it is all turning horribly sour. We do have a committee but it isn't worth a rotten

---

1 Dobrzhenets, Villik and Gvirtsman, all violinists and all hard up, played in the pit orchestra of the Komissarzhevskaya Theatre; this was presumably the connection. The great actor Vera Komissarzhevskaya (1864–1910) established her theatre in St Petersburg in 1904.

egg: I am supposed to be in charge, Abramycheva the number two. The people really pulling the strings are Nodelman and Gvirtsman, and they seem to be preoccupied by the most trivial matters: thinking up something or other to print for the committee, devising the format of the tickets. Everyone seems far too lazy actually to learn their parts. Feona has called a rehearsal for Sunday, but we still must have another rehearsal on our own tomorrow in order to get a bit more proficient in our roles. All this is terribly aggravating.

Our marks for the last quarter were recently announced. I got 5 for History, 4+ for General Literature, 4+ for Russian, nothing for Physics but yesterday I got 5 overall. No other student has higher marks than me: Piastro and Dobrzhenets got 5, 4 and 4 with no pluses.

The wedding of Mitya Maksutov[1] took place today: the Prince is marrying Princess Obolenskaya. Mama attended the ceremony. Papa arrived this morning having spent time in Moscow on the way. My godfather's health is improved, there is hope for his leg, but there is still cause for concern.

I listened to the *Siegfried Idyll* – what a delight!

15 November

There was an evening of music by Taneyev on the 14th, to which Papa and I went together. We met Sergey Ivanovich[1] downstairs at the cloakroom taking off his coat, and exchanged a few pleasantries.

'Good evening, Sergey . . . excuse me, I don't remember your patronymic . . .'

'Oh good gracious, Sergey Ivanovich! You always used to call me simply Seryozha, so please go on doing so!'

Taneyev then asked how my musical activities were progressing, and I told him what a pleasure it was for me to have had the chance to hear him performing, which I had never been able to do before. What a nice man he is, and how different from Lyadov – they are chalk and cheese!

23 November

It is odd how variable my moods are! Mostly I am very cheerful, but from time to time something like a depression settles on me, I don't know what causes it. Usually, so I have observed, it happens after I have been sitting at home all day, or I have been reading something boring, or something has not gone well for me and made me dissatisfied with myself, often something completely trivial. Well, so be it. Today I am in good spirits. I played Old

---

1   The Maksutovs, a princely family, were connections of Alexander Rayevsky, Prokofiev's uncle by marriage.
2   Taneyev.

Maid with Arseny Stepanovich Belanovsky (a priest from Yekaterinodar, the son of our old priest at Selidovka and brother of Stefan), who has come to St Petersburg to present a petition. Old Maid is a very enjoyable and fashionable card game for four players which I have adapted for three by eliminating all the low-denomination cards up to sixes. I have got pretty good at it and often win.

My chess match with Struve ended on the 19th in a draw: 4–4 and 2 draws. We are going to start another, the winner being the first to win five games, and this time it will be serious, not more than one game a day and with unlimited time to think. I want to buy a control clock. I am absolutely confident of winning this second match; in the first one none of Struve's victories were achieved according to the rules of correct play, I was always missing things and making fatal errors. Two of my wins came through his errors, but the other two were properly planned and executed by me according to established precedent, and I do consider myself the stronger player (as does he, in fact).

Matters with the Conservatoire theatre production have taken a turn for the better. We had a rehearsal with Feona on Wednesday and he completely changed the direction of the show. My relations with the girls have never been better.

2 December

On Thursday there was a student concert in the Conservatoire: a student orchestra conducted by students, with student soloists. The most interesting work on the programme was Korsakov's Concerto, performed by Lemba:[1] I joked that 'Malko[2] conducted while Lemba played'.[3] Lemba was not bad, although sometimes he lacked power. Towards the end he was overcome by nerves and started to play fistfuls of wrong notes, and he completely fluffed the octaves at the end, when his hands seized up altogether. I relayed all these comments to him and he entirely agreed with them. A lot of people felt that I was being too severe, and one of the girls said, 'You'll make a real newspaper critic one of these days!' On the whole I was pleased by this remark: I could indeed become a good critic, and a right bitch to boot, and then they would all catch it. The music in Korsakov's Concerto is extremely beautiful

---

1   Artur Lemba (1885–1963), pianist, composer and critic, later professor at the St Petersburg Conservatoire.
2   Nikolay Malko (1883–1961), conductor with a distinguished international career. Until he left the Soviet Union in 1928 he conducted at the Kirov Theatre and in 1926 in Leningrad undertook the sensational premiere of Shostakovich's Symphony No. 1. From 1956 to 1961 he was chief conductor of the Sydney Symphony in Australia.
3   Prokofiev makes an untranslatable play on words, based on the way Russian verbs alter their endings according to the gender and number of the subject. 'Lemba' appears to be feminine; 'Malko' neuter.

and original, not at all like many other concertos. I asked Winkler to let me play it in due course, and he said he would do so.

After that came Saint-Saëns's *Suite algérienne*, a piece I had analysed fully in Tcherepnin's score-reading class last year. But this was the first time I had heard it played by an orchestra, and I had no idea how marvellously it was orchestrated, simply astounding! There were not many people at the concert, except for a lot of students who get in free. I did, however, see an old acquaintance there, Yury Frolov. I had met him at the Pavskys two years ago but since then had not seen much of him except occasionally at concerts. At one time we used the intimate form of address, but then for some reason reverted to the formal style. He knows a lot of the girls at the Conservatoire and is close friends with some of them, particularly in our sixth form.

The day before yesterday I went to *Kitezh*. In the spring, when it was new in the repertory and there were only four performances, I went to all of them, but this was the first one I had attended this season. I have a deep love for this opera; its beauties are of course beyond praise, but I must say that Tcherepnin, who was conducting this performance, was quite extraordinarily bad!

Struve and I have begun our second match and so far it is going very well for me; I have won the first three games. Myaskovsky considers my Fourth Sonata has more material than the others but is spoilt by the lack of an overall structure; I agree with him and may revise it.

10 December

What can this mean – am I getting tired of my Diary? No, not at all, but there has simply been no time, and also I have been subject to mood swings and changes of opinion, so that from moment to moment I might set down completely different views on the same subject.

On Friday there was a concert of music by Glazunov. The background to it was that, as part of the Conservatoire's having been granted its independence, it was allowed to set up a canteen which would be completely managed by the student body. Elections were held in the approved manner and a committee formed to run the restaurant. The committee did a first-class job, and everything was going splendidly until it was discovered that the enterprise had run up a substantial debt. How precisely this had come about was not clear, but the decision was taken to organize a concert in honour of Glazunov, the proceeds from which would go towards clearing the debt. At this point a serious rift developed between two opposing groups of elected student officers: those on the Canteen Committee and those on the Senior Students' Committee. Each group wanted to demonstrate its authority and its untrammelled right to wield despotic power. There were quarrels and a great deal of abusive language; nevertheless the concert took place and thanks to the presence of such names as Glazunov, Sobinov,[1] Barinova[2] and Malmgren[3] the hall was filled to capacity. The main work on the programme was Glazunov's Seventh Symphony, a work that can give pleasure even after repeated hearings (Rimsky-Korsakov adores it), but is not especially distinctive or individual. 'Assembled, rather than composed,' as Rozovsky[4] put it. Glagoleva was at the concert, the first time I have seen her at one. She is undoubtedly very beautiful.

I sometimes find it very strange: how and why it is I don't know, but I have not yet started courting any girl in particular. Thinking about this, I have come to several conclusions. In the first place I have a tendency always to seek out a person's least attractive characteristics; normally one does just the opposite: looks for the positive qualities and lets them balance the negative. As a result I seldom, if ever, find anyone who satisfies me completely. In the second place, there is a very large female population in the Conservatoire, so it provides an *embarras de richesses*, furthermore while forbidden fruit is always the most desirable, here one can do whatever one wants. In the third place I have a horror of battening on to anyone, of becoming a disagreeable companion or of being a burden. My feelings on this subject are so fastidious they amount almost to a phobia. And finally, I do not want to jeopardize the position of prestige I have secured for myself in the Conservatoire. The girls here regard me as so unshakeably independent that in theory I could sustain this view of myself indefinitely. I have even got used to holding it myself. Recently, however, I have resolved to conduct myself in a kinder, gentler manner.

Now on the subject of the conductors' class. The only people Tcherepnin ever allows to conduct are Saminsky and Kankarovich, no one else gets a look-in. Furman was once given one-eighth of a symphony to conduct, that is to say half of one movement, while Orlov, Kolomiitsev and I are completely left out in the cold. And even the two first-named are unhappy at having been allowed on to the podium no more than three times. Eventually Kankarovich composed a submission to the Artistic Committee of the Conservatoire. It was a very good document, well written, correct and to the point, but it included one charge to which I felt unable to subscribe because it was so brutally tactless: 'We cannot but be aware that Mr Tcherepnin lacks competence, and indeed on several occasions has discredited himself...' etc. I succeeded in persuading people that it would be better to omit this

---

1 Leonid Sobinov (1872–1934), famous tenor, soloist at the Bolshoy Theatre in Moscow and guest star at the Mariinsky Theatre; La Scala, Milan, and other leading opera houses.
2 Maria Barinova (1878–1956), pianist who studied with Busoni, later professor at the St Petersburg Conservatoire.
3 Yevgraf Malmgren, cellist.
4 Solomon Rozovsky (1872–1962), composer and teacher.

sentence, and at the present time the deposition is being made in a fair copy so that we can all affix our signatures.

At the last lesson I asked Tcherepnin when I should be allowed to conduct something. He replied, not before Christmas. After the class we surrounded him in a body and began to complain about the wretchedness of our position, but Tcherepnin is a consummate diplomat and politician and an expert at crushing his opponents in the subtlest possible way. I recall one occasion when he was late for his class. Saminsky, with his usual brashness, without waiting for permission or even giving it any thought, mounted the podium and began to conduct the symphony. Tcherepnin suddenly made a belated entrance, stood stock still for a moment and then clapped his hands several times to stop the orchestra. Then, turning to Klimov,[1] he said in a loud voice, 'Mr Klimov, Mendelssohn *Meeresstille* if you please!' Lobster-red, Saminsky gathered up his score and stole surreptitiously down from his elevated position.

The other occasion was just a few days ago. After the fruitless discussion we had had with Tcherepnin, the conductors were grumbling quietly away that they were still being given no opportunity to conduct. The grumbling grew to a crescendo when Tcherepnin himself started waving his arms about on the podium. We decided we would register our protest by ostentatiously leaving the class, but could not agree exactly when to carry out this manoeuvre. Eventually we realized it would soon be time for the break, so we decided the best time for our demonstration would be when we reconvened at the end of the break. Tcherepnin carried on conducting for ages, very slowly and repeating virtually every bar three times. When at last he finally finished, he turned to the orchestra and said, 'Gentlemen, we shall not be taking a break today, the class is now terminated.' We all just sat there: we had planned to make a fool of him, but instead he had made a fool of us, and moreover had not given any of us a chance to wave our arms about for the whole of the class!

Coming back to today's events, after talking interminably and expertly manipulating the conversation, he smoothly extricated himself from the snare we had attempted to set for him by sweetly bidding us good day and leaving. Before that he had declared emotionally, 'Now, gentlemen, I shall continue to supervise my students Klimov and Malko until the spring, see them through their graduation, and perhaps after that I shall step down.' At this point he bashfully lowered his eyes, while we covertly smiled at one another in blissful anticipation. 'But then again, I may stay on a bit longer, I don't know,' he went on thoughtfully. Our faces fell.

When Tcherepnin had gone, I brought back into focus one of the phrases

---

1 Mikhail Klimov (1881–1937), choral conductor, later professor at the St Petersburg Conservatoire.

he had uttered: 'Well, if you like, you may work out your own timetable!' I urged that we do exactly this, and the idea gained support. We decided that three people would conduct at each lesson, and proceeded to draw up a list. If this comes off it will be excellent, otherwise Christmas will come and I shall not have conducted once, which would be terrible! In reality, however, had he asked me to conduct during the autumn I would have disgraced myself badly, never in my life having held a baton, but for the last three weeks I have been practising at home, in front of the mirror, and have got the hang of it pretty well. So now when the time comes for me to have to perform I shall be perfectly calm and confident, and I warrant I shall be no worse at it than Messrs Saminsky & Co.

17 December

A few days ago I received an invitation to attend a gathering of 'emerging composers' at the Conservatoire with the intention of putting together a programme for a concert to take place in the Small Hall in January. Anyone with compositions, chamber music, vocal, ensemble or piano to their name could submit and perform them, following which there would be a secret ballot and the works receiving the most votes would be performed in a concert. The idea came from Mme Ranushevich, a pianist and composer who graduated last year from Solovyov's[1] class. Ranushevich is an educated person of indeterminate age somewhere between thirty and sixty, and it is not impossible that she has some qualities as a composer. As many as fifty people had been invited, but only seven turned up. Four offerings were performed: some songs by Ranushevich, of which one ('Two Little Clouds') was good, another tolerable and the rest feeble. Abutkov, who graduated alongside Ranushevich in the spring, sang and played some interminable and utterly unmemorable pieces, compared to which a song by Saminsky actually appeared beautiful. After that I played some of my piano 'doggies':[2] 'Reproach', 'Eastern Song', 'Tragedy', 'Humoresque démoniaque', 'Fairy Tale' and 'Phantom'. They were a great success, eliciting a variety of reactions. It was agreed that we should meet again in a week's time, in what was hoped would be greater numbers. For interest's sake the other six balloted on my pieces: 'Fairy Tale' got 6, 'Humoresque démoniaque' – 4, 'Eastern Song' – 3, 'Reproach' – 2, 'Tragedy' – 0 ('Phantom' was not voted on). Initially 'Tragedy' was much liked, but then people found fault with the major thirds in the second subject and it dropped out of favour.

1   Nikolay Solovyov (1846–1915), composer and critic.
2   The nickname (because of their 'bite') given by Vasily Morolyov, the Sontsovka veterinary surgeon who encouraged the youthful composer's musical ambitions, to his more developed but still juvenile piano pieces, several of which were later revised for his first published opuses. 'Fairy Tale' and 'Phantom' are two of the *Four Pieces for Piano*, Op. 3.

The other thing that has completely fallen from grace is *Portrait of a Summer*, thus fulfilling my prediction. The decision was taken to put on a concert instead.

My chess partner, Struve, went away 'for a couple of days' to Yurev,[1] but he has not been here for two weeks now. I miss playing chess very much. In January I must absolutely join the Chess Society.

On Friday I went to the student concert, only my second time in four years, something people found it hard to believe. It was a terribly long and boring evening, and there were not many people I knew there. On top of it all someone stole my galoshes. When I complained about this, people cried, 'That's nothing! Ysaÿe had his violin worth sixty thousand stolen at a concert, poor fellow, now there's a real tragedy for you!' But others objected that it was probably just a publicity stunt, to which the Ysaÿists retorted that their man was in no need of publicity.

25 December

Christmas Day and Mama's birthday. Our family all seems to have notable birthdays: Mama was born on the same day as Jesus Christ, while my birthday is a hundred days into the year, 11 April being the hundred and first day of the year. I got one very interesting present today. Recently Nadya Petrova was given a toy, a shaggy-haired teddy bear. I was immediately attracted to him and started to play with him myself. 'Do you really like it?' I was asked. 'He's really lovely!' 'Well, you just wait, we might get one for you since you love him so much.' 'All right, all right, don't tease!'

And now suddenly, today, on a huge great tray, Mama, Papa and Aunt Tanya, laughing triumphantly, brought in a great big furry bear! An enchanting animal; everyone who came fell for him, and Andryusha Rayevsky declared, 'I'm going to get my Sasha one just like him.' In short my bear is a great success and now sits in my room on the table, looking slyly about him out of his beady eyes.

A few days ago I finally wrote out Bessonova's pieces for her, a waltz and a 'Pas d'Espagne'. Of course they are completely worthless, in the first place because they are dances and have no independent existence, and in the second because all she has done is filch whatever she could from her friends. Nevertheless I must admit that they sound quite good and are not as elementary as one might suppose. Their structure is plausible, the music flows quite logically. The last piece demonstrates a real musical feeling, all the more surprising since Bessonova is terribly lazy and knows nothing of elementary theory, not to mention harmony. She cannot even write out her

---

1   In Estonia, now (and before the nineteenth-century Russification of the Baltic provinces) known as Tartu.

own work. She had imagined this would be just as much of a problem for me as well, and was astonished that I made it all look so easy. Now she is of course delighted and even more insistent that I must come and visit her. Her name-day is on the 24th, but it will be celebrated on the 25th, so I was invited for that evening. Naturally I thanked her very much and said how touched I was, but regretted that I would not be able to come as it was the birthday of my Mama.

The second meeting of the 'emerging composers' took place on the 23rd and, ye gods, was even worse than the first one. This time nine people were present, all of them, practically without exception, the personification of dullness. To be fair, the one exception does have undoubted talent: Rastropovich. The others are, musically speaking, neither fish nor fowl nor good red herring, neither listeners nor serious musicians but something in between: they would like to be the latter but in truth most of them are little more than the former. Once again there was a secret ballot, and the results for my pieces were: 'Fairy Tale' – 6 (out of eight), the song 'The boat cast off'[1] – 5, 'Humoresque démoniaque'[2] – 4, 'Reproach' – 2, 'Processional', 'Eastern Song', 'Fête sacrée' – 0. We shall reconvene once more. A legend about me is already in circulation: that Prokofiev cannot bear to hear two consonant notes in succession!

---

1 Setting of a poem by Alexey Apukhtin, later revised and published as Op. 9 No. 2.
2 This may be the piece identified by Samuel Shlifshteyn ('S. S. Prokof'yev: Materialy, Dokumenty, Vospominaniya', Moscow, 1956) as 'Humoresque in F minor' composed in 1907, the same year as 'Eastern Song' and 'Reproach'. None of these pieces was published with an opus number. There seems to be no information about 'Processional', 'Fête Sacrée' or 'Tragedy'.

1908

1 January

Happy New Year! Indeed! Because of it I had eight calls to pay today, and there are still two to do tomorrow. Looked at from a vertical perspective, this amounts to fifty-eight flights of stairs ascended and descended. However it was all interesting, because everywhere I went I was made very welcome. I spent the holiday quietly, going to only two parties. As usual we saw the New Year in with the Rayevskys. Aunt Tanya was feeling unsociable, not because she had quarrelled with anyone or anything, she simply wanted to stay on her own in her room.

Tomorrow at last is the day of our famous Conservatoire ball, which has dominated the dreams and ambitions of our class for half a year now. The ball is to be preceded by a concert: (1) two pianos – Anisimova and Ospovat; (2) recitation (without music) – Glagoleva; (3) solo piano – Sadovskaya; (4) trio – Gvirtsman, Zimbalist[1] and myself; Interval; (5) violin – Villik; (6) solo piano – Shvarts; (7) a concluding trifle, a piece by Glinka to be played by our trio. The concert will be followed by a ball. There are six organizers: the four committee members plus Fliege and one other person, distinguished by red bow-ties, while the other, second-class, citizens will have to make do with blue ones. It's a real shame that it conflicts with an invitation to the Pavskys, who really want me to be there, but since their do will start at seven while the first of my items in the Conservatoire concert is not until a quarter to ten, I shall be able to go the Pavskys first and then on to the Conservatoire.

4 January

Accordingly at half past seven I arrived at the Pavskys, where the company was really nice: a quartet of Frolovs, a duo of Skalons and a little later on the Dobryshins. It promised to be generally a very jolly time because they were all old friends. Lyolya Skalon has grown prettier and is turning into a very beautiful young lady, although lacking the last ounce of refinement. I managed to secure her for a long dance and talked to her of old times, teasing her gently about Riga, where she seems to have a perpetual hankering to go, and about her plans to become a writer. At twenty past nine Mama and I set off

---

[1] Not the celebrated violinist Efrem Zimbalist, but the cellist Solomon Zimbalist (b. 1892).

for the Conservatoire. Originally only Papa had intended to come to the concert, but in the end on the spur of the moment Mama and Aunt Tanya came too. Mama and I had just entered the room when five or so students descended on me from the top of the stairs like snow falling on my head, crying, 'Prokofiev, hurry up! Prokofiev, we've been waiting for you!' Apparently Zimbalist had not yet arrived either, and in fact he turned up ten minutes after I did. I had hardly entered the green room when Gvirtsman launched into: 'Do you have the nerve to go on stage and announce a change of programme?'

'With the greatest of pleasure,' I said, and before I knew what was happening found myself on stage addressing the audience. It all happened so quickly that I cannot now remember exactly what I said, although I remember that I spoke with feeling, more or less made sense, and did not rush my words. The first few items did not require my presence. First were Anisimova and Ospovat in 'Gnomes',[1] not too bad, beta minus. This was followed by Glagoleva reciting Nadson's 'Life'.[2] Nerves affected the start of this, so I was told, but she got better as she went on, so had a success and had to encore it. Next was Sadovskaya giving a rather colourless perfomance, and then Villik, who was excellent. Shvarts was ill, and after the interval we played our Mendelssohn trio. We played well and were highly praised; people who had heard our final rehearsal were amazed because then we had been appallingly incoherent having had only three rehearsals; but now we were really concentrating, were not nervous at all, in full possession of our faculties so had no memory lapses, and in consequence gave a splendid performance. Straight away after the Mendelssohn we did Glinka's 'Doubt',[3] also impeccably, but it is of course complete rubbish as music. This ended the programme, but suddenly up popped Glagoleva to play the pieces Shvarts was supposed to have contributed; they were not in any case very interesting pieces and the way she played them was uninspiring, so the net result for her was that she lost more than she gained from performing.

The concert over, we adjourned to have our photograph taken in one of the classrooms transformed for the occasion into a drawing room. While we were arranging ourselves on the seats, the audience milled about at the doors and peered in, their noses pressed to the glass. 'Look, gentlemen, we're making a menagerie of ourselves!' someone exclaimed, pointing at the crowd. At last the camera shutter clicked open and the magnesium flared. Afterwards I

---

1 Grieg's 'Procession of the Gnomes', No. 2 of Three Pieces For Piano (1860), evidently in a duet version.
2 Much anthologized poem written in 1886 by Semyon Nadson shortly before his death from tuberculosis.
3 'Somneniye' ('Doubt') is a well-known song by Glinka to words by Kukol'nik; it also exists in a version for piano trio.

walked back with Bessonova to the green room, but it was empty. All at once Glagoleva came in, followed by her mother. Glagoleva introduced me in a most flattering manner, we chatted about this and that, and then at Mme Glagoleva's request, since no one else was there, I played one of my little pieces, 'Reproach'. Mme Glagoleva is a very charming lady, but as for her daughter, I have lost much of my liking for her, first because of her misguided decision to perform in place of the absent Shvarts; second, although many people found her particularly beautiful today, her beauty is not of a type I particularly admire; third, she behaved all evening in an irritatingly lackadaisical manner, spending all the time in the artists' room languidly inclining her head to those around her.

The dancing began. I sat out the first waltz, because waltzes always make my head spin, then danced the next few dances with Bessonova, with whom I also spent the intermissions, so generally, it could be said, I was with her. She dances well but extremely passionately, too passionately in fact, so that it is hard not to be thinking 'one can have too much of a good thing'. Bessonova has hundreds of admirers: the little dears stand a discreet distance away, casting envious glances at her. This species of *signor* is beyond me, they seem to have no respect for themselves and so deserve none from others. Bessonova was goading them by spending more than half the evening with me. Early on she was her usual cheerful self, but little by little her mood darkened and she adopted a fretful and difficult air: probably she was a victim to that absurdly strung-up frame of mind in which one feels something is missing without being able to say what it is.

However, at that moment we encountered Bessonova's mother, who promptly engaged her daughter in conversation. Seeing my chance, I smartly absented myself and found myself in the middle of the dance hall. After dancing with two or three girls I asked Esche senior for a dance. She is very nice, in every sense superior to Bessonova, although suffering from a tendency to be pretentious and to put on airs; there is a lack of simplicity there. I spent quite a long time with her, and was most of all struck by the fact that she is only sixteen but looks at least eighteen.

After that I danced briefly with Bessonova again, and at half past three, although the evening was still not over, took myself home. My general impression of the ball was much better than I had expected.

11 January

I shall not go to the Chess Club today, I'll go on Sunday. I was there last Friday and saw Malyutin, but one has to be twenty-one to join the Society. Also, it costs 15 roubles for the privilege, plus 50 kopecks entrance fee each time, but tournaments are open to non-members. I managed to get permission from Mama and Papa to visit the Society (the 'Club', as they call it) but not more than once a week.

The tournament starts on the 15th, and there are categories for Levels 4 and 3, which Malyutin recommended I enter for. I am trying my hardest to persuade Struve, but he has exams coming up and will probably want to duck out of it.

Our complaint against Tcherepnin has been investigated, following which there was a lengthy round-table discussion with him, distinguished by interminable political wrangling, but he himself was quite amiable. The upshot is that there are now officially only five of us in the class, which means it should be easier to get some practical experience. Any more radical changes will have to wait until next year. In the meantime he promised to let Kankarovich and Saminsky conduct at a student concert, and recommended us all to attend the opera class. This is putting on three operas: Cui's *The Snow Prince*, Nicolai's *The Merry Wives of Windsor*, and an opera by one of our students, Galkovsky, called *The Gypsies*. It's admirable of the Conservatoire to put on an opera composed by a student, except that (by all accounts) this particular one is not a very good example of the genre . . . in the style of Tchaikovsky, but ten times more primitive.

I went to the opera class for the first time today because I had to play the piano for *The Merry Wives* while Brauer conducted and the whole class sang. He took a terribly fast tempo, and I had never seen the score before, so I had to strain every nerve and deploy all my skill to avoid falling flat on my face. I seem to have managed since it all went off well and people were amazed at my sight-reading prowess. Now I am supposed to coach some of the male and female singers in their roles.

Not long ago, in one of the General Subject classes, I had to write an essay of my choice on one of six topics about *Onegin*.[1] I chose the most difficult: 'Onegin as an example of the Superfluous Man',[2] and at first could not get to grips with it at all. But I followed the rules, made out a plan of the essay, and structurally it worked as a composition. My marks for the second term were: Physics – 5, History – 5 minus, General History of Literature – 5.

The photograph taken on the 2nd has been developed and can now be seen. Some people (including me) came out really well, but the general impression is hopeless, because the camera was too big and too near, so the perspective is completely distorted: the people at the front are the size of handkerchiefs, those at the back no bigger than a 10-kopeck piece.

---

1 Prokofiev means Pushkin's verse novel *Eugene Onegin* rather than Tchaikovsky's eponymous opera based on it.
2 The name given to a seminal character type found throughout nineteenth-century Russian literature, derived from Byron's *Childe Harold*, exemplifying a man alive to social, political and moral issues but too hidebound and disaffected to act on them.

The wedding of Katya Rayevskaya and Palya¹ Ignatiev took place on the 9th. I was the number-two best man of eight – Shurik² being number one. It was the first time I had fulfilled this role, and at a high-society wedding to boot. But everything passed off all right, and I even managed my particular job of leading the party round the analoy³ without treading on the wedding dress's train. The couple were married in the Engineers' Castle,⁴ in the very room where the Emperor Paul was strangled. Mama was the proxy⁵ mother of the bride, the proxy father was Tobizen, the Governor of Kharkov. The bride looked incredibly beautiful this evening.

13 January

Chigorin has died. Poor, poor man! To tell the truth, the real Chigorin, Chigorin the Great, died some years ago; in recent years there have been no more than occasional flickers of his former greatness to be seen. All the same the death of a Russian champion is something to be mourned, because 'the citadel is abandoned – the citadel entire, the idol overthrown – the God destroyed', as was said of Steinitz when he lost to Lasker. Such is the fate of all champions: Zuckertort lost his power before he died, Steinitz was overthrown by Lasker in his last five years, and even if Chigorin was never actually overthrown his was still an abandoned citadel. No one defeated him, but all his challengers gradually grew mightier than he. The year 1903 was the last time he showed himself to be the true Chigorin: he carried off the First Prize in Vienna with a successful challenge to the Rice gambit, won the majority of his games as black against Lasker, and was the victor of the Kiev tournament, but later, after a respectable win at Cambridge Springs, he joined the ranks of the least successful among international players. True, he took Fifth Prize and a victory over Salwe at Nuremberg – these were victories, but not great ones! At the last Łódz tournament, when Chigorin was lying on his deathbed although many people thought he was merely evading taking part, he would not have won the First Prize: the winner was Rubinstein while the older Russian master would not have made more than third or

---

1 Pavel Ignatiev, an army captain in the Guards Engineer Regiment. The marriage was unhappy owing to Ignatiev's profligacy and boorish arrogance, and ended in divorce after three years.
2 Prokofiev's first cousin and the bride's brother, Alexander Rayevksy.
3 High lectern on which holy books or icons are displayed.
4 The magnificent Mikhailovsky Palace was dedicated on the feast day of the Archangel Michael in 1800 as the official residence of Tsar Paul I. Paul's guardian angel did not, however, protect him from being murdered in his own bedroom soon after taking up residence. In 1823 the building was taken over by the School of Military Engineering, hence the name it is still known by today. It is now a museum.
5 Traditionally in a Russian Orthodox wedding the bride's parents do not attend the ceremony but appoint proxies.

fourth. After that, had there been a title match for the chess crown of Russia, the venerable Russian idol would have certainly been dethroned and brought down. Now Rubinstein has the crown by inheritance. He is worthy of it, and will bear it as nobly in Europe as Chigorin did ten or twenty years ago. The crown indeed may well become a worldwide one, for the young champion promises much, and sooner or later, in life or in death, Lasker will be forced to yield. Although said to be the best of men, Rubinstein will never earn that instinctive support and love, his triumphs will never be taken so much to heart, as the great Russian master, the subtle analyst and chess player of genius, Mikhail Ivanovich Chigorin.

27 January

The day before yesterday my concert grand piano was delivered. Our German & Grossman, bought four years ago at auction for 285 roubles, has recently given unmistakable signs of giving up the ghost, and I have long been promised a concert grand. So now we have acquired one, a Ratke, costing new 1,300 roubles, but as this one has been used a few times for concerts it was on offer for 1000, and confidentially to us for 900. Our old one was taken in part exchange for 275, so altogether it will have cost us 625 roubles. It's a fine instrument, of course, but the sound is much softer, although they say it will get more brilliant as it is played, and in any case it will sound bigger in a bigger room. Myaskovsky is coming on Wednesday to 'see the piano'. When he was here ten days ago we played through Beethoven's Ninth Symphony; he told me it was the first time anyone had managed to get to the end of it with him. In general he is a friendly and straightforward person, and conducted himself much more graciously when he visited than I expected him to. Zakharov was also here at Christmas, and I also went to his house, but we have not yet quite managed to hit it off. Mikhail Mikhailovich Chernov[1] came to see us today; he looked through my latest compositions and generally approved them. He said he would try to arrange for some of them to be played at one of the 'Evenings of Contemporary Music'.[2]

---

1 Mikhail Chernov (1879–1938), composer, musicologist and teacher, who gave the young Prokofiev some lessons in counterpoint when he first came to St Petersburg and later introduced him to the organizers of the 'Evenings of Contemporary Music'.
2 The 'Evenings of Contemporary Music' shared with Diaghilev's *Mir Isskustva* ('World of Art') magazine not only some of its founding members but a generally non-academic, art-for-art's-sake aesthetic. The five founders of the 'Evenings' were the 'Nevsky Pickwickians' as Alexander Benois dubbed them, the cultivated dilettantes Walter Nouvel and Alfred Nurok, both close to Diaghilev, the critic Vyacheslav Karatygin, and the pianist–composers Ivan Kryzhanovsky and Alexander Medem. The 'Evenings', which began in 1902, were conceived as a radical alternative to the largely mainstream repertoire of the Conservatoire, the Russian Music Society and Mitrofan Belyayev's Russian Symphony Concerts.

I am going to the Chess Society today, to play with Traubenberg[1] (Baron von Rausch von Traubenberg). I have not mentioned him before, but have thought about him a good deal. He is a young student who enrolled in the Society at Level 5 in the autumn, rising rapidly until he has now almost reached Level 2. Struve says, 'Traubenberg's laurels give you no peace!' The last time I was at the Society I beat his friend, who is not quite as strong as Traubenberg, and now I am about to play the man himself.

3 February

Arensky's *Nal and Damayanti*[2] is a thoroughly bad opera! So far I have found a total of three beautiful moments in it, and they are really beautiful, but most of it is pure note-spinning! Worse than Asafyev! Apparently it is not doing very well and will soon be taken off.

Alpers is a very nice person (although childish). She seems to be a good friend of the Frolovs. We must talk about this some time.

6 February

On Monday I finally got to conduct. When Tcherepnin turned to me and said, 'All right, why don't you have a go at the first movement?' I was so stunned I had to ask him to repeat it: 'What did you say?'

I climbed on to the podium, forgot my score, came down again to get it, went up again, and began. At first it was rather tentative, but things soon fell into place and it all went smoothly. Of course my total lack of experience for example made it hard for me to distinguish one woodwind instrument from another, so when I had to indicate specific entries I couldn't tell where was the oboe and where the clarinet, all I could do was gesture vaguely in the right direction. I also found it hard to pick out the sounds of the different instruments, somehow I couldn't hear them properly, and on one occasion when things started coming apart it was four bars before I could identify the culprit who had come in early. All the same it went off very well and Tcherepnin, who usually drew novices off to one side to berate them, said to me, 'Well, not a bad beginning, not bad at all', and sent me off with his blessing.

The other conducting students congratulated me on a successful debut

---

1 Baron Konstantin Rausch von Traubenberg (1871–1935) was an artist and sculptor who exhibited at the 6th Exhibition of the Society of Russian Artists and at the Paris Exhibition 'New Arts from Russia' in 1908. Nikolay Gumilyov, writing to fellow poet Valery Bryusov (from whose novel Prokofiev was to draw the libretto for *The Fiery Angel*) had this to say of Rausch's work: 'The sculptor Rausch von Traubenberg did not have many works in the show, but displayed great taste and a loving attention to the lessons of the past.'
2 Composed in 1904.

and said they had not expected me to turn in nearly such a lively display. The work I conducted was Schubert's 'Tragic' Symphony.

24 February

For too long I have been neglecting my diary, and have accumulated a mass of things to write about. There was an incident with Balalayev. What happened was that whereas I have never particularly taken to him, he for some reason likes me: he recently gave me a 5 and a verbal commendation for my essay on *Boris Godunov*.[1] Before that there had been quite an amusing incident: he had set us a passage from *The Miserly Knight*[2] to learn by heart, and the moment he called out 'Prokofiev!', I picked up on the final line and announced in a loud voice, 'Baron, you lie!' Balalayev spun round in his chair, thinking I was about to say something cheeky, but seeing that I was calmly continuing, the whole class burst out laughing. I got a 5 for that recitation as well. Anyhow, at the start of one lesson, not having noticed that Balalayev had already begun lecturing, I was still whispering to my neighbour. Balalayev, who was in a bad mood and who in any case had a penchant for threatening people with exclusion from his class for making a noise, rounded on me, shouting, 'Listen you: either leave the class or stop talking!' – an unnecessarily rude and unjustified rebuke. I did not leave the class there and then (although I later regretted not doing so), but decided to cut the next five classes. At the next one Bessonova announced that Prokofiev would not be attending any more.

'I know he has been annoyed with me for some time now,' said Balalayev. 'It's all because I gave him only a 4 last term. Petty, very petty! . . .' And later he said to another student, 'Well, I'm not angry with him any longer, so he can call it off now.'

I stayed away for five lessons. However, wanting to keep abreast, I asked one of the girls, Alpers, to let me know by postcard what had been covered in the lessons, which she was kind enough to do. She was in fact very generous about it (not that it caused me to alter my former opinion of her). In the course of quite a long conversation I asked her about the Frolovs. She said that she knew them well, they were frequent and welcome visitors at her home, and she had heard about me from them. It ended up with me being invited to her house on Saturday. At her request I got her two passes to the general rehearsal – the first favour I have done for a girl in our class. Later I met her at the Maly Theatre with the Frolovs. Both her beaux were invited into the box; I sat in the sixth row with her mother and father.

The next event was the opening of *The Ring of the Nibelungen* at the

---

1   The verse play by Pushkin, not the opera by Musorgsky.
2   Another verse drama by Pushkin also the basis of an opera, this time by Rachmaninov.

Mariinsky Theatre. Those who had subscriptions last year could renew them; I renewed our two stalls in the fifteenth row. But I wanted to hear the whole cycle twice. I got nothing in the first open subscription draw, so I tried again for the third. In order to improve my chances, I took along Elena and Masha. However, by the time the queue got down to them they were unsuccessful. Twice I managed a place in the draw, and was lucky both times with a 25 and a 64. However behind me there were two women, each of whom drew three times and got six zeros. All in all it took me four and a half hours, but at the end of it I got a seat in the fourth row, near the left gangway, which I consider one of the best seats in the theatre.

On Thursday 14th M. M. Chernov at last introduced me to the 'Evenings of Contemporary Music'. I took along some of my short piano pieces, volumes two and three (up to and including 'Entreaties'[1]). Only four people were there: Nurok,[2] Nouvel,[3] Medem[4] and Senilov.[5] Mikhail Mikhailovich gave me a very warm recommendation and I sat down to play my pieces. The first was 'Snow', which at once grabbed their attention and pleasantly surprised them: original, descriptive, logical and beautiful were some of the adjectives they used to describe it. They very much liked the other pieces as well, and afterwards they all came rushing up and enfolded me in their embrace. 'You must absolutely come to our Thursdays and bring whatever you have written!'

Medem (for a long time I did not realize he was a teacher at the Conservatoire) asked me, 'Did you graduate from the Conservatoire as a pianist?'

'Excuse me, I'm still on the Junior course!'

'The Junior course?? You have such a marvellous technique, and your octaves are so good.'

'You may not believe this, but, I've just come from a lesson with Winkler, where I really came to grief with my octaves!'

Later on Myaskovsky greeted me by saying, 'Nouvel tells me you created a furore at the "Contemporaries" with your pieces!'

2 March

On Thursday I again went to the 'Contemporaries', taking my Sonata No. 4 (in D minor)[6] and once again the third volume of my short pieces. Of the Sonata the first movement was the best received, while the short pieces

---

1 'Molby' ('Entreaties'), one of Two Pieces for piano (1908). 'Snezhok' ('Snow') is the first of the Two Pieces.
2 Alfred Nurok (1860–1919), critic and writer, musical editor of *Mir Isskustva* magazine. He also wrote criticism for *Apollon* magazine.
3 Walter Nouvel (1871–1949), critic and writer, a close associate of Serge Diaghilev and Alexander Benois.
4 Alexander Medem (1871–1927), pianist, composer, professor at the St Petersburg Conservatoire.
5 Vladimir Senilov (1875–1918), composer.
6 The Sonata No. 4 (1908) in the juvenile catalogue, not the later Sonata No. 4, Op. 29.

repeated the success they had enjoyed before, especially 'Snow', 'Reminiscence' and 'Elan'. Kryzhanovsky[1] said, 'Leave out the triads: they really don't sound right among your harmonies.'

There was general agreement that they would like to hear the pieces performed in a concert. Since this would be against the rules for a student still at the Conservatoire, a pseudonym was suggested, for example Sergeyev. However under pressure from Papa (with whom in fact I agree) I shall probably ask them to put it off until the autumn: once I've finished the Fugue course I won't be so worried about any possible unpleasantnesses with the Conservatoire!

The Conservatoire, with student forces, is putting on an opera by a student, Galkovsky: *The Gypsies*, along with Cui's short opera *The Snow Prince*. As I predicted, *The Gypsies* is terrible. It has practically no material to speak of, and contains so little of interest that one can only pray for deliverance from it! It does have two beautiful but unrelated leitmotivs: Aleko's and the betrayal theme, but the main Gypsies theme has simply been plagiarized and the rest is all either dull or stolen, and sometimes both. I have already had some intercourse with the composer, but it has usually ended with him getting angry and walking away. I hear that Glazunov, Klimov and the rest, in fact all concerned, are unhappy with the opera, except for Korsakov who loves it and knows it practically by heart. There is no man so wise that he cannot make a fool of himself! A feeble opera by a feeble talent! For God's sake, they'd have done better to put on my *Undine*, which is lying unfinished at the bottom of the sea!

3 March

Zakharov came yesterday, and we played Scriabin's *Divine Poem*.[2] What a joy! I adore this work. After dinner we went together to the dress rehearsal of *The Gypsies*, which was due to start at eight o'clock. Galkovsky's opera is pretty worthless, but Cui's was actually worse. By this I mean that although it has more, and better, material, the overall impression is so lacking in individuality (not helped by a terrible production) that God preserve us from the like. I stuck out *The Snow Prince* to the end, but ran out of patience with *The Gypsies*. Remembering that Tcherepnin had once said that above the stage was a good place to listen to opera, I decided to give that a try. I asked Sadovskaya[3] if she wanted to come with me, and she said she had never been

---

1 Ivan Kryzhanovsky (1867–1924). Although a doctor by training, having spent some time in the laboratory of Ivan Pavlov at the Imperial Medical Academy, Kryzhanovsky studied composition with Rimsky-Korsakov and was admired as a critic and teacher – Myaskovsky studied harmony with him.
2 Symphony No. 3 (1904).
3 Yevgenia Sadovskaya, piano student at the Conservatoire.

up there, so we clambered up a mass of straight and spiral staircases almost up to the roof of the building, and there, from the wooden walkways across the fly gallery above the stage, we listened to Galkovsky's ill-starred music and feasted our eyes on Platonov far below us on the stage, gesticulating like a little insect in his Onegin-like costume.

Then we came down the way we had come, but decided that rather than go back to the stalls of the Great Hall we would try listening from the balcony. Although the Conservatoire has its own electricity supply, it is very stingy with it, consequently even though there was a dress rehearsal going on, only one and half lamps were burning in the foyer and upstairs there was total darkness. Sadovskaya and I decided to press on nevertheless, and at the top of the stairs found ourselves in complete blackness. Feeling our way and tripping over steps, we searched hand in hand for a door into the balcony. We found one – locked. We found another – also locked. By now our eyes had got accustomed to the gloom, and by the flickering light from the moon outside we saw another door right over on the other side. We ran over; by good fortune this one was open, and thus we found ourselves in a completely deserted balcony. This was perfect: we could listen to the music if we wanted to, or talk if we wanted to without disturbing anyone, and no one would come and bother us. We made good use of it and spent the whole opera chatting in a very friendly and open way about all kinds of trivia, what we thought about things, and I paid her several rather bold and pointed compliments. The rehearsal ended, we successfully found our way downstairs and said goodbye, and Zakharov walked home with me.

10 March

On Thursday when our History teacher appeared for the class he was in the foulest of moods. Normally he jokes around with the girls, but today he announced stonily that he would be going round the whole class testing us on our set task: the Emancipation of the Peasants, about which we were all supposed to know everything there is to know. One after another everyone got 2s, only the best got a 3, or 4 minus at the most. I was almost the last to be called, but finally it was my turn. I had been sitting quietly, thinking that I knew the subject well enough to count on at least a 4. But suddenly I was struck with an inspired thought, and when my name was called I collected up five history books from other students, opened them at the page which dealt with the Emancipation of the Peasants, and piled them up on the table where 'Ginger Whiskers' was sitting. Unhurriedly I laid them out on the table and was about to give my answers. But before I could utter so much as word, he asked abruptly, 'Just a moment! What's the meaning of this?!'

In my most innocent tone of voice, I answered, 'It's so that if I forget something I can look it up . . .'

He lost his temper: 'Get out! I never thought to see this from you! The girls, now, they're always making a row and larking about, but now you're doing the same thing, acting the fool! I did not expect it of you, not at all!'

Impassively I set about collecting up the five textbooks and returned to my seat.

'I never thought you would play the fool like this, I really did not!' he called after me.

'But I do know the lesson well,' I replied, with an air of unholy innocence.

'I don't want to hear it! I don't want anything to do with you!'

He made no entry in the register, not giving me either a 2 or a 5, nothing but a little dash. Obviously he will grill me up, down and sideways at the next lesson, which means I'll have to revise the entire History course. Whatever possessed me to do what I did? I can't say. Probably I just wanted to see what would happen. Anyway it greatly amused the whole class.

12 March

Glagoleva buttonholed me on Wednesday and asked me if I was going to *Valkyrie* that evening. 'No, my subscription tickets are for Wednesdays and Fridays.'

'Well, I'm going this evening.'

It so happened that I had on me a little book with the libretto of *Valkyrie* in German and a note of the leitmotivs. I gave the book to her, saying that before hearing the opera she really should have some idea of the leitmotivs. After the lesson the conversation again turned to *Valkyrie*. I sat down at the piano and played Glagoleva some of the most important themes. Everyone crowded round at first, but then gradually drifted away, leaving just the two of us. Glagoleva wanted me to tell her the plot of the opera, so I explained that there was not just one single opera but four, all linked. Then I narrated the whole of the *Nibelungenlied*, going into particular detail for *Valkyrie*, and illustrated the musical ideas on the piano. Then we went to the library to get a piano score so that I could demonstrate more specific musical illustrations, but there was not one there so we returned empty-handed and I played what I could from memory. Little by little we branched out from the Nibelungs into other topics, discussing Korsakov and the fact that Steinberg[1] was about to marry his daughter.

'Is she attractive?' asked Glagoleva.

'Yes, she has an interesting face.'

'What do you mean – interesting? There are beautiful faces and there are ugly faces, but I don't think I know what you mean by an interesting face ...'

---

1 Maximilian Steinberg (1883–1946), composer and teacher. Much loved by his teacher (and eventual father-in-law) Rimsky-Korsakov, he never fulfilled his early promise as a composer but became a highly respected teacher of composition in the Rimsky tradition, numbering Shostakovich among his pupils.

'I mean a face that is neither beautiful nor ugly but one that makes an impression when you see it, and makes you want to know what sort of person lives behind such a face.'

Glagoleva was bowled over by *Valkyrie*; I gave her Sviridenko's *The Ring of the Nibelung* to read.

22 March

At four o'clock today I played the piano on stage for *The Snow Prince*, since there is to be a repeat performance of it along with *The Gypsies*, and then at two minutes past five went to the canteen. Bessonova introduced me to Lesnenko. We chatted briefly about this and that, and she said she was sorry I could not come on Sunday. Then she said to me, 'We go in the same direction, don't we?' Lesnenko left, and Bessonova and I walked out together.

30 March

On Wednesday I heard Galkovsky's *The Gypsies*, which was receiving yet another performance. It was really the first time I had listened to it properly, and overall I suppose it was just about acceptable, but still pretty worthless. M. M. Chernov said to me afterwards, 'Shamelessly bad music; I wouldn't swap a single piece from your notebooks for both these entire operas!' I bowed low in acknowledgement.

It so happened that I hardly knew anybody who was at this performance and the intervals were very long, so to relieve my hellish boredom I sought out Esche junior. I wanted to restore our former good relations, as her indifference had greatly upset me. I didn't expect to be able to do much about this here, as she would probably make her usual fuss and anyway would be bound to be flanked by her two girl friends, so having nothing better to do I thought I would just keep an eye on her from a distance. However, all the way through the interval Esche junior appeared to have vanished into thin air, so I was just about to return to my seat in a thoroughly bad temper, when whom should I run into in a deserted corridor but my quarry, alone and glancing from side to side as if looking for someone. This was an unexpected piece of luck, so I went up to her and started a conversation about nothing in particular, the opera and other things. Seeing that I was not going to be nasty to her or make caustic remarks, she did not try to make her escape, but we did not talk for long because her friend soon made an appearance. At the end of the performance she showed herself more than willing to chat to me, and so harmony has been restored. I am very pleased about this.

Academic lessons finished on Friday. I did not go to the last History lesson, and the great historian, no doubt mindful of the famous incident with the five history textbooks, did not call my name. I was sitting listening to the rehearsal for the Sheremetyev[1] concert, when suddenly Dobrzhenets appeared: 'Alexei Stepanovich[2] wants to see you in class.'

My first thought was to ask Dobrzhenets to say that he had not been able to find me, and then make myself scarce, but he would not let me do that, so after abusing him roundly (at which he took considerable offence) I moved off in the direction of the class. On the way I met Palechek:[3] 'Are you free at the moment? Good, then please come quickly to the opera class; they are desperate for an accompanist!'

Naturally I was delighted, and went to the opera class. But when 'Ginger Whiskers' got to hear of it he became extremely annoyed and declared that since Prokofiev was not willing to come and be examined he proposed to mark me down from 5 to 4 for the whole year. However, if I wished I could come tomorrow and be tested outside the class. Since I had had nothing but 5s and no nils (i.e. no response) for the whole year, I decided not to be tested, on the grounds that he has no right to give me anything less than a 5. But the following day as luck would have it I ran into him in the corridor when he was sitting on the windowsill questioning Bessonova. Catching sight of me, he called me over and asked me a ridiculously easy question. I began my answer, but without letting me finish he said, 'I always knew you would know that!'

At the end of the class the committee convened to settle the year-end marks. It was announced that anyone having more than two 2s (that is to say, anyone with three 2s out of the four marks) would not be allowed to participate in the public examinations. Gvirtsman and Fliege fell into this category, and appeals to Glazunov, it seemed, would be of no avail. In conclusion, Rusinov[4] declared that in all his experience he had never come across such a rowdy and disobedient class, especially the girls.

To my astonishment, my marks were a nice round 5 for all subjects, without even a single minus. The same was true of Osipova. Today the sixth form had its photograph taken with money left over from the ball on 2 January. Although the photographer Fliege engaged on that occasion had made such a brilliant success of his magnesium photograph that nobody was able to get a single copy from it, we still gave him another try. I would rather it had been just the class, and lobbied hard for this, but other voices insisted on inviting Glazunov and Nikolay Ivanovich Novich, and all our teachers and even some of the former teachers. We'll see how it turns out.

1 Count Alexander Sheremetyev (1859–1919), conductor and musical organizer who founded a concert series in St Petersburg.
2 Petrovich, the History teacher.
3 Josef Palechek (1842–1915), Czech-born bass singer, soloist and producer at the Mariinsky Theatre, responsible for premiere productions there of Rimsky-Korsakov's *Mlada* and *Servilia*, Professor of Opera at the St Petersburg Conservatoire.
4 Rusinov was the Inspector (Head) of the Conservatoire's Academic School and also taught Physics.

3 April

I had been very on edge at my recent lessons with Winkler, because the prospect of imminent examinations always makes him jumpy and impatient, behaving more like a Stinkler than a Winkler.[1] But surprisingly enough the lessons proceeded with great good humour, and for the final one he set up a mock exam and made me run through the whole of my technical programme. When it was over he observed, not without an element of surprise, that it had been not bad, and he considered I was ready for the examination. This meant more to me than anything; for two days I did not practise at all, then played for an hour and a half, and then on the day of the exam just for half an hour before setting off, full of confidence. Thanks to Winkler's approval I was hardly nervous at all and ran calmly through my scales, arpeggios and thirds (the latter, unfortunately, not too well although they are my speciality), then a pretty decent, brisk account of the Clementi octave study. The exam finished with Czerny's A flat Study in trills; this went very well indeed and brought forth applause from the other examinees and listeners in the hall, which is not supposed to happen. In general the exam went very well for the class, Winkler was beaming, we distinguished ourselves (Burakinskaya 4.5, Troitskaya 5 – although she did not play as well as I did and was herself heard to say, 'If I get 5, Prokofiev should get 6.5!'). It's clear that I do have abilities as a pianist, since I practised very little this winter owing to lack of time, to the extent that I would be reluctant even to put a figure on the number of hours. I've been telling Winkler that I practise two hours a day ('Not enough, not enough . . . !'), but in truth it was rare for me even to do a full hour, and often I did nothing at all. Of course I'm not counting all the rest of the time I spend at the piano in composition, reading through scores and so on.

Now the public examination on the 25th is looming, which judging by the pieces that I have to play should go even better. If so then the way to Yesipova should be open to me, although I am getting on so well with Winkler that I shall be sorry to leave him.

Recently I have been voraciously stuffing myself with Wagner: two subscriptions to *The Ring*, and on top of that more of his music in the concerts by Sheremetyev and Nikisch, this year being the twenty-fifth anniversary of the composer's death. I've heard eleven Wagner performances in the last few days, and there are three more to come. After him I find I don't want to hear any other music, and I don't even have any inclination to compose – he seems to have percolated right through my fingers and into my pen. Because of him my C minor Sonata (No. 5)[2] has ground to a halt. This is the sonata I decided to compose in case I needed something to show Lyadov; from the

---

1 An untranslatable pun: 'Winkler turns into Svinkler' – *svinya* is Russian for swine.
2 Subsequently the first and third movements of the Sonata No. 4, Op. 29 (later marginal annotation by the composer).

perspective of the 'Evenings of Contemporary Music' it may appear a retrograde step, but the purity of its form and texture appeals to me very much. I told Myaskovsky that I had made a start on a sonata, and a little later he informed me that he had himself begun an A flat major Sonata, No. 3 (that is to say his seventh) and had got as far as the development. So, not to be outdone, I carried on to the recapitulation, but soon he let me know he had finished the first movement. I started my Finale, but Myaskovsky then told me he would be putting off writing the other movements of his sonata until the summer. I have his sonata here with me now, but I don't like it at all, especially its harmonic language.

18 April

Examinations, examinations! Lord, what I've had to do to prepare for this wretched History exam (tomorrow) – Papa arrived, and made me cram the whole syllabus. I've spent all Easter on it. But what is interesting is that while before I could not bear the thought of the Conservatoire, I miss it now I'm not going in to it. I've grown used to you, my love! I suppose it's only natural. I'm spending the holidays very quietly and unobtrusively, swotting my history, no outside interests, so of course that's the reason for my fond memories of the Conservatoire. A day or two ago, dropping in for some unimportant reason (to find out the exam timetable) I sat on the windowsill and chatted for an hour and half to Sadovskaya and Esche junior.

The thing about Alpers is that I really like her; she and I often walk back from the Conservatoire together as half of our way home is along the same route. On the first day of the Easter holiday I received a postcard with a picture of a small girl picking a bunch of huge flowers – much bigger than the girl – with this inscription: 'So many pretty flowers I see, how beautiful they are! (*Kitezh*)'. And on the reverse, 'Christ is risen!', with no signature. Such a witty card really impressed me. I thought it might be from Zakharov, because this is his favourite passage from *Kitezh*. And who but he would know the opera so well and would have a copy of it to quote the text exactly? I copied out the music from the passage in question and sent it to him, also without a signature. I thought of putting, 'He has risen indeed', but Mama said that it would be understood without that.

A few days later I had a reply in which he thanked me for thinking of him and for *Kitezh*, but he would not after all be able to come and make music with me, as he had promised, because he was so busy. It was obvious that either the flowers had not come from him, or that he did not want to admit it and was playing the innocent. There was no doubt that it had come from someone in the Conservatoire; it was not addressed to me by the usual first name and patronymic. I ran through the female students in my mind, and remembered that I had kept a card Alpers had once sent me about Balayev.

I looked it out and compared the handwriting. To my astonishment, the one was an exact replica of the other. So that was it! I did not expect such a thing from her, but how nice that someone was thinking of me! When I see her I must contrive some reason or other for exclaiming, 'My God, how many pretty flowers, how beautiful they are!' while maintaining an air of innocence; her expression will soon tell me whether it was really she who sent it, and at the same time betray her surprise that I have guessed the truth.

23 April

I have passed three of the General Subjects exams and a fourth, written one. So far I have the highest marks of anyone and am at the top of the class. Only Physics remains, which terrifies most people, but not me, at least not so far.

On the subject of the flowers, somehow I have not yet managed to tax Alpers with them. Two questions concern me: how much do I really like her? And specifically, what are her good qualities, those that make her truly stand out? Nothing particular springs to mind. What about her less attractive side? Nothing much there either. I believe there are three main reasons why I am drawn to her more than most other girls: (1) she is a very sweet person in herself, she cannot help being so, it is an integral part of her personality; (2) she is also, unlike most people especially in the Conservatoire, straightforward and unaffected, not remotely given to posing or showing off; (3) she is close to the Frolovs. Of late she has lost some of her looks because of her freckles, but before that she was very pretty; seen from behind, especially in her blue and white dress, she looks very graceful.

Relations with Glagoleva are as good as ever: we have grown used to one another and respect one another.

Bessonova failed two of her exams and did not turn up for the third. With me she continues to be guarded but amiable, but I honestly do not care for her. I tell myself that the only plus about her is her unchanging friendliness to me.

With Sadovskaya I'm on the best of terms. A little while ago I took her history book and crossed out in it all the things she could afford not to bother learning for her exam, and suggested that she come to hear me being examined on the 25th.

'Write the date down in the margin here, so that I don't forget.'

I wrote the date down on one of the pages, and while we were talking inscribed arrows on all the remaining two hundred pages, pointing in the direction she should turn to find the note.

'Good God! What on earth made you do that?'

'Well, wherever you open the book, you'll find an arrow there. Follow the direction it points in, and you'll see another one. Go on doing that until you get to the note reminding you to come to the exam.'

She told me this made her laugh all the time she was revising her History.

28 April

On Friday I played my public piano examination. It went very well. The test étude by Kessler, in F minor, which nobody could manage to get their fingers round properly, went well, and Yesipova, whose choice it was, listened with evident pleasure, nodding her head in time. The Bach fugue (C minor, from Book II), received, in Winkler's words, an impeccable performance, and finally Schumann's *Traumeswirren* was fast and accurate, with an expressive middle section. In short, I was awarded a 5 (Winkler beamed), a mark matched only by one other, a girl named Dubyago. After the exam Medem was trying to say something to me, but couldn't get the words out and had to content himself with gripping my hand firmly. Mama and Aunt Tanya told me that when I came on stage, Yesipova leaned over to Glazunov and whispered, 'Is that him?'

'Yes, that's him.'

Intriguing!

Aunt Katya arrived late for the examination, and ran into Professor Miklashevsky, a rising star, downstairs in the foyer: 'Can you tell me please, is this the examination for Winkler's class?'

'It's over.'

'It can't be! Tell me, how was Prokofiev?'

'Very good. Very talented. Only one fault: he has a most peculiar way of arranging his legs under the piano!'

'I'll certainly pass that on. So you say he was good?'

'Not just good – very good. I gave him a 5.'

Myaskovsky came to the exam. I was touched by a chap troubling to come from the other ends of the earth, all the way from Peskov, especially to listen to me. No one would do such a thing. The programme Winkler has given me for the summer is very interesting: a Schumann sonata and the Korsakov Concerto. I twice heard the concerto during the winter (played first by Lemba and then by Kreutzer[1]) and it enchanted me with its refinement, clarity, simplicity and sincerity. I remember telling Winkler that I would like him to let me play it as my graduation concerto from the Conservatoire.

'Well, no, for that we ought to choose something else. But we'll definitely do it some time.'

So now, when he was thinking about the programme for the summer: 'A concerto . . . what about a concerto for you?' I smacked my lips and half in jest suggested, 'What about the Korsakov!'

'All right then, do the Korsakov, since you are so keen.'

I really had not expected this.

---

2 Leonid Kreutzer (1882–1953), pianist who studied with Yesipova. He had already left Russia in 1906, settling first in Germany where he taught at the Berlin Hochschule, then in Tokyo.

3 May

The academic exams are all finished. I was quite brilliant in Physics and was the only person to get a 5.

Our group photograph is ready. It's come out well. I look good, slightly as though I am about to burst into tears, but with a mockingly confident expression. Almost everyone is collecting signatures on their copies of the photograph.

The cat is now out of the bag with the flowers. We were sitting and chatting on the windowsill after the exam, while Alpers and some of her friends kept passing to and fro along the corridor. Eventually she must have got fed up with our heated conversation because she kept coming up and asking Glagoleva stupid questions. When I went over to the door to see what was going on in the exam, she could bear it no longer: 'Did you get Fevroniya?'

'Fevroniya?'

'Didn't you get her?'

'I did. But you're too impatient; I thought I'd make you wait until I mentioned it . . .'

Afterwards, when we left the Conservatoire together, I went back to the flowers, saying that I had liked them very much, and they had made me spend long hours playing through *Kitezh* again.[1]

1 July

The exam for Tcherepnin's conducting class took place on the evening of 4 May and proved to be my least successful of the year. Although I am a very good sight-reader I only got a 4 for score-reading, and 3.5 for the actual baton-waving. The last was perhaps only to be expected, since I had conducted only once during the year! The orchestration exam was the following day. My assignment was one I found quite interesting: Grieg's D major *Humoresque*. My instrumentation was not particularly imaginative or colourful. Checking it, Lyadov and Tcherepnin both for some reason agreed that I should be given no more than 3.5. The oral questions I had to answer were trivial in the extreme, for instance I had to give a detailed description of all the percussion instruments. I got 4.5 for that. As for Korsakov, he was ill and did not attend the exam, but his class report for the year (I got the chance to sneak a look at it) said, 'Talented; did not produce much work; not many successful pieces; 3.5.' Perfectly true. Last year I attended all his classes diligently and brought work in punctually, which was well received.

---

1   Prokofiev kept the card. Nearly half a century later he produced it when Vera Alpers visited him at his dacha in Nikolina Gora, and asked her, 'What made you preserve your incognito then?' (Article by Vera Alpers written in 1961: 'Iz proshlogo' ('From the Past'), published in S. S. Prokof'iev, *Stat'i i Materialy*, edited by I. Nestyev and G. Edelman (Moscow: Muzyka, 1965).

1908

This year I missed quite a few lessons, taking advantage of the fact that because Rimsky-Korsakov had a lot of students, he had suggested we submit work only every other week. In the event my submissions were even less regular than that; after all, this year I had almost no time for anything! I myself was dissatisfied with much of what I produced; theoretically I had completed the orchestration course, but did not really feel that I knew much about it. No matter, thought I, it won't take me long to pick it up.

Overall exam results so far were: myself 4, Kankarovich 4, Saminsky 4.5, Myaskovsky 5. The last one, on 6 May, was Fugue, the one I had been dreading. The fugue subject we were given was a nice one, we had ample time to work on it with no time constraints, so all was set fair. I wrote with great care, always keeping in mind the Lyadov *desiderata* and not allowing myself to indulge in anything 'interesting'. It was pretty dry, and I made sure to put in plenty of sequences of secondary dominant sevenths. Myaskovsky looked through it and made several suggestions for minor improvements, most of which I incorporated. The further I got into it, that is to say the nearer I came to the denouement, the more relaxed I became; this often happens to me. After approximately eighteen hours of work, spread over three days, I handed in my fugue.

Mama and I were leaving on 18 May, all our things were packed and the tickets bought; the train was due to depart at 6.30. That morning I would learn the fate of my fugue, and so I went to the Conservatoire. It transpired that they had started with the Harmony assessments, then they would move on to Counterpoint, and only after that would they get to the Fugues. That meant, as far as we could work it out, that they would have to get through more than a hundred and fifty works before starting on the Fugues! God only knows how many talentless drones there are in the world who end up bearing the honourable appellation of music teacher! After considerable effort I managed to put in an application to have my fugue assessed before my train left. Suddenly out rushed Lyadov: 'Prokofiev, you play chess, don't you?'

'Yes, I do play.'

'How good are you, a strong player?'

'Pretty strong.'

'Well, how strong, approximately? What level?'

'Level 3.'

'Level 3! Oho!'

'What about you, Anatoly Konstantinovich? How good a player are you?'

'Well, I belong to two clubs. And I've been friendly with Schiffers (pronouncing the 'e' with great emphasis) and Chigorin!'

'What level are you?'

'Level 4, I'd say, although that's only in theory, I'm not so good at openings.'

'Do you go to the Chess Club, Anatoly Konstantinovich? We could have a game there.'

'I don't know about that! After all, you're better than me, you see!'[1]

At this point Glazunov appeared, and spoke to Lyadov.

'What's all this about? There's no doubt about his passing and going on to the next stage, is there?'

'No, but Sasha, he wants to know what mark he's getting.'

'4.5, I think. All right?'

So that was it, I had a 4.5. Glazunov said (both of them were very friendly) I had not made any mistakes and everything was very good although the counterpoint could have been more interesting and in better taste, but the fugal entries were all very beautiful. I started to stammer out something to the effect that I should like to be excused the study of form next year, but this was met by a categorical refusal, I must complete the course in form, and that was that. We parted, Lyadov firmly clasped my hand and inclined his head significantly, and I went off to catch my train. It was a more successful outcome than I could have expected. I heard that six weeks ago Asafyev met Lyadov somewhere and asked him how thing were going in his class. In particular: 'And Prokofiev?'

'We–e–ell! . . .' and Lyadov gestured briskly.

But as it was, everything was fine. I later found out that the whole class had done well: Myaskovsky, Elkan and Akimenko[2] 5, Kankarovich, Rozovsky, Saminsky 4.5. Zakharov and Asafyev (who had hardly attended at all because of his university course) were deferred until the autumn. That's Lyadov all over! Next year, for instance, when he was asked, 'Why do you keep not turning up for your classes?', he would reply, 'My students still get 6s in their exams, don't they?'

This took place on the 18th of the month, but before that, on the 9th, there had taken place the Conservatoire Graduation Concert. Mama decided she absolutely must attend – how could it be that her son had been at the Conservatoire for four years and she had never attended a Graduation Concert! So I had to get hold of a ticket for her, but these were allocated only either to those who were graduating or who were actually taking part in the concert. This seemed to rule out the possibility of obtaining a ticket. But then Kankarovich came up with a good dodge.

'Why don't we play the drums, then they'll give us tickets!'

This was at the general rehearsal, and Lemba's Concerto did indeed

---

1 In his *Autobiography*, Prokofiev attributes this exchange to an evening a year or so later in the hospitable environs of Nikolay Ruzsky's apartment. In the later version Prokofiev is at pains to point out that he did not part from Lyadov on bad terms.
2 Presumably a son or nephew of the composer Fyodor Stepanovich Akimenko (1876–1945).

include a tam-tam, which I said I would play, while Kankarovich took the cymbals. I had never in my life even been near a big drum, but we boldly took our seats and set about counting bars. We only had to bang once, just before the end. We counted and counted, but we must have counted too much because by the time the concerto ended we still had not banged. Nevertheless, we decided we would play in the concert, asking Malko to give us the clearest possible cue with his baton at the right place. And that was how we got our tickets. As usual for a Graduation Concert there were thousands of people attending, and the closest row in which I could get a seat for Mama was the fifteenth. I then rushed round telling everyone, including Anisimova, Sadovskaya and Dima (Abramycheva's cousin, in his final year at high school), that they must watch out for my appearance in the first piece after the interval. When they asked in astonishment, 'Doing what?', I replied calmly, 'Playing the Turkish drum.'

The interval over, Kankarovich and I took our seats and started counting bars. Finally, with one eye on Malko and one eye on the music, we counted to the right number and clashed and banged. Evidently it was the right place, but a lot of people thought we had not bashed sufficiently *forte*, and were expecting us to make more of a noise. But however much of a joke we thought it was to bang a drum, it was still a cause for satisfaction to have got it right and not have a disaster on our consciences. The moment the concerto was over I rushed to embrace and congratulate Lemba, and to ask him, had I played well? 'Very well, very well,' he replied, obviously paying no attention. I rejoined my own friends.

The next day we left St Petersburg and Europe.

26 July

On 18 May Mama, Aunt Tanya and I left St Petersburg for Sukhum[1] to stay with the Smetskoys. Olga Yuryevna Smetskaya was an old school friend of Mama who had married the millionaire Smetskoy but had kept up a close friendship with Mama ever since. On a visit to St Petersburg during the winter she had pressed us to come and stay with her, and it was to her that we were now on our way. We took the train as far as Novorossiisk, and then the steamer from Novorossiisk to Sukhum, where we arrived late in the evening to the fragrant smell of honeysuckle and a myriad fireflies.

I shall not give a detailed description of our stay in Sukhum, I already

---

1 Sukhum is the capital of Abkhazia, formerly part of Georgia but at the present time a self-declared independent republic. Sukhum is the Abkhazian name for the city called by the Georgians Sukhumi, but Abkhazians regard it as an offensive appellation. Although this was not a political issue at the time, Prokofiev always uses the local variant of the name, Sukhum.

have two months of my diary to catch up on, so at the moment it's not much of a diary at all! I'll confine myself to a brief account. We were welcomed with exceptional warmth and kindness. The countryside is astounding, but somehow I did not find myself as overwhelmed with its beauties as others have been even though I did like it very much. We spent three weeks and three days there, and by the end I was getting bored. This was understandable because there were no musicians there, nobody with whom to play chess, and indeed hardly any young people at all (our hostess's neighbour and distant relation O. P. Dmitrieva had three children, the eldest daughter Olya being fourteen years old, an entirely uninteresting girl although impeccably brought up). As for musicians, there was only Mme Metelyova, who in her day had been a celebrated violinist under her professional name of Prokopovich; she was indeed a magnificent player and an excellent musician but she was all the time away or bedridden with rheumatism. And not a single chess player in sight.

Aunt Tanya and I left on 18 June (Mama stayed for a further week) and went together to Rostov, after which I went on alone. This was my first solo journey, but I was already such an old hand at travelling by train that it did not make a great impression on me. While we were in Sukhum we made frequent sightseeing trips to view the attractions. The longest of our journeys was to Novy Afon[1] (24 versts), the most interesting to the Venetian Bridge. The trip to Novy Afon involved two carriages. We looked round the monastery, where I posed as an English journalist and wrote down all the information we were given in a notebook, and then to the dismay of our monastic guide loudly and with feeling declaimed German poetry whenever we reached a particularly noteworthy point. In the caves I cut myself a walking stick, which I christened my Holy Staff, but it turned out so monstrously ugly that the only thing I could use it for was to go swimming. The Venetian Bridge was where, according to legend, the Venetians repulsed Tamerlaine. That is the only interesting thing about this bridge, but what I did find truly impressive was the gorge below it. I was enthralled and fell into a silent reverie in which I saw myself walking, hand in hand with someone but otherwise alone, through this wonderful place, about which few people even in Sukhum seemed to know.

Incidentally, I have remembered that just as we were embarking on the steamer at Novorossiisk to come to Sukhum, whom should I meet but... Piastro. The dear fellow was going from Sebastopol to Tiflis with his father and sister. The sea was like glass, which I always love, and I felt like declaiming:

---

1 Novy Afon (New Athos), monastery situated on the shores of the Black Sea with a cathedral built over a shrine said to contain the bones of the Apostle Simon the Zealot (Simon the Canaanite).

Unfathomable sea, azure sea,
I stand entranced above your abyss![1]

as to our disgust we had drummed into us by Balayev. But now with Piastro I recalled it with pleasure.

His sister was a typical Georgian with a face of great beauty but otherwise distressingly fat and sluggish. Somehow all Georgian women seem to have something crude about them. As soon as the passengers realized we were musicians, they badgered us to play. I at once said I would, but Piastro, and especially his father, made such difficulties and started to put on such revolting airs that the pair of them drove me to distraction. 'Our music is down below, but our new bespoke concert clothes are up above, and it's a long way to have to go, and we don't want them to get creased . . .' Eventually the public got tired of asking and gave up. After a quarter of an hour Piastro *père* appeared, triumphantly bearing a pile of music, and portentously announced: 'Found it!'

'Maybe, but I'm no longer interested in accompanying!' I said, to his evident dismay.

The net result of this was entirely satisfactory: we didn't play together, but I played on my own. I don't think Piastro minded at all. Afterwards we played chess, which I won 4–0–0. He told me he had played two games with Lyadov, one of which he lost and the other was a draw.

3 August

I was glad when halfway through June I finally arrived at Sontsovka and could immediately settle down to write my Symphony. As long ago as last autumn, September even, I had decided that I would compose a symphony during the summer, but would not start it until I got to Sontsovka. I held firm to my resolve all through the winter but now it was time to throw myself into it with fervour.

In the spring, Myaskovsky had planned to compose a quartet, but I advised him to write a symphony, so he was now also engaged on composing a symphony. It was our intention to have them both finished by the autumn, and then to show them to Glazunov in the hope that he would agree to let them be performed at one of the student concerts. I am taking extra care over mine, devoting much time and effort to refining the themes in order that they should be beautiful, have good style and most importantly of all, character. Mostly I am pleased with them. When I composed the second subject, at first it excited me beyond words, but I am now beginning

---

1 Slightly misremembered first two lines of Zhukovsky's poem 'The Sea'; the sea should be 'bezmolvnoye' (mute) rather than 'bezdonnoye' (bottomless).

to have doubts that I may have stolen it from somewhere. Myaskovsky and I have been corresponding intensively, and he has reassured me on this score, although he finds its shape reminiscent of a quartet by Brahms. I don't know any of Brahms's quartets and I really don't want to change anything, so it's going to stay as it is. My Symphony will be as short as possible (after all, what can be worse than a long symphony?) and in three movements, with no scherzo. A scherzo has to be brilliantly orchestrated, and I'm not yet ready to risk that. In any case, a scherzo is not really my style.

Later on, however, the thought came to me: perhaps a *Scherzo satanique* – but by then it was too late, that will have to wait for another time. My first fear was that I would not manage to complete the Symphony in time, and my second that it would be no good. But, as is my wont, the more I got on the more relaxed I became. Myaskovsky likes my themes very much (unfortunately I cannot say the same about his).

I'm playing my Winkler piano programme quite respectably now. I feel as though I really made progress during the late spring and early summer, and therefore I enjoy practising now. The Korsakov Concerto is not nearly as daunting a proposition as I thought it would be. The great composer died on 8 June. When I was passing through Novorossiisk on 17 June and had eight hours to while away in the station, I happened to open a newspaper and read the headline: 'Funeral of Rimsky-Korsakov'. It is such a common name, and he was so far from my thoughts at that time, that I paid no attention. But when I looked more closely and saw '. . . the composer N. A. . . .' I realized what had happened, and was really shocked and upset. Korsakov had died, and I never had the opportunity to study with him. I know, I attended his course in orchestration, but only after a fashion. I remembered the last time I saw him. It was in the Conservatoire, on the second floor,[1] on the stairs. Opposite was a conference room, in which an exam in Russian was apparently taking place. I was standing talking to Abramycheva, and off a little to one side was Rimsky-Korsakov deep in conversation with a very short person. Cheerful, good-humoured, a figure of extraordinary attractiveness, he was in the middle of an impassioned account to his diminutive companion of something that had happened in connection with the production of his *Snow Maiden* that was then in progress in Paris. I watched him with admiration thinking: there is a great man who has achieved fame and glory. And now he is dead.

I remember his last triumph, at a Belyayev[2] concert where the Intro-

---

1 Russians, like most Continental Europeans, number the storeys of their buildings from one (the ground floor) upwards; this 'second floor' was therefore what an Englishman would call the first floor.
2 Mitrofan Belyayev (1836–1904), millionaire timber merchant and passionate music-lover, had since the 1860s almost single-handedly determined the future course of Russian music for several generations by his support of a handful of composers, notably Rimsky-Korsakov,

duction and Wedding March from *The Golden Cockerel* were performed. The Introduction was not particularly well played, but I really loved the Wedding March, whose orchestration absolutely stunned me – never had I heard such brilliant colouring – although I was embarrassed by the banality of the Introduction's middle-section theme. When applause rang out at the end of the performance, it was more of a thunderclap than a storm, but a thunderclap that never seemed to end, neither swelling nor diminishing, the entire hall standing and applauding to a man. Korsakov sat in the third box on the left, dressed in a long grey frockcoat. For some time he sat motionless, and then came down to take a bow. The Wedding March had to be repeated.

15 September

THE BLESSED SERGEY: Just one more page, the last to finish writing
And then at last my symphony is done ...¹

The last page is written, my Symphony is done, my first work composed in real hopes of a performance. Previously I had set my sights on an opera and worked on *Undina*,² but when during the autumn I started seriously thinking about the implications of an actual performance, I came to the conclusion that this was more likely to be achieved with a symphony. Thinking I might not have the time to do it during the winter, I determined to wait until the summer. Seeing performances of orchestral pieces by Lemba and Galkovsky included in student concerts and productions has convinced me that it should not be too difficult to get mine performed, since surely I am not inferior to them as a composer. My resolve grew steadily, and in fact I was subject to very strong urges to start composing the Symphony, but I would not allow myself to do so, reasoning that I would not achieve very much and indeed might even damage the work. From time to time, when feeling disconsolate at the older female students' indifference to me, the thought would come to me: 'Just you wait, in a year's time the other students will all be engaged on my Symphony, and I shall be the composer ...', although I would

---

Lyadov, Glazunov and Scriabin. The influential music publishing-house he established in Leipzig (because Russia was not a signatory to the Berne Convention on copyright) and the seasons he organized of orchestral concerts, chamber music evenings and Glinka Prizes, were all exclusively devoted to Russian composers. The membership and activities of the 'Belyayev Circle' became the benchmark of establishment music-making, and continued after the deaths of Belyayev in 1904 and Rimsky in 1908 under the artistic direction of a conservatively minded artistic committee consisting of Glazunov, Lyadov and Artsybushev.

1 A paraphrase of Pimen, the aged monk in Pushkin's *Boris Godunov*: 'One final legend to relay/And then my chronicle is done.'
2 Unfinished opera, written in spurts between 1904 and 1907, to a libretto by Maria Kilshtedt after a poem by Friedrich de la Motte Fouqué adapted by Vasily Zhukovsky.

usually have enough sense to realize that, in the first place, there was no guarantee of this, and in the second, it was all a long way off.

I set to work feverishly, spurred on in the main by the prospect of a performance. If someone had told me my Symphony would not be performed, I would hardly have been able to finish it. There were moments during both the composition and the orchestration when I would get stuck in a tricky or tedious place, but by then I was so acclimatized to the thought that I would be returning to St Petersburg in the autumn with my Symphony that I simply could not imagine appearing without it. I had my moments of despair, when one or another theme refused to come, or I could not overcome some difficulty in the development or balance an orchestral tutti, and at such times my anger would get the better of me and I would swear never in my life to write another symphony. But for most of the time the work went smoothly and pleasantly.

Our departure for St Petersburg is fixed for the middle of September, and lo and behold it is the 15th of the month and I have finished the Symphony. 'The work is done . . .', now I have to wait for the performance. Now it's finished I can take a more detached view of whether or not it will be played – perhaps yes, perhaps no. I look on the possibilities as I would on a game of two players in competition: either may prevail, and the victory of either will not surprise me; all that remains for me is to be overjoyed or cast down. I believe my Symphony should have a good chance: the music is beautiful – no one, I think, will be able to deny that; the form is correct, the harmony also is beautiful, the tunes striking, they combine together well and although the counterpoint may be a little cheeky no one can say it is not there . . . the one thing I am not sure about is the orchestration. I am very much afraid that some of the tuttis have not come out as they should, and this sometimes colours the affection I feel for my bulging score. I am reassured by the thought that I shall be showing it first of all to Glière, and he will certainly have things to say about it. Myaskovsky will also have suggestions to make, and Glazunov will correct anything that needs it. Finally, whether it is played or not, it is still good that I have composed a symphony. Ultimately it will be valuable, both from the point of view of technique, and for other reasons. I can say with confidence that my summer has not been wasted.

I have not written anything in my diary about the first chess tournament I ever competed in. It began earlier this year, on 1 February in the Chess Club, an open tournament for players of all levels. I thought that all levels would participate, but as it turned out the majority of the competitors were Level 2 players with a sprinkling of Level 1s and Level 3s, so bearing in mind my lack of experience I was one of the weakest to participate. I remember waiting at the club on 5 February for it to begin, sitting in the room next to the playing hall chatting to Malyutin.

In came Chudovsky[1] proffering a fan of white tickets and inviting me to draw my lot. 'I shall be most interested to see whom this pits me against,' I said, drawing number 4. A moment later he came back, took my hand and led me into the playing hall. 'Well, you can begin now,' he said. 'Here is your partner.'

We were introduced. The chessmen were laid out on a separate table beside us, with the clock, some paper and a pencil. We sat down. 'What level are you?' asked my opponent, Demchinsky.[2]

'Level 4 ... 3,' I replied diffidently.

'Shall we begin?'

'Please.'

It was all very solemn and ceremonious. I was terribly nervous. I had long dreamed of taking part in a tournament, and now I was doing so. Play began, and I almost lost the power of thought altogether. Trying to make notes my hand shook, and I could do no more than scrawl. And the game itself was somehow not what I expected. Viennese – I had never played the Viennese convention. I could remember the principle – get out one's pieces as soon as possible; and the Lasker technique: knights first, then bishops. I tried to let my opponent lead. From time to time I looked at the clock, and to calm myself chewed a sweet. While my opponent was thinking, I rose from the table and went over to Chudovsky, who was at a long table slantwise from me, playing against Budberg.

Leaning over them I peered at his notes. 'You're looking a bit red and anxious,' smiled Chudovsky.

I heard the ping of the clock and hurried back to my game. I had the impression I was gaining the advantage, and began to think up a strategic movement that ran somewhat counter to theory. After an hour and a half I was in difficulties, and then I lost a pawn. I came out in a hot flush – there is no other word for it. Next I feinted an attack, but then my opponent suddenly said: 'See now, mate in one move ...'

'How?'

He indicated F8.

'Oh, yes, I see ...'

But now I was not so disconcerted, because the actual blow had fallen

---

1 Valerian Chudovsky (1882–?1938), philologist and critic, chess player, regular correspondent of *Apollon* journal, notably on poets and poetry. He was arrested during the purges of the 1930s and is believed to have died in a labour camp.
2 Boris Demchinsky (1877–1942), philologist and writer. Prokofiev was much attracted to his personality, wide-ranging literary interests and knowledge, and later enlisted his help with the librettos for *The Gambler* and *The Fiery Angel*. 'Still a young man of about thirty, he spoke in tones of great evenness, a slight smile playing about his lips. I thought to myself: what interesting things could be heard from such a man!' (*Autobiography*.) Demchinsky perished tragically of starvation during the 1900 days of the Leningrad blockade, 1941–44, imposed by the Germans.

earlier with the loss of the pawn. I went into the next room, where Traubenberg, who had already lost his game, was sitting writing out a league table of the tournament.

'Did you lose?'

'Yes. But that's good; it means I'll win all my other games.'

'Oh, is that so? Well, I lost as well, so we are companions in misfortune.'

I lost my next game too, in fact I did not have much success throughout the tournament. But in almost every game there was some point when I managed to gain the advantage, even if sometimes a slight one, only to lose it subsequently by exposing a piece or simply by a poor move. But I was always left with the hope of winning the next game. This hope was nearly justified.

In my last two games I was drawn against Level 1 opponents. I almost won against Lyuts, and finally gained a victory over Potyomkin, in this way compensating for the bitterness of defeat.

25 September

We returned to Piter[1] today. I went into the Conservatoire, where the first person I met was Ivanova, a Winkler fellow student. 'Congratulations on the professorship,' she said.

Alexander Adolfovich[2] has, it seems, been made a full professor, and we are all delighted by this promotion. The next person I met was Saminsky, who informed me that the Form course is to be taken by Wihtol.[3] This is what always happens: we have got used to pouring vituperation over Lyadov, take that you miserable so-and-so, and now we shall miss him and shed tears over him. Lyadov will be teaching the higher course in Practical Composition, Kalafati[4] Harmony, in short God only knows what will come of all this. Went to see Myaskovsky to clarify the situation and to unburden my soul. A little later, in floated Alpers from somewhere or other, and we greeted one another with joy (more perhaps on my part than hers). She is taller than she was and has become, I think, less attractive, as she has adopted a grown-up hairstyle that does not suit her at all, and generally I feel she could make much more of herself. We chatted for about ten minutes. By the end I could not hold back any longer and took to teasing her gently.

1   Affectionate, universally understood nickname for St Petersburg.
2   Winkler.
3   Isof Wihtol (Jazeps Vitols) (1863–1948), prolific Latvian composer, teacher and critic, student of Rimsky-Korsakov, an influential member of the Belyayev circle and as critic of the German-language *Sankt Petersburge Zeitung*, implacably hostile to progressive tendencies.
4   Vasily Kalafati (1869–1942), composer and professor at St Petersburg Conservatoire. Among his pupils were Asafyev and (privately) Stravinsky.

Our conversation was ended by the arrival of Kankarovich, so I said goodbye to Alpers somewhat abruptly and went off with Kankarovich to the opera class, where I stayed for about a quarter of an hour and saw Platonov. He is a monstrously ugly fellow, although I am gradually coming to the conclusion that he is enormously clever.

On my way through Moscow I had called on R. M. Glière[1] and shown him my Symphony. He approved of it, the second movement most of all, but his favourite theme was the work's opening one. What gave me most satisfaction was that he found the counterpoint adequate and the orchestration not bad at all, in fact very well done. These were the things I had been most worried about. Musically he liked the work, although he preferred the piano pieces ('Snow', 'Scherzo', 'Fairy Tale', 'March', etc.) 'This is what you should be writing,' he said to me. 'This music has a future.'

He firmly recommended doing everything I possibly could to get the Symphony performed, as nothing is more valuable than having the opportunity to hear one's own work. On my arrival, his greeting was: 'How handsome you've become! What a good-looking young man! Very dangerous for the Conservatoire girls.'

Mama put in: 'That's what I keep telling him: don't run after the girls, let them run after you ...'

1 October

Went to see Myaskovsky. I was very much put out to discover that he had already given his symphony to Glazunov a week ago.

'Why didn't you wait? I'd been imagining this idyllic scene where we would go and see him together ...'

He told me candidly that to do this would have been the height of stupidity from his point of view, because I am capable of actually playing my Symphony, which he is not, and therefore his Symphony would have inevitably lost ground had we gone there together. Even so, however much Glazunov might be put off that the composer was not himself capable of demonstrating it to him, the fact remains that he has submitted his symphony. I could see it was time for decisive action.

The following day at one o'clock I presented myself with my score at Glazunov's door, but he was not there. I did the same thing at seven o'clock, only to find that they were at dinner and had guests. The next day, at eight o'clock, I was there again. 'Knock, and it shall be opened unto you ...' I caught sight of Glazunov. He was in a hurry to go somewhere, but after a

---

1 Reinhold Glière (1874–1956), composer, Prokofiev's first real teacher; he spent the summers of 1902 and 1903 with the family in Sontsovka.

brief exchange I came away with an audience for Sunday at five o'clock. 'I simply don't have a moment just now, no time at all. Could you wait until Sunday?'

Now I must scratch out and paste corrections into my Symphony and wait for decision day on Sunday. On Thursday I shall probably go with Myaskovsky to the 'Evenings of Contemporary Music', and I will take my new-born child along with me. Myaskovsky said they are thinking of putting together an orchestra, and if they do that could be a way forward.

Zakharov greeted me warmly, but I'm no longer so fond of Saminsky and have begun to fall out with him. Winkler has a new student, Volodya Deshevov.[1] I first met him two years ago and occasionally see him at concerts. He is going to continue living out at Tsarskoye [Selo] and will come into the Conservatoire four times a week. Winkler told him, indicating me, 'That's the person you should learn sight-reading from; Mr Prokofiev is an excellent sight-reader.'

Myaskovsky told me that when Deshevov played the C minor Fugue, Winkler said to him, 'I wonder if you heard Mr Prokofiev's performance of the fugue at the examination? Take his playing as a model: his was a first-class fugue performance.'

I am very glad that Deshevov has entered the Conservatoire. The first time he played for Winkler he played études by Rubinstein and Chopin, and Winkler was delighted. 'You have complete mastery of this piece,' he said of the Rubinstein. 'You should perform it at a student concert, it would be very effective.'

I was late for the Chess Club tournament, but started a game with Chudovsky, who had taken First Prize in the previous contest. To my astonishment he now proceeded to lose all his games one after another. I could not understand it, and felt sorry for him, regretting the formerly invincible Chudovsky. He lost the first game of his match with me as well. Such is the way of things.

Like it or not, I must train myself to stop teasing the girl students at the Conservatoire and make myself as agreeable as I can. I will be triply rewarded. It's amusing to tease people, but not so amusing when they try to run away as soon as they see you coming.

4 October

Saw Sofia Esche in the Conservatoire again yesterday while she was making a telephone call. I bowed as I passed, and she responded with a smile. When she had finished speaking I went up to her and started a conversation,

---

1 Vladimir Deshevov (1889–1955), pianist and composer, mainly of operetta and theatre music.

reminding myself of my vow to avoid teasing or being sarcastic. But this is not an easy matter where Esche is concerned: being herself something of an *enfant terrible* she positively invites it and therefore makes it hard to carry on a conventionally polite conversation. But thanks to some politesses on my part the spikiness of our intercourse soon softened and we had a very friendly talk. She imparted the following information: her sister Esche senior has left the Conservatoire to enrol in a Drama course where she is showing signs of considerable talent. Esche junior has abandoned her General Subject courses and now attends the Conservatoire only twice a week for piano lessons. I was not much interested in the first item of news, but the second was cause for real dismay: Esche junior has really blossomed, grown up and become a beautiful, cultivated and well-mannered girl only to vanish, to all intents and purposes, over the horizon. Actually this was only to be expected: it is not often that one encounters such superior types within the Conservatoire purlieus.

She then mentioned that the Esche family home is the meeting place for a very interesting group of artists, and after associating with them 'it is positively disagreeable even to look at the Conservatoire students, so many of them are just bumptious smart alecks whose hand I don't even want to shake', and so on. In a word she has matured, which is good, but the consequence is that she has moved away from the Conservatoire, which for me is a pity. Saying, 'you have become such a rarity for us here now', I asked her her timetable for being in the Conservatoire. We talked for about a quarter of an hour, and then parted with great civility, all of which left me with the most pleasant impression.

12 October

Yesterday I met Esche in the Conservatoire again, as two days previously, but this time she was not alone; her elder sister was with her as she evidently has enough feeling for the place to drop in to the Conservatoire from time to time. We were pleased to see one another, and had a long chat. I asked a lot of questions and she told me a lot of interesting things about her Drama course. Generally, both sisters were charming and friendly. I suppose the elder is more mature and self-possessed, the fact is she is just that little bit older, but the younger sister is the one I like more. The former is more artificial, more inclined to play a role; the latter much more natural. The conversation turned to composition. Some time ago I had mentioned to Esche senior that I was interested in writing songs, but was having trouble finding suitable texts. 'Why don't you ask me?' she asked, and began reciting some verses. Yesterday, seeing her again, I reminded her of her promise. 'I'll write it out for you by heart if you like,' she replied, and quickly going over to the window, she knelt down and started writing. This was 'Blacksmith, forge chains for my heart'.[1]

I set to work at white heat. I don't quite know the reason, but so far I have simply not succeeded in bringing it off. It may have been because I have never written a song before, or because I so badly wanted to write something that would give immediate pleasure, or I was not in the right mood, or I could not concentrate, but the result is that I am now in a catastrophic state of mind, although this may also be because I feel bereft of friends, of love, of all attachments ... I have no close friends, never yet have I truly loved anyone ... oh, what rubbish I have begun to talk!

17 October

A few words on musical matters. On the 11th Glazunov recovered from his illness and departed for Kiev for two to three weeks to conduct concerts of his own works. This upset me greatly, because now my Symphony will have to wait for ever. The day before Glazunov left, Myaskovsky lay in wait for him for five hours at the Conservatoire and managed to ask him to return his score. Glazunov replied that he had not had time to look through the whole work, but what he had seen had given him great pleasure. He asked to see the score again on his return. Of course I am happy for Myaskovsky (I believe his symphony is good) but at the same time I am not a little envious and fear that this may mean curtains for my own work. Glazunov recognizes in Myaskovsky's work something of the style of Taneyev and indeed himself, whereas mine lacks this colossal skill in counterpoint and (in this sense) beauty of design, even though everyone assures me that my music is not in fact deficient in contrapuntal argument. My strong suits are beauty, inspiration and form; but Glazunov is a contrapuntalist through and through, and that is why he finds in Myaskovsky's work stylistic resonances with his own. This puts me at a disadvantage. In any event, we shall see what happens. Although I rate Myaskovsky very highly, and dearly love his songs 'Circles' and 'Blood', I remain convinced that he will not become a great composer: he is a supremely literate musician and his music is often beautiful, he composes a great deal, but he lacks that necessary element of brilliance and compelling originality.

The 'Contemporaries' accorded polite acknowledgement to my Symphony and were complimentary about it, but on the whole received it coolly. It is not their style, although they were very enthusiastic about the last two piano pieces, 'Humoresque' and 'Suggestion diabolique'. When I played the latter,

---

1 Presumably from Zhukovsky's poem 'Svetlana': 'Blacksmith, forge for me a new garland-crown of gold, and a golden ring.'

there were certain passages that made them laugh out loud and jump up and down in their seats. They want to have them performed at the end of November, but for that I shall need Wihtol's permission.

18 October

Saw Sofia Esche today after not seeing her for a week. She seemed delighted to see me and altogether she clearly welcomes my attentions and finds me interesting. Nevertheless I have reverted to my earlier, springtime feelings about Alpers, and am very attracted to her. She is a sweet, uncomplicated person to be with, she has an educated understanding of music, and we are good friends. I have softened the first impression I had of her this autumn, at that time she was not showing herself to advantage, and although one could not quite call her pretty, she is not at all bad looking.

25 October

If only Glazunov would give his consent to my Symphony being performed, the whole question could be settled very easily. In a few days he will return from his trip, and once again I shall be knocking at his door. Also, I need to obtain permission to perform my piano pieces, since Wihtol says it is the first time in his experience that a student has asked for such permission, and he is uncertain how to respond. Consequently, I must apply to Glazunov. The 'Contemporaries' want me to programme seven of my piano pieces in their concert at the end of November. I played them all to great acclaim at one of their Thursday meetings. Saminsky (at Myaskovsky's suggestion) also appeared in the same session with two of his songs, hoping that they also might be included in the concert.

At the end of my 'Suggestion diabolique', which was greeted with noisy approbation and which had genuinely sounded very effective, Saminsky shyly stole along the wall to the piano, and to his own very tentative accompaniment sang his songs in a quavering, husky little voice, full of hesitations and wrong notes, for which he kept apologizing. He sang one song, to no perceptible reaction, and then another... the response was the silence of the grave. The song concluded with an augmented triad, of which he was manifestly very proud. Nobody paid the slightest attention. Saminsky then said, 'Well, that's it', once again provoking no response. Trying not to attract attention to himself, he inched his way back along the wall, and vanished. I felt genuinely sorry for him that evening; it was a most uncomfortable occasion to witness. I stood to one side and tried not to catch his eye.

I had in any case been planning to show my pieces to Winkler, who is in general very pleased with me, when in the middle of a lesson he suddenly turned to me: 'Medem has been telling me that you are going to perform your pieces . . . please let me have a look at them first. In any case I shall be most interested to see your compositions.' I shall bring them to the class on Thursday.

1 November

On Thursday I attended the memorial concert for Rimsky-Korsakov, an event that left me with the most favourable impression, especially the last act of *Kitezh* which was given in a concert performance. *The Maid of Pskov* was also good, in fact everything was good except for an execrable performance of Rimsky's Piano Concerto by Drozdov (the brother of the more celebrated Anatoly Drozdov). Only now can I fully appreciate the refinement of Lemba's performance last year. I arrived at the concert without a ticket, but managed to get hold of a pass from Mlle Alpers, so I was lucky. It has been entertaining for me to discover that her friends (Anisimova, Abramycheva, Fliege, Nodelman) who are always around her as they were this time, have decided that I am paying court to Verochka, and therefore devote the most delicate ingenuity to leaving us alone together as much as possible. I have only to come near the group for them to start peeling off to right and left, and a moment later I find I am on my own with Alpers. At first it was amusing and rather pleasing, but now it has begun to annoy me.

Esche and Glagoleva were not at the concert. How often have I pondered: which is the better, Esche or Alpers? But I always come to the same conclusion: it is not possible to compare them. They are at opposite poles: the good qualities of the one are precisely the deficiencies of the other. If you were to imagine a non-existent ideal, in which the best qualities of each replace the void left by the defects of the other, you might end up with Esche and Alpers. But if I was obliged, as a matter of urgency, to choose one or the other, which would it be? The answer is, of course, neither.

5 November

Solution to the previous conundrum: Alpers is a far better person than Esche, but Esche is incomparably better looking.

10 November

After ten attempts to track down Glazunov, the eleventh finally brought success and I showed him my Symphony. He approved the first movement least, the second movement more so and the third still more. The first movement was too dissonant for him, particularly the second page of the exposition.

The third movement is almost dissonance-free. 'Of course it may be that your ears are different from mine, after all you are at least twenty-five years younger than I, but even taking that into consideration I think dissonances like this would be more effective if they were used more sparingly, just occasionally.'

His overall impression was that I had injected a good deal of fire and passion into the Symphony as a whole, especially towards the end. Its form was good and the 15/8 bars in the last movement particularly successful. When I asked him how he found the orchestration, he said that from what he had been able to see everything was in place. His final judgement was that I clearly possessed technique and a measure of compositional experience. As I left, I asked, 'Alexander Konstantinovich, might it not some time be possible for our student orchestra to try out the Symphony?'

'You will have wait for a while; I am really too busy at the moment to answer this question. I have to go to Moscow, but when I come back you can show it to me again and we will examine it movement by movement.'

We parted. Generally it had gone very well – provided, of course, I achieve my ultimate objective of a performance.

13 November

One day around four o'clock, after a lesson with Winkler, I went into the canteen for a glass of tea. There were not many people there, but among them was Sofia Esche, who seemed to be well known to most of the people present. She was behaving quite dreadfully, like the worst kind of Conservatoire miss, making eyes in all directions – presumably including mine – talking too loudly, running about all over the canteen and laughing affectedly, scattering flirtatious glances on every side. She was wearing a kind of green dress, extremely *décolleté*. I sat to one side with a disapproving expression on my face, and eventually grew so angry I went home. The following day Vasily happened to offer me a pass for the dress rehearsal of *Judith*[1] with Chaliapin at the Mariinsky Theatre, which had just begun, and Esche happened to be there. 'Why don't you come with me, I'll take you,' I said.

At first she was reluctant, saying that she would not be allowed in, but soon allowed herself to be persuaded and we set off. We got in without too much difficulty, and sat together in the stalls. I was bored to tears: the opera is dreary beyond words and Chaliapin was not singing well. Esche was not concentrating, spending most of her time ogling the best-looking of the singers. When the third act started I went home. I've almost completely lost interest in Esche.

1   Opera (1862) by Alexander Serov (1820–1871).

22 November

Since nothing much has happened in the meantime, I shall set down some biographical particulars I have ascertained.

Alpers. One of her forebears was... a Spaniard. Hence she fancies herself as Donna Alperes. Her father was born in Little Russia,[1] an engineer and a railway constructor, so that in her time Mlle Alpers has travelled quite a lot. She herself was born in Nikolayev, and has lived in Feodosia, Tomsk and Kostroma, although this was when she was very young and for the past eight years she has been living in St Petersburg. She was first enrolled in the Institute,[2] but later 'at the insistence of Rimsky-Korsakov' transferred to the Conservatoire. All her family are musicians; her mother sings and her father invariably takes all his scores away with him to Kostroma, where his job is. The family stays behind in St Petersburg and touchingly writes to him every day. The family additionally consists of a grandmother and two younger brothers, the elder of whom I know. Alpers performed recently at a student evening, without making much impression. I saw Yury Frolov there on this occasion and didn't recognize him at all – he was wearing an awful pince-nez. The Frolovs are very close friends of the Alpers, they spent a summer together at a dacha in Pavlovsk. I don't think he is courting her, but that I am is already regarded as a signed and sealed matter. In fact I do very much enjoy spending time with her, I see her almost every day as she has taken to coming to Aesthetics on Tuesdays. All in all she is the best of the bunch, but it is a pity there are none better than her.

Esche (senior, I mean). There is something mysterious about her genealogy. Her mother is the Princess Khodanskaya and her father has a double-barrelled surname. One of these barrels is Esche, the other is something baronial, I cannot remember what, but in any case for some reason the daughters have only the one name. As for her nationality, 'Esche' in German means an ash tree, as far as I know, and people say that in Finnish it means an ass, but in fact I think she is of Polish descent.

7 December

Last time I wrote up my diary I was complaining that nothing had happened, but now I can say the opposite. The most important event was the second appearance of my Symphony before Glazunov. This time it was easier: I got through to him at only the third attempt. I presented myself at

---

1   Ukraine was at that time known to Russians as Malorossiya ('Little Russia').
2   The only university-equivalent academic training available to women in Russia at the time was through private educational institutions, the best known of which was the Bestuzhev Institute.

Kazanskaya Street by appointment at half past one. 'Well, I think we should look at the movements individually, shouldn't we?' said Glazunov.

'In that case, Alexander Konstantinovich, I'd like to begin with the third movement. That is the one you liked best and it has the fewest dissonances,' I replied. Glazunov had no objection to this, sat himself down at the piano and proceeded to play from the score while I sat beside him. He made a few observations, confining himself to details of scoring, and stopped in only two or three places where he found the harmony too pungent. At two o'clock Myaskovsky arrived, having been asked to come at that time to show his songs (he needs a recommendation for Jurgenson[1] to publish them), but Glazunov carried on with me until a quarter to three. When he had finished reading it through to the end, he said, 'The conception is very good. But the way you have realized it . . . is harsh, very harsh . . . and as for trying it out . . . I honestly don't know how to go about that . . .'

We talked round the subject for quite a long time, Glazunov weaving the threads of the discussion in such a way that I cannot now disentangle them. The gist was that the Symphony has much that is good in it, but too many dissonances; also I have been very cavalier in my treatment of the part-writing. For this reason he thinks that if I were to present my Symphony as it is, it could do me harm. Obviously he was anxious to encourage me and have something of mine performed, but the dissonant nature of the Symphony was in its disfavour. He asked me, 'Do you have another work that would be easier to perform?'

By the end of the discussion matters began to resolve themselves a little. There are three possible orchestras: the Court Orchestra, Count Sheremetyev's and the Conservatoire's. The first is probably the best quality, but I never hear anything about their concerts, and I think it would be a cul-de-sac that would not lead anywhere. As for the other two, both have approximately the same reputation orchestrally speaking, but the Conservatoire concerts have a higher profile and are generally more interesting. I tried to press for the latter. In the end, Glazunov decided that the last movement was suitable for performance, and promised to look again at the other two. 'We'll have to ask Malko or someone to learn it and conduct it,' he said. 'Just make the corrections I mentioned to you and then we'll look at the second movement.'

---

1   The music publishing firm of Jurgenson was founded in 1867 by Pyotr Jurgenson with the help of Nikolay Rubinstein, whom Jurgenson had assisted with the organization of the Moscow Conservatoire, and published the majority of Tchaikovsky's works. Jurgenson missed a trick in rejecting Balakirev's proposal that he should publish the music of the young Glazunov, thus affording Mitrofan Belyayev the chance to step into the breach and found his own publishing enterprise. After Pyotr Jurgenson died in 1903 the business was carried on by his son Boris. There was also a lesser publishing concern in St Petersburg, run independently by another member of the family.

I thanked him, said goodbye, and left. The Symphony, thank God, will be performed, although everything had been left so vague that I could not visualize with any clarity what exactly was to be done, or how. Now I must get on with touching up and patching it. Although he had not made a great number of corrections, it all takes a tremendous amount of time and is slow, tiring and tedious work. But if it leads to the Symphony being performed . . . !

The other event was my first appearance at a students' concert. I performed the First Chopin Etude, Brahms's Rhapsody and the C major Etude of Rubinstein. I was not very confident about the first piece with its horrible arpeggios, because the slightest trace of nerves is apt to derail it. I therefore decided I would play it only if and when, being actually on stage, I was sure of being completely at ease. I was a little anxious beforehand, but I calmed myself, sat down at the piano, and the étude went well. I knew the other two pieces inside out, and played them for all I was worth. I was applauded warmly and at length. Overall my success was greater than anyone else's that evening, despite the fact that two pupils of Yesipova's class were taking part. Yesipova was there listening, and Zakharov, who transferred to her class in the autumn, is going to ask her privately what she thought of me. All year my determination to leave Winkler and join Yesipova's class has been undergoing a steady crescendo. When Winkler was my Junior-course teacher I was quite happy with him, and he taught me my scales and studies extremely well. But now that I am moving up into the higher echelons where artistry must come to the fore, I am less satisfied.

Generally I have a passionate desire to move ahead; in any field I invariably seek the company of those whose accomplishments are superior to my own and from whom I can learn. But when I myself reach their level, my interest in them wanes. Now when I come for a lesson with Winkler, I find he has nothing new to give me. Either I know everything he is going to say in advance, or I have already forgotten it in the course of learning the work. What is the point of my sitting for another two or three years to stay effectively in the same place, when I feel that I have great potential for the piano and my ambition is to be a good pianist?

The advice I am hearing on all sides is to move to Yesipova.[1] The only

---

[1] One wonders whether Prokofiev knew exactly what he was taking on. Here is George Bernard Shaw, writing as 'Corno di Bassetto' in *The World*, reviewing Mme Annette Essipoff's performance at Steinway Hall, London, on 17 May 1894: 'No technical difficulties trouble her enough to rouse her: sometimes she is interested and interesting, sometimes cold and absent, always amazing. The cobbler's wife may be the worst shod woman in the parish; but Leschetitsky's wife is undoubtedly one of the greatest exponents of his technique in Europe. If it were possible to believe that she cares two straws about what she plays, she would also be one of the greatest executive musicians in Europe. But she has discovered that all this is vanity, and so, with her indifference cloaked by a superb habit of style, and by the activity of her unerring mechanism,

person opposed to it seems to be Papa. And on a personal level I should be very sorry to harm or offend Winkler. To which Myaskovsky objects: 'When your eyes are fixed on your goal, it's no good looking at the difficulties you have to overcome.'¹ I shall probably move to her class in the spring or autumn.

But to return to my evening. Naturally many of my Conservatoire friends and acquaintances were there. My performance was right at the beginning of the programme, so that the rest of the evening was free for me. I gravitated once again to the company of Mademoiselle Alpers (and her brother). She is very nice, of course, but has really absolutely no personality, and she is beginning to bore me.

19 December

Yesterday I performed some of my pieces ('Fairy Tale', 'Snow', etc.) at the 'Evenings of Contemporary Music' in the dual capacity of composer and interpreter. My entry on stage was greeted with a scattering of applause, which pleased me since after all I was making my first appearance there. I was quite calm and played well. There was applause after almost every number and at the end. It would be untrue to say that the applause was wildly enthusiastic, but that is the nature of the audience and in any case people clapped my pieces more than the other items in the programme. I heard that after I had left the stage there was a great deal of muttering, noise and vigorous exchange of opinions. In general, even if not everything I did met with universal approval, different pieces were liked by different people, and I was listened to with great interest, which is what I need.

Three of Myaskovsky's songs were also performed. Although they are probably his best examples, they met with little success. He was not present himself as he has fallen ill with influenza, or perhaps he was simply too nervous. I like very much his song 'Blood', but it failed to please the audience. One or other of the 'Contemporaries', it may have been Karatygin,² delivered himself of the provocative opinion that Myaskovsky's music has already

---

she gets through a recital as a queen might through a drawing room.' (Bernard Shaw, *Music in London 1890–94*, vol. II, (London: Constable & Co., 1932).)

1   I quoted this maxim in a letter to Papa. His response was: 'But sometimes those dead bodies can rise up and strike you on the back of the head.' (Note by Prokofiev.) In the *Autobiography*, Prokofiev quotes Myaskovsky's advice as being rather more brutally expressed and in line with his father's comment: 'When you are marching towards your goal, it's no good looking at the corpses you have to walk over.'
2   Vyacheslav Karatygin (1875–1925), composer, also one of the most knowledgeable and perceptive critics of new music, admirer of Stravinsky, Schoenberg and Prokofiev. Karatygin's review of the notoriously scandalous premiere of Prokofiev's Second Piano Concerto at Pavlovsk is, for example, a model of intelligent and far-sighted commentary.

dated. I interpret this as meaning that until recently the newest trends in music were those Myaskovsky is following, but they have already moved on whereas Myaskovsky continues to write in the same style and it therefore appears dated. This analysis may well be correct.

This was then my debut appearance in public as a composer. All the same I can't attach too much importance to it; it is my Symphony that is preoccupying my thoughts. And Glazunov, as luck would have it, has started another drinking bout. Devil take it, perhaps I should make a donation to the Temperance Society...

On 3 January, so I hear, there is to be a Conservatoire evening organized by my academic classmates from last year 'just like the one we did then'. I think I should like to go.

1909

10 January

Activities are starting up again at the Conservatoire. I'm glad about this; I had a most disagreeable Christmas, hardly went anywhere, and Papa, who had come for the holidays, fell ill with influenza on the third day and spent the whole time in bed. For the first time we saw the New Year in at home – previously we have always been at the Rayevskys. The outlook for my Symphony is turning sour. On the 31 December I saw Glazunov at a rehearsal, but all he did was pontificate: 'Be patient, let me get this concert over first...'

And now he's started drinking... Maria Pavlovna Korsak[1] says that she has some influence with a certain Ruzsky[2] (he owes her 2000 roubles). This same Ruzsky is a friend of Glazunov's and therefore in turn has some influence with him. She thinks this may be a way to get something moving with the Symphony, although I don't have much faith in it. So, patience, patience, patience...

I've been playing piano duets with Mlle Alpers. I got hold of Glazunov's Fifth Symphony yesterday in the Conservatoire, which she has mentioned a few times and which I love very much, and tried it out with her. She is, it turns out, a terrible sight-reader. Just as I expected!

20 January

I finally met Mlle Glagoleva in the Conservatoire yesterday. I was going along to Winkler's class, absorbed in my own affairs, when I suddenly met her coming in the opposite direction along the basement corridor, arm in arm with her friend Popova. She has grown up, become very slim and is more beautiful than ever. She greeted me in the nicest possible way and we chatted for ages. She told me she had spent Christmas in Yelizavetgrad, and that she had been studying with Meyerovich but was now changing to Drozdov. Meyerovich is Yesipova's star pupil and is likely to end up with the prize concert grand and gold medal. Glagoleva said he had been chasing her

---

1 Maria Korsak (d. 1915), a friend of Prokofiev's mother and Aunt Katya Rayevskaya, was married to Vladimir Korsak, the Chief Public Prosecutor at the St Petersburg Palace of Justice.
2 Nikolay Ruzsky (d. 1927), a wealthy amateur cellist for whom Prokofiev subsequently wrote the *Ballade* for cello and orchestra, Op. 15. Ruzsky was noted for his lavish hospitality, which Prokofiev enjoyed on numerous occasions despite prickly relations with Ruzksy's daughters Irina (Ira) and Tatyana (Tanya).

assiduously, so she was surprised when he suggested she should study with him. But he behaved throughout with impeccable correctness and the lessons went very well. Today is her first time for a lesson with Drozdov, and she was nervous as anything – her knees were shaking and buckling under her. I was delighted to have seen Glagoleva; I felt proud to be in her company and to be able to feast my eyes on her. It did wonders for my self-esteem to observe the way in which, without interrupting her conversation with me, she would nod an acknowledgement to the obeisances of passing students who either were acquainted with her or would like to be. What tact, what delicacy, what gracious self-possession in addition to her good looks! Of her type, Glagoleva is perfection. The impression she made on me was tremendous. Nevertheless, I am not the slightest bit in love with her. There is no question of this, and in any case there would be no point. I conclude by adding the opinion I expressed to Bessonova and Ospovat after my encounter with Glagoleva (which naturally I am hoping will be passed on to her): 'Yes, Glagoleva has really blossomed in beauty and intelligence.'

24 January

I saw Glagoleva again on Thursday. She greeted me with the words: 'You're just the person I'm looking for!' What it is about, and it seems to be urgent, is that she has a dancing partner of some kind with whom she wants to perform an Assyrian dance in Assyrian costume, and there is accordingly a need for some Assyrian music to dance to. Hence her appeal to me as a knowledgeable and competent person in such matters.

I said she would have perfectly fine Assyrian music if she could just get hold of an old frying pan, and that would fit the bill quite satisfactorily, but she objected reasonably enough that the Assyrians featured a lute or something of the sort in their music. Could I not dig up some Assyrian motif and then write some music based on it? I explained that just a motif on its own would not be much use since it would need some harmony to go with it, and the Assyrians evidently lacking any concept of harmony, one would have to cobble together some conventional Oriental harmonies. So would it not be easier to get hold of some music that already existed? I made enquiries of a Sacchetti[1] student who happened to be passing (say what you like, but Sacchetti does have a first-class knowledge of the history of music) and he pointed us in the direction of *Empress of Saba*,[2] which we found straight away in the Conservatoire library. I started to play it and picked out a few

---

1 Livery Sacchetti (1852–1916), cellist, historian, musicologist and professor at the St Petersburg Conservatoire.
2 Opera (1861) by Charles Gounod. To English speakers, 'Saba' is 'Sheba'. In the *Autobiography* Prokofiev attributes the suggestion to the Conservatoire's librarian, Friebus.

places while Glagoleva listened. We soon alighted on the Processional March in the first act, which sent Glagoleva into raptures both about the music and about my playing of it – sight-reading, if you please, and so beautifully! It was exactly what she needed, and of course nobody but me would do to accompany her. I declined. Glagoleva started to plead, politely making sure she had my first name and patronymic and so on correct. After all, we would only need four rehearsals of an hour and half each, over in Petersburgskaya Storona![1]

I was inexorable. 'Cross my heart and hope to die, I have a chess congress starting in a few days!'

'Well, please come on Sunday. That way the three of us – you, I and my partner – can at least work out how and what we are going to dance!'

I remained unmoved, enjoying the sensation of resisting this beautiful girl whose slightest whim was obeyed by all at a wave of her hand. 'I suffer from chronic allergies that give me a cold in the head and I am forbidden to go anywhere near Peterburgskaya Storona. Come to the lesson on Monday, I'll be there as well, and bring your partner along. We'll be able to sort something out then!'

Glagoleva consented, and that was how it was left between us.

31 January

Maria Korsak invited me to her house at the same time as Ruzsky and that was how I met him. I played him my Symphony, which he liked, especially the last two movements. He found them very original and said he would speak to Glazunov, and not only that, he thought it would be good for me to become acquainted with the well-known critic Ossovsky[2] and with Alexander Ziloti.[3] The introductions were performed three days later at a Belyayev concert; both gentlemen were very amiable and said they would be glad to listen to my baby in a few days' time. But two weeks have passed since then without sight or sound from them. Glazunov started a heavy three-week drinking bout on the 3 January, and emerged from his terrible affliction only about four days ago. Meeting him in the Conservatoire I immediately launched a full frontal attack: 'Alexander Konstantinovich, when is the orchestra going to perform my Symphony?' Glazunov muttered

---

1 Literally 'Petersburg Side' – an area of the city of St Petersburg, a little out from the centre but not very far. Now known as 'Petrogradskaya Storona'.
2 Alexander Ossovsky (1871–1957), prominent musicologist and critic, composition student of Rimsky-Korsakov, professor at the St Petersburg Conservatoire.
3 Alexander Ziloti (1863–1945), pianist, conductor and concert organizer, cousin of Sergey Rachmaninov. Ziloti had been one of Liszt's favourite pupils; Prokofiev states with relish in the *Autobiography* that Liszt used to call him 'Zilotissimo'.

something under his breath and then began speaking in his customary inaudible, inarticulate fashion, completely evading the point that interested me. He drifted vaguely on to the subject of Scriabin's *Poème d'Extase*, but I headed him off and managed to steer the conversation back to my question. Eventually Glazunov said, 'Have a word with Nikolay Nikolayevich Tcherepnin, show him your Symphony, and see what he has to say. Maybe then we will play it.'

I approached Tcherepnin, tiptoeing on eggshells: 'Would you be so kind as to look at my Symphony? I've already shown it to Glazunov, you see, and he said it would be important to know your opinion.'

Tcherepnin was exceedingly gracious, listened to the Symphony and pronounced his verdict: 'If this work was anything like a conventional student composition, such as for example Galkovsky's *The Gypsies* or Lemba's Symphony, I would certainly recommend it for performance. But your piece goes way beyond the limits of normal student work, it is harmonically too complex for our orchestra and they won't be able to play it. You would flee in horror at the first rehearsal. Not only that; I'm not sure there are going to be any student concerts this year. But if you succeed in arranging something with another orchestra, that would be very good; I support the idea and will do what I can to help.'

While we were speaking Glazunov came up and said he was arranging for the Symphony to be played by the Court Orchestra at the end of February, and that I should get the parts copied.

So that's settled. But it doesn't satisfy me: of all the concert series this is the one that gets least publicity, and the hall the orchestra plays in is awful. What a pity I have already outstripped the abilities of the Conservatoire orchestra! . . .

The orchestral parts for the Symphony are now being copied.

4 February

I now meet Glagoleva regularly on Mondays and Thursdays in the Conservatoire. Bit by bit the saga of the Assyrian dances unfolds. The Glagolevs are holding a masked entertainment on the 7th, at which Glagoleva will perform. She has been putting tremendous pressure on me to accompany the dances.

At first I was quite sincere in my refusal. I did not want to, and I was too lazy, but eventually I gave in and agreed. We started to rehearse. At my insistence, the first rehearsal was in the Conservatoire. Glagoleva produced her partner, B. E. Petri, a nice young man; we settled the details of the music and worked out a preliminary plan for the choreography. Yesterday we had a proper rehearsal at her Institute and worked admirably from nine until half past eleven. First we invented steps for her alone, then with Petri, and then put it together with all three of us. It has actually begun to shape up quite well.

Incidentally, there is something about Glagoleva, I am not yet sure exactly what, that is beginning seriously to put me off. I already find her beauty boring.

Now to another theme. On 30 January Zakharov performed at a student evening; he played well, but not as well as he can do. Mme Alpers and her daughter were both at the performance and issued the most pressing invitation for next Sunday. 'Unfortunately I won't be able to; at eight o'clock sharp I must be at the opening of the chess congress!'

'Well, come after the congress, then.'

'I will if I possibly can.'

As I said goodbye to them I was firmly resolved to pass up the invitation. But after ten minutes or so I felt a strong desire to go, and when Sunday came, soon after eleven o'clock, as soon as the chess session ceased to hold my interest, I called a cab and went to their house on Shestaya Rota Street.[1] When I rang the bell the door was opened by the elder brother, then Verochka darted out followed by her younger brother, so I was greeted by all three of them.

The evening passed in a relaxed, informal way: some of the time at the piano (Verochka sang in a small, quiet voice), some dancing – in a word very pleasantly. Mme Alpers (I still don't know her name and patronymic) is an enchanting person, extraordinarily gentle, with wonderful eyes and teeth. Everyone was very friendly. Once when Bessonova addressed me as 'Sergey Sergeyevich', Alpers objected, 'Oh, how terribly formal!' and several times herself called me 'Seryozha', a name she obviously likes. I don't know why, but I pretended not to notice, maintaining formality by continuing to address her as 'Vera Vladimirovna'. But I very much like being in their house: they asked me to visit without ceremony.

1 March

Glazunov speaks – and his bidding is done. On 23 February the Court Orchestra played my Symphony. True, it was only a private rehearsal – Glazunov evidently does not want a public performance of my Symphony in case it might damage me – although in fact I don't see how it could. Either he is opposed to me appearing before the public in a half-baked state, or he wants to avoid the risk of my works being performed prematurely. Goodness

---

[1] 'Shestaya Rota' means 'Sixth Company Street' – in the military sense. The Prokofievs later moved to Pervaya (First) Rota.

only knows the real reason, but it has not made my life any easier. Hardly had Keck finished copying the parts for me and relieved me of 54 roubles, and hardly had I finished proofing all five hundred pages (although this task was greatly lightened by the help of Myaskovsky and even my mother), when the day came for the rehearsal at which it would be performed.

A few days before I met Glazunov: 'Alexander Konstantinovich, would it be a good idea for me to take the score to Warhlich[2] a couple of days beforehand?'

'Yes, all right, take it to him.'

'Alexander Konstantinovich, perhaps it would be best if I played the score through to him?'

'Well, do play it to him, then.'

'Alexander Konstantinovich, would you be so kind as to give me a card of introduction to him?'

'Here you are, then.'

In fact he was good enough to give me a complete letter in which he asked Warhlich to receive me and let me play the work through to him, recommending me in addition as an 'excellent pianist'.

I called on Warhlich.

'No one is at home.'

'But I have a letter from Glazunov!'

'The thing is, you see, he is unwell and has given instructions that no one should be admitted. If you wish, I can give the letter to him.'

Evidently the letter was read.

'They have recovered, and will receive you now.'

Warhlich was extraordinarily courteous, listened to the Symphony, finding the orchestration of the first movement not colourful enough but having high praise for the second movement and approving of the third. In general he made it clear that the work interested him and he was happy to conduct it. As I left I apologized for disturbing him, but he replied that he was happy to be of service to an emerging composer, and on that note we parted.

On Monday 23rd at a quarter to ten I was in the Court Orchestra's rather uncomfortable hall. Also present were seven of my closest relations, plus Myaskovsky and Zakharov. I did not invite anyone else, not being sure how appropriate it would be to inundate a private rehearsal with members of the public. Warhlich appeared at ten o'clock, and a quarter of an hour later, Glazunov. I had not known in advance that he would be coming, and I found his presence very disconcerting. It is true that after my Symphony the orchestra was due to rehearse his *Elegy*, so he would have had to be there for

---

2   Hugo Warhlich (1856–1922), German-born violinist and conductor of the St Petersburg Court Orchestra.

that, but surely he could just have put in an appearance for his own piece.

In any event Glazunov appeared and the orchestra began my Symphony. My family were sitting on the right, Myaskovsky and Zakharov on the left near the front while Glazunov sat diagonally across near them, even closer to the front. I positioned myself behind him. Glazunov rose from his seat to say something to Warhlich, but then turned and came to sit beside me. Warhlich raised his baton and announced: 'Symphony.' I was not the least bit anxious.

They began. Everything appeared to be in place, except that it sounded rather loud. The brass chord in the ninth bar blared somewhat, but otherwise everything was fine. The main theme and its extension sounded right. Zakharov shifted about in his seat murmuring approval of the sequence of dominant-seventh chords. Eventually we arrived at the second subject, and this seemed all right too, not too loud as some people had warned me, except that the trombones were very strident. Glazunov got up and asked them to play *forte* not *fortissimo*, and *legato* not *staccato*. I sidled up to Warhlich and asked him for a shade slower tempo.

Everything went smoothly after that, and even the trombones quietened down. The transition to the final theme and the theme itself did not sound as effective as I had hoped, somehow the seams showed even though this is one of the most scrupulously designed passages in the score. I blamed the orchestra and the awful acoustic of the hall. Start of the development. The trombones underscoring the opening subject – an addition I made only yesterday – sounded wonderful. We reached the climax of the development. Almost nothing could be heard above the brass: all my combinations of textures simply disintegrated. I shall have to broaden out the themes and make the brass play more quietly.

There followed, as Andryusha put it, a bit of a hole: the flute could not be heard at all and the clarinet only feebly. Of course this is partly due to the hall, but they will have to be doubled. The pedal point also vanished: I don't know what was going on at that point. And finally, the last chord obviously needs lengthening. Thereafter everything was fine; the second subject sounded splendid in the recapitulation. The first movement came to an end.

The opening of the second movement sounded better and softer than I had expected. All went well until the bass-clarinet theme at the very end of the movement, which could not be heard no matter what the player did. I asked Glazunov if he thought this was due to the orchestration or the acoustic of the hall? Glazunov muttered something into his beard but then added, 'All the same, it could do with strengthening, it needs something . . .'

'Bassoon, perhaps?'

'Yes.'

Incidentally, I was amused to see how Glazunov disliked the unresolved ninth at the very beginning before the entry of the strings. He quickly turned to me: 'Is that right?'

'Yes,' I replied. But I can see that until one gets used to it, this chord can seem strange.

The opening theme of the Finale sounded coarse; it should be more *legato*. The imitation in the bass clarinet could not be heard – with all the racket going on this was true generally of this instrument. Warhlich and the orchestra just could not make this passage work although they stopped and tried again a couple of times. The second subject was all right. The development sounded coarse, mainly because of the performance, but the parallel fifths were very good. Later on, however, the *fortissimo* at the very end of the development section sounded watery, which is a great pity. Here the orchestration is definitely the culprit. In the coda, the four horns swallowed their theme, and the transition to G major was unconvincing, it would be better simply to repeat it. Further on all was well, but the return of the opening theme, which is designed to be an impressive moment, passed without making much effect; the trombones blasted out *staccato*, and generally the moment went for very little although by all appearances it ought to have sounded splendid. The last page sounded a bit rough.

In general the movement I liked most was the second, which was to my ears near immaculate.

The Symphony ended, to be followed by the break. At this point Baron Stackelberg[1] appeared, resplendent in the uniform of a general. Glazunov whispered to me, 'You should thank him', and thereupon presented me to him. 'How young he is!' exclaimed the Baron.

I started to express my thanks.

'You'd better wait though, until we've heard it,' responded Stackelberg.

I did not understand what he meant, but just then the orchestra assembled on stage again after their break, and began to tune up by running through some of my themes.

'A bit late in the day!' smiled Myaskovsky.

On came Warhlich... and suddenly I heard an E minor chord with a fifth above it, and my Symphony started again. This was a completely unexpected and joyous surprise. This time everything went far more smoothly and sounded twice as good as the first time: the orchestra was making an effort in front of the Baron and really playing for all it was worth.

I was absorbed in the music, following attentively the integration of the themes, the counterpoint, the part-writing, even though the first hearing had made me pretty tired. This is the only way I can account for the fact that

---

1 Baron Konstantin Stackelberg (1848–1925), Director of the Court Orchestra, and incidentally owner of an extensive collection of musical instruments.

although the Symphony was played right through without a break, I had absolutely no impression of it as a whole, merely an assortment of separate fragments and individual passages. It distressed me for some time afterwards that I had not come away with an idea of what sort of work I had come up with; I had to ask everyone what sort of impression it made on them. The *Andante* I more or less understood, and hearing it the second time I liked it the best of the movements because of its fullness, its lovely harmonies and overtly seductive passages. The Finale could and indeed should sound much better, and as for the first movement I don't know what to say as I have no clear impression of it at all. Myaskovsky, Zakharov and all my relations liked it very much. When a week later I got the score back, I found that I liked it too.

At the end of the Symphony Warhlich presented me to the orchestra: 'Gentlemen, this is the young composer whose Symphony you have just played.'

The orchestra tapped their bows on their music stands, I bowed and thanked them as Glazunov whispered I should, saying something like, 'You played it very beautifully', and then I thanked the administrative triumvirate and listened to Glazunov's *Elegy*. Then I said goodbye and left. Stackelberg said to me, 'Fine, fine . . . only you know, the way you orchestrate is not very colourful' – i.e. repeated word for word what Warhlich and Glazunov had said.

Ziloti returned to St Petersburg from abroad on 1 March. On Sunday I visited M. P. Korsak and she asked me what Ruzsky had done for me. Since the answer was nothing, she promised to telephone him to ensure that my Symphony will at least get to Ziloti. It seems unlikely that he will want to perform it next season, but at least it is important he should get to know the work.

Now here's another thing. Nurok has arranged a concert of music by young Russian composers to be played at the artist Makovsky's[1] Salon exhibition, and has included three pieces of mine: 'Fairy Tale', 'Despair' and 'Suggestion diabolique'. They were to have been played by Pyshnov[2] but have now been passed over to Yovanovich,[3] a pianist known for his skill at sight-reading and for the possession of a fine soprano voice. Yovanovich was supposed to demonstrate how well he had learned my pieces by playing them through to me at Karatygin's house, but all he did was play 'Fairy Tale' execrably, and 'Despair' and 'Phantom' not at all. I made the appropriate remarks

---

1 Sergey Makovsky (1877–1962), poet, art critic and founder of the Makovsky Salon, established in emulation of the Paris Salon. A close associate of Alexander Benois and other *Mir Isskustva* acolytes, Makovsky founded *Apollon* magazine in 1909 and remained its editor until 1917.
2 A more familiar spelling would be Pouishnoff, the name by which the Ukrainian-born Leff Pouishnoff (1891–1959), a student of Yesipova, subsequently became well known in the West as a barnstorming virtuoso.
3 Mladlen Yovanovich, Serbian-born pianist.

to him, in a fairly forthright but light-hearted manner, but Yovanovich took offence. Next day Nurok sent me a letter in which he asked me to apologize to the pianist. I wrote Yovanovich a charming but unapologetic note, having in fact rather taken offence myself at Nurok's attitude. As a result my pieces were not played and I ceased to attend the 'Evenings of Contemporary Music'.

Winkler, who did attend the concert, said it had been a very unsuccessful event and that Yovanovich's performance of a work by Medem had been disgraceful. Kankarovich said he had met Karatygin somewhere, and Karatygin had told him that I was very talented, more even than that, but that I lacked restraint both in my music and my character, and that I had a very high opinion of myself – so there!

12 March

The second rehearsal of Glagoleva's dances took place a few days after the first one. Petri was ill and did not come, so Lyosochka[1] and I rehearsed alone. We did not do so for long, however, and adjourned to drink tea in her sister's empty flat just across the landing. Tea was *tête-à-tête* in the little dining room, after which we did a little more dancing, I played her something of mine, 'Despair', I think, which sent her into raptures, and then I accompanied her home and we parted. It was all very lively, gay, pleasant and correct, but rather like being in the company of a miniature iceberg. This seems to be how it is with Glagoleva. She is certainly very gifted, extremely so, but I cannot help wondering how nice a person she really is.

On Saturday, 7 February, I presented myself in accordance with strict instructions at nine o'clock. The guests had been bidden to arrive at ten; the ball was being held in the Institute.

Everyone including myself – much to my distaste – was in fancy dress and wearing masks. I am not used to wearing a muzzle and found it very inhibiting to my speed of thought. However, since everyone recognized everyone else anyhow, the masks soon came off. I knew hardly anyone so stood by myself in a corner to observe the proceedings, which earned me a rebuke from Glagoleva: 'You behaved like a composer, not like a clown; I'm very displeased with you.'

I danced a short *Pas d'Espagne* with Glagoleva, and left it at that. She dances as if performing a holy rite, making every step with the utmost precision and not uttering a word, whereas I am the complete opposite, I make no effort to do the dance correctly and chatter away nineteen to the dozen. The centre of attention was Petri who, dressed up to the nines, energetically directed the dancing and noisily enlivened the company.

1 Affectionate diminutive of Glagoleva's Christian name Leonida.

The Assyrian Dance did not begin until about three o'clock in the morning, when apparently the Meyeroviches[1] arrived. Glagoleva simpered, uttering affected little cries of protest, but eventually began. The dances themselves seemed to go off all right, perhaps they were very good, Christ only knows. Of course they were applauded and there were calls for encores. About that time tea was served, and only then did the atmosphere really begin to liven up.

Most of the time I was acutely bored, coming to life only towards the end when I danced enjoyably *avec entrain* with Mlle Meyerovich, talking throughout and even managing to knock over a chair. I went home at six, but I heard the party went on until eight.

26 March

Recently I have grown accustomed to the Conservatoire and become very attached to it. The person I see most often there, regularly I should say, is that lovely, dear girl Verochka Alpers. On Mondays and Thursdays I have a Winkler lesson at three o'clock while she has Ossovsky at the same time, so we often meet; on Wednesdays and Saturdays at half past twelve I finish History of Music with Sacchetti, and not long after she comes in for Harmony. I usually hang about in the Conservatoire for a while and then meet her. Finally, on Tuesdays at half past eleven we are both there for Aesthetics and sit together through this class. We play noughts and crosses or I correct her harmony exercises, sometimes we cut an india-rubber into little pieces – the class goes by not too boringly although we don't always have much idea what Sacchetti has been talking about. On Fridays and Sundays we don't meet. At the moment the opera class is working on a production of *May Night*,[2] so after the piano lesson we often go over to listen to the rehearsal, but she is always in a hurry to get home for dinner, afraid to be late.

Not long ago Mama renewed her friendship with Yekaterina Lyashchenko, with whom she had been in a state of hostility for eight years, not so far as I know for any good reason but because of some intrigue of Aunt Tanya, who still refuses to meet her. Yekaterina Ippokratovna is actually quite a good musician, who at one time studied with Mama and now plays the piano quite reasonably. When we met, she said to me, 'We have some mutual friends: the Alpers family', and launched into a whole dithyramb about them.

She introduced me to Kalinovsky, another musical gentleman and friend of the Alpers household. It's possible that this chain may lead to Mama meeting the Alpers, so that the two families will establish a connection. Not that I care much, it's all the same to me.

---

1 Alfred Meyerovich was a pianist and former star student of Yesipova.
2 Opera (1878) by Rimsky-Korsakov.

I am not in love with Verochka, but I do like her very much. She may not be so attractive as a woman, but she is an exceptionally dear and gentle person. Her mother, in her day, was probably even nicer, but her father – although I do not know him very well – I do not care for as much; his manner tends to be rather crude, although he cares passionately for music and is the dominant musical force of the household.

Verochka has a saintly personality; it is rare to encounter a character such as hers. In spite of my being so highly strung, in spite of my neglectful treatment of her, sometimes abandoning her in the middle of a rehearsal to seek the company of another female student or to meet Myaskovsky, she never gets angry with me, never shows the slightest hint of disapproval, never gives vent to the mildest reproach.

Since Papa could not be with us at Easter, Mama and I came down on the Monday of Holy Week to Sontsovka. But because I have an Aesthetics exam on the Friday after Easter, I will have to go back on my own to St Petersburg – my first solo trip. It's horrible here, cold and damp, and the garden is decidedly dank. Still, it is good to prepare for Aesthetics, and think about St Petersburg. Went to see the Rebergs – a complete non-event as far as I was concerned.

8 April

And thus on the second day of the holiday week I left Sontsovka and returned to St Petersburg. It was a good journey, although on the way I lost an opera *scena* I had written for Wihtol. When I got back to St Petersburg, therefore, I had to write out again all twenty pages of the music, which I did, and presented it to Wihtol yesterday. Having listened to it, his verdict was that it made no sense whatever to him, a wonderful reward for all my toil. The examination is on Sunday, and I shall be interested to see how the panel views my *scena*. For myself, I like it very much.

The Aesthetics and History of Music exams were on the 5th. Verochka Alpers ducked out of them; she had no time, she said, having to practise for her forthcoming piano exam to allow her move up to the Senior course. When we met we were like old friends.

On Saturday there was a Conservatoire party, to which I went. The difference between these parties and the parties the Academic classes lay on (at least those I have attended in the past) is, first, the latter happen only once a year whereas there are three or four of the music Conservatoire parties, and secondly, the former are rather more enjoyable. In any case I went along, not because I had any special reason for going, as on the last occasion, but just to pass the time. The first impression was ghastly, a terrible noise and anyone I might have the slightest desire to dance with conspicuous by their absence. But then I met Alpers, and although I don't normally like to be with just one girl all evening, this time I was happy to as she seems to have no other young men dancing attendance on her. It was good fun. We spent the rest of the evening with Berezovskaya, quite pleasantly, then Akhron and I took her home, and I went to bed at four o'clock.

14 April

At ten o'clock today there was an examination for wind players, at which I accompanied the trumpeters and clarinettists. Released from that, and knowing that my History exam was due to start at one o'clock, I decided to stay around the exam room in the hope of meeting Mlle Kuzovkova. She was not there, but during the break, while I was standing in the Small Hall talking to someone, she sat down behind me with Mme Vasilieva. I turned round to speak to her: 'Mlle Kuzovkova, did you pass into the Senior course?'

'I did!'

'Brilliantly, I expect?'

'Four and a half.'

'It's amazing, they're letting children into the Seniors these days!'

However, I then changed the subject to the excitingly topical one of the impending History exam. Vasilieva, who sat there giggling from time to time, I rather ignored.

15 April

I met Kuzovkova on the stairs again today, a tiny creature with a sly smile and terribly attractive. Verochka Alpers is under threat. But I saw her too today, and after a gap of five days was very pleased to do so. Although she was hurrying to a lesson, I dragged her off to listen to the exam performance, where we sat by ourselves chatting in the balcony.

But then, suddenly realizing that she was now more than half an hour late for her lesson, she insisted on going to it. All my attempts at persuasion proving in vain (she is always remarkably firm about such things) Verochka departed, leaving me glowering disapprovingly.

She has begun to dress very well: out on the street she wears an elegant navy blue suit with a white boa and hat, while indoors she wears a dark blue dress, also very nice. Another point in her favour.

26 April

A week ago we had our exam in Form, which consisted simply of assessments of the work we have produced during the year. I presented my opera *scena*, a couple of songs, a chorus, a sonata, an Andante, a few pieces –

thematic fragments and outlines. If I had also brought some variations, a genre I can't abide, I would have produced more work than anyone, since no one else had done an operatic *scena*.

I was asked to play the sonata: the whole of the first movement, half the second and half the third, then 'Thou wast meek but dangerous',[1] and finally the opening of the operatic *scena*. I was told that would be enough.

Elkan still had to play after me, following which the professors began their deliberations. We were outside the door, but could still hear the odd snatch of discussion. The greatest indignation was aroused by my compositions, Lyadov voicing the strongest objections. 'What is your view?' he was asked.

'I have nothing to say!' he shrieked. 'Nothing to say, and not one of them will I have in my class. No harmony, no form, no music – nothing whatsoever! Monsters, the lot of them!'

Everyone then talked at once, followed once again by Lyadov: 'They're all trying to be little Scriabins. Scriabin took twenty years to get where he is, but Prokofiev thinks he can write like that straight out of the cradle!'

This was met with silence. Then Lyadov again: 'It's like a procession of elephants!'

'Prokofiev undoubtedly has talent, but the stuff he's writing – the devil only knows what it is!'

Glazunov was tactful enough to be absent, as he was needed for another examination. After about an hour and a half we were brought the verdict: we were all given 4.5, but Lyadov refused to accept anyone in his class for the future except Akimenko and possibly Rozovsky.

Kankarovich left because he was conducting that evening and Saminsky was not there. Wihtol dropped a hint to Elkan that there was little point in his staying any longer, and Myaskovsky had taken offence at Lyadov's comments, so the only one of us determined to pursue the matter was myself. However, I managed to persuade the other two to wait at least until Glazunov appeared, and when he did, I led the charge.

'So, Alexander Konstantinovich, what are we supposed to do then?'

The plump, pot-bellied fellow mumbled in his usual indistinct fashion, that, umm, you see, he couldn't force Lyadov, and, you see, he couldn't take us himself, because he was absolutely full up, so perhaps we should approach Sokolov[2] . . . and so on and so on.

---

1 This song, written at the suggestion of Yelizaveta Esche, seems to have disappeared. It was a setting of a poem, 'The Song of Love', by Mirra Lokhvitskaya (1869–1905), who is said to have had a passionate and poetically inspirational affair with the Symbolist poet Konstantin Balmont. Balmont's poetry was already well known to Prokofiev, although the two men did not meet personally until 1915; it was a favourite source of texts for Prokofiev's songs and choral settings, and provided the title of the *Mimolyotnosti* (*Visions fugitives*) collection of piano pieces published as Op. 22.
2 Nikolay Sokolov (1855–1922), composer, teacher and prominent member of the Belyayev Circle.

Elkan said nothing, Myaskovsky said nothing, and then someone else came up to Glazunov and our attempt collapsed around our ears. Gradually everyone dispersed until only I remained. I waited for Lyadov and mounted a full frontal assault on him: 'Anatoly Konstantinovich, is it true that you don't want me in your class?'

'Oh, for pity's sake, what is the use of discussing it . . .'

'But how can you do this when I studied with you for four years, and then for some reason a year with Wihtol; almost everything I know I learned from you and now that I am coming up to graduating you don't want to let me continue with you!'

'Yes, but what is there for me to teach you? It's not I who should be teaching you, but you me!'

Out of the blue, up rushed repellent Professor Petrov and started jabbering away: 'Yes, yes, that's quite right what he says, it's not he who should be studying with you, but you with him! Quite right, absolutely right . . .' and then lapsed into silence.

Lyadov continued, 'The monstrosities you have given birth to are so appalling, how do you expect me to teach you now?'

I replied, 'If that is the case, if I am as you say on the wrong path, now is precisely the time that I should be corrected and brought back into the way of truth. You seem to be saying that as I'm now a trained composer I should accept my diploma and make myself scarce from the Conservatoire! In the first place, not all my music is of that sort; if you like I can show you my Symphony, there is nothing too terrible in that . . .'

'What about the seconds?'

'What do you mean, the seconds?'

'Well, at the "Evenings of Contemporary Music" didn't you play one of your pieces that is full of seconds? Seconds, seconds, seconds . . .' and Lyadov, waggling two fingers in the air, graphically illustrated the interval of a second.

'Well that's the way the people there compose, after all, so it was in the nature of an experiment, and they liked it . . .'

'All right, write something during the summer that you can show me in the autumn, and I'll see about taking you then.'

'You mean there's hope for me?'

'Yes, go on and write something.'

We shook hands firmly, and parted.

Myaskovsky was subsequently envious of the result I had achieved, and after questioning me in detail also spoke to Lyadov. The latter said that up until the examination he had been intending to accept both Myaskovsky and me, and it was only the examination that had so upset him. He now agreed to take Myaskovsky as well.

Later on I heard that the entire Solovyov class, four or five students, had failed the exam in Form, among them the mature students Alexeyev, Osipov, Rukin and others.

7 May

Concerning Max. Some time during the winter, at a student concert as I recall, Mademoiselle Alpers, Madame Alpers and I were sitting together in the balcony. On to the stage came two students from Ossovskaya's[1] class to play a two-piano piece, and along with them another student to turn the pages. He sat between the two in a remarkably easy and relaxed manner, and I was fascinated by the way in which he rose to turn the pages to right and left.

'That's a clever chap, look where he's positioned himself,' I said to Verochka.

'That's Max, one of Ossovskaya's students,' she explained.

Later I saw him again in the Conservatoire. I mentioned this to Alpers: 'I do like the look of that fellow-student of yours.'

'Yes, he's got rather nice, regular features. And he's very musical . . .'

'Does he play well?'

'Not particularly at this stage, he's still on the Junior course, but he knows everything there is to know about the repertoire. Sometimes I disagree with him, even quarrel with him, because he is so certain he is right about everything. He even knows Papa's songs.'

I found this interesting, and it sparked a desire to get to know him which, however, I soon forgot about.

Now that the exams were going on and I often found myself in the company of Miss Alpers and her friend Kamyshanskaya, Max as a classmate of theirs often attached himself to us. He seemed anxious to get to know me as well. Soon we started talking, and thenceforward the four of us always sat as a group listening to exam performances. Afterwards we would go home together, as we all lived in the same direction.

More often, however, there were just the three of us, without Kamyshanskaya. Usually Max and I would walk Verochka Alpers to her home on Shestaya Rota, then go back to Pervaya Rota, at which point Max would turn right and I left to the Pokrov,[2] near where I lived. These walks were very enjoyable, we had the liveliest conversations and Max was often very funny.

The weather was lovely, the scent of spring was already in the air, and one day we took it into our heads to walk further afield, for instance to the

---

1   Varvara Ossovskaya (1876–1942), pianist and teacher, wife of the critic and musicologist Alexander Ossovsky.
2   The Church of the Protecting Veil, near the Prokofievs' apartment on Sadovaya Street.

Summer Gardens. No sooner said than done. We fixed the day, met at the Conservatoire as a threesome and set off. We went on foot as far as Nikolskaya, and from there took a tram to the Troitsky[1] Bridge. We decided it wasn't worth going into the Summer Gardens, and instead boarded a boat going to the Saviour of the Blood.[2] We didn't go in, but when we reached Kamennoóstrovsky took another tram and went to Novaya Derevnya:[3] nobody knew what this place was like, and we were interested to have a look and find out. When we got there we walked around for a quarter of an hour and ate some chocolate I had brought along. On the way back we took the boat and went back to the Summer Gardens, where again we took the tram and so back to the Nikolsky Market. Then we walked Verochka home and separated to our own homes.

Verochka was thrilled by our excursion, I was happy with it, Max said it had been 'all right'. Max is a very skilful conversationalist and towards the end, when I was getting a bit tired from our trip, even began to annoy me a bit with his predilection for verbal nuances. I was feeling too lazy to think up ways to compete and score points off him, and I felt stung by this. Max rose greatly in my esteem.

There and then we agreed on another excursion, a bigger one. I suggested going even further afield, out to the edge of the city, but in the end we decided that we would take a boat to the Islands,[4] as far as the boat went, and then walk along the shore. The company expanded to include Kamyshanskaya. Whom else would we like to invite? We couldn't think of anyone.

13 May

Two days later there was a general rehearsal for the Graduation Day concert. Alpers and Kamyshanskaya were there; I said hello to them and we exchanged a few words. For most of the time I sat with Max, who genuinely does know a great deal of, and about, music. I like inflicting on him things like some frightful *Fairy Tales* of Medtner that he didn't know, or Scriabin's latest works. However, I was not always successful in surprising him with Mr Scriabin.

---

1 Troitsa – 'The Trinity'.
2 The great Russian-style church on Konyushennaya Square, recently restored, where Alexander II was assassinated.
3 Suburb to the north of the city on the far side of the Neva.
4 The city of St Petersburg consists of forty-seven islands in the Neva delta, with its maze of tributaries, canals and connecting bridges. When Petersburgers refer to 'The Islands' (Ostrová), however, they mean the group of three islands called Kamenny Ostrov, Yelagin Ostrov and Krestovsky Ostrov that form the north-east boundary of the old city, bounded by the Neva as it flows into the Gulf of Finland on its journey from Lake Ladoga in the east through the city into the Gulf of Finland. On the far side of the river the suburbs begin.

The Graduation Concert took place the following day. The whole idea of Graduation Day at the Conservatoire is inextricably bound up with appalling crowds and interminable performances. I positioned myself in the balcony, right at the end near the stage, and sat leaning against the wall on the red velvet rail overlooking the stage. It was a good spot from which to observe the stalls. First, there was a splendid view of the doors into the hall when they opened between the various numbers of the programme to allow latecomers to stream in through them. People flowed like lava in through the doors to coalesce at the crossings as they sought to pass further along the gangways. The mass of humanity heaved and oozed until eventually all the gangways and seats were filled so that it would have been impossible to find room to drop so much as an apple into the hall. Then there was the absorbing spectacle of the whole audience straining up in their seats at the end of each number in order to see what was happening on stage. At such times the mass grew in height by about an arshin[1] and resembled nothing so much as a saucepan of milk coming to the boil.

At first I saw no one I knew, or at least no one I knew in whom I was interested. But the programme would be going on for six hours, so I could relax knowing that sooner or later I would see everyone I might want to, and such was indeed the case. Bored, I walked along the long corridors that lead to the teaching part of the Conservatoire, and in an otherwise empty corridor I bumped into Alpers wearing a new and very striking white dress.

'What are you doing here?'

'Waiting for Papa. We heard that one of his songs is going to be sung, so we telephoned him, but he may be late!'

Other people I met later included Alpers's brother, Zakharov, Myaskovsky and his sister, Kamyshanskaya, Kuzovkova, Deshevov, the Kalinovskys, Ye. I. Lyashchenko, Ziloti, Piastro's father, Kobylyansky and finally, after the interval, Yelizaveta Esche. She was just there by chance, dressed not particularly extravagantly but very interestingly. If there is any one of the female students who could unquestionably count me among her admirers, it would certainly be Yelizaveta. In January, when saying goodbye to her after the Ball, I had asked her to provide me with some verses for a song, and three days later had written to her reminding her of my request. It was not long before her younger sister handed me in the Conservatoire her reply, accompanied by a good choice of poetry. I chose 'Thou wast meek but dangerous' and, as I wrote to tell Esche, quickly completed the song. She did not reply. Meanwhile I realized that I did not like the song very much, and wrote another. In the event, however, the first proved to be good, and the second much less so. I did not see the elder Esche sister in the Conservatoire, but from time to

---

1 An arshin is about 70 centimetres, so the image is of something rising just over two feet.

time met her younger sister, who always asked about the song. I would reply that I didn't have it, I must have given it to someone, and so on.

Eventually, at the beginning of March, Sofia Esche pressed me most insistently to bring it to a rehearsal she was going to attend the following day. I did so, but when she asked me, 'Have you brought it?', I answered evasively, something to the effect that, 'I don't know . . .' At that moment Yelizaveta came up and said that she had received my letter, apologized for not having replied, and asked me to show her the song. I then played it; both sisters fell into raptures over it and begged me to transcribe it for them. I did so, inscribed it with the initials 'E.N.E.', and sent it to Esche. Again I got no reply, and only at the Easter evening concert at the Conservatoire, where I met her hand in hand with Alpers, did she trill, '*Merci* for the song!' and that was all.

I was offended. I didn't see either sister for some time after that, but finally met Yelizaveta at a concert in the Glinka Museum. 'Let's go in,' she said, 'I really want to hear Lomanovskaya. But there's such a crowd.'

'Why don't I take you into my retiring room? It's so comfortable in there, and you can hear everything very well!'

I took her into the retiring room next to the Tsar's box, which is naturally out of bounds to hoi polloi. But some time before I had succeeded in getting into it when I found a door leading to an under-stage corridor, into which you could also get access from one of the rooms beside the green room. So now I tried my luck again by opening that door, thinking that way I could get Esche into the retiring room. Lomanovskaya had already started to sing, so we had to hurry, and Esche and I almost ran along the corridors, up stairs and down stairs, across landings, taking wrong turnings, before finally bursting into the retiring room. Before our eyes appeared Gabel[1] and Dzhiarguli,[2] upon which we instantly turned round and fled back down the staircases the way we had come. It was very funny, we were shamefully hot and flustered, behaving like naughty schoolchildren. All the same we did want to hear Lomanovskaya, so I took Esche back to my perch by the balcony rail. We were fine there and settled down happily for the next hour and a half.

Meyerovich, our First Prize-winner, played, and played extremely badly, why I don't know. I think he is an excellent pianist, with a good technique and great power, but on this occasion his playing lacked equally refinement and delicacy on the one hand, and fire on the other. I cannot help wondering if this is really how he is? Piastro played well, as did Mikhelson,[3] and to my amazement Drozdov's performance of Tchaikovsky was also good. Esche left after that.

1 Stanislav Gabel (1849–1924), bass singer, professor at the St Petersburg Conservatoire where he directed the opera class.
2 Dzhiarguli was an official of the Conservatoire, akin to a theatre house manager.
3 Irina Miklashevskaya (née Mikhelson; 1883–1956), later professor at the Leningrad Conservatoire.

I have at last received my diploma and now have the status of a Free Artist. Completing the course in Form and passing all the mandatory subjects has given me the right to a Diploma in Composition Theory. If I remain as a Practical Composition student of Lyadov, as I am doing, I may if I wish delay taking my diploma for another two years; provided I come to agreement with Lyadov I would have the opportunity of improving my final marks (currently 4.5 for Form and Fugue, 4 in Orchestration) and get a medal. But my father wanted me to take the diploma now whatever happened, to be quite certain of it, and so I had told Gabel that I wished to have it now. They read out my name from the stage and called me up to be formally presented with the piece of paper, but I did not go up – where would be the pleasure in that without the medal? Gabel handed the document to me straight after the concert. I don't quite know why Papa was so insistent, but insistent he was and so I was forced to take the diploma. Naturally I would have preferred to leave it and can see only one advantage in having it now, that I achieve at least a certain status which will give me more freedom to disagree with Lyadov.

27 May

In this way the conclusion of the Graduation Day performance also brought to an end my subservience to the Conservatoire, and there was in theory nothing to stop me taking off to whatever of the four corners of the world I wished. Mama had to remain in the city until June, because after intensive searches, furious arguments and protracted hesitations we had found a new apartment and were planning to move to Troitskaya Street, but I had no such restriction and could go to Sontsovka any day I pleased.

However for the first time in five years I did not feel especially drawn to the country, and so took my time over such matters as ordering a new suit, getting new hubs for my bicycle, music for the summer, etc. In this way passed a further ten days in the city, and I left for Sontsovka only on the 20th.

A couple of days after the Graduation Day concert I went into the Conservatoire, where I caught a fleeting glimpse of Alpers. Later that day, towards the evening, I went back again to rehearse with a singer whose exam performance I was accompanying. Once again Alpers and Kamyshanskaya were there. Verochka was sitting her Harmony exam that day, and from morning till night had been being tormented by her examiners. We talked about this for a while and I learned that Max had fallen ill with influenza, which is why he had disappeared from view as far as the Conservatoire was concerned.

In the days that followed I was often in the Conservatoire, listening to the exam performances which went on every day. Progressively fewer and fewer people came in, and if I did not find what was going on in the examination hall particularly absorbing, I got bored.

The liveliest event was Rozanova's class exam, at least in respect of the audiences it attracted. This teacher had a good many students from the current and former Academic classes, so there were a lot of young people coming to listen to their friends. The hall was flooded with sunlight, everyone was dressed in their best for spring, and altogether the atmosphere was relaxed and happy. Yelizaveta Esche appeared in a lilac suit with a long tulle streamer on her hat that went right down to the floor. I bowed to her in greeting.

'I've come in to hear my sister, but needless to say I was late.'

'I also came to hear your sister, and of course I was late too,' I confessed.

Esche is already appearing at the Maly Theatre, admittedly in minor roles, nevertheless it is something to be appearing on that stage. She is touring the Volga during the summer to enliven the whole region with theatrical performances.

'If I had stayed at the Conservatoire,' she said, 'I would still be scraping away on a fiddle. But now here I am, an artist of the Maly Theatre!' She could hardly believe that I was now myself a Free Artist.

Meanwhile, I was getting into trouble at home for disappearing so frequently to the Conservatoire, and I stopped spending so much time there. The last time I was there was on the 20th, when I went to hear Ossovskaya's class exam in order to hear Max, who I thought by now would have recovered and would be playing a Beethoven concerto. Also, he was planning the following day to go to the Crimea, and I wanted to see him before he went.

However Max was not better, did not play for the exam and was nowhere to be seen in the Conservatoire. I went up to Verochka Alpers – I remember, I was wearing for the first time my European suit and light yellow shoes, having finally discarded student dress. Verochka had been taken to see the doctor, who had ordered her not to play the piano, to rest in bed for two hours in the afternoon, and to eat eggs in the morning – in short, to look after her nerves and take care of her health generally. It was now time for her to go home and have lunch. We went out together. She was obviously reluctant to part from me, and suggested that we go as far as Nikolsky Gardens together, where she broached the subject of our corresponding over the summer.

Usually during the summer I correspond with a wide circle, but it is mainly about chess or music. This time I had decided I could also afford to write to a small number of my student girl friends. As for Alpers, I had never imagined that such a modest little girl would be given permission to write to a young man, so had not included her on my list. But now, as we walked through Nikolsky Gardens, she twice dropped hints that she would welcome an exchange of letters with me. Whether accidentally or on purpose I don't know, but I did not react at the time, and it was only as we were saying goodbye that I decided to say, 'Well, all right, do write to me if you like and you've nothing better to do.' So now, standing on the corner of Sadovaya and Voznesensky Streets, she said, 'Shall we write to one another then?'

Naturally I agreed enthusiastically, and asked for her summer address. A pencil was produced – no paper. I turned out my briefcase, which contained a Scriabin sonata, and stood holding it in front of her like a desk. She wrote it down, complaining how illegible her writing was. So there we were, standing outside Fillipov's pâtisserie,[1] I on the pavement and Verochka down on the street. It must have made a most original scene.

The address safely written down, we clasped one another's hands firmly, said goodbye and went our ways. I was very happy with events, and left St Petersburg that evening.

About Glagoleva. After the Assyrian Dances I stopped meeting her in the Conservatoire. Once she gave me back my briefcase, which I had left at her house after the ball and which no doubt she had thought I had done as a pretext for having to go back to retrieve it . . . When subsequently I was giving a performance of the Schumann *Toccata* at a student concert, I wrote to her. She replied merely that she would certainly come if I could procure a pair of complimentary passes for her. I did this, and she did come and hear my *Toccata*. I naturally felt flattered by this, and so on 2 May, when I was to play the Korsakov Concerto for my concerto exam, I wrote again to tell her about it. This time she did not appear, but three days or so later I got a letter from her saying she was sorry not have been able to come, but hoped very much that I would drop in to see them some time, and . . . that was all.

On 14 May I had several calls to pay, among them the Glagolevs. When I arrived, everything was upside down, the floors were being polished, the chairs were up on the tables, it was almost impossible to get in to the drawing room. Lyosenka appeared after about five minutes, in a somewhat dishevelled state. 'Why weren't you here yesterday?'

'Yesterday?'

'I'm off to Italy soon, we had a farewell tea party yesterday. I wrote to you.'

'I didn't receive anything . . .'

'Oh, that's a shame. Please excuse the mess we're in here. We'll be leaving soon and I didn't go to bed until six o'clock.'

I stayed for about twenty minutes, and then left. As I was saying goodbye she presented me with a rose, apologized for her mother not being able to come down to see me, told me the expression on my face was just like a disappointed little boy, and said that if they got a group together on Sunday to go boating she would invite me. She would write and let me know. Two days later a letter arrived in the negative; I wrote her a rather pompous and offensive reply, she responded to that, and thus of its own accord a sparky correspondence started up.

1 Well-known pâtisserie and coffee shop on Troitskaya Ploshchad (Trinity Square). It had a sister establishment in Moscow.

31 May

At present I'm in Sontsovka writing a Sinfonietta. This is how the idea of the piece came into being. Scriabin's *Extase* was being played at a Belyayev concert, and at the rehearsal it was being dismembered section by section, each excerpt being repeated several times. When they got to the end, I assumed there would be a complete run-through from the beginning, but instead ... suddenly they launched into Rimsky-Korsakov's Sinfonietta. It was such an unexpected contrast that Myaskovsky and I could not help looking at one another and bursting out laughing. After Scriabin's elaborately majestic music with its colossal layers of complexity, its maelstrom of confusing tempi, its gripping climaxes culminating in ecstatic outbursts, Korsakov's Sinfonietta appeared so small, so self-effacing, but at the same time transparent as water, and so lovely! It was a delightful little scrap of a child side by side with a monstrous giant.

It came to me with blinding clarity that both kinds of music could be good, and could be enjoyed; both compositional genres were valid. And gradually I arrived at the conclusion that what I should do during the summer was compose both a large-scale work and a little Sinfonietta. It had long been my intention to compose a large, descriptive symphonic tone-poem. The previous year I had written a symphony rather than a tone-poem simply because a symphony had more of a definite structure than a symphonic piece bearing a descriptive title, and since writing symphonically was new to me as a composer. I felt I needed a clearer framework.

Now, however, I resolved to tackle programme music, even though I had not settled on any particular subject. But in the meantime, during the spring, in between other activities, I had begun thinking about themes for the Sinfonietta, so that when I arrived in the country almost all the material was ready in my mind, and within a week I had written out the score of the third movement. Everything went very smoothly and easily. My first plan was to compose a single-movement work, but then I had second thoughts and turned it into three. Then it occurred to me that it would be good to repeat the first movement at the end, strengthening the unity and bringing a fresh and original touch (Myaskovsky, however, is sure that someone has already done this and it doesn't work at all). Eventually, when the contrasts between the second movement and the scherzo turned out to make them seem more like an opening movement and a finale, I decided to intersperse them with intermezzi in a style corresponding to the first movement, and thus ended up with five movements. But the whole work should not last more than fifteen to twenty minutes.

An important spur to the Sinfonietta was the following circumstance. After numerous obstacles Kankarovich had succeeded in being given *May*

Night to conduct at the Conservatoire. He proved to be really rather a good conductor and has received an invitation to conduct in Voronezh this summer. When I jokingly asked him if he was planning to include any Prokofiev in his programmes, he readily agreed to do so. We agreed that he would perform my Symphony this summer, and my Sinfonietta too if I finished it. I'll enjoy going to hear them. I am well aware, however, that although Kankarovich thinks I am talented, he cannot bear my music.

4 June

There has been an important development with my piano studies: I have changed from Winkler to Yesipova.

When I came back to St Petersburg in the autumn I was firmly convinced that I would go on studying with Winkler and that I would graduate from the Conservatoire as his student. But everyone, and I do mean everyone, started asking me if I wasn't planning to transfer to Yesipova. Why are you still with Winkler? Change over! Make a move! He's not giving you anything any more. You'll never become a virtuoso with him – and so on, and so on. Although I defended Winkler, the more I continued my lessons the more I gradually began to lose confidence in him. Earlier, when I was still in the Junior course, I could see that there was an unbridgeable gulf in understanding between us, but as time went on I became much less aware of the difference, he ceased to give me any new ideas, he often repeated himself and was not coming up with interesting new insights. Sometimes I would challenge him, sticking up for my own opinions and as often as not prevailing; occasionally I could even show him nuances he had not thought of. In short, our relationship had moved beyond the normal relationship between a professor and a student. It was a constant source of amazement to the class that Winkler and I managed to stay on good terms.

By December, but only after a prolonged and disagreeable period of hesitation, I had definitely decided to leave Winkler. Nevertheless, I decided to put off the actual deed until the spring, and so when that time of year came round, I commissioned Zakharov to open negotiations with Yesipova.

I was worried that she might refuse me: it was not easy to join her class, she was inclined to be very capricious, and so on. She might agree to hear me, but if she did, and even if she liked me, she might still not say straight away that she would accept me, but only that she would 'think about it'; her decision could be delayed until the autumn, and only if she has a space then will she say yes. I was very anxious not to fall between two stools, that is to say to leave Winkler before I had been accepted by Yesipova. As a demonstration piece I prepared the Schumann *Toccata*, which I had successfully performed – with no input from her of course – at a student concert.

Zakharov took time to bring himself round to raising the subject with her, but eventually, one fine day in April, he announced that, you see, well, there's my friend Prokofiev, one of Winkler's students, and it has long been his dream to come into your class, and he would be so grateful if you would listen to him. Yesipova said, 'I know him, I heard him play at a student concert and in his exam, and I'll take him. But I know that Winkler is proud of him, and I will only do so if Winkler asks me himself.'

A propitious response, but the last requirement looked unachievable.

I sent Zakharov back with a new commission. 'It doesn't seem very likely', he said to her, 'that Winkler is going to take the initiative and ask you about Prokofiev ...'

'Well, what do you expect me to do about it? I'm not about to fall out with Winkler. You know, what you should do is ask your friend to approach Glazunov, he'll know how to deal with it.'

I immediately approached Glazunov.

At my opening words our soft roly-poly's currant-bun eyes bulged, and he muttered reluctantly that he knew for a fact Yesipova would not accept anyone else into her class, and continued in that vein. When I reassured him that she had already promised to take me, Glazunov changed tack, becoming very friendly and saying that of course while Winkler was a first-class musician, Yesipova was a pianist and he (Winkler) was not; and if my ambition was to become a pianist then of course I should study with a pianist, and so on.

Next, he said that I would have to rely upon Winkler's discretion; he was a gentleman, and surely he would let me go without making a scandal. He promised to take the matter up with both Yesipova and Winkler, and on that note we parted.

The following day Glazunov told me that he had spoken to Yesipova and she had confirmed that she would indeed accept me. Now there remained only the most difficult part: to talk to Winkler.

'Here he comes,' I observed, 'perhaps you ...'

But Glazunov anxiously began fluttering his hands and his belly: 'No, no, one can't do these things just on the fly. This must be carefully thought out, prepared ... and then ...'

Several days went by and I did not see Glazunov. When I could wait no longer, I sought him out, and asked if there was any news.

'No, no, I haven't spoken to him,' replied Glazunov. 'You know, it's rather awkward for me, as Director ... it might be seen as an order ... it would really be better if it came from you ... why don't you have a try ...'

I could see there was no help for it, and the best way forward would be for me to ask Winkler straight out, as though it were a perfectly normal request and there was no other way.

Calmly, almost cheerfully, I went up to Winkler. 'Alexander Adolfovich, you have taken me right through the Junior course and now I'm through to the Advanced. May I now have your permission to leave you ... with grateful thanks ... and go to Yesipova?'

'But will she take you?'

'Apparently so.'

'In that case I can't possibly hold you back.'

'You mean you will sign a card for me giving your approval?'

'If it is necessary, yes,' and here Winkler for the first time showed some annoyance. Whereupon he proceeded to take me through the Korsakov Concerto with scrupulous care. He maintained impeccable command over himself, his voice cracking only once or twice.

My exam was on 2 May, and I played the concerto quite respectably; Winkler himself played the accompaniment and gave me a 5. Glazunov and Winkler were full of praise; the audience was not large but my family were there in force, all eight of my relations, and among other friends Ye. I. Lyashchenko, Myaskovsky, Zakharov, Alpers, Max and a chess player called Kudrin.

The exam over, Glazunov had a long discussion with Winkler, round whom his students then clustered, wanting their programmes for the summer. Feeling somewhat guilty I hung back behind the others. One by one, Winkler gave out the assignments and then, turning to me: 'And for you, Mr Prokofiev, here is your passport.'

He handed me a certificate of permission to leave his class and join that of Yesipova. I thanked him in words of sincere appreciation: he had given me technique, had set me on my feet, he had always been attentive to my needs; we parted friends. Mama also went to him and thanked him for his kindness towards me.

20 June

The Winkler question was now resolved. But I still had not met Yesipova, and did not know what I should be practising during the summer. At the exam performance of Kalantarova's[1] students, Zakharov introduced me to her. While the exam was going on Yesipova, tired of listening, went out from the hall to smoke a cigarette and stood by the door into the hall talking to Nalbandian. Zakharov led me up to her.

'Anna Nikolayevna, this is your student Prokofiev. He would be glad to know what he should be working on this summer ...'

Yesipova looked me up and down and extended her hand. I took it, and repeated Zakharov's request.

---

1 Olga Kalantarova (1877–1952), pianist and teacher, assistant to Anna Yesipova and eventually Professor of Piano at the St Petersburg Conservatoire.

'First of all, has Winkler released you?' asked Yesipova.

'Winkler has released me. Our parting was very amicable. He gave a note of permission to come to you.'

'Perhaps you could show it to me?' said Yesipova.

'Unfortunately I do not have it with me. But I can tell you word for word what it says: "I have no objection to my student, Sergey Prokofiev, joining the class of Professor Yesipova. A. Winkler."'

To this Yesipova said nothing. Then: 'During the summer, I should like you to work on the classics: Bach, Handel, Mozart, Beethoven. Practise the classics.'

'Thank you.'

We exchanged salutations and parted.

Interestingly the whole conversation was conducted in a discreet *pianissimo*, so that neither of us could actually hear much of what the other was saying.

And thus – hooray for me! – I had moved from Winkler's class to Yesipova's, and to be fair, had managed it brilliantly. Many very talented pianists who, like me, wanted to come to her, had to undergo the ordeal of playing for her, shaking with fear before the dreaded audition in her apartment. I had none of this, and the most alarming aspect of the affair had been my conversation with Winkler, which in the event proved to be more than amicable.

Among others who were joining Yesipova's class along with me I should mention the very young Malinskaya. A student of Vengerova,[1] she had moved up to the Senior course in the spring, gaining a 5+ in the technical part of her test. Since those moving to the Advanced course include a lot of people who aren't really up to much, this five star greatly intrigued me, so I went to hear Malinskaya's repertoire exam. I met her on that occasion and was able to calm her down before she went on stage. She did indeed play marvellously: most lively and convincing. So now we are fellow students of Yesipova!

23 June

As soon as I settle into rural existence, my diary tends to go into a decline, and if I do write it up it's not more than once a month. After all, this out-of-the-way spot does not give me much to write about.

I'm writing my Sinfonietta and practising the piano, sometimes with good results and sometimes not, and I spend two hours with Papa on drawing, for which I seem to have developed some facility, and mathematics. Correspondence plays a big part in my life when I am in the country. I divide it into

---

1 Isabella Vengerova (1877–1956), pianist and former Yesipova student. In 1924 she moved to America and took up a professorship at the Curtis Institute of Music in Philadelphia, where her students included Leonard Bernstein and Samuel Barber.

three categories: chess, music, and purely pleasure. I am playing – quite successfully – in two 'Niva' chess tournaments. In the first of them I am confident of winning first prize; I am not so well placed in the second although it too is beginning to look good. My main musical correspondent is Myaskovsky, and in the pleasure category Alpers, Schmidthof and Glagoleva.

Alpers's letters were really a surprise to me: long, full of interesting content, fluent and well written. She is very good at describing her summer pastimes, and gives a rounded picture of her life in Pavlovsk; in a word, reading them one gets a complete and satisfying impression. The correspondence with her has become the one I most look forward to, to the extent that – so far as I can calculate – I should have received a letter from her a week ago but there has been none. I wait eagerly for the post and am disappointed and upset when there is nothing from her; it quite spoils my mood. The post to and from Pavlovsk seems to take two and a half weeks!

At first Glagoleva wrote spasmodically, and her letters were just brief notes. But three days ago I got my first long letter from her. But my God, what a letter! I could hardly make out any of it, either the handwriting or the subject matter. Glagoleva always so perfectly in control, Glagoleva the very incarnation of correctness – and now, suddenly, her handwriting all over the place, crooked, muddled, full of crossings-out, incoherent, obscure . . . she is in France doing nothing, sunk in idleness, idleness, idleness.

Lastly, Max and I hurl short, fiery epistles at one another, battlefields for our wit and verbal jousting.

Kankarovich wrote from Voronezh that he could not guarantee a performance of the Sinfonietta because the police were persecuting the Jewish orchestra and it was not certain whether it would be allowed to give concerts or not. However, his next letter was more reassuring; the business with the police had settled down. I started to step up the pace with my Sinfonietta, giving myself a deadline of 25 July to get it finished. That meant I must get a serious move on. It was still looking as though I would simply have to battle on through all the obstacles regardless, when Kankarovich solved the problem very simply: he quarrelled with his Voronezh impresario and left the city showing him a clean pair of heels. Voronezh was thus left with no Kankarovich and I was left with no Sinfonietta, because I abandoned work on it before getting to the end. Of course I will finish it in the autumn, but for now it can stay where it is, as I have no desire to compose it at the moment!

This turn of events did not depress me at all, in fact I was happy that I no longer had to finish the work by 25 July. Working under such pressure was beginning to wear me out. I am almost certain I shall be able to place the Sinfonietta in St Petersburg, where it will get a better performance than it would have in Voronezh. As a work, it has turned out to be more complex than I originally thought, and I was in any case starting to worry that Kankarovich and his orchestra would not be able to cope with it.

It would be altogether too boring to sit here in the country until autumn, and I'm not going to. Mama has gone to Yessentuki to take a cure for her rheumatism, and so instead of going to Voronezh I'll visit her. It will be nice to go to the Caucasus.

21 August

I arrived in Yessentuki on 2 August. This is my first time at a resort. The crowds of elegantly dressed people walking all day in the park were good to look at. It was pleasant to watch beautiful women with their well-dressed cavaliers and at the same time to feel that I too was no less of a well-dressed gentleman, not someone from the lower orders. Even so I was aware of a slightly chilling sense of alienation: these were not my people, not remotely, and I felt very alone without my friends. How was it that in spite of everything the crowds at Conservatoire parties could evoke in me such a pleasant, warm glow? The answer is that I knew so many of them personally, or at least knew something about them; they were my people, I knew their characteristics and how they behaved.

I stayed with Mama in a hotel called the 'Kazyonny Barracks'.[1] In the room opposite ours there was a lady called Varvara Nikolayevna Brandl, whom Mama had got to know on the train to Yessentuki. They then roomed together, took the cure together and so on. When Mama got food poisoning from some roast lamb she had eaten and became really ill, this Varvara Nikolayevna devotedly cared for her and nursed her so that she soon got better. Mama told me all this in a letter, I was touched by this concern, and when I replied sent my greetings to Varvara Nikolayevna.

I had no cause to repent of having done so because Varvara Nikolayevna proved to be a young and rather beautiful woman, tall, well formed if perhaps a little full in the figure ('a Yessentuki beauty' in the words of N. N. Smetskoy), vivacious and high spirited, quick off the mark, relishing the attentions of her admirers, a little given to caprice but on the whole very nice indeed.

We instantly became friends, not that I was running after her or anything though. We signed up for an excursion to Beshtau,[2] going as far as the mountain by horse and carriage. There were three of us in our carriage: Varvara

---

1 The 'barracks' that had been acquired from the all-Russian Exhibition in Nizhny Novgorod and were brought to Yessentuki to be re-erected as a hotel. 'Kazyonny' means 'belonging to the State or Government'.
2 A mountain with five summits near Pyatigorsk. (The name comes from the Turkmen language meaning 'five mountains', as does the Russian name Pyatigorsk.)

Nikolayevna, a girl from the Conservatoire, and I. (The Conservatoire girl was called, I think, Syropyatova, one of the countless pianists studying there.) It was terribly uncomfortable sitting on the little seat in front; I twisted and turned, to and fro, until I finally managed to get settled a bit.

This was how it was for about half the way, after which we went up the mountain on foot. Eight people altogether had signed up for the excursion, Mama not being one of them. Varvara Nikolayevna was soon bringing up the rear of the party, groaning and stopping to drink water and slowing us all up. This irritated me, and the girl from the Conservatoire and I were first to the summit. We had a very lively conversation, and I met her a couple of times subsequently in Kislovodsk. But I started to be perhaps a little neglectful of her, and when once I turned up late for a duet session we had arranged in Kislovodsk, she decided that I was insufficiently respectful towards her, and badgered me with tales of how she frequented Court and belonged to the highest echelons of society. I was less than impressed by this arrogant display and teased her mercilessly, which enraged her. At our parting she was furious and I was laughing, even though her insufferable arrogance left a disagreeable aftertaste.

But this is all by the bye.

When we came down from Beshtau, we split up. Varvara Nikolayevna was tired, and went to Zheleznovodsk by carriage, taking three other ladies with her. The remainder of the party boldly decided to walk to Zheleznovodsk. Having covered these five versts we still felt so full of vim that the Conservatoire girl and I went off to have a look at Zheleznovodsk park. But the way we were dressed and our long walking sticks aroused such amused attention that we beat a hasty retreat. It was only when the whole group reconvened at the train at eight o'clock that fatigue began to take its toll. All the same, when we got back to Yessentuki, Varvara Nikolayevna and I burst into our room so energetically that Mama, who had been expecting us to be worn down to the ankles, was first amazed and then horrified at how much we had caught the sun.

We had immediately to wash ourselves with sour milk and lemon. Having neither one nor the other, Varvara Nikolayevna and I went out to buy a lemon and two portions of yoghurt, rushed back home, cut the lemon in half, divided the resulting mess, smeared it all over our faces, and went to bed.

On the 9th Varvara Nikolayevna left to go to Yalta. I had to go to Zheleznovodsk to discuss our departure plans with Katya Ignatieva, and so went as far as Beshtau station with Varvara Nikolayevna. I arrived at Yessentuki station a few minutes before the train was due to depart. Varvara Nikolayevna was already there, surrounded by a throng of people who had come to see her off.

In a quiet moment I said to her, 'Mama begs to be excused, but she is having a massage; she asked me to bid you farewell and kiss you goodbye . . .'

'Well,' said Varvara Nikolayevna, with a smile, 'hadn't you better carry out her instructions?'

'I don't think one should rush things!' I replied.

The train came in, amid scenes of indescribable chaos. The second class was already full to bursting. The porter who had her bags tried to get them into a first-class carriage, which quickly filled up with bags literally up to the roof. Noise, crush, swearing at the guards, the final whistle, and to crown it all a blustery wind.

Eventually the train started, the passengers packed in like sardines. I lost sight of Varvara Nikolayevna and had to fight my way through the passengers to find her. Only when we got to Pyatigorsk did I succeed: she was in a third-class carriage and rather the worse for wear: she had been shoved and jostled, the feather in her hat was broken, her things were spread all over the train goodness knows where, it was all, in a word, too terrible. However her natural gaiety soon reasserted itself.

When we arrived at Beshtau it was time for us to make our farewells. On the third and final bell her train pulled out, and I crossed the platform to my train, which was already waiting there.

One other feminine face fleetingly passed before me at this time, one that left me with sweet memories. It happened on the second day of my visit. Some cadets staying at Mineralnye Vody had organized an event in aid of some good cause or other, a concert to be followed by a ball, and Varvara Nikolayevna was selling tickets for it. The concert programme did not look particularly inspiring, also there was no one to play the accompaniments. Varvara Nikolayevna suggested that I do it. At first the cadets were too shy, but eventually they came to me in a body and asked for my help to get them out of difficulties. I said I did not want to play any solos, but would be glad to accompany.

After the interval, standing in the wings of the theatre, I felt quite at home. I had got on very well with my soloist Gorsky, who graduated from our Conservatoire only a couple of years ago, and we made a good job of three songs. Then there was some kind of recitation, and finally a lezginka, with which the concert programme ended.

The lezginka dancer was a very small, very young girl, about sixteen years old, very pretty and delicate, in a pale blue blouse and black skirt, and an expression of sheer terror on her face. We talked for a while, I calmed her down and cheered her up, laughing and joking as I was used to doing in the artists' room at the Conservatoire. When she went on stage I sat opposite.

I didn't much like the dance itself, but I found the music really attractive. It consisted of repeated four-bar phrases supported by a primitive kind of harmony. Just before it ended I got up and went to join Gorsky in the artists' room. From there I could hear that the lezginka was being encored, and then he and I went in to the hall, reminiscing about the Conservatoire.

In the hall, the ball was beginning. I hate dancing, I am no good at it and am afraid of it, so of course I had no intention of dancing myself. Soon I went to find Mama, who was also not having a very good time, and we decided to go home. Mama went to get her coat from the ladies' room and I was waiting for her sitting in a chair when my pale blue blouse happened to pass by with a friend. Seeing me, she asked, 'Why aren't you dancing?'

'No good at it,' I replied.

Mama came back and we went towards the exit. On the way I again glimpsed my new friend and she threw me a glance. I then left, sure that I should soon see her again, perhaps in the park.

However it was five days before I saw her there. I have two deplorable characteristics: the first is not remembering the faces of people I have met; the second is not greeting anyone unless I am absolutely sure we are acquainted. On this occasion both qualities manifested themselves in spectacular fashion.

My pale blue young lady – actually brown this time – was walking arm in arm with her friend. Not sure whether it was really her or not, I looked her carefully up and down, and walked on by. At the crossing, just near the exit from the park, I saw her again, this time standing in the middle of the path, right in my way. I cannot explain how this happened, but again I looked at her long and hard, almost as if to interrogate her – and walked past without bowing to her.

'What can he mean by that?' I seemed to hear her say to her friend – or perhaps it was merely the expression on her face.

I was extremely angry with myself.

Three days later we went to Kislovodsk, and I never saw her again. And so a charming little cloud disappeared from view over the horizon.

10 September

Max Schmidthof is a truly interesting person.

I have already described how we first met in April earlier this year. I remember I was sitting with Verochka Alpers in the balcony of the Small Hall listening to an exam performance. With us was Kamyshanskaya, whom I had recently got to know.

The performance was about to start, but none of us had a programme. 'Wait a moment,' I said. 'I'll get one from your friend.'

Max was sitting across the gangway with a miniature score in his hands. Of course it looks good to be sitting with a score, but why on earth should one need one for a Beethoven trio, particularly one for violin, viola and cello?

I went over to him and asked to look at his programme.

After the interval Max came and sat behind us, or rather behind Kamyshanskaya. He obviously wanted to get to know me. I knew him by sight, and he had probably heard about me from Verochka, so as I was now in the company of his classmates it was natural that he should come and sit near them, even though the girls were between him and me.

I don't remember how we first got into conversation or what we talked about, I only remember I did not pay a lot of attention, he seemed just like all the others. As we talked I recall silently taking the Beethoven score out of his hands, turning over the pages, then giving it back to him with a smile.

We continued to meet at exam performances, after which he, Verochka and I would make our way home together. The first time we did so, Max did not exactly shine; it was left to me to drive the conversation forwards, which I did in my usual unstoppable way, Max saying very little. I was wearing my new spring overcoat but Max still had on his winter coat. He must have been very hot in it, so he kept it unbuttoned, and I felt a bit sorry for him.

The first time he made me laugh we were walking back from the Conservatoire, and as we came out of the Nikolsky Market into Sadovaya Street we turned towards Vosnesensky. On top of the fire station there is a clock. 'Max,' I said, 'can you see what time it is?'

'I'll just have a look,' he answered, and then, surreptitiously taking his watch from his pocket, said, 'Five minutes to two.'

'My goodness,' said I, 'what fantastic eyesight you have!' but at that moment I spotted him replacing his watch. The penny dropped, and we burst out laughing.

By the time we went on our expedition to Novaya Derevnya, Max's tongue had loosened and we spent our time arguing over the most ridiculous things. When we had walked enough and got tired enough to start for home, we took the tram at Troitsky Bridge and sat in the rear carriage, which was completely empty. I don't remember what we were arguing about, only that Max won the debate hands down. I also remember being put off by the deafening rattling of the tram and hearing Max say, 'Yes, of course, with the tongue I've got, no one ever gets the better of me in an argument!' I stared at him in silence, my brain a complete void, unable to think of a single thing to say in reply.

When I got back home, I began to think: can it really be true that Max's skill with words means I shall never get the better of him? I was accustomed to think of myself as having a pretty quick tongue, and my self-esteem was injured. I told myself it would not always be like this: it had simply been a lucky shot, the result of my being tired. Max was certainly resourceful but not exceptionally so, and in any case he was not noted for quick repartee. In our group the first place always belonged to me, not to him.

After that walk Max and I met every day and became the closest of friends. This was at the beginning of May. Even Myaskovsky noticed our closeness, and would break off our discussions to say, 'Look, there's that chap you're always knocking about with . . .' 'You would be amazed how much he knows about music,' I returned. Indeed I was satisfied that Max really was extremely well informed about music, especially the piano repertoire. He was not nearly so well up in symphonic music, and in this was the exact opposite of Myaskovsky.

On 7 May, at the rehearsal for the Graduation Day performance, Max and I met up for what proved to be the last time before the summer break, sitting together for most of the rehearsal. In front of us were Kuzovkova and her friend, and I very much wanted to go and sit with her. During the interval I decided I would put my plan in operation, and went up to speak to her. At that moment Max came up and said, 'Well, goodbye, Prokofiev, I'm off home.'

He had come up with so decisive an air that I had no choice but to break off the conversation I had just started with Kuzovkova, and say goodbye to Max, which I did in a rather brusque, offhand way. Max then went home.

Soon afterwards I heard that he had fallen ill. I frequently checked his coat peg to see whether he was in or not, but he stayed away and did not come in to the Conservatoire at all. Finally, on the 20th, I came intending to hear his exam performance, but he did not turn up for that either, so I went home not having seen him at all.

I sent him a short note from Sontsovka, to which he replied very affectionately and wittily without a trace of malice. Our correspondence took off once again, both of us setting all kinds of tricks and traps for each other – I more enthusiastically than he. The subsequent letters he sent were not as entertaining as his first one, and sometimes had a sense of strain. And then in August, on my return from the Caucasus, I received a letter of a totally unexpected kind.

It was an extremely rude letter, deliberately designed to cause offence, tactless, aggressive, and yet again not without a touch of wit. The gist of it was: 'When you started writing to me, I thought you would have something sensible to say. But in the event, your letters contain nothing but cheap witticisms that hold no interest for me at all. I am therefore not giving you my new address. I leave here today.'

My first reaction was one of utter astonishment. I had not had the slightest intimation of such a radical alteration in the status quo, indeed all the evidence from the last letter Max had sent me was that neither had he expected his next letter to be in such a vein.

My second reaction was to wonder what I should do now. He had not given me his address. I remembered that in the spring he had said he planned to visit the Crimea. Should I send a letter to Sebastopol, to be called for? But after all there was a lot more to the Crimea than Sebastopol. I decided to write to his old address and hope that it would be forwarded. But what to write?

It should be short, clever, and insolent enough to wound.

I could have worked out something of the sort, and it would not even have been too difficult. But the result would have been a thoroughly abusive quarrel that would probably damage our relationship beyond repair. This was not what I wanted.

As long ago as May I had decided that Max and I were on the way to becoming truly close companions and the best of friends. I had never had a particularly close friendship with anyone in my life; the closest would be Myaskovsky, but the significant difference in our ages was always there to be felt. Thus, even though Max was now insulting me, my aim was to do my best to make peace with him, while still contriving to hold my own banner aloft. This was not as hard as it might seem.

What could have been the cause of Max's outburst?

On my side it must have been that I had provoked him beyond endurance with my continual teasing and facetious remarks. And what were the qualities in Max revealed by his outburst? Inconsistency. Lack of manners. Lack of self-control. Max, in short, had behaved like a spoilt child. So, I reasoned, if I were to adopt the tone of a grown-up chiding a naughty child, explain the position and show myself able to rise above the petty squabble, I would be able to emerge from the situation with my head high, and at the same time avoid the risk of a permanent breach.

However, I could not achieve this without writing a long letter, and sensible as this might have been, a short response was more flattering to my self-esteem.

Besides, there was the problem that if I wrote to the old address my letter would either reach Max, or would fail to reach him. This was most important, because my position would be completely different depending on which of the two possibilities came about. A third possibility was that Max could receive my letter, but pretend that he had not. In that case my position would be extremely complicated.

Indeed, Max's letter occupied my thoughts all day, putting me distinctly out of sorts, and I even thought it would keep me awake at night. But I slept well, and the next day I made a sketch of a mushroom that I had taken from a botanical atlas, and on the reverse wrote, 'Eat some of this, silly boy, it will do you good!' and sent it off to Max. I wrote to Verochka Alpers telling her the story, and saying that we had called our new-born puppy Max. At least that will get the rumour circulating in St Petersburg.

By the time I am writing this, the affair has begun to lose some of its sting, and I am able to look on it almost as a dispassionate bystander. It will be very interesting to see how things are when Max and I meet in October. Probably he is already constructing tragic scenes and rehearsing crushing verbal exchanges ...

22 September

Many guests came to Sontsovka in September: Aunt Tanya, Aunt Katya, Uncle Sasha, Katya and Palya Ignatiev. It was a bit of a squash, superficially very jolly but in fact rather boring. Everyone was very nice, there was much affectionate kissing and games of vint,[1] but when the 19th came I was glad to get away and head for Piter. The rest of the family was to stay in the country for another ten days or so. I arrived back in St Petersburg today and installed myself in the Rayevskys' apartment on Sergievskaya Street, because our new apartment on Bronnitskaya is empty and boarded up, and in addition to that had been broken into and burgled during the summer. (However our things were recovered and the thieves sent to prison.) About one o'clock I went in to the Conservatoire, as I had been missing it, not any one person in particular, but the Conservatoire itself, the idea of the place. Oh, horrors – there are four hundred new students this year! But it will be interesting to see some new faces.

At the entrance I met Orlov, and there on the stairs was Zakharov, hurling a disproportionately furious stream of abuse at me. The cause of this was our summer correspondence and the wildness of my letters. A little more and we would have really fallen out. I tried to steer the conversation into less contentious paths, and learned that Yesipova was about to come into the Conservatoire and begin her first class. I had arrived just in time! I had not yet registered, so I needed to catch her and present myself. A few minutes later Myaskovsky turned up. I am terribly fond of my dear Kolechka. Over the summer we had been writing to one another in a precise and businesslike way. The poor fellow had been sitting out the whole summer in the dust of the city. He has completed a symphonic tone-poem called *Silence*. We agreed to meet this evening at his house.

We were interrupted by Yesipova's appearance at the bottom of the stairs. I went towards her and bowed, she extended her hand to me in gracious welcome. I plunged straight in: 'Anna Nikolayevna, may I come and see you in your class?'

'With pleasure.'

---

[1] A popular card game, mixing elements of whist and preference, involving the classic procedures of trumps, bidding, tricks and the successful or unsuccessful achievement of a contract by the end of each hand. The name 'vint' (in Russian 'screw') derives from the clockwise bidding procedure and the technique of inducing one's opponents to increase ('screw up') their bids to the point at which they will fail to meet the contract.

I was very relieved. Such a capricious queen, but all seems to be going well.

'Prokofiev, I'm putting you down for Fridays,' said Yesipova, when everyone was in the class and she consulted the register.

A student hopeful of joining her class started to play, quite well but not particularly brilliantly. Yesipova listened, Glazunov beside her. When the student had finished, Yesipova said, 'That was good. But unfortunately I have no room in my class, so I cannot take you . . .'

All the unfortunate girl could do was get up from her seat and leave the room.

After her, Shubert played Beethoven's *Appassionata*. It was all right, but I would not put it higher than that. Then another couple of girls . . . I sat and listened, reflecting that my own playing was capable of being both good and bad. I could be brilliant, but I could also lose confidence, and be careless over details. I had prepared Mendelssohn's E minor Prelude and Fugue, and now I was going to have to play it on Friday . . . To regain my confidence enough to bring it to Yesipova, I would really have to spend the intervening two days getting the piece off perfectly and then play it through first to Zakharov.

After I had heard the two girls I left the class. It was about three o'clock in the afternoon, the Conservatoire was quiet and not many people were about. It seemed strange, this calm, when an hour ago everything was boiling like water in a kettle and you couldn't get through the corridors for the crush.

I was not yet ready to leave, and sat on the windowsill chatting to one of the music-theory people. Suddenly Yesipova appeared, having finished her teaching. Having left her class before it finished I felt uncomfortable about her seeing me sitting right opposite her room. I jumped up and made a dash for the staircase in the opposite direction, where I bumped into Verochka Alpers.

She was delighted to see me, and I her. All in all, Verochka is the sweetest person in the whole Conservatoire. If only she could add beauty to her other charms, I would be head over heels in love with her. She has matured and she looks a bit better than she did.

Trying to avoid Yesipova, I dragged Verochka down the stairs with me, and we talked for about an hour. Her reaction to the incident with Max was one of interest and amazement. I was laughing about it and saying that I was very curious, when Max came into the Conservatoire, to see how he would behave.

'Shame on you for replying to him like that!' she said, thinking about the mushroom.

She told me that Nodelman had died in Yevpatoria from typhoid. I am very sorry this has happened. I did not get on especially well with her, and I never felt that she liked me, even telling Verochka things like: 'He's not really to be trusted.' All the same she was a clever person, practical, energetic and lively. As it happened I had thought of her several times during the summer.

At half past three Verochka and I left the Conservatoire and went together to Pervaya Rota, where we parted. I looked in at our apartment and then went back to Sergievskaya Street. It is now evening. I was tired and so did not after all go to Myaskovsky's. I'm writing my diary and practising for Yesipova.

26 September

The day after my arrival, Wednesday, I did not go into the Conservatoire until five o'clock, when I found it completely deserted and so I came home again, slightly dispirited. At home I practised and prepared for my Yesipova debut, and thought frequently of Verochka Alpers, whom I had missed and whom it had been so nice to see again. Myaskovsky came to see me, and I went to visit M. P. Korsak, who took me to her house in her carriage. Nothing else to report.

On Thursday at around noon I went into the Conservatoire to play my Mendelssohn Fugue to Zakharov. This time the Conservatoire was seething. Myaskovsky was there, and I caught a glimpse of Kuzovkova and Berezovskaya . . . We looked for an empty classroom, and I played my Fugue to Zakharov. He gave me a very hard time; I thought I had made a good job of it but he said it was very inartistic and Yesipova would be very critical. Up till that moment, because of all the work I had done on preparing the Fugue, I had felt I was on solid ground for my entry into Yesipova's class. Now, however, listening to Zakharov's criticisms and bearing in mind the high quality of the students in Yesipova's class, then thinking back to her queenly manner during the deferentially whispered conversation I had had with her, I began to feel rather nervous. Nevertheless, practising the Fugue once more at home restored my confidence that I did know it thoroughly, and the following day I set out for my lesson in a calm frame of mind.

But I will come back to that later. Yesipova teaches four days a week, starting at one o'clock, and when I had finished playing the Fugue to Zakharov we went to today's class. The lesson had already started and when we entered, Malinskaya, my acquaintance of the spring, had just finished. The fact that she also was in the class interested me; I consider her a very accomplished pianist, and of course being a newcomer she was in the same position as I.

It so happened that the only available seat was next to her, so I sat down.

'Well, how was it?'

'Seems to have been all right.'

'I hear she tends to bawl one out?'

'No, on the contrary, she was very gentle.'

'Well, splendid.'

Just to sit in on this class is pure pleasure. The students play very well, Yesipova's comments and explanations are fabulously interesting. Overall it is on a much higher and more intelligent plane than other, 'ordinary' classes; one has the impression that the best talents in the Conservatoire are collected here, even the room and the pianos are better quality. It is like being translated from the depths of the countryside into the cream of Petersburg society . . .

After teaching for an hour and a half, Yesipova went to have a break and a smoke. Everyone poured out of the classroom in her wake. Yesipova vanished into the committee room, while we dispersed along the corridors and mingled with the crowd.

I talked to Malinskaya about the impression Yesipova's class had made on her, about how she felt she had got on that day, about how it might go with me tomorrow, about whether it was true one was sometimes required to play technical studies and double thirds, the sort of thing Zakharov and Akhron and I had already long forgotten.

Verochka Alpers came up. She had just played for her teacher Ossovskaya, and was surprised to have been let out so quickly. This time I liked her much less. Compared to the impression she made on me at our earlier meeting, she seemed already to have lost some of her looks. She said that Glagoleva must be back from Paris, as she had already been to see Fliege, but Fliege was intending to leave the Conservatoire. Anisimova was even tinier than before, but had become very fashion-conscious and thought even more of herself than previously. Bessonova has clearly decided to transform herself into a beauty.

At this moment Yesipova passed by on her way back to the class. Verochka went to look for Berezovskaya to get back a book she had lent her, and we Yesipova students returned to the class. However, I did not go in but after stopping and listening at the door for a little while, turned back. Downstairs I caught a glimpse of Bessonova in the distance, but then had to pass Abramycheva sitting on the windowsill in the middle of a group of male and female students. As I came up to her I saluted her with great courtesy but walked on past without saying anything. This may have offended her. Back around 10 September, not knowing by what date I should be back in St Petersburg, I had asked Zakharov, Myaskovsky and Alpers when Yesipova would be starting her classes. Just in case I also wrote to Abramycheva, who lived near the Conservatoire, to let me know the same thing. As I later discovered, she answered my letter, although hers did not arrive in time to catch me in Sontsovka. Never mind, I will thank her another time.

Verochka came and we left the Conservatoire together. She was on her way home and I wanted to go to our apartment on Bronnitskaya to see if any letters had come for me, so I accompanied her as far as Vtoraya Rota.[1]

---

1 'Second Company Street'.

That evening and on the following morning I practised hard for Yesipova, and at noon was already in the Conservatoire. I went into her classroom. Everyone due to play today was there: Zakharov, Akhron and Vinogradov were thumping away at three pianos simultaneously, each playing their own pieces. I stood for a moment and then headed for the door. Zakharov called out, 'Where are you off to? This is just up your street, isn't it, all these lovely juicy dissonances!'

I threw my music case at him and went out.

I was halfway through the door when I was surprised by an unexpected encounter – unexpected . . . but also very welcome. For slinking along the wall, not two paces away, was Max Schmidthof. For a couple of moments we looked at one another. He approached along the wall, and I stepped out through the doorway. He waited, uncertain how I would greet him, and I rapidly ran through my options. After a moment, I went up to him, smiled, and said hello in a very friendly way: 'What's this? I thought you said you weren't going to be here until October.'

'Well, I'm back now.'

'Been back long?'

'Yesterday. You?'

'About four days ago. I've just come out of my class for a moment. This is great timing; I'm about to go in to my first lesson with Yesipova. Very frightening, but you can take my mind off it.'

We sat on the windowsill by the library.

'Listen, what made you send that crazy letter?'

'Well, after your letters . . .'

'In the first place, it was so terribly illogical and inconsistent!'

'Well yes, inconsistent it may have been in relation to my other letters, but if you think of yours, you must admit you were asking for it.'

'Did you get my reply?'

'Your reply? No, I didn't. I left there the next day.'

'Pity. It was rather a good reply. I thought you must have got it.'

'Was it a long one?'

'No, very short.'

'Well, can't have been very interesting, then.'

'On the contrary, it was very interesting. Yours was such a long letter that the only possible way to respond to it was to keep it short.'

We moved on to other subjects. I asked him, 'What did you compose during the summer?'

'I wrote a ballade.'

'Oho! For orchestra?'

'No, for piano. And some songs.'

'You will show them to me, won't you?'

'Possibly.'

'Who are you afraid of? Yourself, or me?'

'Myself, of course. How about your Sinfonietta? Did you finish it?'

'Not completely. It's in the last month of pregnancy. But I wrote some études for Winkler! And a sonata for Lyadov, except I've lost it.'

'How did you manage that?'

'I must have left it behind in the country. They'll send it on. It's the second time I've lost a piece, it's scandalous, really.'

'What about your heart? You didn't lose that?'

'What, down there in the country? It's dead and alive, you can't find a single soul with a pulse. No, my heart's still in one piece.'

'That's good. You'll need it during the winter.'

Shandarovsky came up, but I soon got rid of him. Max and I talked for about another quarter of an hour. Then he took out his watch.

'Well, goodbye,' he said. 'I've got to go to lunch.'

'How do you mean? Have you already had your lesson?'

'No, I just happened to be passing.'

'Is this the first time you've been in?

'Yes.'

'I'll come downstairs with you.'

When we were downstairs I asked him, 'Did you learn the *Toccata*?'

'I did. I'm going to play it to Ossovskaya.'

'What are you going to learn next?'

'I don't know yet.'

'If I were you I'd try Medtner's *Fairy Tales*.'

'Why?'

'You'll be following in my footsteps. After all, you always try to learn what I've just learned!'

Max was lost for a reply to this. It was quite a successful little dig.

When he had got his coat on, I asked, 'When shall we meet again?'

'I'm coming in for my lesson on Monday.'

'I'll be here on Monday as well. So we'll meet then.'

'I don't suppose you'll still be around then. I don't come in until five or seven o'clock.'

'No, probably not . . .'

'Well, goodbye.'

A firm handclasp, and we parted.

I'm pleased with this encounter. I like Max so much, and he will think about me now. I believe I will have produced quite an impression on him, what with the blitheness of my tone of voice when we met, the fact that he saw me emerging from Yesipova's class, the points I scored off him, also perhaps the elegance of my smart grown-up grey suit (he was in his black student jacket). What a shame I won't be seeing him again for some time. On the other hand, perhaps it's a good thing.

And so, having parted from Schmidthof, I went into the class, and the lesson soon began. Akhron was the first to play. He was note-perfect, loud and confident, like a gramophone record, but without much artistic feeling. After him came Zakharov. He played well, and with insight, but all the same something was missing; it all had a kind of smoky miasma over it, and Yesipova was dissatisfied.

'You didn't do much work this summer, did you?' she said.

'On the contrary, I worked very hard . . .'

And indeed, Zakharov had made strenuous efforts all summer, but with wretchedly poor results.

Then it was my turn to play my Fugue, which I did by heart. She let me play the prelude right through without stopping, only once or twice reminding me '*crescendo*' or '*forte*'. But when I had finished she told me that my accompaniment had been uneven, and made me play the whole thing slowly and loudly, pointing up some delicious nuances on the way. She stopped me more often during the Fugue, mostly to criticize my tempo when I speeded up, and sometimes my accuracy, which suffered from haste, and most importantly of all my pedalling, which at one point even caused her to cry out in dismay. But all in all it passed off pretty well, on the level of a 4, or at least a 4 minus, and Zakharov was very pleased with me. My next assignment is Beethoven's Thirty-Two Variations. I have bought the music and have started work on them with great diligence.

4 October

When I came into the Conservatoire on Tuesday, the first person I met was none other than Leonida Mikhailovna Glagoleva. She greeted me delightedly and was very affectionate. She loved the letters I had written to her during the summer, finding them unusual and original, nobody had ever written to her like that, in short Monsieur Prokofiev's style was altogether unique. Then she told me all about her travels and chatted on generally, and when we parted she begged me not to forget old friends. We spent two hours together.

I have not altered my opinion of Glagoleva: she is beautiful and interesting, but she exudes a cold sort of quality. In general, though, I am happy with the way I am passing my time: everything is going well and on an even keel. This autumn is far more full of interest than the same time last year; I remember then seeing Ye. Esche on one occasion and saying in response to her question whether I was getting on all right that my main feeling was one of boredom. No doubt there was an element of posing in this, but there was some truth in it as well. Now, when I wake up in the morning, I know that ahead of me lies a day full of interest and even if, exceptionally, today is not so interesting, tomorrow is certain to be.

11 October

So far I have only had two lessons with Yesipova, but Zakharov finds that I have already made progress. Whether this is so or not, merely to be studying with Yesipova is pure joy. Whenever I am preparing for my lesson I take the greatest pains to refine and polish the piece, to make it sound immaculate, clear and intelligent. What a blessing that I came to her from Winkler!

Nevertheless, the memory of Winkler is sacrosanct. During the summer, in memory of the good years I had spent under his tutelage, I composed four studies especially for him, dedicating them to 'my deeply respected teacher.' I brought them in to Winkler the day before yesterday, so tomorrow I must contrive to meet him 'accidentally' in the Conservatoire to find out how he likes them. Myaskovsky considers them a great success and a step forward. Personally, I think they are a little crude, a first attempt at this form, but still they are more successful than I thought they would be when I first began writing them.

For Lyadov I revised my old Sonata.[1] I am very fond of it: the freshness of its themes, the absolute clarity of its part-writing and the pianistic way it is laid out for the instrument. Myaskovsky was cool towards it; he found the cadences too old-fashioned, but overall it was a success. Vinogradov heard it and promised to learn it and play for Yesipova's class, not immediately, but later on. This is very interesting to me. As for Lyadov, he will see it tomorrow.

Tcherepnin has started off his activities with great energy. He has set up a conducting timetable and has already gone through several scores with us. It will be excellent if it all carries on like this, and everyone will get a chance to conduct once a week. My turn will be tomorrow for the first time, so today I am industriously studying my scores and enthusiastically waving my baton about. My spine is hurting from the unfamiliar activity.

On Thursday I again saw Lyosochka Glagoleva in the Conservatoire. When she heard I had written a sonata, she insisted on my playing it to her, going into ecstasies when she heard it. She then surprised me by revealing that she had been asked to join the Conservatoire chorus, an invitation she intends to take up. It will be interesting to see how she sings in the choir.

That same day I saw Max again, and we had a good conversation. I told him I was sorry he was so seldom to be seen in the Conservatoire, and this is the truth. It is a great pity.

The person I am seeing most of is Vera Alpers. She is obviously getting

---

1 A reworking of the first movement of the Sonata No. 2 of 1907 into a single-movement sonata, eventually published as Sonata No. 1 in F minor, Op. 1.

more and more attached to me, and I do very much enjoy being with her. On one occasion in the Conservatoire I waited for her to finish her class with Steinberg so that we could leave together. But after a while, thinking she might have already left, I put on my coat and went to Jurgenson's to buy some music. However, as I was crossing the square, I thought perhaps she had not left after all, so turned back, making as if to collect some music from the Conservatoire. I looked high and low for Verochka but still could not find her, and eventually left again. Now, when I got to the same place I had turned back from before, it occurred to me that it would be easier to go to Johansen's rather than to Jurgenson's, and I seized on this thought because it meant I would have to retrace my steps and pass the Conservatoire yet again. Probably a little ashamed of my indecisiveness, this time I avoided the front of the building and went round the side – a longer route but one that increased the likelihood of meeting Verochka. And lo, just as I was approaching the statue of Glinka, there she was. How pleased I was to see her!

Naturally she was surprised to see me coming from that direction: 'Where have you sprung from?'

'I was on my way to Jurgenson to buy some music, but then I changed my mind and thought I would go to Johansen instead.'

'Oh, I need to get some as well . . .'

And so off we went together, and had an incredibly nice time. We spent some time in Johansen's, and then went together to Liteiny Street, where we said goodbye and I put her on a tram. She is such a lovely girl, Verochka. Sometimes I have a great longing to put my arms round her and kiss her!

15 October

Being in Yesipova's class has brought me new friends. Generally, I must say, the class has been extremely friendly and welcoming, although I blush to record that I simply cannot remember the faces of all twenty girls in the class: one day I say hello and talk to a girl and the next day fail to recognize her and bow to her as I should. Of the men, the one I am most taken by is Vinogradov. He is a very talented fellow, young and rather lacking in sophistication, but extraordinarily likeable. When he chanced to hear the Sonata I wrote for Lyadov, he said he would like to learn it for Yesipova. But when he mentioned the idea to her, she told him not to, but she did say she would like to hear me play it. According to Vinogradov, Yesipova has heard a lot about me as a composer, so much so that when someone said to her, 'What talents you have in your class now!' Yesipova replied, shaking her head sagely, 'Yes, yes, yes . . .'

I won't play her the Sonata, but I shall get Vinogradov to learn a couple of the new studies. However, I don't want him to say anything to Yesipova for the time being.

The other interesting student in her class is Borovsky.[1] At the exam performances in the spring I heard him give an outstanding performance of the Schumann *Toccata*. At the time I did not want to accept that he played it better than I did, because I think my performance is also very good. But little by little I became persuaded of his superiority, and since then I have had great admiration for Borovsky as a pianist. By contrast he is only just beginning the Theory course and looks up to me for having completed it and graduated as a Free Artist, thus our relationship started off rooted in mutual admiration. He is a very nice person, and an excellent pianist.

Among the female students, not counting Malinskaya and Berlin, my friends are Terpelevskaya and Hoffman. Terpelevskaya was in the Aesthetics course with me last year. She is twenty-one years old, with wonderful hair, a graceful appearance and rather a pretty face. But the most wonderful thing about her is her eyes: they contain her whole being. They are large, beneath strongly defined eyebrows, very dark, alive and penetrating, like those of a wild animal, the very first thing you notice about her. As a person she is simple, kind and merry, occasionally a little over-excitable, veering almost towards Bessonova territory – except that Bessonova is almost a caricature whereas Terpelevskaya is someone one can really take to.

Hoffman – what can I say about her? She is certainly very talented. But despite her seventeen years she is so tiny and so plain that involuntarily she excites sympathy. She is obviously interested in me. She has an attractive friend from the General Studies sixth form but I don't know anything about her, not even who she is, but she must also have joined the class this year because I only noticed her a few days ago. I must get to know her. She is extremely pretty, and not only that, I have a feeling she would be nice.

23 October

Last spring Verochka was always inviting me to her house, but I refused, making one excuse after another, and never once went there. This year the invitations were renewed, albeit in rather general terms: 'Do come', or 'Drop by some time.' Finally on Saturday a maid brought over a note with a particularly pressing invitation for that evening. I collected some of my scores and set off.

Kalinovsky was the only other guest. I played my pieces, and then some Mozart sonatas in a two-piano arrangement by Grieg, followed by a suite for piano duet by Mr Alpers himself. The only sour note was the continual sparring between Mr Alpers and Kalinovsky over trivial matters, such as whether

---

1 Alexander Borovsky (1889–1968), pianist with a distinguished career in the West. He emigrated in 1920 and eventually settled in Boston, US, where he was much admired by Koussevitzky, making frequent appearances and recordings with the Boston Symphony.

or not Grieg had a right to add a second piano part to what Mozart had written. In every other way it was extremely pleasant and warm.

As I was leaving, Mr Alpers asked me, 'Are you at all interested in criticism?'

'Yes, of course,' I replied.

'Then please come and see us again on Thursday and bring your compositions. Ossovsky will be here, and so will Belsky.'[1]

I thanked him, and naturally said I would come. Accordingly on Thursday, taking my Sonata, a couple of studies and the first movement of the Sinfonietta I once again found myself in the pleasant environment of Shestaya Rota Street. This time the door was opened by the maid, not as usual one of the brothers. Directly opposite the front door was a study in which Mr Alpers was sitting writing out some music. I went in. Next door, in the drawing room, Verochka was trying out something on the piano, and from time to time her little brother peeped in at the door as he passed. I found the scene an attractive one.

After a quarter of an hour there was a ring at the doorbell and Mr Alpers went into the hall. I went into the drawing room and greeted Verochka. Belsky entered with his wife. I was very interested to meet him, as I knew his wonderful librettos for *Kitezh* and *Petushok*.[2] He proved to be a quiet, taciturn gentleman with a big bump on his head. Then appeared Kalinovsky and M. and Mme Ossovsky. They were the most important of the guests, and I had been anxiously awaiting their arrival.

Music-making began after tea. A young lady sang – appallingly badly – a couple of songs, then the company turned to me, asking me to play my compositions. I suggested beginning with Scriabin's Fifth Sonata, which was enthusiastically agreed. I had been with Zakharov the previous evening and played it very successfully to him. As it was a genuinely rare event to hear such an unconventional work, the sonata elicited a sensational response.

I then played my own sonata. It went down well, although the studies had a greater success, especially No. 4, which I had to repeat. Lastly I played the opening movement of the Sinfonietta, which was also well received; it was found to be 'quite new music' but very accessible and 'ought to find its way straight into the Belyayev concerts'. However, the management of this concert series is a mess at the moment: Artsybushev has taken over the reins from Rimsky-Korsakov, and he is a very strong personality who has all the power and makes all the decisions.

Ossovsky said, 'With your permission I will mention your Sinfonietta to

---

1 Vladimir Belsky (1866–1946), librettist. As well as the operas mentioned, he wrote the libretto for Rimsky's *Tale of Tsar Saltan*.
2 Rimsky-Korsakov's opera *Zolotoy Petushok* (*The Golden Cockerel*), composed in 1907 but banned by the censor on account of its implied criticism of the concept of absolute monarchy, and not produced until 1909, after the composer's death.

him, and it might be that he could squeeze it in to this year's programme. He usually acts on my suggestions, at least he has always done so in the past.'

I said I would be deeply grateful, and such kindness from him was more than I could possibly have expected. Nevertheless the suggestion was only made in passing and was not referred to again. Ossovsky's other generous act was to offer me his pass for Ziloti's rehearsal, knowing that I did not have one myself.

This man has a uniquely wide knowledge of musical life. No wonder that he is a permanent fixture among the 'highest circles' of the establishment in the musical world. He is a first-class raconteur and was a fund of fascinating information.

Mme Ossovskaya was also very kind to me and asked a lot about Yesipova. I asked her how Schmidthof was getting on. She said he usually came for his lessons at seven o'clock in the evening, and that this year his playing had gone downhill in terms of technique. When he came back after the summer his fingers were all over the place, so she had had to set him the most elementary exercises. He had come to Ossovskaya two years ago at the urging of Ziloti, hardly able to play anything. As a performer he was nothing special, but very capable, hardworking and conscientious, and deeply interested in music. Both Monsieur and Madame said very nice things about him.

'I'm always holding you up as an example to him,' said Ossovskaya, 'because of your technique and your understanding of how things should be played.'

'That's probably why he wrote me such a cross letter in the summer.'

'From what I hear it may have been the other way round. Perhaps you were at fault this time,' replied Ossovskaya, who must have heard something of our famous correspondence, or at least had got an inkling of the touchiness of my character.

I went home well pleased with the evening. If Ossovsky can really arrange for my Sinfonietta to be played, that would be a development I had hardly even dreamed of. Reason told me not to count on such a triumph, but it was a flattering thought and at least made me get on with and finish the Sinfonietta.

I have been getting very pressing invitations from Glagoleva as well as from Verochka. I said that the next free Sunday I had I would visit her, to which she replied that it did not have to be a formal visit, she would simply be very glad to see me one evening. Eventually the penny dropped that her mother had gone to Yelizavetgrad leaving her alone and bored, thus in need of my consoling company.

That Sunday evening I presented myself at Glagoleva's. Her sister, Sonya, was there. Sonya's husband had died during the summer and she was now living with them. Also present was a student who seemed to be some kind of cousin, a deeply uninteresting, lanky youth.

I was greeted with quotations from my letters, which seemed to delight not only Lyosochka but her sister, and we had a generally very enjoyable evening chatting. I played my pieces and the Scriabin sonata, and Lyosochka revealed that she adored the text of Scriabin's *Poème d'Extase*, which I had given her a little while earlier, and which she now planned to learn by heart in order to recite.

By the time we said goodbye, we were delighted with one another.

I repeat that there can be no comparison between this autumn and last. Then I was not even feeling well, I was tired and anxious and for a time suffered from insomnia, I was constantly frustrated over getting my Symphony performed, and was often depressed. But typically for me, the first half of this year I was hoping for better things, always expecting the next month to bring greater riches, success and interest. As it turned out I was right, for after the turn of the year I did begin to feel better, my insomnia ceased, the Symphony was performed, I made new and interesting friends. An exciting event was the international chess tournament in St Petersburg. In short, by the second half of the year I was feeling much happier.

This year, the high point began from the day I returned to St Petersburg, with my initiation into Yesipova's class, the success of my studies with a marvellous new professor who motivated me to work with enthusiasm, an interesting class of fellow students, the excitement of my conducting studies, which last year had been so disappointing, a crowd of interesting new personalities, a much closer relationship with Verochka and with Glagoleva thanks to my summer correspondence with them.

No longer do I have to console myself with thoughts of life getting brighter in future months – I simply have no time for such distractions. The present time has so much to give and be enjoyed that I could wish for nothing more. At all events that is how I feel. I haven't been in a bad mood since the day I came back, not a moment's depression, and no intention of suffering any.

Last week provided particular satisfactions. I much enjoyed my visits to the Alpers and the Glagolevs (where I was able to show off my new, grown-up suits) and where everyone was extremely civil to me; I conducted for Tcherepnin; everything went well for Yesipova – and on top of all that, there was Ossovsky's suggestion that my Sinfonietta should be performed – and where indeed? Nowhere else but the Belyayev concerts! This was the high point, and on my way home I could not help reflecting that the intensity of such impressions crowding in on me and the sheer variety of life must surely slacken for a time, they could not long be maintained at such a pitch. There is just not enough material in the world to allow that . . .

So, time now to ease off and take a break!

27 October

Sometimes life brings especially good days. Such a one was yesterday.

It began with the conducting class. It was my turn, and I was beginning Schubert's C minor Symphony.[1] I started somewhat uncertainly, but then it got better, and by the middle of the movement something clicked with the orchestra and they began to play really well. When I finished and stepped down from the podium, I saw Glazunov sitting in the front row. He had come to see what was happening in the class.

The class finished about one o'clock. I met Kamyshankaya and we talked for a while, then Verochka came up and asked about tomorrow's rehearsal for the symphony concert at which Sobinov was due to sing, and which was also to include a performance of Tchaikovsky's Fifth Symphony.

We went off to find Dzhiarguli to ask for passes, but instead of him ran into Glazunov who was being asked the same question by two of the Theory-class students. 'Sokolov must have the tickets, but he is not here at the moment', said Glazunov. 'Let's go into the office; we'll probably find them lying around somewhere on the desk.'

We went in, and Glazunov rooted around in the desk and took out a bulky package. 'This must be it,' he said, and slit open the packet with a big knife. In it was a thick folder with lithographed passes for the following day's rehearsal. Glazunov stood turning the parcel over in his hands and then said doubtfully, holding it out to us, 'Well, gentlemen, perhaps you could give them out to your colleagues?' And with that he went out.

The effect was as though someone had suddenly dropped a pile of gold on the table in front of us. I am sure the same thought flashed into all our minds: on whom would we choose to bestow the precious passes? But we assumed an air of sober responsibility as we approached the bulging package. 'We should all take only as many as we need for our class, and give the rest to Dzhiarguli so that we don't get into any trouble,' said one of the theoreticians.

'There are ten in my class, so I'll take ten,' said another.

'I'll take nine, then,' said the first.

'Well, I'll take fifteen, for the Theory people and for the conductors,' said I, taking care to get hold of at least twenty-five. 'But mind they go to the Theory people, not to the Conservatoire girls,' I added sternly.

By the time I saw Verochka again someone had already given her a pass. 'Let's go somewhere where there's no one about; I've got something to show you,' I said to her.

When we found ourselves on a deserted staircase, I showed her my haul. 'How many would you like?' I asked.

1   Symphony No. 4 ('Tragic'), D.417.

She took a pair, just in case. But as I had some time on my hands, I busied myself handing out passes to the Theory students.

Then I went in to Lyadov's class for my second lesson with him. In the first lesson he had asked me next time to bring the exposition of my quartet. It caused a furore and drove him into a complete frenzy. He consigned me to perdition, to Richard Strauss, to Debussy, to the devil, anywhere at all provided I left his class in peace.

The furious assault lasted a full hour and a half, in the course of which I succeeded in establishing my right to submit another quartet, and after that to disappear from the face of the earth.

So this time I had brought a more Lyadov-friendly quartet, telling him I thought he would find it more acceptable.

'I'm sure it won't have any music in it!' declared the maestro, opening the score. But it proved to be quite conventional and he even liked some passages. Although other places made him groan, at least there was no talk of Strauss or Debussy. When he had completed his inspection, Lyadov bowed in a friendly manner to Myaskovsky and to me, and said, 'Gentlemen, please carry on.'

So that was another success for today.

I still had several rehearsal passes in my pocket. I must give one to Glagoleva, she is a fan of Sobinov.

'Are you going home?' asked Verochka Alpers, appearing from nowhere.

'Yes, I am.'

'Let's go together.'

I put on my coat and went outside. Verochka had still not come out, so I walked slowly to the corner of the street and waited there in front of a poster, then I saw Vinogradov and started talking to him.

To my surprise, there was Lyosochka Glagoleva's green fur coat on the opposite corner of the street, heading towards the Conservatoire. This was indeed my lucky day! She was of course delighted to get a pass for the rehearsal.

On the far side of the statue I stopped at the stop to wait for a tram. But none came, and I kept looking over towards the Conservatoire hoping my companion would come. When the tram was almost upon us, she appeared, but from the other direction. I heard a voice behind me say, 'What are you doing, waiting for a tram?'

'For a tram, and for you. What happened to you?'

'I forgot my gloves so I'll have to go back to the Conservatoire and get them.'

'But wherever did you get to?'

'Actually I was very quick today.'

'But you still forgot your gloves. Never mind, take mine; I've got two pairs in my pocket.'

After some hesitation she accepted mine, and we happily set off home. When I finally got back to my own apartment, I was so tired I could do nothing but lie down and go to sleep.

And thus ended a really good day.

20 November

My diary seems to have taken on an airy, romantic cast, as though I were a completely irresponsible fellow and never think of anything else at all. In reality, though, people who talk endlessly of their love affairs and who they are sweet on at the time irritate me. As far as my diary is concerned I don't want to be too hard on myself, since this emphasis is purely fortuitous. My life generally, and this autumn in particular, is awash with impressions and events, and I am keen to include them all into the diary. But it is much easier and more pleasant to write about amorous adventures than about other, drier, matters. Besides, one always wants to talk to people about the new developments and events that occur in one's life, while the romantic aspects, private to oneself, can only be poured out in a diary. So it is natural that this element should predominate, while much of the remainder would be a boring, dry recitation. This is why my romantic associations with girls occupy so much space. But this is by the bye, in the nature of a brief prelude. It is so long since I have written anything that a million things have happened in the meantime, and it is hard to know where to begin.

I'll start with the conducting. I have been on the course for three years now, and during the first two I conducted precisely three times. This year I resolved to be super-energetic, to make my presence felt and become a thorn in everyone's side, in a word to go on banging my head against the wall until I was allowed to conduct. Circumstances conspired to fulfil my desire: we had a good orchestra, we now had a proper schedule, everything in short was set fair.

On first ascending the podium, I felt most peculiar. Although I knew the score thoroughly and knew what gestures to make, I was terribly ill at ease. I had no basis from which to launch the music. Tcherepnin heaped abuse on my head, commenting that my conducting reminded him either of a corpse or a lunatic. The second time was better ('less bad', as Tcherepnin put it) but still far from good. Tcherepnin said he felt sorry for the orchestra having to play under my direction.

After this I decided to go and see Kankarovich. Although he had invited me some time ago, I had never been – but this evening I hastened along. My first question was about a particular fermata, but there and then on the spot he gave me a complete lesson, a proper outline of conducting technique.

An entirely new horizon opened before me. I discovered the fundamentals of conducting and learned a mass of specific techniques, such as what to do with the left hand, how to hold my elbows, how to give a firm downbeat. In a word, I became a conductor, and my second debut would be a world away from what had gone before. I visited Kankarovich several times, and studied his gestures.

Even so I found myself among those rejected for the Jubilee concert. It was obviously not going to be possible for all eight of us to conduct in the same evening, especially on such a special occasion, so four were chosen and four rejected. As a consolation, we rejects were told that we would get to conduct at student concerts.

So it was that on 6 November I made my conducting debut. Tcherepnin had not a shred of confidence in me, but he still had to give me my chance. I conducted the first movement of Schubert's 'Unfinished' Symphony. During the general rehearsal Tcherepnin so exasperated me that I all but slapped his face, going so far as to give serious consideration to the consequences of such an action.

However, this was to be the evening when, in the words of my classmates, I 'broke the record' for confounding expectations.

I was on first, arriving with two minutes to spare. I had decided that, whatever my feelings, I would put into practice my theory that one should drink a glass of water before going on stage. I did so, and went out. I raised my baton, noting with satisfaction that I could hold it steady.

I began. I was probably the only person in the hall who had any confidence at all in a good outcome, but in the event it went tremendously well. Tcherepnin enfolded me in an embrace after the performance and told me that Glazunov was also very pleased. But sly old Sasha,[1] despite my trying hard to catch his eye, said nothing. No doubt he didn't want to spoil me.

Now I have been assigned to coach a choir in a number from *Oprichnik*.[2] On Fridays a female choir drawn from piano students meets to learn a work for later performance at a student concert. The first conductor to have this job was Shteiman,[3] and now it's me. It is quite a large choir, consisting of about fifty girls. We rehearse in the Small Hall, with Tcherepnin and the Class Inspector in attendance, so the girls behave and pay attention, and the work goes smoothly and easily. Nearly all the girls I know sing in this choir. This is another way for my conducting to make progress, and it promises well.

My relations with Yesipova are good. People tell me she likes me because I am quick at grasping what she tells me. One day, leaving the class, I heard her call me over: 'Prokofiev!'

1   Glazunov.
2   Opera (1872) by Tchaikovsky.
3   Mikhail Shteiman (?–1949), conductor. He was later to become Principal Conductor of the Ukrainian National Opera.

I approached.

'When are you going to play something you have written?'

'Anna Nikolayevna, I didn't know you were interested.'

She inclined her head.

'Not only that, but I would be playing them as a composer, not as a piano student.'

'That's all right, you may play them as a composer.'

'With pleasure.'

I settled down to learn my Sonata and the Fourth Etude with great thoroughness. For the first time in my life I am learning one of my own compositions hands separately. On 13 November I brought her the Sonata and the Etude. Yesipova was teaching at home that day, and Zakharov, who was much interested in the Sonata and had already begun to learn it, came to hear me play it, and to see for himself Yesipova's reactions.

I played the Sonata no worse than I played it at home, and to my surprise was not at all nervous. Yesipova followed my performance with the score.

'Very interesting music,' she said, 'but I should like to hear it played by someone other than yourself. It's all very well to have accents, but you mustn't play *fortissimo* all the time. And you constantly overpedal. Leave the score with me and I will put in the pedal markings.

I thanked her, gave her the Sonata, and left. She was less keen on the Etude. 'Too decadent,' she said.

Zakharov congratulated me on my success, because praise from Yesipova, and moreover her request to keep the score, meant a great deal. And when, after five days or so had passed, Yesipova saw me, she smiled very pleasantly and said that so far she had only had time to mark the pedalling on four pages. Then, a week later, that is today, when she was again teaching at her home and I was playing Beethoven, she handed me my Sonata so thickly covered with pedal indications that I caught my breath in admiration. She added that if I did not agree with her suggestions, she would revise them. I naturally thanked her very much, and said that I had been asked to play the Sonata in Moscow, and therefore would be very grateful if she would agree to give me a lesson on its performance. To which she responded, 'With pleasure.'

A propos Moscow, R. M. Glière has written to me that my piano works have been proposed for performance at the Musical Exhibitions organized by Deisha-Sionitskaya.[1] In our recent exchange of letters he has been telling me I should meet Leonid Nikolayev,[2] who joined the Piano Faculty of the Conservatoire this year. He knows Deisha and has on occasion been on the

---

1 Maria Deisha-Sionitskaya (1859–1932), dramatic soprano, teacher and organizer of a series of chamber-music concerts in Moscow under the title 'Musical Exhibitions'.
2 Leonid Nikolayev (1878–1942), influential pianist and teacher at the St Petersburg Conservatoire. He was also Shostakovich's piano teacher.

jury for her concerts; he is a knowledgeable musician and a very nice person. Reinhold Moritsevich said he would like me to get to know him better.

When I approached him in the Conservatoire, saying that Glière had recommended me to him, he was extremely kind, saying he had heard a lot about me and was very glad to meet me. He came to see me on Wednesday and listened to my compositions. He liked the Sonata and the Etudes, but not 'Suggestion diabolique', and the pieces for the 'Evenings of Contemporary Music' even less. He advised me to play the Sonata and a selection of smaller pieces in Moscow. By the way, Myaskovsky and Zakharov are planning to come to Moscow with me in January, to see a performance of *Petushok*, the former also to have a look round and the latter to see his brother.

I'm very glad to have got to know Nikolayev: he is charming and well informed.

I have had two lessons with Lyadov but I'm not going to any more for the time being; I've simply no time to compose anything for him, and not much inclination either.

21 November

Often I come home from the Conservatoire in company with Verochka Alpers, usually in the early evening just as it is getting dark. We invariably take a little stroll through the Nikolsky Gardens and take a couple of turns round the church before continuing on our way. It is quiet by the church, and there is nobody about, the snow lies white and it smells of the trees. One time I offered her my arm, and since then we have been arm in arm – it is nicer and closer like that – reverting to a decorous distance apart once we emerge from the park.

All the same there is a certain formality to our relationship. From time to time the question plagues me: why is it that I have never loved anyone nor been loved? After all, I have seen, and continue to see, a great number of girls, but they all slide past me with indifference. Sometimes this grieves me, and I look with envy on the loving couples I see. What is the reason? Surely my character cannot be so horrible, my behaviour so repellent, that I drive them all away? It is true I am demanding: the object of my affections must possess an attractive appearance, cultivation and depth, but I sometimes I begin to doubt whether I am ever going to have any success.

No, love is a matter of chance. Suddenly, out of the blue, there it is – one person falls for another person, and it's love. No amount of courting or attention can compete with pure chance, the simple play of fate, to bring you to your goal. I have refined this thesis to a state of great clarity.

In the last few days I have been applying myself seriously to work, practising the piano a lot, composing my Sinfonietta and working on my conducting.

7 December

Last Sunday there was a student production that included two acts of *Ruslan*[1] and one act of *Faust*,[2] accompanied by two pianos instead of orchestra. In January it will be done with orchestra. Kankarovich, Tolstyakov and Kolomiitsev conducted the two-piano version and the other student conductors, myself included, played the pianos. I have not been to a single opera class this year, so could make no claims to be one of the actual conductors, but I was very happy to be playing for it. We took the score and by mutual agreement divided the piano score into two parts, moved two pianos into the pit to form the orchestra, while the conductor occupied his usual position, and we played, so we thought, splendidly. But the general feeling was that we did not play splendidly at all, very badly in fact, and afterwards we came in for a lot of criticism.

On Thursday I bumped into Max and was very glad to see him. It transpired that Alpers and Kamyshanskaya had happened to meet him in the Conservatoire and inveigled him into a committee to get a birthday present for Ossovskaya. They were due to meet today to go together and buy it.

Max and I went down to the second floor and walked about chatting near the library and Yesipova's classroom. Things brightened up when Berezovskaya appeared in the company of a pretty, dark-eyed blonde.

'Why are you so red in the face?' demanded dark-eyes.

'I've just been conducting *Slava*.'[3]

And indeed I had just emerged from this ordeal and had not yet fully come to myself. The conversation turned to conducting; I showed them the score of *Slava* and read out some of its ridiculous text. I then showed them a miniature score of Scriabin's *Extase*, which I had lent to Glagoleva and which she had just returned to me via the concierge. She had loved it, and I, looking at it, fell in love with it again myself.

20 December

The Russian Musical Society,[4] having been in existence for fifty years, is now celebrating its jubilee. The celebrations lasted three days: Friday, Saturday and Sunday, 18, 19 and 20 December. On the 18th at two o'clock the opening

---

1 *Ruslan and Lyudmila*, opera (1842) by Glinka.
2 Opera (1859) by Charles Gounod.
3 Chorus from Rimsky-Korsakov's opera *The Tsar's Bride* (1898).
4 The Imperial Russian Musical Society was in existence from 1859 until its dissolution in 1917. The classes in music instruction instigated by the Society in St Petersburg in 1859 formed the basis for the later Music Conservatoire, hence the Jubilee Celebrations. The Conservatoire's own Jubilee was three years later.

ceremony consisted of deputations and speeches, concluding with a performance of Rimsky-Korsakov's *Slava* (our choir of female piano students had been learning it but in the end the performance went ahead without them). On the 19th there was a concert conducted by Glazunov and featuring major heroes and heroines: Auer,[1] Verzhbilovich,[2] Yershov[3] and our own Yesipova. Yesipova! This was a great event. Our class collected 150 roubles and presented her with a huge bouquet of white flowers, while we pelted her with more flowers from our vantage point in the balcony. I had a hand in arranging all this. Finally, on 20 December in the afternoon, there was a concert by students of today playing the same programme as fifty years ago. In the autumn, partly as a result of the heated disagreement with Tcherepnin and the deputation to Glazunov, our class had secured an agreement that the orchestra playing for the concert would be the student orchestra and the conductors would be members of the conducting class. But as decreed by Tcherepnin and Glazunov, only four conductors were chosen and four rejected – the latter being myself, Orlov, Furman and Shteiman. The chosen ones were Kankarovich, Saminsky, Tolstyakov and Kolomiitsev, with Kankarovich taking the lion's share and the others sharing the crusts. I was not one of the chosen. But what could I do? It was already a familiar story for me, and in any case it may have been no bad thing, since it was only recently that I had begun to get the glimmerings of how to conduct.

The general rehearsal for Saturday's concert was on Thursday morning; since tickets for the concert were by invitation only and since my mother badly wanted to hear Yesipova, I promised to take her in to the general rehearsal. That morning Mama and I got into a cab and set off. As we were passing Nikolsky Park I spied in front of us a cab with Katya Borshch (whom I was very glad to see) and Nadia Popova in it. We all arrived at the same time at the entrance to the Conservatoire; I bowed to the girls, and they disappeared into the entrance. Mama and I made our way to the Great Hall, where Glazunov was in the middle of conducting Rubinstein's Symphony.

Yesipova played marvellously, and when she had finished and come out into the foyer, her whole class made a bee-line for her. She was extremely nice to me and introduced me to her son Ilyin, asked about my Sonata, and

---

1   Leopold Auer (1845–1930), celebrated violinist, conductor and teacher, professor at the St Petersburg Conservatoire; his pupils included Jascha Heifetz, Mischa Elman and Efrem Zimbalist.
2   Alexander Verzhbilovich (1850–1911), cellist and professor at the St Petersburg Conservatoire, trio partner of Yesipova and Auer. Among his pupils were Leopold Rostropovich and Semyon Kozolupov; Mstislav Rostropovich, who was a pupil of both the latter, is therefore his musical 'grandson'.
3   Ivan Yershov (1867–1943), dramatic tenor, leading soloist of the Mariinsky and Bolshoy Theatres and one of the most famous singers of his day, professor at the St Petersburg Conservatoire.

enquired – quoting my words back at me – whether I was learning it as a composer or as a pianist. 'Both hands separately', I answered.

When the rehearsal was over I took Mama back to the concierge of our building, then myself returned to the Conservatoire where pass-fever was again raging. Obviously everyone wanted to attend all three concerts, but the number of passes was limited. Of course all Yesipova's students had a guaranteed place, but one pass per concert was not enough for me.

However, I qualified for two passes, one as a conductor and one as a pianist, because they were given out from different sources. At this point the dark-eyed blonde – her name was Mlle Rudavskaya – turned up, and of course took possession of my spare pass. Overcome with gratitude, she vanished. The other spare pass, for the opening ceremony, I gave to Verochka Alpers, who already had one but needed another for her mother.

I found Myaskovsky sitting on the windowsill on the main staircase, and went to join him. He appeared to have little interest in the jubilee. At this moment Borshch came flying up the stairs and vociferously demanded a pass from me. Laughing and teasing, I said I would not give her one. She went off, and Myaskovsky started talking about something else.

'Don't you think she is pretty?' I asked.

'She has nice eyes, very dark and passionate – but no, I'm not very keen.'[1]

The following day at two o'clock I arrived at the opening ceremony, attired for the first time in my new dinner-jacket. The first person I met was Wanda Yablonskaya, and as I could not see any of my other friends, I sat next to her. Five minutes later, however, I was delighted to catch sight of Glagoleva sitting in the balcony opposite. Verochka and her mother Lyudmila Vasilievna came and sat beside her, so I moved and went to join them, next to Glagoleva.

After a while, the two girls and I decided to leave the balcony and go down to the stalls, where there seemed to be plenty of empty seats, but we found it was not so easy to get in. Nevertheless, the usher guarding the entrance did not raise too many difficulties in allowing passage to two elegant young ladies in white dresses with their cavalier, and so we settled ourselves in seats in the stalls. Very good. But there was still better to come: sitting a few rows behind us was Glière, who was there as a member of a delegation from Moscow. I decided that greeting my former teacher was sufficient justification to leave my two ladies for a moment, and so I went to see him.

Saturday afternoon saw the general rehearsal for Sunday's concert and another bout of pass-fever. Max was there, and Alpers, and Merimanova. This Merimanova, a pretty little monkey with a pince-nez and a great

---

1   This appears to have been the only conversation I ever had with Myaskovsky on the subject of female beauty. [Subsequent note by author.]

favourite of Glazunov, wheedled a whole pile of valuable passes out of him for that evening's concert. I do not much care for her, but she evidently does for me, because she gave me three passes for the concert, on condition that I call for her before the concert and take her to it.

After the rehearsal there was a terrible crush and hubbub, everyone trying to get passes and besieging Glazunov in his office. Since it was known that I had a pocket full of them they descended on me and practically tore me limb from limb. Eventually, having given a pass apiece to Glagoleva and to Max, I went out with the latter discussing the vexed question of shaving, something I would not be able to put off addressing for much longer: should one go to a barber, or was it an operation one should carry out oneself at home?

That evening, Merimanova and I arrived at the Conservatoire to find anxious preparations already in train to ensure everyone had flowers for Yesipova and the presentation of the bouquet had been organized.

The concert started. Auer played the Tchaikovsky Concerto simply magnificently, although afterwards some of his students were very critical. For my part, I listened with rare enjoyment.

During the interval I was very busy and preoccupied dealing with the flowers. Yesipova was due to play next, and we had to be in position to shower her with flowers from the balcony. A hundred and sixty posies lay in three shallow baskets; we took them out and laid them on the red plush rail of the balcony.

This time I could not pay as much attention to Yesipova's playing as my mind was on other things. The moment she finished, the flowers rained down on her from above. They lay around her on all sides, and one of them even landed on the train of her concert dress, so that she swept out with it to the artists' room.

Yesipova had a huge success, and played two encores. Needless to say, we yelled and screamed like madmen. Down below in the stalls, Pyshnov and Zakharov, immaculate in full evening dress, carried up to the stage with Hoffman and Merimanova our enormous basket of white flowers.

Afterwards the whole class went backstage to see Yesipova and lined up to congratulate her. It was so nice: all the male students bent to kiss her hand, she kissed the girl students and they also kissed her hand. 'These are all my fledglings,' she said to a heavily decorated general standing beside her.

By Sunday afternoon's concert, when it was our conductors' turn to perform, jubilee fatigue had begun to set in. I came and sat in the front balcony with Smirnova, Tietz and some other students from Yesipova's class so that we could hear Borovsky's performance of the Concerto by Rubinstein.

Our conductors did not acquit themselves badly; at least nobody disgraced themselves. But I cannot say that Kankarovich shone as much as he had hoped to.

1910

1910

8 January

I celebrated Christmas according to the new calendar.

Because she had been preparing for her own concert, we had not had any lessons with Yesipova since the beginning of December. In Tcherepnin's class, preparations for the concert had also meant no real activity had been going on there either. I had not attended any of Lyadov's classes since the autumn. Thus no work in the real sense of the word had been done, even though the time had flashed by.

A pre-celebration mood had spread throughout the Conservatoire; everything was geared to rehearsing for the concerts, and the longer it went on the more this mood dominated. When the final three days devoted to the concerts themselves came to an end on the 20th, I returned home exhausted by concerts and distraction and bustle; I had had enough of girls and of not doing enough of my own work. I wanted to get back to work, to get on with something worth while, to move forward and to immerse myself in another world.

I had no particular plans for entertainment during the holidays, and happily planned the following programme for myself:

- work intensively for Yesipova (Zakharov had more than once nagged me for not practising enough);
- thoroughly learn the programme for Moscow;
- finish the Sinfonietta, otherwise it would never be finished;
- compose a chorus for women's voices.

After all, there I was working with a female chorus in the Conservatoire, and if I wrote something for them, presumably they would sing it. I hinted as much to Tcherepnin, and his reaction was encouraging – 'only be sure and show it to Glazunov' – and so I set to work on composing it.

I can say in all conscience that the programme I set myself over Christmas I fulfilled in its entirety. I did practise for Yesipova, maybe not with furious application, but diligently enough. I worked hard on the programme for Moscow. I completed the Sinfonietta, and composed the women's chorus.

I was less excited by the finished Sinfonietta than I had expected. The choral piece, however, I like very much, and the score looks good. My only worry is that Tcherepnin and Glazunov may find it too difficult for our young lady pianists and that will prevent it being performed. I worked with enthusiasm, saw no one from the Conservatoire and did not miss any of them. On 27 December there was a costumed ball at the Conservatoire.

That same evening I was invited to the Alpers; it was pleasant but nothing exceptional. On the 25th we had guests at home. For the first time Myaskovsky was invited, to come without formality and play vint; he was put at a table along with Uncle Sasha and V. Ye. Korsak.[1] Myaskovsky sat there, quiet and serious, and seems to have emerged with dignity from the ordeal. The Yablonskys were there also, with the very attractive Wanda: it was a jollier evening than some we have had in the past.

New Year we celebrated by custom at the Rayevskys, quietly and traditionally. When midnight struck everyone raised their glass, silence fell, the women prayed on their knees, and I remembered that this was the moment when one was supposed to think of one's beloved. Three years ago thoughts of Lyolochka Skalon had brought a smile to my lips; the year before last I could not think of anyone one; last year I thought tenderly of Verochka; and now? Many girls, and dear ones too ... a smile came to my lips once again, but no one seemed proper to the occasion.

On New Year's Day I paid calls – twelve in all, including the Ruzskys, Tobizen, Korsak, the Alpers and the Glagolevs. I enjoyed my visits; they were fun. With the Alpers I spent a chic, formally correct five minutes. Verochka was very sweet and looking good. It was seven o'clock by the time I got to the Glagolevs. I don't particularly care for Mme Glagoleva, although there is no doubt she is a highly intelligent and educated person. I had a 'clever' conversation with her, as a result of which I earned a subsequent description of myself as 'a good musician and interesting company'. The conversation touched on the Conservatoire evening that was due to take place on 3 January. On an impulse I said to Lyosenka: 'Leonida Maximovna, why don't you and I go?'

Until that moment I had not definitely decided myself whether I wanted to attend the event: for some reason I had decided that there would not be 'anybody' there. Lyosya began to see some merit in this: 'Why not, it's a good idea! Let's go and see what they get up to!' No sooner said than agreed. There were mild objections from Mama, but as I said I would come and collect Lyosya at ten o'clock, it was agreed we would go.

Fearful nevertheless that the matriarchal influence might after all prevail, the next day I despatched a glowing letter which, as it seemed, produced the desired effect.

On the 3rd I had to attend a children's party at the Pototskys, and at half past nine set out from their house, accompanied by Kostya Skalon.[2] As we

---

1 Vladimir Korsak, Public Prosecutor in the St Petersburg Courts of Justice, and husband of Maria Korsak.
2 Konstantin, the brother of the three Skalon sisters.

drew nearer to Peterburgskaya Storona I began to have some doubts about Glagoleva: she might come or she might not, at the very least I was expecting at least some hesitation. But everything turned out better than I had expected: Glagoleva immediately put on her coat and we set out.

'You have so much youthful energy,' said Glagoleva. 'I wish I could take just a tiny bit from you.' 'Ma vieille amie!' said I in response.

First impressions on arriving at our destination were that the occasion was better organized and more elegant than we had expected. The concert part of the evening had just finished, and the dancing had begun. We took a couple of turns round the room, and it soon became apparent that I had forgotten what skills I ever possessed. The band struck up a polka. I had not the faintest idea what I was supposed to do in this dance. Glagoleva insisted that I try; I declined equally insistently. When a student came up and asked her to dance, she looked interrogatively at me, I looked back at her, and they disappeared into the crowd.

I stood in the hall for a while and then went out into the corridor, aware of a mild sense of pique mixed with a rather stronger one of relief. Glagoleva was less interesting than I had anticipated and ... she was too old for me.

The polka over, she emerged from the dance hall with her cavalier. Now she was extra attentive to me, and her squire was extremely nice. The three of us strolled about the corridor, but at this moment the crowd thinned and there was Berezovskaya all alone. I asked her to dance. Berezovskaya was more animated than usual: she was the main organizer of the whole event so was by way of being in charge. She felt in her element, and this made her good company.

Following our old custom we went up the stairs and found ourselves on the top floor. It was fairly dark there, but still there were plenty of people about. We soon took possession of a splendid window seat near the library.

Berezovskaya had a large amount of money in her purse, which she had just got from Kirlian,[1] and eventually she handed the purse to me for safe keeping. 'The party is going to make a huge profit, you know,' she said, giving me the bulging purse. And then, seeing one through the window, 'Look, a car! We ought to go for a drive.'

'Let's do that!' I egged her on.

'No, seriously, we'll do that when the party's finished! We'll get up a group ...'

'Not more than four, though.' Glagoleva? No, Glagoleva wasn't the right person. 'I know one couple who would jump at it: Biryulin and Kuzovkova.'

Kuzovkova being her best friend, Berezovskaya jumped at the suggestion. After searching for some time we found them on the ground floor. Naturally

---

1 Another student at the Conservatoire.

they fell in with the idea. Biryulin drew me to one side and asked who would be paying for the trip, since he was completely out of money.

'Berezovskaya has plenty of money,' I replied. 'For goodness' sake, I don't know who'll pick up the bill, but don't worry, in any case it won't all be on our tab.' We went off to make the telephone call, to which the answer was that a car would collect us in a quarter of an hour.

I dashed downstairs and got my coat. The girls were ready and waiting and the weather was marvellous. The car had not yet arrived. We were happy and excited; as a group we all liked and understood one another. We were young, it was the first time in our lives any of us had done anything of the kind, the excursion presented itself to us as a uniquely interesting and seductive enterprise!

'Listen, listen! I think it's coming,' exclaimed the girls, straining their ears. We peered all around as the sound grew clearer and clearer in the still of the night, until finally an automobile appeared from the direction of the Torgovy Bridge and clattered noisily up to us.

'Car for Berezovskaya?' I asked the chauffeur. He replied in the affirmative as the car had been ordered in her name. We settled our ladies in and took our seats opposite. It was an ordinary taxi; at least the girls were quite comfortable even if we weren't, but who cared? We asked for the hood of the car to be open, and the driver went to sit up on his box.

'Where to?' he asked.

'To the Islands,' I said, as the girls clapped their hands in glee.

The car emerged on to the embankment and then crossed the Troitsky Bridge and scorched round Kamennoóstrovsky. I felt a twinge of envy at the love-birds Biryulin and Kuzovkova, who were petting amorously.

After traversing Kamennoóstrovsky we plunged into a forest of dark side streets. It was quite light from the moon, but the girls became a little nervous. Then we passed some ice-covered slopes. Hills! Of course! Since they are there we must sledge down them!

We scrambled up but when we reached the top were overcome with terror. I had never sledged downhill, Kuzovkova categorically refused, and Berezovskaya also took fright. We asked for a four-man sledge, and were given a terribly uncomfortable one.

'Let's go, just the two of us!' I said to Berezovskaya. We sat on the sledge and pushed off, clinging fast to one another. It was the most terrifying moment of my life. The sledge moved slowly over the edge and rapidly gathered speed on its downward trajectory. I pressed Berezovskaya to myself as hard as I could.

As we made our way back up again we crossed the path of another sledge: our junior partners had summoned their courage to have a go. We shouted a greeting to them, but they had other things to think about, and only Biryulin called something in reply.

Regaining the car, we continued our journey. When we reached the Strelka[1] we got out of the car and started walking. Biryulin and Kuzovkova, however, preferred to stay *à deux* in the car, so Berezovskaya and I wandered about the square and sat on a bench by the sea.

I opened my coat halfway and we sat companionably leaning against one another. This was very nice: the beautiful Berezovskaya, such an attractive, pure and lovely girl, sitting cosily cuddled up to me, and all around us complete silence, the wide, white square lit by electric lamps and the moon, and far away on the left hand side the two bright lights of our automobile.

Nice as it was, we did not want to sit for long. After all, we were not lovers. Snow-maiden Berezovskaya, cold as ice, not made for love.

All the same, it was wonderful, and we enjoyed it. We started to fool about and essayed a snowball fight, but the snow was too dry and crumbly, so we returned to the car where the more passionate pair awaited us.

Then we went back. It was after two o'clock in the morning, and we had to catch the end of the party. I tried to hurry the driver, and at last we swept up to the Conservatoire. We gave the driver 12 roubles, and went inside to disrobe.

We sped into the dance hall, where the ball was coming to an end. The hordes descended on Berezovskaya: how could the organizer and Mistress of Ceremonies voluntarily absent herself from her own ball! But we insouciantly brushed away the objections and their grumbles subsided.

For the first time in my life I actually enjoyed the process of dancing, and began to understand people who are able to carry on dancing endlessly without exchanging a word. Berezovskaya even thought I was showing some improvement as a dancer. When she wanted a turn with Akhron, I went up to Verochka Alpers. 'Oh no, I'm far too tired . . .' she began, but her objections lapsed and she immediately consented.

I danced two dances with her; she said she had enjoyed the evening and had danced until she dropped. I embarked on a brief, vague outline of our outing to the Islands, but the last waltz ended and in the valedictory march I led her back to her friends.

I took Nyura Berezovskaya back to her house, kissed her hand and was presented by her in her capacity as organizer of the ball with a handful of chocolate bars. I went to bed at four o'clock.

The next day I thought of Glagoleva. I thought she would have taken umbrage at me, but wanted to avoid a quarrel with her, for the following reason. Some time ago I had been walking along Morskaya Street with her

1 The 'Spit', the easternmost point of Vasilievsky Island that juts out into the Neva. The colonnades of the early eighteenth-century Stock Exchange flanked by the two Rostral Columns served as beacons to guide ships into the two arms of the river whose confluence is at this point.

and we were talking about skating. Five years ago, at Sontsovka, I had learned how to do this, and although by no means an expert I was quite capable of looking after myself on the ice. But in Petersburg I had been skating only a few times, although Mama was very keen that I should, skating being a healthy pursuit, and had even made me a special warm jacket. But I found it boring, and so little came of it.

Recently, however, skating kept on cropping up in conversation: so-and-so skated, so-and-so did as well, and every now and then I regretted that I could not do it. I had never been much good even when I was doing it regularly, and now I had forgotten what little skill I formerly possessed. Glagoleva told me she had a rudimentary knowledge of the art, but always had to be supported and could not do it on her own.

'Let's learn together!'

'All right, let's!'

So in this way I acquired a companion, and a very desirable one to boot. We made serious plans to begin our skating instruction, but somehow kept putting it off.

I wrote to Glagoleva pointing out that it was only after she had abandoned me at the party that I left her. And if only she could only have known what a splendid and jolly trip we had, she would readily have forgiven me everything!

I got no reply, and therefore could not be sure whether Lyosenka was angry with me or not. I was pretty confident that our relationship was strong enough for any coolness, if coolness there be, not to last long, but I did worry about possible damage to our skating plans. Also I could not help feeling rather like a guilty schoolboy.

Some days later I was sitting at home thinking over my various romantic affiliations, and it occurred to me that it would be an original idea to list them and place them in order of their respective attributes: length of relationship, good qualities, likeability, etc.

Whom would I place at number one?

This was the most difficult thing to decide. Yet, strange as it may seem, I came all of a sudden to the clear and certain conclusion that the palm must go to Yelizaveta Esche. In the first place, it belonged to her by virtue of longevity; since before the days when I started to keep a diary, when I did not know a single girl in the Conservatoire and would blush at the mere thought that I might be seen talking to one, I had picked her out among her peers, had often followed her from a distance and dreamed of her.

No. 2 was Glagoleva. No. 3 was Alpers.

Fourth place went to Katya Borshch. This was where she belonged.

No. 5 was Rudavskaya. She was so pretty, so extraordinarily pretty! And a star for all the orchestral musicians in the Conservatoire; Kankarovich was smitten by her and continually danced attendance on her but she was in love with Kirlian, a rather boorish youth who rejoiced in his nickname of 'the herring', but of whom I personally had a rather low opinion. Now, however, his improved circumstances raised him in my estimation.

After the evening of 3 January I abandoned the pursuit of Rudavskaya. She has admirers and to spare as it is. This is not because I lack boldness or self-confidence, I simply feel it repugnant and a betrayal of my self-esteem to be one of a crowd; in such circumstances the game loses all interest and the only result is wounded pride.

No. 6 is Berezovskaya, and quite right too. And No. 7 is little Kuzovkova, with whom for a long time I could not get along, but finally it has come all right.

31 January

This winter I am a happy man. My life is filled with interest, I feel I am living it to the full and taking from it everything it has to offer. When I was asked the traditional New Year question, what I would like people to wish for me, after a moment's thought I answered quite sincerely that I lacked nothing. And this is the truth: everything is good, and as life goes on it will get better still. Since last autumn the stimuli in my life have grown colossally. All of a sudden everything seemed to take off at once: my piano playing, the music I was composing, my composing career, my circle of friends. There is so much diversity in the way I spend my time: I can be absorbed now in one activity, now in another, turn and turn about.

Yes, I am tremendously in love with diversity, everywhere and in everything. Without it, life palls.

My work for Yesipova comes in bursts. When I am in a Yesipova phase I practise carefully for two hours a day, making good use of this time and concentrating hard on what I am doing. This phase will go on for roughly ten to twenty days. At times like this I make good progress, but then enthusiasm cools somewhat and I find my attention turning to something else.

Over Christmas I composed a lot, but now am almost wholly focused on a transcription I am making of Scriabin's Symphony. Today for example I spent five hours on this without noticing how the time was passing.

At the moment I am less interested in conducting. This may be because I am genuinely not really so attracted by this activity, or it may be because I don't find it very stimulating – after all, how could I? – being obliged to pursue it in a class – and what a class! – under the direction of the dreaded Tcherepnin!

Aside from all this, the Conservatoire is a great place to meet girls, and very pretty ones too. Last year I was complaining that I had no one except

Verochka Alpers, but now I have truly lots to choose from. And this is the one field above all where I love variety, perhaps because I do not have one particular individual who loves me in the true sense of the word. But collectively they all love me, and so I can be free and easy and enjoy being with them. From time to time what might be called 'holiday periods' occur in the Conservatoire, when, for example, people are busy preparing for a production or a concert and there is a whole series of rehearsals. At these times everyone is absorbed in what has to be done, but at the same time there is time for idling and just hanging about. These are happy times in the Conservatoire!

But once the production or concert, or whatever it is, is over, one tires of the relative inactivity: it is not a surfeit exactly, more that one can have too much of a good thing, and then one feels drawn back to the work that has been temporarily abandoned, bringing with it a renewed surge of energy and a desire to get back to work with a will.

What could be better than that?

Now to return to my chronicle of the Conservatoire, which, as I recall, I left in the middle of the skating saga.

Glagoleva responded to my automobile *tour de force* with truly angelic sweetness, so much so that I was abashed, and we pursued our plan to go skating. I insisted that it should be just the two of us, with no third party. As skaters we were ideally matched, neither of us being capable of much more than standing up precariously on the ice ... We arranged a twice-weekly visit to a sparsely populated rink at the First Cadet Corps, gradually improving and enjoying ourselves.

I showed Tcherepnin and then Glazunov my chorus *The White Swan*,[1] composed during the Christmas holidays. Never had a composition of mine found its mark as quickly and easily as this one did. Tcherepnin approved, Glazunov approved, they went to the class administrators and announced that on the following Friday they should assemble their 'ducklings' in order that the composer could take them through his new chorus, with a view to its being performed at an evening concert accompanied by the orchestra. Fantastic!

A little later I started rehearsals with the girls. They liked the piece and enjoyed singing it; I was transmogrified into 'the composer', 'the maestro', my stock in the Conservatoire rose rapidly, and I became a well-known figure within its walls, just as I had dreamed of before writing *The Swan*. I was 'a composer' who had written a 'very beautiful' chorus.

Glagoleva said to me, 'I have this feeling that every day that goes by, every time you step into the Conservatoire, you advance a further step along your

---

1 To words by Konstantion Balmont, later published as Op. 7 No. 1.

musical path.' Her words were prophetic: the very next day was to bring not a step, but rather a whole leap forward.

Verochka Alpers was performing in a student concert. She played not badly, a little pallid, but it was quite successful. In the same concert I was accompanying another of Ossovskaya's students, a girl. Ossovskaya herself was not present because she was ill, but she had asked Verochka and Max to call in afterwards and tell her how it had all gone. It was not a long concert, and finished about eleven o'clock. Vera wanted Max to go on his own; he in turn wanted Vera to, thus at this stage neither was intending to be the one to go. The three of us spent the evening together. 'Oh, for heaven's sake, let's all go together,' I said. 'One of us will go in for a minute or two, and then we can go on home. It's on our way for all of us.' I may have had a faint hope, just at the back of my mind, but if so it was no more than a fleeting possibility.

Everyone was happy with this plan, and off we went. It was decided that Verochka should go up for a minute while Max and I waited downstairs with the concierge, and this is what happened. But upstairs they wanted Verochka to stay, which she said she could not do as her companions were waiting for her downstairs, at which Ossovsky himself rushed down to drag us back up with him.

It is rare to come across welcoming hospitality such as the Ossovskys then offered us. But even more was in store for me: Ossovsky, far from forgetting about my Sinfonietta, had spoken to Goldenblum[1] about it and arranged for it to be included in Count Sheremetyev's concert season, and next season my offspring was to be included in a real, live subscription concert series!! This amazing turn of events was the completely unexpected and brilliant culmination of the evening of 22 January, and when I got home I sat down, hugging myself, to play through the lovely piece.

To return to the chronicle. My chorus was performed at the 28 January concert. This was rather short notice, necessitating a compressed rehearsal schedule, but there was no possibility of delaying it, because the next student concert was not until the 12 February, at which time I would be away in Moscow, and the one after that would not be until March. When the orchestra played through its part at rehearsal it sounded wonderful, and I was quite satisfied with my orchestration. But when the orchestra was combined with the choir the result was such an utter mess that it was impossible to hear anything; neither group was used to the other so that both made mistakes both separately and together. In spite of this the choir had no opportunity for any more rehearsals with the orchestra, as the orchestra was simultaneously involved in productions of *Faust* and *Ruslan* (rehearsals for both of which I had from time to time accompanied), so they simply had no time. In the end

---

1 Moritz Goldenblum (1862–1919), conductor and critic.

matters got so bad that Tcherepnin disbanded the orchestra altogether, engaged an outside one for the opera, leaving my chorus with nothing to accompany it. 'My dear Prokofiev, I have had to let you down!' was the way Tcherepnin greeted me one day.

But he was arranging another, later concert in the Great Hall for the conductors' class, and promised that the chorus would be performed on that occasion, not by the original choir of female pianists but by one made up of the real singers in the opera class. 'Perhaps you could write another little piece for chorus . . .' For this concert, however, the accompaniment would have to be on the piano, not orchestra. In fact it had all become such a terrible mess that on the whole I was relieved, relations having not been particularly harmonious with the orchestra, which had not had time to learn the piece properly.

The day of the student concert came. I was excited to be recognized in the Conservatoire as a composer. My piece was the first item in the programme, and among the full house to listen to it were Yesipova and many friends and members of my family. I conducted, and Tcherepnin accompanied (very badly). The choir itself sang well enough and made a real effort, although quite a number of the lady pianists were not there, having defected to go to Hofmann's[1] concert. Although warmly applauded, the work had only a moderate success. I had expected more, but the lack of an orchestra, the rather impoverished vocalizing of the singers and Tcherepnin's feeble accompanying all had their effect. The triumph I had anticipated turned out to be no more than a success. It was a pity, but I could not grieve too much: the real performance still lay in the future, and this evening's exercise was more in the nature of a dress rehearsal. Yesipova praised the work, and Glazunov was drunk.

Among those who were present was Ye. Esche . . . my 'number one'. Her sister had mentioned to me that she was also planning to come, and I was very interested to see her again – we had not met since May. Although she had not greatly changed, something about her seemed to have coarsened: too much hair fluffed up all over her head, some thespian mannerisms borrowed from the boards, the face as pretty as ever but the whole ensemble likewise tinged with a certain blowsiness in the hands, in her dress, in her gestures and in her face. A pity: this was no longer the Esche who two years ago had borne herself so bravely. She was now an actress, on whom the backstage mores of the theatre had imprinted their sorry traces.

On Saturday *Faust* and *Ruslan* had their dress rehearsals. I found myself chatting to Rudavskaya and having a very pleasant time. She wanted to see

---

1 Josef Hofmann (1876–1957), Polish pianist, student of Anton Rubinstein, with a worldwide reputation, especially in Europe and America.

the stage. 'What about a bird's eye view, from the top balcony?' I suggested. 'How about that?'

'Can one really get up there?'

'Of course one can!'

We climbed up and listened happily to the rehearsal from that vantage point.

Rudavskaya was very sweet, very simple, and very flattering in her attentions to me. What could have impelled her to draw close to me? A wish to supplant Berezovskaya? Or had my *White Swan* done the trick? Did she just like me? Probably a mixture of all these things. In any case the result was as delightful as it was unexpected. My number five was smiling upon me: Rudavskaya, thought by many to be the most beautiful girl in the Conservatoire.

For some reason I had always regarded her as rather empty-headed and silly, but up here high in the balcony she revealed aspects of herself I had not remotely suspected. She was studying in the gymnasium, but had been tempted to the Conservatoire by Miklashevsky. She was in the General Subjects sixth form of the Conservatoire but was due also to take her gymnasium school exams in the autumn. She has an interest in botany, has put together a herbarium, and knows all the Latin names of the plants. She has studied anatomy. She takes part in athletics and has splendid muscles. She plays the piano for three hours a day, and models for two painters and a sculptor. In order to achieve all this she goes to bed at midnight and rises at seven. She lives in Peterburgskaya Storona in the building above the Eilers flower shop, and in their spare time they all rush about throwing flowers at one another. All in all an enticing picture, even if half of it was made up. And on top of it all, the most enchanting face, alive with energy and strength!

I was very happy. I really liked Rudavskaya, her vivacity, the brightness of her attitude to life. I cannot exactly say that I was carried away by her, even a little, but there must have been something, because the influence of my silvery-eyed 'good genius' immediately made itself felt: I took to rising punctually at half past eight; by nine I was already sitting at the piano where I would work without stopping for two and half hours, concentrating on being genuinely productive. Then I would make a start on composing. In short, I worked happily and meticulously, and achieved much.

6 February

Recently my attention has been attracted by a tall, slender, elegant blonde with a pince-nez, Mlle Hansen.[1] Previously I had scarcely noticed her, in fact

---

1 Elfrieda Hansen (1893–?), piano student of Yesipova and sister of the violinist Cecilia Hansen.

I had confused her with another pince-nez-wearing student, Mlle Golubovskaya,[1] and neither of them had made much impression on me. But for the last month I have been noticing Hansen more frequently in the Conservatoire in the company of Misha Piastro and a beautiful black-haired friend.

I had a strong desire to get to know her. In the same concert as my chorus was performed, Hansen was playing the piano accompaniment for two students from Auer's class. I thought this would provide a good opportunity to meet her in the artists' room, but this did not happen so our acquaintance had to wait for another day.

Last Monday, talking to Kamyshanskaya, I saw Hansen again and then, a few minutes later, a group consisting of Hansen, Kamyshanskaya and Shvarts sitting and talking on the windowsill. The thought flashed through my mind that I could join them on the strength of knowing Kamyshanskaya and Shvarts, but just then an even more propitious circumstance occurred: Alpers came up to the group. I made my move, greeted her and started talking to her about something or other. Alpers, still carrying on her conversation with me, seated herself next to the others on the windowsill. Kamyshanskaya was next to join in, and soon I contrived to make myself part of the whole group's conversation, not paying particular attention to Hansen but at the same time always trying to include her in the discussion. Little by little she began to respond, at first to her girl friends and eventually to me. An hour later, by which time Shvarts had already left, Alpers and Kamyshanskaya got to their feet and announced that it was time for them to go home.

But Hansen decided to stay put!

'You and I don't know one another at all,' said Hansen.

At this point I felt I should stand up and introduce myself to her. But I did not do so; after all it was obvious that she knew perfectly well who I was, and I already knew her. So, somewhat sheepishly, I said, 'I had the honour of admiring you during the concert, when you were accompanying Lednik and Piastro.'

I like Hansen very much. I don't exactly know precisely in what way or for what reason, but the simple fact remains that I have taken to her. I now meet her almost every day in the Conservatoire, we spend a good deal of time together, she is exceptionally nice and straightforward with me. I am not in love with Frieda Hansen, it's not even that I find her particularly attractive, but I simply like her company tremendously, and at the present time she is the girl in the Conservatoire who most interests me.

---

1 Nadezhda Golubovskaya (1891–?1975), pianist and harpsichordist, student of Sergey Lyapunov, later professor at the Leningrad Conservatoire.

9 February

On the 5th we heard a concert by Medtner. It was an interesting event, even though it consisted solely of piano music by a single composer. The *Sonaten-Triade* was rather boring, but the smaller pieces were very attractive. He plays well, although his right hand lacks power and I swear that you can hear him breathing as far back as the sixth row.

I met Sergey Taneyev, who was in St Petersburg to play his [Taneyev's] Trio. He was extraordinarily kind to me, insisting that I turn pages for him in the Trio and asking many questions about my forthcoming visit to Moscow. He introduced me to Medtner.

I leave today for Moscow, where I am to play my Sonata and three of my Winkler Studies in Deisha-Sionitskaya's Musical Exhibition. These 'Exhibitions', apparently, have a good reputation in Moscow. Not only this, but to judge from what I hear, Moscow musical circles already know something about me and people are waiting for me to come there. This makes it a pleasant prospect.

I have completed the piano transcription of the first movement of Scriabin's *Divine Poem*, and checked it meticulously against the orchestral score. I think it has turned out successfully. Scriabin is in Moscow. Shall I have a chance of showing it to him?!

Altogether I have high hopes of Moscow.

My Danish friend Elfrieda Genrikhovna Hansen is very, very nice.

And so, gentlemen, it is time to say farewell for a week!

15 February

It so happened that the train on which I went to Moscow was the same as the one on which Taneyev was travelling. And embarrassingly enough I was in second class while he was in third, which was shameful. As you may imagine, I sat with him the whole time and he was kind enough to keep me talking until half past midnight. It is hard to describe the sheer quantity of valuable information he imparted to me during those five hours; by the end he was so carried away that he delivered a complete lecture on composition theory, on voicing, on musical line, on how to write in variation form . . . altogether in the space of a few hours he taught me ten times more than Wihtol and Lyadov had managed to do in a year and a half. I saw him twice more while I was in Moscow. He liked the Sonata and *The Swan* very much, the Etudes less, he was cool about the Sinfonietta, and once again he opened up for me a treasure chest of fascinating insights into the theory of composition. That's the kind of person one should study with!

As for the Deisha-Sionitskaya performances, they were postponed until

21 February, so I was asked to come back ten days later, travel costs being borne by the Exhibition. Accordingly I went back to St Petersburg the following evening, quite relaxed about this turn of events.

The most interesting thing that happened in Moscow was my visit to Scriabin. Taneyev had given me a letter of introduction to him, and so, taking my transcription along, I went to call on him. I was quite nervous on the way there, but not wretchedly so, and I thought to myself that this was a moment I would long remember.

Scriabin lives in a detached house belonging to Koussevitzky.[1] As I stepped over the threshold I was conscious of being quite 'the gentleman', and my nerves evaporated. My main worry was that Scriabin might not be there, especially as this was the day after his own concert. But the footman assured me he was at home, and I asked him to deliver the letter, saying that I would wait for a reply. In his letter, Taneyev had recommended me as 'a young composer and pianist from St Petersburg' who has made a transcription of the *Divine Poem*, and asked him to look at the transcription, 'by which you would infinitely oblige your sincerely devoted . . .', etc.

A moment later Scriabin darted out, a small, puny, delicate man. His face was extraordinarily beautiful, a hundred times more so than any of his photographs, with wonderful eyes, fine features and a unique, irresistible charm. A few wrinkles below the eyes and a sallow complexion could have been the result of the previous evening's concert. I could not take my eyes off him, although I don't think he would necessarily have been aware of this from the way I spoke.

An irresolute, questioning figure, Scriabin stood at the bottom of the stairs. I stepped towards him and announced my name. Scriabin responded by giving his own name, and we shook hands.

'You see, just at the moment I cannot do anything . . . we are just going out to visit relations . . .' he said. 'Perhaps if you were to come back tomorrow?'

'Unfortunately that would be difficult; I have to return to Petersburg today.'

However it transpired that Scriabin would himself be coming to St Petersburg on the 16th or 17th, and he asked me to telephone him at the Hotel Mukhin.

'Although it's possible I may not stay at the Mukhin. In that case Glazunov will know my address.'

'Glazunov is not well at the moment.'

'Perhaps he will be better by then?'

'I doubt it. I left St Petersburg the day before yesterday, and there was no talk of his being better then.'

---

1 According to his daughter Nina's memoirs, this was the very house on Glazovsky Lane acquired by Alexey Meshchersky in February 1917 when he left his wife and moved to Moscow to set up house with Yelena Isaakevna Grevs (N. A. Krivosheina, *Chetyre treti nashey zhizni*, YMCA Press, Paris, 1974).

'But how can he be ill? He has to conduct my Symphony on the 20th!' naively expostulated Scriabin.

I picked up my portfolio, which was lying near by on a chair, and took out from it my transcription. The portfolio itself was bulging with a mass of other music, but the only thing I took out from it was this one slim score.

'Is that all?!' cried Scriabin in wonder.

'I've only done the first movement.'

Scriabin began leafing through the music.

'If you like I can leave the score with you for the time being,' I said.

'Is this the only copy?'

'Yes, I just have the one.'

'Then I can't possibly take it. Suppose any of it were to be lost.'

'But that couldn't possibly . . .'

'No, no! You know what happened with Conius's transcription? He sent it to Leipzig and something happened to it on the way. He had to do it all over again from the beginning.'

'Anyhow, I would much rather play it to you myself.'

We began to say our farewells.

'When would you like me to telephone you?'

'Well, I think some time on the 17th.'

'Very good. But perhaps it would be simpler if you were to telephone me, to 237–61, to let me know when you are free. I live at 7 Bronnitskaya Street.'

'Yes, that will be fine.'

Scriabin made a note of the number and the address, said goodbye in a very friendly manner, and I left. While looking through the music, Scriabin had observed that the difficulty with transcriptions lay in making sure everything could be heard while at the same time being transparent.

It was three o'clock when I left the house, and my train was due to leave at seven. After my visit to Scriabin there was nothing of interest to hold me in Moscow, and I wanted to get back to St Petersburg. I was a little disappointed we had had to postpone a proper examination of the manuscript, but I was charmed by the courtesy that the maestro, this man of genius, had shown me. I returned to the Glières, where I had been staying, and from there left for Petersburg.

On Friday morning I was home again. I practised the piano and at one o'clock was at my place in Yesipova's class. She was teaching at home that day, and I met Ilyin,[1] who invited me to play vint with them that evening. I had long hoped for a social invitation from Yesipova, but she had been steadfast in not issuing one, sticking to her small chosen clique consisting of Zakharov, Shubert, Borovsky, Pyshnoff and Friedrich. Now at last I was to be included in the company.

---

1 Anna Yesipova's son.

That evening I had intended to attend the student concert to listen to Katya Borshch and to spend some time with my friends after my trip. But of course I now altered my plans and went to Yesipova's. It was all very nice but actually rather boring; we played vint – herself, Ilyin, Shubert and I. Ilyin is very good at the game, Yesipova pretty bad, so she loses, but she plays with much passion. At eleven o'clock the party broke up and we went our various ways.

Life is generally good, the only fly in the ointment being Frieda Hansen. On Saturday my lesson was at four o'clock, but I arrived at the Conservatoire at two, knowing that Hansen usually came in at about that time. I met her on the ground floor, looking particularly attractive. We were glad to see one another, and were enjoying our *tête-à-tête*, but then Kirlian came on the scene with some books and various business matters to discuss, and I stood to one side. They were soon deeply engaged in conversation, so I turned on my heel and went away.

A couple of days later I met Hansen with Piastro senior. I have nothing against him at all, in fact I am very fond of him, but for some reason I was stupid enough to confine myself to a quick, muttered greeting and then hurry away, even though I was not in fact busy and had nothing special I needed to do. When I came back – alas! – Hansen was once again with her two dreadful friends, and I was forced to stand and talk to Nikolayev.

26 February

After this, and before my second visit to Moscow, I twice met Hansen in the Conservatoire. On both occasions she concentrated her attention almost wholly on me and her hooligan companions were sidelined, so there was no occasion for conflict. I merely expressed surprise that she should wish to be seen in the company of such dubious individuals as these two, and quickly sketched a cartoon showing her out walking, every inch the proud Empress, flanked by two black slaves, one on either side.

That seemed to settle matters. Hansen likes to walk continually round the corridors, and I went with her, so that by the time I got home my feet were as sore as anything. We played a duet version of Liszt's *Mephisto Waltz*; she is a good sight-reader and I enjoyed playing with her. She says herself that she has a natural technique, and indeed it is very good. She is proud and touchy, however, and whenever she goes wrong (especially if I start laughing), her face turns red.

On the 19th I left for Moscow, promising to write to Frieda.

Moscow was a mad whirl of activity. I stayed with the Glières; Goldik[1]

---

1   Glière. The nickname derives from his first name Reinhold, which since Russian has no 'h' sound would be pronounced Reingold – c.f. Gorovitz (for Horovitz), Gansen (for Hansen).

was conducting his Second Symphony so the whole family was in an uproar, the children were bawling, everyone was rushing madly up and down. Eventually the performance took place, and the post-concert supper went on until four o'clock in the morning, even though I had to perform the following day. In the morning I practised, and in the afternoon lay down for three hours, in order to be fresh for the evening. I did not suffer from pre-concert nerves, but did get a little fatigued from all the waiting.

The piano was a marvellous Bechstein, gorgeous to play. I played well and took great pleasure in it: the Sonata and three of the Etudes. I had a great success, and was called back three times. Taneyev, Lavrovskaya and Deisha-Sionitskaya all sang my praises and said that I excelled as a performer. This was particularly pleasing to hear, since my Petersburg friends are always criticizing me for being such an atrocious interpreter of my own works.

My thoughts are now turning to finding a publisher for these pieces, or rather I should say I have been thinking about this ever since the autumn and have now decided I must put the plan into operation. I shall twist Ossovsky's arm to help me get an introduction to the Russian Music Editions.[1]

The day after my concert I paid some calls, dined with Taneyev, ran around all day and in the evening returned to St Petersburg.

About Scriabin. Before I went to Moscow I saw him twice in St Petersburg, talked with him, sat with him at rehearsals and again fell under his spell – but did not succeed in showing him my transcription. The maestro was having two symphonies performed at the same time, so dashing between rehearsals like a cat on hot bricks he simply could not find the time. And that was how it had to be left: I left to go to Moscow, and he went abroad.

I came back from Moscow to St Petersburg. Although it was February weather, freezing and dusty from there not having been any snow, I was terribly glad to see Piter again. When I met Hansen we were friends again: the oboist has been given his final *congé* and is keeping his distance. Kirlian makes an appearance from time to time. All this is splendid. At the moment Hansen has a bad cold, although she still goes to bed at two o'clock. Last time I saw her she was not herself at all, dull and ailing.

And what about Rudavskaya and Berezovskaya? They have completely dropped out of sight. A pity, of course – they are such attractive girls!

---

1 Music publishing house originally founded by Sergey Koussevitzky and his wife Natalya specifically to publish the works of Russian composers. It soon became known as the Russische Musikverlag (RMV) since, like Belyayev, Koussevitzky based the enterprise in Berlin for copyright reasons.

14 March

From 1 March the Conservatoire moved into spring mode, symbolized by the start of examinations in the Small Hall. The place takes on an atmosphere of highly strung energy, palpably anxious but at the same time frivolous.

I was amazed when I counted up the time Hansen and I had been friends and realized it was at least a month. I thought it had been more like a week, perhaps two, but certainly not as long as six weeks. I do not seem to be having a great deal of success although I devote so much time to her: she is very friendly to me, just as she was the first day we met, but I cannot claim that we have become as close as one might have expected. In the last few days she has been rather cool towards me, while for my part I have begun get slightly bored – in other words I am experiencing a bit of a lacuna, spreading outwards from my feelings about her towards the Conservatoire as a whole.

This week I have been working very hard at my second chorus, *The Wave*,[1] finishing the score in order to present it to Tcherepnin.

In my last diary entry I referred to Berezovskaya and Rudavskaya. The fact is that spending the whole of February in pursuit of Hansen I lost sight of these two girls. Now that March was here they have reappeared in my thoughts and as I start to draw away from Frieda, I have been making approaches to them.

Here are my conclusions. Berezovskaya is extremely beautiful, but terminally dull. This phrase sums up her entire personality.

Rudavskaya is sweet, full of fun, and small. God forgive me from saying that she is empty-headed or vapid, but all the same . . . something is missing. She is just a trifle bland. Everything slides past, nothing sticks. She is still very young, seventeen . . . But a really nice girl. The day before yesterday, having not seen her for some time, I met her at a student concert. To my surprise she was alone, standing in the balcony. When I came back to the balcony she was still on her own, so I went up to her. She gradually warmed up and talked to me, and eventually we made up a foursome consisting of Rudavskaya, me, Sadovskaya and an army doctor, and we happily fooled about half the evening.

1 April

My father was ill all the way through the month of March, and this cast a shadow over everything else. There were some days when the doctors considered his situation hopeless, and at these times total gloom descended. His condition is now a little better, and in consequence my mood is lifting.

There is not much of importance to report in the Conservatoire. Yesipova has also not been well and my studies with her have to some extent slackened

---

[1] Words by Konstantin Balmont, published as Op. 7 No. 2.

in intensity. Tcherepnin's class is working up to a concert at which it seems I am to conduct Glazunov's *Lyric Poem*. This should have been when my two choral works were also performed, but the singers are too busy with the opera. However there is a chance that they may be included in Count Sheremetyev's concerts next season, so I am not too chagrined that once again my choruses are not being performed at the Conservatoire.

One evening the ex-'Contemporaries' did me the honour of coming to my house – Medem, Nurok, Kryzhanovsky, Nikolayev. They listened to the Sinfonietta, the Sonata, the Etudes, and liked them all even, to my surprise, the Sonata. Nurok promised to 'warm up' Ossovsky about getting the Sonata published. I must pay a call on the Ossovskys.

As for my Conservatoire girl friends, I have little in the way of concrete developments to report. At the head of the list are Rudavskaya, Palasova and Hansen. I see them all, not all at once but in turn: the enchanting Antoinettochka,[1] the interesting and unusual Greek Palasova, and Frieda Hansen who is, when all is said and done, very much to my taste.

One other person whom I have not so far mentioned is Mlle Khaslavskaya-Golubovskaya, or just plain Golubovskaya. At Rozanova's examination last spring she played Glazunov's *Variations* quite impeccably, and then in the autumn Sadovskaya introduced me to her. After that we lost sight of one another, but recently we have begun to meet with great regularity. I enjoy her company very much; she has an exceptional musical intelligence, every kind of intelligence in fact, and is always interesting to talk to.

12 April

On the 10th I played some of my works at a concert organized by Nurok for *Apollon* magazine. Others taking part were Medem, Nikolayev, Stravinsky and Karatygin, all playing their own compositions. Apparently Scriabin had played at the last *Apollon* evening.

A few days before this event E. A. Znosko-Borovsky[2] invited me to spend an evening at his house. I had never visited him before, but was always meeting him at the Chess Society. I like him very much, and also our discussions about chess tournaments had always been carried on by correspondence, so I was pleased by the invitation and went willingly. What was my

---

1 Antonina Rudavskaya.
2 Yevgeny Znosko-Borovsky (1884–1954), journalist, literary and theatre critic and chess player. '"Ooh, that Red," said Andrey Rayevsky, "a Social Revolutionary!" I did not know precisely what a Social Revolutionary was, but Andrey so rolled his eyes that I thought to myself, "Such a nice young man, to be such a desperate revolutionary! Interesting, and dangerous."' (*Autobiography*.) A naval officer decorated for gallantry in the First World War, Znosko-Borovsky emigrated to Paris in 1920 and became well known in the West, partly as a fine championship chess player but mainly through books such as *The Middle Game in Chess* and *How Not to Play Chess*, the latter containing as the first of its useful maxims: 'Avoid Mistakes'.

astonishment when I arrived, to find that the company consisted not of chess players but was exclusively artistic. It transpires that Znosko-Borovsky is the secretary of *Apollon*, and most of his guests were associated in some way with the journal. It was the first time I had found myself in such company and I was fascinated to observe the way in which gentlemen of an artistic bent conducted themselves: wandering through the rooms in groups arm in arm, gentlemen and ladies all mixed up higgledy-piggledy, with great freedom but at the same time the utmost decorum. It was all especially interesting since much of my future life was destined to be spent in similar society.

And so, on the 10th I played my Sonata, 'Fairy Tale' and an Etude (a short one) to this gathering. The room was not large, the setting intimate, with about a hundred and fifty listeners, all invited and all from the artistic world. Among musicians, the 'Contemporaries' group was represented by Tcherepnin, Steinberg, a few critics and others.

Tcherepnin has recently come round to believing in me as a composer and musician. This happened after he heard my choral pieces and, most importantly, the Sinfonietta. Our relations have now altered dramatically for the better and he is doing yeoman service for me, broadcasting golden opinions about me in the highest musical circles.

My success exceeded that of all the others and my virtues extolled by the musicians present. Even Steinberg was complimentary. And some of the critics, including Timofeyev, who the year before had written of me that 'in among the welter of sounds may occasionally be discerned glimpses of talent', came to me and introduced themselves. One or two people – Nouvel, Myaskovsky – were not very enthusiastic about the Sonata and advised against publishing it as Opus 1. But I think this sonata would be an ideal first opus for me. Nouvel went so far as to say that it should not even be Op. minus one. But I hold to my opinion.

Another person who came to hear me was Sofia Esche. She was impressed by the 'menagerie' of girls I had succeeded in accumulating from the Conservatoire. How did I manage to accommodate simultaneously so many beautiful girls, including Lyosochka Glagoleva, who according to Sofia was far from indifferent to me? 'You're all the rage at the Conservatoire just now!' she decided.

Sofia Esche has the physical attributes to be an extremely interesting woman, but sometimes she gets herself up in such extravagant dresses and hats that it is positively embarrassing. She is highly intelligent, but has been spoilt by the backstage world of the Maly Theatre. Even before, she was something of an *enfant terrible*, with a tongue sharp enough to skin one alive. She and I clash in impassioned verbal skirmishes, and there are times when she can floor me so completely with an unexpected turn of phrase that I quite lose the power of speech to respond. And, my God, the barbs she launched at the 'menagerie' were so vicious – the only ones who escaped the lash of her tongue were Glagoleva and, up to a point, Alpers! I had been avoiding her all winter, but her response to my neglect was invariably one of friendliness and courtesy. From time to time her dress sense seemed to be taking a turn for the better. But the thing that really attracts me is the devastating machine-gun of her tongue. She was warmly enough disposed towards me the other day to come halfway home with me.

It is now Holy Week, and the Conservatoire is closed. I am staying at home and practising, although not terribly diligently: Papa's illness has put me off my stride. Usually the months of April and August (that is to say, the final months of my Petersburg and country sojourns respectively) are the most productive of the year so far as work is concerned.

23 April

Easter was horrible. Papa was very ill at the end of Holy Week, and we spent day and night at the hospital. On Easter Day he was a little better, and at the moment is not too bad. But none of us can feel very cheerful.

I stayed at home on Easter Day, and the following day dined with the Rayevskys. Before that I called on Glagoleva. She was not well, so I did not go in but sent up a friendly note. She did not of course reply, and I heard no more; I have now heard the whole family has gone to Finland.

I am enjoying being made a fuss of by the Ruzskys; they are good company and I like being at their house. Ossovsky and Ziloti are working on getting my Sinfonietta into the Sheremetyev concerts. We shall see. As for getting the Sonata published, Ossovsky recommends sending it to Moscow to the Russian Music Editions. Both gentlemen were present at the Ruzskys, as was also the daughter of the famous Yershov, a not bad-looking but rather fidgety girl of seventeen.

The next evening I went to a party, although without much enthusiasm because of Father's illness. The party itself was most depressing; I was bitterly disappointed in Hansen, who was boring, disinclined to talk, capricious and plainly in love with someone else. Without emotion I crossed her off the list, and when I awoke the following morning even experienced a certain pleasure at the space that had been cleared.

In the afternoon I went to play the piano for Auer's class. He has examinations coming up, and had asked Glazunov to provide him with accompanists: Shubert, Katya Borshch and I were detailed to do this. Hansen also regularly accompanies this class as her sister[1] is a student of Auer's, and when I arrived

---

1 Cecilia (Tilya) Hansen (1897–1989), violinist with a renowned European career, later the wife of Boris Zakharov. Often referred to as 'The Queen of the Violin', she usually wore a white dress for performances and (doubtless not only for that reason) was described by the young

she was already there. She greeted me coldly, no doubt as a result of my having left the previous evening's party early. But when I turned in a rather flamboyant accompaniment for my violinist, reading from sight, and Auer showed that he was pleased, she changed her tune and became sensitive, refined and amiable, happy to converse and pay attention to me. In a word, she became again that same Hansen whom I had, 'without knowing why', so liked formerly. In the class I chatted quite neutrally with her, but as I was going home I realized that I was not at all indifferent to her and that in spite of everything she was one of my favourites in the Conservatoire.

Rehearsals for Sunday's concert began on the Thursday. I had been assigned Glazunov's *Lyric Poem*, a good choice for me because while the orchestra may have no respect for Beethoven or any other composer, it does have a lot of respect for the Director and therefore takes a lot more care with his pieces than with any others. Also, to conduct this piece gave me the most enormous pleasure and satisfaction, without a trace of nerves, and this was very important for my conducting debut.

Alpers was there; I had not seen her for a long time. It was not a very interesting encounter: our close relationship is obviously a thing of the past. Hansen's judgement was: 'Verochka looks like a mangy cat.'

This was out of order: certainly she was looking rather drab, but it was an unjust and cruel observation. However, by now I was used to the way the Conservatoire girls make catty remarks about one another, so that if one believed everything one heard one would have to wash one's hands of the lot of them!

Here is my current list, in order: 1. Hansen 2. Glagoleva 3. Rudavskaya 4. Palasova 5. Sofia Esche (!) 6. Merimanova (!!) 7. Alpers.

Berezovskaya has been crossed off the list.

30 April

It has been a week since I last made an entry in my diary, and a week that has seen a sharp crescendo in intimacy with Frieda Hansen.

Tosya Piastro has gone to Kharkov, where he has taken a position as concertmaster of the orchestra for the summer. He went at the beginning of Easter; Hansen was upset and worried, and I'm told even shed tears. The time I had seen her at the party was just when her spirits were at their lowest ebb.

But as is the way in such matters, the sharpness of the initial pangs subsided and Hansen found that life went on without Piastro. As a result, the primary object of her affections being absent, I, who had been in second

---

Yehudi Menuhin as 'an angel'. Spending her last years in London, she continued to play into her ninth decade.

place, moved up to the main spot. My suit was helped by the success I had conducting the *Lyric Poem* on the 25th, my equally successful accompaniment in Auer's examinations, and my status just then at the height of fashion within the Conservatoire. There seemed no doubt that my continual and assiduous siege of Hansen was not unwelcome, so why on earth should she not console herself with me? And so it proved. On the 25th, after I had finished my podium antics with *Lyric Poem*, we listened to the rest of the concert together, and then went for a walk along the embankment and into the Alexandrovsky Gardens.

The following day we took turns to play the accompaniments for the class: once we had gone out on stage we did not leave but sat there for an hour and a half. While she was playing I turned pages for her, and vice versa. Afterwards we spent the whole day wandering about the Conservatoire. In the evening she had an external Physics exam, so I went with her to it and we sat together. Today, when she came into the Conservatoire, she asked Bessonova to find out if I was there or not. We walked out together, and found ourselves at random emerging on to a deserted Korabelny Embankment. It is the sort of place, alternately deserted and swarming with the lower orders, that Hansen found mildly alarming, but we walked arm in arm and had an enjoyable time.

The intimacy of our conversation and our relationship is also growing – exactly that intimacy whose absence I was so much regretting a month ago.

On the 25th I conducted Glazunov's *Lyric Poem* in a Conservatoire student concert. There were no disasters, and both Glazunov and I had a success(!). This formed part of the conductors' class exam. The marks we obtained were: Kankarovich 5, Shteiman and I 4½, Saminsky 4, Kolomiitsev 3½. Kankarosha[1] won the silver medal, which marked his final graduation from the Conservatoire. Saminsky and Kolomiitsev were also deemed to have completed the conductors' course, leaving only Shteiman, Tolstyakov and myself for next year. Apparently no new students will be accepted. We shall be able to do whatever we want!

I'm seeing a lot of Sofia Esche. Things between us are as they were; her tongue fires a continual barrage to right and left.

The name 'Esche' works well musically: all its letters correspond with musical notation.[2] One day I composed a pleasant little piece and presented it to Esche. Today she was dancing around and calling out to me: she had obviously worked out the meaning of the composition. All the same, I still prefer Hansen's company.

1 Kankarovich.
2 In Latin script and German notation, 'S' being E flat, 'H' being B natural. Here, Prokofiev spells the name ESCHE in Latin script, following German transliteration and notation. But see p. 8 n. 3.

6 May

On 1 May the Conservatoire was deserted. There were no exams, and classes had wound down. But I still went in, knowing that Frieda would be there about four o'clock. I pressed her to come out for a walk with me.

It took some time to persuade her, but eventually we went. 'I'm not going anywhere but Nikolsky Gardens,' said Frieda.

'Oh no, let's go to the Neva!' I said.

More disagreements, but I still got my way. We came to Vasilievsky Island and turned left on to the embankment. At the end of the embankment we came out on to Bolshoy Prospect, and I made Frieda go right to the end of that, right up to the sea.

2 May was Sunday. I stayed at home, practised the piano for my exam, and pined for Hansen.

The rehearsal for Yesipova's class exam took place in the Small Hall on Monday evening. I had finished practising my programme in the afternoon and so had some free time. Frieda had said she would be in the Conservatoire that evening. When she left to go home I went with her, and at the corner of Voznesensky Street quietly suggested that instead of turning right, the way to her house, we turn left towards Morskaya Street. We lingered a little in Alexandrovsky Gardens, then went on to the embankment, but it came on to rain so I put her in a cab and retraced my steps to the Small Hall.

The following day was the day of my piano examination. Following a suggestion Taneyev had made to me while I was in Moscow, I played a Buxtehude fugue, and Tchaikovsky's *Scherzo à la Russe*, Op. 1 No. 1. I transcribed the Buxtehude organ fugue, which is out of print virtually everywhere, for piano, and learned it thoroughly. Yesipova had almost no criticisms to make. I titled the piece *Prelude, Fugue and Postlude*, and asked for the date of his birth to be inserted after the composer's name: 1637. I also gave a lot of thought to the way I learned the *Scherzo*, and it went well, with clarity and above all much gaiety. I had wanted to play Medtner's *Fairy Tale*, Op. 8, and during February and March made good progress with it, but Yesipova did not care much for the piece and eventually conceived a hatred of it. Finally she went so far as to shout at me and went on grumbling for quite a time afterwards.

Yesipova's class exam was spread over two days: on the first day it was the turn of the newcomers and three of the weaker existing girl students. The remainder were to play on the second day. I was supposed to be number 5 on Day Two, but as at the rehearsal I had played the fugue and the *Scherzo* so splendidly – as I was told – I was put as the last to play on Day One, which afforded me incredible satisfaction. However one looks at this, it marked me out from the others, and was more than flattering to my self-esteem.

So it was that I played on the 4th. I was calm, it was a good performance, and I was awarded a 5. I had not expected less, in fact I had been half-hoping for 5½. Only eight people played on that day, so the exam was rather abbreviated. There was a large audience, although the hall was not completely packed. Yesipova extended her hand to me and said, 'Very well done.' Glazunov expatiated on who Buxtehude was.

Everything was fine, but . . . there was a but. To begin with, I only got a 5, while Malinskaya and Kuznetsova both got 5+. That was the first thing. Then everyone else also got 5, even though they did not play as well as I did. That was the second thing. Then it was a little disappointing to find when I came out, having spent too long after my performance chatting in the artists' room, that Hansen had already gone home. And lastly there were several people not in the audience who I had hoped would have come to hear me play: Glagoleva, Rudavskaya, Esche, Myaskovsky, Winkler, Nikolayev. Aside from this all was well, and Ilyin said to me, 'Your stock has risen greatly in my eyes: I thought you were just a composer who played the piano a bit, but you clearly have the ability to turn into a marvellous pianist.'

As for the second day, which was truly the triumph of the Yesipova class, Borovsky and Hofmann[1] were both awarded 5 with two stars(!), Berlin 5+, and most of the remainder 5. Borovsky's account of the Brahms *Paganini Variations* was that of a truly consummate, finished pianist. Akhron and Zeiliger,[2] who last year had 5+, this year had to be content with georgeless[3] fives and their tails drooped between their legs.

On this second day of the examination I was completely free and sat up in the balcony with Frieda Hansen. Frieda was slender, elegant, piquant and altogether enchanting: I sat and feasted my eyes upon her. In the opposite corner of the balcony from us sat Myaskovsky. When the exam performances finished, Frieda went into a little sulk, and by the time we parted on the way home had definitely drawn away from me. The next day was a holiday, and I asked her to telephone me. I am now sitting at home repining; she has not telephoned although I am waiting for her to do so.

10 May

Frieda was supposed to be performing her piano examination today, but her teacher Dubasov is suffering from neuralgia and so there is to be no exam today.

For the last few days Frieda has been very out of sorts. Her nerves are

---

1 Yelena Hofmann, not the celebrated pianist Josef Hofmann.
2 Alexander Zeiliger (1892–1959), pianist, student of Anna Yesipova.
3 A straight 5 without enhancement.

strained to the limit, and on top of that I am pretty sure that she is missing the elder Piastro terribly. My stock with her has fallen recently, and probably stands only a little higher than it did a month ago. It may have risen with Ilyin, but in Denmark it has fallen. What price the international market?

Am I jealous of Piastro? The answer is no. I am almost certain that he does not reciprocate to the same extent, that he returns to her only a tenth of what she devotes to him. Piastro stands quite high in my estimation, and I do have respect for him. He has intelligence, he is an interesting person in his own right, and has both talent and reputation as an artist.

When Hansen bestowed favour and approval on Kirlian and the oboist Petrov I was beside myself, since these two nonentities were totally unworthy of so much as one drop of her attention, and I could not bear the thought that they were receiving any. I cannot say the same of Piastro; he has the right to be loved by Hansen. With him it is useless to enter the lists, and if at some time in the future I prevail, it will be at the cost of many humiliating defeats.

In any case, it is only this year that I have achieved any notable status in the Conservatoire; last year hardly anybody knew me and I'm sure I would in any case have lost out to Piastro then.

Needless to say, of the thousands who came to the Graduation Day concert I could find no one I wanted to see. The programme was very dull. Still, Shubert soon pointed out Frieda to me, and later, strolling through the corridors with Golubovskaya I came across her in the company of Misha Piastro and Nyura,[1] and exchanged bows with her. The people I wanted to see were Ziloti, Rudavskaya and the elder Esche sister, and besides that of course I was a little put out with Frieda – I certainly did not want to join her group. And when just before the end I tried to seek her out she was nowhere to be found.

So I did not see her there. Today I am sitting at home and plan to do the same tomorrow, although Frieda has an oral exam in Harmony and will be expecting my presence in the Conservatoire. The day after tomorrow are the examinations for Drozdov's and Ossovskaya's classes: that means Glagoleva and Alpers. I imagine that Hansen will put in an appearance at these. This will be an interesting day for me. A week ago Frieda sent me a photograph. It is quite enchanting. I often look at it, and my heart melts.

22 May

On the 12th I attended Glagoleva's and Alpers's examination performances. Frieda was not there at the beginning, but a little while later came in and sat near the front. I listened to Verochka's playing. It was all right, quite good, she has made progress, as I told her in a very friendly way.

---

1 Palasova.

Then I went into the artists' room, where Lyosya was moping about before going on stage to play her number. 'I'm going out to Sestroretsk today for the start of the season,' she said. 'Why don't you come?'

I was delighted. We agreed that I would come to their house at five o'clock, have something to eat, the company would then assemble in order to leave at six. Glagoleva played rather routinely, but made a perfect stage entrance.

Just before five I visited Papa in hospital, and left some time after five. The weather was marvellous and I felt my mood lightening. There was only three-quarters of an hour before Glagoleva's train left, so I jumped on to a tram and went straight to Novaya Derevnya station. The tram got there three minutes before the train was due to leave; I looked everywhere but could see no sign of Glagoleva, then the train jerked into motion and I with it. I searched through every carriage on the train without finding any of the promised company, and concluded that they must be coming on the next train. I knew nothing whatsoever about the resort of Sestroretsk, except that, as it turned out, it was more than hour's journey away.

I began to be bored, standing on the outside platform of the last coach of the train. The weather was divine, and all around was green, tranquil and sunny. I thought what a jolly excursion it should have been, and how sad to be on my own.

Melancholy descended. This was a stupid situation: there seemed no point in going anywhere. What on earth was I to do in Sestroretsk when quite possibly Glagoleva, expecting me to come and dine at her house, had called off her party and not come at all? Meanwhile it would be an hour's journey back to St Petersburg, and then another hour on the tram to get home.

It was getting more than I could bear. I tried to force myself to go on to the resort, but failed. At the last station we coincided with the train going in the opposite direction, so I jumped over to it and . . . returned to Piter.

Next day I went to see Myaskovsky, not yet having decided whether to go to the singers' exam or not. But he said that Asafyev would be accompanying, so I dragged him out and we went together. This suited me very well, because I cannot abide going to something on my own when I don't really know what I am doing there. We slipped inconspicuously in and sat together in the balcony.

And all of a sudden – bang! – down below appeared Rudavskaya, lively as quicksilver and pretty as a picture. This was a new thought for me, as some time ago she had vanished from my life; at the Graduation Day concert I had only glimpsed her from afar. Before that, in the good times, we had agreed to write to one another during the summer. I had not expected to see her again, but wanting nevertheless to ensure my stable of summer correspondents, I had put Rudavskaya right at the top of my list, and fearing that she might disappear somewhere for the summer had dropped her a little note, a neat piece of verbal tight-rope walking.

It seemed that the note had produced the desired effect. She had received it yesterday, and came into the Conservatoire today. Then Max, who was already in the balcony, appeared and announced that he was soon leaving to go to the country. I went downstairs with him, and we agreed to play chess (!) by correspondence, since it was clear that we could not rely on carrying on a normal correspondence after last year's debacle! Incidentally, in his exam he played wildly, was very nervous, got lost and made mistakes, but still got a 4.

The exam was soon over. I met Antoinettochka, who promised to come tomorrow and immediately fluttered away again, and then Frieda Hansen. We walked home together, but Frieda was cool, having seen me together with Rudavskaya.

The next day was the examination for Rozanova's class. Rudavskaya was enchanting and spent all the time with me. We parted the best of friends. Antoinettochka promised to write to me soon and to give me her portrait; if the weather was good we would go out somewhere together, in other words the usual mass of enticing prospects that would doubtless evaporate without trace.

The next day, the 19th, was the day of Nyura Palasova's exam. Frieda Hansen was almost out of her mind with worry for her. She told me that she might be going back to Moscow the following day, and might not be returning to Petersburg at all until the autumn, or alternatively she might come back after a few days.

20 June

The end of June. Day by day the summer is passing, and I am still sitting in Petersburg. If anyone had told me beforehand that it would be like this I would have been appalled. But this is how it is. Papa is still ill, and evidently beyond hope. The surgical side of his illness was all dealt with successfully, it seemed that the cancer had been removed and the cure was complete, but his strength has been so depleted by the three-month struggle that his heart is giving out, he has no appetite – and this is the only thing that can save him. Mama is in torment, day and night she has not left his side for a moment since March, while I, although I can do little to help, must stay miserably in the city. It was such a wonderful winter! – but the kinder months of the year have been far from crowning it.

I am working, but not as seriously as I should. I play the piano, working on my sound, keeping my fingers curved, practising the Saint-Saëns Concerto and the *Mephisto Waltz*. I've finished *Dreams*.[1] I've composed a lot of material for the Concerto. I'm writing a sonatina.

---

1   *Sni* (*Dreams*), symphonic tableau for orchestra, Op. 6.

And yet the atmosphere is not right.

By my own efforts I organized a postal [chess] tournament for prize-winners in which I am myself playing with much pleasure. I won a match +2–0 = 1 against P. P. Saburov for the championship of the Conservatoire (!). My chess is evidently improving.

Petersburg is empting itself of people, leaving only the stones behind. Zakharov is in Terioki, Myaskovsky has gone to Siverskaya, Golubovskaya is also there, Alpers is in Pavlovsk, Max in Pushkin, Borovsky in Sergievskaya Pustynya, Glagoleva in Sestroretsk, Rudavskaya in Terioki, Borshch in Yelizavetgrad, Palasova in Yekaterinodar, and Hansen in Kamenska.[1]

Hansen! In May she went to Moscow, but soon came back. Came back, and fell ill, with a cold, with her nerves and from the White Nights. I had many letters from her and we kept up an intensive correspondence, but she was only in the city for ten days and we did not see each other once. I wanted to very much, I missed her, but Hansen was like a block of wood and with a rare indifference contrived to do without me. On the way to Kamenska and when she was there she sent me four letters: I did not reply to any of them. Farewell, Frieda.

Meanwhile Rudavskaya, who naturally did not keep a single one of her promises, vanished into the blue yonder. I waited for a long time and then decide to dash off a letter to her, full of pretty jokes and word-play. What was my surprise when the next day Antoinettochka called me on the telephone. She would be waiting for me at the Conservatoire in half an hour, she had somewhere to go on business, would like to see me, and had time for a stroll. She was still in Petersburg and had not yet been away at all. I was delighted, and immediately set off. She was already on the square, the darling, in a hat with a rose-coloured bow on it, a rose-coloured tie and a rose-coloured rose below that. We went to her dressmaker and then to one of her friends, and walked in the gardens on Vasilievsky Island. I then walked her home convinced that Antoinettochka was a very, very sweet girl.

The next day she left for Terioki,[2] from where she wrote me the loveliest

---

1 Siverskaya, Pushkin, Sestroretsk, Pavlovsk, Terioki (now Zelenogorsk) are all resort areas within reach of St Petersburg. Pushkin (Tsarskoye Selo) and Pavlovsk are imperial palaces and parks to the south of the city, Sestroretsk and Terioki to the north west along the north shore of the Gulf of Finland. Yelizavetgrad (later Kirovograd) is in the Ukraine, south of Kiev; Yekaterinodar (later Krasnodar) is in the Caucasus. Sergievskaya Pustynya (Pustynya = desert) is on the site of a monastery dedicated to St Sergius, the holy fourteenth-century ascetic, on the south shore of the Gulf of Finland. Stamits Kamenska, birthplace of the Hansen sisters, was a Cossack settlement near Rostov-on-Don.

2 After the construction of the railway line from Petersburg to Vyborg in the 1860s, the whole 'kurortny rayon', 'resort area' along the southern shore of the Karelian isthmus became during the nineteenth and twentieth centuries a favoured dacha destination for the Petersburg middle classes, artists and intelligentsia. At the time Prokofiev was writing, the names of the settlements were all still Finnish; after the Russo-Finnish War of 1939–40, which resulted in Finland

letter. I replied straight away as requested to the poste restante, but it is already a week and I haven't heard from Tonechka. I do understand that there could be too many things getting in the way for us to have a regular correspondence, so am not in the least offended by my charming friend. For the last three Tuesdays I have been going to Pavlovsk to listen to music: the Alpers are staying there. I've been getting there some time after three, then going for a walk with Verochka, playing some music and then at half past eight going to the concert, leaving to come home again at eleven. What is remarkable about the Alpers family is how united they are – a unity expressed not least in the whole family's great affection for me. It is a delight to be with them. And Verochka is lovely – maliciously I must add, when there is no one else.

In any case, let the others be – if they're not there, they're not there and that's an end of it. Last time we walked for two full hours, leaving the town behind us, first along the road and then across a field into the forest. In the forest I took Verochka's arm. It was marvellous in the forest! Seldom have I penetrated so deeply into one. This solitude *en deux* [sic], with no one else for miles around, nothing but the dense, half-dark woods, was strangely seductive.

But it was damp among the trees: we soon came out again into the meadow. There we sat and rested for a while, then returned home. I have the happiest memories of that walk.

---

ceding Karelia to the Soviet Union, names were changed into Russian, including the much prized resorts of Terioki (to Zelenogorsk), Kuokkale (to Repino), Kellomyaki (to Komarovo). The two last named became official Artists' Rest Homes under the Soviets (Shostakovich holidayed and stayed in dachas in Repino, Sestroretsk and Komarovo). An eye-witness account from 1894 of Terioki and its railway station, so important to Prokofiev, contains the following delightful description:

'Continuing by train beyond Beloóstrov towards Vyborg, we come to Terioki, where the trains wait for about half an hour. In summer, besides tradespeople hawking bread, Vyborg pretzels, bottles of mineral water, etc., crowds of dacha residents flock to the station to wait for the arrival of the train. As the visitors emerge from their carriages they climb sedately into gigs that bear them contentedly off along the smooth, broad road in the direction of the town and its dachas, which start almost at the station and go down towards the seashore.

'Terioki is a small town consisting of dachas constructed in the Finnish style, with gardens and balconies. Peasant cottages belonging to the local Finnish population are scattered over the whole area, but the building of the dachas has caused the formation of many streets and alleys leading off the main road to the station and the surrounding villages. These are strung out right along the seashore, a few paces from the road.

'The landscape around Terioki is flat and sandy, and encircled by pine forests extending on all sides for several versts. This part of the Gulf of Finland, being a sandbank, has a sandy beach strewn with granite boulders and dotted with rush-matting bathing cabins from which the dacha residents bathe. There is no river in Terioki, so the residents draw water from wells. The town has a Finnish primary school, several butcher shops and greengrocers, a brewery supplying the local settlements, and a small hotel which offers passable meals and accommodation. The majority of permanent inhabitants are Finns, who offer services including transporting visitors from the station into the centre of the town, and renting their cottages for summer lets.'

Yesipova is spending the summer in Gungerburg.¹ Zakharov and I made the journey there to visit her, as she is always pleased when her students come to see her. Boris arrived early in the afternoon, and I got there later the same day. It is a six-hour train journey to Narvi, and not a very interesting one. But to my great surprise Kostya and Lyolochka Skalon were also on the train, and we had such a nice time that we were almost sorry to arrive at Narvi so soon. I was in good form and talked non-stop.

At Narvi I migrated to the river steamer and forty minutes later disembarked at Gungerburg to be met by Borya. We put up at an hotel. From noon until evening we spent with Anna Nikolayevna, who was very nice to us, and in the mornings and evenings Borya and I strolled about the gardens and the beach. Anna Nikolayevna was almost on her own there: only her student Schweiger and one of her dependent relations were with her. We played vint and draughts and similar pastimes. I very much enjoyed the evenings with Zakharov and became close friends with him, as much as is possible with someone with as closed and egotistical a character as his. We drank tea with milk to celebrate our *Bruderschaft*.²

An amusing experience was when, wanting something to drink, we went into the Kursaal. Offered a sherry cobbler³ and not knowing what it was, we said yes. But as soon as we started to suck the heady stuff up through the straw we were both appalled and had to rush outside to the beach to breathe in some fresh air.

Two days afterwards we left for home together, I to Petersburg and Boris to Terioki. He very much wanted me to go to their dacha with him, and I was sorely tempted by the invitation. It was not just that I wanted to be there with him, there was also the attraction that Antoinettochka was somewhere in the vicinity, and as soon as I was released from home I did get myself together and went out there.

10 August

I am writing this from Sontsovka. Papa died on 23 July, after exactly four months in hospital. For a long time after the surgical operation to remove the cancer from his intestine, there was little change in his condition. By rights he should have improved, but he did not. Either his organism was not strong enough to recuperate straight away, or the root of the disease had not in fact been cured. Indeed some tumours did appear in the liver, so the

---

1 Town in Estonia, today known as Narva-Yiesuu.
2 The ritual (usually more commonly accompanied by alcohol) in which Russians cement their relationship by addressing each other in the intimate second person singular – what the French call 'tutoyer' and the Germans 'dutzen'.
3 Cocktail consisting of sherry, orange juice and red curaçao.

cancer had spread there also, and we knew then there was no salvation. In his last days Papa was not conscious, and if he did regain consciousness for some moments it was a consciousness drugged with morphine, and so he died not knowing that he was dying.

His actual passing was not a blow to me. The blow had fallen on 27 March, when the doctors confirmed after the first operation that Papa's condition was hopeless. From that time onwards there were only slight fluctuations of improvement or deterioration, so that I did not believe he would get better and even at times hoped for a quick release for him.

Did I love him? I do not know.

Were anyone ever to insult or do him harm, I would have gone to any lengths to defend him. As for loving him, in the past six years I had grown away from him. We had little in common, and not a single shared interest.

In winter I saw him only in those brief interludes, four times or so a year, when he came to Petersburg. And then our main point of contact was the study of algebra, geometry and drawing, which although it was sometimes enjoyable was sometimes less so because of Papa's tendency to excessive pedantry.

In any case I feel that at the present time I have not yet arrived at a true appreciation of my father's undoubtedly noble personality. He served me, his only son, unstintingly, and it was thanks to his tireless work that I was provided for so long with all my material necessities.

May you rest in peace, the fitting reward to a good and noble man!

11 August

I now take up the story where I left off.

Three days or thereabouts after I left Gungerburg, which must have been around 23 June, I went to Terioki to stay with Zakharov.

I was delighted to be there. I like Boris Zakharov very much indeed, he has many excellent qualities that bind me to him. He is far from stupid, has a strong personality, is not without wit, and is excellent company, always the gentleman not simply at heart but in his manners and in the way he dresses; he is good-looking, serious and practical. The truth is, there are not so many people in the world who would justify such a description. And I am sure he has yet more qualities than those I have just listed. Finally, I seem to have been aware of all his admirable qualities since we first got to know one another, even though our friendship grew slowly and gradually.

The first time I saw him was four years ago, in October 1906. He had just turned nineteen, whereas I was fifteen and a half. I was in Lyadov's Counterpoint class; I remember him coming into the class and I also remember that on that first day we left the Conservatoire building together. Most of all I remember his enormous peaked student's cap, which had an unusually dandified air about it.

We got on well together right away, although we had no particular need of one another and I did not at that time regard him a very solid musician. Even so, by the following year, or even by the end of that first season, our relationship was already of the closest.

The fact that we were both in the Fugue class brought us together much of the time, and in the Form class something of a regular triumvirate gradually established itself: Myaskovsky, Zakharov and me.

There is one undesirable aspect to Zakharov's character. Although it is perhaps not correct to describe it as undesirable, it cannot be counted among his good points. I mean his egotism, which is related to his strength of character. There are other less attractive qualities: a despotic inclination and an unfeeling heart, but I shall say something about this later. In consequence of his egotism, Zakharov can be interested only in what at any given time touches him personally. For this reason he often disappeared completely from Myaskovsky's and my view, and this did not make it easy to maintain a stable and harmonious relationship with him.

Meanwhile, Myaskovsky and I found ourselves in full accord with one another, and despite the ten-year difference in our ages on very good terms. I admired him as a superb musician and as a serious composer, constantly working. For his part he found me an interesting composer and probably a reasonably good musician: we showed one another our compositions, played four-hand music together and enjoyed one another's company.

For the past eighteen months Zakharov has very much wanted to be one of our company, but something has always got in the way even though we were always very glad of his presence. Each time we were together at Myaskovsky's house or at mine, as sure as fate something would come up to prevent his joining us, and he was constantly letting us down in this way. Whenever we did manage to gather as a threesome, he would often complain that he felt excluded from whatever was of burning interest to us at that time: we would be discussing the music of Reger, or of Strauss, and this was not music he knew.

I am deeply grateful to him for what he did last spring, urging me to come into Yesipova's class and making it possible for me to do so. This was a wonderful service to perform for me, probably the most notable service anyone has ever done for me. I will always be grateful to him for it.

By last season our relationship had begun to grow into something recognizably like friendship, and when I started to study with Yesipova it blossomed into the real thing. Some time around the end of May this year he telephoned me to say goodbye and tell me that he was going to his dacha at Terioki. I replied that I was probably going to have to stay in the city for at least half the summer, at which he was very sympathetic and said that I must absolutely come and stay with him at Terioki and he would be very offended if I did not. I agreed with joy. In the meantime we agreed to make a joint trip to visit our grandma (Yesipova).

The result of all this is that from the day of our first meeting right through to our final parting at Terioki station our friendship has undergone a steady crescendo, and there is no reason to expect any diminuendo now! I can only repeat that I am exceedingly fond of him and could not be more happy at the situation.

12 August

And so, I was very happy to be arriving at Terioki. The Zakharov family is very large indeed: six brothers, two sisters each with a husband, plus two wives of two of the brothers, making twelve in all. There is no mother; the father does not live in Terioki and makes only occasional visits. The whole Zakharov tribe is grown up (Borya is almost the youngest) and operates as a republic with perfect unanimity. This is wonderful! The environment confers a great feeling of freedom.

The dacha is luxurious, 'villa' would be a better description, furnished and equipped in irreproachable comfort, and all its residents are extraordinarily agreeable, straightforward, young and gay.[1] It was not many days before I had got to know them all, liked them all, and felt at home as a fish in water. Croquet, tennis, piano duets, sea-bathing, walks – a continual round of pleasure.

Not every member of the family was there at this time, three of the brothers were missing and were due to come in July. There was an annex to the Zakharov tribe in the shape of the Karneyevs, a family living two dachas away of whom the two most notable members were the two daughters Lidusya and Zoryusya, with their younger brother Lyova, nicknamed by me Simpoponchik, and a gaggle of smaller fry.

Lidusya was seventeen and a half, and a nice-looking girl, slim and supple with lovely eyes, a cheerful soul, uncomplicated sometimes to the point of silliness but atoning for this by her extraordinary charm. 'Lidusya li dusya?'[2] she babbled continually, to which everyone was glad to assent.

---

1 'The house stands ... on the corner of "Zakharov Street", leading to one of the grandest dachas in Terioki – the Zakharov dacha. This was a building of more than thirty-six rooms and an enormous parquet-floored hall; all the rooms were lined with carved-wood panelling' (P. F. Mirolyubov, *Raznoye o zhizni v Teriokakh* (*Aspects of Life in Terioki*), unpublished memoir). Between 1917 and 1939, while Terioki was in Finnish territory, the house became a headquarters for the Finnish Schützkorps, or volunteer Home Guard, and thus played a significant part in Finnish Resistance to Stalin's Winter War invasion of 1939–40.
2 Untranslatable play on words involving 'dusya', a term of endearment. 'Lidusya's a little darling, isn't she?'

Zoya was two years younger. She also possessed a charming little face, a little more childish and doll-like, if one may put it that way, than Lida's. But in fact, even though the child in her often peeped through, she had a more serious and reflective side to her than her sister.

All the same, I preferred Lidusya to Zoya. Simpoponchik was an attractive thirteen-year-old schoolboy, delightful in his boyish charm.

We all met the first evening I was there. It was the eve of St John Baptist's Day[1] and we all went down to the beach with candles to light. I was fairly unexcited by the prospect of meeting the Karneyev girls, but in the interests of general sociability decided I would make myself agreeable to them.

It was a most attractive picture when for several versts the whole length of the coast was lit up with a chain of campfires. Borya quickly organized his own fire, collecting a gang of children to help, getting everyone running around in a frenzy, and – Borya of all people! – teasing Lidusya and Zoryusya and good-naturedly flirting with them, to which they responded with such infectious willingness that I was immediately drawn into the fun.

I am usually quick to make friends with people, but this was exceptionally fast work even for me, so much so that the very next day someone was asking us how many years we had known one another. Relations in both directions were as free and easy and straightforward as could be, and could only possibly have reached the level they did by virtue of the untarnished uprightness of Zakharov's own character. As his closest companion I was immediately accepted on trust.

We argued and chaffed and squabbled (Zorka was particularly adept at this), and sauntered around with our arms round each other's waists. But there was never a trace of anything coarse or vulgar in this, it was all just simple fun and happiness. It never occurred to the girls that we might take advantage, and they were always quite ready to play the fool with us. For our part Zakharov and I were just as happy to join in all the teasing and flirting, and loved being with them, although we agreed between ourselves that nice as they were to have fun with, once out of sight they would also be out of mind.

We had no hesitation in awarding Lidusya the palm over Zorya. Zoya was 'a big little girl' while Lidusya was 'a young lady', part of whose enchantment lay in the fact that despite her unruffled surface, a hint of more complex depths could sometimes show itself.

When Borya was with her, Zorya would attach herself to me, and when I was with Lida, Borya would take up with Zorya. Such realignments did not worry us in the slightest. On the contrary, it was all the more amusing, and when we were walking out in the evenings, we made an inseparable quartet of Lidusya, Zoryusya, Boryusya and Sergusya!

Borya taught me to play tennis while we were at Terioki, and I took to this

---

1 St John Baptist's Day is Midsummer Night, the summer solstice.

splendid game with enthusiasm. They also taught me a game called 'ninth wave',[1] which we played on rainy days for 5- and 10-kopeck pieces. I wasn't very keen to play but did not want to refuse, so tipping out all the loose change in my purse on to the table staked 70 kopecks. The result of the game itself was quite a surprise: when I got up from the table I had 18 roubles in my pocket, although I hadn't enjoyed playing it at all. But a great expert, Dr Khaikin, lost 25 roubles.

I set up a croquet championship, a proper tournament, which so caught the fancy of the whole company that for two whole days nothing else was talked of. The gentlemen removed their jackets and the ladies their corsets in order to allow themselves greater freedom to play. Nikolay Stepanovich, Borya's brother, broke his mallet when he lost a game to me. First prize was won by Borya, who brilliantly destroyed all opposition. I won the second prize.

16 August

When I decided to go to Terioki I knew that Antoinettochka Rudavskaya was living at a dacha somewhere near by. But how to track her down was another matter, since I had received no reply from my response to her letter, and had heard nothing from her since. I told Zakharov that one of my Conservatoire girl friends was staying in Terioki.

'I know, I've seen her several times at the station,' he replied.

'She's the prettiest girl in the Conservatoire,' I said.

Zakharov said he did not find her particularly beautiful. And so, although when I arrived at Terioki I was desperately anxious to find her, life with the Zakharovs so turned my head that three days went by during which not only did I not find Rudavskaya, I did not even attempt the search. Meanwhile, my family had given me leave to go away only for three days, promising however that if Papa's state of health permitted it, I could return again. The three days passed in what seemed like three minutes, and already it was time for me to go back to Petersburg. Boris accompanied me to the station, and on the way I was grumbling that they had given me such a good time I had let Rudavskaya slip through my fingers. But as we were nearing the station:

'Look over there, to your right! There she is, your girl from the Conservatoire!' cried Zakharov suddenly. I looked round to see a chubby figure, and turned away much disgruntled.

'Are you out of your mind?' I said.

'No, of course I'm not, it's definitely her, look, sitting over there!' Boris was overjoyed. 'Go and say hello!' and without further ado he swept off my hat and bowed low in a parody of salutation.

---

1 Card game of skill and chance in which the banker plays against the other players who stake on the cards they draw against the bank's selected nine cards, the last one, if successful, paying out the stake ninefold. Seafaring lore has it that the ninth wave will be the biggest and most powerful.

'Oh, do shut up, it's nothing like her! That's someone else – it's Popova!'

I was discomforted and annoyed at the unwelcome substitution. Meanwhile, the girl was approaching us, and so we had to bow and make ourselves known to her, whereupon I immediately bombarded her with questions about Rudavskaya. It did not take long for her to get the point, and she was able to confirm that indeed there was a pretty girl from the Conservatoire Academic class staying there, and that she was often to be seen at the station.

'Well, for God's sake,' I concluded, dashing for the departing train, 'if you see her again please do tell her that in the first place I send her my very warmest greetings and would very much like to see her, and also tell her that I am probably coming back here tomorrow, so where would I be able to catch her?' saying which I left.

In Petersburg I discovered that the cook had been let go and the apartment closed up, so the family would be very happy for me to go and base myself with the Zakharovs. The Zakharovs were equally happy, I was trebly happy, and seeing that Papa was feeling reasonably well, I prepared to return to Terioki for a more extended stay, promising to come back to Petersburg and see my parents every three days.

At the station I encountered Popova, who this time joyfully informed me. 'I did see your lady, and asked her to be here tomorrow at noon precisely.'

I was radiant, and the following day haunted the station minute by minute.

Antosha did not come, but I could not be too annoyed with her. I did not believe this was coquetry on her part, nor ill manners, but rather inexperience: a young girl would very likely be apprehensive, or unable to get away from her mother, or something of the sort, but whatever it was I did not think that she would deliberately stand me up. Even so, the net result was that the connection with Antosha was once again broken. How was I to see her now? Several times I bicycled over to the station and saw Popova, but she had no more of any consequence to tell me.

One day towards evening I persuaded Boris to come over with me to the station to post some letters. After an initial reluctance he eventually agreed. For some reason he did not want to take the bicycles actually as far as the station, but waited with them in a nearby wood while I took the letters and went on to the platform.

And . . . zip! Out of the blue, there was Antoinettochka. Sweet as ever; there was just no way in the world she could have come out to meet me earlier, but she was glad to see me now, it was so dull here, there was no one she knew.

Unfortunately I could not linger and spend much time with Antoinettochka then as Zakharov was waiting for me. We arranged to meet the next day just before eleven, by the casino on the beach. When I emerged, Zakharov was already coming towards the station, wheeling my bike alongside his.

The next day at half past ten the same thing happened as before, and I was left standing around. Devil take it! Strangely, I was not upset at Antosha this time either. But it was rather humiliating to be led by the nose like this, and in front of Borya too. And the worst of it was that once again the thread had slipped from my fingers, and I had no way of catching up with Antoinettochka. One day there was a big fire in a building in Terioki: I was there watching, and I took to going to church on Sundays – but all to no avail. Antosha was in hiding.

In the meantime Borya and I were awaiting the arrival of Myaskovsky, to whom we had written at the beginning of my stay and who had promised to come as soon as he had seen his father off to Vladivostok. His father left on 5 July. On the 8th I was due to be in Petersburg, since that was Papa's birthday, and so I had written to Kolechka that if it suited him we could meet on the evening of the 8th and travel to Terioki together. As I saw my parents twice a week I was also there on the 5th. Getting back to Terioki in the evening, whom should I see at the station among a great crowd of people, but Boryusya.

'What are you doing here?'

'Oh, I just came to send off some letters. I'm glad I've seen you; your girlfriend is wandering about here somewhere . . .'

'What?' and I rushed over to Antosha.

'Every morning I'm on the beach,' she confided. 'I'll be there from eleven o'clock tomorrow, come then. I'll be sitting there before you get to the casino, where there are three benches.'

This time the arrangement sounded a bit more reliable. Antoinettochka did not want Zakharov to see us together (why not?) and for my part I did not want to keep him waiting, and so in expectation of the following day's meeting, we soon parted.

We went home through the forest, and the conversation turned to Myaskovsky. Suddenly Borya said, not in relation to anything in particular, 'Well, anyhow, we all know Myaskovsky's a lousy musician!'

I looked at him in amazement. He said, 'We'd better run on now, otherwise it will take us for ever to get there.' I started to run, Borya behind me. Suddenly I heard him stop and call out, 'Eh, Seryozha! Stop! Seryozha!'

I turned round, and there behind me were Zakharov . . . and Myaskovsky, looking small and grey. I could hardly believe my eyes. I rushed to embrace him, and only then learned that he had arrived in the afternoon, and the two friends had come back to the station to meet me. They had met the earlier train, and then waited more than hour for the next one. They had spotted Antoinettochka, but Zakharov still considered my other one – Hansen, I suppose – superior. Kolechka had gone into the woods, either so as to leave the field clear for my encounter with Tonya, or possibly simply in order to ambush me; in any case we all laughed heartily over it. Altogether we rejoiced in the reunion of the triumvirate, and were in the best of spirits.

The only problem is that Myaskovsky has no existence apart from music, and his presence can be like a silent shadow. He is a strange being. His lack of sociability, especially when women are around, is impossible to describe. But where music is concerned he is quite another person, one for whom nothing else exists. Such is Myaskovsky. Within our triumvirate he is pleasant, talkative, sometimes even charming.

The next day, at eleven o'clock, I made my way to the beach and on one of the three benches found the delightful Tonyusha, deep in Daudet's *Sappho*.[1] We walked along the beach, I took her to the Zakharo-Durdinsky Park next to the water's edge, a neglected woodland into which, as a matter of fact, the public was not supposed to go. We strolled along, picking wild strawberries, and came across a heap of torn-up scraps of paper, evidently some sort of document which we gathered up and, sitting on the grass, tried to restore to its original form. It turned out to be a list of names of the dead for whom prayers were to be said in church. We were mildly scandalized.

Just then, in the distance, along a path, I spied a lady in a white dress with a red parasol, and thought I recognized Borya's sister-in-law Zinaida Eduardovna Zakharova. Tonya and I were sitting on the grass with the scraps of paper on our knees; so that we would not be seen I lay on the grass behind Tonya, and fortunately the lady passed on by.

The time was approaching one o'clock. It was time for me to go in to lunch, and so we parted until the following day. I got back to the dacha just as everyone was sitting down to the meal. Our rendezvous had been observed, it appeared, and I was immediately subjected to a fusillade from all sides. I was teased mercilessly about my tryst; I defended myself with courage and skill, but could not prevail. For most of the meal I was the butt of their good-natured baiting. After dinner I even thought to ask Kolechka: what had it all been about?

'Just a bit of fun,' he smiled.

I was not to be put off, however, and frequently repaired to the beach. I went for many walks with Antosha, not long ones although we always planned to go further afield, but even so I have the happiest, most cloudless memories of that blessed time in Terioki.

Tonya appeared one day wearing a quasi-brooch of fake gold, which it was then very fashionable to wear with a piqué collar, which she had snatched from me on one of our first meetings.

This went on for about ten days. But then it came on to rain, and the thread was once again broken.

---

1 *Sappho, moeurs parisennes* (1884). Alphonse Daudet's novel has no connection with the Greek poetess beyond the heroine's name.

On Saturday morning, it must have been 17 July, I set off soon after nine for the station with a letter in my hand, although my main objective was to see if Antosha might be there. And indeed there she was, on the platform, a tiny little thing in a crimson Japanese scarf surrounded by a multitude of her relations. I could do nothing but bow politely and move on, a huge white tobacco flower blooming in my buttonhole. I sat on the platform among the crowd, a few seats away from the source of my magnetic attraction, and settled down to wait. I had to wait a long time, but when at last the group broke up to go home, Tonya managed to return my glance with a smile. I cheered up, and went home myself. I was going to have to get up early – well, relatively so – because I had met my friend E. A. Znosko-Borovsky, who was spending a couple of days in Terioki, and invited him to come to the dacha the next day at around ten o'clock.

It was wonderful weather that day, Sunday, and everyone was in holiday mood. Some days are like that.

Znosko arrived, we spent an hour or so at the chessboard and then talked. All the others had gone to church, and some time after eleven o'clock we went too. Evidently he had someone to meet there, and I of course was going in search of Antoinettochka. The church was so tiny that the stragglers had to pray on the pavement outside. I sat and waited expectantly on a bench.

Eventually the crowd poured out. The Zakharovs went off, Znosko went off, and I continued to sit on my bench. Tonyusha was almost the last to leave; she saw me, inclined her head and came over to me. We went down to the beach, fittingly as bosom companions.

After dinner I got completely carried away playing tennis with Zinaida Eduardovna and then went for a swim. I had another brief reunion with Antosha, then had another game of tennis, and at nine o'clock received a telegram: 'Come at once, Father very ill.'

At half past midnight I was in Petersburg, in the hospital.

21 August

A terrible time then ensued. It was clear that all hope for Papa was lost. The cancerous tumours in his liver had started to break up and his whole internal organism was disintegrating. Externally he looked dreadful, a truly lamentable sight. Only with difficulty could Papa recognize those around him, and eventually he ceased to have any conscious understanding at all. 'Sit down,' he would continually plead, almost unintelligibly. He moaned softly, his head turned to one side on the pillow, his right hand endlessly passing over his face, touching his ears, stroking his moustache and his close-cropped beard. There was no respite – how could there be? – we simply had to wait for him to die. Oh, the hideous irony of having to sit and wait for someone you love finally to die!

Aunt Tanya and I slept at the apartment, Mama and Aunt Katya, summoned by telephone, at the hospital.

On 23 July, at five o'clock in the morning, the telephone rang. 'Papa has died,' was all Aunt Katya said.

'The kingdom of heaven be his,' I said. I put on my clothes and went to the hospital.

Now came the miserable time of the funeral and the interment. Oh, it was a bad time. Only at such times does one appreciate a life free from pain and trouble.

22 August

Before my last trip to Terioki I had written to Tonya – from whom I had received a couple of sweet but incoherent letters of sympathy – to say that I would be arriving back on the 29th at eleven o'clock in the morning, and wanted very much to see her.

I had scarcely hoped that Tonka would be at the station, but when I arrived in Terioki she was the first person I saw on the platform. She poured out her sympathy to me, said that she had thought of nothing but me all this time, and now would be with me as much as I wanted. We walked along the road for over an hour deep in the most loving conversation. At half past twelve we returned to the station, as I had to be at the Zakharovs by one o'clock to dine. We arranged to meet next day at ten, and perhaps to go together on the train to Petersburg, since Antosha said she would do that, the only obstacle being her mother's agreement. She came with me halfway through the woods belonging to the Zakharovs, then I kissed her hand and exactly at one o'clock arrived at the dacha, where the Zakharovs welcomed me with the utmost tenderness.

After dinner a croquet tournament was announced, similar to the one I had organized previously. The battle raged for several hours, during which no one left the croquet lawn, but finally we all got a little tired and I badly wanted to go and play tennis. Eventually I departed with Zinaida Eduardovna for the tennis court.

In the evening we played music and strolled about; Lidusya and Zoryusya came too. Borusya was exceptionally kind and loving to me.

At nine o'clock the next morning we all got up and gathered round the piano in the big hall. We were all laughing and carefree, but outside it was grey and gloomy, damp and unwelcoming, the rain falling ceaselessly, sometimes in a real downpour. I shared in the general merriment, but my heart was grey and full of tears to match the rain outside the house.

This continued until dinnertime. About two o'clock we rose from the table. The weather had brightened up. My original plan had been to leave on the five o'clock train, but when talking yesterday with Rudavskaya we had decided, if she was successful in arranging matters so as to come with me to Piter, to go at half past three. All was to have been resolved at our ill-starred meeting.

I decided I would leave at 3.30 in any case. Seeing Antosha at the station would be my last chance, otherwise I would lose her until the autumn. I gathered up all the things I had left behind from my last stay, and began my goodbyes. Then I remembered that I had left a pair of trousers to be altered in a shop in the town, and I would have to go and collect them. Luckily Boris's sister-in-law was going that way in her carriage, so she willingly gave me a ride to the shop and Borya promised to go directly to the station.

Ten minutes before the train was due to leave, Boris and I were pacing up and down the platform. I looked up and down in all directions but could see no sign of Rudavkskaya. It was all going horribly wrong. But then, when I had completely given up hope and mentally said goodbye to my dear one, out she darted from a hitherto unnoticed gap on to the platform, Rudavskaya, my darling Simpoposhka, making straight for me.

Truthfully – unless she was lying – she had been at the station that morning for our appointed tryst, and had it not been for the rain was ready to go for a long walk with me and even, if I wanted her to, to come down the line with me to the next station.

'Antoinettochka, my angel, I implore you to come with me now: we'll just go as far as one or two stations, then get out and have a walk there, and then we can each go our separate ways.'

Antosha was on the point of agreeing, but kept urging me to return to Zakharov; I also wanted to spend the last few minutes with him, but could not bear the thought of losing the precious time with Tonka, while she was reluctant to be introduced to him. Finally, all but persuaded to come with me, she crossed over to the other platform where my train was at that moment coming in, and I went back to Borya, who had just met some friends coming off the train from Petersburg. Borya and I went through this train to the platform where my train was drawing in and where Antoinettochka was standing. There, amidst the din of the approaching train and the hissing of the engines, I introduced her to Boris.

She stood in the entrance to the carriage and I on the step below, with Borya below that on the platform. Borya needed all his resourcefulness to keep the conversation going; Rudavskaya responded reluctantly and distractedly while I felt out of my element and could not find an appropriate topic. Altogether it was a relief when the third bell rang, Borya and I affectionately said our farewells and I disappeared behind Antoinettochka into the carriage. It was almost empty, with only one other person in it.

Rudakvskaya and I sat side by side talking happily, our cares for the time being behind us. I persuaded her to come as far as Beloóstrov[1] so that we could make use of the time on the Customs inspection.

The time sped by like a bullet; the stations flashed past like telegraph poles, and in an instant we were at Beloóstrov, where I handed in my packages to the Customs officials. There were two hours to wait until the next train, so Antosha and I walked off arm in arm to go – where? Wherever our fancy might take us.

What bliss it was to be with one's dearly beloved somewhere one has never been before, where everything, all roads, are unfamiliar, where one knows nobody and is unknown to anyone, to have two hours of freedom in which to wander wherever and look at whatever one likes, all cares cast aside.

We walked along the road, still wet from the morning's rain, which sometimes prevented us from going arm in arm. At first the road was lined with fences and buildings, but later these thinned out to be replaced by dachas and open spaces and woods. In the distance could be seen the gleam of lakes, and finally the dachas ended and there was nothing but the harmonious composition of lakes, meadows and forests to please the eye. No more mud and dirt, all was bright and lively, the sun was shining and we were happy.

At length we came out on to a small peninsula dotted with trees going down to the shores of a lake. Here there was no one about at all, just the lake, the trees, Tonyusha and I. We stood by the water's edge; I covered her dear, pretty, glowing face with passionate kisses. But all the time we never left off talking about quite other things: Tonya remarked that the lake was very deep but I said that the water had a yellowish tinge to it which meant that the bottom was showing through, and one could go right to the middle of it without fear of drowning even if one could not swim.

So passed a time out of mind, and I cannot say how long it was before we turned back. Now all the talk was of future plans, where letters should be sent to, would Tonyusha be able to come in to Petersburg next day, we must be careful not to miss our trains. Thus deep in conversation we arrived back at the station, where I bought a ticket for Tonya. Both trains – mine to Petersburg and hers back to Terioki – were already in and waiting, but mine left later and I stood by Antoinettochka's carriage until she left, promising to do her best to be at the Alexander[2] at three o'clock the next day. Five minutes later my train also left, carrying me to Petersburg.

That brought my time with Tonyusha to a close, for she was not able to

---

1 Beloóstrov was the border railway station between Russia and Finland which, although at this time forming part of the Russian Empire, was administered as an autonomous region.
2 A furnished apartment building on Nevsky Prospect.

keep her appointment at the Alexander with me the following day, and the day after that Mama and I left to go south by the Sebastopol train.

19 September

These lines are being written in Sukhum.

From Petersburg we arrived in Sontsovka, where we had the task of winding up all Papa's affairs, sorting out and deciding what to do with all our domestic goods and chattels. One way and another my parents had lived a whole lifetime in Sontsovka.

Now we had to say goodbye to Sontsovka. I was very attached to it, it had been my home, yet I could not regret leaving it – what was there to value in this run-down, deserted spot? Six years ago, when I had first left Sontsovka for no more than half the winter I had almost wept, so closely was my childhood bound up with the place. Then Petersburg was interesting, but alien. But now everything I cared about was centred on the city; Sontsovka was like an elderly relation to whom, as happens with elderly relations, the ties of life had slackened and no longer bound me closely.

The sorting out and packing up held little interest or emotion for me. I concentrated on music, walked in the fields and generally felt detached from my sojourn in Sontsovka.

For a few days I went over to Nikopol to see Morolyov. Vasili Mitrofanovich Morolyov is one of the most passionate lovers of music I have ever encountered. He got to know us about five years ago when he was appointed veterinary surgeon in our Bakhmut district. Discovering that I was a musician and pianist, he so attached himself to me that whenever he was at Sontsovka he would literally not allow me a moment away from the piano. (I remember that the first time this happened the *pièces de resistance* were the A flat Sonata of Beethoven[1] and Scriabin's *Poème satanique*.) On my side I recognized in him a chess player, and that was what most of all drew me to him. I challenged him to a match but was beaten (+5–8 =1). Later there were a whole series of matches, five or six, in which I gradually prevailed, so that eventually I was able to give him a knight.

Whenever he came to us we bargained like gypsies: I had to play him thus and thus pieces of music in return for him playing me thus many games. And in this way many days were spent in 'play'. He is in general a most cheerful and amusing person, and despite the difference in our ages we became the closest of friends and even addressed each other in the intimate form.

Three years ago he was transferred to Nikopol, but I still went to stay with him every summer. I made no mention in my diary of my summer trips to Nikopol, probably because for the three or four days that erupted into my

---

1 Most likely the Sonata No. 31 in A flat, Op. 110.

life on those occasions I inhabited a completely different world from my other activities: we would spend entire days at the piano and at the chessboard, I lost several pounds in weight, only to return home and fall into my accustomed rut.

This summer I went as usual to him for four days or so. I played him my Sonata, Op. 1, a revised version of my Sonata No. 2, which I had dedicated to Morolyov. It was with great pleasure that I was able to dedicate this version to him too.

On 7 September I left for Sukhum, to the Smetskoys; Mama and Aunt Tanya arrived two days later. It is beautiful here of course, and comfortable – but truth to tell, boring. It is hardly a case of acute boredom though, as I am practising hard in preparation for the autumn, and going for lots of walks. And I shall be here for only ten days altogether. But I still miss Piter, the music, and the Conservatoire, which I expect is already seething like a kettle of boiling water. Tantalizing newspaper announcements of the subscription concerts with their programmes tug at the nerves, especially when I read of Scriabin's Fifth Symphony. What? His Fifth! Or could that be a misprint? It's high time to head north, to the beloved north!

Tonya Rudavskaya has been writing to me pretty regularly and often at some length, although not always perfectly grammatically. Her letters are full of details, and always tenderly expressed. I usually responded, always with great pleasure and expressions of equivalent tenderness. Now I very much want to see my dear Pomponchik, my Tonechka. For the last two weeks she has been strangely silent and has not written to me. Well, never mind – although I often dream of her.

Zakharov is a lazy correspondent, but is a delight when he does write. Kolechka Myaskovsky wrote praising my last orchestral piece, which gave me great satisfaction.

And so, to Piter. I am looking forward to an especially active, productive and pleasant winter.

29 September

On the 26th my train carried me swiftly towards Piter. I had spent my nameday, the 25th, wandering around Moscow engaged on various musical affairs. I saw Cooper,[1] who confirmed his promise to play *Dreams* in Moscow this winter.

The Russian Music Editions, to whom I had sent my Sonata, Op. 1,

---

1 Emil Cooper (1877–1960), distinguished Russian symphonic and opera conductor. He rose to prominence in the West from 1909 with Diaghilev's Paris and London seasons, and later conducted regular series of symphony concerts in Moscow. Cooper emigrated in 1923 and settled in America, conducting the Chicago Lyric Opera and becoming Music Director of the Montreal Opera Guild.

returned it with a rejection slip, which did not, however, cause the world to come crashing about my ears. I already knew this excellent music publishing house to be distinctly partial, publishing only a narrow circle of its favoured composers, making it virtually impossible for an outsider to be admitted. Glière's advice is to get fixed up with Jurgenson using the good offices of Taneyev.

(I heard, incidentally, that Myaskovsky had had some songs accepted by the Russian Music Editions. Bravo, Kolechka! He is the first Petersburg composer to get his foot in the door there. Am I envious? Hardly at all, well, perhaps just a little. He is a good musician, and any success he enjoys as a composer will be fully deserved. But I have faith in myself.)

When leaving Sontsovka to travel to the Caucasus I had written to Rudavskaya letting her know to the minute the time of my arrival in St Petersburg and asking her to meet me. I had heard nothing from her for the past three weeks and did not know whether she would come to meet me or not. This would be a significant test of our relationship. Most likely she would not. Although sometimes it seemed more probable that she would. All the same, approaching Petersburg I inclined to the negative. In Sukhum one day I had found a camomile flower, and the message of the leaves as I plucked them off one by one, was 'no'.

But there on the platform of the Nikolayev station was Antoinettochka to meet me, and the first thing she did was present me with a bouquet of roses. We had a lovely hour talking and catching up, and then she went home while I went to the Rayevskys on Sergievskaya Street, where I planned to base myself until Mama returned from Sukhum in three weeks or so.

That evening I called Zakharov and went to see him. He made no secret of his pleasure at seeing me, which I fully reciprocated; such was his joy that he even seemed a little embarrassed by it. I telephoned Kolechka, but he had disappeared somewhere.

The next day in spite of the wind and the dampness of the weather I had a rendezvous with Antosha in the Summer Gardens. We walked for near enough two hours, got our feet soaked, caught cold, were very loving with one another and on parting agreed to meet the following day in the Conservatoire.

There is no question Antoshka has been won over by my letters! It was definitely the right thing to do to send her punctual and sweet letters, despite her unreliability and even though it was sometimes annoying to write without getting a reply, in the hope that it might still pay off in the autumn. And here was the proof that I was right.

After saying goodbye to Rudavskaya in the Gardens I went to the Conservatoire.

I felt very different from the same time last year, when I had gone in to the Conservatoire champing at the bit to immerse myself in a world that held so much interest for me, in whose personalities I was so engaged, to absorb all the new developments that had occurred in my absence, to see the many people whom I liked and found interesting. Now, I had already seen Zakharov, my best friend, and Rudavskaya, pride of place among my sweethearts. I had caught up also with all the news. Everything else would be secondary. Yesipova was teaching that day, but not my group. Anna Nikolayevna had only just started work and was teaching at home.

I saw Lyonochka Nikolayev, Sashenka Borovsky and Volodochka Deshevov.[1] They are all great fellows and friends of mine, I was glad to meet them all again and we kissed and embraced. Borovsky had competed in the Rubinstein Competition and received an honourable mention, on the strength of which he was said to have put on airs and to be charging 15 roubles for a lesson. Even so, he is a nice person. Nikolayev is gaining great popularity in the Conservatoire as a teacher. Zakharov mockingly said that all one heard in the Conservatoire these days was: 'Who are you going to?' 'Yesipova.' 'What about you?' 'Nikolayev.'

As a composer, Deshevov is less interesting. I have heard some of his things; they are on the rough side, but not totally devoid of good music.

I next saw my oldest acquaintances, who all seemed to have lost interest in me. Alpers passed by without noticing me at all, or at least pretending not to. Just before leaving to go to the country I wrote to her telling her of Papa's death, telling her my address and saying I hoped she would write much and often. It took her the best part of a month to get around to replying; her mother had been ill. Nevertheless I was hurt by this and did not write again for three weeks, when I sent belated congratulations on her name-day. My letter was rather curt and indifferent in tone and, despite a surface courtesy far from friendly. All the same, she is a sweet girl and her family are very nice.

Returning to the Conservatoire on Tuesday, I first met Tonya Rudavskaya, as she had promised. I had nothing to do there, as Anna Nikolayevna had asked me to play on Thursday rather than on Tuesday. Antosha had also finished whatever she was doing there, so we left the building together and I said I would accompany her to Chernyshev Lane.

2 October

I had my first lesson with Anna Nikolayevna on Thursday the 30th. The previous day I stayed in and practised; the only other thing I did was look in on Kolechka Myaskovsky in the evening. It transpired that of the eight songs he had sent to the Russian Music Editions they had accepted only one, so it was

---

1 Leonid Nikolayev, Alexander Borovsky, Vladimir Deshevov.

not as good a result as I had thought. I looked at the sketches for his Second Symphony – acceptable, but not much more than that. Of course, its contrapuntal accoutrements are wonderful, and in that respect it will be undoubtedly very interesting. I am simply making the observation that in its present state it is not particularly interesting or original.

Coming into the Conservatoire on Thursday for my lesson with Yesipova, I played Beethoven's 'Aurora'[1] Sonata. I thought I had learned it thoroughly, but from the beginning Yesipova stopped me several times for trifling criticisms, and then made me play it terrifically fast. Personally I like the way I played it, and consider that since last year I have made really solid progress.

Coming out of the class I saw my dear Tonka, who had been listening to me play from outside the door. Hansen was also walking by with Abramycheva. Hansen looks considerably less attractive than she did; a lorgnette now dangles on a black ribbon round her neck, and she constantly fiddles with it. Probably this homely appearance is just a passing phenomenon, nevertheless it cannot be denied that she is no longer the bewitching Frieda of those springtime days. I felt that her attraction for me had passed, even though the memory of it remained. We had a rather detached conversation during which I was ironically critical of her desire to finish her Conservatoire training this year.

The next day was the Feast of the Protecting Veil, so of course there were no classes, but Antosha and I came into the Conservatoire to meet and go for a walk. I dragged her off to Vasilievsky Island and the sea. Tonyushka boldly took my arm, insisted when we got as far as the sea that she was not at all tired, and chattered happily all the while. In spite of the brightness of the day, the sea was dark grey, almost the colour of lead, and little waves rippled over the surface. Tonyusha and I stood and watched them, but then the wind began to freshen, and Tonya had to dash off somewhere, so we walked quickly back to the tram and returned to the city.

14 October

Two weeks have passed. I attended the Conservatoire regularly every day and spent, as I had foreseen, a lot of time in the opera and conducting classes. I conducted the orchestra twice and was extremely pleased with myself.

I see Tonyusha a lot, almost every day, in fact it is rare for two days to go by without our seeing one other. We took a fancy to go to Kronstadt, a fancy I enthusiastically supported. But first Tonya's mother was not well, then she herself got the sniffles and a sore throat, then the weather turned cold, and our fantasy had to remain unrealized.

---

1   In Russia Beethoven's 'Waldstein' Sonata, No. 21 in C, Op. 53, is known by this name.

Aunt Tanya has come up from the Caucasus and moved into the apartment; she arrived today and I have not yet seen her. She told me on the telephone that Mama is not well with influenza, and in general is little improved, her nerves are in a bad state and she cries a lot. I am desperately sorry for Mama. Now I begin to appreciate what a truly gifted human being she is. Six months of the troubles she endured so devotedly would break the spirit of anyone. I hope that her natural strength will enable her to transcend it all.

I am playing telephone chess with Golubovskaya, which is entertaining. She has joined Yesipova's class, and this is a very good move for her.

I am taking part in the St Petersburg Chess Championship, facing stiff competition. Of course I shall be made mincemeat of, but I don't mind, I enjoy the play. Tonyusha gave me a victory talisman: a pretty little sliver of gold with a diamond set in it that she used to wear around her neck, and added to her gift a good luck kiss. I wanted to hang my talisman round my king, but my opponent Rausch's hackles rose and I had to remove it. I was very near to winning my game, but in the end lost it. No matter. Next time I shall be on the point of losing but will then win . . .

I am not doing any composing at all, there's no time. A pity. (Pfui, what indolence!)

3 November

I am horribly busy and a vast amount of time goes on the conducting class. We are putting on *The Tsar's Bride*[1] and *Romeo*[2] and this means I have to be virtually full time in the opera class; this is absolutely necessary seeing that I have decided to study opera conducting technique. It is not easy, and sometimes it is deadly boring, especially when one has to sit through such appalling music as *Romeo*, but I believe I shall soon get the hang of it, more or less. As for orchestral conducting, of course I can no longer complain of the dearth of practical opportunity I suffered last year, but there is still less of it than I would like, bearing in mind how few people there are in the class. Tcherepnin himself conducts a good deal, and Shteiman does a lot. He deserves it, as I can see; his gestures are brilliant and he shows every promise of becoming a first-rate conductor (although his level of musical development is not especially high). Kolomiitsev, who is in the process of becoming a Russian citizen, gets to conduct quite often, although with no more talent than he had before, and Kobylyansky continues to be a big fat zero.

I began this year with a quite reasonable conducting technique and even

---

1 Opera (1878) by Rimsky-Korsakov.
2 *Roméo et Juliette*, opera (1864) by Charles Gounod.

thought I was doing pretty well, but for some reason my technique fell apart in Tchaikovsky's *Italian Caprice* and it has since gone downhill. Generally Shteiman has comprehensively outstripped me, something I had not expected but now must accept as an established fact. It is clear that I am not doing enough to perfect my abilities in this field. Is it because I do not care passionately enough about the technical craft of conducting? Or am I simply not capable of mastering it?

In any event, a great deal of time goes on this, and there is not much left for piano practice. Zakharov is always telling me off about this, and quite rightly: he says if I go on like this I will simply wither away and go to seed *à la* Shubert or Shmayevsky, and will not amount to anything.

Meanwhile there are other powerful forces coming up, ready to obliterate me. One of these is Shtember,[1] a very serious pianist who is said to promise great things. With such reports ringing in my ears I went in fear and trembling to my next lesson with Anna Nikolayevna, but she had praise for my Liszt *Feux Follets*, which cheered me up greatly.

No! Shteiman is not my superior, either in talent or understanding! Surely he will not prevail simply by working harder?

Shtember, Borya and I have enrolled in the Sokol Gymnastic Club. My mother has long wanted me to join, in the belief that it is extremely important to develop one's physique.

I resisted for a long time, partly from laziness and partly not wanting to devote the time to it. But in August, in Sontsovka, D. D. Sontsov[2] succeeded in persuading me of the value of gymnastics and also how much energy exercise gives a person. This was timely advice, because I detest feeling miserable or in low spirits, which sometimes happens to me, perhaps because I have been growing very quickly in the last few years, or for some other reason. In any case I cannot bear not feeling on top form; the more vigorous I am, the happier I feel generally. My ideal of physical energy is a fly on a summer's day. Ridiculous it may be, but I often think of this when I watch them in summer: there is the pure undiluted life-force, free from the merest hint of listless inertia.

On my return to St Petersburg I enthusiastically set about interesting Zakharov and Myaskovsky in the idea. Kolechka soon dropped out, but Shtember independently joined the Sokol, so that three representatives of Yesipova's class are now enrolled in this institution.

Shtember is a young man of about twenty, not very good-looking and very serious. He is modest but extremely resilient, generally a nice fellow although not without a few rough edges to his character. He is incredibly

---

1 Nikolay Shtember (1892–?), pianist.
2 Dmitry Sontsov, the owner of the estate managed by the composer's father at Sontsovka.

taken with the Sokol. Altogether the three of us much enjoy being there together, and it plays an important part in my life.[1]

6 November

I believe that it is unhappiness, rather than happiness, that most firmly attaches a man to life. To put it another way, the man who is unhappy is more likely to place a greater value on happiness. By analogy, two people who live together not always in perfect harmony but sometimes quarrelling will thereby come to appreciate each other more – provided, of course, the discord stays within bounds. Tonya Rudavskaya and I have had an amazing number of squabbles over the last few days, but they have only served to bring us closer together in friendship. Or perhaps this is just how it seems to me.

Yesterday we were together at the first student concert of the season. Shtember played a Chopin *Ballade* (less well than I had expected). As well as Shtember, Borshch and Hansen were due to play (the latter the *Mephisto Waltz!*) but for some reason both cried off.

Antosha and I had a really good evening together. The programme was so colourless as to be not at all interesting, and I begged Antosha to come out with me and wander round the Conservatoire, as I could no longer bear the stuffy hall or the noisy foyer and wanted to be alone with my Tonya. She was not keen, and despite my pleading she categorically refused. But I went on insisting until she got tired of it and went into a sulk. When, later, we were sitting in the balcony pretending to listen to the music, I said to her that I knew what I ought to do was to get up and leave, that is what anyone in my position would do, but I lacked the resolve to do so because it would mean parting from her without knowing when I would see her again, and the thought of not seeing her again for a long time was deeply upsetting to me. I said all this very seriously, and my very seriousness evidently touched Tonka. 'Seryozha,' she said, ' I'm not angry with you now.'

We softly squeezed one another's hands. The angrier our quarrels, the sweeter were our reconciliations.

Today she promised to ring me and confirm whether or not we could go to Pavlovsk tomorrow (another of my fantasies apparently not to be realized), but she did not telephone.

---

1 The Sokol movement ('sokol' is the Russian – and Czech – word for 'falcon') was a youth and gymnastics organization founded in Prague in the 1860s by Miroslav Tyrš. Its *mens sana in corpore sano* ethos allied to growing anti-Habsburg sentiment caused it to spread rapidly through the entire Slav world, being to some extent a counterpart of Baden-Powell's Scouting movement. Bolshevism effectively suppressed the Sokol clubs in Russia, although elements of their ideals and teaching found their way into the Pioneers. However, the movement continued to flourish elsewhere in the Slav world, rising to about three-quarters of a million members during the inter-war years. It still exists today in much reduced numbers and influence.

27 November

On 9 November Shteiman told me that following the death of Lev Nikolayevich Tolstoy a committee had been formed within the Conservatoire to establish an award in his name, and the proceeds from a student production or concert in the Great Hall were to be devoted to raising funds for the award. Therefore we conductors should lend our enthusiastic support to the proposal by organizing a concert in which we could appear.

My immediate thought was that I could present *Dreams*, which Tcherepnin had independently promised to perform, and also I could play my Sonata. This would be a marvellous opportunity for me. Shteiman and I got to work.

There was a great amount of fussing and intriguing because too many different elements were involved in organizing the concert. The committee's job was to ensure the box-office income and the distribution of the tickets; ours was to come up with the programme. To provide the ultimate seal of authority it must then be approved by Tcherepnin and Glazunov. Dzhiarguli must book the hall and get permission from the city authorities. Gabel must nominate a singer, Auer a violinist. God knows, everyone was flying his own kite and trying to influence matters to his own advantage. Shteiman wanted to conduct the March from *Götterdämmerung*, purportedly appropriate to Tolstoy. I was trying to promote my own compositions. The committee wanted it prominently stated in the programme that the concert was in memory of Tolstoy. Dzhiarguli was firmly convinced the city authorities would not allow the concert anyhow because of the disturbances.[1] We wanted it to take place as soon as possible, while everyone was still full of enthusiasm for it. Tcherepnin was dragging his feet because he wanted more rehearsals. Glazunov, on the contrary, was in a hurry because he was going to Moscow on the 24th. Dzhiarguli was also slowing the process down, arguing that time would be needed for official permission and for the tickets to be printed.

---

1 Prokofiev is referring to the unrest following the 'Bloody Sunday' massacre in the square in front of the Winter Palace in January 1905, which led to a general strike supported by the students and some of the faculty of the Conservatoire, notably Rimsky-Korsakov, Lyadov, Glazunov, Yesipova and Verzhbilovich. Odd man out was Auer, who later suffered much obloquy for his support of the Conservatoire's Government-friendly directorate. The dissident professors were dismissed, and Prokofiev himself signed a general letter of resignation in protest, although it later transpired the letter was never handed in. In any case the Conservatoire was closed and the examination schedule effectively disrupted, although private tuition continued in the professors' homes (for Prokofiev special piano with Winkler and Counterpoint with Lyadov). Only in the spring of 1906 were the rebellious professors finally reinstated and the Conservatoire resumed operations with Glazunov as Director. As for Tolstoy, during the last three decades of his life his increasing anti-authoritarianism and anti-clericalism had made him an object of deep suspicion both to the Government and the Russian Orthodox Church, which excommunicated him in 1904 (despite repeated appeals, this has never been rescinded).

At last the concert was scheduled for the 22nd (which clashed precisely with Scriabin's concert). Both my pieces were included – hurrah! This is how it happened: the Sonata's duration is about eight minutes, and *Dreams* roughly the same. 'All right then, so we'll give Prokofiev a quarter of an hour!' exclaimed Tcherepnin, and Glazunov inclined to this as well, saying that he would first listen to the pieces and if he found them acceptable would include them in the programme.

The next day I went to see him to play him *Dreams* and the Sonata. It was my first appearance before His Highness's penetrating gaze since I had pestered him two years ago about my Symphony.

Glazunov liked both works. While I was playing the Sonata Lyadka[1] suddenly appeared from nowhere, the selfsame Lyadka from whom a year ago this Sonata had called forth a paroxysm of condemnation.

As Lyadov insinuated himself into the room, Glazunov said, 'Look, Anatole, would you, you know, perhaps, have a listen . . . to this Sonata, you know . . . Prokofiev . . .'

Anatole ran his eyes over the score and, wrinkling up his nose, drawled, 'Oh, it's that one in F minor . . .' But when he heard it, he had good things to say about it. Evidently he has grown in wisdom during the year.

And thus my bold plan was crowned with brilliant success: I shall appear in the Great Hall in all my capacities simultaneously, as composer, conductor and pianist.

I was happy, proud and busy as can be. Proof-reading the parts was tremendously time-consuming. Then came the rehearsals: four in a row. *Dreams* was allocated much of the time, because the other works had all been more or less studied in the course of the autumn. Even so, the piece proved difficult for the orchestra, which continually perpetrated errors and played diabolically out of tune. But by the time of the concert they had pulled themselves together and played extremely well, although other opinions held that the playing was execrable. I conducted – tolerably, but well this side of genius – and I must admit, hand on heart, that it was not flawless. The reaction was mixed: some people found the whole experience thrilling, others (the majority view) found the music thrilling but not the orchestra; I also heard that there were plenty of people who found nothing to like at all.

However, I played the Sonata well. Even the most inveterate critics of my pianism, Myaskovsky and Zakharov for instance, had nothing but praise for my performance. The public liked the Sonata well enough, and I was called back to the platform. While learning it for the concert I made a good many changes, mostly refinements of detail, and made a fair copy that I shall now send to Jurgenson along with Taneyev's recommendation.

---

1 Anatoly Lyadov.

28 November

As a student conductor I had been presented with a free subscription to Koussevitzky's concerts in good five-rouble seats. About two weeks ago (at just about the time that the notion of the student concert was being canvassed) I invited Rudavskaya to come with me to one of the Koussevitzky concerts and promised to get hold of a ticket for her, which I managed to do without too much difficulty. Tonya thought about it and agreed to come. I loved having her with me at the concert, although to be honest she understands next to nothing about music. But she did not distract me from listening to any of the serious and interesting works, and at least I was not bored with her company during the tedious parts that are to be found in all concert programmes. It was all very pleasant and comfortable.

When the concert finished, we put on our coats and went out. Taking her arm I proposed that we walk to her house, and we got ourselves into a real muddle with our pronouns, mixing up 'thees' and 'thous' and 'yous' until we simply used them indiscriminately so that it became a joke. By the time we said goodbye at the entrance to her building and I kissed her hand, we had firmly settled on 'thou', and I got a letter two days later written throughout in *Bruderschaft*[1] terms.

Several days passed. There was still a week to go before the student concert and I was up to my ears in proof-reading parts, rehearsals and practising the Sonata. Although I was longing to see Toshka and was missing her, I was probably doing so less than she imagined.

I was happy with the way the Sonata was going, but the orchestra was having a lot of troubling learning *Dreams*. They could not grasp the problematical harmonies, and I found I had to put accidentals before each note. However, at the general rehearsal they played not badly. Not many people were present at this rehearsal; only Mama and Aunt Tanya came from my family. My dear Kolechka Myaskovsky was at every rehearsal though, assisting me with all the proof-reading and generally being of the most tremendous help to me.

Before the concert I was not nervous at all; I was completely calm and even arrived for the beginning of the concert even though my first appearance was not until the fifth item on the programme. All my relations came, ten in all. (How this concert would have thrilled my late Papa!) Then there were Myaskovsky, the Conservatoire directorate *en bloc*, Cui, Nurok, Nouvel, the Zakharovs (Boryusa and Vasyusa), the Karneyevs (Lidusya and Zoryusya), Wanda Yablonskaya, the Alpers, Borshch, Golubovskaya, Tonyushka of course, Max, Borovsky, Deshevov and others. Those who were

---

1 See p. 164 n. 2.

not present included Nikolayev, Winkler, Glagoleva, Lyadov, and as far as I could see Hansen and Palasova.

Dreams was preceded by a solo appearance by Lenochka Hofmann and half the orchestra had wandered off, having to be recalled only a few minutes before I went on stage. Zakharov came backstage to have a few words with me and embrace me, then he left. Up jumped Tcherepnin to say that the orchestra must tune before playing, but this they failed to do properly. Just before going out I suffered a very disagreeable twinge of nervousness, but all I needed to do was come out on stage to forget all about it: there was so much to do. Vasili adjusted the conductor's stand, where a lamp was getting in the way of turning the folio pages on which I had written out the score of *Dreams*, while I painstakingly committed to memory the disposition of the orchestra, since at the rehearsals the platform had not been set up; now it was on the stage of the Great Hall the layout was quite different.

The piece went smoothly. Once or twice I probably did not give decisive enough cues, and once or twice I heard the bassoons fudge their entries, but when during the applause I shook the leader's hand and turned to leave the stage I had the impression that the orchestra had played with a good deal of temperament. This impression has now faded, because so many people have told me that the orchestra was all over the place.

My piece was followed by the interval. Many people came back to see me, among them Tonka, who stayed out with me for the second half.

When I asked him about *Dreams*, Glazunov mumbled, 'Muddy ... muddy ... and then, when you have an E major triad on top of a C major triad ... that was muddy as well ...'

I had no recollection of having written an E major triad over a C major triad, but Myaskovsky explained it as follows: I had an E major chord over a C bass note, and someone in the orchestra had played a G natural instead of a G sharp, resulting in an E major triad over what had now become a C major chord.

The second half of the programme began. Tonya stayed out with me and we sat on a bench behind the colonnade surrounding the main staircase hearing the occasional *fortissimo* floating out from the performance in the hall of Liszt's *Preludes*. At the point where there were eight bars of the piece still to play, I counted down 'eight, seven, six, five ...' and giving a farewell kiss to Tonya made my way back to the artists' room. I was super-calm, and absolutely confident about the Sonata.

The last person who came to see was Max Schmidthof. 'I think you ought to play with a bit more power, otherwise it may not project,' he said.

I went on stage. The piano was a good one, but for some reason instead of the usual stool it had before it an unattractive-looking ordinary chair, and not only that, it was so low that it felt as though the keyboard was about the height of a dining table.

I remembered Max's advice and indeed did have the impression that the piano was not sounding very bright. But my misgivings were misplaced; it was quite loud enough. The Sonata went very well; there was a lot of applause and I was recalled to the stage. Deshevov came backstage, and Myaskovsky with his brother-in-law. Tcherepnin was delighted. Glazunov was clapping, but I did not see him to speak to afterwards.

After the concert I was surrounded by a crowd, those lovely girls Lidusya and Zoryusya Karneyeva, Golubovskaya, Seryozha Sebryakov[1] with Nadia, and others.

Saying my farewells to all, I went in search of Totoshka to take her home. We went part of the way on foot, and part by tram, kissing in the deserted streets of Peterburgskaya Storona until I brought her to her door at half past twelve.

At home I told them I had been to see Shteiman. My family were all delighted by my debut and congratulated me. I went to bed at three a.m.

29 November

The following day, on our way home after the Koussevitzky concert, sitting on a bench near the Troitsky Bridge, I asked her, 'Do you love me, just a little?'

Tonka blushed and said, with a smile, 'What a thing to ask a girl . . .'

'I asked you because you're signing your letters to me "your loving . . ."'

'I always write the truth.'

'All right . . . but I don't believe you, all the same.'

We have got used to not believing one another.

21 December

Glagoleva is getting married. One day in November she invited all her admirers to her house, and during dinner her mother announced the betrothal. The assembled company greeted the announcement with the silence of the grave, only the family echoing her mother's toast to the happy couple. The whole incident was very typical of Lyosechka's style. I was invited, but did not attend, out of laziness. I am glad I did not.

Her fiancé, the engineer Vladimirsky, is an intelligent man, very persistent and a strong character, but not remarkable in any way. It always surprised me how uncomplainingly he put up with all Lyosochka's horrendous capriciousness, which at times exceeded all normal bounds. To play with him as Glagoleva has done is quite unprincipled. It was no great surprise that she

---

1 Sergey Sebryakov was the son of Dr Tatyana Sebryakova-Zhitkova, Prokofiev's mother's cousin.

settled on Vladimirsky; things had looked as though they were heading that way, although I did not expect her actually to do the deed, and was mildly disappointed that Lyosenka would in the end make such a . . . I can't say bad, simply uninteresting, match.

22 December

December proved to be a rough month. I felt terribly sick; I was not actually ill, but ached all over and had to sit about at home. This is how I spent the time from the 7th to the 14th, and now from the 20th I have once again been confined here. This time the reason is a boil that erupted on the back of my head, which grew so big that I have to go to the hospital where Papa was in order to have it dressed. As a result all my neck and my head are swathed in bandages, as though at the very least my skull has been smashed. They tell me I must go about wearing this nonsense all week.

Covering it as best I could with a starched collar I doggedly attended At Homes on three evenings in a row at the Ozarovskys, the Ossovskys and the Ruzskys. The Ossovskys have announced that they are At Home every other Saturday evening, and they have invited me very pressingly to attend. I am delighted to do so, since the company they keep is of the greatest interest to me. I've been twice. I met Lyadov there, the first time this has happened in a private context. Mme Ossovskaya even went so far as to ask me, as she greeted me in the hall, 'Lyadov is here. Is that all right with you?'

I reassured her on this score, and my old adversary and I talked – with some animation – about chess. Tcherepnin was also there; I had met him before at the Ruzskys. It turns out that the enchanting Tcherepnin is now entering the lists foaming at the mouth in support of my compositions and doing his best to persuade one and all of my huge talent. Truly, he has turned from being an implacable foe into a diehard friend. However this may be, my musical affairs have not been prospering much lately. Cooper in Moscow is tight-lipped, saying nothing. And Jurgenson, despite the persuasive appeal of Taneyev's letter, has rejected my first two opuses, something I did not expect. I am not yet allowing myself to be depressed by this, but even though I know plenty of people I do not know where to try next.

On the 16th I played at an 'Evening of Contemporary Music'; the series has been revived. I played three of my Etudes, in D minor, E minor and C minor. I played effectively, although not by the sternest critical standards as impeccably as I had played the Sonata in November. My Etudes and I both had a success, succeeding in rousing the audience from the torpor in which they had heard the other works in the programme, not excepting two lovely songs by Myaskovsky which were played next to my pieces. Those critics and musicians I knew there showered praise on me.

Morolyov was also at the concert. Morolyov! That was a turn-up for the books, him coming suddenly to Petersburg. I cried out with astonishment when he burst into my room without warning. It was bad luck that I was ill the whole time he was there, and did not once go out with him during the almost two weeks he spent in Petersburg. He is the most awful peasant, but for all that a great and profound musician, and the most wonderful friend I could have.

Anna Nikolayevna Yesipova has now declared that my Sonata, Op. 1, the very same work she described a year ago as 'good music', has no music in it whatsoever. And when Boryusya played in her class my 'Gavotte', which is dedicated to him, that blameless little G minor Gavotte, she pulled a face and said to Zakharov, 'Don't you have anything more interesting in your repertoire than pieces by Prokofiev?'

'Do you not like it, Anna Nikolayevna?'

Her answer was a second grimace. Clearly in her eyes my image as a composer has assumed a monstrous aspect. God be with her! Although, of course, it would have been better if the image had the face of an angel . . .

One day I brought to her class Glazunov's Second Sonata. This is a lovely work, as good as his First Sonata and even more original. But as well known as No. 1 is, so is No. 2 ignored and forgotten.

Anna Nikolayevna made a great to-do about 'exotic' repertoire, but listened to the Sonata before declaring that it would have been better for such rubbish never to have been written. I replied calmly, 'Unfortunately, Anna Nikolayevna, Glazunov is never liked on first hearing.'

The shaft went home, and Yesipova was quick to retort, 'It is by no means the first time I have heard it. So-and-so played it for me, and so did so-and-so. Now I want you to bring me some Beethoven and some Schumann!'

23 December

I want to be quite clear about what sort of person Tonya Rudavskaya is. Zakharov was wrong in describing her as a conventionally pretty girl. Her beauty is of a different order, and a higher one. It is not consistent from day to day: sometimes it is more, sometimes less, but at all times Tonya Rudavskaya is herself. She is not obsessed by her beauty, doesn't flaunt it or use it to flirt with, and she doesn't use it as a weapon to bend people to her will. There is not an ounce of coquetry in Tonya Rudavskaya, even when it could be very useful to her. At home she is kept on a very strict rein, especially by her father. She comes from a good family and is very well brought up. She does not have an especially brilliant or penetrating mind; in this she is like most people.

That she is undeveloped is as clear as the living day. The ordinariness of her intellect and the relative immaturity of her mind are the reasons why her company can sometimes fall short of enchantment. She is beautiful and a sweet person; I love her very dearly for these qualities, but I cannot be deeply and seriously in love with Tonya Rudavskaya; she knows it, and so do I.

27 December

At the beginning of December, *Romeo* was staged in the Conservatoire. To my surprise I simply cannot get to the heart of this opera business. It would be a most useful and interesting accomplishment, indispensable to me as a conductor and ultimately there is no reason why it should not be an open book to me. But for the time being I can only tiptoe round the edges and am unable to find my way to the heart of it.

I played no part in the production; all I did was accompany from time to time in the class and attend the general rehearsal. The next production will be *The Tsar's Bride*, and this is something I have been thinking I could engage with seriously. Although I will not be assigned to conduct the opera, at least it would be good to study it and prepare it in depth.

During the dress rehearsal of *Romeo*, Toshka and I sat first in one corner of the hall, then in another, and then in a third, where we quarrelled. When I met her a few days later I was distant and reserved with her, for no other reason than that I was already getting ill, but she was her usual sweet and tender self and even came with me to Yesipova's house (she was teaching at home that day) and waited on the pavement until I appeared at the window.

After that I stayed at home for a week. Antosha wrote me an unequivocal declaration of love, which made me extraordinarily happy. In reply I thanked her for her 'loving and tender little note' and sent her a little Mazurka, dedicated to Antoinettochka.

1911

10 January

I did not enjoy Christmas. The whole time until New Year I had that accursed boil, and generally was not feeling well. The work was not going well either, and my mood was at best mediocre – not more than 3+. My 'Nettochka'[1] needs a thoroughgoing revision to make it fit for performance – but here I am already halfway through January and I have not yet done with it. I left the second movement unchanged; the first movement I filled out somewhat and cleaned up the orchestration; and the third movement I fundamentally revised, making significant changes to the counterpoint and re-orchestrating it, while nevertheless leaving the structure unchanged. I still have the fourth and fifth movements to do, and have not yet looked at them. I shall dedicate the work to Tcherepnin, and do so with great pleasure. Seemingly he places it above *Dreams*, and loves it very much.

I am very anxious to go to Moscow, mainly on account of Jurgenson. Also, I must try for another invitation to play at the Musical Exhibition; I have plenty of repertoire for this.

The day after Christmas I had a visit from Tonya. We sat in the entrance hall and chatted, then I wrapped a scarf around my neck and we set out for a walk around Piter. We walked just about everywhere, including to Vasilievsky Island, and for the first time for a long time did not quarrel.

New Year was celebrated quietly with the Rayevskys at their home. They taught me to play bridge. On 1 January I went visiting and made fourteen calls.

On the 2nd I was at the Ruzskys, where I now feel completely at home. Nikolay Pavlovich is the nicest person in the world and adores me, his daughters are also good friends, although I sometimes cross swords with Ira Nikolayevna. I played trios with Nikolay Pavlovich and Kolakovsky, a new professor at the Conservatoire: it was all very good. On the 6th we went to see Konshin,[2] the Director of the State Bank, who had been at the Ruzskys and had invited us to call on him so that I could play to him; now I am scaling the heights of society.

The next day Boryusya and I went out to Tsarskoye[3] to Anna Nikolayevna,

---

1 The Sinfonietta.
2 Alexey Konshin (1858–?) had been appointed Director of the Russian State Bank in 1910, in which capacity he served until the outbreak of war in 1914, after which he became President of the Russian Commercial-Industrial Bank.
3 Tsarskoye Selo.

who was spending the Christmas holiday there and who had invited us to visit her. We played vint, naturally; it was pleasant and dull.

On the return journey, standing on the outside platform of the train, Boris and I fell to philosophizing. I said to him, in relation to something or other, that he was a dry old stick: dry and callous. His response was to give me a notably objective and comprehensive analysis of his own nature.

For him, music is the ultimate goal of life, and the service of music his most important task. But mastery, he feels, can be achieved only by unremitting work. Meanwhile he is aware of possessing the happy quality of attracting people to him, both men and women, and therefore, did he but wish it, could have a wide circle of friends. But since he has a tendency to get carried away and become addicted ('if I start drinking I can never be sure that I won't end up getting blind drunk . . .') he keeps himself strictly in check and often in his cold, dry way deliberately snubs people in order to protect himself from being distracted from his main task, which is music. Sometimes he does experience loneliness, but the musical progress he feels he is making goes some way to compensating him for his sacrifices, and this satisfies him.

I replied by saying that he might well be right, I would not contradict him, but such a programme for conducting one's life was quite alien to me.

11 January

By tradition the annual party arranged by the Academic classes of the Conservatoire takes place on 4 January. I put on my dinner jacket, white waistcoat, brilliantly shiny shoes, found myself to be the epitome of style, and went to the party.

Tonya Rudavskaya desperately wanted to go too, largely of course on my account, but her virulently anti-Semitic pater would not give her permission and so I had to relinquish my Tonya, and Tonya had to relinquish her party. It was not a very interesting occasion. Of course it would have been much more enjoyable if I could have had such a charming companion as Tonya on my arm. Nevertheless, since Tonya has been the exclusive object of my attentions all autumn I have dropped all my other ladies, and I thought that if I were to be at the party on my own I would at least be able to recall them to mind. The period of my infatuation with her has passed.

20 January

There is a most delightful girl at the Conservatoire, called Marusya Pavlova. She looks like a brunette, although she is not really one; her figure is flawless and her face enchanting. Still, I have not yet studied her face in detail – is this because I have a poor memory for faces? Or is it – and this is more probable – because I was not the first to notice her? Zakharov, Kankarovich, even Borya Alpers, have all mentioned her in passing as very pretty.

I decided to strike up acquaintance with Pavlova at the party where, as she was taking one of the Academic courses, she was bound to be. Strolling about the corridors and the hall, I soon came across her selling flowers and confectionery together with Kirlian and some other young people. When I saw the throng of admirers surrounding her, I felt my desire wane, and judging that it would be better to wait until another time made my way home long before the end of the evening.

In the meantime Kankarovich has come up from Simferopol to St Petersburg for two weeks. He now has a position in Simferopol as Director of the Institute of Music, but strains every nerve to get back to Piter. I remember him taking as his motto five years ago something I once said about him: 'Either I shall be a conductor, or I shall put a bullet in my brain.' But Simferopol has no orchestra, and in any case Maestro Kankarovich needs something better than a provincial band. He has come to see and be seen by the leading musical lights here.

30 January

On the 26th I had a conversation with Pavlova and Levitskaya. I was standing by the doorway into Yesipova's class; Zeiliger and Zeberg were hanging about there as well, and the two girls came up to them with a question about something. Adopting an air of supreme delicacy and restraint, I tentatively inserted myself into the conversation. Soon afterwards I went down with both the girls in the refectory for lunch, and by the time we shook hands to say goodbye we were, if not friends, at least on good terms.

Pavlova is studying singing . . . and this surprised me in view of her extreme youth. But this is in itself very attractive . . . Levitskaya is a boisterous individual, not stupid, but a little coarse. After our initial meeting we now see each other almost every day.

31 January

On the 28th Glagoleva married Vladimirsky. I was one of her Attendants,[1] number three of eight. Number one was Dernov, number two Petri. Curiously enough I almost missed the wedding altogether. Originally it was to be on Sunday the 23rd, but then the date was changed to the 28th; I had mis-

---

1   In the Russian Orthodox wedding ceremony both bride and groom are supported by a number of nominated attendants who take part in the ceremony, as do, in Catholic and Protestant services, bridesmaids, pages, the best man, the bride's father, etc.

takenly taken the 28th also for a Sunday, but in fact of course it was a Friday.

When I realized my mistake I rushed about as if someone had just lit a fire under me. My tailcoat was at the tailor's, my white waistcoat at the laundry; nowhere at all could I find the right sort of tie. I had to go to the Rayevskys and borrow Shurik's[1] glad rags. I just managed to get to the bride's house by a quarter to eight, the wedding being at eight in the church of the Ministry of Home Affairs not far from the Alexandrinsky Theatre.

The bridegroom is a dull, rather colourless fellow. Lyosya was radiant in her devilish beauty, a dress of magical simplicity showing off to perfection her flawlessly sculpted form. During the wedding ceremony I was much occupied with my role; I was in any case very interested in the procedure, never before having been this close to it.

The crowns[2] were brought in and placed over the heads of the bride and groom. When it came to my turn, Lyosya suffered a slight mishap, a startlingly unpropitious accident! Just at the moment when the priest was bringing to her lips the chalice containing the consecrated wine, she was reminded of something funny. She succeeded in stifling her laughter enough to fasten her lips round the cup, but either she was again overcome by the giggles or she choked, splashing the wine all over her sleeve and on to the carpet. Lyosya made a grab with her left hand, which was clutching the lighted candle,[3] and in so doing set fire to her veil. In a flash bride and dress were ablaze, the burning candle flew out of her hand on to the floor, where it rolled along the carpet, and Lyosya spun round. All her attendants rushed to beat out the flames, and the blaze subsided as quickly as it had begun.

Calm was soon restored and the interrupted ceremony proceeded on its way. But hold! The ring has disappeared! Where can it be? We all hunted high and low, but could not find it anywhere! The congregation shuffled their feet to enable the carpet to be lifted up; the bride was asked to move to one side. There was the ring, under her feet! The ring was placed on her finger, and the marriage concluded without further incident. I was the first to lead Lyosya around the table.[4] We celebrated with champagne and then went to dine at the bride's former home.

1   Alexander Rayevsky, the author's first cousin.
2   The Russian Orthodox marriage ceremony itself has many symbolic and ritual aspects. Crowns may be wreaths or made of gold or silver, and symbolize both the creation of a new 'kingdom', the household, of which the husband and wife are King and Queen, and martyrdom, denying themselves former freedoms and pleasures in order to devote themselves to one another and to their children.
3   Bride and groom both hold candles throughout the ceremony, recalling the Wise Virgins of the New Testament whose prudently filled lamps contained enough oil to receive the Bridegroom, Christ, when He came in the darkness of the night. The candles also symbolize Christ, the Light of the World, who will illuminate the couple on their journey together through life.
4   The bride and groom take their first steps as a married couple around the table on which are placed the Gospel and the Cross, the first representing the Word of God and the second the Redemption by the Saviour.

Lyosya held herself very much at arm's length from her young husband: she called him by his surname using the formal style of address, and when we all cried 'Bitter! Bitter!'[1] she would not. Finally the groom's father, a venerable old priest, came up to the young couple and said with great gentleness, 'Now, my children, time to seal your union with a kiss! . . .'

'No!' replied Lyosya with a graceful movement of dismissal – and refused. The old priest gloomily retired to a corner, and when it was time for the guests to leave he merely shook hands briefly and without much warmth with his wild new daughter-in-law.

Weddings!

13 February

A few words about my musical activities. In January I put more pressure on Ruzsky to speak to Glazunov about the Sinfonietta. Nikolay Pavlovich was only too happy to do so, but left for a two-month trip to the country before he had a chance to see Glazunov.

Meanwhile there began to be talk in the Conservatoire of organizing a concert of compositions by students in March, with works by Lvov, Spivakovsky and Mehrwolf[2] already on the bill. It was perfectly clear to me that my works should have a greater share of the programme than those of anyone else, if only because I was also a student on the conducting course.

I collected up my Sinfonietta, secured an audience with Glazunov and showed him the work. He liked some of it, especially the first, third and fifth movements, and even singled out for praise the counterpoint in the second movement, but he could not understand the passages in which the interval of a second is held in the bass with a fourth above it, and he found the harmonies in the C–A–C–A episode muddy; in fact there was much that appeared to Glazunov's ageing ears muddy, or provocative, or incomprehensible. In any case, there could be no question of giving so complex a work to a student orchestra. Tcherepnin, happening to come in to the room at this time, concurred with this opinion. On the other hand, Tcherepnin was very supportive of the idea of my two choral pieces for female voices, *The White Swan* and *The Wave*. It was therefore decided that as soon as work on *The Tsar's Bride* was completed the women choristers would be free to learn *White Swan* and *Wave*. As for the Sinfonietta, Tcherepnin would have a word

---

1 It is a tradition at Russian wedding breakfasts for toasts to the newly wedded couple to be made with a cry of 'Gorko!' ('Bitter!'), on hearing which the couple must kiss. Sweet wine is called for at the same time. The origin of the custom is not clear, but probably has something to do with symbolizing on the one hand the contrast between the sorrow of solitary life and the sweetness of union, and on the other the future sharing of life's burdens.
2 Rudolf Mehrwolf (1887–1942), composer, whose later career in Soviet Russia was mainly in music for the cinema.

with Khessin, who was now the conductor of Count Sheremetyev's orchestra.

I was getting to work on correcting the choruses, particularly *The Wave*, when without warning Gabel declared that the choristers had had quite enough to put up with in *The Tsar's Bride* and would be let go immediately afterwards, so there could be no question of even thinking about my pieces. Damnation! Hell and damnation and seven-striped devils!

Well, if the choruses had fallen by the wayside, I would have to try to appear playing my own works on the piano, for example those on which I was working for Moscow. After all I was the only real composer in the Conservatoire, the others no more resembled composers than Siberian deer, but I was being bypassed! Where was the justice in that? What was required, of course, was students who wrote like students; anyone who wrote like a composer rather than like a student would find no place in student concerts!

I have taken to meeting Pavlova and Levitskaya frequently, practically every day. Pavlova is a flirt; paying court to her is a difficult and risky business. I decided that initially at least it would be better to have the status of a good companion, so when we meet I am pleasant and straightforward, I chatter about whatever topic happens to come up, and pour out a stream of witticisms that provide a constant source of amusement to both girls.

We often leave the Conservatoire together after four o'clock, walk over to the Mariinsky Theatre to read the posters, then Pavlova goes off, usually escorted by someone, to go home to Vasilievsky Island, while Levitskaya and I go to the Nikolsky Gardens before parting to go our separate ways.

After a while I succeeded in myself being the one to escort Marusya Pavlova home, on the pretext of having to visit my tailor, who genuinely does live on Vasilievsky Island. We had a lovely walk together there. She talked a great deal, every word a lie. I repaid her in the same coin. A few days ago the three of us came from a rehearsal at the Court Theatre back to the Conservatoire; a snowball fight was in progress on Nikolsky Square – the greatest fun.

I see less of Rudavskaya, the letters have ceased and telephone calls are rare. But not long ago I did telephone her and invited her to come for a walk. She came at once, and we spent two hours or so wandering round Piter on a frosty and windy evening, dropping into a pastry shop for warmth. The last time I saw her we again quarrelled.

Vera Alpers on Pavlova: 'She is a sweet person, and such a simple soul . . .'
'Well, not as simple as all that,' I replied.

22 February

1

Tonya's face is beautiful,
But in between the ears

There's empty space. It's laughable
Were it not too sad for tears.

2

Tonya's beauty can't conceal
The fact that she's an imbecile.

19 June
Sukhum – Kale

I have written nothing in my diary for four months. 'The man has got completely out of hand' as the saying goes – and I have got completely out of the way of writing my diary. It happened because I fell prey to various *ennuis*, which sometimes cannot be avoided in life, in consequence of which I lost my customary emotional equilibrium. As this oscillated so did my mood, and when my moods are unstable I lose the inclination to keep up my diary; in any case, anything I wrote would not have been truthful. I would certainly not have been sincere at this time.

My basic attitude to life is temperamentally easy-going, life does not impinge on me deeply but tends to slip with an unruffled surface. Even during my *ennuis* this happy quality was evident! Besides this, I have far too extensive a reserve of *joie de vivre* for it to be seriously depleted, and this worked overtime to restore my emotional balance so that bleak moments would alternate with my usual cheerful disposition. Thus life flowed on its way with its ups and downs, the blacker moments first brightening, then appearing less often, and finally ceasing altogether.

Generally speaking my diary deals with facts rather than with moods: instead of wandering off into a labyrinth of dreams and fantasies it is real life that I love, and I am not much given to soul-searching. At this point I will bid adieu to my nebulous character sketch: that's quite enough of that. I said earlier that life flowed on its way with its ups and downs, and now what I want to do is give an account of these ups and downs during the past four months. I have long wanted to sit down to my diary, but lack of time caused me to put it aside until I could take it up in the peace and quiet of Sukhum.

To begin with more serious matters, here is an account of my musical activities.

In the end, nothing at all came of the student concert in which I had first wanted to present the Sinfonietta, then my choral pieces and then some of my works for piano – nothing as far as I was concerned, I mean. Tcherepnin went away to Monte Carlo, and Glazunov, to whom I appealed with a request to be allowed to play my own pieces, declined on three grounds: (1) my compositions represented a fundamental departure in character from

Conservatoire norms, there was no objection to their being played at any other concert but not at Conservatoire concerts; (2) opportunities for performance should in the first instance go to students who were still taking the Theory of Composition course, which I was no longer doing; and (3) since I had taken up almost half the last concert, it was right that others should have a chance now.

I was thus outflanked on all sides, and the concert took place with no involvement from me. At first I was angry, but then I didn't care.

The pianist was Kobylyansky, who played his own sonata, as I had done at the last concert. He plays quite well (he graduated from Yesipova's class) but not as well as I do, his playing lacks passion and on one occasion he lost his way and had to stop, his embarrassment as a performer communicating itself inevitably to the audience. The sonata itself does not make much impression of organic unity and neither is it very original; there is evidence of talent but the composer's musical taste is not very highly cultivated.

Of the three orchestral compositions that were played, the overture by Mehrwolf was talented; he should certainly have a career. Spivakovsky's overture was total rubbish ('To my dear teacher A. K. Glazunov'... what a treat for Glazunov!) Lvov's Symphony, the fruit of seven years' labour, deserves some consideration; occasional passages show talent, but elsewhere the music is painfully feeble, for instance the conclusions of all four movements. Limp-wristed Lvov will plainly never make a composer.

It being now clear that I could not expect my works to be performed at the Conservatoire, I began to look for other avenues and other contexts. I reasoned as follows: if I made a list of all the well-known Petersburg conductors (there are five), collected together all my scores (there are also five of them) and showed my five scores to the five conductors I would end up with $5 \times 5 = 25$ chances that one of them might get performed. Surely my compositions cannot be so bad that out of twenty-five attempts not one will get anywhere?

My five scores were: the Sinfonietta, *The White Swan*, *The Wave*, *Dreams* and *Autumnal*. The five conductors were Wahrlich, Goldenblum, Ziloti, Koussevitsky and Khessin. Unfortunately *Autumnal* I straight away had to eliminate from the list: in September, when I had just finished it, I had given it to Cooper to look at when I was in Moscow on my way back from the south to St Petersburg. He took it willingly, and promised to return it to me within two weeks, but in spite of my writing to him several times about it the wretched man kept it all autumn, all winter and all spring. Thus I was unable to show *Autumnal* to any of my conductors. The two female choruses, *The White Swan* and *The Wave*, were also not very suitable, because while conductors always have an orchestra at their disposal, they rarely have a choir. So the main choice for the way forward fell upon *Dreams* and the Sinfonietta.

Of my five conductors I knew three personally: Ziloti, Goldenblum and Wahrlich. Tcherepnin had promised to introduce me to Khessin, and Ossovsky was in a position to introduce me to Koussevitzky.

Ziloti had already seen *Dreams* and rejected it, since he is against choral works on principle ('too expensive'). There seemed little point in showing him the Sinfonietta, and I did not have *Autumnal*. Tcherepnin had little good to say of Goldenblum; moreover a year ago I had shown him the Sinfonietta, to which he had reacted coldly, and I did not particularly want to approach him again even with another work.

I therefore went to see Wahrlich at the Court Orchestra. He absolutely loved *Dreams*, and with no beating about the bush said that he would perform it in the Court Orchestra's next concert of new works. He was less enthusiastic about the Sinfonietta, but still he did like it. We decided that this work would be better left until the autumn, nevertheless with a promise that it would be performed, if not at a public concert at least at a private one. I went away delighted with my success.

A month passed, and then in the middle of April Wahrlich's assistant, Belling, came bearing a request to give him both the score and parts of *Dreams*. I was not at home, so he left a note in which he stated that the first rehearsal would take place tomorrow, and the performance a week later. I was very proud. Myaskovsky came with me to the first rehearsal, and for the first time – during the performance in the Conservatoire I had not been able to hear anything – I heard my *Dreams*. And what pleasure it was, after the Conservatoire, to hear a good orchestra capable of playing everything properly. The only cause for criticism was that the tempi were not exactly right; also nothing could be done about the horrible acoustic of the Court Orchestra's hall. 'But the music is good,' I said in all sincerity to Myaskovsky, as we listened to *Dreams*. He agreed.

However *Dreams* was not destined to be performed in this concert. A couple of days later Wahrlich informed me that they (who?) had wedged a second soloist into the concert, and *Dreams* must therefore be postponed until the autumn. I was not too concerned by this. Zakharov told me later he had heard from Belling the reason *Dreams* was omitted was because it had not been liked (again, by whom?). Nevertheless I was satisfied that at least I had heard it, and as for the future, time would tell.

Meanwhile Tcherepnin gave me a glowing letter of recommendation to Khessin, who had recently been appointed Chief Conductor of Count Sheremetyev's orchestra. For some reason it took me some time to bring myself to go and see him, and when I eventually did I found him on the point of leaving for Rostov-on-Don, where he was conducting the summer season. I succeeded in persuading him to listen to *Dreams* and some movements of the Sinfonietta. *Dreams* had an even greater success with him than it had had with Wahrlich, and the Sinfonietta also intrigued him. (In his letter Tcherepnin had laid most stress on the Sinfonietta.) Khessin promised his best efforts to have the works performed in Rostov, and then departed, visibly impressed. Since my plan was to spend the summer in Sukhum and Rostov was on the way there, this was a very timely proposal.

As for the fifth of my conductors, Koussevitzky, I asked Ossovsky to introduce me to him. Ossovsky promised to do so, but then informed me that although he had seen Koussevitzky and spoken of me to him, Koussevitzky was going to Moscow for some time. When he returned, a disagreement of some kind had arisen between them, so for the time being the plan had to be put in abeyance.

Such were my perambulations around my five conductors. To them should be added a sixth: Kankarovich – incidentally the first student I sat next to, sharing a desk, when I entered the Conservatoire. He and I had together joined Lyadov's Harmony class in 1904. Throughout the intervening six years we had maintained good relations, completing the Composition Theory course and entering the conducting class side by side. But here he raced ahead of me and graduated last spring. In the autumn he was appointed Director of the Simferopol Musical Institute, where he is still in post. This summer he has been invited to conduct three concerts in Pavlovsk, in which he proposes to present my *Dreams*. A few days ago I received a letter from him confirming his promise.

Last winter, after giving the matter some thought, I had made serious attempts to find a publisher for my works. I sent the Sonata and the Etudes to the Russian Music Editions and to Jurgenson, but both rejected them. The way into the Belyayev publishing house is barred to me because of the make-up of the editorial board (Lyadov, Glazunov and Artsybushev), and in any case they have no money. The remaining publishers, small enterprises, did not much appeal to me. I resolved to make another attempt to come to an agreement with Jurgenson, this time not in writing but in person. In any case I wanted to go to Moscow this winter, as I had been invited to perform my compositions at Deisha-Sionitskaya's Musical Exhibition concerts, along the lines of the previous year. But the series kept being postponed, from January to March, then from March to April, and in the end they did not take place at all. This motivated me to take action on my own account, and as soon as the Yesipova exam was over I took the train to Moscow, having armed myself with a magnificent letter of recommendation from Ossovsky to Jurgenson. Arriving in Moscow in the morning I went straight to the Glières and dropped off my suitcase there, as I planned to spend two days in Moscow; in such circumstances I always stay with the Glières.

I was fascinated during lunch to listen to Mme Glière trying obliquely in various ways to put me off the idea of Jurgenson becoming my publisher: it would be very difficult, he pays very little, he is very slow to bring things out, he does not like young composers, in short – try any publisher in the world but him. The fact of the matter is that Jurgenson is her husband's publisher and currently holds him in high favour, little deserved though this is: Glière writes rubbish by the cart load, Jurgenson publishes it by the cart load, and pays handsomely for it. I don't know why – probably it sells well in the provinces. La Glière is clearly anxious that no young rivals should appear to queer the pitch, and makes strenuous efforts to scare off young pretenders.

Nevertheless, I wrote to B. P. Jurgenson[1] asking him to grant me an interview and 'permitting myself to enclose' Ossovsky's letter. Meanwhile I went to see Cooper to get back my score of *Autumnal*. I met him on the street; he was full of apologies and wanted to bring the score round to Glière's apartment, but I told him I would prefer, if he did not mind, to call on him around seven o'clock.

Returning home I found that a messenger had brought a reply from Jurgenson to the effect that Mr Jurgenson would expect me in his shop at four o'clock. I put on a frockcoat, collected my portfolio and set off. After excusing myself for troubling him, I said that I should like to show him my compositions and seek his advice on publication. I went over to the piano and played through the Sonata, a couple of Etudes, 'Reminiscence', 'Elan', 'Jest' and 'Fairy Tale'. He obviously liked much of it, but since he does not understand much about music, the greatest effect was produced by Ossovsky's letter. When we went back into his study, he told me that he was prepared to publish my works, and asked me for my specific proposals. I said that I would like to publish my Sonata as Op. 1, the Four Etudes as Op. 2, and I also had a collection ready to make up Op. 3 consisting of 'Fairy Tale', 'Jest', 'March' and 'Phantom'. I had additionally identified a collection for Op. 4, but had not yet finished the revisions that would be needed for publication: 'Reminiscence', 'Elan', 'Despair' and 'Suggestion diabolique'.

'How much are you asking for the four opuses?' asked Jurgenson.

I replied, 'In the first place I should like you to be the publisher of my music. For me this would be a sufficient honour, and the fee is of secondary importance. Accordingly I should prefer you to tell me how much you consider appropriate.'

Ossovsky had warned me that Jurgenson pays new composers either pennies or nothing at all, one must be prepared for this and not take offence. I remember once when talking to Leonid Nikolayev about publishers, he picked up my Sonata, turned it over in his hands as if judging its weight, and said with his half-smile, 'Jurgenson would give you about fifteen roubles for this . . .' I took it as a joke and did not pay much attention. But later, when I was thinking more about publishers, I found it infuriating to think that I would be paid so little for my first published opuses, and in particular for the

---

1 Boris Petrovich, son of the business's founder, Pyotr Jurgenson.

Sonata which, sooner or later, would undoubtedly enjoy wide circulation and make a heap of money. Later still I calmed myself, after all I had come to Moscow thinking: just publish me, the money doesn't matter. When all's said and done, is it really so important whether I get two or three hundred roubles more or less?

Mama has shares in the North Donetsk Railway and various other stocks and shares, and sees them fluctuate in value to the extent of five to eight hundred roubles every day. Financially we are not so much on the breadline that we have to strain after every hundred roubles. Mama even offered to pay the cost of having the Sonata published privately. All the same, it is depressing to be paid so little for one's work. But what's to be done, one just has to put up with it; after all, Jurgenson does not yet know anything about the composer he has agreed to publish, whether he is a genuine talent or an also-ran.

In response to what I had just said, Jurgenson covered his eyes with his hand and did some mental calculation. A couple of minutes later he pronounced, as if hesitating, 'I can offer you one hundred roubles for them.'

'With pleasure,' I replied firmly.

He immediately took a form of agreement with conditions attached, and wrote it out. I received a hundred roubles, for which I signed away my rights. The detailed conditions were simply outrageous and I would never have signed them had they not been printed and therefore evidently standard for all composers. There and then I left the Sonata with Jurgenson, but as to be put into publishable form the other pieces all needed work, promised to send them very soon. Jurgenson undertook to bring them out by the autumn, and with that we parted.

I took a cab and went to call on Taneyev. On the way I thought over the publishing deal and was not sure whether I should be rejoicing or not. It was certainly galling to have been offered so very little: a hundred roubles for the Sonata plus another twelve pieces! Fifteen roubles for the Sonata and seven roubles apiece for the smaller pieces! Surely in a few years' time I would get fifteen hundred roubles . . . but to hell with such miserly accountancy! Jurgenson said that once he took on a composer for publication he would also publish complete orchestral scores and parts.

Taneyev was not well; he had dislocated his foot and was in bed. He still welcomed me very courteously and at once said he was extremely sorry that in spite of his, Taneyev's, recommendation, he had not managed to see Jurgenson after the latter had ignored the compositions I sent him in December. I replied that the matter was now concluded, and relayed to him what had transpired with Jurgenson.

I showed Sergey Ivanovich *Dreams*. Unfortunately the piano was five rooms away, and it was hard to hear the piece from such a long way off. The score of *Dreams* was written in pencil, and Sergey Ivanovich found it hard to make out without the piano, not to mention that it was impossible for him to get an overall idea of the piece. At first he made one or two very apposite remarks on points of detail, but then started to carp at all the innovative ideas he found, and even to poke fun at them. For example, in the second theme, why should the bass harmony stay in C while the melody itself modulated to C sharp?

Not wanting to let him go on looking through *Dreams*, I played him Etude No. 3. He praised my piano technique and my way of performing the work; as for the music he neither applauded nor castigated it, and added that from five rooms away it was difficult to hear the rapid harmonic progressions. Then I showed him 'Reminiscence' and was once again subjected to a hail of mocking gibes. I took out my watch – it was a quarter to seven, I was due at Cooper's at seven, and Cooper lived half an hour away. I quickly jumped up and began to take my leave.

'Don't be angry with me, Sergey Sergeyevich, that I've been so . . .'

'Good gracious, Sergey Ivanovich, what are you thinking of! It was very interesting . . . only I've promised to go and see Cooper at seven o'clock . . .'

'Come back tomorrow if you're not going away.'

'With the greatest of pleasure, Sergey Ivanovich, provided I don't return to Petersburg tonight.'

I went to see Cooper. I got back my score of *Autumnal*, and a second copy of *Dreams*. Cooper was his usual kind self, and suggested I go with his personal recommendation to see Mme Kerzina[1] with a view to performing my piano pieces in her chamber music concerts, but said not a word about conducting my works himself.

From Cooper I went to Saradzhev.[2] For some time Mme Glière had been saying that I should approach him as a good conductor with a penchant for new works. This summer he is conducting symphony concerts in Sokolniki,[3] and during the spring he had come to St Petersburg to ask Kryzhanovsky if he knew any new composers and new works. Kryzhanovsky pointed him in the direction of Myaskovsky's *Silence*, which Saradzhev undertook to perform at the end of May, but for some reason said nothing about me.

Saradzhev was not at home, so I left him *Dreams*, *Autumnal* and the

---

1   Maria Kerzina and her husband A. M. Kerzin, wealthy Moscow music-lovers, organized series of chamber music concerts. They had been notable supporters of the young Rachmaninov.
2   Konstantin Saradzhev (originally Saradzhian) (1877–1954), Armenian-born conductor who had studied with Nikisch. The previous year, Saradzhev had founded, in partnership with Vladimir Derzhanovsky, a Moscow version of the Petersburg 'Evenings of Contemporary Music'. Both men had an acutely discriminating ear for new music, and Saradzhev regularly programmed new works in his open-air summer concerts in Sokolniki Park. After the Revolution Saradzhev had a distinguished roster of students at the Moscow Conservatoire, where he was Director from 1936 to 1940.
3   Sokolniki Park, originally laid out as the hunting ground of the tsars, is an enormous park a little to the north-west of Moscow city centre. In Soviet times it was an important site for exhibitions and trade fairs.

Sinfonietta, along with a letter, and then returned to the Glières. It was ten o'clock in the evening, and I managed to catch the mail train back to St Petersburg.

Ten days later Glière came himself to Petersburg, and at my request brought with him the scores I had left. He told me that Saradzhev would not perform them as the programme was already settled for the whole summer. Well, if they won't be played, then they won't be, but it is a great pity.

Another ten days, and Myaskovsky went to Moscow to hear his *Fairy Tale* (*Silence*). I went with him to the station and was overjoyed to see Kolechka so happy and youthful. For economy's sake he had meant to travel third class, but the train was so full that he had to go first class.

In Moscow he was welcomed with great pomp: Saradzhev, Derzhanovsky[1] (the publisher of *Muzyka*) and others came to meet him. Anything Myaskovsky had to say was treated as the pronouncement of an oracle, and he proclaimed my virtues from the rooftops, going so far as to say that history would brand them with ignominy if they failed to promote me ... to sum up, three days later I received a letter from Myaskovsky asking me to send *Autumnal* and *Dreams*.

It turned out that Saradzhev had not actually seen my scores when I left them with him; it had been someone else, I cannot remember who, a composer and general nuisance, who looked at them instead. I sent off both scores, and when he returned, Myaskovsky told me he could guarantee that *Dreams* would be performed this summer, indeed both pieces at some point (unfortunately not in the same concert as they are both in E minor and share a similarly misty and reflective cast).[2] Next year I would be invited to perform my Concerto, which is not yet written. Grateful thanks to Kolechka. Astonishingly enough, his *Fairy Tale* was a great popular success, and he is himself near enough satisfied with the piece, although he has declined to have it published by Zimmerman.

When Zakharov and I were visiting Anna Nikolayevna at Christmas, she informed us that she was beginning to put together the examination programmes for the members of her class. I asked for a little time, because at first I did not know what I wanted to play. Then I bethought myself of Liszt's sonata, and it came to me with blinding clarity that this was the very piece I should learn and perform at the exam: it very much fits my style and is the perfect work for me to demonstrate my powers in their best light! I informed Anna Nikolayevna of my choice, but she was strongly opposed, saying that she could not abide this sonata, and since I was not able to suggest anything

---

1 Vladimir Derzhanovsky (1881–1942), influential critic, editor and founding publisher (1910) of the magazine *Muzyka*.
2 Saradzhev conducted *Dreams* in Sokolniki Park but was indisposed for the later performance of *Autumnal*, for which the stand-in conductor was Alexander Medtner, brother of the composer.

better, I must play the second and third movements of Grieg's Concerto. As much as was possible in the circumstances, I protested, and managed to get permission to bring to the class both the Grieg and the Liszt so that a choice could be made between them. But the length of the Liszt so appalled Anna Nikolayevna that I had to take the Grieg.

I learned the Grieg and twice brought it to a lesson, even though my heart was wholly with the Liszt. But when I came to the end of March, the Grieg was suddenly replaced by the Liszt! I was mad with joy and set to work with a completely new attitude. I said to Anna Nikolayevna that I considered this work preparing for the exam to be the most productive of the whole year; in it all paths converged towards optimum mastery, and I could make more progress than at any other time, therefore it was all the more important that the repertoire should be interesting, demanding and lie close to my heart.

However Anna Nikolayevna was not really happy for me to play the Liszt, and an incident occurred that almost brought about a rift between us. The background to it was that, a short while before, Lenochka Hofmann played her graduation recital, some of it good and some of it less so, and I rather incautiously tore to shreds the less successful aspects of her playing, in the presence of some who were close to Anna Nikolayevna, such as Schweiger and Kalantarova. This enraged Anna Nikolayevna. It so happened that my critical remarks coincided with my request for permission to accept an invitation to play my big C minor Etude, 'Jest', 'March' and 'Phantom' at the revived Evenings of Contemporary Music. For this I needed Anna Nikolayevna's permission. She had never before raised any objection and it was on the very last day that I made my request, at the class she was teaching in the Conservatoire, although not of the group I was in. Anna Nikolayevna turned down my request and would not give me permission to appear in the concert. Why ever not?! Because the concert was one for a paying public, and on top of that I should not be wasting time and effort on appearing anywhere in public when I was not making any significant progress myself but merely criticizing others; I would be better employed on being rather stricter with myself. And finally, there were other professors in the Conservatoire besides Yesipova and I was welcome to choose any of them I liked. And she turned on her heel and went into her class.

I was in a horrible position. The programme had already been printed, and I was due not only to appear myself but also to accompany other artists, hence my absence would harm others as well. I decided to wait until the break, and speak once again to Yesipova. The intervening two hours of waiting were most disagreeable. Worst of all, she might now cut me off with a complete snub: 'I've given you my answer, have I not? What are you pestering me again for?'

But Anna Nikolayevna condescended to listen to my impassioned arguments, and then proceeded to read me a lecture about criticizing and berating everyone else when I had no right to, and so on and so on. I heard her out without complaint, reasoning that if she was tearing a strip off me like this it meant I had not been written off entirely. After listening patiently to the end of the lecture, I enquired if I could still play in the concert?

Anna Nikolayevna said, 'I am not giving you permission to play. But if you do play, I will not make any trouble for you.'

'Excuse me, please, Anna Nikolayevna, but . . . I do not fully understand what you are saying . . .'

'You may play,' said Anna Nikolayevna, 'but without my permission.'

I bowed and left, still somewhat at a loss.

Besides the four pieces of my own, I was due to play piano works by Schoenberg, a new Viennese composer. When these compositions appeared for the first time on Nurok's desk three weeks ago, we were all appalled, perplexed and repelled at the hideous absence of music and senseless dissonances. Not only that, but with their mass of notes and markings of all kinds it was almost impossible to work out how they should be played, and one after the other all the pianists participating in the Evenings declined to perform Schoenberg: Nikolayev, myself, Medem, Richter.[1] Without wasting time on any of the others, Nurok came straight back to me and persuaded me with the following argument: since the *raison d'être* of the 'Evenings of Contemporary Music' was to present to the public new works that have attracted attention both in Russia and abroad, they had an obligation to include the works of Schoenberg without passing judgement on their quality, but simply on account of the stir they had caused in Vienna. I agreed to play two pieces. I found it intriguing getting to grips with them. Although I could not see any music in them, here and there were glimpses of atmosphere, or something very like it. I determined to draw out this atmosphere in my performance.

I asked for my own pieces to precede the Schoenberg pieces, because I was afraid that the Schoenberg might precipitate a scandal. But Nurok mixed up the order of the programme, and in the event I had to play the pieces the other way about. Before I went out to play, he asked me what reaction I thought Schoenberg might provoke in the audience. I replied, 'I promise you that after the first two minutes the audience will be listening to it as real music . . .'

On stage, I announced in a loud voice, 'Works by Schoenberg', in order to prevent, God forbid, anyone thinking that I had composed them (my only previous appearances at the 'Evenings' had been as composer–pianist). At first when I started to play the audience listened very attentively, as to 'real music'. And indeed, at the very beginning of the piece I contrived to create a

---

1   Nikolay Richter (1879–1944), not his more famous Moscow colleague Sviatoslav Richter (1915–1977).

mood of sombre restraint with overtones of savagery and lamenting. This lasted for about two pages, then someone in the hall burst out laughing. The laughter grew and grew, as did the noise level. The second of the two pieces was short and loud, and so managed to drown the noise in the hall. But when I finished playing the din and the guffawing in the hall were tremendous. The only thing that saved Schoenberg was the seriousness and obvious commitment with which I performed the music. And the strange thing was that the more my ears became accustomed to the discordances the less I felt them, and the music appeared to me wholly and irreproachably admirable; whenever an occasional consonant harmony appeared in place of the expected dissonance, it struck my ears as an equivalent dissonance.

And so, to the jeers of the audience I made my way from the stage. But by the time I approached the door to come back again, applause was suddenly ringing out in the hall, acknowledging the seriousness of my performance. I bowed gratefully. Hardly had I finally left the stage when I was surrounded by an ecstatic group of the principal organizers of the evening. My performance had caused a sensation among them; they had not anticipated that it would be possible to make of such pieces, no three bars of which any of them had had the patience to work out, something that would be listened to as 'real' music.

A few programme items further on I played my own compositions, pretty well, especially the difficult Etude No. 3, which went down a storm with the audience; I was called back three times. During the interval all the musicians were very complimentary, praising both my music and its performance, but as for the Schoenberg they merely smiled and shrugged their shoulders.

The following day it was with some misgivings that I went to my lesson with Anna Nikolayevna. But she had not a word to say about the events of the previous night, and all went smoothly. I applied myself with great zeal to the Liszt sonata. It was curious that a month before the exam seemed to be plenty of time, but when only three weeks were left it suddenly seemed to be upon me. Anna Nikolayevna gave me no pointers at all while I was learning the sonata, so I worked on it entirely unaided. The more time went on, the better the sonata became, and most importantly, the playing increased in intensity all the while. At the general rehearsal in the Small Hall I played really well, except that my breathing was rather noisy and I exaggerated the *fortissimo* passages. I was quite rightly criticized for this, and told that a powerful *fortissimo* is good, but it is unpleasant if allowed to become harsh.

The 4th of May dawned, the day of the exam, exactly the same date as the year before, only this year twenty-four pianists were playing, all on the same day. I was allocated the eleventh slot, not a particularly high place but with the advantage of closing the first half of the programme, which moreover included a galaxy of very good young players: Akhron, Shmayevsky, Shtember and Vinogradov. This position was very flattering to me.

I had very few pre-performance jitters, fewer than I had expected. Sitting at the piano I had a pleasing sensation of calmness and complete control of myself. The performance went well; I felt the work I was performing was an interesting one. In the fugue I worried about losing my place, and had prepared in advance a few safety nets to which I could skip should I come off the rails. However, I successfully negotiated all the hazards of the fugue, only to get lost the moment it was safely past. But I modulated in the style of the music without spilling a drop, and emerged on to the right road. In the reprise I went wrong again but this time found my way to the following section of the music so adroitly and stylishly that it afforded the listener nothing but pleasure, and no one in the audience – I swear – noticed anything amiss. At the conclusion of my twenty-five-minute sonata I left the stage to resounding applause, and the interval began. My emergence from the stage to the front of house was greeted triumphantly: among those who congratulated me and said how marvellous I had been were Shtember, Rudavskaya, Myaskovsky, Hansen, my relations (six of them) and Golubovskaya, who particularly stayed in my memory. Yesipova was full of praise, Ilyin too of course; Glazunov also paid me compliments but thought I had taken the fugue too fast. Getting a bit lost mattered not at all, it was even a good sign that I had managed to recover myself. (A curious episode: Mama came face to face with Yesipova, introduced herself, and in the most flattering phrases thanked her on my behalf. Anna Nikolayevna extended her hand (the left hand) and said, 'He is doing very well, I am very pleased with him.' Hmm! . . . Not exactly what she was saying a month ago.)

And so my exam performance left nothing to be desired: the carefully thought out plan had been superbly realized. But a disappointment awaited. When the Class Inspector read out the marks, it appeared that out of twenty-four candidates twelve had received 5+ (Zakharov, Shtember, Zeiliger, Berlin, Kuznetsova, Dubiansky, Benois, Livshitz and some others). I got a straight 5. Why so? I do not know. It spoilt my subsequent outing with a dozen or so of the students to a restaurant and then on to the Aquarium. But Borovsky, who before he went on to perform had been heard asking himself, 'Now, shall I get a 5++ or just 5+?' was in an even worse plight: he got the same as me. However I soon consigned my marks to the devil, deciding that no one in the Conservatoire understood anything, when suddenly Yesipova, who had been very favourably disposed to me ever since the exam, murmured something about 'your 5+ . . .'

'Straight 5,' I corrected her.

'No, 5+,' replied Anna Nikolayevna.

'I also saw it put down as 5+,' confirmed Ilyin.

I was more angry than pleased, and resolved to make a big fuss with the Class Inspector over her incorrect announcement of the marks. Ten days or so later I was accompanying students from Ossovskaya's class in their exam, and when the Class Inspector began to read out the results, I declared loudly, 'Gentlemen, if any of you have a low score, do not be too upset. Olga Borisovna usually reads out something different to what is written there, usually a lower mark.'

Olga Borisovna turned to me, thinking this was a joke in rather poor taste, whereupon I rapped out sharply, 'I got a 5+ in our exam, but you read out a straight 5.'

She was angry, but collected herself. 'I read out exactly what is written, and if your marks are altered later, that has nothing to do with me!'

Anna Nikolayevna's parting words to me were that I should play more Beethoven: my playing needed to acquire more serenity.

As for my composing activity this winter, the results are rather paltry: nothing except a few corrections to and revisions of existing works: the Sonata, the choral piece *The Wave*, the Sinfonietta, and the Op. 3 and Op. 4 pieces. All the more reason, as the summer approached, for me to settle down to work. In plan was the famous 'big concerto' for piano, which I had already started, but which I could not get around to continuing. And then, in the spring, a little concertino had sprung into being from somewhere or other, a pendant to the difficult large-scale concerto. As well as these, a symphony had begun to shape itself in my mind, for which the exposition was already composed in outline. I longed to get on with all these in the summer.

One March day, in the opera class, there had been a discussion about the operas that were to be studied in the Conservatoire next year. From the international repertoire Mozart's *Don Giovanni* had been identified, but nothing suitable had been found from the Russian repertoire. Shteiman said, jokingly, 'Why doesn't Prokofiev write us an opera, and we'll put it on!'

This had a galvanizing effect on me. That very day I had an exceptionally spirited discussion with Shteiman, in the course of which I heard myself saying that I was tremendously excited by the notion of writing a one-act opera, and that I would have it finished by the autumn. I asked him to propose the idea, but in a more serious vein, to Tcherepnin. Tcherepnin expressed interest, and although he obviously did not believe that the plan to compose an opera and have it performed would really come off, he agreed that a precedent had been set in Galkovsky's *The Gypsies*. He gave me a good deal of useful and specific tips about opera composition, notably on the choice of a subject, which must be the starting point for everything that follows. For a first attempt at opera, the subject should be as simple as possible, intimate and not too exotic, without over-ambitiously aiming at anything too original. The most important thing for an opera is that it should have plenty of life and movement, otherwise the characters run the risk of simply turning into wax figures. Tcherepnin listed a few possible sources for subjects:

Coppée,[1] PortoRiche,[2] *The Decameron, The Thousand and One Nights*. He then left for Monte Carlo.

Everywhere I went from then on I asked people on every hand to find me a subject for my opera. Never have I been as excited about my future work as I am now. I even expatiated on my need for a subject sitting in the artists' room at the 'Evenings of Contemporary Music' when I was playing the Schoenberg pieces and my own works, and a Mariinsky Theatre tenor, Andreyev[3] happened to be there and heard me. A day or two later he sent me a note saying that he had a subject for me, and would I like to read through it with him? I went to see him and he read me a one-act play by Baroness Lieven:[4] *Maddalena*. At first I was not very interested and found it hard to concentrate, but by the end I was absorbed by the beautiful, if conventional, tale. I still did not intend to write an opera on this subject, however, but I took the play home with me to read it through once again when I had time.

In the meantime none of my other sources had come up with a subject which seemed to fit the bill, and *Maddalena* had the advantage that it had been written as a drama and therefore would not need a great deal of alteration to be transformed into a libretto. If alterations were needed, the author was alive and living in Tsarskoye Selo, so the changes could be made in collaboration with her. I read through *Maddalena* once more, and this time something hit me right between the eyes: *Maddalena* was not a play for the legitimate theatre, it was a pure-blooded libretto crying out to be set to music. To elaborate: it contained many passages which in a theatrical production would not be interesting and would pass unnoticed, whereas treated operatically and set to music they would gain enormously in interest. For instance, the beginning of *Maddalena* the play is not particularly exciting; it seems frankly superfluous . . . But operatically it could evoke a marvellous atmosphere, a magnificent canvas on which to portray the character of Maddalena: beautiful, inconstant and remote. The whole of the opening section would be transformed into scene-setting, both interesting in itself and crucial for the listener's understanding. Then, in the play the scene between Gennaro and Maddalena is attractive and interesting, but the audience still cannot see why it should be there at this point in the action,

---

1 François Coppée (1842–1908), French poet, novelist and playwright.
2 Georges de Porto-Riche (1849–1930), French novelist and dramatist whose plays about love and passion were extremely popular at the time. His best-known play was *Amoureuse*, a highly charged emotional vehicle for the celebrated Gabrielle Réjane.
3 Nikolay Andreyev (d. 1919), tenor soloist of the Mariinsky Theatre and a regular principal in Diaghilev's opera productions.
4 Baron (not Baroness) Lieven was the *nom de plume* of Magda Gustavovna Lieven-Orlova,who, as Prokofiev described her in his 1941 *Short Autobiography*, was 'a young lady of fashion, more agreeable in society than talented in the theatre'. (Semyon Shlifstein (ed.), *S. S. Prokof'ev: Materialy, dokumenty, vospominaniya*, op. cit.)

and I am certain will be indifferent to it. In the opera, on the other hand, it will be transformed into an impassioned love scene, which thanks to the music will transfix the audience: the listener will already have been alerted to the musical character of Maddalena in the first scene, her music will have engendered a particular mood, a recognizable link between listener and heroine, while the appearance of Gennaro extolling the virtues of Maddalena only serves to strengthen the link and make her still more appealing to the audience.

In the drama, by contrast, all that is achieved by Gennaro's entrance is the introduction of a new character, thereby arousing the spectator's expectations of what is to happen in the succeeding scene, which in turn can only explain its predecessor when it takes place. I pondered all this as I read through Maddalena again, this time with much greater enthusiasm than I had when I first read it with Andreyev. The concept of 'beautiful evil', which is the theme of the play, is an interesting one in itself, and the whole play is written with such 'cinematographic' speed of action that there is no time for it to become boring for the composer to write music for, nor boring for the audience to listen to. Also, the initial characterization of Maddalena and the need to create a mood right at the beginning of the opening scene presented me with an immediately interesting task. I sat down at the piano and started to improvise, coming up at once with the first theme. I liked it, and thus was *Maddalena*'s fate sealed.

The libretto divided the opera clearly into four scenes and produced an exceptionally elegant structure:

Scene 1   characterization of Maddalena;
Scene 2   characterization of Gennaro (interwoven with the preceding, i.e. Maddalena);
Scene 3   characterization of Stenio (interwoven with the preceding, i.e. Gennaro);
Scene 4   all three combined, each with his or her own passions.

What could possibly be more elegant as a plan for a one-act opera?!

I therefore set to work on *Maddalena*. Intensive work on it, however, I postponed until the summer, restricting myself for the present to composing its material between whiles. In June we left Petersburg to go to Sukhum. I had already composed all those parts of the first scene in which Maddalena is alone on stage, and a good portion of the material I needed for the second scene. In Sukhum I worked intensively on the opera, and in the course of three weeks composed the second and third scenes.

On 26 June I received a postcard from Derzhanovsky letting me know that *Dreams* would be performed in Sokolniki on 1 July, and *Autumnal* some time between 10 and 20 July. Midway between the performances of the two pieces was the date on which Kankarovich was to conduct *Dreams* in Pavlovsk, so I happily left Sukhum on the first steamer out. But the steamer was taking on a cargo of peaches, which delayed it for six hours, and by the time I got to Novorossiisk all the trains had gone. I have a twenty-one-hour wait in Novorossiisk, so I have taken a room in an hotel, and am now sitting there writing my diary.

29 June
Novorossiisk

(Note: I remember that when I was a child in Sontsovka, this day, the feast of SS. Peter and Paul, was a day of great village celebration and pomp, as St Peter and St Paul were the patron saints of the church in Sontsovka.)

Over the last fifty pages I have been setting down the musical events that took place in my life during the four months since I last wrote my diary. Now I want to recall what has happened with my friends and other people I know. I might as well start with Marinochka Pavlova. Between February and May our relationship did not change much. But the onset of spring brought with it the end of General Subjects classes for both her and Levitskaya, interspersed with a few exams, and our regular encounters ceased. One day she invited me to play the piano accompaniment for her singing exam, and I was delighted to agree. Although she repeated the invitation, when I proposed coming into her class so that we could try out our repertoire together, she took fright and chased me away. As the exam approached, I could see that Pavlova was torn between wanting me to be her accompanist and not wanting me to hear her sing in, so to say, an informal situation. Without telling her, I therefore went directly to Professor Ivanov-Smolensky, for whose class I had never before accompanied, and proposed that I should be the accompanist for the exam, a suggestion the old man was delighted to accept. On my part this was a heroic act, because it meant taking on my shoulders the burden of more than ten singers of both sexes, with four lengthy rehearsals.

I saw Marinochka at only two of them. She proved to have an enchanting voice, with a lovely timbre, but like herself, rather small. Her phrasing was refined and intelligent, and Ivanov-Smolensky says that the voice will develop and she has a great future. At the exam itself (which was on the day before my own) she was terribly nervous, and was at such pains to tell me that I must not let her down, and would have to extricate her from any difficulties she might get herself into, that she even made me nervous, so once on stage I assumed what I hoped was such a reassuring air of blithe serenity that I was in danger of hitting wrong notes. She received a 4+, but as I did not wait for the marks to be read out, and she was not able to come to my Yesipova exam the following day, I asked her to telephone me to tell me her marks. The dear girl did in fact ring, but unfortunately I was not at home when she did.

The next time I met her was two weeks later, when I took her home from the Conservatoire, talking inconsequentially about this and that. She was planning to stay in Petersburg for a while, and then go for the summer to Luga.[1] With that we parted; I sent her greeting cards when I was away in Moscow and Terioki.

Meanwhile the late northern spring had arrived, and the few trees Petersburg boasts were beginning to turn green. I felt a strong pull to get out of the city and go somewhere into the country round about.

And so the excursions began. The first was to Kronstadt,[2] where for almost a year I had been meaning to go with Tonka. The attraction for me was that to get there one had to take the steamer and make a sea voyage to another town . . . this was exciting. But for one reason or another we never succeeded in organizing the trip, until one warm April day we made an arrangement by telephone to meet at noon on the pier by the Nikolayevsky Bridge. At first Tonya irritated me by being terrified that someone might see us going to Kronstadt, and so spent the whole time hiding in corners. But then we ventured on deck together, where as we imperceptibly neared our destination a general of some kind attached himself to us. The reason we struck up an acquaintance was that he was sitting beside Tonya and me as I embarked on an outline of the opera I was intending to write. The general listened and listened until he could contain himself no longer, and then announced importantly, 'If one is going to write an opera, one must first be a composer.'

He was greatly upset by seeing some upstart pipsqueak turning the head of a pretty young girl all too ready to be taken in by him. I explained to the general that I was indeed a composer. Our general, it appeared, was a poet. We talked, and the general took it into his head that I must set his verses to music. He would write a poem about our meeting. He entertained Tonya with sweets and paid her compliments; she was immensely pleased. When we arrived at the jetty, Tonya and I got into a cab and set off.

Kronstadt turned out to be a horrible little place, bare and dusty. We had two hours to kill, so we lunched in an hotel and sent postcards to our friends, took photographs of one another, walked round the town for a while and

1 Town much favoured by dacha owners about a hundred kilometres south of St Petersburg, on the main railway line to Warsaw.
2 Kronstadt was established by Peter the Great as a fortified naval base, defence and outer port for St Petersburg. Strategically placed on the island of Kotlin in the Gulf of Finland about twenty-five kilometres from the centre of the city, it is ice-bound for several months of the year. Having played a significant role in the Revolutions of 1905 and 1917, it rebelled once again against Bolshevik rule in 1920, only to be savagely suppressed by the Red Army, although the strength and dignity of the sailors' demands were influential in persuading Lenin to institute the New Economic Policy.

returned to the jetty in time for the ferry back. The route back was different; we disembarked at Lisi Nos¹ and from there by a little train. This was also very enjoyable as we sat reading the *Satyricon*.² On Kamennoóstrovsky Prospect we said goodbye.

A few days later the general sent me some long-winded verses describing our meeting on board the ferry. As poetry they were dreadful, but they afforded Tonya and me huge pleasure. We never saw him again.

The second trip was also by steamer up the Neva, towards Schlüsselburg.³ Schlüsselburg itself was too far, so after two hours we disembarked at a village called Ivanovskoye,⁴ somewhere in Ust-Tosna, and went for a walk. It was a cold and rather misty day, and while we were on the boat we froze to death. Ivanovskoye was knee-deep in impenetrable mud, but once we were out of the village it was better although the landscape was mostly factories peopled by hordes of workers, and the way they stared at a pretty young girl from the town began to make us feel rather uneasy. Further out we came to some fields, in fact a rather beautiful landscape of woods, fields and a river. We went into the forest and ate our sandwiches, bananas and chocolate. We kissed and were very affectionate. We almost missed the steamer back, but returned contentedly to Petersburg.

A third jaunt, out to Peterhof,⁵ was less successful. Another time when we were wandering round Novaya Derevnya⁶ and along the Primorskaya road, we again fell to squabbling again, so much so that we even went home separately. But on one other occasion, in almost exactly the same place, we had a wonderful walk, the nicest of all.

We went on the little train as far as the station at Kellomyaki,⁷ and set off with no particular destination in mind. At first it seemed a dull enough place, and I dragged along grumbling to myself. This was the first place we had come to at Tonya's instigation.

We crossed a deserted field several versts wide, and then I persuaded her

1   Literally, the 'Fox's Nose', a resort on a headland jutting out into the Gulf of Finland from the north shore opposite Kronstadt.
2   *Satyricon*, satire by Gaius Petronius (?27–66), *arbiter elegantiae* to the Emperor Nero.
3   Fortress town at the head of the Neva river on Lake Ladoga forty-five kilometres east of St Petersburg. The fortress was captured from the Swedes by Peter the Great in 1702 and renamed Schlüsselburg (German 'Key Town') to balance Peter's companion fortress at the mouth of the Neva west of the city, which he similarly captured and called Schlotburg ('Lock Town').
4   A small settlement on the south bank of the Neva river, about halfway between St Petersburg and Schlüsselburg.
5   A complex of magnificent palaces and parks laid out by Peter the Great as his official summer residence on the south shore of the Gulf of Finland. Peterhof (in Russian Petrodvorets) is most celebrated for its fountains, modelled on those created for Louis XIV at the Château de Marly.
6   A suburb on the north bank of the natural boundary to the city formed by by the Bolshaya Neva river.
7   See page 165, n. 2.

into the woods. But at first it was more undergrowth than actual trees, and turned into such a marshy swamp that it was only with difficulty that we extricated ourselves from it. On top of that Tonya saw a snake, which put the fear of death into her. We beat a hasty retreat back to the field, and you should have seen how she clung to me seeking protection from the snake. I pacified her as much as I could, savouring the sensation of her trust in me as a protector. Emerging from the forest we lay down on the grass and ate our bananas for lunch. Eventually, our arms entwined around one another, we made our way back to the station.

The last of our rambles was round St Petersburg itself. It was towards the end of May, and the weather was hot. Instinctively drawn towards the cool of the sea, we nevertheless avoided our usual Vasilievsky Island, where we had been several times and were now tired of, and went instead to the south part of the Fontanka. We walked along the Fontanka and on to Yekaterinhof[1] (of whose existence we were unaware and which was a great surprise), then by some unfamiliar streets on the outskirts of the city to a tumbledown bar, which at least had no one in it and where we drank some lemonade. We pushed on further and eventually, leaving the town behind us, came into open country. It was strange one moment to be in St Petersburg and the next to be in the country. The ground must have been very low-lying and susceptible to flooding, for all around there were dykes reminiscent of Holland. However this expedition was not as successful as the one to Kellomyaki, because on the way back we managed to get thoroughly disenchanted with each other.

The day before I left for Sukhum I was sitting with Tonya in the square that lies between the Summer Gardens and the Engineers' Palace. Tonya, clearly upset that I was going away, was extremely sweet and loving, and kept on saying, 'Our last time together, our last time . . .' She promised to write to me often, and was as good as her word.

14 August
Kislovodsk

I believe Borya Zakharov to be one of the most talented people I have ever come across. Talented in life (but not in music). He is a rare being, of a type that infinitely appeals to me. I am keenly aware of how much I love him, but oh! how upsetting his coldness can be, and the way in which he can repulse a person coming to him with outstretched arms. On my side, I am frighteningly quick to take offence; and then my love turns into intense hatred. Whichever way it is, it is rare that I am indifferent to him. The conversation

---

1 Eighteenth century park originally laid out along the banks of the Fontanka river for the Empress Catherine I, Peter the Great's wife, in the south-west part of the city.

we had in January on the train from Tsarskoye to Petersburg, and the self-analysis he shared with me on that occasion, plainly affected him as well, for he several times recalled it.

After that, we did not see much of one another. We were both at Anna Nikolayevna's name-day party on 3 February – the first time I had been invited to one of her *grandes soirées*. It was a lavish affair, dinner suits and evening dress, and most of the guests were from the professorial faculty of the Conservatoire, while from the student body were Borya, myself, Shubert, Borovsky, Berlin, Benois, and Schweiger. The evening had its intriguing side, but was for the most part rather boring.

On Shrove Tuesday a trip to Terioki was organized. Borya had been saying for a long time that he wanted to get everyone together to go to Terioki at some point during the winter, and when I several times reminded him of this, finally it was arranged for this day. 'Only make sure that you're free for the whole day,' said Borya. 'We'll leave in the morning and come back late in the evening.'

'I've already crossed out the whole day from my life,' I replied.

The group that assembled was a large one, about twenty or twenty-five people: Borya, Vasya, Styopa[1] and Georges Zakharov; Vera Stepanovna and Zinaida Eduardovna with her brother and sister (Volodya and Nadya Markus); Lidusya and Zoryusya; myself; Kokochka Shtember; Sofochka Kapustina; Nina and Kira Durdin; A. Danilov; Esper Lukich, and many others. Sofochka paired up with Georges, Borya was the chief organizer and linked particularly to Nina and Kira; I had not seen Lidusya for a long time and was very happy at the chance to be with her again, so paired up with her for the whole expedition.

I was in uncommonly good spirits that day, in fact it was one of the jolliest times I can remember; the whole trip to Terioki was an incredibly happy one! The weather was glorious, with the snow lying white and brilliant on the ground. From the station a gang of us walked to one of the Zakharov dachas (the main one was closed for the winter) where a delicious meal was waiting for us. Then we went on five separate sleighs to a hill several versts away down which we could toboggan. Zinaida Eduardovna drove our sleigh, and I sat behind her with Lidusya and Kokochka Shtember, hurling snowballs at the other sleighs and misbehaving disgracefully with Lidusya.

After the tobogganing session we set off for home again, Stepan Stepanovich taking charge of the sleigh with the most mettlesome of the horses. Firmly imprinted on my memory is the image of him dashingly adjusting his gold pince-nez as they glinted in the sun, lending a deliciously piquant air to his chubby cheeks as he masterfully took hold of the reins. 'Who's going to come with me?' he asked.

---

1 Stepan.

Lida and I followed him into the sleigh with Zinaida Eduardovna, who was in a hurry to catch a train, also Kokochka, who had no intention of being left out. A touch on the reins, and we were off like a rocket, dashing along the road at a furious pace. But things took a turn for the worse whenever we encountered oncoming traffic on a road that was too narrow to allow two sleighs to pass. Continually at risk of a collision, we whooped and hollered at approaching sleighs which in terror and astonishment were forced off into a snowdrift. Still worse was to come when we met, not a lightweight Finnish sleigh, but an enormous contraption consisting of several tree trunks bound together and supported on two tiny little sleds. The five in our sleigh were a pretty tight squeeze, Lida and I sitting on the right-hand side with our legs dangling over the side, so the prospect of huge tree trunks bearing down on us from the opposite direction was a distinctly dangerous one. And indeed, the next time we met one, we were lucky not to come to grief altogether. There was no way round it, and for one moment I thought my legs were going to be chopped off by a log, or at least my knees would be shattered; luckily, however, I suffered only a slight graze. But at that moment I felt our sled overturn, and I went head over heels into the snow.

I scrambled to my feet and saw the horse running off with our sleigh on its side, while Stepan Stepanovich, still hanging on to the reins, ran alongside through the snow trying with all his might to get back into the sleigh and stop the runaway horse. They disappeared round a bend, and I turned to see Lida by my side. The log which had struck me had fallen right on to the poor girl and bruised her side, her arm and her knee. She stood there pale as death, her face contorted with pain, and I expected her at any moment either to fall down in a faint or to erupt in hysterics. But the dear girl pulled herself together, merely removed from her wrist her watch and bracelet, which had been broken in the impact and pieces of which were digging into her hand, and hurled it into the snow. The bracelet buried itself deep in the snow, Kokochka crawled about looking for it, while I stood beside Lida attempting to calm her down.

The largest of the sleighs and its coachman turned back, and out jumped Borya, very anxious about Lida. She was put into the big sleigh, and they moved off. Lidusya soon recovered herself and was able to smile at the comic mishap, although for a time she lay there quietly and a little crestfallen. I went after our ill-starred horse, which by now had been caught and subdued.

When we returned to the dacha we had supper. Vasya Zakharov and I drank to our *Bruderschaft* then went skiing along the shore. Later we drank tea, and raised the roof with our racket as we danced with whomever or whatever came to hand (including the chairs). I seem to have been the wildest member of the party. At midnight, completely exhausted, we all returned to Piter.

On the way back, Borya and I found ourselves *tête à tête* on the outer platform between the carriages, and he asked me, 'Well, what do you think, was this a day to be crossed out from your life?'

'On the contrary, it is inscribed in letters of gold,' I replied with emotion. Borya was very pleased.

Soon afterwards Borya went off somewhere for three weeks; I could not reach him anywhere by telephone, but later I discovered that he had not been in Petersburg at all but had gone with Vasya to the family's country estate near Staraya Russa.[1] Later I heard that he had not at all had a good time there, had fallen ill with something or other, but what he did not say. I still don't know what happened to Bobosya at that time.

On his return we met at an afternoon concert in the Hall of the Nobility, for the first performance of Rachmaninov's *Liturgy*.[2] He was delighted to see me, was affectionate and charming, and that evening came to my house. I have seldom known him show such warmth and pleasure in my company.

Thereafter we resumed our association as it had mostly been hitherto, our meetings being neither frequent nor rare but as they happened; from time to time we would speak on the telephone. Originally our telephone at home had been down in the front entrance hall of the building, but now we had one in the apartment itself. One of the most frequent callers was Lidusya; we had become close friends after the expedition to Terioki, and she took to calling me almost every day, sometimes several times a day. Around this time she was having some difficulties with her parents, and although the causes were trifling the problems they raised were serious. At home she had been virtually sent to Coventry; nobody would speak to her, and this was happening at a time when she was working for her graduation exams. She was just a girl, quite frail moreover and not always in the best of health, with no one to turn to in her hour of need. I was her sole friend and support; I listened patiently to her woes and we went for walks together. I felt genuinely sorry for her.

Some time later, at Easter, the problems over and peace with her parents restored, I dropped in at the Karneyevs on my way to the Ruzskys to pick up a walking stick I had left there. Now there was a new misfortune: her father, who suffered from a terminally weak heart, had been out with friends, had drunk too much, and was now in bed in a critical condition. The house was

---

1 A spa town in Novgorod Province, between St Petersburg and Moscow.
2 Rachmaninov's *Liturgy of St John Chrysostom*, Op. 31 (1910). This was not in fact the work's first performance, since it had been performed the previous November by the Moscow Synodal Choir conducted by Nikolay Danilov. The performance Prokofiev attended was the Petersburg premiere at a Ziloti matinee concert at which the composer conducted the Chorus of the Mariinsky Theatre. The Liturgy of St John Chrysostom is the Eastern Rite equivalent of Holy Communion.

as quiet as the grave. Lida and I sat on a sofa in the entrance hall; such was her unhappiness that I put my arms around her, and she clung to me so tightly that I could do nothing except kiss her time and time again. This became a habit with us, so that we were always kissing one another.

But this is all I want to say about Lida: as for Borya Zakharov, an incident arose between us at the beginning of April.

I came to Anna Nikolayevna's class in order to ask her permission to play at a concert for the 'Evenings of Contemporary Music' on the evening of the same day. I was not expecting any difficulty in obtaining her permission, and was asking her really only for form's sake. But Anna Nikolayevna's reaction was extremely hostile, and she refused to give me permision.

Our conversation took place at the door into her classroom, and after it was over for some reason Anna Nikolayevna went out into the corridor, while I remained inside the room. I was in a state of shock, feeling as though the ground had been cut away from under my feet. Borya came into the class, and I leaned over to him: 'Borya, listen, what on earth am I to do . . . ?'

'I really don't know what to tell you,' he replied dismissively, and began to talk to someone else.

At the time I did not fully absorb the implications of his behaviour, merely feeling myself rather alone, but later on, and especially when the matter had been resolved, I could not get over the callous lack of humanity with which Borya had treated me at such a time. When next he rang me up I taxed him directly with it, ending the conversation with a well-aimed, and eventually notorious, parting shot that became like a label tied round his neck: 'You are a good person to have when you are not needed, but when you are needed you are loathsome.'

After that, for a time we did not speak to one another.

Naturally, in time all was smoothed over. He came to hear me play the Liszt sonata in class, and concluded that I had made good progress. Then one time he was appearing in an amateur play (he is an excellent actor), and he very much wanted me to come and see him in it, which I did in company with all his family and the Karneyevs. After the show there was a ball, but I left fairly early on in the proceedings. I will, though, add a few words about one revealing little scene: at the end of the performance Borya appeared in the hall resplendent in full evening dress, and as many of his friends were there he was surrounded by people congratulating him and telling him how wonderful his performance had been – Sofochka Kapustina, quite overcome, presented him with a bouquet. Borya was, in a word, several feet off the ground and felt himself quite the hero of the hour. When the music for the ball struck up, nobody took to the floor except for one officer jigging about on his own. Borya has only the vaguest notion of how to dance, but since he was in a manner of speaking the host, he felt it his duty to set an example.

He therefore asked a girl to dance and moved out with her on to an empty dance floor. He did not know any of the steps, but so graceful and gentlemanly, so urbanely affable was the effortless impression he conveyed – befitting indeed the hero of the hour – so courteous his colloquy with a partner who was all the while conscientiously performing all the correct steps, that the illusion of an accomplished dancer was complete!

(Chronological correction: this particular evening in fact preceded the Terioki expedition. I was mistaken.)

When it came to the Yesipova class exam, Boris was the last but one to play, and did so magnificently. His performance was of Rachmaninov's First Concerto; this work was really too undemanding for him and for the prestigious position it occupied in the programme, something for which I more than once criticized him. To follow such a difficult work as the Glazunov sonata, which he had played the year before, with the Rachmaninov Concerto was actually rather shameful. One evening after the exam, dining at Yesipova's house, we were discussing Zakharov's performance and I said of the Rachmaninov Concerto that it was properly a piece for the Junior course. Anna Nikolayevna was furious: 'What nonsense you talk! You talk the hind leg off a donkey, but never have anything worthwhile to say!' This occasioned such a roar of laughter from the table that Anna Nikolayevna had no choice but to turn her wrath into tolerant good humour.

Before the exam I several times played the concerto through with Borya and made a few suggestions. He accepted them, and I think they played a significant part in his performance of the work. He played the concerto marvellously, had a huge success, and was awarded a 5+ star. When he heard his mark, he said, 'Well, it's very nice to get a 5+, the first time I have had it,' and beamed with pleasure.

After the exam we went in a group, twelve of us in all, to a restaurant and then on to the Aquarium. It would all have been quite delightful had I not just heard that my own mark was a straight 5, not a 5+, and this spoilt my enjoyment of the post-exam celebration.

3 September
Moscow

During the second half of May Borya twice invited me to stay with him in Terioki. On the first occasion the only people there were Borya and Vasya, the remainder of the family having stayed behind in Petersburg. The main dacha had still not been made ready for the summer, so we stayed in the smaller No. 6 ('Ward No. 6',[1] as I dubbed it). I was there for two or three days,

---

1 The title of one of Chekhov's most famous short stories.

and the time passed most enjoyably with rambles all over the area; Lida and Zoya came and we went with them to Lake Krasavitsa. It was a heavenly time.

A few days later I came back to Terioki, by which time the family had moved out from Petersburg for the summer and were staying in the big dacha. Borya and I spent the evenings philosophizing. Since he considers I have keen powers of observation, I exploited them to analyse his character. There is nothing in the world Borya likes better than hearing about himself.

I told him he was not a good comrade. He agreed, but said that he was closer to me than to anyone else. He said he had never yet encountered anybody whom he felt to be unquestionably superior to himself, yet to find such a person would be for him the culmination of happiness, and only to this person could he be a true friend. I said that I also felt closer to him than to anyone else, but probably this was because I had not yet met anyone with whom I could have an even closer relationship. My truest friend would have to be someone exactly like myself.

I charged him with callousness, and he said that if there was a streak of this trait in him it was not premeditated but involuntary, it simply came of its own volition and was a genuine expression of something external to himself.

He said that many people had tried to analyse him, but nobody was willing to understand him as he truly was. I objected: 'You mean that nobody wants to understand you as you would like them to. For instance, I believe that I do understand you, but my understanding may well not be to your liking.'

Borya said. 'You accuse me of being callous, cold and indifferent to people. I have had many disappointments in life and cannot be open and trusting towards people. More than anything else in life I love art, and music. You know that I am not a recluse. I do not hide from the world; I love to enjoy myself and to be with people, but more than any of this I love art, and I cannot allow anything at all to distract me or stop me concentrating on or serving my art. May I tell you something, even if you find it callous?'

'Well?'

'Do you remember, when we were playing croquet today, we were concocting a telegram to send to Paris?'

'Well?'

'And then we were arguing about it costing five kopecks more or less . . . But this was the one person in the world who is dear to me.'

The person we were speaking of was Mlle Bastian for whom, as I had heard several times, Boris harboured tender feelings. A very beautiful girl, she was about to get married in Paris. Without stopping to think, I replied, 'The reason she is so dear to you is that you are not dear enough to her.'

Borya did not reply, and silence descended. All the same, what he had just said offered such a new and, if one may put it thus, such a striking insight, that it made a great impression on me. 'Tell me, please, is she marrying an Englishman?'

'Yes. And she does not love him at all.'

'Is he rich?'

'Yes.'

I put a few more questions to Borya, but was reluctant to torment him any more. As this was our last evening, it was also our last conversation, and I left the next day. I still harboured feelings of resentment towards Borya, however, and *en route* to Sukhum, on the steamer, I sent him a caustic and mocking letter which I hoped was witty enough to hit its target.

The next day I went back to St Petersburg to attend Lilia Konshina's wedding, and then set off with Mama for Sukhum, to compose my opera *Maddalena*.

One phrase Boris said to me I found very flattering. We were sitting in the hall of their dacha: Borovsky, Boris, I, the Karneyev girls and some members of the Zakharov family, discussing whether or not our Yesipova was really as wonderful a teacher as she is reputed to be. Borya said she was, and for his clinching argument declared, 'Even Sergey praises her, and since he criticizes everyone and acknowledges no one, you may be sure she is good!'

And when some of those present queried this statement, he added with the utmost seriousness, 'I say this in all sincerity.'

1912

2 March

S. Esche is sitting on a chair and bending down low. Standing next to her, I notice that a button on the back of her dress is undone. I do it up. S. Esche spins round.

'Don't be alarmed,' I say, 'I'm not undressing you, I'm dressing you.' She replies, 'The second often costs more than the first!' and laughs. Very witty. So much so that at first I didn't get it.

13 April

One day this summer in Pyatigorsk, S. I. Taneyev said to me, 'Where, Sergey Sergeyevich, do you think your predilection for dissonances comes from?'

'Well, you know, Sergey Ivanovich, when I was eleven years old and I brought you my first symphony, you listened to it and said with a smile, "Very good, very good; except the harmony is painfully primitive..." Those words burned themselves into my brain, I became ashamed of my primitive harmony, and tried in every possible way to make it more interesting. This ambition has never left me, and as my musical powers developed I was always aiming at ever more complex harmony, until some piano pieces I wrote in 1908 arrived at such a peak of uncompromising harshness that since that time I have retreated to more consonant configurations.'

Sergey Ivanovich laughed. 'Well, imagine that! I never knew it was I who had set you off on that path...!'

21 April

Some dates relevant to *Dreams*:
- Second subject (C–F–G–A flat) composed in 1905
- Remaining material – autumn 1909
- All material organized and score begun in May 1910
- Score completed 16 June 1910
- Revision incorporating some suggestions by Tcherepnin completed on 21 October 1910
- First performance, Conservatoire, 22 November 1910
- Second performance, Sokolniki, Moscow, 1 July 1911
- Third performance, Pavlovsk, 9 July 1911
- Further revision completed, 21 April 1912

18 August 1912
Kislovodsk

I left Yessentuki on 21 July to perform my Concerto[1] in Moscow and Pavlovsk. On 13 August I came back with Mama to Kislovodsk.

Here in Kislovodsk I spend my time as follows: in the morning I drink coffee in the park and then go to Tsintsinator's chemist's shop, where I am renting an upright piano in a very comfortable little room where I work until one o'clock composing my Sonata Op. 14. It is going well and I am absorbed in it. Then I bathe in Narzan spa water and go home to dine with Mama and the Smetskoys. After that either Max and I have arranged beforehand to go into Yessentuki or Pyatigorsk, or I do something with the Ruzskys, or I go and play chess in the park.

I gave the first performance of my Concerto Op. 10 on 25 July in Moscow, and then again on 3 August in Pavlovsk. These were my first appearances with orchestra, but rather than being terrifying experiences they proved on the contrary extraordinarily agreeable. I knew the solo piano part thoroughly, but the orchestras, playing from handwritten parts, were not very good. In Moscow I was accompanied by Saradzhev, who was so completely *au fait* with the tempi that I had not the slightest worry. In Pavlovsk, however, I did worry: Aslanov[2] was not on top of the tempi and the orchestra made a great many errors. Also, there were many people I knew at the Pavlovsk performance, and altogether it was a more important occasion for me than Moscow, all of which amounted to a great strain on the nerves.

I had a great success both in Moscow and in Pavlovsk, playing two or three encores each time, and I got a dozen or so press notices. Although Sabaneyev[3] wrote such a scathing review it was laughable, the others all acknowledged my talent; even though some of them were inclined to grumble, others praised me to the skies. There is no doubt that these appearances have established me as a 'real' composer with an enviable position relative to the musical hoi polloi.

The history of the composition of the Concerto is as follows:

At the start of summer 1910 I conceived the idea of writing a concerto. I worked out some splendid and very ingenious passages and composed the material for the exposition – admittedly not at this stage completely integrated.

---

1 Piano Concerto No. 1 in D flat major, Op. 10.
2 Alexander Aslanov (1874–1960), conductor, artistic director of summer season of concerts in Pavlovsk.
3 Leonid Sabaneyev (1881–1968), critic and composer, author of biographies of Scriabin and Taneyev. His passionate enthusiasm for Scriabin's music prevented him from forming objective judgements of the value of the new generation of Petersburg composers, including Stravinsky, Myaskovsky and Prokofiev.

The basic concept was an effective one, and it evoked a favourable reaction from those people I played it to.[1] But later that summer I was concentrating on *Dreams* and *Autumnal*, and put the Concerto on one side. I returned to it in the autumn, composing the material for the Andante and the Finale, and adding to what I had already composed for the first movement. I was enraptured with the music I had composed, but so far had not written a note of the score. The Concerto promised to be exceptionally difficult to play.

Then another thought entered my head: how good it would be to compose a light, transparent and uncomplicated concerto, capable of being played by anyone. It could be performed in the Conservatoire; I decided to dedicate it to 'emerging talents'. And thus in parallel to my serious, demanding Concerto, I planned a light, attractive Concertino, full of *joie de vivre*. This was in the spring of 1911. A marvellous theme for the Introduction came to me immediately, and for the main subject I took a theme from a little piano piece, 'Carnaval', which I had written in 1908 and dedicated to Myaskovsky.[2] I also quickly composed a bridge passage in C major. But then I called a halt, occupying myself instead with *Maddalena*, on which I worked all the summer of 1911. From time to time, to have a break from the opera, I tried to compose more material for the Concertino, but little came of these attempts.

In the autumn, however, matters proceeded more rapidly. What seemed to be emerging was quite a lengthy movement, a large-scale blazing Allegro. Was this going to be suitable for a concertino? And this was not all; it was turning out to be anything but the simple, straightforward piece I had envisaged – my original idea was receding further and further into the distance. Might it not be better to include the Andante, expand the whole work and make the result into not a Concertino but a full-blown Concerto? It would be a more solid construction, in fact better in every way. Added to that, my feelings had cooled sharply towards the earlier concerto from the previous year.

Inserting the Andante into the Concertino worked very successfully, as did the scherzo-like development section, and in this way the Concertino was transformed into a Concerto. At Christmas I set to work on the orchestration, and in February 1912 the Concerto Op. 10 was finished.

Among musicians the Concerto had a great success; I cannot recall any who did not like it.[3] I was particularly interested in what Tcherepnin would

---

1 From this material the passage in parallel triads (alternating between the right and left hands) was eventually used in the first movement of the Piano Concerto No. 3. [Subsequent note by author.]
2 The piece, one of Prokofiev's 'doggies', as Morolyov had dubbed the composer's 1907 piano pieces because of their 'painful bite', has disappeared. From the Prokofiev–Myaskovsky correspondence, however, it was clearly composed in the summer of 1907 and sent to Myaskovsky, who gave it its title of 'Carnaval'.
3 Glazunov apparently did not; I was so incautious as to stumble through for him on the piano a version based on a sketchy outline of the piece. [Subsequent note by author.]

think of it. He declared it to be my best composition, vigorous, lively and marvellously rhythmic. Another flattering opinion was that of the French critic Calvocoressi, who was on a visit to Russia at that time. According to him my Concerto was the most interesting work he had encountered in St Petersburg. The performances in Moscow and Pavlovsk somehow seemed to arrange themselves of their own accord; I also wanted to give it to Ziloti, but Ziloti condemned it in the most abusive language, placing it on a par with the works of Schoenberg, a judgement that caused more than a little indignation among my supporters, headed by Tcherepnin.

The Concerto's form.

The canvas on which the basic formal design is drawn is sonata form, but I so far departed from it that my Concerto cannot possibly be described as being in sonata form.

A massive Introduction in D flat major, which by virtue of its material is of great importance in itself, moves into C major and is then followed by a transition from C major to the main subject, which is of course also in D flat major. This is extended and leads to the second subject, in E minor. A short cadenza for the solo piano introduces a new theme in E minor, which has some of the characteristics of a concluding section and may be thought of as the first concluding section. This is followed by a second concluding episode in E major. Although it too has a feeling of cadence about it, it does not in fact bring the exposition to a close but modulates back to the theme of the introduction, and it is that which concludes the exposition section of the work.

The notion of interpolating between the exposition and the development of a theme previously heard in the introduction can already be found in Beethoven, albeit in a more reticent fashion, for example in the 'Pathétique' Sonata.

My Concerto then proceeds, not by the expected development section, but by an entirely new theme in the style of a rondo of the fourth and fifth types.[1] This theme is a completely self-contained Andante dropped in, as it were, at this point. It is followed by the scherzo-like development based on the second of the two concluding sections, into which the orchestra weaves references to the second subject, while the solo piano contributes an echo of the transition passage to the main theme. There ensues a dialogue between piano and orchestra based on the interval E–A, taken from the first concluding

---

1 A rondo of the fourth type has two episodes between three refrains of the main subject and concludes with a repeat of the first episode in the tonic. The fifth type interposes a concluding episode of new material, usually in the dominant, before the first refrain of the main theme, and then once again to conclude the movement, this time in the tonic. Development of an episode brings the form closer to that of sonata rondo. In the work under discussion, the importance of the *Andante* as effectively the Concerto's slow movement gives it considerably more weight than a conventional rondo episode.

section, and against the background of this interval appear glimpses of the principal subject. The orchestra brings the development section to a close, after which the piano embarks on an extended cadenza reprising the main subject, with a note of freshness introduced by omitting the C major to D flat major modulation, the theme being instead succeeded by another extension. The orchestra enters with the second subject, and while the piano contributes some freely contrapuntal material, sets out one after the other the two concluding sections. Piano and orchestra join together for a statement of the second concluding section, which as before leads back to the theme of the introduction, and this brings the whole work to a close. It is the threefold repetition – at the beginning, in the middle and at the end – of this powerful thematic material that assures the unity of the work. Leonid Nikolayev, however, says that the Concerto is not an integrated whole but a series of fragments that relate well one to another and have been skilfully stitched together. Oh, really?

While composing the Concerto I took pains to ensure that the piano would at all times be heard and would always be pleasing to the ear when combined with the orchestra. In this I was successful, but there are places where from a purely pianistic perspective the piano part is not particularly interesting. Nevertheless to the listener it sounds effective and impressive.

3 September
Kislovodsk, the Ruzskys' dacha

On the subject of the rift with Zakharov and my growing friendship with Schmidthof.

There is no doubt that my friendship with Zakharov was more than a conventional association between comrades. I admired his intellect, his wit, his independence of mind and his refined manners: all qualities that are close to my heart. He was three years older than I, but in maturity and experience of life there were considerably more than three years between us. He had a strong influence on me. Three years ago, even before we went to Terioki together, I went to considerable lengths to become friends with him, to win his affection and to strengthen the bond between us. This continued throughout, right up to the break between us. The first time I went to Terioki I was bowled over by the sum of all the impressions I received there; up till then I had spent all my time in the uninspiring confines of my family, summer in the monotonous life of Sontsovka, winter in St Petersburg. Here I was pitched into a magnificent dacha in the company of my most beloved friend: complete freedom, every imaginable entertainment, glorious girls, and on top of all that, Zakharov himself. The brilliance of this new world altogether dazzled me. After I had left, we exchanged a number of warm-hearted and amusing letters, and when in September I returned to Petersburg, losing not a moment to see him on the very day of my arrival, my return was welcomed with the greatest possible affection. This was the high point of our friendship. Even though it may have seemed that we grew still closer after that, the spark was not there to the same extent.

But Zakharov also possessed certain traits that coming into collision with my own character were bound to cause conflict. The closer I got to him and the more I tried to win him over, the more our natures in fact showed themselves to be incompatible, and the more I ran up against the negative side of him. This process continued for a year and resulted eventually in our parting company.

Zakharov's self-sufficiency stemmed from his belief that he was superior to the general run of people, including his own family, to such an extent that it became an indissoluble part of his flesh and blood and gave rise to a complex of highly individual character traits: a dogmatic refusal to accept any point of view not in absolute conformity with his own; a strong personality with a tendency to degenerate into despotism and the stubbornness into which a despotic nature is inclined of itself to degenerate; and finally an unconscious but all-embracing contempt for the remainder of humanity.

While I was less intimately bound to Zakharov these qualities were not particularly noticeable, and even held a certain attraction beneath the elegant plumage and general address of a personality whose independence and self-confidence owed nothing to anyone. But when I succeeded in my aim of becoming closer to him and penetrating below the 'plumage', which no longer held any appeal for me and had receded, so to say, into the background, I fetched up against these proclivities as though against a hedge of thorns through which I could not pass.

My own temperament has its own longing for freedom and independence, and is also not without an element of despotism. But whereas in Zakharov these qualities manifested themselves in an immovable, adamantine rigidity, in me they were generally more mutable, inchoate and latent. However, moments of extreme passion could lead to an outburst that could be far more intense and deeply felt than Zakharov's. I am capable of yielding to someone in whom I have faith, am conscious of loving and – once I have satisfied myself as to his superior qualities – can put him on a pedestal, content to acknowledge his pre-eminence. In many respects I did subordinate myself to Zakharov. But when blind despotism led him to impose his will at all costs, when everything he did could be on no other terms than his own, when he would brook no explanation from me simply because it had become a habit not to listen or pay attention to explanations from anybody, it became so disagreeable to me that I would flare up in a rage that burned much hotter than my love for him. And the very fact that at this time I was not completely a free agent, had no other friend to turn to, could not simply turn my back and walk away, could not in all conscience relieve my feelings by lashing him with my tongue – all this served to fan still more the flames of my temperamental predisposition to take offence which is, in any case, abnormally acute.

The first time I exploded was after I left Terioki at the end of my second summer staying there. I had been there in all for ten days at the end of May, and was on my way to Sukhum with Mama. On the steamer I wrote him a letter with all the wit and humour of which I was capable, poking fun at him in a sharply sarcastic way. The letter relieved my own pent-up feelings, serving to avenge the offences I had suffered and to dissipate the anger I felt towards him. When his reply came, I was afraid it would show how angry my dreadful letter had made him. But his letter was a model of restraint, and my next letter to him was a very sweet one. When in July I came north because of the performances of my works, I spent two more weeks as a guest of the Zakharovs. And once again the crazy collision of our two characters resulted in everything becoming overlaid with an atmosphere of conflict, more notches on the blade of our irreconcilable differences.

This time I relieved my feelings not in a letter but by not writing at all, vanishing into thin air from the moment of my departure. The Karneyevs wrote to me that my silence had astonished and upset Zakharov. But as before, I succeeded in sublimating my own resentment, and when I returned to Petersburg at the beginning of September I spent another week at Terioki. The family was very fond of me and to all outward appearances relations with Boris were perfectly harmonious, but somewhere deep down – with me, at all events – there now existed a perceptible rift. Our friendly intercourse persisted through the first half of the autumn, but the rift steadily grew, and in November came the rupture.

The immediate cause, the straw that broke the camel's back, was so trivial that it is hardly worth recalling. The summer before last I had been in hot pursuit of Rudavskaya and during the following winter she and I were inseparable, but then we tired of one another. Thereafter we did not meet very often, but whenever we did we took pleasure in one another's company, mulling over old times and sometimes kissing. Zakharov had never made any secret of his hostility to Rudavskaya, but one day she told me that from time to time he himself had not been averse to dallying with her, providing some facts that supported the story. I exploded and resolved that the time had come to break finally with this person, and did so.

What I had in mind was to replace our former friendship with the conventional relationship between two students at the Conservatoire who are obliged to meet once a week at their lesson. I took to avoiding meeting him as much as possible, and confining myself to brief and grudging exchanges when we did meet. If he telephoned me I answered monosyllabically. At first, Zakharov could not understand what had come over me; when he did understand, he also distanced himself. We settled into the relationship I wanted, aloof, meeting rarely and when we did so exchanging only the politest of salutations.

I could not say at the time whether this was a final break, or a temporary one. But I experienced no emptiness at the loss of my 'best' friend, and had no desire to renew the intimacy. A year has now passed, and I still have no resurgence of any such desire, indeed it is foreign to me. During the year four unusual incidents are worthy of note: (1) Two or three months after our rift there took place the wedding of his brother Vasya. I was not invited to the wedding, clearly as a direct result of the quarrel. I was surprised and hurt, because I had maintained an excellent relationship with Vasya and this seemed to me too brutal a demonstration of hostility. (2) Anna Nikolayevna's name-day was in February, and as usual there was a collection to present her with the traditional gift from the members of her class. But most of them were so indolent that the only people prepared to take it upon themselves to collect the money and choose the present were Zakharov and I. This entailed more frequent meetings than we were used to at this juncture, and when the whole group went to buy the present, which was an aquarium, we both enjoyed acting up for all we were worth the role of truly bosom friends: we laughed, we heatedly discussed the gift, we were both on top form, ceaselessly cracking jokes and laughing at each other's witticisms whether they were funny or not. Everyone regarded us as once again inseparable, but the name-day party passed and, having enjoyed the comedy, we again went our separate ways. (3) I was seriously ill with pleurisy at Easter. Zakharov got to hear of it and wrote me a letter of sympathy. I replied facetiously. (4) In May, Zakharov moved out to the dacha at Terioki and said to the Karneyev girls, 'It's very sad that Seryozha won't be with me at the dacha. Please tell him I said so.'

The Karneyevs were the point of contact through which we both heard regularly about each other's doings. I saw them frequently and was on very good terms with them, as was he. However our positions *vis-à-vis* the girls differed from one another: while I never denied the things I found good in Zakharov, I mocked his weak points and never missed a chance to lampoon him. He, by contrast, never uttered an ill word of me. My attitude was the more active one, while his was a façade of nobility.

Such is the story of our relationship. Sadly, I must postpone my account of how my friendship with Max Schmidthof began; there is no time at the moment. At this stage I shall simply note that neither my former nor my present friend can stand one another. Two years ago Zakharov said of Max, 'Oh, that's the fellow with a face like the bottom of a barge . . .' For his part, Max can hardly bear to hear Zakharov's name mentioned.

7 November
St Petersburg

This summer I had intended to complete the score of *Maddalena*. But the work went less easily than I had expected, and by the end of June I had finished only forty pages, the first scene. Throughout July and the first half of August I led a nomadic existence with my Concerto performances, and composed nothing, but at the end of the summer I resolved to get down to work again on three projects: (1) make another attempt to finish the score of *Maddalena*; (2) re-orchestrate and revise my old C minor Symphony[1] to give it new life as my new 'Symphony No. 1'; (3) to write out the score of the sonata I had begun.

I discarded the Symphony, deciding to retain only the Adagio, which I published separately as Op. 5 [sic]. The choice of what to work on fell on a Sonata, such as I had been writing in Kislovodsk. Its origins were as follows: some years ago I had written a Gavotte in G minor, which was invariably a great favourite with audiences, and people were always asking me whether I was going to publish it soon. It was a nice little piece, and I had nothing against the idea of publishing it as it stood. But it had to have some companions to make up another opus. I had a smart little unfinished Scherzo, fairly simple music. An idea for a sonatina was beginning to germinate (I always had a penchant for such things!) and that could make the third piece. In this way Op. 12 was coming together. In May I wrote to Max in Pyatigorsk to tell him that I was planning to dedicate this Sonatina to him, as I had long wanted to write a small but serious piece for him.

The Sonatina progressed slowly, but by the time the summer was half over it became clear that it was going to be far too big for a sonatina, and that musically it was far from simple. It was at that point, still in Kislovodsk, that I decided to write a sonata, and fell to with enormous enthusiasm. As material for the scherzo I took a Scherzo I had written for Wihtol when I was studying form with him, but the trio was new, as were all the other movements. I was delighted with my new Sonata; it was also well received by Max and by N. P. Ruzsky, to whom I played it while it was in course of composition.

The Sonata finished, I turned to a *Ballade* for cello for Ruszky. I had been promising to write him a cello piece for two years now, but not feeling particularly drawn to chamber music I found it hard to get down to delivering my promise.

---

1 Prokofiev seems here to refer to the symphony played through by Hugo Wahrlich and the Court Orchestra in February 1909. But that work was in E minor, and the slow movement is marked *Andante*, not *Adagio* (as is the slow movement of the Sinfonietta, Op. 5).

When I was twelve years old I wrote a Violin Sonata, and it had a very attractive main theme that I decided to exploit for the cello *Ballade*, extracting five bars from it. Just at the time when the composition of the Piano Sonata was coming to an end in Kislovodsk, Mama was leaving to go to Sukhum and I moved to stay with the Ruzskys, where there were naturally questions about when I was going to get down to writing the *Ballade*, stimulating me to improvise on my old theme. In short, once the Piano Sonata was finished, the material for the *Ballade* was already composed in my head and I was able to realize it quite easily. Actually putting it together involved a fair amount of work, but I managed to do it before leaving Kislovodsk, so that before I left for Petersburg a complete sketch of the *Ballade* was ready.

All the same, however equipped I was to write for the piano, and although I had good instincts and a sound grasp of orchestration, I was not well prepared technically to write chamber music. Bringing the cello and piano parts of the *Ballade* into good order and balance cost me much labour, but the more the work continued the easier it became. Aside from this there was a mass of things to do in Petersburg, and so it was the end of October before I finished the piece. The Sonata Op. 14 and the *Ballade* Op. 15 were thus the fruits of my summer work.

27 November

It happens that today I do not need to go into the Conservatoire, and I have the whole day at my disposal. I am taking advantage of this to experiment with making a daily entry into my diary. I don't suppose the reserves of energy will last long, but at least let's give it a try.

The day was not wasted: I looked through the Sonata Op. 14 one final time in preparation for sending it to Moscow and Jurgenson. In my covering letter I asked for 200 roubles, and I think he will pay that. It is said that hunger is the best spur to work. I am not starving, but I do have a shortage of pocket money, and that prompted me to check through the Sonata and, finding it satisfactory, to get it ready to send off. Usually I keep my compositions for longer than this to give them time to mature, and for any revision they need.

As well as the Sonata I did some work on the Piano Concerto (No. 2) and moved it forward.

At eight o'clock I am going to the student concert. Señora Umnova[1] has promised to be there, and I am far from indifferent to her.

---

1 Lidia Umnova, singing student of Professor Aktseri at the Conservatoire.

28 November

I spent the whole of yesterday's student concert with the delightful No. 17A.[1] We flirted and generally much enjoyed one another's company, and afterwards I took her home. This was the first time we had been out together. During the evening all the electric lights went out, much to the delight of all the young people. Two candelabras with stearin[2] candles were brought on stage and the concert continued.

This morning at nine o'clock I went to the small orchestra class. I tried my best to winkle out of Tcherepnin the results of the competition that had been held among the singers to participate in the jubilee celebrations, only to be told that the results are not out yet. This is of interest generally, but also in particular because Umnova is very anxious to know about Lel.[3] All I know is that I shall be conducting the second cast, and therefore my hope is that those to whom I am especially partial will have done badly enough to end up in that cast as well. During the class I had to conduct the student orchestra the whole time, that is to say two and a half hours without a break. Exhausting, but useful. Mozart's G minor Symphony, Glazunov's Wedding March and Glinka's *Night in Madrid*.[4]

After that there was a play-through of Weber's *Konzertstück*, to be performed on Saturday, which had been assigned to me to see what I made of it without any professorial advice. I was going to go home after that, but I met Max and stayed in the Conservatoire talking to him for another hour.

At four o'clock there was a rehearsal of *Judas Maccabaeus*,[5] the first time with massed choirs, and therefore a terrible crush and chaos.

Tcherepnin informed me that he had spoken to Gabel and Glazunov, and I shall probably be given *Ivan The Terrible*[6] to conduct at the Jubilee. Evidently my *démarche* to Tcherepnin was not in vain. It does not amount to much for my participation in the Jubilee, but it is better than nothing. It's an interesting challenge for a conductor, but it sounds pretty awful. In comparison with the wretched *Ivan The Terrible* the *Spanish Caprice*,[7] which Tcherepnin has reserved for himself, will be a blaze of brilliance, not to mention that it is something one can conduct with one's foot. Oh Tcherepnin, you're nobody's fool, are you!

Today I was inside the new Great Hall of the Conservatoire for the first

1 Lidia Umnova.
2 Solidified fat used for making candles.
3 The shepherd boy character in Rimsky-Korsakov's pantheistic opera *The Snow Maiden*, sung by a contralto. Lidia Umnova was competing for the role.
4 Overture: *Reminiscences of a Night in Madrid* (1851).
5 Oratorio (1747) by Handel.
6 Opera (1873) by Rimsky-Korsakov, more usually known as *Pskovityanka* (*The Maid of Pskov*).
7 *Capriccio Espagnol*, Op. 34 (1887), by Rimsky-Korsakov.

time. Fascinating as it was to see it, I was disappointed: the stage is small and uncomfortable, it has become a purely theatre space with cheap-looking chairs in the stalls ... and I miss our old hall, so light and white and beautiful, long and spacious, and so full of memories!

It always used to remind me of a huge dock into which a great ship could be brought. True, it was hopeless for lyric theatre productions, but as a concert hall it was far and away more roomy and accommodating than this new 800,000-rouble box. Thank God they have left the entrance foyer with its white columns, the best place in the Conservatoire.

(1) I played my Sonata Op. 1 to Vera Meriin;[1] she liked it very much. (2) Tcherepnin says that Gabel is very fond of me. (3) I have to study *Ivan The Terrible* for tomorrow's rehearsal.

29 November

Yesterday evening I stayed at home; Max came round and we wrote some of the 'Yellow Book'.[2] This morning there was a rehearsal of *Terrible*. It went quite well, and it is all coming together. But Tcherepnin gave me a real dressing-down for my frightful gestures and my contorted body: when I'm concentrating on the music I forget about what I look like. He suggested that is something I should pay more attention to. Glazunov then conducted the accompaniment to his Piano Concerto. Boryusya[3] came in to listen, but no one paid any attention to him. Tomorrow they will rehearse together and at that point Boryusya's star will rise over the horizon.

An interesting proposal was made by the bassoonist and the leader of the orchestra: to present a repeat performance of the opera two days after the Jubilee to raise funds for the orchestra, to be followed by a ball. This would be to my advantage, since obviously I would conduct this performance.

I had a lesson with Yesipova today, after an interval of a month. She greeted me very kindly: 'What happened to you? Have you been very busy?'

It would appear that word has reached her of my activities as a conductor. I played the Tchaikovsky Concerto for her, and was praised for it.

In my spare moments I am reading Korsakov's autobiographical *Chronicle of My Life*[4] and the biography of Tchaikovsky by his brother Modest.[5] I am

1 A student at the Conservatoire.
2 The 'Yellow Book' was a small notebook with a binding of thin yellow wood, into which Prokofiev entered the answers given by various notable and interesting people he encountered to the question: 'What are your thoughts on the sun?' The book is preserved in RGALI, the Russian State Archive of Literature and Art.
3 Boris Zakharov.
4 N. A. Rimsky-Korsakov, *Letopis' moyey muzykal'noy zhizni* (*Chronicle of my Musical Life*), first published St Petersburg, 1910.
5 Modest Tchaikovsky, *Zhizn' P. I. Chaykovskogo* (*Life of P. I. Tchaikovsky*), 3 vols (Moscow, 1900–1902).

reading them in parallel, a year at a time, and find this a fascinating method. The books are a strong stimulus to compose, but unfortunately at present there is little time for this. All the same, I am happy to be so intensely busy at the moment, and only having occasional opportunities to compose can sometimes produce better results than when I have unlimited time.

30 November

Yesterday evening I stayed at home desperate to sleep, because for the past two nights I had not slept well at all. I tried to work on the Concerto, but was too tired and nothing came of it.

This morning there was a rehearsal of *Maccabaeus* with orchestra and singers. It went well, although I had to yell at them from time to time. Boryusya was there; the first time he had seen me conduct. He then played the Glazunov Concerto. Yes! That's Zakharov's playing all over, the same awful insincere emotion as always! Glazunov accompanied appallingly.

The orchestral musicians' plan to repeat the Jubilee programme to raise money for the orchestra has won Glazunov's approval. The authorities openly regard me as the *Kapellmeister*; I say nothing, but rejoice inwardly.

Running down the stairs after the rehearsal, I saw No. 17A in conversation with Bobrovich.[1] I joined them, but after a minute or two Kruglovsky and another singer attached themselves to us. Seeing that no one was paying much attention to me, I turned and left.

At half past two there was a service of dedication for the new hall.

'Service of dedication?'

'You mean a requiem?'

'Service of dedication for the new hall?'

'Requiem for the old one?!'

The General Subjects classes, both boys and girls, were all sitting in rows. When Max and I came into the dedication service and walked quickly past, the boys – most of whom were playing in my orchestra – bowed to me. I acknowledged them in a way that showed I was not taking it seriously, but still it was quite an effective moment. This time I liked the hall better.

No. 17A came to the service and then sat right through the rehearsal of *The Maid of Orleans*[2] in the Small Hall. She nodded to me during the rehearsal – but hadn't we already greeted one another? Probably I had not been attentive enough to her when we met earlier in the morning. That would be unfair, she is very nice and there is nothing to reproach her with, but it will do no harm.

Myaskovsky's letter-writing style has much in common with Tchaikovsky's (as far as I can tell from the biography).

---

1 Voice student (tenor) at the Conservatoire.
2 Opera (1878) by Tchaikovsky.

I am in a completely disastrous financial state, having completely run out of pocket money. Max owes me 50 roubles, but all he has is a few coins. Even so we took a taxi today.

1 December

In the evening we had a vint party, our first in the new apartment: the Rayevskys, Mme Yablonskaya and Kolechka Myaskovsky. Kolechka was very charming, although it was not a very exciting evening. He found my latest version of 'Suggestion diabolique' spectacularly good, and also liked the opening of the Second Piano Concerto. He said, 'It feels a bit lazy, but that's all to the good.'

In today's class with the small orchestra I accompanied a piano concerto for the first time. Tcherepnin had given it to me to prepare entirely on my own. Because of this I had quite a swelled head, but when it was over I came in for a lot of criticism for all the things that were not just so. After the lesson Tcherepnin went through *Ivan The Terrible* with me, specifically from the point of view of appearance. His comments were interesting and perceptive, but now I have the 'pleasure' of assimilating them and incorporating them into my own conducting technique.

At the evening rehearsal I could not find Lel anywhere, but then 17A[1] suddenly drifted in, such a lively, dear creature, an absolute delight. She was immediately called to rehearse; I sat in a very obvious place with nothing to do, and she likewise was standing in full view, but I paid her no attention and did not once look at her. She probably understood why I was doing this; she tried her best to melt into the background and finally disappeared so that I did not see her go. Dear Lel, how wonderful you are!

I have invitations to two balls this evening: the Konshins and the Meshcherskys. But I am staying at home; I cannot be bothered to go to the Konshins, nor to the Meshcherskys, although I very much enjoy being at their house and would have gone had they repeated their invitation, but it was a month ago that they asked me! I hardly go out anywhere at the moment, I am too happy with the routine I have adopted and the things I am busy with: our opera productions, my conducting, composition, my pursuit of targets[2] numbers 9 to 17, and Max. This is my life, my sphere of activity, where I feel at home, the domain of which I am king. I have no desire to wrench myself away from it and enter another, it is too good here. Of course it would be very pleasant to be present at a grand occasion and ball, but apart from anything else I rise very early (half past six this morning) and by the evening I am already nodding off.

---

1 Both 'Lel' and '17A' refer, of course, to Lidia Umnova.
2 Girls.

2 December

Max came this evening; we did some writing in the 'Yellow Book', and discussed what is happening at the moment and particularly 17A. This morning I lazed about until after ten. Then I worked on the Concerto, concentrating on the first movement's A minor theme. The first two bars are good, but I cannot get any further. In the afternoon I was in the Conservatoire: Gabel asked me to coach a duet that is to be performed at the student concert. The only time he seems to be happy is when I am accompanying. Then I went into the Small Hall, where they were learning Glazunov's *Jubilee Cantata*, in which the entire voice contingent of the Conservatoire is taking part: students and faculty. Umnova was not there. I looked up the address directory and found Ivan Ivanovich Umnov, a hereditary holder of the title of Honoured Citizen.[1] I had always thought Umnova had an aristocratic background, Max on the other hand was sure that the derivation of 'Umnova' was ecclesiastical. It proved to be neither one nor the other, which I am very glad of.[2]

Natashka Goncharova is a very sweet girl and tremendously affectionate; we are good friends and call each other 'thou'! In *The Snow Maiden* she has a costume as Kupava (Kupava appears in Act III but does not sing), and indeed as a person she is very Kupava-like[3] ...

When I got home I read more of *The Life of P. I. Tchaikovsky*. I am entranced by this book, mainly because I find it such a tremendous spur to composition. I have begun the scherzo of the Concerto.

3 December

I spent the evening at the Shtembers. The young members of the family are all going for Christmas to their estate near Tula, and want me to go with them. I like the idea of having a week off in the country and taking a break from the hurly-burly of the city, but I shall not give a definite answer just yet, I am too choosy over the company I keep. 'Quite interesting' is not enough for me; it must be 'very interesting'. So I am saying neither yes nor no to the Shtembers. Max and I had a plan to go to Nice for Christmas (I badly want to go to Monte Carlo to try out my 'system') but neither of us has any money

---

1   Honoured Citizen ('Pochotnyi Grazhdanin'): a hereditary honour, conferred municipally or locally on prominent citizens, usually in the professional or mercantile sectors; it exists to this day.
2   Max may actually have been nearer the truth. The name Umnov (meaning 'clever one') is often formed by aphaeresis of the initial syllable of 'Igumnov', a name that in turn derives from the word (*Igumen*) for the Father or Mother Superior of a monastery.
3   Kupava is the Snow-Maiden's rival in love, first with Mizgir and later with Lel, whom Kupava marries at the end of the opera.

at the moment, nor are we likely to have, so this is not going to happen.

Today we had our first opera rehearsals in the new hall: the powers that be were listening from every part of the hall to check the acoustics and the ensemble between orchestra, chorus and soloists, but were unable to tell what sounded good and what did not. One thing is certain: the orchestra is hard to hear on the stage. Tcherepnin was conducting and will continue to do so until 'things settle down'. I am reconciled to this. I wandered about the stage and the auditorium, and chatted to the singers, mostly to Natashka Goncharova. Once again Umnova was not there. A rotten trick, Lidia Ivanovna! A whole week has passed since our delightful evening together at the student concert, and we have still not seen one another again. How can this be?

They also rehearsed Glazunov's *Cantata*, a work of stupendously little talent. The way he has borrowed the theme from Rubinstein's Fourth Concerto is just inept and stupid. However, the billing and cooing of the trumpets with the clarinets just before the entry of the chorus is not bad.[1] The choral section is quite short and rather good, it sounds truly triumphant. I would very much have liked to hear the Rubinstein theme ringing out in triumph on the brass against the background of the massed choir, that would really have been effective, but it loses its point when Glazunov presents it at the beginning of the work, so much so that one blushes for the *Cantata*'s composer.

As well as this theme, Glazunov has pinched so much for this piece that when I met Lyadov I told him that I very much approved of the concept underlying the *Cantata*: beginning it with a theme from the first Director of the Conservatoire, winding up with one from the latest holder of that office, and in between a theme from its first student. 'Whom do you mean?' asked Lyadov in surprise.

'Tchaikovsky. From *Romeo and Juliet*.'

A gesture of disbelief.

I: 'I mean, I don't suppose it was done deliberately . . .'

Lyadov (embarrassed): 'No doubt, no doubt . . .'

Things are cooking nicely with our orchestral enterprise; it is bound to be a financial success now the Jews have become involved. The idea of repeating the complete production has been rejected; instead it will be a concert, part of which I will obviously conduct. What about the soloists? Lazerson has been suggested as violinist. The pianist? The proposal is to have the same soloist as for the Jubilee concert, and it looks is though this will be Zakharov. No, *merci*, I don't want Zakharov at all, and therefore made the suggestion that we should have a pianist whose name will draw the crowds. This suggestion was taken up, so that put paid to Zakharov. All the organization is

---

1 This later gave me the idea of combining trumpets and clarinets in the sunrise section of the *Scythian Suite*. [Subsequent note by author.]

devolving on to a committee of three: the bassoonist and the leader of the orchestra, and I have been brought in as the third member. This is flattering, but exhausting.

4 December

In the evening I composed some of the Concerto, then Max came round, we chatted and wrote some of the 'Yellow Book'.

This morning saw a great triumph: Jurgenson has sent me his offer for the Sonata, offering me 200 roubles for it. I am delighted and cock-a-hoop. This was the figure that I told him I wanted when I sent him the Sonata, but I had been dreading the possibility that he might try to 'meet me halfway' by coming up with another figure, as he did with the *Toccata* (where he initially proposed 50 roubles instead of 100 and then, meeting me halfway, 75). Myaskovsky laughed, supposing that it had been the Sonata, rather than Jurgenson, coming to meet me halfway, but hurrah! I got exactly the amount I had demanded.

Today we were rehearsing *The Maid of Orleans* in the Great Hall. Once again Tcherepnin conducted, and I wandered about. No. 16A was very sweet, of course: Goncharova and I are as loving as anything when we are together (she says that her temperament has both sanguine and choleric elements), but the one I needed was 17A, and she was not there. She appeared later and sat together with a lady in a hat. I bowed impassively and decided to wait until she was alone. The lady in the hat did indeed take her departure quite soon, leaving Umnova on her own, and I made a dive towards her. I asked tenderly, 'Well, and how is our dear Lel today?'

'All r–i–i–ight,' she drawled. 'And you?'

'All r–i–i–ight,' I drawled back.

We then had a lovely conversation. I told her that I had been thinking about her often; she returned that on the contrary she was sure I had forgotten all about her. Unfortunately she was soon summoned to sing in the choir of angels.

After the rehearsal, the 'Committee of Management for the Concert and Ball', i.e. the bassoonist, the leader and I, had to tackle Glazunov about reserving the hall and other matters. I suggested that the bassoonist should do most of the talking, and I would confine myself to the occasional brief comment. While we were talking, 17A passed by, and I, without shifting my position, surreptitiously caught hold of her hand and gave it a squeeze. She responded likewise, and went off. Kruglovsky, who has a habit of hanging around when he is not needed and especially when I have something going with Umnova, noticed this and pestered me mercilessly afterwards. When the interview with Glazunov was over, very satisfactorily from our point of view, I swiftly excused myself to go and find 17A, with a view to asking her to come with me to that evening's student concert. On the way I was intercepted by one of the Conservatoire staff: 'Please go to be photographed with Anna Nikolayevna's class!'

I brushed him off and went on my way. I had already been photographed with Yesipova's class, but nothing worth having had come out. Now I could not be bothered and anyhow I had no time; I have no particular affection for the class and it was much more important to me to find Umnova. She was waiting for me and herself beckoned me over to relay the following conversation she had just had with Palechek on his way past:

'You'd better look out and sing well on Thursday.'

'Why? Whatever the outcome I shall not be singing in the show.'

'Wouldn't you like to know who is going to be singing in the Jubilee Concert?'

'Go on, then.'

'Umnenkaya!'[1]

But as he does not speak Russian all that well, he called her 'Umnen'kaya', as if he had a plum in his throat.

I congratulated her with all my heart, although naturally I was disappointed that she would now not be singing in the second performance and had accordingly been 'taken away from me'. Although she very much wanted to, she could not come to the student concert because today was the name-day for Varvara, and that meant she had to see her godmother. I jokingly complained that up until now she had been a sweet girl, but now that she had had such a success no one would be good enough for her and she would even not comply with requests from me.

I don't quite know why, but Umnova's success has put me into the most wonderful mood, and I am as sincerely pleased at her victory as if it had been my own.

When I saw Zakharov, I handed him back his handkerchief, which I happened to pick up from the floor of the cloakroom this morning. He was very surprised: 'Where did you get that?'

I, laughing: 'It's a memory of things past. Please take it, and bury the memory with it!'

We then talked for a while about current matters. Catching sight of Max I deliberately broke off our conversation in mid-word, said, 'Excuse me!' and quickly went over to Max. Max and I then visited Varvara Ossovskaya (because of the name-day) and then separated to go to our respective homes.

---

1 A pun on Umnova's name: 'Umnaya' means 'a clever woman' in Russian, the diminutive Umnenkaya means 'clever little girl', a sobriquet Prokofiev makes much use of for this particular object of his affections.

5 December

After dinner I went to the student concert. I accompanied the difficult duet from Ippolitov-Ivanov's *Asia*,[1] sung by Feinberg and Bobrovich. The music is terrible, but the performance was outstandingly good. Our piano class favourite, Raya Livshitz,[2] played Chopin's Third *Ballade* wonderfully, but the piece is third-rate rubbish. In general there was not much of interest in the programme, and Max and I would have been very bored if I had not had several accompanying jobs to do on stage and if we had not been so entertained by the spectacle of a morose-looking Boryusya, who obviously cannot reconcile himself to our inseparability.

We went home afterwards in a crowd; I with 16A, Max with his young sister and her two girl friends. Katya Schmidthof[3] finds 16A very pretty indeed, which pleased Max.

This morning I practised improving the fluidity of my gestures in front of the mirror while studying *Ivan The Terrible*. I conducted the rehearsal at one o'clock. Glazunov and Gabel came to watch, ostensibly to see whether I was up to the honour of appearing in the Jubilee Concert. I conducted with the whole of my trunk in Olympian repose, as directed by Tcherepnin, even though I managed to knock my hand against the desk hard enough to draw blood. The VIPs praised my plasticity, but Tcherepnin had a couple of comments to make on matters of technique.

There has been a suggestion that the Introduction to Ippolitov-Ivanov's opera *Ruth*[4] should be performed in addition to the other works in the Jubilee programme, and Tcherepnin wants to give this to Tsybin.[5] I have nothing against Tsybin, but it's annoying to have him stuffed into the Jubilee Concert.

News: the pianists who have Rubinstein's Piano Concerto No. 2 (?!), which is also in the programme, in their repertoire are Zelikman and Ariadna Nikolskaya. Ariadna is a celebrated beauty; I remember her appearance over the Conservatoire horizon two or three years ago, when she was still only a young girl. She industriously set about the conquest of the more interesting male students; she would have very much liked to add me to the list, but from stubborn contrariness I avoided being introduced to her and did not

---

1 Opera (1900) by Mikhail Ippolitov-Ivanov (1859–1935), based on a short story by Turgenev.
2 Raisa Livshitz (1898–?), piano student at the Conservatoire.
3 Max Schmidthof's sister.
4 Opera (1887) by Mikhail Ippolitov-Ivanov.
5 Vladimir Tsybin (1877–1949) trained as a flautist, had been principal flute in the Mariinsky Theatre, and in 1923 became Professor of Flute at the Petrograd Conservatoire, playing a leading role in establishing the Soviet school of flute playing. Also a composer, Tsybin and his singer wife founded in 1920 a charitable music academy for homeless children in the town of Pushkino, near Moscow.

bow to her, even though to all intents and purposes we had been introduced on two occasions.

Nowadays Nikolskaya is not much in evidence, preferring the company of the Corps of Marines and the Navy to that afforded by the Conservatoire. Last summer Max and I decided that there was no reason not to make the acquaintance of such an attractive young lady, the more so as her intellect and vivacity were very highly spoken of. Nevertheless, I did not want to be the first to make a move, and left it to chance. And now, suddenly, it appears that Nikolskaya may be performing in the Jubilee Concert! She will be at her apogee, and on a pedestal. The conductor is Tcherepnin. We shall see, this is all very interesting. I shall do all I can to avoid making her acquaintance, and it will make it all the more piquant that I cannot possibly avoid meeting her since after Tcherepnin I shall be the most prominent figure in the arena where she is now to appear.

After the orchestral rehearsal there was a piano rehearsal of the opera in the Great Hall, which I conducted. I hoped to see 17A, and in fact she turned up at the end of the rehearsal. I had a headache and was not feeling my best. I caught up with 17A downstairs, and passed on to her that Glazunov had been very complimentary about her, saying she was very graceful. She is terribly nervous at the prospect of having to sing with orchestra tomorrow for the first time.

When I ran off down the stairs, there at the bottom stood 9B with some friends from the General Subjects class, all shifting about humming and hawing in a vague kind of way. 'Go on, go on, don't be scared,' I heard one of them say, and a girl shyly approached me and offered me a ticket to a party. I said that I would take two in the first or second row. But first I need to get some money from Jurgenson.

I went home with my headache and with tears starting in my left eye. I slept for an hour, but the pain in my head did not go away. In the evening I went into the Yusupov Gardens, which have recently opened to the public. Although it is not yet freezing hard, I went skating. Now I am writing my diary; my headache is better.

Yesterday I played my cello *Ballade* with Abashidze.[1] He played like Ruzsky, that is to say he managed all the notes, but not very well. Once again I felt convinced that the cello sounds good and that the *Ballade* is a very fine piece.

This morning, while I was at work on the Piano Concerto, Mama said, 'How horrible that sounds, just as if you had no ear at all!'

My answer was to shut the door. She has no understanding of my music whatsoever.

The day before yesterday, talking to Max, there popped into my head the

---

1 A cello student at the Conservatoire.

idea of writing a humorous scherzo for four bassoons that could be played at a student concert. It could be very amusing!

Another fine idea would be to compose a 'Eulogy to Glazunov' for bass, timpani, two bassoons and double-bass, in which the bass would sing a doleful, funereal melody based on Glazunov's works, to the accompaniment of a theme from each work together with the original work from which the theme was stolen; the timpani meanwhile marking the divisions between one episode and the next with the same incredible obtuseness that distinguishes the conclusion of his *Jubilee Cantata*.

6 December

I stayed at home in the morning and learned the Tchaikovsky Concerto. In the afternoon there was a rehearsal of *The Snow Maiden* including 17A's debut with orchestra. She was in a complete panic and sang a few wrong notes, and some of her top notes were out of tune. This was partly a result of the stupid configuration of the new hall, whereby on the stage it is practically impossible to hear the orchestra, especially in piano passages. Generally Umnenkaya has a good voice that projects admirably from the stage, and as her appearance is radiantly graceful and really stands out from the crowd, she is well able to command the stage. When she had finished singing I thought I would not seek her out immediately, because our relationship has already been observed by many people who will seize on the slightest opportunity for malicious gossip. By the time *Snow Maiden* was over there was no longer any sign of Umnova.

Mme Tcherepnin[1] was at the rehearsal, and at the end of the act we both went back to see Tcherepnin at the same time. She said to him (referring to me), 'He's much better looking than he used to be.'

I: 'Thank you.'

She: 'How shall I put it? You have become more *sculpté*.'

I: 'That is due to the efforts of Nikolay Nikolayevich. He made me work so hard on making my gestures more plastic when I am conducting that I could not help becoming more *sculpté*!'

She: 'Kolechka, are you ever going to come home?'

He: 'No, no, no! Leave me alone!' (*Laughing*) 'Sergey Sergeyevich, do please take her away!'

From the rehearsal I went to the Ruzskys to celebrate Nikolay Pavlovich's name-day, where as usual there was a great crowd and a mountain of refreshments. They scolded me for forgetting them completely. Tanya tries to avoid noticing me, and I take my revenge by not saying goodbye to her when I leave.

---

1   Tcherepnin's wife was Marie Benois, the niece of the *Mir Isskustva* painter and stage designer Alexander Benois.

At home I discovered that Umnova had telephoned twice. Alas!! I waited impatiently for her to call again, which she did. She was in despair over her debut earlier, she would die, she would throw herself into the Fontanka. I tried to convince her that, on the contrary, she had sung extremely well, but she would have none of it and was in great distress. Please would I come round and console her? I said that I had promised to go skating today. We said goodbye until the following day.

I set off for the Yusupov Gardens. I adore skating and filling my lungs with fresh air, but today there was hardly anyone I knew there. When I got home I wrote Lidia Ivanovna a reassuring letter in which I did my best to convince her she had been a success. I am such an idiot not to have gone to her. She needed me today, needed me particularly, I was indispensable. But I failed to seize the moment, and now it has gone. Fool, fool, thrice-damned fool!

8 December

I did not write my diary yesterday. So that things do not get out of order, I will repair the omission now.

Friday

In the morning I practised the Tchaikinson[1] Concerto, and also worked on composing my own. The first movement promises to be excellent when I've finished it. Then I went to our rehearsal. Vocal training had just finished and everyone had been sent over to the Great Hall. There was a huge scrum of people, the kind of scrum I love. For some reason Yesipova was being extremely affable and talked to me for a long time. I could not see Umnova, but eventually she appeared, surrounded by so many friends and her teacher Aktseri that I could not get near her. Natasha Goncharova was as loving as could be, and we sat together on a sofa behind the columns. Her lips were rouged with lipstick which I made her wipe off.

Only towards the end of the rehearsal could I get to sit with 17A. I had not expected the poor girl to have been reduced to such a state by her debut performance yesterday. She is ready to abandon the Jubilee, the stage, the Conservatoire, everything. This was no affectation but true, unadulterated terror such as a child feels. All my exhortations came to naught against the impenetrable wall of her stage fright and the booing and catcalls of 'Disgraceful!' her imagination so vividly conjured up. All this was because of two or three notes that she sang slightly sharp. I accompanied her home and persuaded her to come to the student concert with me.

1 Tchaikovsky.

Correction: Nikolskaya is not playing in the Jubilee concert. There was a competition for this and she had to yield the palm to Zelikman. Ah, Ariadna, happiness was so nearly within your grasp! ...

The Rayevskys dined with us, and at eight o'clock Max called for me and we set off for the student concert. First on the bill was the gorgeous Ariadna, who having been eliminated from the Jubilee Concert was now playing her concerto at the student concert. At nine o'clock, as we had agreed, the delightful 'English Rose'[1] arrived, and we passed the whole evening together delightfully sitting in the balcony. No. 14A (Litvak) was also in the programme, and her playing finally put paid to the shaky fascination she had once exerted over me.

We next heard a throwback to my past, Elfrieda Hansen, who was excellent. Nikolskaya's playing was fine: Max said that during the interval everyone was commenting on her magnificent eyes and powerful fingers. He was disappointed that I had not been around in the interval to witness Nikolskaya continuing to bestow her attention on him despite being the centre of attraction. But I was up in the balcony happily flirting with 17A until half past eleven when I took her home, only to come back again to the concert to see whether Alpers might be playing. All of her saintly family was there, baffled by the lack of notice Max and I took of them. Alpers played well, a performance that augurs well for her future. When Hansen passed by I put my fingers together as though to applaud her for her performance, and was quite unprepared for the effect this produced: Hansen stopped, came up to me quickly, extended her hand, and said, 'How can this be? Are you actually applauding me, after two years of nothing but criticism? This is praise indeed – the greatest pleasure I could possibly have from this evening.'

I replied, 'I am merely returning to you some of the pleasure you gave me with your playing.'

Saturday

In the morning I worked at Tchaikin's Concerto to go some way towards justifying the good standing I seem to enjoy at the moment with Anna Nikolayevna. After that I improved the 'plasticity' of some of my gestures for *Ivan The Terrible*. At one o'clock I went to the Conservatoire for the rehearsal. But I was not on until half past three, so I filled in the intervening time wandering about with Max. No. 9B was sitting at a little table selling tickets for the party, but we were unable to buy any because Jurgenson is not sending any money until seven o'clock.

Our orchestral project has had to be postponed until January; something went wrong with the booking of the hall. Tcherepnin has gone back on his

---

[1] Another nickname for Lidia Umnova.

word and is not letting me have a single opera rehearsal in the current period. He says after Christmas, when preparations get under way for the second performance, I shall be master of all I survey, but for the time being it is not a good idea because the soloists should not have to face different interpretations from two different conductors. On top of that Gabel and Palechek are so on edge that to be anywhere in their vicinity is like sitting on a powder keg; they are liable to fly off the handle for no reason at all. I do not agree with him, but acquiesced with uncharacteristic meekness. Tsybin conducted the overture to *Ruth* and received an ovation from the orchestra. Why? *Ruth* is such a simple piece a dog could conduct it with its tail. My *Terrible* was on at half past three; it went just fine and Glazunov was pleased. Greatly daring, I asked him if he was happy with the adjustments he had wanted me to make to my conducting technique the last time he had seen me, which I said I had made efforts to absorb. He said he had already noted the improvements and that I had carried out all his recommendations. As in fact I remember nothing at all of what he told me, and am unaware of having taken any action in response, I am unclear as to what he can have observed.

I almost got as far as kissing Goncharova. She agrees with Mme Tcherepnin about how much better I look on the podium, and generally showered me with compliments.

Max came round in the evening. Tomorrow I shall drag him out somewhere, perhaps to Imatra. At eleven o'clock we went to the Warsaw Station to find out the times of trains, and as they seem to suit very well we shall go. I wrote a letter to Umnenkaya to tell her that there would no rehearsal on Monday but that there would be one on Tuesday. Her ordeal has been postponed by a day.

10 December

Yesterday morning I left the house at a quarter to nine and went to collect Max from 63 Nevsky Prospect, from where we went by taxi to the Finland Station. There was a good express train leaving at 9.45, and we sat in a comfortable restaurant car until Vyborg, getting out at Terioki to walk about the platform and bring back many memories for me. At Vyborg we changed trains and went on the branch line to Imatra where we arrived some time after two. We were instantly surrounded by a bunch of hotel agents, and the one to whose blandishments we yielded took us to some vile inn. To start with we went by sledge to Malaya[1] Imatra, about six versts away. In the city

---

1 There are two settlements, Bolshaya (Great) Imatra and Malaya (Small) Imatra. The waterfall on the river Vuoksa, part of the great system of lakes and rivers flowing into Lake Ladoga, is a famous tourist attraction.

it is thawing and everywhere is deep in mud, but here the snow is pure white and the air wonderful, although it was drizzling a bit and that spoilt the enjoyment. When our sledge had brought us to Malaya Imatra we discovered that to get to the ice-clad slopes one has to go on foot; this was not easy, but we had fun doing it. Both Imatras are interesting and beautiful rather than awe-inspiring, something like a mountain stream swollen after a downpour of rain.

Returning from Malaya Imatra soaked to the skin from the rain, we had dinner at our squalid hotel and wrote a quantity of postcards, nineteen in all. At six o'clock we returned to the station at Bolshaya Imatra to post our letters and to book our tickets for the return journey. Then we paid a visit to the Grand Hotel 'Cascades' for coffee and Benedictine (a rare pleasure) and to read the newspapers. At nine o'clock we went to view the Falls illuminated by floodlight, not a particularly impressive sight, and went for a walk along a deserted woodland path. We had supper at the 'Cascades' and at midnight caught the direct sleeper back to Petersburg.

This excursion gave me a great deal of pleasure and I found it very refreshing after the intense activity of the Conservatoire. I love the peace and wonderful air of Imatra, and I liked the 'Cascades' Hotel as well. After the second Jubilee Concert performance, when I shall probably be very tired, I shall come here for a week and finish my Concerto.

Will it ever be finished? Or shall I have expired from boredom first?

We got back at nine o'clock this morning. I changed my clothes, practised the piano and then went to the rehearsal. *Terrible* is going very well indeed, and Tcherepnin is in ecstasy(!). Glazunov is also being very friendly; I have clearly made my peace with the directorate. I made two innovations in *Terrible*: (1) I took the opening considerably faster; (2) in the middle tuttis there were long sections that I did not conduct at all, merely giving a strong downbeat from time to time, mostly on the general crotchet rests before the syncopations. Both ideas were approved.

Nikolayev's student Zelikman played Rubinstein's Second Piano Concerto splendidly (the piece itself is not bad either). He will be my rival at next year's graduation. I feel the impulse to practise more growing ever stronger. Tsybin completely fell apart in *Ruth*.

While I was talking to Natasha today, up came Umnenkaya, but by the time our conversation was over she had vanished. I found her drinking tea near the buffet, but she was surrounded by a group of girls I did not know, so I did not manage to have a proper talk with her. She looks quite green with anxiety about her forthcoming performance. She does not want to sing in the Jubilee Concert. I told her if she did not, I would break off relations with her.

Tcherepnin mentioned to me his idea, since we have a decent orchestra at the moment, of arranging a concert in the latter half of the season featuring new composers such as Wagner, Brahms and similar. 'No Russian composers, just European ones.'

'Thus placing Russia firmly in Asia,' I said, somewhat baffled by this persecution of Russian composers. I had been counting on a chance to present my First Piano Concerto in the second half of the season. 'Wouldn't it be good to do Scriabin's First Symphony, seeing that we have a chorus available!'

Tcherepnin mumbled something vaguely negative in reply, but I was very taken with the idea of Scriabin No. 1, and will revert to the subject later.

Tcherepnin has formed the conclusion that my musical *Weltanschauung* is not decadent at all but classical: I am attracted by precision in thematic material, clarity of exposition and integration of form. This is true.

11 December

Yesterday evening I went with Max to Scriabin's concert. Absurd as it may seem, I have not been to a single concert so far this season; the Scriabin concert is literally the first I have been to. I did not think much of the 24 Preludes, Op. 11, but I was fascinated by the Seventh Sonata. The sonata is deeply interesting, it has more substantial material than the Fifth, not frightening and ultimately without aggression. A defect is that there is quite a lot of rehashing of material from earlier opuses. I was most interested to hear his account of the *Poème satanique*[1] which was masterly except for those passages that call for powerful sound and grandeur.

Half of the audience could not understand the sonata at all; the other half was making a great effort to understand it.

At the concert I met Boris Petrovich Jurgenson at the concert. He was very nice. He said that each time we met I seemed younger to him.

'So that soon I shall turn into a little boy again?'

'No. But your compositions are somehow more profound than seems possible from someone of your age, and that is why whenever I meet you I am astonished at your youth.'

When I got home I learnt that Umnova had telephoned me. Her family has finally had a telephone installed, and she wanted to let me know the number. It was eleven o'clock in the evening, but I called her back right away.

Umnenkaya was in a state of terminal panic about tomorrow's performance, could not sleep, and would go straight out to Imatra (in the postcard I had sent her from there I had said it was an ideal place to commit suicide: quick, effective, fashionable and painless). On the subject of my letters: 'Oh, Sergey Sergeyevich, if you only knew how nice it is to get your letters every morning!'

---

1 *Poème satanique*, Op. 36 (1903).

This morning I practised Tchaikovsky, and in the afternoon went to rehearsal. On entering the hall I heard the start of the third act of *The Snow Maiden*. Umnova was already on stage and singing in the first ensemble. She appeared graceful, but distraught. I wished I had come earlier so that I could have helped her to calm down.

'Max, do something to make her see me.'

'Go and sit in the front row.'

I went down and leaned over the rail towards Tcherepnin as if to ask him something, and stayed there. Umnenkaya did see me then. She sang Lel's aria accurately, in tune, but her fright made her sing very timidly. The other Lel was then brought on, but she made a botch of the whole aria, singing half a tone sharp. I went up to Gabel and said with a smile, 'Stanislav Ivanovich, she sounds like a D flat clarinet!'

'You think the first one was better?'

'No comparison. Twenty times better. She is just terribly nervous, but that will pass.'

'Yes, yes, that's what we'll do.'

And indeed, the rival was soon eliminated and Umnova restored.

12 December

I slept late, then practised the Tchaikovsky and also worked on the new sketches I had made for my Concerto. In form and construction my Second Piano Concerto is going to be a consummate piece of work.

In the afternoon, another rehearsal for the Jubilee Concert. We did not rehearse *Ivan The Terrible* because I had told Tcherepnin it was in good shape, and in any case other pieces were in much less satisfactory condition and therefore should have the time devoted to them.

Zakharov played the Glazunov Concerto well; I would give him a 4 or even a 5. But the concerto is written in such a way that it the pianist has very little opportunity to shine in the first movement (the only one the programme had time for). However, this suits Boryusya's playing. Zelikman is riding high; Polyakin is playing magnificently. The teaching staff was wheeled out for Glazunov's *Cantata* (Auer led the orchestra, Gabel was principal double-bass, Ferni-Giraldoni,[1] disintegrating from decrepitude, was the soprano soloist, and so on). This medley of venerable talents resulted in an atrocious mess, and the unfortunate luminaries were punished with a rehearsal lasting over an hour.

As had by now become our custom I met Umnenkaya at the end of the

---

1 Carolina Ferni-Giraldoni (1839–1923), Italian prima donna with a distinguished career at La Scala (Norma, Rossini's Desdemona). She also had a solo career as a violinist.

rehearsal; we talked – not for long, no more than ten minutes, but as always delightfully. A few rows away sat a morose-looking Boryusya, on his own. I thought, he really should not be alone while he has performances coming up.

On my way home I went into the Yusupov Garden to skate for half an hour. In the evening we were visited by Balin, from Alfyorov's office. We talked about the stock exchange. He advises me to make a complaint about the fraudulently inflated price I had to pay for the Iron-Cement shares, which he thinks I would be able to prove. That would get me 500 roubles back.

13 December

During my piano practice in the morning I was satisfied that I have got the second and third movements of the Tchaikovsky Concerto to a good state, but in the afternoon lesson with Yesipova they did not go so well. I am prone to lose confidence in her presence, and when that happens everything collapses. The lesson was at her house; after the lesson Anna Nikolayevna offered a cup of tea. I declined, pleading the need to attend a rehearsal and asking for permission to visit her over Christmas.

The rehearsal was in costume. Backstage all was gaiety; everybody knew everyone else but could not recognize them, just like at a fancy dress party. Lel was enchanting: a slim, elegant boy, perfect for the part. He[1] was less nervous and sang rather better, but still not especially well. Feinberg (Snow Maiden), Molchanov (Thibaut) and Levitan (Bertrand) were all excellent, the last named being my favourite on account of his impassioned performing style, dramatic gifts and outstanding voice.

I spent a whole hour sitting with Umnenkaya. Needless to say our *tête-à-tête* was discovered by Kruglovsky, who proceeded to bore us witless. Umnenkaya was bewitching, but why did she not say a word about my letter? I had sent her one yesterday evening which, referring to her gloomy intention of dying, included a humorous account of her funeral rites. Perhaps, I wrote, as she lay in her coffin I would place a kiss on her 'cold, decomposing forehead' in the final moments before it was closed?

Marusya Pavlova is dancing a Bacchante in the 'Dance of the Skomorokhs'[2] which for some reason has been choreographed as a kind of Bacchanalia. Boryusya's eyes followed her every movement, and the instant the

---

1 Meaning 'she' of course: Lel is a breeches part.
2 The skomorokhs, the Slav equivalent of the harlequinade or commedia dell'arte, were troupes of wandering players, tumblers, minstrels and jesters, and a feature of Russian life from the twelfth to the seventeenth centuries. Their music was played on a variety of traditional instruments such as the domra, the balalaika, the gusli (a form of psaltery), the gudok (a kind of rebeck), bagpipes, tambourines, etc. Banned as blasphemous by the Russian Orthodox Church towards the end of the seventeenth century, their art gradually died out.

dance ended he leapt from his place, but the entire corps de ballet was summoned into the Small Hall to go through their steps. I was asked to play the piano for them, while Boryusya, having missed Pavlova, went home.

Glazunov is suffering from an abscess in his ear and a burst eardrum. It looks as though he will not be able to conduct, and Tcherepnin is taking over from him. It will be recorded in the history of music that the composer of the *Cantata* managed to burst his own tympanum. A fitting and highly significant verdict on the work.

Tcherepnin revealed that Glazunov had been very complimentary about my conducting of *Ivan The Terrible* and my technique. I said that no doubt this was because I had taken so much to heart his comments on my gestures(!). Tcherepnin laughed heartily. He is no lover of Glazunov as a composer and despises him as a conductor.

I stayed at home in the evening, and Max came round.

15 December

I rose late and did little during the morning. I looked through the score of *Terrible* and then went to the rehearsal for our concert. There was a noisy hubbub in the Conservatoire and the hall was full to capacity, in short the Conservatoire was present *in corpore*, the way I like it best. The rehearsal started with *Terrible*; I went on the platform (that is to say the stage; there being no platform the orchestra had been set out on the stage, which made it sound dreadful), but some rearrangement of the desks was going on, so I sat waiting on the lid of the piano with my back to the hall, a pose in which I rather fancied myself. I was quite confident about *Terrible*, and was not nervous in the slightest. It did indeed go well. Tcherepnin praised me for my 'well-thought-out' interpretation and then took over for the rest of the programme, my part being thus over. The *Capriccio*[1] sounded dull in this hall. Zelikman played decently, and Zakharov, except for his opening chord, very well indeed, better than I had expected and without any of his off-putting Zakharovesque tricks. Max and I sat up on the top balcony to listen.

In the interval Tonya Rudavskaya buttonholed me, looking not quite as nice as she had before, but attractive all the same. We went to drink some milk and spent the interval happily together. After the Glazunov Concerto (conducted after all by the composer) I went up to Zakharov's family and complimented them on his performance. I did not speak to Zakharov himself, even though he told me how excellent *Ivan The Terrible* had been. I wanted to see 17A, although it was a problem to find her in such a crowd. When those singing in the *Cantata* were called to the stage, I scanned the

---

1   Rimsky-Korsakov's *Spanish Caprice.*

stream of people pouring on to the stage from my vantage point in the balcony, but still could not find her. Max went off to a ball in Kronstadt, so I descended to the stalls, where I saw Zakharov sitting at the far end of the row next to Rudavskaya; they were chatting amiably.

At that moment Tcherepnin walked through the hall; I ran after him and caught up with him just at the moment when he was passing Zakharov and Rudavskaya, but I did not look at them and went out of the hall talking to Tcherepnin. I went on to the stage in the hope of finding Umnova, but could not see her anywhere. But she was singing in the chorus, and so once the chorus had finished all their rehearsals we finally got together and took ourselves off to the balcony for the remainder of the rehearsal. She had received my letter and had been amused by it.

Many people complimented me on *Ivan The Terrible*, including Nelli Frantsis, who air-clapped me from a distance as I had done to Frieda Hansen. I went up to talk to her, and we chatted about nothing in particular for a while.

As we parted, she said, 'Thank you!'

'What for?!'

'For coming and talking to me!' (Meaning, I suppose, appreciation of the honour done to a lowly General Subjects student when so elevated a personage as a conductor condescends to bestow some portion of his attention on her.)

We had guests in the evening, three tables of vint, including a clutch of Rayevskys (six), Myaskovsky, Korsak, Gadlevich (i.e. Godlevsky) and Mme Yablonskaya. Since this was the first appearance in our home of Shurik's new wife,[1] we had champagne to welcome her officially into the family circle and to accompany the ritual of *Bruderschaft*. I played vint, and enjoyed it.

Myaskovsky is receiving more and more invitations to write for the press, among them requests for articles on Stravinsky and Prokofiev. We disagreed about whether compositions should be given opus numbers. I said I thought it was essential, but he is resistant to the idea of doing so for his works. After three glasses of champagne we decided that we would wait another year, until 1914, to drink to our own intimate friendship, when we would go through the *Bruderschaft* ritual and become 'brothers'.

16 December

As it had been half past three before I got to bed, I slept until eleven. At one o'clock Mama and I went to the Conservatoire for the general rehearsal of our operas. Having seated Mama in the balcony with V. O. Yablonskaya, I went back down and after half an hour found my dear Lel, looking utterly ravishing. When the *Snow Maiden* rehearsal began I sat in the front row.

---

1 Alexander Rayevsky, Prokofiev's cousin, had married Nadezhda Meyendorf.

Umnova sang Lel's aria neither badly nor well, but Tcherepnin made her do it again and this time it was not bad at all. In the final analysis Umnenkaya does not have a particularly big voice, but the timbre is good. Her agitation was such that it transmitted itself even to me; anxiety on behalf of others, however slight, is a greater torment than for oneself. All around I heard people whispering how lovely she looked.

I met Umnenkaya towards the end of the interval. As soon as she saw me she broke off the conversation she was having and wafted over to me to ask me what I thought of her performance today. Again she was in despair; I reassured her, while Steinberg, Gladkaya and Kedrov all told her to her face how good they thought she had been. After this came the rehearsal for *The Maid of Orleans*.

Lintvaryova[1] gave me the glowing review Karatygin had written in *Apollon* of my D flat major Concerto. In return she wanted me to let her read through the manuscript of the Concerto, which I did.

Vera Alpers greeted me coldly, saying she was surprised that I do not always acknowledge her or bow to her, and that she would like an explanation.

17 December

On Sunday Max came and the three of us – with Mama – went off about one o'clock to the launch ceremony of the Conservatoire's Jubilee. The stage, decked out in green cloth, looked very smart. At the front of the stage a table stretched right the way across, and behind it sat the most highly esteemed professor and members of the directorate. Behind them was the orchestra, and further back still an enormous choir dressed in white. The scene was ablaze with light, greenery, palms, flags and tricolour banners. The elegant audience was resplendent in white gowns and evening dress.

The proceedings began with a telegram from the Tsar and a series of tedious speeches, and then Glazunov's *Cantata*, played twice (not that bad, in the end). Then distinguished visitors (about eighty of them), telegrams and S. Orlov's[2] *March*, which failed to make much of an impression. The story behind this *March* is that a competition to write it was announced to students in the spring and aroused a good deal of interest. I myself considered writing one but lost interest when I realized the lengths I would have to go to in order to please the Conservatoire's directorate. In the autumn three of the marches were presented for consideration. One showed no talent at all, one was illiterate, and the third, a little less bad, was Orlov's. Glazunov rewrote it and re-orchestrated it, and that is the story of Orlov's *March*.

---

1 Voida Lintvarova, a fellow student in Anna Yesipova's class.
2 A student at the Conservatoire.

As an event, the celebration ceremony was interesting and quite fun. Jurgenson, Tcherepnin and I had quite a long conversation during which Tcherepnin said nice things about me. Jurgenson spoke about S. I. Taneyev: 'One of the most touching of our great musical figures, as blameless as a young maiden from the day of his birth until the present day.'

I saw Khessin, who always says he is very interested in my compositions but never has the time to look at them. He promised to call on me.

While the ceremony was in progress I came up to the balcony several times to see Mama and Max; from there I could see the chorus through the binoculars and with some difficulty made out 17A. She and I met during the interval, but the delightful Sakhnovsky, a friend of Nikolayev's, attached himself to us and so persistently and blatantly ogled Umnova that I could bear it no longer and removed myself to go and talk to Jurgenson. While I was putting on my coat to go home at the end of the ceremony I spotted 17A in the crush, but did not feel like approaching her.

At home I did not trouble to take off my tails because it would soon be time to go back for the concert. I was not nervous; naturally my mood was a little elevated but it would not be right to describe it as nervousness. I had a quick look through the score of *Terrible*, but this was not really necessary as I knew it backwards. I practised bowing from the stage in front of the mirror, then called for a taxi and Mama and I set off for the concert. I was on first. Tcherepnin was walking round all the orchestra desks getting the instruments to tune with an enormous 'Viennese' tuning fork. After a telegram from the Princess[1] had been read out, I went on stage, calm and with a sense of enjoyment. The performance of *Terrible* was better than at any of the preceding rehearsals. I was universally considered to have conducted well; only Khessin was heard to say that after all I was a composer, not a conductor. I was satisfied that I had done the best I could. There was just one place where I nearly slipped up, and it was not a difficult passage at all: I somehow got it into my head that the orchestra was playing the first beat of the bar when I was indicating the second beat, so I altered the direction of my baton but immediately realized that this was not correct and now I was out. Just at this point there was a tutti entry, so I gave a mighty downbeat in tempo, and everything righted itself. The rhythm at this point was so strongly accented that the orchestra hardly noticed my mistake, but it threw me into a complete panic. However, I quickly pulled myself together and the performance continued without incident. The applause was cordial but not prolonged, the work itself being of such excruciating tediousness. Thus concluded my part in the Jubilee Concert of the Conservatoire.

I went out into the foyer and was walking up and down in order to cool

---

1 The Grand Duchess Princess Yelena Georgiyevna of Sachsen-Altenberg, the Conservatoire's royal patron.

down after conducting when I came across Zakharov, also pacing up and down in anticipation of his turn in the spotlight. He suggested that we go to the buffet to have some lemonade, so we went and sat at a little table in the deserted buffet. It felt strange to be sitting together drinking lemonade after a year and a half of being estranged. We talked about this and that, mostly the Jubilee celebrations, but our conversation, which was carried on more by me than by him, was inevitably marked by a certain constraint and awkwardness. I went to pay for the drinks; he did not want me to treat him and pulled out some coins from his pocket, but I did not take them and they were left lying on the table.

Then I went upstairs to join Mama and Max, aware that Umnova would be sitting not far away. There was not a seat to be had on the balcony, so I stood in the gangway scanning the audience for a sign of Umnenkaya. Suddenly someone grabbed my hand and I heard 'Congratulations!' – it turned out that I was standing right next to her seat. I remained there waiting for the piece to come to an end, when Kruglovsky suddenly appeared out of nowhere and, seeing us together, mumbled something ironic. This riled me, and as soon as the music stopped I left and returned to my seat.

Tsybin gave *Ruth* a decent performance that was well received out of respect for its routinely workmanlike composer. Tsybin's conducting style is fluent but unnecessarily expansive. Zakharov played extremely well. For the last work in the programme, the *Capriccio*, I went upstairs to the balcony.

Following the concert I repaired to the Small Hall, where the professors, distinguished guests, soloists from the concert and other representatives of the musical world had been invited to a banquet. The hall had been transformed, but very tastefully so, and looked quite different from its normal self. Nikolay Ruzsky asked me to sit at his table, where there were already Gabel, Mme Gabel and some other people of no particular note. But altogether it was a lively and interesting occasion. People went from table to table laughing and clinking glasses. Gelever[1] said warm words about my compositions, to which Ruzsky added that the pianist Romanovsky[2] had also been excited by them. I was home soon after two o'clock.

On the morning of the 17th I went to the morning chamber music concert, although it promised little of interest. Golubovskaya played delicately. Tilichka Hansen[3] is very decorative, and her hands are bewitchingly graceful in play. Zakharov was sticking like glue to both the Hansen sisters, but I declined to bow to Frieda who seemed very much put out by this.

The opera performances took place that evening. Although I was not

---

1 P. Gelever, a Professor of Piano at the St Petersburg Conservatoire.
2 Gavriil Romanovsky (1873–1941), distinguished pianist, student of Anna Yesipova and a noted interpreter of Scriabin's piano works.
3 Cecilia Hansen (1897–1989), celebrated violinist, sister of Elfrieda Hansen, later the wife of Boris Zakharov.

involved this time, the fact that next time I would be playing a leading part aroused my liveliest interest. *Maccabaeus* went well on the whole; there was the occasional incident, but nothing developed into a major calamity. Andrienko was good; Arakina also but less so than usual. Kruglovsky was good, Rapp-Kleze awful. The chorus sang well and the orchestra managed all right without the first trumpet.

I went backstage after *Maccabaeus* and looked around in search of Lel. Suddenly I heard Palechek: 'Quick, come over here to this side of the stage!' I went over, but could not understand why he had summoned me there. Lel's dressing room was there, but surely that could not be the reason?! I caught sight of Lel in the distance, peeping round the door.

Waiting in the wings just before the start of *The Snow Maiden*, I found Umnenkaya already in her position for the 'Khorovod'.[1] She was nervous and smiled guiltily. I spoke a few words to her, shook her hand and then left, as the action was about to begin.

N. P. Ruzsky had a seat for me next to his in the third row. He questioned me about the cast, particularly about Umnova, of whom he had heard from somewhere. She sang sharp in her first stanza, but the second and third were absolutely fine. Her success was great, and she could have sung an encore, which would have made it even better. Feinberg scaled the heights as the Snow Maiden.

At the end of the interval Glazunov addressed the audience from the stage, thanking all those who had taken part in the celebrations: the highly esteemed organizers Osip Osipovich,[2] Stanislav Ivanovich,[3] Nikolay Nikolayevich,[4] and the students 'beginning with the greatly talented conductors, soloists, chorus, orchestra and ballet . . .' Greatly talented conductors!! Oho, do you mean Tsybin and me? Bravo, Sasha,[5] just carry on like that!

During *The Maid of Orleans* I either wandered round the foyer with Max or prowled backstage lying vainly in wait for 17A. The opera came to an end to the traditional ovations for Glazunov, Gabel, Palechek, Tcherepnin, more vociferous this time than ever before. This brought to an end the celebrations: a huge crowd of students shouting 'Slava!'[6] carrying Palechek shoulder-high and behind him, raised up with considerable difficulty, Glazunov.

I searched for a long time for 'Glupenkaya'[7] to take her to the banquet at the 'Cuba' restaurant where about a hundred and fifty people were going,

1 Round Dance.
2 Palechek.
3 Gabel.
4 Tcherepnin.
5 Sasha is the usual short name for Alexander, Glazunov's first name.
6 Literally 'Glory!' – the conventional acclamation of a hero or victor.
7 Another nickname for Lidia Umnova based on the meaning of her surname ('clever'): as Umnenkaya means 'the clever one', 'Glupenkaya' means 'the stupid one'.

more or less the same people as the previous day, except that today one had to pay for one's meal. Zakharov went off arm in arm with Pavlova; I presumed he had chosen her as his supper companion, which made me want all the more to take my 17A along. But she was nowhere to be found, so I went alone.

It was the first time I had been to a dinner like this in a restaurant. Nikolay Pavlovich again had me sit at his table, but I stayed only a couple of minutes as when we went into another room to get our savouries, Tcherepnin accosted me: 'Seryozhenka, we'll sit together, won't we?'

I was delighted to agree, and we went off together to the other end of the hall. We had a good talk about the opera performances that had just taken place, about music generally, and other things as well, including a hint that when I had completed my Conservatoire training he would be able to secure some interesting conducting opportunities for me. The toasts began, and we circulated, clinking glasses with all and sundry. I moved to the next table, where Mme Benois[1] was sitting. Zakharov was there as well; he had arrived late, without Pavlova. Scarcely had I left that table to move on when he called out, 'Seryozha... Seryozha!'

I turned round to see that he was holding his glass aloft in an invitation to clink. From where I was standing I also raised my glass and waggling it slightly in the air, immediately walked off towards Ruzsky at the other end of the room. 'Who's this fellow suddenly turning up, then? I don't know who you are, move along please!' I unleashed a stream of apologies, explaining that I had been bidden by my professor to sit with him and could not refuse. Then I went back to look for Zakharov, but by that time he had gone off somewhere. I regretted this.

After several toasts, Glazunov raised his glass to the students and the others who had taken part in the celebration, then for some reason went specially to clink with Berlin, one of the female students, presumably because she is very pretty. He then came up to me, and asked, 'Where is Zakharov?' Zakharov was found. Clinking glasses with him, I smiled: 'Well, it seems we are under orders to drink to our respective healths!'

After a little more small talk he invited me to sit down at the now empty table. I lit a cigarette, and we started. It was a long talk, all about the 'abnormal' relations I had recently instigated. It is not easy to give a coherent account of what was said, as the conversation proceeded in a rather disjointed manner. Zakharov confessed to having wanted a serious talk for some time, and it was obvious that he had been giving our relationship a lot of thought, had studied it from all angles, reached several very wise conclusions and formulated a plan designed to achieve a specific objective. I on the other

---

1 The first wife of Alexander Benois, and the mother of his children, was the painter Anna Karlovna Kind (1869–1952). This was his second wife.

hand was talking for the sake of talking; I had no plan and no objective in view. I was not even sure what tone I should adopt, but I was extremely curious to see how the interview would develop, and could not help being aware of keenly enjoying the process. Never in my life having smoked before, as I sucked away at papirosa[1] after papirosa my head began to swim from that and from all the wine I had drunk, but the gist of our discussion was perfectly clear.

Zakharov first asked what had been the cause of my abruptly breaking off our relationship. I replied that the actual cause was entirely trivial, but the cup had been so full that the smallest drop made it spill over.

'But it would still be interesting to know what that drop was?'

'The same as all the other drops that filled the cup.'

Zakharov: 'I have never said anything bad of you, but I know that you have often spoken ill of me in front of people who know me. But surely, if they know me, then there was no point in abusing me, was there? You would not be able to blacken me in their eyes.'

'I don't deny that I have spoken badly of you, but it was never my intention to harm your reputation.'

Zakharov: 'I consider you to be an incredibly talented and very clever person . . . you have a fine mind, but in truth you are still just a child . . . a child! You must agree that you are still a child!'

'Agreed. I am much younger than my years, and glad of it.' (*Laughing*) 'I even look young for my age!'

'Well preserved,' smiled Zakharov, using a phrase usually said about old men.

Later he said, 'The way I see it, your initial impression of me was one that did not correspond with reality. When you got to know me better you found I was not precisely as you had imagined, and that caused you to be disappointed.'

'The image I formed of you was as a seed-bed with lovely flowers, beneath which were fresh green leaves, and beneath them the earth – but when I dug deep down into this earth I found dung.'[2]

'You always did have a gift for disagreeable imagery! But now I want very much to put an end to the unprecedented relations that have arisen between us, and if the friendship that once existed is no longer possible between us, at least let us have the appearance of normal relations that two musicians would have with one another. As a musician I rate you extraordinarily highly,

---

1 The traditional Russian cigarette, which has a cardboard tube between the smoker's lips and the tobacco.
2 A Russian would detect a clear additional nuance in the above exchange, in which Zakharov continues to use the intimate form of address as between family or close friends, whereas the author has abandoned it and reverted to the formal second person plural.

I have the highest opinion of you as a composer; as a conductor you are not very gifted, neither will you ever amount to much as a pianist, but you will be a great composer. I believe that now you similarly look on me as a true musician. Before, you did not do so, and at that time you were right, but I am not now as I was. Surely you do regard me as a musician?'

'Well yes . . . I'd put you about 4, I suppose . . .'

'All right, a 4 mark, so be it.'

At the same time as aiming at complete honesty, I was also seeking a way of encouraging him: 'You sometimes have very perceptive judgements, for instance you once wrote of Rachmaninov's symphony that it was like a long corridor with every now and again windows opening out on to a wide vista.'

'Well, yes, but I'm not speaking of letters just now. Your letters, for example, have everything very deliberately thought out, you have every telling expression off by heart! But now let us drink to our new relationship, even if it is only on the surface, because I tell you, I cannot continue as we are.'

'All right, but you cannot alter the reality of the position which is, to speak allegorically, that I left you to pass into another room, and now having closed a glass door behind me it is only through that door that I can look at you.'

At this moment Tcherepnin passed by. I pulled out my watch and saw that it was twenty to four in the morning. 'Nikolay Nikolayevich, what about going on to the "Donon"?'

'Yes, yes, let's go!' – and saying goodbye to Zakharov we went to the restaurant.

Tcherepnin was tipsy, but very good company. Quite a crowd of people had said they were going on to eat at the 'Donon', mostly people from the opera production. Initially I had not been sure where would be the best place to go for supper; having perused the list of 'Donon' diners beforehand and not finding any names that attracted me, I had decided on balance it would be better to go to the 'Cuba'. But now at the 'Donon' we – that is to say mainly Nikolay Nikolayevich – were greeted with delighted shrieks of 'Hurrah' and plied with champagne, and Tcherepnin was urged to make a toast. Everyone gathered round and silence fell. 'To the health of young talent,' he said . . . and crash!! on the final syllable dashed his champagne glass to the floor.

The effect was tremendous. The evening continued with Spanish piano music and dancing and general uproar. Gauk[1] draped himself round the shoulders of an extremely *décolletée* lady; timid Solovyov smiled his baffled-looking smile; Kruglovsky and Bobrovich were in their element. It was the

---

1 Alexander Gauk (1893–1963) became one of the Soviet Union's leading conductors, holding a range of distinguished musical directorships including the Moscow Bolshoy Radio Orchestra and the USSR State Symphony Orchestra, whose first principal conductor he was. An outstanding teacher, he numbered among his students Yegveny Mravinsky, Alexander Melik-Pashayev and Yevgeny Svetlanov.

first time I had been in anything like this sort of situation, and I observed the scene with great curiosity. Not that I was merely a passive onlooker: I threw myself into the gay spirit of the evening and even danced, but I could see that this was not the life for me, not my style, not my element, and after a little more than half an hour I went home after an unsuccessful attempt to drag Tcherepnin away with me – he, on the contrary, was well away with the drink and having the time of his life.

19 December

Yesterday I awoke at eleven o'clock, and in spite of such a short night and the amount I had drunk the night before, felt wonderfully well. All work at the Conservatoire had finished for the term, I was a free man and could settle down to my Concerto. That afternoon Max and I strolled along Nevsky Prospect. We went into a photographer's studio and I told him everything about the previous evening, leaving out only a few details of my conversation with Zakharov. I bought a copy of Tcherepnin's concerto. While we were at supper Tcherepnin had told me it was one of his favourite children, but for some reason nobody is interested in it. His muse is not at all original, but everything he composes is interesting and sounds beautiful. I was very interested to have the score of the concerto, especially as I had heard it five years ago and had not thought much of it then.

In the evening I went skating. Although there was music and a lot of people, the only person I knew there was Borya Alpers, who demanded an explanation from me. What on earth is all this about? Every evening I seem to be faced with nothing but 'explanations' – last night Zakharov, and before that Mme Ozarovskaya.[1] I am very fond of Borya, a schoolboy who rather charmingly affects the most stylish externals of good form. This evening his preoccupation with good form was seriously to the fore, the heart of the matter being the offhand way I am supposed to have acted towards his family on the evening of the student concert at which his brother had performed (I attempted to persuade him otherwise on this score), and towards his sister (I did not bother arguing this charge). As is my wont, instead of defending myself I attempted to muddle the issue while at the same time making it clear what a very nice young chap I think he is. It ended by the young man losing his temper, turning his back on me and skating off.

This morning I slept like a log until half past twelve. From tomorrow I'm going to start getting up early, otherwise I shall sleep right through Christmas and not get my Concerto written.

---

1   The Ozarovskys were friends of the influential composer and critic Vyacheslav Karatygin (1875–1925), one of the first to herald and promote Prokofiev's genius.

In the afternoon Mama and I visited Papa's grave at the cemetery. I then went into the Conservatoire to pick up the scores of the operas; I want to look through them from time to time to keep my memory of them fresh in view of the forthcoming performance. If there is anything I fear about this concert, it is its sheer length: I could get tired and lose concentration. The Conservatoire was deserted.

I wrote a reply to Calvocoressi in Paris. He is proposing to perform my D flat Concerto in Paris, and wants the score. Having checked right through it and made a few corrections, I have sent it off for copying and will send it to him as soon as I get the copies back. To have the Concerto performed in Paris is very flattering, but I would much prefer it to be heard in Piter.

This evening I am going to Umnenkaya's house, an invitation to which I am greatly looking forward. She telephoned me yesterday expressing surprise that I had not come backstage to see her after her performance, to which I replied that I had done little else but look for her everywhere. She had not been allowed to go to the dinner, and much regretted this, because it meant that for her the celebration had felt somehow unfinished.

20 December

It was very nice at Umnenkaya's. The family lives in patriarchal style, with elder married sisters and a Papa of mercantile demeanour, *un peu style* Zakharov *père*. They are clearly well off, but Umnenkaya herself is extremely sweet and the sisters seemed nice as well. But seeing Ivan Ivanovich side by side with Lidochka one would be hard put to it to guess that she was his daughter. All the newspapers gave Umnenkaya a good review, so she flitted about happily, all trace of her former terror gone.

I still slept until eleven this morning, but did get some work done on the Concerto. In the afternoon I went into the Conservatoire, where we were all presented with Jubilee badges, not terribly pretty, but acceptable. I saw Umnenkaya, but sadly only a glimpse, because Tcherepnin got in the way with his final pre-Christmas lesson. He had some important information to impart, though. First, there are to be two performances, on 20 and 27 January – this will be excellent practice for me. Secondly, the opera for next semester will be *The Stone Guest*.[1] I don't know this opera, but look forward to it with the greatest interest. Thirdly, as well as *Guest* the programme will include excerpts from *Rigoletto*[2] and *The Queen of Spades*[3] to piano accompaniment. *Rigoletto* has been allocated to Tsybin, and *The Queen of Spades* to

---

1 Opera composed in 1872 by Alexander Dargomyzhsky.
2 Opera (1851) by Giuseppe Verdi.
3 Opera (1890) by Tchaikovsky.

me. Tsybin's assistants will be Kreisler and the two Solovyovs, while I shall have Skorunsky and Dranishnikov.[1] Generally, it is accepted that *The Queen of Spades* is a more serious proposition than *Rigoletto*, and the more experienced conductors have been allocated to it. As far as the symphony concert is concerned, it is still up in the air.

I shall have to study all this music, not to mention the classical works for the small orchestra, over the Christmas holiday. But the most important thing is to conduct well on 20 January.

'Get all three scores and swallow them with lots of butter!' was Tcherepnin's advice. And as well as garnishing them thus he recommended practising conducting all three of them straight through one after the other, as training for stamina. I bade farewell to Tcherepnin for the holidays, and Gabel even kissed me – we are having a real love affair!

When I got back home I telephoned Umnenkaya. She has been allotted Polina[2] to sing; I am delighted.

Dined with the Konshins: a good dinner, but enveloped in a cloud of mild boredom. After playing some four-hand Mozart and Beethoven, I hurried home. Tomorrow I shall rise at nine o'clock and – to work!

21 December

Got up a little earlier than yesterday, and by ten minutes to ten was already at the piano composing the Concerto.

In the afternoon Max and I went for a walk along Nevsky (my new vogue), bought postcards, for which I have a great weakness, and also scores of the operas *The Stone Guest* and *The Queen of Spades*. When I got home I played through the latter with passionate interest, especially the dramatic passages. I dined at the Ruzskys and played my *Ballade* with him; he likes it more and more and promises to learn it properly so that he will be able to play it really well. Meanwhile his intonation is cruelly out in the Andante. I pay no attention to the girls, and they do their best to return the compliment, but they are at a disadvantage: their Papa keeps praising the *Ballade* to the skies, so they can't very well ignore me.

---

1 Vladimir Dranishnikov (1893–1939) became a leading Soviet conductor of opera and ballet, holding posts at the Kirov Theatre, where he was Chief Conductor from 1925 to 1936, and the Shevchenko Theatre in Kiev. In Petrograd/Leningrad during the 1920s he was responsible for many first performances in the Soviet Union, among them Prokofiev's *Love for Three Oranges* (1926), Berg's *Wozzeck* (1927), Strauss's *Rosenkavalier* (1982), as well as the first Soviet production of Musorgsky's *Boris Godunov* (1928).
2 In *The Queen of Spades*.

22 December

Sitting at the piano again by half past ten. At night I dreamed about Tonya Rudavskaya, Ariadna Nikolskaya and Umnenkaya. The first named telephoned me today and very nicely asked me to go for a walk with her on Wednesday. Well, why not, no harm in that. I'd like to very much.

The Concerto is slowly inching its way forward. After lunch I played through *The Stone Guest*. It's interesting, although a bit on the dry side and the material is not especially distinctive. Still, it is interesting, and should be very effective on stage. Some of the climaxes have a marvellous sense of upward striving.

In the afternoon I went to the Yusupov Garden and skated; there was no one about. I cannot go through a whole day without filling my lungs with fresh air. Afterwards I played through *Queen of Spades* and once again marvelled at it, despite the fact that it has become so hackneyed.

A letter from Morolyov: he is sending 1000 roubles towards our joint venture on the stock exchange.

A postcard from 16A consisting of a single letter of the alphabet and the address.

23 December

Although I did not get up very early, I still worked seriously at the Concerto, and it is moving forward. Work was interrupted by lunch at one, and afterwards I could not compose any more, which put me in a bad mood. I read Tchaikovsky's biography. Taking it a teaspoonful at a time every other day, I have now got as far as Volume II. As much as the first volume stimulated me and made me want to work, so does the second depress me with its whining. I find I get sucked in to this whining, and it spoils my mood.

In the afternoon I had to go to the Yablonskys by reason of Madame's birthday. We talked about the dramatic aspects of opera.

After that I went skating. Since there was absolutely nobody I knew there, to relieve the boredom I set myself a challenge: to go round all the ponds a certain number of times without stopping. Yesterday I managed six circuits, and then after a rest another six. Today I managed eight. To go round the whole circuit is quite a long way, and tiring. Just as I was leaving I caught sight of Borya Alpers in the distance, but God spared me from meeting him.

Back home I have the whole evening free and am alone in the house. It is an ideal situation for working, but I feel rather weary. The Concerto is not coming together; I'll play through *The Stone Guest*.

24 December

As I decided yesterday that I was too tired to compose, instead I opened my diary and started perusing some of my old entries. I came across the idea I had had of writing a scherzo for bassoons, was fired with enthusiasm and spent the whole evening on it. I began it at eight o'clock and by half past midnight the Scherzo was complete and written out with all the finishing touches in place.

I was lucky to have this experience which Tchaikovsky describes – when the material flows of its own accord and all one has to do is make choices. I worked with feverish absorption and did not notice how the time was passing. Although I have never felt drawn to quartets, in this Scherzo I found myself quite at home with the quartet idiom. I shall send it to Tcherepnin at New Year.

Afterwards at night I could not get to sleep for a long time, my nerves were too stretched, and for that reason slept until twelve. Even so, I managed to finish part of the Intermezzo of the Concerto.

At half past three I met Max at Winter's store. We had agreed that lateness at the rendezvous would attract a penalty at the rate of a rouble a minute. This made us both punctual. We walked along Nevsky; there were throngs of people as it is Christmas Eve.

We met V. and S. Alpers.[1] Max bowed, but I did not. It was a great moment: we collided at the precise instant that I was explaining some stock exchange project I had in mind: '... and then I'll open a credit line for twenty thousand...' The Alpers will have heard this.

We also met Myaskovsky looking in the Russian Music Editions shop to see whether Scriabin's Sonata No. 7 had been published. I introduced him to Max. Kolechka has bought himself a new piano, and is very pleased with it. His opinion of *The Stone Guest* is that it is boring rubbish.

In the evening I stayed at home and wrote out a fair copy of the Scherzo. This morning I found I did not like it so much, but now I like it again.

I sent Nina Kirsch a card congratulating her.

Umnenkaya has disappeared from view and is nowhere to be seen. Evidently she really is 'Glupenkaya' after all.

25 December

Christmas Day, also Mama's birthday, but she does not like to talk about it.

Because it was a holiday I rose at midday. Mama gave me some scent, and a gold ten-rouble piece. I did not feel like composing, so played through

---

1 Vera and her brother Sergey.

Guest to the end. Interesting. The use of whole tones to suggest horror is absurdly trite, but up to a point it does produce an effect of some kind. And how daring it must have seemed at the time!

In the afternoon I went for a solitary skate. Today I completed sixteen circuits, a veritable feat. A colonel with a young cadet and some ladies stood watching my patient circumnavigation. A light drizzle came on; the ice gleamed, producing a watery reflection of the trees, the sky and my flying figure.

In the afternoon we had visitors: Aunt Katya, Katya, Andryusha and Shurik[1] with his wife; A. P. Maksutova came to dine; she is a princess and wears the decoration of the Order of St George.[2]

In the evening I played through *Queen of Spades* and read Tchaikovsky's biography. It is deeply interesting, but the unadulterated melancholia that washes over everything percolates into me as well.

26 December

Just before waking I dreamed of Tchaikovsky; I was walking with him somewhere; he was so kind and gentle and made me feel so sad that I woke up in a very distressed state.

I worked quite well until lunchtime on the cadenza of the Concerto. It is complete in plan, but working out the details is taking a long time.

In the afternoon I went to see Kolechka to show off my Bassoon Scherzo and to inspect his new piano. The Scherzo was a huge success, the only criticism being to enquire why there should be a modulation to D major before the trio. He is very unhappy with the recently published Etudes by Scriabin on the intervals of the ninth, the seventh and the fifth and considers they are not worth performing. In my 'Suggestion diabolique' and especially 'Snow' he considers my use of parallel ninths incomparably more successful. I don't like the Scriabin Etudes myself. As for 'Snow', I seem to have lost the manuscript. I played him a little of my embryonic Concerto, and he liked what he

---

1   The Rayevsky family, except for the father, Alexander senior, Prokofiev's uncle by marriage.
2   Alexandra Maksutova and her elder sister Yekaterina were distant connections of the Rayevskys. This is an occasion when Prokofiev seems to have confused his chronology, since A. P. Maksutova is known to have died in 1905. The error also appears in the *Autobiography*. Unlike the British George Cross, which is awarded for civilian gallantry, the Military Order of the Saint Grand Martyr and the Triumphant George was an Imperial Russian order of chivalry created by Catherine the Great for exceptional valour in the face of an external enemy. It has four degrees, the highest of which has only ever been awarded to twenty-five persons, mainly members of the Russian Imperial Family and foreign Commanders-in-Chief. Clearly the holder of this award, in one of the lower degrees, was not the Princess Maksutova herself but her late husband, Admiral Prince Pavel Maksutov, a naval officer who had taken part in the Battle of Sinope, one of consequences of which was the Crimean War. The Order was abolished after the October Revolution but reinstated by the Government of the Russian Federation in 1992.

heard. On the title page of his *Alastor* is the inscription 'To Sergey Sergeyevich Prokofiev'.

From Kolechka I made my way to the Yusupov Garden, but it was closed on account of the thaw. Returning home I played through Act I of *Guest*, and at eight o'clock Mama telephoned from M. P. Korsak's house asking me to go over and listen to a singer called Maria Pavlovnina. I put on a frock-coat, called a taxi and went.

28 December

Yesterday I did not manage to write anything in my diary. Rising not very early as is my custom at present, I settled down to the Concerto and worked slowly on the cadenza. At the moment I am working on the Concerto less enthusiastically than before; this does not mean that the quality of the present outcome is any less good, especially since the bulk of the three movements is already composed; what I am doing now is welding it all together and adding the finishing touches.

Max and I met at Winters at half past three and walked along Nevsky talking as we went, and then along the Embankment. We ate blinis at Peretz on the corner of Morskaya Street and washed them down with a glass of chartreuse. He promised to come and see me in the evening. At home I was dining with less gusto than usual, when Max telephoned suggesting that we go to the Artistic Opera Company, which had rented our Conservatoire Hall and was presenting *Eugene Onegin*.[1] I dressed in a hurry, Max called for me in a taxi, and we got seats in the sixteenth row. This company's production of *Onegin* moved me to tears: Tanya and Olya were seventeen-year-old girls with plaits down to their shoulders and simple dresses; Lensky was a fiery nineteen-year-old youth, and Onegin an ice-cold, reserved gentleman. The settings were enchanting, the *mise-en-scène* irreproachable, the ball scenes and the final scene so stylish and the whole look of the third and fifth scenes so beautiful that they provoked a storm of applause. The performance was of a studied simplicity, with some musical and scenic details that gave particular pleasure. It seems to me that the production as a whole must have been very much like what Tchaikovsky, to judge from his letters of the time, wanted so passionately (but hardly dared hope for) when he was writing *Onegin*. Vocally, the principal singers were not remarkable, but they were all decent. Among the details I noted particularly the quarrel between Lensky and Onegin, when the former calls the latter a dishonourable seducer and Onegin retorts, 'Be quiet, or I shall kill you!' Usually Onegin rushes at Lensky as if to attack him, the pair then having to be dragged apart. But in this

---

1 Opera (1878) by Tchaikovsky.

production he preserves the contemptuous bearing of a gentleman, rapping out the words in such a way, or so I understood, as to suggest that the killing he refers to is not at that moment but will be on the morrow. This interpretation is far more arousing, as it makes clear that this is the moment when he decides that, come the duel, he will not spare Lensky.

But overall, the aspect of the whole production that gave me the greatest pleasure was the composer Tchaikovsky, and I was overwhelmed by the genius of this opera.

During the interval Max and I met the delightful trio of Lida and Zoya Karneyeva with Zora.[1] I had not been in touch with the Karneyev girls for a month and a half – we have simply been taking a rest from one another. It was nice to see them, but Zora ... I was simply enchanted to be seeing her again! It had been six months since I last saw her in July, and before that there had also been a six-month gap, since the January before, which was in fact when we became acquainted. Whenever we spoke on the telephone it was never for less than half an hour, and sometimes an hour. Zora is a terrific flirt, sultry and interesting, and by no means devoid of musical understanding. I always liked her, but Lida did not welcome our encounters and was inclined to be jealous.

And so it was today, when my attention was so obviously centred on Zora. She was in a box with other members of her family but was clearly unbearably bored, escaping downstairs at each interval. We had very interesting conversations each time, and then it turned out that Lida and Zoya were going somewhere on Krestovsky Island for the rest of the evening.

'We have a car; can we take you there?' we asked, receiving a joyful assent. In point of fact our taxi had promised to come back for us at the end of the performance, but the rascal let us down and we had to take the first car we came across, which as luck would have it was a very luxurious one. The girls were delighted, and pressed us to come and visit them, so it all went splendidly and Max and I were very pleased. It was a pity that Zora went off with the rest of her party, and I have no idea when I shall see her again.

Friday

I had gone to bed late, so naturally did not get up too early. I did not do much with the Concerto. Katya Ignatieva came to talk to me about my scheme to invest. I need capital, so I propose that I do the work and we split the profit equally. She provides the money, I play the stock exchange, we ought to get a return of 60 to 80 per cent over the year and that will provide

---

1 Zora Grevs, or Graves (the family was originally from England), a friend of the Karneyev family, whom Prokofiev had met when a summer visitor at Terioki.

each of us with a tidy income. Katya agrees, and will come up with three thousand; she is already dreaming of going to Paris. Morolyov will chip in a thousand, Mama likewise but merely in order to increase the equity and to add value to my enterprise, not to share the income, which will all go to her. I agree with this and am pleased that my project is taking shape, as it should provide a decent amount of money for my day-to-day expenses, the more so as in view of the murky political situation shares are currently low in value. The only snag will be if we miss the point at which they will go up sharply, but just at the moment it is too risky to buy because of the threat of war.

In the afternoon I went skating, but did only seven circuits today. Borya Alpers was reasonably civil, and I did my best to be affable to him. A pretty fifteen-year-old girl was also out skating today, whom I had noticed last winter. She had run out of patience with her friend, who was barely able to stand up on the ice, and I was bored too, so there was a rapport between us. But we did not meet; I lack courage in such situations.

29 December

Max, Katya Ignatieva and a trio of Yablonskys visited us in the evening. Max and I were disenchanted with the company, which was preventing us from going off into a corner and writing the 'Yellow Book'. A gypsy woman told me my fortune, forecasting all kinds of terrible disasters.

I went to bed at two o'clock and rose at midday. The scherzo of the Concerto is as lively as one could wish, but the middle section is not yet up to scratch. I had a nice card from Calvoshka:[1] he is interested in the Second Concerto but is still waiting for the First.

In the afternoon I went to the International Bank to find out if they would let me have an on-call account there. On Nevsky Prospect I unexpectedly met Max, who had some business of his own there but was not in any great hurry. Fate had clearly decreed that we should stroll along the street together. Max is very short of money for the holiday, and I decided to let him have some of mine. We went into Alfyorov's office, and although I had already withdrawn all the money I had made from my stock exchange dealings, I drew out 200 roubles on credit, giving 100 to Max and keeping 100 for myself. Of my fee for Op. 14, 70 roubles is left (100 has gone on living expenses, 25 given to Max).

Then I went skating. After a brief glimpse of yesterday's delectable vision she vanished. But Vera Alpers was there, so I went over to her and began making complimentary noises. She, however, echoed her little brother by demanding that I explain myself, declaring that if I did not do so our acquaintance would be at an end. I replied that the decision lay in her power, but that the burden of sin would lie on her conscience. Laughingly I pro-

---

1 Calvocoressi.

posed that we make a final break in order not to have the awkwardness of acknowledging one another in the future. She said that that was not what she meant, but I replied that it was precisely what she was saying. I then bade her farewell.

This evening I am going to a New Year party at Zherebtsova-Andreyeva's.[1] I am looking forward to it, as all of her class will be there. How attached I am to the Conservatoire and all its denizens!

30 December

While on my way to the Andreyevs I reflected that Zakharov was also a friend of theirs and might well be there. I found this an interesting and slightly disturbing prospect, but my supposition proved to be false.

The company was not particularly exciting, but I was not bored. An unexpected pleasure was the presence of the Meshchersky girls, whom I was delighted to see. To be honest, in their simple dresses they did not look very remarkable, and the elder sister was more attractive than Nina, but I am very fond of Nina because of the inexhaustible fund of mischief buried within her. I soon lost sight of her, to my chagrin.

Our prima ballerina, Mlle Petz, who had been such a success in the 'Dance of the Skomorokhs', turns out to be a student of Zherebtsova and therefore was also present. I fell out with her because I told her, quoting Berendey's[2] injunction to 'turn somersaults and show off, you fools', that she had been dancing 'a fool', and that generally I thought the choreography inept and Presnyakov,[3] who had directed the dance, stupid.

The actress Bedrinskaya made quite a stir with her recitation, her skill and feminine charms succeeding in turning nonsense into art.

I played the Scherzo from my Op. 14, Etude No. 4 and the Gavotte, all of which went down well especially the Gavotte (dubbed 'Rigaudon' by the Meshcherskys) which had to be repeated. People wanted to hear the 'Fairy Tale', but neither I nor the gifted Yovanovich, who also plays it, knew it by heart and there was no score there.

Today I got up at midday and put the finishing touches to the piano part of the Concerto. When you are writing a concerto, if you conceive of it as a

---

1 Anna Grigorievna Zherebtsova-Andreyeva (1868–1944), mezzo-soprano, much favoured by Anton Rubinstein, with whom she often appeared in concert. Gave many first performances of works by Stravinsky and Prokofiev. The tenor Nikolay Andreyev was her husband.
2 Tsar Berendey in Rimsky-Korsakov's opera *The Snow Maiden*, to the composer's own libretto based on a verse play by Nikolay Ostrovsky. Prokofiev's current inamorata, Lidia Umnova, sang the part of the shepherd Lel in this opera, in which the 'Dance of the Skomorokhs' also occurs; it is this to which Prokofiev alludes.
3 Valentin Presnyakov (1877–?), Professor of Movement at the St Petersburg Conservatoire and stage director of the opera class.

combination of piano and orchestra, the pianistic side of the solo part will always suffer. This has happened in about half the passages in my Concerto No. 1, where the piano–orchestra combination is effective but not particularly interesting for the pianist to play. When composing the Second Concerto I paid a great deal of attention to the challenges of the solo part, but even so there are times when the composer–musician in me prevails over the composer–pianist, and I have not been able to avoid dull or, so to say routine, passages for the soloist.

What would be the ideal way to compose a concerto? It occurred to me today that it would certainly be interesting for a pianist to be presented with a concerto that had had its origin in a technically challenging sonata and subsequently been transformed into a concerto. The solo part would be bound to be interesting pianistically, while the sonata itself would benefit by the reinforcement and embellishment of a skilfully added orchestral texture. Brilliant idea! Supposing I were to take my Sonata Op. 1? No, that would not work; in the first place I have progressed musically since then, and also one should not disturb the bones of works that have appeared in print. But I do have a nice Sonata in A minor, also a perfectly good C minor Sonata,[1] and suppose I were to put together a crisp little concerto from that? I am most attracted by this idea. Whenever I am engaged on a major piece I always have an urge to attach to it a little pendant, something a little lighter. So I could have a Concerto No. 3 to go with my Concerto No. 2, although the musical material of Concerto No. 3 would be somewhat anachronistic even if not in conception and compositional technique.

During my afternoon skating session I was on fire with my new plan, and since both sonatas, in A minor and C minor, were with Max, I telephoned him and asked him to bring them over to me.

31 December

Max called for me in a taxi in the evening and we went to the Artistic Opera Company's production of *Meistersinger*. Playing through the piano reduction earlier in the day I had been overwhelmed by it and even thought it Wagner's best opera. But now, seeing it on the stage for the first time, I experienced a slight feeling of disappointment. First of all, it is so unbelievably long that fatigue and boredom inevitably set in, particularly in the first act where the material is less absorbing than it is in the succeeding acts.

---

1 These sonatas, composed in 1907 and 1908 respectively, were eventually recomposed in 1917 and published as Sonata No. 3, Op. 28, and Sonata No. 4, Op. 29. However, since the theme of the Andante had also been used for the slow movement of the E minor Symphony given an airing by Hugo Warhlich's Court Orchestra in 1909, it also eventually re-emerged in orchestral dress in the composer's 1934 transcription for orchestra of the Fourth Sonata's slow movement, Op. 29A.

Secondly, there is the almost total lack of dramatic action and the long-winded clumsiness of the libretto. Thirdly, the vocal writing for about half the opera is routine (as is the music), so why do these passages need to be there? Fourthly, the humour is apt to be coarse and heavy, and the role of Beckmesser could have been written, if I may so put it, with less artificiality and more refinement. As for the basic musical material of which the opera is composed, it is on such a level of genius that after *Meistersinger* there seems hardly any need for another note of music to be composed. I have always said as much, and this is what is so seductive in the vocal score.

This morning I wrote letters to Umnenkaya (my precious), Goncharova and Klingman. I also sent a card to Wenzel[1] (just to cheer him up), and a registered packet to Tcherepnin with my Bassoon Scherzo along with a much loved epigraph: '... the strangulated wheezing of a bassoon ...'[2]

At noon I went to the International Bank to find out if they had accepted me for an on-call account, as they by no means accept everyone. But me they did accept, thank you very much. After my bank visit I went with Maria Korsak, Mme Miliant and the singer[3] to the People's House so that Figner[4] could hear the latter. Maria Pavlovna had especially asked me to accompany her. I was very happy to have the chance of meeting Figner and to see how it would all turn out. In fact nothing very remarkable occurred; the singer sang splendidly and Figner, it seems, will take her.

For the time being I shall have to forget about my Concertos, the Second and the Third, as the spectre of 20 January is looming. For that I must be on absolutely top form.

By tradition we saw in the New Year with the Rayevskys, this must be the seventh or eighth time in a row. Uncle Sasha is not well, and the household was therefore rather subdued. We had a game of vint and I improved my knowledge of bridge. After we had welcomed the New Year, Andryusha and Shurik bashed their way cheerfully through the overture to *Carmen* and then asked me to play something. I sat down and played Lel's aria from *The Snow Maiden*.

1   Vladimir Wenzel, Professor of Piano at the St Petersburg Conservatoire.
2   Quotation from Griboyedov's comedy *Woe from Wit*.
3   The singer Marina Pavlovnina, whom the author had been summoned to meet some days previously.
4   Nikolay Figner (1857–1918), tenor, the original Herman in *The Queen of Spades*, Director of the People's House. Figner was well known enough as a tenor to figure in a quatrain Prokofiev tells us in the *Autobiography* he set to music at the request of the Rayevsky children's governess:

No no, not Figner, neither Yuzhin,
The only one I truly need
(The others are a dime a dozen)
Is Leonid, O Leonid!

David Yuzhin was another well-known singer, but Leonid Sobinov (1872–1934) was, along with Ivan Yershov, the most admired tenor of his generation.

General consternation. To pacify my public I played the Grieg Sonata, which they all wanted to hear, and we all went home at half past one.

A note on the dating of entries in the diary.

Until now I have been heading my entries with the day and the time that I wrote them. But reading through my diary, I have come to the conclusion that it would be better to note the day to which the entry refers, rather than identifying the date and time it was written. If my diary were one that concerns itself with abstract propositions – my inner, spiritual life, leaving more concrete events relatively unexplored – a record of when the observations were written would be more relevant. But since my inner world depends to a great extent on what happens in real life, I am mostly setting out the facts, describing the day as it goes on from the morning through to the evening. Henceforward, therefore, I shall note down the date of the day about which I am writing.

1913

1 January

As I was in an agitated state yesterday I needed physical activity today, so after getting up a little earlier than usual and playing through the themes I had been thinking about yesterday (with which I was pleased) I went out skating. The Yusupov Garden was deserted and windy. I practised the 'Dutch Step'[1] a bit: this exercise strengthens the legs and helps one to proceed more smoothly. Lunched at home and then went to the Conservatoire, where I went through with Tcherepnin Haydn's 'Paukenschlag'[2] Symphony. It had never occurred to me before that its name derives purely from one drum beat in the sixteenth bar of the Andante.

There were not many people of interest to be seen in the Conservatoire. The younger Rozhanovich sister ran past, which sent Tsybin into ecstasy. Saw 16A in the distance, but this failed to give me much of a thrill. I had a postcard from her today with a rather bad picture of a restaurant. The person I wanted to see was 17A, but after her telephone call, to which I have not reacted, she has fallen silent. I must be patient, I was the one at fault.

Today is Lida Karneyeva's birthday. Last year at this time I was with them, brought chocolates, and went with them and Zora to the theatre in the evening. This year I confined myself to a telegram ('warmest congratulations, very best wishes and a thousand greetings, Sergusya'); it's not that I don't want to spend the evening with them, but Zakharov will probably be there, and I don't want to be obliged to make myself agreeable to him, while it would hardly be good manners to sit there with a scowl on my face. That is why I contented myself with a telegram and avoided visiting or telephoning.

In the evening I finally got down to revising the D flat Concerto. I did so with great enjoyment, which should help to make the revision lead to a successful outcome. I am happy with the orchestration except for a few places where I want to make changes. If the orchestration works out well I shall not delay any longer but send it to Jurgenson.

In the evening I looked out of the window: a clear frosty night and a full moon. I thought about 17A.

---

1   The basic manoeuvre of skating on one leg at a time, alternating the body weight from side to side while leaving the outer leg in the air in order to produce the graceful swaying movement that generates speed. It was developed in Holland in the fifteenth century to facilitate rapid transit along the canals.
2   Known in English as the 'Surprise' Symphony, No. 94 in G major, Hob. 1:94.

10 January

There is talk of peace in the Balkans, causing an upward lurch in the stock market. In the morning I went to the International Bank and opened a withdrawal-on-demand account with the 4000 roubles I had accumulated, leaving instructions for twenty-five Nikopol-Mariupolsky shares to be purchased. The general mood in the bank was excited and cheerful because of the rise in value and the resulting profits. After that I busied myself with revising the Concerto, and just before three went to the Conservatoire.

Collided with Vera Dmitriyevna[1] who, being responsible for arranging male and female singers for the opera class and being also a stupid woman, invariably gets everything muddled up and flies into a temper with me when I present her with evidence of her incompetence. At the time I was carrying three heavy scores of the operas currently in the repertoire, and all but crowned her sagacious head with all three. I continued on with my burden so as to remove myself from any temptation to excess, and seeing Elena Klingman, attached myself to her. To give her her due, I spent a pleasant twenty minutes chatting to 16A.

In the opera class we worked on *The Snow Maiden* – we could not do much, as the male singers had to remind themselves of what they had forgotten over the Christmas holiday. Mme Leschetitskaya (Yesipova's daughter) came in to listen to her Popova. It was the first time she had been present when I was conducting; I tried to make my attitude as peremptory as I could, with a view to this being passed back to Yesipova. She was exceptionally friendly to me.

The evening papers carry reports of the substantial rise in the stock market, which makes very pleasant reading for Mama and me. Returning home I tinkered with the Concerto and read a long letter from Max about his adventures in Simferopol. He is most punctilious in writing to me every day.

Spent the evening with the Konshins, not a particularly entertaining time, but nice all the same. I left at eleven.

11 January

Slept badly. In the morning went to the International Bank and instructed them to buy twenty shares in Parviainen.[2] But my debut in playing the market has not been terribly successful: the Turks are threatening war and stocks have taken a downward turn.

Lunched at home, and after playing through *The Queen of Spades* went to Tcherepnin. Vera Dmitriyevna, greeting me, did not shake hands. So that's

---

1 Vera Dmitrievna Petrokokina, one of the Class Inspectors at the St Petersburg Conservatoire.
2 A major iron and steel concern in St Petersburg, with two factories known as the Old Parviainen and the New Parviainen.

how it's to be, is it, Mme Petrokokina? All right, war it shall be, but it will cost you blood, and if you have any left at all afterwards, it will be bad blood.

Tcherepnin considers the scene in the Countess's bedroom one of the greatest passages in all opera. I agree wholeheartedly with him. As we went through the scene today, I playing and Tcherepnin breathing life into it, Tsybin sat in the corner with tears coursing down his face.

Not many people attended the Ensemble class today, and half of those who were there had sore throats. God only knows how they are going to get the show fit for rehearsal.

In the evening Aunt Katya and Uncle Sasha came to us, also the singer with whom we went to see Figner and who had been so touched by my accompanying her performance.

At first I was reluctant to play for her again, feeling I had had enough music during the afternoon, and this evidently annoyed Aunt Katya, but in any case I eventually gave in because she does in fact sing extremely well.

Yesterday the following conversation with 16A took place:

'I noticed some of your compositions among the music belonging to one of the teachers in Dvinsk.'

I: 'You don't say! I'm even beginning to have a presence in the provinces!'

16A: 'Don't be rude about our Dvinsk, please. It's nothing like the back-water you might think!'

In the afternoon I met Volodya Deshevov in the Conservatoire, not having seen him for a long time. Much affection on both sides, but we were both in a hurry. I am extremely fond of him, and he is the only one to whom I made a *Bruderschaft* proposal (I had wanted to with Max and Zakharov, but in the event waited for them to propose it). Deshevov had met Tanya Ruzskaya somewhere or other and found her very attractive.

12 January

I am so happy Max is coming back. At 10.40 I was at the Nikolayevsky station[1] to meet the train from Sebastopol. We went together to his place at 68 Nevsky Prospect, left his suitcase with the concierge there, and set off down Nevsky. He did not even go in to say hello to his family, putting that off until several hours later. Of course this mark of attention to me gave me great pleasure. Indeed, Max appears to be very seriously attached to me. We drank coffee in the Andreyev patisserie and strolled along the Prospect. Max talked non-stop about his stay in Simferopol, where he made quite a splash and attracted much attention because of the way he carried on. He had great success there but not, alas, with his heroine and the main reason for his journey, Marusya Lyutz.

---

1 The station now known as Oktyabrsky (October).

By half past twelve we had by no means exhausted his stories, but had to separate until the evening. I went to have my photograph taken, then to Tatyana Sebryakova[1] to give her good wishes for her name-day, and then to the Conservatoire. There I was supposed to be conducting a gala singing practice for the whole chorus and soloists, but less than half of them turned up. The practice over, Tcherepnin said, 'I have good news for you: the performance scheduled for the 20th is postponed until the 27th, so we have plenty of time for rehearsal and will manage to get everything done.' I cannot say I was overjoyed by this, because it had about it a smell of the third performance being cancelled altogether. As far as today's rehearsal was concerned, Tcherepnin thought I did not insist enough and lacked control over the large forces. Eventually I asked him about the Bassoon Scherzo: 'Nikolay Nikolayevich, why haven't you said anything about my Scherzo?'

'Why, yes, it's very nice . . . very good . . . we should get it played some time . . .'

This was certainly not much to get in return for the Scherzo, which merits considerably greater praise than that.

I had hoped to see 17A today, but she did not come to sing. This is a bad sign, as it suggests that she is going to hide herself away until 5 February, when all the present productions are shelved and we move on to preparations for *The Queen of Spades*. I miss her, but I shall not telephone.

Met Sharoyev[2] on my way back from the Conservatoire, and as he likes me made him come along with me.

At home I scratched out and pasted in corrections to the First Piano Concerto until Max came at eight o'clock. The evening flew by in talk about all that had happened to us while we were apart. I played him parts of the Second Piano Concerto: he likes the third movement and especially the first movement cadenza. The Finale elicited vociferous approval; I had to repeat the opening theme three times.

13 January

In the morning I had another look at the D flat Concerto. In the afternoon went skating with Klingman at the rink by Krasny Bridge. She is a mediocre skater, and in comparison with the aristocratic environment of the Yusupov Garden the rink has too many small fry rushing about everywhere falling head over heels.

In the evening, since she had given me a ticket for it, I went to Zherebtsova-Andreyeva's concert. These are always interesting events

---

1 Prokofiev's mother's cousin. Being a doctor, she sometimes acted as the family doctor.
2 A fellow piano student in Anna Yesipova's class.

because of her intelligence as a performer and the intriguing novelties and beautiful rarities from the past she puts into her programmes. A group of songs by Tcherepnin was very attractive, a tasteless excerpt from Strauss's *Ariadne auf Naxos* horrible beyond belief, and the latest songs to come from the pen of Taneyev simply not good, the music having no relationship to the words. I was astonished. Tcherepnin's view, apropos these songs, was: 'You must remember, this is a man who has spent his whole life never going outside his room; he doesn't mix with people, doesn't drink wine, doesn't have anything to do with women; his only strength lies in being able to produce counterpoint!'

Magda Orlova's elegance and refinement attracted universal attention, and afterwards everyone wanted know who was the enchanting woman with me. I answered that she was 'the mother of my daughter'.[1] The Meshcherskys invited me for Friday; I accepted with pleasure.

Tcherepnin: 'Bring your Sinfonietta in to the class. We have a good orchestra at the moment, and they should play it.' When I got home I looked through it. Will it really sound good? To have any chance of doing so, it will need a scrupulously nuanced performance, which it is hardly likely to receive from our orchestra. Nevertheless, Tcherepnin's suggestion filled me with joy.

14 January

It was good to be made to get up early. At ten o'clock there was a rehearsal in the Small Hall of all the operas, with full chorus, soloists and orchestra. But since the first performance has been put off for a week the zeal of those taking part has lost some of its edge: some of the instrumentalists were missing, only half the choir was present and not more than a dozen of the soloists. We went through *Maccabaeus* and bits of *The Maid of Orleans*. It was all right, I got quite tired but not excessively. Tcherepnin was not happy with some of my tempi and some of my gestures, and wants to discuss them at tomorrow's class. He said we should show the Bassoon Scherzo to Kotte, the woodwind professor, as it must certainly be played. This is a better reaction.

Klingman says at least half the female choristers have a strong partiality for Tcherepnin. I can believe this, he can be charming when he wants to be.

Max came towards the end of the rehearsal. We went off to lunch at Peretz's restaurant, on the corner of Morskaya and Nevsky. Our cash is running out, so we have to deny ourselves more sumptuous fare. Here we had some delicious sandwiches and pies. We both had a fancy for a glass of light wine, but when it came it was not a glass but half a bottle, and not

---

1 Magda Orlova, writing under the pen name of Baron Lieven, wrote the libretto for Prokofiev's opera *Maddalena*.

particularly light either, quite heavy in fact. Nevertheless the walk back to the Conservatoire in the frost was enough to clear the fumes from our heads.

In the Conservatoire I met Natasha Goncharova. I am, it seems, very nice, I have become very handsome, my greeting was original, and in conclusion, since she is learning Italian, 'jo t'amo' [sic]. Thank you very much. After that, the opera class, and then, glowing from my encounter with Natasha, I went home.

A letter from Lintvaryova with her comments on my D flat Concerto, which I had given her before Christmas. She liked it.

Have been thinking of an interesting project: in order to develop my mastery of instrumental colour in my scores, I should write a series of concertos, one for each instrument, consulting in each case the relevant orchestral musician so as to explore all the technical possibilities of that instrument, and then write in such a way as to exploit its maximum strengths and virtuosic capabilities. Having done that, to listen critically, amend as necessary, and listen again. Composing these pieces would not be particularly difficult since the point will not be to plumb the depths of musical profundity or to create intrinsically valuable material, but by concentrating on the technical aspects to achieve a workmanlike result that is attractive to listen to. The opus would consist of ten concert pieces, one each for flute, oboe, cor anglais, clarinet, bass clarinet, bassoon, horn, trumpet, trombone and tuba.

In the evening continued revising the D flat Concerto and thought about Natasha Goncharova.

15 January

Getting up in the morning is so much more pleasant in January than it is in December: then one is woken by the fire being laid and lit, but now it is the sun shining in. I love getting up early, but if I don't have anything special to do I find it difficult to be out of bed earlier than noon.

At ten o'clock I was at the bank to see about the new issue of shares in Parviainen. By half past ten I was in the Conservatoire where we were supposed to start work on *The Queen of Spades*, focusing in particular on the role of Polina. But I need not have hurried: not only was our Polina not there but the work we were studying was *Rigoletto*, so after deputing the conducting to Dranishnikov I went out of the class. Met 16A and had a long talk with her, at the end of which we were joined by a rather attractive girl from the chorus, Zina Lenkina (or as I call her, Lena Zinkina). There was a tremendous buzz and excitement in the corridors today because of an Aesthetics exam. One of those drifting about who had come to keep an eye on this exam was a pallid-looking Boryusya.

Lunched in the Conservatoire canteen and had a lesson with Tcherepnin (the Canal Scene from *The Queen of Spades*, the Haydn symphony and *Maccabaeus*, sorting out yesterday's shortcomings). Then in the ensemble class I put on Tsybin (or as Mama calls him, Tsypin[1]) to conduct and myself went home.

Finished reading the second volume of Tchaikovsky's biography, a book that is giving me the most tremendous pleasure. Max came round in the evening and we went together to the student concert. It was not much of a programme and the audience was small, no one of great interest having turned up. Kätchen Borshch played well; she has made great progress. Zakharov was there; my inseparability from Max evidently grates on him and he soon disappeared from view.

I was home at eleven.

16 January

The first session of the small orchestra since the break, therefore I was in the Conservatoire at nine o'clock, to find the fellows listlessly gathering. Tcherepnin did not greet me, and neither Dranishnikov nor Tsybin were there. I had to conduct the whole time, going through Haydn's 'Paukenschlag' Symphony. Not that I have anything against this.

After so much conducting I felt exhausted and wanted to leave the building. Sitting on a chair by the cloakroom I studied those coming in, thinking for some reason that I might see Umnenkaya even though I knew perfectly well there was no reason for her to be here at this time. This quiet angel, whom I found I was missing seeing, certainly has character.

Returning home I had lunch and continued reading Tchaikovsky's biography. Today is Zoya Karneyeva's birthday. Max and I said we wanted to go and wish her happy returns – she was flattered, but would not be at home. We therefore composed a 100-word telegram of great pomposity and spelling out all the punctuation in words ('semicolon', 'dash') that made us laugh when we read it out. Zoya subsequently telephoned us and invited Max and me to dinner.

At four o'clock I went skating and then completed my revision of the D flat Concerto; it is now ready for two copies to be made, the first to be sent to Paris and second as soon as it is ready, to be sent to Jurgenson. In the same period I must also complete 'Despair' so that I can send Jurgenson the whole of Op. 4 together with the Concerto; it is eighteen months since he paid me for the work and to my shame it has still not been despatched.

This afternoon a society was making a collection for a memorial to Tchaikovsky. I subscribed 3 roubles.

---

1 Derived from the Russian word for a chicken.

Max tells me that his aunt is sending him to Pyatigorsk to deal with some business left over from last summer. If I succeed in selling the Concerto I should love to go with him, or if the stock exchange rises and I get some money, depending also on whether I can take a two-week break from the conducting class once the opera performances are over. We could go on the Georgian Highway to Tiflis.[1]

17 January

Tcherepnin is ill and I had to do the rehearsal today without him. But it was more of a shambles than a rehearsal: a failure of communication about the rehearsal meant that none of the singers came, and it was very unsatisfactory trying to rehearse the orchestra without them. After a difficult half-hour persuading them to go through *The Snow Maiden*, I dismissed them. The flautist, Shifrin, was messing about and playing the fool the whole time, and when at the end of the rehearsal I remonstrated with him, he apologized. I then went to see Tcherepnin, who had asked for a report on how the rehearsal went. He made me play my Scherzo, which made him laugh, and asked me to make parts for it so that it could be performed.

I did not go to Yesipova's class, as the Chopin B flat minor Sonata is not yet ready. Generally I am not doing much piano practice, but Kalantarova said she had heard me play for Yesipova before Christmas and thought I was making great progress.

Max has a sore throat and did not come. I went on my own to Peretz, ate there, and to kill time before the lesson walked back along the Embankment and past Umnenkaya's house.

Met Wenzel in the corridor and talked to him. It was break time for the General Subjects classes and a lot of girls were promenading up and down the corridor. Three girls arm in arm walked past us, and hearing us calling each other 'thee and thou', stopped as if rooted to the spot. But their ears were not deceiving them, I was sitting on the edge of a table with Wenzel standing before me in an apparently exalted state of mind, and we were indeed conversing intimately. An entertaining moment!

As I walked home along Nikolsky Lane it suddenly occurred to me, I don't know why, that behind Umnova's broad smile is indifference ...

In the evening Max and I took a car and went to the People's House[2] to

1 Tbilisi.
2 The idea of People's Houses or People's Palaces – 'A palace of pleasure and imagination around which the people may place their affections and which may give them a home on which their memory may rest' – as Lord Rosebery declared on opening the People's Palace on Glasgow Green in 1898 – spread from Britain and Continental Europe to arrive in St Petersburg in 1899 with the opening of the People's House in Alexandrovsky Park. January 1912 saw the addition of a magnificent and suitably large new opera house, with a stage and fly-tower larger and

hear *The Queen of Spades*. I found the new hall in the People's House very impressive in its spaciousness, its large capacity and airy feeling. Beside it our Conservatoire theatre is a poor relation. I had been greatly looking forward to *Pique Dame*. The opening scene did not quite live up to expectations, but beginning from the second right through to the final scene I enjoyed it thoroughly. The last scene is inept, and ruins the overall impression. It should start with the appearance of Herman: everything that precedes this should be discarded as detracting from the drama. 'What is our life? A game!' sounds strange and is superfluous, as is the final page of the opera. It is a matter of regret that the music accompanying the first meeting between Herman and the Countess does so little to reflect and enhance it. Altogether the opera has much that is long-drawn-out and superfluous, not just from the dramatic but also from the musical point of view. Even so, the scene in the Countess's room is pure genius from first note to last, and it is not the only one.

Max and I talked at length and with passion about the opera I intend to get down to as soon as I finish at the Conservatoire. It occurred to me that it could be madly interesting to write an opera whose hero would be, not a fictitious character about whom no one really cares, but none other than Pushkin himself!! His glittering life, his passionately dramatic end, together with the utterly irresistible charm of his personality, beloved by all, could be made into a libretto of irresistible attractiveness. And what a stunning scene Pushkin's letter to Heeckeren,[1] a historically verifiable letter, could be! Tatiana's letter would pale by comparison. And the whole era! Glinka, planning *Ruslan*!

18 January

This morning, in the best of spirits and putting on my tie from Brussels in the hope of meeting Umnenkaya, I set off for the opera class. The class was full, and seething with activity. I was greeted with much respect, a chair was provided for me and I was invited to conduct, as without a conductor nothing

---

higher than the Mariinsky Theatre, intended to outdo anything in Europe. The architect G. I. Lyutseradsky employed the latest ferro-concrete materials and construction techniques to boast of the building's complete impregnability to fire; needless to say it was badly damaged by a huge conflagration (fortunately at night) two days after the grand opening and remained closed for many months. The building is now known as the Music Hall.

1 Georges d'Anthès, the widely presumed lover of Alexander Pushkin's wife Natalya Goncharova, whom Pushkin felt obliged to challenge to a duel that ended in the fatal shooting of the poet, was originally brought to St Petersburg by the Dutch Ambassador to the Court of Tsar Nicholas I, Baron Heeckeren. Heeckeren later adopted d'Anthès as his legal son and heir, who then took the name of Georges-Charles d'Anthès Heeckeren. The letter Prokofiev refers to was an insulting one written by the poet to the elder Heeckeren, accusing him of acting as a pander for his adopted son.

can start. 'Tsypin' was not present, so even though *Rigoletto* was not my responsibility I took his place to conduct it. The work went with a swing and I soon took charge of the action. Unmnenakaya sat throughout, but the moment the class came to an end she got up and left. I concluded that she had either left the building altogether or was drinking tea in the little kitchen upstairs. Went upstairs – not there; came downstairs again – not there either. On the bottom landing I met Man-del-baum, who battened on to me with questions about something or other. At that moment I caught sight of Umnenkaya coming out of the cloakroom and quickly leaving the building. Upset at missing her I pictured myself out on the street just at the right moment to catch her. At this point Man-del-baum clumsily terminated the conversation, saying: 'Yes, well ... I mean ... must go now,' and dived into the cloakroom. I realized that to catch up with Umnenkaya would necessitate an undignified chase, and thoroughly annoyed took myself off into a classroom to study the score of *Zauberflöte*. Happily, the score soon diverted me and the next hour I spent absorbed in it, after which I went to have lunch in the canteen. The weather, as bad luck would have it, was wonderful – a sparkling bright day with a light frost, what a wonderful time to be in Yukki![1]

This was followed by Tcherepnin's class, in which we tediously ground our way through the third act of *Faust* with piano accompaniment. At four o'clock, ensemble practice. The first work was again *Rigoletto*, and knowing that it would be half an hour before we got to *Pique Dame* I went out into the corridor, to make Umnenkaya think I had left the Conservatoire altogether, as yesterday. Had some tea, strolled about the corridor, and after half an hour came back into the class. When *Pique Dame* started I had expected to see Umnova on the stage, but she had been taken off into another class where, to save time, several girls assigned to the role of Liza were working separately with Klimov, leaving me with Gabel and the remainder. Somewhat crestfallen, I nevertheless worked with a will for an hour, after which Klimov came bustling back in and announced that he had finished and sent everyone home. Umnenkaya must therefore have gone, and so I went home myself.

Max came at eight o'clock. He was in a bad temper, but I was delighted to see him and have someone to whom I could relate the events of the day. I then put on my dinner jacket and we left together, he to go home and I to the Meshcherskys. They were entertaining, and there was quite a crowd there. Romanovsky, a gifted pianist and great admirer of my compositions, told me that he had been invited next autumn to give a concert of Russian works in Rome, for which he had been asked to supply a conductor. He suggested that I should be that conductor, with a full programme of Russian works including some of my own. This is not yet confirmed, and is a secret.

1 Spa resort to the north of St Petersburg.

If he is to be the only soloist he could play two concertos, in which case one would have to be my D flat. Unfortunately he does yet know this work.

As for the Meshcherskys' musical evening, it included a quantity of chamber and solo music. The only thing I played was the Scherzo from my Op. 14, but it was decidedly a success.

19 January

Although the small orchestra began at nine I did not come in until eleven, purposely staying in my bed through the boring commencement of the class. I conducted Glazunov's *Processional*[1] and afterwards met Max, who had come in especially for the Senior course exam. We had lunch at Peretz and then I returned to the Conservatoire for choral practice. The chorus arrived late and unwillingly, but it did come. There was no sign of Umnova.

Gabel suddenly showed up and after a whispered conversation with Tcherepnin announced loudly that the choral singing was so out of tune and the chorus members so lazy about turning up that not only should singing practice be abandoned for the day but the performance would be cancelled altogether. Everyone then dispersed, and Tcherepnin explained the true reason to me.

The Conservatoire, having built itself a new theatre, has rented it out to the Artistic Opera Company, reserving for itself a certain number of days for its own rehearsals and performances. Mengelberg[2] had taken six rehearsals for his I.R.M.S.[3] concerts, and as a result there was no time left for us. The Conservatoire was behaving like a streetwalker offering herself to the nearest bidder, and despite possessing a theatre whose sole purpose was to provide a home for the Conservatoire's productions had now contrived to get itself into a position where it was obliged to cancel them. And this in its Jubilee year! The tragedy is that Glazunov is a hopeless drunk, Artsybushev is in Odessa, Gabel is senile and unable to say 'Boo' to a goose, and the result is that I and all the soloists who have worked all through the autumn and winter now have to come to terms with the disappointing and demoralizing situation of realizing that thanks to our disintegrating administration, our efforts have been completely pointless. I was all for tackling Tcherepnin head on, but he explained that there would be no point in this as he was not himself a member of the Conservatoire's administrative team. If he were to raise any questions about it, the first thing that would happen is that he would be asked what business was it of his, seeing that the administration itself was silent on the subject?

1 *Wedding March* for orchestra, Op. 21.
2 Willem Mengelberg (1871–1951), Dutch conductor, Musical Director of the Concertgebouw Orchestra in Amsterdam continuously from 1895 until 1945 but with several periods working with other orchestras.
3 The Imperial Russian Musical Society.

To sum up, therefore, I shall now have no opportunity to conduct anything right up to the time when I shall have to conduct *The Queen of Spades*. It is infuriating and stupid, devil take the lot of them!

I immediately resolved that on Monday I would find out the schedule for future classes, and that very day leave Petersburg for a week or two, either for the Crimea or for the Caucasus. I need a change of atmosphere, to travel, to blow away the cobwebs; only then will I be able to settle down to work once more. That same evening Max and I had an intensive confabulation on the subject of our trip. He is ready to go whenever it suits me – the mark of a truly priceless friend! These are our possible projects: (1) the Crimea, with or without a detour to Nikopol: ten days, 150 roubles per head; (2) Pyatigorsk and Tiflis, or perhaps a circuit via Tiflis – Batum to Sebastopol: two weeks, 200 roubles each; (3) Paris: two weeks, 250–300 roubles each.

No. 3 soon fell by the wayside on grounds of expense, fuss and bother with passports, and we were not especially drawn to it in any case. Max favoured Pyatigorsk – Tiflis – Batum – Sebastopol, and it was indeed tempting, but the rough sea crossing from Batum to Sebastopol put us off. There remained the Crimea or Pyatigorsk and Tiflis; we hesitated between these two and left the decision open for the time being.

Mama was not keen on the idea in any form, but refrained from putting her foot down in protest. I persuaded her that while we were away she should go to Moscow. She is bored with all our acquaintances here, but Moscow has the advantage of the Smetskoys being in residence. I think that is what she will do. As for my financial situation, the D flat Concerto is now ready to be sent to Jurgenson, and I hope he will give me 250–300 roubles for it. On the strength of that Mama will lend me 300 roubles: I do not need as much as that, but will have to lend the money to Max, who does not have a *sou* to his name.

20 January

Got up late, not in a very cheerful mood and therefore sluggish at leaping out of bed. At two o'clock Max and I met at the photographer's. This scoundrel has been an eternity producing his pictures: Max and I have been haunting his shop in pursuit of them since November. Today we kicked up a real fuss.

After that we walked along the Prospect discussing our trip, but still without coming to a firm conclusion. In reality we do not have to decide until we physically arrive at the Nikolayevsky station: the express to Sebastopol (No. Kr. 1c)[1] leaves at 9.30 in the evening, and the Black Sea Express to the Caucasus at 9.45; we can get on either.

---

1 'Kr' stands for 'Kuriersky', that is to say a 'courier' or express train.

At four o'clock I went in to see Myaskovsky. He was as nice as ever, but his room and the general surroundings in which he lives have a depressing effect on me. *Alastor* is nearing completion. My second subject in the Finale of the G minor Piano Concerto pleased him very much, but he did not endorse my idea for a Third Piano Concerto, on the grounds that there is a complete break between my old and my new styles of composition; they have nothing in common with one another.

One of the orchestral musicians had made a comment to him that I was hard to follow as a conductor, and when there is a climax I make the mistake of demanding everything the orchestra can give long before the peak, so that when the real climax comes it is not heard.

I dined at the Ruzskys, whom I have not visited for a long time. The atmosphere was not too wonderful there: Nikolay Pavlovich was away, and Tanya was still on her way back from Kiev. I tried to be pleasant to Ira, but she still cannot bear the thought of Max and takes every opportunity to castigate him. Returned home about eleven o'clock, and spoke to Max on the telephone. We decided we would go to the Crimea; as a destination it is not as far and generally has more attraction. So, our journey is settled, always provided tomorrow's conversation with Tcherepnin does not introduce any unforeseen complications.

21 January

Natasha Goncharova rang up at nine o'clock. When it is no longer of any importance, everyone becomes very punctual and precise. She wanted to know whether there was to be a rehearsal, and at what time. I told her the production had been cancelled, and that I was off to the Crimea. Astonishment, followed by: 'Well, at least please bring me back a branch of myrtle!'

'I'll bring you back a block of ice, because it's all frost and snow there at the moment,' I replied and, saying goodbye, went back to sleep.

In the afternoon I went to Alfyorov to draw out 300 roubles, and then to buy an indelible pencil for writing letters on our travels. They sold me the most basic kind available. In the Conservatoire Tcherepnin said that all was not necessarily lost with the production: Glazunov had emerged from his drinking bout, the Princess was currently in St Petersburg, and it might just be that all the problems would be resolved. He supported the idea of my going away and gave me a week's leave, but asked me to delay my departure for a couple of days until the question the performances could be settled.

A big concert is in prospect for the spring: Beethoven's Seventh Symphony and Violin Concerto, the Overture and Bacchanale from *Tannhäuser*, Berlioz's *Cellini* and a piano concerto. Any reason why it should not be mine?

Max came in the evening. We had only just settled ourselves comfortably in my room when the telephone rang with an urgent appeal from Korsak to go over there. The invitation was couched in such insistent terms that, cursing, I went.

22 January

In the morning I composed a rather attractive theme, destined probably for the Andante of the Third Concerto. Around two o'clock I went to the Conservatoire, where I found to my chagrin a notice stating that the student concert for that evening had been cancelled. Tcherepnin's class was working on *Faust* and *The Magic Flute*, followed by the opera ensemble class, into which I looked briefly. Tcherepnin discussed my trip with Gabel, who said that if the performances were indeed going to take place they would not be before 3 February, so there would be no problem in my having ten days' leave of absence. Delighted by this, I returned home. Max and I will set out tomorrow! But what a disappointment that there was to be no student concert! However, Umnenkaya was presumably unaware of this, so I devised a ploy which worked like clockwork.

At seven o'clock I went to Nikolayevsky station to post a letter to the Rebergs letting them know I would be passing through Kharkov. I then took a car and went to the Conservatoire, which as a result of the cancelled concert was deserted. After waiting for twenty minutes I saw Umnenkaya, a sight to gladden the eyes, and told her the evening had been cancelled. Telling each other how disappointed we were, we emerged on to the street, at which point I proposed to her that we go skating instead. Horrified at the idea, she declined the invitation, whereupon I mentioned that the car was waiting in any case, and if she liked I could take her home in it. She was rather mistrustful of this, and indeed the driver, instead of going down Offitserskaya Street[1] went along Glinka Street, then Morskaya, then along the Embankment and across the bridge. We drove around the Islands for some time and then, without getting out of the car, came back. We parted at the entrance to her building, and she promised to write to me in Sebastopol. The glove she forgot and left in the car will go with me in fond memory of delightful 17A.

23 January

Felt rather poorly. At a quarter to nine was in the Conservatoire for the Small orchestra class. Solovyov was making his debut today. He is a reasonable conductor, but so timid and so browbeaten by misfortune that one cannot help feeling sorry for the poor fellow.

---

1 This street is now called Ulitsa Dekabristov (Street of the Decembrists).

Said goodbye to Tcherepnin, met Max at the city ticket bureau and bought tickets for today's Kr. 1c, collected the photographs from Kaspari, drew out money from the International Bank, renewed my subscription tickets to the Mariinsky, looked in at the Conservatoire, and was home by four.

As I write it is eight o'clock and my suitcase is packed. Max rings up to say that he will call for me in a taxi. We will go to Romanovsky's concert for half an hour, and then go straight from there to the station. The train leaves at 9.30. We will break our journey for one day at Nikopol and then continue to the Crimea, where we shall be until 3 February. I close this diary entry now, as I must spend a little time with Mama before leaving. Tomorrow she is herself going to Moscow.

At this point my diary breaks off for the duration of our trip, to be replaced by travel notes written along the way partly by Max and partly by myself, taking turns. Their light-hearted tone testifies to our excellent holiday mood; altogether the trip was a great success and was an exceptionally enjoyable and restorative experience. Max and I not only get along famously, we are becoming indispensable to one another. It happens only rarely that two people of such greatly similar outlook find one another. But this is what has happened to us.

What follows is our travel notes.[1]

Chapter 1: Departure

Max: 'There go our happy wanderers,' exclaimed the young ladies. 'Have a good journey,' obsequiously added the well-tipped porters, bowing and scraping.

I: When the whistle went, kissing hands right and left we transferred ourselves from the station platform to the open platform of the train, and gently steamed out of St Petersburg.

Chapter 2: The Journey

We had had visions of new rolling stock on the train, and our dream came true, because the whole train was brand new ... with the exception of our carriage. Throwing scarves round our shoulders we left our compartment and made our way to the restaurant car to drink tea and write postcards.

Chapter 3: Nikopol

Max: Emerging from the station at Nikopol our first thought was that we would need a boat to take us to Morolyov, but it transpired that this town's

---

1 The travel notes are not reproduced in full. [Subsequent note by author.]
2 A fairly primitive horse-drawn cart-like conveyance, without springs.

resemblance to Venice is only partial: although it consists exclusively of canals overflowing with mud and water, the gondolas hereabouts are four-footed ones. Cautiously we boarded a tarantass[2] and set off. After traversing almost the whole town we disembarked at the doorway of a stone house. The clicking of a Kodak was heard, upon which Morolyov embraced Sergusya in a hug and informed us that out triumphant entry through the gates had been immortalized on film. Vasily Mitrofanovich urged us to the table, where he regaled us with pies and apricot brandy. Himself he enthusiastically downed several glasses of vodka, firing off a stream of talk and bustling about, creating a most welcoming atmosphere.

Seryozha was hardly allowed time to swallow the last mouthful when he was sat down at the piano by Vasily Mitrofanovich to begin his Nikopol sentence of hard labour, which differed from the Egyptian variety by lasting not one day but one and half. Seryozha played through entire volumes of music, one following another until almost the complete Morolyov library was piled up on the piano desk. Around four o'clock Seryozha begged Vasily Mitrofanovich to release him so that he could have a shave, a request the latter reluctantly acceded to as he sorrowfully opened the door while already relishing the prospect of the lengthy evening concert he was villainously envisaging.

By half past ten Seryozha, pale as death, was lying on the sofa having his temples rubbed with vinegar as he helplessly sipped water and wine. But the implacable Vasily Mitrofanovich was unmoved by this pathetic sight and continued to insist: 'Now, Seryozha, at least just play the first movement and the finale! After all it's child's play to you, but for me it is pure pleasure ...'

But Seryohza was egotistical enough to deny Vasily Mitrofanovich his pleasure and instead 'gathered up his sash and hat and quickly left the scene'.[1] We wandered about the waterlogged streets while Vasily Mitrofanovich entertained guests at home with supper and Rachmaninov's Serenade. Deciding that we must get away tomorrow by the twelve o'clock train, and formulating a crafty ruse to achieve this, we returned home where Vasily Mitrofanovich put us to bed and we sank instantly into the deepest sleep.

26 January

I did not wake up until nine o'clock, but Seryozha enjoyed hearing the innocent voices of the children going to school at seven. At ten we summoned Vasily Mitrofanovich and revealed our artful scheme: he was very near taking offence but was at least partly mollified by the second and third movements of the Rachmaninov Concerto and the whole of the Prokofiev Concerto. He was dubious about the work by Sergey Prokofiev, but was once

---

1 Russian folk expression.

again transported by that by Sergey Rachmaninov, and having been presented with a card bearing the somewhat barbed inscription, 'To his dear friend Vasily Mitrofanovich from the unhappy victim he tortured on 25 January 1913', sent us on our way with his blessing.

Chapter 4: Simferopol

I: Simferopol welcomed us with fair weather, but at first glance the town is no more than mediocre, at least up to the level of the Hotel Europa, which fully lived up to its name. Here we changed our clothes and sallied forth looking appropriately European, walking around the handsome streets, having something to drink, making the occasional purchase and most importantly looking for a car to take us on the expedition we were planning for the morrow. At our first attempt we were left smiling wryly at the price demanded, a 'Katenka',[1] and continued the hunt at another garage, now with the help of Alyosha Karsky, a fat schoolboy we happened to meet at a crossroads whose girth as far exceeded his height as his unprepossessing appearance did his mental capabilities. Max from political considerations made friends with him, whereas I yielded to Christian imperatives and teased him so ferociously that he may even have become a little thinner.

The three of us did the rounds of garage proprietors, becoming in the process expert in the distinction between a limousine and a landaulet, but failed to find what we really hankered after, an open-topped car. We hired a landaulet for the following day and then went to the matinee performance at the theatre. Conducted into what seemed to be a private box, we found it occupied by a trio of young children, one of whom turned out to be Kisa, the younger sister of the very Miss Lyutz with whom Max had a certain understanding. We left the theatre some time before the end of the show, Max to pay a call at Aksakovskaya Street where Lyutz lives, while I returned to our hotel.

After that we went for a walk, changed, and went to a concert of chamber music by Tchaikovsky. Pyotr Ilyich's Trio gave us great pleasure, enhanced by a thoroughly excellent performance. During the interval I made the acquaintance of the Lyutz family and formed the opinion that Mr and Mme were fine people, their elder daughter Klava was unworthy of attention, while the object of Max's attentions, Marusya, was a curious, slim girl, rather nervous, with red hair and an unusual face. Quitting the concert to revisit the theatre and then coming back once again, we savoured to our great enjoyment Tchaikovsky's First String Quartet. Before we finally left the concert Mme Lyutz extended an invitation to visit them.

---

1   A 100-rouble note, so called because it bore a portrait of Catherine the Great.

28 January

Chapter 5: In the Car

Max: Our red landaulet stood throbbing at the door. Climbing in, we first called in at the post office, where I sent off 5 roubles,[1] after which we set off on the highway that leads to the pass. The weather was wonderful, the automobile purred along in fine fettle, and we were as happy with the one as with the other. As we approached the mountains the scenery grew more picturesque. We crossed the Salgir river several times. The first signs of snow began to appear, increasing in depth until eventually the wheels of the landaulet started unambiguously to skid. We stopped for ten minutes at Taushan-Bazar for the chauffeur and his assistant to fit chains to the wheels. These had the opposite effect to that usually expected from such encumbrances, as far from slowing us up they allowed us to proceed further. We sped over the pass (2,350 feet) and, enjoying the warm breeze and the blue of the sea, began the descent to Alushta.

Alushta was warm but uninteresting, so after a walk along the promenade we continued our journey, gradually becoming aware that another red car containing two passengers was following us. Before long we realized that the mysterious strangers were intent on overtaking us. Our driver in a patriotic fervour urged our machine on to the limit, giving us the thrill of our lives as we hurtled round the steep bends of the highway overhanging the precipice. The race went on almost until the final bend on the approach to Gurzuf. We were shaken about like kittens and the trunk on the roof performed the dance of the seven veils. When it shed its final covering the chauffeur's assistant crawled with chimpanzee-like agility up on the top of the car and lashed everything down firmly again. But all these heroic efforts were in vain, and to the deafening screech of the other car's horn we were overtaken and reduced to turning into Gurzuf and the consolation of lunch at the Second Hotel.

I: The beluga we had consumed was pickling itself nicely inside us and restoring our good humour in its suspension of cognac and white wine, until the smooth blue surface of the sea tempted us on to a boat. Resisting the blandishments of a Turkish felucca we installed ourselves in a Russian boat and sailed off into the welcoming sea. Pushkin's grotto was very nice, and the one next to it, slightly smaller and dubbed by local wits Madame

---

[1] The note accompanying the money transfer read: 'Dear Sir, in accordance with the instructions of my friend Seryozha Prokofiev I have the honour to transfer to you the sum of 5 roubles which should be added to the amount collected for the gift to A. N. Yesipova. M. Schmidthof, Simferopol, 28 January 1913.' [Subsequent note by author.] This coolly provocative note was sent to Boris Zakharov.

Pushkin's Grotto, made me think of Natasha Goncharova.[1] We then put in at the rocky Oddolary cliffs and tried to land in order to walk on them, but as soon as we reached the shore we had to leave again quickly as the sun was about to set. We left the park unvisited and our indefatigable motor conveyed us to Yalta. By this time we were accustomed to the speed of our motion and passed the time calmly chatting of this and that.

We very much liked the famous town of Yalta. We took a room at the Rossiya Hotel, but were then faced with the disagreeable necessity of reviewing our financial situation, which was threatening to deny us any possibility of ever getting back to St Petersburg. After an anguished discussion we decided we would have to economize on food, cutting out the luxurious delicacies we enjoyed so much. Having written a stack of postcards we went out to post them, and then went for a walk along the promenade to enjoy the delights of Yalta.

Chapter 6: *The Troika*

The journey to Alupka was enjoyable but, in comparison with our motorized dash, intolerably long. The weather took a turn for the worse, becoming cold and rainy. The palace at Alupka is a fine place but the park is positively enchanting, and the temptation to come back and visit it again in summer was irresistible. The sun came out, blessing us with its southern warmth, and inclined us as we settled back into our carriage to vote Alupka the jewel of the south coast.

Max: Describing an incredible series of spirals we ascended to the Baidar Pass, where again we encountered snow. Seryozha wrapped himself in his cloak and we longingly went over in our memory the fast drive we had enjoyed the day before. It was already quite dark by eight o'clock when at last we saw bright lights and the carriage clattered through the arch into our so-called hotel.

30 January

At seven o'clock in the morning some kind soul with our interests at heart woke us up to look at the sunrise. This morning, however, the resplendent god's ascent to the Empyrean had bashfully concealed itself behind a cloud.

We decided a brisk walk down to the church at Foros would be in order, taking in a couple of good Baidar steaks at the same time. We then continued our journey to Sebastopol. It took us four hours on a boring highway to

---

1 Pushkin was married to Natalya Goncharova, the namesake of the Conservatoire student who had caught Prokofiev's fancy. Neither should be confused with the great Cubist painter.

reach the 'White City', during which we saw the last of the sea and felt the last of the warmth. On arrival we went to the railway station, where we had lunch. A visit to the post office produced no more than a miserable teapot.[1] Then we walked down Historic Boulevard, carefully examined the famous fortifications, drank chocolate in a patisserie and ended up back at the station, where finally we dozed off in the train bearing us to Simferopol.

Chapter 7: Simferopol Again

I: Embraced by the soft beds of the Europa Hotel, the dust of our journey cleansed by our well-appointed washbasin, our cheeks freshly shaved by an obliging barber, our long-suffering suitcase refilled with clean linen, we revelled once again in the pleasures of civilization and slept halfway round the clock. The other important event was our invitation to dine with the Lyutz family.

Around three o'clock we made our *entrée* into the house on Aksakovskaya Street (in the provinces the morning is hardly over before it is time for dinner). The comfort of the surroundings and the deliciousness of the meal were in sharp contrast to the provincial manner of the way it was served, as was the gentle courtesy of the parents to the wildness of the children.

But the train would brook no delay, and so at the height of the revels we had to tear ourselves away – the capital beckoned. Collecting our suitcase we bade farewell to the Europa Hotel, and half an hour later the noble express was bearing me away from cheerful southern climes to the cheerful north, while reckless Max, unable to part from his fragrant flower, stayed behind in Simferopol to play out the final act of his drama.

Chapter 8: My Return Journey

Compensation for my unavoidable departure came in the form of the long-awaited new rolling stock. Gratefully I stretched out on the bunk as outside raged a snowstorm of such ferocity that my nose froze the instant I stuck it out of the window.

2 February

The weather next morning was as brilliant as it had been the day we came from Petersburg to Simferopol, except that the Réamur thermometer was

---

1 A 'teapot' is Simferopol schoolboy slang for something going wrong. We had been expecting a pile of letters but there were only two. Nos. 17A and 18A, the Karneyev girls, Dranishnikov and others had all let us down. [Subsequent note by author.]

now showing –16 degrees, a piquant contrast to the +16 it had been in Yalta.[1] At Kharkov the Reberg girls chatted away to me, and during dinner two ladies from Simferopol plied me with questions about my impressions of their city. After a good night's sleep alone in my four-berth compartment I finally set my foot on the pavements of the capital. St Petersburg was enjoying mild winter weather as a white taxi carried me home to Pervaya Rota.

3 February

I reached home at eleven o'clock in the morning, half an hour after Mama arrived from Moscow. She had had a wonderful time there, and had been delighted by my present to her for her name-day. It consisted of an album of snapshots taken by me five or six years ago in Sontsovka that had then been forgotten about. I had dug out the negatives and given them to the Kodak shop to develop and print. Before our departure I had given the printed photographs to a Moscow aunt of Max's who was on a visit to St Petersburg at the time, asking her to send them to Mama in her hotel on her name-day. The plan worked without a hitch.

Until two o'clock I played a piano version of Beethoven's Seventh Symphony, which I had been learning at odd moments during our trip, and at two went to call on Anna Nikolayevna to celebrate her name-day. As usual on this occasion her drawing room was full of students of both sexes, the majority of whom did not know how to behave. Boryusya greeted me politely but thereafter avoided me, evidently offended by the 5 roubles I had sent via Max. Hansen, to whom I could not after all avoid saying hello, started flirting with me. Lintvaryova, Shtember, Sharoyev, Zeiliger and Raya Livshitz were all very nice. There were about twenty new students there, half of whom I did not know at all, while the other half reacted to me with unconcealed hostility, presumably because of my equally manifest indifference to them. Yesipova herself was very nice but did not invite me for the evening (perhaps there was not going to be one at all?). If there is, and I am not invited, who will be, besides Zakharov?

I went to see Tcherepnin, but he and his wife had been so careless as to go out. Their son came to the door, and stammeringly passed on the message that Papa would like me to go straight to the orchestra class. I went home, passing Umnenkaya's house on the way, and occupied myself with writing my travel notes in this notebook. Telephoned the Ruzskys, who pressed me to go and see them. I did so; although not a complete waste of time I did not

1 The Réamur scale goes from zero degrees (freezing) to eighty degrees (boiling) of water at normal atmospheric pressure. Sixteen degrees above or below zero would therefore be twenty degrees centigrade.

particularly enjoy myself. When I looked at Tanya I could not help remembering Kislovodsk. Nikolay Pavlovich was as delightful as ever, and full of praise for the *Ballade*. We will play it together in the next few days.

4 February

At ten o'clock I went to orchestra class to be welcomed affectionately by Tcherepusha, who insisted he had been missing me. There has been another change in plans for our current activities. Naturally nothing was said about *Maccabaeus*, and the proposed concert with Beethoven's Seventh Symphony also seems to have gone up in smoke; the new idea is a concert to celebrate the centenary of Dargomyzhsky's[1] birth, in two weeks' time, no less. Tcherepnin was already reading through *Kazachok*[2] this very day as well as the *Finnish Fantasia*,[3] some choruses, and other pieces. *Kazachok* presents a highly attractive sound world, and reawakened in me the notion of composing some serious and stylish dances for orchestra. I conducted Vyshnegradsky's[4] *Andante* based on a glorious Chuvash melody.

Wenzel attempted to engage me in a lengthy conversation, but I evaded it. While away on my trip I had sent more than eighty postcards, one of which was to him. He was touched by this and regretted that he had not known where to send a reply. Since Yesipova was teaching at home and there were not many congenial faces in the Conservatoire, I initially went into the class for the express purpose of learning new Dargomyzhsky scores, and then went to Peretz for something to eat.

When I returned I saw Natasha Goncharova, who on seeing me exclaimed, 'Oh, how wonderful to see you!' A girl she knew happened to be coming towards her just as she said this, and taking the exclamation as meant for her rushed to fling her arms round Natasha's neck. A farcical scene ensued, and the girl quickly took herself off. My meeting with Natasha was joyful and full of affection.

The opera class greeted me in a very friendly manner. Kruglovsky sprang to his feet and adopted a humorous pose; the Rozhanovich sisters were cheerfully demonstrative. I did not stay long; the performances were

---

1 Alexander Dargomyzhsky (1813–1869), composer who lived and worked in St Petersburg. His two best-known operas, *Rusalka* and the posthumous *The Stone Guest*, after the poem by Pushkin, orchestrated by Rimsky-Korsakov, are still in the repertory.
2 *Malorossiiski Kazachok* for orchestra (1864). A Kazachok is a dance from the Ukraine.
3 *Chukhonskaya Fantasia* (*Finnish Fantasia*; 1867), the second of Dargomyshzky's three orchestral fantasies based on folk material. Finland was an autonomous grand duchy of Russia until 1917.
4 Ivan Vyshnegradsky (1893–1979), at this stage strongly influenced by Scriabin but following his emigration to Paris after the Revolution more interested in avant-garde techniques, particularly the use of quarter-tones. At one time he made a serious attempt to interest the piano manufacturers Grotrian-Steinweg in building a piano to accommodate them. Vyshnegradsky later married Alexander Benois's daughter, Yelena.

slack and in any case with Glupenkaya absent they lacked colour for me.

At home I went back to Tchaikovsky's biography with a keen sense of anticipation and read a dozen pages or so, burying myself in another, and enchanting, world. Composed some material for the Finale of the Concerto, melted over my Sonata Op. 14 and revised the song 'The boat cast off'.[1] Wrote my diary and took a bath.

I have not had any letter from Max, although I would have expected one. A letter was forwarded from Sebastopol but I did not recognize the handwriting. Could it be from Umnenkaya, or perhaps from Dranishnikov? The envelope was fairly crude, so probably it was from Dranishnikov.

5 February

In the morning I studied the score of *Kazachok*. At half past eleven I went to the Conservatoire and caught the end of the opera class, where they were going through *The Queen of Spades*. Chided Gauk for wrong harmonies. The role of the Countess was being taken by another singer also called Umnova: her singing was respectable, but her looks were inferior to 17A. Saw Nikolskaya in the distance. We had sent her two postcards from our trip, both with a very fancy representation of two gents in an automobile. On one was written: 'They went to the Crimea', and on the other: 'They are driving round the peninsula.' The cards were not signed, but we had not made any attempt to disguise the handwriting.

With Tcherepnin we went through the Dargomyzhsky pieces. The chorus of the Eastern Hermits[2] is wonderful.

At home I found a clutch of five letters, three from Max. One of these contained a hilarious account of the evening after I left, another was a postcard, and the third a long lament occasioned by the failure of his suit of 7B. I had foreseen this, and advised him that there was no future in staying on longer.

In the evening I went to a student concert, but found nothing there of any interest whatsoever. Golubovskaya played the Korsakov Concerto well; she is the most intelligent of our female students. Dubyansky[3] was pretty bad.

A telegram from Max: he is arriving back tomorrow at eleven on the Black Sea Express. I shall try to meet him, it will be interesting to talk.

In the Russian Music Editions I found a postcard with a picture of Tchaikovsky, showing him not as an old man with a grey beard but as a man of about thirty-five. It was fascinating, and strange, to see him in this way. I never saw Rimsky-Korsakov other than as a greybeard, but presumably he must also at some time have had a rather different appearance!

1 Published as Op. 9 No. 2, to words by Alexey Apukhtin.
2 From *The Stone Guest*.
3 Alexander Dubyansky (1900–?), piano student at the Conservatoire.

6 February

At nine o'clock small orchestra. This group is shortly to make its debut at a student concert in a Haydn symphony, Mozart's *Magic Flute*, the Weber *Konzertstück* and the *Wedding March* of our revered Director. The Weber will be played by Gauk or by a pianist from outside the class. After consulting with me, Tcherepnin apportioned the conducting as follows: I will do the symphony and the *Konzertstück*, the *Flute* goes to Tsybin and the *March* to Dranishnikov. Tcherepnin is lavishing attention on the last named, hoping to make a conductor out of him. Gauk and Solovyov made a hash of their debuts.

This morning I rehearsed the symphony until half past ten, and then dashed in a taxi to Nikolayevsky station to meet Max off the Black Sea Express. I knew he would be in a distressed state from his failure with 7B, I wanted to know how it had all turned out, and indeed I simply wanted to see him and talk to him. Our friendship is too close for us not to have perfect understanding of one another, the worlds we inhabit are the same worlds. I started off by complaining that 17A was avoiding me, whereupon he cheerfully gave me chapter and verse on the finale of his Simferopol hopes. As we had done the last time, we took his suitcase to his home, he kissed his mother, and we went to Leiner's restaurant to have lunch.

Saying goodbye to Max I went back to the Conservatoire to work with the chorus on repertoire for the Dargomyzhsky concert.

At home I read more of the marvellous Tchaikovsky biography and studied Dargomyzhsky's interesting, albeit complicated and slightly absurd *Finnish Fantasia*. A vague feeling of despondency overtook me, but it was soon dispelled by telephone calls from Max and from Vera Meriin asking me to give her an account of our Crimean voyage.

7 February

The morning saw interesting work with the large orchestra on the forthcoming Dargomyzhsky concert. I then went to Anna Nikolayevna for a lesson, the first for two months. She was extremely friendly and went through two movements of the Chopin B flat minor Sonata with me. She had many valuable things to say, but all the wrong way round. I played reasonably well. Saw Kolka Shtember, who was making rather crude jokes. Met Natasha at the entrance to the Conservatoire: exclamations of joy, at which I took her arm and walked with her to the tram stop.

Went to eat in the canteen. On the stairs met Zinka Lenkina, who bore down on me asking me not to misrepresent things she says. Commiserating with her yesterday on the criticisms voiced by Vera Dmitriyevna, I had overheard her saying she was in such a rush to get somewhere else that 'feathers were growing on her calves'. I informed Klingman that Lenka Zinkina had vouchsaved the information that hairs were growing on her calves. Klingman was aghast, turned bright red and today passed on to Lenka Zinkina what I had told her. I was subjected to a stiff lecture from her that the phrase 'feathers are growing on my calves' is to be found in Chekhov.

Because Palechek is ill, Klimov has been put in charge of the musical side of the opera class. I put Skorunsky on to conduct while I sat idly by waiting for Umnenkaya. It was a great moment when the door opened and she appeared. I immediately went to sit next to her. 'Nice to see you are still alive. I was beginning to wonder.'

'Have you been back long?' she asked.

'Yes, I've been back in St Petersburg for a week now.'

This was a deliberate exaggeration arising from my irritation at her taking so long to appear in class. I asked if she was going to sing Polina today, but it appeared that this was out of the question: she was hoarse, and besides, she was due to sing in a concert on the 9th. Where? 'Oh, a long way away.' What was she singing? 'Tchaikovsky's "On the Golden Cornfields".'[1] We were not able to spend long together, because Klimov had to go off to a lesson and asked me to take his place. I spent an hour and a half working on the ensembles, adopting a rather discreet approach to the singers, which they seem to have appreciated – at least, they all came up to me before leaving to thank me for the way I had worked with them. Hardly anyone was left by the end of the class, as everyone wanted to go off and study the part of the Countess. But Umnenkaya sat it out until the very end.

In the evening I had planned to play the *Ballade* with Ruzsky, but he is going away to Vilnius and the idea had to be called off. Visited the police station to report the loss of my passport during my trip to the Crimea. The police officer wanted to know how it had come to be lost. I said I thought it must have fallen out of my suitcase.

Max came round in the evening. We reminisced about our trip and looked through my letters from 1911, which I had recently got back from the binders.

We wrote a card to schoolboy Karsky with a teapot on it and added a note to the effect that 'Katya will not be coming'. He had been very keen that Max's sister should come and visit him in Simferopol.

8 February

In the morning I made some progress with the Finale of the Concerto. Around one o'clock I went into the Conservatoire. Nelli Frantsis said, 'Oh,

---

1 No. 2 of Six Songs, Op. 57, to words by A. K. Tolstoy.

how wonderful the Crimea is! When you go again, do take me with you!'

In Tcherepnin's class we looked in detail at the Finnish *Fantasia* and, for some reason, *Sadko*.¹ The first scene has such energy, it goes as if on wings! And the fourth scene is a really interesting challenge to bring off; the only thing is, it is so incredibly long drawn out. After Tcherepnin I thought of going into the opera ensemble class, but there was no Umnenkaya and it was so dull even the flies were expiring from boredom. I turned on my heel and went home. As I walked along I thought to myself that after all she was at heart a pig: I had sent her four letters and not only had she not replied, she had not said a word about them when we met yesterday. But in the end I decided it was not worth bothering about.

In the evening Max and I wanted to go to the theatre, but there was nothing decent on. We did not feel inclined to sit at home, so went out to see what we would see. We rang up the Karneyeva girls, in whom our sixteen postcards sent from the road – each one outdoing the other in refinements of wit – had produced a sensation. The girls said they would very much like to see us. We strolled along Nevsky and went into the station to renew our acquaintance with the Sebastopol Express, for which we had developed a great affection. We drank cups of chocolate at Filippov's and were home by eleven. For some reason I was in the gayest of moods all evening. I thought of Zakharov.

9 February

Because Umnenkaya is singing somewhere or other at a concert today and without doubt will be spending the day in an agony of apprehension, I wrote her a letter filled with the most amiable nonsense.

Nothing much happened in the small orchestra class and I was home by one o'clock. I should have liked to show my compositions to Koussevitzky with a view to his performing them, but he had given his last concert and was on the point of leaving. Bad timing. Vera Dmitriyevna has been complaining to Tcherepnin that I do not bow to her and am generally impolite.

At home I revised 'Despair'.² The original version, whose middle section I am dissatisfied with, has been lost. I restored the opening from memory, making it a bit more interesting, and for the middle section found some very attractive material in a piece I had written and dedicated to Myaskovsky in 1907, contemporaneously with the little *Carnaval* from which I drew the main theme of the First Piano Concerto.

1   Opera (1897) by Rimsky-Korsakov.
2   Originally composed in 1908 and revised for publication as Op. 4 No. 3.

In the afternoon I went skating with Kolya Ruzsky. Tomorrow there is a big group going to Yukki, in expectation of which a mountain of three hundred sandwiches has been prepared, and I am invited. At first I was not very keen, but then I thought I should like to go. I do so love the fresh air!

At ten o'clock I put on my tails and went to the Meshcherskys, who were holding a grand ball. A blonde girl with whom I had had a sharp exchange at supper last time rather attracted me this time around, but I simply could not remember her surname, Lanson perhaps. On seeing me she inclined her head, but when in the quadrille it fell out that she and I would have to waltz together she cried out, 'What, with you? No thank you! Not for the world!'

I responded, 'Well, I don't want to either', and then started dancing with her. But she tore herself away and ran off. Later on in the evening she came up to me and said, 'Sergey Sergeyevich, play me something from the *Feuerzauber*.'[1]

I replied laughingly, 'I don't want to play you the *Feuerzauber*!'

'Oh but please, well, something else, then!'

'I'm not going to play you anything!'

'Why not? Well then, let's go and sit somewhere and talk.'

'Be off with you, please. I've no desire to talk to you!'

Silence. Then, disappointed: 'Well anyhow, it wasn't you I was interested in, it was just Wagner's music . . .'

'And when I asked you to dance, it wasn't you I wanted, it was just a woman to dance with!'

She laughed. Silence. Then she turned on her heel and left.

At the ball I made the acquaintance of the Kavos sisters, glorious girls; they had known about me for some time. They are friends of Borovsky and especially of Zakharov, and for this reason I tried to be extra charming to them. They gave me their telephone number, asked me to call them and generally to deepen our acquaintance. At a quarter past three I dragged myself away to go home, although I did not really want to. But I have to get some sleep before Yukki tomorrow.

10 February

Got up at a quarter past nine, put on my white skating outfit with a lightweight overcoat on top, felt boots, and went to the Finland Station. Besides the Ruzsky girls and their mother there were Tata Konshina with her brother and B. N. Yastrebov, and a dozen or so people I didn't know. Although the thermometer was showing −9 degrees, the sun was shining so brightly and

---

1 Magic Fire Music from Wagner's *Die Walküre*.

the weather generally so marvellous that half Petersburg was making its way out to Finland and the train was so packed it seemed as though it would literally burst open. In Levashova we got sledges, and for some reason Ira Ruzskaya insisted on sharing one with me. I had no objection. It was a little dangerous to begin with, but then became extremely pleasant. It was a very jolly ride, but I kept thinking of Umnenkaya and deciding that some time I really must bring her here. After sledging down the hill eleven times we went to have lunch in a dacha specially reserved for the occasion, where a servant put out a delicious spread from the baskets we had brought with us. After lunch we went out for a sleigh drive. It is a beautiful area; the sun dazzlingly bright and the snow like the down of a feather bed. Three times we tumbled out of the sleigh, enjoying ourselves hugely, got lost and ended up in Pargolovo.[1] There we messed about for an hour, getting frozen stiff with the cold, and as soon as we found our way back to Yukki came inside to warm up again. As a result we were all very merry as we hurtled back to the station. Our sleigh made the trip without incident, but one of the other sleighs tangled with one coming in the opposite direction, turned over and broke a shaft, tumbled the horse into the ditch and had to pay a fine. On the way back the Ruzskys invited me to their house, but I had slept less than five hours the previous night and felt so sleepy that I went straight home to sleep. In the evening I had another invitation from the Karneyeva girls, but again was so tired that I declined, as I did Max's suggestion that we go to a chamber music evening in memory of Tchaikovsky. I stayed at home, idly leafing through Tchaikovsky's biography, and at eleven o'clock turned in.

11 February

The copyist charged 15 roubles for copying the score of the Concerto; it looks beautiful, but there are some mistakes and I face a horrendous task making the corrections.

In the morning the orchestra class studied the *Finnish Fantasia*, an interesting piece. I then returned home, buying several newspapers on the way to see if I could find any reviews of the concert in which 17A was singing. Indeed I found one in the *Petersburg Gazette*: she had been singing somewhere at the Gunpowder Works[2] and had worn a pink dress. That was all the critic had to say about her.

At half past three I went to the opera class. Umnenkaya also came, but

---

1 Small inland town in hill country to the north-west of St Petersburg.
2 The Gunpowder Works was established as a private company by Imperial Decree in 1884, the Russo-Turkish War having conclusively demonstrated the need for copious and reliable supplies of gunpowder for munitions. The factory was situated on the banks of the Neva near Schlüsselberg.

found a hidden corner to sit in. I had to play for the whole class as Skorunsky, when he learned I would be there, declined to turn up. The last time at the Ensemble class I rather curtly forbade him to leave the room when he got up suddenly from his seat. He paid no attention, went all the same, and on top of that seems now to have taken offence.

Leaving the class I ran into Lida[1] in the doorway. She thanked me for the note I had sent her on Saturday, saying that it had helped to reassure her. Evidently my calculations had been accurate, my note had arrived in time and had been welcomed. She had sung well and celebrated happily until five in the morning. Umnenkaya was utterly charming, flirtatious, and of course this was all delightful for me. I told her I had been missing her, and she said the same about me. She thanked me for the letters I had sent from the Crimea, and in return I thanked her for the letter she had promised to write to me and that I was still waiting for. She promised next time to write without fail. Then I shall have to go away again soon! I accompanied her to her next class, she said she would be there again tomorrow, and I went home walking on air.

In the evening Max and I went to the 'Crooked Mirror'[2] and laughed ourselves silly. On the whole he is disenchanted with life because of the dashing of his hopes of 7B he had suffered in Simferopol. In addition, at home they are continually criticizing him because of the trip, and he is not being given enough money to live on. 'It would be a fine thing to shoot myself.'

12 February

Made some progress with the Finale of the Concerto in the morning, composing the concluding material. Had the idea of writing an orchestral suite in the summer, designed to be attractive and musically not too difficult, rather as Tchaikovsky 'serendipitously' wrote the *Serenade for Strings*. Then I went to be shaved, and on to Alfyorov to take out 50 roubles, to Skhefals about my shoes, and to the Conservatoire.

With Tcherepnin we went through strictly technical points in the Weber *Konzertstück* in preparation for the orchestral performance coming up. This was followed by the chorus, and then the ensemble class. Umnenkaya arrived and took her seat. Klimov was tearing one unfortunate Liza to shreds with insupportable pedantry, while I sat having nothing to do except get infuriated by his denseness. But just then a happy thought struck me: I went over to Umnenkaya and the red-haired Natasha (the English rose and the English horse) and suggested to them that we go off on our own and work

1 Lidia Umnova.
2 A satirical topical revue theatre with a high standard of writing, established in 1908 in the Theatre Club of the Society of Dramatic and Musical Authors in St Petersburg.

somewhere else. They willingly agreed, we found an empty classroom and starting going through Polina and the Countess. Umnenkaya was in high spirits and sang with gusto. She has a strong voice, the timbre struck me as too thick to be entirely pleasing, but she herself is a delight. Redheaded Natasha sang well.

After that we returned to the class, where Skorunsky continued to accompany and Klimov to pick holes in everything. Gabel sat near by. The scene in question was the one by the canal in which Herman sings of seeing the Countess's ghost. Skorunsky simply could not work out the rhythm, contenting himself with a vague tremolo. I went over and gave him the beat so that he could see it. Gabel rushed over as well and started playing the notes on his back and then on the keyboard, getting frightfully excited and getting it wrong himself. I stretched my arm round Skorunsky's shoulder and played two bars with mathematical precision. Gabel shrieked joyfully, 'Yes! That's it! Of course, just like that!' Skorunsky, much embarrassed, tried to strum something, but still could not manage it. I went back to my seat where Umnenkaya whispered to me, 'Foo, how shameful to be so bad!' I was delighted to have made such a good impression on her and treasured her words.

In the evening Max and I went to the student concert. We missed Nelli Frantsis's performance, but saw her afterwards surrounded by friends. The only word to describe Vera Alpers's playing is awful. Seryozha Alpers was not bad. I approached their parents with praise for Seryozha without paying any attention to Verochka, but when Madame opened her mouth to say something and began, 'Sergey Sergeyevich . . .' I briskly went over to the door, and saying good night, disappeared.

13 February

At nine o'clock the junior orchestra, which is also preparing for the concert. I went home after that, not to do anything in particular, and around three o'clock went to Tcherepnin's class. There we went through Beethoven's Fourth Symphony, which we are going to play later with the small orchestra. At half past five I returned home intending to spend the evening working, particularly on tomorrow's lesson with Yesipova, but Zoya Karneyeva telephoned asking Max and me to come and dine. I looked in my book and saw that today is her name-day.

Something untoward occurred with the box of chocolates I took with me as a present: we were greeted by Lida and by Madame in the entrance hall, the sound of guests could be heard in the drawing room, but Zoya was nowhere to be seen, so I left the chocolates in the hall and entered the drawing room. Having found Zoya I went back into the hall, but the chocolates were gone. After dinner, in response to requests, I played Op. 1, the 'Gavotte' from Op. 12 and the *Scherzo* from the Op. 14 Sonata. In connection with the 'Gavotte' it came up in conversation that it was dedicated to Boryusya. I said, 'You probably imagine that "Boryusya" is Boryusya Zakharov. Well, the 'Gavotte' certainly is dedicated to Boryusya, but not that one!' Incidentally, he rang up to congratulate Zoya. I brought Max back home with me, and after chatting for an hour we parted, well content with the events of the day.

14 February

Finnish Fantasia and *Kazachok* with the large orchestra, after which Tcherepnin sat discussing a questionnaire on 'whether music is harmful'. There is no doubt that Mozart died from exhaustion brought on by an excess of creativity, Schubert died from the irregularities of his way of life, Schumann was generally an unhappy man, introverted, solitary, and took to drink from loneliness. But Liszt, Wagner, Haydn testify to the fact that music does not necessarily have any effect on longevity.

Until two o'clock I stayed on in the empty classroom playing the piano, and then at two went to Yesipova. The day before yesterday, at the student concert I had been to with Max, I came to the conclusion that overall Yesipova had done me more harm than good, putting me off performing on stage and taking away from me much of my love for and joy in the instrument.

Now, I played her the March and the Finale of the Chopin Sonata. Her comments were arcane, but not uninteresting. She recommended me to study an Adagio from a Mozart sonata for the next lesson. But the most important thing she said was that I would be equipped to graduate next year. I was thrilled to hear this, since I had already firmly resolved to sever my links with the Conservatoire next season, and feared that Yesipova might put some obstacles in my path.

After a meal in the canteen I went to the opera class. No. 17A came, but so late that I was already getting bored. At the end of the class she and I lingered together at the door of her piano class and spent an enchanting half-hour, never taking our eyes off one another and talking about everything under the sun. I would absolutely love to take her to Yukki on Sunday, but am not mentioning this just at the moment.

In the evening Max grumbled that he was too lazy to want to do anything, but I forced him to come with me. As we entered the concert hall we heard Nikolskaya producing a brilliant ending to whatever piece she had been performing. This was a great surprise to both of us. After hearing another performance we left the hall to find Ariadna strolling along the corridors past the mirrors with some fellow in a frock-coat.

15 February

At nine in the morning, a special session for the small orchestra. We took the strings desk by desk through virtually the whole of the programme for the concert. I became completely exhausted and at half past twelve went home, asking Tcherepnin to be so generous as to give us another class in the afternoon, which he gladly agreed to do. At home I read a little of the Tchaikovsky biography, wrote up some of my diary, and around four went into the ensemble class. Since Klimov was taking them through *Faust*, I suggested to the *Pique Dame* cast that we go into another classroom, where I spent two hours working with them. Umnenkaya was among them, but I did not work with her until just before the end, having to devote more attention to the others. After our work I did not get much chance to talk to Lida, as other people kept getting in the way. In the evening I stayed at home thinking out 'Despair', writing my diary, and reading *Satyricon* and the biography.

Yesterday morning I went with Tcherepnin into Kotte's class to show him the Bassoon Scherzo. There and then it was tried out with four of the students. The students scratched and squeaked their way through it rather inexpertly, but what surprised me was how splendidly and entertainingly it came out. This time Tcherepnin was delighted with the Scherzo, and Kotte undertook to study and perform it properly. What a pity the student concerts are over!

16 February

At nine o'clock a serious rehearsal had been laid on with the small orchestra. This orchestra does not play particularly well, and the Weber accompaniment was frankly bad. Tsybin is ill and his work was given to Dranishnikov.

After this class we went to the general rehearsal of *Elektra* at the Mariinsky Theatre. The Conservatoire had three boxes allocated, one for the opera class, one for the Theory students and one for the conductors. I had been put in charge and so had to act the mother hen with her chicks, settling them all in their seats in the boxes and chasing out intruders. When I had done that I took the box ticket and went down into the stalls, where I thought I might find Umnenkaya and where there are always interesting people to be seen. I did indeed find Umnenkaya quite soon, but she was sitting so far along from the gangway, engaged moreover in conversation with someone, that I simply went up, shook her hand in greeting and went on my way. I wanted to catch Wahrlich, but he was dancing attendance on acquaintance after acquaintance with such a business-like air that I felt I could not interrupt. Aslanov was friendly, asked me to come and see him (he lives near me) and wanted to know if I had any works suitable for children. Then we settled down to listen to

Richard's work. What most interested me was his concept of scenography, by which I mean the representation of the action and the text in the music.

There were places where I experienced the keenest satisfaction, although I did find it strange that the inner workings of the mind of a small woman lost in the remote vastness of a gigantic stage should generate such an explosion of noise from the brass and the bass drum that the roof seemed about to cave in. True, I do not know the story very well, and am therefore not so moved by the developing passions of the characters. As for the music itself, some moments are highly dramatic and powerful but some are of the greatest vulgarity, there is a superfluity of note-spinning, a total absence of any vestige of form, and the piece is inconceivably long. Generally, the music is curious but not genuine, as fake gold does not ring true.

Extremely tired and dissatisfied, I returned home through the cold and the wind and ten degrees of frost. Umnenkaya telephoned as promised at five. In spite of the cold I had been hoping for her agreement to our trip, but once again she refused: tomorrow she would not be allowed out; it would be cold; it was too far away; and it was the name-day of her small niece. So it came to nothing, and I was left alone to console myself after yet another refusal by Glupenkaya. Either because things had not turned out as I wanted, or because it had genuinely promised to be an enjoyable excursion, I was terribly disappointed.

Instead I stayed at home playing chess with Mlle Roblin, my governess of years ago, who had come to stay with Mama for a few days. I was delighted when Max telephoned; he had a free evening and so I invited him over. Before he arrived I went to the police station again about my passport, and learned to my great satisfaction that my old one had been found in the compartment of the Sebastopol train. It had been sent on from Sebastopol and could now be returned to me. Max and I wrote in the 'Yellow Book' and talked over the student concert.

17 February

In the morning the thermometer was showing minus twelve. This helped to dispel my irritation with Umnenkaya, as to go in such cold would not be possible in any case. But then the sun came out, light flooded into my room, the temperature rose to minus seven, and again I regretted our lost day. However, I got over it with a prolonged spell of work on the Concerto, composing successfully today. But as a composer it must be admitted that I work slowly – nowhere near the rapidity of Tchaikovsky, who could turn out an entire opera scene in two days or thereabouts. One explanation of this could be Tchaikovsky's relative indifference to the harmonic aspects of his music: it takes much less time to write a melody than it does its harmonic accoutrements. But I am always absorbed in the latter, with the result that after three hours' or so productive and uninterrupted work there can still be less than a page to show for it.

Some time after four I went to call on the Rayevskys, whom I had not seen since the New Year when they were all ill. The weather was mixed frost and sunshine, and I had a wonderful walk there and back, covering more than ten versts in all. I caught it in the neck from the snobbish Rayevskys for coming muffled up in a white skating cap. I was piqued by this: the temperature was ten below and my ears would have got cold.

In the evening I went to a charity evening at the Konshins. It was an unbelievably elegant do, with ministers, Kokovtsov[1] and mandarins of such ilk. The men were wearing full evening dress although I, not having anticipated this level of grandeur, was only in a dinner suit, which made me feel ill at ease. Despite the participation of such luminaries as Ziloti, Yershov and others, the greatest success belonged to Yelena Popova, a young singer from the Imperial Theatre still studying at the Conservatoire. She and I are on friendly terms, and I could not have been more happy at her success.

18 February

As I walked over to the orchestra class this morning I had a feeling that because of Shrovetide nobody would show up. So it proved, and after struggling on until eleven Tcherepnin dismissed the half of the orchestra that had come. Then they played a rather silly quartet by Vyshnegradsky for three flutes and harp, after which we went through excerpts from *A Life for the Tsar*[2] in view of the tercentenary of the Romanov dynasty.

On Thursday there is to be a solemn afternoon concert with anthems and excerpts from *A Life for the Tsar*, which I have to conduct and accompany.

Following this, at Max's request I renewed my acquaintance with the younger Hansen sister.[3] He finds her attractive. Marta Shverlein[4] told me her music teacher from Dvinsk had sent her a letter overflowing with praise for my compositions and saying that she gives them to all her pupils to play. What an agreeable thought, that with no effort on my part at all, my music is being played in the provinces. Oh, the world is not totally devoid of good people!

1   Count Vladimir Kokovtsov (1853–1943), politician, prime minister from 1911 to 1914.
2   Opera (1836) by Glinka. In Soviet times the opera was renamed *Ivan Susanin* (which was, in fact, Glinka's original title) after the eponymous hero who sacrifices his life by deliberately leading the Polish forces hunting the newly crowned Tsar astray in order to save his life.
3   Cecilia, the violinist.
4   A somewhat back-handed nickname for Yelena Klingman. In Gounod's (and Goethe's) *Faust*, Marthe Schwertlein is the heroine Marguérite's morally compromised duenna-like neighbour whose amorous hobnobbings with Mephistopheles facilitate Faust's conquest of Marguérite's virtue.

Around two o'clock I met Max Anatolievich[1] at Peretz's and we ate pancakes. We then went together to the Conservatoire. Paying no attention to the minus ten degrees Max had on only an autumn overcoat. In the Conservatoire we went up to the third floor to wait for Umnenkaya, but the moment she appeared Gabel caught hold of me and started talking about something, so I had to let her pass us by.

In the opera class I both accompanied and conducted. I had a mild contretemps with Palechek over tempi, but later we sorted it out and with the help of the piano score reached agreement. He poked me affectionately in the ribs and said I was 's–s–stubborn'.

Stayed home in the evening, practised Mozart, wrote my diary, and was delighted by a very friendly letter from Yurasovsky,[2] who wrote in response to my request to tell me that if I wanted to see Koussevitzky the best thing would be to come to Moscow on the 24th. I'll go like a shot.

19 February

At ten o'clock there took place the general rehearsal for today's concert by the small orchestra. Tcherepnin was in a state of incredible nerves, but when I drew attention to this he replied mildly that, on the contrary, he was feeling exceptionally calm. The beginning of the rehearsal was a disgrace, but after a while they pulled themselves together and began to play quite well. The Weber, which I had been especially nervous about, also went well. For the first time the piano was in its proper concert position; for the earlier rehearsals it had been stuck somewhere at the back, miles behind the orchestra. I love to see a grand piano with the lid open, in position on the stage in front of the orchestra, ready for the concert. I felt this surge of affection in the summer when I played my Concerto, and now, as I stood on the podium with the instrument open behind me, I felt it again. The thought came to me that in the course of my life I should no doubt be both playing and conducting a great many concerts. Which of these activities would I be doing more often, it would be interesting to know?!

I hardly had time to go home and eat some bliny when it was time to return to the Conservatoire and go through the excerpts from *A Life for the Tsar* with Tcherepnin, and to rehearse with the chorus the National Anthem and Glazunov's *All Hail!* The intention had been to have *God Save the Tsar*[3]

---

1 Schmidthof.
2 Alexander Yurasovsky (1890–1922), composer and conductor. A student of Glière, he was more successful as a conductor than as a composer, founding in 1929 and subsequently directing the Smolensk Symphony Orchestra.
3 The Russian national anthem from 1833 to 1917, music by Alexey Lvov.

sung with piano accompaniment, but I had the brilliant notion of having it accompanied by the organ. The idea was accepted, and indeed it now sounds very good.

At half past seven the four of us – Mama, Mlle Roblin, Max and I – got into a hired car and were driven to the concert. We were there early, at ten to eight there was no one in the hall and it looked as though we would be performing to a non-existent audience. The orchestra had annexed every nook and cranny of the artists' room, my heart sank at the chaotic noise emanating from there.

The first item on the programme was the *Magic Flute* overture conducted by Dranishnikov. The concert started slightly late, so that by the time I went out on stage the hall was all but full. Just before going out I had a twinge of apprehension, quite a pleasant feeling, something like the start of a journey. The orchestra played the symphony quite decently for 'junior course' students, but pretty unsatisfactorily for anyone with any sort of discrimination. For my own part, so far as I could judge there were no mistakes (except for one time when I omitted to call for a *forte*). The consensus of listeners was that I conducted very correctly, perhaps too correctly; Glazunov found all the tempi exactly right. Tcherepnin said that everything had been fine and it was now possible to talk to me conductor to conductor. All of this was very pleasant to hear, especially as I have heard times without number from Myaskovsky, Zakharov and not so long ago from Tcherepnin himself, that I would never make a conductor, their judgements invariably expressed with a coldly determined air of damning finality!

The symphony was only moderately well received, probably because people were bored. It was followed by Weber's *Konzertstück*, which Gauk played well in places, but with an awful lot of mistakes. I accompanied carefully and accurately. The orchestra got lost sometimes in the innumerable pauses, but got through to the end successfully. Gauk had a huge success, clearly not on account of his playing but of his pretty face. Dranishnikov then conducted the *Wedding March* to the accompaniment of trumpets and drums and calls for the Director to take a bow. I sat in the buffet drinking lemonade with Max. (A pleasing parallel: this is exactly what I was doing with Zakharov after *Ivan The Terrible*).

For the start of the second half I went up into the balcony where I found Umnenkaya on her own and was able to spend the whole evening with her. As always in such circumstances it was quite lovely. We talked of this and that, of how bad-tempered I am, of who 'Marta Shverlein' really is, of how much she wants to study this role and on Thursday Krasovskaya, Bobrovich and Man-del-baum(!) are coming to her to rehearse the quartet from *Faust*.[1]

---

1   Marguérite, Marthe (a mezzo-soprano role which Lidia would be singing), Mephistopheles and Faust.

In the interval we descended to the ground floor. Mama saw her, and found her very attractive. Umnenkaya had to go home at half past eleven, and in spite of all her protests, I accompanied her there.

20 February

Spent the morning going to the International Bank, to the photographer (who has still not produced anything) and to Alfyorov to draw out 100 roubles: 50 for my trip to Moscow and 25 each for Max and myself.

I then worked at home writing out a fresh score for 'Despair' and generally reading Op. 4 for publication. It felt good to sit and slowly leaf through a complete manuscript! There is a bit of bother about what to call 'Navazhdeniye' in French.[1] I have been pestering Mlle Roblin, but so far have not come up with the right title. ('Fantasmagorie' is not quite it, although it sounds good.) Proof-read and corrected the Paris copy of the D flat Concerto.

At seven o'clock I visited A. V. Ossovsky to ask him for a letter of introduction to Koussevitzky, because there are so many people wanting to see Koussevitzky he might well not admit me. Two years ago Ossovsky had written me a splendid letter of recommendation to Jurgenson, and I now wanted another. But Ossovsky was not at home. Half expecting this I had prepared a note, which I left, promising to return tomorrow. I was actually quite glad not to see him, since it is never very pleasant to have to ask a favour in person; such things are much better done in writing. Also I know that when I sent my F minor Sonata[2] to Koussevitzky's publishing house and the jury there turned it down, Ossovsky supported it, and when the jury still would not accept it, Ossovsky resigned from it.

21 February

The tercentenary of the Romanov dynasty. Celebrations on the street and announcements by the Mayor that the public should be cautious, and not even venture on to the streets at all, better to celebrate privately at home. We had an afternoon concert in the Conservatoire.

I called in to Ossovsky's on the way, and he very kindly gave me a letter for Koussevitzky, less extravagant than the previous one to Jurgenson, but skilfully persuasive especially where he simultaneously requests help to get my works performed and expresses his gratitude for fulfilling the request.

I arrived at the Conservatoire in time for the public service of prayer. Umnenkaya was standing there taking part in the service. We shook hands and I left.

---

1 Ultimately to be entitled 'Suggestion diabolique', published as No. 4 of Op. 4.
2 Sonata No. 1 in F minor, Op. 1.

After the service we all went into the Small Hall, the chorus arranged itself on the stage, and I conducted the National Anthem twice through to the accompaniment of the imposing organ and the two pianos. After that someone read something very long and boring, then Frantsis recited, not very inspiringly, some passages from *Ivan Susanin*,[1] and then the chorus sang numbers from *A Life for the Tsar*. The event closed with me directing a performance of Glazunov's *All Hail!* after which everyone dispersed.

In the evening we hired a car and went to look at the illuminations: Mama, Mademoiselle, Max and I. These were nothing special, but there was such a crowd of people and carriages on Morskaya and Nevsky that we spent more time stationary than moving. Dropping the ladies back at home we went to the station to post a letter to Koussevitzky, along with Ossovsky's recommendation and a request to receive me on Sunday. We took the letter to the Nikolayevsky station because I love those machines that dispense stamps and accept registered letters, and after that we wandered back along Nevsky, where the illuminations had been extinguished, and parted to go home, at peace with the world.

22 February

At night I dreamed of the stock exchange, money, and trying out my brilliant system in Monte Carlo. In the morning I went to the station to get my train ticket to Moscow, yielding to Max's arguments that I should go first class.

Returning home I wrote my diary and at three o'clock went to Myaskushka to see him and to get back my score of *Dreams*. He was very annoyed with me, complaining that I should have been to see him long before this, but had disappeared. And he had some justification, for he had made a transcription of *Dreams* for piano four hands, as well as completing *Alastor* in full score and piano reduction. We played *Alastor* in the duet version. I liked it very much indeed, more than any of his other things. It has a clearer construction and is more distinctive and beautiful than his previous compositions. I am very happy that such a serious and interesting work is dedicated to me. One noteworthy feature is that whereas the opening theme of *Alastor* does not appear to bear any relationship to the opening theme of my G minor Concerto, a correspondence between the two themes emerges during the development.

His transcription of *Dreams* is meticulous, perhaps too much so, as there are places where the texture needs to be lightened. It was interesting to play one's own work in a new arrangement and in a completely new sound world. My new version of 'Despair' appealed to Myaskovsky, who declared the piece

---

1   The poem by Konstantin Ryleyev, on which Glinka based his opera *A Life for the Tsar*.

to be very much to his liking. 'Elan', on the other hand, he did not like at all.

From Myaskovsky I went on to the Ruzskys. Nikolay Pavlovich roared that I had neglected him and no longer loved him. I retorted that it was just the opposite: it was he who had fallen out of love with me; no sooner did I arrive than he would be off to Vilnius. We played the *Ballade*. Perhaps I was tired, but his performance gave me no pleasure. Stuffing the music back into my case, I went home.

23 February

At half past one, lunch with Max at Leiner's restaurant, where we enthusiastically demolished half a bottle of Cordon vert. Then we went for walk, and parted to go home. I forced myself to look through the Paris copy of the Concerto and made some corrections to it.

I telephoned the Karneyev sisters, hoping they might come to the station to see me off, but they said they were busy this evening. Zoya was nice, but Lida was unwarrantably cool, probably still brooding over my refusal to accompany them to the theatre on 13 February. I also rang up Natasha Goncharzon[1] – a long chat crammed with affectionate exchanges.

Then I packed my things, revised four bars of 'Suggestion diabolique' and two of 'Elan', and at half past ten Max called for me in a taxi and we went together to the station. I shared my two-berth compartment with a spherical gentleman, a Mr Leonov, returning home to somewhere near Ryazhsk[2] after attending the tercentenary celebrations in St Petersburg as a delegate. He gave an entertaining account of the festivities. At Lyuban[3] I wrote postcards to Max and to 17A, the latter lovingly and elaborately calculated to produce an effect. At the ball I had shown her a glimpse of my ticket and provoked her importunate curiosity by refusing to tell her where it was for. Previously I had let her know I was tired of St Petersburg and was longing to go off somewhere else. In a word, I had sowed the seeds, and now was suddenly departing, leaving a question mark over how, where and for what reason. I added to my note her favourite music from *The Queen of Spades*, a phrase which always made her laugh: 'I don't want to sleep in a bed, a berth in a small compartment is far more desirable than the room of which I've tired.' On the other side I wrote: 'Farewell, Lidia Ivanovna!' and left it at that.

1 Goncharova.
2 A town between Ryazan and Tambov in Ryazan Province, south-west of Moscow.
3 Station on the main line to Moscow, halfway between Petersburg and Novgorod.

24 February

I slept reasonably well in the upper bunk, and arrived in Moscow at ten o'clock. Posting the cards to Umnenkaya, Goncharova, Mama and Max I took the hotel carriage and went to the Boyars' Court Hotel. There I reserved a room, changed into a frock-coat and went for a quarter of an hour to call on the Smetskoys, who are leaving today. Then I collected up my manuscripts and put them in my case, and made my way to Yurasovsky, who had invited me to do so when he wrote to me.

The story of how I got to know Yurasovsky is as follows. This summer I played my Concerto in Moscow, and in the same programme there was an orchestral work by him, *In the Moonlight*. It was well laid out for the orchestra but not particularly memorable or original, and in contrast to my Concerto, which was warmly applauded, got curtain calls and provoked a lot of discussion, it did not have much success. After the concert four of us – Yurasovsky, Derzhanovsky, Shenshin and I – went together in a cab to Yavorsky's to have supper. We had a good laugh about the expected mauling we would get from Sabaneyev in his review. When I left to return to Petersburg I asked Yurasovsky to send me the reviews from Moscow, which he did. The press's reaction was very different from the audience's: Yurasovsky came off all right, but I was damned comprehensively. Later in the autumn Yurasovsky came to St Petersburg to promote his compositions, met all the top people and according to him had a great success everywhere. He came to lunch with me, when he talked loudly and at great length, and then played me his *Phantom*, which struck me as quite an interesting piece. He heard me play my Sonata No. 2 and said that while of course it was very interesting and inventive, it had not a scrap of real melody in it, just a series of 'tigerish leaps'. This annoyed me, and when he said that the movement he liked best was the Scherzo, I retorted, 'Well, I take just the opposite view, that's my least favourite movement . . .'

'Why?'

'Because the other movements are all more subtle; the Scherzo is targeted at a less discriminating taste.'

I was very much astonished when Yurasovsky brazenly admitted the following: 'I had intended to compose a symphony. But then I thought, no, that will take too long, I'll make do with a single movement and give it an attractive-sounding title. So I rooted around for a bit and came up with a quotation from Victor Hugo, and called the piece *Phantom*. And you see how well it's turned out: everyone thinks it was written to fit the programme!'

In January I had a letter from him asking me to find out what I could about the Court Orchestra. I did as he asked, and in return said I would be glad if he would let me know when Koussevitzky would be in Moscow. In answer I received the friendliest imaginable letter recommending me to come to Moscow on the 24th, inviting me to lunch and offering me a ticket to Koussevitzky's concert in the afternoon. That was the reason I had come to Moscow on that date, and was now appearing on his doorstep for lunch.

The Yurasovsky residence is an imposing apartment; his parents are clearly well off. He is very envious of my success with Jurgenson (200 roubles for the Sonata). He played me his embryonic piano concerto – not worth any attention – and then we went to the Koussevitzky concert. It was a lovely programme: Rachmaninov's *Isle of the Dead* and Second Piano Concerto, and Scriabin's *Extase*. I adored the last named, especially the place where the high moaning of the woodwinds is doubled by the horns down below, a marvellous passage. Nikolay Orlov[1] accosted me in a very friendly fashion at the concert, saying he had tried to buy my Concerto but it is not on sale; he had acquired my first Etude but had not managed to negotiate its difficulties. I met Tamochka Glebova,[2] who wreathed her face in smiles at the sight of me, no doubt recalling how she had snubbed me in January. But I had not forgotten either, and the coldness of my bow to her soon wiped the smile off her face. Before the concert Yurasovsky introduced me to Koussevitzky: he was extremely friendly and said he had long been interested in my compositions, he would be very, very glad to listen to them and made an appointment to do so at five o'clock tomorrow. I was already familiar, from Yurasovsky's expert parody, with his unusual speech mannerisms, drawing out each word to about a mile long.

After the concert Yurasovsky and I went to see Glière, who Yurasovsky said was always at home to musicians on Sunday afternoons, but there was no one there worth bothering about. I played 'something new' – the *Ballade* – on an atrocious piano. Yurasovsky, Glière and Bryskin[3] listened but had nothing to say, not understanding much about it. Glière himself was charming, as always. His wife is in bed, having borne him a second pair of twins.

I left Glière's at eight and went back to the 'Boyars' Court', in good spirits. I had supper in my room, wrote my diary and went to bed at eleven.

25 February

Rose at nine, walked over to the town station and got a ticket for the relief express train. Returning to the hotel, I telephoned Jurgenson and asked for a meeting at one thirty. When I got there we talked for a solid hour, but our conversation led nowhere and my hopes were dashed. He demonstrated to

---

1 Nikolay Orlov (1892–1964), pianist, pupil of Konsantin Igumnov. Orlov left the Soviet Union in 1922 and had a successful career in the West as a Chopin specialist.
2 Tamara Glebova (1892–?), harp student at the St Petersburg Conservatoire.
3 Arkady Bryskin, conductor.

me how it would cost him two thousand to print my Concerto, and how was he expected to recoup the money? Suppose the Concerto would not sell, then he would have lost his two thousand entirely. To cut a long story short, he offered me three hundred roubles, but only after a hundred copies had been sold. 'And even then,' he added, 'it will not be a profitable venture for me since, for example, it might take twelve years for those hundred copies to sell.'

Nettled, I said, 'Well, if it takes twelve years to sell a hundred copies I wouldn't take a fee at all!'

We proceeded to make a note of the agreement. I offered him my *Ballade*, and he accepted it in principle but preferred for the time being not to make a specific agreement because in view of the queue of works waiting their turn it would in any case be several months before anything could be done with it. For instance, the *Toccata* had been waiting since October and had gone to be engraved only a few days ago, while December's Sonata was still in the queue. In short I left not a cent better off than I had come. As I left, I said with a smile, 'All right then, Boris Petrovich, now I shall send you the score of *Dreams*. Last autumn you promised to publish the work, so now you will be able to have the two scores engraved simultaneously.'

'If I did promise, then . . . well . . . I keep my word,' he replied, having obviously failed to take account of this circumstance, which was going to cost him another eight hundred to a thousand roubles.

After that we said goodbye. Outside it was a marvellous day, little streams gurgled past, and I had two and a half hours before my appointment with Koussevitzky. I took from my pocket my 'best friend in Moscow', the plan of the city, and went on foot. Still, I was a little cast down to be returning without any money, and to find all my efforts and powers of persuasion foundering against the stony face of the businessman.

However, I soon recovered my spirits, went into the post office to collect a letter from Max and then to Filippov's for a drink. There I enjoyed reading Max's letter, and following his advice despatched a postcard to Nikolskaya. One side I left completely blank, and on the other wrote, 'To read what is written on the reverse, lightly moisten it with the following mixture: caustic potash 10 gr., citric acid 5 drops, pure spirit 100 gr.' Let her try to work that one out!

From Filippov's I went to see Koussevitzky, in the same building in Glazovsky Lane as three years ago I had tried to meet Scriabin. Sergey Alexandrovich received me with great courtesy, and said that he was most interested in my Concerto which he knew had been performed last year with Saradzhev. He offered tea, while I told him about my years in the Conservatoire, past and present. We then moved to another room. 'What I should really like to hear is your Concerto,' said Koussevitzky.

'In that case you will understand the threefold pleasure it gives me to play it to you,' I returned politely.

He: 'Do you have any objection to playing on a Steinway?'

I: 'On the contrary, this make has the Nobel Prize for pianos!'

He: 'Myself I prefer Bechstein, but if you would prefer to play on a Bechstein we would have to go upstairs.'

I played my D flat Concerto pretty well, with conviction and enjoyment. He sat following the score with great attention, occasionally quietly conducting a phrase. When I had finished, my Concerto elicited praise exceeding anything it had previously attracted. 'Your work has brought me to a state of ecstasy. This is true music, magnificent, magnificent, magnificent music! I am grievously sorry that my subscription series for next season is already planned in detail and I cannot include it in the programmes, but I shall definitely include it in one of the non-subscription concerts for the general public. But it requires a great pianist to play it – yourself, perhaps. I hope that you will agree to perform it this winter in a public concert, and the season after next in the subscription series in St Petersburg and Moscow: either this concerto or whatever else you may have composed by then. Please forgive an intrusive question, but how old are you?'

'Twenty-one.'

'You are very, very young. To have written such a thing at your age, so alive with tension! Of course, Scriabin composed his concerto at the age of eighteen, but it is not to be compared with yours!'

I asked him how he thought pianists would find the Concerto from their point of view, to which he replied, 'I tell you, it is magnificent, magnificent, magnificent music!'

I then played him *Dreams*. His verdict was that it was a beautiful work that should certainly be published and would be performed (but not, as he made clear, by himself). However, being an earlier work than the Concerto it could not have the same importance. He then asked me who was publishing my works; had I submitted them to the Russian Music Editions? I said I had, but they had been rejected and now Jurgenson was publishing them. When he heard that I had just offered the Concerto to Jurgenson, Koussevitzky expressed regret, also that I had not sent other works to the Russian Musical Editions. I said I was not sure whether it would now be etiquette in respect of my regular publishers Jurgenson to send my works to another publisher. After this I stood up to take my leave, and Koussevitzky said his concert bureau would send me an official engagement to appear in a public concert next season.

Leaving the hospitable environs of the house on Glazovsky Lane, I went to call on Saradzhev and then Derzhanovsky, but neither were at home, so I returned to the 'Boyars' Court', dined and at nine o'clock took the hotel carriage back to the Nikolayevsky Station, leaving Moscow at ten. Despite the fact that men and women are supposed to be in separate sleeping-car accommodation, I discovered in my compartment a rather unprepossessing woman and a young lady with some resemblance to Lida Karneyeva. Opting for comfort rather than feminine charms, I transferred to an all-male compartment where I slept soundly until morning.

26 February

In Petersburg it was raining, mixed with snow. A white taxi took me swiftly to Pervaya Rota, where although it was by now eleven o'clock everyone was still asleep. I left my suitcase and asked the taxi to wait for me so that I could go on to the orchestra class in the Conservatoire. But this had apparently been postponed until the following day, so instead I went to the opera class. The first phrase I heard being rehearsed was none other than the famous 'I don't want to sleep in a bed!' Palechek demonstrated admirably the dying moments of the Countess. After an hour I left, rang up Max and met him on Nevsky for lunch at Leiner's. From Leiner's we went back to the Conservatoire in hopes of seeing the delightful Ariadna,[1] but she had already gone and I went to Tcherepnin's class.

Back at home I slept, and when I got up played chess with Mlle Roblin, wrote my diary, practised for Yesipova Mozart's Variations and his C major Sonata, the one Umnenkaya scratches her way through with her long, polished fingernails.

27 February

Although today is normally small orchestra class, because of the impending Dargomyzhsky concert we had the large orchestra. Max came after the class and we went to lunch at Peretz. Before the choral class we had what seemed like an interminable conversation with Zeiliger, to whom, as a rival to Zakharov, we were very attentive. Zakharov and Zeiliger had both reserved recital dates in the Small Hall in October, but Zakharov had been overcome by indecision and had withdrawn.

A recovered Tsybin turned up for the choral class. Tcherepnin announced the order of the programme for the concert: *Finnish Fantasia*, *Kazachok* and some lengthy accompaniment to me; the *Rusalka*[2] dances and 'The Little Golden Cloud Passed the Night'[3] to Tsybin; the choruses and Laura's

---

1   Nikolskaya.
2   Opera composed in 1856 by Dargomyzhsky.
3   The first line of Lermontov's poem 'Utyos' ('The Rock'); of all lyrics perhaps the one most often set to music by Russian composers, and the inspiration for Chekhov's short story 'On The Road', in its turn the basis of Rachmaninov's orchestral fantasy *The Rock*.

arias[1] to him, Tcherepnin – why? By what right? No right at all, that's just how it is. The teacher's right to take the bread from the mouths of his students.

At home I worked on some details in the Finale of my Second Concerto. Wrote to Koussevitzky thanking him for his 'generous attitude' to my music. The graduating students' exams begin tomorrow, and Lavrov's class will be performing.

28 February

Because the Small Hall is now taken up with exams and the threat of the Artistic Opera Company has for the time being receded from the Great Hall, today we were rehearsing there. We were visited by Glazunov, Gabel and Vyshnegradsky. We played the Andante from the latter's symphony, which we had studied with the orchestra in between whiles.

Vyshnegradsky is a member of the Conservatoire Directorate and a composer of minor talent but serious and technically proficient. For some reason Glazunov had wanted the orchestra to perform the Andante from his symphony, apologizing for the fact that it would have to be done without the celesta since the Conservatoire did not possess such an instrument. Vyshnegradsky exclaimed, 'Then allow me, please, to donate a celesta!'

The instrument was ordered from Paris, and Vyshnegradsky's bank was sent a bill for 500 roubles. Tcherepnin was terribly proud of having thus earned the Conservatoire a celesta, and told Glazunov all about it. Glazunov mumbled, 'We don't have a tuba either . . .'

And so, today we were playing his Andante. Tcherepnin conducted first, followed by me.

After the orchestra class I went to Offitserskaya Street (almost opposite Umnenkaya's apartment) for my lesson with Yesipova. But when I rang the bell, out bounded a dog, followed by Kalantarova and then Yesipova: they were going for a walk. To keep them company I had to walk along Offitserskaya as far as the Kryukov canal. I spoke proudly about my developing relationship with Koussevitzky, but this made no impact on Yesipova. Anna Nikolayevna is not impressed by any developments that take place without her involvement. As for today's lesson, she was occupied solely with her students who were graduating; lesser mortals were postponed to another day. I returned to my place of learning and lunched with Max in the canteen.

After that we went to hear Lavrov's class give their exam performances. The interval was enlivened by the appearance of a whole *pléiade* of girls from

---

[1] From *The Stone Guest*.

the fifth General Subjects class, including Damskaya,[1] Khantsin and two very pretty girls. The *pléiade* began by milling aimlessly about, but then settled into a semi-circle around one of the windows in the foyer. As I passed, one of them called out something. I spun round to them and, making a gesture of surprise, said, 'My God, the whole class all together in one place! All that's missing is someone to give you a lecture!'

'Give us one! We want one!' they chorused.

I sat down and started a long conversation with them, the girls making plain how delighted they were to make my acquaintance. Eventually they all drifted away, only Damskaya still clinging on with a plea that I should write a harp piece for her to play. I promised I would, and went into the opera class, but today they were doing *Rigoletto*.

At home I started on a Prelude for harp, which came together quickly and promised to sound effective. Max came at nine o'clock and dragged me out. We walked along Nevsky and Morskaya and dropped into Filippov's for a cup of cocoa, discussing the attraction of the Islands in such glorious weather and how nice it would be, once the Neva thaws, to take a boat out to Schlüsselberg.

At home I sat up until a quarter past one finishing off the Harp Prelude, after which I played it through five times and, hugely delighted with myself, went to bed.

1 March

In the morning I set out with the intention of composing some more of the Concerto, but instead improvised for a projected set of ten 'easy pieces' for piano, in which I would include a version of the harp piece. I ended up not doing very much at all, and at twelve thirty went into the Conservatoire to listen to the exam performances in the Small Hall, which proved to be deadly dull. I went into Tcherepnin's class and spent the best part of four hours there, hearing a sad piece of news: *Pique Dame* is hanging by a thread. First, the orchestral musicians are also taking their exams, so rehearsals and exam performances are bound to get in each other's way. Second, we do not have a Herman: Brudno is frankly deplorable and Kuklin, although good, is

---

1   Eleonora Damskaya (1898–?), a harp student at the Conservatoire with whom Prokofiev maintained a friendship and correspondence throughout his time in Petersburg, Petrograd, his years in the West and after his return to the Soviet Union. Friendship and correspondence lapsed between 1927 and 1948, apparently because of Damskaya's perceived unwillingness to help trace the prize grand piano Prokofiev had to leave behind in Petrograd in 1918, but contact was then resumed and continued until shortly before the composer's death. Several letters from the correspondence, which is unpublished, have been translated by Harlow Robinson and included in his *Selected Letters of Sergei Prokofiev* (North Easter University Press, Boston, 1998).

suffering from a 'diplomatic illness' by reason of singing Parsifal at the Sheremetyev. Once again the Conservatoire has disgraced itself. As for me personally, it matters very little either way: I am bored to tears by the whole thing!

I found Umnenkaya up on the second floor talking to a Jew with an extraordinarily large face. She saw me afar off and nodded to me. Max and I approached, but the large-faced Jew was not about to give up so easily, and kept butting in to the conversation, paying no attention to Umnenkaya's evident lack of enthusiasm for his company. 'Look over there,' he said. 'There's Professor Zurmüllen. She's in tears: it's so cruel, they've just failed one of her students!'

He had begun to irritate me. With cool bravado, I said, 'But I'm always happy when someone fails,' – general astonishment – 'because so many people these days are scraping in to qualify as Free Artists that the status is beginning to lose its value, therefore it should be a matter for rejoicing when unnecessary ballast is kept out.'

He started to object, but just then Ossovskaya walked past, and Max said, 'She'll be able to tell us.' He went up to her, and I followed. Ossovskaya was friendly as always, and told us that the student, so far from failing, had in fact got a 5, while Zurmüllen had been so anxious about her that the relief had reduced her to tears.

I returned to the group. 'Zurmüllen is weeping from joy, not from grief. Her student did not fail, but unexpectedly got a 5.'

The Jew was a little taken aback, but continued to protest that she had failed.

My attention was diverted by Tcherepnin, who walked past at this moment and said there would be no ensemble class for *Pique Dame* today. Umnenkaya said she would go home then, at which I suggested we go out for a walk. She then invited me to her house so that I could play her the C major Mozart Sonata, so we went out together into the glorious weather. I dragged her along Morskaya Street and the Moika canal.

My rival today proved to be one of the members of the chorus, a longstanding admirer of Umnenkaya and the one who had looked after her muff while she was rehearsing Lel. While I went off to speak to Tcherepnin he told Umnenkaya that he wrote for one of the papers and just you wait, when that Prokofiev conducts *The Queen of Spades*, I'll scratch his eyes out in my review. Excellent critic! I suspect that the paper he writes for is one of those rags they sell on the street in front of the theatre instead of programmes. The only problem is that, sadly, it looks as though *Pique Dame* is not going to happen!

Stayed at home in the evening, doing nothing in particular and playing chess with Mlle Roblin, who is leaving later today to go to Pskov.

In the Conservatoire today I met Mme Ossovskaya, arm in arm with Mme Yesipova. To the former I expressed my gratitude for her husband's assistance in my Moscow affairs. After I had gone, Varvara Alexandrovna extolled my 'exceptional talent' to Anna Nikolayevna, who chewed her lip affectionately and said: 'Puppy!'

2 March

Rehearsal for Dargomyzhsky at ten o'clock in the Great Hall, consisting mainly of Tsybin worrying away at his *Dances* and Tcherepnin at the pieces he has carved for himself out of the programme. I conducted the *Fantasia* and *Kazachok*, taking pleasure in what I was doing because I now feel myself to be quite a decent conductor. After that I went to Gabel to go through with him and Bobrovich *The Wedding* in the Glazunov orchestration, which I am also to conduct in the concert. This proved to be an interesting challenge as far as the accompaniment is concerned, and I am very glad Tcherepnin let me read it through with the orchestra as well as himself.

At two o'clock Max and I attended the exam performances of Barinova's class. The hall was full, because one of the contenders for the grand piano prize, Rabinovich, was playing. Zakharov and Zeiliger both came to listen, their noses in the air.

Rabinovich's playing was brilliant, but without depth. When we emerged it was raining, but I kept Max company as he was walking Shalyt to her home on Torgovaya Street. Max then came home with me to get a copy of a Chopin *Ballade* and stayed until evening. We happened on an old programme of a concert by Zherebtsova with the text of the duet from Strauss's *Ariadne auf Naxos*, containing the following lines:

> ARIADNE: Were I to find myself
> in your embrace
> I would drown in bliss!
> Secrets lie hidden
> in the breath from your lips.
> Tell me, what has happened?
> What has become of Ariadne?

This passage we cut out and pasted on to a card depicting a beach at the seaside with an appetizing girl resembling Nikolskaya sitting with her back to the viewer, and a sailor standing beside her tenderly holding her hand and shoulder. Putting the card in an envelope and shrieking with laughter we sent it to the delectable 13A.

Then I was visited by a cadet called Muftel, who brought with him his composition, a melodrama to which the text has sadly been lost(!). It was a familiar story: a composer devoid, not completely of talent, but of musical education, with the result veering between ineptitude and vulgarity. In addition, Cadet Muftel was not too bright; Max amused himself disgracefully at his expense. After half an hour the composer took his leave.

My own piano exam will take place in exactly a year's time. If I have any cause for concern, it will be from an unexpected lapse of memory. I have lost confidence in playing from memory, probably because I never play anything without the score. I now feel that if I attempt to play a long programme and am at all subject to nerves, I shall certainly forget and make errors. In truth it is not so much that my memory is poor as that it is overstrained with anxiety. I must take steps to deal with this disagreeable condition before it is too late. From today onwards I shall play by heart!

Mama says that Lyubov Yakovlevna Firsova, Olga Smetskaya's sister, is planning to sell her estate, for which she will get about 300,000 roubles. She would like to move in with us as she is now quite alone in the world. We shall have to take a larger apartment, which we can divide with her. Mama will find life much more pleasant like this, and in addition Lyubov wants to invest in the stock exchange and is asking Mama to take charge of this. Naturally, this should prove profitable.

3 March

Worked on the G minor Concerto in the morning. I am totally in thrall to it, but, my God, when will I ever finish it?

Waited for a phone call from Lida Umnova hoping that she would explain her dereliction of yesterday, but this did not happen. I telephoned her instead. Once again we had a delightful conversation accompanied by an invitation to visit her this evening. I promised to be there at ten o'clock, and felt a thrill of pleasure.

Paid a thank-you call on the Ossovskys, and sounded out the ground as to whether I should send *Dreams* and the *Ballade* to the Russian Music Editions. The answer seemed to be yes. The jury consists of five people: Koussevitzky, Ossovsky, Rachmaninov, Medtner and Struve.[1] The first two will be 'for' and the next two 'against'. All will depend on the fifth, but I have a feeling it will be passed. As for Jurgenson, he should not feel offended, seeing that I have already offered these works to him and he rather turned his nose up at them.

Dined with the Ruzskys. I did not particularly want to, but Nikolay Pavlovich himself telephoned me to find out how things had gone in Moscow, so I felt I had to go. As usual the parents were delightful and the daughters as prickly as she-devils. Nikolay Pavlovich is going to Yekaterinodar and asked for a copy of the *Ballade* so that he could give it to a talented cellist he knows

---

1 Nikolay Struve (?–1920), director of Koussevitzky's Russische Musikverlag, as his Berlin-based Russian Musical Editions publishing concern was known.

there, who is arranging a concert in St Petersburg in the autumn and wants to include the piece.

At half past nine I said goodbye, took a taxi, and after a pleasant drive along the Embankment and Morskaya Street arrived at Umnenkaya's. At first I was disagreeably surprised by the number of guests, who filled the drawing room, but on further investigation they turned out all to be family: a brother, three sisters, their husbands and a couple of outsiders. I spent two very enjoyable hours and felt in excellent form, telling many stories to which Umnenkaya and her sisters listened with evident interest and gales of laughter. I then played the Mozart C major Sonata, my performance eliciting a furore: used to hearing Lidochka stumble through it they were accustomed to thinking of it as a boring and unattractive work. I then played my 'Gavotte', the 'Harp' Prelude and the Scherzo from Op. 14. Lidochka asked me to play something that would make her stay awake all night thinking of me, to which I said that she ought to be doing that anyway. At midnight I took my leave and went home.

4 March

Rose early, looked through Dargomyzhsky's *The Wedding* and was in the Conservatoire by nine, but Tcherepnin did not appear until half past and the orchestra did not assemble before ten. Orchestra class over, I went downstairs where I met Max, and we went together so that I could buy a bowler hat, after which we had a meal at the Kvisisano[1] restaurant and then back to the Conservatoire for the exam performances.

These were boring to the point of stupefaction. By half past three I could stand no more of the Conservatoire and was ready to go home. Max suggested a walk, so we strolled along Offitserskaya, the route we knew Umnenkaya would have to take on her way to the Conservatoire. Sure enough, there she was, running up to us and blushing. I said I was on my way to Yesipova to take her some music, and she said she was going to Jurgenson to buy music. After a quarter of an hour of polite chitchat I accompanied her to the corner of Voznesensky and Offitserskaya Streets, my reward being a stroll in highly agreeable company.

At home there was a letter from Morolyov. He wants to withdraw his thousand-rouble investment in our stocks and shares project. I had to reply, setting out all kinds of arguments why this was not a good idea. Max rang up in the evening, but I resisted all his blandishments: he is leading me into spending far too much time in idle pursuits and this evening I really must

---

1 There was a Kvisisano restaurant in St Petersburg and one in Moscow. The name is a transliteration of Italian 'Qui si sano' – 'Here one is healthy'.

stay at home and work. I practised the Mozart (playing it by heart) and wrote my diary.

Tonechka Popova[1] has the most wonderful perfume. I fell in love with it before Christmas, but it all got used up before I could find out the make. Then Popova herself vanished. Today both Popova and her perfume suddenly reappeared out of the blue, and I relieved her of her handkerchief. Mama thinks the perfume smells like the fresh melted water you sometimes get in the middle of a patch of ice, but I must find out the name of it tomorrow and buy myself some. There are times when I am very much drawn to a strongly aromatic scent. I remember the first time I was in Sukhum I could not get over the smell of the gardenias.

5 March

Waking up in the morning I could still smell the subtle perfume wafting from the handkerchief on the table beside the bed. My spirits immediately soared. I got up, dressed and made some corrections to the *Ballade*. In the score of *The Queen of Spades* I came across the marking *piangendo*, which appeared most apposite to a particular episode in the *Ballade*. The copyist arrived and took away the score to make the copy for Yekaterinodar, and I went to the Conservatoire. On the ground floor I ran into 17A – what was she doing there? There was no reason I knew of, and if there had been, she should have left half an hour ago. Max says she was hanging about the corridors for twenty minutes or so doing nothing, so it looks as though she must have been waiting for me. Kruglovsky then appeared and stared at Lida, which immediately made her blush. When he caught sight of me he giggled and went away, accompanied by my promise to get a pistol and fire corks at him.

When Lidochka had gone I met Antonina Popova and returned her handkerchief to her, demanding in exchange the name of her perfume. She said it was Guerlain Coty, so when Max and I went off to have lunch at Peretz we went into a parfumier only to discover that Guerlain and Coty are equally names of different perfume houses, each of which has fifteen or so varieties. Guerlain Coty is a nonsense, so either Popova was deliberately putting me off the scent or was having a joke on me. We went to Alfyorov and I drew out 100 roubles, 25 of which I gave to Max. Spent 60 kopecks on a taxi back to the Conservatoire to hear Barinova's class exam, Katya Borshch in particular. Kätchen has talent and temperament, but is very uneven: sometimes she is splendid, at other times she simply splashes about.

Ran into Popova and taxed her with misleading me about the make of

---

1 Antonina Popova, singing student at the St Petersburg Conservatoire.

perfume. She promised to make enquiries at home, and I said I would telephone her at eight o'clock.

When I got home I rang Popova. Amused at my persistence, she told me the make was Guerlain Cadine. I immediately went round chemist shops and parfumiers in the locality, asking for it by name in three of them, but nowhere could I find this perfume. I again decided that Tonechka was deceiving me, but when at last I telephoned a big store on Nevsky they did have it. I was thrilled. It's not cheap: 10 roubles for a small bottle.

Max came in the evening and we composed and wrote the 'ultimate witty letter' for Ariadna. The letter was written on fine grey paper with quotations in red ink taken from music she plays. It looks magnificent. The letter's construction is in the form of a dialogue, the conceit being that on presentation of a Chinese banknote we will be authorized to receive letters addressed to us at the Central Post Office, and declaring that for just one signature by Ariadna we are ready to sacrifice our lives. Setting all this out in the most elegant manner we amused ourselves mightily at all the details of the letter and, highly delighted with ourselves, sent it to her address.

6 March

I did not go to the small orchestra class today because I was bored with it and in any case they would probably not turn up. Instead I composed some of the third movement of the Concerto. This is undoubtedly a less striking movement, but it has much good music in it and is impeccably put together.

At half past twelve I went to the 'plumber'[1] to have my teeth plumbed. Then I went to that rascal of a photographer, who still has not got anything for us. But I did find a group picture of Lavrov's class with Radochka[2] leaning forward roguishly, which I bought to hide away in my desk. I then bought a bottle of Guerlain Cadine and am luxuriating in this scent, despite nagging doubts that it may after all not be the same as Popova's.

Max and I went in the evening to Borovsky's concert. He usually plays very well, but is occasionally not completely convincing. It was a success, with encores, flowers and so on. Afterwards Mme Borovskaya invited me to their house to dance, but I politely declined.

---

1 A complicated pun: Prokofiev calls the dentist a 'plombír', which is a sort of ice-cream filled with candied fruit (French *plombière*) while 'plómba' is the proper Russian name for the material with which a dentist fills a cavity.
2 Ariadna Nikolskaya.

7 March

Dargomyzhsky rehearsal in the morning. Tcherepnin kept changing his ideas about tempi in the *Fantasia*, resulting in horrible distortions. He then criticized my gestures. *Kazachok* went well though. Then Tcherepnin, considering that I had not made a good job of conducting *The Wedding* last time, took it over himself and did it in his own way, which was quite at variance with my own good intentions. Following him on to the podium, I attempted to bring it back to its previous form, at which Tcherepnin protested and we crossed swords mildly. Having finished, I sat down with Bobrovich to talk through *The Wedding* once again and clarify for him my conception, while an infuriated Tcherepnin screamed at the orchestra. Later on, at four o'clock, Tcherepnin had a fatherly word with me, during which he assured me that he always had my interests at heart whereas I always seemed to want to pick a fight with him. Presumably his annexing of Laura's arias and the choruses was just another expression of his concern for my interests. After the orchestra class I went to eat in the canteen and then returned to the Conservatoire to listen to the Dubasov class exam.

In the evening I meant to accomplish all sorts of useful tasks, but actually did very little: wrote my diary, read Maupassant's *Pierre et Jean* and had telephone conversations with Umnenkaya and Zoya Karneyeva.

8 March

Before orchestra class, while I still had a clear head, I read through the *Finnish Fantasia*, and having fixed all the gradations of tempo in my brain went in to rehearsal. This time the tempi were praised without reservation. Tsybin's efforts in 'The Little Golden Cloud Passed the Night' were condemned as hopeless, and indeed he is generally not much of a conductor at all. Thanks to the breathing points I had marked in the score and the exhaustive pains I had taken to absorb all the rhythmic details of the vocal part, *The Wedding* was beyond reproach as far as accompanying the soloist was concerned, but Gabel was indignant at the difference between the tempi chosen and those he had wanted. Tcherepnin, who (because of yesterday) was mainly to blame for the muddle over the tempi, at once retired into the background, while I demonstrated my innocence in the matter. Bobrovich was suitably castigated, *The Wedding* had its original contours restored, and when we repeated it all went well. My confrontation with Tcherepnin thus ended in a victory for me. Under his lucid direction the choruses sound truly excellent, the Laura arias as interpreted by Vasilieva less so. I had a flaming row with this same Vasilieva today, which ended with her demanding an apology from me. I replied, 'Most willingly', since I had no desire to insult her, and peace was restored.

Max arrived towards the end of the rehearsal. We left the building immediately it was over and went to have lunch at the 'Vienna' restaurant on Gogol Street. We did not care for the 'Vienna' as much as Leiner's. For me personally the 'Vienna' carries associations with Yesipova's class and in particular with Boris Zakharov: I have been there three times before and always in connection with the Yesipova class exam.

After lunch we went back to the Conservatoire where I listened to the Drozdov class exam. The talented Bai was playing: he was very good. During his performance I thought about my own programme for the following year. The pity is that the more I study particular works the more I get sick of them, ultimately to the extent that I can no longer bring myself to play them . . . I thought it would be better to learn two programmes, with two different works by each composer, so that before the exam I would have a choice of whichever I found least antipathetic at the time. The programme is provisionally taking shape as follows: Bach – C sharp major Fugue; Beethoven – first movement of his last sonata; Schumann – Sonata in F sharp minor (complete), Chopin – Polonaise in A flat and something gentler; Liszt – *Mephisto Waltz*; Russian composer – my *Toccata*.

At home in the evening we, that is to say Mama, had guests (six people), and we played lotto. It was fun, although I do not really like family evenings.

9 March

The general rehearsal started at nine o'clock. There was not much of an audience to begin with, but later a respectable crowd turned up. The *Fantasia* and *Kazachok* seem to be fine, and Tcherepnin's numbers are also good. Tsybin's are mediocre. My own contributions over, I sat in the darkened hall with Umnenkaya and Max. However, I then returned to the platform to conduct *The Wedding*, which this time survived without critical comment. Umnenkaya stayed sitting beside Max, continually drawing attention to the elegance of my appearance on stage. At the end of the rehearsal I enjoyed considerable success with the female elements of the Conservatoire, notably with 22A, who is an incredible flirt, a singer (from the opera class) of only moderate physical charms but a gifted interpreter of the role of the Countess in *The Queen of Spades*.

Max and I then went off to lunch at Leiner's, where we had half a bottle of delicious Graves, and then parted, he to see his aunt on business and I back to the Conservatoire to see about tickets. Gabel, from whom I had boldly requested ten tickets, gave me a note for Friebus,[1] requesting him to give me whatever I asked for (!). I got an additional eight from Annenkov. After furnishing 'Target Girl' No. 21 with three tickets, I went home. Learned the Mozart by heart, wrote my diary, then at half past nine Max came round and we allocated and sent the tickets to Umnenkaya, Myaskovsky and various relations.

Max stayed with me until two o'clock. By the end we had got round to discussing with great enthusiasm a trip next summer, departing on 20 May and covering the following itinerary: St Petersburg – Vologda – Yaroslavl; Yaroslavl to Nizhny Novgorod by boat; thence another steamer to Astrakhan; then a third steamer across the Caspian Sea to Petrovsk. Then by train to Vladikavkaz and the Georgian Military Highway; several days in Tiflis; Borzhom;[2] on to Batum (necessarily in daylight); Batum – Sebastopol; on foot to Alushta taking it in stages over a week via Balaclava, Baidari, Alupka, Yalta, Gurzuf and finally to Alushta; by automobile to Simferopol via Bakhchisarai; and finally express train back to Piter. It will take a month, and we will be back in the capital by 20 June, the date on which Max comes of age and takes possession of his 1,500 roubles, while I shall try to arrange a performance of *Dreams* in Pavlovsk. The programme for the rest of the summer will depend on circumstances, but whatever happens I must find a comfortable little town somewhere in the provinces where I can bury myself and get on with my work.

10 March

After a good night's sleep I rose at eleven and got on with proofreading the copy of the *Ballade* the copyist had brought me. I made corrections to one bar and then put it in a printed-paper-rate wrapping to send to Yekaterinodar.[3]

At a quarter to two Max called for me in a taxi and Mama joined us to go to the Conservatoire. The concert opened with a lengthy address by Sacchetti, which lasted three-quarters of an hour, after which it took some time for the audience to fill the hall. Untroubled by nerves, I spent some of the time in the artists' room and some with Myaskovsky, talking about his transcription of *Dreams* (he had taken the score back to revise some passages in accordance with my suggestions). He does this work with extreme conscientiousness and meticulous care; too much so in places, where he could be more imaginative in compressing and simplifying the texture. All the changes

---

1 Alexander Friebus, head librarian of the St Petersburg Conservatoire and subsequently at the Mariinsky Theatre. A small, hunchbacked man, his nickname among the students was 'Diminished Fifth'.
2 As with Sukhumi, a more acceptable spelling to present-day Georgians is Borzhomi.
3 At the request of Nikolay Ruzsky. See p. 333.

I suggested in *Alastor* he has incorporated, which is very flattering to me.

Sacchetti having finished his speech, I was summoned to the podium for the first item, the *Finnish Fantasia*. A few people started clapping as I walked on, but they were not supported and the hall soon subsided into quiet. I thought I conducted the *Fantasia* very well. It had a moderate success, and was followed by a trio conducted by Tsybin. I returned to accompany Bobrovich in *The Wedding*, which did not go quite as well as at the rehearsal, but Bobrovich and I, and Tcherepnin and Gabel, were all satisfied. Bobrovich and I acknowledged one another, and I came back on to conduct *Kazachok*. This went with a swing and had a great success; Tcherepnin's verdict was that I had done well and had succeeded in convincing a lot of people today of my talent. He went on to deliver himself of the following nonsense: 'Not so long ago people were saying it would never be possible to make a conductor out of you, but I stood firm and was the only one to defend you, and now you see how my words have been justified.'

The truth was the complete opposite: there were many who had great hopes of seeing me become a good conductor, and it was Tcherepnin who with incredible persistence kept telling me my hands were no good, my gestures useless, I would never be a conductor even if eventually I would just about manage to conduct my own works...

Interval. Max informed me that 17A was in the audience, 11A also, and listening very attentively, apparently in a state of some excitement. We went out into the foyer, to encounter 17A with her brother and sister coming towards us. We made a lively group: Max, I, and the three Umnovs. The interval soon came to an end, however.

The second half consisted of a whole selection of songs with orchestral accompaniment conducted by Dranishnikov. We conductors and assistant conductors sat in the buffet drinking tea with Tcherepnin. This evening he is off to Kazan for a week, and wants us in the meantime to work with the small orchestra. As the senior member, it will be my job to look after the juniors, make sure Gauk gets some opportunities to conduct, and generally oversee the satisfactory progress of his work. But my most important task will be to get a grip of the orchestra, exerting my authority to exclude from the class anyone who is disobedient, in collaboration with the orchestra manager's assistant. In short, for the duration I am to be invested with the dignity of Tcherepnin's own office. The opera repertoire will be two acts of *Rigoletto* and one act of *Faust*, to be performed in two weeks' time with piano accompaniment, either by Tsybin and myself, or just myself.

In the second interval I chatted with my relations, and once again with Umnenkaya, with whom I strolled up and down deep in conversation, raked by the critical gaze of the elder Alpers. I exchanged bows with an extremely elegantly turned out Mme Umnenkaya.

In the third half of the concert I sat with Max near my relations. Student Tcherepnin conducted the choruses smoothly. Tsybin, rising and squatting on his haunches and waving his arms like a Ukrainian, brought the concert to a close with the dances from *Rusalka*. Afterwards Tcherepnin kept me back for a long conversation, so that by the time I wished him a good journey to Kazan the hall was deserted, except for Max who, loyal friend that he is, had waited for me. We decided to go somewhere for dinner with half a bottle of Cordon vert, and having settled on the modest Leiner's, sat there until well after eight.

Later that evening I read a little and wrote.

11 March

At last a free morning, and I can do some composing. Settled down to the Concerto, but did not achieve much – was interrupted by a questionnaire I had been sent about my musical biography for a new publication by Engel of Riemann's Dictionary.[1] Since the questionnaire has been circulated with a musical journal, it is by no means certain that the publishers are specifically seeking information about me; it has been sent to all musicians and only those considered worthy of attention will be included in the publication. Since I do not know whether I am yet in this category I feel disinclined to send my biography for it to be pitched straight into the waste-paper basket.

After lunch I went to my 'plumber' and then by arrangement met Max. We went to the Central Post Office to see whether any reply had been received from Ariadna to our last missive. Approaching the window where *poste-restante* letters are claimed, I enquired for anything addressed to: 'Bearer of a Chinese Note of Exchange.'

'What number?'

'I'm not sure what number . . . it will be in Chinese . . .'

The girl made a thorough search but no letter could be found. We had scored, as they say in Simferopol, a teapot, and somewhat chagrined made our way to the Conservatoire.

I met Natasha Goncharova, who said the usual things very pleasant to hear, and listened in her company to a female student of Nikolayev. Then I went to the opera class, because the imminence of the production, even though it is only to piano accompaniment, seriously demands attendance. We went through Act III of *Faust*. I am not very familiar with this music,

---

1 Hugo Riemann (1849–1919), German scholar and musicologist. His *Encyclopaedia of Music*, considered at the time the standard work, was published in German in five separate editions between 1882 and 1900, the last edition being translated into Russian and originally published by Jurgenson.

and although I was conducting, I was mainly concerned with listening, absorbing and committing to memory.

Home for dinner, after which I put on my dinner suit, took a car and went to pick up Umnenkaya. For some years now we have had a season ticket for Wagner's *Ring*, two stalls seats in the fifteenth row. I have grown tired of it over the last few years, so Mama and I have been in the habit of not taking up our seats but passing them on to others. But this time I decided to make use of ours for Umnenkaya, and a week ago proposed our going together to *Die Walküre* today. Umnenkaya had agreed, and so at seven minutes to eight I was ringing the bell at her door. She had worried that I would not come and regretted that I was so late: she was on her own and had thought we could sit quietly and talk. She was looking wonderful all snuggled up in her furs as we descended the fantastic staircase of No. 60 Offitserskaya Street. 'Carrrr!' ordered the freshly tipped doorman, darting out on to the street, and we rolled happily away to the theatre. We barely had time to leave our coats and go into the auditorium before the lights dimmed and *The Valkyrie* began.

While recognizing Wagner's genius I never cease to be amazed at the sheer quantity of unnecessary music that dilutes the episodes of pure genius. Listening to Wagner is indissolubly linked in my mind with a sensation of incredible, black boredom. If half of it were to be cut and the opera ruthlessly pruned, the result would be an incontrovertible masterpiece. It was a long time since I had heard a performance of *Valkyrie*, and this evening I listened with genuine pleasure, the best being, as before, the second part of Act II. The sound of Hunding's horn offstage sent me into ecstasies. As for the tedious bits they were greatly relieved by the presence of such a charming companion as Lidochka. At the end of the first act I said to her, 'There you are, Lidochka, that is the way in which, five years from now, I shall arrive on your doorstep and wrest you away from your future husband . . .'

Silence.

'Agreed?'

'Agreed.'

'Make sure you have the sword ready for me!'

The whole evening went by in the pleasantest manner. I was walking home with her, when she said, 'What gave you the happy idea of taking me to *Valkyrie*?'

I replied that she had declined so many of my happy ideas that I had almost decided not to invite her to *Valkyrie*.

At home, Mama said, 'That was Lidia Ivanovna you were out with, wasn't it?'

'Yes.'

'Just look at you, your head's still in a whirl . . .'

And certainly, lovely though the thought of marrying Lidochka is, I know we would be deliriously happy for half a year, and then after another half a year we would separate. This second phase would not be so difficult – I have a great technique for parting with people. Dear Lidochka!

12 March

In the course of the morning I finished the sketches for the third movement. Everything has fitted together splendidly. I am happy.

Around two o'clock I came in to listen to the Yesipova class examinations. This is a 'big day' in the Conservatoire. Among those graduating this year are Poznyakovskaya,[1] Zeiliger and Zakharov – all of them good, none of them outstanding. The examination, which took place in front of a packed hall, lasted from 2 p.m. until 6 p.m., and was an extremely exhausting event. The result was as before: Zeiliger has talent, Zakharov is more intelligent and harder working. Much of Zakharov's playing was of great refinement, but it lacked brilliance of technique, temperament and warmth. He failed to electrify the audience, and at the end of his programme people started to leave, although all agreed that he had played well . . . well, but blandly.

I went into the artists' room while Poznyakovskaya was on the platform, drawn there more by curiosity than any special sympathy or antipathy. Sitting there were Zeiliger, two of his friends, and Zakharov, yellow as a piece of old parchment. Zeiliger was thumping out something on the piano with the practice pedal down, while Zakharov responded rather reluctantly to my remarks. I had no real purpose in being in the artists' room, but I persuaded Zeiliger to play me two Scriabin Etudes. After that he got up and went out of the room, whereupon Zakharov said: 'I'll now play you a study by Lyapunov.'[2] I listened to the étude, made some irrelevant remark about his cuffs, and left.

At home I was plunged into a bad mood, brought on by tiredness and a slight indisposition, but by evening it had all vanished, so I studied Beethoven's Symphony No. 4 in preparation for conducting it tomorrow.

13 March

At nine o'clock in the morning I was in the small orchestra class, discharging the responsibilities of Tcherepnin *in absentia*. I read through and started

---

1 Natalya Poznyakovskaya (1889–1981). She was later, in May 1925, to give the first performance in the Soviet Union of Prokofiev's Piano Concerto No. 3, at a concert organized by the Association for Contemporary Music in Leningrad (although the pianist originally proposed for this event was Samuel Feinberg; it seems he did not succeed in learning it in time).
2 Sergey Lyapunov (1859–1924), composer, pianist, conductor and professor at the Conservatoire. A disciple of the 'Mighty Handful', he was particularly associated with Mily Balakirev. An extant piano roll recording of him performing his *Elegy on the Death of Franz Liszt* (Etude No. 12) reveals him to have been a prodigiously powerful pianist.

work on the second and third movements of Beethoven's Fourth, both of which the orchestra found difficult. Tsybin was not there, Dranishnikov had hurt his hand, so I put Gauk on to conduct. He has evidently been practising his conducting technique at home, and is capable of something approaching a decent conducting style, but the orchestra refuses to pay attention to him. Generally the orchestra behaved rather badly and I had to shout at them, but I was reluctant to resort to the stricter measures Nikolay Nikolayevich sometimes employs, such as excluding certain musicians from the orchestra.

Tired, I went home, had lunch, and went to the dentist. But the dentist was ill and had gone to the doctor, so the session was cancelled. I did not want to go back home, as the weather was good, so I continued on to the Conservatoire to listen to the singing exam. In fact I was quite keen to hear some of my friends who were graduating, and sat through all the performances. Damskaya played me my Prelude on the harp; it sounds much as I envisaged it, but she did not play well. I played it to her on the piano to illustrate how I wanted it; she showed enthusiasm and promised to learn to play it as it should be played.

At home I practised the piano and wrote my diary. The fine weather drew me back outside, and at eight o'clock Max and I met and walked along Nevsky, then along the Embankment and past Umnenkaya's house along Offitserskaya. From the Mariinsky Theatre back to my home we took a car, discussing excitedly the trip we were planning to make during Holy Week to the Caucasus (Tiflis and the Georgian Military Highway). To do this Max would need at least 150 roubles from his grandfather, and as for me, I need the stock exchange to go up. I have sold 'Iron-Cement', which I had inauspiciously bought last August, at a loss of 1,250 roubles, but made a profit of 700 on 'Nikopol'.

14 March

In the morning I studied the third act of *Faust*, because last time Palechek had convinced me that I did not know it sufficiently well. I played for Yesipova, and then at half past one Max and I met to go together to the Central Post Office. But the only letter there was for us was the one we had sent ourselves to test that in fact letters sent by this method really did get there. Walking past the new 'Astoria' Hotel, Max pointed to the windows looking out over the corner of Morskaya Street and St Isaac's Square, and said, 'What a *chic* place to have a room that would be!'

It was announced in the opera class that there were to be no performances at all, not even with piano. This has not greatly upset me, in fact I am quite glad: to conduct an opera without an orchestra is not a particularly enjoyable experience, set against the vast amount of time it takes to prepare it. But

I am beginning to notice something: whenever I am assigned an opera to conduct, it immediately gets cancelled. (1) the repeat performance of the Jubilee Concert; (2) *The Stone Guest*; (3) *Pique Dame*; (4) *Rigoletto* and *Faust*.

At seven o'clock I went to old man Saburov's to dine *en famille*. The day before yesterday he rang me up – at eight thirty in the morning, no less – to invite me to dinner. Among the guests was N. S. Tereshchenko, of the wealthy family that plays a prominent role in the musical world, particularly opera. I was very happy indeed to make the acquaintance of any member of this family. Tereshchenko said he liked my Sonata Op. 1 very much; he is a knowledgeable composer himself and given to bashing away merrily on the piano.

Before going to Saburov I called on Myaskovsky. He gave me his unambiguous opinion that I shall never make a conductor, I don't have the hands and arms for it, my rhythm is erratic, etc., etc. I jokingly replied that such a judgement merely confirmed that the depth of his knowledge of music is matched only by the depth of his ignorance about conducting. He has incorporated some of my suggested changes in his *Dreams* transcription, and left other passages as they were. The transcription is very good, merely a little awkward in places.

In the biography of Tchaikovsky I have reached 11 April 1981. On the day of my birth Pyotr Ilyich was in the middle of the Atlantic Ocean on his way to America. A storm was raging and he was tormented by terror and seasickness.

15 March

I meant to do some composing in the morning, but did not; instead practised Schumann for Yesipova.

Went in to the opera class at eleven, not to work, but to meet Umnenkaya. Also, although the performance has been cancelled, Gabel asked me to drop in from time to time to check on the musical side of the class. Lidochka was there.

At home, practised Schumann. Rang 17A, who was surprised that this morning I had disappeared without warning, and said that not having seen me for some time she was missing me. This put me in a wonderful frame of mind. Met Max at the box office of the Maly Theatre, and we saw *As It Happened*, a lively and amusing play. I don't go to the theatre very often, but enjoy it when I do. On the way back I got a speck of grit in my eye, which I tried for a long time to get out, but the eye continued to be painful and was still hurting when I went to bed.

16 March

Got up early and went to the small orchestra class. There were so few musicians there that after waiting forty minutes I conferred with the assistant orchestra manager and dismissed them.

Damskaya, whose heart I have evidently won, played the 'Harp' Prelude again, this time, after the suggestions I had made, much better. Whatever mote had got into my eye still seemed to be there, so I went to the eye clinic (on our staircase) and there they removed a beam. Immediately I could see properly again, a blissful feeling. After lunch I visited the dentist and the photographer, with whom I finally reached agreement, and he promised to develop and print the pictures I wanted.

Home again I had every intention of working, but Yurasovsky appeared, having for some reason come up from Moscow. As usual he talked in a very loud voice, frowned as he listened to excerpts from my Second Piano Concerto, confessed that he found my muse unsympathetic, and finally played me an astonishingly bad Scherzo from his Trio. I told him I thought the Trio might sound all right but the music in it would consist of complete rubbish. Yurasovsky cheerfully agreed with this evaluation. On the other hand, the choir he conducts is extremely talented. Bidding him goodbye, I attempted to dissuade him from further claims on my society.

In the evening I pasted into my black notebook my reviews and critiques that have been accumulating since the summer.

Read through my diary entries for November and December, those that referred to Umnenkaya. Very interesting. It appears that no one else has managed to sustain such a prolonged and constantly warm relationship with me as my dearest 17A.

17 March

Worked intensively and productively on the Finale of the Concerto until half past two: a particularly successful passage has finally begun to flow in the development.[1] The main thing is that up until now I have not been able to get the form of the second half of the Finale completely clear in my mind: this has been causing me a great deal of trouble and inhibited all desire to compose. But today the form manifested itself with great clarity down to its details. True, it does not conform to the best of the old traditions, but in itself it is entirely logical and complete, and that is all that matters. I have great respect for the old forms, but I also have complete faith in my own

---

1 Evidently the place where the orchestra has the second subject and the piano has a variation of the main theme. [Subsequent note by author.]

instincts for form, and often give myself licence to depart from convention.

After two o'clock I had lunch, and then my head began to ache from the intensive efforts I had been making all morning. I telephoned Max and suggested that as it was such a glorious day we should go for a walk. We wandered about for two hours, through the Summer Garden, then the Embankments, along Morskaya, drank a glass of Graves at Peretz, and then took a taxi, I to the Meshcherskys and Max to go home. The Meshchersky family was very pleased to see me. They are planning to be in Yessentuki in the summer.

From the Meshcherskys I went along to the Nikolayevsky station to see off Yurasovsky (returning the courtesy he had shown me in Moscow), but he had left by another train. He telephoned me when he returned home to tell me that he had received a fee of 300 roubles for six of his songs from Zimmermann. Bravo, but all the same it does not mean he is destined to be a great composer.

18 March

Had a good composing session on the *Finale* in the morning, a continuation of yesterday's. To the dentist at one o'clock. Max joined me there at two, and we went to the Conservatoire to hear the exam performances by Auer's class, but it turned out that his class had played this morning, and what was happening in the afternoon was boring rubbish. X-A (Khantsin)[1] was in a long dress today, and looked ravishing. Our conversation was as long as her dress. She invited us to visit her in Kerch.[2] Max left to walk Shalyt home, and I went in to the opera class, where I was delighted to see Umnenkaya. After I had finished my work with the class I went up to her, but hardly had I uttered ten words and received the information that instead of her nose healing she had managed to scrape her cheek, when in the distance I observed Tcherepnin making haste straight towards me – he had just returned from his trip. While he plied me with questions, Lidochka turned away and went to her piano class, Tcherepnin continuing to wear me down with his account of not getting as far as the Caucasus but being bogged down in Moscow.

When I finally extricated myself from the clutches of my over-affectionate professor, I decided I would wait for Umnenkaya to come back, and my patience was eventually rewarded. Lidia Ivanovna and I went for a lovely walk, first along the Moika, then back again as far as the Field of Mars, then along the Embankment, just wandering about until after nine in the evening.

1 Isabella Khantsin, a piano student at the Conservatoire. Prokofiev calls her X-A because her surname begins with the letter 'KH', which in Russian is spelt 'X'.
2 Ancient town on the eastern edge of the Crimea, between the Black Sea and the Sea of Azov.

As delightful as ever. Thanks, it seemed, to the efforts of one Boris Konstantinovich, she would be singing at Peterhof and would thus have to decline my invitation to *Siegfried*. This Boris Konstantinovich is apparently a suitor for her hand, a student by the surname of Olshansky, said to be a 'good chap', tall and gangling according to her, but very clever. He was at her party and we were introduced: he seems extremely nice.

Returning home I dined late and then practised for my next lesson with Yesipova. I still have the Mozart Variations, which I have not touched for five days, firmly in my memory by heart, and I can also play from memory the Schumann Sonata, which I am learning at the moment, so evidently my memory is not as terrible as I had begun to persuade myself it was.

Came across some reviews of Umnova's appearance as Lel in December. (1) 'Lel's aria was well performed by Miss Umnova (class of Prof. Aktseri), the best singing coming in the second couplet of the aria' (*Rech (Speech)*); (2) 'We should note also Miss Umnova who gave a good account of the role of Lel and was acclaimed at the end of her performance' (*The Stock Exchange Gazette*); (3) 'A student, Umnova, who appeared in the role of Lel, has a beautiful voice, but is as yet undeveloped material...' (*St Petersburg News*). All good ones, no stinkers. Bravo!

19 March

Did not compose in the morning, instead practised Schumann for the Yesipova lesson and read through my diary of the Crimean trip, which I have promised to show to 17A. Then Tcherepnin's class at two o'clock. From September until late spring Tcherepnin always goes about in a beaver fur coat with the collar turned up, and is therefore always getting a cold. Today he appeared in an autumn overcoat.

I: 'Nikolay Nikolayevich, how is it that you are not wearing your fur coat?'
'Well, you know... it doesn't seem so bad today... quite warm, really...'
'Mind you don't catch cold: it's only +18 today!'

I had nothing to do in the class so went home, practised for Yesipova, went to Alfyorov to draw out 100 roubles (40 for Max, 60 for me) and round about five o'clock went into the Conservatoire.

In the evening someone rang up, and when I went to pick up the telephone, a voice said, 'Listen to what's being played.' I heard my Gavotte. The call was from the Meshcherskys, who adore this piece. They asked me to dine informally on Friday.

Sensational news from Ruzskys, all of whose property in their apartment has been distrained on account of some debts, while Nikolay Pavlovich is away. *Quel scandale!* I'm sure this has something to do with Tanechka and the high and mighty way she always carries on!

20 March

At nine o'clock I was in the orchestra class with the small orchestra, the large orchestra having been stood down until the Graduation Concert. Tsybin was going through the Andante desk by desk, and the tedium and gloom were of such Stygian proportions that I went home to compose my Concerto.

I was reading yesterday how deeply absorbed Tchaikovsky had been in the composition of his Sixth Symphony, and this fired my own inspiration. I worked right through until seven o'clock in the evening with no more than an hour off to go to the dentist, completing the coda of the Finale and the trio of the Scherzo. To my own great surprise the Concerto seems to be nearly finished: there remain the first movement cadenza (which I already sketched out in plan), and then all the gaps still needing to be stitched up, where I know what I want but not how to get it. This is primarily a matter of technique. I do not expect the orchestration to take very long: I want to keep the accompaniment simple and transparent. The coda in the Finale is very convincing and appropriate, but I don't expect it will please those who take pleasure in decoding this Concerto. On the other hand, the Scherzo's trio is as charming as can be.

Yesterday I finished reading Tchaikovsky's biography. It has taken me five months, and given the greatest satisfaction. Not to mention that in any case I love detailed descriptions of real life, this book is in itself one of the most interesting I have ever read.

21 March

In the morning practised Schumann for Yesipova, wrote my diary, was not moved to compose. About two o'clock met Max in the Conservatoire: he had a lesson with Ossovskaya and I with Yesipova, but neither teacher was in fact working as they were both attending the exam performances of Vengerova's class. This is really quite a disgrace: since the New Year I have had all of three lessons! I hear that Akhron has moved to Dubasov. Although I do not much like Akhron, I approve the step he has taken.

Bought the score of Tchaikovsky's Sixth Symphony, and reading it in the evening found myself utterly captivated by the stunning beauty of its emotional power. A thrilling work. According to Tchaikovsky, the work has a programme, 'but what the programme is will remain an enigma to all who hear it'.[1]

Worked on the composition of the Concerto (first movement cadenza) until four o'clock. As a bonus I also had a marvellous idea for the conclusion

---

1 As related by Diaghilev. [Subsequent note by author.]

of the first movement, but I cannot work out the end of the cadenza itself, that is to say how to connect the cadenza to the new idea. The join must be seamless, as this is a key point.

Visited the Meshcherskys, where Yershov was surrounded by a cluster of girls for whom he signed autographs on postcards bearing his likeness. Before that he had been posing for some of the girls to sketch his portrait.

However, I was soon asked to sit down and play the Scherzo from my Second Sonata, which hereabouts ranks with the 'Gavotte' as my most popular piece. It was a success, and a contented Yershov, with typical egocentricity, declared: 'A t–talented . . . devil . . .!' This expression, in turn, created an effect and was greeted with acclaim; and then we went in to dinner. I sat next to Nina. After dinner Madame and I played the Tchaikovsky Trio on two pianos (came off splendidly).

23 March

Small orchestra in the morning, Beethoven Fourth Symphony and a talk with Tcherepnin about the unpleasant impression created by Rimsky-Korsakov's autobiography. It has so much poison and small-mindedness, as though it came from the pen of an insignificant, commonplace individual, not of the great man Rimsky-Korsakov was. Tcherepnin compared Rimsky's literary style with that of Tchaikovsky's letters, to the advantage of the latter. Could it be that while Tchaikovsky's life was a series of triumphs, Rimsky-Korsakov lived in the shadow of the dazzling fireworks detonated by Pyotr Ilyich?

At home, after another visit to the 'plumber', who presented me with a bill for 35 roubles; I did some work and then put on my frock-coat to go with Max (he came to call for me) to congratulate both Lidias on their nameday. While I was at Umnenkaya's, Max stayed in the car. Lidochka was dressed in her best and looking very pretty. There were a lot of people there, but all of them were relations, the sisters and their husbands with – oh horror! – children, a nobly served buffet table in the dining room, and chocolate. I stayed for no more than ten minutes, but all of them were spent chatting to Lida, while the sisters did their best to leave us alone. Lidochka wanted Max to come up too, but I said that was not convenient, made my farewells, and left.

We bought chocolates and by half past five were at the Karneyevs, where we had been invited to dine. There we encountered a representative of the enemy camp in the shape of Georges Zakharov. When he was introduced to Max the sullen hostility between the two camps erupted. Max and I managed a swift defence of our position by launching into a flamboyant description of our forthcoming May trip, whereupon their mother jokingly asked us to take Zoya and Lida along with us. Georges was ill at ease, and even complained to Lida. But he pulled himself together at dinner, was friendly and funny, although most of his witticisms derived from Boris. He left soon afterwards, but Max and I stayed until ten, and then walked home.

24 March

All morning and until half past three composed the Concerto. To be precise, all the material is now composed, but there are substantial sections where although the thematic material and the harmony are in place, and the layout is there in principle, these sections are still represented physically by white, largely empty pages. To fill these spaces with the details that will realize the conception I imagined while I was composing the material, is for me a task integral with the composition of the work seen as a whole.

Today I filled in all the central episode of the first movement and worked with such intensity that I quite forgot to have any lunch. By three o'clock my head was beginning to ache, then Max came round and we went out for a walk.

Our walk today took us round the suburbs, with the following route: Pervaya Rota – Zarotnaya, Ryzhsky – Staro-Peterhofsky – Bumazhnaya – Yekaterinhof – Volynka – Tentelovo – Yemilyanovka, from which we emerged into a Low Countries-like field partitioned by dykes, presumably against flooding.[1] Two years ago I was here in the same place with Tonya Rudavskaya. The reason Max and I do these long walks is to get into training, which he especially needs as he is not a good walker, and on our summer expedition I am proposing a six-day walk from Sebastopol to Alushta. Part of the way from Yemilyanovka we came back on foot, part in a rickety horse-tram, and part in a tramcar that was in comparison the height of luxury.

In the evening my headache returned, not having been completely flushed out by the walk, and I went early to bed. In the morning I had had two telephone conversations with Umnenkaya: it appears that *Siegfried* is being performed not on Monday, as I thought, but on Tuesday, so I went to great lengths to persuade her to come with me, claiming that *Siegfried* had been postponed until Tuesday as a result of my urgent request. Umnenkaya made a fuss to begin with, but eventually agreed, presumably after she had been given permission at home.

25 March

The morning went by on some polishing of *Dreams*, and at noon I went to see Aslanov to talk about the summer concerts. Despite his invariably friendly

---

1 Areas to the south-west of the city. From the map this walk cannot have been much less than twenty miles.

and courteous manner, and his goodwill to me, I cannot say I am particularly partial to him. He lives in a small but exceedingly comfortable apartment two steps away from me, 'bachelor quarters' as he terms it, with a young housekeeper – an ideal set-up, in a word. I told him I should like to play the Second Piano Concerto towards the end of the summer (before then I won't have learned it), and should also like to hear *Dreams*. He readily accepted both works, and was only concerned that he did not have a fifth and sixth horn for *Dreams*.

We agreed if necessary to share the cost of the extra players between us, 16 roubles, and fixed the date of 2 August for the Concerto and 25 June for *Dreams*. There would be no concerts before 20 May, and from then until 20 June Max and I would be on our travels. I deliberately settled on the date for *Dreams* on my return, in order to have a reason for coming back to St Petersburg. Mama was at first horrified at my thus having to travel back to St Petersburg twice, but I convinced her that there was no other way, and the subject was dropped.

In the afternoon I took *Dreams* to the copyist to prepare the parts so that there would not be any delay in sending the score to the Russian Music Editions, requesting that it should be considered and returned to me no later than the beginning of June. Then I went on to Myaskovsky's, with whom Aslanov had asked me to have a word concerning a performance of *Alastor*. For some reason Kolechka is not all that keen on the idea; he would rather his old C minor Symphony. When I got home, I carried on for a while composing the Concerto.

26 March

Composition work on the Concerto. Had a completely new idea for the end of the first movement, which I think will be very good. At half past one came into the Conservatoire, where because of exams going on I was surrounded by all those crowds and energy I love so much. For half an hour I hung around waiting for Tcherepnin's class and caught sight of a pale-looking Boryusya and his rival Zeiliger, masking his ambition under a cloak of counterfeit friendship. Zeiliger had spent the night in the 'Stray Dog' café and was about to sit his General Knowledge exam with a head full of cottonwool.

Tcherepnin came and went through Glinka's *Kamarinskaya*[1] with us. He then outlined to us his thoughts on the music of the future, predicting the demise of the piano, the quartet and sonata form. Comparing myself to the fantasies of Tcherepnin, I already see myself as a *passé* musician.

After dinner I put on my dinner-jacket and headed towards Offitserskaya

---

1 *Kamarinskaya: Scherzo on a Russian Dance Tune* (1848).

Street to take Umnenkaya to *Siegfried*. I stayed for half an hour in pleasant conversation with Lida and her sisters, then we went to the theatre. She has a new coiffure, and as always looks most elegant. The box to our right was occupied by the Ruzskys, sitting in the one to the left was Volodya Deshevov, hence Lida and I were subjected to a crossfire of curious glances. Throughout the first act we were so buried in the piano score that I got a stitch in my side from the awkwardness of my position, so for Act II we 'shut up shop'. During the intervals we strolled about, and it was nice, but not as nice as it had been when we had come to *Valkyrie*. I also do not like *Siegfried* as much as *Valkyrie*: despite the wealth of fabulous episodes – the Introduction, all Siegfried's entrances, the comedy of Mime, the cheerful forging of the sword, Alberich's abuse of Mime, the opening of Act III and the entr'acte – everything takes such an interminable time, is so needlessly long drawn out, that I literally begin to suffocate with boredom.

While I was taking Umnenkaya home we had a slight tiff, which was immediately smoothed over, and when in the course of saying goodbye I kissed her little paw, she promised to telephone me tomorrow. Walking home, I asked myself: can it be that my affection for Umnenkaya is already on the wane?!

27 March

In the orchestra class I conducted a disgracefully half-present small orchestra in the last two movements of Beethoven's Fourth Symphony, after which I passed the baton to Tsybin and Dranishnikov and went to meet Max. He told me that Ariadna was in the building to sit her exam to move up to the senior course. We later heard from Nikolayev that she had not done particularly well, that she was suffering from anaemia(?!), her health was not good and she had not lived up to expectations.

Walking home we regretted not having the cartoonist's skill to be able to draw something representing a well-nourished Radochka above a comment referring to her anaemia and her lack of success in the exam. But I was then struck by a brilliant notion, which we spent the rest of the day executing. From the photograph of our group we cut out Radochka's impassioned physiognomy and stuck it on to the body of another, fatter girl, then attached the whole thing to a silhouette of a grand piano I cut out of cardboard. It worked splendidly, and resulted in a well-upholstered Radochka sitting convincingly at a piano. Lavrov[1] we cut out complete from the same group photo, and Nikolayev (who had been Nikolskaya's examiner) from

---

1 Nikolay Lavrov (1861–1927), pianist and professor at the St Petersburg Conservatoire. Lavrov was Ariadna Nikolskaya's teacher.

another group we acquired from Kaspari especially for the purpose. But because in this photograph his trunk was masked by students, I took just his bust and so arranged it that it looked as though Nikolayev was sitting at a table. The whole ensemble was then pasted on to dark green card, with Radochka sitting on the right at her piano, and Lavrov next to Nikolayev, who was smiling at her apparently in thrall to her charms. Above this was written: 'Professor (*to Examiner*) – Oh, my dear colleague, please do have pity, give her a 5! After all, she suffers from anaemia . . . See how thin she is . . . (*whispering in his ear*) and how pretty! (*Aloud*) When her health permits she must walk along Morskaya and enjoy herself in all kinds of distractions and not tire herself out at the piano, the cause of her disgraceful performance!'

Below, written in Max's hand: 'But the incorruptible Examiner disdains to succumb either to these honeyed words or to the feminine wiles, and with iron justice awards a mark not quite equivalent to 5+.'

So feverishly did I apply myself to this work of art that I almost came down with a headache.

At seven o'clock I went to dine with Saburov and to play in various chamber groups. The diplomat Persiani is very knowledgeable about music, and old man Saburov really surprised me by sitting down at the piano and giving a most energetic account of the *Kreutzer* Sonata. I tried to get away as early as I could. As I was leaving, Saburov promised to get me an introduction to the aristocratic musical Zinoviev family.[1]

I walked home from Spasskaya Street, and when I got there looked with pleasure at the brilliantly successful caricature we had made for Ariadna. Then with equal enjoyment I read through my diary entries for the month and, pleased with life, went to bed.

28 March

In the morning practised for Yesipova and wrote my diary. My mood was so-so. At half past one went to the Conservatoire, which was again very crowded because of the grade exams for the higher course.

Made my way to the 'chemist's' – the building where Anna Nikolayevna lives has a chemist's shop in it. She was in a bad mood, and ranted mercilessly at the female students, but with me she was for some reason very gentle, calling me by my first name and patronymic and even giving me two tickets for Drozdov's[2] concert tomorrow. I played her Chopin's A flat Polonaise. Just as

---

1 The Zinovievs had been prominent in the higher echelons of St Petersburg society since Peter the Great's time. A. D. Zinoviev was Governor of the city in the early years of the twentieth century.
2 Anatoly Drozdov (1883–1950), pianist and teacher, professor at the St Petersburg Conservatoire.

I was about to begin, she said, 'Oh, not those polonaises again! There's no music in them, nothing but banging and crashing.'

I could not refrain from taking up the cudgels: 'How can you say such a thing, Anna Nikolayevna! There is much good music in among the banging and crashing...'

'Well, just play them *piano*,' Yesipova stamped her foot.

Back at the Conservatoire I met Max, saw a lot of people I knew, and examined how the sound of arrows being loosed is achieved in *Antar*[1] (I need a similar effect in the Scherzo).

In the evening Max and I went to Aktseri's concert and met Umnenkaya there. The concert was fairly boring and in every respect inferior to Zherebtsova-Andreyeva's, with the exception of the floral tributes, which entirely covered the stage.

Afterwards I took Umnenkaya home. From the Kryukov canal onwards I took her arm, and in spite of her protests did not release it until we reached the entrance to her building. She said she was so displeased that I had not sought her out in the intervals of the concert she would never go anywhere with me ever again.

29 March

Completed the first movement cadenza, all but six bars, that have been composed but still need the figuration filling out. The end of the cadenza, at the entry of the orchestra, is technically a little rough, but effective.

Mama is planning to go abroad with her friend Lebedintseva at the end of May. She would like me to accompany her, but I am holding out for my Russian expedition with Max. If Mama stays in France all summer, then I will join her for the month of July. The idea of travelling round Russia appeals to me much more than going abroad, not because I don't want to go there but because I know that in time this will happen of its own accord.

At one o'clock Max and I met up in the Conservatoire, to be there when the 'express', i.e. Ariadna, came out. Surely she must have received the caricature by now. But the 'express' was sour-faced and paid us not the slightest attention. Accompanied by her teacher, Nikolskaya shuttled between the Director's room and the Class Inspectors' desk, engaged in some ploy with both of them, presumably concerning the upgrading of her marks.

At this juncture Leonid Nikolayev appeared, and a whole scenario unexpectedly developed. After the customary amiable exchange of courtesies, Nikolayev was about to come and sit with Max and me on the windowsill

---

[1] Rimsky-Korsakov's Symphony No. 2, Op. 9, is subtitled 'Antar'. The work was originally composed in 1868; this is more likely the composer's third revision, carried out in 1897.

when a poster on the wall suddenly attracted his attention and he darted over to look at it. As the poster was positioned low down he squatted on his haunches, balancing himself with his hands on the floor. I did the same, parodying his pose, and also stuck my nose into the poster. Nikolayev burst out laughing like a maniac, and I also found the situation very funny. We stayed there for half a minute, shaking with laughter, while the passers-by stared at us in amazement. As I got up I saw Ariadna at the bottom of the stairs, standing watching us like a pillar of salt. Preumably she will now realize the source of my detailed information about her exam. Nikolayev went away and Tcherepnin, who had also appeared, led me into his class.

We discussed the Graduation Concert. Tcherepnin is not planning to go away at all beforehand. This is a pity, as it means I will not be in full charge. He told me he has higher hopes of me than of the other conductors. The inference is that Tsybin and Dranishnikov will also be sticking their oars in. Ideally I would prefer to be the only one, but all the same, to hell with them!

In the evening I donned tails because I was going on to the Konshins later on, and went to the Drozdov concert. Max, to achieve matching stylishness in our apparel, also put on tails, and so amid the drab audience we stood out in dazzling splendour, which as a matter of fact I found very embarrassing. Drozdov plays with great intelligence and has a good command of tonal gradation, but he bangs too much and try as he may cannot get the audience in the palm of his hand. I was bored, and soon left to go to the Konshins.

Invitations to the Konshins are always very grand affairs, and full evening dress is *de rigueur*. There was music today, singing, some young people and some older ones, dancing and vint. At first I did not find it very interesting and did not know where to put myself; I was forced to play the Chopin Polonaise and my 'Gavotte', both of which went down very well and caused some young ladies to come up to me and ask all sorts of questions. But I did not care for them and gave them short shrift in my replies. As soon as I sat down to play vint, however, I cheered up. I have been playing this game since I was twelve years old and seem to be pretty good at it; today I had luck with the cards. Tanya Ruzskaya was also there, but we did not see one another until after supper. Not without a touch of malice, she asked me, 'Have you been a Wagnerite for long?'

'Ever since I found an interesting companion to go with.'

She had not expected such a direct response. 'But not so long ago you were very condescending about Wagner?'

'I've never been condescending about Wagner, but he is so long that one can only sit through him if one has pleasant company.'

Nikolay Pavlovich is back, and has apparently invited me to come and see him on Sunday. Not a word was said, needless to say, about the debt situation, and to my disingenious question how they were getting on, Tanya replied: 'We're getting on fine.'

30 March

At a quarter past nine I was in orchestra class for the small orchestra, not having had quite enough sleep. It is really high time to disband this orchestra, but Tcherepnin has decided to keep it going for another week. All the better players are sitting their exams, and the only ones left are the dross, which makes it impossible to get anything done. I studied Glinka's *Kamarinskaya* with them. The score of this work, that is to say this particular copy of the score, is remarkable for having been presented to me by Glazunov before I entered the Conservatoire, and is inscribed: 'To my dear colleague Seryozha Prokofiev from A. Glazunov'. To think that once upon a time I was on such terms with Glazunov!

Afterwards I stayed in at home and notated the Concerto. In the evening I went to the Maly Theatre with Max, who had been presented with complimentary seats in the second row by his grandfather. The play was *An Ensign of the Reserves* by the actor Tarsky, about wartime life in a provincial town, in the style of Kuprin's *The Duel*. It was long and wordy and not very interesting, but worth seeing for the picture it painted of life at that time.

31 March

Worked on composing the Concerto until two o'clock, and then decided to walk with Max to Ligovo[1] – a notion that had occurred to me during our previous excursion to the village of Yemilyanovka.

Because this evening the Mariinsky Theatre is presenting Tcherepnin's *The Pavilion of Armida*[2] and a staging of Schumann's *Carnaval*, we were very interested to try to get tickets. But the performance was sold out, so at three o'clock we set out for Ligovo. The weather was mixed, now fine and sunny, now foul, sometimes turning to a horrible slushy snow that melted as it fell and after half an hour stopped us walking any further. It was not very warm either: four degrees or so above zero.

As far as the Narvsky Gate we went by tram, from Narvsky to the Putilov Works[3] on the top deck of a horse-tram. It was terribly cold in the wind, and

---

1 Dacha resort on the south coast of the Gulf of Finland.
2 One-act ballet first produced at the Mariinsky Theatre in 1907 to a scenario by Alexander Benois, who also designed the settings, and choreography by Mikhail Fokine. The first manifestation of what became the *World of Art* conception of *Gesamtkunstwerk* ballet, it was taken to Paris by Diaghilev to open his 1909 season there.
3 One of Russia's oldest manufacturing concerns, the Putilov Works dates from 1801. By the

by the time we got to the Putilov Works we were frozen stiff. Deciding that it was really not walking weather at all, we turned into a low dive of an inn and asked if they had any cognac. 'We have everything!' replied the landlord.

'In that case, please let us have some Benedictine.'

'Certainly, sir,' he said, plonking an eighth-litre bottle down on the counter. The Benedictine was not the genuine article, but some sort of ersatz brew. However, we drank a glass each and felt the warmth flow through our veins. Stuffing the rest of the bottle into our pocket we went out into the street, and just as we did so it started snowing again. But we boldly paid it no attention, the snow soon stopped and the sun came out. We hoped the road would lead us either into a wood or into some fields, but we were mistaken: it was lined all the way along by dachas, small settlements and dwellings of various kinds, while the wooden planks of the pavement continued under our feet. This pavement was no bad thing, by the way, because whenever we came to a gap in it we sank up to our ankles in the mud. At difficult moments we consoled ourselves with a shot of Benedictine, and when we had drained the small bottle dry pitched it into a puddle in the grounds of Count Sheremetyev's dacha. At six o'clock, in good spirits, we reached Ligovo station and ordered ourselves dinner. Hunger is the best cook, so the dinner was delicious and we ate it all without stopping. We dropped three postcards (to Umnenkaya, the Karneyev girls and Khantsin) in the letterbox and joyfully disposed ourselves on the crimson seats of a first-class carriage. Outside there was a snowstorm, but we were snug and very happy.

I was home by eight o'clock and abandoned my intention of going to the Ruzskys, preferring to occupy myself with my diary. Remembering that tomorrow Novikova was taking her exam, for which she had to produce a composition, I tried to find the sketches I had made for myself under similar conditions five years ago, and riffled through the 'archive' box in my desk drawer, but no to avail. But I did find a whole pile of old things I had written on all sorts of subjects, some of which were amusing, and one about a duel I even read to Max over the telephone.

1 April

After yesterday's walk I slept until eleven, then practised the piano and went into the Conservatoire. I got there at five to one, at the precise moment when the candidates from the sixth class were being asked to take their seats

---

beginning of the twentieth century it was a vast enterprise embracing iron and steel mills and factories producing railway lines and engines, ships and armaments. After 1934, renamed Kirov Works, it concentrated on turning out tractors and steam turbines for the power plants needed for the electrification of the Soviet Union.

for the Composition exam. As well as the Conservatoire's own students there were a number of external candidates, so there was a great deal of noise and bustle.

In the evening I pressed on with orchestrating the Concerto. Previously I had wanted to delay making a start on this until all the music, in particular the solo piano part, had been composed in detail. Now, however, with only a few short passages remaining to be written out, I decided not to wait any longer but to start on the instrumentation, intending to complete the unfinished passages in between whiles. I started writing the score with immense satisfaction. While going through the composition process I had already been working out in my imagination the orchestral texture I wanted, so there was no difficulty in laying out on the pages of a full score the light and transparent accompaniment I envisaged, nor the notation of the solo piano part. A very enjoyable process.

In this Concerto I made two discoveries: the first is that the orchestra is given no material whatsoever to present independently, and the pianist, once having started to play, does not cease until the final bar. This is surely no bad thing; on the contrary, I feel that it creates a certain tension in the listener and fixes his attention irrevocably on the soloist. Secondly, the score turns out to be shorter (fewer pages) than I had imagined, the orchestral accompaniment being of such transparency that each page can accommodate more than one line of full score.

Today is 1 April, a manifestation of which occurred when, during the evening, I received a caricature of myself and Max. The likeness was not at all convincing, but it was nicely drawn. It depicted two stylish fops in tails, with our names below, and on the reverse this bit of doggerel:

Why bother with the gossip-woman's tales,
When gossiping yourself so seldom fails . . .

I should like to think that it came from Ariadna, but could not be certain of this however hard I tried to examine the drawing, turned the envelope over and over, looked at the postmark and even sniffed the paper.

2 April

By nine o'clock I was already sitting down to the score of the Concerto. It's the first time this winter that I have jumped out of bed so early without a rush to get to the orchestra rehearsal.

In the afternoon I went to the Tcherepnin class but he did not come, and there was nothing really to do there. Returning home I sat down again to the score. Around nine I felt I had done enough and telephoned Max, suggesting a walk. He replied 'with pleasure' and we wandered about for a couple of hours, downing a glass of Chartreuse apiece at Peretz. He came back to my house for tea and together we worked out from the handwriting of some of the letters that the caricature was the work of the Karneyev sisters, and the postscript referred to our habit of poking fun at people.

Natasha Goncharova rang up to invite me to her *soirée* on Friday. She lives with her sister, who is married to an officer in the Horse Guards, von Glazenap. As if to underline, as she always does, the fact that she belongs to the aristocracy, Natasha this time prefaced her invitation with a hint to the effect that I would no doubt be surprised at her being willing to invite me to her house. This annoyed me, and I'm not at all sure that I will go.

3 April

A letter I received this morning in a hand I did not recognize, although it was quite similar to my own, proved to be from Ariadna Nikolskaya. The douche of cold water we had suffered on our visits to the Central Post Office ended in an unexpected triumph. The letter announced that the writer was going away to Kiev and, in order to avoid the consequent risk of 'your excellently witty letters, which afford me the greatest possible pleasure, remaining unread by me there', supplied her address.

At half past nine I came to orchestra class but, as might have been expected, the orchestra consisted of three students and so was dismissed until the autumn. Tcherepnin talked at length to us about orchestration, and then Dranishnikov played his Variations, a mish-mash of styles brilliantly laid out for the piano and totally lacking in individuality. When Tcherepnin and Dranishnikov had gone I discovered that there was to be a public performance of chamber music involving those pianists who had gained 5+ in their exams. I decided to wait for this and telephoned Max to let him know. Zakharov played well, but with a certain lack of boldness (Franck sonata); Rabinovich with authority and conviction. Zeiliger was good. Max and I then went to our respective homes and I sat until evening working at my orchestration, changing to the piano reduction when my brain refused any longer to conjure up orchestral combinations.

4 April

Orchestrated until eleven, and then had to stop to practise the piano and get three movements of the G minor Sonata into some sort of condition to play at the lesson with Anna Nikolayevna. At one o'clock went to the Conservatoire, but Anna Nikolayevna was teaching at home today. At the lesson I was preceded by two girls who played so badly that my sonata seemed good by comparison.

At home I worked for a while, but it was soon time to go to Saburov, who has taken to issuing frequent invitations to me. On the way I called in at the Shtembers to collect the copy of the 'Gavotte' I wanted to take with me to the Meshcherskys. Kokochka opened the door.

'Ah, Serge!'

Out ran the sisters: 'Serge! Serge!'

Mamasha: 'Serge!'

Papasha: 'Serge!'

Din and uproar, but I was in a terrific rush and, quickly wrapping up the 'Gavotte' and trying to respond simultaneously to everyone, promised to come back 'very soon, definitely, absolutely promise'.

There was nobody very interesting at Saburov's, and it was tedious. But, thank God, it was over quite soon and by ten I could be gratefully back at my score. Old man Saburov impressed me all the same by belting through a lot of music by heart, not easy stuff either, ending up with some Variations by Henselt that he had read through with the composer himself all of fifty years ago.

5 April

Went on orchestrating all morning and until half past two. I am proud of the fact that the orchestral texture of the Concerto is so transparent. I had difficulties with one passage where the brass section of the orchestra drowns the soloist . . . but strange as it may seem, I particularly like this place.

At three o'clock I was at the 'plumber' (the old man has engaged a very attractive young assistant) and then returned to my work. Copying out the cadenza was fun at first, but eventually seemed rather a pointless activity.

I decided I would not go to Natasha Goncharova's, and instead went to the Belyayev Concert. I don't remember the last time I was at a symphony concert, it was so long ago, and therefore I found all the little trivial things enjoyable: seeing people I know from the world of music, even simply going up the staircase to go into the hall.

Scriabin's *Divine Poem* is a wonderful work, even if open to criticism for its occasional longueurs, indecent length and orchestration that is not always impeccable (for example, the lame attempt to reproduce the billing and cooing of doves; the opening of the second movement, and the grandiose repetition of the same theme at the end of the movement, where the strings do something incomprehensible instead of exploiting their timbre to breathe life into the brass's flaccid trumpeting of the theme.

The other items in the programme were a complete antidote to this work, in that they were marvellously orchestrated but utterly devoid of any inspiration in their content. They were: Glazunov's *From Darkness to Light*,

Lyadov's *Apocalypsis* and some songs by Weisberg.[1] I felt ashamed for the composers.

Wenzel, stammering and diffident, asked me if I would accompany his graduating student in the Schumann Concerto. I was delighted to agree, and said I would come to his class tomorrow to discuss it. After all, Lyuda Novikova[2] will be having her last lesson with him before Easter tomorrow, and I will take care to arrive just as she sits down at the piano. It will be my only opportunity to catch the 'elusive Princess Lyudmila'.

6 April

At half past ten I went to Wenzel's class in the Conservatoire for 'discussions' – but my real purpose was, to put it bluntly, to see Novikova. I made a most impressive entrance into the class because as I came in Wenzel leaped up and lisped something to me using the intimate form, to which I responded loudly and importantly. But . . . Novikova was not in the class today. I suggested a play-through with his student on Monday at noon, that is to say when the invisible princess would be sitting her Russian language exam, and left the room rather disgruntled.

In the corridor I was grabbed by Steinberg and Karnovich. Karnovich is graduating from Steinberg's class in Practical Composition this year, and Tcherepnin has suggested that I should conduct his *Variations for Orchestra* in the Graduation Concert. The two of them now handed me a bulky manuscript with a request to consult with Tcherepnin about cutting some of the variations. I talked to the composer, then went to Tcherepnin's home, came back, offloaded the score to have the parts made by a copyist, and did not get home myself until three o'clock.

I wrote out one page of the cadenza until Max came and we went for a stroll as we had done the day before. Ariadna did not leave yesterday; I was talking to Borovsky in the Conservatoire today and saw her, looking very pretty indeed. She made straight for me, then suddenly stopped, turned about, and vanished.

Our ratiocinations today produced the same result as yesterday. Either Ariadna had not got the tickets, or she was mocking us.

7 April

I finished the six bars in the cadenza I had left uncompleted, and by sitting and working until three finished orchestrating the first movement. At three

---

1 Yulia Weisberg (1878–1942), composer of conservative inclinations, subsequently to join the editorial board of the journal *Musical Contemporary* (*Muzykalny Sovremennik*), founded by Andrey Rimsky-Korsakov and Pyotr Suvchinsky.
2 Lyudmila Novikova, piano student of Vladimir Wenzel at the Conservatoire.

Max and I went to have a look at the Palm Sunday festivities. His cousin, Volodya, who is still at school, caught up with us.

'I was behind you all the time,' he said.

'No, you weren't,' we objected.

'Yes I was.'

'Well, if you were, what were we doing at Potseluyev Bridge?'

'Talking to a young lady.'

That made us chuckle, because I had indeed at Potseluyev Bridge met and talked to . . . Anna Nikolayevna Yesipova.

At half past nine in the evening I went to see off the Meshcherskys, who are going to the Crimea for Easter. That mischievous little imp Nina is my favourite: we joked and flirted all the time at the station. Then I took a car and went on to the Ruzskys, where this time everyone was friendly and loving, even Ira, with whom I spent a pleasant half-hour sitting out on the balcony. They invited me to stay with them in their dacha on the Volga in the summer.

8 April

The copyist has brought back the parts from *Dreams* and seems to have done a good job. I trust him, so I shall not proof-read it. I packed up the scores of *Dreams* and the *Ballade*, and sent them to the Russian Musical Editions. If they do not accept them for publication, I can always send them to Jurgenson, but if they do agree so much the better. First, I will get some money for *Dreams*; second, they will do it quickly; and third, I am really tired of hearing Jurgenson grumble about how he will make a loss on *Dreams* and how it would be better not to rush with the *Ballade* . . . When he does take something he sits on it for ever; he had the *Toccata* in November, it is now April and I still do not have the first proof. He's worse than that photographer rascal, Kaspari!

At noon I came into the Conservatoire to rehearse the Schumann Concerto with Wenzel's student, and when that was over went out into the corridor where all the sixth General Studies class was milling about waiting for their Russian language exam. Novikova was walking in my direction with a friend, so I went up to them. We had a few pleasant words, then I beckoned over Shalyt and asked them both if they would accept our invitation to go for an automobile ride today. They agreed, leaving us to decide the destination.

Delighted with this I let them go to take their exam, and having telephoned Max, met him at Alfyorov's as we needed to draw out some money. We then went to pick a car, an exercise which took us more than an hour and a half. Eventually we settled on a 'tourist' taxi, whose driver agreed to stop the meter and take us to Pavlovsk for a fixed price of 25 roubles. While he was getting the car ready we went to buy sandwiches and cakes. But on the way I got a piece of grit in my eye, such a fine, healthy example of the genre that I was forced to take another taxi home to the eye clinic above our apartment. There they removed the offending irritant, but my eye was still red and swollen, so while waiting for Max I lay down with a Goulard lotion[1] compress. Max arrived twenty minutes later, my eye was better by then, and after stopping to collect our ladies we set off for Pavlovsk.

I have known Novikova for more than a year, and always liked her, but since Shalyt introduced us we have seen one another only occasionally. I was curious to know what she was really like, as hitherto I have only been able to judge from appearances.

The car made rapid progress through the city and ran out along the Pulkovo highway, and we chatted merrily as we sped along. We had a marvellous walk in the park, but were just about to turn into the station when the rain came on. Milochka[2] and I ran for it and were the first to reach the car, but all of us got soaked to the skin – especially Max and I, since we were only wearing jackets. The car roared back along the road to Petersburg, the rain did not let up and dripped cold trickles on to us through a hole in the landaulet roof. We ate our sandwiches and cakes and made a good deal of noise. Shalyt very much took second place to Lyuda, and stayed in the background, but Novikova was thoroughly enjoying herself talking to me and to Max. She comes from a military family in Volhynia province,[3] and lives in Petersburg with an elderly cousin, knows very few people, is lonely, and evidently this excursion with us was a big event in her life.

After the car had taken us to her house on Kanonerskaya Street, we said goodbye and went on to deposit Shalyt at her place of residence. Then we went to my house to drink cognac and dry out.

Kolechka Myaskovsky, whose birthday it is, was already waiting for me at home: we were due to go together to see Aslanov to 'force-feed' him with Myaskovsky's Symphony No. 2, proposed for performance at Pavlovsk. Supplying Max with a pile of books, some cognac, the sofa and a pillow, I went off with Myaskovsky to Aslanov. In spite of two glasses of cognac I played the four-hand piano version of the symphony quite respectably and an hour later was home again. The symphony contains much good music along with much that is boring, but until I hear it in its orchestral colours I shall reserve judgement.

1 Goulard water (*eau de Goulard*, also known as *eau blanche*), named after the eighteenth century French surgeon Thomas Goulard, is a solution of sub-acetate of lead, used as a lotion to combat inflammation. Judging by this, it seems to work.
2 Lyudmila Novikova.
3 One of the oldest Slav settlements in Europe, in the north-west of the Ukraine, formerly part of Poland.

At home, Mama had been talking to Max and secretly trying to get him to talk me out of going down the Volga and going abroad instead. Max, needless to say, gave me a full account of the conversation and made no attempt to persuade me to go abroad.

9 April

Did not feel like starting to orchestrate the Scherzo. Played through on the piano the first movement of the Concerto and was enraptured by the splendid sound of the cadenza, the first time I had been able to play it right through. Wrote my diary, and played from memory the pieces I had been working on with Yesipova. Collected my photographs from the photographer, who had had them since November. Some of them are not bad, especially one where I am propping up my chin with my hand.

Bought the Lizst E flat Concerto in case it should come up at the Graduation Concert. I know it well, but have never looked at the score. It has a good deal of wit in it, not just the musical ideas but also the manner in which they are presented, but it has no depth whatsoever.

After dinner I went for a walk with Max. We looked in the shops for good walking sticks, but they all cost at least 25 roubles, which I think is too much money. Max objects that the concept of 'too expensive' is intrinsically inapplicable to any given object; the only valid concept should be: can I or can I not afford it?

In the evening I wrote my diary, which I have neglected for the past three days.

10 April

Spent all morning orchestrating the Scherzo. At two o'clock went into the Conservatoire to rehearse the Schumann Concerto with Yatsyno, Wenzel's student. I must have earned her respect, because while completely ignoring Wenzel she kept asking my advice about her performance. I responded with some caution, not wanting to offend Wenzel. After the rehearsal he told me that he considered himself immeasurably in my debt for the great service I performed in accompanying Yatsyno. I said that in return I would be grateful if he would assign another work to Novikova for her examination piece than the Mendelssohn B minor Etude (she had been complaining about it in the car and I had promised to try to help get it changed).

Returning home I wrote out more of the score until seven o'clock and got as far as the trio of the Scherzo. After dinner Max and I got a taxi and went to the corner of Kamennoóstrovsky and Bolshoy Prospects, and from there went walking round the Islands: Kamenny, Krestovsky and Yelagin. We covered about twelve versts and some time after eleven o'clock made our way home.

11 April

Today is my birthday; I have lived on this earth for twenty-two years. I feel myself to be much younger than this number; I should like to be no more than nineteen, and regret being as much as twenty-two. I spent today like any other day, not celebrating my birthday in any particular way. I got a lot of the score written – eight pages, that is the whole trio of the Scherzo. I also thought out the reprise, which I have not yet composed.

The Karneyeva girls and Max sent me telegrams. Vera Alpers sent a letter. The poor girl is suing for peace, she has been the first to extend the hand of friendship, as since the skating incident I have not bowed to her. Kolechka Myaskovsky brought me a present himself: Korsakov's *Orchestration*, which has recently been published in an edition by Steinberg. I am very touched. (Incidentally I have established that one episode in the first movement of his C sharp minor Symphony was taken from Rubinstein's Second Concerto. That's the source to borrow from!)

At seven o'clock Max saw his mother off on her way to Moscow. At five minutes past I arrived at the station and we went for a walk. This time we sat on the top deck of a steam tram, and warmed by the steam from the funnel went as far out as the village of Murzinka, and then on to Rybatsky. We sat by the shore of the darkly flowing Neva, then returned to the station and took the express back to Piter. Max talked to me about Schopenhauer's philosophy and told me something of his life, which I found deeply interesting.

By half past eleven I was home and got down to writing Easter messages. A sealed letter to Tcherepnin, postcards to Goncharova, Rudavskaya, Novikova, N. Reberg and Vera Alpers in acknowledgement of her birthday greetings; visiting cards to Wenzel, Nikolayev, Pavlinov, Morolyov, Kachenovsky, Glière, M. M. Sezhenskaya,[1] the Lyutzes, Yurasovsky, Mlle Roblin. To Anna Nikolayevna Yesipova I shall send the customary telegram.

12 April

Felt disinclined to work in the morning, but still managed three pages of the Intermezzo. I have put the Scherzo aside for the time being, until I have composed the reprise.

After lunch I went with Mama to buy flowers and took them to Papa's grave. Then I called for Max and we went to buy ties and hats. Max wants a

---

1 Maria Sezhenskaya, a distant relation.

'Spanish' hat because they are so elegant. Took the Easter greetings to the General Post Office, but because of its being Good Friday it was closed from eleven o'clock onwards. Max has had himself new visiting cards made, and so is sending them to everyone whether appropriate or not.

When I got home again my head was aching, even though I had not done much work today. I really must have done too much yesterday. Took a lemon vanilla powder and the pain went away. At seven o'clock went to Anna Nikolayevna to get my programme of summer work, and in view of my final graduation next year, we mainly discussed today the programme for my graduation performances. I am determined to play my own works in these categories: (1) the concerto; (2) chamber music; and (3) work by a Russian composer. I was very afraid of a firm 'no' from Yesipova, because of the history of her attitude to my compositions, which is as follows.

She was undoubtedly aware of my composing activities before I came to her as a student, and when I first began to study with her boasted of the kind of student that was now coming to her, composers no less. However, the composer in question came to her lessons as a pianist, saying not a word about his composing activities. Then she herself asked me to play her something I had written, and I played her the Sonata Op. 1. She praised it and offered useful suggestions about pedalling, which I was overdoing mercilessly. I still possess the manuscript with the pedalling meticulously marked throughout in Anna Nikolayevna's hand. Soon after this I started bringing to the class pieces by Medtner and Scriabin, and acquired a reputation for being a raging 'modernist'.

The result of this was that Anna Nikolayevna decided I too must be a modern composer, that is to say, according to her reckoning, whatever I compose was bound to be rubbish. This led in turn to a change of heart about the Sonata; Zakharov was informed one day that there was no music in it, no real music at all ... When I heard this I announced that from that day forth not a note of my music would Anna Nikolayevna hear, and I have kept my word until today. Last summer I played my Concerto in Pavlovsk and said nothing to Anna Nikolayevna, allowing her to find out about it from the newspapers. By law she had the right to exclude me from her class for appearing in a public concert without permission, but she said nothing.

And so to today. Anna Nikolayevna was very friendly and announced that in all ten of us would be graduating, among the men Tietz, Shneye and Mindlin. They are all good, but none of them are 5+. Of the girls, Berlin and Tseitlin are worthy of attention; besides, they are both very pretty and enjoy the special protection of Glazunov. In answer to the question what Bach I would choose, I mentioned *The Art of Fugue*, which was approved with the recommendation that I choose a fugue with more than three voices. As for Mozart I had no opinion, and was put down for the C minor Fantasy (not the one associated with the Sonata), which I do not know. As for Beethoven, I mentioned something about the first movement of the big B flat major Sonata,[1] but this has already been given to Shneye and I had to be content with Op. 111. For Schumann I declared a preference for the complete F sharp minor Sonata, which was accepted. About Chopin there was much discussion and searching through the notebook, but no firm decision was arrived at. For Lizst, Anna Nikolayevna tentatively suggested *Mazeppa*, but I held out for *Tannhäuser*, which after a lot of grumbling – it's so long ... it's overplayed ... was accepted. Now came the big moment: what would I choose for a work by a Russian composer? I was absolutely astonished when Anna Nikolayevna readily agreed that I should play something of my own – even enquiring what. And what about the concerto? After a cautious preamble I proposed my No. 2.

'Now really, that would mean your piece followed by your piece: that's not very discreet. Make a choice: either the concerto, or the solo piece in the recital programme!'

'But it seems to me a good thing that I have a range of weapons at my disposal.'

However, I quickly agreed that I would play the Concerto and choose another composer for the Russian work in the recital programme. I am sure with a bit of diplomacy during the winter I shall be able to finesse a solo work of mine. And for chamber music I must go in a couple of times to Blumenfeld's[2] class; I think I shall be able to come to an agreement with him that I should play my *Ballade* for cello.

Anna Nikolayevna graciously dismissed me and went to the bath house. Delighted with the success of my project I went home, where I found Max already waiting for me so that we could make a detailed itinerary for our May journey in the light of a guidebook that had recently been published. We soon became absorbed in a long and precise travel plan down the Volga, to the Caspian, the Caucasus, the Black Sea and the Crimea, setting it out day by day and even hour by hour, and fixing the day of our departure as 22 May (the day following Umnenkaya's exam, Max's exam and the first Pavlovsk concert, an interesting combination), returning on 21 June.

---

1 Presumably the 'Hammerklavier', No. 29, Op. 106.
2 Felix Blumenfeld (1863–1931), pianist, conductor and composer. As a conductor at the Mariinsky Theatre he had been responsible *inter alia* for the premiere of Rimsky-Korsakov's *Legend of the Invisible City of Kitezh*. Blumenfeld was a prominent ally of Rimsky-Korsakov, Glazunov, Lyadov and the student body against the Directorate in the events of 1905 that led to the temporary closure of the Conservatoire and its re-opening under a new autonomous statute.

13 April

Decided not to do much work today, so as not to risk getting another headache. At half past ten Max and I went to the Central Post Office to post our Easter greetings, then to Frehlich to order summer outfits, then to Leiner for lunch (car, Curaçao, Graves), after which we had an hour and half spare until three o'clock. We went to his house, drank tea, and then I went to the Conservatoire to accompany Wenzel's student (the girl has blossomed, has become flirtatious and laughs a lot), and finally home.

At home I read with great interest my 1912 correspondence, which I have just got back from the binders. The wretched man has muddled the chronology of the letters up to April. I also received the long-awaited proof of the *Toccata* and, to my astonishment, Op. 4, except, for some reason, the first piece, 'Reminiscence'. I wrote to Jurgenson reminding him of this.

How should 'Navazhdenie' be spelled?[1] It would be more logical with an 'o' but when I played the piece four years ago at the 'Contemporaries' someone said it should be with an 'a', from the word 'vaditi', 'povadka'. That is how I have written it ever since, but other people object that it should be written with an 'o', from the word 'vodit', 'navodit'. My manuscript has 'a', but in the proof someone first corrected it to 'o', which was then crossed out and the original 'a' substituted. Whom should I consult? Balayev?[2]

Some time after eleven I put on tails and white waistcoat and went with Max to the Conservatoire to the Easter Mass. Mama, who does not like the huge crowds at Conservatoire services, went with Aunt Katya to another church. Max and I were hoping to meet one or two of our girls. But none was there – the female students were being unpatriotic and were all celebrating the Mass in other churches. Boryusya, whom Max cannot bear, was there, as was Glazunov, with whom I was obliged to exchange the traditional three-times Easter kisses. When I ran into Vasily Zakharov, he immediately asked me, 'Have you heard the news?'

'No, what?'

'You must have?'

'No . . .'

'Christ is risen.'

---

1 This discussion concerns the Russian title of the piece known in the West as 'Suggestion diabolique'. The English-speaking reader may not find it very illuminating, but Prokofiev's ear for language, especially descriptive language, is so precise that it seems wrong to omit it.
2 Nikolay Balayev, Russian language and literature teacher at the St Petersburg Conservatoire.

14 April

Easter. While I was still thinking of getting up, the clock struck twelve. I still managed four pages of score, however. Mama gave me a present of Fleur amie perfume, but I'm not changing my Guerlain Cadine for anything.

At four o'clock Max came in a taxi and we went out paying calls. The first was to the Karneyeva girls, who were both very pretty and charming. Five minutes, a rouble tip to the servant, and on to the next. Max still had to go to Ossovskaya, but was keeping me company.

At the Ruzskys I asked Nikolay Pavlovich about the Volga, a subject on which he knows everything there is to know. They were followed by the Sebryakovs (four minutes), the Yastrebovs, the Orlovs and the Ossovskys, but none of these were at home.

The Andreyevs expressed much interest in my new Concerto and asked me to play it through to them and their musician friends as soon as it is finished. They had been at the Meshcherskys before they went away, and Romanovsky had played my 'Gavotte' to general acclaim.

The only person at home at the Umnovs was Lidochka, everyone else was out. My four-minute visit produced little of significance in the way of conversation, because some tow-haired Junker or other was visiting at the same time. But . . . was it possible that Umnenkaya had stayed at home and not gone out with the rest of her family in hopes of seeing me? In my most recent telephone calls I had been very firm about not accepting any invitations from her – but today perhaps, knowing my devotion to the conventions of social life, and having accepted their hospitality during the winter, might I not consider myself under obligation to pay an Easter call?

Max went to see his aunt, and I went back to collect Mama, who had taken a fancy to a ride in a car, and we went to the Konshins, to Saburov and to Korsak. Regretting the absence of the Meshcherskys in the Crimea, we went to dine at the Rayevskys.

15 April

In the morning and until two o'clock worked on the scoring of the Intermezzo, keeping it light and completing eight pages. At half past two called for Max at his house at 63 Nevsky Prospect, and proposed a long walk to him. We went through the Summer Garden, then all the way down Kamennoóstrovsky Prospect, then Kamenny and Yelagin Islands and Staraya Derevnya until we came out on the main road to Sestroretsk. Seeing two amorous young men teaching a pretty young girl how to drive an enormous great car, our interest was fired not so much by the girl as by the car. I said that not this summer, but next, we absolutely must make a car trip round

Russia; it would be a colossally interesting, new and romantic project, and would not necessarily be terribly expensive: we ought to be able to buy a second-hand car for, say, two thousand, and afterwards sell it for fifteen hundred. Max said it was a mandatory trip to make, and if he comes into his inheritance we would obviously be able to buy a magnificent car.

When we got to Lakhta[1] we were pretty cold, as despite the fine weather the Réamur stood at only 11 degrees, and we had on only summer jackets. After a glass of Martel we pursued our schedule and got the train to Sestroretsk, from where we walked on to Beloóstrov. But we lost our way, and it began to grow dark. Climbing up a small hill we could see in the distance a proper road, which when we got to it led us safely to Beloóstrov just as the light went completely, and then took the express train back to St Petersburg. On the way we passed by the place where in 1910 I had for the first time in my life exchanged kisses with a girl – Tonya Rudavskaya. But the area had since been built over and now looked different, and although this poetic spot could not have been more clearly engraved on my memory, I could not see it now.

Sitting in the restaurant car swallowing steaks we quickly arrived at 'Pietari'[2] and looked for a taxi. But there was none to be had, so we set off nothing daunted to find our way home on foot, having walked (including our accidental detour in Sestroretsk) all of twenty-five versts and got ourselves not a little tired in the process. I slept wonderfully.

16 April

In the morning I achieved four pages of the Intermezzo and treated myself to a play-through of the first-movement cadenza, which I much enjoyed doing. It is beginning to come together, and lies very well under the fingers.

Around two o'clock I went to Raya Livshtiz's concert, mainly because Max wanted to. Raya has a superb digital technique, but as for the rest it is worthless, she should not be given concerts at this early stage and this one was unbearably boring.

At home I read a little of Artsybashev's *At the Brink*;[3] he is an excellent writer with good style. Later I wrote my diary.

In *Muzyka* there is an incandescent article by 'Misanthrope', i.e. Myaskovsky, about the Belyayev Concerts, in which he tears into the managers and

---

1 Small village on the Karelian shore of the Gulf of Finland.
2 Piter, i.e. St Petersburg.
3 Mikhail Artsybashev (1878–1927), novelist influenced by Nietzsche, concerned with themes of free love, sex and death. The characters in *At the Brink*, published in 1912, are caught between their desires for sex and for death, and often end by committing suicide. Artsybashev was expelled from the Soviet Union as an undesirable in 1923 and lived in Poland until his death.

the untalented composers whose works are programmed. He concludes by asking the question: why are composers like Tcherepnin and Mehrwolf and the like not being played, including 'the young, ebullient Prokofiev' . . .

In the evening I went to the Shtembers, whom I had promised to visit over the holidays. Sonya and Nadya were not there, Kokochka embarked on long, serious conversations about music, while Papa and Mama Shtember treated me with great consideration and even love. I was there for an hour and a half, and then left.

17 April

At ten o'clock I went in to play the concerto accompaniment for Wenzel's girl Yatsyno. It went very well. Glazunov was remarkably cheerful and even permitted himself a pleasantry at my expense: while I was waiting for the exam to begin I was sitting at the table where the programmes are usually sold, and on this table was a metal plate for the money, although as yet there were no programmes there. Glazunov, seeing me as he passed by, laughed and said, 'What's this, we've got a new girl selling programmes, have we?'

I responded in kind: 'I'll sell anything you like, except that there aren't any programmes!'

'Well, here's a rouble for you anyway!' said he, and a rouble tinkled on to the plate as he passed on. A few minutes later I went into the artists' room, where I found Glazunov again. He repeated his witticism, saying here was the new programme-seller. He then enquired with great courtesy if it would acceptable for Yatsyno to play a little later instead of straight away. His good humour is a bad sign: it means he's drinking!

After lunching at Leiner's I went home, since I long to get on with my Concerto. However, I did not do much of the orchestration, producing instead a sizeable portion of the piano score. I am laying this out leaving a space for the solo piano part so that the copyist will be able to insert it from the full score. When the piano score is published the solo part must be clearly marked (pianoforte) in brackets, and the accompaniment (orchestra) in brackets, so that the eye will instantly be able to distinguish which is the orchestra and which the solo piano.

At seven o'clock I went to dine with Saburov, who has obviously taken a great fancy to me. The only other person present was his son. The old man played Henselt's transcription of *Coriolan*, a very good overture, an excellent transcription, and for a seventy-five-year-old player a very powerful performance indeed.

18 April

Did very little all morning: three pages of the *Intermezzo*; it's a terribly long movement. Max and I had arranged to meet in the Conservatoire at two o'clock for the final exam performances by Nikolayev's class. Nikolayev has shaved off his beard and looks very funny. Miklashevsky, who I had never thought had much time for me, came up and with deferential curiosity wanted to know if it was true I had composed a second concerto. I satisfied his curiosity on this point and politely agreed to play both concertos to him.

I came back quickly, having borrowed Liszt's Concerto No. 2 from the library, and Max and I followed in the score the performance by one of the girls in Nikolayev's class. I did not know this concerto before: it has an enticing opening theme, but looking at the work as a whole one does not get much sense of any climaxes. No doubt they are there when one hears it with orchestra. The piano style is very interesting, but some passages are very dull for the pianist. I merely state this fact to reassure myself.

After the Lizst Concerto things became much more boring; there were no attractive people around, and I went home to get on with writing out the Concerto, managing another five pages. Went out for a walk with Max at nine o'clock; we went as far as the Strelka, and then back to the corner of Kamennoóstrovsky and Bolshoy Prospect. Long walks are child's play to us now, and we thought nothing of going the whole way on foot. Then we took a fine-looking 'tourist' taxi and went to our respective homes.

19 April

In the morning and until two o'clock orchestrated the Intermezzo. Thank God, the end is in sight, and tomorrow I should finish it. But my God, what a long piece it has turned out to be! This was not my intention at all, but I cannot cut anything out of it, otherwise the form will be lost. The idea of it is that the music moves from G minor to somewhere else and arrives at the trio, while the reprise returns to G minor at the same time as most of the melodic ideas, both their general shape and their treatment, go from high to low pitch and from *forte* to *piano*, whereas at the beginning of the movement the general tendency is from low to high and from *piano* to *forte*.

In the afternoon Max and I went to Frehlich to order our summer suits. We want them to be made of red material. The Rayevskys expressed outrage at this when I told them, but in any case at the moment Frehlich does not have any suitable cloth. He has promised to look for some.

In the evening we entertained guests at home, principally the Yablonskys and a young lady who is renting a room from them, a strikingly beautiful Armenian studying singing with Zherebtsova and who, although she has been attending the Conservatoire only since the autumn already has an impressively comprehensive grasp of all the gossip. She knows all about me from Zherebtsova-Andreyeva, and today was enthralled by my playing and by the liveliness of my personality. At first I did not take to her very much, finding her rather coarse, but later felt attracted by her. Her eyes have a naturally languid, weary expression that reminds me of 19A, but the latter is more refined and elegant, and better.

Mama heard the Scherzo from the Op. 14 Sonata for the first time, and was thrilled by it.

20 April

Rather than carry on with the orchestration I felt like composing a piece for Op. 12, which I plan to consist of ten pieces in a slightly more popular vein than my other opuses. The Meshcherskys have always called my 'Gavotte' a 'Rigaudon' and I started thinking about what actually distinguished a gavotte from a rigaudon. Digging around in Petrov's book[1] I discovered that they are almost the same thing, except that the gavotte starts with two crotchets to the bar and the rigaudon one. Without really meaning to I found myself starting to compose a rigaudon, and then dropped it. But today the same material composed itself into a rather nice little rigaudonlet into which also inserted itself a theme I had formerly envisaged for the Concerto, and which consisted of a pretty sequence of consecutive triads and sevenths. After a while the 'Rigaudon' was finished.

In the afternoon, to get some air, I went into the Conservatoire and sat with Max listening to the final exam performances of the external students ('external to music', as Nikolayev describes them). What a glorious work Rachmaninov's First Concerto is (the first movement)! Even allowing for the thinness of the musical material and a certain immaturity, how lovely is its representation of sincerity, tenderness, and a general feeling of delight. On top of that its pianism is beyond reproach and it is utterly free of routine or uninteresting passages for the soloist. I am speaking here of the first movement; I do not know the second and third movements but apparently they are not so good.

I sent Umnenkaya a story by Muizhel[2] I cut out of *Ogonyok*.[3] The heroine

---

1   Text book of musical anaylsis by Alexey Petrov (1851–1919), Professor of Composition Theory at the Conservatoire.
2   Viktor Muizhel (1880–1924), novelist, short-story writer and playwright. He became a distinguished war correspondent in the First World War.
3   The most famous and long-running Russian politically non-aligned arts and society journal, first published in 1899 in St Petersburg as an illustrated supplement to the *Stock Exchange Gazette* (*Birzhevye Vedomosti*). It is still published today, albeit as a result of a recent (2004) publishing buy-out, in a more commercial format than previously. 'Ogonyok' means 'little flame'.

reminded me very much of a slightly caricatured Lidochka, abandoned by the hero for another girl who bubbles over with life. Above the title I wrote in blue pencil, 'This story is surely dedicated to you, my friend!'

In the evening I went with Mama to the Korsaks, who are always very nice to me, my attendance being required to preserve the proprieties. From them I went to the Ruzskys, who were having a party for young people today. There was nothing of interest to me there, and in fact I do not much enjoy their gatherings for the young, I much prefer the grown-ups, i.e. musicians. With the Meshcherskys I love the girls and don't care much for the parents, but with the Ruzskys it is just the opposite: I am extremely fond of the parents and have no interest in the children.

The Meshchersky and Ruzsky families cannot abide one another, but they have several mutual friends, like the Kishinskys: two girls and their brother. I knew the elder Kishinskaya, but before today had never picked the younger one, Varya, out of the crowd. She is a friend of Nina Meshcherskaya at the Obolensky High School, and Volodya Deshevov splutters with excitement when he describes her charms. She herself came up and spoke to me today, and we had a long talk about the Meshcherskys. I went home some time after one o'clock.

21 April

Spent most of the morning idling about, and then went out for some air, to show Max the designs for our suits that the tailor had brought round. I stayed with him for a while so that by the time I returned home it was already one o'clock and I did not after all manage to finish the Intermezzo today, since Max and I had arranged to go for a walk at four.

Umnenkaya rang up in a state of high dudgeon about the story I had sent her: some elements in it might apply to her, but the rest was grossly exaggerated. She was extremely put out, and demanded my agreement that she was nothing at all like the heroine of the story. On the contrary, I said, I thought the character traits of the girl in the story were mild compared to her own. Umnenkaya had been shocked by the briefness of my Easter visit, she had hardly caught more than a glimpse of me, and was missing me. The faint whiff of my perfume from yesterday's envelope had overjoyed her and, in a word, I must come and see her this very day. I replied that this was out of the question; my behaviour would probably serve only to upset her further. Umnenkaya got very cross at this. In any case, I said, I was about to go for a long walk. Where to? To the cholera cemetery. She was horrified by the idea and begged me to choose another destination lest, God forbid, I should catch an infection and die. Then she would be very sorry.

Saying goodbye to Lida, I went to Max's and we started off on our intended itinerary. After half an hour we remembered that we had left the map lying on the table, but we did not want to go back for it so carried on without it. First, we lost our way in the Volkov Cemetery, which we should have gone straight across, but instead wandered about its precincts, jumping over graves that were sliding down the bank into the canal. When we eventually found a road, we went on it as far as a railway branch line, which caused us some perplexity as we had expected it to be the main Nikolayevsky line. Suppressing our doubts we pressed on, expecting to follow the railway line past the cholera cemetery, then turning away from it towards Obukhovo. But we were not on the line we thought we were, and ours proved to be a disaster, taking us through a bog and sometimes disappearing altogether, with an icy wind freezing us to the marrow. Our main difficulty was that we had no idea which direction we were heading in. Eventually we found ourselves at the Farforovsky Halt on the Nikolayevsky permanent way, which we followed as far as Obukhovo, and from a little bridge over the tracks watched the Kislovodsk express thundering through. We warmed ourselves up with tea in a cabbies' pull-in and ogled the local 'targets'. Finding them quite acceptable, we thought what a good idea it would be to take a top-quality example away with us to somewhere in the vicinity. Then, loading ourselves into a train, we came back to St Petersburg.

I telephoned Umnenkaya to reassure her that I had not met my end in the cholera cemetery, and we had a long, amicable conversation.

22 April

Today is a great day in the Conservatoire: the final exam of those graduating from the piano class. Eight people were performing, all of whom had been awarded marks of 5+ for their recital programmes. This year, because of the Fiftieth Anniversary Jubilee, they were competing for three prizes of a grand piano; in normal years there is one piano for the winner of the first prize. Max and I were there at ten o'clock to find an already packed hall. We were counting on seeing a good number of 'targets', but the competition itself held such interest for us that we soon forgot about them. Well-tipped ushers made a way for us to the front of the hall, where we had a little more room to sit.

The first to play was Bai, a student of Drozdov, in the Tchaikovsky Concerto. This was a good performance, with very fleet passage-work, power and temperament and as much expressivity as one could wish. In places he rushed the tempo to the detriment of the phrasing. He was followed by Katyusha Borshch – my love of long ago – who played Chopin's E minor Concerto very nicely, but after Bai and Tchaikovsky the effect was somewhat insipid and dull. After her came her colleague from Barinova's class,

Rabinovich, a pianist with sensational fingers and nothing whatsoever between the ears, who gave a sparkling account of the Lizst Concerto. I was ready to bet that he would get one of the prizes. Rabinovich's performance was followed by a short pause, and then we rather reluctantly listened to two girls: Lapina from Dubasov's class and Zurmüllen's student Motseikovich (she who had earlier evoked tears of joy from her professor).

Lapina played truly badly, Motseikovich was fine except that Glazunov's Concerto sent everyone to sleep. Next came the long interval, with a myriad acquaintances in the audience: a slew of Zakharovs, brothers, sisters and wives; Lidusya and Zoryusya, looking marvellous; Saburov; Myaskushka. Not many 'targets', I like 19A but don't know her. Rudavskaya told me she had a damaged lung, and Marusya Pavlova was in a very bad way: she has galloping consumption and is in a sanatorium somewhere in Finland. I am truly very sorry for Marinochka. Since seeing her leave the Jubilee Concert hand in hand with Zakharov I have not seen anything of her at all, and could not understand what had become of her. I suspect Rudavskaya's 'damaged lung' has an element of coquettishness about it, but perhaps it really is so. The crush during the interval was inconceivable, and it was virtually impossible to get to the buffet. Zoya wanted something to drink, and Max performed some sort of miracle in getting her a glass of milk, which he kindly bore aloft to her right from one side of the Conservatoire to the other. She was touched.

After the interval came the most interesting group participating in the competition: Yesipova's class. Poznyakovskaya performed Saint-Saëns's C minor Concerto with exceptional refinement and brilliance, and elicited a storm of applause. Her playing invariably draws praise, but I have always remained rather sceptical. After her came my ashen-faced ex-friend Zakharov, to whom two princesses of the royal blood had come to listen. He was an authentic candidate for the prize of the piano, as Yesipova had always pushed him. I did not consider him a worthy winner, as I had always said – to his face, when we were friends – that he was more gifted in life than in music. Max listened with hostility, the Karneyev girls with reverence. Zakharov was clearly suffering from nerves, his face whiter than the milk-coloured organ forming the background to his performance, and more than once his hands slipped right past the keyboard. His playing was dry and harsh, without so much as a drop of the warmth, languor or passion Rachmaninov calls for. The audience greeted him with less than moderate enthusiasm, and Zeiliger followed him on to the platform. I thought to myself: surely they're not going to give the prize to Zakharov? Are Poznayakovskaya and Rabinovich really inferior to him? Or am I simply biased? I tried to examine myself honestly: would I be afraid to enter the lists against Rabinovich? Or Zakharov? No. But even so, they are probably going to award him a prize. Zeiliger played the same concerto as Rabinovich, the first half with more depth but the second with less brilliance.

Everyone had to leave the hall while the professors considered their verdict. Myself, I would have awarded the prize pianos to Poznyakovskaya, Zeiliger and Rabinovich, but the Areopagus[1] decided otherwise: the first prize did indeed go to Poznyakovskaya, but the other two were awarded to Bai and Motseikevna.[2] The hall listened to the unexpected result in silence, and Borusya slipped out almost as soon as the rumour began to spread that he had been passed over. I had no quarrel with Zakharov's wings being clipped, the more so as his talent is not so great as to justify his being put on a pedestal. On the other hand his fall did arouse in me more sympathetic feelings towards him.

Went home at seven o'clock feeling extremely exhausted, but still managed a couple of pages.

23 April

Made a start on orchestrating the Finale. I really had not expected the orchestration to drag on for so long. After all, the reprise and the Scherzo are not finished yet.

At two o'clock went into the Conservatoire for a meeting with Tcherepnin about the Graduation Concert. I am to conduct three piano concertos: Tchaikovsky, Glazunov and Saint-Saëns (C minor). In addition I have to conduct two works by graduating composers: Karnovich's *Variations*, which I already got some idea of from before Easter, and the overture to a ballet by Shaposhnikov.[3] I heard about Shaposhnikov in the summer, as Saradzhev performed his ballet suite in the same season as my Concerto. Myaskovsky likes him.

If there are some lightweight vocal numbers in the Graduation Concert then they will be given to Tsybin or Dranishnikov. Nothing was said about any symphonic works; presumably Tcherepnin wants to keep them for himself.

After this discussion I joined Max and we went to choose material for our suits. We want them to be red, the same red as Max had seen his uncle, an artist, wearing. But the tailor could not find this shade anywhere and so we went off ourselves on an independent search. After a trawl round eleven shops we came to the conclusion that this red was not to be found, and went back to our apartments.

1   The Council of Elders of Athens in pre-classical Greece; the supreme court sitting in judgment on criminal matters.
2   Ironic declension of her surname as if it were a patronymic.
3   Adrian Shaposhnikov (1887–1967), composer of operas and ballets, eventually became a leading figure in the musical bureaucracy of Turkmenistan.

At home I studied the scores I had borrowed of the Tchaikovsky and Glazunov Concertos. The orchestration of the latter is appalling! All the parts are doubled and trebled, everything so lush and ponderous that the poor soloist will have difficulty making himself heard. It is so dispiriting to see an attractive phrase from the piano and realize that it will be completely covered by the strings, and by the wind on top of the strings, and sometimes also by the brass on top of that.

Towards eleven I went to the Warsaw station to say goodbye to Yesipova, who was going abroad. It was a piquant sight to observe Zeiliger and Zakharov. All year they have been wary of each other, in competition for the piano, and both ended up without one. But on the station platform they bravely kept up appearances, assuming expressions of carefree insouciance, Zeiliger whispering gossip into Drozdov's ear, both of them chortling with amusement, while Zakharov tried manfully to enliven the company with jokes and pleasantries. Yesipova commissioned me to take good care of Poznyakovskaya at the Graduation Concert. Poznyakovskaya snorted, 'You'll have to watch out; I can be a very awkward customer', to which I replied, 'Don't worry, I can be twice as awkward as you.' Then the train pulled out to a great waving of hats and I went home.

Max and I exchanged walking sticks. I had always liked his, and he had taken a fancy to mine. The swap was his idea but I was more than ready to agree. His is the more stylish, mine the more original.

24 April

By around two o'clock I had had enough of work and by agreement went to meet Max at the Conservatoire. But there was nothing of interest happening there, only a tedious cello exam with no one particularly attractive in attendance. We went to the 'Samolyot'[1] company to find out sailing dates of various boats. Nikolay Pavlovich had provided us with a list of vessels that would be good for our trip, and ones we should avoid. On the way we went into Alfyorov's and I drew out 100 roubles, 40 for Max. The unrest in Scutari had settled down and the European Powers had occupied Albania, therefore the stock market was rising along with my hopes of a profit.

At home I did more orchestration and then went to the Maly Theatre. When, in the autumn, I had asked Rudavskaya to get me tickets for the Navy Ball, I promised in return to get her complimentary tickets for the Maly

---

1   Although the Russian word 'samolyot', literally 'self-flying', is now universally used to mean an aeroplane, it has an older application to any device involving self-propulsion, particularly a ferry-boat anchored in mid-stream whose keel is so angled against the current as to induce the craft from one side of a river to the other. It is doubtful whether in 1913 anyone would instinctively have associated this travel agent's name with air travel.

Theatre (through the good offices of Max and his uncle). She had recently reminded me of my obligation and Max had got four stalls seats, so we went as a quartet: Max, myself, Rudavskaya and a friend of her choice. Before going to the theatre I shaved my head down to a Number Nought haircut; I always shave it smooth in the summer and this year did so a month earlier than usual because my hair was getting very long. At the theatre everyone had great fun at my expense on account of my bald appearance, persistently making facetious complaints about being seen with such an eccentric-looking companion. Rudavskaya was extremely boring and strangely jealous in her efforts to keep me away from her friend Tamara, a cheerful chatterbox with a deliciously pretty little face. The play – *The Dancer* – was quite amusing for the first half, but became boring after the interval. After the show Max got hold of a car and we took the girls home, chatting away happily, to Arkhiyereiskaya, where they live.

25 April

In the morning there were still a few passages in the Finale to finish, after which I only managed to orchestrate a couple of pages. I am beginning to wonder anxiously when I shall ever finish the Concerto: the Finale is pretty long, then there is the two-piano version to do, and all this with the Graduation Concert coming up for which there is going to be a mass of work.

Around two o'clock I went into the Conservatoire to hear Auer's pupils. I try not to go on working after half past one, as I start getting a headache if I do.

I saw 22A (the former 22A has now been re-numbered 14B; the one I mean is the new one). We are not acquainted, but I do find her very attractive. I did not get to hear Auer's students as Nalbandyan's class played first, and at four o'clock I had to go to see Tcherepnin about the impending Graduation Concert.

Shaposhnikov played through the Introduction and Dance from his ballet which bored me to tears. It is very modern, cheap, intricate stuff without a trace of music. It's not difficult to conduct, but there will be a lot of work involved in learning the score, which is very floridly presented and about a square arshin[1] in size. After this Karnovich played his *Variations*. This music is not at all modern in style, well crafted without being particularly talented, witty in places and on the whole, it must be admitted, very nice. Four of the ten variations were cut, and the composer will bring those that are to be played to me on Saturday evening. The first rehearsal is on Sunday, no less. Altogether I have a ton of work for this Graduation Concert. My poor, lovely G minor Concerto, when shall I be able to finish you?

---

[1] Seventy-one centimetres.

Returning home I settled down to orchestrating, but the tailor came for a fitting, and Max came as well to see what the material for my new suit looked like, so that he could order the same for himself.

Studied Shaposhnikov's ballet and loathed it. Max approved of the 'Allemande' and the (as yet unfinished) 'Rigaudon'. By autumn I would like to have all ten pieces for my Op. 12 composed and published, having sold the complete opus to Jurgenson for 1000 roubles. Max objected that to be prepared to put down a wad of cash of that size he would have to have sold out of all my previous works. He then came up with an ingenious suggestion: that we should ourselves buy up all the copies of my Sonata No. 1. Tomorrow he will go to the shop and request two copies, these he will send to his sister and his cousin, next I will go in, and so on.

What trash this ballet of Shaposhnikov's is!

26 April

I have laid aside my diary for three days and therefore today had to devote the morning to bringing it up to date. In between I played Shaposhnikov's ballet and cursed the composer.

Around two o'clock I went to the International Bank to put some money into Parviainen. These wretched shares did go up, promising a yield of 800 roubles profit (to my combine), but I did not manage to sell them again in time before they went down again.

After that I went to buy myself a Spanish hat, as Max had recommended, a very natty pair of shoes, and two copies of my Sonata, which I want to present to Wenzel and Winkler. I then went to the Conservatoire for the final exam performances of the singers who were graduating. There was a great crush, both *beau monde* and general public. My shaven head continues to be an object of astonishment, exclamation and exasperation; several people did not recognize me at all. Frantsis raised her shoulders and eyebrows as high as they would go and whispered, 'What do you look like?! . . .' Katyusha Borshch's reaction was even worse: she came running up to me, stood as if rooted to the ground, snorted, turned on her heel and called out to her friends, 'Come over here at once! I've something very funny to show you!'

Tcherepnin asked, 'How can you even think of conducting the Graduation Concert like that? Turn round . . . well naturally, everyone will think you have gone bald!'

Altogether there was no end to the gasps and clamour and exclamation. Yesterday Max suggested that I would soon get to the stage of hitting anyone who mentioned my coiffure:

'What have you . . . ?'

'All right, how about a sock in the jaw?'

I saw Natashka Goncharova at the exam today, a delightful vision of loveliness, but sadly, having asked me to change a three-rouble note, she dashed off somewhere and vanished, not, however, before calling over her shoulder, 'My idol! ...'

Klingman was sitting next to 22A, and later told me that her name was Belokurova, and that she was a student of Fohström.[1]

With Tcherepnin I went through the Tchaikovsky and Glazunov Concertos, and that done, went home. By that time the singing exam was over.

In the evening we entertained the Rayevskys and played vint.

27 April

Hardly had I woken up when a letter from Max struck me like a blow to the head: 'I must give you the latest news – I have shot myself.'

I thrashed about in and out of bed, rushed round the room, went over to the mirror, ran into the next room. My first semi-conscious thought was why, why, cut the cord of a life so joyously taking shape?! He said several times that to shoot oneself was a very easy matter, even that it was 'the last word in *chic*'; sometimes he would contemplate the way in which it might be done ... and I knew that he valued life as not worth half a kopeck. For him it would be no more to shoot himself than it would be to down a glass of Benedictine at a single gulp, finding that too 'the last word in *chic*'. Horror gripped me at the sheer likelihood of the event – and yet at the same time I wanted to think that something made it not so.

At this point his aunt Sofia Ivanovna telephoned and in a frightened voice asked if I knew what could be the meaning of the letter she had just received. Max had written to her that he had decided to end his life; he would seek out a secluded spot in order to spare his family the fuss and bother of funerals, police enquiries and so on. He would not write to his mother as he could not bring himself to do so.

What reason could lie behind this?

No reason. 'Reasons are not important' had been his wry comment in his letter to me. I summoned a car, dressed hurriedly and went to Sofia Ivanovna. After a brief and fruitless attempt to penetrate the cause and meaning of the catastrophe, we went to the police station to make a report, and then to the Missing Persons Bureau. Everywhere we went we requested

---

1 Alma Fohström von Rodé (1856–1936), known as the 'Finnish Nightingale' (presumably to distinguish her from her senior Swedish rival) was a prima donna at the Bolshoy Theatre in Moscow as well as a star in European opera houses before settling in St Petersburg. Two of her most celebrated roles were in Glinka operas: Lyudmila in *Ruslan and Lyudmila* and Antonida in *A Life for the Tsar*. After the Revolution she returned to Helsinki and eventually taught in Berlin.

that any information resulting from enquiries be given not to Max's mother but to Sofia Ivanovna. Next we went to the Finland Station to verify the postmark on the letter: it had come from Finland, but the postmark was completely illegible and it was impossible to discover the place from which this terrible news had come.

As we went, we began to uncover the reasons that lay behind Max's action. After the death of his father, the family was left in some poverty and continually had difficulty in making ends meet for the bare necessities of life. Max despised work, Max was ashamed of being poor, for Max everything had to be 'the last word in *chic*', people must be dazzled by having dust thrown in their eyes. But although Max had little enough for the ordinary necessities of life, he needed to splash money about extravagantly, therein lay his happiness. And all the time at home there was grinding poverty.

The first step on the slide into the abyss was in the summer of 1911, when Sofia Ivanovna put him in charge of her theatrical business in Pyatigorsk. He performed the task admirably and Sofia Ivanovna's takings increased; naturally he was trusted and large sums of money – all the box-office receipts – flowed through his hands. He spent them regardless, and was 'the last word in *chic*'. Next summer, that is the one just past, the same thing was repeated, except that this time we also became friends, and this friendship contributed to his ruination. He was extremely attached to me, and before whom should his brilliance shine if not before me? In Yessentuki I had money – 350 roubles for six weeks – and as I had no other friends spent it all, and quite freely, in Max's company. His extravagant habits were highly contagious, and more than once I squandered sums of 25 roubles on nothing – the only thing that mattered was to look *chic* in his eyes.

Autumn came, and whereas Max's prosperity came to an end my situation, although the stock market had plunged, was still quite flush. Max would not capitulate, however: he kept telling me about his wealthy relations and said that his mother was a woman of means, and if he was short of ready cash this was only because his mother felt it was politic to rule him with a rod of iron. I had no conception of the straitened circumstances in which the family lived, believing them to be rich and accustomed to spending money without regard to the consequences. When we dreamed up the idea of going to Imatra (and Max was always mad on travel) Max revealed that his pockets were completely empty. I said I would lend him the money, but at first he declined, saying that he did not want to get into debt. 'What's all this about debts?' I objected, accustomed to Max spending roubles like water.

He badly wanted to go to Simferopol at Christmas, and although he had some money, it was not enough. I gave him 100 roubles, he was delighted, and went. At the end of January we went together, and once again I stood treat. He invented fables about getting 500 roubles from his mother in the summer, and 1,500 roubles from Sofia Ivanovna on attaining his majority. This was followed by a fairy tale about his dying grandfather, who was leaving him a legacy of 100,000 roubles. And so on. Needless to say, I believed every word and thought of him, if not as a rich man, at least as someone more than adequately provided for. At home and at Sofia Ivanovna's there was consternation at his extravagant way with money, his way of life with cars, restaurants, and so on . . . But there too he was weaving a web of fantasy. According to him, Prokofiev had an income of 25,000 roubles a year, was awash with money and gave to him, Max, freely.

Thus Max, growing up poor, contemptuous of honest toil, straining with all his might towards the allure of glistering gold, festivities and *chic*, becomes a prisoner in the enchanted kingdom from which he cannot any longer escape. Telling me about the hundreds of thousands of roubles coming from his rich relations, at the same time he is telling them about Prokofiev's millions. Drawn inextricably into the affluent world existing only in his imagination, he no longer has the power to return to the real world of hardship. Step by step he approaches the crash, the inevitable moment when the lies, the whole fabulous fairy-tale castle built of cards, will come tumbling down. But he attaches no value to life, does not cherish it, the idea of penury so appals him that life obliged to be lived within its confines is not worth having, to sacrifice such a cheap possession for the chimera of gold is a bagatelle. And Max light-heartedly allows himself to be carried away by the current he has himself generated, he believes in his own lies, he luxuriates in his castle in the air, he is carefree and gay, he knows he will not have to savour the sour taste of poverty, that death will rescue him from this misery. And what is death compared to beggary? A mere nothing! So Max unconcernedly continues delighting in the pleasures of his imaginary castle of gold.

The summer brought the first signs of impending catastrophe as the date grew ever nearer of our departure for the Volga, the Caucasus, the Black Sea and the Crimea, the journey we had talked about all winter. It began with our need for a summer wardrobe, we would have to spend money on expensive tailoring, and then we must buy the tickets. Max went on talking about the one and half thousand roubles from his aunt; to his own family he spoke of Prokofiev assuming all the expenses of the trip. Things began to unravel: there was no money, the tailor was waiting for a sample of the material Max wanted for his suit and was already making mine, I was urging Max to get on and buy his summer shoes and hat. Max was pinned to the wall. Nowhere could he get the money he needed, but to reveal the true state of his indigence was unthinkable: a scandal, a disgrace, a comprehensive collapse. No longer would he be Max the carefree epitome of style, but a pitiably exposed braggart down on his luck, patiently submitting to the jeers of the vulgar and forced to scratch a living at some despised occupation. This was terrible, this was more than he could bear ... And it would be so simple to evade this fate, so easy, all he had to do was shoot himself. And if his death could be surrounded with some mystery, if the act could be invested with a wild beauty, my God how 'last word in *chic*' would be the end with which he would conclude the poem of his life!! ...

The previous day Max had been in the best of spirits, with not a care in the world. Then in the morning he got up, dressed with unusual care in his best suit, his patent-leather shoes, a dress shirt, a tie identical with one of mine, probably lit a good cigar and settled himself in the car he had ordered. Feeling himself to be from head to toe a gentleman of fashion, he entered a first-class compartment and wrote two stylish letters, to his friend and to his aunt: 'begging to inform you of the latest news – I have shot myself', 'so that there should be no tedious bother with the police I shall find a remote spot where no one will find me ...'

At some station in the depths of the country in Finland he left the train and plunged into the forest. He walked for ten versts or so into the silent thickets and the backwoods. On the shore of some deep lake, or in the middle of a marshy swamp, there he shot himself, to sink without trace into the abyss, beautifully and enigmatically. I am sure that when he placed the muzzle of the revolver into his mouth and curled his finger round the trigger ready to loose off the bullet, he felt with exalted clarity the lacquered shoes upon his feet, the dense forest all around him and beneath him the bottomless abyss – and with a final thought of 'the last word in *chic*' cut through the cord of life.

Is that not a better end than lying contorted with pain in a rumpled bed, drenched in sweat, the eyes rolling helplessly?

And so Sofia Ivanovna and I arrived at the station. It took me much time and trouble to ascertain the source of the postmark on the envelope, and it was only when I tracked down a particular postal worker whom we woke up at home in his apartment that we discovered it had been franked in the post van of a train – but which train, no one knew. By this time we realized we could no longer avoid going to tell Max's mother what had occurred. We decided to say nothing about the letters. On the way we constructed all kinds of theories: I was convinced Max would have left the train at some tiny wayside halt and disappeared into the forest. Sofia Ivanovna said that if this were the case, he would definitely not have done away with himself near the station but would have continued on foot for as long as his legs would carry him. Perhaps he was even now still alive, and still walking ... This thought struck me like a thunderbolt: could it be that, putting off from moment to moment the actual act of self-destruction, he had eventually put aside his intention and was now seeking out somewhere he would be able to hide himself away from the world? Perhaps he was making his way to Sweden to disappear in an alien land? Perhaps he had not wanted to kill himself but to hide himself from the eyes of the world to earn his bread, but not bread from prosaic lessons in St Petersburg or the drudgery of playing in a cinema, but bread spiced with the poetry of adventure, always on the move from one place to another, in search of fortune, and glimpsing from occasional newspaper reports the doings of a Petersburg that had long ago buried all memories of him.

Some details did support such an interpretation: leaving that morning, he had put on clean linen and a good suit of clothes; he took with him my letters, that he loved – what else could they be but memories of his former life? He had taken a little bottle of anti-callus lotion I had given him the day before. I began to hope.

God alone knows what his mother suffered that day. Katyusha's[1] cheeks were suffused with tears. Sofia Ivanovna and I did what we could to comfort them, and then I went home. My Mama greatly sympathized with my grief and went with me to the Finland Station where I wanted to continue my investigations into the postmark. I did not find out much: the letter had been posted on a train coming to Petersburg yesterday evening, but at what point the letter had been handed in and franked no one could tell us. I went back to see Sofia Ivanovna, where I found also Max's uncle, a well-known actor. In his view what had happened was evidence of a psychic abnormality.

In the evening Sofia Ivanovna and I went back to the station taking with us a picture of Max, and sought out the conductor of the train which we worked out Max had probably taken. The old man recognized the picture as that of a first-class passenger going to Terioki. This gave a completely new line of enquiry. Why Terioki? Terioki was the home of someone Max hated – Zakharov. I immediately telephoned the Karneyevs and, without saying anything about Max, got embroiled in a fruitless conversation. Zoya soon let me know that Boryusya had been in Terioki yesterday and was today safe and sound on his way back. It was clear that there was no question of Max having gone to shoot Zakharov and then turning the gun on himself.

With that our search ended for the day, I went back home and lay down to sleep. Feeling too alone to stay in my isolated room I preferred to sleep in the dining room.

Max's mother was not married to his father. Max was illegitimate and had no claim to the nobility to which he pretended. His name was not Schmidthof but (through his mother) Lavrov, and his patronymic was not even Anatolievich but Ivanovich.

---

1 Max's sister.

28 April

Next morning, lying in bed, I felt myself so alone I was close to despair. Yesterday the pain of loss had been alleviated by bitterness at the deception: every single thing my friend had told me about himself, that I had believed implicitly, had been false! But now I forgave him everything in the face of the horror of the loneliness to which I was now condemned. True, the magnificent Max, as he had depicted himself to me, had never existed, but I had no regrets in discarding the myth and easily accommodated myself to the sham of his brilliant exterior. But Max had perished, Max was no more, I was alone, and my God how powerless and helpless I felt myself to be!

This dreadful feeling did not survive the arrival of Karnovich to play through to me his *Variations* that were to be performed at the Graduation Concert. Thank God the first rehearsal was postponed from Monday until Tuesday, otherwise I should simply have had to refuse to conduct them.

I was much cheered by going for a walk with Umnenkaya: it was an easy, pleasant and even happy time with her, even though we managed to quarrel over her disinclination to go to the Islands. I spent the evening with Myaskovsky and played him the not quite finished Concerto. It was not easy to play it without any preparation, and at some places in the Finale I simply had to stop and rest my hands. He liked the Concerto and Kryzhanovsky, who was also there, went into ecstasies over the Intermezzo. I shall dedicate the Concerto to Max's memory.

During the afternoon Sofia Ivanovna was at the Missing Persons Bureau and gave them Max's picture. She had been seen by the officer in charge, who had promised to carry out a search with the utmost energy.

Driven by the extremity of my loneliness I decided to re-establish good relations with Zakharov. Boryusya is the only person whom I can imagine filling the void left by Max's fate, and to be alone is beyond my powers. I happened to learn from the Karneyevs that tomorrow is his last exam before graduating, and the day after he is going away to the Volga. Tomorrow, therefore, I shall go to the Conservatoire to have a serious talk with him.

29 April

I slept well and was not too unhappy when I woke up: there was no time, I must go to the Conservatoire to talk with Zakharov. When I ran him to earth, he came towards me with a smile, occasioned by my shaven head, but even so I felt it was a happy start to our friendly discussions. He was waiting his turn to go in to be examined in the History of Music. I decided it would be better to wait until he had finished his exam to broach the serious matter that was on my mind, and in the meantime wandered with him around the downstairs corridor making small talk about current Conservatoire events and the way the examinations had been going. When Zakharov had finished his unimportant exam we walked together out of the building and I asked him where he was going.

'Home.'

'Let's go and have lunch somewhere.'

'No, I can't. I must go home. I promised my sister.'

Then, after walking twenty paces in silence, I came straight to the point. 'You see, the fact of the matter is, that I should very much like to revert to a conversation you may remember we had last winter at the "Cuba". At the time I had a rather strange attitude to our discussions, and there were reasons for it, because there was a wall between the two of us. I am referring to Max Schmidthof. Today that wall is no longer there . . . He has shot himself dead.'

'Shot himself?'

'Yes. And I should like to clear up as unequivocally as I can the causes of the strange relations that existed between you and me.'

'You mean, because now Schmidthof has gone there is a vacancy?'

'No, not because of that.'

'Then, to be friends again until a new Schmidthof turns up!'

'Why can't you look it at another way: after Zakharov came Schmidthof, until such time as Zakharov returned?'

'All right, but there is not, and will not be, a new Zakharov, and you persuaded yourself the old one was no good, so there doesn't seem much point in us becoming friends again.'

I do not remember the details of the conversation that ensued: after a few more brief exchanges Zakharov suggested we go to the 'Vienna'. I liked the idea of this, because it signified his agreement to having a serious talk. We got into a cab and set off. Naturally we postponed the nub of our conversation until we had reached the 'Vienna'; in the meantime we talked of other things. Zakharov said he could never understand what had bound me so closely to Schmidthof; he considered him unquestionably inferior to me, and as far as Zakharov had been able to observe, all my friendship with Schmidthof had consisted of was trying to make an effect, often a cheap and unattractive one, centred around cars, clothes, throwing money about and affecting one pose after another. I replied that with him I had experienced true and unadulterated comradeship, and that I valued him for his mind, his wit and his visionary dreaming.

When we were sitting at a table and had ordered lunch, I opened the proceedings by setting out my views on our relationship. I recalled Zakharov's phrase, uttered at the 'Cuba', that I had ascribed to him all possible qualities and when I found some of them wanting I had been overtaken by bitter disappointment. Now I wanted to put before him another interpretation. I said that all the attention I had lavished on him had been reciprocated with very much less from his side. This had resulted in something akin to an unpaid debt, which had preyed on my keen sense of self-worth to such an extent that it had obscured and pushed into the background my perception of the totality of his good qualities, so that the qualities evaporated leaving behind only the sense of injustice. We began to quarrel and I picked all kinds of fights with Zakharov. Then came Max Schmidthof, and between Zakharov and me a wall grew up. Only when this wall collapsed did I see clearly that my former hatred was no more – it had been neutralized by my attacks on him, and consequently all those qualities of Zakharov that I admired were no longer concealed from me and had regained all the force of their former attraction. It would be silly and childish if I were simply to say: 'Now, Borenka, let's kiss and make up and go and play with our toys!' but in view of my renewed affection for him I wanted to set out for him how matters stood with as much clarity as they now appeared to me and explain to him the processes that had caused my change of heart.

Zakharov replied that relations between us could no longer be as simple and unclouded as they had been before, because even when it is over, a quarrel always leaves behind a fissure. I objected that it was wrong to think in terms of fissure: a quarrel, like a thunderstorm, cleanses the relationship. At the start there would inevitably be a certain artificiality, but that would soon pass.

Zakharov then said that I had set him a very difficult task which he would have to think carefully about and which could be finally resolved only once everything had had time to settle a little ... and what a pity it was that only the death of Schmidthof had impelled me to seek a reconciliation with him. He wanted to believe that the wall had been made of nothing more than cardboard, but why was it that I had taken it for stone?

With these words our elucidatory discussion concluded. When we took our seats on the tram, it seemed to me that already we were feeling the old affinity for one another, but mistrust still separated us. Tomorrow Zakharov and his sister and brother-in-law are leaving to go down the Volga as far as Saratov, returning on the 12th. As we parted, I said, 'If in the midst of the wide expanses of the Volga you are visited by any happy thoughts, please send me a couple of words.' We shook hands and I got off the tram.

What were my feelings at this time?

Mixed, but on the whole glad. When I am convinced of something I am a forceful and serious person, but the stronger the conviction the less frequently it occurs. When on the other hand I am prey to doubts, my God how weak and helpless I am, and how terrible is my loneliness. A friend is indispensable to me, a friend on whom I can lean, whom I trust utterly and whom I love. When I have this, there is nothing I cannot do! Zakharov could be for me such a rock.

30 April

When I awoke in the morning, lying on the sofa in the dining room (where I have my bed made up now rather than in my room) I was ready to give myself up to gloomy thoughts, but I was not given the opportunity to do so because I was immediately handed the score of Karnovich's *Variations*, brought round by the composer. Evidently I am becoming more accomplished as a conductor, because previously I would never have dreamed of conducting something I had only looked at so superficially. But now I went through the whole rehearsal, taking the orchestra through each variation, note by note for three whole hours, and earning praise from Tcherepnin. Generally I have been lucky with the Graduation Concert: I am conducting six items in the programme, that is almost the whole concert. Tsybin is apparently being given nothing, and is in fact leaving before the concert takes place; Dranishnikov may get a couple of vocal numbers to accompany. All this is very pleasant to contemplate, although cast down as I am by the dreadful event I cannot put my cares aside and rejoice.

At home I practised the piano. I was seized by grief and apathy, and above all horror at the apathy. But the mood passed and I started thinking how to spend the evening so that I would not have to sit at home on my own. Solitude, bringing in its train black thoughts, fills me with panic. My God, what will it be like in the summer? All my plans for travelling have disintegrated, I shall have no choice but to go abroad with Mama, to foreign parts, where I shall be even more alone. This thought provoked such an onslaught of aching melancholy that I resolved for the time being to think of it no more, especially as Mama had not brought up the subject.

I thought of going to the Chess Club, but then remembered that at eight o'clock that evening Zherebtsova-Andreyeva's class would be giving its exam performances. This cheered me up and I decided to go, for there would be plenty of people I knew there. Not only that, but there might be a chance of seeing Goncharova and Mlle Belokurova.

In this I was disappointed and sat instead with Klingman, who displays towards me the most incredible submissiveness. Umnenkaya also attended the examination, but needless to say sat where there was no possibility of my approaching her. From a distance she inclined her head to me. When I was at home once more she telephoned me, and our talk was light and pleasant balm to the soul. Dear Umnenkaya!

1 May

Next morning I proof-read Op. 4 and Op 11,[1] packed them up and sent them to Jurgenson. I was so absorbed in this occupation I did not notice the time flying by. In the afternoon I went to Auer's class exam, but there was not much of interest there. I had not said anything about Max's death in the Conservatoire, not wanting it to turn into one of those inconsequential tidbits idle students chatter about when they have nothing better to do.

When I returned home I felt once again that I was alone in the world. The Karneyevs telephoned to say they had heard from Terioki that a young man wearing a bowler hat had been seen at the station, looking and acting in such a confused manner that he had attracted the attention of the police. Since he refused to give his name and had no passport in his possession he had been arrested. After several days in the local police station, on the grounds that he stubbornly kept silence and appeared not to be in his right mind, he was transferred to the prison at Vyborg.

This information plunged me into deep depression. A young man wearing a bowler wandering about the station at Terioki behaving like someone who had lost his wits might well be Max having failed to screw himself up to accomplish the deed of shooting himself. Half mad, cooped up in prison, forced to crawl back to Petersburg to face a mother half dead with grief, a failed suicide, ashamed to meet his relations – what a downfall, what a disgrace!! . . . Picturing the scene to myself I was seized with horror, and if at that moment someone had told me that Max really had shot himself I would have shaken his hand in gratitude. However, as it was, soon afterwards the Karneyevs were able to refute the story as they were informed that the young man in question was fair-haired and wearing a lambskin coat, and furthermore he had been picked up not on Friday but on Wednesday.

I was reassured. I spent the evening at home looking through the scores of the Tchaikovsky Concerto and Shaposhnikov's ballet, and writing my diary.

I lay on the sofa and remembered Max as he had been last summer. A small, supremely elegant figure with an alert expression on his handsome and interesting face, invariably dressed in fastidious style, with a yellow rose in the buttonhole of his light-coloured suit, he went about with an air of brisk efficiency, light on his feet and always on the job: taking money at the box office, arranging the theatre company's travel to a neighbouring resort, issuing instructions backstage, signing passes for those who needed them. At any given moment his expression could be one of gaiety, or if something untoward occurred, knowing and impudent, and if he was spending money, disdainful. Always lively, always vibrant, graceful and attractive, competent

---

1 Four Pieces for Piano, Op. 4; Toccata for Piano, Op. 11.

and gay, an excellent manager and the best possible company, he seemed in every way to be a person in need of nothing, insouciant and very happy with life.

2 May

At ten o'clock I visited the Missing Persons Bureau to talk to an officer there, Mr Ivanov, who had been assigned the job of searching for Max. From my conversations with this official I formed the conclusion that few if any hopes could be placed on results coming from this department. I asked him if it would be of any use for me to go myself to Terioki. He replied that it could be helpful, and that if I felt it likely that Max had gone to Terioki, it would be best if I were to make a report to the local Landsman.[1] I decided to go there tomorrow.

Back home I had another look at Shaposhnikov and at two o'clock went to rehearse the Graduation Concert, where the orchestra had been set out on the stage of the Great Hall. Rehearsing Shaposhnikov's ballet proved to be extraordinarily difficult, because the inexperienced orchestra had to struggle to work out the dissonances of 'contemporary' music from the pen of a not very talented composer. When that was over I still had to plough through Karnovich's *Variations*, after which I was completely exhausted.

After the rehearsal Ossovskaya, to whose ears vague rumours had already come, asked me to come to her classroom, and I had to tell her the sad news. In this way Max's death became part of Conservatoire currency. Then Tcherepnin and I listened to Bai's playing of the Tchaikovsky Concerto and settled various details of the performance. Bai plays extremely well.

At home gloom settled once again; I was seized by anxiety and fear for the future. My mood lightened when I went out to go to see the Karneyevs, whom I had promised to visit this evening. Both girls were uncommonly kind and affectionate, and we talked long about Max. I recalled our summer together at Mineralnye Vody, and related various things that had happened during the summer. I read them the diary account of our January trip to the Crimea, which they liked very much. Asked Zoya if she would go with me tomorrow to Terioki, and she all but agreed to do this. I do not want to go on my own, and while I should really have liked to go with Katyusha Schmidthof I am not sure how appropriate it would be to ask her.

I went home calmed in spirit and happy with the evening.

---

1 The Landsman was the local police chief in the Finnish Autonomous Grand Duchy (this was the status of Finland within the Russian Empire from the Frederikshamm Treaty in 1809 that concluded the war between Sweden and Russia, until the October Revolution, following which Finland declared independence).

3 May

Rose at eight and got ready to go to Terioki. Zoya telephoned and said that her mother was not well and she would not be able to come with me. I was upset, because the last thing I wanted was to go on my own, but I pulled myself together and set off. I just caught the fast train, and on entering the carriage was hailed by Georges Zakharov, who was also on his way to Terioki. I was much cheered by this meeting and we talked happily all the way to Terioki. Georges invited me to lunch, an invitation I readily accepted. I have very warm feelings about the Zakharovs' dachas; even last summer, when I went to spend a day with the Karneyevs and was hardly on speaking terms with Boris, I could not resist calling in for a ten-minute visit just because the sight of their dacha aroused such a desire to be there.

Leaving the station at Terioki I went into the gunshop to make enquiries as to whether anyone had purchased a revolver the previous Friday. Max's picture was passed round all the salesmen, but produced absolutely no recollection with any of them. I then went back to the station and asked at the ticket office if anyone had bought a first-class ticket to Vyborg, or any other north-bound destination, on Friday. They said quite definitely that no one had bought a first-class ticket, only second-class. I went to the magistrate and made a full and detailed deposition to him, laying particular stress on carrying out a search in the environs of Terioki. The Landsman took the matter very seriously, clearly taking a great interest. Taking the photograph he ordered it to be reprinted and distributed to all the neighbouring police stations. He kept me for three-quarters of an hour and used up a whole sheet of paper in notes. He promised to let me know any results his men came up with.

I then went to Zakharov for dinner. He fed me a range of extraordinarily fresh and delicious country produce, and I missed two trains by walking down to the sea before I said goodbye to Georges and headed back to the station. It was wonderful, warm weather; nature was smiling despite the struggling northern spring. As I walked through the forest my heart was light and my soul was easy after the mental anguish of the week I had gone through. I felt able to contemplate making a long journey alone.

I dozed in my first-class carriage and thought of Umnenkaya at Kuokkale.[1] On arrival in Petersburg I jumped into a taxi and went to the Conservatoire. There I sought out Motseikevna and introduced myself to her, saying that as Tcherepnin was not able to come personally he had asked me to go through her concerto with her (this sounded very impressive). We went into a classroom by ourselves and sorted out tempi and other conceptual points for the performance, in other words we 'sang it through'.

---

1 Resort on the Karelian coast of the Gulf of Finland.

The Karneyev girls telephoned and suggested going to the cinema. At first I declined, feeling too tired, but then changed my mind and went, spending a nice evening *à deux* with Zoya; Lida was with her future fiancé, a Captain Second Class. We walked for a bit and then went to the cinema.

4 May

Next morning I practised the piano, wrote my diary and composed a bit more of the 'Rigaudon'. It is settled that in the summer I shall accompany Mama abroad; a few days ago I would have been in despair at the prospect, but now I have no objection, in fact I can even say I am looking forward to it with a certain amount of curiosity. If I get very bored I reserve the right to come back to Petersburg for *Dreams*, and in any case I shall return at the end of July.

I rang up Natasha Goncharova and we had a good talk. I had seen her yesterday, such a glorious creature, but did not get a chance to go up to her. Worked with Poznyakovskaya much as I did yesterday with Motseikovna. Saw the slender 19A in the distance and felt a keen desire to get to know her. At home in the evening I caught up on my diary, which I had neglected for a few days, and talked to Umnenkaya, inviting her for a walk tomorrow. She said she would like to come.

5 May

I read in the newspapers that today is the opening day of Pavlovsk. Rather than walk with Umnenkaya in Petersburg, wouldn't it be better to take her to Pavlovsk? Although, of course, she would be very nervous and probably would refuse. Anyhow, I rang her up. As expected, at first the idea frightened her, but I told her to go and ask her elder sister, telling her that we would keep away from the worst of the crowds, that we would get there before the main influx of people and leave before they left, and would have a lovely walk in the park. Ten minutes later she rang back to say that, yes, she could come.

At twelve o'clock Karnovich came to see me to give me a whole series of notes about his *Variations*, and then we went together to rehearsal. On the way he demonstrated his speciality: singing and whistling simultaneously, enabling him to produce a contrapuntal effect of two voices.

I started the rehearsal with Shaposhnikov's ballet and then got down to detailed study of the *Variations*. Tcherepnin then arrived and we went through the accompaniment to the Tchaikovsky Concerto, with me playing the solo part on a dreadful upright piano.

Home again, I put on my light suit, a black tie with a red stripe, took Max's walking stick – as a benediction – and in a rather frisky cab went to collect Umnenkaya. I decided against a car, so as not to alarm her. Umnenkaya was still very hesitant, so I had to employ all my powers of persuasion to reassure her that all would be well. Finally, just a few minutes before the train was due to leave, we arrived at the station, leapt out of the cab and scrambled into a carriage after the second bell had gone. Lidochka was appalled to see that it was a first-class carriage, and wanted to move into second class. When we got to Pavlovsk we went straight to the park and strolled happily about until nine o'clock. Returning to the station we went into the concert hall and heard a snatch of whatever music was being played at the time, then it was the interval, which plunged us into the most almighty crush. Umnenkaya went to freshen up in the washroom while I waited for her by the door. At that point I met Mama, who had also come to Pavlovsk with a woman friend. Successfully evading their claims on me, once Umnenkaya appeared again we walked in the park for another hour and then went to the train, but it was so full we would have had to stand. There was another one in a quarter of an hour. The return journey was full of tender endearments: Umnenkaya squeezed my hand and thanked me for a lovely day out. She asked me to telephone her and come to see her, saying that she would always, always, be glad to see me, and when she asked me, when would I stop paying her such notable attentions, I replied, 'As soon as I fall out of love with you.'

'So shall I have no peace until then?'

'Not for a single moment.'

6 May

Got up at half past ten, sat down to 'Rigaudon' and finished it. I was tempted to start writing it out, but decided to wait for a less busy time.

Glazunov was supposed to be coming to the Graduation Concert rehearsal today; Tcherepnin had told me that the composer wanted to conduct his concerto himself. At first I was perturbed by this: were Zurmüllen and Motseikevna up to something? But it transpired that Glazunov had from the very beginning intended to take the baton, so I relaxed. Tcherepnin saw some advantages in this, in that the presence of the Director would encourage the orchestra to pay more attention to what they were doing. Today Glazunov rehearsed just the orchestra without the soloist, at enormous length, taking up the whole rehearsal. I sat talking amicably to Motseikevna.

After the rehearsal I was at home and then went to call on Kolechka[1] for half an hour, after which I dined and spent the evening at the Rayevskys, it being Uncle Sasha's birthday. We played vint.

---

1   Myaskovsky.

7 May

Dreamed of Max: he was preparing to shoot himself; I attempted to dissuade him, but he explained so clearly and logically the vanity of his life that I was talked into supporting his decision.

In the morning I went to Gelever's class's exam in the hope of hearing or at least seeing 19A, whom I should still very like to meet. But she did not play and was not even there, so I returned home empty-handed.

Wrote my diary and around two o'clock went in to rehearsal. I had to conduct a lot today, mainly the Karnovich and Shaposhnikov pieces. I also went through the Tchaikovsky Concerto just with the orchestra. It is a wonderful feeling to conduct this work. An incident occurred during the rehearsal of Karnovich's *Variations*. The principal flute did not turn up at all to the previous rehearsal; this time he was there but played a lot of wrong notes and in one place failed to play the theme. Tcherepnin screamed: 'What's this, are we short of a flute again?'

I responded, from on high, 'We have one, but he cannot play!'

The flautist got very angry and growled, 'You watch what you're saying!'

This was an intolerable situation for a conductor to be in. I was on the point of making a great scandal 'calling in the Director' but on reflection decided that this would be in no one's interests and that I had better resolve the situation myself. I sternly informed the flautist that he did not know how to behave in an orchestra, that he had no right to be insolent to the conductor, and that by so doing he merely revealed his own lack of manners. I shouted very loudly, slapping my baton down on the score, the orchestra fell silent and the rehearsal proceeded.

Rumours about Tcherepnin leaving to take up the position of Director of the Moscow Philharmonia[1] have begun to circulate in the Conservatoire. Well, I never! The place will be a desert without my dear Tcherepusha ... Although for some reason it would give me huge pleasure to see him as a Director. But who could replace him here?!

In the evening I worked on the two-piano score of the Concerto. Rang up Umnenkaya to ask her if she would come with me the day after tomorrow to the opening of the season in Sestroretsk. As usual her immediate reaction was to be appalled at the idea, and she refused. But I am not giving up hope, boring though it is that she is such a timorous little thing.

---

1 In Russia a Philharmonia is a civic music organization rather than an orchestra. It can employ musicians and orchestras, promote concert series, own and run concert venues.

8 May

Next morning, with some reluctance, I studied Brahms's Violin Concerto which I am to conduct at the Graduation Concert. At rehearsal I conducted Tchaikovsky's Piano Concerto with Bai as soloist. It was very enjoyable, although I was not completely successful in managing the orchestra chords that fall in the gaps between the soloist's headlong octaves. This was followed by Karnovich and Shaposhnikov.

One of the orchestral musicians, an old friend, told me that the orchestra had held an investigation into my confrontation of yesterday with the flautist, the conclusion of which was that I had been in the right and the flautist in the wrong.

Tcherepnin, to whom I confided my intention to go to Paris, was very supportive of this and said I was doing exactly the right thing in going there.

When I returned home, Mama had some important news for me: the Terioki Landsman had telephoned to say that Max's body had been found. The matter is therefore settled: Max had not vanished abroad in search of happiness there; Max had not disappeared without trace, engulfed in the lake or in the swamp. Everything was clear, simple and definite: Max had shot himself and his corpse was now lying on a table. Coincidentally with the news came a letter from Morolyov enclosing a photograph of Max and me arriving at Nikopol, with a note from Morolyov apologizing for not having replied to Max's Easter greeting card 'as I am not sure of his address'... Alas, his address could not now be more simple.

At five o'clock the Landsman (or rather his assistant) came in person to tell me the facts as he knew them. Reading in the Finnish newspapers that the body of a suicide had been found in the Vyborg area, he asked his Vyborg counterpart for any distinguishing marks on the body, all of which coincided with those of Max. The discovery of his visiting card in a pocket removed all remaining doubts. The body had been found three days ago in the woods near the railway station at Syapnye, the first station on the line between Vyborg and St Petersburg. The corpse was already beginning to decay and had been placed in the morgue at Vyborg.

I informed Sofia Ivanovna of the tragic discovery. We decided we must tell his mother: this would in any case have to be done sooner or later. Sofia Ivanovna wanted me to be the one to give the news; she would be there to soothe and comfort, but her tongue refused to pronounce to his mother the words: 'Max is dead.' I called for Sofia Ivanovna and the three of us (with her close friend Gurko) went together to see Alexandra Nikolayevna. Sofia Ivanovna had truly dreaded this moment; she asked us to go in and say what we had to say without her, while she went to a shop to buy some liquid ammonia. We entered Alexandra Nikolayevna's room, I leading the way and

Gurko following. I was almost calm, and in response to Alexandra Nikolayevna's surprised look said in a firm voice, 'Alexandra Nikolayevna, there is bad news about Max.'

'Have they found him?'

'Yes.'

'Is he dead?!!'

'Yes.'

She uttered a cry and fell to the floor beside the chair. We raised her up and carried her to the bed. Sofia Ivanovna burst in and we frantically tried to bring Alexandra Nikolayevna back to consciousness. She alternated between sobbing wildly and relapsing into unconsciousness. Gurko and I sat by the window and spoke of Max. It appeared that shortly before his death Max had asked Gurko to speak to Sofia Ivanovna to see whether he could spend the summer living in her apartment, as he wanted to stay there for the whole summer and work. Obviously Max, in his efforts to find some way out of the vicious circle in which he was trapped, was going through some kind of mental crisis. He was trying to start to work, to give up his dreams of the high life, to face up to his straitened circumstances, but . . . the prospect was of so un-*chic*, so humiliating, so boring, so hopelessly drab an existence that in the end he chose the bullet. It was simpler. Looking at his weeping mother, Gurko said that Max had always been ruthless. This is true.

'You said a letter – did he leave me a letter?' asked Sofia Ivanovna. I replied that in his letter to me he had written that he could not bring himself to write to his mother.

'Please show me that letter!'

But I could not let her see the half-joking tone in which he had written to me and so I lied, saying that the letter had been given to the police. After this I felt there was nothing more I could do, and so I went out. Following Max's disappearance his family had left their apartment and moved to furnished rooms in 126 Nevsky Prospect. Coming out of the entrance just now and seeing No. 124, I was struck by the irony of fate: how many times had Max and I passed No. 124 and looked up at its windows, wondering on which floor the delectable Ariadna lived?

I had had no dinner today; it was nine o'clock and so I went for a snack at Nikolayevsky station. Again this brought back memories of Max: he loved coming here, for any reason or no reason. And how often we had been here together, leaving for the Crimea, or one of us meeting or seeing off the other, or simply coming to watch the departure of some express or other.

Lost in sombre thoughts I went to see Myaskovsky, having promised to play his Symphony through four-hands to Aslanov. Saminsky and Shaposhnikov were there as well, everyone was talking about music and were immersed in the subject. I suddenly felt how lovely it was to plunge into this world and forget all the sadness outside. It worked, and I became cheerful again. We played Myaskovsky's Symphony, and then I played *Dreams*, and then to conclude, the Scherzo for Four Bassoons, which went down extremely well. Aslanov said he would programme it next summer. My sunny mood persisted even when I left Myaskovsky's to go home.

9 May

The morning was spent on studying the score of Brahms's Violin Concerto and Saint-Saëns's Piano Concerto, and at one o'clock I rehearsed them with soloists and orchestra. Neither concerto went particularly brilliantly: for both Poznyakovskaya and Lipyansky it was their first time playing with an orchestra, consequently they made mistakes and played unrhythmically. Neither was my accompaniment up to much, and the orchestra did not know the music. After the rehearsal Tcherepnin took me aside into another classroom and went through both concertos with me very precisely. The conversation turned on his departure for Moscow. There seemed to be a good chance that he really would go, and then the conductors' class – the child to which Tcherepnin himself had given birth – would wither on the vine. Personally, I would of course be permitted to finish the class, but after that it was very questionable whether later conductors would flourish. Who could succeed Tcherepnin? God forbid it would be someone who himself has ambitions to be a conductor, because then the students would not get very much practice. Tcherepnin's own opinion was that the best person to replace him would be Blumenfeld: an excellent musician and personally the soul of probity; in his time a fine conductor who had had to step down from the podium after becoming paralysed. Although he had recovered he was not fully fit, one leg still dragged, and he would not be able to conduct much if at all. But he would direct the class admirably, and the students would conduct.

As for the Moscow Philharmonia, Tcherepnin's responsibilities would include conducting two concerts of music by new composers. As soon as possible Tcherepnin proposed programming my Concerto, and if at any time I needed to earn money, he would always be glad to welcome me as a teacher of piano.

At the end of the rehearsal I felt exhausted, and wanted to get some air by walking to the Islands. From the Conservatoire I telephoned 17A, but she grumbled that she had to go and meet some woman, and then go with her sister to Tsarkoye Selo. Having wasted over half an hour in this telephone conversation I came to the conclusion that there was going to be no joy with Umnenkaya, so I went home.

I was too restless and bored to stay at home doing nothing, I wanted company and air. All of a sudden the Karneyev girls telephoned and asked me to go with them to Pavlovsk: Lida, Zoya and Zora were all going. This was far better, and off I went to Pavlovsk in the company of three charming and interesting young ladies. It would have been perfect if the stubborn 17A had been travelling to her Tsarskoye Selo by the same train, but this was not to be. In Pavlovsk we walked a lot and listened to a little music. All three girls were as tender and doting on me as one could wish, vying with each other to flirt and play the fool, in general making a complete contrast with the incredibly strait-laced Umnenkaya. The evening slipped by and I even felt a touch of pride that I should be surrounded by three such interesting and attractive girls. Aslanov, whom I went in to see for a moment, told me that Shenshin[1] was looking for me. He had come from Moscow to show Aslanov his compositions.

'I feel sorry for you,' I said.

'But why do you say that, Sergey Sergeyevich,' returned Aslanov, reasonably. 'I'm prepared to be bored by ten Shenshins; if among them I should find one Prokofiev, I'll be very happy.'

I thanked him for his courtesy, and boasting to my three fair companions of the above-reported conversation, took them for sandwiches and then back to the train. The train was packed to the gunwales; we ensconced ourselves on the open platform, but even here we found ourselves under attack, and when I ruthlessly defended our position one gentleman who had not succeeded in forcing a way on to the train angrily jabbed me in the arm with his stick. The girls were terrified, the other passengers indignant, and I was amused by the impotent rage of the man left on the platform. After I saw the girls home I telephoned Sofia Ivanovna.

Earlier this morning she had gone to Vyborg. I would most certainly have gone with her to fulfil my last duty to my friend, but could not do so because of having to rehearse for the Graduation Concert. Perhaps this was for the best, to avoid needlessly torturing my nerves still more.

Max had been found by some children. He was lying near the forest, on some stony ground. A good quality Browning lay beside him. The children ran to get some shepherds, and the shepherds called the police. Max was taken to Vyborg, to the morgue. He lay there with a peaceful expression on his face, his eyes wide open, blood on both temples. His hair was dishevelled, but probably this had happened while his body was being carried. His suit had been removed in the morgue and he lay just in his underclothes. They were spotlessly clean, and this proved that he had shot himself the day he disappeared. Sofia Ivanovna went through all the formalities with the police. Max was buried with a bleak absence of ceremony, no burial service, in the Vyborg cemetery. Sofia Ivanovna, it seemed had not waited for the inter-

1 Alexander Shenshin (1890–1944), composer and conductor.

ment. I had asked her to buy 25 roubles' worth of flowers in my name, and Sofia Ivanovna confirmed that she had done this.

'Eyes open and both temples soaked in blood . . .' Max had been sure of himself: he had not batted an eyelid and his hand was steady. The bullet went straight through the right temple and out through the left. A good shot. Bravo.

Returning home I inscribed on the score of the Second Piano Concerto: 'To the memory of Maximilan Anatolievich Schmidthof.'

Tomorrow I shall put on a black tie and wear it in mourning for my friend.

10 May

Getting abreast of the concertos, with which I had so much trouble yesterday, occupied all morning. I telephoned Lidia Ivanovna, inviting her to go for a walk this evening.

After the day I had had yesterday, I was tired when I went to rehearsal, and it was not long before my head began to ache. The Tchaikovsky Concerto went well and I enjoyed conducting it. But then things began to go awry, and became unpleasant. Korguyev, the violin teacher, who had not been happy with the way I conducted yesterday, asked for this concerto to be assigned to Tcherepnin to conduct. Then Poznyakovskaya ran to Glazunov with the same request. This infuriated Tcherepnin, who considered they should have appealed to him, and he took my side. A confused rumpus ensued which came to my ears, my head hurt, I was angry and upset. Tcherepnin eventually negotiated that I should conduct the Brahms and Saint-Saëns Concertos again today, and if they were considered again to be unsatisfactory then I would be taken off them. Glazunov and Korguyev sat in the first row of seats while Tcherepnin sat next to Glazunov attempting to persuade him at every favourable opportunity that I was, in fact, conducting perfectly well. I cannot say that it was a very pleasant experience to conduct both these concertos under these circumstances, but they ended in a victory for me; both went well, and a beaming Tcherepnin congratulated me by leaving the conductor's baton in my possession.

I left the rehearsal to go to the Requiem service for Max, which took place at six o'clock in the chapel at Zagorodny near Pyat Uglov. After standing all through the service with true feelings of love for Max I emerged on to the street with those few relatives of Max who were present, and walked back alongside Katyusha, a very nice girl to whom I felt it natural to transfer my love for Max. She presented me as a keepsake with his sapphire ring, which Max always wore, and said that tomorrow she was leaving St Petersburg and moving to Moscow. I asked her to write to me and not to forget me wherever she and her mother went. It seemed to me that by keeping in contact with Katyusha I would in some way also be maintaining contact with Max, and if they were to disappear entirely from my life no one would be left who was close to him, and the last remaining links would abruptly and painfully be broken for ever. Not only that, but the Schmidthof family interested and attracted me as a reflection of my friend.

And so, both of us promising to write to one another, I parted from Katyusha and her mother. I slipped the ring on to my finger but then when I wanted to take it off again it would not come off as easily and I skinned my finger. Then I thought – perhaps the ring had been for ten days on Max's corpse and I could get an infection from the poison in the body . . . but of course this was nonsense and if it were the case that Max had shot himself while wearing the ring it was doubly precious to me. I put it away for now, so as not to exacerbate my nerves, but in time I shall wear it in memory of him.

When I got home my head was aching, and I slept.

The concierge passed me a note from Borislavsky, a Sokol member, asking me to come to Sokol-3 about my March. Another Sokol member had written some words for a marching song that had been set to music by various people, including a composer called Shollar and even the veteran Cui. When I was shown them, I declared them to be rubbish. Back came the very reasonable objection that it was all too easy to criticize, but could I do any better myself? I said, 'Of course I can!' So I wrote them a March, a silly and derivative piece but lively and good fun, with a catchy tune. They liked the March, I presented it to Borislavsky, and forgot about it. Now Borislavsky was telling me that a new Sokol branch had been formed, Sokol-3, and wanted me to visit it to make an agreement that it should become the new branch's official theme tune. I was happy to agree; now the music had to be passed by the committee, and in the meantime I was to be made a member of Sokol-3. In the past I had been an enthusiastic member of Sokol-1, although I had not been there once this winter and had got quite out of the way of it.

The Karneyev girls telephoned and very kindly invited me to Terioki; they are going there tomorrow. They also asked most insistently if they could have my photograph.

I think that justice demands I should play my Piano Concerto No. 1 in the Belyayev concert series. I therefore went yesterday to see Glazunov to ask him if he would be prepared to let me play my Concerto to him. He was more than ready to agree to this, and even asked if I meant the First or Second Concerto, thus demonstrating that he knew of the existence of No. 2, and suggested that I remind him at the Graduation Concert so that we could make an appointment to meet.

11 May

Slept until eleven to get some rest after yesterday's excitements, and then went to the general rehearsal. The first work to be gone through was the Saint-Saëns Concerto, and it went well, and after that everything was fine. Now that all the disagreements had been ironed out my fatigue left me, my head stopped hurting, and I felt in top form. A photographer took a picture of us; I thought the photograph was meant to be only of those graduating and therefore stood to one side, but Glazunov turned to me and said, 'Sergey Sergeyevich (the first time he had addressed me by name and patronymic), you should be up there on the conductor's podium!' I stood up, only to be surrounded by a lot of loutish orchestral musicians. But I was wearing my light-coloured suit, and so stood out very prominently.

There was quite a big audience for the dress rehearsal, but not many people I wanted to see. No. 19A sat for a while, but then left; I gave 21B and 21M a ticket each for tomorrow's concert. After the rehearsal the heavens opened and the rain poured down; everyone crowded into the entrance to the Conservatoire but the rain was so heavy it was impossible so much as to poke one's nose outside. Tcherepnin turned up his coat collar and bravely ventured out.

'Sergey Sergeyevich, won't you come with me?' he said.

'I can't, Nikolay Nikolayevich, as you can see I'm in nothing but a light suit.'

'Well, you'll just have to stay put then. Serves you right for being such a dandy!'

When I got home I telephoned Umnenkaya and invited her to the Graduation Concert tomorrow, but she grumbled and made all sorts of difficulties about a rehearsal for her exam at half past three in the afternoon. I still sent her two tickets.

Went to the Ruzskys and played Nikolay Pavlovich my Concerto. Some of it was too much for his comprehension, but what he did understand he liked, especially the first and third movements. He is a kind man and was very sympathetic about Max's death. His daughters, who had never liked Max, sat without saying a word.

12 May

I am used to conducting now, so this morning the prospect held no terrors for me. Mama's friend Mme Pavskaya came at half past twelve and we went together to the Conservatoire.

Following an exhaustingly long recitation by Gabel of the year's activities, I opened the concert with Karnovich's *Variations*. The orchestra played badly, and in the event the variations proved to be rather uninteresting: there are some nice things in the piece but Karnovich is not going to become a significant composer. This was followed by the Tchaikovsky Concerto, which except for the inevitable shortcomings of a student orchestra went very well indeed. For instance, at one point Tcherepnin had asked for a tremendous *sforzato* from the timpani, so I indicated this with a particularly vigorous gesture that produced nothing at all: the timpanist sat calmly with his arms folded looking with interest at the audience in the boxes. It looked extraordinarily stupid. I happen to be particularly fond of this place in the score; I even had a dream about it last summer, in which the music appeared to me as I rushed headlong down a mountainside, ever faster, more impetuously and more enraptured by the sound . . .

Afterwards I was visited in the artists' room by Ziloti and Aslanov, both of whom paid me compliments about my conducting. This was a pleasant surprise, since I had expected Aslanov to say much the same as Khessin had benignly advised in the winter: that I should give up the idea of conducting. The Brahms and Saint-Saëns Concertos also went very respectably. Then came the interval.

I went to the buffet, where I accidentally shook hands with Vera Alpers, whom I do not usually greet in this fashion, saw my family and also Myaskovsky, who was as always sceptical of my conducting abilities. He finds me lacking in rhythmic stability. Rozovsky, smirking, said that watching me he was sure he was witnessing the birth of a second Ziloti. At that point I remembered that I had sent a ticket to Zora and went to look for her. She was very loving, although less attractive-looking than usual. Promising to come back and see her after the next item in the programme, I went to find Glazunov. When I succeeded, he gave me an appointment for the 20th, at ten thirty in the evening.

Next I conducted the Introduction and Dance of the Maidens from Shaposhnikov's ballet *The King's Feast*. It sounded all right with all its tricks of orchestration, but musically it is thin stuff. When this was over I had finished my stint on the podium, so went to find Zora, and because there was no seat free next to her made her come back to the fourth row with me. There we sat until the end of the concert and throughout the presentation of diplomas. Motseikevna played quite well, but went wrong a few times, much to the alarm of Glazunov, who was conducting. Presentation of diplomas over, the freshly minted graduates assembled decoratively on the platform to be photographed. Zakharov, Zeiliger and Rabinovich, of course, were not among them. Zora was being nice, but cattily observed that we did not seem able to produce a single beautiful girl. As a matter of fact, there was one sitting right behind us, Marusya Pavlova, whom I had not seen since the winter Jubilee Concert, when she made a fleeting appearance on the arm of Zakharov. She was recuperating from incipient tuberculosis and for the sake of her health was going to spend the summer near Ufa. We did not have much to say to one another, but it was pleasant all the same.

The Graduation Concert came to an end and I took Zora down to the foyer. She was full of praise for my conducting, was very affectionate, and promised to telephone me and when there was an opportunity to come with me to Pavlovsk.

After this I came home. Usually after such events, Graduation Concerts, opera productions, concerts and the like, everyone involved gets together and goes off somewhere for dinner or supper, or on the razzle. I have never enjoyed this sort of thing much, probably because I don't find the company particularly congenial. I always used to go home on my own, not without a certain feeling of emptiness. But the last occasion, after the Dargomyzhsky evening, Max was with me; we walked and dined together and I did not feel bereft, I was happy in the company of the one person I wanted to be with. Now I feared to be alone and away from the celebrations, but for some reason today they did not happen and there was no gathering, so although I went home solo I did so contentedly, even happily.

At home a package from Jurgenson was waiting for me, containing the second proof of Op. 4 and Op. 11, so I took them with me in the evening to Myaskovsky's. He played both opuses through to me, winkled out several errors and listened to the new 'Rigaudon', proving to me that it is not a rigaudon at all because the music should be in a fast tempo and *alla breve*, whereas this piece has a quite different character. So there!

I learned *en passant* that Zakharov had returned today from the Volga, that he had rung Myaskovsky and some time in the next few days they were to meet and make music together. In answer to Myaskovsky's question as to whether I had thought it had been right not to award Zakharov the prize, I said I thought it had: musically he was superior to the other contestants, but technically he was not as finished. The prize was given for qualities as a pianist, not as a musician, and therefore the jury had been right to give the prizes to rival candidates with more brilliant, purely pianistic gifts.

13 May

Spent the morning making the two-piano version of the Concerto. At one came into the Conservatoire to say goodbye to Tcherepnin, who is leaving tomorrow for Paris. Walking along Offitserskaya Street to the Conservatoire, I met a whole group of Bai, Zeiliger and Zakharov coming in the opposite direction. I stopped, and we had a very amicable conversation about this and that. The ventilation holes in my hat provoked much hilarity, and then I asked Zakharov if he had enjoyed his trip down the Volga. That was the end of the conversation, and I went on my way regretting that I had had so little chance to talk to Zakharov, it now being uncertain when or how we would meet again to continue our 'peaceful negotations', which might now have to put it off until the autumn. He was friendly and joking today, but he did not write me any letters from the Volga. This may indeed have been quite the right thing to do, but I do not feel inclined to make any more overtures towards reconciliation, and probably he does not want to either, for fear that I might throw myself at him just to save myself from the agony of loneliness. Now I am able to reflect calmly on the whole situation and put it all into perspective.

Arriving at the Conservatoire I waited for Tcherepnin. While I did so I read the reviews of yesterday's concert; mostly they simply reported the fact of my having conducted without going into any detail of my or the soloists' performances. In two papers I received a measure of glancing praise.

Tcherepnin dashed into the Conservatoire for a minute and now had to do the rounds of the banks in preparation for his trip abroad. He suggested I keep him company, and as I was free I gladly agreed. We discussed my future and Tcherepnin spoke approvingly of the 'armaments' with which I had equipped myself for embarking on the stormy seas of life, advising me to concentrate on my activities as a performer and not to coop myself up in the world of teaching. It is not yet settled whether he is going to become the Director of the Moscow Philharmonia, but if this does happen then without question the best person to replace him would be Blumenfeld. As his health is not good and he sometimes has to take time off for sickness, he would need an assistant, who could be a former student, for instance Shteiman or myself. I said goodbye to Tcherepnin at the Mayor's Office in the hope of meeting him in ten days' time in Paris.

Later that evening I was at the elderly Saburov's; we played chess.

14 May

Next morning, the two-piano reduction and the diary. Telephoned Lidochka at three to ask her out for a walk, but she could not as she was seeing off her sister to Kuokkale.

'All right then, I'll meet you at the Finland Station and come back with you,' I said, and set off for the station.

I duly met Glupenkaya seeing off her sister, and we walked along the Neva Embankment. At the steamer pier I tried hard to get her to board a steamer and go to the Islands. Lida was frightened, said she wouldn't and fought against it for a long time, but eventually gave in and we went. It was a holiday and the steamer was packed with people, the sun was shining brightly and the banks were green, but a cold wind was blowing. We walked around Yelagin Island, Umnenkaya invited me to stay at Kuokkale, and we listened to the frogs croaking. Listening to them, Lida found for the first time (just like the other Lida, Karneyeva) that their singing was beautiful, and peered everywhere trying to see them. It was a nice walk, but in my soul something was not right.

In the evening I went to the station with the Ruzskys, who were going to the Volga, where they have rented an estate or a dacha, to which they also invited me. They are buying a car to use in Petersburg. *Chic.*

15 May

This morning, after a struggle with myself, I accomplished an important task. I felt very proud of myself.

In the afternoon I wrote my diary and worked on the two-piano score. In the evening I wrote to Katyusha Schmidthof.

16 May

In the best of spirits. Worked on orchestrating the Finale.

At three o'clock went into the Iretskaya[1] exam, which was distinguished by a lively and festive atmosphere. Just before dinner Lidia Karneyeva telephoned; she had come from Terioki on business and also to see her doctor, who lived opposite us. I invited her in and she came to dinner, after which I hired a car in which we went round several places she needed to visit, and I then took the delightful girl to the station and she went off to Terioki, not before extracting a promise from me to go and visit them soon. But what most interests me is: is Zakharov in Terioki at the moment?

At home I telephoned the Meshcherskys to find out when and where they were going away for the summer. The answer was that they were leaving in a few days' time for Gurzuf, where they planned to stay until the end of the summer, but in the meantime they were at home and would be very pleased to see me. I put on a coat and went. There were not many other people, two or three at most, among them one Zaitsev, a gentleman with a little Mephistopheles beard who talked knowledgeably about Paris. I spent the whole evening there and enjoyed myself very much. I like Nina – an exceedingly attractive girl. They invited me to stay during the summer, and by the time I went home I was walking on air, delighted with the invitation; the Crimea is exerting its pull on me. The only fly in the ointment was that my tooth was hurting.

---

1 Natalya Iretskaya (1845–1922), coloratura soprano who had studied with Pauline Viardot and appeared in recital with Anton Rubinstein. From 1881 she was Professor of Singing at the St Petersburg Conservatoire.

17 May

Went to have my tooth looked at. Doctor Ulanovsky, or Ulanovich as I call him, had gone out to Terioki yesterday, and now was curious to know the identity of the pretty girl I had been seeing off at the station. He himself has a very attractive, dark-complexioned assistant.

At home I finished off a page of score and then went to hear the exam performances of Leschetitskaya's[1] students. Natasha Goncharova was in a desperate state of funk and sang appallingly; Tonechka Popova, black-haired and elegant, very well. I sat with Umnenkaya and her girl friend Natasha, a flaming redhead. Umnenkaya wanted to know where my perfume came from. 'From her,' I said, indicating the singing Popova. 'Foo, I've gone right off it now!' exclaimed 17A.

Vera Alpers appeared. Her figure is most elegant, but her face is beginning to droop. After the performance I went up to Natasha Goncharova, little by little recovering after the ordeal of being on stage. 'I'm going to Berdyansk[2] tomorrow,' she informed me.

'Oh, that's not possible. I very much want to see you before you go.'

'And I you. Shall we go to the Islands tomorrow?'

I was thrilled. Promising to call for her tomorrow, I relinquished her to the attentions of her adoring suitor Chuprynnikov[3] and went off to find Umnenkaya. I was afraid she might already have left, but she hadn't; probably she had been waiting for me. We went for a walk, starting with the Kalinkin Bridge and then on to the sea, or more accurately to the mouth of the Neva river. But this was not far enough for us, so we continued to Yekaterinhof, where I showed her the palace. It was empty and unlocked, so I persuaded her to come inside with me. The rooms were small and cramped and uncomfortable.

On the way back we talked about Max. I told her about the final word in the last letter he wrote to me: 'Farewell.' What a wild, fantastic cargo of meaning was borne by that commonplace word, the very last one he directed towards his only friend immediately before leaving this world never, but never, to return!

---

1 The daughter of Anna Yesipova and Theodor Leschetitsky, who taught singing at the Conservatoire.
2 Port on the north coast of the Sea of Azov.
3 Mitrofan Chuprynnikov (1866–1918), tenor soloist taking character roles at the Mariinsky Theatre.

18 May

My visit to the Meshcherskys had reawakened in me the desire to compose a rigaudon. The one I thought I had written was not in fact one, because it was in a slow tempo. I now set to and began to write a quick, lively piece.

At three o'clock I ordered an open-topped car and went to pick up Natasha. She was alone in her married sister's luxurious apartment, where she had been staying all winter. Today Natasha was not looking quite so beautiful, but she was still extremely nice, and told me that the reason she liked me so much was that I was such an uncomplicated person. The car proved to be a satisfactorily sporty one, and it was also pleasant going round the Islands. We parted with expressions of great tenderness and promised to write to one another.

19 May

By 9.45 in the morning I was already speeding up the line to Terioki on the excellent Finland Express, greatly looking forward to my visit. In the restaurant car, where I went to have a cup of coffee, I encountered Captain Second Class Barkov, Lida's admirer. At first he was evasive, not wishing to disclose where he was going, but eventually it became clear that he too was on his way to the Karneyevs. Lida and Zoya were dressed in their best as they met us at the station, and we were a happy party as we walked to their dacha. Boris Zakharov has not yet arrived in Terioki; a pity.

The Karneyevs have evidently come into some money recently: the hospitality was lavish, with all kinds of liqueurs and much conviviality. We had a nice expedition in two phaetons to Chornaya Rechka,[1] Zoya and I in one and Lida and Barkov in the other. I talked a lot about Max. Zoya listened and commented with great interest and sensitivity. Then we played croquet, in the course of which Lyova, the 'representative of the Croquet Club' suffered defeat at the hands of Zoya and me, which induced in him paroxysms of rage. I nearly missed my train home; Barkov was staying the night. I got a piece of grit in my eye, from standing on the outer platform of the train. My eye swelled up and tormented me all night.

20 May

Next morning I went to the eye surgeon whose office is above our apartment. Wrapping some cotton-wool round a sliver of wood and dipping it

---

[1] Chornaya Rechka ('Black River') is a riverside spa just outside St Petersburg. It was the site of Alexander Pushkin's fatal duel with Georges d'Anthès.

into some kind of liquid, he skilfully turned back my eyelid and in a trice lifted off the offending grit. The sore eye immediately subsided, but I had hardly slept and so was not in good shape to work. Telephoned Umnenkaya. She is in a state of panic about her impending exam and was going to see her friend, a classmate and companion in distress.

In the evening I was at M. P. Korsak's, which was boring. 'You must definitely go to the Meshcherskys,' she pronounced authoritatively, learning of my invitation. I shall go.

21 May

Finished off my jolly little 'Rigaudon', also managed to work out the episode in the Finale of the Concerto where the first movement theme is repeated. This has hitherto resisted my efforts.

Went to our dirty, cramped and stuffy Mayor's office to put in an application for a foreign passport. From there went to the Conservatoire in order to be there for Umnenkaya's exam. Her father, brother and sisters were all sitting in the hall, visibly nervous and craning their necks every time a new student appeared on the stage. When Lidochka appeared, sparkling with diamond earrings, she looked magnificent. Her singing, however, was not on a par with her appearance, although she sang the wife's aria from *Sadko*[1] not at all badly. The voice is good, although nerves make her sing sharp.

In the interval I rush round, mutter a few words to her sister, do not manage to get in to see 'her' in the artists' room and dash off to catch a train. Kolechka Myaskovsky and I have a *rendezvous* at the Tsarskoye Selo station to go to Pavlovsk, not just for the concert but to have time for a walk beforehand. I must try to meet Zakharov, as I am sure he will be there. Indeed, a Zakharov did join us in the train, but not that one: his brother Vasily, a fine fellow if inclined to be a bit rough in his manners. On arrival at Pavlovsk, Myaskusha and I went for a walk. He writes in *Muzyka* under the pen name of 'Misanthrope', and his recent overview of the Belyayev Concerts has delivered so blistering a castigation of the management for their failure to honour the founder's wishes in terms of programming works by new composers (including myself), that apparently this same management (Artsybushev, Glazunov and Lyadov) has seriously taken fright and now proposes to enlist the help of Ossovsky and Pogozhev. This is very timely for me: I want them to programme my concertos and am about to start actively working to achieve this end.

Before the concert I went into the artists' room to see Aslanov. He had

---

1 The wife of Sadko, the singer and psaltery player in Rimsky-Korsakov's opera, is Lyubava Buslayevna.

been impressed by my conducting at the Graduation Concert and now proposes that I conduct *Dreams* at Pavlovsk myself. Zakharov was not there, but Myaskusha said that he would be seeing him in Terioki tomorrow.

Listened to the *Divine Poem*. It is wonderful music, but how shapeless the first movement is! Say what you will, but with its inordinate length and absence of any landmarks, the form is diffuse to the point of haziness. The opening of the Finale is magnificent, but why follow those sprightly and attractive pizzicatos with yet more meandering music?

Debussy's *Chambre magique*[1] sounded good but there's not much music in it. There is more in Stravinsky: his *Infernal Dance*[2] is simply excellent. Afterwards I strolled around for a while among the numerous, fashionably dressed audience. Met 'the Pillow'[3] from Yessentuki and had a nice talk with her. I felt good in my smart light suit, gracefully pirouetting hither and yon and remembering how Max used to do the same in Pyatigorsk.

22 May

Composed a coda for the little 'Rigaudon', and got a lot of orchestration done. Telephoned 17A to catch up on yesterday's exam. She is soon going out to their dacha. I should have liked to see her, but the way things are she has no time today. So I just stayed in all day except for a short outing to Alfyorov to draw out 100 roubles. But I got a lot of the orchestration done.

Received a package from Katyusha Schmidthof containing a song by Max to words by Lermontov: "Tis dreary and gloomy . . .' I studied the song with the greatest possible interest and found in it signs of real compositional ability, with temperament, expressive means, much intelligence . . .

And life, when it's seen in the cold light of day,
Is naught but an empty and futile cheat.

This concluding phrase was set to music of such unfeigned pathos that I was at once overcome by sadness. And indeed, Lermontov's bitter phrase, the melancholy ending of the song and the image of Max's bullet-ridden corpse came together in a despairing but beautiful unity. Oh, to have this phrase on the headstone of his grave!

What was it that prevented Max's talent from developing? He never spoke of his own work, indeed in later days he gave up composing entirely, affecting complete indifference to those productions of earlier years to which this song belonged. Did he himself sense that nothing would come of his gifts?

1 Symphonic Fragment No. 3 from *Le Martyre de Saint Sébastien*.
2 'Infernal Dance of Kashchey's Subjects' from *The Firebird* Concert Suite (1911).
3 Clavdia Sheintsvit, a brief romantic interest from the summer of 1909.

Did he fear ridicule, the casual wounding of ignorant criticism? Or was it simple laziness? Or the constraining effect of being alongside me and my parallel, albeit swift and sure, development? If he had nurtured his own composing, perhaps he would not have wanted to end his life!

In the evening I continued working. Had a long telephone conversation with Lidochka, and when it was over, longed for more.

23 May

Ascension Day. Spent the morning on the Finale of the Concerto. Exhaustive and circumstantial conversation with Mama about investments. It turns out the situation is extremely positive: if we were to dispose of all our stocks and shares we would have capital assets of 72,000 – we are almost wealthy!

Telephoned Umnyashka, suggesting a trip to Pavlovsk in view of the wonderful weather. 'No, no, no!' was the inevitable response.

While I was still attempting to persuade the recalcitrant mule, it started to rain. 'You see, you even manage to upset the weather!' I said. But by four o'clock the weather had got over its umbrage and the sun was shining once more. I went to the Umnovs and took tea with them. The family is charming; the father, who had presumably been sleeping, appeared. Generally he seems to be a bit of a rough diamond, and occasionally uses vulgarisms like 'in this day and age', but today he was resplendent in dazzling white linen, which I found very pleasing. Eventually I succeeded in dragging Lidia Ivanovna out for a walk; the weather was quite irresistible. We crossed over the Nikolayevsky Bridge and after prolonged discussions embarked on a steamer. The wind whipped my hat off and tossed it all over the boat, narrowly escaping sending it over the side. Fortunately someone captured it and restored it to my head. We went as far as Okhta[1] and got out to walk. Our intention was to get out of the city and find the green of the countryside, but the wooden pavements[2] stretched out interminably. By the time we eventually crossed over the branch line joining up with the main Finland railway line and got into open country, Umnenkaya was already beginning to complain that she need to get home. This would have been a fine place for a walk, but Umnenkaya dug in her heels, guests were coming at eight o'clock, she would need to hurry and indeed was already probably late. We walked home. She walked as fast as she could, all the time gripped by panic that the guests would arrive and she would not be there. And in fact it was ten o'clock by the time we arrived back, and I laughed to see how she raced up the stairs. Still savouring the delights of our excursion, I returned to my Pervaya Rota.

1   District of St Petersburg on the right bank of the river Okhta, a tributary of the Neva.
2   At this time pavements, and many of the roads, in the city were constructed of wooden planks.

24 May

Thank God, the Finale is almost finished. After lunch I telephoned Lidia Ivanovna; tomorrow she is off to Kuokkale and is very busy packing, also she was about to go and visit her mother's grave in the Smolensk cemetery. I said that I very much wanted to see her and would meet her at the gates of the cemetery so that we could go for a walk. When I arrived at the gates I found her there, not yet having been to her mother's grave, and she suggested we go together. We did so, stayed there for a while and then returned. The grave is of good workmanship and carefully tended. They called her mother Matrona; her parents were not members of the intelligentsia, but had money. How could the coarse-featured father and Matrona-mother have managed to produce as delicate and aristocratic a daughter as Lidochka?! We walked on to the Tuchkov Bridge, where I got 17A on a tram, but going in the opposite direction, away from town, and persuaded her to come with me to Novaya Derevnya, where we could walk in the country. But there was nowhere nice to walk there, so we boarded a horse-drawn tram and went as far as Lanskaya, from where we could get into Udelny Park. This was quite a long way, but it was green and lovely there.

In the evening I telephoned Sonya Esche, who had dropped out of sight for a long time. She was stunned by news of Max's death, and I talked for a long time about him. I was very touched by her sympathy; she told me she had always liked Max. After the conversation I felt very downcast.

25 May

Caught the 11.30 train to Terioki. It was very nice, but not as exciting as the last time I had been there. The Zakharovs are in Pavlovsk listening to Cecilia Hansen. A shame.

It came on to rain, but by evening it had stopped. Zoya and I walked by the sea; it was oppressive and very tiring. We got back to their dacha at midnight; everyone was asleep, but Lida woke up as we cautiously climbed up the stairs to the top floor. I crept into her room, and Lida sleepily turned over in bed. I made the sign of the cross over her and kissed her. My bed was made up in the next room.

26 May

Awoke to the sound of torrential rain. Outside it was damp and grey and there was little incentive to get up. In any case, no one gets into the dining room earlier than eleven in the Karneyev household. We talked for ages to the girls on the other side of the wall, and then finally went down to have coffee. Lida and I went out to look at a piano for sale in one of the other dachas, but the rain, which had ceased for a time, now began to pour down again, and we had to take shelter in the first building we came to, which turned out to be a laundry. Lida told me about the Stieglitz school where she was studying drawing, and the progress she was making there. I looked at her, thinking how beautiful she is, and what an irreproachable figure she has. Forgetting about the piano, which was still some way off, we turned for home again. The weather was very damp, but at least the rain had stopped. We were sitting on the veranda when there was a knocking at the gate and Borya and Georges Zakharov appeared. The girls fluttered off to meet them while I stayed on the steps of the veranda. After a warm handshake we played croquet: Zoya and I against Lida and Borya. Georges went to play with the little ones.

We managed only a few strokes of the game when the rain came on again and we had to flee to the veranda, where we sat and chatted, the conversation assuming a slight air of artificiality. Boris and I were the centres of attention, each of us trying to show off our wit. Meanwhile the rain stopped once more, and we went out to continue our interrupted game. But fate was against it: the housemaid appeared to tell the Zakharov brothers that their Durdin cousins had arrived; Boris put down his mallet, excused himself and left. The rest of us returned to the veranda, where lunch was served. The sole topic of conversation over lunch was the relaunch of the 'Croquet Club'.

Three years ago, when I was a guest of the Zakharovs, I had organized several kinds of croquet competitions. These had produced a powerful impression on Lyova; he had established a croquet lawn at his own dacha and organized a championship. The Zakharovs teasingly dubbed this institution the 'Terioki Croquet Club' and referred to Lyovka as the 'President'. Each spring there is a ceremonial 'opening of the Club', and each autumn an equally ceremonial 'closing', to which guests are invited and jollifications ensue.

This year's opening was due to take place today at three o'clock. We had hardly eaten the last mouthful of lunch when crowds of assorted Zakharovs, Durdins and others appeared at the gate, at least a dozen people in all. At their head was Boris, carrying something wrapped up in paper, behind him Georges and his sister with bread and salt,[1] all three decorated with absurd insignias of various grandiose orders. Boris bared his close-cropped head and came to a halt in front of the veranda, on the steps of which stood Lyova.

'Deeply respected and highly esteemed Mr President!' he began . . .

Various Zakharovs, impersonating reporters and Pathé News cameramen, clicked their Kodaks. Boris spoke of the high merits of the Croquet Club and in conclusion begged to be allowed to present to the Club a croquet mallet of historic antiquity that had lately been discovered in the course of

1 The traditional symbol of hospitality.

archaeological excavations in South America. So saying he removed the wrappings and withdrew the shattered fragments of an incredibly old and utterly useless mallet. I laughed until I cried. The President accepted the priceless gift with due reverence and in his response expressed his gratitude for the honour shown to the Club. The bread and salt was then offered and accepted, and everyone repaired to the croquet pitch. A loud firecracker was set off, symbolizing the firing of a cannon, and at the same moment the flag was unfurled on a flagpole. The season thus opened, and the proceedings commenced with a comic match featuring the most incompetent players (Lida, the Durdins and others). Everyone else disposed him or herself on benches round about, the 'Kodaks' clicked merrily away, the hosts brought out drinks, there was a lot of noise and laughter, most of all from Boris, who was inventive, quick-witted and gay and who was enjoying being the centre of attention. He paid no attention to me whatever; I might as well have not been there. I found this very unpleasant, but I could do nothing about it, I could not leave, or even appear to notice. I perfectly understood the game that was being played out, and no matter how disagreeable it was resolved to hold my ground and give no sign of being aware of the boycott. I could console myself with the thought that if it was in fact the case that the comedy was being played for my benefit, I must be the most important person present. The cod match finished, and another more serious one was organized to follow it: Zoya and I against Georges and Lida. Borya was asked to play, but declined, saying he did not want to. 'Look, you've already got a four: Zoya, Sergey Sergeyevich . . .' This was the first time he had ever used my name and patronymic; always before it was just my name on its own.[1]

Our match was played without much enthusiasm, and then the Zakharov family prepared to go home. The lawn emptied and I was alone with Lida and Zoya. I suggested a walk down to the sea, which the high winds had whipped into exciting motion. The girls changed their clothes, and we set off. On the way we met again the Zakharov contingent, which had gone straight from the Karneyevs to the beach; they were now on their way back. I walked between Lida and Zoya, arm in arm with them both. We stopped, the girls embarked on an interminable conversation, but I could see that Boris and I had nothing to say to one another, and so with me trying to hurry my companions along we said goodbye and went on our way. As we did so I heard Boris promising he would try to come back and see Lida this evening.

On the seashore the wind was truly piercing, the waves were enormous and some barges had been washed up on to the sand. Soon enough we got sand in our eyes, and decided to go home. It was getting dark. We had supper and a slight gloom descended; even so I decided I would miss one more train and wait for Zakharov to come.

1   In other words, a more intimate form.

I was right to wait: Georges appeared, and then Borya and the Durdin sisters. We sat round the table on the veranda and played cards, silly games but with lots of gusto, especially one called 'Pigs'.¹ The noise grew, and the laughter. Borya laughed at my jokes, and we began to talk more, a certain rapprochement in the air, which made me very happy. But . . . the train would not wait, and the time for me to go grew ever nearer. For a while play came to a halt, as Lida, who tomorrow morning at dawn had to leave for Petersburg to sit a drawing exam, was sent off to bed. Everyone crowded on to the veranda, and then went into the house after Lida. I remained alone with Boris, but what was there to say? Mechanically I too went inside, took my coat and hat and began saying my goodbyes. With Zakharov – who was perfectly aware that I was going abroad for the whole summer – I deliberately confined myself to airy persiflage.

Zoya came out with me to the gate and would have come further, but I would not let her, instead sending her back to look after her guests, and walked in semi-darkness to the station. At the turn in the road I looked back towards the Karneyev dacha, and recalling Chekhov's 'A Dreary Story', said 'Adieu, my happiness, my joy,' addressing thus Zakharov.

Once on the train I stood on the outside platform of the last coach watching the speeding rails and thinking my thoughts about Zakharov and about Max.

But I shook off these thoughts and when we reached Kuokkale sent off a postcard to Umnenkaya, with the object of mystifying her over my presumed presence there.

Arrived home very tired but quite tranquil.

27 May

I awoke with a heavy heart and a feeling of emptiness. In three days' time we would be leaving to go abroad. I had not the least desire to bury myself in some remote country house in a foreign land, when even here at home I felt myself terribly alone. But there was nothing for it but to get up and busy myself with all manner of things that had to be done: getting tickets to Paris, putting in an application for a foreign passport, changing money. Gradually I got going, and as I did so became absorbed in these tasks, energetically pursuing all the preparations for a trip abroad. By the time I got back home with 100-franc train tickets in my pocket, I was already looking forward to getting abroad.

1 A simple game of dice in which the player tots up the sum of as many throws as he chooses, with the aim of being the first to reach a hundred. The risk is that if a one is thrown the entire score of that turn is wiped out and the die passed to the next player.

Esche rang up. Hearing that I was about to go abroad, she cried, 'Oh, you must go, you must go,' and talked on and on about how interesting and valuable it would be to move in artistic circles there.

At four o'clock I finished the Finale of the Concerto. Apart from the trio of the Scherzo, the work is complete.

That evening it poured with rain. I wrote some letters: to Natasha Goncharova and to Nina Meshcherskaya. I wanted very much to establish a correspondence link with Nina, but initially was uncertain what tone to adopt.

28 May

Next morning I went to the Mayor's Office to collect the foreign passport I had requested the previous day. There were about two hundred people waiting to get their passports, and the queue spilled out of the Mayor's stuffy rooms far into the street. After walking around a little I found a messenger willing to stand in my place for 60 kopecks an hour while I went for a walk along Nevsky Prospect. Soon it came on to rain, generously irrigating those passport-seekers less resourceful than I, while I sought refuge in the Kvisisano. After an hour and a half I replaced my messenger, and ten minutes later, the passports safely in my pocket, returned home.

Later in the day I was going to Pavlovsk, and while initially I was reluctant to make the journey alone, I reflected that it was after all not very far to Pavlovsk and I would find plenty of people I knew there. The conductor today was Glazunov, and when I went to see him in the artists' room he courteously invited me to take a seat. I asked if I might show him my Concerto, and on learning that I had booked to travel abroad the day after tomorrow, he gave me an appointment for tomorrow in the Conservatoire. I thanked him and went into the auditorium to listen to the concert. Glazunov was conducting his Sixth Symphony. I know this work well and on this occasion listened to the first movement with enjoyment. The second and third movements are uninteresting, but the finale is really good. But if I were to write a symphony, I would not want to construct it brick by brick, as Glazunov does with the patience of a bricklayer stolidly building a substantial wall . . . my symphony would be a savage whirlwind, a vast, elemental succession of hammer blows of fate!

Interval. I saw Aslanov and we decided that *Dreams* will be performed on 2 August, in the same programme as the Concerto, and that the conductor of *Dreams* would be myself. After seeing him I met Umnenkaya's brother and then the Scheintsvit family, in whose company I heard Glazunov's *Dance of Salome*.

29 May

Next morning, before taking my Concerto to Glazunov (I am referring to the Concerto No. 1, which I wanted to play to him with a view to its being performed in the Belyayev Concerts), I played it through by myself. I have not looked at it for some time, and have matured in the intervening period; at least there are many places that, as it now seems to me, could do with revising. This is particularly true of the middle Andante.

Preparatory to going abroad, Mama and I visited Papa's grave. It is marked with a beautiful and very visible black cross that I had chosen for my father. Mama said, 'My name will be inscribed below his here, and should anything happen to you, yours will be too . . .'

I began to think about my death, and did not want to die now, before I had composed anything of real importance, as I felt convinced I would do before long . . . And then my thoughts took another turn: after we are both dead and gone I do not want our capital to go to our relations. No, no, a thousand times no! Either to charity or to music.

We returned home and I went to Alfyorov and took out from my account a couple of hundred roubles for personal expenses, which I then took to the Crédit Lyonnais to change into francs. There I studied the faces of French people, among whom I would soon find myself. Interesting physiognomies. In return for my roubles they gave me 600 francs. No! Dreadful faces: hair black as pitch, eyes darting everywhere, dark bags under the eyes . . . what on earth has possessed us to go abroad?!

Went into the Conservatoire which, to my surprise, was not completely deserted but peopled by one or two professors, attendants, clerks from the office. My dear friend Vera Dmitrievna was for some reason hanging about as well. Glazunov received me at once and listened to my D flat major Concerto. He approved of the form, the logic, the technique, found much temperament and admirable sonorities, but the music itself . . . strange . . . incomprehensible . . . of course, your ears are different from mine . . . but all the same . . . It turned out that Glazunov must have heard from somewhere or other of the existence of the Second Concerto. I played him the *Intermezzo*.

'Very interesting. Splendidly done. But the music . . . very strange . . . especially the middle section.'

I explained the logic of the middle section, and then played him the first movement. Glazunov liked the mood of the opening and generally considered the Concerto to be a significant development over the First. Very individual and interesting piano style, but the music! . . .

As I left, I enquired whether there would be any chance of including the Concertos in the programmes for the Belyayev Concerts? He replied that the artistic direction of the Belyayev Concerts was the responsibility of a special committee of three, consisting of himself, Lyadov and Artsybushev. If I wished my Concerto be considered I should submit it to the committee at the beginning of September. As for his personal opinion, Glazunov advised me that he was the most progressive of the three: Lyadov and Artsybushev having an even more sceptical attitude to music of such modernistic tendencies.

I said goodbye and left. Glazunov promised that he would come to the concert on 2 August if he was anywhere near St Petersburg at the time.

30 May

Spent the afternoon packing my cases, and in the evening Sonya Esche persuaded me to go to the Luna Park,[1] where I had never been. I very much enjoyed riding round the American mountain ranges, and Sonya was most amused: 'Look at him letting his hair down like that!' It was true, I was having a splendid time and Esche proved to be a delightful companion.

An hour before the train left I was back at home, ready to leave Russia with pleasant memories of the mountains.

Mama and I left St Petersburg by the eleven o'clock night train, which had the disadvantage compared to the alternative seven o'clock departure that we got to Berlin at six o'clock the next morning and to Paris at eleven o'clock at night. But all tickets for the 7 p.m. train had been sold until 8 June, so we had to be grateful for what we could get. We were travelling with a European amount of luggage, by which I mean that we each had one trunk in the luggage van and one case with us in the compartment, a very different matter from the thirteen pieces of luggage without which Mama was incapable of travelling within Russia.

And so, we locked up the flat and climbed into a cab, each of us with rather different feelings. Mama had been wanting to go to Paris for ten years, and was now on the point of fulfilling a dream especially cherished during the loneliness of her years buried deep in the country at Sontsovka. I, on the other hand, tended towards lazy indifference with perhaps a dash of curiosity, aware that I would be going abroad many times during my lifetime, it would always be something before me, and therefore this time it was of no consequence if I did not find it particularly interesting.

However, even at the station we encountered familiar faces. Going to drop a postcard to the Karneyevs in the town letterbox, I met Man-del-baum and had a chat with him. When I went into our compartment I found that we

---

1 Modelled on the Luna Park fairground on Coney Island, New York, St Petersburg's Luna Park opened in 1912 on the site of the public pleasure gardens on Offitserskaya Street created in the eighteenth century by the deeply eccentric philanthropist Prokofy Demidov. Luna Park had rides, carousels, a switchback railway and a simulated Wild West mountain range.

had as a travelling companion as far as Vilnius Wanda Yablonskaya, an unexpected pleasure. Wanda was cheerful and interesting company, and we passed an agreeable time together before going to sleep.

31 May

I love sleeping on trains, and although my rest was not completely undisturbed, I enjoyed it. I woke up after we passed through Dvinsk and went into the restaurant car – which had rather surprisingly been attached to our train – to drink coffee. Wanda and I talked until we reached Vilnius, and looked out of the window at the green countryside, which is much more attractive than that along the line to Kursk.

Vilnius already had a whiff of abroad, with Poles, foreigners of various kinds, a large map of Europe's rail network all contributing to a sense of the approaching border. Further on, the sound of German and French being spoken alongside Russian in the restaurant car added to the sense of strangeness, and we heard talk of Customs, of Bettkarten,[1] our arrival time in Berlin. Also unfamiliar from the Russian experience were the tunnels and the fact that we travelled on the left side of the track.

Just before Verzhbolovo[2] we were relieved of our passports and told that they would be returned to us after the second bell. Needless to say, this aroused the naive question of what would become of us if they were not, after all, returned? At Verzhbolovo we waited for more than an hour, changed money and had something to eat, during which for some reason Mama decided to bid a temporary farewell to the Russian tea she likes so much. I wrote postcards. The second bell went near enough half an hour before the train's departure. Thereafter we all had to stay in our compartments where, of course, we had to show our restored passports twenty-five times. After the third bell we slowly moved off and crossed the border. Uncle Sasha had told us that we would cross over a bridge, half of which was in our country, the other half in Germany. I had imagined that this bridge would be at least as big as the one over the Dnieper or over the Volga, but in fact it was a weedy little thing over a skinny stream we could easily have jumped across without the need for a bridge.

I crossed the border not without a tremor of respectful circumspection: there I am at home while here I am in alien surroundings; there I can converse in my mother tongue while here no one will understand my Russian

---

1 Sleeping car reservations (German).
2 Verzhbolovo (Lithuanian Verbilis, German Wirballen, Polish Wierzbołowo) was on the border between what was in 1913 the southernmost Baltic province of Russia and the German province of East Prussia. The border is today between Lithuania and Poland.

language; there everything is familiar while here everything is strange and other – laws, regulations, people, trains.

Wanting to be European-style travellers we dispensed with the services of a porter and each took our own bags through Customs. While Mama stayed on guard over our luggage as it lay there on the Customs counter, I went to the reservations clerk and, nervously trying out my unfamiliar German, obtained two sleeping-car places to Berlin. When I rejoined Mama I found that the Customs officials had barely glanced at our things, stuck labels on them, and we were free. But we did not realize this and waited for a long time for the bags to be inspected, until we thought to enquire and learned that as we were booked through to Paris it would be the French who would look at them, the Germans thinking it no concern of theirs.

An imposing German with Kaiser Wilhelm moustaches and a helmet held a folder containing all our passports and called out the Russian surnames in a heavy accent. As soon as Mama and I had received our passports we collected our cases and emerged on to the German platform, where a beautiful, immaculately clean train welcomed us into our compartment. But it was not long before we fell victim to a false alarm: someone said that the train on the other side of the platform was also going to Berlin, but via Königsberg,[1] whereas ours was going by another route. As we apparently should be going via Königsberg we had got on to the wrong train. Mama panicked and began to drag out our cases, while I went off to check which train we ought to be on. It turned out that we could go on either train, but since our sleeping-car reservations were not via Königsberg, we should stay put. I helped Mama put our cases back where they belonged, much put out by the fuss and bother with which we had paraded our primitive inexperience. I then realized there was still half an hour to wait until the train left, so went to write more postcards.

I was surprised to discover an unusual degree of pleasure at being abroad. It was a quite new feeling of joy, excitement and curiosity about the unfamiliarity of everything surrounding me, all of which evinced a flavour entirely different from what I was used to in Russia. I took huge pleasure in a whole series of trifles: buying German postcards, paying in marks and pfennigs, asking in German for ink, putting 'Russland' instead of the accustomed address, affixing a strange stamp, posting the letter in an unexpectedly massive postbox, having first taken the precaution of asking, 'Bitte, wo ist der Briefkasten?'[2] And the people swilling beer and the babble of voices in German completed the impression.

After this, knowing that there would be no warning bells Russian-style, I

---

1 Now Kaliningrad, Königsberg was the capital of what was in 1913 East Prussia.
2 'Where is the letterbox, please?'

returned to our meticulous, comfortable compartment. But even this absence of the familiar was something to be relished: as the seconds tick away to the appointed moment when the train will smoothly pull away from the platform, is this lack of warning bells not itself an expression of German punctuality, a cultural norm according to which no one needs to be goaded by a succession of ringing bells, but simply understands that at 5.42 precisely the train will leave and one had better be safely on board by then?

Leaving Mama to strike up a conversation with her neighbour, a lady from Switzerland, I made my way to the restaurant car, ordered a bottle of real German beer and took my first look through the window at Germany. Even though we were at most a verst outside Russia, the difference was already noticeable: all the fences were neat and in good repair, the fields clearly divided one from another, the roadsides planted with trees.

My good mood stayed with me until evening, which itself did not last long for at ten o'clock, in view of our arrival in Berlin at six o'clock the next morning, we went to bed. My sleeper companion was a nice old gentleman, Mr Zakharchenko, who was an experienced traveller abroad and who gave Mama and me many useful pieces of advice. He persuaded us to spend all day tomorrow in Berlin, since he considered it a sin to pass through such a remarkable city without seeing it.

1 June

German sleeping cars are exceptionally comfortable, but it was very warm up on my top bunk and I did not sleep particularly well. We were woken at five o'clock, and were amused to observe that as we approached Berlin we passed through a whole series of Berlin stations – Berlin-something-or-other, that must be ours, no, must be further on, then Berlin-something-else, no, this still isn't it; finally Berlin-Friedrichstrasse, and we had to scramble out quickly as the train waited there only for two minutes before continuing to yet another Berlin-something.

We left our suitcases in the left-luggage bureau, and as the station is right in the centre of the city, walked out in search of coffee. We were joined by the Swiss lady, Mama's companion of the night, who had also decided to spend the day in Berlin. We were glad of her company, finding ourselves for the first time in our lives in a great foreign city and not having much of an idea where to go, but although she had undertaken to act as our guide she turned out not to know anything either, got lost and thoroughly confused.

Narrow Friedrichstrasse at six o'clock in the morning was completely deserted, and any impression Berlin made was muted. The cafés all seemed to be closed until we found the 'Bauer', which is open day and night. Having satisfied our hunger we took a taxi and went to see the town. Berlin taxis are cheap, comfortable and splendidly appointed. In an hour and a half our magnificent machine had taken us all round the city at a cost of no more than eleven marks.

By now Berlin was certainly making a great impression on us: a mass of splendid buildings and monuments and many fine streets. The Tiergarten is a most substantial and impressive park, with broad, straight avenues very much in the German taste. Then we went along a wide highway to Charlottenburg, but we found this less interesting and retraced our steps.

The ladies visited Wertheim, which is like our Muir and Merrilees[1] on a grand scale, while I savoured the luxury of being on my own for three-quarters of an hour of freedom. I wandered up and down the humming, bustling Friedrichstrasse, went into some of the automat buffets, posted a couple of cards, had a shave. Then I went to find Mama and the Swiss lady in Wertheim; the latter had things of her own to attend to, and Mama and I did not quite know what to do with ourselves. Mama complained of feeling tired, sightseeing in Berlin was so fatiguing. We sat for an hour on Unter den Linden and looked at the inhabitants of Berlin, who were out on the street in droves, the hour having already passed midday.

Soon after one we met up again at the restaurant in the Kempinsky Hotel, as we had been told that at one o'clock half Berlin would be lunching there. This proved to be correct: it was packed with people, and we had an excellent meal: lobsters, half a bottle of champagne, wild strawberries, and so on. Mama and I then visited the Zoo, one of the things for which Berlin is celebrated. The Zoo is stupendously well kept, and there is an abundance of animals, also maintained in excellent condition but many of them with such a dispirited air that it saddened the heart to look at them. It was also quite a painful experience to go round the Zoo with Mama, because she kept feeling tired and wanting to rest.

From the Zoo, partly on foot and partly by tram, we went back to the Friedrichstrasse station where I left Mama to wait for the train, she being quite worn out by all the running about we had done. I was also quite tired, but was so happy at being free again that I took a taxi and went back to the Tiergarten, which I had liked this morning when we briefly passed through it. Leaving the car, I plunged into the little paths running everywhere through the shady park. Comparing the Tiergarten with our own Islands I came to the conclusion that of course the Islands are more beautiful and more poetic, thanks to the Neva, the sea and the ponds; somehow they have

---

1 The Scottish merchants Andrew Muir and Archibald Merriles established their shop in St Petersburg early in the nineteenth century. By the end of the century, however, the shop had relocated in Moscow, where it still exists in the shape of TSUM, the big department store beside the Bolshoy Theatre housed in the magnificent art-nouveau building by Franz Shechtel.

a more elegant aspect. But the Tiergarten is so beautifully laid out, so shady and imposing, so Germanically impressive, that I found it simply enchanting. I walked along the paths for a long time, crossing over from one part of the park to another. There were many courting couples strolling in the avenues, but I did not see a single German girl of any beauty. Thoughts of Umnenkaya and Max came to mind. At length I came to some ponds, reminding me of the Islands. I sat for a while and scrawled some cards, and then set off for home, that is to say, to the station. An unattractive German woman with a pince-nez was sitting on a bench with her lips greedily clamped to those of the soldier she was kissing. A revolting spectacle. I overtook two young girls who assumed a negligent air and snorted behind my back: 'Ein fremde Pschüt!'[1] I quickly turned round and stared at them.

At nine o'clock I was back at the station, and at 9.42 we left for Cologne, taking with us the most positive impressions of Berlin. Another comfortable sleeper and I, dog-tired with a full day on the go, slept like a log.

2 June

Just as with Berlin, we arrived in Cologne just as it was getting light, at seven o'clock in the morning. We had half an hour before the train left for Paris, so Mama and I decided we would have a look at the famous cathedral, which is right by the station. This vast Gothic structure undoubtedly impresses with its beauty: we tried to go inside, but the Sunday service was in progress and when Mama exclaimed loudly at something she saw, a man dressed in red and carrying a staff came up to us and said that we were welcome to look round the cathedral between twelve and two, but now we should leave. I was very angry at Mama as we stumbled hastily back to the train.

This time, being a day train and not a sleeping car, the compartment was not nearly as spacious. At some of the stations where the train stopped, hawkers came to the windows with trays of delicious ham sandwiches in fastidiously clean wrappings.

We were not troubled with Customs at the Belgian frontier, and sped through industrialized Belgium, which seemed to be entirely covered in factories, mills, railways and highways. There were plenty of mountains, forests, fields and beauty spots to be seen, but there was also more than enough smokestacks, coal and grime. The train plunged into tunnels and forever seemed to be stopping; at the stations and on board the train the French language gradually began to prevail over the German. At Liège I ran out into the station buffet, but it appeared to be indecently bad. We halted there for a quite a while before being hooked up to the Nord-Express (it was

---

1 'Bloody foreigner!' Or at least Prokofiev's interpretation of this exclamation.

a pleasant and entertaining sight to see imperious Russian women and old men unsteady on their pins sitting in stately splendour in the spacious compartments of the Nord-Express) and proceeding on our way.

In one of the compartments of the adjoining carriage I came across Mme Benois, the young wife of the elderly painter, a former student of Yesipova and the object of the amorous attentions of Borovsky and of Zeiliger. We were delighted to see one another, to sit and chat. At one o'clock we crossed the French border and rushed onwards to Paris. I had never before experienced such velocity: the train must have exceeded a hundred kilometres an hour. We swayed and shook about in all directions, the countryside flashed by with cinematographic speed, while the train seemed to be going faster and faster until I was brought to a state of ecstasy.

We went to have lunch in the restaurant car and sat down at a table with two foreign ladies. An amusing Babel of languages ensued: one of the women, a lively and energetic personality, spoke German and French while the other, an attractive girl sitting next to me, spoke German and English. I could speak French and, with some difficulty, a little German; Mama understood German but could speak only French, and to cap it all Mama and I spoke Russian to one another. It was terribly funny, as we were all talking at once, constantly getting into a muddle, addressing one another in the wrong language, correcting ourselves, translating and giving orders sometimes in German, sometimes in Russian, to the waiter, who could not understand a word of anything but French. The jolting of the train made the plates determined to fall off the table on to the floor, and it was impossible to pour out the water, let alone drink it.

After lunch we went back to our hot and stuffy carriage. The green and pleasant countryside of France was pleasing to the eye: I looked out of the window, my thoughts returning to Max, of whom I had dreamed with uncanny clarity the previous night. Then I went back to the restaurant car, drank some water and some Cointreau, wrote a letter to Umnenkaya, and gave myself up to the pleasure of the swaying motion of the train. At five o'clock we began to pass through the outskirts of Paris. Then the Eiffel Tower loomed up on our left, something I had always wanted to see. Next we passed through the fortifications erected to defend the city against the Germans, which made me think of the bombardment the latter had inflicted on Paris, and finally we pulled in to the platform of the Gard du Nord. After obtaining with great difficulty the services of a porter we waited in line for a long time to have our luggage inspected by Customs, a procedure that gave rise to questions about whether we had any tobacco in our possession, and eventually were able to load ourselves and our luggage into a taxi and emerge into the streets of Paris. 'Well, here it is, Paris,' said Mama as we came out through the gates of the Gare du Nord and she looked around her. 'Nothing special, though.'

She was right. The streets in this outlying part of town are narrow; the shops, as it was a Sunday, closed and the pavements deserted. We were not yet able to appreciate the beauty of the Parisian houses, all built of the same grey stone, and our route to the hotel that had been recommended to us on the Rue Helder did not take us through any of the wider streets.

We were given two rooms *au troisième au-dessus de l'entresol*, i.e. what we in Russia call the fifth floor, since here the ground floor is not counted and our *bel étage*[1] goes by the name of the *entresol*. The rooms themselves would have been acceptable – after all, what does it matter where one sleeps? – except that they were impossibly stuffy and noisy from the street.

Mama, tired from the journey, drank some tea and went to lie down. As soon I had washed and changed my clothes I went out to inspect the town. I felt drawn to the streets, and in any case I wanted to find my friends: Tcherepnin, Nikolay Andreyev, Shteiman; all were in Paris. I had no address for the last named; Tcherepnin had told me I could enquire for him at the Théâtre Astruc[2] on the Champs-Elysées. Andreyev had given me his address as the Nouveau Théâtre, Opéra Russe, Avenue Montaigne. Feeling somewhat alone in an enormous foreign city I wanted to seek out my Petersburg friends as soon as I could. Most of all I wanted to see Tcherepnin.

As soon as I reached the corner of the Rue Helder I found myself on the noisy central Boulevard des Italiens. The first thing I saw was a café with a mass of tables outside on the pavement. I was immediately approached by a Frenchman who sold me a plan of the city, a dozen postcards with views of Paris, and offered me from under the counter a packet of indecent pictures. Somewhat embarrassed I said that I was in no need of the last of these, and going off into a quiet corner unfolded my map. This proved to be a tourist map showing all the most famous buildings of the city, and it was just what I needed. There were no little streets on it, just the main thoroughfares. It did not take me long to find the Boulevard des Italiens and thus to establish my present whereabouts. I then rather dubiously tried to find the Champs-Elysées, fearing that since they were fields, they were probably somewhere a long way off, out of the city. To my joy I discovered that these particular 'fields' were the very heart of the city, and no great distance from the Boulevard des Italiens. Consulting my map at each corner I came to, I made my way thither on foot. I very much liked the noise and bustle of the

---

1 Russians use the French expression for the equivalent of the English first floor or Italian *piano nobile*.
2 The year 1913 saw the opening season of the Théâtre des Champs Elysées, established by Gabriel Astruc, journalist, publisher, theatrical impresario and close collaborator of Diaghilev in the Paris Ballets Russes seasons at the Théâtre du Châtelet of 1909, 1911 and 1912. The inaugural season in the splendid new theatre proved financially ruinous and Astruc resigned, apparently never to recover enough to resume his activities as an impresario, although he did mount a spectacular *Fête merveilleuse* for the Ballets Russes at Versailles in June 1923.

boulevards, which only confirmed the famous liveliness and gaiety of the French people.

I had to walk quite a long way down the Champs-Elysées before I found the Théâtre Astruc, which turned out to be the same institution as the Nouveau Théâtre of which Andreyev had spoken. But the doorman could not tell me where either Tcherepnin or Andreyev were staying, and the only address I could find out was that of the director of the company, the celebrated Diaghilev. Although I was not acquainted with him I set off to find him at his hotel in order to track down the addresses I needed. His hotel was terribly grand, and sinking into an armchair I despatched a *garçon* with my card, on which I had written: 'I most humbly beg your indulgence in informing me of the addresses of N. N. Tcherepnin and N. V. Andreyev.'

Diaghilev was not in, but his secretary kindly came down to tell me that Tcherepnin had apparently left a few days ago to return to Russia. Andreyev had left the following address: until Monday, Hôtel Terminus, thereafter 7 rue Marbeau. I thanked the secretary and, somewhat disconsolate at having missed Tcherepnin, decided to seek out the Hôtel Terminus. Noticing that the Eiffel Tower was not far away, I walked over and stood at its feet, feasting my eyes in excitement on the sight, and then took a taxi to the Terminus, rue St Lazare. There was no Andreyev there, but they told me there was another Terminus, near the Gare du Nord. However, it was now eight o'clock and I needed to go home to have dinner and to see how Mama was faring.

Mama, fatigued by the journey, had decided to do without dinner and go straight to bed. I therefore took a taxi and went to find the Hôtel Terminus at the Gare du Nord. Andreyev was not staying there either, but I discovered there was third Terminus – at the Gare de l'Est. This was not far away, so I walked to it. No Andreyev there, but it appeared there was yet another Terminus, this time at the Gare de Lyon, indeed there would be a Hôtel Terminus near every station. At this I lost heart, and went home.

I dined in the noisy and uproarious Café de la Paix, finished the letter to Umnenkaya I had begun on the train, and went to bed, but not before I had spent a long time in search of a letterbox. When I eventually found someone to show me one, I still could not work out where it actually was: a small slit let into a wall, with below it the times of collections in tiny print. There are some more obvious letterboxes, built into bollards rather like lamp posts, but even they are not so visible as to dispel the suspicion that the French regard letterboxes as such shameful objects that they must as far as possible be disguised!

3–8 June

Next day I took a taxi and about twelve o'clock went to the Rue Marbeau to try to find Andreyev, as that was where he was supposed to be moving to from Monday, that is today. It transpired that he had been there for two weeks, that is to say not from this Monday but from Monday goodness knows when, which is why I had not been able to find him at any of the Hôtels Terminus I had tried. Besides Nikolay Vasilievich,[1] his wife was also in Paris, our Conservatoire teacher and the nicest woman in the world. They were both overjoyed to see me and welcomed me with outstretched arms, told me I had done absolutely the right thing in coming to Paris, and urged me to bring Mama over to their pension, which was inexpensive, comfortable and, thanks to being situated on the edge of the Bois de Boulogne, benefited from excellent, pure air. Because the Andreyevs are such kind people and Mama would be bored if left alone in Paris, I needed no second bidding. In a week's time they, together with the rest of the Diaghilev company, would be moving to London, and they suggested I go with them for three days or so as a tourist. This was a splendid idea, and I grabbed it with both hands. At four o'clock Mama and I moved across to the rue Marbeau and took two cosy rooms next to the Andreyevs' in their pension. The Andreyevs are extremely fond of me, they and Mama soon took to one another and I am equally attached to them, so the week passed in a state of enchantment.

The same evening Nikolay Vasilievich presented us with two seats for *Khovanshchina* at the Théâtre Astruc. The Diaghilev Company's productions of the Russian repertoire were having a colossal success: Chaliapin's name was on everyone's lips, the Russian chorus was everywhere admired, the Russian Ballet outdid the French in refined perfection, and the operatic subjects from the era of Ivan The Terrible were stunning in their representation of the life of those times.

Our visit to the theatre was of absorbing interest. Apart from anything else I was interested by the external aspects of Parisian *chic*: one is not admitted to the stalls except in full evening dress; during the interval the men wear top hats. I did not have one, so Nikolay Vasilievich lent me his; tomorrow I shall have to buy a *claque*.[2] I was much taken with this notion, as this fashionable headgear is not much worn in Russia and it had not occurred to me that I might have to wear one. The theatre audience was a great source of fascination, the women all in the latest Paris *modes*, and not least the theatre itself, which had only recently been completed. It was most

---

1 Andreyev.
2 A *chapeau-claque*, i.e. an opera hat, a silk topper that could be collapsed flat when not on the head.

elegant, finished in salmon and gold with grey marble, the women dressed in the height of fashion and their escorts in tail coats and top hats. The effect Chaliapin makes is tremendous: I consider him a performer of genius and an interpreter of incontestable authority. All the singers were excellent, Andreyev very good in his minor role. In a word, the performance was quite glorious, and even impressed Mama, who is always extremely hard to please. The only weakness was the conclusion of the opera, but that is a matter for the conscience of Rimsky-Korsakov and Musorgsky.

I went backstage in the interval, to Andreyev's dressing-room and met Maria Briand there, recently graduated from the Conservatoire[1] under her rather less euphonious real name of Shmargoner; she told me that Shteiman had gone to London to prepare for the arrival there of the whole troupe. Returning to my seat in the auditorium I threaded my way through our corps-de-ballet, about to go on stage to dance the Dance of the Persian Slave-Girls in the next act. They were all so modestly made up, such a choice selection of slender, miniature figures, so pretty and so scantily clothed, that the tail coats and top hats that had managed to penetrate backstage clung to them like leeches.

Next day, in the same theatre, I heard Stravinsky's *Petrushka*. I was most interested to see and hear this ballet, which has not yet been seen or heard in Russia, and went to the performance with the liveliest curiosity. The way it was staged sent me into ecstasies, as did the orchestration and the wit constantly displayed, so that my attention did not flag for a moment, so engaging was it; but the music ... I thought about it a great deal, and finally came to the conclusion that there is ultimately something not real about it, despite its many talented passages. But my God, what an avalanche of padding it contains, music not needed for the sake of the music but purely for the stage. A week after hearing *Petrushka* I set out in a letter to Myaskovsky a more exhaustive statement of my thoughts about Stravinsky and my verdict on him.[2] *Petrushka* is a short work, and so it was followed this evening by Ravel's *Daphnis*.[3] I have never been much interested in modern French music, and hearing *Daphnis* did little to win me over to it. Undoubtedly this music possesses its own attractive aroma but there is so much water in it, its

---

1 With the Conservatoire's Gold Medal. Maria Briand (1886–1965) had a distinguished career as a lyric soprano at the Mariinsky Theatre, excelling in Tchaikovsky's heroines.
2 See Introduction, p. xxii, where Prokofiev's letter to Myaskovsky is quoted.
3 *Daphnis et Chloé* (1912), ballet from which Ravel later extracted two orchestral concert suites, the form in which the music is most often heard today. The original ballet had choreography by Mikhail Fokine, sets and costumes by Léon Bakst. The scenario, which Prokofiev (and others) found so unengaging, was adapted by Fokine from a romance by the third-century Greek writer Longus, in a sixteenth-century translation by Jacques Amyot, *Les Amours pastourales de Daphnis et Chloé*, the twist being that the total sexual innocence of both parties precludes their having any idea what to do about their burgeoning feelings for one another.

contours are so diffuse, that all in all it is not worth listening to. On top of this, the story of Daphnis is not very interesting, and Ravel has no notion of how to illustrate what is happening on stage. As long as we are dealing with poetic maidens and forest glades the music is affecting and relates to the images on stage, but when we get to dramatic incidents or Bacchante dances the impotence of the composer is all too clearly demonstrated.

On the third evening I saw the staged version of Rimsky-Korsakov's *Sheherezade*: quite successful, very gorgeous and exotic, like the music. What happens on stage is in full accord with the score, with the exception of the very end.

Schumann's *Carnaval*, orchestrated by a whole *pléiade* of Russian luminaries (Rimsky-Korsakov, Glazunov, Tcherepnin, Arensky), proved to have been rather tediously and unimaginatively staged. I had expected better, since this music offers such wide vistas for the imagination. It was interesting to hear how it had been orchestrated, although the more pianistic the number, the less successful it was in its orchestral guise.

Among the sights of Paris we saw were the Louvre and the Salon. We happened on a very experienced guide in the Louvre, a former professor who had evidently taken to drink. He was very helpful in that he knew the Louvre like the back of his hand and was able to talk knowledgeably about all the major works of art there. Dates, names and historical information poured out of him in an uninterrupted stream. I looked respectfully at venerably time-ravaged statues and age-darkened pictures; at the beginning I found it interesting, later on boring, and eventually excruciating.

The Salon enchanted me. Never had I seen anything more beautiful than this vast, softly lit room, entirely filled with wonderful marble sculptures half hidden among the greenery. The most entrancing view of the hall is from the balcony of the picture gallery.

Then we visited the Eiffel Tower. It is something that has fascinated me since I was a small boy of seven, and while this is quite natural for a child I had retained my interest to this day. I had promised all my friends at home in St Petersburg that I would send them a postcard of the tower, so now that I was actually ascending it I sent no fewer than twenty-nine – to every person I considered worthy to receive one. I persuaded Mama to climb up the first level by the stairs rather than taking the lift: this was fun and quite dizzying, as the narrow staircase winds its way upwards quite out in the open, and the ground seems a long way down. Mama, worn out by the climb, stayed on the first level to drink tea, while I continued up on foot. Disappointed that this next section of staircase was enclosed, and still not feeling particularly tired, I reached the next level. Above this the stairs were not accessible and one has to take the elevator, which has enormous windows on all sides. As it slowly and smoothly glides up, the body of the tower is so airy one has the feeling that one is ascending in a balloon. On reaching the third level I found it to be an enclosed balcony, hot and crowded on account of the numbers of tourists crammed into it. Discovering that there was one more level, I climbed up to it and found myself completely alone, none of the other tourists having realized it was possible to do so. The view from here was illimitable, stretching out until it disappeared into the mist. The height is colossal, but not so as to make the head spin. I thought of Max: this was the place to end one's life by suicide. A terribly *chic* and even pleasant way to achieve it. I asked a guard if there had been any instances of people throwing themselves to the ground. He said there had not been, but this may have been the answer he had been instructed to give. After sitting for a while in my eyrie and looking at Paris, I descended, found Mama, and we returned home.

The Louvre, the Salon and the Eiffel Tower were the main attractions we visited. The Bois de Boulogne is interesting not so much for itself as for the people it attracts. Altogether Paris, as a city, is astonishingly beautiful, alive, gay and seductive. Naturally I did some shopping, chose perfume at Guerlain, staying nevertheless with my favourite Cadine, ordered a very smart black suit with black-and-white-checked trousers, bought a *claque* and some very elegant and inexpensive linen. I much enjoyed going into cafés, experimented with whisky and soda (not bad at all), but not once did I go into any of the bars or night-clubs for which Paris is famous: in the first place I am completely inexperienced and unenlightened about such places, and in the second I was staying *en famille* (with Mama and the Andreyevs) and in such a context the prospect did not arise. For moving about the city I made frequent use of the nimble little taxis, and even succeeded in finding my way around the underground Métro, a transport system that gave me huge pleasure.

Some news reached me from Russia: Natasha Goncharova sent me a long and affectionate letter; Katyusha Schmidthof wrote me six very insightful pages, Kolechka Myaskovsky was kind and generous as ever, Nina Meshcherskaya wrote asking me not to forget about coming to Gurzuf, and finally Umnenkaya allowed herself a short missive, quite nice, I marked it four out of five. The Karneyevs did not write at all, even though I bombarded them every day with some amusing card or other – but that was mainly on account of Borya, to make them talk about me to him.

All in all I had the best possible impression of Paris, I felt on top of the world there, surrounded on all sides by novelty and interest. The Andreyevs could not have been kinder, the city was beautiful and lively, our pension cosy, my room comfortable, its double bed – my first – pleasurably stimulating my imagination.

I had brought a quantity of manuscripts with me, counting on

Tcherepnin to help me make them known to musicians in Paris, but Tcherepnin had gone back to Russia and so my manuscripts stayed in my trunk. Calvocoressi was extremely busy and I managed only one meeting with him. I played both my Concertos to him and his friend, the pianist Robert Schmitz.[1] The First Concerto they already knew, and appreciated (although they pointed out that the main theme had been taken from Balakirev), the Second they could not make much of. They promised to try to get Chevillard[2] to perform the First Concerto next season. This would apparently be very prestigious, and God willing it will happen, although I do not place much reliance on their promises.

9 June

Travelled with the Andreyevs to London: they will be there singing for three weeks; I will spend three days or so with them simply as a visitor. The previous day was occupied with packing trunks, especially for the Andreyevs, who accumulated such a huge quantity that we could barely fit into two taxis to take us to the station. Here also there was pandemonium: the porters, not generally very sturdy fellows in France, heaved and strained themselves to breaking point and muttered angrily, but eventually we got ourselves on to the platform and took our places in a small and over-crowded compartment with a door opening directly to the outside world. With fifteen minutes to wait before the train left I strolled along the platform and could hear nothing but Russian voices. This seemed odd for Paris, until I realized that practically the entire Diaghilev contingent was on the train, including many of the soloists and the chorus.

At 8.25 the train pulled out of the station. It was still early in the morning, but we bustled about and settled down to enjoy our breakfast, ingeniously arranged in a box sagaciously bought in advance by Nikolay Vasilievich at the station. He carefully divided everything into three and generously fed us. After this we all lapsed into a contented doze until after a

---

1 Elie Robert Schmitz (1889–1949), pianist, voice coach, writer, impresario, physiologist and tireless propagandist for new music, had one of the most varied and fruitful musical lives it is possible to imagine. In Paris, as well as coaching singers such as Maggie Teyte for her role as Mélisande in collaboration with the composer, he founded and directed the Association Musicale Moderne et Artistique, which became one of the leading vehicles for new music in all genres. Moving to America after the First World War, Schmitz continued to perform as a pianist and also founded the international Franco-American Society, later Pro Musica, Inc., which brought to America for the first time such figures as Ravel, Bartók and Respighi and also exported American composers to Europe. The list of the composers sponsored by the Society in America, including Prokofiev, embraces many of the leading figures in European music.

2 Camille Chevillard (1859–1923), composer, conductor and son-in-law of Charles Lamoureux, direction of whose orchestra and concert he assumed in 1881.

three-hour journey we arrived in Boulogne to gaze nervously at the sea in anticipation of the rolling of the ship and our consequent seasickness. But the Channel was calm, and we settled ourselves on the first-class upper deck of the little steamer that was to carry us obligingly over the straits.

The boat cast off, to my great jubilation. The weather was perfect, the sun bathing us in its gentle warmth, while up in the bows of the ship one could feel the stiff breeze coming off the ocean. The deck was furnished with deckchairs on which English ladies in check suits stretched out in the sun. Typical English gentlemen, the genuine article, strolled up and down; even the servants were English. In short, everything was so utterly different from Russia, everything so perfectly accorded with the descriptions in accounts by travellers to England and America, that I felt I was truly in a new world: I experienced the keenest desire to travel, to go far, far away, to America. Indeed, in Russia one speaks of America as of somewhere so remote that one will never actually go there, as it might be to the moon. But here it all seemed quite natural, near at hand, one could almost stretch out one's hand and touch it. Look, out there to our left stretched out the limitless expanse of the Atlantic Ocean, and there, crossing our path, was an enormous liner confidently ploughing its unruffled way to New York, where it would dock five days from now. Sitting beside Anna Grigorievna[1] I talked enthusiastically to her about going to America.

An hour and a half later we were nearing the shores of Great Britain, at Folkestone. The London train was waiting on the jetty. Once again the voices of Russian singers ... oh, these Russian barbarians, neurotic artists, dimwitted choristers, fussy, anxious, ignorant of so much as a word of English, calling to one another up and down the platform with desperation in their voices at the thought of getting on the wrong train – how they amused me!

At last we were all settled and started our journey. With us in our compartment was another Andreyev, a baritone. I knew him slightly, and we all talked merrily. I knew that he was a friend of Zakharov's, and this made him interesting to me, but I did not bring up his name in our conversation.

Another person who attached himself to us in our compartment was one of the choristers, a Chaliapin acolyte and the wag of the whole company. He was really quite a comedian, all the time sticking his head out of the window and calling out to his compatriots 'senk-yew' – the only two words of English he knew. But on the whole it was a tiring, hot, dusty and stuffy journey, not improved by the many tunnels and the associated, irritating soot. At last an endless sprawl of suburbs signalled the onset of London, then we crossed the Thames (a pitiful little stream) and pulled in to Charing Cross station. There matters took a turn for the worse: action was called for, but not one of the

---

[1] Zherebtsova-Andreyeva.

three of us could speak English or had any idea how to proceed. Anna Grigorievna had a few disjointed phrases culled from *A Russian in England*, Nikolay Vasilievich remembered one and a half words from last year's visit, while the only contribution I was able to make was 'jockey-club' and 'water-closet.'

We stood stupidly on the platform, surrounded by a mountain of luggage, trying in futile dumbshow to attract the attention of a porter. At this juncture a certain Maria Ivanovna came rushing up to us, a woman formerly from Russia who adores Anna Grigorievna and had come to meet her. She broke into a torrent of fractured Russian, the porter loaded our bags on to a trolley, and within a few minutes we were rolling through the London streets in a taxi. As a town London is all very well, but it is not the equal of Paris.

We were staying in a quiet street, Clifton Gardens, in a small hotel where Maria Ivanovna lived and where we also put up. Because it was a Sunday it was the servant's day off, so it was up to us to shift our heavy cases ourselves. Maria Ivanovna had temporarily relinquished to the Andreyevs her charming room with windows looking out over the garden, and I was given an upstairs room, not particularly nice, but it scarcely mattered where I would lay my head for three nights.

Locking the door, I removed my clothes and savoured the delicious prospect of washing the soot and sweat of the journey from my body. But a disappointment lay in store for me, instead of a washbasin with running water there was only a basin and a jug, moreover the jug was empty. I was forced to make myself decent again and go in search of a servant, no easy task. When I eventually found one I took her up to my room and handed her the empty jug, which she took away and soon brought back full. But alas! the water was hot, almost boiling; the idiot assumed I wanted to shave. There was nothing to be done: I tipped the water into the basin, waited until the temperature became bearable, and washed myself in warm water, consoling myself with the thought that at least afterwards the temperature of the air would seem cooler.

Washed and changed, lobster red as if from a hot bath, I went downstairs to find them all drinking tea. 'Well now,' asked Maria Ivanovna ceremoniously, 'how are you liking the most civilized city in the world?'

'That's hardly the word I'd use: no washbasin, no water, no bell to ring, no electric light, no chairs . . .'

'What do you mean, no chairs?!'

'Just what I say, there is only one chair in my room, and it is full of holes.'

'I'll get a chair sent up to you,' she said quickly, somewhat disconcerted by my initial impressions of London.

After this exchange Nikolay Vasilievich said he wanted to go and sign the book honouring the Dowager Empress of Russia, who was at that time visiting London. I was very ready to keep him company, so as to have a look at the city. But as it was Sunday, the city was empty and lifeless; it is a peculiarity of the English way of life that practically nothing happens on a Sunday. We were not out long before coming back to have dinner, after which I took myself on my own to Oxford Street, in its way a fine street and extremely long, but not especially distinguished. When I had walked enough I hailed a taxi and with some difficulty explained to the driver where I wanted to go, painstakingly spelling out to him my address. At half past ten I was back, to general alarm that I might have got lost in London . . .

10 June

In the morning I strolled along the main London streets Oxford Street and Regent Street. They are fine, but Paris is more beautiful. Horses have all but disappeared, everything now is motor traffic. A peculiarity of London is that there are no trams, instead there are swarms of omnibuses, which rush along at great speed and with great dexterity, overtaking one another so that it is a miracle they do not collide! Most inconveniently, traffic drives on the left rather than on the right: it is hard to get used to this and know instinctively from which side a bus is going to leap at you, from the right or from the left, especially at crossroads, where they come from all sides.

At eleven o'clock Nikolay Vasilievich proposed that I should go with him to a rehearsal of *Boris Godunov* at the Drury Lane Theatre (I kept stumbling over the pronunciation of this word when I first started to say it). The theatre itself is not much to write home about, although the orchestra was wonderful. I sat in the auditorium listening to *Boris* with the greatest enjoyment. Around me the Russian chorus members recounted to each other the vicissitudes of finding accommodation in London, and the peculiarities of the places they eventually ended up in. Andreyev One greeted me with the greatest courtesy; the producer Sanin[1] was also very charming; I met Petrenko,[2] a lady of great style and a marvellous singer, and the conductor Cooper. We were all together in the most friendly manner during the interval, but it was not the time or place for any talk of specifics.

I was delighted to meet Shteiman again; he is now one of the company's junior conductors. We lunched together after the rehearsal and talked a great

---

1 Alexander Sanin-Schoenberg (1869–1956), actor and producer. Sanin had been a key figure in the pioneering days of the Moscow Arts Theatre but had been eased out in 1902 because of financial re-structuring. Drawn to the lyric stage, he soon joined the Diaghilev entourage, having in the meantime married Lika Mizinova, the woman in Chekhov's life most feared and detested by the doyenne of the Moscow Arts Theatre, Olga Knipper-Chekhova, who became Chekhov's wife.
2 Yelizaveta Petrenko (1880–1951), mezzo-soprano, soloist at the Mariinsky Theatre and noted interpreter, among other roles, of Dalila, which she studied under the direction of Saint-Saëns.

deal: he is very happy to have a contract with Diaghilev, which at the very least has afforded him the opportunity of travelling all over Europe and seeing how music is made in the different capitals. He gave me news of Kankarovich, whom he had seen in Dresden. Poor Kankarovich is disappointed with the way his career both as conductor and composer has failed to take off. He is vegetating in Dresden with nothing particular to do, repining, languishing and gradually losing any desire to carve out a path for himself. Alas, this is the worst thing of all.

Back at home I found Mme Andreyeva had taken to her bed, all the packing in Paris having made her ill. An elderly lady, Mme Smith, a Russian married to an Englishman, was sitting in their sitting room: she decided that I, as a visitor, should be looked after, and so invited me to dinner, and on the way I could see something of London. Essentially, however, I saw little new to add to the streets I had already visited. Her house was comfortable but dull; her son Petrushka was only able to mangle a few words of Russian and her good-looking twenty-four-year-old daughter disappeared soon after my arrival.

Getting back to the hotel at nine o'clock I sat in my room upstairs and wrote letters to Ninochka Meshcherskaya and Lidochka Umnova. I had not previously had any experience of gas lamps, and the devil alone knows how one is supposed to put them out! It took me twenty minutes of fiddling before I succeeded in extinguishing this frightful contrivance!

11 June

Wrote a long letter to Myaskovsky with my comments on *Petrushka* and then left my little room to go out with Nikolay Vasilievich, who had to pay a call on the Russian Embassy while I went to look at Hyde Park. *En route* we went in to several of the Oxford Street stores and when Andreyev went off to the Embassy, instead of going into the park I kept on along Regent Street and Piccadilly, window-shopping at the big shops there. My eye kept being caught by the abundance of shipping-line offices, whose plate-glass windows were dignified by huge and artistically represented models of ocean-going liners, some of them with sections cut away so as to show the internal construction and layout. There were also brilliantly coloured images of India and America, with piles of the appropriate guidebooks and brochures. Such appetizing displays, beckoning from afar, are not to be found in St Petersburg, or even Paris, and they make London seem somehow more closely connected to the world, so that a trip to India or South America, which seems to a Russian a virtually impossible fantasy, here appears a relatively normal, even simple undertaking. Another difference I found between serious London and frivolous Paris is that in London it is almost impossible to find a shop selling good-looking postcards, whereas in Paris they are on every street corner.

Without meaning to I found myself at Charing Cross station, and judging that it was time for lunch seated myself on the upper deck of an omnibus, a system I had learned to make use of as I had the Paris Métro, and went home. After lunch I was sent off to look at Westminster Abbey. Figuring out from the map that I could get there via Hyde Park and St James's Park I decided to walk, although the distance was about six versts.

Striding heartily through Hyde Park I came across a large crowd and a line of soldiers keeping them back. It transpired that they were waiting for the cavalcade of the King and the President of France, who was on a state visit to London. I waited for half an hour, partly out of curiosity but mainly because I could not in any case get any further, and was rewarded by the spectacle of King George and President Poincaré passing by in magnificent antique carriages. The crowd welcomed them with cheers while the band thundered out the Marseillaise, breaking into the English National Anthem after three bars.

Passing through the charming St James's Park I came into the sombre shade of Westminster Abbey. Here below its tombstones lie kings, dukes, generals and the great figures of England. Serried ranks of artistic monuments adorn all the walls and many side chapels of this elaborately constructed building. I was especially struck by the recumbent memorials, in which the former potentates lie in the full glory of their raiment as if at the very moment death took from their beds. Beside them lie their wives, carved in stone. I could not repress a feeling of awe as I wandered among these memorials to former greatness, now in their graves but breathing yet in every fold and nuance of their marble incarnations. I stood for a long time by the memorials to Handel and Shakespeare, and walked round the church, overwhelmed by its grave beauty. Westminster Abbey produced a profound impression on me.

Then, from the bridge across the muddy waters of the Thames, I looked at the beautiful Houses of Parliament, and took a cab back to the hotel. Those nice horse-drawn cabs special to England, having two large wheels and a coachman up above with his back to the passengers, are rapidly dying out in London to be supplanted by the quick and comfortable taxi. But I love the cabs, splendid and cosy as they are!

After dinner Andreyev invited me to Drury Lane for the premiere performance of *Boris*. All the tickets had been sold at astronomic prices, but it would be possible to listen from the wings. This was very interesting to me, and so I went. As an outsider I had great difficulty in gaining admission, however, and had to fend off several attempts to eject me.

Chaliapin is an artist to whom I bow the knee. He was very nervous, since this was his debut performance before an English audience. He paced about the wings like a wild beast in a cage before going out on stage. But his success was colossal. I sat in the wings with Shteiman, and we agreed that we would see London and its environs together, since neither he nor I had yet had a chance to do so. Also, since neither of us could speak the language, it would be less alarming if we were together...

In the interval I went out into the foyer to gaze upon the audience, the cream of society in the height of fashion. Nothing in the world is more fashionable than a London premiere! And indeed, the audience shone with unexampled brilliance, especially the London gentlemen. If Paris outshines London in the matter of the feminine *toilette*, it must yield second place to the impeccably turned-out English cavalier. I thought of Max.

Boris is a superb opera. Musorgsky's feeling for the stage was unerring, his is an ideal model of how to write for it. I have a tremendous desire to write an opera. My opera will be a good opera, a true one!

12 June

Before lunch I went with Nikolay Vasilievich to one of the big stores, where I agonized over trying to explain to the assistant what I wanted. I made several English purchases, among them some shirts, a good tennis racquet, tennis shoes, and writing paper.

After lunch, as we had agreed, I went to call for Shteiman. Our idea was to go out to Windsor, but now Shteiman was pulling a long face and wanting to put off our excursion until tomorrow. Today we might go to the Zoo, for which London is famous. I seem to be fated to visit zoos: in Berlin we were also packed off to the Zoo; but I did not protest, and so off we went.

London Zoo is a good zoo, but not as good as Berlin, although in essence it is much the same. Here what most struck me were the snakes in the reptile house, the toads, the lizards, and all manner of ill-favoured amphibians, inexpressibly revolting to the eye. I studied the snakes with the keenest interest, starting with the huge boa constrictor and ending with the scuttling little snakes that played on the nerves and made one involuntarily keep looking at the floor for fear of something unpleasant crawling down there, and shiver with fear at the touch of anything cold. We stayed at the Zoo until fatigue overcame us, then parted until tomorrow and went to our respective homes.

In the evening I wrote postcards to my friends – greetings from London – and went to bed, not before having a good look to check there were no snakes in it.

13 June

At ten o'clock I went to the post office where there was a public telephone, and called Shteiman to find out if he could get away from the theatre to come with me to Windsor. Going up to the telephonists, I boldly announced: 'Please, Miss, GERrard seven-free-four-o!'[1] They looked at me for a brief moment, then at each other, snorted, and began to laugh uncontrollably. Embarrassed, I thrust a paper at them on which Shteiman's number was written. Still laughing, one of them read what was on the paper and called up the telephone number. When it answered she shouted incomprehensible phrases into the receiver for about five minutes, then hung up and turned back to me with another unintelligible English utterance. To my feebly mimed objection that I could not understand, she repeated her statement, but with the same result. Thereupon she mimed to me the information that it was not possible to speak on the telephone. I could not understand why: whether her telephone was out of order, or whether Shteiman's was, or whether it was simply busy and if I waited a minute it would be clear and I would be able to speak. I thanked her and went out into the street to find another public telephone. There was one quite near, on Formosa Street, and this time I did not try to inflict my pronunciation on the telephone girls but like a dumb man simply handed them my piece of paper with the number on it. I was quickly connected with Shteiman's hotel; he was free and was waiting for me, so I took a taxi and a quarter of an hour later was at the Morton Hotel, where he was staying. Shteiman was for some reason all for substituting somewhere nearer for our excursion, but I really wanted to see Windsor and after some minutes' diplomatic manoeuvring we set off. In the notebook I carried I had made a preliminary note that the station from which trains went to Windsor was Paddington. The taxi driver – I was getting used to this by now – refused at first to understand where we wanted him to take us; eventually we simply said 'Vindzor' and demonstrated the motion of a train. Eventually it dawned on him, and he took us to the station. Our next task was to work out from which window to get a ticket to Windsor, as there were several of them. Boldly I approached the first one and said: 'Vindzor?' 'Yes,' answered the clerk. I bought two first-class return tickets and we went on to the platform. Next task: where was the train and which platform did it leave from? We asked the first railway official we came across and by dint of showing him our tickets and saying 'Vindzor?' made gestures indicating our hopeless inability to know where we should go. He pointed towards a bridge over the platforms and said something in which we

---

1 Until the 1960s London telephone numbers consisted of three letters of the alphabet representing the particular district (GERrard, FLAxman) followed by four digits. A GERrard number would have been somewhere in the West End.

caught the word 'four'. Deducing that we would find our train departing from Platform Four, we climbed the stairs, crossed the bridge and down again the other side on to the platform marked with the number four – and we were not mistaken. Leisurely we sat down in a carriage, and at that moment the train started: we had arrived precisely on time. Now that we were safely ensconced in our enclosed box and moving swiftly to our destination, a new worry arose: where should we alight? It would be fine if the train went straight to Windsor, but what if we needed to change somewhere? We had no idea.

After about forty minutes the train stopped, but this was not Windsor. We were intending to continue further, but happily enquiries revealed that we should indeed change here. We crossed over to the indicated platform, where we found, not another train, but a large electrically driven carriage. Still unsure whether we were going in the right direction, we boarded the electric carriage and suddenly after rounding a bend there in front of us was an ancient and remarkably beautiful castle, and we realized that we had arrived in Windsor. The station was directly opposite the castle, and getting out of the carriage on the left-hand side we ascended a long and picturesque flight of stairs to find ourselves within the outer fortifications. Inside, the castle is just as fine and just as redolent of antiquity as it appears from the distant vistas from the train. As we climbed up on to the high stone walls, looked down into the moats and got lost in the labyrinthine passages of the castle, we thought about those olden times of sieges, assaults by battery, stormings, huge boulders hurled from catapults, pourings of boiling oil, the complex plan of defence of the town and its impregnable castle. Unfortunately we were not able to see everything: perhaps the most interesting part of the castle, the centre, was closed to the public because of the visit of Poincaré, and there were guards in front of the doors.

Emerging from the castle we went to have lunch in the hotel. This was a delightful session: Shteiman told me all about Tcherepnin, who had apparently come to Paris in the hope of conducting for Diaghilev, but in this had been unsuccessful. He had had supper with Shteiman and had been in a supremely light-hearted mood, relating his exploits with no fewer than three lovers during the winter, Armashevskaya and two others.

I know Armashevskaya, who studied at the Conservatoire and has no talent at all. But she was always hanging around Tcherepnin, and I had suspected there was an ulterior motive. We finished lunch, and having discovered from a French footman that the park was near by, set out to find it. Soon we were approached by a coachman who agreed to drive us round the park for four shillings. We had hardly got inside it when he stopped the carriage, and pointing first to the left and then to the right, embarked on a lengthy discourse. Assuming that he was giving us some kind of historical overview, we tactfully nodded our heads and pretended to understand something of what he was saying. But then we kept hearing references to 'five shillings' as he pointed in one direction and 'six shillings' in the other, and we deduced that he was offering us a more extensive detour, which we declined by waving our hands dismissively, and he continued the way we were going.

The country round Windsor is nice to look at, but not at all remarkable, somewhat like central Russia, and not really worth the effort of going to see it. But the castle, which we now approached once more from the other side, is incredibly beautiful when viewed from a distance.

By five o'clock we were back in London, and Shteiman suggested spending the evening together. I said I would call for him at eight o'clock, and dropping off my card to Mme Smith on the way, went home.

I played Nikolay Vasilievich at 'sechsundsechzig'[1] and won, and asked him about Zakharov, whom he said he knew because for some reason Zakharov was on the invitation list for evenings at the Konstantin Konstantinoviches,[2] although this year, because of the illness of the princes, there had not been any evenings and so he had not seen him.

After dinner I went to see Shteiman. He wanted me to see a girl from the depths of Africa, the special fire in whose eyes he expressly pointed out to me in such a way that it was obvious he wanted to pursue her, but he did not know in what language to converse with her.

He, I and a good-natured German working as assistant to the conductors in the Russian company visited one of London's many music-halls where the programme consists of songs, dances, conjuring tricks and humorous sketches. It all goes on for two hours without an interval. The theatre is luxurious, the seats soft, the orchestra first class, the production lavish, the chorus and ballet contain a choice selection of pretty women, several very talented comics – such are the characteristics of a typical music-hall. We had a wonderful time and laughed uproariously despite not understanding a single word. We left, absolutely delighted with our evening, and after sitting

---

1 A card game ('Sixty-six') for two or three players of the 'marriage' type, that is to say in which the object is to win tricks and earn bonus points by melding matched pairs of kings and queens. Also known as *mariage*, *Schnapsen* and *Gaigel*.
2 The Grand Duke Konstantin Konstantinovich (1858–1915), who wrote poetry and plays under the pen-name of 'K.R.', was the grandson of Tsar Nicholas I. Although his inclinations were homosexual, as his remarkably candid and moving diaries posthumously revealed, he dutifully married and fathered nine children, of which the fourth, born in 1881, was a son named Konstantin and was therefore like his father Konstantin Konstantinovich. As well as being a gifted writer and translator, K.R. was a good musician, served as Chairman of the Russian Musical Society, and was a generous and effective champion of the arts generally. Dying in 1915 he was spared the terrible retribution visited on most of the Romanov family; not so his children, three of whom (including Konstantin) were murdered in 1918 by their Bolshevik captors in the Urals town of Alapeyevsk within twenty-four hours of the murder of the Tsar and his immediate family in Yekaterinburg.

for half an hour in a crowded café, separated to go our various ways home.

There are a great many pretty English girls, in fact I should say that one is more likely to encounter a beautiful face in London than in Paris. I resolved to learn English; it will be essential for my future travels.

14 June

At eight o'clock in the morning I called my goodbyes through the door to the Andreyevs, thanking them for having brought me to London, loaded my cases into a taxi and went back to Paris. My ignorance of the language landed me in all kinds of trouble at the station with booking a ticket and consigning my luggage, but a resourceful porter got me together with a Frenchman, a hotel representative, and with his help I quickly got everything sorted out and even managed to buy a Russian newspaper, which whiled away the rather uninteresting journey to Folkestone, where we arrived at 11.50. There I boarded a cross-Channel ferry, on which I repeated my experience of sunning myself in deckchairs on deck surrounded by English passengers. Again the limitless expanse of the Atlantic, again that irresistible pull to cross trackless oceans in search of other lands, different from ours . . . the boat begins to pitch and roll, a slight sensation but enough to make me fear the spectre of seasickness, as I see some of the women turn pale and assume an attitude of helplessness in their deckchairs. But it is really nothing, so I take a chair, place it firmly in the sun and, frowning, jam my hat down over my eyes and give myself over to dreams of America. There is no question of 'feeding the fishes', an expression Andreyev is fond of using.

Boulogne. Oh, what a joy to be able to speak and be understood without any problems. There is not an Englishman in sight; everyone has suddenly become French! Thanks to having only one case I was not held up in Customs at all, and was the first person on to the train. I took a corner seat by the window, had a snack at the station, changed my shillings into francs, and sped swiftly and without stopping into Paris.

In Paris I had to wait in line half an hour for my case to be inspected by Customs, but they did not go through it, and I took it myself to a taxi, enjoying glimpses of the Paris streets as I crossed the city, stopping on the way to collect my letters. There was only one, from Lida and Zoya, and by seven o'clock I was at rue Marbeau, where Mama was very pleased to see me.

15 June

Lida wrote asking why I had not taken her with me to London. When I woke up in the morning, half dozing I had sweet visions of going on a journey with her.

At Mama's insistence I went to see Mme Lebedintseva, whom I do not know, but with whom it has been proposed that we should go together to the Auvergne. Mme Lebedintseva is a very nice woman; in five days or so she is going to Royat, but in the meantime is thirsting to see Mama. Then I went to see Mme Guyonnet, the wife of an automobile manufacturer's representative. She and her husband had been in St Petersburg in May, and had met Mama at the Rayevskys; I was getting my letters through them. Mme Guyonnet, an absolutely charming woman, suggested taking us on a trip tomorrow by car to Versailles. I was thrilled by the idea, and in gratitude was happy to play a Beethoven sonata for her.

After the call on Mme Guyonnet I went to buy stockings for Sonechka Esche, Lida and Zoya. The pretty shop assistant was highly amused when I explained to her that I needed the most fashionable articles, and moreover for three different pairs of legs, assuming that I must have an entire harem. I blushed crimson, but nevertheless bought the stockings and proceeded to another department, where I acquired a beautiful walking stick made of snake-wood with a knob of polished stone. All this time I had not parted with Max's stick, but by now it had almost disintegrated. In London, when people were trying to get me to leave the wings of the theatre I had had to dodge about so quickly I had damaged it still further, so not wanting to ruin it completely I now put it away until I was back in St Petersburg and could have it repaired.

In the evening Mama had planned to visit Mme Lebedintseva, but since the taxi-drivers were on strike and Mama was nervous about going in the Métro, I walked with her to the Quartier Latin. I did not go in to Lebedintseva's, but while Mama was with her I went to a café and downed a beer, sitting at a table right on the boulevard.

16 June

At two o'clock a six-seater open-topped car drew up outside our hotel, with Mr and Mrs Guyoneet and her son from her first marriage at the wheel. Pierre de Fonbrune is a delightful young man of twenty whose appearance is spoiled by a stubborn rash on his face, neck and hands. We sped through Paris and then out through the suburbs. Altogether it was a superb expedition. Arriving at Versailles we looked briefly round Louis XIV's palace, and if I did not pay much attention to it, it was only because I kept being rooted to the spot by the fabulous vistas from its windows. From the Palace we walked to the Trianon Palace Hotel, where we had tea in great luxury. Looking out at the lovely Versailles park and its palaces I remembered what Tcherepnin had said: 'Come to Paris, go out to Versailles and spend a few days there.' Quite right. One day I will do just that.

After tea we sat in our nice car and went to St Germain, where we marvelled at all Paris spread out before us, and then returned to the city through the Bois de Boulogne, delighted with our excursion and all that we had seen.

In the evening I yielded to the entreaties of the landlady and some of the ladies in our pension, and improvised on various themes they picked out. I played them all kinds of nonsense, but they were full of admiration. I do not like improvising, and do it only rarely, perhaps once a year. The process of composing at the piano has nothing in common with improvising: composition consists of intensive, urgent searching, in the course of which the composer divides himself into two people: the creator and the critic. The first rapidly clothes his thoughts, one after the other, in snatches of music; among this throng there will be a number of purely automatic reflexes, but buried deep in them will be ideas of true originality. It is like sifting through gold-bearing sand and occasionally coming across a nugget of something valuable. The composer–critic instantly evaluates the mass of musical fragments the creator has produced, and unceasingly rejects, rejects and rejects until the moment he detects a hint of something original, fresh and beautiful. Then he fastens on to it like a hook and stays with it, while the composer–creator immediately sets to work to develop the embryo, to enlarge it in all possible directions. The composer–critic criticizes what his alter ego is doing, continuing to reject the attempts to develop the material. If a nugget is detected in the sand he quarries away hoping to find an ingot, but all too often the result is that the nugget crumbles away leaving nothing but more sand. The scrap of idea that started it all off turns out to be worthless. But if, on the other hand, it can be crystallized into an original idea meriting some attention, whether it be a theme or a harmonic idea or simply an interesting musical turn of phrase, then the objective has been achieved and the gold bar has been found. It may consist of just a few notes, a sequence of two chords, or even a long idea lasting several bars. Now it can be written down, perhaps to be put aside for a day, or even a month. The precious ingot has been found and carefully salted away; now it is time to look for others, and when several have been unearthed the task of linking them together to make a chain can be undertaken.

This is all down to the power of the imagination, to which the material in question is submitted and by which, depending on its value or otherwise, it is more or less successfully exploited. But as for improvisation, this is more a question of a sequence of ideas which must be made to follow one from another, the most important thing being that no interruption to the flow may be allowed. The composer–critic may not call a halt to a thought he does not like and insist on another, because this will constitute, however briefly, a break in the chain. The composer's critical voice is stilled in the face of the imperative to keep going, the imagination is forced to work on the first idea that comes along, and the improviser himself cannot avoid feeling that he is composing less good music than he is capable of. This is like panning sand which to the uninitiated eye seems to sparkle in the sunlight, but which hardly ever contains true gold. I can state that it never happened to me that I discovered any useful material for my compositions by means of improvising.

17 June

Getting up early in the morning, I took the Métro and went right across the city to the Gare de Lyon to get tickets and reserve our places for the train. I returned home the same way and became very tired from the noise of the underground trains.

I then packed my cases and at 12.30 we left Paris, catching the train by the skin of our teeth. The train was cramped, stuffy and tiring, and I was quite done in by the time we reached Royat, which we did at 7.30 in the evening. The hotel car met us and took us to the Grand Hôtel des Sources, as recommended by Mme Lebedintseva. This was not a particularly expensive hotel, but it was not a particularly good one either. I took a critical look at Royat, a place where I was destined to spend a month, having been brought there without consultation by Mama, who herself knew nothing about the resort beyond what she had heard. A hole, or not a hole? I fear, a hole.

18 June

Next morning I went to walk in the park, which at a little over a hectare in size brings you to its boundary almost as soon as you step out. Round about there are either hotels or other buildings, or hills, so it does not appear that there is anywhere to go for a decent walk. There was not a soul in the park. The tennis courts were poor, and no one was playing. I am used to Kislovodsk and Yessentuki, and this place is a hole, a complete and utter hole!

I am extremely discontented, and told Mama that I might just stay for a couple of weeks, but God forbid any longer!

19 June – 7 July

In the end I stayed in Royal for three weeks. I procured an upright piano from the neighbouring regional capital of Clermont-Ferrand, and worked.

Royat is a spa resort for elderly people of between fifty and seventy years of age. Young people are a rarity here. I felt sure that spending time here would depress me, and in order to have some moral compensation for the sense that my time was being wasted I would work as hard as my strength allowed me to. And indeed, I spent never less than six and a half hours, and often as many as eight or nine hours a day working. This was no doubt laudable, but my nerves, instead of calming themselves, became more and more frayed. What was bad was that, since I did not have the strength to work the entire day without stopping, I did not know what to do with myself when I did take a break. My days were spent in the following way: I would get up at eight in the morning, drink chocolate in the dining room and go for a ten-minute walk. Until lunch I sat at the upright piano learning my Second Piano Concerto, nothing else, just that. Lunch was at half past eleven in the dining room. At our table, besides Mama, sat Mme Lebedintseva and two of her friends: an elderly but very lively Frenchman and a woman who hardly spoke. Lunch consisted of a good many dishes and lasted almost an hour. After lunch I walked for about an hour, and then worked again until dinner: either the two-piano score of the Concerto or tidying up Op. 12, or transcribing the more important orchestral parts of the Concerto, since I did not trust the copyist. I spend another hour practising the Concerto, then had another half-hour walk before dinner, which was at half past six, and I was glad even of the company I found there. Dinner would be followed by a couple of hours writing my diary or some letters, and at ten I went to bed.

In this uneventful way three weeks passed. Episodes that broke the routine were as follows: I discovered in the casino a form of roulette called 'petits chevaux'; it is not as good as roulette because the odds are distinctly unfair. I sat at the table, immediately won a lot of money, and then lost an even bigger sum, so that the outcome of the first evening's play was to be down 120 francs. I did not regret this, merely deciding that next time I would stop after I had lost 20 francs. On that occasion I won 50 francs, but over the next two days lost them and thereafter ceased to visit this unprofitable institution.

An important event was writing a letter to Zakharov, which I had decided (before I left St Petersburg) to do as soon as I got to Royat. I had to let some time elapse after his strange behaviour in Terioki. I wrote to him by registered mail and posted the letter on 20 June.

Because it was a registered letter the envelope had the sender's address on it. I had not been counting on a reply, but one came much sooner than I could have expected even if I had been waiting for it. Zakharov acknowledged my skill at persuading him of my sincerity, extended his hand to me, and hoped that my handshake would soon be as welcome to him as it had been in former times. I was overjoyed and greatly heartened to receive this letter, to which I did not send a reply as it did not seem to need any.

As for my other correspondents, for the first week and a half, as if by common consent, there was no word from them. Then the letters began to arrive with some regularity. Volodya Deshevov wrote twice, friendly but insubstantial letters; he is someone I had always liked very much without in fact spending much time in his company. Now I felt I should like to see more of him. Myaskushka and Katyusha Schmidthof both wrote, but I heard nothing from Umnenkaya or from Goncharova. Probably they had been offended by something cheeky I had written to them . . . or perhaps they had got married. It was some time also before Nina Meshcherskaya broke her silence, but then she spread herself over four pages and generously invited me to Gurzuf, which I shall be very happy to do as soon as I have played my Concerto in Pavlovsk.

Mama, seeing that I was taking it out on her for Royat and that I was working till I dropped, suggested that I went for ten days or so to Switzerland, while she would stay on in Royat and later join me in Berlin. I found this an appealing idea, so I bought a map and studied train timetables, and Joanne's delightful *Guide to Switzerland*,[1] and soon became absorbed in planning the details of my trip, working it out down to the last minute. The prospect was most alluring, and I would still be back in St Petersburg in time to do two weeks' work on the Concerto. This was proving to be such a demanding and complex piece to learn that I was beginning to be worried that I would not master it in time for the Pavlovsk performance. I was hoping that it would respond well to the ten-day intermission I was imposing on it for my travels around Switzerland, and that the two weeks in St Petersburg thereafter would be enough to bring it up to a condition where I would be able to play it decently in Pavlovsk.

As for my composing activities, despite the intensity with which I had been working, the results were not very impressive: the two-piano score was still not finished, I had transcribed only five of the orchestral parts, and Op. 12 was still not ready. This last was all the more regrettable, since I had a feeling it was destined for great success, and should be published as soon as possible. The last piece in the set was to be a set of variations on a lovely theme I had composed on the day Max and I left for the Crimea. Max had always admired it, considering it one of my happiest inspirations and on a level with the best of the Second Piano Concerto. But all I managed to do was polish the theme itself and sketch out four variations, without actually composing any of them. I did compose for Op. 12 the 'Legenda', a little piece on the subject of a poetic image now buried in oblivion. I love this piece very much. I have been unable to finish the Op. 12 'Scherzo' for a year and a half now, and still cannot move beyond its sticking point. I want to dedicate it to Volodya Deshevov. The 'Mazurka' was composed three years ago, when it was dedicated to, and a fair copy made for, Myaskovsky. Since then both he and I have contrived to lose it. I have remembered it now, but still have not

---

1 Adolphe Joanne was a prolific French writer of travel guides. The first edition of his *Itinéraire de la Suisse* was first published by Hachette in 1841.

found the time to write it down. I have revised Boryusya's 'Gavotte' and added one or two things, and am now very happy with it.

I decided to re-orchestrate and partly revise the First Piano Concerto, and this was another thing I had intended to do in Royat, but in the end did not manage. My God, when am I going to get all this done?! I sold the Concerto to Jurgenson as long ago as the spring, but still have not sent it to him to have it 'cut'.[1]

9 July

Got up at 7 a.m. My things were already packed, the bulk of them going with Mama via Paris, so all I was taking to Switzerland was a small case with the bare necessities. Bidding farewell to Mama, I carried my case on to a tram and set off for Clermont, whence I would take the through train to Geneva. What a joy to travel light, with not so much as an overcoat over my shoulders! I felt generally on top of the world, a mood partly accounted for by a long letter from Lidochka Umnova that I received ten minutes before I left. It was a long letter, coquettish and distinctly amorous, and the overall effect was extremely agreeable in spite of the twenty-six mistakes she made in it. The letter occupied me for more than half the journey to Geneva: I daydreamed happily about Lidochka and looked out of the window at the pictures flashing past, and felt content.

Nearer to Geneva the permanent way improved but my mood worsened. Nevertheless I ferreted about with interest in Joanne's excellent *Guide*, a most intelligently and thoughtfully contrived, and rather touching, compendium for the tourist, going into great detail about what to look out for from the train; which side of the carriage to sit; which hotel to stop at; how much to tip – all set out with great care and foresight.

Although we were constantly disappearing into tunnels, all the time on our right-hand side was the beautiful fast-flowing Rhône. It was growing dark by the time we arrived in Geneva. Firmly gripping my suitcase I was walking into the Hôtel International just opposite the station when I noticed a spare, ramrod-straight American gentleman of about forty-five with glasses, a sun-tanned face, a small bald patch in his grey-streaked hair. He had been in my compartment on the train from Royat, and was also evidently making for the Hôtel International. But the hotel was full, and we were offered a room to share. A quick glance at one another and we agreed, he from practical necessity, I because it is more fun with two people.

We washed, put on clean collars and went out to inspect the town; the American had visited Geneva four years ago and therefore to some extent

---

1 Engraved.

acted as guide. As I had to equip myself as an Alpine tourist, we tried to locate the appropriate shops, but as the hour in Geneva was by then nine o'clock in the evening all the shops were closed and all I could do was note where they were so that I could make my purchases the following morning. Passing the rather insignificant Jardin des Anglais from where, however, one has a splendid view of the dark-coloured lake, we found a café where, as we had not eaten earlier in the day, we ordered supper.

In the meantime the weather had taken a turn for the worse, a wind had got up and it had begun to rain. The *garçon* stoutly maintained that it never rained in Geneva, and this was just an aberration. I agreed with him, saying that very probably they did not have much rain, but on the other hand water was apt now and then to descend from the sky. After supper we waited a little until the rain eased off, and then walked briskly over the attractive Mont Blanc bridge and went back to the hotel. The American marched at a great pace, holding himself as upright as a pole, and told me that he was going on to Lucerne, moreover that Geneva was full of *cocottes*, but that 'he did not go with women very often'. He said that Europe was a much more interesting place than America; Americans, of course, must regard Europe much as Europeans regard America. At eleven o'clock we went to bed, at which point I announced to him that I would be getting up at five.

10 July

I did not sleep particularly well, but still felt refreshed when I woke up. The sky was overcast but the American, poking his nose out of the window, opined that the weather would clear up and that he was going to Lausanne on the steamer. Parting amicably from him, I emerged on to the street and went to the station to get the *abonnement général* I had ordered yesterday, a ticket allowing me to travel anywhere in Switzerland for a period of fifteen days. It was six o'clock in the morning Paris time, seven o'clock in Geneva, the shops opened at eight and the train left at nine. I spent the hour walking along the quaysides and having a mug of chocolate. I did not go right into the centre of the city, but judging by the promenades along the lake shore it is a small but pretty place. Altogether Geneva was not looking its best, because the sun was hidden behind the clouds and the atmosphere was grey, the general flavour would have been reminiscent of our Neva had it not been for the entrancing smell of the lime trees in flower and the extraordinarily gentle expressions on the faces of the inhabitants.

Between eight and nine I succeeded in buying for myself in three different shops: a suit, boots, a knapsack, a stick, dark glasses, and socks; to attire myself in my purchases; to take a taxi back to my hotel; pack my old clothing and equipment away in my case, keeping what I immediately needed in the knapsack on my back; despatch my case right through to Lausanne; and go myself to the other station, called Des Eaux Vives, for the train to Chamonix.

I cannot say why, but the three hours it took for our agonizingly slow progress to Fayet-St Gervais passed almost imperceptibly, even though especially at the beginning the view from the windows of the train was short on enchantment. At Fayet we transferred from the steam locomotive to an elegant electric-powered one. This one-hour journey to Chamonix is ravishingly beautiful and the bridge across the Arve, fifty metres above the water, awe-inspiring. I left the train at Chamonix, fuelled myself with a sandwich and in accordance with my pre-determined itinerary went on foot to Montenvers, a pretty steep climb of more than two hours. In defiance of my American's prediction and the morning indications that the weather would lift, thick clouds lay over the summits of the mountains, and the general feeling was grey and overcast. It was warm, however, and I soon found it pretty hot work going uphill. All around was quiet and still, the pine trees framing the symmetrically ascending twists in the road somehow adding to the sense of peace. It did not seem very like July, more like autumn. Below lay the beautiful valley of Chamonix with its cluster of little houses, and behind it reared up the sheer faces of the forest-clad mountains, slashed by two grey streaks of the glaciers and crowned by clouds pressing low upon their peaks. I walked slowly but without stopping, a gently growing lassitude from the long ascent accompanying my sense of well-being and a contented soul at ease.

It was a long and fairly monotonous climb, but I gained a lot of height: Montenvers stands at the same number of metres as the year we are in – 1913.

Far below lay the valley of Chamonix, and by now the clouds were down alongside the road. It began to spit with rain. A building came in sight round a bend – the hotel. 'All right now, go ahead and rain all you like!' thought I, carelessly. Obediently the downpour commenced, whereupon I found that the hotel was considerably further away than I had thought, and by the time I reached it I was soaked to the skin. The weather now finally broke: the hotel was enveloped in wind, cold and rain. I decided to abandon temporarily my planned itinerary, which called for a half-hour rest before pushing on, and instead stay at the hotel until evening or even for the night. This was itself an interesting proposition, for a rare sight extended immediately in front of the hotel: a glacier. I was sopping wet outside from the rain and inside from my dash to the hotel, and this is an easy way to catch cold, so I drank down two glasses of rum, booked a room, and taking off my wet clothes collapsed into bed.

It was five o'clock in the evening by the time I awoke. My room was warm enough, but the rest of the hotel was gripped by cold and the only way to keep warm was to drink grog. I returned to the warmth of my room and applied myself to my diary.

Outside the rain lashed down, and even turned to snow. The snow-covered glacier, the fluffy clouds lying on the mountaintops and floating in the ravines down below gave the scene a wintry appearance. Downstairs in the hall a fire crackled merrily in the grate, while a tourist attempted to pick out a tune on the terrible little upright piano in the sitting room. This was in the South of France in July!!

At dinner I talked to a cheerful French doctor, who evidently took a liking to me and treated me to a glass of Benedictine.

11 July

I was woken with chronometric precision at a quarter to five and informed that the rain had stopped and the weather was fine. Within ten minutes I had dressed, swallowed a cup of chocolate and was out in the fresh air. A wintry landscape was spread before my eyes: during the night snow had fallen on the mountains, the glacier glistened at my feet, and down below the mist eddied like cotton-wool. The air was clean and crisp, and I was none too warm in my English clothes. I kept up with the guide as he quickly preceded me down to the glacier, and before long I was warm from the pace he set. We crossed over the heaped-up stones that separate the glacier from its shores and moved on to the ice. The surface of the glacier itself is a series of icy waves, the ice not glassy smooth and slippery but soft, like snow that turns to ice as it freezes. At the point we were crossing the going is not difficult or dangerous: there are no deep crevasses and the inclines not particularly steep. All the same I was very grateful for the nails in my boots and the spike on the end of my stick. One detail I found entertaining was that everywhere on the ice and round about were lying quantities of torn and tattered stockings, some of them very good quality, but now either frozen into the ice or trampled into the mud. I saw scores of them and could only imagine that it was a tradition to cross the glacier in stockinged feet and then toss them aside as no longer useful.

As soon as we reached the pile of stones on the far side of the glacier my guide informed me his job was done, and having accepted his five francs and told me to turn to the left, left me alone. This was quite frightening at first, because I had to leap from one huge boulder to the next with no sign of any path. But the rocks began to decrease in size, soon a definite path emerged, and I increased my pace: it was still a good way to Tines but not long before the train was due to leave – a little over an hour. After half an hour I had got as far as Mauvais *pas*, the irony of whose nomenclature I had not anticipated. Into an almost sheer rock face a semblance of dubiouslooking narrow steps had been cut. It seemed impossible to traverse them, slippery as they were from the mist and the rain, but salvation lay in an iron rail attached to the rock with hooks. Holding on to this rail made it not only possible but quite easy to cross Mauvais *pas*, even though the sheer precipice below offered little in the way of comfort in the event of a slip or fall. It is not a short hop either: taking it step by step and holding on to the rail took at least ten minutes. I do not consider myself brave, but I managed the traverse without feeling terrified; on the contrary I rather enjoyed the unconventional method of progress. From the other side of the pass to Tines there was a good path descending into the valley.

According to the guidebook it would take another hour to walk there and I was obviously going to be late for the train, but some shepherds I met said it would take no more than half that time. I tore along at the speed of an avalanche and to my surprise after a fifteen-minute scramble down the hillside reached the station with twenty minutes to wait before the train left. On the other hand, I was as wet as a goose. It was raining, the weather was cold and grey, and the mist was all around. I sat in the train and, as it moved off, felt my shirt clammy and icy as I cooled down. A certain recipe to catch cold. Going into an empty first-class compartment I did some gymnastics to warm myself up; this helped and after three minutes' exercise I felt a blessed warmth stealing through my veins. As soon as I felt I was getting cold again I repeated my exercises, visiting the empty compartment three times during the hour it took to reach the Franco-Swiss border. There was a buffet here, and I drank a glass of Kirsch, almost choking on the strength of this terrifying but nevertheless delicious stuff, and felt not so much warmth as sparks coursing through my veins.

We changed trains to enter Switzerland, and at once the views through the windows became extraordinarily beautiful, the mountains higher, the gorges deeper, each moment revealing an ever more interesting vista, the whole scene so magnificent that one could only gasp in delight. The line clung to the steep mountainsides, often at such a height above the sheer green abyss below that one shuddered to think what would happen to us were we to go crashing down. But a train crash here would be unthinkable: the result would be hundreds of thousands of tourists deserting Switzerland, and in any case the Swiss engineers have deployed all their genius to make this railway absolutely safe. Sometimes the mist would either creep down or float up like a great blanket and obscure the panorama for a time, but then it would clear to striking effect. The rain was kind enough to cease, but the grey weather persisted and where the guidebook indicated the Alps, there was nothing but cloud to be seen.

Plunging into tunnels and spiralling down, the train now descended an incredibly steep decline to the station at Vernayaz. I got out of my carriage and walked over to see the Trient stream which, encircled by two huge rocks leaning above it, rushes foaming into the valley. Light wooden platforms are hung on wires attached to the rocks by metal hooks, and by walking on them one can penetrate this savage corridor and look down on the endless twists and turns of the water below. After viewing this interesting spectacle I was accompanied back to the station by a somewhat uncouth German tourist, and took the train to Lake Geneva, approaching it from the other side to the one I had been on before. Although the rain was now pouring down once more, the lovely lake preserved its naturally mild appearance, and its shores, adorned by an incredible variety of fresh, luxuriant vegetation and dotted with attractive-looking hotels, only served to enhance its beauty. Following my itinerary I alighted at Montreux, 'jewel of Lake Geneva', and to escape from the rain had lunch in the hotel opposite the station. But this was the rain's farewell appearance, and after it the weather began slowly but surely to improve. I looked round the handsome town of Montreux following the route prescribed by Joanne, and then walked along the shore to Clarens where I looked at the cemetery, which has an outstanding view and is more like a garden than a cemetery, with white memorials peeping out from the foliage. I saw several Russian graves and wondered why it was ever necessary to write more or better than 'E. I. 1910' which I saw modestly inscribed on one splendid white stone nearby . . .

I then descended to the lake, boarded a steamer and an hour later was in Ouchy, which is the landing stage for Lausanne, the town itself being not on the waterfront but higher up the hill. A stupid Russian sitting with his family near me, made an unsuccessful joke: 'Lausanne is up above, but its Ushi,[1] you see, are lower down!'

The funicular railway took us up into Lausanne proper, and I took a room in a hotel, lugged over from the station my suitcase, which I had sent on straight from Geneva, found a postcard from Mama at the *poste restante*, changed into lighter shoes and went out to look at the town with the Joanne guidebook in my hands. The ink on the binding had begun to run from all the time I had been clutching it in my hot hands, and had stained them red.

Altogether I am being the complete tourist: I don't waste a minute, look at everything quickly, punctually follow the dictates of my itinerary and take particular pleasure in outdoing the English who are here in droves, for example by writing my postcards with a fountain pen while they are reduced to pencils, watching them stagger about with their luggage while I have had the foresight to send it in advance directly to where I am staying, watching them screw up their eyes against the sunlight while I am comfortably hidden behind my dark glasses.

And so I looked round Lausanne, although the most interesting sight I saw there was the two Russian girls I met on the street. As a town it has little

---

[1] 'Ushi' is the Russian word for ears.

to recommend it, not even a decent restaurant, and I was hungry, it being by then nine o'clock. And then I remembered that Ouchy had produced a rather pleasant impression on me when the steamer docked there, so I took the tram down to dine there. And indeed it is a very nice place, with the waters of the lake taking on a soft, rosy hue in the rays of the setting sun and plashing gently against the shore. After dinner I went back up to Lausanne, and having written a few pages of my diary, slept the sleep of the dead.

There are an incredible number of Russians in Switzerland; one can hardly go a few steps without meeting one. Russian speech is heard much more than any other except, obviously, the native tongue. Each time I hear it, it gives me pleasure.

12 July

I asked to be woken at six, so as to be able to go and see Le Signal de Lausanne, a look-out point on the mountain from where one has a splendid view over the town and the lake, before I caught my train. There I drank my morning chocolate before hurrying down to take the eight o'clock train to Yverdon, on Lake Neuchâtel. I had been told that this lake was not interesting enough to warrant a visit, but I somehow liked the look of it on the map and decided to include it in my itinerary anyway. Going down to the lakeside from the station I was met by a fierce wind, and the lake presented an unexpected aspect: waves topped by white horses pounded on to the shore. Lake Neuchâtel had none of the serenity of Lake Geneva and, now that I think of it, it had on the contrary a hard-edged outline, an aggressive character and was a dark blue colour, blending here and there into green. I went so far as to ask a sailor if passengers ever got seasick in such weather, but he assured me with a smile that they did not. With two other passengers I embarked, and we sailed off into the 'open sea'. Whenever we turned broadside on to the wind, the boat was tossed about so violently that the benches on the deck overturned and I, stubbornly perambulating from bow to stern and back again, staggered about like a drunk man, thoroughly enjoying the experience. I had not a twinge of sickness, which pleased me very much bearing in mind the future voyages I plan to make to America.

Soon the boat turned to head straight into the wind, and the pitching and tossing ceased, also the wind decreased in strength. Undoubtedly Lake Neuchâtel is less picturesque than Lake Geneva; with the dark blue colour of its waters and the character of its shoreline it recalls the Black Sea. After two and a half hours we docked at Neuchâtel, which has a delightful aspect when seen from the lake. I had some lunch, bought gloves, looked round the town and after an hour and a half entrained for Berne. Despite the fact that the clock said three o'clock in the afternoon, I felt so overcome by the desire to sleep that I had difficulty in keeping my eyes open to look at the beauties of Lake Bienne, by the shore of which the train ran.

I arrived in Berne at four o'clock and allowed myself with the open Joanne guidebook in my hand to look at the town. I think the words Berne and Bear must have a common root, otherwise why should there be such a cult of this animal in the city? Everywhere you look there are postcards depicting the animal, stuffed examples and even a large pit cut into the rock with live bears in it. For all that Berne is the capital of Switzerland it is a small town, quite handsome, compressed into a horseshoe formed by the river Aap which runs along the bottom of a deep ravine on the sides of which the houses disappear into the greenery, linked by beautiful, high bridges. The Kornhaus Bridge and the area round about are so lovely it is hard to tear one's eyes away from them. An amusing feature in the centre of the town is the clock tower which presents a complete performance every hour on the hour and draws a crowd of curious onlookers.

From Berne I went on to Thun, on the lake of that name. The sun was already setting, the weather magnificent, making the lake inexpressibly beautiful. It resembled neither the rough Neuchâtel nor the smilingly southern Geneva. Dusk lent the water the colour of steel, and the combination of this surface of polished steel, the dark green of the shores and the pink-tinged Jungfrau on the horizon made a harmonious ensemble that was nothing less than a *chef-d'oeuvre*. As darkness fell we passed by a lofty mountain near the jetty at Spitz, and when after a while I looked back at it I saw at the very top what looked like a huge diamond radiating with light. It was explained to me that there is a hotel on the summit of the mountain, whose name is the Niessen. I could not take my eyes off this diamond shining so brilliantly through the dark, and after long searching through Joanne found the information I wanted about the mountain and its hotel. I came to a decision: my itinerary provided for two nights in Interlaken; the second one I would spend on the top of the mountain.

We approached Interlaken through a picturesque canal, and the moment you step off the jetty you are in a square framed by half-a-dozen welcomingly illuminated hotels. This produced a most cheering effect, and having booked in at one of the hotels I collected my case from the station, had supper, and fell sound asleep, covered not by a blanket but by a light feather duvet.

13 July

Joanne states firmly that to become acquainted properly with Interlaken takes four days, and gives a detailed timetable for each day. All I had was one day, and that only until half past three, at which point I had to leave to get to the top of the mountain with which I had fallen in love. In the end I abandoned all pretence at a proper inspection and spent the morning and early afternoon walking around Interlaken and the hills closest to it. It is a pretty little place, consisting almost entirely of hotels and guest-houses. Among its visitors seem to be an overwhelming preponderance of Russians. By two o'clock I had had enough of Interlaken, and in any case I was dropping with fatigue. I boarded a steamer, followed by a train, followed by a funicular which ever so slowly bore me aloft towards the summit of Mount Niessen, which is more than 2,300 metres high; the funicular took over an hour for the ascent. This climb has everything: crossing an elegant bridge to begin with, the line then curves round with precipices on either side, tunnels, and a long incline straight as an arrow. At first I was as thrilled as a child simply to be going up so high, climbing up so far that the end was far out of sight. But after a while it became boring, and my good humour evaporated. However, when I eventually found myself on the summit I cheered up at the throng of tourists; I love tourists, especially older ones, guidebook in one hand and binoculars in the other, marching purposefully along looking from side to side lest an important detail demanding attention should inadvertently be missed. On the summit, however, they were thin on the ground, and soon went back down again, although the last funicular, departing at seven o'clock, brought a fresh crop of a dozen or so replacements. All at once the scene became noisier as they invaded the upper square, unfolded their maps and pointed out landmarks with outstretched fingers and upraised walking sticks, pronouncing the while the strange-sounding names of the surrounding peaks and rivers. Truly, the view was almost limitless, except where it disappeared into mist and haze. Two lakes, Lake Thun and Lake Brienz, lay at our feet, Thun clearly visible with a long chain of snowy peaks to the east that changed from pink to blue to grey as the sun sank slowly down. Clouds billowed below us, sometimes obscuring one or another part of the view, and occasionally advancing on to our summit so that we ourselves were engulfed in a thick mist. Near the hotel snow was lying in places, but this was because of an unusually cold summer; normally at this time of year there is none.

After dinner, when it was completely dark, I went up again to the upper square. It was illuminated by about a dozen electric lights, and it was these that had produced the gleaming diamond that had so enchanted me down below on the lake. But up here the effect was very different, and actively unpleasant: it hurt the eyes, and prevented anything below being visible at all. I returned to my room to find that a German had been squeezed in to share with me. But he was nice enough, settling down to sleep straight away after assuring me that the longer I stayed up to write the more soundly he would sleep. I thanked him and sat down conscientiously to write my travel notes, although my head was longing for its pillow even more than my neighbour.

14 July

At four o'clock there was a hullabaloo and racket in the hotel for all the world as if a regiment of cavalry were charging up and down the corridors. Outside it was pouring with rain, grey and unwelcoming, so the German and I closed the shutters and slept on until six o'clock. When I went down to the dining room I saw that there had been a comprehensive take-over of the hotel in the shape of a large excursion that had been climbing on foot up the mountain all night. As tourists must take the weather as it comes, they were soaked through, muddy and tired, and they filled the dining room, the corridors and even half lay on the staircase. But they were chattering happily and at such a high volume that at first I could hardly think straight. A pretty waitress took me under her wing and with extraordinary rapidity produced chocolate for me to drink, after which I took one more look at the square with its boundless view and at 6.44 took the funicular back down the mountain, taking an hour for the trip. I sat and thought about Max, comparing him with Zakharov, but without coming to any definite conclusion.

There were two more trains after the funicular, until at nine o'clock I was back in Interlaken by the shore of Lake Brienz. Trains in Switzerland are not troubled by the incredible German mania for punctuality and are often late, but on the other hand they wait for one another. So it was on this occasion: the steamer waited for the arrival of our delayed train. Lake Brienz is longer, deeper and surrounded by higher mountains than Lake Thun. There is in fact some resemblance between the two, but it was difficult for me to compare them since I saw Thun at dusk while I was now seeing Brienz in the full glare of the morning sun. It being Sunday, a military band was playing on the deck of the steamer, there were a lot of passengers, and the voyage had a happy, holiday atmosphere.

When the *Titanic* went down, the ship's orchestra was ordered to play cheerful marches in order that the passengers should not be gripped by panic, and the *Titanic* slipped into the deep to the sound of music. Now as I thought of this dramatic event I could see the point of this terrible conception. After Lake Brienz, the train again ascended a long gradient, at the end of which there opened up a view of the delightful small, dark-hued lake known as the Lungernsee. Another lake, the Sarnersee, proved to be larger but not so attractive, and after a two-hour journey we descended to the Vierwaldstatter See and stopped at Alpnachstadt. Here I left the train, preferring to continue my journey by boat.

If Lake Geneva is the gentlest of the lakes, Lake Neuchâtel the roughest, Lake Thun the most poetic, the Four Cantons Lake has to be the most interesting because of the intricacy of its features and the height and steepness of its shores, which in many places plunge sheer into the water. Even with the map spread out on my knees it was not always possible to work out in which direction the steamer was heading at any given time. We passed the cottage in which Wagner lived while he was forging his *Ring*; fascinated, I devoured it with my eyes but it was an ordinary-looking little house, quite pleasant, but I wished it had a more bardic aspect. We docked at Lucerne, strikingly laid out on the inclined shores of the lake. Lucerne has many fine buildings and a marvellous, shady promenade along the quayside. I badly wanted to walk around the town, but at that moment the heavens opened and the rain poured down. Caught out by this I took shelter under one of the leafy trees of the boulevard until the rain eased off enough for me to pay it no heed and race along looking at the town on my way to the train station. I had read in Joanne that a few hours away from Lucerne by train was the famous Devil's Bridge, scene of Suvorov's[1] heroic crossing in 1799, and I was so interested in this historic place that I resolved to go immediately to see it. The four o'clock express would get me quickly to Göschinen, from which Devil's Bridge lay six kilometres further on along the highway. After the rattling and shaking carriages of the Swiss trains it was pleasant to sit on the comfortably upholstered seats of the Milan express rushing forward without stopping every five minutes. We were plagued with tunnels, of which there are as many as eighty on this line, and we plunged into one almost every minute. Neither did the weather offer much consolation, as it was grey and cold, and the rain came intermittently. Passing through Brunnen we ran along the side of the lake, which despite the weather looked splendid. Leaving the lake we started to penetrate deep into the mountains, the line twisting and turning in labyrinthine complications, now spiralling upwards, now describing great curving loops. We went through tunnel after tunnel after tunnel, and in between had glimpses of wild scenery that recalled the journey from Chamonix.

We arrived at Göschinen, and I watched my comfortable train disappear into the twelve kilometres of the St Gotthard tunnel as I remained on the rainswept platform. But the tourist can pay no heed to the weather, so I climbed into a carriage and went to Devil's Bridge. I would soon have become wet through had it not been for the elegant rug covering the horse, with whom I took turn and turn about, wrapping myself in the plaid while on the move and returning it to its owner when we stopped. Devil's Bridge has a savage beauty about it, thrown over a foaming waterfall plunging into a wild ravine, the whole scene picturesque in the extreme. Nearby is a large

---

1 In September 1799 Marshal Alexander Suvorov, the 'Russian Hannibal', resolved on a desperate strategy to extricate his hugely outnumbered and exhausted army from certain annihilation by the French at the St Gotthard pass by taking them across the Alps. The gamble almost came to grief at the Teufelbrücke, a narrow bridge over a waterfall high up on the river Reuss, but Suvorov beat back the French forces barring his way and eventually led the great majority of his 20,000 men to safety.

cross, about fourteen metres wide, carved into the rock of the mountainside, commemorating Suvorov's troops. We returned to the town, the weather worsening all the while. I stayed the night in a small hotel.

15 July

By seven o'clock in the morning I was already on the train, and at eight boarded the steamer at Flüelen, precisely on the opposite side of the lake from Lucerne. The weather, which at first had showed signs of lifting, now suddenly thought better of it and poured down again, threatening to ruin my trip, but then just as abruptly substituted kind-heartedness for its former rage, the sun shone brightly and remained thus until evening. This was a marvellous journey: a beautiful lake, a crowd of well-dressed passengers, good weather and a holiday atmosphere. Several kilometres away I caught a glimpse of Wagner's cottage, and at that moment it gleamed with brilliant light like the hilt of the magic sword Notung in *Die Walküre*. No doubt the cause of the refulgence was the same, except that Notung reflected the fire whereas the windows of the cottage were reflecting the sun.

Tying up at wonderful Lucerne, the steamer deposited me on the quayside, now no longer awash with water but radiant in the sunshine and alive with the colour of the gaily clothed population. I walked around, had lunch in the hotel by the side of the lake, collected letters from Mama and from the Karneyevs, who expressed themselves as puzzled by my long silence, and after spending three hours in Lucerne took the train to Zurich. It was a hot, stuffy and rather boring journey until we got to Rapperswill, a town on the southern shore of Lake Zurich.

I did not look at everything on the Vierwaldstatter See I was recommended to by Joanne: I did not go up Mount Piri, from where one has a view over all the bends and convolutions of the lake. Joanne notes that this excursion is a classic and not on any account to be missed, but like Leporello in the wake of Don Giovanni I was tired of being dragged hither and thither (especially up funicular railways!) and, like Leporello, cried, 'I now would be the master' and gave this mountain the go-by.

And so I came to Rapperswill and boarded another steamer which crossed the lake to bring me to Zurich. By comparison with the Vierwaldstatter See, Lake Zurich is unimpressive, lacking towering mountains, intricate bends and bays and peninsulas. It is plain and simple, but agreeable for all that, and the little island just off Rapperswill is very nice. It was also a wonderful evening. After two hours we drew into Zurich, also less dramatic than splendid Lucerne. Without going into the city centre I went into a park on the edge of the town where I walked, dined, watched the waters of the lake gradually darken in the dusk and at nine o'clock sought out a hotel for the night near the station. The town was noisy, brightly lit and full of life, Banchofstrasse very reminiscent of Paris. I collected my case from the station, got a room in a hotel, bought a Russian newspaper from the kiosk, and having read it fell into the bottomless sleep of the tourist.

16 July

The first thing I did was to go to the Post Office and to Thomas Cook's. *Poste restante* had for me a letter from Mama, the fifth by her reckoning but only the third I had received. Where the others ended up I have no idea. Then there was a card from Marinochka Popova, to which I hastened to respond. Thomas Cook & Sons sold me a ticket to Berlin with a sleeper reservation as far as Nuremberg. To be precise, Cook's took my money and promised to deliver the ticket to the station, but such is their reputation that I trusted them without a receipt, and my faith proved justified. Then I went back to my hotel, packed my suitcase and at eleven o'clock went off to Neuhausen to view the falls on the Rhine. These are not so impressive at first glance, but when I climbed up to the platform at the very top of the falls, a mass of water thundering down boiling and foaming into the depths below, splashing me as if from a giant watering-can, I appreciated the mighty power of the Rhine waterfall. I wondered why no one had invented some form of armoured tube in which connoisseurs of extreme experiences would be able to descend through the falls themselves? One's body could be encased in a steel torpedo, the head could be protected by a helmet like a diver's and a steel cage to ward off any flying rocks. It would be so exciting to hurtle down through the torrent and then be fished out of the water far below! I gazed at the falls from all angles, then went out in a boat on the river below the falls, tossed about by the waves they created, then lunched and drank a whisky and soda at Schböschen Worth. As I still had plenty of time I went to look at the neighbouring town of Schaffhausen, which according to Joanne is of all Swiss towns the one that has most completely preserved its medieval atmosphere. Unfortunately this atmosphere also contained a large quantity of dust, and I was thankful to emerge into the relatively shady square. There I killed an hour reading through my travel impressions, after which I got back on the train and returned to Zurich soon after nine. I walked back along the brightly lit streets and quaysides and turned into a busy, cheerful café on the Banchofstrasse, where I swallowed some supper and enjoyed feasting my eyes on a pretty girl serving the tables. In fact she was not all that pretty, but when I saw her standing in profile at the green fence in conversation with someone the other side of the fence paying her compliments, she was so elegant, so full of grace and charm, that I could not take my eyes off her for fear of missing a single one of her movements. Awarding her a two-franc tip by way of acknowledging her especial gracefulness, I took myself off to the station where, bidding farewell to Switzerland, I boarded the train for Nuremberg.

I was alone in my splendid compartment of the International Company's train. In the neighbouring compartment, sharing with mine a washbasin, was a woman, also travelling alone. Her inability to master the technicalities of the sliding bolt occasioned some entertaining encounters between us, after which I slept soundly practically all the way to Nuremberg.

17 July

We arrived at Nuremberg at half past nine in the morning, and the Berlin train was due to leave at eleven, so I had an hour and a half to look round the famous old town. I took a taxi, and taking my seat beside the driver, asked him to show me the town. Certainly the ancient houses, leaning crazily from the perpendicular, framed equally crooked streets, and all this was very curious and interesting, and even in its way beautiful. The building that most interested me was Hans Sachs's[1] house, at which I spent a long time looking with interest almost amounting to reverence. The leitmotifs of Wagner's opera never left me for an instant. Then we drove at random for a while round the town, finishing the tour half an hour before the train's departure.

After seven and a half hours travelling through the uneventful German countryside I finally arrived in Berlin. This is a city I like, and I was happy to spend what was left of the day there. I reserved a room at the Hotel Metropole and then after walking along the rackety, buzzing Friedrichstrasse, lunched at the Kempinsky. Afterwards I took one of the luxurious taxis of which Berlin can justly be proud, and went to the Tiergarten. I walked there for an hour and then returned to the hotel, where my besetting misadventure befell me: I got a piece of grit in my eye, which began to torment me mercilessly. All too depressingly aware that until I could have it looked at by a doctor this unwelcome guest would continue to plague me, I consulted the hotel concierge. He sent me to a nearby clinic, where the grit was removed and drops of some noxious fluid put into the eye. The psychology of this ailment decrees that the moment the offending cause is removed, a mood of unparalleled *joie de vivre* descends, and thus it was that I, carefree as the wind, proceeded along the bright lights and teeming crowds of Friedrichstrasse. But after a little while I became aware of a strange discomfort in my eyes, and finding a mirror to look into saw that one eye was unnaturally enlarged while the other had shrunk to a point.

Ascribing this phenomenon to the dubious liquid the clinic had dropped

---

1 The cobbler hero of Wagner's *Die Meistersinger von Nürnberg*.

into my eye, I judged my best course of action to be to go bed and sleep, a plan which I immediately put into operation.

A couple of hours later I was awakened by a knock on the door: it was Mama, arrived from Paris. We spent a joyful half-hour telling each other our experiences, and then she went back to her room. It was one o'clock at night and we had to be up betimes in the morning.

18 July

Next morning we were on the platform at eight o'clock, half an hour before the train was due to depart, eyeing the trains as they arrived every minute, either disgorging or swallowing armies of passengers before proceeding on their way with a deafening clangour. A man from the hotel procured good seats for us. The train was bound for Verzhbolovo, or as the Germans call the place, Wirballen, and hence we began hearing more Russian spoken than German. We felt we were almost home again, in Russia. The train covered this distance in ten hours, and at seven o'clock in the evening we arrived at Eydkuhnen, where the passengers changed their marks into roubles and hawkers proffered all kinds of books prominently labelled 'Banned in Russia'. We crossed the border at a leisurely pace and stopped at Verzhbolovo to see a characteristically dirty, clumsy-looking train the other side of the platform. We had heard such dire warning about Russian Customs that we were in a state of some trepidation, even though we had absolutely no contraband whatsoever. Our passports were taken away and the contents of our cases piled up on the Customs counter. Twenty minutes passed in silence, and then officials bearing passports in their hands appeared, and coming round the enormous pi-shaped[1] counter, which was completely covered with heaped-up belongings surrounded by their owners, began in a stentorian voice to call out names. Once called, the passenger had to identify and present himself for inspection. We were unlucky and had to wait interminably, until one of the officials at last called out: 'Prokofiev!'

'Here! Here!' we cried joyfully from the opposite end of the counter. Our cases, unlocked and opened, lay in front of us. The officer and his female assistant, the 'bloodhound', came over to us. The bloodhound plunged her expert hands into the cases and nimbly ferreted through them – and the inspection was over. Our bags had green pass labels affixed to them, our passports were returned to us and, tails borne proudly aloft and clutching our seat reservations, we entered the Russian carriage. Casting a jealously critical eye at our surroundings, to establish whether Russia was really so much worse than abroad (it was a little, but not much), we set off. It grew dark and we wanted to sleep.

---

1 In the shape of the Russian letter п or the Greek π.

19 July

In the morning we discovered that the train was delayed an hour because an axle in one of the carriages had overheated and needed to be replaced. I looked out of the window and tried to imagine the impression Russia would make on someone coming from abroad. What mostly struck me were the lack of habitation and the number of peasants going about barefoot. The train rolled gently along, without the noise and bumps of its German counterparts, but more slowly.

We arrived in St Petersburg at half past twelve, poured ourselves and our things into a taxi and stopped outside our door in Pervaya Rota. Petersburg was oppressively hot and dusty, the roads everywhere dug up, and the city in its July dress was extraordinarily unappealing. Our flat was also not its usual welcoming self: the sofas were covered in dust and there was a smell of paint, the redecoration having taken longer than it was supposed to. We quickly decided we would go and spend two weeks in the more comfortable surroundings of the Rayevskys' apartment and so without delay moved over to Sergievskaya Street. I wasted no time in getting back to work, until six o'clock when I went to the Tsarskoye Selo station to get the train out there. The air in Tsarskoye, unlike Petersburg, was fresh and dust-free as I went in search of Volodya Deshevov at his dacha. He in his customary affectionate way was very glad to see me, friendly and charming. He had been very touched by my card from the Eiffel Tower and made me promise to come out and visit him in the winter to go skiing.

In company with his brother we went to Pavlovsk to hear the concert. Kajanus[1] was conducting, so sadly Aslanov was not there. I did not meet any friends or acquaintances there, but we still enjoyed ourselves. Volodya is a very nice fellow, but perhaps a little jejune when compared with Max?

The orchestra librarian told me that they do not have a single available copyist in the orchestra. I will have to look for one in St Petersburg. Sibelius's *En Saga* has many interesting passages, but it is too long and lacks shape.

20 July

And so we installed ourselves in the Rayevskys' apartment near the Tauride Gardens. Because of the antediluvian sound of their piano I decided to practise on my own at Pervaya Rota, so I rose at eight o'clock, walked across the city and by nine o'clock was seated at my own piano, which I must admit was likewise grotesquely out of tune. As might be expected, my attempts at the Concerto were extremely rough today. The Scherzo was especially hard to

---

1 Robert Kajanus (1856–1933), outstanding Finnish conductor and Musical Director of the Helsingfors Philharmonic, friend and champion of Sibelius.

play, and my hands became numb with fatigue. But I did play through the whole work by heart, and that was good. I worked until one o'clock and then returned home, that is to say to Sergievskaya Street, and had lunch. Afterwards I scoured the town for a copyist, and then spent the evening with Myaskushka, who had already chastised me over the telephone for not going to see him the previous evening.

He showed me the manuscript score of Stravinsky's *Sacre*, sent to him by the composer, probably in gratitude for Myaskovsky's favourable notices of the work. Myaskovsky picked out all kinds of particularly interesting passages and considers Stravinsky to be a gifted innovator, even though he raises an eyebrow at his cacophony. He was most insistent that I take my *Maddalena* to Moscow with a view to having it performed at the Free Theatre,[1] a new enterprise in which Derzhanovsky and Saradzhev were playing an active role). My reaction to this idea was fairly muted for the following reasons: (1) *Maddalena* needs orchestrating, and this would take up a huge amount of time that I simply am not going to have during the autumn; and (2) my ideas about opera have advanced considerably in the two years since I composed *Maddalena*, which now in many respects fails to satisfy my present demands. I played Myaskovsky my new pieces, 'Rigaudon' and 'Legenda'; the first he liked, the second also, with the exception of the end.

Today I received from Jurgenson copies of the just-published *Toccata* and Op. 4. I am always apprehensive on first opening such volumes, because my eye invariably falls on some infuriating misprint or other, and so it was today. One place in the *Toccata* has semiquavers instead of demi-semiquavers. But both works are beautifully produced; in this respect Jurgenson is exemplary.

21 July

By nine fifteen I was at Pervaya Rota and at the piano working on the Concerto. I worked until one, but not without a few short pauses, interspersing learning the Concerto with the composition of the Etude for Op. 12. This is the last piece of the ten in this opus: it was composed two years ago, but somewhat inadequately: now I am in the process of recomposing it from the

---

1 Derzhanovsky and Saradzhev were indeed deeply involved, but the prime mover of the Free Theatre was Konstantin Mardzhanov (Mardzhanishvili) (1872–1933), Georgian by birth. Renowned as actor and director of the plays of Chekhov and Gorky, he arrived in Moscow in 1909 to join the Moscow Arts Theatre, where he came under the influence of Gordon Craig. In 1913 he left to found the Moscow Free Theatre, under a banner of synthesizing all aspects of lyric and dramatic theatre genres. Sadly the Free Theatre folded after one season, for the usual reasons of financial insecurity and artistic disagreements, but in that one season in 1913–14 it presented several gound-breaking and influential productions, among them a mime production based on Schnitzler's *The Veil of Pierrette*, to a specially commissioned score by Dohnányi, that launched the career of the great director Alexander Tairov.

beginning, using only elements of the original material and leaving its character unchanged, everything else is new. I am thinking of dedicating it to Romanovsky, a first-class pianist, charming person and a devotee of my muse.

At half past one I returned to Sergievskaya Street, had lunch, changed into my new suit with its check-patterned trousers, almost unheard of then in Russia, and went to Terioki to see the Karneyevs. During the first part of my foreign travels I had sent them a quantity of cards, one a day, until I discovered that they were tardy about replying, so I abruptly stopped writing to them and did not send them anything at all during the latter half of the trip. Now, as soon as I appeared, there were cries of: 'Sergusya!! Where have you sprung from? What happened to you? Why didn't you write?'

Both girls were, as usual, fresh and pretty as paint. After half an hour's chat about abroad, we went down to the sea. Passing the Zakharovs' bathing-place, Lida spotted Boris Zakharov riding his bicycle along the wooden boardwalk down to the shore. Both girls hallooed to him and ran over to the boardwalk, while I and another young man, Savenko, stayed where we were. Then we all met; I greeted Zakharov politely, taking off my hat, and he said, 'Hullo, welcome back.'

Lida and Zoya chattered on about how Sergusya had suddenly appeared today out of the blue, we looked out and there he was! Then the conversation turned to some party they had been to the previous evening, and when Zakharov asked where we were going, we said we were first going to play tennis, and then to the cinema, and why didn't he come with us? But he said he could not, because they had a house full of guests, at which I interposed: 'Well then, all the more reason to come to the cinema with us, because then the house won't be so full.'

But he replied that he would only come if all the guests decided they wanted to as well, and with that we parted, Boris this time politely raising his hat. We continued on our way. On the tennis court we met Boris Alpers, who always makes an elaborate fuss of greeting the Karneyevs, and is obviously playing a game of some kind. My own greeting to him was rather cold and brusque. I was even ruder to Seryozha Alpers, merely offering him my left hand in passing. After tennis we went to the cinema (Zakharov did not come) and then dined at home, with the usual lavish amount to drink, and at ten o'clock I returned to Piter after promising to see them on Friday.

Zakharov is going away to visit the Grand Dukes on Wednesday, and when he returns plans to come on 2 August with the Karneyevs to Pavlovsk to hear me.

22 July

In the morning I again practised at Pervaya Rota. The *Scherzo* is improving. In the breaks I read Otto Weininger's[1] *Sex and Character*.

After lunch Mama and I went to the Novodevichi Monastery to visit Papa's grave, after which I did some shopping and then wrote my diary. In the evening I went to the People's House to see what sort of a place it is. I liked it very much. Around the building is a large park with all kinds of attractions like the Luna-Park. There were crowds of people there, not the commonest sort, but somewhere between the intelligentsia and the common folk, a good many attractive female faces among them. There were students, high-school pupils, and some citizens evidently bored and looking for adventure. There were footmen and chambermaids, swapping origins and backgrounds: 'Where be you from then?' 'We'm from Tula.' There were some respectable citizens out with their wives, behaving like tourists. Altogether I approved of the institution and resolved to come back another time, but this evening I went back to Sergievskaya Street at ten and went to bed.

23 July

Next morning I again practised the Concerto, breaking off from time to time to read Weininger. I also played through some fragments of *Maddalena*. I was not very excited by the early passages in the opera, but the dramatic story of Stenio so gripped me that I was afire with the notion of revising *Maddalena* and having it performed. There is no doubt that much of it, all the vocal parts, need to be rewritten, but *Maddalena* does have the makings of a good opera. The terrible thing is, though, that it will have to be orchestrated, and I simply have no time to do this work. Even to complete the vocal score and bring it to a state suitable for a student production at the Conservatoire would take all winter, and if I were to embark on the task of orchestrating the whole opera I would be in danger of failing my last year at the Conservatoire, not to mention all the other work I have to do. But how nice it would be, all the same, to have *Maddalena* produced and performed! Perhaps Myaskovsky would give me a hand with the orchestration!

At eleven I went over to see Aslanov, as he lives near me. We must settle a time for him to get to know my Concerto. Aslashka had a surprise for me. The Concerto performance had been scheduled for 2 August, but in the

---

1 Otto Weininger (1880–1903), Austrian philosopher whose flamboyant suicide at the age of twenty-three in the house where Beethoven had died made his book *Geschlecht und Charakter* a *cause célèbre*. As a Jew who had converted to Christianity, Weininger's contentious views on race, gender, religion and genius, influential though they were on writers and thinkers such as Strindberg and Wittgenstein, were profoundly misogynous and anti-Semitic.

meantime a terribly important benefit concert of some sort had been arranged for the 3rd, and since this would need a great deal of preparation some rehearsal time had been taken from the preceding concert, i.e. mine. For this reason Aslanov suggested postponing my Concerto until the final concert of the season on the 23rd of the month. I was on the point of flaring up at this high-handed approach, but just in time it occurred to me that all could work out to my advantage. In the first place, I was far from ready to perform the work and the 23rd would give me time to learn it properly. In the second place I could immediately go to stay with the Meshcherskys in the Crimea, returning on the 20th. I therefore agreed to Aslanov's suggestion, and we there and then re-scheduled the Concerto and *Dreams* from the 2nd to the 23rd. Also, there would probably be a bigger audience in St Petersburg on the later date.

Going back to Pervaya Rota, I again opened *Maddalena* and became absorbed in considering what changes I would make and what a splendid opera would result. I then went to Sergievskaya Street for lunch and informed Mama of the new date for my performance and of my intention to go tomorrow to Gurzuf. Mama had no objection, and herself proposed to go the day after to Yessentuki, where the Smetskoys were expecting her.

After dinner I went to see Myaskovsky in the hope of casting out an exploratory line about the orchestration of *Maddalena*. I began by telling him that I had played through the opera today and had been exceptionally pleased by it. He was thrilled. 'How marvellous! Now you must revise and orchestrate it, and then we will get it performed in Moscow.'

This was my cue to begin complaining that however tempting a prospect this was, it was unachievable, since come the autumn I would be completely overwhelmed by work in the Conservatoire...

'Three weeks' hard work would be enough to orchestrate *Maddalena*,' objected Myaskovsky.

'Three weeks?!' I gasped.

'Three weeks.'

'Well, you do it then, if you think it will only take three weeks to orchestrate a complete opera!'

'Give *Maddalena* to me, and I'll do it,' smiled Myaskushka.

'You'd be my greatest benefactor,' I replied half jokingly. 'We can cobble together a four-hand version, you can orchestrate it, and I'll do what Borodin did, paint it all over with gelatine and hang it out to dry!'

In this way we roughly sketched out his participation in *Maddalena*. Myaskovsky then told me how much he liked 'Legenda' and said he would not give it back to me, I must present him with it. We went to Shreder's shop so that we could play my Concerto on two pianos, where incidentally N. Ya. M. was severely critical of my piano reduction of the orchestra part, saying that composers were never much good at transcribing their own works, and making many valuable suggestions. It was the first time I had played the work with a second piano and I made a good many mistakes listening to what the other piano was doing. Altogether it was a very interesting experience, although the Scherzo was diabolically tiring to play.

After an hour playing through the Concerto with Myaskovsky and hearing his considered opinion that it was better than the First Piano Concerto, I went out to Tsarskoye Selo to find Volodya Deshevov and go with him to the concert at Pavlovsk. But he was not at home, having already set out for Pavlovsk as it was already nine o'clock. I went there on foot and arrived at half past nine, in time for the interval. I met the 'Pillow' and her delightful married sister. I poked my nose into the auditorium but still could not find Volodya Deshevov, and soon left to come back to Petersburg with Karatygin, with whom I had an interesting conversation about music. Among other things, when I asked him what he knew about the Free Theatre, he said that he had authority to propose operas for the repertoire there, and if I wished to propose *Maddalena* he would support it, so I hastened to assure him that I did indeed so wish.

24 July

I had a lot of things to do today, but the most important was to get myself to Gurzuf. In the morning I drew money out of the bank, looked in on Kolechka, went to the Town Hall to exchange my foreign passport for a Russian one, and went to the ticket office in the town for a train ticket. However, they would not sell me one, saying that on the day of travel tickets could be bought only at the main station. But I did run into Kolechka Shtember there who, as it turned out had also been abroad but was still as disorganized as ever. I told him I had just received the printed version of the *Toccata* with the dedication to him, and suggested he come with me to Pervaya Rota to get a copy of it. We did this, and while I quickly got together what I needed for Gurzuf, he tossed off roulades on the piano. When I happened to mention something about Tonechka Rudavskaya, he said, 'How funny those childish infatuations seem to me now!'

We said goodbye, and with my case stuffed full of all sorts of minor impedimenta (but forgetting my famous London tennis racquet) I went back to Sergievskaya. After lunch I quickly changed my clothes and rushed to the Finland Station to go out to Kuokkale. I did not want to go away without having seen Umnenkaya, and had in any case sent her a postcard saying I would be coming out today. I wandered about Kuokkale for ages looking for their dacha, when suddenly I heard a cry: 'Sergey Sergeyevich!' and saw

Lidocka coming towards me. She was staying in a dacha with her married sister, was looking very pretty, and as soon as her sister left the two of us alone together she said all kinds of heartwarming things, that she had thought she might never see me again, that she was terribly happy to see me now, and so on. In her last letter she had written something very mysterious about us possibly seeing one another in Gurzuf, which was a very pleasing thought although I did not place much reliance on it. Now it transpired that if she did go to Gurzuf, which was in any case doubtful, it would not be before September. She was disappointed that I was going away this very day, especially as I only had a few hours to be with her before going back to St Petersburg to pack. I did not want to leave her either; I felt a strong desire to stay there with Lidochka, to kiss her, to marry her . . . but I was hard as flint and the seven o'clock train saw me on my way back to Petersburg. There I had to rush round like a madman getting my things together, packed both my cases, I hoped without forgetting anything, and caught the eleven o'clock express train to Moscow.

Zakharov was, I knew, also on his way there today to see the Grand Dukes. I had a flicker of hope that I might meet him on the train, but it was neither a very strong nor a particularly eager expectation.

25 July

At ten o'clock next morning, at half past ten local time, I was in Moscow. I had all the time in the world, until eight o'clock that evening, and nothing to do except see Derzhanovsky and play through *Maddalena* to him and to Saradzhev.

I drank a leisurely cup of coffee at the Nikolayevsky Station, having ascertained to my disgust that there was no chocolate to be had, and then took a tedious stopping train across town to the Kursk Station. I then occupied myself with writing my diary, first at the station and later in a pub, until three o'clock when I presented myself at Derzhanovsky's. As we did not have much to talk about I started to play *Maddalena* to him in expectation of Saradzhev's expected arrival at five o'clock. Hardly noticing what I was doing I played the entire opera to him. It seemed to be to his taste, and he said that when I had revised it, especially the vocal parts, it would be most suitable for production at the Free Theatre. Derzhanovsky himself has no specific relationship with the theatre, but he will be influential with Saradzhev and via Saradzhev, the theatre's principal conductor, on the management. Saradzehv himself did not hear the opera since I saw him only for five minutes when I called briefly on him.

As well as our discussion about the opera, Derzhanovsky had much to say about the chamber music concert he was arranging in November of works by Myaskovsky and myself. The performers would be the celebrated (as Derzhanovsky described him) cellist Beloúsov[1] (my *Ballade* and Myaskovsky's Sonata), Derzhanovsky's wife (Myaskovsky songs) and myself (Piano Sonata No. 2 and the Myaskovsky Sonata). Having to play the piano part in the Sonata for the cellist meant that in effect I would not be getting up from the piano stool all evening. It was all very interesting, but I was concerned about having the time to learn so much material. I suggested that Zakharov be the pianist for the Myaskovsky Sonata, but he (Derzhanovsky) is not an admirer of Zakharov's playing.

In connection with this concert I have to send Beloúsov my *Ballade*, but since the score is still in Petersburg and Mama is leaving tomorrow morning, Derzhanovsky and I rang Mama up. At first she was alarmed by a telephone call from Moscow, but when she calmed down we had a nice talk and everything was quite distinctly audible despite the six hundred versts that separated us.

At eight o'clock I boarded the Kislovodsk express which would enable me somewhere along the line to catch up the fast train to Sebastopol. I had supper and disposed myself for slumber, but for a time could not get off to sleep because of some kind of nervous condition that had started when I was in Royat. Nevertheless I was in good spirits.

26 July

Next morning my Kislovodsk express caught up the Sebastopol train at Kharkov, and as I had made an International Class reservation for that train, I transferred to it. Just as the train moved off I remembered that I had left my overcoat in the Kislovodsk train, so I had to telegraph the gendarmes, but all ended well as they undertook to retrieve the coat and send it on to Gurzuf.

Although the train was packed my International compartment was empty, the train crawled along in tandem with the hours of the day, and I was bored. Lacking anything else to do, I subjected my face to a close examination and discovered little creases under my eyes and at the corners of my mouth. I decided my face was losing its pristine freshness, generally I was feeling faded, and I must seriously attend to my physical condition. This winter I shall be assiduous in following my Sokol exercise regime, and before

---

1 Yevsey Beloúsov (1881–1945), cellist sonata partner of Alexander Borovsky, gave many first performances including Myaskovsky's First Cello Sonata. He left Russia in 1922 and settled in New York, where he continued to perform, becoming professor at the Juilliard School of Music.

that, this summer I shall go somewhere in the country and work in the fields from morning till night.

Towards evening we crawled into Alexandrovska, where thoughts of Max and our winter journey came into my mind. After that the carriage filled up with people and I lay down to sleep.

27 July

At eight o'clock the next morning we were in Sebastopol. I got myself a place in a five-seat motor car, and half an hour later was on my way to Yalta. My companion was a nice elderly lady, and we chatted happily all the way.

Exactly half a year ago I had covered this same route in the opposite direction, not in a car but in a horse-drawn cab, and with Max. Now Max's features and my memories of him did not leave me for an instant. As the remembered hills, ravines, the buildings, the twists and turns of the road passed before my eyes, I could not help clearly recalling all sorts of trivial details from these winter scenes: the grey scarves we were both wearing, the coachman's broad, ruddy back encased in his English overcoat, the subjects Max and I discussed. Here we had laughed until we cried at the vacuous expression of the cows chewing the cud; here we had shivered from the icy wind blowing off the mountains, when I was freezing cold and muffling myself in my scarf while Max twitted me for making such a fuss; here we had talked about the conflict with Boryusya; here was where the coachman had watered the horses and we had stopped up our noses because of the smell; that was the hill where Max had told me interesting facts about a battle between the Russian and English forces. And so it went on during the whole drive. The thoughts came crowding in one after the other of their own volition, and I could only struggle with the melancholy aspects they were bent on assuming.

The car soon arrived at the Baidar Gates, where we stopped briefly before continuing. The moment when the car comes through the gates and suddenly the boundless sea is spread out before one's eyes is certainly a memorable sight. In Alupka, which I found as attractive a place as I had done before, we dropped off a General in a steep, narrow street where there was no possibility of turning round, so we were forced to continue up the precipitous incline. Our progress attracted a crowd, we puffed and panted, hooted, all but slipped back down the slope, and it took us a good half-hour of awkward manoeuvring before we managed to break clear and press on towards Yalta. Our speed caused the axle to overheat, and the car filled with smoke just as we were approaching the entrance to Yalta, so my travelling companion and I did not linger getting out of the vehicle. Since this had occurred two steps away from her dacha she invited me in for a cup of tea while the car's problems were attended to. But the car proved to be beyond hope, so I got hold of a cab, put myself and my things into it, and went down to the pier. Here I boarded a steamer small enough to get quite severely tossed about by the waves, causing several of the ladies to turn pale and throw up over the side. But I successfully avoided paying my dues to the sea, and after an hour disembarked at Gurzuf. Accompanied by a porter staggering under the weight of my two cases I appeared at the door of Dacha No. 14, but nobody appeared to be at home. I had not been expected until the evening, and I had to wander about until I found the maid. Vera Nikolayevna was unwell and in bed, and the girls were out playing tennis. I left my luggage in the room I was told I would be sleeping in, and went to find the tennis players.

I was wearing my suit from Switzerland and a hat that came down low over my face. The girls, absorbed in their game, did not notice me and for about ten minutes I stood by the railings watching them before coming on to the court and greeting them. They were pleased, even excited, by my arrival; we went back to the dacha and after dinner visited the cinema. I was in the best of spirits, laughing and joking and talking all kinds of tomfoolery, and putting the whole company in a good mood.

28 July

A few words on the Meshchersky family. Vera Nikolayevna is an exceptionally interesting woman, clever, energetic and far from shallow. Coming from impoverished gentry stock near Malamo, she married Meshchersky, an engineer, and thanks to her brains and her husband's great abilities they carved out for themselves an outstanding career, so that Meshchersky now directs several factories and substantial enterprises, with an income of 150,000 roubles a year not counting what he rakes in from investments on the stock exchange. This spring the doctors discovered symptoms of tuberculosis in Vera Nikolayevna and recommended that she spend the summer months in the Crimea. All summer she has been ailing, and this has made her captious and irritable, so that not a day passes but she rounds angrily on her daughters, with Nina taking the brunt of her displeasure.

The elder daughter Talya is an interesting young woman of eighteen, slim, languorous and very good-looking. But it is the younger one, Nina, whom I prefer: small, with black eyebrows knitted together and a look of sly devilment in her eyes. Both daughters are good musicians and artists, so the piano was weighed down with piano reductions of Wagner and all the rooms were cluttered with tubes of paint.

Besides the host family several guests were staying; Vera Nikolayevna's sister and her daughter, both utter provincials; Oleg Subbotin, a young man-about-town of considerable charm; the artist Bobrovsky,[1] about thirty-five years of age with an air of prosperity and success about him, somewhat bored by life in Gurzuf, in whom Talya was obviously taking a romantic interest; Serge Bazavov, the girls' cousin, a delightful student on whom the affairs of the household had devolved by reason of Vera Nikolayevna's indisposition; and finally Yevdokia Silvestrovna, a close friend of Vera Nikolayevna.

The environment in which I found myself was as follows: a detached villa standing in the grounds of a beautiful State-owned park, the blue sea, brilliant moonlit nights, and Nina, who from the moment of my arrival was ready to come for walks with me and engage in all sorts of antics, for which she continually risked incurring the wrath of Vera Nikolayevna. For these three weeks I consciously idled, except for the forty minutes I devoted each day to learning the Concerto. I played some tennis, learned to play billiards, bathed and sunbathed, as a result of which my body turned first crimson, and after the skin peeled off acquired a nice brown tan.

The next day we went in a party for a walk up a nearby hill and there kicked up such a racket that we could be heard by Vera Nikolayevna sitting at home in the dacha. When we got back she read us a stern lecture that our bad behaviour was letting the side down.

In the evenings I often went out walking with Nina and her cousin Vera. Both girls made it clear they liked me, because Nina would exclaim: 'America is losing ground!' and Vera would chime in: 'So is Australia!' Evidently 'America' and 'Australia' were soubriquets of former romantic attachments.

I did not particularly care for Vera, but for Nina I certainly did. On one occasion she brought me her autograph album and asked me to write something in it. This is approximately what I wrote:

'The following is an account of events that took place in Gurzuf on 31 July 1913. "Bring me 'Rigaudon' this very instant," squealed Nina shrilly. Obedient to her command I brought the manuscript, played the piece, and enquired whether it would be a good piece to play as an encore at Pavlovsk, should the occasion demand it. "Don't bother, it's such rubbish!" Nina decided. "Nobody will like it anyhow." Ready always to bow to the enlightened opinions of great musicians, on this occasion too I tremblingly accepted the rebuke, and in order to acknowledge in a worthy manner my gratitude for this worthy judgement by presenting a worthy object, resolved to

---

1 Grigory Bobrovsky (1873–1942), a noted artist who had exhibited in numerous group shows since 1899. He won gold medals at the Munich Internationals of 1911 and 1913, and at this time was teaching at the St Petersburg Society for the Encouragement of the Arts.

dedicate "Rigaudon" (secretly, of course) to: "Ninochka Meshcherskaya".'

Nina's first reaction on reading this was to be angry, but later she was flattered by the dedication and even tried to play 'Rigaudon', although not quite managing to master it.

Five days after I got there, Talya's friend Nadya Planson came, a blonde girl to whom I had taken a fancy during the winter. She was now, it appeared, engaged to be married and the wedding would take place in two weeks' time.

2 August

Yesterday I agreed with Nadya Planson that we would go for an early morning walk: I would get up at half past seven and call for her in the next door dacha where she was staying. However, it was not yet seven when little pebbles began striking the door of my room, one after the other at regular intervals. I leapt out of bed, opened the door – and there was Nadya, standing and laughing. I called out to her that I would be ready in a moment, and hurried on some clothes, making such a noise that the maid came down from Vera Nikolayevna upstairs and asked me to be quieter. Somewhat abashed, and anticipating the wigging I would be getting later, I completed my toilet and set off with Nadya in the direction of the hills. We had a nice talk about Switzerland, about England, where Nadya had lived for some time, and about her forthcoming marriage. Finding a mountain lake we drank tea at a wayside hut (my God, what disorder compared with Switzerland!) and then came back down again, where we separated, Nadya to her dacha and I to go and bathe.

Vera Nikolayevna hired a boat, and we went to Suuk-Su, a quiet little place with a good hotel and restaurant about two versts from Gurzuf. While everyone was sitting around in the garden outside the hotel, Nina, Nadya and I went inside to inspect the interior arrangements.

On the way back some of us, myself included, sprawled out in the stern of the large boat, gently rocking to the rhythm of the waves as we sailed along. After dinner Vera Nikolayevna and I played a duet version of a Beethoven symphony (she is a useful pianist and over the time I was there we played all the Beethoven symphonies twice over), and I then went for a walk. Talya wanted to walk round the Tatar village at night, but had not been given permission to do so. Today, however, she got hold of me, and we stealthily slipped away. The villages stretched away up the hillsides, looking with their crooked little streets and strange-looking houses in the bright moonlight like illustrations from a fairy tale. Talya's artist heart responded, and she was in ecstasy.

When we came back home we found Nina slumped in the depths of an armchair on the veranda. She had a headache and looked down in the mouth. When I asked what had brought on her headache, she replied, 'I get them sometimes. Papa sometimes suffers for weeks on end with migraine. It's a degenerative disease. Later on it can turn to epilepsy.'

I sat on the arm of the chair and announced to the assembled company: 'Gentlemen, Ninochka is degenerating!'

When I went to my room, Nina appeared at the window. 'Good night,' she said.

I responded likewise.

'Kiss you,' she added, then blushed and quickly disappeared.

I found someone had sewn the blanket on my bed to the mattress. It took ages to unpick. A little present from Ninochka, I suppose.

3 August

They were getting ready for morning tea. I sat and read Chekhov's letters, inexhaustible in their humour, and then went for a swim, although the sea was not completely calm, the waves were running and someone was even drowned yesterday. On the beach I met Bobrovich, the tenor from the Conservatoire. He was very good company, seems to be having a wonderful time in Gurzuf, and was boasting about some girls who have come down from St Petersburg. I suggested that he organize an expedition for us all to go to Alupka: I wanted very much to go there, but could see that nothing was going to come of the idea with the stay-at-home Meshcherskys.

At lunch, everyone was very gay. I read out from one of Chekhov's letters a description of a menagerie in Naples, containing the following phrase: 'Seeing an octopus guzzle another animal is a truly revolting spectacle.' The expression was seized upon, and the moment someone started tucking into an appetizing morsel or stuffing a juicy water-melon into their mouth, there would be heard from the other end of the table, 'guz–z–zling octopus', the adjective being pronounced with noisy relish.

After lunch Nadya Planson finished off her portrait of Talya, a most successful likeness. I really liked this portrait and was always praising it. Planson suggested that I sit for a study she wanted to make of me. I agreed readily, but the sketch proved to be no good; I could not recognize myself at all.

Myaskovsky wrote to me praising my Second Piano Concerto to the skies and calling it a classic. I was very pleased with this and told Nadya all about Tcherepnin, whom she knows. Nadya listened avidly, laughing with all her heart.

4 August

Today is Yevdokia Silvestrovna's name day, so there were flowers, champagne and caviare. Even I was dragged into presenting her with flowers, even though my only relationship with her has been one of crossing swords. Planson was always asking me to play something for her, and as she is very nice, after lunch I sat down at the piano and began to play her the Second Piano Concerto, and before I knew what I was doing had played the whole of the first movement. After that, by popular request I played the other three movements. To my great surprise, the Concerto was a great success, and everyone now goes about humming the opening theme. Nina said she wanted to paint my portrait. I sat for her, Nina opened all her tubes of paint, assumed an expression of great seriousness, and started to paint. For an hour and a half I was forced to sit quite still, not even being allowed to read Chekhov's letters. Nina has the most marvellous teeth. After an hour and a half, when Nina allowed me my freedom, I glanced at the canvas and saw such an idiot staring back at me that I got quite angry. Nina pacified me, saying that it was still only a sketch and all the detail would come later.

Released from my obligations as a model, I joyfully immersed myself once again in Chekhov's letters, and was thrilled to find in them a note of Tchaikovsky's visit to him,[1] by which Chekhov had been very flattered.

Nadya Planson finished her excellent portrait of Talya. Once again I complimented her on it, and declared that she must now rehabilitate herself, so far as I was concerned, by making another study of me, more successful than yesterday's. She said she would not have time to do this before leaving, but if I came to see her this winter she would paint my portrait properly.

After dinner the whole company decided to take a boat out to sea. The scene was one of great loveliness: the moon hiding itself behind beautiful clouds, the sea steel grey and mirror smooth. We all gaily piled into the boat, and pushed off, our two oarsmen enthusiastically propelling us into open sea. The village of Gurzuf glittered as a terrace of lights, while in the distance far out to sea the big ferry steamed past on its way to Batum. I lay back, comfortably propping my head on Talya's knees and let my hand trail in the warm water. We attempted a sing-song, combining the tune from *Meistersinger* with 'Toreador'. This is not as easy at it sounds: we made mistakes and sang out of tune, but after a few goes it began to work. A street cry I used to hear in Terioki: 'Stur–r–r–geon from the Vol–l–l–ga!' that for some reason I blurted out in the boat made everyone laugh, but Vera Nikolayevna at that moment recollected herself and through her laughter told us all to behave

---

1 In October 1889, when Chekhov asked for and received permission to dedicate his story 'Gloomy People' to Tchaikovsky.

ourselves. While we were walking back from the sea to the dacha, all the young ones broke away and ran as fast as they could.

Tired, I went to bed. I sat at the open door of my room, my soul at peace, and looked at the moon, the sky and the scudding clouds, drinking in the stillness of the night.

5 August

Nina and I smiled at one another as we passed; there was no trace of yesterday's capriciousness. The morning passed in bathing, playing the piano and reading Chekhov's letters. After lunch, Talya and Nadya sat opposite one another and took turns sketching each other's portrait. Nina abandoned yesterday's attempt to get my likeness and decided to sketch my profile in charcoal. An hour's work produced a rather grubby portrait, but a good likeness. At tea Nina once again repeated what she had said before, something along the lines of: 'Of course, you are a very nice young man, but you don't inspire the kind of feelings that "America" did!' I got angry at this, turned my back on Nina and during the walk that followed ignored her. We had our photograph taken as a group in various poses, and I always contrived to be at the opposite end of the group from Nina. When the photos came out, you could see the furious expressions we both had on our faces. After that I went home to practise the piano, returning after some time with Bobrovsky to rejoin the rest of the company on the beach and fool about with them. This was to be Nadya's last evening with us; early tomorrow morning she leaves for Sebastopol to be married.

6 August

Today was in comparison a bit flat. Nadya Planson had left, also Alexey Pavlovich,[1] Nina and I were having a row which went on all day. In the morning I followed my usual routine of bathing, practising the piano and reading Chekhov's letters. All the sunbathing I have been doing is making my skin peel off and my body itch all over. After lunch I performed a disappearing act and went to visit Bobrovich. He was very nice and I much enjoyed the time I spent with him. After tea I stayed at his place continuing work on the Concerto.

We went for a walk: Talya, Nina, Bobrovsky and I, Oleg staying behind to develop the photographs taken yesterday. Talya was sulky, having received a ticking-off; Nina was pouting, in a bate with me; 'Uncle Grisha'[2] also had

---

1 Nina Meshcherskaya's father, a captain of industry known in some quarters as 'the Russian Ford'.
2 The artist Grigory Bobrovsky.

something on his mind and was not his usual ebullient self. Sitting on a bench with them I looked at the three scowling profiles and started to laugh, but all the same it was not much fun. Later on, however, at eleven o'clock at night when everyone had been packed off to bed, Oleg and I stole off to the seaside, to the profound envy of the girls. We walked along the beach and talked all kinds of irrelevant nonsense. Oleg is a dear, an extremely nice young man.

7 August

For a long time I had had a plan to go to Alupka, a place I had liked ever since my winter journey with Max, and I had talked Oleg into coming with me. Today we decided to put our plan into operation. Setting out at eleven o'clock we tussled with each other at *Sechsundsechzig* until we got to Yalta, and then looked at the lovely shoreline. The view of Alupka is especially beautiful, but the place itself is also a delight, much more attractive than Gurzuf although it seemed rather deserted (perhaps because it was the lunch hour). While we were having lunch we sent an urgent telegram to Talya and Nina:

> We're here in Alupka, enjoying the view,
> How sad, oh my doves, that we're here without you!

After our meal we felt a little sleepy and went to play billiards, because in Gurzuf it is always very crowded and one has to wait for ages to get a turn. Cautiously enquiring how much it would cost if we were to tear a cloth (25 roubles) we began to play. Unfortunately we got completely absorbed and went on for two hours, leaving only an hour to look round Alupka. But that proved to be enough, since at five o'clock there were not many people about.

We went all round the park, and I recalled with uncanny clarity all the avenues and shops Max and I had visited in January. Then we took the steamer back to Yalta, which presented a totally different scene, throngs of well-dressed people, lots of pretty faces, and we had a pleasant time of it walking along the promenade, the beach and the park.

The last part of the journey back from Yalta to Gurzuf was a delectable trip in a very skittish cab by the light of the rising moon. I felt a great yearning to travel, far away, to America, round the world . . .

When we arrived back at the dacha everyone was sitting down having evening tea, and the conversation was lively. I am still not speaking to Nina, an attitude she reciprocates.

8 August

After lunch Talya thought she would like to make a portrait of me in oils, which I agreed to sit for. Nina stalked about with a cross look on her face, unapproachably keeping herself to herself. Oleg and I cleave to Talya, Talya to Bobrovsky – and Serge to everyone. Nina cried, 'Oh, how I wish Sasha would come soon!' Sasha is a cadet, the brother of Vera who departed today, and he is expected in the next day or two.

In the evening the whole company went to play billiards, where there was a mass of people of all shades and classes, including a hairdresser. Vera Nikolayevna played with Bobrovsky, not without a certain style. Afterwards Talya, Nina, Oleg and I went down to the sea, I arm in arm with Talya singing in counterpoint with her, having spent part of the day explaining the rudiments of this art to her. When at eleven o'clock we all went to bed, I deftly pocketed the cards from the table, a ruse that enabled us (Oleg, Serge and me) to play vint in my bedroom until 2 a.m. I have not played for a long time, and enjoyed myself hugely. After two o'clock struck we stood up, straightened our backs and stretched our numbed limbs. Oleg went off to his dacha, Serge and I to our beds, only to hear before long a cautious tapping at the door. It was Oleg, who had not been able to get into his house and who had come back to sleep on the sofa in ours.

9 August

At half past eight, still bleary-eyed from lack of sleep, but casting knowing glances at one another, we went in to tea. Vera Nikolayevna suspected nothing. The girls, to whom we had whispered hints about our 'gambling den', were indignant but consumed by secret envy.

After a subdued lunch, I posed for Talya. Nina sat down at the piano and played a Rachmaninov song, 'How fair this spot',[1] that I had brought back from Yalta. I went over to her and corrected a wrong chord she had played. She had not expected this and in a hoarse voice asked, 'What?' I showed her where the mistake was and went away.

Sasha arrived this evening. At tea I argued with him about everything, teased and provoked him and told him all sorts of ridiculous cock-and-bull stories that he believed. Everyone laughed except Sasha, who said not a word. Nina, sizing up the situation, said coldly to her cousin, 'Well, you don't seem to have got any cleverer than you were!'

After eleven o'clock we again played vint, this time with Sasha making a fourth. We went on until three o'clock, fortified by a delicious watermelon

---

1 No. 7 from Op. 21 (1902).

that Oleg had craftily purloined from the kitchen. Oleg stayed on the sofa again.

10 August

Our appearance next morning was met with icy reproof from Vera Nikolayevna, to whom the walls and doors had carried information about our nocturnal misbehaviour. The cards were confiscated and vint forbidden. Talya smirked, seeing Serge's ashen face.

In the evening I took Nina's arm and asked her if she would like to come for a walk. She at once said she would, but Oleg attached himself to us and rather inhibited the occasion, two being company where three is none. The moment of reconciliation after a long-drawn-out quarrel would have been delicious, had Nina and I been on our own, but in the circumstances it was just an ordinary walk. A pity, a great pity!

We visited a skittle alley and then returned home. At tea Nina suddenly came out of her shell and became happy, laughing and chattering with all and sundry. Tea was a rowdy, boisterous affair, just like old times.

11 August

In the cool of the evening we walked along an avenue of cypresses. Nina and I peeled off to go to the sea, and after walking some distance sat on a big boulder jutting out into the water, the waves rolling in around us and every so often splashing us. She was wilful and coquettish, and we became so absorbed in one another that we forgot the time until we realized we would be late for dinner, and then had to run fast. By the time we got back we were in a somewhat dishevelled state, and received a stern ticking-off from Vera Nikolayevna, while the others teased us relentlessly about our flushed cheeks and disarranged hair.

12 August

Went swimming in very rough waves, holding on to a rope and continually getting struck from behind by waves and stones. Later we went to the billiard hall to see Sasha (by his own account the best player in Yekaterinoslav) take on the hairdresser (the champion of Gurzuf). The contest had to be kept secret from Vera Nikolayevna, who could never in her life have contemplated the thought of her nephew playing against a hairdresser. Sasha was defeated, to our enormous satisfaction.

Today a tennis competition had been planned for the summer dacha visitors, but the Englishman who was making the arrangements got sunstroke and the whole thing collapsed. To my regret, I did not make use of Gurzuf's amenities for this noble sport. Oleg and I did once make an attempt, but we were terrible, everyone laughed at us, it was baking hot in the sun, and we dropped it.

At dinner Nina received a packet of letters that clearly upset her. We joked that if letters were the cause of the upset they ought properly to be described as laxatives.[1] On the presumption that the letters were in some way related to her former romance, I decided to make peace and behave towards her in a calm and friendly way: I even lent her my fountain pen to write her reply with.

When everyone went to bed, Oleg and I on the pretext of finishing our game of *Sechsundsechzig* took the cards down to our rooms and there set up a session of *vingt et un*. We started in the approved way with stakes of 20 kopecks, but ended up with gold pieces and banknotes. Early on I won 35 roubles, but at the end was a mere 10 roubles up. Serge lost an equivalent amount, Oleg also lost, but the most annoying part of it was that Sasha won 28 roubles!

13 August

After dinner we lolled around in the garden, occupied like boa-constrictors in digesting what we had just consumed. I made a serious but unsuccessful attempt to persuade people to come for a walk, but in the end only Nina and I went, which was of course the most delightful possible outcome. She wanted to see what a whisky and soda was like, so while she waited on the garden seat I went into the drawing room and asked for half a bottle of soda, poured two glasses of whisky into it, and hiding it under my jacket went back to Nina. Under cover of the darkness of the avenue we drank, I enjoying every mouthful, Nina spluttering with disgust and protesting that the precious fluid tasted of salty, soapy water.

We got into terrible trouble from Vera Nikolayevna for our unchaperoned walk, while our whisky-tasting session, when it reached the ears of the young people, caused a sensation. When everyone dispersed for the night I played chess with Oleg on a board the factor had brought from Yalta, and won the game although it was not an easy victory.

In bed I was exasperated with myself for the stupid way my relationship with Nina had played out in the course of the day. I felt diminished in my own eyes, kept waking up during the night, and suffered a thorough lowering of the spirits.

---

1   The Russian word for 'disorder' or 'upset' is also used colloquially for 'diarrhoea'.

14 August

The morning passed uneventfully. At lunch Vera Nikolayevna sharply remonstrated with the girls for their behaviour, calling them 'guttersnipes', which caused them no little distress. In the autumn they are to be put under the charge of a strict English governess. After tea in the afternoon Serge, Oleg and I went riding. Serge's mount was a fiery thoroughbred, Oleg was on a skewbald and mine was an elderly little grey. Our departure attracted quite a crowd. I mounted my horse in the most inexpert way, while Serge's thoroughbred was restive and shot away champing at the bit, Oleg and I at full pelt in pursuit. No misadventures befell us on the way to Suuk-Su, but we got tremendous pleasure from the ride. The return of the ungainly equestrians was awaited with great curiosity, but we arrived back in good order and avoided falling flat on our faces.

After dinner Vera Nikolayevna and I played through the Ninth Symphony right to the end. Later in the evening we laid out patience and played chess.

15 August

An hour after finishing lunch I went to bathe, and on the way back looked in on the somewhat disorganized boat races that had been arranged on account of today being a local holiday. The whole town had come out because of the holiday, and in the park there were a concert and games.

After dinner Vera Nikolayevna and I executed Beethoven's Eighth Symphony, and then we all gathered on the terrace with nothing particular to do. 'You could at least go for a walk,' remarked Vera Nikolayevna.

'Yekaterina Nikiforovna!!' I hollered.

Yekaterina Nikiforovna (or Fyodorovna) was the housekeeper, and since the day before yesterday when Nina and I had been scolded for disappearing on our own for the whole evening, it had been decreed that our walks must be chaperoned by the housekeeper. But today this duty was entrusted to Uncle Grisha Bobrovsky or, as we young ones called him behind his back, simply Grishka. We went to see the firework display, but had hardly got as far as the beach when we came to a quick agreement with Uncle Grisha where and when we would rendezvous to go back to the dacha, and paired off to go in different directions, I of course with Nina.

16 August

Nina grizzled that she could not come to my concert, which she very much wanted to. I said that it did not matter, as there would be plenty of other girls to take her place.

Lunch was accompanied by a lively discussion about a billiards contest today. I said I considered I was now good enough to play matches with the 'grown-ups', for instance with Nina. I don't know why this notion had not occurred to me before, but now it was deeply interesting to me and to Nina. We excitedly made plans, and having secured permission from on high, set out for the billiard hall as soon as lunch was over. I told Nina the stakes we were playing for would be kisses; she did not protest. I played better than usual today, twice winning a game with a particularly effective winning stroke and so being awarded a kiss from Nina.

After tea everyone else went for a walk but I stayed behind to practise the Concerto as yesterday I had not practised at all and the date of the performance was now getting very close. After an hour I went to find the rest of the party walking in the avenue of cypress trees and Nina, who was missing me, at once proposed a wager; was that the Hippopotamus sitting on a bench down there, or was it not? ('Hippopotamus' was the nickname I had bestowed on Serge, which everyone now called him.) Since I knew for certain that he was still at home, I readily agreed to the wager (also for a kiss, whereby those 'lost' at billiards might be reclaimed) and thus won a second round. Nina, to my huge delight, exclaimed, 'Oho, "America", you're losing ground!'

My triumph is complete.

17 August

Although the boat sailed early in the morning, everyone got up to come down to the pier to see me off. I was leaving along with the cadet Sashka, who was on his way to Yekaterinoslav. Bobrovich came as well. At last the steamer docked, the cadet and I embarked with our luggage, and we were borne away from hospitable Gurzuf. For a long time we waved our handkerchiefs and hats.

The boat rolled, but not very much. Passing the *Standard*, the Tsar's splendid yacht, we dropped anchor at Yalta where we transferred to the larger steamer bound for Batum. The first-class areas were jam-packed with people; there was not a seat to be had on any of the benches on deck; it was hot and sticky and exhausting. I ate some lunch and then went up to the bow, where at least there was a breeze, but even here it was swarming with passengers. I climbed up on to a pile of ropes, and comfortably coiled up watched the coastline slide past. All the time I was thinking of Max, and a shadow of melancholy clouded my thoughts. I dozed for a while, and awoke refreshed.

We rounded the southern tip of the Crimean peninsula. The coastline, bare of vegetation, plunged abruptly into the sea. Nearer to Sebastopol the coast was lower and flatter; although there was still no flora to grace it, the bright sun and the blue sea combined to soften its unwelcoming aspect. We entered the bay, and passing a line of naval vessels, tied up at the port. It took an eternity to unload and disembark, after which we took a cab and went straight to the railway station. There were three hours to wait until the train left; the cadet went off to wander about on his own and I, glad to be relieved of his company, ordered a drink and settled down to write to Vera Nikolayevna to thank her for her hospitality at Gurzuf. After six o'clock we were allowed to board the train, at which point I discovered to my horror that my compartment was already occupied by two ladies and, not only that, but they had spread themselves and their belongings all over the entire compartment, the seats, the luggage racks, with an assortment of parcels, packages, umbrellas and baskets of fruit. I was transported with rage, did battle for my space, which I eventually cleared, and then departed for the restaurant car, staying there until late at night – much to the relief of the ladies, who presumably thought I had stayed behind in Sebastopol.

At Simferopol I walked up and down the platform, thinking that perhaps I might meet someone I knew from my winter travels with Max. But this hope, of course, remained unfulfilled.

18 August

Next morning I was in Kharkov and saw Nina and Zina Reberg,[1] whom I had alerted by postcard to my arrival. We had a few minutes' lively conversation, but the train did not wait long and we soon had to be off again. By midnight I was already tired of travelling. When we got to Moscow, I walked up and down the platform in the hope of seeing Myaskushka, who was staying with Derzhanovsky and to whom I had written suggesting he travel back to St Petersburg on the same train as me. But as I later discovered, my letter did not arrive in time, and so I returned to my compartment and left Moscow regretting that there was no Myaskuna to cheer me up. But at least the ladies got out in Moscow, and that was all to the good. I slept soundly all night.

19 August

Arrived in St Petersburg feeling on top of the world and settled into the empty Rayevsky apartment, that is to say empty except for a servant whose presence alleviated the feeling of a completely deserted household that our own apartment would have induced. I changed my clothes and went to play my Concerto to Aslanov. I am not convinced that he understood the music, but he said that it was not a difficult work to conduct, and generally took a favourable attitude to it. 'But oh! what a pianist we've lost in you!' he cried.

---

1 Two of the three daughters of Dr Reberg, doctor, family friend and neighbour from Sontsovka.

I asked why he would say that. Either I play well, in which case the world has not lost a pianist; or I don't, when it follows that I am not a good pianist hence there is no loss to regret. He explained that what he meant was, I am so burdened with my composing and conducting activities I do not have the time to perfect my keyboard technique, and as a result my capabilities as a pianist suffer from being insufficiently cultivated.

For the performance of *Dreams* we lack a fifth and sixth horn and a second harp. Perhaps it would be better to postpone it until next summer? My answer was that I preferred to perform it now, and would pay for the necessary extra instrumentalists.

Returning home, I telephoned Umnenkaya. Her sister answered, and she invited me to visit them in Kuokkale. I said I would come out in a day or two.

20 August

Rose at eight and went to Pervaya Rota to work on the Concerto, the piano at Sergievskaya Street being so antediluvian it is impossible to practise on it. The Concerto is definitely coming together! I also learned some encore pieces: the Harp Prelude, so as to astonish the audience with C major after all the harmonic imbroglio of the Concerto; the Etude No. 4, and Nina's 'Rigaudon'. Visited Myaskovsky, who came back today from Moscow, and played through the Concerto with him on two pianos in Shreder's shop, after which we went to dine at the 'Vienna' restaurant. I found it easy to relax in the company of my dear Kolechka.

In the evening I went to Pavlovsk to hear the concert devoted to the works of Tchaikovsky. Saw Clavdia Sheintsvit[1] and her charming sister. Revelled in Tchaikovsky's Sixth Symphony and went into ecstasies over its closing pages, their sonority and the expressivity of their mood. I issued a proclamation: 'Down with dryness in music!'

Met Karatygin and told him I have become more conservative and am now an aficionado of Tchaikovsky.

21 August

Today is the day of the first rehearsal, so I rose early and went to Pavlovsk, calling for Myaskovsky on the way.

After a boring suite by Kazachenko,[2] rehearsed under the baton of the elderly but pleasant-looking composer, it was time for my Concerto. I advanced gleefully on the piano waiting on the platform with its lid open. I

---

1 The 'Pillow'.
2 Grigory Kazachenko (1858–1938), composer and (mainly choral) conductor.

adore the concert grand piano, standing so fair and ceremonious on the stage in front of the orchestra! But first, and quite properly, Aslanov wanted to go through the Concerto with the orchestra alone. It sounds good, as I envisaged it, and the orchestra also managed it pretty well without too many wrong notes. Having played through the piece from beginning to end, Aslanov then repeated it with me playing the solo part. The weather was not hot, and it was quite cool inside the hall; the piano was damp and my fingers were stiff. Because of the cold the left hand muffed the accompaniment at the beginning. In the middle of the first movement I could barely manage the octaves, and I could hear nothing of what was going on in the orchestra. We left out the cadenza and proceeded straight to the Scherzo. To my surprise and delight, Aslanov asked for a slower tempo, saying it would sound better like that. The violin harmonics in the trio squeal and drag; they should have the piccolo added to them. In the Intermezzo I was nervous about getting lost in the innumerable modulations, but went wrong only once, which I found very reassuring. The leaps in the Finale were very fleet, but the second half of the movement was not so good.

The rehearsal over, Aslanov and Myaskovsky proffered all kinds of advice about details; Myaskovsky's for the most part sensible, Aslanov's for the most part not. All three of us travelled back to St Petersburg together in the train, except that I stopped off at Tsarskoye and went to try to find Volodya Deshevov, which I succeeded in doing after a certain amount of effort. He was as nice as ever; he had not written to me because he had been going through a period of internal struggle with himself on religious issues, but he was now more settled in mind and also more cheerful. I found it very attractive that he was a prey to struggles of this kind.

Returning to St Petersburg I went to Pervaya Rota to practise there. Wrote out the opening of a Concertino for violin, an idea that had occurred to me the previous evening. It is a beautiful, tender theme that gives me much pleasure. In the evening I had intended to visit Myaskushka, but he was going out somewhere else and I spent the evening in the Sergievskaya Street flat, enjoying myself writing up my Gurzuf diary. It is clear to me that Nina (Fyaka[1]) is pursuing me.

22 August

There is no rehearsal today and I was on the point of going out to Kuokkale, when I was surprised by a telephone call from Umnenkaya who, it appeared, had moved back to St Petersburg. This is a shame; I should have liked to see her in Kuokkale. We had a long talk, but without any endearments. Lidochka

---

1 Prokofiev's private nickname for Nina Meshcherskaya.

promised to come to my concert tomorrow. I dined with the Andreyevs, who were heart-warmingly affectionate and kind, so that I felt myself to be among old friends. We reminisced much about Paris and London; I told them about Switzerland and particularly enjoyed relating my time in Gurzuf.

Anna Grigorievna happened to mention a mutual acquaintance with the Meshcherskys, one Zaitsev, 'who is by no means indifferent to Nina'. He is in Terioki at the moment. At this moment the penny suddenly dropped and I realized that this gentleman was none other than Nina's 'America'. He had been staying at Gurzuf just before me, and I had seen his portrait, painted by Nina, hanging in Serge's room. I had met Zaitsev at the Meshcherskys last spring: a small, dark man of around thirty. So this is 'America'! This is the man who stands in my way! I left the Andreyevs, my head reeling from the discovery.

Sat with Myaskovsky and with his kind and experienced help made a number of corrections to the score and parts of the Concerto, the need for which had surfaced during yesterday's rehearsal.

23 August

Went to the rehearsal again with Myaskovsky, and we were joined at Tsarskoye by Volodya Deshevov. I was stupid enough to travel without an overcoat; it was unbearably cold and before going on to play I warmed up with gymnastics and a glass of rowanberry vodka. I asked Aslanov to make more of a pause before the second movement: after the exhausting cadenza it is physically impossible to go straight on and play the even more demanding Scherzo. The tempo of the Scherzo was not too fast, and they took it, as Myaskovsky recommended, absolutely *piano*. Thanks to this, the Scherzo went without problems. The Finale went better than yesterday.

Returning home after the rehearsal I made various corrections to the orchestral parts, sitting with Myaskovsky, who offered me coffee. Dressed in tails, at a quarter to seven I was at Tsarskoye station to join the group going from there to hear me in the concert. Lida and Zoya were there, but Boris Zakharov, who as I heard had also intended to be part of the company, wasn't; he would come by a later train with the Hansen sisters: Tilya, the famous violinist, and Frieda, the former object of my affections. It was a pity they were not coming out with us.

In Pavlovsk I met the Andreyevs, Deshevov, the 'Pillow' and her sister, and many musicians whom I knew. The concert began with Kazachenko's Suite; everyone piled into the hall except me; I strolled around the deserted grounds waiting until it was time for me to go on. Was I nervous? In the fullest sense of the word – no, but it would of course not be true to claim that I was completely relaxed. I went into the artists' room, where I found

Andreyev talking to somebody; he had come in to help calm my nerves. Aslanov was rubbing his hands with glee because so many critics and musicians had come today. Just before going on, I was handed a telegram. I was amazed, it came from Serge, my Gurzuf friend, writing from Oryol to regret his inability to attend the concert. This cheered me up no end.

At this point an attendant came to inform me that Aslanov had already been on the podium for some time, so I hurried on to the stage, my entrance being greeted with applause. I was quite calm at the beginning of the Concerto, but in the middle of the cadenza began to lose my nerve, and went wrong in the *colossalo*. In fact it sounded fine, but the truth is I was improvising whole passages rather than playing exactly what I had written. There was some applause at the end of the first movement, so I got up and bowed. Aslanov, as I had requested, made a long pause between the first and second movements, smoothed down his hair, wiped his nose, and eventually under cover of his handkerchief smiled at me and asked if it was all right to continue. I inclined my head. The Scherzo began at quite a slow tempo and was easy to play, and following Myaskovsky's advice I played the whole thing *pianissimo*. In the trio I again became nervous and made mistakes, but after running up and down some chromatic scales instead of my written passages I quickly got back on track, so that nobody noticed the blunder. I was extremely worried in the Intermezzo that I might modulate to a tonality I did not mean to, and indeed this did happen, resulting in a highly disagreeable moment when I heard the orchestra coming in in a different key to the one I had landed on. Nevertheless I quickly managed to extricate myself, and in the Finale I was quite calm and it went better.

Following the violent concluding chord there was silence in the hall for a few moments. Then, boos and catcalls were answered with loud applause, thumping of sticks and calls for 'encore'. I came out twice to acknowledge the reception, hearing cries of approval and boos coming from the hall. I was pleased that the Concerto provoked such strong feelings in the audience. I was presented with a large laurel wreath with blue ribbons, which delighted me. Coming back for the third time, I played the 'Harp' Prelude as an encore, again greeted by a mixture of applause and catcalls. I then played the Etude No. 4, with the same response. Everything soon quietened down and I opened the envelope pinned to the wreath, nothing having been inscribed on the blue ribbons. Inside the envelope was an amateur snapshot and there looking at me were all the dear faces of my friends from the Gurzuf dacha. I was very touched.

At that moment the Andreyevs appeared in the dressing room, and hardly had I passed them the photograph to look at when in rushed Lida and Zoya wth Volodya Deshevov, followed by a crowd of the 'Contemporaries'[1] with

---

1 People connected with the Evenings of Contemporary Music in St Petersburg.

Karatygin at their head, all expressing their delight and congratulations. Asafyev, Myaskovsky and Aslanov came in and all were full of praise. I apologized to Aslanov for the trouble I had caused and thanked him for his accompaniment, and we kissed. He said that someone had just come rushing up to him angrily muttering, 'Thank you very much, but you're welcome to keep that!'

I went outside. The Hansen sisters came up to speak to me, but Zakharov did not appear and this upset me. There was no sign of Umnenkaya either. The Karneyevs beckoned me back into the hall to listen to *Sheherezade*; clearly they wanted to be seen with me as the hero of the evening. At the end of *Sheherezade* the audience began streaming out through the exits and at that moment we bumped into Zakharov and the Hansens. I greeted Zakharov, our two groups exchanged a few words, and then we moved on. Before long Deshevov joined Lida, Zoya and me, and we went to the buffet for a light supper, after which on the train going back we found ourselves in the same carriage as Zakharov and his girls. We were sitting not far away from them, and the girls exchanged a few words, but then each group talked among themselves and paid no attention to the other. For some reason Lida moved to another spot, Zoya went to sit behind her and Volodya behind her, leaving me alone. I then turned to the Hansens and said, 'Perhaps you wouldn't mind if I came and sat with you?'

The response was: 'Please do', and they all moved up to make room for me. Zakharov immediately addressed me with exceptionally flattering comments about the Concerto. I really had not expected him to like it so much. General conversation ensued all the way to Petersburg. Arriving, we said goodbye and started out along the street, I arm in arm with Lida and Zoya. At the Zagorodny we looked back and saw that behind us was a likewise configured group of Zakharov with the two Hansens. We hallooed to them, and they asked where we were going, to which we replied that we were going to look in at my apartment, where I was going to change out of my tails, and then I was going to take them to Vasilievsky Island to stay the night with their friend.

'But what if she can't have them to stay?' asked Zakharov. 'What will you do then? I'd better come with you, otherwise I won't rest easy. But I must take Tilya and Frieda home first.'

I said, 'You take them, then, and afterwards come back to me, we'll wait for you there. No. 4, Pervaya Rota.'

This was decided upon, and the Karneyev girls and I went to Pervaya Rota. The concierge, woken from his slumbers, looked askance at the two women I was bringing home at one in the morning. We went up to the empty flat, where the electricity was not working, and all the illumination we had between us was a single candle end which we stuck in a milk jug.

Summoning a taxi by telephone, I left the girls in the drawing room and hurried to change my clothes in my own room. I had hardly managed to throw off all my clothes when Zakharov arrived.

'Today is a good day for me,' he said. 'I'm once again in your home!'

'Yes,' I replied, looking at him.

He stretched out his hand to me and said, 'Well then, Seryozha, let us forget all that has passed between us!'

We kissed one another, and from the next room there were cries of joy from the girls at our reconciliation. Going out to the street we all piled in to the car. Lida had developed a headache, Zoya was complaining of toothache, Zakharov also said his head hurt, and I was the only one to feel completely happy and content. We took the girls to Vasilievsky Island and then found ourselves alone in the car.

'We shall long remember the 23rd August, Seryozha!' said Zakharov.

In answer I gripped his hand. He told me that he would be leaving Piter in two weeks' time for the whole of the winter and was going to study in Vienna. I expressed regret, but was not in fact too upset: for me the spiritual connection between us is more important than the physical companionship of frequent meetings. We spent the time on the way to his house talking about Vienna. Tomorrow Lida, Zoya and I are going out to Terioki, and we decided we would all go together with Borya.

Well satisfied, I returned home. It was almost three o'clock.

24 August

Usually I sleep well, but last night, after the emotional excitements of yesterday, less so. Next morning I went out to buy newspapers, but there was only one review, in the *Petersburg Listok* – a mixture of good and bad.

The weather was fine and I walked in the Tauride Gardens, and enjoyed writing a detailed account to Nina Meshcherskaya of the previous evening's performance. Then I went by car to collect Lida and Zoya and took them to the Finland Station. It was already after three o'clock and the evening papers were out, so we looked at the reviews in the car. Boryusya joined us at the station. We are cautious with one another; the simplicity of our former relations has not yet been fully re-established.

That evening in Terioki we all went out together in a party.

25 August

Everyone always sleeps late at the Karneyevs, and so it was eleven o'clock before we had our coffee. Emerging into the outside world we saw Zakharov's sister's husband, who called out to us that there was a wonderful review in *Rech*. We hurried off to the station to buy the papers, and there encountered Zakharov, who had come to meet Myaskovsky. Myaskovsky was late, so we spent the time reading a whole crop of concert reviews. Karatygin, in *Rech*, gave praise with his customary forthrightness. The *Petersburg Gazette* had an amusingly written article, which I liked very much. We had fun collectively reading the German newspaper, expecting Lida and Zoya as former students of the Peterschule to be expert translators, but they pleaded that although they could understand the drift of what was being said, they could not translate word for word.

The whole noisy entourage went home, meeting on the way the Alpers family, who are also living in Terioki. I bowed my greetings to them.

In the afternoon we played croquet at the Zakharovs' and had tea there. And so, once again I am in this dacha! The whole family was very nice to me, especially Luiza Alexeyevna, the wife of Boris's elder brother, who seemed to be giving a cordial welcome to my reconciliation with Boris. In the evening we went to the cinema. Boris and I tied to our legs, underneath our trousers, the kind of little bells dogs wear on their collars. Tinkling away in the darkness of the cinema, we loudly expressed our concern that there might be a dog somewhere who would be crushed in the crowd. Some of the audience worried in sympathy, others got angry at the interruption. We were highly amused.

26 August

Next morning, Zoya and I walked in marvellous weather as far as Kolomyagi,[1] while she regaled me with all kinds of silly stories. We came back from Kolomyagi by train, and at five o'clock I returned to Petersburg on the train, seen off by Borya and both Karneyev sisters. I called in at Pervaya Rota, where I found a little note from Nina: 'Without you all is quiet and sad . . .'

In the evening I went to see Myaskushka. The 'Sergey Koussevitzky Concert Bureau' had sent me an official invitation to appear in a performance of my First Piano Concerto at their public concert on 16 February. This is exactly how Koussevitzky made the offer to me when I saw him in the spring. This marvellous news justified my confidence at the time that my concerto would go down well, and that it would open the door to the Koussevitzky concerts.

---

1 Village, then in open country but now a suburb, to the north of St Petersburg.

27 August

In the morning I worked at Pervaya Rota and revised the 'March' for Op. 12. The 'March' had been composed five years ago and dedicated to Morolyov, and in its day used to have great success under its title of 'Morolyov's March'. Then it disappeared, only to resurface when it came unexpectedly to mind at Gurzuf, where again it was heard to general approbation. Now, by adding some spicy harmonies and incorporating an episode I had composed recently, I had a completely new piece, moreover one that gave me much pleasure. I shall include it in Op. 12 in place of the E minor Etude, which is still far from ready.

At six o'clock I was at Myaskovsky's, who had summoned me by telephone because of the unexpected arrival from Moscow of Saradzhev. At their request I took with me *Maddalena* and the Second Piano Concerto. I was particularly anxious to play *Maddalena* to Saradzhev, the Free Theatre's principal conductor. However much Myaskovsky and Derzhanovsky kept up the pressure, any decision to produce the opera would in the end depend mainly on Saradzhev.

Maddalena produced an impression on him, although there was a lot of it he did not understand. But he was not impressed by the vocal aspects of the music. I objected that since I was well aware that all the opera's vocal parts needed comprehensively recomposing, he should not be misled by their present form. The Concerto he liked very much indeed. As we walked back from Myaskovsky's he took my arm in a friendly manner and offered me the position of assistant conductor of the Free Theatre. Without either agreeing or declining, I attempted to find out how much work the position would entail. 'That is difficult to say with any precision . . .'

'But some idea, all the same: three hours a day, or six, or ten?'

Even six would be too much, because it would encroach on my composing activities. The likelihood seemed to be something in the region of six hours.

The journal *Muzyka* has a section presenting opinions and comments on recently published new works. Contributors include Myaskovsky, Karagichev,[1] Saradzhev and others. Derzhanovsky has now sent me, via Myaskovsky, some compositions by Sabaneyev to review. I relish the delicious piquancy of the moment: this was after all the same Sabaneyev who systematically used his columns to annihilate me after every one of my Moscow appearances!

---

1 Boris Karagichev (1874–1946), composer, critic and teacher, himself a pupil of Taneyev.

28 August

Worked partly at Pervaya Rota and partly at Sergievskaya Street. Finished the 'March', practised some classical repertoire I am learning for Yesipova, and looked through the compositions of Sabaneyev and a young composer called Stanchinsky.[1] I've already finished my comments on Stanchinsky; as for Sabaneyev I will have to think more deeply. In view of our particular relationship I shall have to be circumspect.

At eight o'clock I called on Volodya Deshevov, but he was not at home. After waiting half an hour for him, I returned to St Petersburg.

29 August

I had promised to go with Myaskovsky on the eight o'clock express to Terioki. But Myaskovsky could not go because of Saradzhev's visit, and the pouring rain and implacably overcast sky were other reasons to dampen my enthusiasm for going. But it was a dull prospect to sit on my own in Petersburg, so I nevertheless struggled into my Swiss suit and went. There were problems getting my ticket at the station, and I only got in to the train two minutes before it left. As it happened, the weather improved, and by the time I disembarked on to the platform at Terioki an hour later, the sun was shining.

Lida, Zoya and Borya met me, we took two cabs and raced one another to the dacha. After an hour the Hansen sisters arrived at the Zakharov dacha, and we combined forces (I was staying with the Karneyevs) to go for a truly excellent, long excursion. In the evening the men dressed up in women's clothes and the women in men's. Lida in my Swiss suit looked such a handsome young boy that I called her Dorian Gray. Tilya Hansen and Zoya, especially Zoya, made completely convincing schoolboys, Borya an imposing matron with a bosom. I was the very image of a woman of easy virtue, painted and powdered, my head crowned by an enormous hat. We went together down to the beach, attracting startled glances from those we encountered on the way. Afterwards we danced in the hall of the Zakharov dacha, the newly fledged cavaliers inviting their similarly fledgling partners to dance. We had supper there and then played party games. The Zakharov family lavished attention and affection on me.

---

1 Alexey Stanchinsky (1888–1914), composer and pianist, pupil of Taneyev for composition and Igumnov for piano.

30 August

Next morning Zoya and I went on a long walk along the shore as far as Tyursevo, a spot I wanted to see since I knew that Nina's 'America' lived somewhere near there. And indeed, on a tin sign somewhat the worse for wear, I read: 'Zaitsev Dacha.' Hell!

After our wonderful walk we came back in a cab, then in the afternoon we gathered at the Zakharovs' and walked down to the sea. Luiza Alexeyevna took photographs of us all, especially wanting to capture me together with Boris. We presented a happy picture, with me leaning my elbow on his shoulder. One photograph should come out particularly well and provide a lot of amusement: Borya, Zoya, Lida and me snapped with our arms flailing in a fierce discussion about what poses we should strike for the picture.

We sat on the sand beside the sea and then walked further on along the beach. Zoya and I went again to the Zaitsev dacha, and even a verst or so further. Lyova has developed a talent for comic verse, and today composed an amusing and malicious poem about me, Borya and Georges.

We laid out patience Gurzuf-style, which I taught to Lida and Zoya. I talked a lot about 'Fyaka'.

Later that evening I went back to St Petersburg.

31 August

In the morning I practised at Pervaya Rota, and at one o'clock went to see Karatygin to recover my score of the Second Piano Concerto, which he had taken away to look at immediately after the performance. He asked me to come back and see him on Tuesday, because Nurok, Nouvel and some others wanted to have another opportunity to listen to my Concerto. Ziloti was also planning to come. Ziloti! Oho! ... Taking my score, I went over to Kolechka; we looked through it together and pencilled in some corrections to the orchestration.

Towards seven o'clock in the evening I went to Tsarskoye to see Volodya Deshevov, who was expecting me in his splendid apartment. Also present were two nice young men: his brother Seryozha, a rather nervous gentleman, and his cousin. The Borodins also came, acquaintances of the Ruzskys and descendants of the composer. Volodya displayed his talents as a raconteur and played havoc with our nerves by telling us ghost stories. His time is taken up until the 10th, preparing for his Fugue exam, but thereafter we plan to renew our closer acquaintance. He was full of praise for my Concerto and believes that I have found my true path as a composer, while he is still struggling unsuccessfully to find his.

In the train going back to Petersburg I ran into Aslanov. 'My dear fellow, there is a review about you in *Theatre and Art* at which one can only tip the hat!' He followed his own prescription and was extraordinarily kind and agreeable for the whole journey, evidently pleased at having secured for Pavlovsk a novelty that had aroused such widespread interest.

1 September

When I enquired what impression Saradzhev had taken away from *Maddelena*, Myaskovsky said that after some discussion of the opera, Saradzhev had formed the view that a production would be possible. Today I therefore set to with enthusiasm to revise the opera, beginning with the third scene, the one closest to my heart. It seems to be going well: half a day's work has produced half a scene. I rang up the Ruzskys to see if I could visit them this evening, but there was no reply, so either the apartment is still unoccupied or the telephone is out of order. I stayed at home and caught up on my neglected diary, completing seventeen pages. Telephoned Umnenkaya and had a long talk with her. But she declined the invitation to go for a walk when the weather is fine, coming up with a long list of reasons why this would not be possible.

2 September

Today is the day the Meshcherskys return from Gurzuf. I made efforts to dress as elegantly as possible, and felt surprisingly nervous at the thought of going to meet them. The *chic* thing to do, I thought, was to arrive precisely four minutes after the train was due to arrive, but in the event the train was twenty minutes late and I had to wait on the platform. We were a welcoming party of eight, including Meshchersky himself, Serge and ... yes, Zaitsev, wearing a stylish light-brown English overcoat that, however, did not go well with either his suit or his hat. Our greeting to one another was civil. I talked breezily to Serge, turning every now and again to Zaitsev, who from time to time would interject: 'Well, when I was in Gurzuf ...'

The train belatedly and slowly drew in to the platform; first on to the platform was the diminutive Nina, who rushed to embrace her father. 'Hello, octopus,' she said, extending her hand to me.

Behind her appeared Talya, Vera Nikolayevna with Mushka[1] and Yevdokia Silvestrovna. I cannot give an account of the ensuing conversation, since everyone was talking at once exchanging the latest news. They all knew every detail of my concert, having received from various acquaintances all the reviews – including some I had not seen myself – as well as eye-witness

---

1 The dog.

accounts. I did not try to monopolize Nina, for fear that she might after all find Zaitsev more interesting. But I still talked to her more than anyone else did, and Zaitsev only made his approach to her when I went away to find out about the luggage.

It must be admitted that it is pretty grand to have one's own house, a large two-storey apartment, and nevertheless decide to put up at a hotel. But that is what the Meshcherskys are doing because of uncertainties as to whether their own apartment is in the appropriate state of readiness to receive them.[1] They are staying at the Astoria, the new hotel that has recently opened and is the height of fashion. Inviting everyone to visit them this evening, they got into a car and departed. I took a taxi and went to the Conservatoire.

The Conservatoire was seething with a mass of mainly newcomers up for their entrance exam; there had apparently been over eight hundred applications. It was interesting to see all these new faces. I met several friends who had already heard about my appearance at Pavlovsk. I was amused by the way those who had read the critical notices in *The Day* and *New Times* either avoided saying anything or offered words of encouragement and consolation, whereas those who had read *Rech* were fulsome in their praise and congratulations.

I wandered around the Conservatoire for a while and then went to Pervaya Rota intending to carry on with the revision of *Maddalena*, but the mood was not on me and I did not achieve anything. I was debating with myself whether to go to the Meshcherskys this evening or not. The wretched Zaitsev would be there again, and if Nina showed a preference for him, it would not be very pleasant for me. The Andreyevs had asked me to let them know when the Meshcherskys were back, so I decided I would ask them if they were planning to go to the Astoria, and if they were, to join their party. The presence of allies would help me either to go on the attack or, if it proved necessary, to defend myself. They said they were indeed going, and so pretending to have some business in the part of town where they lived, I said I would call for them and we could go together, to which my dear Andreyevs cordially assented.

No sooner said than done. At eight o'clock I was with the Andreyevs and we set off, a merry little group. The three of us squashed into a cab, with me squatting on my haunches in place of the non-existent seat. Giggling at the absurd picture this presented we arrived at the Astoria. The Meshcherskys had taken a suite of several rooms with windows opening on to Morskaya Street on one side and St Isaac's Cathedral and the statue on the other. I could not help marvelling that I found myself in the very room that Max had dreamed of one day occupying! We found the Meshcherskys just finishing a late dinner. There were several not very noteworthy guests; Zaitsev and his

---

1 The Meshcherskys were doing up a large and luxurious two-floor apartment at No. 22, Kirochnaya Street.

mother came a little later for half an hour. The conversation was lively, revolving mainly round my Concerto, life in Gurzuf, and plans to visit London and Paris. The Andreyevs and I formed the centre of attention. Nina, to whom I paid no particular attention, asked me several questions, calling me Seryozha. When Zaitsev arrived and everyone went into the next room, Nina and I stayed where we were while the servants were clearing away the dinner. Nina told me all that had happened in Gurzuf since I left. Then we went into the main room, where Nina sat by my side, continuing our animated conversation. 'What is "Kuokkale"[1] up to?' she asked.

I said I had not seen her at all.

'Well, "America" is coming apart at the seams!' said Nina.

Zaitsev was sitting just by us, but evidently does not know who "America" is.

In short, Nina made me feel as happy as could be. There was not enough room for everyone to have tea in the dining room, so Nina and I sat in the hall eating watermelon. When we came back into the dining room, I sat on the arm of Anna Grigorievna's chair while she fed me pieces of pear. Nina sat beside Zaitsev but continued talking to me. The Andreyevs stood up to take their leave, and so did I. Everyone came out to say goodbye, and as she did so, Nina said to me, 'I will find out whether the hotel has anywhere we can play billiards, and then I'll ring you.'

As we went down the stairs, Anna Grigorievna said to me, 'Nina has become so pretty: those lovely eyes . . .'

'I'm always telling her that she has beautiful . . . fangs,' I said.

I am invited on Friday to the Andreyevs: Zakharov will be there, and the Meshcherskys have also promised to come. It will be interesting to see how the Meshcherskys and Zakharov get on!

3 September

The morning went by on going to meet the Rayevskys at the station, hanging about waiting for the late arrival of the train, fussing around with the luggage, and so on.

Coming back to Pervaya Rota, I had just settled down to work when one of the Conservatoire guards came to tell me that the Director was requesting my presence to play accompaniments for the entrance examination. This was an interesting proposal, so after dropping in to the Tsarskoye Selo station, where I am in the habit of having my lunch these days, I went to the Conservatoire, which was again bursting at the seams. The exam I was asked to play for was for people wanting to join the singing course. I had very little to do, but looking at the poor girls nervously choking back their anxiety was good entertainment.

---

1 Lidia Umnova.

Tcherepnin appeared and took me aside, saying with a laugh, 'I'm going to sue you for 12 roubles. I was told you were in Gurzuf and I specially went there, but couldn't find you!' This must have happened after I left. We (Tcherepnin and I) had a most enjoyable conversation for about an hour. The news is that he is going to stay on at the Conservatoire for another year, and we shall have a new student in the class, someone with the reputation of an educated musician. Just at that moment this person came up to be introduced: around thirty years old, with a pince-nez, dark, and rather awkward in his movements. I don't remember his name.

Then I walked past the Astoria and went to the 'Alexander'[1] where I put in Max's walking stick for repair, and went in to the photographer's opposite, where I ordered an enlargement of his portrait to hang on the wall of my room. At the Rayevskys I talked a lot to Katya, who loves me and always flirts in conversation with me. I showed her the photographs from Gurzuf; she liked the look of the Meshchersky girls. She had herself been in Gurzuf the year before, and I enjoyed the thought that she had been there. She was appalled by my check trousers.

In the evening I went to Karatygin's house, where a group of musicians had gathered to listen to my Concerto. Present were Nurok, Nouvel, Tcherepnin, Braudo,[2] Senilov, Gnessin[3] and a good many others, including Tamochka Glebova, towards whom I harbour feelings of resentment and whom I pretended not to notice. Ziloti did not come after all; this is not surprising as he is apt to lose his temper at the mere mention of my name. The Concerto was met with tumultuous acclamation, people described it as the most interesting event of recent times. I am considered to be a modern classic. According to Tcherepnin, 'Nurok has spent his entire life in the service of new music . . . now all-seeing God has sent him in his old age Prokofiev!'

The 'Harp' Prelude and Nina's 'Rigaudon' were also loudly acclaimed, especially the last named. 'How fresh it is! What rhythmic vitality!'

4 September

I usually sleep well, but of late have taken to waking up early, seven or eight o'clock in the morning, and not wanting to go back to sleep. Six to seven hours every twenty-four is not enough. I am getting as jumpy as a cat.

1   A building of furnished apartments on Nevsky Prospect.
2   Yevgeny Braudo (1882–1939), musicologist, teacher and writer on music.
3   Mikhail Gnessin (1883–1957), composer and teacher. As well as professorial posts in both Moscow and Leningrad Conservatoires he collaborated with his sister Yelena in the foundation and direction of a music conservatoire in Moscow that as the Gnessin Institute, later the Gnessin Russian Academy of Music, became, and is to this day, second only to the Moscow Conservatoire in importance.

In the morning I stayed at Pervaya Rota revising *Maddalena*, losing myself so much in the work that only at half past two did I remember that I should go to the Tsarskoye Selo station for lunch. Afterwards I carried on working, but it was less productive. I was hoping for a telephone call from Fyaka to suggest a game of billiards, but there was silence from her.

In the evening I went to the Ruzskys, who have been back for three days now. Nikolay Pavlovich was incredibly kind, Tanya's and Ira's complexions have turned pink and white. I made myself agreeable to them; Tanya hardly spoke to me, but Ira was very chatty. On the subject of her complexion, I told her she had been transformed from a lemon into an apple.

At night I slept well.

5 September

More *Maddalena*: after strenuous efforts scene III is now finished. Rang up Myaskovsky to see whether he would be in this evening, as I wanted to show him the revised music for this scene, also my Sabaneyev review, which I have finally forced myself to write. I wrote according to my conscience: rigorously and to the point. At six o'clock I walked back to Sergievskaya. I wanted the telephone to ring and for it to be Nina, I wanted this badly, but Nina is a law unto herself and one could wait for ever.

Myaskushka was engaged elsewhere this evening so I could not see him, and after racking my brains I could not think of anywhere else to go, so I used the evening to write up my diary of the Gurzuf visit from scraps of notes I had made while there. Many of these had to do with Fyaka, and writing out the narrative gave me much pleasure.

I have a new approach to life, which I am finding has a very beneficial effect: when I start doing something I continue with it and do not allow myself to be distracted for a moment. Interruptions, I now realize, are very unhelpful: one should work without lifting one's head from the page at all, that way work will be finished more quickly and leave more time for other occupations.

6 September

This evening I am going to the Andreyevs, where Zakharov and the Meshcherskys will also be present. As soon as I woke up this morning the prospect filled me with pleasurable anticipation.

Had a letter from Mama saying that she is coming back tomorrow.

Worked at Pervaya Rota on scene II. Almost the whole of the first half of the scene is new. I am totally absorbed by *Maddalena*. The success of my Concerto has given a real boost to my creativity.

When I was too tired to work any more, I reread Max's letters to me and mine to him. He was a rare, a nonpareil friend! It was a gauge of the strength of our friendship that I never encountered any side of Max that was antipathetic to me; his qualities were those craved by my soul, he answered all my emotional needs and as a person he was closer to me than anyone else in the world. He is no more, and I am overcome by grief. But this grief must be fought and vanquished, as must thoughts of Max himself. The past cannot be brought back, so what purpose is served by harking back to it?

Having dined at Sergievskaya Street, had myself shaved and coiffed, I went with keen anticipation to the Andreyevs. In the drawing room sat the Andreyevs themselves, with Nikolay Pavlovich's brother and Boris Zakharov. The meeting was cordial, I handed over a letter the concierge had given me to bring up, sat down at the opened card table and suggested a quick game of *Sechsundsechzig* to Nikolay Vasilievich before we got down to bridge. At this point the doorbell rang, and through the open doorway into the hall could be seen Talya and Nina.

'Here come the octopi!' I cried gleefully, but immediately had to ask pardon for my outburst because the parents were following just behind their daughters as they came into the room. Vera Nikolayevna sat straight down at the card table. Nikolay Vasilievich fanned out the cards and organized the bridge, inviting Meshchersky and Zakharov to play. This surprised me as I had not known that Zakharov was a bridge player. Vera Nikolayevna exclaimed, 'Before we begin, can Prokofiev play us something! It's a long time since I heard him. Sergey Sergeyevich, Nina's "Rigaudon", if you please!'

'The dedication to Nina is being removed. When I played the "Rigaudon" to her she declared it to be rubbish. But only a few days ago I played it to a group of musicians, and they told me it was a splendid piece.'

Nina: 'You know, you've become much better looking than you were.'

'Naturally. I've just come from the barber's.'

'No, I'm serious. It's really quite noticeable, even compared with Gurzuf.'

She then related to me how she had been tormenting some fellow today by describing how we spent our time during the summer, and quoting to him my comment about how the best kisses of all were those on the bridge of the nose, especially with knitted-together eyebrows like hers. The poor chap was of course consumed with jealousy and now hates me with every fibre of his being. From something she said later it would appear that 'America' has been banished into such distant realms of outer darkness that the relationship is likely soon to be all over, in the most satisfactory (for me) sense of the word.

We went back into the drawing room. Zakharov had finished his bridge game and soon said goodbye and departed. I walked out with him into the hall, asking him if he planned to spend an evening with Kolechka. He replied that all his evenings were taken up, but he would try to arrange a time, and would telephone me. I said I would be playing *Maddalena*, and he expressed great interest in hearing it.

The evening flew by quickly. The Meshcherskys offered to take me back in their magnificent car. Meshchersky himself sat with the driver, and I sat beside Nina. At the Astoria they all got out, giving orders to take me on to Sergievskaya. I climbed out of the back and went to sit with the chauffeur, the octopi laughing to see my figure installed in their automobile, and waving to me as we drove off.

7 September

In the morning I received a telegram from Mama informing me that she would not after all be arriving back until the 12th, so I dashed to the Nikolayevsky station to get a letter off to her by the ten o'clock express, as it is some time since I wrote to her. Somewhere in the station I lost my Paris walking stick; it was a good one, elegant, and it had cost twenty francs, but ... I did not grieve too much: after Zaitsev's snakeskin cane mine had rather come to disgust me. In exchange I got back from the repair shop today Max's now mended 'historic' walking stick.

At home I worked intensively on *Maddalena* and got a lot of the second scene done. Although she had promised to, Nina did not ring, the wretch. On the way back I had dropped in to Myaskuska to show him my comments on Stanchinsky and Sabaneyev. The first he approved of, the second he thought was too harsh and needed toning down.

In the evening I had intended to go and see Lida Karneyeva, who suffered a heart attack a few days ago, but it turned out that she had recovered completely and had gone to visit the Hansens, where Zakharov would be as well. So I was left with a free evening, which I used to finish my Gurzuf diary and revise my article on Sabaneyev. Both these tasks I completed.

8 September

It was wonderful autumn weather, a cold day but sunny. I walked over to Pervaya Rota and immersed myself in *Maddalena*. As usual the work went well and the second scene is now almost finished.

At long last I have received the proof copy of the Sonata No. 2. Oh, what a delight is my little Sonata! It looks so sweet, and is a joy to play. To play the whole work from beginning to end from the proof copy was one of the most enjoyable things I have done recently. That's good, well-written piano style for you – no need for all that dashing up and down the keyboard from one end to the other, or those rhythmic perversions Sabaneyev goes in for!

After this I walked in the fine weather along Voznesensky Prospect, Morskaya Street (past the Astoria), Nevsky and Liteyny Prospects and Kirochnaya Street to Sergievskaya.

Nina rang up at eight o'clock. They had been to Tsarskoye by car to choose a winter dacha. She asked me what I was doing in the evening. 'Nothing much, probably just sitting and correcting proofs.' I would have been glad to spend the evening with them, but Nina said nothing about it. We could not talk for long, because her chatter was distracting her father from his work. Damn the girl! I like her so much; I am sure I am not in love with her, but the way she switches from right to left, blows hot and then cold, is utterly maddening.

I spent the evening in the Chess Club, where I have not been for a long time. There were not many people there, it being a Sunday. I played with Gelbak, who is a strong player, and our game went on for about three hours. I was on the point of winning, but ... in the end I lost.

9 September

At Pervaya Rota I finished the second scene, but immediately I did so I had to leave to go to the Smolensky Cemetery because of the Requiem Mass being said for Aunt Tanya, who died a year ago today. At one o'clock I was in the Conservatoire, to see what excitements were going on there and what was planned for our work programme. Met a lot of people. Tcherepnin took me to lunch and explained his plan for our studies. There would be four in the conductors' class: I as the senior, Tsybin the number two, Dranishnikov and ... oh God, what is his name? ... Shtrimmer, the juniors. Gauk, Solovyov and Kreisler will stay on, having the status of 'supernumerary unpaid secondments'. I am very pleased that the small orchestra programme has a lot of Bach, Handel and Gluck, because I have begun to lose interest in the diet of Haydn, Mozart and early-period Beethoven we have been having recently.

Had a very affectionate letter from Natasha Goncharova after a silence lasting three months. She is coming to St Petersburg tomorrow. I telephoned Nina at the Astoria, and we talked about trifles, and about the family's plans to go abroad for two months, a prospect that fills Nina with horror. We agreed that she should ring me the day after tomorrow.

I dined early in order to be at Myaskushka's by seven o'clock, because Zakharov had said he would come. But then he telephoned to say that he was forced to cry off. This is often the case with him so neither Myaskovsky nor I were unduly surprised. I played Kolechka the second and third scenes of *Maddalena*, and received high praise for them in their revised form. 'Splendidly done. I'm really beginning to envy you your gift for harmony.'

I dropped a hint about orchestrating the work, but Myaskovsky said he thought this was something that could be done only by the composer. I put on my most pathetic voice and said that the poor opera would be condemned for ever to hide its light under a bushel, because this particular composer was never going to find the time to orchestrate it. Silence. Myaskovsky: 'Well, it would certainly be an interesting challenge, to orchestrate a thing like that! If you died and *Maddalena* were still not orchestrated, of course I would produce a score for it.'

'My dear fellow, hand me a revolver and I'll shoot myself straight away, as long as you promise to take on *Maddalena*!'

He laughed.

10 September

Walked to Pervaya Rota. Having spent a whole week immersed in work on *Maddalena* I did not feel like doing any more today. The proof copy of my lovely little Sonata was lying on the desk and I set to work on it with joy in my heart, working without a break until two o'clock.

At half past two I telephoned Umnenkaya and after long and boring pleading on my part we met at the Conservatoire to go for a walk. Everything went very well, the weather was beautiful, and Lidochka said she had been missing me. But on the Embankment, down at the pier where the Finland steamers go from, a real rupture occurred. I had set my heart on going on the steamer, but she flatly refused. Neither of us would give reasons for our stance. The altercation ended with me remaining on the jetty and her walking away from me back along the Embankment.

Well, this is goodbye. I have lost my liking for you, Lidia Ivanovna...

I returned home alone, feeling of course rather disconsolate. I finished my proof-reading and had an affectionate telephone conversation with Natasha Goncharova, now back in Petersburg.

11 September

At Pervaya Rota I worked on a Mazurka for Op. 12. I brought it back it from memory, wrote it out, polished up some details, and then revised it. Fyaka telephoned at three o'clock. I had been waiting for the call and was thrilled when it came. 'Seryozha, come over and we'll go for a walk: Talya, you, a law student we know, and I. The law student will go with Talya and you will come with me.'

'All right,' I said, and went off to the Astoria.

We walked along the Embankment and Kamenoóstrovsky Prospect, gossiping about everything under the sun. Nina said she had woken up once in the middle of the night and seen the abyss that was in her soul, and the emptiness in her heart. That is why she is so ready to flirt with 'America' and with me. But it was a pleasant walk and Fyaka is very dear to my heart.

In the evening I visited the Karneyevs, who have moved to a new apartment, and a very nice one too. The girls had been quizzing Boris as to what Fyaka was like. He had told them that she was small, dark, not at all pretty, and continually calling out 'Seryozha!' My conversation with Lida and Zoya was about whether Boris was really beginning to go bald. I first noticed the tell-tale gleam on his head about two weeks ago, and felt a twinge of melancholy. Lyovka has already made up a satirical verse, including the following sally:

> ... heads or tails? Whichever way,
> Isn't the bald spot here to stay?'

Borya unexpectedly came in at half past ten. We all talked together for a while, and then, as he evidently had some sort of important private business with Lida, they went and sat by themselves for a whole hour. When Boris said goodbye I went outside with him, and we were both very friendly, although there is still a wall-like sense of strain between us. And this wall is on his side. A strange character!

12 September

Stayed in at Pervaya Rota and finished the Mazurka. At one o'clock went to the Conservatoire, partly to have a walk and partly to take a score out of the library for Tcherepnin's class. At the entrance I met Golubovskaya. She said, 'What a coincidence seeing you. I have just been playing your Op. 3 pieces, and I learned the "March" in half an hour. The pieces were given to me by an admirer of yours, who was in raptures over your concert at Pavlovsk.'

At that moment the admirer in question turned up and paid me many compliments, although I did not remember her face. Coming out of the Conservatoire I met Shteiman and we reminisced happily about London, where Shteiman had spent another month and a half being bored. He wished he had heard about my trip to Switzerland, because he could have joined me. He and I have two things in common: (1) we both like travelling; (2) neither of us likes travelling alone.

Before dinner I called on Myaskushka and gave him the new version of the Mazurka.

'How is *Maddalena*?' he asked.

'On the shelf. Abandoned. What's the point if she hasn't been orchestrated?'

'You mustn't think like that. I've left some time free for her.'

'You can't mean it?!' I exclaimed joyfully, and made haste to leave, as I had taken him away from his dinner.

At eight o'clock that evening Mama arrived on the Kislovodsk Express. Aunt Katya, Katechka and I met her. Mama had recovered her strength and was looking tremendously well. I was very happy for her. We all got into a car and went to our own apartment. At ten my aunt and my cousin left, leaving Mama and me to share all our news until half past twelve at night.

13 September

All morning I made a piano transcription of the Bassoon Scherzo. All this actually meant was putting on to two staves what had previously been on four, but it was finicky work and I did not mange to finish it. On the other hand, somewhat unexpectedly, I did finish off the 'Scherzo'[1] for Volodya Deshevov, which had a long time ago come up against an impasse. I am pleased not only to have got it moving again but completed it.

Since Mama had brought some magnificent pears and apples from Sukhum, I felt I must follow the tradition established in previous years and take some to Yesipova. She has been back in St Petersburg for a while but is suffering from bronchitis and is not leaving the house. I called on her at five o'clock but she was not seeing any visitors. I left my card and the fruit. My God, I am graduating this year and since March have hardly put one finger in front of another for a lesson with her! From Yesipova I walked home along Morskaya Street and Nevsky Prospect.

In the evening I went to the Sokol for gymnastics. I'm out of practice and got terribly tired.

14 September

Finished the orchestral Intermezzo that links the third and fourth scenes of *Maddalena*. I am happy with it. Up till now this section has had quite a different character, and was not successful.

Suggested a project to Zoya that I had dreamed up during our Terioki walk to the Zaitsev dacha: a long walk of twenty-five versts. Zoya agreed, and at 12.49 pm we set out on the road towards Yukki. We walked along a couple of streets in the Vyborg district and then crossed the main Finland railway line, got slightly lost despite the map I had with me but nevertheless found our way to Lesnoy, approaching it from the south-east. We pressed on, leaving Udelnaya on our left and did not stop until we reached Poklonnaya Gora[2]

---

1 No. 10 of Ten Pieces for Piano, Op. 12.
2 'Greetings Mountain', a hill to the north of St Petersburg, so called because it is supposed to be

from which we had a grand view over Ozerki. The town gleamed dazzlingly in the sunshine but we pushed on, now walking along the road to Vyborg. About four o'clock, having walked for three hours without stopping, we made a brief halt at Pervoye Pargolovo.[1] It was a bright, clear autumn day. We bought postcards, apples and chocolate and rested in a small boat tied up to the bathing stage there. We were, not so much tired, but a little less overflowing with energy than we had been when we started out. The only thing Zoya complained about was that her shoe was beginning to chafe, but in herself she was hale and hearty, rosy-cheeked and full of go, and looking very pretty.

Once when Lyova and I were playing chess at Terioki, I said sententiously as I made my move, 'As in Lasker v. Tarrasch', to which Lyovka, not a whit disconcerted, replied, 'As Boyle said to Mariotte.'[2] I found this very amusing, and that evening when I was out walking with Zoya we called each other Boyle and Mariotte. Now, resting in our boat, we wrote a few postcards (to Borya, Lida, Zorya[3] and Fyaka) signing ourselves Boyle (Zoya) and Mariotte (me). The postcard to Nina was addressed to: Fyaka, Room 217, Astoria Hotel, St Petersburg, and the text read: 'Boyle and Mariotte arrived safely in Pargolovo after three hours and ten minutes' walking. Continuing on (to Yukki). By wire from St Petersburg Telegraph Office.' On the other side was a view of Pargolovo, and below it a drawing of Boyle and Mariotte striding along. Above was their conversation: 'My dear Boyle, I see Yukki in the distance.' 'Oh yes, dear friend Mariotte, but we are not the least bit tired.'

We continued. The way from Pargolovo to Yukki is not easy to find because it is a maze of twisty little roads and paths, but God sent us a little girl to guide us, who showed us the way so that we got there with no trouble. At seven o'clock, bright as buttons and delighted with ourselves, we found ourselves at Yukki beside the mountain down which we had so gloriously sledged last winter. It was getting cold and dark, so we took a cab and reached Levashovo just as it became completely dark. After waiting an hour for a train we installed ourselves in the comfort of a first-class carriage and returned to St Petersburg, at which point the indefatigable Boyle went on to

---

the spot from which Swedish heralds were despatched to Peter The Great to sue for peace at the end of the Russo-Swedish War.
1   A complex of three villages, First, Second and Third Pargolovo, on Count Shuvalov's estate. From the middle of the nineteenth century it had been home to a reclusive colony of German farmers.
2   In Britain the law stating that the volume of a gas varies inversely as the pressure is known as Boyle's Law, after its discovery in 1662 by the Irish natural philosopher Robert Boyle. However, the principle was discovered independently and published by the French physicist Edmé Mariotte in 1676, in consequence of which elsewhere in the world the law is known, more accurately, as the Boyle–Mariotte Law..
3   Zora Grevs.

visit friends while Mariotte went home, had something to eat, took a bath and collapsed into bed.

On this day a year ago Max, Lida, Zoya and I had gone on an expedition by car to Krasnoye Selo, and in the evening Max came to my house on Bronnitskaya Street. Mama was in Sukhum; we stoked up the fire, pulled up two deep, soft armchairs, and sank into them before the blaze. We brought in pears, bananas, liqueur chocolates and shamelessly indulged ourselves. Max smoked a cigar. We called up our friends on the telephone and made entries in the 'Yellow Book'. The evening had been such a joy that we repeated it the following day, and then again and again, meeting up at Bronnitskaya Street, almost every evening until the end of September, when Mama returned. I still have vivid memories of our cosy 'Evenings by the Fireside at Bronnitskaya'.[1]

15 September

Wrote my diary, practised the 'Scherzo' from Op. 12 and some of the Schumann Sonata for Anna Nikolayevna, and talked on the telephone to Boyle. Boyle was in good form, except for minor complaints about her heart. Sonya Esche called, and I much enjoyed talking to her.

By five o'clock I was tired of sitting at home, so I walked to Karatygin's to retrieve the score of my Concerto, and then to Ruzskys for dinner. Nikolay Pavlovich had just returned from Kiev; Tanya and Ira had just left for the same place. It was quite a pleasant evening. I beat Kolya ten times at chess.

16 September

Borya Zakharov telephoned to thank me for the postcard from Yukki and to ask who my companion had been. I told him, and said I hoped we should be able to meet before he went away.

Made corrections to the Concerto, touching up the places Myaskovsky and I had identified. Most of them are minor, but it is a terrible business physically scratching out and then pasting in changes to the score.

Tomorrow is Vera Nikolayevna's name-day. She said that for her present she would like me to dedicate a piece to her. So be it. I've begun writing it, but it will not be finished by tomorrow. Not that it matters, because there is no piano in their hotel suite. I am not sure whether to include the piece in Op. 16[2] or Op. 12. If Op. 12, I will remove the Variations and extend them to make a separate opus, as the theme is such a lovely one.

---

1 Ironic reference to Gogol's *Evenings on a Farm near Dikanka*.
2 *Sic*. Presumably at this stage it had not been decided whether Op. 16 would be the Second

At one o'clock I went into the Conservatoire to ask Glazunov where and when I should send the scores of the two Concertos to be considered for inclusion in the Belyayev Concerts. I found out the answer, and then had a long talk with the 'admirer' to whom Golubovskaya had introduced me. It turned out that three days before my Pavlovsk appearance she had sat beside me looking over my shoulder at the score of Tchaikovsky's Sixth Symphony. Now I remember. I promised to present her with the score of 'Despair'.

Anna Grigorievna Andreyeva has been promoted to a full professorship. Mama spoke to her on the telephone today, and Anna Grigorievna was asking why I had not been to see them. She finishes work at seven o'clock and would be pleased to see me any evening. And so this evening at seven o'clock I went to offer her my congratulations and had a wonderful time there. At nine o'clock Nikolay Vasilievich, his brother and I all went to the Astoria, where we found the Meshcherskys entertaining several guests, among them the very nice Romanovsky and Zaitsev. I studied Zaitsev closely: he is really quite uncouth. For the first time I felt annoyed, and paid Nina no attention. Could it be because I am upset that the Meshcherskys are going to be abroad from September until January? We sat down to bridge, Meshchersky politely going from one table to another. Seeing my notes, he enquired, 'Why do you put it down under the letter "F" when Nina loses a point?'

'Because F is Nina: "Fyaka".'

'Did you say "Fyaka"?'

'Fyaka.'

'Listen, Nina . . . in that case there was a letter for you this morning . . . addressed to "Fyaka". I sent it back telling them it wasn't for us . . .'

Nina dashed out of the room . . . I announced to general amusement that this letter must have been my postcard from Yukki. A bellboy was summoned and commissioned to look for the letter. Vera Nikolayevna called me a crazy man.

I explained to Alexey Pavlovich that 'Fyaka' was a perfect description for Nina, who always says 'Pfya!' when she is annoyed about something, in other words she pfyaffs, and also the word suggests 'byaka'.[1]

The bridge game proceeded on its way. I am really getting the hang of it, Talya has some skill, Nina not much, and when Vera Nikolayevna comes and begins giving her some pointers, she gets completely flustered. I laughed and said what I love about her is the glassy-eyed, blank look of total incomprehension that comes over her at such moments . . . Nina got very angry, and

---

Piano Concerto or the five pieces collected together as *Sarcasms*. Eventually the Concerto was published as Op. 16 and *Sarcasms* as Op. 17. The 'Capriccio', as this piece was eventually called, was published as No. 5 of Op. 12.

1 Baby talk for a mess or a mishap.

said, 'What I love about you is your perpetual cheerfulness. Just like a Borzoi puppy.'

'Oh, don't try to be witty, for God's sake. It's so painful to watch someone near death trying to make jokes!'

'Who says I'm near death?'

'You are for me, since you are going abroad until January.'

17 September

Made corrections to the Concerto and continued composing yesterday's piece. The material is good.

At two went to the Conservatoire for the start of the conductors' class. All the conductors and assistant conductors were present. Tcherepnin made a long speech outlining our responsibilities and our authority, the programmes for the small orchestra, the large orchestra and the opera class. For the last named there are to be three scenes from *Falstaff* and two from *Rigoletto* to mark the centenary of Verdi's birth. I as the senior shall conduct *Falstaff*. Altogether Tcherepnin is being extraordinarily nice to me, and it looks as though this year I shall be gobbling up all the best plums. After this discussion Tcherepnin and I had a long talk.

Afterwards I went to the Astoria to wish Vera Nikolayevna a happy nameday. I presented her with the dedication of the new piece, but as the score is not ready yet I gave her a notice of the dedication, written out on one of my cards with the theme of the piece on it. I was at the Mescherskys for only five minutes, after which I went to the Konshins. Next summer they are hiring a whole boat and taking a big party down the Volga. They invited me, and I am very tempted. Then I went to the Shtembers, where there was a good deal of noisy talk and laughter. Why had I not come to Dubrachek? I played some of my pieces. They were liked, but my performance of them was not. I said, 'Well, you may all be very critical of the way I play, but please bear in mind that all the reviews call attention to what an excellent pianist I am.'

Papa Shtember: 'Well of course they praise you. You play so . . . loudly . . .'

Returned home and rang up Sonya Esche to congratulate her as well. Spent the evening at the Sokol. Today they were marching to the strains of my Sokol 'March', which everyone seems to like.

18 September

Finished the piece I was writing yesterday.[1] I like it very much. I wanted to write it out in a fair copy, but laid it aside and instead made more corrections

---

1 Eventually the third of *Sarcasms*. [Subsequent note by author.]

to the Concerto. Practised the Schumann Sonata in preparation for the lesson with Yesipova, and played through *Falstaff* ready for Tcherepnin. The opera is an enchantment, wonderfully achieved, and if one is not too demanding, the music is attractive. It will be very interesting to conduct.

In the afternoon Mama and I went to buy some cufflinks for my nameday. They are very nice indeed, semi-precious ruby, or rose quartz as it is called. Home again, I carried on working until nine o'clock, when I went to see the Karneyevs, who were entertaining besides me Zakharov and Captain Barkov. Zakharov had been to Yesipova's recently; her toady Sasha had been to my Pavlovsk concert and reported back that I had performed the devil only knew what, played it the devil only knew how, disgraced her class and been booed off the stage. Anna Grigorievna was indignant, and when Zakharov attempted to give a more accurate version of events, told him he was wasting his time sticking up for his classmate. A nice state of affairs! It is beginning to look as if I shall not get to play my lovely Concerto at the final exam. I must ask my supporters among the professoriat (Tcherepnin, Medem, Nikolayev, Andreyev) to congratulate Yesipova on my success. Otherwise goodness only knows what will happen.

19 September

Made corrections, more corrections and still more final corrections to the Concerto and in between played *Falstaff*, Tcherepnin having asked me to put on a show for the edification of the younger students.

At two I decided to go into the Conservatoire and incidentally to try to enlist the support of my friends among the professors to build my defence against Yesipova. In fact I did not see any of them, but I did have a long talk with my Pavlovsk admirer, Mlle Bushen. She had spent two months in Gurzuf, leaving there only a few days before my arrival. This gave rise to all kinds of happy memories about places we both knew, and I enjoyed telling her all our Gurzuf pastimes. She knows the Meshcherskys by sight because of playing tennis, but is not acquainted with them. After quite a long conversation, as I was leaving I ran into Seryozha Alpers, the only member of the family with whom I am on reasonably good terms. Seryozha has moved across to Blumenfeld's class and up to the fourth General Subjects class. He has improved noticeably.

Home again, I telephoned the Meshcherskys, and when the servant enquired whom I would like to speak to, Talya or Nina, I answered 'Talya'. I told Talya that I had received a letter from the 'compensator'[1] to the effect that Yesipova was ejecting me from her class, and that the piece I had written for

---

1 Refers to Boris Zakharov.

Vera Nikolayevna had proved to be a monstrosity, with each hand playing in a different tonality. We both laughed at that, and said goodbye. In the evening I wanted to go and visit the Andreyevs, but they were not at home.

Finally finished the corrections to the Second Piano Concerto. I picked up the score of the First and leafed through it. For a long time now I have been dissatisfied with the instrumental layout of the Andante, and for that reason have not sent it to be engraved, because I was hoping to be able to come up with a satisfactory revision. But the answer to what I needed obstinately refused to come. Today, however, the moment I looked at the score I suddenly saw with absolutely clarity what was required, and the movement itself assumed such a lucid and logical form that I straightaway set to work in a state of some excitement. By the end of the evening the Andante in its revised form was complete, needing only some finishing touches and orchestration.

I will have to keep up the pressure on myself, but it will be ready by Monday, the day on which the Belyayev Committee meets to decide its programmes.

20 September

During the morning I put the finishing touches to the Andante and transcribed the sketches I had made. Now I am orchestrating them.

At a quarter to two I came into the Conservatoire and went through *Falstaff* with Tcherepnin. This opera is so full of life and entertaining. The harp teacher, Mme Walter-Kühne,[1] asked me to compose something for her instrument. I replied that I had already written a Prelude for harp, dedicated to one of her students. Mme Walter-Kühne asked me to bring the Prelude to her class and promised to have it performed at a student concert.

Returning home, I continued orchestrating. In the evening I enjoyed a gymnastics session at the Sokol and played the members my 'March'. An unattractive Sokolette asked me to come half an hour earlier and play it for her female colleagues.

21 September

Still orchestrating the Andante. As I am now too late to send my Concertos to the 'Board of Trustees' by post, I went today to 50 Nikolayevskaya Street and asked whether it would be acceptable to deliver the manuscript by hand on the day of the meeting, that is to say the day after tomorrow. A polite lady who lives in the apartment where the meetings take place said it would be

---

1 Yekaterina Walter-Kühne (1870–1931), harpist. She left Russia after the Revolution and lived abroad for the remainder of her life.

acceptable, and the committee room itself is secure and comfortable enough for it to be safe to leave the manuscript there. Returning home, I finished the Andante, so both Concertos are now ready for submission to the committee. But I cannot be confident of success: Glazunov has little sympathy for my compositions, Lyadov actively considers me to be pernicious, and the chairman, Artsybushev, is in the same camp, although to what extent is not certain.

In the spring I began reading a novel, *At the Brink*[1] but had abandoned it in the middle. Today I picked it up again and found the place where I had stopped reading before. It was the scene in which Krause commits suicide, and it induced in me a dismal feeling of depression. Three numbers, 10–5–4, written in indelible ink in the margin, in Max's hand, at precisely this point in the book, gave food for thought. I knew Max did not have such a pen, but one had been lying on my desk. So Max, on the eve of his death, sitting on my sofa, had leafed through this book and made notes. Were these numbers just random, or did they have a hidden meaning?

I telephoned Nina Meshcherskaya and said I would like to see them. Nina said they were going to dine at the 'Pivato' restaurant and afterwards going to the cinema; would I like to join them? Although I don't usually go to the cinema except when I am in the country, never having time to do so in the capital, I quickly agreed and after a quick dinner at home joined them at the 'Pivato'. The Meshcherskys, in a body, plus Romanovsky, were occupying a separate private room; my entrance was greeted with shouts of joy, loudest of all (which really surprised me) from Alexey Pavlovich. I was found a place, sat down and took over the conversation, freely talking about any subject that came up.

Dinner finished, and two cars were waiting for us at the entrance to the restaurant. I went in the big car with Alexey Pavlovich and the girls, Vera Nikolayevna and Romanovsky in the other car. Alexey Pavlovich laughed indulgently at Nina's propensity for picking a bone with me on the merest trifle. We arrived at the cinema and took a box. The programme was rubbish, but we all enjoyed ourselves laughing at those things we privately found amusing, and then went back to the Astoria to eat watermelon.

22 September

Completed the Andante. Both concertos are now completely ready. It gives me enormous pleasure to look at the scores in all their ample glory.

Having prepared for Tcherepnin the next scene of *Falstaff* (we are doing the second scene of Act I and the first and second scenes of Act II), I went to

---

1 See p. 371, note 3.

the Conservatoire, where Tcherepnin, despite the holiday, was teaching his class. Idly leafing through the pile of class registers, I opened Yesipova's and to my astonishment found my name missing from the complete list of her students. I was deeply offended. Oho, so Yesipikha[1] is spiteful enough to consider crossing me off her list of pupils. In theory she does have the right to exclude me for having made an unauthorized appearance in a public concert; I don't believe she will actually do this, but she is capable of causing me all kinds of difficulties with the administration.

In order to have the matter cleared up without delay, I armed myself with my most benevolent disposition and when Tcherepnin's class was over went to see Anna Nikolayevna. To my surprise our meeting could not have been more friendly, and not a word was said about the Pavlovsk concert. To be quite clear about it, I therefore raised the matter myself, at which Anna Nikolayevna was a little shocked, but not excessively so, and asked, 'Surely you are not intending to play this Concerto for your exam?!'

If I replied in the affirmative, that could spell the end of my Concerto. At the last moment, I decided to be diplomatic. 'If you do not wish me to, then I can choose a classical work.'

Yesipova had not expected this. I added, 'My Concerto does have this advantage, though: it is much more difficult to play than any of the others, and will give me an opportunity to display a technique the others will not find it possible to match in their concertos.'

'Yes, I have been told it is extremely difficult. Zakharov was defending it one day, and almost got into a fight with one lady . . .'

We parted amicably. My day for a lesson with her will be Tuesday. After seeing her I went straight to the Warsaw station to bid farewell to Borya Zakharov, who is going to Vienna. A lot of people came to see him off: his relations, the Karneyev sisters, the Hansen sisters. We kissed each other as we said goodbye. I was glad to see him, but I am not grieving over his departure. Since our reconciliation, relations between us have been artificial and not straightforward. His going away and our subsequent correspondence may smooth things out.

In the evening I did not feel like working. Mama went to the Rayevskys; I stayed behind, and then went to see Kolechka Myaskovsky. He approved my new version of the Andante from the First Piano Concerto, and also the 'Scherzo' for Volodya Deshevov, which I played to him complete for the first time ('a marvellous piece'). I was chastised, more in sorrow than in anger, for not having yet completed the revision of the fourth scene of *Maddalena*.

---

1   The way this nickname has been formed is clearly intended to be pejorative rather than affectionate.

23 September

Played for Yesipovna, wrote a covering letter to accompany the Concertos, made up one package of the lot, and took it myself to the 'Board of Trustees'. The lady who lives there, whose door is now adorned with a notice saying 'Board of Trustees for the Encouragement . . . etc., etc.' said that the first meeting was not in fact taking place today, but in a week's time. I nevertheless decided to leave the Concertos there and, handing them with their covering letter to the lady, departed for the Conservatoire.

Gave Walter-Kühne my Harp Prelude. After casting her eye over it she appeared rather dissatisfied, giving me to understand that it was too simple and the texture too light. I replied that that was precisely the effect I was aiming at. She said she would take it home to look at it properly. I then met Klingman, who has put on weight and looks awful. She told me again of the popularity my compositions enjoy in her home town of Dvinsk; four girls from there have recently entered the Conservatoire and the first thing they did was ask to have Prokofiev pointed out to them. In return for the excellent publicity she is creating for me I promised her 4 per cent of the net profit from my next concert in Dvinsk.

Met Mlle Bushen and presented her with a copy of 'Despair'; we were joined by Golubovskaya and we all went on talking for about an hour, sitting on the windowsill. When they boasted of how they loved walking and how far they could go, I there and then suggested a walk to the Islands. At the end of September, when the leaves turn bright yellow, red and brown, the Islands take on such a ravishing appearance it is hard to tear one's eyes away from them. The girls agreed. As far as Kamennoóstrovsky Prospect we took the tram, and then continued on foot. By the Antique Theatre[1] we ate sandwiches Golubovskaya discovered in her muff, and I told the girls the story of this theatre, which I had read at some point in *Ogonyok*.[2] We then continued to the Strelka,[3] gazed our fill on the multitude of wonderful colours the leaves displayed, and the slanting rays of the setting sun. Freezing cold and tired, we turned for home. When I got there I drank two 'sergeant-major's[4] glasses of rowanberry vodka to warm myself up, which made my head spin. I lay down, curled up in a warm blanket, and slept. Some time after nine I went to

---

1 The Antique Theatre was the creation of the theatre historian and administrator Baron Driesen von Osten, who persuaded many eminent actors, directors, academics, designers and musicians, including Sanin, Roerich, Benois, Sacchetti and Glazunov, to collaborate with him in his dream of re-creating authentic mediaeval mystery and miracle plays. The Antique Theatre opened for one season in 1907 but then closed again until 1911–12, when it was revived for a season of Spanish plays by Cervantes, Lope de Vega and Calderón.
2 See p. 374, note 3.
3 See p. 141, note 1.
4 A good, stiff measure.

our dear Doctor Bogdanov-Berezovsky[1] to get something for my chronic cold.

24 September

During the night my watch for some reason was two hours slow, so when I looked at it on first waking up I went back to sleep again until after eleven. When I realized my mistake I sat down in a panic to study *Falstaff*, so as to make at least some attempt to prepare the final scene for Tcherepnin. From two until four we went through it with him, and then from four to six the principal singers came for their first class on the opera. Everyone was there, Gabel, Palechek, Tcherepnin, all the conductors and many of the singers. Tcherepnin and I played through all three *Falstaff* scenes we were working on, Gabel becoming so absorbed in the music he sang along and banged with his palms on the lid of the piano. After that the singers were allocated their roles, and assigned to one or other of the conductors. This year Tcherepnin had instituted a new procedure whereby the cast was divided among the student conductors and assistant conductors, who would then be responsible for coaching the singers in their roles. Tcherepnin distributed them as follows: I had all the *Falstaff* women, Dranishnikov all the men; Gauk was to be my assistant conductor, Shtrimmer – Dranishnikov's. Tsybin had all the *Rigoletto* singers, both men and women, with Kreisler to assist him. *Merci*, Tcherepnin, for giving me the ladies!

Returned home exhausted after four hours' work without a break, and looked forward greatly to relaxing at the Sokol. It may seem strange, but one does relax while doing gymnastics. At first I don't pay much attention to what I am doing, but then I get into it and really enjoy it. After our exercise session everyone gathered round the piano to sing my 'March'. Home again I rang the Astoria, but it was Alexey Pavlovich who answered the telephone and the conversation went no further than mutual expressions of their desire to see me and my desire to visit them.

25 September

My name-day. I told Mama I was not going to celebrate it. Will guests be coming? Relations? No, thank you!

Settled down to revising the fourth scene of *Maddalena*, but I did not get much done: at twelve o'clock Aunt Katya came, and she and Mama and I went to the Novodevichi Cemetery. I am always glad to visit Papa's grave, but today it was not very pleasant because of the cold wind and rain.

---

1 Dr Mikhail Bogdanov-Berezovsky was a specialist in otolaryngology and problems of deafness. Valerian Bogdanov-Berezovsky, the composer, musicologist and close friend of Dmitry Shostakovich's youth, was his son.

In the afternoon a stream of relations and friends of Mama's came, so that the day evaporated in pointless intercourse of one kind and another. I received a long letter from Derzhanovsky with all sorts of interesting ideas for the November concert. I shall be very interested to hear the *Ballade* played by such a highly praised cellist as Beloúsov. But I was extremely annoyed at Derzhanovsky's refusal to print my review of Sabaneyev's music. His reason was that Sabaneyev would sever his relationship with *Muzyka* if *Muzyka* were to publish an article so derogatory to him. At first I was inclined to retaliate by withdrawing from the November concert, but then decided it would not be worth it. My review of Stanchinsky appeared in the preceding number of the magazine, and I became quite agitated reading it.

Not all my friends know when my name-day is, and I did not receive many letters. 'My dear Boyle' sent a telegram. Lidka[1] is annoyed with me for something rude I said to her and is not congratulating me. Damskaya rang up to congratulate me and aroused my curiosity by mentioning a 'dark blonde girl' who is in love with me and is dying to get into the opera class in order to be near me. In the evening I played telephone chess with Golubovskaya and checkmated her twice. The day before yesterday, after our walk to the Islands, she stayed the night with 'Shurik' (Bushen), who had woken her up in the morning to the strains of my 'Fairy Tale'.[2]

26 September

Today I had time seriously to get on with recomposing *Maddalena* and did a sizeable portion of the fourth scene. I also looked through Bach's organ *Passacaglia* in someone's orchestral version, which the small orchestra is going to do. A wonderful work; however, to judge from the score it is painfully long and will be exhausting to play. At five o'clock went to see Myaskusha to complain about Derzhanovsky, but Myaskusha went to great lengths to pacify me. On the desk of his piano I saw the scores of Scriabin's Ninth and Tenth Sonatas, and played some of them: the first glance showed me that there is much wonderful stuff in them, and the main thing is they are less complicated than I had expected. After the convolutions of the Sixth and Seventh Sonatas I was afraid he was going to climb higher and higher towards the 'heights of negation'.

After dinner I telephoned the Astoria and spoke to Nina. She invited me to come with them to the 'Crooked Mirror' tomorrow.

Visited the Andreyevs and showed them my old song 'There are other planets'.[3] I love this song, and the other day, inspired by the example of

---

1 Lida Karneyeva.
2 Op. 3 No. 1.
3 Op. 9 No. 1, to a poem by Konstantin Balmont.

Maddalena, made some revisions to the vocal line. It is now a good song, and Anna Grigorievna liked it very much. She wants to include it in her recital programme in December. I noticed on her piano some songs by Myaskovsky that for some reason I did not know before, except for the lovely, melancholy 'Circles', but they are all good.

27 September

Next morning, I worked successfully at *Maddalena*. I had written to Vera Nikolayevna asking her to command one of her 'subjects' to ring me if they had managed to get an extra ticket for me. Nina telephoned. She laughed and said it was an outrageous way to write, as if to suggest that she was not capable of doing it herself. 'Why is your voice so angry?' she asked, suddenly.

'First, because I am in the middle of composing; and second, because I'm generally angry with you.'

'Well ... you shouldn't be angry with me, because "America" has been sent to the same place as "Kuokkale".'

I did not react in any way to this piece of information, and quickly terminated the conversation. Even so, it was pleasant to hear of 'America's' downfall.

Tcherepnin's class in the Conservatoire went through the magnificent *Passacaglia* of Bach; it will be a real pleasure to learn it with the orchestra. No. 19A, slim and elegant, stood and watched me. Like Seryozha Alpers she has moved this year into the sixth General Subjects class. The Karneyevs told me they saw her in Terioki in the company of the Alpers family. Interesting.

In the evening I put on my dinner suit and went to the 'Crooked Mirror'. At curtain-up only Kessel, a friend of the Meshcherskys, was there, the others all arrived late. They were accompanied by Serge Bazavov and Bobrovsky, and I was delighted to see both of them. Last of all came Zaitsev, and as Nina was sitting on the edge of the group, he sat next to her. I remembered how heartily Max and I had laughed at the 'Crooked Mirror' in the spring. This evening the programme did not seem quite so good. In the interval all the young people drifted into the foyer, but I deliberately stayed behind with Vera Nikolayevna, coming out only at the end of the interval. In the second interval we all went out together. Nina was upset at my lack of attention to her. There was a small *contretemps* just before we went back in: Nina came up to me in the presence of Serge and Zaitsev, and said, 'Seryozha, please come with me ...'

I laughed in her face and said, 'Why should I want to come with you and listen to all the gibberish you talk!' and went off with Talya and Bobrovsky.

At the end of the show we all went down to get our coats. I had put my coat on, and winding my famous grey scarf round my neck went up to say goodbye to the assembled company. Then I started off down the staircase. Nina caught hold of my scarf, and when I looked round, she hid. I walked home, deciding that Nina is not worth bothering about.

28 September

In the morning, my beloved *Maddalena*, and then at two o'clock to the Conservatoire, for my first session with the *Falstaff* ladies. But not many of them turned up, also there was a muddle over the texts – there are two different versions. Nevertheless we worked for an hour and a half, and afterwards Mama and I went to choose an overcoat for me for the winter. However, we could not find anything we liked.

In the evening I practised the piano, wrote my diary and looked through the second proof of the Sonata. At night I had an extraordinarily vivid dream about Max, it was just as though I was meeting him again after his suicide. I was lying on the sofa plying him with questions while he, collarless and with his hands stuffed in his pockets, walked up and down the room telling me everything that had happened. I asked him the reasons for his suicide. He replied that first of all, it was because of his illegitimate birth and the tragedy of his different names: Schmidthof – Lavrov – Alexandrov. Secondly, there had been difficulties and violent arguments at home. I asked him whether, on that last evening that he spent with me, he knew he was preparing to shoot himself on the morrow, and what his feelings were at the moment when he came to the irrevocable decision that that was what he had to do. He replied that the decision had already been taken before that evening, and therefore his attitude towards it was perfectly calm and indifferent. Then I asked him to tell me everything that had transpired from the moment he boarded the train to Vyborg until the moment of his death. He agreed readily, but asked me before he did so to play him something on the piano. I went over to the piano, and seeing on the desk the proof of the Sonata I had dedicated to him, thought that he would most of all like to hear this work he loved so much. I sat down and started to play, and with that woke up.

29 September

In the morning, *Maddalena*, on which I could have spent all day; I started out well but by lunchtime was tired, and since I did not have anything planned for the afternoon, telephoned 'my dear Boyle' and suggested a walk to the Islands, as the weather was good. Zoya agreed and we set off at three o'clock. At that precise moment, as if to mock us, it began to snow heavily, thick, wet snow. But we persisted, and snow-encrusted, white and damp, ploughed on. By the time we had walked the whole length of Kamennoóstrovsky Prospect, the snow began to ease off and soon stopped altogether. We shook it off the sleeves and collars of our overcoats and turned on to the embankment of Kamenny Island. In recompense for our ordeal the green trees, still in their raiment of snow, looked magical, and a special enchantment was the view of the Countess Kleinmichel's[1] dacha from Yelagin Island. We went as far as the Strelka and then went over to Novaya Derevnya, where we took a taxi from the Primorskaya line station there and went to our respective homes. My feet, shod in thin half-boots, were wet through, and to protect myself from the threat of pleurisy, as soon as I got home I rubbed them with eau de Cologne and put on my thick Swiss socks.

30 September

Slept in, so it was eleven before I sat down to *Maddalena*. At three o'clock went into the opera class to see what they were doing with *Falstaff*. Palechek had all the singers sitting in a row and was making them read their lines with plenty of expression but without the music. Then I went with Mama to get a winter overcoat, but since again we could not find anything ready-made, ordered one bespoke from a tailor.

Lyovka Karneyev, whom we all used to regard as just a little boy but who in fact is now seventeen years old, has developed quite a talent as a satirical poet. He has a whole gallery of pen-portraits of his acquaintances, including Boris Zakharov, me, and quite a few others. Yesterday, via Zoya, I got some of them. Of course, there are some awkwardnesses and rough edges, but they also have a good deal of wit. Here are excerpts from the portrait of me:

> Set at large on life's high road;
> Began to think himself a swell;
> Acquired a wardrobe, latest mode,
> Assumed the world's ways very well.
> Sergusya's he of whom this ditty
> Paints a portrait, very pretty,
> Or rather, properly expressed,
> Reveals the truth and damn the rest.

> Although he has some savoir-faire
> His manners often let him down;

---

[1] The Kleinmichel dacha on Kamenny Island, rebuilt in striking Gothic style in 1904, was home to the Countess Maria Kleinmichel and the setting for her glittering salon frequented by the social, cultural and political elite of pre-Revolutionary St Petersburg. After fleeing Russia in 1918, the Countess, a woman of great charm and wit, wrote an engaging memoir, *Memories of a Shipwrecked World*.

> A childish streak is sometimes there
> When he squires ladies round the town.
> His tongue is not at all averse
> To scorching people with a curse,
> But woe betide the man who tries
> To do it back to Serge: he dies.
>
> I wouldn't wish on anyone
> To be beyond Sergusya's pale –
> I've been there, and it is no fun;
> I barely lived to tell the tale.
> He digs away and tries to find
> Your weak points, which is most unkind;
> He'll talk and talk, till as a rule
> He shows himself to be a fool.

And later:

> A famed composer Serge appears,
> His music tortures people's ears,
> Alas. A schoolboy nihilist,
> He bashes like a pugilist.
>
> Serge early learned to cut a dash:
> Cars, first-class carriages, the more as
> They cost him money – made a splash.
> He readily discards 'Auroras'
> As quickly as a worn-out glove,
> And cuts off any burgeoning love
> The instant there's the slightest sign
> Of wedding bells along the line.
>
> His wit is razor sharp, for sure,
> But often out of place, alas.
> He can't resist the chance to score
> So often ends up seeming crass:
> 'The bark of that tree, on inspection,
> Resembles Yesipova's complexion!'
> He once said, laughing fit to bust.
> But now I'm tired, so stop I must.

In reply I sent him this quatrain:

> Behold the frown, the furious glare,
> With which he snarls and damns to black all

Men. A beast, but lower down the stair,
No Leo,[1] but an evil jackal!

I don't know whether he received it or whether I made a mistake with his new address, but Zoya telephoned me today and did not mention my response.

I rang the Astoria to find out when they are going away. The answer is on Saturday. Nina answered the telephone. I replied curtly, 'Well, thank you for the information. I shall be at the station on Saturday.'

Obviously not expecting the conversation to come to such a rapid termination, she quickly added, 'Wait a moment... Perhaps you'd like to come to *Boris Godunov* with us tomorrow?'

'Tomorrow I cannot, I'm going to the Sokol. You always invite me when I have a session there,' I said, and turned the conversation to other matters.

1 October

Another morning on *Maddalena*; the end is in sight. Towards two, still not having learned the simple but lengthy Haydn symphony, I went to Tcherepnin's class: he was at work today in spite of the holiday. I skated through the symphony sight-reading it, then worked with my singers, of whom ten had turned up today. The fact that Palechek troubled to come was very nice. Tcherepnin made a list of when the conductors should attend the opera class, but the list did not include me on the grounds that I have a standing invitation to go whenever I choose to check that everything is going as it should.

Pleased, but rather tired, I went back home. However, around eight o'clock I suffered an attack of nervous exhaustion that was extremely disagreeable. But it passed off during my Sokol gymnastics and by the time I got home afterwards I felt once again calm and in control. 'Free-style games dispel our gloom, transporting us to far-off bounds...' as the Sokol song proclaims.

While we were having tea I told Mama that some Sokol members were going to Helsingfors[2] and had suggested I go with them. 'Good idea, it will be interesting,' said Mama.

2 October

Finished the revision of *Maddalena* and made a note at the end that this second version was dedicated to N. Ya. Myaskovsky.

---

1 Lyova (Lyovka, Lev, Leo) is also the Russian word for lion.
2 The Russian name for Helsinki.

In the afternoon I practised the piano, went to the dentist, had myself measured for a new overcoat, and wrote some letters. As the Meshcherskys are leaving on Saturday I rang up to find out when they would be at home to call on them before their departure. I was glad that Talya answered the telephone. She said they would probably be at home tomorrow evening, and that the Andryushes[1] were also planning to be there. This would be confirmed by telephone tomorrow.

I also had a telephone conversation with Zoya, but we fell out because when she exclaimed: 'See what a clever girl I am!' I told her she had an admirable brain for an environment the size of a chicken coop.

In the evening I went to see Myaskovsky with a portfolio bulging with scores. The scores in question were *Maddalena*, my old E minor Symphony, which Myaskun had for some reason said he would like to see, the proof of the Sonata which I wanted to give him to play through (with his amazingly meticulous eye he always spots any mistakes), the song 'The boat cast off' and the 'March' from Op. 12, which I was a little nervous of showing him.

Maddalena was approved, the dedication welcomed and the manuscript left for Myaskovsky on the piano desk. He looked through the Sonata and found, not one mistake, but a whole heap of them. He praised the song and also the 'March'. In short, a very pleasant and productive evening.

3 October

With no *Maddalena* to occupy me, my free morning seemed very long. I had a letter from Derzhanovsky: 'Are you angry? You have every right to be . . .' and asking me to let him know immediately what I would like to include in my programme for the concert.

I thought the following: (1) Sonata No. 2; (2) Etude Op. 2 No. 3; 'Fairy Tale' and 'March' from Op. 3, 'Despair' and 'Suggestion diabolique' from Op. 4; 'Prelude', 'Rigaudon' and 'Legenda' from Op. 12. I suggested that these pieces be immediately followed by my cello *Ballade*, and I asked to be excused from performing the rest of the programme, the *Toccata* and the Myaskovsky Sonata, especially since I had the impression that the composer was not particularly anxious for me to perform his Sonata.

I packaged up the corrected proof of my Sonata, and practised 'Suggestion diabolique'. Fyaka telephoned and invited me for the evening, asking me to be a little more polite and attentive than I had been at the 'Crooked Mirror'.

Went into the Conservatoire, where the news is that *Falstaff* has been cancelled, because Palechek thinks the women will not be able to cope with it. And whose idea was it to do *Falstaff*, if not Palechek's? What idiocy!

1 Andreyevs.

At half past eight went to the Astoria, keyed up by a feeling of great anticipation. All the Gurzuf contingent were there: Serge, Uncle Grisha, Zaitsev and his mother, the Andreyev brothers but not Anna Grigorievna, Romanovsky, and another four or so people. They were all sitting in a semicircle, but there was nowhere for me to sit down, so I sat on the windowsill, and since conversation seemed to be flagging when I arrived, I at once took it over. When the party separated into tables for bridge I took Serge aside and proposed a revival of our 'card den' with the 'compensator'; we could get together some time, perhaps at my house, to play vint. Serge agreed this would be a good idea.

There were three bridge tables. At my table were Serge, the lawyer Count Rostopchin and Nina. I grumbled that it was hopeless to play with Nina – even though she is sometimes helped by her Papa. Serge yielded and partnered Nina, who laid down her cards as dummy. I laughed and said, 'How nice to see Ninochka in her true colours!'

For the first half of the evening Nina was laughing and happy, but later a cloud came over her. I could see that she was miles away, but did not know the reason. Ninochka assumed a wistful air, withdrew into herself and responded listlessly to all around her. I liked Nina this evening, but seeing that she had something on her mind unrelated to the present company, I adopted a mocking tone with her and when we said goodbye I did so matter-of-factly. I shall go to see them off at the station on Saturday.

As we emerged on to the street, Romanovsky said, 'I'm going to the "Vienna", I have someone to see there. Shall we go together, gentlemen?'

'Yes, let's do that,' said Andreyev.

His brother and I both said we would go as well. The 'Vienna' was crowded, airless and smoky. I had eaten half a box of chocolates at the Meshcherskys and the smell of food now turned my stomach. A modest mug of ale, some people I knew from artistic circles, a few drunken faces, and we all went home. As a healthy, active person I am not much of a frequenter of places like the 'Vienna' at night.

4 October

Slept until half past ten and then practised 'Suggestion diabolique' and the Sonata, after which I went to Tcherepnin's class. When I woke up in the morning, I was sad at the thought of the Meshcherskys going away. Never mind, there was plenty more material in the Conservatoire, so today I went in half an hour before the start of the lesson to have a look round, but did not find anything particularly to attract me. In the class we rehearsed the Bach *Passacaglia* and a Handel organ concerto. I enjoy very much working on the 'old masters'. One of the female students gave me a copy of *Apollon* containing a round-up of the summer season by Karatygin. Most of the programmes had no more than a cursory mention, except for my concert, which was described over two columns of perceptive, laudatory and flowery prose. The same issue had an article about Merezhkovsky by Chudovsky,[1] at one time a great admirer of mine. The article was so muddled and overstuffed that it was sometimes difficult to grasp its meaning at all . . .

In the evening I went to the Sokol and enjoyed punishing myself on the rings and the vaulting horse. My new English overcoat is made of soft, thick, reddish-brown material, and I am very pleased with it. I must get myself a dark-blue velvet suit.

5 October

In the morning I collected from the post office a letter I had been urgently waiting for, and was relatively happy with its contents. I then practised the piano until four o'clock: my own works for Derzhanovsky and others, and other composers' for Yesipova. Finished writing out the revision of the old 'Gavotte' for Op. 12. At four went out for a walk and to pay a couple of calls: to Saburov, who I found had not yet returned to St Petersburg, and to M. P. Korsak. When I got back I had dinner and then went to say goodbye to the Meshcherskys. I arrived at the station five minutes before the train left and found about thirty people in the farewell party, so that I could hardly find the departing travellers in the crush. However, almost at once I ran into the small figure of Nina, deep in conversation with Zaitsev and Romanovsky. I wanted to sidle past, but Nina spotted me and started to ask me if I would write to her. I stood with her for a few minutes, and under cover of the crowd we held hands tenderly. I felt very loving towards her. Nina said, 'I shall write you such despairing letters!'

But I soon tore myself away, saying that I must say goodbye to her parents. Alexey Pavlovich and I kissed. Then I saw Nina again. At the second bell the family boarded the train. 'Seryozha, you must shout "hurrah" as the train pulls out,' Nina said.

Puffing and panting, Yershov hurried up with a bouquet of flowers, and for a time made himself the centre of attention. Zaitsev stood some way off among the crowd. The third bell sounded, and the train glided away from the platform, quickly gathering speed. I yelled out: 'Hurrah! They're off!' Vera Nikolayevna wagged her finger at me deprecatingly.

Serge Bazavov said we should watch the wheels as they disappeared. I said, 'If you look at the wheels, all you'll see is the buffers . . .' Yershov exclaimed, 'How strange it is to think that the link that unites us all here is suddenly vanishing from our midst for three months.'

---

1 See p. 60, note 1.

I agreed with Serge and Oleg that we should not lose sight of one another, and we should get together from time to time to play bridge. Oleg invited me to play this evening, with 'a real Englishman from London', but I had to hurry off because Myaskushka and I had planned to go and hear *Boris Godunov*. I said an affectionate goodbye to Bobrovsky. At the entrance to the platform, I ran into the Andreyevs, who had arrived late. Anna Grigorievna invited Zaitsev to come and play bridge some evening. 'You're a bold sort of fellow,' she said. 'Just ring up and say you're coming!'

Zaitsev laughed and indicated me. 'He's the bold one, not me . . .'

I asked Anna Grigorievna if the day after tomorrow would be a possible time to come and play bridge, and this was agreed. I said goodbye and returned to the platform in order to see off Katya Ignatieva, who was leaving for Odessa twenty minutes after the Meshcherskys' departure. (That will be piquant, bridge with the Zaichik![1]). Katya and Aunt Katya had got themselves in a muddle over their tickets and were dashing towards the exit, getting excited, then rushing back along the platform and barely got themselves sorted out in time. We didn't know whether to laugh or cry.

From the station I hurried off to the Music Drama Theatre for *Godunov*, where Myaskovsky was already waiting for me. The conductor, Bikhter,[2] prides himself on his originality, and in desperately seeking something new to say so distorted the themes that it was positively unpleasant to listen to. Myaskovsky informed me that Leonid Sabaneyev had written an article in the *Moscow Gazette* about modern composers in which he threw a good few brickbats, among them some in my direction, while praising Stanchinsky(!). Dear Stanchinsky, I imagine he will be greatly gladdened and comforted by this. I said to Myaskovksy, 'My dear friend, please suggest a good subject for an opera!'

He answered without a second's hesitation: *The Idiot*, by Dostoyevsky. *Sic*!

6 October

As I need to learn 'Fairy Tale' and prepare thoroughly Etude No. 3 and other pieces for the Moscow concert, I bought several volumes of my own music from Jurgenson and settled down to them today. I also did some work on the Schumann Sonata and then felt I wanted to go for a walk.

Telephoned Golubovskaya proposing that she and I and 'Shurik' should walk somewhere to the outer reaches of the Islands. But Golubovskaya could

---

1 'Zayats', the root of Zaitsev's name, means a hare, so 'zaichik' means a little hare.
2 Mikhail Bikhter (1881–1947), pianist and conductor, was Musical Director of the Music Drama Theatre. Bikhter was a piano student of Yesipova and a conducting student of Tcherepnin. As a pianist he appeared in recital with singers such as Chaliapin and Zabela. From 1933 he was a professor at the Leningrad Conservatoire.

not come, and suggested I get in touch directly with 'Shurik' (Mlle Bushen), which I did. She responded enthusiastically to the proposal, and at two o'clock we set out from the Nikolayevsky Bridge, near where she lives. We walked right across Vasilievsky Island, then Petrovsky Island and on to Krestovsky Island. This is where the Batareyny Road starts, the far end of which – and indeed Krestovsky Island itself – is outside the limits of the St Petersburg town map, and therefore intrigued us. We ventured off the map and before long found ourselves nearing the sea. The road ended, but between us and the sea there was still land, so low-lying that whenever there is even a light breeze from the west it floods. However, at the moment there was no wind, and the ground was just a swamp. We resolved that, come what may, we would get right to the sea itself, so leaping from tussock to tussock we trudged on by means of a board we found and dragged along with us. It took the best part of an hour, but we got there in the end and experienced a glow of satisfaction even though our feet were irreversibly soaked through. We walked back again.

At home I rubbed my feet with eau de Cologne, but it cannot have been a wholly effective remedy as for the next week I had a cough and a cold and was afraid of developing pleurisy.

Mlle Bushen is a splendid and very charming walking companion, and anything but stupid. She is deeply interested in my music and all my musical activities and, I venture to say, in me.

The St Petersburg Chess Society is organizing a series of tournaments to mark its ten years of existence. One of these is a tournament for Higher Educational Establishments, and a meeting was to be held today to which I had been invited as the representative of the Conservatoire by the President of the Society. I was happy to agree, and the meeting took place this evening in the Chess Club. The contest itself will take place at the end of January and involve roughly thirty to forty people, two or three from the Conservatoire. After the meeting I played three games, winning to my great satisfaction all of them.

7 October

The 'Board of Trustees for the Encouragement of Russian . . . etc.' returned my Concertos with a polite refusal on the grounds that it would not be possible to present my Concerto as part of its Belyayev Concerts Series because there were already others in the programme. I was prepared for this and not at all surprised.

In the evening I went to the Andreyevs. I played them my song 'The boat cast off', and it was very well received. Afterwards Nikolay Vasilievich, his brother, Zaitsev and I played bridge. I have learned something about the technique of this game, and am now capable of playing quite a decent hand. Outwardly relations with Zaitsev are friendly; in any case I have nothing against him even inwardly; to judge from the scene at the railway station it is pretty clear that I have prevailed. When we had finished our game we wrote a long, witty letter to the Meshcherskys in which Zaitsev and I formally testified to the fact that the Andreyevs had formed part of the farewell party but had been late in arriving. I wrote, while the others clustered around and dictated what I was to say. I signed the letter: 'By the Grace of God Free Artist Sergey Prokofiev', and Zaitsev: 'Former Yogi and Cardmaster Kirill Zaitsev', after which he added, 'I'm sure they will understand there why I am a former Yogi . . .' I knew that in Gurzuf a book had been doing the rounds about Indian yogis (wise men). If Nina, in the shady Gurzuf avenues, had been in the habit of calling Kirill her yogi, I could well understand the biting sarcasm with which he acknowledged his resignation from that post . . .

8–23 October

The important musical events that happened during this period were as follows: Tcherepnin, to whom Artsybushev had conveyed the information that there was to be a third Belyayev Concert and that he, Tcherepnin, would be invited to conduct it, had asked Artsybushev why my Concerto had not been included, bringing forward a raft of arguments in its favour. Chief among these was that I would be performing it for Koussevitzky. To cut a long story short, the discussion ended with an agreement that if a third concert did indeed take place, my Concerto would be programmed, otherwise Tcherepnin would decline to conduct. For the time being this is a secret, and I am to tell no one about it.

I went to my first lesson with Yesipova. 'What are you talking about, the whole Schumann Sonata?' she asked in horror. 'To bring such a complex piece up to examination standard would take all our time and leave none for the remainder of the repertoire!'

All the same, I played her two movements and they were obviously very much to her taste since her conclusion was as follows: 'Well, all right then . . . bring the whole work to me for the next lesson, and then we won't need to touch it again until the exam.'

This hardly tallied with what she had said earlier, but never mind! After this she went off to Kiev and Odessa for a concert tour with Auer, and there were no more lessons for three weeks.

During this period the people I saw most frequently were Myaskushka, whom I visited several times, and Mlle Bushen, with whom I had several very pleasant encounters. I also talked on the telephone to Damskaya, who has taken to ringing me up for no obvious reason. One Friday evening Mama had guests in, among them dear Nikolay Andreyev. He, Kolechka and Oleg – I had invited him – made up a vigorously contested bridge four, which was very enjoyable. I had also telephoned Serge and Zaitsev(!) but neither of them was able to come. Fyaka sent me three short letters and received the same number in return. They are in Berlin at the moment, and their postcards of familiar places gave me great pleasure.

I have not seen or heard anything of the Karneyevs. Zakharov sent me a card some time ago, but I am not going to write back to him at the moment: caddish and silly it may be, but I do not want to write a letter of aimless small talk, and I don't feel in the mood to write anything more significant. Speaking of moods, what desperate moods I suffered during this period!!

On Saturday the 19th at 8.20 in the evening I got on a train to Vyborg, spending the night there. The following morning I went in search of the cemetery where Max is buried, but went to the wrong one. Max's lies seven versts outside the town and I had no time to get there, since I had to continue my journey. That evening I went on to Helsingfors, where I stayed until the 23rd, returning that evening to Piter. My mood had improved considerably, I had done what I set out to do, and by the time I came back I was blithe and anxious to get on with life.

Vyborg is a sprawling, provincial little town. Helsingfors is a foreign city, a mini-Berlin, very interesting and well-favoured. On the train I read through the score of Berlioz's *Benvenuto Cellini* Overture; what an abominable welter of transposing instruments! You can spend half an hour working out what all those trumpets and horns in different tonalities are supposed to be playing, and in the end what you find is a common triad! All the instruments in my scores will be written in C.

Oh, how I adore travelling!

On my return to the city, for ten days or so I did not write my diary. I will briefly summarize the period.

24 October

Arriving for the large orchestra class I learned from Tcherepnin that a concert had been arranged for 3 November in which I was to conduct Beethoven's Seventh Symphony, also his Violin Concerto, and Liszt's Second Piano Concerto. Tsybin would conduct the Overtures to *The Flying Dutchman* and *Euryanthe*. Tsybin is also graduating this year so I was quite ready to accept the way this programme was divided up.

And so, out of the blue I was suddenly plunged into a frenzy of activity: I had to learn both concertos and do all the rehearsals, as well as practising the solo part of my First Piano Concerto, which is how I spent the evening.

25 October

Studied Liszt's wonderful concerto in the morning. In the afternoon I went through it with Tcherepnin and attended the Requiem Mass marking the twentieth anniversary of Tchaikovsky's death.

At home I finished composing and tidying up my *Musical Letter to Zakharov*.[1] I had had the idea for this in Helsingfors, working out all the text and music as I walked along the embankments and sat in a Finnish café. The music is of course not serious, but it is, I think, the first time that I have composed away from the piano.

Don't laugh, it's not at all a bad method. When I got back to St Petersburg and sat down to play on the piano what I had written, to start with I hated it, but a day later I already liked it.

In the evening I enjoyed a session at the Sokol.

26 October

It is six months since Max died. When I had finished practising the D flat Concerto and written a long covering letter to Jurgenson with detailed instructions for its publication, I decided that evening I would show Myaskushka my piano reduction of the orchestral part. But he was planning to go to the Ziloti concert, and he was also being pestered by Saminsky and Shaposhnikov, so although he played through it he had no particularly cogent observations to make. Anyhow, I think the transcription is more or less in order.

I went back home, to be called on by Borovsky. He is making a quite successful career as a pianist and is soon leaving for a twenty-four-concert tour of the great cities of Russia that will take him right up to Christmas. I am very happy for him, and the thought that he will be spending two weeks at the end of dismal November in the warmth of Tiflis, where he has five concerts, makes me positively envious.

Borovsky had come to listen to my Second Piano Concerto, to which his attention had been drawn by Karatygin's reviews. I played the concerto to him, and the Sonata No. 2, and some of the smaller pieces. His comments were very perceptive; it is clear that he has a very good appreciation of my music and is altogether a very experienced musician. The music I write is very much to his taste. He asked me to send him in Tiflis the score of the Second Sonata as soon as it is published.

---

1 *A Musical Letter to B. S. Zakharov in Vienna from S. S. Prokofiev in St Petersburg* for voice and piano, *sans* op.

27 October

The funeral of Liza, the Rayevskys' elderly and long-time servant.

In the afternoon I went to the production of excerpts from *Onegin* and *Faust* in the Small Hall, done to piano accompaniment. The Conservatoire does possess a theatre but it is let, so student productions are corralled into a hastily adapted stage in front of the organ in the Small Hall. Gabel was rubbing his hands with glee: 'What a marvellous little stage we've made of it!' But many of the audience are justifiably incensed by this 'little stage' since it is, to all intents and purposes, a pathetic pile of rubbish.

Tcherepnin asked me long ago if I wanted to conduct the performance with piano, but I thought this would not be very interesting and would not justify the length of time I would have to spend on rehearsals. The conductor's baton was therefore on this occasion passed to Dranishnikov. The show went very well.

In the evening I thoroughly enjoyed playing vint at Oleg Subbotin's house, and won a rouble and a half for the car journey back. Oleg has almost completely recovered from his paralysis, but still the doctors are sending him to a warm climate, to Nice. He is leaving in a week's time, which is a great pity as he is the most delightful young man.

28 October

Sent the full score and piano score of the D flat Concerto to Jurgenson with a long covering letter. I also despatched the *Musical Letter* to Boryusya. Immediately after writing it out I did not like it so much, but now I find it good, and amusing.

29 October

At the moment I am working on my programme for the Moscow recital on 24 November. I want to play this programme really well.

Yesipova has returned from her concert tour, and today I 'returned to a state of grace' as Bushen puts it. Once again, it started with the same old discussion: surely I could not be planning to play the whole of the Schumann sonata at the exam?! Today I played the Finale, not particularly successfully, but for some reason got well praised for it.

I missed out going to the Sokol and instead attended the first of this season's student concerts. I love these events anyway, and on this occasion Ossovskaya had asked me to accompany her student in the Grieg Concerto. In the same programme, one of Winkler's students, Dudar, was playing, a most lovely-looking girl. Today she got lost in the Schumann *Toccata*, kept stopping, and finally ran off the stage and into the corridor, where she broke down in such a terrible fit of hysterics that it simultaneously tugged at one's heartstrings and reminded one of a dog howling. She was spirited away into a classroom where with difficulty she was brought back to a state of reasonable equilibrium.

30 October

Practised the piano. Went into the choral class, where they are keen to get going on *Aida*. Tcherepnin, needless to say, is actively working with the 'ladies'. Belokurova is not in the chorus.

In the evening I went to the Sokol party, which consisted of a small display of the best members, both male and female. I had to provide music for the exercises, some of which have their own special music (Czech, and rather good), but for others I had to improvise something in waltz rhythm, and since nobody wanted any serious waltzes I brought shame on my grey hairs by playing *Songe d'automne*.[1] They then marched to my 'March', in the course of which the audience (mostly themselves members of the gymnastic club) clapped along merrily to every beat in the bar. With the whole room thumping in rhythm, it was very effective. When the Sokol sisterhood was performing their exercises to my accompaniment, they behaved in a particularly cheeky manner; I repaid them in kind. I could not get out of my head a phrase from *Rheingold*: 'How stupid you are, silly sisters!'[2]

31 October

The concert has been postponed for ten days, until 14 November: Glazunov is drinking; Auer is away on a tour and cannot nominate a violinist, and the pianist has fallen ill. Thus the immediate urgency has somewhat abated. Today in the orchestra class I went painstakingly through the Seventh Symphony, each part in turn, having with Kreisler's help the previous evening marked in the phrasing, especially in the wind instruments to eliminate all the unbearable natural harmonics, and also singling out those places where the theme in the double-basses is hard to hear and needs to be brought out (one of Beethoven's shortcomings).

In the afternoon I practised the piano, and then put on my dinner-jacket as I had been invited to dine by the Ruzskys, whom I had not seen since goodness knows when. I am told that Ruzsky has sold his copper business in

---

1 A popular waltz by Archibald Joyce, the 'English Waltz King'. Harold Bride, a survivor of the *Titanic*, recalls it being played by the orchestra on deck at the moment when the ship went down.
2 Flosshilde's ironic rebuke to the other Rhine maidens in the opening scene of Wagner's *Rheingold*.

the Caucasus and got a million for it; this may be false information. In any case he was as charming as ever, and his appearance is fresher and younger than it was. I did not talk much with Tanya, but sat next to Ira and we chatted away the whole time. The Konshins were also there; they asked me to dine on Wednesday. As usual with the Ruzskys the wine flowed, as did the champagne, liqueurs and vintage brandy. After all that I had my work cut out to concentrate enough to play a Schumann trio.

1 November

Slept in a little, then practised my programme for Moscow and also for Yesipova. In the afternoon, in Tcherepnin's class, I went through the Beethoven Violin Concerto. Sokol in the evening, followed by telephone calls from both Damskaya and Bushen relating how they had fared in the student concert this evening. Damskaya was the first to ring, and I asked her about Bushen, so that when the latter also rang I was able to tell her everything about her performance. When she exclaimed in astonishment 'Je n'en reviens plus! . . .',[1] I said that I had been sitting up in the balcony and she must have failed to notice me. She believed this.

2 November

In the presence of Lyapunov (St Serge, as Bushen calls him referring to his exceptional piety and the nobility of his countenance) and Tcherepnin, I played the orchestral piano for Shkarovskaya. She can play the Liszt concerto quite well, but is apt to go to pieces and puts on the most incredible airs. She is the type of well-off, fairly pretty and extremely bumptious Odessa girl who says things like: 'Ooh, now, could we possibly just have a tiny, tiny ritenutochka on this wee notochka?'

A postcard from Zakharov to say how delighted he was by my 'talented illustrations of Petersburg life', and a longer letter would follow in a few days. I am very pleased.

In the evening I went to the second performance of the *Onegin/Faust* programme and sat with Shurik Bushen, which made for a very pleasant evening. Gabel sat by the piano the whole evening, making no effort to conceal his anxiety and making it hard for Gauk to play. Not only was he tapping his foot loudly on the first beat of the bar, but his shoes were squeaking, which I found exasperating. During the interval I went up to him and jokingly said, 'Stanislav Ivanovich, Gauk here and Tsybin and I are getting up a subscription to buy you some rubber galoshes!'

1 The phrase ('I'm not coming back any more!') is neither grammatically correct nor appropriate to the context, so may be a misunderstanding or a slip of the pen.

'?!'

'Well, it's just that your shoes are making such a noise banging and squeaking! . . .'

'They're not really squeaking, are they?'

'Like a Ukrainian[1] ox-cart.'

Stanislav, being a good-natured sort, just laughed.

The violinist to play in the concert is announced as Tilka Hansen, which is very good news.

3 November

Today I agreed with Bushen that we would do a really long walk, of the kind that both she and I have a penchant for. The weather was grey, overcast, foggy and dirty-looking, but it was not actually drizzling, so we set off. We walked right across the Islands: Vasilievsky, Petrovsky, Krestovsky and Kamenny, and emerged on to the Strogonov Bridge. Then on to Novaya Derevnya and the mud of the Lansky Highway, where we got well and truly bogged down until we finally reached Udelny Park. Here I wanted to sit down and eat the chocolates and pears I had in my pocket, but all the benches were wet and the tireless Shurik was itching to press on. And sure enough, turning to the left we came upon a wonderful open area with a beautiful forest, water, and even a hill. Soon after this we came to the main coastal railway line (the branch line to Ozerki) and walked back along the tracks to Novaya Derevnya, eating the chocolate and pears as we walked along and not sitting down to rest.

But this was not a long enough walk for Shurik, and she asked what I would think about going on to the Strelka? I would really have liked to rest, but did not want to be seen as giving up, so on to the Strelka we went. The Islands were dark and deserted, but we made it to the Point, after which we returned to Krestovsky Island, boarded the horse tram to Vvedensky and then a whole series of trams back to the centre, where we parted because we were each dining with an aunt: she with hers on Rasezhaya Street and I with mine on Sergievskaya Street. Mlle Bushen is no slouch at conversation either; hers is much enlivened by her spectacular knowledge of French and German.

At the Rayevskys I had dinner and then played vint, in which game I am finding that my knowledge of bridge has a good effect. But around ten o'clock I was beginning to feel diabolically sleepy and my temples were hurting, so I hurried Mama up and we went home.

---

1 Prokofiev's word here is 'khokhol' which is a slightly contemptuous Russian word for a Ukrainian.

4 November

I had a wonderful sleep last night. Next morning I went to rehearse the programme for our concert. The finale of the Seventh Symphony[1] is so badly orchestrated it is torture to learn it with the orchestra! Shkarovskaya was late for rehearsal and St Serge was in an agony of apprehension. Nikolay Nikolayevich[2] was obviously also much put out, and when he saw her after the rehearsal forgot his usual air of debonair gallantry and flew at her in a rage.

When Bushen arrived at her aunt's, she told me, she had immediately gone to sleep in a chair in the corner, and when she woke up played my compositions on the piano.

Playing by heart is one of the things I find most difficult to do. But today an inspiration came to me of how to do it without ever having to fear memory lapses again and fixing the music indelibly in the mind. When a piece has been sufficiently learned with the music, one must try to remember it away from the piano, imagining the sound of the music in parallel with the way it is written, that is to say recalling the music through the ears at the same time as remembering how it looks to the eyes. This must be done slowly and meticulously, reconstructing in imagination every detail of every bar. This is the first stage. Stage two consists of recalling all the music aurally while training the visual side to recall not the score but the keyboard and the individual keys which are employed to produce the sound of the music in question. The transition from stage one to stage two is not easy, because the more one tries to visualize the keyboard, the more the printed notes seem to appear before one's eyes ... But the more one gradually succeeds in absorbing into memory the keyboard alongside the music, the more one can be sure that the piece is irrevocably stored in the memory, since when it is reproduced all three sorts of memory are combined: musical, visual and digital, each of them having first been exercised separately and only later integrated.

Today, going to the Sokol, I experimented: on my way there I rehearsed in my memory the first movement of the Schumann sonata by imagining the notes in the score; and coming back, the keyboard (this I found quite difficult and exhausting), and when I was at home I played the complete movement without hesitation, whereas before undertaking this exercise I had hardly ever managed to play it without stopping or hesitating.

A practical advantage is that one can practise anywhere at any time: walking along the street, sitting in the tram, waiting in a queue, anywhere indeed where one would be bored without this activity to engage the mind.

---

1 Of Beethoven.
2 Tcherepnin.

5 November

Practised the piano and brought Yesipova the Second Fugue from *The Art of Fugue*. My idea was to play each entry of the fugue subject *forte* and all the secondary figures *piano*. Anna Nikolayevna approved of this principle, and generally had no adverse comments to make. 'What are you going to play in the category of Russian composers?' she asked.

'I haven't chosen this section yet.'

'Well, you seem to be so fond of these moderns: Medtner, Scriabin . . . choose something by one of them.'

'Very good, Anna Nikolayevna, I will.'

After the lesson, which was in Yesipova's house, I went to the Conservatoire. I still had three-quarters of an hour to wait before Tcherepnin's class, so I sat and chatted with some of Yesipova's female students about musical current affairs. Then I went through Beethoven's Violin Concerto with Tcherepnin and Tilya Hansen, who is very nice and plays magnificently. I behaved in a very restrained, serious manner with her. The Hansen sisters and the Karneyev sisters are now close friends, and I am sure Tilya will tell them she is playing with me and that they will come to listen on the 14th.

Before the rehearsal with Hansen, Tcherepnin played some excerpts from *Carmen* so deliciously that I was seized with a desire to hear this opera, the more so as many people have said what an excellent production of it is now to be seen at the Music Drama Theatre. But alas, tonight the performance was of *Sadko*, not *Carmen*.

I should have liked to go to the Andreyevs, whom I have not seen for some time, but Nikolay Vasilievich was singing in the opera. I rang up Mlle Bushen and invited her to come with me to the theatre, any theatre. We went to the Maly Theatre, but the play was awful, stupid rubbish. We walked back afterwards while Shurik expatiated on Wagner in a long, eloquent stream of discourse.

6 November

I have not been into the small orchestra class for some time, but today I came in to conduct Bach's *Passacaglia*. The orchestra had forgotten what they ever knew about the piece, and conducting it was torture. All the same, Tcherepnin is proposing that the orchestra should appear in a concert on 22 November, and that the *Passacaglia* should also be played in its original form on the organ by a student from the organ class. This will be very interesting.

At home I practised the piano and started reading Dostoyevsky's *The Gambler*. I've known this story for a long time, but it came into my mind recently as a good potential subject for an opera. Now that I myself have played roulette, which I did in the summer, this magnificent story with its clumsy, awkward yet terrible atmosphere, engages me extremely.

Soon after six I struggled into my tails and went to the Konshins for dinner. As always it was a very smart affair: full evening dress, the table decorated with gardenias, and so on.

Ira Ruzskaya and I (we are friends now) went back to the Ruzsky flat by car and brought back the cello so that Nikolay Pavlovich and I could play together. Afterwards many of the young people, among them the Konshina sisters and the Ruzskaya sisters) went to the Navy Ball. I would have been quite interested to go too, but was not sure whether, if I expressed a wish to go, there would be a ticket, and as I had an early start and a demanding rehearsal tomorrow I kept quiet about it.

7 November

The Scherzo from the symphony did not go very well, and according to Tcherepnin I was to blame. However, I was given high praise for the Finale, which I had studied intensively before the rehearsal. Cecilia[1] arrived, and we made a very good job of rehearsing the Beethoven Violin Concerto, after which we had a nice talk.

There followed the interval, and then Shklyarovskaya[2] interpreted the Liszt concerto with a sense of rhythm that can only be described as wayward. An over-excited Lyapunov, a nervous Tcherepnin, a large number of listeners in the audience, a rehearsal lasting almost an hour and a half – it was all exhausting, but interesting.

The Director of the Vilnius branch of the Imperial Russian Musical Society, Treskin, has invited me to appear there in Tchaikovsky's Trio and some of my pieces, at a time of my choosing. A hundred and fifty roubles fee. I agreed, and after discussion we settled on 28 November. He will send a telegram to reserve the hall for that date.

I then went home, where I found Yurasovsky had arrived from Moscow and was waiting for me. He is very full of himself, but a nice fellow. All the same, to have to play him 'Suggestion diabolique' and other pieces after an exhausting rehearsal, and then to listen to his compositions, was not the easiest thing in the world.

'You're playing in Moscow on the 28th, aren't you?' he asked.

'I am, but it's on the 24th.'

'No, it's the 28th. Derzhanovsky has changed the date of the concert. If you look in the latest number of *Muzyka* you'll see: it's the 28th.'

---

1 Hansen.
2 Properly, Shkarovskaya. This nickname has a faintly pejorative nuance.

This shook me. What was I to do about Vilnius? I'd already given my word to the Director, and he had telegraphed to reserve the hall. I rang the Conservatoire, but no one knew where he was staying.

Today I avidly went on reading *The Gambler*. The story excited me, and disturbed me, beyond words. How stupid it is, how clumsy ... and how true. I do not know whether it can be made into an opera; I did not even think of that as I was reading. And yet, to find a way of representing the roulette table, the crowd of players, the terrible visage of chance, was irresistibly fascinating.

Today I found out from the assistant manager of the orchestra why it was that I had not seen 'my friend' Wenzel recently. The answer, alas, is that he has progressive paralysis and is in hospital, having all but lost his reason ...

8 November

As soon as I got in to the Conservatoire I told everyone I met that I urgently needed to find Mr Treskin, so that the moment he appeared someone would come to find me. Eventually we did find one another, talked over the problem and postponed Vilnius until January.

Went through the Liszt concerto with Shklyarevskaya and Tcherepnin and sorted out a number of details. Tcherepnin was very agitated and even flew at me when I dissented from his suggestion that I should conduct a particular passage first in two and then in four, changing the beat every four bars.

After the rehearsal I did not go straight home as there was a Requiem Mass for Anton Rubinstein and after that a rehearsal for the third performance of the *Faust/Onegin* programme, the one being done to piano accompaniment. After that I did go home, practised the piano for Moscow, had dinner, and went to the student concert in the company of Kokochka Shtember, who called for me. The student concerts this year have not yet caught fire: they are not well attended, the programmes are short and generally have a somewhat drab character. Had it not been for Kokochka I would have expired from boredom ... I was delighted when, towards the end of the interval, Shurik Bushen appeared, her hands importantly plunged into her pockets. We spent the remainder of the evening together and thus avoided boredom. She has also read *The Gambler* and is excited by it. Golubovskaya is reading it now. Lintvaryova, another Yesipova student and a very nice girl, played some Scarlatti very well indeed at the concert.

I am going to write my autobiography. The title will be: *My Life (With Details)*.

9 November

I had myself woken at half past seven as by nine I must be at rehearsal, which today looked like being a complicated one. It began with the Bach *Passacaglia* played by the small orchestra which we were preparing for the student concert at the end of November. The organ professor also attended and we repeated the performance, this time with him playing the organ. However, he played very quietly and without making any changes in registration, so the performance did not produce any particularly impressive highlights. The large orchestra came in at ten o'clock and joined the small orchestra to play *Euryanthe* under the baton of Tsybin. This meant a free hour for me so I went into the Great Hall where Safonov was rehearsing his programme for a concert in memory of Tchaikovsky, less in order to listen to the music than to observe the public, which because it was a general rehearsal was present in large numbers.

Returning to the Small Hall I rehearsed the Liszt concerto. The piano was now in its proper position by the conductor's stand, Glazunov came in to listen, the orchestra girded up its collective loins – and the concerto went really pretty well. Glazunov said to Tcherepnin that I had made great strides as a conductor. This was very pleasant to hear, and when the rehearsal was over I went round the Conservatoire chatting and joking with the Rozhanovich sisters and looking at Belokurova, who today was adorning the corridors with her presence. I think she should be singing in the chorus (she did last year, at least). I then returned home and went to sleep on the sofa.

In the evening I attended the concert. These days this is something of an event for me, as I have practically given up going to concerts since the spring. I thought how silly I had been when I entered the attractive Hall of the Nobility[1] and saw the crowds of music-lovers, among them many people I know, the whole environment giving me the greatest pleasure. I heard *Prometheus*[2] which, for the greater enlightenment of the dull-witted audience was played twice – an enterprising and not necessarily stupid procedure.

My impression of *Prometheus*: tedious, lacking in climactic points, the endless trills and splashes become wearisome, the form is diffuse. In all other respects *Prometheus* is a highly remarkable work.

I met Shteiman at the concert and was delighted to see him. Walked Shurik Bushen home.

---

1 Now the Great Hall of the St Petersburg Philharmonia.
2 Scriabin's *Prometheus, Poème du feu*, Op. 60.

10 November

It being Sunday, I slept in and did not do much piano practice. Went to the third performance of our piano-accompanied opera programme. Umnova did not sing the role of Siébel, whether because she was too nervous or because she had been taken off for singing sharp I do not know, and was replaced by Rozhanovich. Dranishnikov, standing in for Gauk, accompanied excellently. Molchanov has a wonderful voice. During the interval I was sitting on a sofa in the foyer and, spotting Klingman, beckoned her over to sit beside me. She obeyed, and we gossiped about everything and everybody.

I paid a call on Saburov; the old man received me very graciously.

In the evening the Andreyevs, Mama and I went to the opening of an exhibition of Cubist paintings by young artists. If I am a musical cubist, how far I have lagged behind them! For example: a large canvas, entirely covered with a multi-coloured mosaic, with no hint whatever of any outline of an identifiable object. It is entitled *Orchestral Conductor*. Any connection between a conductor and the colourful rug represented here escapes my understanding. But I don't wish to mock; I would sincerely like to appreciate the ideas underlying the way the artist has chosen to express himself.

At the exhibition I met the charming young Radlov[1] and also my former admirer Mr Chudovsky.

11 November

The last rehearsal before the general rehearsal. The symphony went pretty badly and I ran out of steam trying to bring it into some kind of order. Nevertheless, Mme Tcherepnin complimented me on the progress I have made as a conductor, producing a flood of allusions to Greek mythology which, to my shame, I am ill equipped to interpret. Tilya Hansen plays wonderfully and with exemplary rhythm, she is easy to work with; Shklyaryevskaya is a more difficult proposition although this performance also went well. The main question mark is over the symphony. In proportion as my strengths as a conductor increase, the closer to my heart become works I

---

1 The Radlov brothers were Nikolay (1899–1942), an artist and cartoonist and – the more likely encounter on this occasion – Sergey (1892–1958), a gifted theatre director and disciple of Meyerhold who would play a large part in Prokofiev's plans for future stage works. Radlov was responsible for the 1926 staging of *The Love for Three Oranges* at the Leningrad Academic Opera and Ballet Theatre (Akopera) as the Mariinsky was by then known before being reincarnated as the Kirov, and the following year was planning a joint production with Meyerhold of *The Gambler*, but this was aborted because of political and bureaucratic machinations. In 1934 Prokofiev saw Radlov's Studio Theatre production of *Romeo and Juliet* translated by his wife Anna, and this was the impulse for the ballet, Radlov himself providing the first (not very satisfactory, as it turned out) draft of the libretto.

perform, and I very much want the symphony to have a good performance.

At home I got a letter from Fyaka, which made me very happy.

It really is time I composed a symphony! I am, in fact, beginning. As I walked home from *Prometheus* a snatch of melody occurred to me, and from it a theme has now developed. In time some episodes will appear. In the first instance I shall try to accumulate as much material as I can, and then get down to composing the complete work.

Shurik Bushen telephoned in the late afternoon: I had asked her during the morning if she was going this evening to Artsybushev's *Jealousy*, which is currently having a successful run at Nezlobin's theatre.[1] She said she would think about it, but now said she would let me know in an hour's time, prevaricated, and could not make up her mind. I decided to forget about Artsybashev and go instead to the Sokol, also to go to *Carmen* tomorrow and not invite Shurik, as a punishment for her capriciousness.

At the Sokol there were not many people taking part in my session, so I had to work harder than usual: my exertions almost crippled me!

12 November

Dawn was hardly a glimmer in the sky when I was woken by the insistent ringing of the telephone. I was frightened at first, then irritated, and decided not to answer it. Some while later the cook informed me that it had been Mr Saburov, inviting me to dinner. When I asked what time this had been, she told me: half past seven. Saburov doesn't sleep much, so he is quite liable to ring up before dawn.

In general nothing much interesting happened today. I went into the Conservatoire and afterwards dined with Saburov, played chess with him (+1–1) and played the piano. He promised to acquaint me with the music-loving Zinoviev family, whom he had mentioned last winter.

Was home by half past eleven and went to bed.

13 November

The general rehearsal. Tilya Hansen sent a message that her cheeks had swollen up and she would not be coming to the rehearsal. This will not matter; I am quite relaxed about this piece and it will leave more time for the

---

1 The impresario Konstantin Nezlobin had launched his private theatre enterprise in 1909 in Moscow, where among the talented directors to be given their introduction to the metropolitan stage was Konstantin Mardzhanov. From 1911 Nezlobin was also active in St Petersburg, renting for his 1913–14 season the Panayev Theatre on Admiralty Embankment, later to be destroyed by fire during the October Revolution.

symphony. I therefore applied myself with every ounce of energy at my command to this work. We stopped, repeated passages and worked away at it until noon; it was not like a general rehearsal, but the symphony refused to catch fire and blaze into life, although the third and fourth movements were all right. All went well also with Shklyarevskaya, but Tsybin's pieces were better. The audience was quite numerous, as is usual for a general rehearsal.

Following the rehearsal there was a general distribution of tickets, and then I walked along Morskaya Street and Nevsky Prospect with Bushen. Went to draw out 50 roubles from Alfyorov and they gave them to me, but advised that only just over 200 roubles were left in the account. I do not know how they calculate this, but it is not much considering that at one time 4,400 roubles had been deposited. Came home at four o'clock tired, hungry and in a very bad temper. Had something to eat then went to sleep on the sofa.

In the evening Mama and I were at the Andreyevs and played vint. It was a lovely time because of the great mutual affection that exists between us.

14 November

Overslept, which I should not have done seeing that I was not late going to bed, and this always gives me a headache. Mended the lock on my cupboard and preened myself on this achievement. Otherwise did very little, put on my tails, shaved and went to the concert, which was timed to start at one o'clock. Hansen has mumps and telephoned to say that she could not take part; this is much to be regretted as her performance would have been the best in the programme. I was in an excellent mood when I arrived backstage: I am not nervous before appearing as a conductor, but the mood was promptly spoilt by learning that Jascha Heifetz was to be an emergency replacement for Tilya, and because of the last-minute nature of this substitution, Tcherepnin would be conducting, reading the score from sight, instead of me. But as it turned out the new arrangement failed to come about at all, and I need not have been upset. Even so, the start of the concert was delayed for forty minutes, causing some of the audience to become disgruntled. While we were waiting, I saw Myaskushka, my fellow 'Sokol' Borislavsky, and Bushen, to whom at her request I lent scores.

At last the concert began. I went to the podium not from the forestage but through the orchestra, threading my way around the stands. However, my progress was spotted from the balcony, and was greeted by applause. I ascended the podium, bowed, then asked Vasily to re-seat the clarinets, who for some reason had been put among the bassoons. This took some time, and then I began. The opening chords sounded marvellous, and after that all went smoothly, better than yesterday. I felt myself to be fully in control although, naturally, not everything was as perfect as I would have wished. But to achieve refined nuances in a performance by a student orchestra is a virtually impossible task. By the Finale I was getting tired, and drops of sweat rained down from my brow on to the score. The audience applauded each movement, and I was called back to take another bow at the end. Glazunov said I had made huge strides; Tcherepnin praised the performance and was heard to say to someone, 'A fine display of carving by our little Seryozha!'

During the interval I talked to Myaskovsky, who as usual found a whole cluster of imperfections and left me in no doubt that I was no conductor, even though he acknowledged an improvement over last year. Among the audience were Mama with Aunt Katya, Kokochka Shtember, Shteiman – whom I was very glad to see – and old man Saburov. In the distance I caught sight of the slender form of 19A.

In the second half of the programme the small orchestra joined forces with the large orchestra, producing a sea of musicians on the platform. Tsybin conducted *Euryanthe*, not a difficult piece but it did go tremendously well and was a great success with the audience, Tsybin being called back several times. After this came the Liszt concerto. Shklyarevskaya was very nervous and went badly to pieces. To perform a difficult work with an unrhythmical soloist is not a situation calculated to make anyone feel secure. We were escorted on to the stage as if going into battle: 'It'll be fine, God willing, it will go well . . .' 'Whatever happens, the most important thing is not to get lost . . .' and so on.

As soon as I found myself on the podium, I found it quite funny. There were in the end no disasters in the concerto performance; Tcherepnin found three places to criticize, but these were not serious and from my point of view almost all unavoidable. Glazunov was full of praise. The concert ended with the Overture to *The Flying Dutchman*, conducted by Tsybin.

I had to weigh up what I should do after the concert, and eventually walked back along Morskaya and Nevsky with Shurik Bushen. At home I rang up Shteiman, who had positive things to say about my conducting. I was tempted to suggest that we go to have dinner somewhere together and then to the theatre, but he was already engaged. I therefore decided to spend the evening at home, partly because in any case I was feeling extremely tired. I made some telephone calls and played the piano. Yesterday I had a prophetic dream that I was giving my examination performance next spring, and the piece I had chosen in the Russian composers' category was a fugue by Taneyev. Of late I had completely forgotten his existence, but today, remembering my dream, I looked out this fugue and found it an enchanting piece. I shall definitely learn it for the examination.

15 November

It is now time to get down to the operas: Tsybin is conducting two scenes from *Rigoletto*, I three scenes from *Aida*.

In the meantime I bought the newspapers and looked through them to see if there were any reviews of yesterday's concert. The *Petersburg Listok* was lukewarm about me but very complimentary about Tsybin. The *Petersburg Gazette* and *The Day* were both very critical of me but praised Tsypa. At first this upset me, but then I laughed it off; later on I imagined the glee it would arouse among some of the lumpen Conservatoire drones and this made me angry; and finally I completely recovered my good humour and after a walk made my way back to the Conservatoire. Nothing very remarkable was going on there.

In the evening I played through *Aida* and went to the Sokol. On the three last occasions I was there I had been in the second group, which not many people go to, but today I was once again in the first group and enjoyed being in the midst of a busy, lively throng of people. We had our photograph taken.

16 November

A serious conflict broke out in the Conservatoire between Tcherepnin and Palechek, in the course of which the former flew at the latter in a passion because his singers were said to have insulted the junior conductors, and one of the women singers had been rude to mild-mannered Tsybin yesterday. Palechek got very excited, his ears turned first red, then lilac and eventually blue, and I began to worry he might have a heart attack. Eventually it all calmed down and Tcherepnin, already visibly regretting his outburst, tried to make amends by himself playing the piano accompaniment for *Aida*. This suited me very well, as I was able to make a note of his tempi. There is a wonderful Amneris in Morenschild, who sang the title role in *The Maid of Orleans* last year. True, her voice has a certain artificiality, but the intonation is true and she has great dramatic gifts. The theme from *Aida* has been pursuing me all day, driving me to distraction.

At four o'clock went to see Myaskushka, who had Beloúsov with him at the time. Myaskovsky has succeeded in persuading him of the merits of my *Ballade*, and today we played it through twice. This was the most tremendous pleasure for me: the first time I had heard my piece played as it should be. Beloúsov played all the notes accurately; the upper register of the cello sang and keened; the intonation was impeccable, as firm as if it were on a keyboard; all the climaxes and thunderous crescendos were in place – in a word, I was in ecstasy. Among other things he suggested that the second subject should be played *pizzicato*, an idea of which I approved.

But the Moscow recital, it appears, is going to have to be postponed because of the singer's illness, and the unfortunate thing is that the singer is Derzhanovsky's wife[1] and without her the recital cannot take place. Beloúsov is busy all December, so if the concert is to be postponed rather than cancelled altogether it looks as though it cannot now be before January. I am very much put out by this.

My notes about the publication of the D flat Concerto provoked not only discussion in Moscow but also some reservations, because Jurgenson, via Derzhanovsky and Myaskovsky, wants to query some allegedly unplayable notes and also wants all manner of transpositions (as it stands, the parts for some instruments are written one way in the full score and another way in the orchestral parts). Without letting me know any of this, Myaskovsky had replied that the concerto had already been performed twice, everything had been played and sounded correctly as written, and there should be no question of transposition as the composer wanted it the way he had notated it and would not give way on this point. Quite right, bravo, Myaskusha!

His own D minor Sonata has been published. At one time it was dedicated to me, but the dedication was subsequently withdrawn because of some cross words between us. It now seems to be dedicated to a certain Hofman,[2] an old friend of his who has played the sonata to him on many occasions. Well, devil take the pair of them, but at all events I'm very glad to see the sonata in print. In the summer of 1911 I used to play it a lot and sent the composer a long letter with a whole list of minor changes. At the time he rejected almost all of them, but now I see he has made the changes according to my suggestions. His other published sonata, the Cello Sonata, I am less fond of.

After dinner I wanted to go to Ziloti's concert, particularly to hear Debussy's *Jeux*. The tickets had all been sold, so I went to the backstage entrance and sent up my card to Ziloti with the following inscription: 'SSP begs of Alexander Ilyich the very great favour of granting him a pass, so that he may hear the performance of Debussy's *Jeux*.' Ziloti ordered a pass to be given to me, and so I got into the concert.

Jeux is an interesting and poetic piece without much content. 'Well, no, you won't find a lot of meat in it,' agreed Tcherepnin, who himself finds other things besides meat to admire in the French composers he loves so much.

I met Luiza Zakharova[3] at the concert. She told me that Godowsky[4] had heaped praise on Boris and was predicting his triumph in the New World as

---

1 Yekaterina Koposova-Derzhanovskaya.
2 The pianist Nadezhda Ludwigovna Hofman.
3 Boris Zakharov's sister-in-law.
4 Leopold Godowsky (1870–1938), the celebrated pianist and composer.

well as on the Old Continent. 'So Borya is already practising his English in preparation for America,' I put in.

'Yes, he must be. He isn't going to stay too long in Vienna,' continued Luiza, 'but you can see that he shouldn't come back to Russia before he has garnered some laurels from abroad.'

This is true. Although, Beloúsov has managed to scrape up laurels from every corner of Europe without finding much success in Petersburg.

From the concert I went to the house-warming of Erasmus, a very nice gentleman, a friend of Seryozha Sebryakov.[1] I made his acquaintance in Moscow when I played at Deisha-Sionitskaya's Musical Exhibition. It was not a particularly lively occasion, but he himself is very charming, entertained us with card tricks and served us with delicious drinks. The evening dragged on until three o'clock, however, which I detest.

Earlier, in the afternoon, I had run into Marinochka Pavlova on a tram. But for some reason I thought she would not be very interested in me, so confined myself to two or three phrases and hastened on my way.

17 November

Stayed at home and worked, except for an hour or so in the middle of the day when I went for a walk in the warm, windy, damp weather. I have almost finished composing the E minor piece for Op. 12. I don't want to call it an 'Intermezzo', but have not yet settled on 'Capriccio' as a title.[2] I love it very much, but the second half has been resisting coming together. Now it has, and I must finish it as soon as possible and send it to Vera Nikolayevna in Berne, because she is still there, not in good health and bored.

Later, I found a second subject for the concertino, and also some more material for the projected symphony. In general, my immediate composing plans are: a concertino for violin (lyrical, elegant); a symphony (menacing, tragic, full of unrestrained striving); a set of variations (delicate) already sketched out; a set of songs (six); of which I already have two, and the rest will be written for Anna Grigorievna.

In the evening Shteiman and I went together to *Carmen* at the Music Drama Theatre. This theatre is really worth paying attention to: the scenic side, the productions, the care and attention to detail – these are all admirable, often marvellous. The conductor was not Bikhter, as a result of which the music was free of perversions and distortions. I listened to *Carmen* with the greatest possible pleasure; it is in many respects a model of what an opera should be. And how splendid to have an operatic work filled with such vivid thematic material!

1 The son of Dr Tatyana Sebryakova, Prokofiev's mother's cousin.
2 Eventually published as 'Capriccio', No. 5 of Op. 12.

18 November

On the 29th the Conservatoire will celebrate Lyadov's jubilee year[1] with a small concert of his compositions, conducted by Glazunov, Tcherepnin and even Gabel. Today all of them were conducting, so I went in to listen for half an hour. After that I went home, where I did a lot of work and in the evening went to the Sokol. There I met Yury Frolov, whom I used to meet in the old days at the Pavskys and the Alpers.

19 November

It is Boris Zakharov's birthday today: he is twenty-six. To mark it I sent him a card three days ago.

In the morning I assiduously practised my examination programme. I do intend to learn it thoroughly but, my God, it will be an exhausting matter to play the whole programme through from beginning to end!

In the Conservatoire after lunch I went through *Aida* with Tcherepnin from the point of view of the conductor, and after that conducted it for Palechek's opera class. The score is in manuscript with the violin staves on top and the flutes below them, the bassoons between the trumpets and the trombones, repeated bars are not written out but simply numbered – in short, it would be hard to imagine anything less intelligible... The only saving grace is that both music and orchestration are on such an extraordinarily simple level.

Went with Mama to the student concert, as she also wanted to hear how Shtember plays. The attendants conducted her with a polite bow to the front, while I went up into the balcony thinking I would have a more entertaining time there. Shtember is an excellent pianist.

20 November

I have received an invitation to perform my works at some sort of private concert for a higher-education institution for women, which is supposed to showcase contemporary literature and music. This will take place on the 24th. I agreed.

Practised the piano, composed a little for the symphony, and went for a long walk. In the evening saw Myaskovsky. I played him my now finished 'Capriccio'; it may not have made much of an impression on him, but I love it. Mme Derzhanovskaya is still not well and it is not certain whether the Moscow concert on the 29th is going to take place or not. Derzhanovsky is not saying anything, and Beloúsov and I find it rather exasperating to be left in the dark.

---

1 Lyadov joined the teaching staff of the St Petersburg Conservatoire in 1878, so 1913 marked the thirty-fifth year of his association with the institution.

21 November

Anna Nikolayevna Yesipova and Leopold Auer are giving their customary pair of sonata evenings, as a result of which for the third week running we have no lesson. The collection to buy flowers to present to Anna Nikolayevna has been mishandled by the incompetent Benditsky, who succeeded in scraping together no more than 35 roubles, for which sum this morning Benditsky and I ordered a basket of flowers, albeit quite a large and elegant one. In the afternoon I did some piano practice and then, although it is a holiday, went to the Conservatoire to work on *Aida*. At seven o'clock I went to the Ruzskys, who were having a dinner today with a guest list of musicians: Ziloti, the Ossovskys, Romanovsky, the baritone Andreyev, Pogozhev[1] and others.

I had had a little telephone *contretemps* with the daughters, as a result of which they were not really speaking to me. The parents, however, were extra kind, and the guests were all old acquaintances, so it was all very splendid. Dinner was accompanied by champagne, sherry, and liqueurs, so my head was swimming; we rose from the table at midnight. Romanovsky plans to include my F minor Sonata in his concert in March, and is full of extravagant praise for it. Because of this I was made to play it; although my head was spinning I managed to play the Sonata with some vivacity. The First Sonata over, the Second was demanded, which I also played with some success (especially from Ossovsky; Ziloti had already gone by then). The pieces, 'Legenda', 'Rigaudon' and 'Prelude' had the biggest success of all.

22 November

As I did not get to bed until half past three, I slept late this morning. Wrote a letter to Katyusha Schmidthof to tell her that I would not be performing in Moscow on the 24th, as she had been expecting. She has been very much looking forward to seeing me. In the afternoon, to the Conservatoire. I announced that tomorrow I would be coming in to the choral class, to see how they had been getting on learning the repertoire without me. Myaskovsky telephoned to say that Derzhanovsky was postponing the concert until January. This is very disappointing. I shall in any case have to make a trip to Moscow: for negotiations with Jurgenson, to discuss *Maddalena*, and to see Koussevitzky about the Second Piano Concerto.

Tsybin came to see me; he will have a summer season either in Rostov or in Baku, and for this reason wanted to borrow a stack of fourteen scores

---

1 Vladimir Pogozhev (1851–1935), theatre historian and amateur composer, chief administrator of the Imperial Theatres.

from me. In the evening I went to the Sokol. They want to produce postcards with my 'March' printed on them by a photographic method, and therefore would like me to make a neat copy of the score.

23 November

If I do not have to be somewhere by a certain time I find it impossible to get up early: this is disgraceful. This is what happened today: it was eleven by the time I sat down at the piano.

The postponement of the Moscow concert means that I can devote all my efforts to the Yesipova repertoire. At one o'clock I went into the Conservatoire to study the score of *Aida*, which they will not allow me to take home with me. At half past two, the choral class. Gauk was going to conduct, but I asked him to play the accompaniment and myself took the baton. Evidently the chorus has become accustomed to not working very hard under Gauk, talking and not paying attention to the singing. I at once took them in hand, introduced a whole lot of phrasing, tapped loudly with my baton whenever their attention wandered, shouted at them from time to time, generally cracked jokes and made them sing well and with some character.

Nikolay Nikolayevich came in towards the end and evidently approved what I was doing. Then we rehearsed with the men the offstage chorus of priests which Kreisler, to my great surprise, had prepared extremely well.

Nikolay Nikolayevich whispered in my ear that it seemed the business with the third Belyayev Concert was looking promising (his *Narcissus* and my D flat Concerto), which news filled me with joy.

After the Conservatoire I ran in to Myaskovsky, whom Derzhanovsky had asked to pacify me. 'Don't be angry with him,' said Myaskovsky, soothingly. 'Things are not going at all well with his *Muzyka* magazine.'

I decided I would go to Moscow on the 29th, and asked Derzhanovsky by postcard if Jurgenson would be in Moscow on that date, and if I should bring *Maddalena* with me. Myaskovsky, however, is deeply engaged in orchestrating his Third Symphony, and in addition is making plans for a fourth and fifth, so it seems unlikely he will be able to do anything about orchestrating *Maddalena*. In the evening I stayed at home playing the piano and finishing the piano transcription of the Bassoon Scherzo. Somewhat embarrassed, I played Myaskovsky the Sokol 'March', but to my great surprise he liked it.

24 November

Slept late, then went for a walk along Morskaya and Nevsky. Stayed in all day composing a theme for the symphony and practising the piano, then after dinner suddenly began writing a tender, languorous waltz.

Sonya Esche rang up with some sensational news: after a fierce battle with herself she has joined the Operetta where she is acting, dancing the tango, wearing glamorous costumes and all with a great success, receiving bouquets and getting a good salary. She fears it will all too soon come to an end because she does not sing, although she is taking private singing lessons to remedy this. She invited me to come and see her perform.

It was most enjoyable to talk to my old flame, spoilt and crazy though she is, but very intelligent.

In the evening I went to the Rayevskys for the name-day of the Yekaterinas, with guests and vint. At half past ten a student in a car came to take me to the evening of contemporary literature and music at the Bestuzhev Institute.[1] When I got there, Igor Severyanin[2] was reading – or rather mumbling – his verses. The students raved and howled in ecstasy, endlessly demanding encores.

After the interval I played my pieces, on a fairly dreadful piano whose *forte* was tolerable but whose *piano* was execrable. Yulia Weisberg[3] had warned me to choose a reasonably accessible repertoire for these musically non-specialist female students, so I played the 'Fairy Tale', the 'Gavotte', the 'Prelude', and the Scherzo from the Sonata. Wherever any of these pieces demanded a lyrical sound from the piano it was awful, so bad that I could hardly bring myself to play. But the Scherzo sounded crisp and full of bite, provoking applause, whistles and cries of 'encore' from the hall. I took my time coming back on stage, but when I did and bowed, it was strange to see a hall full to bursting with nothing but female faces – there was not a single male to be seen. As an encore I played the Etude No. 4 and the 'Rigaudon', and was stunned by all the whistling and cries for more encores; someone demanded the Sonata (I was extraordinarily gratified to learn that my 'literature' is getting so well known . . .). My performance was followed – with considerably less success – by some rather odd songs by Stravinsky performed by his brother,[4] and then some witty little pieces by Karatygin.

Debussy is conducting in a few days' time in the Koussevitzky series. On Thursday *Apollon* magazine is inviting the French composer to visit them. Karatygin has invited me to play some of my works.

1   The Bestuzhev Institutes offered pioneer university-level academic courses for women only, from the time when women were not admitted to universities.
2   Igor Severyanin was the pen-name of the poet Igor Lotarev (1887–1941), whose aping of the Italian Futurists' celebration of technology and the speed of city life, allied to a sensuous command of rhythm and language, made him extremely popular, especially with young people.
3   Yulia Weisberg (1878–1942), composer and journalist, was Rimsky-Korsakov's daughter-in-law, being married to his son Andrey, and was on the editorial board of the conservatively inclined journal *Muzykal'ny Sovremennik* (*Contemporary Music*).
4   Probably the two Verlaine settings 'Un grand sommeil noir' and 'La lune blanche', Op. 9. Stravinsky wrote the songs for his younger brother Gury, who was at this time embarking on a career as a singer (baritone).

One of the students on the course was enthusing about the wit and erudition of Chudovsky. I was amused by her panegyric, and objected that in reality he was a mere lightweight, the only thing he was any good at being chess. She in turn was surprised by what I said, and told me that Chudovsky has now become terribly serious and spends whole days in the public library and whole nights working, has turned against Scandinavian literature, and on top of that . . . has got married!

25 November

Towards noon I went into the Conservatoire to hear the Lyadov works being rehearsed. Unfortunately I was too late to hear Anna Grigorievna's account of the songs, but I did hear the chorus in an excerpt from *The Bride of Messina*.[1] It sounded nice, except that the chorus had forgotten all the phrasing I had tried to teach them.

At home I had lunch and then walked back to the Conservatoire to rehearse *Aida*, to piano accompaniment but in the Great Hall and with the chorus. Since the doors of the Great Hall were locked and remained so for some time there was a huge crowd outside in the corridor on the second floor, a real gathering of the clans: the chorus, many of the soloists, students from the General Subjects classes who happened to be out on break. I love this sort of agglomeration of humanity. Out of Fohström's class suddenly leapt Belokurova, looking wonderful in a light-coloured shirt. Then the doors were opened and the whole *Aida* contingent surged *en masse* inside the Great Hall. *Aida* is going really well.

In the evening I had a gymnastics session at the Sokol. On the 8th they are having a gala and have asked me to perform in the concert section of the evening. That is the date of the matinee *Aida* performance, and I never know what to do with myself in the evening after such events, so I was glad to agree.

26 November

Practised Beethoven Op. 111, studied the score of *Aida*, and composed some material for the symphony, none of these for very long. At one o'clock took Op. 111 to Anna Nikolayevna for my lesson with her. The poor lady is struggling with a terrible cough: she is not allowed out, and even indoors she is forbidden to move about the apartment, confined to one room. The lesson was conducted under somewhat exotic circumstances: I played in the draw-

---

[1] Lyadov's setting of the final scene of Schiller's play *Die Braut von Messina*. Lyadov's score had been written as his own graduation composition from the St Petersburg Conservatoire.

ing room while she sat in state in her bedroom and Poznyakovskaya ran backwards and forwards passing on instructions from Anna Nikolayevna to try such and such phrasing. Anna Nikolayevna's opinion was that my performance of the sonata was uneven and lacked control, but all the same she thought the work suited my temperament and eventually I would be able to play it well.

Then I went through the score of *Aida* with Tcherepnin. Since we do not have very much rehearsal time, he is not going to do the preparatory work with the orchestra but hand it straight over to me. I like the idea very much, but will really have to pore over the score in detail. In fact I shall have almost no chance to do this, but I ought to be able to get to know it well enough.

In the evening I went to the student concert; it did not look like a particularly interesting programme, but all the same I love these occasions. For the first part I sat with Damskaya and her rather beautiful sister, so I was not bored. I had not realized that Umnenkaya would be singing: she was warmly applauded but did not actually sing very well. I did not see her during the interval, but ran point blank into her papa, who to my great astonishment greeted me with every kind of endearment. In the second part of the concert I sat with Volodya Deshevov, whom I had not seen for a tremendously long time. He was, as usual, very nice, is working seven hours a day but even so will not graduate this year and is delaying his final exams until next year. Among other things he told me that Tamochka Glebova had married an actor in a civil ceremony, and she and her new husband had gone to their estate in Ryazan. At first I found this rather comic, but then I decided bravo! Well done indeed, Tamochka!

Bushen appeared during the second half and moved from seat to seat five times so that I would notice her, but despite all her efforts I decided to pay no attention.

27 November

I telephoned Koussevitzky repeatedly today at the Europa Hotel, about ten times, but could not get through to him. Because he had received me so kindly in the spring, I wanted to take advantage of his presence in St Petersburg for his subscription concert series and show him my new compositions. In the evening I went to the concert, which consisted of works by Debussy, conducted by Claude himself. Much of Claude's music is interesting, but it is all very similar, and in that sense is boring. Koussevitzky was very gracious, but asked me to show him my new work either on his next visit to St Petersburg or when I come to Moscow. I said I would be going to Moscow the day after tomorrow, but this was not a convenient time for him. So everything was left up in the air, and he proceeded to praise Debussy's music to the skies. Makovsky, the editor of *Apollon*, said he was glad that I was appearing tomorrow at the magazine's reception in honour of Debussy. I replied that I had received his invitation and would be happy to attend. 'What do you mean, "attend"?' We are expecting you to play some of your works! Debussy is most interested in you, Koussevitzky has told him a great deal about you, and we have been recommending you as 'le compositeur russe qui a le plus de talent'.

I was deeply flattered. Chudovsky also took it upon himself to approach me and tell me my *Apollon* appearance had aroused a great deal of interest. I responded vaguely and coldly. It is true that he has got married, and to a rather attractive wife.

Caught sight of Shurik Bushen in the hall, and wanted to find her so that we could leave together, but she vanished somewhere. I returned home content with life.

28 November

The general rehearsal for the Lyadov Jubilee Concert. Although I am not taking part myself I came to the start of the proceedings; first to hear the programme; and second because there is always a lively atmosphere at general rehearsals. Gabel was greeted with a storm of applause as he mounted the podium, and then successfully carved his way through the *Polonaise*. Anna Grigorievna sang some of his Russian songs, delicately but too *piano*. Lyadov's art is insubstantial, while being in its way palatable and comforting. On the whole, my attitude to the anniversary celebrations of my former professor–oppressor is one of indifference.

Met that chatterbox Sadovskaya, whose married name is now Bokhanovskaya, my erstwhile companion in the General Subjects class; we use the intimate form of address to each other, I'm not quite sure why. Seeing Klingman I asked her how the Dance of the Slaves was going, which the movement class is preparing for *Aida*. Some time soon I intend to exert my rights as conductor to visit the class, to see what they are doing and to settle the tempo.

Caught a brief glimpse of Ariadna Nikolskaya, heroine of last year's romantic escapades with Max, since when I had not seen her. Now I caught sight of her darting out of the movement class, so I presume she is dancing one of the slave boys. I returned to the Small Hall, where I found Shurik Bushen. She was all set to cold-shoulder me for failing to notice her at the student concert, but I soon sweetened her up and she gave me a playful box on the ears. She went off to St Serge's class, and I went to drink a glass of milk. In the meantime the rehearsal came to an end and everyone dispersed.

At four o'clock I was due at *Apollon* for the Debussy reception, where I was to play my Etude and 'Legenda'. But for some reason, before going there I found myself wandering back into the Conservatoire, where I ran into Belokurova and Klingman. I went into the Great Hall with Palechek and the whole opera class, just as they were about to rehearse *Aida*. I blithely said to Klingman, 'Yelena Maximovna, why don't you come into our chorus, just for old times' sake!'

She replied that even if she wanted to, she would not be allowed in. Belokurova, seeing that we were in conversation, stood to one side, but Klingman called her back to introduce us. And thus everything resolved itself neatly and simply. I was very pleased, although affecting not to react with too obvious an interest in my new acquaintance. Belokurova is a most attractive personality: elegant, vivacious and feminine.

I went to *Apollon*. There was a large crowd of musicians and artists there, among them many I knew and was happy to see. Debussy, accompanied by the Koussevitzkys, arrived late. He was welcomed by a speech from Chudovsky, in French of such arcane refinement that I could understand very little of it; some of it may have been beyond Debussy himself. There followed a stammering address from Sacchetti. Polotskaya-Yemtsova[1] played Musorgsky's *Pictures from an Exhibition* and Anna Grigorievna, who was extremely nervous, sang two of the same composer's songs. Another singer, and then I was on with my Etude No. 3 and 'Legenda'. Rather nervously and with slightly stumbling fingers, I played them. The audience listened with attention, and applauded in approval. Debussy rose, came up to me and praised the pieces and the individuality of my technique. Nikolayev was complimentary about my performance. Karatygin was delighted by 'Legenda', a piece he had not heard before. Koussevitzky uttered not a word, to my chagrin, but his wife, sitting in state on Debussy's right-hand side, applauded with a will. Everyone then went to drink tea, after which the speeches and the music continued at inordinate length, to the mortal affliction of Claude and the diminishing interest of the audience. I had an enchanting conversation with Tamara Glebova's mother, was introduced to Mme Chudovskaya, an attractive woman, an artist, who showered me with compliments, and made the acquaintance of Professor Kal.[2] After that I went home; it was eight o'clock and I was tired.

At home I found a postcard from Derzhanovsky saying that *Maddalena* and I were awaited at the Free Theatre at noon tomorrow. My plan had been to travel tomorrow, but now I would have to go right away. Fatigue had so sapped my energy that I regarded the journey with something like panic.

---

1   Sofia (Sara) Polotskaya-Yemtsova (1878–1957), pianist, was a particularly favoured musical associate of Makovsky and Karatygin, closely associated with the international musical, artistic and literary aspirations of *Apollon*.
2   Alexey Kal (1878–?), critic and Professor of Music History at the University of St Petersburg.

Nevertheless, I reminded myself that the best place of all to sleep is on a train, quickly organized everything I needed, called at Myaskovsky's to collect the score of *Maddalena* and just caught the eleven o'clock express to Moscow. The bright moonlit night and white snow made the scene through the carriage window irresistibly attractive.

29 November

The train arrived in Moscow at half past ten; I went straight to Derzhanovsky, who made telephone calls both to Jurgenson and to the Free Theatre. The latter I went to straight away, while Boris Petrovich[1] would expect me at four o'clock. Saradzhev welcomed me extremely affectionately and took me into a piano rehearsal of *Kashchey*,[2] which had not quite finished. I enjoyed listening to this lovely opera. When the rehearsal was over, Saradzhev led me into the comfortable office of Mardzhanov, one of the theatre's principal managers and producers, to whom I took a great liking. We were joined by more producers, assistant conductors, singers of both sexes, a dozen or so people in all. Then we returned to the room in which the *Kashchey* rehearsal had been taking place, and I sat down at the piano.

My first task was to outline the plot of the opera. At first I stammered and had to cast about for words, but as I warmed up the narrative began to flow more entertainingly, I quoted some phrases illustrating the action on stage and indulged in some digressions on the psychology of the characters. When I had completed my outline, there were expressions of approval of the opera's subject.

I started to play the music of the opera. I must admit that since I had done my revision and given the score to Myaskovsky in September I had not set eyes on my manuscript, and had forgotten much of it. I made some unforgivable mistakes, sometimes alighting on adjacent chords and leaving out whole bars. But more than anything I wanted to maintain the dramatic pace and passion of the opera. This I succeeded in doing, and when I finished, Mardzhanov exclaimed, 'I am greatly impressed by the temperament and psychology of the characters, but I will leave assessment of the musical content to Konstantin Solomonovich.'[3]

Saradzhev was more than ready to give his backing to the music. Members of the company came up to me, asking me to play again one passage or another. Tired and hungry, I gratefully drank tea and ate a sandwich. It was clear that the orchestration would not be completed in time for inclusion in

1 Jurgenson.
2 *Kashchey The Immortal*, one-act opera (1902) by Rimsky-Korsakov.
3 Saradzhev.

the repertoire this season, and it would have to wait until next autumn. We discussed whether Jurgenson would publish the vocal score with piano, and then they invited me to this evening's performance. After courteous farewells I went to the town ticket office to get a ticket for the midnight train, and then went to see Jurgenson to try to sell him Op. 12. He was affable, talked of this and that, and made an offer of 250 roubles for the opus. I said that even 500 would be a very small fee, demonstrating to him that this was a collection of my most marketable and popular pieces. Jurgenson proposed 350 and then 400, but I would not give way and produced ever more weighty reasons why even 500 was not really enough.

'All right, we'll try it . . .' he said lethargically, and reached over for the paper on which I would assign him the rights.

I signed, and received 200 roubles in cash (300 to follow by post), and decided not to persist with the *Ballade* at the moment but to leave that until February. Saying goodbye to Jurgenson, I went to have dinner with Saradzhev. Another dinner guest was the talented actor from the Free Theatre company Chabrov, who had been touring Europe and had interesting tales to tell of Spain and Budapest. I rang up Yurasovich:[1] 'You must really have a friend at court!' he cried, when he heard about the 500 roubles.

Then, as I was very short of time, I went to pay a call on Katyusha Schmidthof. She was living on the far side of Moscow from where I was, and when I finally ran Nizhny Tagansky Lane to earth, I found myself in a terrible slum area of disgusting houses and drunks on the street. I looked at my watch and saw that I had almost run out of time to get back to the Free Theatre, where they had particularly asked me not to be late. And so much did I want to avoid alarming the poor family, so anxious was I to get home myself, although I knew they would be glad to see me – that I got on to a tram and hurried back to the theatre.

They gave me a seat in the front row and I watched and listened to a mime performance: *The Veil of Pierrette*, based on the one-act play by Schnitzler with music by Dohnányi. I was asked (by Mardzhanov, Saradzhev and the actors) what I thought of this art form, clearly in hopes that I would agree to write a score for a mime production. During the interval they took me backstage and generally looked after me most attentively. My conclusion was that as a genre mime can be successful so long as the action is continuous and every bar of music corresponds to a specific action on stage. But if a long stretch of music is used to illustrate the drama on a large scale without descending to detail, the result can be tedious and rather silly.

Taking my leave of Saradzhev, I asked him how I should realistically regard the chances of *Maddalena* being produced? He replied that the omens

---

1 Yurasovsky.

were very positive, but the direction of the theatre was still undergoing all manner of 'revolution'. The way forward would be much clearer in a week's time or thereabouts, and he would let me know. I said that only when I had a contract in my hands would I start work on the score.

I had fifty minutes left before the train left, so took a cab and went to the Nikolayevsky station. The cabbie took me down all sorts of unknown back streets and eventually drew up outside a station that bore little resemblance to the Nikolayevsky. The idiot had brought me to the Brest station, right on the other side of town. I had half an hour. I leapt into another cab, promised the coachman a rouble tip, and had him make a dash for Nikolayevsky. I was there at six minutes to midnight, managed to gulp down a sandwich and got into the carriage as the third bell went.

30 November

Arrived in Petersburg at the same time as I had the day before in Moscow, half past ten. I was sleeping so soundly that I almost slept through my capital city. Went home, had a talk to Mama, studied the score of *Aida*, composed a theme for the symphony – a little rough, but very good all the same – and at three o'clock went to the Conservatoire. Today was the day for the singers to compete for their roles in the Number One cast. Once again a huge crowd had congregated on the second floor outside the hall.

Belokurochka appeared from somewhere and stood right in front of me with a welcoming smile on her face. I greeted her politely but formally and passed on, inwardly hugging myself that I had seen her.

The competition was open, so there were a great number of hopeful participants in the hall. There is a school of thought that says competitions like this are a bad thing, but I love them because of their manifest excitement and sense of nervous strain, and the way everyone hates everyone else, the professors (male as well, but especially so the female of the species) strung up to such a pitch of excitement that they are ready to do battle on behalf of their students. There are always little scandals and arguments and internecine conflicts among the 'authorities'; all this is highly amusing and entertaining. As far as it concerned me, the result of the competition was that my Amneris will be the gifted Morenschild; Aida the respectable Seleznyova, Radames Vikinsky, who is very musical and reliable (*hors de concours* as he was the only candidate).

In the evening I went to Rachmaninov's concert. *The Isle of the Dead* is, except for the over-extended opening section, a wonderful work. I also greatly admire the Second Piano Concerto, but Ziloti dashed it off at such a speed that the listener was alternately alarmed and repelled. After this came Rachmaninov's new work, *The Bells*. I was stunned by the wealth of deeply interesting and endlessly inventive ideas, not always a characteristic of Rachmaninov's music, the mass of fascinating devices he employs, and many unexpected delights. The third movement, *The Tocsin*, brought me to the point of ecstasy with the elemental power of its expression. I came firmly to the conclusion that this is the best thing Rachmaninov has ever written, applauded deliriously and quarrelled with our modern-music aficionados who simply dismiss him. When I got home I telephoned Myaskovsky, but alas, he also tore *The Bells* to shreds: not a single melody, a mass of sham window-dressing, a total dislocation between text and music . . .

1 December

Sent the 'Capriccio', dedicated to Vera Nikolayevna Meshcherskaya, to her with some notes at a couple of places in the margins of the score – (1) next to the title 'Capriccio': 'The afore-mentioned title, which has no character associations whatever, is offered with the aim of promoting characterization in performance, as well as representing a tribute to that of the person to whom the work is dedicated' – in other words, a slightly veiled piece of cheek; (2) just before the second trio: 'The following passage, which the composer considers to be the noblest part of the work, may be perceived by the player who is fearful of looking into the future as something to be endured, and is accordingly presented to any such unfortunate individual with the option of leaping from this point directly to the indicated star.' The 'star' was drawn by hand at the beginning of the final reprise.

In the afternoon at the Conservatoire there took place the first orchestra rehearsal of *Rigoletto* and *Aida*. Tcherepnin and Gabel were both in attendance and seemed to approve my handling of the music, finding only that I have a tendency to exaggerate the tempi, and when I get too absorbed in the score I forget the need for proper gestures, making them in an intolerably slapdash manner. When I got home again I stayed in, practising the piano, writing my diary and talking interminably on the telephone to Shurik Bushen telling her about my trip to Moscow.

2nd December

At orchestra class in the morning I completed my first full play-through of the *Aida* excerpts, and Tsybin did the same with *Rigoletto*. Things seemed to go better with me than with him; at least after the rehearsal Tcherepnin disappeared into another classroom with him. I chatted to Luiza Bluvshtein, one of Gelever's students, next to whom I had once sat at a concert, went for lunch in the canteen and then came back into the Conservatoire for a meeting with Gabel, who has a soft spot for me and wants to determine finally the tempi in order to avoid any *contretemps* later on. The corridors then filled up with all those taking part in *Aida* and *Rigoletto*, and we went into the Great Hall for the final piano rehearsal: tomorrow will be with orchestra.

In the evening Nikolay Shtember called for me and we went together to the Sokol.

3 December

Today there should have been a Yesipova lesson, but she is ill and confined to bed. I am not too upset about missing this lesson, as what with all the *Aida* rehearsals the Chopin sonata has rather gone off the boil. Someone had even suggested to me at the rehearsal yesterday that I write to Yesipova saying that I was ill. I said, 'It's more serious than that. I'll tell her I've been put in a lunatic asylum!'

In the morning I composed some more passages of the violin concerto. I want this to be a lighter, more delicate work.

Towards three o'clock I went to the first stage-orchestra rehearsal of our operas. We began with *Rigoletto*, which ran into trouble from the very first bars. Naturally, it was Tsybin's first experience on the podium for an opera, but he was less to blame than the orchestra, which had no idea what it was doing. And the reason for this was that Tcherepnin had been blithely spending all his time on the Lyadov Jubilee Concert and had not left enough time to prepare the orchestra. All they had had was one brief run-through of the opera scores, and were now comprehensively covered in obloquy. Stopping every minute and getting completely out of step with the singers, Tsybin struggled on for more than two hours. There was no time left for *Aida*, because those orchestra musicians who were playing for the cinema and other more entertaining assignments now wanted our rehearsal to finish. Tcherepnin took their side, but Palechek got very excited and said that if this happened we would not manage to get through our work.

'But if we keep them back now,' said Tcherepnin, 'they will all have to pay a fine[1] and no one at all will turn up for rehearsal tomorrow.'

Palechek blew up, started spitting blood, forgot his Russian, and spluttered, 'If they don't show up, so they . . . we . . . throw them out them from Conservatoire.'

'Well, you can throw me out along with them!' Tcherepnin hit back.

This struck me as such an inept response that I entered the fray. 'Nikolay Nikolayevich,' I said, 'it has never been accepted that opera rehearsals last only two hours. Our orchestra is so undisciplined and their performance today has been such a disgrace that it is simply not right to defend them and take offence on their behalf.'

---

1 Presumably for missing the cinema assignment.

My unexpected intervention, and above all my use of the word 'disgrace', proved fateful. Tcherepnin's parting furious words to Palechek were: 'In my opinion such discussions should take place in the privacy of our office and we should not be arguing in front of the whole Conservatoire!' and with that he went out.

The rehearsal ended, with *Aida* postponed until the following day. I went home having wasted two and a half hours.

In the evening I attended the student concert, but there was nothing of any interest in the programme, nor were there any interesting faces to be seen in the audience. Met Shurik Bushen and it was nice to talk to her. At last I have a good, long letter from Zakharov. I'm very pleased with it.

4 December

Slept long; as all the rehearsals are in the afternoons I decided to allow myself to stay in bed in the mornings so as to dispel my nerves. I looked through some *Aida* recitatives, congratulated Ossovskaya on her name-day, and some time after two came in for the *Aida* rehearsal. Mounting the podium with feelings of the keenest pleasure, I began in a business-like and resolute manner. Pretty good! *Aida* went much better than *Rigoletto*. It may well be an easier proposition to conduct, but on the other hand it is more interesting and has a range of 'attractions' that Tsybin's *Rigoletto* excerpts lack: a chorus, a ballet, a wind band, and a chorus of offstage priests. Due to the inexperience of the singers I could hardly hear them, and often was reduced to following their lips. In any event, the rehearsal must be counted a success, since the management generally declared that it was satisfied with *Aida*. Tcherepnin was morose and taciturn with me, although he was laughing and joking with the girls.

Feeling rather tired, I spent the evening at home, playing telephone chess with Golubovskaya. She won one of the two games, much to my surprise.

5 December

Slept until noon. My Sonata No. 2 has been published and today I received my regular five copies. I am greatly attached to this sonata, and contemplating it in its printed form afforded me much satisfaction. I am also happy that this work I love so much is dedicated to Max. When I came into the Conservatoire for rehearsal I showed off the sonata, and played it for Golubovskaya and Bushen, the former making some very pertinent comments. Tsybin says that there is now a complete rift between him and Tcherepnin, and it is so serious that Tsybin may leave the class.

The *Rigoletto* rehearsal began, leaving me again to kick my heels in waiting. I don't know how matters stand between Tcherepnin and Tsybin, but there is no doubt Tcherepnin is extremely angry with me. At last *Rigoletto* ended, then there was an interval, and then *Aida*. The stage now took on a festive air, filling up with the chorus and the ballet as Presnyakov brought on his 'slave boys', all of whom were young and pretty girls, appetizingly decked out in black tights. The orchestra musicians took their places and all the otherwise unoccupied men as if by accident made a bee-line for the stage and the wings, headed, needless to say, by Tcherepnin and Chuprynnikov. I assumed a serious, business-like air and perched on my conductor's stool, but there was such a noise coming from the orchestra that it was impossible to begin. I had to shout at them so loudly that even Gabel became embarrassed and grabbed my arm. But the orchestra at once fell silent, and I was able to turn my shriek into a joke.

Aida went not too badly, not many sins could be laid at my door, except that at one point I was paying too much attention to what was happening on stage so that my gestures were too broad to achieve a *piano*. At the end of the rehearsal I encountered Tcherepnin, who abruptly blurted out, 'The orchestra is always too loud! And that is your fault! All students of the conducting course are taught how to indicate *piano*!! Goodbye!!' and went out.

Somewhat perplexed by this rocket, I was standing talking to some students of the Theory class. Suddenly, out of nowhere, there was Serafima.[1] I went over to her and started a conversation. Belokurova had her hair pulled back smooth and did not look nearly as attractive as before. I looked at her and found her unappealing. Had she always been thus, had this goddess existed only in my imagination?! If so, it is a sad day. I took my leave and went home, my mood soured by this unwelcome discovery and the rocket from Tcherepnin.

Went rather reluctantly to the Sokol but unwound there and did my exercises with great enjoyment.

All the same, Belokurova is very dear to my heart!

6 December

Slept long. The rehearsal today is in the Small Hall because something else is happening in the Great Hall. This is exasperating, as I have only just got used to hearing the sound of the singers' voices, and now this will be a completely different acoustic. Also, today's rehearsal is with the second cast, and so there were many occasions on which we had to stop. At the end of the *Aida* rehearsal, I asked Tcherepnin about my gestures. He did not reply. I then said, 'I asked you because yesterday you criticized me on this point. I worked on it at home and should now like to know whether I have made any progress.'

---

1 Belokurova.

Tcherepnin muttered something I did not catch, and I moved away. Tsybin began *Rigoletto*, at which point Tcherepnin came up to me and said, 'Are you surprised I did not answer your question? You permitted yourself to shout at me with Palechek in front of the whole Conservatoire! If I set any store by my career as a professor in this Conservatoire, I should have reacted to your rudeness in a very different way. I have seen a great deal in my time, and nothing surprises me any more! I might have expected such behaviour from Tsybin next March; I should certainly not have expected it from you until at least May, but it has happened now!' And with that he turned on his heel and went out.

I had certainly not expected this second explosion from Tcherepnin. I found it deeply hurtful in any case that he should have been expecting some act of insolence or hostility from me after May,[1] and resolved to have the question of our relationship out with him at the earliest opportunity. In a state of some distress I went to congratulate Nikolay Andreyev on his name-day. Mama was there; although it was the middle of the afternoon we played vint and had an enjoyable talk. From the Andreyevs I went on to the Ruzskys, where there was a crowd of guests, noise, gaiety and Nikolay Pavlovich, whose name-day naturally it also is, was a beaming host, the table groaning with champagne, liqueurs and fruit. N. P. was his charming and affectionate self: 'Sergusya, Sergusya . . .', Ira could barely bring herself to offer me her hand. I met many friends there, among them Marusya Torletskaya, *née* Yershova. We were delighted to see one another, chatted and smoked. At seven o'clock I took myself off home, the parents saying goodbye in a friendly way but not asking me to stay for dinner, presumably because of my quarrel with their daughters. This hurt me a little. At home I found a dozen or so of my relations having dinner. I played them the Sonata No. 2, which went down very well. They were all very kind and promised to come to *Aida*.

7 December

The day of the general rehearsal, to which I set out with keen anticipation, although two things were spoiling my pleasure in it: (1) the Tcherepnin incident could not simply be brushed aside, our relationship must be clarified; (2) the opera is by no means secure and could go badly today.

In the Conservatoire there was an air of great excitement, and the moment the doors of the Great Hall opened it filled with people. After a long delay, *Rigoletto* started. I had nothing to do and did not want to listen, so I

---

1 By which time Prokofiev would have graduated and would no longer officially be subject to the discipline of being a student of the Conservatoire.

wandered aimlessly about hither and thither. I went into one of the side boxes where the chorus and ballet were sitting. 'You're not allowed in here!' said Vera Dmitrievna.

'Why not?'

'Because if everyone comes barging in here there won't be room to turn round!'

'Who is "everyone"? There is only one conductor of *Aida*, and that is myself!' I objected.

The girls tittered, Vera Dmitrievna, unable to bear my presence, went out instead. I had a nice chat with the chorus.

My Mama and Mme Yablonskaya were among the audience sitting in the hall, being kept company by Anna Grigorievna. Not far away from them sat Sonya Esche, who had come to see how I did. But she was not looking her best, her eyes and lips over-emphasized. Marusya Pavlova, when I went up to her, responded politely to my greeting and expressed surprise that I had not shown any interest in how her voice was developing. I said I had written a song dedicated to her, but I had not shown it to her because there was no point: she would not understand or appreciate it. I am referring to the song 'The boat cast off', written to verses[1] suggested by Marusya, that at one time I had thought of dedicating to her.

Aida began. I felt wonderful on the conductor's rostrum, and indeed the opera went very well, twice as well as the previous day. I had to stop the orchestra once because of a wrong entry leading to confusion by the violins, once I had to shout at the yawning and half-asleep timpanist, and once had to bring the orchestra back to order when the musicians were making a noise and climbing up on their chairs to get a better view of what was happening on stage during the offstage chorus. However, apart from being an enjoyable experience, the rehearsal was of little help to me.

Tcherepnin sat in the front row throughout the rehearsal, paying me no attention. But when it was over he climbed over the rail and said quite kindly that tomorrow I should come early and try not to be too anxious. I said I would like to have a serious talk with him, to which, presumably thinking I was going to apologize, he responded by mumbling something in a patronizing tone of voice. At the end of the rehearsal Gabel spoke to me at length and with affection; Tcherepnin joined us but I said nothing to him.

Tired, I went home, did nothing and then went to the Yusupov Garden to get a season ticket for the skating and to find out what had happened to the boots and skates I had forgotten there since the spring. They were still there, safe and sound.

---

1 By Alexey Apukhtin.

8 December

Slept soundly and long. When I got up, I played my Sonata No. 1, shaved, dressed in my tails and arrived at the start of the performance, that is to say for *Rigoletto*. I felt on top form, as I always do when I am going to conduct, and if there was a fly in the ointment it was the incident with Tcherepnin. An army of relations had come, and not in vain, for it proved to be an excellent performance. *Rigoletto* was not as good, but *Aida* was even better than at the general rehearsal. I was secure in my conducting and fixing my gaze on any musician from whom I wanted to extract more than he was already giving. It was the first time I had made use of such hypnotic techniques, and they yielded tremendous results. There was only one potential disaster: Aida came in half a bar early, but by this time the orchestra had the score off by heart and I was able to restore order without difficulty. The orchestra applauded me at the end of the performance.

Before beginning *Aida* I sat in the box first with the chorus and then in the make-up room with the 'slave-boys', where the poor girls squealed as they applied a mixture of soot and beer to their faces, designed to turn them into Negroes. They were all very polite to me.

I went down to Morenschild's dressing room, where Aktseri[1] promised me a box of chocolates if I prevented the orchestra from drowning her. And sure enough, in the interval I was presented with a box of delicious chocolates which I handed round to everyone, the directorate included (Tcherepnin declined; we seem not to be on speaking terms, although at the end he reminded me of his Tuesday class at two o'clock). Morenschild had the most tremendous success. At the end of the performance I came to her dressing room. Iretskaya expressed her gratitude to me, Morenschild presented me with one of her flowers, Aktseri a whole bunch of violets. As happy as could be, I went home.

Gala evening at the Sokol. I have no particular desire to go, but I must, because I promised to play my Sonata (No. 1) in the concert part of the programme. While I was playing something suddenly happened to the upright piano and it ceased to make any sound. I looked inside to see what had happened to the mechanism, and people in the hall began to laugh. I myself thought it was quite funny, and announced in a loud voice, 'Can't be helped, the piano doesn't want to play', and left the stage. Somehow the piano was mended and I got through the sonata to the end. Afterwards I spent a pleasant hour with Mlle Dobrotina, her brother and a girl from the Conservatoire, Duvidzon. At one in the morning the party broke up and we all went home.

---

1 One of the Professors of Singing at the St Petersburg Conservatoire.

9 December

Walking past the Conservatoire I looked in, partly because I was counting on meeting Tcherepnin to sort out our differences, and partly because it was pleasant to see and talk to people: after yesterday I felt myself something of a hero. Shurik Bushen related her visit yesterday to the Borovskys, where on hearing someone refer to me in sceptical terms, she launched into a passionate defence of my talents. This provoked the malicious comment: 'Well if that's your opinion of him, how lucky you are to be a fellow student of his at the Conservatoire . . .' to which Bushen retorted: 'The Conservatoire has nothing to do with it, we hardly ever see one another there, but I am glad to be living at a time when compositions such as his appear.'

'Oho! You talk exactly as though he were Beethoven or Tchaikovsky!'

She shot back: 'Yes, but some people are so unfortunate as to be born in the gaps when there is no Beethoven, no Tchaikovsky and no Prokofiev!'

All present were stunned by this. Mme Borovskaya murmured, 'I wish my Shura[1] had such a passionate admirer as you!'

The Alpers family was also present silently listening to this exchange.

In the Conservatoire I played the piano for the *Aida* rehearsal with the second cast. Shteiman was very nice, and said that he had heard of my success yesterday with *Aida* and regretted he had not known about the performance.

In the evening I had a session of gymnastics at the Sokol. At night I dreamed of India and was overcome with a desire to travel, to go on a really long journey, right round the world. Some day, this will happen. It is decided. I have even worked out the itinerary: Nice – Barcelona – Madrid – Lisbon – New York – Washington – Niagara – Chicago – San Francisco – California – Panama – Cuba – Brazil – Rio de Janeiro – Buenos Aires – Chile – New Zealand – Australia (south to north) – Manila – Malacca – India – Ceylon – The Red Sea – Constantinople – Odessa – St Petersburg.

It would take a year, or perhaps more. Papa once long ago made me a present of six thick books – a kind of world geography reader. At the time I did not appreciate them, but now I am going to look them out and read everything that has a bearing on my itinerary.

10 December

Practised the Chopin sonata, but Yesipova is still not well enough to teach and once again there was no lesson. Tcherepnin had called a class for two o'clock. I went to it, and as soon as he entered the room, said that I would like to speak to him. Tcherepnin growled, 'I don't have time now!'

---

1 Alexander Borovsky.

'Fine,' I answered, 'then I'll wait until the end of the class.'

I did not go into the class, Tsybin was not there either, nor for some reason Dranishnikov, and so Tcherepnin was forced to work rather aimlessly with two of the junior year conductors. Our having-it-out session took place at the end of the lesson. We removed ourselves to a dark and secluded staircase leading up to the Small Hall. I lent against the wall with my arms folded across my chest and my head lowered. Tcherepnin paced backwards and forwards, excited and shouting, more at himself than at me.

Our clean breast of the situation led to the following. My point of departure was the offence I had taken at Tcherepnin telling me what he 'expected from me in May'. ('All my students think it their duty to give me a kicking once they have graduated from my class.') What possible reason did he have for thinking that I would want to 'kick him' when I graduated from his class?

His point of departure was simple indignation that I should have allied myself with 'an embittered old man' (Palechek) and raised my voice to him (although in fact I did not do this at all), accusing him of letting the orchestra play and behave in a scandalous manner.

We were in fact talking at cross purposes. He was not the least bit interested in whether I was offended at his accusation of 'May'; I in turn was not much concerned about his spat with Palechek. I spoke in a serious, restrained but offended tone of voice; Tcherepnin got excited, used a great many fanciful turns of phrase including French expressions, and talked a lot of nonsense. I said that if he honestly thought that in May, when I finished the course, I would turn against him and start 'kicking' him, it could only mean that he was anticipating some low trick from me; that was why I considered his words insulting.

'If you feel I have insulted you, why don't you ask satisfaction from me? Please! Please! Challenge me to a duel!'

This was getting silly. I said I was sure it was only in the heat of the moment that he had charged me with preparing to 'kick' him and he did not truly mean it; that was why I had asked for this meeting. If we were unable to come to agreement on this point I frankly would feel unable to continue my studies with him.

'If you wish to leave my class, of course I cannot prevent you. But I do not advise you to take this step,' said Tcherepnin. And a few sentences later: 'No, sir, I did not expect, did not expect at all that you would ally yourself with Palechek to attack me!'

'That is precisely what I hoped to hear you say,' I said quickly.

'But please do not think you have trapped me!' Tcherepnin corrected himself.

In the end the conversation could not be brought to a satisfactory conclusion. All I could take away from it was that we were talking about different things, and that Tcherepnin was probably more deeply wounded than I was. We shook hands and parted down different staircases.

I returned home dissatisfied and discontented. My ill humour came out in the second of my sarcastic pieces,[1] the first section of which (in other words all the material I had at this stage) I had composed a long time ago. Now, unexpectedly and very sarcastically, the second part came into my mind. Compensation for the conversation I had just had! I am very happy with the piece.

The student concert that evening was not a very lively affair, but it was nice sitting next to Tanya Maslova. When she laughs, very pretty laughter lines appear on her face. I told Golubovskaya and Bushen that a fashionable duel was being fought in the Conservatoire. 'What with?' asked Golubovskaya. 'Conductor's batons?'

11 December

Having sat up until half past two writing out the *Sarcasm* piece, I slept in this morning, but once I was up I played it through on the piano, and some other pieces as well. At two o'clock there was an orchestra rehearsal in the Small Hall for the second cast; the orchestra was lackadaisical and did not play well. They are bored with the operas. Tcherepnin is now taking more of an active role in the rehearsals, and was of some help to me. However, our relations on both sides are dry and official. When Tsybin ascended the podium, Tcherepnin got up and walked out.

Returning home, I became absorbed in reading my bulky geography books. My round-the-world trip takes up most of my thoughts these days. I am reading about places on my route, at the moment New York and Washington.

In the evening I attended the Koussevitzky concert, partly to hear the music and partly to see him, since on his last visit he had asked me to remind him about my Second Piano Concerto the next time he would be in the city, that is to say now. This is not a very enjoyable task, and in addition Koussevitzky was conducting himself this evening, so he was too busy for me to speak to him. Glazunov's Seventh Symphony is a piece I know well. It is not bad, but still-born. Scenes from *Petrushka* cheered me up and reminded me of Paris. Risler[2] gave a wonderful performance of Liszt's A major Concerto, compared to which Shklyarevskaya's performance was a belch after eating rotten meat. Koussevitzky accompanied with a calm authority that I could only envy. Liszt's *Préludes*, written for a modest orchestra, simply do not sound opulent enough.

NB: never write for double wind – it must be treble, or quadruple.

---

1 *Sarcasms*, five pieces for piano, Op. 17.
2 Edouard Risler (1873–1929), French pianist, later professor at the Paris Conservatoire.

12 December

Tcherepnin, pleading illness, did not attend the rehearsal at all. We were in the Great Hall, and I was mortally afflicted with boredom while Tsybin plodded through *Rigoletto* despite the efforts of Bushen and her enemy Damskaya alternately to engage my attention. The singers today were only marking, singing at half-voice, the orchestra played abominably although they were indignant when I shouted at them. The basses and cellos were not there at all, and Annenkov thought it would be a good idea to replace them with temporary substitutes who had not the slightest idea about *Aida*. They played so many wrong notes that I sent them packing and asked Tvordovsky to play their parts on the piano. In short, nothing of any value was achieved today; it merely served to demoralize. Returned home and 'went to America', reading about Chicago, Niagara and San Francisco.

In the evening went to the Yusupov Garden where I much enjoyed my skating. There was a tremendous crowd there, all chattering away in German, just like in Berlin. However there was no one I knew there. Bushen is zealously learning to skate in order to be able to keep me company.

13 December

General rehearsal of the opera production. It is all beginning to nauseate, especially with such a rabble of an orchestra. Tcherepnin sent word that he was still unwell and for the second day running did not attend the rehearsal. The chorus was slack about assembling: many of the girls sat in the stalls and seemed disinclined to come up on stage. But a general rehearsal is always an event in the Conservatoire and the audience soon filled the hall. *Aida* went neither well nor badly; I hope she will pull herself together for the performance.

During *Rigoletto* I scanned the hall for signs of Serafima, but unsuccessfully, and only as the crowd was dispersing did I catch sight of her in the distance, picking her out because of her height. But she disappeared, and I ran into Vera Alpers, who once again hailed me.

'Sergey Sergeyevich,' she said, 'let us make up and be friends again . . . Or . . . don't you want to?' she added, with the most winning smile of which she was capable.

I thought for a few moments, while she waited, and then said, 'Very well, it's all the same to me, but let us if you want to', and giving her my hand, walked on. This cheered me up, although the truth is, I acted like a swine.

At home I practised the Chopin sonata and in the evening went to the Sokol.

14 December

No rehearsal today. Looking into the Conservatoire on my way past, I ran into Kreisler, who insisted that I play him my Second Sonata. To get rid of him, I did, and he went into raptures over it, which I had not expected. We then had quite a long talk, during which he told me of his interest in antiquities and in monasteries both in Russia and abroad. He is far from stupid. He was been very active all through the production of the operas, preparing the men's chorus outstandingly well and taking his backstage duties very seriously. We are on very good terms now: I call him my right hand, he calls me his torso.

Went into Jurgenson's asking for copies of my D minor Sonata so that I could send it to Zakharov, to Morolyov and to Katyusha Schmidthof, but he does not yet have it in the shop as the copies have not arrived from Moscow.

At eleven o'clock in the evening, tails, white waistcoat, new patent-leather shoes, for the ball at the Konshins. It is a long time since I have been in the *beau-monde*, and today it was very nice to drink in the fashionable elegance of the Konshin establishment. At first it was a little strained, but by and by the atmosphere became gayer. I danced a lot, and drank a lot. I danced a quadrille with Tanya Ruzskaya, even though our relations are still far from easy, and Ira gave me an unbelievably sour greeting. After twirling about until I was in a state of exhaustion, I went home. It was almost four by the time I got to bed, but that was long before the end of the ball.

15 December

To recover after the previous night's ball, I slept until I had to get up for the performance, but still arrived to conduct exhausted and out of sorts. I was bored during *Rigoletto*, but in the interval Shteiman appeared and then Telyakovsky[1] came into the artists' room, accompanied by Glazunov, Gabel and Tcherepnin. I was at the time standing in the wings. Glazunov came up to me and said, 'Come with me; I'll introduce you to Telyakovsky.'

I followed Glazunov and while the introductions were being performed, studied Telyakovsky with some curiosity. He is a shabby functionary with nothing remarkable about him, but he has a good sense of his own importance. Tsybin was also sent for, and Tcherepnin was generous in his recommendation, emphasizing the fact that he had risen from the ranks of orchestral musician to conductor. Evidently Tcherepnin and Tsybin have managed to settle their differences. For Tsybin, being presented to Telyakovsky was a great event: a fellow spends his whole life humbly tootling on the flute in the

---

1 Vladimir Telyakovsky (1861–1924), Director of the Imperial Theatres until the Revolution.

pit of the Mariinsky Theatre, and all of a sudden he is being presented to ... of all people ... none other than His Excellency himself, Director of the Imperial Theatres!

The performance of *Aida* was the equal of the first performance, except that at the beginning the new Amneris, a student of Zherebtsova-Andreyeva called Pavlinova,[1] dragged. I reasoned that if the tempo drags, the conductor will be blamed, and if the ensemble with the singer is bad, then the conductor will likewise be blamed; so the least worst course of action is to keep up the tempo, and I made sure the chords came in advance of the voice. This helped, she picked up the tempo and all was well.

During the interval Tcherepnin told me that my performance had sent Figner, the Director of the People's House, into ecstasies. It seems to be Theatre Directors' Day. However, Telyakovsky left after the first act of *Aida*. I had met Figner before at Korsak's and at the Meshcherskys'. Shteiman told me he approved of the way I had handled the opera. Quite a number of the orchestra musicians (those who are not my enemies) applauded me at the end.

Came home and went to sleep on the sofa, to be woken up by a telephone call from Sonya Esche. I yelled at her that she was disturbing my rest, replaced the receiver and then went back to sleep. Stayed at home in the evening, and practised the piano.

16 December

Today's rehearsal for the third performance was not a full one, because there were only minor differences between the second and third casts of singers: a new Gilda in *Rigoletto* and a new Aida for me. Consequently all the numbers that did not involve them were omitted. Only half the orchestra and a quarter of the chorus turned up. But even so, a dress rehearsal for the third performance is still a dress rehearsal, and there were plenty of people in the hall to listen. Serafima was not among them, and I saw her only after the rehearsal, coming up the stairs towards me. She acknowledged me first, and then disappeared.

In the evening I went to the Sokol. I gave Yury Frolov a ticket for tomorrow's performance.

17 December

The third performance was an evening one, therefore I did not feel like doing any work during the day. Generally the Conservatoire was empty, everyone

---

[1] Marina Pavlinova, whom Prokofiev had reluctantly coached at the insistence of Maria Korsak.

is disappearing for the holidays. I was about to go myself, when Serafima suddenly appeared. Joyfully I went up to her (the first time I have done so) with a polite smile and jokingly invited her to sing in the *Aida* chorus. She laughed and said that nothing would persuade her to sing, but she would like to come to the performance if I would give her a ticket. I gave her one for a seat in the tenth row, and then proceeded to tell her various amusing things that had happened during our opera production. We walked along the deserted corridors, laughing and talking, and had a very cheerful time.

I then came home and by eight o'clock was back in the theatre. Up till now the opera performances have been in the afternoon, but today is an evening show, and there was more of an atmosphere, people were dressed up, Glazunov in evening dress.

At the beginning of *Aida* there was a small *contretemps*: the harps got confused and went wrong, but quickly recovered and after that all went well. There were several small slips, but nothing to worry about, and the performance generally went smoothly enough. At the end of the opera, as I was going out from the orchestra, I caught sight of Belokurova standing in the box about the orchestra pit and smiling at me. As I walked past the penitent harps I pulled a disapproving face.

Glazunov said to me, 'Bravo, bravo, *Kapellmeister!*'

And so, *Aida* is off my shoulders, and I have done a decent job of work. I felt as though I was walking on air. We all made up a party to go to the 'Vienna' for supper, and invited Tcherepnin, but he declined. 'No, Nikolay Nikolayevich has still not forgiven us,' I said, tragicomically quoting from *Rigoletto*: 'I am forever cursed by the old man!'[1]

The party consisted of Tsybin, Kreisler, Tvordovsky and me. I was in the highest of high spirits as we reserved a table for the four of us. The Andreyevs were also in the 'Vienna', having come there to eat oysters after the dress rehearsal of Parsifal. Anna Grigorievna said that Pavlinova had been accepted for the Mariinsky Theatre; I congratulated Anna Grigorievna (her teacher) on this success, and then rejoined my own table. We ate bliny and drank wine and liqueurs. Tsybin told a stream of *risqué* anecdotes. A toast was drunk to me, not as a conductor (deliberately) but as a composer. Kreisler raised his glass to Tsybin, and to the junior conductors. At three o'clock, the stories still in full flow, we went home. I slipped and fell on the ice; everyone guffawed and pulled me up by the arms, although my fall had had nothing to do with what I had drunk.

'S.S., we'll give you a hand.'

'But that's not the reason I fell down.'

'Never mind, we can still give you a hand.'

---

[1] 'Quel vecchio maledivami' from Act I of Verdi's *Rigoletto*.

18 December

After the 'Vienna', needless to say, I overslept. When I got up I practised the piano, and at three o'clock went skating in the Yusupov Garden with Bushen, who is frenetically learning the art, to the extent that she is already quite steady on her legs and in time will overtake me.

Around seven I went to dinner with Luiza Alexeyevna Zakharova, where I met a good many people I know. Vasily Zakharov had met Tcherepnin somewhere or other, and Tcherepnin had told him that I had conducted *Aida* magnificently(?!). Frieda Hansen made some caustic comments. Lida Karneyeva and I kept well away from one another, although I had a nice, neighbourly conversation with the younger Kavos sister, a very beautiful girl.

At ten o'clock I attended one of Baron Driesen's[1] Wednesday *soirées*. Not many people were there and the subject of the lectures was not one especially close to my heart: 'Everyday life in the plays of Ostrovsky'. Nevertheless, to hear it being debated by the likes of Sologub,[2] Volkonsky[3] and others was interesting, and the humorous *resumé* of the evening's proceedings by Sladkopevtsev[4] was a delight.

19 December

Went into the Conservatoire to get scores from Friebus for the February concert: *Shereherezade* and *The Tempest*,[5] also the vocal score of *The Marriage of Figaro*, which we are going to do in the second half of the year. The Conservatoire had emptied of people; I saw Glazunov, who was very nice. Damskaya turned her back on me (because of the incident with the harps). When I returned home she rang up, trying simultaneously to tell me off and to make peace. I learned the Chopin sonata by heart according to my new technique, first imagining in my head the notation of the score, then the keyboard, and then carrying out in my head a harmonic analysis (although this

---

1 As well as his enthusiasm for re-creating mediaeval and other early theatre, Baron Nikolay Driesen von Osten (1868–1935) was literary censor to the Directorate of the Imperial Censors. He emigrated to Paris in 1919.
2 Fyodor Sologub, pen-name of Fyodor Teternikov (1863–1927), one of the leading Symbolist poets and novelists whose Manichaean vision contrasted the ugliness of the real world with the ideal purity and beauty of the world of the imagination.
3 Prince Sergey Volkonsky (1860–1937), literary, dramatic and cultural critic, was the grandson of his Decembrist namesake. A close friend of Marina Tsvetayeva, he dedicated to her his book *Life and Being* in return for her dedication to him of poems from her 1921 collection *The Student*, one of which is addressed to him. From 1899 to 1901 Volkonsky was Director of the Imperial Theatres; among the appointments he made was a short-lived one for Sergey Diaghilev to be Artistic Adviser to the Moscow Theatres.
4 Vladimir Sladkopevtsev (1876–1957), actor.
5 Tchaikovsky's Symphonic Fantasy *The Tempest*, Op. 18 (1873).

would be better done at the outset than later). Because I have not accustomed myself to this technique I found it mentally very tiring, although I am convinced it is the right way.

I am terribly pleased with my sarcastic pieces.

Went skating in the Yusupov Garden with Bushen, but she is still very shaky and stumbled so much that I lost patience with her.

20 December

Went into the Conservatoire, again to Friebus for the scores, and also to hear Damskaya (with whom harmony has been restored) play my Prelude on the harp; she is working on it for a student concert. From the Conservatoire I went on to the Andreyevs. Anna Grigorievna is leaving tomorrow for a singing engagement in London. We played bridge and dined. Karatygin is astonished to find that I am a card player. Later in the evening I went to the Sokol.

Why is it that so few people know Schumann's F minor Sonata?[1] It is a marvellous work, especially the first two movements. If I ever have to give recitals not of my own works, I shall definitely play it. The cerebrally conceived B double flat in the coda of the first movement (= a passing note added to another passing note) is particularly enjoyable. This double flat is something that could never have been conceived at the piano, only in the head.

21 December

Performed a heroic deed: rose at half past seven in order to be at the rehearsal for the symphony concert. Mengelberg is a first-class conductor, and is also a lucky man: he has short arms so can make whatever gestures he wishes without the fear Tcherepnin or I are always subject to, that he will end up flailing like a windmill. Mengelberg presented a vivacious account of Glazunov's Fifth Symphony, a better piece than the Seventh. I know it well, and listening to it gave me pleasure. Strauss's *Don Quixote* is not, of course, music at all. But it has much of interest in it, achieved with skill and humour: the bleating of the sheep, the characterization of Sancha Panza, the episode with the pilgrims.

Did some piano practice, and then at seven o'clock went to the station to see off Anna Grigorievna. At her request I then went to spend the evening with dear Nikolay Vasilievich, who has a bad cold. We had a hard-fought battle of *Sechsundsechzig*. He had interesting stories of Gibraltar, Lisbon and Algiers, which he had visited when serving as a Lieutenant on the *Standard*.[2]

At home I wrote a series of letters, among them to Vera Nikolayevna Meshcherskaya.

---

1 Piano Sonata No. 3, revised version of the *Concert sans orchestra* in F minor, Op. 14.
2 The Tsar's Royal Yacht was called *The Standard*.

22 December

Yesterday I got up very early, but today I slept until half past twelve, later than I have ever done. Practised the piano. Bushen invited me to go skating, which we did. In the evening, just as I was sitting down to write my diary, Sonya Esche telephoned, in a lyrical frame of mind. She told me she had been in love with me for three years, that if it had not been for me she would have been married, and that in her dreams I am her only lover, a notion I pooh-poohed.

My eyesight seems to be deteriorating. Hitherto I have been able to see everything, but now I notice that there are some notices I can't read, names of streets and so on, I can't see the time on clock faces on towers, can't distinguish faces in the balcony when looking up from the stalls. So far it is not causing me any difficulties, but if it gets any worse, it will be a problem.

23 December

Today the men polishing our floors were making such a noise that I could not work, and went to practise in an empty Conservatoire.

Called into Jurgenson's to buy copies of my D minor Sonata. For some reason the copies here have a grey cover, but the ones they sent me from Moscow have a more striking reddish-brown binding. Went to see Myaskovsky. In the evening was at the Sokol.

24 December

Myaskovsky has written of Debussy that on hearing his music one comes home refreshed, as if having taken a deep draught of fresh air from the sea, the woods and the fields.

I also liked this music so much, and music descriptive of nature has such appeal for me, that I felt a desire myself to compose in this style. The second subject of my symphony is certainly very successful, but it is not 'nature' so much as characteristic of a kind of dreamy, mysterious imagery. I very much like this theme; in general, whenever I think of my symphony, I feel a sense of excitement and belief that it will be a wonderful work.

Skated in the Yusupov Garden, but without Bushen. It was freezing, and I assiduously practised my 'Dutch step' and my swerves. At seven o'clock I put on my tails and went to dinner with the Orlovs, who have reappeared over my horizon. Magda[1] is an enchanting person, but not a word was said by either of us about *Maddalena* and I did not tell her about the possible Moscow

---

1 Magda Orlova, who under the pen-name 'Baroness Lieven' contributed the libretto for *Maddalena*.

production. I had a very nice time at the Orlovs, and Nikolay Andreyev, flirting all the time with Magda, kept everyone amused with his vivacity and wit.

25 December

Christmas Day. Slept as is fitting for a holiday: until one o'clock – until my head ached, in fact. Played the piano, welcomed Mama's guests and then went to visit Nikolay Vasilievich, who is still wheezing and keeping indoors. In the evening I wrote to Fyaka and brought my diary up to date for 1913.

Vera Alpers telephoned, wanting to see me. I took fright that she might be inviting me to see her at her home, but she chose a place to meet on neutral ground, the Yusupov Garden tomorrow at noon. I asked her to ring again tomorrow.

26 December

Practised the piano. The Chopin sonata is turning out very well. Most of my programme is proving to be successful, so I am beginning to think I shall play well at the exam. And what if I were to win the grand piano prize?

Using the freezing weather as an excuse, I called off the meeting with Alpers and went to the Chess Club, to watch the Jubilee All-Russia Tournament. The President, Malyutin, confirmed that I should have been made a member some time ago, all the more so as I am now a 'maestro' and people of that ilk are admitted to the Club. I therefore submitted my application and spent three hours there watching the tournament. Saw the famous Capablanca, whom I very much liked the look of. And how unattractive beside him seemed the unshaven, bloated, unsympathetic but also very famous figure of Nimzowitsch!

28–31 December

Over these four days I got up late, at noon, and for the most part stayed at home practising my examination recital programme. (What a horrible structure the Finale of the Schumann sonata has! I found it almost impossible to make sense of these scraps of material that have no more coherence than a pack of well-shuffled cards! In order to learn it by heart I have had to make out an analytical summary and commit the summary to memory.) The Schumann, Chopin and Beethoven sonatas are all more or less on track, leaving the Liszt, Mozart[1] and Bach still to be tackled. To bring off *Tann-*

---

1   It is not clear which Mozart work Prokofiev played for his graduation recital. In April, Yesipova had 'set' the C minor Fantasia (K. 396) (see pp. 367–8), but in the event he seems (pp. 596, 613) to have played one of the sets of Variations.

häuser as it should be done is a diabolically hard challenge and will need all my reserves of strength.

Besides piano practice, I did a little composing during these days. I sent my Sonatas, 'Despair', 'Suggestion diabolique', Etude No. 4 and Op. 3 to Zakharov.

Went skating a couple of times, but without Bushen, who has disappeared over the horizon in protest at my silent refusal to skate with her. Damskaya, on the other hand, is always ready to chat, and we have lively conversations lasting as much as an hour or an hour and a half. She is a fund of gossipy trivialities about herself, her girl friends, what people are saying about me in the Conservatoire, and her telephone calls are never less than entertaining.

The evenings I spent in the following manner: on Saturday I played telephone chess with Golubovskaya. On Sunday played Lotto at Korsaks, where I have not been for ages. On Monday did gymnastics at Sokol. On Tuesday saw the New Year in at the Rayevskys: prayers at eight o'clock, and then we sat down to play vint. At half past eleven we sat down at table *en famille*, and as the clock struck midnight everyone rose with a glass in their hand. I had promised to think of Damskaya, which I did with pleasure, and by association with her, Bushen, then Vegman and Belokurova. No one else.

I completely forgot about Nina Meshcherskaya.

1914

1 January

Slept until one, then practised Chopin and Liszt. At three o'clock spent ages trying to call a taxi – wherever I tried, they were all taken. Eventually a car came and I set off on my round of visits. I had accumulated a number of absolutely obligatory ones, people I had not been to see since last winter. Shurik, Andryusha, the Goldevskys, Saburov and the Orlovs were not at home to visitors. I dropped in briefly to the Konshins and to Korsak. Normally the Ruzskys host a special grand lunch on New Year's Day, lasting until six o'clock in the evening, with lots of guests and much noisy imbibing of champagne, but today nothing was happening; Olga Petrovna[1] was friendly but pale and exhausted-looking, Tanya was in a black mood, and there was no sign of anyone else. They had been seeing in the New Year until eight in the morning, and were only just now getting up. I called on Luiza Zakharova, who was, as always, extremely nice. She told me she had heard that Lida Karneyeva is upset at our quarrel. My last call was on the Ossovskys, a very pleasant visit. According to them, the Ruzskys have become very rich as a result of the discovery of iron ore on their estate in the Caucasus, which is now bringing in a tremendous income. Once I had discharged all my obligations I went to see Nikolay Vasilievich[2] for half an hour, and then went home to dine.

In the evening I went to see the Christmas tree in the Yusupov Garden. I knew nobody there, but still had a good time with the crowds, the merry, rosy faces, the bustle and the fireworks and all kinds of entertainment.

2 January

Practised the piano for a long time, then went skating at the Yusupka[3] and read about America in pursuit of my 'round-the-world' voyage. Today is the day of the Conservatoire ball.

I dressed with care: dinner suit (tails are too formal for a party), smart white Parisian waistcoat, dangerously transparent socks and new patent-leather shoes. I arrived just before half past eight, as stipulated by Damskaya, who had exacted my punctual attendance as a forfeit in a game of *Sechsundsechzig*. In return she presented me with a small phial of excellent, rather

---

1 Nikolay Ruzsky's wife.
2 Andreyev.
3 The Yusupov Garden.

sweet perfume by Coty, taken from her own supply, fed me chocolates and generally showed her attachment to me in the most attentive way.

The concert section of the evening was interminably long, but there were attractions for young visitors in the array of talented and highly decorative female soloists taking part, notably Tilya Hansen. Eleonora[1] performed a piece for harp, and looked most poetic in her ringlets. Katya Vegman, elegant and interesting-looking, was selling flowers. At my request Eleonora took her place for a while, while I danced with Katya.

Although I had not sent any, I received several letters by 'flying post'[2] – two simultaneously just before the end of the evening. This evening I felt happy and gay, I was having too much of a success to notice the proceedings drawing to a close. I should have liked to accompany Vegman home, and by all appearances she would have liked me to, but her family and her mother were there and the poor girl had to go with them. So I set off on my own to go home, and as soon as I got out on the street was about to step into a waiting taxi, but hardly had I got my foot on the step when a schoolboy, closely followed by two figures well muffled up against the cold, ran up shouting that the cab was his. An appeal to the dim-witted driver confirmed that the cab was mine, but at this point I recognized in the bundled figures the Inspector of our Academic School[3] and his wife. Deciding that it would be an act of discourtesy to deprive the powers that be of their car, I declared that although the motor really belonged to me I would be pleased to renounce my claim to the lady. I then took my place in a passing sledge.

3 January

The relations came to dinner. Normally this is a dull occasion, but today I organized a bridge session with Andreyev, Myaskovsky, myself and Shurik Rayevsky – who is by way of being a specialist at the game – and we had a lively time. I was not playing well, and got fleeced. Dear Andreyev got up from the table to go straight to Revel[4] to sing. He has signed a contract for a two-month season in London this summer (with Diaghilev) and would like me to go with him for a month. It would cost about 350 roubles, and I will think about it, that's not bad.

I played my sarcastic pieces.[5] Andreyev loved No. 2[6] and said it was as if the piano was on fire with sixteen hands. Myaskovsky was less taken with this

---

1 Damskaya.
2 A common entertainment at balls, in which people would send one another messages by homing pigeons.
3 Rusinov.
4 The Russian name for Tallin, capital of Estonia.
5 *Sarcasms*, five pieces for piano, Op. 17.
6 Later published as No. 1. [Subsequent note by author.]

one but praised No. 3, which everyone else finds hard to understand. In No. 4 the different key signatures in the left and right hands provoked much lively discussion, likewise the final B flat. I defended it vigorously.

4 January

Settled down to play through the repertoire for my Moscow appearance, and thought about a way an approach to the performance of my Sonata.[1] In the first movement the nuances should be in half-tones, the *forte* passages restrained, likewise the tempo, and the whole movement should be played with a delicate patina of suppressed sadness.

Went skating. At home had a telephone conversation with Damskaya about the party. In the evening learned *Tannhäuser* and wrote my diary.

5 January

Slept outrageously late. Practised repertoire for Yesipova and for Moscow. Broke several strings. Went skating. In the evening caught up with my diary.

6 January
Feast of the Epiphany

Unable to play the piano because of the strings, which the piano keeps on 'swallowing' (as Ratke puts it). Went to see Myaskovsky. *Muzyka* wants an analysis of the Sonata and the *Ballade*. In the evening learned the Bach fugue, which doesn't use any of the broken strings. I played it by heart twelve times. Later played a game of telephone *Sechsundsechzig* with Damskaya. She won one game, I the other. Her forfeit to me is to bring a box of liqueur cherries to the Conservatoire – she has been given a present of five pounds of them – and mine was to read to her the diary of my trip to the Crimea with Max. This reading, which was done over the telephone, gave both of us much pleasure.

7 January

Went in to the Conservatoire, which is slowly coming back to life. Talked to Kreisler, who seems to have spent the whole of Christmas drinking with Torletsky, a friend of his.

Purloined from Damskaya her very warm and soft gloves, offering her mine in return. I now go about in 'damesky' gloves. She thinks this is quite amusing.

In the evening I went to the Sokol.

---

1 No. 2 in D minor, Op. 14.

8 January

Practised the piano. Went to the Chess Club to watch the tournament. I am a member now (and very happy to be so). The tournament ploughs on; today there were no particularly interesting matches. I played with the elderly Saburov; he is getting a bit decrepit now and his memory is beginning to fail, but at the table he is as youthful as ever and after a two-hour battle he had worn down all my resources and I lost. After that I won two games against Palen, an official of the Imperial Court, to whom Saburov introduced me. Around six o'clock Capablanca came into the Club: he is an utterly irresistible person, lively, handsome, quick-witted, and – this is the point – a genius. You should have seen how quickly he showed up the mistakes of our Petersburg masters: on the spot, the instant their games were finished, and right in front of their very eyes! I was entranced.

In the evening I played the piano and telephoned Damskaya to share my impressions of Capablanca. For some reason she takes a great interest in him and knows everything there is to know about him. We talked for over an hour.

16 January

Today, about three-quarters of the orchestra assembled for the first 'reconstituted' orchestra class. Tcherepnin read through *Sheherezade* and worked on individual sections of the piece. Out of boredom I was playing the percussion instruments along with two other young fellows, until Tcherepnin yelled, 'That's enough! I can't hear anyone but you!' After the class I ran into Bushen. She has got used to my not speaking to her, but today I stopped and asked her how she was. She poured out a torrent of news: (1) she is now an expert skater; (2) she has learned my Sonata No. 2, which she loves passionately and is planning to take to 'Lyadya';[1] (3) she has bought my Sonata No. 1 at Jurgenson's. She showed it to me, and there it was personally inscribed from me: 'To N. S. Tereshchenko from the composer as a mark of deepest respect'. That was a turn-up for the book! My works on sale with a signed inscription! I myself had sent it to Tereshchenko, so what was it now doing on Jurgenson's shelves? And even more to the point, how could it have been sold as a new copy? Something wrong here. I explained to Bushen who Tereshchenko was (one of the respected founders of the Chess Club), and could only imagine that when I sent him the sonata in a printed-matter wrapper I must have forgotten to put my own address, and the package was delivered when Tereshchenko was abroad. In the absence of the addressee

---

1 Lyapunov. 'Lyadya' as a nickname suggests 'Dyadya' ('Uncle') used by Russians often with overtones of affectionate condescension.

the package should have been returned to sender, but since there was no address they would have opened the package, seen the name of Jurgenson as publisher, and returned it to the shop. This made sense since I had never had a word of thanks from Tereshchenko, and feeling slightly offended, I had responded rather coldly to his friendly greeting when I met him recently at the Chess Club.

Nikolay Shtember telephoned me in the evening to tell me that he had bought my Second Sonata, liked it very much, understood the logic of all the dissonances and would like to talk to me about the work as a whole. He came at eight o'clock, played through the sonata, and then we went together to the Sokol.

17 January

In the morning I played through and tidied up my Moscow programme, especially the Sonata. Wonderful weather: went for a walk in anticipation of the session with Tcherepnin that evening. We went through *Figaro* and *Sheherezade*. Relations between us have settled down, but are not as affectionate as formerly. Sometimes this irritates me. I still make jokes as I did before, and whenever I don't agree with his explanations, I let him know.

After the class I went to see the Class Inspectors and asked whether Blumenfeld was planning to teach his Chamber Music class. They told me that yes, he was, but they were not sure whether he would accept me, since the class was fully subscribed. According to them his comment, when he looked at the student lists and saw my name there, was: 'Whatever's he doing here?' The administrators, who cannot abide me, were obviously taking the opportunity to spite me, so all I said in reply was that the reason he would have asked the question was that he did not know who I was. Going to see Blumenfeld I was therefore to some extent forewarned, but the good ladies had in any case been talking nonsense, as Blumenfeld could not have been more friendly and when he learned that I had written a Ballade for cello, suggested that I bring it to the class and even that I play it as my examination piece. I was very pleased by this. Gabel told me that the piano exams will now start on 4 March, not at the end of the month as I had thought. Now the cat's among the pigeons! A whole month earlier! But the exams go on for at least twelve days, and Yesipova's class is the last to play, so the earliest I shall have to perform will be the 15th.

The Rayevskys dined with us but I slipped away to the Chess Club for the final round of the championship. The scene was particularly lively, with matches in full swing, players and spectators alike excited and on edge. Nimzowitsch was having trouble beating off Levenfisch's attacks, Znosko-Borovsky was holding firm against Flyamb, who with his usual pallor sat hunched over the board, his face buried in his hands, doggedly squeezing the last drop of advantage from the game. Alekhine manfully attacked old man Alapin. Then came the interval; Nimzowitsch opened the window, thrusting his whole body out into the freezing air – his unorthodox way of refreshing himself. Znosko-Borovsky sat in the next room twitching his leg and reading a newspaper. I went up to him to talk about his match with Flyamb.

'Flyamb looks so pale and grey, yet he can't be as old as all that, not more than thirty-five.'

'He's twenty-seven.'

'Unbelievable!'

Znosko laughs: 'That's what the passions can do to you!'

'But to look at he's such an unassuming . . .'

'Even at twenty-seven the passions can do that to you.'

The interval comes to an end. Nimzowitsch straightens out his position and puts pressure on Levenfisch. I meet Tereshchenko.

'N. S., do you remember we had a musical evening together at Saburov's? I meant to send you a copy of my Sonata, but a strange thing happened . . .'

Tereshchenko: 'What do you mean? I did receive it, and played it with great enjoyment . . . and you wrote such a generous inscription in the score.'

I could not work this out at all, but at that moment a rumour spread through the hall that Flyamb was resigning, so our conversation was interrupted by everyone dashing to the scene of the capitulation. I was sincerely sorry for Flyamb; I had taken a great liking to him today and hoped that he would take the first prize. I did not wait until the end of the tournament, but went home at one o'clock in the morning.

18 January

I get up early these days and immediately go to the piano. The position is serious: there are less than two months until the exam and my programme is anything but ready. It's not enough just to know the pieces; I need to have them firmly nailed into my skull and shall be in a great state of nerves if they are not. At half past eleven, for a change of scene, I went in to the rehearsal of Glazunov's Violin Concerto: half the Conservatoire crams into these rehearsals. Glazunov's concerto doesn't give the soloist much of a chance for display; my own will be a more brilliant affair. The first theme is delicious, but it has been lifted straight from Korsakov's *The Tsar's Bride*. Young Heifetz is an exceptional violinist. Golubovskaya has asked me to accompany her Saint-Saëns concerto in the exam (this is rather piquant, bearing in mind that some people regard us as rivals for the grand piano prize). The 'Piquant Queen'[1]

---

1   A play on words with 'Pikovaya Dama', 'The Queen of Spades'.

was circling around me in an obvious attempt to attract my favourable attention. Damskaya has found out her surname: Spivak. How prosaic! One of our peasants at Sontsovka was called Spivak. Finally Bushen came flitting by, as beautiful, supple and elegant as the very first time I set eyes on her in the autumn. She has changed her hairstyle once again, this time very successfully.

Went home and sat down at the piano. Mama wants to drag me out to the Pototskys' ball this evening, but I have refused as I still need to practise. However in the event I did little except telephone Damskaya, and we set a new record for long phone calls: two hours and ten minutes! I read her my diary account of the trip to Switzerland, and enjoyed myself very much reading it out.

Nurok tells me that because of Medtner's concert our concert has to be postponed from 27 January to 4 February. He also had news for me: Diaghilev wants to meet me. Perhaps he will commission a ballet for his Paris season?! Oho!

There is an item in the *Evening Times* about Zakharov having made a successful appearance at the Palace of the Austrian Archduchess. So Boryusya is starting at the top!

19 January

In the morning I played the piano.

Tcherepnin's class. He says an opera as vocally mobile as Mozart's is made possible only by the simplicity of the harmonic language.

An idea: to write a similar opera on a silly and comically tangled plot, with ensembles, fast-tempo numbers, simple harmonies and instrumentation, but less simple than Mozart's. This could be interesting, since Mozart was not by any means always completely successful in his rendering of the text.

In the evening I planned to go to Scriabin's concert, but in the end decided not to, having had enough music. Then I thought I would go to Nimzowitsch's chess evening, but eventually came to the conclusion that I would rather stay at home. At least I managed to complete the piano score of the Concerto No. 2 and did some work on *Sheherezade*: the second movement needs a lot of study if I am going to be able to get through conducting it without falling flat on my face.

20 January

At the orchestra class Tcherepnin himself conducted the whole time, presumably in revenge for the *Aida* incident.

Tsybin did not show up. He has been hoping to make his debut as a ballet conductor at the Mariinsky Theatre, but has met with no success and is most distressed about it. Kreisler is planning to come with me to Moscow. Myaskovsky leaves today; Beloúsov and I will go tomorrow.

After leaving the Conservatoire I went to see about my ticket, and also bought myself a suitcase. I am very fond of small cases, just big enough to take a tail suit, and a change of underclothes, but light enough to be carried by hand.

Today's edition of *Muzyka* carries both my analysis[1] and Myaskovsky's. The whole issue is in fact devoted to our evening, and discusses our music at length. I went to a lot of trouble over my analysis, including copious music examples in my neat calligraphy, but the photographic reproduction method they used has made them look horribly crooked and uneven.

In the same issue there is an announcement about the Belyayev Concerts. Nowhere does my Concerto figure in the programme. At the time, Tcherepnin had gone to considerable lengths asking for it to be included, insisting that if it were not then he would refuse to conduct anything in the season. But now apparently he is quite ready to accept an engagement even though the Concerto has been left out. Generally, Tcherepnin is a useful back-up when everything is going well without his assistance, but when conflicts arise he is a Jesuit and I now understand why he has so many enemies.

Nikolay[2] came round in the evening and we went together to the Sokol. It is always nice to have a drink after a session there, especially if the drink is champagne. We decided to go into a pub, but they had only two bottles there, both very expensive, so we went instead to the Warsaw station and drank 'Narzan' mineral water.

21 January

Practised the piano.

Nothing of interest at the Conservatoire. Tcherepnin finished his survey of *Sheherezade*, expounding it with passion and with many interesting things to say about it. I talked to Damskaya, who was at the time arm in arm with a girl called, it seems, Solomon, very beautiful and far from stupid.

At six o'clock I got an urgent telegram from Moscow; I was chagrined, expecting news that once again the evening was to be postponed. But all the cable said was: 'Still on. Saradzhev.' I packed my nice new little suitcase and set off for the station. I don't like travelling alone, but this time I was going with Beloúsov, so was in high spirits. Beloúsov was good company and related his experiences on foreign tours. He currently has invitations to Budapest, Norway and . . . Spain. God, that's interesting! The train we were on was the

---

1   Of the Sonata No. 2.
2   Shtember.

Northern Express which has a restaurant car, so we sat there. A year ago this was the very train on which Max and I travelled to the Crimea. I have wonderful memories of it.

22 January

The train was due to wait only eight minutes in Moscow, so we had to take care not to oversleep. Out on the streets it was rainy and slushy, and the first thing I had to do, dandy that I am in my smart shoes, was go to a shoe shop and buy galoshes. Beloúsov took himself off to the Hotel Luxe while I, suitcase in hand, took a tram and went to Saradzhev, calling at Derzhanovsky's on the way. Had a talk with him and Myaskovsky, who was staying with him, and then on to Müller's shop to practise on the Ibach piano on which I am to perform later. I am not a great lover of the make, and this particular example proved to be horrible. However after an hour and a half I got used to it, and began to make it sound reasonable. I then went to the Maly Zal[1] where I found all the participants in the concert and where, moreover, Stravinsky's *Three Japanese Lyrics*[2] (a worthless piece of music) was to be rehearsed. I should have liked to go into the teaching area of the Conservatoire to see how things are done in Moscow, but had no time to do so. As for Moscow's Maly Zal, it is a thousand times inferior to our own Small Hall. Myaskovsky's Sonata sounds wonderful; I particularly like the opening. Myaskovsky, Saradzhev and Derzhanovsky are all ecstatic over my *Ballade*, especially Myaskovsky.

On my way back I called on my relations, and also on Taneyev, whom I had not seen for two years. He was not at home, so I left him a card with an invitation to tomorrow's concert. At home there was more rehearsal with Beloúsov, who is turning out to be phenomenally conscientious. He plays magnificently. In the evening Myaskovsky and I were together at Yurasovky's, who spouted a load of nonsense about music, and this time I found his manner exasperating.

23 January

Slept the night at Saradzhev's, and could hardly stir my stumps in the morning. I went to practise at Müller's and then on to Derzhanovsky to play through the *Ballade* once again. Myaskovsky and I then went together to see

---

1 The Small Hall of the Moscow Conservatoire.
2 *Three Japanese Lyrics* translated into Russian by A. Brandt, for soprano, two flutes, two clarinets, piano and string quartet. The first performance had taken place in Paris less than a month previously.

Yavorsky,[1] a first-class musicologist and well-known Moscow musician. I have known him for some time, and indeed visited him once before after the Moscow performance of my First Piano Concerto. I have not seen him since, although I know from Myaskovsky that he is a great admirer of my music. Myaskovsky is very friendly with him and took me along today for company.

From Yavorsky I went to see Katyusha Schmidthof-Lavrova: I knew they wanted very much to see me, but I was still very nervous about going there. She and her mother are now comfortably installed in Denezhny Lane. Katyusha turns out be a strapping, jolly sort of girl; her mother an ailing lady with the mark of sorrow on her brow. They welcomed me with such unaffected love that I found it almost disconcerting: their love for their lost Max has transferred itself wholly to me. We had much to talk about, everything that concerned Max, although seeing how his mother's face mirrored her grief, I tried not to introduce him directly into the conversation. In any case I was in a rush to get back to Derzhanovsky's to dine, and after half an hour I left, promising to return the following day.

Chez Derzhanovsky all was in a state of pre-concert confusion: Madame busy with the hairdresser, 'himself' oscillating between the telephone and the desk, his mother fussing over the programmes, Myaskovsky attiring himself in his dinner suit. Invitations had been sent to the whole of musical Moscow, but not many tickets had been sold. I twitted Derzhanovsky with a calculation of how many people would actually be there, arriving at an estimated forty definite takers.

I walked over to Saradzhev's (two steps away), put on my tails and went to the concert.

The green room was full of people. I talked to Jurgenson, Yurasovsky and the composer Akimenko,[2] whose brother I know through the Conservatoire. Taneyev had sent me a letter. At last it was time for me to begin, so I went out to a smattering of applause, bowed, and sat down at the Ibach. Although the hall was not full, there was enough of an audience to make a good atmosphere. I played the Second Sonata (its first public performance). I know the piece pretty well; the first movement went all right, I fumbled quite a lot of the Scherzo although it made its effects, the Andante was fine, and the Finale quite excellent. The work was a success; I was called back twice to warm applause. Some Stravinsky songs[3] and then it was again my turn, this time

---

1   Boleslav Yavorsky (1877–1942), pianist, composer and one of the most respected critics and writers on music of his generation. A perceptive champion of new music, he became a close friend and admirer of the young Shostakovich, on whom he exerted considerable influence.
2   Yakov Akimenko (1883–1921), composer and writer on music, whose reviews appeared frequently in *Muzyka*. His elder brother Fyodor, also a composer, was on the teaching staff of the St Petersburg Conservatoire.
3   Two poems of Balmont, 'Forget-me-not' and 'The Dove'; *Trois lyriques du japonais*. The Balmont songs, originally with piano accompaniment, were later arranged for the same combination of instruments as the *Japanese Lyrics*.

with Beloúsov to play the *Ballade*. For some reason I was not so fond of it today, and it did not go as well as it had done in the morning. It was well received all the same, and Beloúsov and I went out to take our bow.

Interval. Quite a lot of people came backstage: Yurasovsky, Myaskovsky, Shenshin, Jurgenson. I talked about the *Ballade* to Beloúsov's former teacher,[1] to whom he introduced me. After the interval Beloúsov and Lamm[2] (known in these parts as 'Khlam'[3] but who proved in fact to be a first-class pianist) performed Myaskovsky's Cello Sonata.[4] I sat in the stalls with Mme Derzhanovskaya and her young half-sister (they have different mothers) Lyolya. Lyolya is thirteen but could easily be taken for eighteen; she is as tall as me with sazhen[5]-wide shoulders. Derzhanovsky calls her the Valkyrie. Belousov finished, to be replaced by Derzhanovsky in the Myaskovsky songs.[6] I sat in the artists' room with Beloúsov and the Valkyrie listening to the Myaskovsky songs, which I adore. The songs were a great success and the composer was called to take a bow, but he hid himself in a corner of the stalls.

Now it was my turn to go on stage again for my solo piano pieces.[7] By now I was almost completely calm, and everything came off perfectly. Some of the pieces elicited applause, which I rose to acknowledge (Etude No. 3, 'Prelude', 'Rigaudon'. But in the last piece, 'Suggestion diabolique', I lost my way and, despite all my efforts to extricate myself, my memory failed and I could not get back on the rails. So I stopped, put my hand to my head, concentrated hard and started again from the beginning. My playing was now rather more circumspect but had great *élan*, especially when I reached the slap in the face of the two glissandos! The audience applauded warmly and I left the stage.

The general feeling was that my memory lapse in 'Suggestion diabolique' had not spoilt the impression I made. A terrible crush in the green room; everyone will be going to Derzhanovsky's for dinner. Myaskovsky, desperate to avoid having to go with the ladies, went with me. I told him how wonderful

---

1 Alfred Glen (1858–1927), through whom Beloúsov could thus trace his cellist ancestry back to Karl Davydov. Glen also taught Gregor Piatigorsky.
2 Pavel Lamm (1882–1951), pianist and musicologist, is probably best known today for his performing editions of Musorgsky's original scores for *Boris Godunov* and *Khovanshchina*. After Prokofiev's return to the Soviet Union he became a trusted collaborator, transcribing and preparing full scores from the composer's short scores of *Semyon Kotko*, *Cinderella* and *War and Peace*. Attendance at the regular gatherings in Lamm's Moscow flat were mandatory for anyone wishing to hear the latest works, often in Lamm's own piano reductions. Here, for example, Sviatoslav Richter turned the pages for Prokofiev when he played the Sixth Piano Sonata for the first time.
3 'Rubbish', 'trash'.
4 Sonata No. 1 in D major for cello and piano.
5 A sazhen is just over two metres.
6 *Two Sketches on Words by Vyacheslav Ivanov* ('The Valley-Shrine', 'Pan and Psyche'); *From Z. N. Gippius*, five pieces for voice and piano.
7 *Four Etudes for piano*, Op. 2: No. 3; *Four Pieces for piano*, Op. 3: No. 1 'Fairy Tale', No. 3 'March'; *Ten Pieces for piano*, Op. 12: No. 7 'Prelude', No. 3 'Rigaudon', No. 6 'Legenda'; *Four Pieces for piano*, Op. 4: No. 3 'Despair', No. 4 'Suggestion diabolique'.

I thought his songs were; he praised my piano playing, especially in the smaller pieces, which he described as beyond reproach. This is the first time I have ever had such praise from him for my pianism; I told him I looked forward to the time when he will approve of me as a conductor too, but at this he shook his head doubtfully.

Supper was a relaxed and cheerful affair; I tried to sit next to Lyolya. She does attract me, but I kept myself on a tight rein out of respect for her tender years. I drew a sign for her on the wrapping paper from a sweet, telling her that if she were to go on thinking about it continually, in five years' time she would understand it. She could not leave it alone, and kept on repeating in a childish lisp: 'Oh, pleeeease tell me!'

I left with the Saradzhevs at four o'clock to go home and sleep.

24 January

A talk with Saradzhev in the morning, who told me the situation with the Free Theatre (concerning *Maddalena*, Mardzhanov and Sukhodolsky[1]). Telephoned Koussevitzky. Sabaneyev's review. Went to Derzhanovsky. Lyolya has been missing me. More 'pleeeease tell me!' Went to see Taneyev, who was impressed by the Sonata, some of which he liked. He made several helpful suggestions, gently chaffing me over my modernistic tendencies. I dined with Saradzhev, and eventually at half past seven Myaskovsky and I got into a cab to leave. Everyone stood at the window and waved. It is the first time Myaskovsky and I have been travelling companions. We have two lower berth reservations, make ourselves very comfortable and lie down to sleep.

25 January

By half past eight in the morning Kolechka and I were in Petersburg and parted to go to our respective homes. As we said goodbye he said in tones of great friendliness that it had been very pleasant spending time with me. When I got home everyone was still asleep, so I went to the orchestra rehearsal in the Great Hall of the Conservatoire – more to see friends than to hear the music. I ran across Marusya Pavlova, whom I always enjoy seeing. She was very nice today, and again expressed a wish that I should hear her sing, so I could see how much she had improved. Then I talked to my devoted Damskaya.

Returning home I practised my D flat major Concerto to my great satis-

---

1 The businessman Vladimir Sukhodolsky, a shareholder in the Free Theatre, created a scandal over what he considered the financial mismanagement of the enterprise, thus helping to bring about its demise after only one season.

faction. In the evening I had planned to continue practising, but Andreyev telephoned and invited me over with such affectionate insistence that I gave in and went. We played bridge and they took 4 roubles off me.

26 January

Today is Mama's name-day, and I presented her with some good writing paper, as what she normally uses is dreadful. In the afternoon I practised my Concerto and the exam recital programme. In general I am concentrating seriously on the piano at the moment. As well as this I studied *Sheherezade* in case Tcherepnin asks me to conduct it tomorrow.

Nurok tells me that Diaghilev has already left; this is a blow because I had already built up in my mind all kinds of fantasies about creating a ballet for Paris and the European fame that would follow. The concert (when I am to play the same programme as in Moscow) has been postponed until the 7th. In the evening we have guests: vint, supper, champagne, in which I make my debut as bottle-opener and pourer-out.

27 January

Went to bed at four and got up at nine, clearly not having had enough sleep. But I had to be at orchestra class in the Conservatoire by ten o'clock to conduct a piece by Yasin, a student who has requested, just as I did five years ago, a 'try-out' of his *Monastère mystérieuse*, a stupendously pointless piece of music although stitched together skilfully enough to sound all right. The piece lasts about ten minutes, and Tcherepnin used the remaining time to take the orchestra through *Sheherezade*. He doesn't give me anything to do – just like old times. I asked Dranishnikov if he would accompany me in my Concerto when I play it for my exam performance. I have had my eye on him for some time, and thought he would be a good choice; he agreed gladly. I went home and had a sleep, and was thinking of going to hear Medtner in the evening, but then decided I did not want to hear any music. What about a Nimzowitsch session then? No, better do some work: press on with the piano reduction of the orchestra part of the Second Concerto, which I did with great enthusiasm, spending all evening on it.

Have to send the Concerto to the RME,[1] before it goes stale sitting at home.

---

1 Russkoye Muzykal'noye Izdatel'stvo: Russian Music Editions, founded by Koussevitzky.

28 January

Practised the Concerto No. 1. It is just as well it has not yet been engraved – a whole series of amendments have occurred to me. In any case, with the passage of time I have outgrown the piece and can now see its defects! We went through *Figaro* in Tcherepnin's class and then afterwards concentrated on the ensembles, where the opera really gets going. These ensembles are not at all easy for the conductor, since the tempi are quick and almost every bar has a cue for one or other of the singers. I lost the place a few times. Susanna is sung by Timofeyeva and another student, somewhat *à la* Popova (from the Mariinsky Theatre) but much more interesting, marvellous in fact, sheer delight! Apparently she is a Sokol member, she belongs to the first group, Sokol I, but her sister is in our group and knows me so now we say hello to one another. Then I went off to Blumenfeld's class, where he introduced me to the cellist Bezrodny, with whom he wants to put me together for my Ballade. Bezrodny's manner was most respectful; he told me he had been playing in the orchestra when I appeared at Pavlovsk.

In the evening Nikolay Shtember and I went to the Sokol.

29 January

Worked all morning practising the piano and conducting, sorting out *Figaro* and *Sheherezade*. Composed the opening of the Adagio of the Violin Concerto, which is fine, very beautiful. Word has already got out about this work and yesterday Professor Nalbandyan[1] went so far as to ask me to show it to him when it is finished. Alas, this will not be before the autumn, at the moment I have no time; most of the material is not yet notated at all, and what there is exists only on odd scraps of paper. In the evening I wrote to Nina Meshcherskaya, who is cross with me for my last, impertinent, letter, also to Mme Saradzheva to thank her for kindly sending me the reviews from my concert in Moscow (which in fact I already had), also to Derzhanovsky, who wants a thematic analysis of my Concerto[2] in view of its forthcoming performance on 16 February.

30 January

In orchestra class Tcherepnin once again spent all the time on *Sheherazade*, and then told me that for various reasons the concert mooted for 12 February

---

1 Ovanes Nalbandyan (1871–1942), violinist who had studied with Joachim and Auer, dedicatee of Lyapunov's Violin Concerto and Wihtol's *Latvian Fantasy*.
2 The First Piano Concerto.

now looks parlous and may well now not take place. If it does take place it will be later, so from now on we shall be concentrating on *Figaro*.

After the class I talked to Bushen (a rare event these days). I then went to see the cellist Rosenstein[1] to play through the *Ballade* for Nurok's concert. I had played with him several times before, four years ago at the 'Evenings of Contemporary Music', and I was not expecting it to be anything like as good as with Beloúsov, but in fact Rosenstein showed a lot of temperament, tone and liveliness: it was a very decent performance and his *pizzicato* was even faster than Beloúsov's. Returned home with a headache and lay down. Persuaded Shtember to go to the Sokol in the evening, where my headache all but vanished. Karatygin has written an article about Medtner and modern classics, in which category he places: (1) Scriabin, Stravinsky; (2) Myaskovsky and me(!). Bravo, Karatygin! I am in no doubt that given time my classic status will be beyond contention, but to have this said about me just now is very useful in opening the door to America.

31 January

Practised in the morning and in the afternoon went through *Figaro* with Tcherepnin, after which I went to the opera ensemble class. After the Tcherepnin–Palechek quarrel none of the conducting students attends the opera class, so Palechek is often left without anyone to accompany the class, which greatly distresses him. Their quarrel has this advantage for us – that is to say for Tsybin and me – that once we get to the stage of serious rehearsing with the orchestra, in other words once Tcherepnin is forced to come into direct contact with Palechek, he (Tcherepnin) will want to stand aside and pass over the orchestral direction to our hands. Now I think the hands in question will mainly be mine, since Tsybin disgraced himself in class today by not knowing his way around *Figaro* at all. Besides, it seems unlikely that Tsybin would get the first performance to conduct, and that is the one that attracts all the limelight; the second is of no consequence whatever. Generally speaking Tcherepnin is more friendly to Tsybin than he is to me (while being perfectly civil to me), and the reason for this is that after the December incident Tsybin pleaded for forgiveness whereas I took the contrary route of essaying a somewhat prickly self-justification.

Struve[2] and Lipinskaya have become bosom friends. Coming down the staircase today I caught sight of them talking to Ozerov. When I cheerfully hailed them, Ozerov called out, 'Serge Sergevich, how do you spell "vetkhii"[3] –

---

1 Yakov Rosenstein (1887–?), cellist, subsequently Director of the Kharkov Conservatoire.
2 Lidia Struve, student at the Conservatoire.
3 'Old', 'ancient'. The first vowel in the word is the one in question.

should it be with a "yat"[1] or an "e"?' Without thinking I replied, 'With a "yat".' When I was later proved wrong, I claimed to have given that answer as a joke.

Struve attracts me more and more, above anyone else in the Conservatoire. My studies there are experiencing a crescendo of activity; I am becoming anxious about the impending examination – although after April I shall be free as a bird. If I succeed in carrying off the grand piano I shall be as proud as a sokol, and if I don't, then I suppose I shall not be terribly upset, I mind less about it than other people would, although of course anyone would relish the thought of coming first!

In the evening I worked, then played vint at Mama's. The Concerto is coming along nicely.

1 February

Set out to meet Anna Grigorievna,[2] but she did not arrive. Played the piano quite a lot. Went for a walk along Morskaya Street. My Sonata is on prominent display at Jurgenson, no doubt as a result of Karatygin's article. In the evening I worked at home and thought how nice it would be to go abroad with Struve and spend the summer in Switzerland with her.

2 February

In the morning played through my recital programme and the Concerto. The latter seems to be going well, not presenting any particular difficulties. Someone rang up while I was in the middle of practising and I went over to the phone in high dudgeon, but as it proved to be Oleg,[3] who had returned yesterday from abroad, I was delighted to hear from him and we had a joyful conversation. He invited me to come round in the evening but I had already planned to go to the student concert and so could not take him up on it. We agreed to meet over the next few days, and I went back to work.

An important thought: when performing in public one must be totally oblivious to one's surroundings and immerse oneself in the music, the music itself and nothing but the music. The performance will benefit and the cause of any anxiety will be removed, since the audience, the source of the anxiety, will be outside the field of attention. 'Immerse yourself in the music' may be trite advice, but it's not easy to achieve. Today, however, I managed it.

In the evening I went to the student concert. I don't know quite what it

---

1 A letter in the pre-revolutionary Old Orthography Russian script, one of three, plus the hard sign in the terminal position following a consonant, abandoned as redundant when the New Orthography was brought in by the Soviets in 1918.
2 Zherebtsova-Andreyeva.
3 Subbotin.

was that put me in such an excellent mood, because none of my 'Cabinet Ministers' were there (Bushen, Struve, Vegman), but I enjoyed being with Damskaya. Zelikman[1] played the second and third movements of the Tchaikovsky concerto most imaginatively: he must surely be a candidate for the grand piano prize. He and I have an amiable, joshing relationship; he treats me with respect, presumably because of my friendship with Nikolayev. Generally speaking Zelikman is a pretty uncouth sort of person. In the evening, as I was going to sleep, I had such an appalling dream of my exam programme not being ready, the Concerto not properly prepared for a concert with Koussevitzky and *Figaro* still beyond me, that I leapt out of bed and had to have a drink of water.

3 February

Yesipova's name-day. Usually there is a kitty of a hundred roubles, but this time everything was in disarray and I bowed out of it. I spent 14 roubles on two dozen magnificent white roses and independently sent them to her myself. In the orchestra class Tcherepnin started on *Figaro*, as the concert has now definitely been postponed. I bought a second-hand copy of the score for 7 roubles, and was following it today. Tcherepnin now behaves more warmly towards me and together we shared our delight in the beauty of Mozart. After the orchestra class I met Vegman and sat with her for half an hour. She is very good in profile: her nose is classical, a fine mouth, she has beautiful hair and eyebrows. She told me she was learning to skate but was always falling and bruising herself. I offered my services as a skating instructor. Then I left my card at Yesipova's and returned home, to practise. In the evening Nikolay Shtember wanted to know if I was going to the Sokol, but I said I wasn't as I wanted to continue playing the piano. Had a conversation with Tonya Rudavskaya, who was visiting them (very nice), and with Nadya, we addressed each other in the intimate form. She was very interested in my Friday concert at the 'Evenings of Contemporary Music' and wants to come with Sonya.[2] Evidently Karatygin's article on Uncle Medtner and me has had an effect.

4 February

Practised until one o'clock and became convinced there is something not working in my programme. That is, the Bach and the Schumann are not bad and I know what I have to do to bring them off, but I still do not have a firm grasp of the Beethoven and the Chopin, particularly the Beethoven: it starts

---

1   A. V. Zelikman, pianist, student of Leonid Nikolayev at the Conservatoire.
2   Nadya and Sonya Shtember were Nikolay Shtember's sisters.

well but then swings from excessive impulsiveness to boring classical restraint and then back again. *Tannhäuser* is not yet technically secure either. At two o'clock I played through my Concerto with Dranishnikov in the Conservatoire. Naturally, reading from manuscript for the first time and up to speed, he was far from impeccable, all the same he is a splendid accompanist and I am happy that I chose him. I know I can be pretty impressive in the Concerto, and Dranishnikov was bowled over by it; I am counting on its having a similar effect on the judges. Lyapunov will mumble away into his knees, Lavrov[1] will want to hurl a chair at me, but there are others who will be genuinely thrilled by it. Conducted *Figaro* in Tcherepnin's class, then Tsybin and I conducted the ensembles. Tcherepnin had a few comments to make about my gestures, but on the whole was kind. Enjoyed a gymnastic session at the Sokol, then went home and played through my programme for the 'Evenings of Contemporary Music'.

5 February

Today I had planned on going through the *Ballade* with Rosenstein but he was ill in bed. In the morning I played through my complete exam recital programme (except the Mozart). By the time I got to *Tannhäuser* I was horribly tired, but I still forced myself to play it. Not surprisingly, it was awful. I was not feeling particularly fresh this morning and had to go for a walk to clear my head in the afternoon. I took to Yesipova's lesson the Mozart variations she had set me for the exam, and on the way dropped into the Conservatoire. There I met Tsybin downstairs, involved in a dispute about his place in the queue for the telephone. With my assistance he won the argument and wriggled his way into the booth. A minute or two later I also slipped in on the pretext of wanting a word with him, and surreptitiously tied his scarf to the door handle. When someone waiting impatiently outside the door yanked it open, Tsybin found himself dragged out along with it, practically throttled by his scarf. This caused general merriment, but Tsybin was very put out, complaining that if anyone but me had done this to him he would have reacted differently, but because of his sincere respect for me he would treat it as an innocent prank.

I went home very pleased with myself and worked until evening: practised the piano, wrote my diary and conducted *Figaro* from the score, which as yet I hardly know at all.

---

1   Nikolay Lavrov (1861–1927), pianist. A member of the Belyayev circle, he gave the first performance of Rimsky-Korsakov's Piano Concerto. In 1915 he was appointed Deputy Director of the St Petersburg Conservatoire.

6 February

Orchestra class: Tcherepnin read through Act II. I sat patiently, it was after all interesting to hear it. At home practised *Tannhäuser*; this is a seriously difficult and demanding piece. Went into the Yusupov Gardens and ran into Bushen there; we talked for about an hour. She was anxious to show me how well she had learned to skate, but I told her she looked like nothing so much as a governess obliged to supervise her charges, which rather deflated her. In the evening, did not go to the Sokol, preferring to study the examination programme. Inevitably, a telephone conversation with Damskaya, who is adept at keeping one interested in her chatter.

7 February

In the morning worked hard at my programme and studied the score of *Figaro*. Came into the Conservatoire at two o'clock, collared Nikolayev and played the Concerto to him. As a debut it was pretty good, a bit rough in a few places (especially where I have made changes), but I am happy about it. I always feel my relationship with Nikolayev is a curious one: his student Zelikman and I are rivals for the grand piano prize. His manner is very friendly, but naturally he won't be shedding any tears if I come to grief in the Concerto, since for his student to win is akin to winning the prize himself. To be fair, Nikolayev is a very kind man and has always given me wise, practical advice on my programme.

At two o'clock Tcherepnin, to conduct *Figaro*. The ensembles are extremely problematical for a conductor until he knows them by heart. At four o'clock went to Rosenstein, who is recovering from his yellow 'flu and wants to play the *Ballade* this evening. We rehearse, his playing is a little limp, but he promises it will be more robust by the evening. Went back to the Conservatoire, conducted the ensembles and then home, completely worn out. I was beginning to get a headache and was in a foul mood, but I still had to perform that evening. I lay down but could not sleep. Then I calmed down and did get some rest, sitting at the chessboard and playing through some old matches. Mama left for the concert earlier than I; I changed, ran through some of the pieces and set out quite fresh for the concert. The first half of the programme had started by the time I arrived: works by various composers. Some Stravinsky songs and a sonata by N. M.[1] were not without interest, but were not well performed.

The second half was devoted to my music, with an invited audience. I played my Moscow programme, to exceptional acclaim. Never before had I

---

1 Nikolay Myaskovsky.

been the recipient of so many congratulations and rapturous accolades, especially for the Sonata No. 2, the 'Harp' Prelude[1] and the Etude No. 3.[2] The *Ballade* was less successful, but this was in part due to a sub-standard performance by Rosenstein and the fact that my accompaniment was too loud. Deshevov called me a genius; Nikolayev praised my pianism; Ruzsky, Nurok, Karatygin, Kryzhanovsky, the Andreyevs, Spendiarov,[3] Tcherepnin, Kobylyansky, Aslanov and Polotskaya-Yemtsova all expressed their pleasure and admiration. My friends from the Conservatoire were particularly enthusiastic: Dranishnikov, Gauk, Damskaya, Golubovskaya and Bushen, whose face, according to Damskaya, was distorted with excitement while I was playing. I was introduced to the celebrated artist Bakst,[4] who talked to me seriously about my feelings about ballet. Again, a whiff of Paris in my nostrils. Karatygin asked me to play at one of his lectures in ten days' time.

8 February

The morning was not very productive, although I did some work and then went to the general rehearsal in the Great Hall of the Conservatoire. It was rather dull, and there was no one particularly interesting in the audience. Struve was not there. However all those I did see continued to rave about yesterday's concert. Chatted to Eleonora, then went home and worked until evening, mainly on *Tannhäuser*. At eleven o'clock went to the Ruzskys, who were holding a grand ball with a great crowd of people and quantities of delicious refreshments. Ira assumed a simulated amiability in place of her usual hostility, to which I responded with a cool reserve. I no longer have much to do with the young Ruzskys, in fact I don't care for them and find them boring. The arrival of Konshin cheered me up, however. Ball and supper went on for a very long time, and when I left at seven o'clock in the morning it was still not over. As I walked home it was strange to see it already getting light, the trams beginning to run and the newspaper boys already on their rounds.

---

1 Op. 12 No. 7, transcription for piano of the Harp Prelude written for Eleonora Damskaya.
2 Op. 2 No. 3.
3 Alexander Spendiarov (Spendiaryan) (1871–1928), prolific composer and conductor. In 1924 he returned to his native Armenia, where he became a leading figure in the symphonic and operatic life of Yerevan.
4 Léon Bakst (Lev Rosenberg) (1866–1924), artist and theatre designer. Founder along with Diaghilev and Benois of the World of Art group and the Ballets Russes, more than any other designer his settings and costumes exemplified the voluptuous exoticism of the Ballets Russes' assault on of all the senses in productions such as *The Firebird*, *L'Après-midi d'un faun* and *Sheherezade*.

9 February

Slept until one, of course not long enough. Spent most of the rest of the day at the piano. Oleg invited me to his place to play bridge, which I was glad to do, and had a marvellous time. Oleg was affectionate and good company.

10 February

When I walked into the orchestra class Tcherepnin was loudly singing the praises of my compositions he had heard at Friday's concert. Today he was rehearsing with the female singers (!) and then informed me that the conductor of the first performance would be himself, the second me, and the third Tsybin. His explanation was that a new rule had been established, that the premiere should be conducted by the professor and the role of the student is to be his assistant. In the past it has always been the other way round. I told him he was taking the bread out of my mouth, that I should be the conductor of the premiere, that even if his new procedure had merit it had never been so before, and it should not be changed for existing students but reformed if necessary for new students next year. He replied that such might very well be the case, but the performances of *Aida* and *Rigoletto* had been so monstrously bad that the risk of things going wrong again could not be taken, moreover Palechek and many of the professors ('Who?' 'Well, Raab[1] for example!' 'Pfui!') had been vocal in their opposition to my conducting the premiere. Furthermore I was not up to the task of conducting such a difficult work, demanding a much higher level of conducting technique than I possessed. In any case it was fruitless to discuss it, the matter was settled, and I would still of course conduct the second performance.

I said that asking me to do so much of the work in the conducting class but giving me so little practical experience was like palming off the creditors of a bankrupt firm with two kopecks in the rouble. Tcherepnin shrugged his shoulders and the subject was closed. I spent the whole day in a fury, but there was nothing to be done, except spit on the whole thing and concentrate on the piano. Sokol, and then a telephone call from Damskaya, who read out to me a very complimentary review by Bernstein, dug up from somewhere or other from last summer, of my Piano Concerto No. 1.[2] Bernstein,[3] indeed!

---

1 Wilhelmina Raab (1848–1917), in her day a famous Mariinsky prima donna taking leading roles in Wagner, Tchaikovsky and Rubinstein operas. She had been teaching at the Conservatoire since 1884.
2 Review by N. D. Bernstein of the first performance of Prokofiev's Piano Concerto No. 1 conducted by A. P. Aslanov, Pavlovsk, 3 August 1912, published in the *Petersburg Gazette*, no. 213 on 5 August 1912.
3 Nikolay Bernstein (1876–1938), a famously hostile critic of the modernist tendency in music.

11 February

Distressed by not having any lessons with Yesipova I telephoned her and she asked me to come to see her today, but when I arrived it turned out that because of the fine weather she wanted to go skating and the lesson was postponed until tomorrow. It is so good to know she is now well enough to go skating.

Saw Tcherepnin in the evening, our conversation was relaxed and free of antagonism. It's stupid and pointless to go on grumbling and cursing, all the same I shall not forgive him for grabbing that first performance. Met Lipinskaya in the Conservatoire and had a long talk with her. She is a very pretty young Polish girl from Warsaw but speaks perfect Russian, which adds to her attractions. On one occasion she saw me talking animatedly to her teacher Vengerova; this made a great impression on a young student terrified to death of her professors, and as a result Lipinskaya now treats me with the greatest respect.

Our *tête-à-tête* was interrupted by Kreisler, who has just returned from Moscow: he came up and could not stop talking. In general I'm on good terms with all the conducting students: I have great respect for Dranishnikov; Gauk is inclined to be a bit of a toady but his understanding of music is good and he has a fine conducting technique; Kreisler is a straightforward sort of fellow; Tvordovsky a reserved, courteous Pole.

I looked in on Blumenfeld's class; he told me that he had played through everything I have written, except the Sonata No. 2, but could not make head nor tail of any of them. Well, thanks for that. Bushen rang up and said that she was planning a Shrovetide escapade to come to Moscow and hear my Concerto, having vowed to be present whenever I have a premiere. True, this is one, being my debut appearance at a major metropolitan concert. I'm beginning to develop a real fan club. In the evening went to the student concert, at which Gauk and Kreisler made their conducting debuts with the small orchestra, as I did last year. Both acquitted themselves with honour in their first real test: Kreisler was a little four-square but Gauk was altogether excellent. I brought each of them a small laurel branch, which made them extremely proud – the first laurels of their careers thus came from me. Tcherepnin was delighted with the small orchestra's performance, and made a speech: 'I contemplate the zeal, the burning ardour with which you apply yourselves to your work, and pray with all my heart that this may long continue. On Wednesday, gentlemen, we shall rest from our labours and there will be no orchestra class.'

Prokofiev's surprise is understandable, given Bernstein's initial dismissal of the First Piano Concerto as 'musical mud' and his claim when reviewing the Pavlovsk performance of the Second Piano Concerto that the cadenzas were 'unbearable ... such a musical mess that one might think they were created by capriciously emptying an inkwell over the paper.'

'Thank God for that!' one orchestra musician burst out.

Then Tcherepnin hauled us off to the buffet and treated us to a glass of beer, talking with unquenchable eloquence, drinking a toast to the health of the debutants and then, for no particular reason, to me: 'for the flowering of your great gifts, greater than of any of us here present, not that this in any way' - gesturing to the conductors – 'inhibits the flowering of your own talents or the great enterprise on which we are embarking together.' Tcherepnin knows he's played a dirty trick on me, filching the opera premiere for himself, so now he feels guilty and is trying to suck up. Oh, the dog knows all too well whose meat he has stolen! I went back to the student concert.

12 February

Yesipova gave me a lesson at half past ten. I played Beethoven and Chopin: she hardly made any comments on the Beethoven but made me repeat several passages in the Chopin. My programme now seems to be in reasonable shape. Yesipova does not look well at all. Afterwards I went to the station to buy a ticket to go to Moscow, and then to see N.M. as I had not seen him for some time. Returning home I played through the Concerto and made a few corrections.

In the evening I went to Koussevitzky's concert. Golubovskaya told me that as she was leaving after the 'Evenings of Contemporary Music' concert, she overheard the following conversation: 'Prokofiev? Very nice young man,' and then, tenderly, 'Terribly cheeky, though!' In Golubovskaya's view, I am the only person to whom such a conjugation could possibly be applied.

I listened to Stravinsky's *Rite of Spring* with heightened attention. Whatever else it is, this work is full of life and all but captures the listener. I was beside myself with excitement at 'The Adoration of the Earth'. But in places it is so shatteringly loud, and in other, quieter, passages such an obvious fake that one is left marvelling that so talented and inventive a musician as Stravinsky appears to have a screw loose! Some in the audience applauded fervently, but most were either bemused or looked round with triumphantly amused expressions as if to say: 'See what disgusting filth these futurists write.'

13 February

In the morning I played the Concerto. At two o'clock Yavorsky came to see me; he was in Petersburg and I had met him the previous evening at the concert. I played him the first movement of my Concerto No. 2 and he appeared to like it, but my sarcastic pieces reduced him to silence. He asked me to let him have the manuscript of *Maddalena*, to which I gladly consented. At four o'clock I went in to the opera class at the Conservatoire, and then stayed at home writing my diary and packing my small suitcase.

Bushen telephoned; she is also going to Moscow tomorrow. That's nice! At a quarter to nine I got my things together, said goodbye to Mama, and took the tram. I thought I might meet Spendiarov at the station, as he was also Moscow-bound to hear his *Three Palms* symphonic study.[1] Spendiarov loves my music, which he heard at the concert on the 7th. He did not turn up, but I met a chess player I know, and we went to the restaurant car where I won a blind game against him. My bunk was the upper one, and as it was narrow and hot I slept badly.

14 February

The first thing I did on arriving in Moscow was go to the RME shop to find out about the rehearsal. This was to be at twelve noon, so in the meantime I went to Saradzhev's house, where his wife received me with great warmth and kindness. The last time I was in Moscow Saradzhev had asked me to stay with him, and I was glad to take him up on his invitation. The conductor Orlov[2] ('a little agricultural, but experienced', as Saradzhev described him), to whom Yurasovsky had fleetingly introduced me a year ago, said that there were to be two rehearsals the following day but there would be no time for my Concerto at the first one. Only at the second, general rehearsal would my Concerto be rehearsed. I pleaded for the morning rehearsal as well, and went away thoroughly disgruntled and almost of a mind to cancel my participation, since the Concerto could not possibly get a decent performance after only one play-through at a general rehearsal. Also, Jurgenson had not managed to engrave the full score, the only printed material was the two-piano reduction (and that not proof-read), and the wind orchestral parts were handwritten. I took away the full score and started to make corrections to it, including the changes I had made while learning the solo piano part. Then I went to see Derzhanovsky.

Everyone was very welcoming, 'himself' was not at home, but I spoke to him on the telephone. When he heard that I had half a mind to cancel, he was excited and saw the opportunity to make a big press scandal, although on the whole he recommended coming to a peaceful accommodation with the situation. I soon left and went back to Saradzhev to continue correcting the score. Spent the evening with the Lavrova-Schmidthofs, reminiscing about the Caucasus, Yessentuki, Pyatigorsk and swapping all manner of

---

[1] Symphonic Study *Three Palms*, after Lermontov (1905).
[2] Alexander Orlov (1873–1948), conductor associated with Koussevitzky and later Musical Director of the Large All-Union Symphony Orchestra.

stories and adventures concerning Max. We were all utterly immersed in our memories; his mother told me over and over how grateful she was that I came to visit them, saying that seeing me she seemed to see Max. As I made my way home I was deeply moved thinking of Max, and the terrible injustice of his never returning to us. For a long time I walked round and round the Cathedral of Christ the Saviour. I want to honour Max's memory by dedicating all my compositions to him.

15 February

Slept well in Saradzhev's cosy study, but was very disinclined to get out of bed and was almost late for the rehearsal. Actually I need not have bothered, since they were not in any case going to work on the Concerto, but Orlov at least managed to get through all the rest of the programme, leaving to the evening rehearsal just one run-through of *Petrushka* and the rest of the time – a minimum of an hour and half – to my Concerto. I settled for this and sat with Spendiarov, who was full of praise for my compositions. After the rehearsal I played the Concerto through to Orlov, to give him an idea of my intentions for the performance. After some time in a café I went to the Hall of the Nobility[1] for the rehearsal. While Orlov was working on *Petrushka* (much of which I find very attractive) I paced out the hall trying to work out which was larger, our Court Hall or their Hall of the Nobility?

Then I settled down to more correcting of the Concerto score, and at once uncovered a mass of mistakes. I was very much embarrassed, because in such circumstances it is the composer who is held to blame. But in fact all the problems were in the first few bars, and afterwards all went smoothly. I was extremely nervous while the errors in the score and parts were being adjusted. But the orchestra got it well ironed out, Orlov's directions to the orchestra were sensible, and now the wheels were finally set in motion it was time for a new worry: that I would not be up to the challenge of playing it well. However as soon as I sat down at the piano the nerves vanished. Nearly all of it went well, the only rocky passages being the changes I had just made. Afterwards I went back to Derzhanovsky's for dinner, and then stayed to practise the Concerto and an encore piece. Lyolya never moved a step from my side.

16 February

Went round to Denezhny Lane in the morning to drop off Katya Schmidthof's tickets for the concert, then came back, ran through the Concerto,

---

1 Known after the Revolution as the 'Kolonny Zal', 'Hall of Columns'. The St Petersburg Court Hall is now the Great Hall of the Philharmonia.

changed into my tails and set off accompanied by Saradzhev's wife, Lyolya and her mother. Met Yurasovsky in the artists' room and followed the performance of Glière's symphony from the score he had with him. What ponderous, boring music it is. As the symphony ground on I grew more and more nervous, as my turn was approaching. The symphony finally came to an end, I paced about the artists' room, Yurasovsky took the piano score to follow it during the performance, and Orlov ushered me on to the platform. My appearance was greeted with applause, I bowed and sat down at the piano which was, incidentally, a horrible instrument.

Before going out, Orlov said to me, 'As you sit down, look at my face, and that will immediately calm your nerves – that's what everyone says.' I took his advice, and indeed the expression on his face was calm, benevolent and slightly stupid. I cannot say for certain that contemplating his person had this effect on me, nevertheless I was not too nervous and my performance of the Concerto was pretty good. That is to say, it had all the brilliance and virtuosity one could wish for, but there were a few wrong notes and smudges. I was not totally sure of the accompaniment, so my playing could not be completely free and sometimes had to follow the conductor. The success was considerable, I was called back several times and had to play three encores: Prelude, Etude No. 4 and Etude No. 3. Before playing No. 3 I was trying to decide between this piece and 'Rigaudon'. I decided on the Etude, but in fact it was the wrong choice: I was tired and could hardly get through it; 'Rigaudon' would have been better.

When I came back into the artists' room I sat down beside Yurasovsky, who had the score of the Concerto open on his knees and started plying me with questions about my performance. Next to Yurasovsky was another man also casting an eye over the score. This proved to be none other than my 'friend' Sabaneyev. When he moved away, Yurasovsky asked me if I would like him to introduce me to Sabaneyev. I replied, 'To hell with him', and left the room.

Bushen appeared and said that it had been 'very, very good'. Spendiarov and several others, some of whom I knew slightly and others not at all, said much the same. After the concert Yurasovsky and I went to a café where he confided in me that he was experiencing disappointment in his career as a composer, and was thinking of becoming a conductor. He asked me if I was really counting on becoming a famous composer? I said that I was, and that I was going to write a very good opera.

Parting from Yurasovsky I went to dine at the Saradzhevs and then went on to the Derzhanovskys, where I was the hero of the hour. Derzhanovsky announced that he had decided to fire Sabaneyev from his magazine, and now regretted not having published my critical review of his music. From Derzhanovskys', lugging my suitcase, I called in for an hour on the Smetskoys, was given flowers and home-made gingerbread, and went to the station to catch my train.

17 February

My train arrived at half past eleven in the morning. I went home for a bit of a rest after all the Moscow activity, not practising the piano because I had bruised my index finger with the octaves in the Concerto.

Went into the Conservatoire to check on things there, and dropped in briefly to the opera class. Everything was going according to plan there, Tsybin conducting away with great energy. In the evening went to Sokol.

18 February

Was woken in the morning by the telephone: Yesipova wanted to give me a lesson today. Ran through *Tannhäuser* and at two o'clock took it to her. I played it by heart, it was quite good but not very refined; Yesipova had no comments on it. Went in to the Conservatoire, and as Tcherepnin's class was going through a Mozart symphony, which did not have much to do with me, talked to Damskaya and Vegman.

Meanwhile it seems there was a conversation going on upstairs along these lines: 'That Prokofiev is a disgrace! He doesn't bother coming to choir practice, or the chamber orchestra, and if he does condescend to come then all he does is criticize, pass comments and make rude remarks.' This was followed by a complete itemization of all the girls I had ever run after. Damskaya relayed all this to me as we walked together out of the Conservatoire, adding that she had asked them to lower their voices. In view of this I resolved to be even more acerbic and tyrannically demanding with the choir.

19 February

Practised. In the afternoon intrigued by yesterday's assault on me, went into the choral class in the Conservatoire, but the choir sang so well that nothing was left for me to say about it. I badly wanted a drink, and as so often in such circumstances nothing would do but champagne. Kreisler and I went to the bar to glug down some Conservatoire booze and drank half a bottle of Cordon Vert with great enjoyment. I would have preferred 'Crystal' but there wasn't any. Returned home and practised my Sonata No. 2 for Karatygin's lecture this evening. At eight o'clock went to the stagecraft class at the Conservatoire. This is a very useful course for singers preparing for a career in opera. They were doing Pshibyshevsky's[1] *Dreams*, a tedious drama not much to my taste.

Tcherepnin was most interested in my Moscow appearance. 'Splendid,

---

1 Boleslav Pshibyshevsky (Przybyszewski) (1892–?), composer and musicologist. From 1929 to 1931 he was Rector of the Moscow Conservatoire.

you're being performed everywhere, and I myself will definitely conduct your Concerto, it's very interesting.' I was privately infuriated by his duplicity: what about the Belyayev Concerts, when he had pontificated that unless they included my Concerto he would refuse to conduct?! Velvety snake! I accompanied Karatygin to his lecture, which was taking place in a moneyed private house frequented, according to Karatygin, by plutocrats. The lecture was very long. Speaking of me, Karatygin said there were indications that I would become a modern classic, but I was still too young for it to be certain what direction I would eventually take. I sat in another room with Kreisler eating sweets. To begin with I did not feel much like playing, but I did, and towards the end began to play well. The Sonata had a success. Belling, the associate conductor of the Court Orchestra, was among those listening, and declared it a masterpiece. I would not say no to an invitation to appear in one of the Court Orchestra's concerts. All the same I went home thinking that, all in all, it had not really been worth playing, except as a gesture of friendship to Karatygin.

20 February

Orchestra class in the morning. I hoped to see Struve but she fled, in a hurry to get to her General Subjects class.

At home I played the piano and then went to offer my congratulations to the Rayevskys on their wedding anniversary. At home I discovered that Meshcherskaya had telephoned. Can this mean that she is back already?! I was not expecting them so soon. In one way I was very happy, but my pleasure was mixed with a vague alarm that at such a busy time, when things were crowding in on one another at such a pace, there should arise yet one more strong magnetic force. Meshcherskaya is undoubtedly a strong force, and magnetically attractive. In any case they were most insistent that I should visit them this evening, so I went. They have moved to a new home in a magnificent and spacious apartment occupying one and a half floors. They all fell on me, headed by Ninka, whose charm certainly does have an element of the devil about it. It was all very jolly, easy-going, shouting and romping about – in a word, lovely. She had brought me a present, said the sweetest things to me, and never have we been such good friends. There was no sign of Zaitsev. I went home happy.

21 February

Played the piano in the morning and looked through the score of *Figaro*. At three o'clock went into the Conservatoire to rehearse the *Ballade* with Bezrodny, the cellist whom Blumenfeld has chosen to play the piece in class and for the exam. Ideas for improvements in the piano part kept occurring to me. I inflicted all kinds of caustic and facetious comments on the girls in the chorus. Tcherepnin, with feigned friendliness, advised me not to pay too much attention to hostile criticism. 'Myself,' he said, 'I never even look at it . . .' Quite right, I thought to myself, when reviews are as terrible as the ones you get, you certainly shouldn't read them.

In the ensemble class Tsybin had already installed himself on the podium although Tcherepnin wanted me to conduct the big ensemble, but I was feeling tired so went home.

In the evening we (Myaskovsky and Saradzhev, who had come to St Petersburg to pursue some conducting project he had in mind) played vint. Saradzhev made himself very agreeable, and Mama took to him. Oleg did not come.

22 February

Played the piano: the recital programme is genuinely almost ready. The best thing about it is that I won't be asked to play all of it – only three works, so I shall not have problems with stamina and getting tired. In the evening I practised some more, had a telephone conversation with Eleonora and played telephone chess with Golubovskaya (the game had to break off at a particularly stimulating and, for me, advantageous position), and pasted in my reviews, which are now beginning to fall like snowflakes. The latest number of *Muzyka* contains no fewer than four mentions of me. Viktor Belyayev,[1] the same who had torn my Sonata No. 1 to shreds with such relish, is now heaping warm words all over No. 2. And a writer from Petersburg (Kryzhanovsky?) reviewing the 'Evenings of Contemporary Music', says that 'Suggestion diabolique' 'bears the stamp of genius'. Nice to hear. Karatygin thanked me for participating in his lecture and gave me 25 roubles for my trouble. Well, I have no objection to earning 25 roubles.

23 February

Since I am now feeling comparatively relaxed about my recital programme, I slept until eleven, and then I had a good long practice. Much of the afternoon was taken up with some gentlemen from the International Bank advising Mama about her shares. In the evening I went to a student theatre

---

1 Viktor Belyayev (1888–1934), critic and musicologist, pupil of Wihtol. Later he played a prominent role in the Association of Contemporary Musicians (ACM), the more liberal and cultivated organization that in 1931 ominously lost out to the militant Russian Association of Proletarian Musicians (RAPM), heralding the era of ideological conformism, artistic repression and the strait-jacket of Socialist Realism.

production, where I saw Golubovskaya and, making use of Nina's present, finished off our interrupted chess game, which I won. Our Conservatoire students produced a lively programme of excerpts from dramas and comedies. I sat with Damskaya, Belokurova was also there; I did not manage to speak to her but luxuriated in the way we saluted one another from a distance. I revealed to Damskaya, who knows I find Belokurova attractive, that I have carried out a 'ministerial shuffle' and now have a new prime minister. Struve is the one I mean, but in spite of all Damskaya's pleading I declined to identify her. Damskaya herself has been moved to the Foreign Affairs portfolio, and when she enquired what post Bushen now holds, I replied that she was a comrade of the Minister for Ways and Communications, thus referring obliquely to our joint excursions and our companionable return from Moscow.

24 February

Orchestra class in the morning, during which Tcherepnin went through *Figaro* with the singers. He plans to let me take the next rehearsal on Monday. Saw Alpers and had a talk with her: she would have gone on chattering for ever and a day. Came home, but lost a part of a tooth during lunch and had to go out again to the dentist. Played through the recital programme and it went very well, I was delighted, and the main thing is that all the pieces are now more or less on the same level of execution, although perhaps the Chopin is not quite on a par, and perhaps also the Mozart, which I have not yet fully mastered. In the evening went to the Sokol with Nikolay Shtember. Nikolay came back with me afterwards and I played him the Beethoven; I did so with some hesitation since I know how critical he can be, but he praised my performance – and that means a great deal!

25 February

Waved my baton through *Figaro* and then practised *Tannhäuser*. At three o'clock came into the Conservatoire only to find Tcherepnin working on *Serbian Fantasy*[1] with the younger conductors. Seryozha Alpers and Nikolayev both performed in this evening's concert; this is the first time Nikolayev has been seen in the Conservatoire this year. Seryozha Alpers has the makings of a serious pianist, he possesses very good instincts although he is still prone to make a hash of things at times. During the interval I caught a glimpse of an entrancing silhouette, but its owner vanished into a part of the hall a long way away from where we were sitting. In the second

---

1 Symphonic Sketch by Rimsky-Korsakov, an early (1867) piece extensively revised in 1889.

half I sat with Seryozha Alpers, Damskaya and an ebullient singer from somewhere or other. Nikolayev's playing was vigorous and full of colour, a lot of people in the hall jumped up to have a better look, but I stayed in my seat. Struve, who I suppose came especially to listen to Seryozha (presumably having met the Alpers family at their dacha in Finland), left the hall but then returned and sat right in front of us, a nice present for me. We were a happy group; I spouted nonsense and told jokes and made everyone laugh, and gradually Struve was drawn into the conversation. Apparently after the concert she was going to Glazunov's study for an exam, as he had been too busy during the day. Struve was nervous about it and soon left, which slightly put a damper on our enjoyment.

At the end of the concert Damskaya and I spied Struve waiting gloomily in the corridor for her exam, so we chatted to her for quite a long time, which needless to say I enjoyed very much. 'You may not believe this,' I said, 'but three years ago your name was constantly on my lips!' Struve blushed and looked bewildered, as she often does when I speak to her. As a tease I explained that six years ago I had played a match with a chess player called Struve, whom I knew quite well at the time but had subsequently lost touch with. The present Struve's manner was wary, as if she was constantly on the look-out for me to be cheeky with her. She takes all my jokes in deadly earnest and replies with grave caution.

She went downstairs, while Damskaya and I looked for the keys to the concert hall and went in. We found the score for tomorrow's exam set work, a Bach chorale, concealed it inside the piano, locked up the hall again and went off. Tomorrow they won't find anything to examine anyone on. When I had seen Eleonora to her house I went home myself, thinking of Struve. I like her looks, her features are not regular but that may be just what appeals to me. In what way they are irregular, I cannot at the moment say with any precision.

26 February

Today I had to take the exam: transposition of a chorale, sight-reading, and learning a new piece. In itself this is not a critical test, but one still has to pass it. On my way in to the Conservatoire I began to worry about the volume of chorales we had hidden, but they had found another one in the library and were using that for the exam. My supervisor was Winkler: smiling, he gave me a chorale to transpose in the Dorian mode. I did it quickly and correctly (I suggested as a joke transposing the right hand up a third and the left hand down a fourth). There were no comments on my sight-reading, then he gave me a Scriabin *Poème* to learn. Five minutes later, having played it through three times, I brought it back. My discovery of two misprints caused a sensation, and by the time I left I had been awarded 5+ for everything. I was pleased – the exam may have been a lot of nonsense, but it was still encouraging to have got 5+. Boasting of my marks to everyone I met, I went home and applied myself to the recital programme, which went well. In the evening there was vint with Saradzhev, N.M., Oleg, Mama and me – a lively session and good fun.

27 February

Figaro in the morning, conducted by Tcherepnin. Timofeyeva said that Golubovskaya had told her about my compositions, she had fallen in love with them, and through them their composer. She wanted to sing a song by me for her examination, if I would let her have one. I promised to bring her 'The boat cast off'.

From Saradzhev I heard that Glazunov had been half asleep at rehearsal yesterday, because he had been up until two o'clock in the morning examining. As soon as I saw Struve I asked her, 'What did you do to upset Glazunov so much?'

'Me–e–e?'

'Well, the morning after he had been seeing you, he came in to rehearsal completely exhausted, complaining of not having been able to get to sleep. Apparently this was the result of some girl who was so indiscreet as to turn up for her examination at two o'clock in the morning!'

Struve exploded and fled, mumbling something like 'what are you talking about'. I came home and practised the piano. Went to see the Meshcherskys in the evening because Nina had said they were upset by my apparent lack of enthusiasm at their return and that I had not been to see them. I was quite surprised by the obvious delight and affection with which they welcomed me. To get some experience in performing it, I played them *Tannhäuser*, about which Vera Nikolayevna had one or two useful comments to make. Then we went into the cosy billiard room to play bridge, Talya and Serge Bazavov versus Oleg and myself with Nina. I actually played the hand, but she sat beside me being terribly coquettish and loving. I am very fond of Talya and Oleg and Serge, so had a nice time in their company.

28 February

Waking up in the morning I recalled something Vera Nikolayevna had said about me the evening before: 'After all, he is a composer; the piano is his second study.' This set me thinking about the way I play, and indeed I found it hard to rid myself of the notion that I am not really a pianist and therefore my performances never transcend the limitations of a diligent but routine crammer. As if to confirm the insight, this morning the programme seemed to have lost some of its edge.

At three o'clock I went to the Conservatoire, because on Monday I have to conduct *Figaro* with the orchestra and singers, and today I needed to conduct the ensembles in order to be absolutely on top of the score. Before the class I joined a pleasant group congregating on the stairs, consisting of Struve, Lipinskaya and Damskaya. Lipinskaya was in a very agitated state saying that she was itching to pull her history teacher's beard. We all laughed and chaffed her. Struve again kept herself rather aloof. After the ensembles I showed Timofeyeva my 'Boat' song, together with some preliminary indications of how I envisage the song: the first glimmerings of morning light, the pre-dawn chill, a leaden, distantly murmuring sea at one's feet, the heart filled with a feeling of bliss unexpectedly joyful but irretrievably lost – all shrouded in the grey mist of breaking day. Timofeyeva evidently liked the song, but was doubtful whether her singing would be able to meet such exacting demands.

In the evening I was at the Sokol. Afterwards I telephoned Damskaya, who talked about some of her friends, including a revealing glimpse of Struve who, as she says, always takes everything too seriously. 'When you mentioned Glazunov yesterday I could see you were teasing her, but she asked me today if what you said was really true.'

1 March

Concentrated on Mozart. At five o'clock left to go to Vyborg.

2 March

Got up at eight, feeling cheerful and bright. The weather was wonderful; I hailed a cab and set off for the cemetery. When I arrived, a caretaker took me to Max's grave, which is in the Finnish graveyard beside the Orthodox one. Rows of poor graves, a white wooden cross with snow all around it and a pencilled inscription on it: 'Maximilian Schmidthof'. I gave the caretaker a few marks so that he would look after the grave when the snow melts, and then stood alone for some time looking at the cross and thinking my thoughts. Here lay what remained of that clever, wonderful head, magnificent Max with his unerringly sure, artistically planned end. Nothing now remained except this modest white cross. I stood before it, and mixed with the sadness of my heart I was conscious of a glow of contentment, of heart's-ease, that I had come here to this grave, which seemed itself in some way to be my friend. It was a fine, sunny day, with a glittering, blinding brilliance, and the neat rows of graves and the noisy shunting of trains in the goods station at the bottom of the little hillside where the cemetery stood, all served to soften the surrounding atmosphere of neglect.

Baring my head, I walked back to the waiting cab. In the train, I stood at the window waiting until we passed the cemetery. It was right there by the track, several versts from the station, and from the train window one had a fine view of it. First to come into view was the Orthodox graveyard, covering one side of the hill with its green church in the middle, and beyond it, separated by a fence, the Finnish graveyard with its neatly arranged graves running down the other side. The graves were easy to see, but the train was going too fast for me to be able make out which one was Max's. Back at home, I collapsed into bed and slept.

Woke up with a headache but still practised the piano for the following day, and turned down invitations from Subbotin and from the editor of *Rech*[1] newspaper, who had expressed an interest in getting to know me and issued the invitation through Karatygin. I looked through my diary to see what had occurred on the same day last year.

3 March

Was in the Great Hall by ten o'clock for my *Figaro* rehearsal with the singers, who were all set out on chairs on the stage. I felt reasonably calm and confident, and did a competent job of conducting the opera. Tcherepnin was satisfied and praised me, not scrupling, however, to point out several shortcomings. I had been afraid I would get terribly tired, but in the event I was not aware of this happening. No one was in the audience except Vegman, hiding at the back of the darkened auditorium.

To cool down after the rehearsal I walked about the corridors of the Conservatoire, but Struve was nowhere to be seen and I went home. I played through the entire recital programme without getting up from the piano, and in the process drove myself to complete exhaustion, although still managing to make *Tannhäuser* sound good.

Kalantarova says that the practice of only playing parts of the exam programme has now been abandoned, so one has to play everything. To train my fingers I have been trying to rent an upright piano with a really stiff keyboard; I looked in all the shops but could not find anything. A pity, but it's too late now, it wouldn't be worth it. A Sokol session, followed by a telephone conversation with Damskaya, who prattled on in her usual way about people in the Conservatoire. Most interesting for me, although I did not let on, was what she had to say about Struve. Struve, it seems, is afraid of me and lives in continual dread of my making her the butt of my teasing and jokes. I must be more gentle with her.

---

1   Iosif Vladimirovich Gessen (1886–1943), lawyer, journalist and publisher of *Rech* (*Speech*).

4 March

Received the proofs of the Concerto, at which I was overjoyed. Got hold of a blue pencil (apparently engravers dislike one using a red pencil for corrections) and settled down with relish to the task. Kalantarova asked me to go for a lesson with Yesipova in the morning. I practised the Mozart Variations and took them along. Anna Nikolayevna has recovered some of her energy, but not to be compared with how she had been formerly: she has lost weight and become somehow wrinkled. She prescribed such a slow tempo for the *Variations* that I despaired, and there was a long discussion about my idea of playing *piano* and with very few accents, in the end making me play *forte* and strongly accented. I was disappointed. Then she asked me to play my Etude No. 3, which went with a swing, at which she smiled and said, 'Reminds me of cats scratching their claws!'

I went on to the Conservatoire, where Tcherepnin itemized all the shortcomings of my conducting of *Figaro* yesterday.

Came home at six o'clock, and had a brilliant idea; to make an orchestral version of my *Sarcasms*. In the evening went with Mama to the concert by Romanovsky, who is playing my Sonata. A million acquaintances, more like a fashionable *salon* than a concert. Two families who cannot stand one other, the Ruzskys and the Meshcherskys, vied for hegemony; both are friends of Romanovsky, both brought along a large entourage of supporters, both presented noble bouquets, and finally both proudly claimed acquaintance with Yershov, who in consequence was obliged to divide his allegiance by seating himself alongside the Meshcherskys while his daughter sat with the Ruzskys. I said to Vera Nikolayevna that Nina and I resembled respectively an elephant and a pug, to which she responded that if such were the case then Nina was a small elephant and I was a very large pug.

Present at the concert were Alpers, Bushen, Kreisler and Damskaya. When Romanovsky began the Sonata they all looked over in my direction, as if to see what I thought about it. At first the attention was welcome, but later it became annoying. Romanovsky played the Sonata well, although there were a few details he did not bring out correctly. Towards the end I grew nervous, fearing that I would be called to take a bow. And indeed, the Sonata being a success, there were enthusiastic calls for the composer and I got up uncertain whether to take a bow on the stage or to acknowledge the applause from the floor. Deciding that the former would be too much '*à la* Sokol' I took my bow by the side of the stage on the floor. Mama was clearly nervous, but happy at my success and invoked the memory of Papa. At the end of the concert I received many congratulations and expressions of praise. N. P. Ruzsky was obviously very pleased, Kreisler declared himself my ardent admirer. The Meshcherskys were delighted.

When I went backstage to thank Romanovsky for his performance a girl in the artists' room made as if to give me an ovation and showered me with questions about my Second Sonata and Concerto. After putting Mama in a cab to return home I went with Kreisler to the 'Pivato' where we consumed half-bottles of champagne.

5 March

Slept in for a while, then practised the piano, and at three o'clock went to the Conservatoire. While Tcherepnin was finishing putting the chorus through its paces I went into the Small Hall, where the fifth day of the examinations was in full swing. Entry into the hall is forbidden while a performance in going on, so I went to the artists' room to listen from there. I was just about to open the door when it swung wide of its own accord, and I found myself face to face with Struve. 'How kind of you to open the door for me,' I said, and went inside. One of Vengerova's students was playing a Schumann sonata (mine), but so badly that I soon went away.

Tcherepnin and I went to the Becker shop,[1] where I played my examination recital programme to him. I was expecting Tcherepnin to have some interesting comments on interpretation, and was not disappointed. He has a rich store of original views on the Bach, Mozart and Beethoven works, and I took them into consideration. Overall he showed great interest in my work, and the session lasted for three hours. On the way back we talked in the friendliest way, just like old times. He even said sorrowfully, 'What a pity, Sergey Sergeyevich, that I did not manage to arrange for your Concerto to be played in the Belyayev Concerts!'

I could not but mistrust this remark; nevertheless I did find his comments on my recital programme very valuable. In the evening Oleg partnered me at bridge at the Meshcherskys.

Talya said she thought my performance of the Chopin sonata was better than Romanovsky's at his concert. Somewhat unexpectedly, I found this very encouraging indeed.

6 March

Tsybin was due to conduct this morning, but I did not go to watch, preferring to stay and practise the piano until I went into the Conservatoire at three o'clock to conduct *Figaro* in the opera class. Just at that moment there was a break in the exams going on in the Small Hall, the hall was being aired and the audience waiting outside the door. There was Struve, talking away to a fellow wearing a jacket. I went back into the Great Hall and con-

---

1 Piano manufacturer and showroom in St Petersburg. The original 'Evenings of Contemporary Music' took place in the Becker shop.

ducted *Figaro*; it was a full rehearsal, but with piano rather than orchestra. In the evening I went to Sokol.

7 March

In the morning, I finished correcting the two-piano score of the Concerto, which I did with great satisfaction in between other work. Went to the opera class, where today the roles were being allocated as between the different casts: who would sing in the first performance, who in the second and so on. This is always a lively occasion generating a great deal of heat, everyone's nerves are strung up to the highest pitch and the air buzzes with mutual recriminations. Today, however, for some reason the decisions were announced discreetly, a word in the ear here and there. I conducted.

The premiere, to be conducted by Tcherepnin, is to be on the 15th, the second (by me) on the 24th, and the third (by Tsybin) on the 30th. All performances are free, with an invited audience. Went home and practised the piano. Signed up for a correspondence chess tournament. Friebus has asked for a copy of the Sonata for the Library: this is very flattering. Today I played the entire recital programme without getting overtired – I'm clearly making progress. In the evening, piano practice and diary.

8 March

Slept until eleven. Practised, and at three o'clock went for a walk along Morskaya Street to buy a copy of the Sonata for Friebus (Jurgenson now has my works on display everywhere, but I shrank from the tactlessness of enquiring how they were selling). Then went into the Conservatoire with the intention of listening to Golubovskaya's exam performance, but it had finished at two o'clock (5+). I sat in the Library while Tcherepnin, who was in an expansive mood, told a story about one of his foreign trips. He had been on a train from Berlin to Paris, and a Russian couple had taken him for a German. In the belief that he could understand nothing of what they were saying, they discussed him in highly disparaging terms, not sparing his presence in the slightest. They ended by offering him a box of chocolates, saying with the sweetest expression, 'Guzzle that, you son of a bitch, go on, stuff it down your throat!' Tcherepnin replied in perfect Russian, 'No, thank you, I somehow don't fancy it.' A pleasing picture.

9 March

Worked intensively on the Bach fugue and the Beethoven sonata, then caught up on my diary. My head seemed rather woolly, so at four o'clock I went out for a walk. Finding myself near the Novodevichy Monastery I looked at Rimsky-Korsakov's grave and Papa's. I love cemeteries. In my mood of quiet reflection, I thought of my own life bearing me inexorably on my journey to old age and death.

Went home and read about America, continuing the 'round-the-world journey' I began a month ago. Oh, how I long to go to America and circumnavigate the globe! Shtember called for me at seven o'clock and together we went to the Small Hall for a rehearsal of the exam recital programme, but neither Anna Nikolayevna nor Kalantarova came. All six candidates were present, however, and we played from the platform to an empty hall. The girls' attitude to me was fairly hostile, while I in turn jeered at them for playing so appallingly. Yesipova had not given them many lessons and had only gone superficially through their programmes with them. The stupid creatures were incapable of working anything out for themselves without their teacher, so their playing was limp, colourless and insensitive. I on the other hand played well, and got through my whole programme in an hour and a half without getting up from my seat at the keyboard. Shtember listened to it all and approved: in the past he has always had a sceptical attitude towards my playing, therefore I place a high value on his praise. I found I could focus my concentration before starting to play, and if I manage to do the same thing at the exam I shall do well there too.

After this I went to Gessen's house. He is the editor of *Rech*, and had invited me via Karatygin. An interesting company was gathered there. I played some little pieces of mine, and then *Petrushka* four hands with Karatygin, parts of which came off splendidly. I happened to catch sight of Reger's sonata, which I had not seen for three years. Heavens, how clear and simple it seems now, but not so long ago it was the densest of impenetrable thickets! How music leaps forward. Karatygin said that he had dropped a hint to Ziloti about my Concerto and Ziloti had asked him to send it to him. Marvellous news.

10 March

Today is the first stage-orchestra rehearsal of *Figaro*, conducted by 'student' Tcherepnin. I went to the rehearsal and sat dutifully through it for almost five hours so as to familiarize myself as much as possible both with the opera and the *mise-en-scène*. I know all the arias and the ensembles, but what I don't yet know is how they fit together. Overall it is a very lively and attractive work, although it suffers from many infelicities, and from the dramatic point of view Mozart could surely have made it twenty times more interesting than he has done. When I come to write an opera I shall not choose an intensely dramatic subject but something light and buoyant, a French comedy with an intricate plot, but it will certainly be an opera with a lot of life about it.

During the interval I went into the teaching side of the Conservatoire and ran into Damskaya and Struve. We talked of my exam, and Struve said she would come. 'Well,' said Damskaya, 'you are bound to get 5+. I think any student expects to get 5+. If I get 5++ I consider it very good, but if I only get a straight 5, it's like a slap in the face.'

Struve suddenly remembered that she had to mug up on her history, and made as if to leave us. I said, 'If it had been a geography exam I would have been able to give you a hand on the subject of America. I've been reading all about it, going on armchair trips there.'

'I know quite a lot about America myself,' said Struve simply. 'I used to live in Canada.'

And went off.

These words struck me like a thunderclap, desperate as I am to cross the ocean and learn everything I can about America. Of course, I didn't show it, but . . . Struve! America! What?! I am absolutely fascinated. After the rehearsal I practised and then later went to Sokol, although people were telling me that it was not a good idea just before an exam, in case I were to damage a hand or a finger.

11 March

Slept well, and then conscientiously ran through my programme. At one o'clock Yesipova telephoned without warning and asked me to go over and play the whole programme through to her. She sat out of sight in an adjoining room, while Kalantarova and Poznyakovskaya ran in and out playing the part of emissaries conveying pronouncements from on high. For my part I was glad to have the chance to play it all to her, because I was still not completely sure about my gradations of tempo in the Beethoven sonata, also about my treatment of the semiquavers in the Bach fugue (the rhythm is maintained the whole time from start to finish). Were they perhaps too massive? To achieve the necessary weight and organ-like sonority I was playing the semiquavers quite heavily while at the same time trying not to overdo it. However my misgivings proved unfounded and there were no criticisms. The Chopin was pronounced by Poznyakovskaya, in a voice laden with emotion, 'very good'. Much encouraged, I played the Schumann sonata 'well' according to Kalantarova, who came into the room to pass on this judgement. The only response to my Etude was a call of 'next!' but the *Tannhäuser* got much praise and Kalantarova's personal opinion that my playing had improved out of all recognition. Tomorrow I shall be the last one to play.

Exhausted, I went to the Conservatoire, where after a piano rehearsal

Tcherepnin and Tsybin were rehearsing *Figaro*. I hung around for a bit, then went into the Small Hall where a Nikolayev student was performing. Good, but not outstanding. Tomorrow it will be my turn to mount the scaffold, but sitting in the hall I felt no nerves. Went home, practised a little for tomorrow, won a telephone chess game with Golubovskaya and went to bed. Of course my thoughts were full of the following day, which I knew to be a very important one, but still I slept well.

12 March

I was so relaxed and comfortable in bed I did not want to get up in the morning, knowing that as soon as I did I should be prey to anxiety and nerves. Rose eventually at eleven and sat down at the piano, beginning from the end of the programme, that is from the Liszt, slowly hammering out the difficult passages. When I had gone through the Liszt, then my Etude, the Schumann and the Chopin, I went out for a walk in the marvellous weather. I walked clean out of the town along the Zagorodny Prospect and then came back by tram. At two o'clock Golubovskaya called me from the Conservatoire, followed by 'Foreign Minister' Damskaya, to tell me that they had now reached the interval following two performances by Kalantarova's students and two by Yesipova's: Hansen (not very good) and Malinskaya (pretty good). I learned that a huge crowd was there, many of whom were waiting for my appearance. I oscillated between nervousness and calm.

I sat down at the piano again to finish playing through the programme: Beethoven, Mozart and Bach. Yesterday evening I had experimented by following my own prescription of writing out the fugue by heart, but when doing this I went wrong at one place and wrote down a figure from another passage. This had made me afraid of going wrong in the Bach. But then I had a brilliant idea: I infallibly committed three specific passages in the fugue to memory, from any of which I could be certain of starting again should I go wrong. I then practised deliberately getting lost and improvising in the style of Bach until I found my way to one or other of these places. Since not many people know this fugue well, a bit of skilful improvising should enable me to get out of trouble with impunity. This device had the immediate effect of calming me down, and I decided I had nothing to worry about: the only thing I had to do, once on stage, was concentrate on the music and ignore my surroundings.

At four o'clock I had a call from the Conservatoire to say that Tietz was beginning his programme, and after him it would be my turn. I put on my overcoat and went on foot to the Conservatoire. At this stage I was in quite an agitated state of mind, but on the way I happened to meet the 'Pillow's'[1]

---

1 Claudia Sheintsvit.

sister, a very beautiful woman to whom I had taken a great fancy during the summer; we had an enjoyable talk in which she chastised me with great gentleness for not having been to see them, and this restored my sunny mood.

All was quiet in the Conservatoire when I got there, the whole world was crammed into the Small Hall. I sat in the stalls; Kreutzer[1] came up to me and wished me well. Going on stage I was not particularly nervous. The hall was bursting at the seams. The panel sitting behind the examining table looked more propitious than I had expected: Glazunov, Kalantarova, Vengerova, Drozdov, Medem, Gabel – all well disposed to me. However on Glazunov's other side sat Lyapunov, an enemy of Yesipova's class and the one whom I most feared, then Lemba and Miklashevskaya.[2] Advancing towards the piano I bowed to the panel and then removed the desk from the piano so that it should not get in the way of my vision, setting it down on a chair by my side. For a moment I sat fixing my gaze on my knees, trying hard to forget the audience in the hall and concentrate on Bach. Feeling that I had got myself into a reasonably calm and focused state, I began the fugue. It went well, and the Mozart also made my heart sing. The Beethoven began well, but in the exposition, where the main theme introduces a contrasting idea, my left hand started to play the theme but my right hand declined to follow suit and I started to lose my way. Calculating that this passage would soon be followed by the second subject, I attempted to progress to it, and began indeed to play it, but in E flat instead of the correct key of A flat. Things were going seriously wrong, but I succeeded in improvising until I got back to the place where I had originally gone wrong – i.e. towards the end of the main subject – at which point I got back on track and everything proceeded smoothly. I finished the sonata well, but all too aware that I might once again make a mess of it.

In the first phrase of the Chopin sonata I missed the keyboard entirely, but I was pleased with the way I played the rest of it, and the greatest satisfaction of all came from the fact that I had conquered my nerves. I felt my performance of the Chopin was better than any I had ever given before.

Before the Schumann I asked Glazunov if I should play the whole sonata, or just one movement. Glazunov consulted with Lyapunov and said, 'Play it all'. This was going to be extremely tiring, especially bearing in mind that I still had *Tannhäuser* to come.

'You mean the entire sonata?' I asked.

'The entire sonata,' Glazunov answered.

There was a burst of laughter from the audience, enjoying the spectacle, and I began the sonata. I was not completely happy with the Aria, but the

---

1 Conducting student at the Conservatoire, not the pianist and conductor Leonid Kreutzer.
2 Irina Miklashevskaya (Mikhelson) (1883–1956), pianist and recently appointed professor at the Conservatoire.

first movement was good and the third and fourth movements positively brilliant. In the Finale, where the left hand crosses the right, I broke a string. Luckily it was one of those strings that has one end wound round the pin and is simply looped over the pin at the other end. When the string broke the whole section with the loop in it jumped off its pin and flew out of the piano and into the audience – an original effect that caused the audience to whinny with pleasure.

At the end of the Schumann people started applauding, but this is not allowed and the applause soon died down. I felt completely drained and was afraid that my fingers would not be nimble enough for my Etude. As for *Tannhäuser*, I did not even want to think about it. I rested for about two minutes – longer would have been unacceptable – and played the Etude. I took a fairly measured tempo, but even so it was fast enough to produce an effect. Then it was time for *Tannhäuser*. Fortunately it begins quietly, and I had time to gather my strength a little. In this piece everything depends on pacing the cumulative effect, it must 'go', and 'go' it did, and I still had just enough reserves of strength for the storm of noise at the end. The final chord was accompanied by an explosion of clapping. As I left the stage to return to the artists' room I was met by Poznyakovskaya, Berlin and Vegman all applauding. Clasping Vegman by the hand I went into the artists' room. Through the open door I could see Struve and Lipinskaya leaving the hall. First to come backstage were Tcherepnin and the conductors Kreutzer and Dranishnikov, all three ecstatic. Shtember's triumphant verdict was: 'Well now! Congratulations! Absolutely splendid!'

Tcherepnin praised everything, Dranishnikov was in a paroxysm of delight. We talked for a long time, and when this group left it was immediately replaced by a new one consisting of Damskaya, the Alpers and others. Coming out of the artists' room I met Glazunov. He congratulated me on a successful examination and said that while there had been many aspects of my interpretation with which he could not agree, as a judge he must preserve objectivity and give due credit to the talent I had shown as a performer. He particularly commended the playing of the fugue: he had been struck by the way I started *piano*, thinking initially it was by accident, but was impressed when he realized I was maintaining the tone throughout. In the Beethoven he found some of my nuances too highly coloured, which detracted from the unity of the whole (?!), but the Schumann was good and the Liszt very good indeed. I thanked him, happy with this directorial judgement. Gabel was especially pleased with *Tannhäuser*, saying that he had found the performance unusually gripping. Catching sight of Lyapunov, I went up to him and said, with a smile, 'Forgive me, Sergey Mikhailovich, for inflicting on you such a thing as my Etude!'

'Well, yes, ha ha! . . . dreadful thing it was . . . quite dreadful . . . but you did play it extremely well, one could hear every last note in it. It was excellent, I gave you 5 with a star; you have great gifts as a pianist.'

'Thank you,' I exclaimed. 'You were the judge I was most afraid of!'

Certainly, to get a 5+ from Lyapunov is a real achievement. He is famous for picking holes in everything, and is no friend to our class. I heard that one reason he gave me 5+ was precisely because I did not play like a Yesipova student.

And so, for the time being a brilliant victory, but we shall see what April brings. Kreutzer, Shtember and I went to the 'Vienna' restaurant to have dinner; we had a nice conversation and Kreutzer proposed that we drink to our *Bruderschaft*, to which I cordially agreed. He predicted that in the Conservatoire this would be regarded as a sensational event. After dinner Kokochka[1] and I walked along Nevsky while he discoursed vehemently on the subject of his own forthcoming final exam. I called in on N.M., had a chat with him, and then went home to tell Mama about the exam and fell into bed dog tired.

13 March

Oof! How good it is to feel the weight of this exam lifted from my shoulders! But the second leg is yet to come. Will my Concerto be my salvation or my doom? Will the judges be repelled by its dissonant harmonies or will they, on the contrary, be stunned by its brilliance and ardour? Perhaps it would be better, while there is still time, to choose another work? No, I still think that I will succeed in giving it the kind of performance that will stun the jury, and that is the route to victory. In any case it will be a first: no one in the history of the St Petersburg Conservatoire has ever graduated performing his own concerto. So, it's settled – I shall play my Concerto. I went into the Conservatoire, where a *Figaro* rehearsal was in progress. According to new rules the examination marks had not been announced, but Gabel smiled his sly smile and said, 'You'll be very pleased!'

Tcherepnin found out from Glazunov that my mark was 5+ and that he, Glazunov, had been especially pleased with the Bach: 'The fugue was played with great insight.'

Tcherepnin repeated his congratulations and is already making plans to include my Concerto in the Graduation Concert. I went into the Kuskova students' exam, where all the girls greeted me as the hero of yesterday's performances. But unfortunately I did not get to hear Galperin, who I was told had given an exceptionally powerful account of *Islamey*, had received 5+ and was clearly a rival for the piano prize. Damskaya says that all the talk is about

---

1 Nikolay Shtember.

whether I shall be the winner of the grand piano. I had to listen to many congratulations on yesterday's performance. In the evening, vint with Saradzhev, visiting again from Moscow, and Kolechka Myaskovsky. We played no more and no less than ten rubbers and had a very lively time of it. I telephoned Oleg asking him to join us but he said that he was too hard at work preparing for his exam.

14 March

At eleven o'clock, the *Figaro* general rehearsal. Saradzhev had meant to come, but evidently overslept after the previous evening's vint. At the start of the rehearsal no one was allowed into the auditorium, but then people were told they could come in as long as they sat no nearer than the tenth row. I was talking to Damskaya, and when the rehearsal began took her to sit with me in the front row. An officious attendant, sticking his nose in where it was not wanted, asked her to leave, but I sent him off with a flea in his ear and he obeyed. The rehearsal went on for five hours because the opera did not go smoothly, which caused Tcherepnin to keep stopping and repeating sections. I listened closely trying to absorb every detail of the *mise-en-scène*. In the interval I went into the teaching part of the Conservatoire, where Struve, blushing and stammering, haltingly offered me her congratulations on my success in the exam.

In the evening I went to the Chess Club, where I played a few games with a Deputy from the State Duma.

15 March

Settled down to revising *Autumnal*. I love this piece very much and believe something very good can be made of it. I have not yet addressed myself to learning my First Piano Concerto, but after so much playing I felt drawn to the piano so played my *Toccata* and my 'Capriccio', which I have learned so that I can play it to Vera Nikolayevna Meshcherskaya and convince her that it is really a good piece. In the afternoon I went to the singers' exam to see how our singers have turned out.

Yesterday Tsybin told me that he had another engagement on the day appointed for his third performance of the opera, and asked me to swap with him and let him take the second performance. I said I could not agree to this and suggested he find some other way to resolve his problem. Tcherepnin came to me today and said that of course I should by rights conduct the second performance, but if Tsybin really could not manage it they would have to appeal to my magnanimity and ask me to relinquish it. This made me very angry, and I said that I found it most objectionable to be appealed to in this way, that it was in any event a disgrace that the first performance had been taken away from me, that I would certainly not give up the second performance and that if this were to be insisted on then I would decline to conduct at all.

In the evening I attended the premiere. Meeting Belokurova, I sat next to her, an enjoyable adjunct to listening closely to *Figaro* and studying Tcherepnin's gestures. Belokurochka was extremely nice and cheered me up, putting me in an excellent mood. She was amazed when I addressed her by her name and patronymic, convinced that no one in the Conservatoire knew what they were. But I had looked up her first name and her address in the Class Inspectors' register, and then found the address in the 'All Petersburg' directory, which gave her father's name. As for *Figaro*, the performance went smoothly, one could even say well. When Tcherepnin was called out to take a bow and accept the plaudits of the audience, he waved his arms deprecatingly and said, 'After all, gentlemen, allow me to say that, thanks be to God, it's not the first time . . .' My entire current 'ministerial cabinet' was present today, as well as those who have been retired: Rudavskaya, Nikolskaya, Hansen and others.

16 March

Worked all day, from eleven to half past four writing out the new score of *Autumnal*, which is making slow progress but coming out marvellously well. Received two proofs of the Concerto, something I always enjoy. I had an inspired idea for a summer project: if I win the grand piano prize and sell my old one, and if Mama will subsidize me, I will twist Kreutzer's arm to travel right round Europe with me: Sweden – Norway – Denmark – Holland – the Rhineland – Switzerland – Milan – the Riviera – Spain – Naples – Venice – the Tyrol – Pest – Vienna – St Petersburg (two months, a thousand roubles). Then in August I can go to Kislovodsk where Mama and the Meshcherskys will be. In the evening Mama and I went to hear Zherebtsova-Andreyeva, who had included my song 'There Are Other Planets' in her programme. I was extremely interested to hear my song, never having heard it performed before. Rather good, although naturally not for the wider public (although actually it was very well received). Anna Grigorievna sang wonderfully, except for her habit of clearing her throat when she finishes singing, but Dulov accompanied drily and he played some wrong notes in the bass. In the interval he said to me, 'Well, I seemed to get your song worked out all right, don't you think?'

I mumbled something in reply.

'Surely there weren't any wrong notes, were there?'

(*Laughing*) 'Quite a few, actually!'

Dulov took offence. 'Well, you know, it was quite a feat to play the song at all, the writing is so tangled and involved! And then your calligraphy is awful, like chickens' feet!'

I laughed. 'So now it's my calligraphy you're criticizing! On the contrary, I write a very neat hand.'

'Anything but. I've read lots of manuscripts . . .' and on and on in the same vein.

When I left he was still pouring odium on my song, so that even Meshcherskaya came to my defence! The Meshcherskys were generally very nice. Afterwards I went to drink tea with the Andreyevs and had a nice conversation with Kal, a music professor at the University. He has taken a great liking to me and told me that earlier in the day he had given a lecture on new music, winding up with me.

17 March

Worked on *Autumnal* (I think the orchestration is turning out splendidly) and at two o'clock went to the Conservatoire to hear Zherebtsova's class in their final exam. Seeing Kreutzer there I shared with him my idea of travelling round Europe, and outlined the itinerary. So far he has no summer plans of his own, but had been thinking of going to the south of Germany to listen to Wagner. My project appeals to him and it looks as though I should be able to persuade him. Naturally I have no intention of going solo.

The exam was not very interesting, none of my 'cabinet ministers' were present, but I had to wait until the end in order to talk over with Gabel and Tcherepnin the rehearsal schedule for the second opera performance. Tsybin has somehow managed to resolve his difficulty with the third performance, and the question of an exchange with him did not come up again. The first rehearsal will be on Wednesday. In the evening I played the *Toccata* and went to the Sokol.

18 March

In the morning studied the score of *Figaro* and dry-conducted it. At three o'clock saw Tcherepnin to talk about *Figaro*, which was very interesting since he was able to share his newly minted impressions from the personal experience of conducting the opera. Then I attended the opera class. Struve darted in but quickly disappeared. Her elegant figure is truly very fetching. Today I outlined to Kreutzer and the other conductors my round-trip plan, but going in the reverse direction, starting in Italy and Spain, then the Rhine and Scandinavia. There was general approbation. Kreutzer is smacking his lips over the chance to see a bullfight.

19 March

At ten o'clock we had the first rehearsal of the second cast with orchestra. Tcherepnin said to me, 'Be demanding, insist on what you want; don't let either the orchestra or the singers get away with anything. This is not to say you should shout at them, but you know all the nuances and all the tempi, so keep them up to the mark the whole time.'

Up on the podium I felt fine, a little nervous here and there of course, and there were a few places where I was not absolutely secure. The ensembles were not very good: for several of the singers it was their first time singing with orchestra, and they either lost their place or failed to look at me. Tcherepnin thought the finales of the second and fourth acts left something to be desired, but on the whole I had demonstrated that I was capable of conducting the whole score very well, the only thing I have to do is get myself into shape. Basically I got very tired – conducting a complete opera is to some extent a skill that comes with experience. In the evening I sat through another rehearsal. Going out in the interval into the teaching part of the Conservatoire to drink a glass of milk, I met Struve and Lipinskaya and promised to get them tickets for the performance. They both cried *'merci'*, their voices radiating gratitude. At six o'clock I went to see Myaskovsky, who checked my corrections to the Concerto and caught a few missed sharps and naturals and also some wrong notes. At nine I returned home and played the piano.

20 March

In the morning I went through *Figaro*, the ensembles and some of the recitatives preceding the arias. Rehearsal at two o'clock, which today went not at all badly and presages a good performance. The only place where things went seriously awry was in the difficult ensemble in the second act, where the singers answer one another and the orchestra provides a background like a sort of indistinct rustling. The singer taking the part of the gardener[1] is the idiot Mandelbaum. He has no concept of rhythm, loses his place, never looks at the conductor and altogether threatens to bring the whole ensemble crashing down. During the interval I met Mme Ossovskaya, who called me 'Mister Laureate' and said it was the general opinion that my playing was more mature and interesting than that of any of my rivals.

After the rehearsal I hurried home, donned my tails and went to the Meshcherskys' box in the Mariinsky Theatre for the premiere of *Meistersinger*. This opera always overwhelms me with the beauty of its themes, even

---

1 Antonio.

though Wagner's approach to composing opera as exemplified in this work is not to my taste, any more than is its great length. Andreyev was very good in the role of David. The Meshcherskys were very kind. Came home much moved by the opera and full of gratitude for the love this music inspires in me.

21 March

Tired out by the previous day I slept in a bit this morning and at one o'clock went to the Conservatoire to rehearse the *Ballade* with Bezrodny. Struve, whom I met on the stairs, talked to me for a long time, which made me happy. She seems to be getting over her fear of me and no longer takes offence at my every word.

Went into the class to rehearse with Bezrodny. He told me how much he likes the *Ballade*; he plays it quite well and I think that with a bit of effort and thorough study we shall be able to give it a good performance. Gabel tells me that there are so many people wanting to come to our *Figaro* performance that not many complimentary tickets can be given out, and I was given only fifteen. When the Meshcherskys telephoned me at home, I had to suggest they try to get tickets through Andreyev. Looked again through the proof of the Concerto, found a few more mistakes, and took it to the Nikolayevsky station to send it express to Moscow. I wrote on it a dedication to N. N. Tcherepnin. This is something I have long planned to do; he loves this work and has always taken an interest in it. It will be my farewell acknowledgement of what I owe him as I leave the Conservatoire, since performing it will be the last thing I do there. But when we had our *contretemps* over *Aida* I wavered in my intention, and for a time could not decide whether to go ahead with the dedication or not. But now I have come down firmly in the affirmative, so I inscribed the final proof 'To Nikolay Nikolayevich Tcherepnin' and added a note to the engraver to be sure to include the dedication.

22 March

Rose early, looked through the tricky passages in *Figaro*, and at ten o'clock was ready and waiting for the general rehearsal. I took with me Nadya and Sonya Shtember, who wanted to get an idea of me as a conductor. The opera went smoothly, except for the chorus in the first act, which made a fair old mess of it. The problem was that I had never worked with the chorus and they had not been at the previous rehearsal, so we had not got to know one another. My tempo was different to the one the choristers were used to, they did not look at me but ploughed on in their own sweet way, while because they were right at the back of the stage behind the scenery I could not hear them very well and did not follow them. In the second act Mandelbaum wrecked the whole scene in which he appears, and it had to be repeated. He is the black spot of the production. In the interval he was heard complaining in high dudgeon that I did not give him his cues, but how can I possibly do that when he invariably comes in long before he is supposed to? In the third act the sextet fell apart, but the fourth act went well.

I was exhausted by the rehearsal and not very happy with the result. I carefully put together and bound the remaining proof copy of the Concerto and today gave it to Dranishnikov, who did not hide the interest and pleasure with which he accepted it. Going after the rehearsal into the teaching area of the Conservatoire I discovered that Zelikman, my rival, was about to play his recital programme, this having been delayed for ten days because of Nikolayev's illness. I ran into Damskaya and Struve, and was happy to sit with them in a pretty full hall. Zelikman played with authority and skill, and was greeted by warm applause from the audience. He has good attack and a fine technique although some of his tempi are too fast to be absolutely even and clean. The playing is refined and the detail interesting, but I was left with the feeling that it was not always perceptive. Schumann's *Carnaval* could have had a better performance.

The performance over, a lively discussion broke out. My supporters declared that his playing was not to be compared with mine, others were loud in their enthusiasm for Zelikman. I talked to Khariton, a Vengerova student who also played today, reportedly well, getting according to some 5+ and according to others 5. He is usually an incredible show-off and self-publicist, but today he was beating the drum both for Zelikman and for me. His view was that Zelikman was certainly a 5++, but that my performance of *Tannhäuser* had been phenomenal. He reported Vengerova's opinion that my performance of the fugue was the best by anyone since the foundation of the Conservatoire. But at that moment Vengerova herself appeared, and when she came to talk to us she was full of praise for Zelikman, somewhat extravagantly so to my ears in what seemed to be an attempt to rile me – although I cannot for the life of me imagine why she should want to do such a thing. To sum up, it now seems that the main candidates are myself and Zelikman, both with an equal chance of the grand piano, both ranked equally although very different in style. Some put it thus: Zelikman is more fluent, I am more interesting. Some preferred me on the grounds of my more broadly based musical education, others preferred Zelikman because he is a specialist pianist, which I am not. In third place I would put Golubovskaya, who is said to have an all-round 5+, and who is undoubtedly an excellent and distinguished player, but lacking masculine authority. Fourth and fifth would be Khariton and Galperin.

I got home at five o'clock, tired, terribly hungry, in a bad temper, had something to eat and went to bed. At eight o'clock I got up and went to the Meshcherskys, where we played through *Kitezh* and *Meistersinger*. I dedicated my piece to Vera Nikolayevna, who still does not like it very much, but I am sure that in time it will grow on her. We played some bridge, but for the most part mucked about. Talya and Oleg referred to Nina and me as 'Mr and Mrs Prokofiev' because we sat side by side at bridge and played the same hand. We quarrelled today: I threw a ball of paper at Nina and hit her on the cheek, she lost her temper and insisted that I apologize. I refused, and she sulked. Probably from tiredness my mood grew worse and worse, and memories of Max and his death only reinforced my depression, so that when I returned home it was in the blackest frame of mind, traces of which were still there in the morning even though I slept well.

23 March

Practised the piano in the morning, working conscientiously on the Concerto. Even if Zelikman does gain the palm, I'm not giving up before I have to. At three o'clock I went for a walk in the glorious weather. Went into a flower shop and sent a dozen white roses to Damskaya for her confirmation, with a card saying: 'R.H.M.F.A.[1] is hereby awarded the Order of the White Roses.' Then I walked along Morskaya Street and Nevsky Prospect, took a ticket for tomorrow's *Figaro* in to Myaskovsky, and returned home. In the evening our Sokol group was presenting a display, but I felt disinclined to go and instead paid a visit to the Chess Club, where I lost two games. The international championship that is due to start in two weeks' time promises to be exceptionally interesting: Lasker, Capablanca, Rubinstein and all the greatest chess masters without exception will be there! If some catastrophe were to strike St Petersburg during this tournament, there would be no chess master left in the world!

24 March

My impending opera performance fills me with less than joyful anticipation. I am worried that there will be some mishap either with the chorus or with Mandelbaum, or with someone else. The only thing that gives me any comfort is the Shtember maxim: 'Just remember, there has never been any such thing as an opera performance in which nothing goes wrong.' Conducting an opera performance that has been prepared by other hands, having to take over other people's tempi and phrasing, is not a particularly rewarding experience. I spent the morning going through the score and satisfying myself

---

[1] Rt Hon. Minister of Foreign Affairs.

that from my point of view everything was in order. In the afternoon I went into the Conservatoire to see if there might be any more tickets going, and looked to see whether anyone worth while was around. I could not get any more tickets, but I did glimpse Tcherepnin on his way to go through the opera with Tsybin in preparation for his performance, which would be the third. I went up to the third floor where I encountered Damskaya and Struve. We had a nice chat, during which Damskaya enquired, 'And how is our Prime Minister?'

'Oh,' I replied, 'I've been feasting my eyes on him today.'

Struve: 'What Prime Minister are you talking about?'

Damskaya: 'The Prime Minister of Sergey Sergeyevich's cabinet.'

Little does she suspect that the Prime Minister was standing right before her eyes!

As there is a party tomorrow in the Conservatoire, I steered the conversation round to the subject and on impulse said to Struve, 'Why don't you come? I'll dance the first waltz with you.'

At this point the door into the Small Hall opened. Struve, who was waiting for her exam to start, rushed to go in, and I went home. I meant to give one of the complimentary tickets to Vegman, but she was not there, so I gave it to Vera Alpers, with whom friendly relations have once more been established.

Went home, dozed for a bit and just before eight went with Mama to the Conservatoire. But the performance was not due to start until half past eight, so I had to wait. Apparently the first *Figaro* performance had aroused a great deal of interest, and today we had a full house. Palechek called for beginners, and I, deep in conversation with Tcherepnin, prepared to go into the orchestra pit. 'Make sure the pianist is there for the opening chord, otherwise you can't start!' came a cry from somewhere up above, and very a propos, since the pianist was nowhere to be seen. A hue and cry ensued, people rushed about looking for the pianist, an excitable Tcherepnin was about to take over the piano part himself, but it transpired that the piano score had disappeared along with the pianist. Gabel came running in, having already been in the hall looking for him. Eventually the score was located, followed by the pianist.

I was delighted to recognize in the leader of the orchestra, who had not been present at the rehearsal, the same who had led the *Aida* orchestra; we clasped hands and saying to one another, 'Well, we old hands at this sort of thing . . .', went to join the orchestra. I enjoyed conducting the Overture so much that at the first *forte* I broke my baton into several pieces. Glazunov, sitting in the front row, saw that there was no spare on the conductor's desk, and sent off an attendant to find me another; he brought me no fewer than three.

All went well until we got to the chorus, but they did not look at me at all, I could hardly hear them and we diverged by a semitone, so they were hurriedly shooed off the stage before the end of their number. During the interval Gabel put the blame on me and I put the blame on the chorus. Altogether it was a most upsetting thing to have happened, and Tcherepnin came round especially to console and pacify me. I began Act II in a foul mood but gradually recovered myself. I was very nervous about the finale of this act, especially on account of Mandelbaum, who as expected sang unrhythmically, forcing me to alternate between speeding up and slowing down the tempo, completely unsettling the pace so that it was a great relief when he left the stage. In this way the second act came successfully to an end, and Gabel was as nice as can be during the interval, presumably to make up for his earlier assault over the chorus. In Act III the chorus watched me attentively, some of the girls grinning broadly when they saw the anger on my face. Act IV also went well; during the last interval I visited the buffet where I met Myaskovsky, who was full of praise for my rhythmic firmness, the way I was directing the chorus and the care I was taking not to drown them. Quite an encomium, coming from him! Hitherto he has never done anything but criticize my conducting, so I was most encouraged.

At the end of the opera everyone was called to the stage: Gabel, Palechek, Tcherepnin, Glazunov, but I was late coming out. I then took my leave of them. Glazunov complimented me on 'the two final acts'. The Countess presented me with a rose from her bouquet and I went home, rather tired and not particularly content – why not, though?

Mama was extremely happy with the performance, as were those of my relations who were present.

25 March
Feast of the Annunciation

I woke up this morning free at last of the opera, and settled down to revising *Autumnal*, spending approximately four happy hours on it. Damskaya telephoned at four o'clock to ask if I would like to go with her to see the Palm Sunday procession. I agreed with alacrity, and off we went. Because it was a holiday weekend and a fine day the crowds were incredible, and we soon turned off on to the embankment and from there into the Summer Garden, where we had a marvellous walk. Today was also the start of the correspondence tournament for Chess Club members, in which I had enrolled; so far not many were taking part but apparently more will sign up in due course. I love playing chess by correspondence and am always ready to join in such projects.

In the evening I went to the party in the Conservatoire, arriving around eleven o'clock just as the concert part of the evening was drawing to a close, to find a full hall. To my surprise all my conducting colleagues were there: Dranishnikov, Kreutzer and Tvordovsky. In fact the public was less interesting than had appeared at first glance, although the evening was to some extent embellished by Klingman and Bluvshtein. A new dimension has been added to our evenings: a cabaret, which commenced at this point, but it was not at all witty, in fact generally tedious and painfully unsuccessful. Everyone was bored by it, including Belokurochka, whom I spotted in a corner with some young man or other, but by the time the ill-fated cabaret came to an end there was no sign of her. I sought her assiduously through all the halls, side rooms and corridors, but she had vanished without trace. There seemed no point in staying any longer, so I went home.

26 March

Slept until noon, then played the piano and made a few changes to the *Ballade*, which Bezrodny and I start rehearsing tomorrow for the exam. At three o'clock I went into the Conservatoire to give my score to Friebus. On the landing of the stairs I met first Vegman, with her enchanting Greek nose, and then Lipinskaya, Struve, and Damskaya – the whole crowd. It transpired out that Struve and Damskaya had time on their hands, and the same was true of me, so I proposed an outing to the Palm Sunday festival. They accepted, and off we went. I ascertained the following: her name is L. N. Struve (I was afraid it might have been Lidia Gustavnovna or Lidia Genrikhovna), she is sixteen years old and is going to be spending the summer living somewhere on the coast. She has lived in Canada and then on Lake Geneva and speaks several languages. She can't pronounce the letter 'r' properly.

As on the previous day there were tremendous crowds for the Palm Sunday festival and so we came out on to the embankment and repeated yesterday's route, walking so far that we tired out the unaccustomed L.N. Alternately turning pale and flushing, she finally pleaded to be allowed to sit down on a bench in the Summer Garden. I enjoyed the walk tremendously. I then went home and played through the Second Sonata in order to attend one of Baron Driesen's Wednesdays and 'illustrate' Karatygin's lecture on new music, as I had done in February. But this time Karatygin spoke about me in greater detail and comprehensively dismissed all of my colleagues without exception, declaring that 'in my opinion we have in Russia today only two modern classics: Medtner and Prokofiev. Young as he is, the latter's place among the classics of today is assured, because . . .' etc., etc., repeating what he had written before in his article about me. I stretched out in an armchair in the next room basking in the approbation. My Sonata enjoyed its usual success, however on this particular Wednesday not many people were present – only about twenty.

27 March

Worked on the *Ballade* and corrected a few things. It plays splendidly now. Tcherepnin has suggested that I give all the professors a copy of my Concerto a week before my exam. First, it will give them a chance to familiarize themselves with the piece, and second, they will see that it has already been published and is in print, and one way and another this is bound to produce a more authoritative impression. Wrote to Jurgenson today asking him to be sure and send me copies no later than 10 April.

At three o'clock went to rehearse with Bezrodny, whose playing I liked a lot. He loves the *Ballade* and plays it really well; all it needs is to be played a few more times. At eight o'clock I went with Mama to play vint with the Andreyevs, and then after an hour went on to the Belyayev Concert to hear Tcherepnin's ballet *Narcissus and Echo*.[1] This is a very interesting work, with a good deal of quite captivating music in it, athough here and there it descends to somewhat derivative, wishy-washy pictorial representation. But on the whole it is an extraordinarily appealing and in places absorbingly interesting work. The ballet had a success, and we conducting students of the composer took along a big bouquet of narcissi, ingeniously chosen by Gauk. When we entered the artists' room, which was packed with people, we congratulated our professor on his triumph. I said, 'That was an incomparable object lesson in orchestration!'

He might perhaps have detected a slight innuendo in this, since Tcherepnin does have a tendency to concentrate on orchestration at the expense of the music. Somewhat defensively, he replied, 'I assure your pedagogic intentions could not have been further from my mind!'

Vera Nikolayevna Meshcherskaya liked *Narcissus* very much, and also had kind words for my conducting of *Figaro*. Her daughters also said they had not expected me to direct such a good performance, and they had much enjoyed the performance. I was sitting next to Kreutzer and thought how good it would be to make a summer tour of Europe and to have him along with me for company.

---

1 Ballet to a scenario by Bakst – who also produced sets and costumes – and choreography by Fokine, first performed by the Ballets Russes in Monte Carlo, 1911.

28 March

Worked in the morning and in the afternoon went into the Conservatoire to play the *Ballade* with Bezrodny for Blumenfeld, who said he could not understand anything about the piece, and even if he could he did not care for it. Nevertheless, he made us play it again, and made a whole series of pertinent comments, touching not only the way we performed the piece but drawing attention to places where bass notes were doubled, etc. He wants us to continue working on it and bring it back to him.

In the evening I went to see the artist Rausch,[1] who had visited me to ask me to play the Sonata at his house, saying that a lot of people wanted to hear it. When he came to my house he had been wearing an old jacket; I wore a dinner suit for his invitation but it turned out that he was having a very smart evening and everyone was in tails. I felt underdressed and uneasy. The Rausches themselves are very nice and straightforward people but I did not know any of their guests. The Sonata was very well received. Not wishing to linger, I left their rather grand establishment at midnight, leaving behind me a noisy crowd of people preparing to dance.

29 March

Tsybin's first rehearsal did not take place owing to the fact that the orchestra had not been got together. Yesterday's rehearsal, however, went well, and today, when I arrived at noon in the Great Hall for the general rehearsal it turned out that this was in fact to be the performance, a 'sudden death' one arising from the fact that, although tomorrow's performance was billed as an exam performance, it had been disallowed by the mayor. Luckily I managed to slip in, but poor old Tsypochka[2] had fallen right into it. Although the hall was about half full of people from the Conservatoire who happened to be there and had come in on impulse, there were no critics, no wider public, no atmosphere of a public event. A good thing I did not swap with Tsybin. He is a fair conductor, but I do not greatly like his work. In the first chorus it was not just a matter of them getting a little out of synchronization with him; the chorus came in a full eight bars early, when the orchestra was supposed to be playing on its own! Neither Tcherepnin nor Glazunov were there.

When the opera finished, at three o'clock, I went to play through the *Ballade*. Bezrodny played very well and, the most important thing, with enjoyment.

---

1 Baron Rausch von Traubenberg; see p. 39 n. 1.
2 Nickname, derived from the Russian word for a chicken.

30 March
Palm Sunday

Stayed in practising the *Ballade*, and made a few changes which will be interesting to show to Blumenfeld. The weather has taken a turn for the worse, and the autumn rain is pouring down. All the same at three o'clock I needed some air, so put on my galoshes and an old overcoat and went out for a walk through the rain and the puddles. I enjoyed walking along thinking of my Violin Concerto. Around seven o'clock I went to dine with Gessen; today is apparently the Jewish Easter and I enjoyed tasting various national dishes and things to drink. There was the usual lively atmosphere in their house, the talk ranging over all subjects under the sun, which makes one somehow feel more connected to the world and its doings.

Gessen was very kind to me, and said that on the following Sunday, the first day of Easter, they would be having some artists from the Moscow Art Theatre; this is a tremendously attractive prospect. Karatygin mentioned to me an 'Evening of Contemporary Music' at which Myaskovsky's sonata was to be performed, and wanted me to appear as well. I suggested my *Ballade* with Bezrodny.

31 March

Came into the Conservatoire at one o'clock to play the *Ballade* to Blumenfeld. He listened closely to it once again and this time was satisfied, with me and with Bezrodny, whom he patted on the cheek, saying that he need not come again. For our part we also felt good about it, and Bezrodny suggested that we try to find Glazunov and play it to him before the exam. As it happened, Glazunov appeared right on cue, so I went up to him and said, 'Alexander Konstantinovich, would you mind very much if we asked your permission to play you my *Ballade*?'

He graciously agreed and promised to telephone the day after tomorrow to fix a time for the audition. We thanked him and went on our way. At home I pondered some chess moves; some of the correspondence matches I am involved in have developed quite intricate situations. In the evening I went to the Sokol, not having been there for all of two weeks. What a splendid establishment it is! Boris has taken my 'March' and is going to have it engraved for publication. I have granted all rights from the publication to the Sokol.

1 April

Rose at nine, and seeing that it was a fine day, rang Damskaya, she rang Struve, and we all decided to make a trip to Pavlovsk. At a quarter to eleven, fifteen minutes before the train was due to depart, I was at the station awaiting both young ladies, but particularly Struve. Damskaya showed up seven minutes before the train left and we waited unconcernedly for Struve until two minutes to eleven when of course we started to worry. At one minute past eleven we were both puzzled and exasperated. Telephoning her at home we learned that she had left half an hour ago. Another half an hour went by, and we decided to wash our hands of her and take the one o'clock train to Pavlovsk. Without Struve I had no particular desire to go, but it would have been stupid to go home. Before departing it occurred to me that it would be a good idea to telephone the station at Pavlovsk and ask the telephonist to look along the platform and see whether a dark-haired girl wearing a grey coat was standing there, and if so, to tell her that we would be on the next train.

When we arrived at Pavlovsk, there was Struve on the platform. What had happened was that she arrived at the station literally one minute before the eleven o'clock train, dashed past the third-class carriages and threw herself on to the train as it pulled out. In Pavlovsk she waited for us on the next train, but when there was no sign of us concluded that we had been playing an April Fool's joke on her, and became very indignant. She was on the point of getting on the next train back to Petersburg, but at that moment the telephonist came running up to tell her that we were on our way. So the First of April had successfully made fools of us all, but it ended happily and we went to walk in the park.

By this time it was three o'clock, and we were all hungry. Both girls had brought home-made ham sandwiches; we selected the driest bench we could find to sit on, I put a block of wood under Struve's feet and we settled down to lunch. Damskaya had brought some chocolates as well as the ham, an excellent move. We then went over to Pavlovsk-2 station for tea. On the way, showing off my Sokol prowess, I vaulted athletically over a ditch but Struve, attempting to emulate me, slipped and fell on the bank and dropped her muff in the water. Helping the former to her feet and rescuing the latter, I led them round the ditch and we went into Pavlovsk-2 station to have tea. Struve had happy memories of Geneva, where she had lived for five years. From Pavlovsk-2 we went on to Tsarskoye Selo, and then returned to Petersburg at six o'clock, all having enjoyed our trip. I was very tired, but when I rang up the Meshcherskys they pressed me to come and play bridge, commissioning me to bring Oleg along as well. It took me a long time to persuade him, since he was working hard preparing for his exam. At that point I noticed a newspaper announcement that Capablanca was offering a simultaneous match session: I very much wanted to take part, but decided that there was no point in taking on Capablanca unless I was absolutely fresh, which was certainly not the case today, so I went to Meshcherskys.

The day after the *Narcissus* performance Vera Nikolayevna had been at a dinner where Tcherepnin was of the company, and had liked him very much. They talked about me, and Tcherepnin had said that he considered me very talented, but he was concerned by the unswerving self-confidence with which I was pursuing my own musical path. Self-confidence to the degree I possess it was not, in his opinion, an appropriate concomitant to talent. Really? We played bridge. Talya and I have recently developed a very close relationship centred around music: playing *Kitezh* together, reading Tchaikovsky's biography, and other such pursuits. And I seem to be having a tremendous success with Vera Nikolayevna: at tea she herself straightened my tie, which prompted me to go down on one knee and sing from *Figaro*: 'Look at the little rascal, what roguish glances, his hands folded before him . . .'[1] My stock in the Meshchersky household seems to be even higher than it was in Gurzuf.

2 April

As requested I rang Glazunov before noon to make an appointment for him to listen to my duo with the cellist, but I could get no reply and so went myself to the Conservatoire. There I was told that Glazunov was not in and would not be coming in. I telephoned Dranishnikov to ask him to come in to rehearse the Concerto, and settled down to wait for him. He arrived, and we rehearsed. He was pleased to have been asked to do it, but complained at the difficulty of his part. The timetable for the exams was posted on the wall: I am the final performer on the final day, a prestigious position that others would give much for. My rivals are also down to play: Zelikman, Golubovskaya, Galperin and Kind. The last two are not really in the running: the serious contenders are Zelikman and Golubovskaya, especially Zelikman. I know I shall have prepared the Concerto thoroughly and that I shall play it well, and that if Zelikman and I give equally good performances the prize will go to me because I have a broader Conservatoire education as a musician. If Zelikman wins the piano it will be because he is a better pianist than I, and therefore I shall not have deserved it.

---

1 Susanna'a aria 'Venite, inginocchiatevi' from Act II of Mozart's *The Marriage of Figaro*, in which Susanna and the Countess dress Cherubino in women's clothes.

3 April

Practised the Concerto and the *Ballade*, worked out some chess moves and towards the end of the lunch hour went to the Conservatoire to get Mama and Struve tickets for the Easter Prime service.[1] Back home, wrote a series of Easter greetings: letters to Morolyov and Tcherepnin, illustrated cards to Katya Schmidthof, Katya Ignatieva, Lyolya Zvyagintseva,[2] Nina Reberg, plain cards to Kachenovskaya, Damskaya, Glebova and Klingman.

At five o'clock I went out for a walk and stood for a long time looking in a window full of foreign travel brochures ('The Sleeping Car', Northern Travel Bureau). Overcome by wanderlust I went in and looked at all sorts of brochures, taking half a dozen away with me.

Called in at Kolya Myaskovsky's; the Russian Music Editions have rejected his Second Symphony. They are still keeping their options open on two more symphonies, a sinfonietta, *Alastor* and several other pieces. Played through with him his First Symphony and persuaded him to let Aslanov have it for the summer in Pavlovsk, it is a splendid work.

In the evening planned chess moves and wrote more Easter greetings. Agreed with Damskaya to go with her and Struve to Terioki tomorrow.

4 April

Got up at eight. The sun was shining and I rang Damskaya. She rang Struve, and at half past nine, fifteen minutes before the fast train, I was at the Finland Station. Damskaya was already there waiting, but once again Struve failed to appear by the time the train left. By the time the next train left, ten minutes later, there was still no Struve. It was at once irritating and amusing that the same story was repeating itself. Again we telephoned her at home, and again were told that the young lady had left for the station half an hour ago. Uncertain what to do we emerged from the telephone booth and ran into Struve on the platform: she was simply late. Such was the innocence of her expression that Damskaya could not stop herself laughing, and I followed suit. Struve had no idea what it was all about, felt foolish and began to lose her temper. At that I also lost my temper at her, and turned on my heel to go and get the train tickets.

In Terioki not all the snow had melted, some puddles still had a crust of ice on them and others were slippery with mud. Going past the Alpers' dacha, the Zakharovs' and the one where Struve had stayed last summer, we reached the sea. But the sea was still frozen, shrouded in corrugated folds of

---

1 Early morning service on holidays in the Orthodox Church, taking place after midnight.
2 Derzhanovsky's sister-in-law, to whom Prokofiev had taken a fancy in Moscow.

snow and ice. I led the girls into the park, where we decided to eat our sandwiches. Struve clambered with great agility on to a pile of timber the Zakharovs use to make a swimming pool in the summer. Some time after three we went back to the station to have tea. There I hired a tarantass[1] and in high spirits we set off in it to Tyurisyavi. I sat up on the box with the coachman, but facing backwards towards the girls. When we arrived I suggested sending a postcard to Lipinskaya, an idea that delighted Struve. Then we put kopecks on the rails beneath a passing train,[2] and sat on a wooden fence at a wayside halt.

Struve told us that she had been born in Frankfurt-am-Main and lived there until she was four, speaking German, then the family moved to Montreal (French and German), then five years later to San Remo in Italy (Italian and Russian), and finally eighteen months ago to Russia. Ye gods, what an interesting life!

On the way back to town I dozed, Struve going to great lengths to avoid waking me up. On the tram we laughed ourselves silly: Damskaya begged me not to have all my hair shaved off, as I had done last spring, saying it made me look hideous. Struve joined in, saying, 'If you do, you will lose all the success you have had in the Conservatoire(!).'

When I got home I found waiting for me a present from Rausch for performing at their house: an elegant crystal goblet. I don't particularly like it, but Mama seemed delighted. Euphoric over our expedition, I went to bed tired out.

5 April

Practised the Concerto and sent off chess moves by post. In the afternoon went with Mama to Papa's grave. Earlier, in the morning, I had obtained tickets for Mama and Struve to the Easter Prime church service in the Conservatoire, which I always love. All my friends come, people dress in their best, there is a huge crush but this does not matter – they are my people. It's a splendid occasion, the men in tailcoats, the place buzzing with actors and singers and suchlike. Mama stood in the church, I stayed down below on the stairs, with Torletsky and Kreutzer. I saw Zakharov's brother, but did not enquire about Boris, because Boryusya is such a swine, he has not written a single word to me. As usual some people fainted, but not many today, only three, one of whom I brought round by giving her water. At the end of the service as I was going up the stairs I ran into the whole Nikolayev brood. Returned home slightly disgruntled that I had not seen Struve.

---

1 An open carriage without springs.
2 A traditional children's pastime: the train wheels squash the coins satisfyingly flat and long.

6 April
Easter Sunday

Although I slept in a little, I managed to practise the Concerto for an hour or so; by now I am almost completely secure in it. Received a card from Jurgenson to tell me that the Concerto has been published and is now available through the St Petersburg shop. Sadly, because of the holiday, the shop will be closed for three days. But in any case I am pleased, this is a fine Egg for a fine Easter Day. This year I have made very few calls, but I always go the rounds at New Year and at Easter. Thanks to the automobile this is not too exhausting. However today I managed to visit only nine homes as, disastrously, they were all at home and all receiving. My first call was to Korsak, where I took Mama, then Saburov, who whetted my appetite with details of the forthcoming chess congress. I stayed for forty minutes at the Meshcherskys, a noisy party was having lunch there, and I felt very much at home with them. Alexey Pavlovich was extremely merry; he leaves today to go abroad and made me play him his favourite 'Battle at Kerzhenets'.[1]

From the Meshcherskys I went on to the Ruzskys where, in contrast, they were on their own and all was quiet. Called on Rausch and thanked him for the gift of the goblet. Nikolay Vasilievich Andreyev was nursing a cough at home. The Konshins were affable, but rather formal. Returned home not at four, as I had planned, but at six, dozed for a while then went out to dinner at Rayevskys and thence to Gessen (without, however, mentioning to the devoutly Orthodox Rayevskys that on Easter Day I was going to a Jewish household). Gessen was entertaining a large and very interesting group of guests: actors from the Moscow Arts Theatre, Stanislavsky,[2] Kachalov[3] and others, Academician Benois,[4] whose acquaintance I was thrilled to make. He is one of the most important pioneers of Russian art abroad, along with Diaghilev and Bakst, and for some reason I have always thought this will be the milieu in which I shall make my career in music. Benois listened to my compositions with great interest, was very complimentary about them, and spoke warmly about how a successful ballet suite could be made from some of my smaller pieces.

---

1 Symphonic picture from Rimsky-Korsakov's opera *The Legend of the Invisible City of Kitezh*.
2 Konstantin Stanislavsky (1863–1938), pioneering actor and director, co-creator with Vladimir Nemirovich-Danchenko of the Moscow Arts Theatre.
3 Vasily Kachalov (1875–1948), the stage name of Vasily Shverubovich, one of the greatest actors of his generation, playing over fifty roles during his time at the Moscow Arts Theatre. He created the roles of Baron Tuzenbakh in Chekhov's *Three Sisters* and the idealistic student Petya Trofimov in *The Cherry Orchard*.
4 Alexander Benois, painter, stage designer and founder with Bakst and Diaghilev of the 'World of Art' group.

7 April

Practised the piano, then went to the Conservatoire to find out what time my chamber music exam would be, but the building was all locked up. Called on Anna Nikolayevna to wish her a Happy Easter and to enquire about her health, but she was not at home to anyone. Would have liked to go for a walk, but my shoe was pinching my foot and I went home instead. Wrote my diary and talked to Sergey Sebryakov, who had called in.

At eight o'clock I went to the opening of the Chess Championship and found myself translated immediately into an enchanted realm, a realm alive with the most unbelievable activity in all three rooms of the Chess Club itself and three more rooms made available by the Assembly Committee. This tournament is a top-level affair, everyone in tailcoats, and here were the masters themselves each surrounded by a crowd of admirers.

Lasker, a little greyer since the 1909 tournament, with his distinctive face, his slight stature and an air of knowing his own worth; Tarrasch – a typically upright German with Kaiser Wilhelm moustaches and an arrogant expression; our own Rubinstein – a coarse, unintelligent-looking face, a touch of the shopkeeper about him, but modest and talented compared to Tarrasch, erratic but dangerous to any opponent; Bernstein, a prosperous-looking man with a handsome, impudent face, shaven head and a colossal nose, dazzling teeth and relentlessly brilliant eyes. Our own gifted Alekhine, with his lawyer's coat and his slightly pinched, slightly disagreeable lawyer's features, self-confident as ever but nevertheless a little subdued by the magnificence of the company. Marshall the American, a typical Yankee, with a touch of Sherlock Holmes about him, ferociously passionate in play but ludicrously taciturn in private life. Yanovsky from Paris, a deserter in his youth from military service and now exceptionally allowed special dispensation to return unmolested for the championship, wearing an exquisitely elegant light grey suit, formerly a famously good-looking breaker of hearts but now in his fifth decade showing his age and wearing gold-rimmed spectacles. The combative vegetarian Nimzowitsch, a typical German student and trouble-maker. Finally two older men, destined to be the victims of all, the portly Gunsberg and, wearing on his face a permanently injured expression, Blackburne, still, despite his seventy-two years, capable of producing original combinations and elegant developments in his conduct of a match. The crowd's favourite, Capablanca, young, elegant, gay and with a constant smile on his handsome face, circulated through the hall laughing and chatting with the easy grace of one who already knows himself to be the victor.[1]

---

1 Emanuel Lasker (1868–1941), Siegbert Tarrasch (1862–1934), Akiba Rubinstein (1882–1961), Osip Bernstein (1882–1962), Alexander Alekhine (1892–1946), Frank Marshall (1877–1944),

Thus it was that I found myself in this irresistibly seductive kingdom, absorbed from the first moment by the forthcoming contest. The speeches began, laying stress on the unprecedented importance of the event with its exceptional galaxy of participants. Journalists from England, Germany, Moscow, Kiev, Vienna, chess masters from Germany, photographers, all added to the splendour of the occasion. The first round begins tomorrow!!!

8 April

Practised the Concerto for an hour and a half, then went to the Conservatoire where I discovered that the chamber music exam is tomorrow. Went to find Bezrodny, but he was not in, so left him a note asking him to come this evening for a rehearsal. Winkler was full of praise for Golubovskaya, describing her as a pianist of great refinement and a serious candidate for the prize. At a quarter to two I was back in my beloved Chess Club. At the barrier erected in front of the playing tables stood a crowd several rows deep (growing eventually to five rows, with many people standing on chairs). To go through the barrier one had to pay a charge of 5 roubles, which I did. At two o'clock the bell went and the masters took their places. I positioned myself at Lasker's table, where old man Blackburne, who had drawn Lasker in the first round, made his first move. Instead of replying, Lasker stood up, strolled indifferently round the room, then returned to the table, moved his pawn and dinged the bell. The great tournament has begun. At the next table Nimzowitsch is playing Capablanca. Capablanca has twice before defeated him, and now plays with a quick, easy elegance. Nimzowitsch cunningly deploys his queen to threaten a pawn, which Capablanca casually sacrifices. General astonishment. In the next room, where a heated discussion of the match is going on, everyone is arguing and shouting, but the consensus is that Capablanca has made a mistake in giving up his pawn, he can gain no advantage from it and even if he can, it is not enough. The ancient Gunsberg develops an obviously prepared but perilous variation of the Evans gambit against Alekhine but fails to gain advantage by it. A murmur in the crowd to the effect that Gunsberg has lost his senses is countered by others claiming that, on the contrary, the move is a subtle one and part of a plan. Alekhine, his ears red, easily beats off the threat. Yanovsky in his magnificent grey suit

---

David Yanovsky (1868–1927), Aron Nimzowitsch (1886–1935), Isidor Gunsberg (1854–1930), Joseph Blackburne (1841–1924), José Raúl Capablanca (1888–1942). The 1914 St Petersburg International Tournament was one of the most eminent gatherings of chess players in the history of the game. It was sponsored in part by Tsar Nicholas II, who inaugurated by ukase the formal title of Grand Master, conferring it for the first time on the five finalists (in order) Lasker, Capablanca, Alekhine, Tarrasch and Marshall, the first three of whom were or became World Champions. The title of Grandmaster is today awarded by the World Chess Federation FIDE.

arrives late to the table to play Bernstein, and from the moment he sits down buries his face in his hands and sits motionless, hunched over the board until the end of the match. Bernstein, in contrast, keeps jumping up, becomes agitated and occasionally shouts at the public not to make so much noise.

All this time the public has been arriving and now fills the whole room. By four o'clock receipts have mounted to 700 roubles, but more and more people keep coming in. Capablanca has now gone on to the attack, and confounding the expectations of all the St Petersburg pundits, has not only won back a pawn from Nimzowitsch but is harrying him mercilessly. Nimzowitsch sits in dismay, hunched over the board, visibly losing his head. Capablanca in complete contrast impresses by the insouciance of his play: getting up all the time to see what is going on in other matches, wandering about the hall laughing. Alekhine has overwhelmed old man Gunsberg and publicly leads an ovation for him, proud of the fact that the first victory in this great tournament has fallen to a player from St Petersburg. Lasker has been playing slowly and reflectively, gradually gaining ascendancy over old Blackburne. The Marshall–Rubinstein game has been a dull one, all Marshall's efforts foundering against the stone fortress of Rubinstein. Even though in the next room D. has maintained his conviction that Marshall has a winning position, this is of no help and the match eventually ends in a draw. Bernstein, smiling, comes up to Saburov and says, 'One can always rely on Yanovsky. As far as I am concerned, he keeps true to himself.' When I ask Saburov what this means, he replies that in the past Yanovsky has always lost to Bernstein. In spite of his attractive exterior there is something not very pleasant about Bernstein, and in my heart I feel sorry for Yanovsky, to whom still clings the seductive aura of his past charm.

At five o'clock I went out, glad to be once more in the fresh air, and went to the 'Vienna' where Kreutzer was waiting for me to dine with him. I am still very keen on the idea of inveigling him into a trip round Europe in the summer. After a good dinner I went home intending to rehearse the *Ballade* with the cellist, but he said that today he was unable to work, however he would be at the Conservatoire at ten o'clock the following morning. Fine, our *Ballade* performance is well under our fingers. In the evening I practised for a while and wrote my diary, feeling rather exhausted, and then spoke to Damskaya on the telephone to tell her about the championship. She was fascinated by Capablanca and wanted to know every detail about him.

9 April

Was in the Conservatoire by ten o'clock although it was not our turn to play until half past two. Bezrodny was not in a good state at all, and we scarcely managed to play the piece through twice. His playing was rather limp, although he promised to pull himself together once we were on the platform. We were rehearsing in the conference hall, next to the Class Inspectors' room, when in burst Yekaterina Nikolayevna[1] and started exclaiming how wonderful the *Ballade* was. I informed her that we were rehearsing and she was disturbing us. She asked if she could stay and listen, at which I lost my temper and closed the score. Flustered, she left the room, saying as she went, 'Well, at least you could let me see the music afterwards.'

'Whatever you like afterwards, but not now, just let us work in peace.'

Today I received my five composer's copies of the Concerto, and of course the first thing I found was two misprints, although not very important ones. I decided to take Tcherepnin's advice and give copies to the professors. So today I handed out copies to Dubasov, Lavrov and Lyapunov. The first two thanked me politely, while on Lyapunov's copy I wrote a long inscription: 'This modest opus submitted to the gracious scrutiny of deeply respected Sergey Mikhailovich in the hope that he will trust to the composer's sincerity and seriousness of purpose in creating sounds that may on first hearing sound peculiar.'

Kolechka Myaskovsky came in after the *Ballade*. In the evening Struve appeared, having now graduated from her General Subjects class, discarded her schoolgirl uniform and put on a white blouse. Since the Easter holiday she seems to have blossomed and become quite the grown-up young lady. We were very pleased to see one another, but had no time to exchange more than a few words. In the *Ballade* my performance went all right, but the cellist was inclined to be tentative and at times lagged behind. I heard that Lyapunov spread out his arms in a gesture of disbelief and Blumenfeld occasionally laughed out loud. The audience greeted and listened to us in complete silence – but then there are never more than twenty or thirty people at a chamber music exam. Still I was a little chagrined, however prepared I may have been for a muted response since, strange as it seems to me, the *Ballade* seems fated not to be understood at first hearing. Our marks were not announced. Mama came to listen, but as she failed to recognize the music of the *Ballade*, which took place at a different point in the programme from that stated, and is so short-sighted she could not see me, she concluded that I had not appeared at all.

In the evening I went to the Chess Club, where the second round was coming to an end. I thought there would be fewer people than yesterday, but this was not the case: all the rooms were full of people with the usual dense throng at the barrier, many standing on chairs. Only two tables were playing; the rest had finished. Capablanca produced a brilliant combination against his countryman Marshall, but the latter succeeded in extricating himself and

---

1 One of the Class Administrators, also known as Inspectors.

the match ended in a draw. Bravo, Mister Marshall, to force a draw yesterday with Rubinstein and today with Capablanca, full marks for holding your own against the favourite. After a fierce, no-holds-barred battle, Nimzowitsch also drew against Lasker. Delighted with this turn of events, he appeared in the evening in a black frockcoat above pale grey sports trousers and a straw-coloured waistcoat – a uniquely glaring lapse of taste! Bernstein took a mere hour and half to destroy Gunsberg, leaving the old man with nothing to do but wander aimlessly round the Club for the rest of the day. Two elegant gentlemen, the veterans Tarrasch and Yanovsky, trudged through a leisurely, uninspiring match, while next to them Alekhine was having to fight for his life to secure a draw with dauntless old Blackburne. He finally managed this, and the crowd applauded while others hushed them so as not to disturb the Tarrasch–Yanovsky game, although nothing could redeem the tedium of its progress. Budarina, a student at the Conservatoire, a lovely girl with whom I had played chess at Yessentuki, came in, stood on a chair and followed the play. In the adjoining room at a large table furnished with paper and ink and newspapers, eight or so journalists were scribbling telegrams, letters and reports for publication not only within Russia but throughout the world.

Wrote to Ziloti today asking him to return my Concerto. He has had it for a month now.

10 April

Received my Concerto and a letter from Ziloti this morning. At first I thought it must be a coincidence, and regretted having written to him yesterday, but it turns out to have been an immediate response. He wrote, not without a touch of malice, that while he was sure I could not possibly be interested in his opinion of my Concerto, for his part he would be interested to know when I was going to 'discover myself'. As a matter of fact, what does interest me is when he is going to discover me. In any case, I spent this morning in a foul mood. In the afternoon I was in the Conservatoire, where I busied myself distributing copies of the Concerto (Steinberg, Blumenfeld, Gabel, Glazunov). On Glazunov's copy I made a grammatical mistake: writing what looked like a gerund for 'from deeply respecting' when it should have been a present participle. I consulted Gabel, who replied, 'Respecting, of course.' Gabel exchanged kisses with me over my presentation to him of the Concerto. Zelikman played very well today (chamber music) and Serafima Kind also turned in a performance of considerable *élan*. I complimented her on her performance, which pleased her inordinately.

I was sitting talking to Damskaya and showing her my Concerto, telling her I intended to play it for my examination performance. At this point I left, but her neighbour on the other side started looking at the score, remarking that he had heard about this composer Prokofiev, that his music was extremely difficult and he found it astonishing that this young man should opt to play this particular concerto for his exam. Damskaya was highly amused, because he obviously had no idea that I, the young man in question, was the composer.

At home I wrote some letters and my diary, and prepared to send the Concerto No. 2 to the RME and the *Ballade* to Jurgenson. Yesterday Myaskovsky argued strongly that I should remove one of the changes I had made – a new sequence of descending chords – and even sent me a letter on the subject today. I bowed to his wishes.

11 April

Today is my twenty-third birthday. Far too many. In fact I don't feel at all like twenty-three, not a day more than twenty. I don't much like celebrating my birthdays and name-days, and am not doing so today. This morning I got a present from Mama: 10 roubles 'to replenish the funds', very timely since I have absolutely no money and it will be at least ten days before I receive any payment for the *Ballade*. Eleonora Damskaya gave me a beautiful gold fountain pen. This was in return for the flowers I gave her for her confirmation. She was given lots of money, and complained that she did not know what to do with it, and now gives me expensive gifts.

Today at the Chess Club the match between Rubinstein and Capablanca was incredibly interesting. I am utterly gripped by the tournament, but it is a bad time for me: I'm either there or at home learning the Concerto, I get extremely tired and today, for example, feel utterly exhausted. At one o'clock I went to the Conservatoire to give copies of the Concerto to Gelever and Kuskova. Found Damskaya, who is agog to see the championship, mainly on account of Capablanca, and took her to the Club. She was naturally a little apprehensive at first going into an unfamiliar milieu, but soon became very interested. Not many women frequent it, but there are perhaps ten who do. I enjoyed pointing out to her various celebrities in the Club, which was full to bursting with onlookers.

We reserved in advance two chairs near the Rubinstein–Capablanca table; the bell went and play began. For the first time I saw signs of nervousness in Capablanca: he was tugging at his eyebrows, grimacing and bent low over the board. He was playing black, and the word in the hall was: 'Pity anyone who has to play black against Rubinstein's queen's pawn opening!' And indeed, it was not long before Capablanca found himself boxed in. Damskaya, who understood nothing of the play, wriggled about all over the place watching Capablanca and asking if he was soon going to win, but I was absorbed in seeing how he was going to disentangle himself from his position. At one point I thought he was skilfully turning the tables, but just then I heard someone behind me opine that he was going to go down a pawn. I concluded this must be a sacrifice, but the other man insisted Capablanca was being irresponsible and missing an opportunity. He proved correct, because Capablanca not only lost a pawn but found himself in a horrible position. With some difficulty I pushed my way into the next room where Yanovsky, who was not playing today, was expounding Capablanca's game, surrounded by a ring of spectators. He thought that whatever Capablanca did he would lose the game, and soon too. I went to look at another match, in which Alekhine and Nimzowitsch, having fallen out with one another, were playing in a cold, unfriendly fashion. Tarrasch, his ears red and an anxious expression on his face (yesterday he lost to Yanovsky) was pressing Gunsberg hard. Marshall was having an excellent game against Lasker, but Bernstein was getting into difficulties against Blackburne and continually shouted at the public, 'Gentlemen! Please keep quiet! It's impossible to play!' complaining angrily to his neighbour, 'They carry on as if they were in a barn, not at a chess club!' What he meant by 'a barn', I have no idea. But the spectators were indeed buzzing like a beehive. Even the other side of the barrier it was crowded and hot. An artist was sketching the contestants.

Eleonora asked me to take her out to the foyer; she was tired and had to hurry off somewhere. Meanwhile Capablanca was holding on with no thought of conceding. I felt sorry for him and in the next room tried to come up with variations that might be to his advantage. He was playing fairly quickly and had plenty of time in hand. Half an hour before the interval he got up from the table and declared that he would stop playing but his move would be recorded at six o'clock. Sosnitsky[1] told me that Capablanca had been boozing until five in the morning at the 'Aquarium', whither he had been dragged by a woman friend who would not leave him alone. Today he was suffering from a bad head and was playing as if his sole aim was to avoid defeat. I was alarmed on his behalf.

Now the crowd was concentrated on the Marshall–Lasker board; both were short of time and the situation was critical. Their anxiety communicated itself to the public thronging round their table, casting worried glances now at the board and now at the clock. But both players succeeded in making their moves, at which the bell went and it was the interval.

Tired, I emerged into the fresh air and went home, lay down and dozed. The Rayevskys came at half past seven to dine. It is after all my birthday. After dinner I put on my tails for an evening at the Meshcherskys, but before

---

1 Vice-President of the St Petersburg Chess Society.

that I went back into the Chess Club where the first person I saw was Rubinstein in conversation with someone and laughing. He must be celebrating having beaten Capablanca, I thought in dismay, and went over to the board on which the match results were displayed. But to my great astonishment and joy I saw ½ – a draw! Hooray, to come back from such a position against Rubinstein and force a draw, this was pure genius. Now I had no doubt that, provided his lady friend did not turn his head too much, he was bound to take the first prize. The other match also ended in a draw; only old man Gunsberg, as usual, had lost his game. There was some disappointment in the Club at so many draws: the championship was in danger of losing excitement. Lasker and Bernstein, surrounded by a huge crowd, were showing each other their matches. Mme Lasker arrived to summon her husband home: a dumpy woman with a rather ordinary face.

I went to the Meshcherskys, where although it was not a grand party and not many people were there, there was dancing. I was still under the spell of the tournament, and if I said anything to anybody it was on the subject of chess. Nina asked me to dance, but I declined. I did meet a beautiful friend of Nina, Mme Filippieva, with whom Nina is going to stay for the month of May. I danced with her, then we talked by ourselves in the study, and sat next to one another at dinner. Went home at three o'clock, my head full of the most pleasant thoughts of the plump and beautiful Natalya Nikolayevna Filippieva.

12 April

Slept until twelve, then practised the piano until half past two, and at three came into the Conservatoire to rehearse with Dranishnikov. Gabel informed me that Tcherepnin was in Monte Carlo and would be returning the day after tomorrow.

'I suppose he'll have lost all his money there?' I asked Gabel, with a laugh.
'I expect so,' he replied.

Glazunov thanked me very nicely for the Concerto. I asked him what he had thought of the *Ballade*. He avoided saying anything directly, but talked about the *pizzicato* passage, perhaps it ought to be transposed an octave higher so that it would be better heard? Everyone seems to be fixated on the *pizzicato*.

Dranishnikov does not yet know his part but is shaping up well and gives me no cause for concern. The Concerto is coming together well and shows every sign of producing a stunningly brilliant effect, more than enough for the purpose. We rehearse in the conference hall. Olga Borisovna[1] comes in; I apologize for being noisy neighbours and say we will go elsewhere. But she

---

1 One of the Class Inspectors.

says it's not that at all, but could she have a word with me? Somewhat surprised I follow her out, and she asks if I do not think that perhaps I might be damaging my chances by choosing my Concerto as my exam piece? My first reaction was that this could be a piece of politicking subtly intended to eliminate my Concerto from the lists, but it soon becomes clear that the conversation is entirely well intentioned and is aimed at helping me win the prize. Olga Borisovna's judgement is that however talented the Concerto may be as a composition, it is too innovative a work for the ears of our professors to accept, they will try and judge the music rather than the performance, and will give the prize to another. Could I not choose another concerto, Liszt, or Tchaikovsky, and start work on it now?

I thanked her for her interest but objected that there was now not enough time to perfect, for example, the Tchaikovsky concerto, and I was not willing to play anything that was not fully prepared. I could not help wondering what could possibly have brought about this sudden concern for my welfare? After all, my relations with the Class Inspectors have hitherto hardly been distinguished by a spirit of cordiality and accommodation. We ended up by agreeing that I should ask Glazunov to listen to the Concerto and give his opinion. At that very moment by chance Glazunov hove into view, and the three of us discussed the matter. Glazunov's opinion was that the Tchaikovsky and Rachmaninov concertos had been played to death, but it would certainly be a good idea to acquaint some of the professors with my Concerto. He therefore suggested I arrange to play it in the Small Hall, for instance next Tuesday at half past twelve, when such professors as would be in the Conservatoire that day could come and hear it. Glazunov added more praise for the way I had played my recital programme, singling out the sound of my *Tannhäuser*. Bravo! It is clear that I am being taken seriously, and after spending the last few days mainly in the company of Golubovskaya, Zelikman and their adherents, who are so confident of their respective candidates' victory that they have made me lose confidence in gaining it myself, I begin once again to scent the prize!

After dinner I went to N.M. to play his Symphony No. 1 to Aslanov in a four-hand version. It's a splendid work; I love the tempo of the first movement, and the Finale is just marvellous (except for the second subject): exhilarating, high-spirited and bright. Aslanov also liked the symphony and will perform it on 20 May in Pavlovsk. This date is particularly good for me, because I will be in St Petersburg at that time and it will be the first time I shall have been able to hear a performance of an orchestral work by N.M. He is very upset at Ziloti's attitude towards me and has written a splendidly venomous article in *Muzyka*, poking fun at Ziloti in the subtlest and most malicious way. Returned home and looked through the Concerto No. 2 preparatory to sending it to the RME.

13 April

On Tuesday, therefore, I face what amounts to an exam. I must give a good account of the Concerto, so have settled down to intensive work on it. I generally feel tired when I wake up in the morning, with pains in my arms and legs, the result of the chess championship and the exam coming at the same time. Not for a long time have I been subjected to such a maelstrom of conflicting demands: whenever I am at the piano, whether in the Conservatoire or at home, I am immersed in my Concerto and the exam performance; but once I get inside the Chess Club, events there absorb me to such an extent that I forget everything else and the exam pales into insignificance besides the struggle of the chess titans.

I nevertheless practised until three o'clock and then went to the Club to watch the Lasker–Rubinstein match, getting there when the game was at its apogee. As usual there was a dense crowd wreathed in clouds of tobacco smoke, and the atmosphere was distinctly stuffy. *New Times* has published a long article complaining about the unsatisfactory playing conditions: the noise, the crowds and the heat. The organizers have been upset by the article and taken it to heart, so that they are now looking for ways to put right the defects in their arrangements. As a first step they have put up large wallboards on which all the moves are displayed instantly, so the public no longer has to jam up so close to the barrier to see what is going on and can follow all the matches from any part of the hall. It also means that all games are fully notated on the boards, each move being added as it takes place.

I arrived about four o'clock, by which time both players had made about fifteen moves. I wanted first to acquaint myself with the progress of the matches, and quickly writing the moves down on a piece of paper sat down at a chessboard and studied them. Then I joined the crowd at the table in the next room that was discussing Lasker–Rubinstein. It was a match of positions, cautious and dry, and had it not been between two such forces it would frankly not have been of great interest. But this was the very Rubinstein who five years before had defeated Lasker, and so we were all fascinated by the game. People were predicting a draw. Elsewhere another game was proceeding without attracting much attention. There was no Capablanca match today, so he was not present to enliven the proceedings. Tarrasch was comprehensively routing Blackburne, while Yanovsky, elegantly concealing his face behind bronzed hands with immaculately shaped nails, snow-white cuffs and handkerchief tucked into his sleeve, was taking his time against Gunsberg. Bernstein and Nimzowitsch were locked in a fierce struggle, while Alekhine, to the joy of the patriots present, defeated Marshall. When six o'clock came and the interval, I went home and spent the evening correcting the Second Concerto to send it to the RME.

14 April

Yesterday evening I had a headache, but this morning I felt fresh and well, and after an hour's practice went to the Conservatoire to rehearse with Dranishnikov. When Olga Borisovna saw me she said, 'Well, how is our hero, all our hopes rest on you (!!).' Just imagine! Who would have thought that I could become a hero to the Class Inspectors! I was excited to see Struve, but she has an exam of some kind today and went off to take it. Not wanting to hold her back I contented myself with wishing her luck. Nearonova called across to me that she was sure I was going to win the grand piano. Then she asked me if I was going to give lessons at the Music Studio. 'What are you talking about?' I asked.

'Well, I have a friend who is dying to be in your class!'

I: 'Well, in that case, do please find out from your friend what and where this studio is, and what Prokofiev's class is. I know absolutely nothing about it.'

Nearonova promised to investigate and pass on the result of her researches.

Rehearsing with Dranishnikov, the Concerto went with a swing. When we got to the end he took some time to recover, and he said that no one with a weak heart should contemplate accompanying it. At home I caught up on my neglected diary (I should like to write more, but there's no time), worked out some chess moves for the correspondence tournament, which I find has a good effect on me: I try to work out the positions in my head and so far am playing well in all of the games I am involved in), and put the finishing touches to the Concerto. Nina Meshcherskaya telephoned to ask when I would be coming to visit them, and said that they would be spending the summer at Kislovodsk – would I like to come? Unfortunately I would not be able to stay with them because the dacha they are taking is too small, but since I am a wealthy man (!) I could rent a room in a neighbouring house. This made me smile.

15 April

Today is a 'big day', as Max would have said. First, I have to perform the Concerto in front of the professors, and second, it is the day of the Capablanca–Lasker match. At noon I was in the Conservatoire and went in to see Olga Borisovna. She greeted me most affectionately and told me that in half an hour's time the professors would be arriving in quite large numbers. And indeed, one by one the professors began to appear in the corridor, so that by the time Gabel and Glazunov turned up there were more than twenty, virtually the entire piano faculty. We were to perform in the Small Hall, so it was to all intents and purposes an exam. I was not excessively nervous, but Dranishnikov was in a complete state of funk. Glazunov seated himself, many of the professors opened the scores they had brought, and I played the Concerto. Dranishnikov accompanied well, and I think I did well too.

When we had finished, I stepped down from the platform. Some teachers nodded encouragingly, others buried themselves in the score, yet others went on talking among themselves. I went up to Glazunov, who asked us to take a short break and then play it again. I went out to have a talk to Dranishnikov, who was going into raptures over the Concerto, drank a glass of milk, and we went back into the hall. We played it through again, after which Glazunov said that they would ask us to retire so that they could discuss the work in private. Quite a lot of students had also been in the hall to listen to the performance, and they were also asked to leave. This resulted in a throng waiting outside the door for the result, but I went upstairs to Olga Borisovna, who quizzed me anxiously on what had occurred. I could not, of course, tell her anything definite. But it was clear that this audition of my Concerto had assumed the character of an important event. All the piano students of those professors who were in the Small Hall were wandering about the Conservatoire talking about the Concerto. Nikolskaya fluttered round me the whole time, fixing her brilliant eyes on me.

At last an attendant came up and said that I was wanted by the Director in the Small Hall. The crowd of curious onlookers still waiting by the door made way for me, and I went in. The whole committee was standing in a group, Glazunov at their head. As I approached, he said, 'This is what I have to say to you, Sergey Sergeyevich – that is your name and patronymic, is it not? We have all listened to your Concerto and come to a decision that it is not in principle an appropriate work for you to perform for your examination, since it is a difficult and unsuitable work on which to judge you as a performer. However, in view of the fact that you will not now have time to prepare an alternative concerto, the committee recommends that you perform the *Tannhäuser* transcription from your recital programme, and following that your Concerto. Naturally you may take a break in between. Does this arrangement suit you?'

I replied, 'Yes, I agree', and thanking the Director and the committee for the great courtesy and consideration they had shown me, I bowed and quickly left the room.

This is absolutely splendid – from my point of view the best possible decision the committee could have arrived at! *Tannhäuser* followed by the Concerto – this is running with the hare and hunting with the hounds.[1] The main thing is, I no longer have to be nervous about my performance in the

---

1   Literally: 'The wolves are satisfied and the sheep intact.'

exam, since I shall be presenting pieces I have already played in public. Some of the professors, meeting me as they left the Small Hall, offered me their congratulations, others politely shook my hand, others were too embarrassed to say anything and could not wait to get away. But I felt myself a hero, and in a state of euphoria made my way to the Chess Club, where the Capablanca–Lasker game had already started.

The champions were sitting at the same table as for the Capablanca–Rubinstein battle, with the usual crowd around them although there were fewer people in the Club than there had been at Easter. The working week had begun: some people were studying, others at work. An electric ozonizer was humming away in a corner, and the atmosphere was generally much cleaner than it had been. After I had familiarized myself with the progress of the Capablanca–Lasker game and had a quick look at the other boards, I went into the adjoining room where Capablanca–Lasker was being dissected and discussed. Yesterday Lasker had crushed Rubinstein, and this victory had caused a real sensation. Everyone now felt that Lasker would be sure to cut Capablanca down to size, but my bets were firmly on Capablanca. His playing is so crammed full of talent that if only he will make the effort he must surely prevail over Lasker.

Lasker was developing a king's pawn opening, and his adherents were jubilant that he was planning a whirlwind assault on the upstart Capablanca. Capablanca pondered for a long time, but eventually turned Lasker's blithe manoeuvre to his advantage and launched a powerful attack of his own. I sat in the next room amid a large group of chess players poring over every move as it was instantly communicated from the field of battle, discussing it from every possible angle, often generating great heat in the process. Capablanca was choosing moves for caution, often not the most startlingly interesting of ploys, but by five o'clock it was clear that Lasker was under attack and having to defend himself. The position was more or less equal as it moved into the endgame. I went back into the hall, where all the boards were showing signs of slaughter: Tarrasch, after working out a lengthy combination, captured Nimzowitsch's pawns after courageously sacrificing his bishops. I watched the Bernstein–Marshall board descending into a state of incomprehensible complexity, with virtually every piece exposed to attack; this sent me into a state of pure ecstasy. But it could not last long: Bernstein lost his queen, smiled guiltily and started to read some letters he had with him. At this point a rumour ran round the hall that Rubinstein had conceded to Alekhine. Sensation. Alekhine, pale and drawn with tiredness, got up from the board. For some reason I find him unsympathetic.

At six o'clock, the interval bell. Tarrasch, having pinned Nimzowitsch's king in the middle of the board, moves inexorably to checkmate him. A truly brilliant mate: Tarrasch is surrounded by admirers congratulating him, people shaking his hand, the applause muted only by the need to avoid disturbing the other players. Tarrasch beams and bows in all directions. Nimzowitsch, a disgruntled expression on his face, rolls up his notes, muttering in fractured German, 'People walking back and forth the whole time, Lasker–Capablanca, Capablanca–Lasker! A man cannot think...'

Went home, and in the evening to the Sokol. I haven't been there for two weeks and have missed it. Yesterday I received the proof copy of my 'March', which they are having published, and having corrected it, gave it back today. I corrected not only the music but the text, putting in the elisions and punctuation marks.

16 April

I dug out *Tannhäuser* and started to prepare it. After my recital programme I had put all the music away in a cupboard saying I would never play any of it again. But fate had decreed otherwise. In any case, I now took pleasure in buckling down to *Tannhäuser*, going through every bar with great care and playing it all at slow tempo, not glossing over any of the technical difficulties. It did not take me long to feel confident that it would go as well as, perhaps even better than, the last time.

At around three o'clock I went into the Conservatoire, where an instrumental concert had already started, but it was dull and hardly anyone was there. Dranishnikov was interested to hear my tales from the chess championship. The Meshcherskys are going to spend the summer in Kislovodsk; in the evening Oleg and I went to play bridge with them. *En route* I went in to the Chess Club, but it's not so interesting to watch the end of a match if one has not seen the beginning. Rubinstein was pressing Bernstein while Yanovsky was deeply entangled with Nimzowitsch. I asked someone to show the Capablanca game in which he had so brilliantly destroyed Alekhine, and was overjoyed at the success of my idol.

I then went to the Meshcherskys; Vera Nikolayevna was not at home when I arrived, but Nina was carrying on a flirtatious telephone conversation with some young man or other. We all fell on her in a group, and during the ensuing altercation the telephone got smashed and pulled out from the wall, and furniture legs were broken. Then we played bridge, Nina and I as usual playing the same hand.

17 April

Today I continued practising *Tannhäuser* interspersed with spells on the Concerto. But I can see that the centre of gravity lies in *Tannhäuser* and that is where I have to concentrate my efforts. The Concerto is going pretty well as it is, and none of the judges will be in a position to evaluate a nuanced performance of great refinement.

Tired, I walked to the Chess Club and followed my usual practice of informing myself from the wall boards of the progress of the matches. Hardly had I taken up my position near the Capablanca–Bernstein board when the latter launched a brilliant combination and, attacking all over the board, had his terrifying opponent on the run. Whatever you may say Bernstein is still a force to be reckoned with, and there are not many who can stand up to him. Next door Marshall sacrificed a piece to Yanovsky. Alekhine had put Lasker in a dire predicament. I went up to Znosko-Borovsky: 'See what happens when you clean up the air and improve the playing conditions – you end up with fifty sacrifices a day!'

Znosko laughed. 'I think we've got too much oxygen!'

The championship is definitely shedding its serious character. People are happy and rubbing their hands with glee.

Interval time draws near. Alekhine has two minutes left to complete eight moves. He looks nervously at the clock and shakes his head demonstratively. I move away from his board and at that moment hear that he has forced a draw by putting his opponent in permanent check. People congratulate him and wring his hand. Pale and limp, he leaves the table. Capablanca has chased Bernstein's king to the edge of the board and mated him in a cunning knight–bishop combination. Whispered congratulations all around and murmurs of 'genius!' At six o'clock I went home.

In the evening I played through the Second Sonata for tomorrow's performance, spoke on the telephone to Damskaya, and worked out my correspondence tournament moves.

18 April

Starting at eleven I practised *Tannhäuser*, then in the afternoon strolled along to the exam performances in the Conservatoire. Had a postcard from Tcherepnin in Monto Carlo replying to my Easter greetings. I much appreciate his attentions to me. At the exam met Damskaya and Budarina (who has been at the Chess Club every day of the championship) and sat with them. However, when I got home bad news awaited me: first, Jurgenson has written declining the *Ballade* (too many other publications in the queue); and second, Myaskovsky relayed to me over the telephone what he had heard from Gabel, that I had lost any chance I might have had of winning the piano by demonstrating my Concerto to the assembled professors. Half the committee completely rejected both the Concerto and me, and the other half was split down the middle, some accepting the Concerto and others not caring about it one way or the other. I could thus count on only a quarter of the votes, and clearly it would have been a better option to have chosen another concerto. But when I had sought his advice, Myaskovsky himself had said I should play my own work?! In any event it was hardly tactful of him to tell me this just now, it was like saying to a consumptive: 'You think you are getting better? Not at all, you'll be dead in three days.'

Myaskovsky's words discouraged me deeply and I spent all evening in a gloomy frame of mind. I played through the Sonata and set off for the 'Evening of Contemporary Music' where Myaskovsky's Cello Sonata was performed (not very excitingly, rather slow and boring). Medem played some of his trivial little pieces. I asked him what he thought of my chances, but his replies, while couched in complimentary terms, were evasive, and he added, 'What do you need a piano for, anyhow?' This similarly struck me as a bad omen. Mme Winkler, whose temperament is to be friendly to all, said she was convinced I would win the prize. Shteiman, whom I met at the 'Evening', is making his debut at the Mariinsky. He has met Coates[1] and spoken to him about my *Maddalena*.

Coates apparently showed interest, and according to Shteiman it could go either way – either impossibly difficult to achieve, or ridiculously easy. Coates is busy composing an opera himself – so why could *Maddalena* not be done as a double-bill alongside it? I played my Sonata, thinking the while about other things: the exam, and Jurgenson. All the same, it was not bad, and had its usual success. As an encore I played my Prelude.

Before the start of the concert, Karatygin made a speech about new directions in music, giving me his usual favourable mention. After the concert I had a word with him about publishers, asking what he thought of Jurgenson in St Petersburg, which is a small press independent of the Moscow one. Karatygin thought this would not be the right answer, preferring Bessel, to whom he will recommend the *Ballade* since his, Karatygin's, opinions carry some weight with him. I told him that I would not consider a fee of less than 200 roubles.

19 April

Woke up still affected by the previous day's depressing conversations about my chances of winning the piano. I was overcome by complete apathy, lost all desire to practise, and wasted time until noon. On top of that I am badly in need of money, and the combination of having the *Ballade* rejected with the failure to win any prizes will reduce my resources to zero. At noon I sat down at the piano and played *Tannhäuser*, which went well enough to restore my flagging spirits. Some tempi are still a bit wayward, but they will come back. Decided to give the Chess Club a miss today, in order not to be distracted. However, wanting a break from working, I went out, taking with me

---

1 Albert Coates (1882–1953), English conductor born in Russia, conducted at the Mariinsky from 1910, Principal Conductor 1914–19. Subsequent international renown in London (Covent Garden; London Symphony Orchestra Principal Conductor), USA and South Africa.

the Sonata No. 2, the 'Fairy Tale' and my opera to Shteiman, who has agreed to send these works abroad to Coates in order that he should get to know them.

Going into the Conservatoire I ran into Tcherepnin, with whom I had an unexpectedly joyful and affectionate reunion. The sun has burned him as brown as an Arab from going out without a hat, and altogether he seemed to be in excellent form. We talked about my Concerto and the exam; he definitely wants to include the Concerto in the Conservatoire's Graduation Concert. To all the doubts I have been a prey to he responded by simply saying, 'Pay no attention to any of that, just go out and play well.' One way and another he restored to me, if not my confidence, at least my energy, and we agreed that on Monday Dranishnikov and I should play the Concerto through to him. He is someone on whom I can always rely for useful comments. I have not yet told him that he is the dedicatee of the work. Last night I dreamt of Zakharov: a bad omen, I won't win the prize.

20 April

Practised *Tannhäuser* and, briefly, the Concerto, and at two o'clock went to the Conservatoire to rehearse with Dranishnikov. I had expected that as it was a holiday the building would be deserted, but I encountered almost all my co-competitors there, practising and taking advantage of the empty halls. Glazunov was also in evidence; people continually went up to him and asked him to listen to them; he assented with exemplary grace and patience to all such requests.

Dranishnikov brought along his sister, a very nice girl, and we started the play-through. It went all right. Then Golubovskaya, Kind and I talked to Glazunov about whether we could get another instrument from Becker, seeing that the one we have is already more or less in pieces. It is interesting that all the serious contestants are talking to one another without a hint of hostility, not as enemies but as partners in a common, difficult, task. The only one to hold himself a little aloof is Zelikman, evidently confident of victory. The others, the 'ordinary' graduands, eye us with a measure of respect, and we told each other how envious we were of them: all they had to do was play well, whereas we were under compulsion to demonstrate our superiority over everyone else! The teachers of the various candidates could not hide their anxiety about their students, sometimes to the extent of passing snide comments on their rivals. I was the only one whose teacher was not present, and so was able to keep myself to myself in the company of the faithful Dranishnikov.

Golubovskaya and I went off together to Becker; I wanted No. 28002, my favourite, the one on which I had played at the Dobychina[1] exhibition.

[1] Nadezhda Dobychina (1884–1949) was a gallery owner, artist representative and organizer of

Golubovskaya also liked this instrument, and they promised to supply it. Golubovskaya and I get on famously well together, and after leaving Becker I took her along to the Chess Club. Just before we got there we saw Yanovsky hurrying past; disappointed that his match with Capablanca had already finished and slightly concerned as to the outcome (since Capablanca had lost to Yanovsky once before) we went in. Once inside the buzz of excitement had reached a new level: 'Capablanca is a phenomenon! Thirty-two moves and there was literally nothing left of Yanovsky.' Meanwhile the other matches were going on all around. Alekhine was mounting a whirlwind attack on Bernstein but he, flushed with yesterday's win over Lasker, was stoutly resisting the fiery lawyer's depredations. Lasker, to my surprise and delight, was having a very bad game against Tarrasch. Rubinstein was in the process of crushing Gunsberg, while Marshall was tussling wearily with Blackburne. Golubovskaya hung over the Lasker–Tarrasch conflict, while I noted down the particulars of the Capablanca–Yanovsky game and took it to a board to study it. Everyone now believes that the first prize is safely in the hands of Capablanca, but this is after all what I have been saying since the first round of the championship. At six o'clock the bell went; Bernstein still has half a minute in which to make two moves. Saburov loudly begins, 'Gentlemen! The Committee ...'

'Don't interrupt the play!' shouts Bernstein, and Saburov stops in mid-sentence, to general amusement. Bernstein finishes his moves and, as he passes Saburov, ticks him off crossly. Saburov, slightly disconcerted but trying not to show it, continues his announcement that tomorrow there will be no play.

In the evening I relaxed, doing nothing in particular and not practising.

21 April

At two o'clock Tcherepnin, Dranishnikov and I assembled in the Conservatoire. Dranishnikov and I settled ourselves at the pianos, while Tcherepnin sat opposite and looked at the score of the Concerto. He said in astonishment, 'Sergey Sergeyevich, I had no idea the Concerto is dedicated to me! My most grateful thanks!'

Dranishnikov and I then played it, Tcherepnin stopping us only at places where the music itself pauses. My expectation of helpful observations from him was not disappointed: he said a good deal more even than I had expected. Most of it was directed at Dranishnikov, but some to me, and some

---

exhibitions, musical and literary evenings. The Dobychina agency existed from 1911 until 1929 as an influential and well-informed dealer of important pictures by artists such as Marc Chagall.

to both of us concerning our ensemble. In short, his comments undoubtedly improved our performance. I thanked him, and he promised to come tomorrow in view of his particular interest. I went into the Small Hall where the graduating pianists were giving their final exam performances, many of them very good, some Yesipova students, almost 'tomorrow's standard'. The audience was large, a full house. Before playing to Tcherepnin I had looked in on the Small Hall, but at that time it had been the interval and the audience was outside in the foyer. As soon as I entered people started noticing me, looking at me and whispering. I am definitely the star turn of tomorrow! Among the crowd I noticed Lida and Zoya,[1] who had come to hear Elfrieda Hansen. Now the Tcherepnin play-through was over, I arrived right in the middle of the Yesipova class performances. Tietz played extremely well; Hansen, Berlin and Tseitlin decently, but not spectacularly. Once again, all eyes were on me. The sensation was at the same time agreeable and disagreeable, since I had so many doubts about tomorrow's outcome. Returning home I hardly practised, looking instead through Tcherepnin's notes. Golubovskaya telephoned, and we exchanged confidences about our respective states of mind. Some days ago I had suggested to her that to take our mind off our worries we should play a telephone chess match on the eve of the exam, but now she said she preferred to work on her concerto. We decided instead to play our 'historic chess game' tomorrow, when the competition is over but while the judges are out considering their verdict. It will certainly be a piquant context for a chess game. Before going to bed I went for a walk. It was a wonderful evening, and the moon shone brightly. That dirty old stream, the Fontanka, rippled and gleamed silver in the moonlight and looked almost beautiful. I wanted to get on a boat and sail away.

22 April

I cannot say that my state of mind during the morning was of the best, dominated by chaotic misgivings over the outcome of the competition, afraid that all this work and striving would come to naught. I played through the Concerto and *Tannhäuser*, and was satisfied with both of them. I was nervous, but not in a state of desperate anxiety. I made up my mind that I was not going to give up for anybody, that a competition is a competition and I would do my level best to play well, forgetting about the audience and the contest all the time I was playing and concentrating solely on the music. That would be my main task. Mama and my relations went to the hall earlier, to hear the start of the competition, and I remained at home alone. I prefer to be alone before I have to perform. But at that moment a workman arrived to polish the floor,

---

[1] Karneyeva.

and in any case I could not sit and relax, so at two o'clock I left the house.

It was too early to go to the Conservatoire as I would not in any event be performing before four o'clock, so finding myself at the Fontanka I got on a boat and sailed off, feeling a twinge of pleasure as I did so. When the steamer arrived at its terminus, at the Kalinkin Bridge, I disembarked on the bank and went on to Peterhof Prospect. Exactly a year ago Boris Zakharov had set off from this very street to go to the contest, proudly hoping for victory. What involuntary promptings had made me come to the same spot today? Did it mean that I also would fail in my bid for the prize? The area was a working-class one, all dusty and dirty; I turned into a little square but it was no better there. There was no green anywhere; only ragged boys and women rummaging in the dirt. One of the less distinguished teachers in the Conservatoire, Puzyrevsky, walked past casting a puzzled, sidelong glance at me. I boarded the steamer again, returned to where I had come from, and then walked from the Fontanka to the Conservatoire, assuming a cold, business-like manner.

In the Conservatoire all was quiet; everyone was at the performance, filling the Small Hall to overflowing, the only exception being those without tickets whom the attendants would not allow in. I went to the artists' room, where I found Malinskaya, another Yesipova student, with Poznyakovskaya. Poznyakovskaya, deputizing for Anna Nikolayevna, was her accompanist. Malinskaya and I have never got on particularly well, and now I asked her to go out and leave me on my own before my performance, a request with which she and Poznyakovskaya, without uttering a word of objection, complied. For the honour of the class, none would gainsay me today.

Altogether there were seven contestants: (1) Kherson, Ossovskaya's student, amounting to precisely zero; (2) Kind, a substantial pianist and a very nice girl, who played radiantly today and produced a great effect by breaking one of the thick lower strings; (3) the student Galperin, who played not badly but without much refinement. Then there were the real contestants: (4) Golubovskaya. When I arrived she had just finished. Word was that she had been excellent. (5) Zelikman, currently on stage. After him would be (6) me with *Tannhäuser*; then (7) Malinskaya, who stood no chance at all, and last of all my second appearance playing my Concerto. This was the first time in the history of the Conservatoire that anyone had made a double appearance at the competition, and it provoked much animated debate. And so, there I was alone in the artists' room. From the Small Hall floated in snatches of rolling thunder from the Liszt concerto, being played, so it seemed to me, as brilliantly as one would expect by Zelikman. The Liszt score lay on the table, and to kill time I leafed through the pages and from the passages I could hear followed the progress of the work.

The final page was drowned by applause in the hall. Then a noise erupted in the corridor separating the artists' room from the hall and there was the sound of people coming out: Zelikman had finished. I opened the door and, seeing Zelikman, thrust out my hand.

'Congratulations, it sounded wonderful, as far as I could hear from in here.'

The response was an outburst of despair. I concluded this must be from an excess of self-criticism and anxiety about the outcome of the contest. The corridor was filled with people who had come running out of the hall. This annoyed me, since there was nowhere I could go to compose myself before going on stage. Khariton came up to me and said, 'I congratulate you!'

'What on?'

'Your main rival is out of the running.'

'?'

'Zelikman came to grief in five places, got lost and smudged the whole of the end of the concerto.'

This information was ringing in my ears as I stepped out on to the platform, but I cannot say whether the effect on me was good or a bad. The bad side was that my chances of success were now greater, and correspondingly so the need for me to play extra well, in which case the piano would be mine. There was applause when I came on stage, and then a long-drawn-out noisy shuffling in the audience. I sat and waited for it to die down in order to be able to begin *pianissimo*. For some days I had been turning over in my mind whether to begin the piece *piano e cantabile*, as Liszt marks it, or *pianissimo* and almost inaudible, as of the chorus of pilgrims heard from afar in the opera. Resolved on the latter, I began very quietly, and heard later that the opening of *Tannhäuser* had been judged the best playing in the whole piece. There followed the bacchanale, during which I began to realize that my hands were tiring fast. The keys were stiff and heavy, and this was that lovely Becker No. 28002, which I had so much wanted and was so delighted when they agreed to supply it especially for the performance! Now I felt I was about to collapse, and all my efforts were concentrated on keeping going until the end while maintaining as much brilliance as I could. The brilliance I did manage, but some of it was rather coarse-grained. My hands were shattered with fatigue. There was loud applause from the audience, mixed with catcalls from someone or other, presumably a Zelikman or Golubovskaya supporter. Tcherepnin, Dranishnikov and Shtember all came back to the artists' room, the first two cordially praising the performance, the last saying that it had been good, but not as good as in the recital programme, after which he departed to Tula. To escape from the mass of people crowding into the artists' room and its environs because of the ten-minute interval, I took Dranishnikov by the hand and we went into a faraway classroom to have a last look at the Concerto and run through some effects I had thought up. On the way I ran into Golubovskaya and asked her advice on how to rest the hands most effectively: is it better to keep the arms high up or low down? My hands were not only tired, they hurt, and I was afraid they would not recover in time for the Concerto.

'Keep them up, of course, let the blood drain from them,' said Bushen and Golubovskaya. Someone else suggested plunging them in hot water, but this was an experiment I was afraid to try. I asked Golubovskaya how she was feeling after her performance, and she replied that she felt all right, although there had been a good many things that had not satisfied her. I went off with Dranishnikov and we looked through the Concerto one more time. Dranishnikov was ecstatic about my performance of *Tannhäuser* and said that Zelikman had suffered an irretrievable reverse. I replied, dubiously, 'If that really is the case, then things aren't looking so bad . . .'

'No, pretty good in fact!' said Dranishnikov.

This gave me my first gleam of confidence in victory. Malinskaya finished, and now it was our turn. Half an hour had elapsed since I had got to the end of *Tannhäuser*, and my hands had still not completely recovered. Walking on to the stage, I saw that many of the professors (there was an army of about thirty of them sitting there) were turning over the pages of the copies of my Concerto that I had been distributing during the week.

The Concerto went splendidly. I was not at all nervous, since I had already performed it in public several times. Dranishnikov's accompaniment was beyond praise: now thundering like a real orchestra, now dropping down to a ravishing *sotto voce*, at all times following the soloist as only someone who sincerely understands and loves this work could do. My basic performance schema – tender restraint for the Andante and unrestrained ferment everywhere else – was strictly adhered to. Overall the performance achieved a rare success, and when it finished there was a terrific uproar with applause and booing, just as there had been after my performance of the Second Concerto in Pavlovsk last summer. My exam was over.

Everywhere masses of people and unimaginable excitement. Many of the professors congratulated me on a 'magnificent' performance. I was encircled by Myaskovsky, Karatygin, lots of other musicians, the Rayevskys and my other relations; for the present the atmosphere was one of triumph. Gradually the crowd thinned, the professors retired one by one into the conference room. Some of the audience went home, but many of them waited outside the door of the conference room to hear the result.

I now proposed to Golubovskaya that we begin our 'historic' game, and took out my pocket chess set. Golubovskaya agreed. Bushen, Shandarovskaya and Golubovskaya's mother also stood round hindering our play – I have evidently fallen into a Golubovskaya camp, that is to say opposed to me, since it is now clear that she and I are the main contenders for the prize, Zelikman having come to grief in the middle of his performance and never recovering enough subsequently to play well. However word is that the judges will not hold his mistakes against him, the more so as this was primarily the fault of Nikolayev, who from a desire to show off was accompanying by heart and apparently was the first to go off the rails.

I let Golubovskaya take white, and the game started. Gradually we succeeded in concentrating on it, and the 'distracting element' evaporated into the conference hall, leaving us undisturbed. Naturally, we could not entirely prevent our preoccupations from interposing themselves every now and again, and at such times the game could appear irrelevant. Sometimes we would catch a sound coming from the committee room and strain our ears to listen, but as time went on the game absorbed us completely and forced us to concentrate all our thoughts on it. I said, 'Don't forget the stakes we're playing for: the piano. If the loser of the game is the winner of the piano, he or she must give the piano to the winner of the game.'

Golubovskaya laughed. 'Agreed!'

The game went on for quite some while. From the direction of the conference hall came a murmuring from the waiting crowd. I said, 'Listen to them shouting: "Zelikman!"'

'Honestly?' exclaimed a startled Golubovskaya.

But it proved to be only an attendant bringing in tea to the judges, immediately fallen upon by the waiting onlookers to find out whether he had heard anything while he was in the room. Meanwhile Golubovskaya made an error and began to lose. After an hour's play she resigned.

We went down outside the judges' room. There was a huge crowd there, many of whom had brought chairs and benches to sit on, and all the way up the stairs. People paced nervously up and down locked in earnest dispute. For the most part they were students of Nikolayev and Lyapunov, that is to say not on my side at all. I looked round to find Kreisler at my elbow, asking me to lend him 25 roubles. 'My dear fellow, I haven't a kopeck to my name. If they give me the piano, I'll lend you the money with pleasure.'

'I'm sure they will give it to you. What is happening just now is they are discussing whether it should be you or Kind, all the others have been eliminated.'

'How do you know that?!'

'One of the professors came out and said so.'

My heart began to beat faster, although I could not entirely rely on what Kreisler said. Soon afterwards I saw a knot of students round their teacher, Professor Kuskova. She emerged from the conference room upset that her student Galperin had not got through to the final voting for the grand piano. 'Well, who has got through?' clamoured the students.

'From those who played today Golubovskaya, and him,' pointing to me. 'And one from yesterday.'

'What about Zelikman and Kind?'

'Did not get through.'

Clearly, matters were coming to a head – the debate had narrowed to Golubovskaya or me. And then Budarina came bustling straight up to me, Damskaya with her. Budarina held out her hand. 'Congratulations! It's yours!'

'What is mine?' I asked, not daring to believe her.

'You've won the piano,' repeated Budarina.

Damskaya offered her congratulations as well. Not wishing, in case of a mistake, to find myself later in an embarrassing situation, I thanked them politely and enquired how they knew all this. They began to explain that Lemba emerged from the conference hall – but at that moment Winkler appeared and I went towards him. He said, 'I congratulate you. It's a splendid result: thirteen votes for you, five against.' A huge majority; I had not expected so much.

I continued on into the judges' room and all the professors came up to me offering their congratulations and shaking my hand. But so thoroughly had I prepared myself for the worst that I could not yet allow myself to rejoice in my victory. Eventually Glazunov appeared, flanked by the class administrators and read out the protocol in a flat monotone. Mumbling, Glazunov announced that the grand piano had been awarded to a student of the distinguished Professor Yesipova, Sergey Prokofiev, then without pausing went on to read out the marks.

When he had finished, some of Nikolayev's and Lyapunov's students set up a *sotto voce* booing. Mutterings of 'unfair!' were heard. My friends came up to me with their congratulations. The booing just made me laugh and think back to Pavlovsk; of course I would have been happier with universal applause, but the Nikolayevites and Lyapunovites were clearly not going to be pleased at the defeat of their heroes. Golubovskaya came up to me and with amazing restraint congratulated me. I smiled and asked her forgiveness.

Damskaya, Budarina, Kreisler and the others were jubilant. I said to Damskaya that if she would like to earn my Mama's gratitude, would she please ring her up straight away and tell her about the piano, as I had to go and find Glazunov and Gabel. Damskaya went off to telephone and I, having briefly thanked Glazunov, left to visit Yesipova. Damskaya and I left together, as it was on her way home.

Arriving at Yesipova's I found Steinberg, Miklashevskaya, Vengerova and Kalantarova already there with flowers and congratulations. But Yesipova's nervous state is such that the doctors were not allowing anyone to see her. The teachers excitedly discussed the voting: Glazunov had been vehemently opposed to me and had not even wanted me admitted to the final vote. However it had been decreed that consideration should be restricted to those who had straight 5+; this left Golubovskaya and myself from today's contestants, and Berlin and Keller (students of Lavrov) from yesterday. The voting was thirteen for me, five for Golubovskaya, two for Berlin and one for Keller. Glazunov was so distressed by the result that he did not want to announce it. He had to be persuaded by the Class Inspectors, who told him that not to make the announcement would be unseemly. Those who voted for me evidently included Steinberg, Miklashevskaya, Vengerova, Kalantarova, Drozdov, Gelever, Lemba, Medem, Winkler and some others. Lavrov and Lyapunov did not vote since they both had students in contention. Dubasov was against me. It was clear that it was my Concerto, not *Tannhäuser*, that had won me the prize.

I went home at nine o'clock to congratulations, champagne, the arrival of the Rayevskys, general acclaim. Constant telephone calls from Karatygin, Myaskovsky, the Meshcherskys, the Andreyevs. Yes, it was indeed a triumph for me, all the sweeter for having been achieved in my beloved Conservatoire, and even more so in that it represented not the pat on the head proper to a model student, but on the contrary the striking out of a new path, my own path, which I had established in defiance of routine and the examination traditions of the Conservatoire.

27 April

Rose at noon seized with the notion of going to London! I conveyed this news to Mama, who did not greatly protest. I could make a whole career for myself in London; the only thing I need to do is learn my own compositions thoroughly. Now I have won the prize I cannot allow myself to play badly, *noblesse oblige*, there's no getting round that! I settled down to learn the *Toccata*, and also composed a little of the Violin Concerto. I will really get on with this work once the Graduation Concert is out of the way. I made my correspondence chess moves and looked at Shcherbachov's[1] score.

To get out of the house for a while, I went to see N.M. He offered me his most sincere congratulations and said that, of course, I had no real competitors: everyone else played like a student, I as a fully-fledged musician. Nevertheless, I have a failing, one that may be ineradicable: a hardness of attack, not just in cantilena, but all the time.

---

1   Vladimir Shcherbachov (1889–1952), composer, studied with Steinberg and Lyadov, professor at the St Petersburg Conservatoire from 1912 until 1948. By training and inclination a composer of the old school and not especially receptive to the iconoclastic ambitions of the younger generation, he nevertheless demonstrated exemplary integrity and courage by abstaining, despite explicit pressure by the chairman, from an infamous Composers' Union Resolution in February 1936 condemning Shostakovich for the crime of 'Formalism' following the the publication of the *Pravda* article 'Muddle Instead of Music' that had savaged *Lady Macbeth of Mtsensk*.

On the way back, went into the *Evening Times* office, where the Chess Championship games are displayed. Today begins Part II of the tournament. In the cramped offices of the newspaper was a crowd of chess players standing in front of the boards with the games on them; the moves being communicated by telephone. Alekhine is having an excellent game against Lasker. I am pleased about that.

In the evening Sergey Sebryakov congratulated me on a new talent: versifying. He finds my quatrain exemplary and irreproachable. At eleven o'clock, when I was already considering going to bed, Ossovsky telephoned to say that he, Karatygin and Tcherepnin had just been having an argument with Ziloti, as a result of which my Sinfonietta would be programmed in Ziloti's concerts this autumn, with me conducting. Varvara Alexandrovna[1] wanted me to go round right away.

When I got there, in addition to the wives of the above-mentioned individuals, I found several recently graduated female music students and a pianist celebrated more for her beauty than for her pianism. After congratulating me on the prize, Ziloti confirmed his invitation and then attacked the 'hooliganism' of Myaskovsky's article. There can be no doubt however that it played a significant role in his change of heart. I am very happy.

28 April

At ten o'clock I came into the orchestra class. We began with Shcherbachov's *Procession*, which the orchestra read through more competently than I had expected. Then Tcherepnin took over to go through it in detail, and I was free. Coming out and going into the teaching part of the Conservatoire I met Struve and asked her about an inscription in French I wanted to write to Calvocoressi, a task to which she applied herself with great seriousness. Then, to my great surprise and delight, I noticed on the programme a song by Myaskovsky, and stayed to listen to it. It was very well sung by my former Aida, a friend of Dranishnikov, and had a great success.

At seven o'clock I accompanied the Meshcherskys (Talya and Vera Nikolayevna) to the station to see them off to Berne. The news of Ziloti's invitation produced a sensation. Talya asked me to write, likewise even Vera Nikolayevna. As they were leaving, Nina and Alexey Pavlovich invited me to lunch and to go with them to the Islands, but I am annoyed with Nina for her rebuke and declined.

---

1   Ossovskaya.

29 April

I am not happy with the Symphony in its present form: there are too many things in it that will not be heard. I plan to revise it all – not just the orchestration but the music as well. This will be my next task. Practised the *Toccata*. At half past one I went to Ratke's factory to see whether he would take back my piano, at a discount naturally, but he said he had nowhere to put it and recommended advertising it in the newspaper. I could get 600 roubles for it.

In the Conservatoire people kept coming up to me and congratulating me. Tcherepnin said that there was yet another hitch with my Concerto. Glazunov did not want it to be included in the Graduation Concert programme and the matter is to be discussed by a committee. I said that if they would not accept the Concerto but wanted *Tannhäuser* instead, I would not play. Tcherepnin agreed with me. I also telephoned Kalantarova, asking Anna Nikolayevna to back me up by saying the same thing.

I then went to see Andreyev, who was in his shirtsleeves packing to go to London. Anna Grigorievna will follow in a month's time. I gave him my Sonata No. 2 and Concerto No. 1 to take to Calcovoressi with the following inscription: '*M. Calvocoressi, en signe de dévouement sincère. Serge Prokofieff.*' Anna Grigorievna is insistent that I should go to London. If I do, then I must spend this month learning English. It is something I have in any case been meaning to do since the autumn. In the evening I went to the Sokol. They had read about my prize, congratulated me and wanted to chair me round the room. I enjoyed my gymnastics.

30 April

Wrote to Zakharov and practised Glazunov's Second Sonata with great enjoyment. I've learned it and will perform it. A strange thing, I do not much care for his music and the man himself is always setting up traps for me, but this sonata gives me a great deal of pleasure. At two o'clock I went into the Conservatoire at Tcherepnin's invitation. We looked through the score of my Concerto, and he gave me some useful pointers. Generally, as he said, the score had made a good impression on him. Saw Zelikman, who evidently has not yet come to terms with his defeat and goes about scowling.

At four o'clock I entered the Astoria Hotel, to which I had received a printed invitation. In one of the hotel's salons two pupils of Isadora Duncan were demonstrating their elegant choreography along with a row of little girls. The beautiful, somewhat revealing, Greek costumes and the plasticity of the dancers' movements were very pleasing to the eye. It was an all-invitation audience, and there were many people I knew among them.

A gentleman approached me and hailed me by name. He introduced himself as representing the Music Studio and asked me about my intention to work with them. The Music Studio is a newly created institution, launched the previous autumn, whose aim is to break down the routine approach prevalent everywhere, even in the Conservatoire. The teaching staff is young: people like Bikhter. I said that (1) I did not want to tie myself down in case of being engaged for concert tours; he replied that I would always be able to go away for a month at a time; (2) I cannot teach courses known, in Conservatoire parlance, as junior courses; he replied that I would only be asked to teach advanced students; (3) I would attend no more than once a week; he said that my wish would be honoured; (4) I did not want to have many students; he replied that I would not have many. The financial conditions would be 75 roubles per student per year, and this is a very decent wage since a senior teacher at the Conservatoire receives 80 roubles a year for two sessions a week. I there and then answered that I appreciated the honour and agreed the terms.

Karatygin has not yet managed to see Bessel. He told me the story of Ziloti and the Sinfonietta: it seems that Ossovsky had been holding a dinner at which Ziloti repeated his indignation at Myaskovsky's article, and most of all at the fact that a 'private letter' had been quoted in it. Karatygin, who was sitting near him, agreed that the private letter should probably not have been quoted, but in essence he agreed with the thrust of Myaskovsky's charge that Ziloti was wrong not to play Prokofiev's music. 'But it's totally lacking in talent! His music has no aroma! Recently I came across a composer (here he mentioned an unfamiliar name) whose music may be incomprehensible, but it does have an aroma, I can sense it, there is talent there. But Prokofiev's music simply stinks!'

Ossovsky, pouring out more wine, leaned over Ziloti's shoulder and said, 'Sasha, I don't agree with you. Prokofiev is very gifted, and you ought to play him.'

And Tcherepnin, sitting opposite and having drunk a lot of wine, announced, 'In my opinion there are only three composers today who are taking music forward: Schoenberg, Stravinsky and Prokofiev, and the most talented of the three is Prokofiev!'

Effective. Ziloti was taken aback, and protested weakly, 'All right, but it means I would have to accompany his concertos myself, even though I find them repellent. Now if he had some symphonic pieces, he could conduct them himself, but as it is . . .'

Tcherepnin: 'I'll take you up on that. He has an excellent Sinfonietta: ask him to conduct that.' Ziloti was thus outflanked on all sides, and gave in. It was at this point that I had received the telephone call summoning me to come.

In the evening I stayed at home, wrote my diary and worked out correspondence chess moves. At the Conservatoire they were meeting to determine the programme for the Graduation Concert, whether my Concerto could form part of it or not. From my point of view it can only work out for the best, because if the Concerto is left out of the programme I shall decline to play *Tannhäuser*, and that will create a scandal. I decided that starting tomorrow I shall learn English, and have asked Mlle Sanb to come and see me. Ten years ago she taught English to all the Rayevskys, since when we have all known her well as a friend of the Rayevsky family.

1 May

Rehearsal for the Graduation Concert. Tsybin is rehearsing Yasin's *Magdal*, music of quite remarkable vacuity. To quote Tcherepnin, it is a well-orchestrated zero. I am rehearsing Shcherbachov's *Procession*, which sounds noisy and authoritative and, after Yasin's music, rich in content. In the end, no obstacles were placed in the way of my Concerto being included in the programme. Tcherepnin says that he will conduct all accompaniments, so the only work I am responsible for is Shcherbachov's *Procession*, which could be conducted with one foot if necessary. This is not much to show for a graduating member of the conductors' class, a point which I do not hesitate to make to him.

Kreisler has decided to go with his mother this summer either to the Crimea, or to the country, or to a Norwegian fjord. I counsel him to go to Norway: London to Norway is not so far, and we could visit one another.

After the rehearsal I chatted with Struve and Damskaya, and we made a plan to go together on Sunday to Schlüsselberg. Timofeyeva got a 5+ for singing, and has been selected for the Graduation Concert.

Mlle Sanb came at six o'clock and I took the plunge into the English language. I think I shall learn it quite quickly, since I am already well supplied with motivation and application. First impressions are of great awkwardness: nothing sounds as it looks. I think Italian would be a lot easier, but in any event I have made a start with interest and enthusiasm.

2 May

Practised the Glazunov Sonata. Pondered alterations to the Sinfonietta; it is shaping up really well, and the best thing about it is that on the one hand it is classical, on the other it is light and gay.

At two o'clock Tcherepnin, Dranishnikov and I met to go through my Concerto, Dranishnikov accompanying and Tcherepnin conducting. Tcherepnin is so interested and is making such efforts that I decided not to make an issue of the fact that he has no right to deprive his conducting students of an opportunity to shine in the Graduation Concert. After all, to conduct an accompaniment, probably badly, is not that attractive a prospect.

At six o'clock another English language lesson – went rather well! I already know quite a few words and took the opportunity to show off my command of them. In the evening went to the Sokol, which I enjoyed as usual.

3 May

There was a morning rehearsal for the Graduation Concert, but since neither Shcherbachov's *Procession* nor my Concerto are on the schedule for today I preferred to stay at home studying English and thinking about the Sinfonietta.

About one o'clock I went into the Conservatoire, where the rehearsal had finished. I asked Tcherepnin if the rehearsal of my Concerto could be postponed from Monday to Tuesday, because on Monday Capablanca was due to play Lasker. I have not been into the Chess Club for some time and I badly wanted to see this crucial game. The girl who had attracted my attention a few days ago was again in evidence today, walking about in a queenly way. I do not like her voice at all, but she is very interesting to look at.

English lesson at five o'clock. Someone rang me up on the telephone, a girl whose name I don't know but find very pleasantly intriguing, and most importantly knew all the results of the chess championship and also spoke English.

At eight o'clock I went to see Nina Meshcherskaya, who had stayed behind alone in their apartment with a German woman. The day before yesterday she rang me up complaining bitterly of boredom, which touched my heart. The company this evening consisted, besides Nina and myself, of Oleg, Serge Bazavov and cousin Sasha. We played open vint, Nina by tradition sitting beside me and pretending to play. She asked me if I would come to Kislovodsk and if I would write to her while she was there. We wrote a letter to Vera Nikolayevna and joked that in three days' time we would get a reply saying: 'Time to go home now!'

I telephoned Damskaya to make arrangements to go to Schlüsselberg.

4 May

At a quarter to ten I was at the landing stage in the Summer Garden. It was a warm day, the holiday crowds were pushing their way on to the steamer and quickly filling it up, but there was no sign of my girls yet. Struve appeared at five minutes to ten, and Damskaya just made it before our departure. It was not a big boat, and the tiny deck was soon full of passengers so that we could hardly find a space for ourselves. The sun was shining and there did not seem to be much air about. It was much more pleasant when the boat pushed off and a fresh breeze got up. We went first along the embankments, then past factories, and it was a good two hours before we reached the natural, un-built-up banks of the river. It was very pleasant to be sailing along, and I was enjoying the society of my two companions.

It takes four hours to get to Schlüsselberg, the first half of the voyage in a south-easterly direction and the second half to the north-east. The sun was baking for the first half, but during the latter half the wind became so strong that we were driven below decks. We arrived at Schlüsselberg at two o'clock after a comfortable and enjoyable voyage. Warmed by the sunshine we inspected Alexander II's canal and lolled on the grass eating our sandwiches, then took a little boat to cross over the canal. Although Schlüsselberg is the administrative capital of the uyezd[1] it is in fact little more than a village and has no resident intelligentsia whatsoever. Because it was a holiday there was a carousel and a pierrot – that was fun. I thought of Stravinsky. We took tea in an awful hotel and at six o'clock re-embarked on the steamer for the return voyage. By this time it had turned cold and we spent most of the time in the cabin watching the amusing behaviour of various couples and threesomes. Back on dry land again we retraced our steps through the heaving crowds of the Summer Garden and parted at the corner of Sadovaya and Morskaya Streets.

I went in to see Myaskovsky. Derzhanovsky is trying all the theatres in Moscow to get my *Maddalena* produced and has kept Myaskovsky up to date with his efforts. Somehow I am not convinced that all of his plans eventually come to fruition.

5 May

Decided not to go to the Graduation Concert rehearsal but went instead to the Chess Club to see the decisive Lasker–Capablanca match. The usual dense crowd was there. Many people now know me, following my *Tannhäuser* performance at the reception, and so I was the object of attention. In one way this is agreeable but in another embarrassing. I am now acquainted with all the masters. Tarrasch is looking a trifle green around the gills: he has lost four matches in a row and only finally managed a draw yesterday. Today he launched a risky variation against Alekhine, but then took fright and started cautiously moving his pieces to build a strong defensive position.

---

1 The lowest-tier administrative district in pre-Revolutionary Russia.

Lasker permitted himself to arrive fifteen minutes late for his match. Unfortunately I missed seeing them sit down at their board: apparently they were frigid with one another and could scarcely bring themselves to shake hands. Lasker was playing white and initiated a modest variation of the Spanish opening, the same with which he won the first game of his match with Tarrasch. The opening of the game was played by both sides at lightning speed, but then Lasker began to take a long time thinking. Capablanca was playing fluently and easily and . . . soon found himself in straitened circumstances. 'That doesn't look very good' was the cautiously expressed feeling round about. Lasker began overtly to apply the pressure, and now Capablanca bent seriously over the board, began tugging at his hair and concentrated hard on extricating himself from his difficulties. Meanwhile Alekhine was taking advantage of Tarrasch's indecisiveness to launch an attack, leading everyone to believe that the game was irretrievably lost. Tarrasch had my sympathy.

The interval began at six o'clock. Capablanca appeared to have devised a way of counter-attacking and ingeniously moved ahead: this delighted some, but others were of the opinion that the advantage was illusory and ruin would inevitably follow. Bashkirov,[1] a very nice young man who had been overwhelmingly impressed by my playing at the reception and invited me to his name-day party (I declined) now asked me to dine with him. He drove me himself to his home in his automobile, and brought me back again to the Club at eight o'clock. With us were his cousin and Rubinstein,[2] who is incidentally a modest man with little to say and that in less than perfect Russian. Bashkirov lives a long way out in the sticks, on the Kalashnikov Embankment, but in a huge apartment with a mother who wears heavy diamond earrings. The master of the household seems to be his elder brother, who went out to dine with some other people without a tie and still wearing his nightshirt, which offended my priggish sense of the proprieties.

By the time we made it back to the Club at eight o'clock the games had already restarted. Those who had had prophesied an unsuccessful outcome to Capablanca's sortie were proved correct: it produced nothing. The game proceeded to a swift conclusion and Capablanca turned over his king. Wild applause greeted the vanquisher of the hitherto unconquered Capablanca. Lasker acknowledged the applause with a wave of his hand, while Capablanca, a haughty expression on his face, ostentatiously strolled round the Club with his nose in the air. The event provoked frenetic discussion: Capablanca defeated!! 'That's the way to deal with a cheeky youngster!' said

---

1   Boris Bashkirov (1891–?), a wealthy young dilettante, wrote poetry under the *nom de plume* Boris Verin. Apart from personal liking, Prokofiev evidently thought well enough of his verse to include one setting ('Trust Me') as No. 3 of his Five Poems, Op. 23.
2   Rubinstein was Polish.

Znosko-Borovsky. 'It's not a good idea to play the fool with Lasker.' Soon after this Tarrasch conceded, but this was no surprise so provoked little comment.

Bashkirov pressed me to return with him, but I was terribly tired and made haste to get home.

Damskaya recounted most interesting doings at the Conservatoire today. Tcherepnin had promised to start work on my Concerto tomorrow, but as Glazunov was absent through sickness Tcherepnin spent a full two hours teaching it to the orchestra, prefacing the work with a long speech to the effect that this was a wonderful composition that would soon be performed everywhere and in every musician's repertoire, and if at first glance it appeared strange, deeper acquaintance would soon render it comprehensible. Damskaya said, however, that despite this many people in the orchestra find the music hideously ugly. The Theory students seem, however, to be very happy. Quite a lot of people were at the rehearsal and listened attentively to my Concerto.

6 May

Seeing that the Concerto had been so ceremoniously introduced and studied yesterday, I had to practise it assiduously myself in the morning in order not to disgrace myself in the solo part, particularly as I had not looked at it since the day of the competition. At two o'clock I went to the rehearsal, where Tcherepnin gleefully announced that as he had already started rehearsing it yesterday, he would begin with it today. While waiting for the orchestra to assemble he sat with the trombones and went through with them some of the interjections made by the brass, which resounded throughout the whole Conservatoire. This produced something like a holiday mood among the listening public in the Small Hall, where the rehearsal was taking place.

Tcherepnin first played through the entire work without me, and then I joined for a complete run-through, which was played without a break. Tcherepnin got carried away and forced the tempi to such an extent that in some passages I had no time to play all the notes. Sometimes he did not follow me, but I decided not to stop him or annoy him with remarks at the time, saving them for later, especially in view of the fact that there are to be four rehearsals for the concert and Tcherepnin has promised to find time for the Concerto in all of them. He is making tremendous efforts, has thrown himself heart and soul into the piece and considers it the most interesting item in the Graduation Concert programme. Amazingly, the orchestra's playing is in no way inferior to either the Koussevitzky or the Pavlovsk performances, and a total of six rehearsals bids fair to guarantee an excellent performance at the Graduation Concert. There were a lot of Theory students listening to the rehearsal, and some of them said to me afterwards, 'Your Concerto is an absolute delight!'

After my rehearsal I went to the Rayevskys to congratulate Uncle Sasha on his birthday; I had been asked for the evening but I wanted to go to the Sokol. On the way I called in at the *Evening Times* office to see what the display boards could tell me about the Chess Championship as all the moves are instantly communicated by telephone. But what was this? Capablanca was several pieces down in his game against Tarrasch. A particularly ingenious sacrifice? No, it was obviously a genuinely bad situation. I was so alarmed by the turn of events that as soon as I left the Rayevskys I hurried to the Chess Club. The crowd was in shock: Capablanca had lost a piece to Tarrasch clearly in an error of judgement, tried to recover but could not and was heading for defeat. Znosko-Borovsky was leaning up against one of the display boards. I went up to him: 'Yevgeny Alexandrovich, do you still think it was a good idea to write a book[1] about a player who keeps on losing games?'

'That's not the half of it,' he replied. 'I've already written another!'

'It's sad to see one's idols dethroned,' said some.

'Nothing of the sort,' objected others, coming passionately to their man's defence. 'Making a mistake going for the wrong rook is hardly being dethroned, you can't say that makes him any worse a player!'

Later I went to the Sokol.

7 May

I'm learning the *Toccata*, and generally starting to practise for London, among other things the Sonata Op. 1, because it seems to me Romanovsky played it better than I do. I want to show that I can play it better than him. In the Graduation Concert Tcherepnin has now turned to the Saint-Saëns concerto with Golubovskaya, but, surprisingly, he does not seem to get on too well with her. Keller, a student of Lavrov, played very well indeed, and that was something I really did not expect, something good coming from Lavrov! When we got to my Concerto there were all kinds of interruptions, since today I did not yield to him in the matter of tempo and wanted him to follow my lead. The Concerto continues to enjoy success, and I was pleased that Golubovskaya in particular found much to admire in it.

8 May

My English is slowly improving, slowly because I have no time to do any homework. Once the Graduation Concert is over I shall have more time. I'm

---

[1] *Capablanca* (1911).

enjoying it very much, though. Tcherepnin decided not to rehearse my Concerto today, because it is in a better state of preparation than other items on the programme. There is a rumour that the administration has decided to discontinue paying wages to the orchestra next year, and as a result many of the musicians are upset and do not want to play. Tcherepnin is nervous and in a bad temper with everyone except me, to whom he continues to be nice. He is extremely dissatisfied with Tsybin and agrees that I was right in my criticism that he is not a conductor, and that simply having good hands is not enough.

At eight o'clock a critic, violinist and writer on Wagner's *Ring* called Walter[1] came to acquaint himself with my Concerto, as he intends to write about it after the Graduation Concert. This is a very agreeable development, and I played the Concerto to him, afterwards discussing it in detail. In the evening I had intended to stay in and write my diary, but Bashkirov invited me to go to his house with such extraordinary charm and insistence that I agreed to go. It was quite enjoyable: I played *Tannhäuser*, with which Bashkirov is completely in love, and then played chess with his cousin. Bashkirov's sister and her husband had a bet of 70 roubles on the outcome, but happily it ended in a draw. Bashkirov had promised to run me home in his car, but it transpired that there was a problem with the tyre, so I called a cab and went off in it, privately suspecting, however, that the tyre was a ruse.

My correspondence tournament is going well and I'm having a lot of success in it; I am benefiting from the international championship. What is less good is that my piano is not sold, the *Ballade* is not being published, and I have no money!

9 May

Practised the Concerto in the morning because I have not done much playing since the Competition, and after all playing with orchestra is not quite the same as playing with a second piano. Not many people turned up at the rehearsal today because it is a holiday, but among those who did come was Glazunov. He has been meaning for some time to conduct the accompaniment for Golubovskaya and Berlin, no doubt as a snub to me, but has not been well. Now he has recovered he is getting to work. The orchestra greeted him with a fanfare. I managed to rehearse my Concerto before his arrival; it went very well, and I think that with any other than a student orchestra it would have been my best performance to date of the work.

I sat with Damskaya and Struve; Damskaya said that she planned to go to

---

1 Viktor Walter (1865–1935), who in addition to being a critic was the leader of the Mariinsky Theatre Orchestra.

the opening of the Sestroretsk season today. I said that if the tournament finished at six o'clock I might like to go too. It would be nice to have a change of scene. Addressing Struve, I said, 'Shall we go?'

'No,' she replied, shortly and without giving any reason. A little while later I repeated the question and got the same answer. I was bitterly offended and very angry with Struve, although of course I took care not to show it. In general, she is not living up to the hopes and ambitions I had of her. All that I had thought of her, seeing her from a distance, has proved to be an illusion. It is true she is not an ordinary or conventional sort of girl, she is very nice, but . . . the fire and ebullience and rebellious spirit that I had thought to detect in her is simply not there, and on top of that she is quite indifferent to me. And so, the Prime Minister will be retired.

I went to the Chess Club for the final round, Capablanca against Alekhine, Lasker against Marshall. Lasker is half a point ahead of Capablanca. When I arrived at five o'clock the games were at their height. Capablanca was playing a high speed, stupendously difficult game against Alekhine, and seemed to have the edge. Just as I got there, Lasker sacrificed a piece. No one could understand what advantage he saw in this but, such is the general belief in the mastery of his play, people concluded, 'If Lasker does this, it can only mean that he is winning.' A buzz went round the room: 'Alekhine has resigned.' I was sitting with Znosko-Borovsky in the next room studying Lasker's game and could eventually see that Marshall had no defence. Everyone rushed to the display boards to witness the final moments of this great chess epic. Marshall gathered his forces for a counter-attack, while Lasker stormed his positions. Eventually Marshall attacked Lasker's king, but the king simply withdrew: Marshall had no further defence. He turned over his king and shook Lasker's hand. The first prize went to Lasker amid wild applause from the whole crowd. And indeed to gain the victory in such company, and in such a way, by scoring seven points from a possible maximum of eight, is truly to show that in the world of chess you are the king. I applauded Lasker, shook his hand and that of his wife. Capablanca stood to one side and talked to Sosnitsky with a fretful look on his face. I left the Club with Budarina; she has spent every day of the tournament within the Club's walls bankrupting herself in the process, but still going. Along the way we met Tarrasch going in the opposite direction towards the Club; I stopped him to let him know the result of the game and how it had ended. To my surprise I found I had enough German to explain the details quite freely, but noticed that interlarded among my speech were some English words I had recently been learning that resembled German ones. With his customary courtesy Tarrasch thanked me for the pleasant news (the defeat of Marshall meant that he would take the fourth prize rather than the fifth) and we parted.

I thought of telephoning Oleg and going with him to Sestroretsk but in the end decided I would rather go to the Sokol and write an article with my impressions about the tournament for the chess column of *The Day* newspaper, which had invited various 'celebrities' including myself to write their impressions of the championship. I was inordinately flattered at the chance to publish my comments on my beloved masters, whom I have known for ten years – not personally, but through the record of their games in different tournaments, over which I used to sit for entire evenings at Sontsovka. I wanted my article to have an international dimension, and went over it in my mind with the greatest care as I walked to the Sokol. As soon as I returned home I wrote it out and sent it to *The Day*.

10 May

The general rehearsal. I decided to put on a bit of a show and dressed in my light-coloured suit, despite the rainy weather. I had worn it at the general rehearsal for the Graduation Concert last year, and it was also raining then. At the start of the rehearsal there were not many people in the hall, but it soon filled up. Glazunov arrived and sat with Sokolov. Nikolayev was quite charming to me; we sat together listening to the various composers' compositions.

Tsybin's symphony is as modest and insignificant as its author. Yasensky has skilfully orchestrated some extraordinarily pointless music. Next on were Tcherepnin and myself to play my Concerto. I knew that the whole audience was waiting for this, and just beforehand was gripped by a kind of insecurity – not about my performance, but simply about how to go on stage. I actually played quite well, and the ensemble with the orchestra was very good. Orchestra and audience applauded. I then conducted my less than noteworthy number: Shcherbachov's *Procession*. The orchestra's attitude to me was friendly and courteous. Owing to the number of accidentals I had put in the parts the performance of *Procession* had a number of wrong notes, but there was no time to repeat it as the rehearsal was in any case threatening to go on until nightfall.

Apparently Glazunov's comment to Tcherepnin was: 'How well it is all turning out', in the specific sense of turning out well musically; this is most flattering. Tilya Hansen played very well indeed. I told her I was going to propose to her: she would be a desirable bride with a dowry, I an eligible groom with a grand piano. After all, we were both prizewinners of the Conservatoire, clearly it was God's will. She laughed and we had a nice talk. Arm in arm with Nikolayev I walked round the corridors asking people their impressions of the Concerto. Nikolayev was full of praise for it. Zelikman appeared and even managed to exchange some pleasantries with me. He has hardly been seen in the Conservatoire since the day of his downfall, and even when he did come in preserved an unapproachably aloof exterior. But God be with him, I've no wish to sneer at him, he is a good pianist. Rest in peace.

In the evening I stayed at home and sent tickets for the concert to all my friends.

11 May

All the same, although I had no fears about how it would turn out, I was nervous before the Graduation Concert. When I came into the artists' room there was an unusual air of expectation: Tcherepnin was fretting because the bass clarinet and the timpanist had not come, Gabel and Frantsis likewise because the official programme had not been ready in time. Tsybin was already on the podium conducting. The hall was full to overflowing. Before long it was time for me to go on to the platform, which I did with only a slight trace of nerves.

My entrance was greeted with warm applause. I enjoyed playing the Concerto very much; although I had some anxiety in one or two places my nervousness never amounted to much. Tcherepnin accompanied well. The Concerto had an enormous success and I returned twice to take a bow. Even Glazunov and Artsybushev were well mannered enough to clap, and the orchestra did as well.

I then conducted Shcherbachov's *Procession*, which the orchestra played execrably, even Dranishnikov on the piano being guilty of mistakes. Then came the interval, and an artists' room full of visitors. There was praise for me from Borovsky, Blumenfeld and many of the professors. Artsybushev came up, complimented me(!), said several nice things and asked about the Concerto No. 2 (sic!). Thanking him for his interest, I tried to convince him that my music has a classical basis. When the interval came to an end and the artists' room and the corridor emptied of people, I met Myaskovsky, Saminsky and Rosenstein, all of whom were very complimentary. I had a verbal tussle with the last named, however, for praising Tsybin's conducting while criticizing Tcherepnin's.

Miklashevskaya introduced me to the pianist Mikhelson,[1] who said she would like to play my Concerto in London next March with Coates, with whom she is on very friendly terms. I was delighted to hear this news both about London and about Coates, who is important to me in connection with the Mariinsky Theatre and the operas I am planning to write. I sat with Timofeyeva, who had earlier sung very well and with great invididuality from *The Golden Cockerel*, and we listened to Golubovskaya. Golubovskaya's playing also had personality, but could not always be heard.

---

1 Confusingly, the pianist and teacher Irina Miklashevskaya was born Irina Mikhelson. This Mikhelson must be another artist.

The concert looked as if it would go on for an eternity, and this evening I had a chess match arranged with Capablanca. I left the hall, removed my tails and stretched out dozing for half an hour on a sofa in the empty foyer. I would have left the building altogether, except that the diplomas were to be given out. But my waiting proved to be in vain; Olga Borisovna read out a long list of names in which my name did not figure; it seems that because I am already in possession of one diploma I am not entitled to another, so I was deprived of the opportunity to display my person before the public. Went into the Small Hall to be photographed. Glazunov, surrounded by a gaggle of girls, did not think to invite me into a position of honour as a prizewinner, but I formed a new row right in the front and sat there with Timofeyeva and Tsybin. The photographic session went on for hours; I was in a very good mood apart from my annoyance at Glazunov. When it was over, the girls lined up to ask Glazunov for his photograph and to bid him all sorts of fond farewells.

Gabel said to me, 'Perhaps I should give him one of mine?! After all, we have worked together!'

Passing Glazunov, I bowed and said firmly, 'Goodbye, Alexander Konstantinovich.'

To my surprise he began to mumble some vaguely friendly words, which I was in no mind to take pleasure in. I therefore abruptly cut off any attempt at a second farewell exchange and left. I was just nearing home when I saw to my horror that it was already a quarter to eight, and the simultaneous match against Capablanca was due to start at eight. Rushing like a madman I threw off my concert clothes, put on a jacket and, not waiting to have anything to eat, dashed in a fortuitously appearing taxi to the Club. Saburov must have already given an account of the Graduation Concert because all sorts of people came up wanting to congratulate me. Lasker asked me to what the congratulations referred, and I told him in German, 'Three days ago you won the first prize here, and today I was also awarded the first prize', and explained the matter. Lasker's comment was that he was a poor judge of music, but I was such a nice young man that he could sincerely rejoice in my success. Dranishnikov, Borislavsky and Budarina all came to watch, so I had quite a crowd behind me, all of whom were anxiously following my fortunes. Capablanca moved from board to board with incredible speed. He started many of the games with the King's Gambit, and I was afraid that he might not do the same with me, but I was lucky. It was a good, solid game; I hunched over the board, trying as much as I could to take no notice of those surrounding me, and the game developed quite well. Soon Capablanca began to press me, but then the game stabilized and continued on an even keel.

Dranishnikov and Borislavsky followed every move in an agony of suspense, and from time to time made suggestions, not necessarily very good ones, however. After two hours of play the game was absolutely even and looked as though it could be heading for a draw. But sadly, by this time only five or six games were still in play, and Capablanca moved at such lightning speed there was no time to think between moves. Somehow he succeeded in breaking through my line of pawns, and won the game. When the results were announced, Capablanca had won twenty-seven games, lost one and drawn two, one of the draws being against old Saburov, a courteous gesture. Bashkirov's game was the last to finish: he had arrived late and although he had the assistance of Rubinstein and Marshall, still lost.

I was a little disappointed by losing, as it was the first time I had ever lost a game in a simultaneous match, and put my name down for Thursday's session in the hope of getting my revenge. As I was leaving I said goodbye to Lasker, who was going home the next day. He was very kind and invited me to his house whenever I was in Berlin, an invitation that made me very proud. The article I had written, drawing analogies between the chess masters and Mozart and Bach, had not yet appeared, but several people seemed to know about it and smiled at me.

12 May

Messed about in the morning and read the reviews. I had promised to go to hear Alpers's and Gauk's exam performances but I had an English lesson and did not go. In the afternoon I walked along Nevsky and Morskaya Street. In the evening Bashkirov called for me in his car and took me back to his house. He said that he and Capablanca were planning to go to London via Sweden – that would be wonderful, we could all go together. I was again pressed to play the piano, and then won a chess game against one of Bashkirov's friends, a very pleasant Prince from Simbirsk.

13 May

Another huge crop of reviews, all laudatory, even the little popular sheets could hardly splutter out enough praise. In the afternoon I went in to Iretskaya's class exam, and felt myself quite the hero of the hour, although there was nothing especially interesting about any of the performances. Dranishnikov and I sat together. Golubovskaya was playing the accompaniment with her usual musicianship. I was critical of the tempo she took for the aria from *Kashchey*, at which she was inclined to take offence, but all was smoothed over and harmony restored. Nearonova squeaked, but Morenschild sang very well.

I went to see Bessel armed with a recommendation from Karatygin, who had already spoken to him about me. The old man received me with great courtesy, spent a long time bragging about his firm, and said that he would be very glad to publish my music, not in the first instance my Second Piano Concerto (I had no intention of offering him this work in any case) but smaller pieces. I proposed the *Ballade*, and he agreed readily enough, but a fee of 50 roubles was the most he was willing to offer. This is too little, so I said that I would think about it and withdrew, greatly dissatisfied with my present situation, in which I am in great need of money but cannot seem to get hold of any.

In the evening I went to the Sokol, where I was fêted with great ceremony. Damskaya telephoned to have a general chat, mentioning among other things that Struve had been talking about me, saying that I seemed to be angry with her. She had produced a character sketch of my personality which had struck Damskaya with its perspicacity. According to Damskaya, Struve sees all my failings but does not consider that I can be accused of overweening pride or putting on airs; according to my lights the way I behave is straightforward. As for the failings, she does not think I am to blame for them, they are the result of my being spoilt and indulged by those around me.

14 May

Aslanov has asked me to let Myaskovsky know that he expects him with me in Pavlovsk today for another play-through, the fourth, of Myaskovsky's Symphony No. 1. This is to be performed at Pavlovsk on the 20th, but Myaskovsky has still not let Aslanov have the score. It was no easy task to track down N.M., as the whole family moved to a new apartment yesterday and I did not know the address. I spent an hour on the telephone phoning everyone I could think of who might know where he could be, and eventually ran him to earth after a great deal of trouble.

During the day I composed some of the Violin Concerto; the first movement exposition is almost clear in my mind now. I am very fond indeed of its themes, and the Concerto promises to be a very affecting work. At seven o'clock Kolechka and I went to Pavlovsk, and I settled down happily to play the symphony through with him in the four-hand version. The symphony was written at the same time as my E minor one and I have long had a great affection for it.

Pavlovsk was green and smelled wonderful. Aslanov lives some way from the station but his dacha is splendidly spacious. The woman who lives with him as his wife is extremely nice and intelligent. I also liked the dog, a French bulldog, although normally I cannot stand dogs. Aslashka was his usual self, self-assured, polite, cunning and not very clever.

Kolechka and I expounded the whole symphony in great detail, and left to come back to town at eleven o'clock. He told me that Saradzhev had serious intentions of mounting a Moscow production of *Maddalena*. He made me an offer to undertake the orchestration of it, as long as I would collaborate with him on it.

15 May

Studied English. In the evening went to the Chess Club for the second simultaneous match session with Capablanca; Dranishnikov, Borislavsky and Budarina again came to watch the contest. With his fourth move Capablanca fell into a kind of trap, which I had refined in one of my correspondence chess matches: 1. D4, D5; 2. K F3, C F5; 3. C4, K C6 threatening K B4. He stood in front of the board for two or three minutes frowning and pulling at his hair. I was thrilled beyond words at having set the champion a real problem. He was down on the exchange, but returned to the attack with such ferocity that I had to engage in all kinds of outlandish diversions to save the game. This went on for two hours. At this point the game settled down and looked as though it was going to turn out all right, but then his queen captured a rook that was protected by my king, and when I took his queen with my king he responded by putting my king and queen in check. 'Oh, you devil!' we burst out, we including Dranishnikov and Borislavsky, who were as avidly engaged in the game as I was. 'Why didn't you put him in check two moves ago, when your queen was on a different square?'

'Yes, that's a real pity, but hang on, we'll move it back to where it was, perhaps he'll have forgotten . . .'

'You can't do that,' expostulated Dranishnikov in a fright.

But I did, and when Capablanca returned, I put him in check. He was about to reply, when he noticed that I had put the pieces back to a previous position, and burst out laughing. He then showed me how he would have been able to win in precisely the same way from that check as well. I was less upset at that defeat than I had been the first time, but still resolved to try again tomorrow, not that I had much hope of retrieving my honour, but it would be interesting to play again.

16 May

At a quarter to nine I was at the station and at nine departed with Kolechka for Pavlovsk. The Andante, with which he began, sounded wonderful, especially the middle section. The Finale was not nearly so successful and not everything came off in the first movement either, as Aslanov dragged out the tempo with excessive ritardandos. I was following the rehearsal with the piano score. I am very fond of this symphony, although of course it would be even better if it had more vigour and more *élan*, and if the orchestration were more colourful.

At one o'clock we returned to St Petersburg, in time for my English lesson. My progress is a little slower than I had expected, as I don't seem to have time to do all my homework. I did not sleep well last night, so yawned like a schoolboy all through my lesson and had to have a snooze in the afternoon. In the evening I went back to the Chess Club for another game against Capablanca. Dranishnikov, my loyal supporter, was less happy with me on this occasion: 'You're not playing seriously at all today.'

But in fact I was playing very seriously. The game started in a similar way to yesterday's, but a little more solidly. Capablanca did not lose an exchange but on the other hand did not win any pieces either. The attack he mounted caused me severe difficulties, but I successfully repulsed it. Capablanca dashingly brought out his other pieces, exposing them to obvious danger, but God save one from the danger of taking them: that way led to certain defeat. Sitting on my right was an apprehensive Budarina, while on my left was the impeccably gentlemanly Yakhontov, Bashkirov's brother-in-law. After two hours of stubborn resistance, I suddenly saw a marvellous combination and said to Yakhontov, 'I'm going to win this game!'

Yakhontov started in surprise, and I showed him the combination, but for the sake of correctness asked Capablanca to make one more move. When he returned to my board, I was in great anxiety because I had worked out a trap that would lead to mate in three moves. I made my move, and Capablanca was about to reply, but suddenly paused, having seen the trap. He stood for a moment in thought, then sacrificed the piece, for otherwise he would not have been able to save himself. I now had the advantage of one piece, and my task was now to exploit it. At one moment I was mortally afraid that he had succeeded in extricating himself from the danger, but he did not succeed and soon capitulated. I savoured the triumph of my victory, and accepted the congratulations of my friends.

Dranishnikov was ecstatic and kept shouting, 'Chair him round the room! Chair him round the room!' Bashkirov invited me home to tea; I said it was rather late but when I found out that Capablanca would be going also I changed my mind and accepted the invitation. The result of today's simultaneous session was: 24 games, 20 won, 2 lost, 2 drawn.

We climbed into the car and went to Kalashnikov Embankment, and Bashkirov drove us right inside the garage, thereby proudly giving himself the opportunity of demonstrating that the family owned two cars. I studied Capablanca with great interest, fascinated to see how he behaved in an informal context. But having gone to bed at eight o'clock in the morning and risen at noon, he looked exhausted beyond words and mostly remained silent, staring into his glass. Bashkirov delivered himself of a long and eloquent effusion about Russian history, to which we listened respectfully. He then asked me to play *Tannhäuser*, which needless to say I was not very keen to do, except that I was curious to see how Capablanca would react to it. He listened with evident pleasure, but confessed to a certain lack of understanding, saying that he thought he must have heard the piece somewhere but could not put a name to it. He was enthusiastic about my 'Harp' Prelude, however.

We went out together on to the street, and when I said that I was going to walk home he said he would too. After exchanging a couple of words about the dawn, I decided to keep silent since he did not seem to want to talk. We stepped out briskly, and I had to make strenuous efforts to keep pace. After about twenty minutes, Capablanca at length broke his silence to ask if it was true that I was going to London via Sweden, and when that might be? He speaks French quite correctly, but with an accent. I answered him in detail, but forbore to ask him if he was making the same journey. After that we talked freely about everything we saw as we walked; Capablanca found the nocturnal population on Nevsky Prospect particularly entertaining. We marched on as far as the corner of Sadovaya and Vosnesenskaya Streets, where we parted, he to the Astoria Hotel and I to Pervaya Rota Street. It was three in the morning, and already quite light.

17 May

Slept late and awoke with a headache. The day was taken up with a visit to the dentist and my English lesson. In the evening I stayed at home and composed my Symphony. The ache in my head passed off as I became absorbed in composition.

18 May

My defeat of Capablanca has created a sensation, my fellow Sokol Borislavsky came to offer his congratulations and to tell me that the Sokol were proud of me and my victory. Today I composed some more of the Violin Concerto and went for a walk along the Fontanka, felt a twinge of anxiety and went to dine with Anna Grigorievna, who is leaving the day after tomorrow for London via Kiev and Paris. We had a good talk; she will arrive in London on 1 June and will set about finding a room where I can stay.

19 May

Rose at eight o'clock and eagerly set off for Pavlovsk with Kolya. I enjoy getting up early and going off somewhere, and in addition there was the symphony to listen to, to which I was much looking forward. Saminsky came with us as well.

Pavlovsk greeted us with its usual lush scenery and hot sunshine. Aslanov displayed his inherent provincialism with a mass of unwarranted ritardandos in the first movement, which I took up with him since N.M. was too reticent to do so. Eventually Aslanov lost patience with me and asked me to take a walk. Just then the Damskaya sisters appeared, so I decided to walk with them. They had just moved to Pavlovsk for the summer. We had a very jolly time talking and laughing. Eleonora is, I realized, the only person with whom I have maintained a close relationship throughout the winter, our constant telephone conversations always finding something interesting to discuss, and never once falling out.

I have made a discovery that I find very intriguing: Damskaya has some things in common with Max. These are: (1) a way of introducing extraordinary passion and conviction into discussions about entirely trivial matters so that one is impelled to regard the triviality as something truly important; (2) a conscious emphasis on style, manifested particularly in throwing money about as if it were of no account. With Max these characteristics were so alluring that I enjoyed them almost without being consciously aware of them. Damskaya is a less vivid version but one that gives me great pleasure because it reminds me of Max.

We walked about until one o'clock and then I returned to Petersburg. Myaskovsky came back earlier, on his own. At home I learned that the great man, Mr Tcherepnin, had come himself to ask me most particularly to be at the Conservatoire at four o'clock. I was curious to know what this could be about. I yawned my way through my English lesson, as I had got up early and been in the fresh air a lot, but was at the Conservatoire by four o'clock. It transpired that Tcherepnin wanted to play his *Red Mask*[1] to Ziloti, who intends to programme it next year. But as it was too much for him to play by himself, he asked me to help him. I was glad to agree, because apart from anything else I had liked *Red Mask* very much since Tcherepnin had played it through to me from manuscript two years ago. He now gave me a proof copy of the printed score, pointed out one or two things, and asked me to look through it at home and then give him a ring. Tcherepnin was extremely pleasant and almost diffident about troubling me. In the Conservatoire all was quiet and deserted.

---

1 Tcherepnin had composed the ballet *La masque de la mort rouge*, based on Edgar Allan Poe's 1842 shocker of a short story 'The Mask of the Red Death', in response to a commission from Diaghilev in 1912. Intended for the 1914 Paris season with Nijinsky dancing Gorsky's choreography, the plan had to be abandoned when Diaghilev and Nijinsky had their falling out, and the ballet was not produced. After the Revolution, when Tcherepnin was living in Paris, he recast the score as an orchestral suite *Le Destin, trois fragments symphoniques sur une nouvelle de Poe*, Op. 59.

20 May

Today I attended the Zherebtsova-Andreyeva class exam. She had asked me to listen carefully to her singers and then give her my opinion. I sat with Damskaya, who had come over from Pavlovsk for a change of scene. She scribbled her observations and graded the singers on her programme. Also present were Nearonova, Alpers and 'The Tigress' – as we had dubbed one powerfully built singer with a predatory expression and sharp teeth, but with a wild animal kind of beauty.

At seven o'clock Mama, Mlle Roblin and I went together to Pavlovsk where we found a large audience for the concert, including Kal surrounded by his musician friends Saminsky, Shaposhnikov, Kryzhanovsky and others. Myaskovsky promised to get my *Ballade* published by Zimmermann with Kryzhanovsky's help, since I do not have so much as a kopeck in my pockets and I refuse to let Bessel have it for 50 roubles. We went into the hall; I sat with my own group, separately from Myaskovsky.

The symphony began very well; the 4/6 passage in B flat sounding splendid, although the Allegro struck me as a little dull. The second subject was ravishing. I had been worried that the public might find the symphony tedious, and certainly it was not helped by the way Aslanov dragged it out at inordinate length. There was rather a lot of substandard instrumental playing. The second movement sounded wonderful, the Finale less good but lively and not boring even though not everything came off impeccably.

To my surprise the symphony was well received, and there was warm applause. I was overjoyed. The green room and all round about was full of musicians. To the critic of *Rech* (*Speech*), who had mentioned in his review of my Concerto at the Graduation Concert that it was in four unequal movements, I said, 'Well, my dear fellow, you stepped right in it this time: my Concerto is in one sonata movement, not four.' He protested weakly but I dismembered him with irrefutable arguments. Then, feeling sorry for him, I broke off the conversation. Myaskovsky was surrounded on all sides by musicians, and was presented by a lady with a rose. I told him I had some detailed observations that I would tell him about later. N.M. was returning to Petersburg with a whole group of people and wanted me to go with them, but I decided I would prefer to go for a walk with the Damskaya sisters.

We had a nice walk and chatted gaily all the time, getting back to the station at eleven o'clock. I spotted Zaitsev and pointed him out to Damskaya, saying, 'There goes my former rival . . .' Then we said goodbye and I got into the carriage, where I found myself standing right next to Zaitsev. We exchanged pleasantries and he introduced me to a tall gentleman of foreign appearance, a conductor from New York called Schindler,[1] after which we all

---

[1] Kurt Schindler (1882–1935), composer, conductor and writer on music. Schindler later worked

sat together conversing in German. Schindler is in Russia as a tourist; he said that because Russian music is all the rage in New York he wanted to see for himself what sort of a country it comes from. He will be in St Petersburg for a few days. I invited him and Zaitsev to come to visit me, thinking that it would be agreeable for a lone traveller to spend an evening in a private home. Also I wanted to show him and acquaint him with my compositions. He agreed gladly and we parted amicably until tomorrow.

21 May

Spoke to Anna Grigorievna on the telephone, and she was very appreciative of my detailed analysis of her students' examination performances. Bashkirov also telephoned, inviting me for this evening, possibly to play chess or perhaps games of chance; Capablanca would also be there. But in the first place I have no money, and in the second Zaitsev and the American are coming to visit me (I am very pleased to be having a real American from New York in my house). They came around ten o'clock. Schindler brought with him a bulging folder of his own songs, splendidly printed by an American publisher.

He played them, and they proved to be well schooled, clever, intelligently put together but for the most part not very original. On the whole I liked them, however. We had tea and various Russian delicacies: sig,[1] rowanberry liqueur – this last went down particularly well. Schindler talked away in French and the conversation took on a lively and unforced tone. After tea I played him the Piano Concerto No. 1 and the Sonata No. 2, the latter sending him into raptures. He said it had an '*asiatische Musik*' cast to it, which he found irresistible. I presented him with a copy of the Sonata and he in turn gave me his entire thick volume of songs. As he left he thanked us for our Russian hospitality and was very touched by Mama's gift of a bottle of the liqueur. He is on his way to the Crimea, and then in a couple of weeks or thereabouts plans to be in London where he plans to spend a month, so we shall meet there. Zaitsev could not praise the Sonata too highly and considers it a huge leap forward from the First Sonata.

22 May

Learning English and piano practice took up all my day. I sent a postcard to Nina Meshcherskaya depicting a gentleman with half-a-dozen girls clinging to him. I think this will annoy her, and that makes me very happy. In the

---

for the publishers G. Schirmer in New York reading and assessing submitted manuscripts.
1 A freshwater fish of the salmon family, much prized by Russians.

evening I went to see Kolya Myaskovsky in his new apartment on Vasilievsky Island, two very splendid rooms. We played through *Red Mask* and found it terribly thin on material. I wanted him to write a review of Schindler's compositions for *Muzyka*, but while acknowledging their literacy, he did not find anything of much significance in them so if he did write anything, it would not be complimentary. We played part of his Third Symphony from the piano score he is in the process of completing; it promises to be very good indeed. I drew attention to several things in the First Symphony that I thought would benefit from revising, but he firmly rejected all of them. N.M. promised (half in jest) to write me a very difficult piano concerto, and I promised to perform it. Matters with Kryzhanovsky and Zimmermann are progressing at a snail's pace, and I still need money badly.

23 May

Wrote to Tcherepnin to tell him that *Red Mask* is now ready to be performed. Went into Jurgenson's shop and looked through his own editions (the Petersburg ones), and mentioned to him, as if in passing, that they were excellently produced and that I would be very happy for him to publish some of my work, for example the *Ballade*. He jumped at the notion and we talked seriously; when I gave him to understand that I was prepared to offer it very reasonably, for 200 roubles, but would not go down as low as a hundred, he asked for time to think. We agreed that I would come back again in three days' time. This is very promising, I think it's all nonsense that he is an inferior publisher.

Home again, I received an unexpected telephone call from Diederichs,[1] who offered me an engagement to conduct two concerts in Sokolniki Park in Moscow on 20 and 22 June. Tcherepnin had originally been invited, but was not able to accept and so had recommended me. My first reaction was to feel flattered: whichever way one looks at it this a very worthwhile invitation, and secondly they are offering me the chance to programme my own compositions. But ... what should I do about London? I would have to abandon that trip, hang about in Petersburg until the 15th, and then not know what to do or where to put myself after the 22nd. Not only that, but with the exception of *Dreams* I did not have anything ready to perform. The Symphony would not be ready in time. The fee was 100 roubles a concert; not a great deal, of course, but in my present impoverished state it would hardly go amiss. I thanked Diederichs for the honour he was doing me, mentally offered up thanks to Tcherepnin for his kindness, and asked for twenty-four hours to consider.

---

1 Andrey Diederichs was co-owner with his brother Leonid of the Gebrüder Diederichs piano factory in St Petersburg.

While I was doing my gymnastics at the Sokol in the evening I thought over the whole proposition – London or Moscow? – and came down in favour of London. Naturally it would be very pleasant to be conducting in Moscow and I could include Myaskovsky's Symphony No. 1 (although I was not sure what I could suggest for the second concert), but when all is said and done, if they asked me once they would no doubt ask me again, while there was no knowing when I would ever again have such propitious circumstances in which to introduce myself to people in London. And surely London offers broader prospects than Moscow!

24 May

In the morning, while I was engaged in my English homework, the telephone rang. Annoyed at being interrupted in my studies, I went to answer it. A male voice said, 'Good morning, Sergey Sergeyevich!'

'Who is speaking?' I asked

'Don't you recognize me?'

'Who is this?'

'Have you forgotten?'

Angry, I put down the receiver. A minute later, the telephone rang again. Mama answered, and called me. I said I was busy learning English. The unknown voice announced himself as 'Zakharov from Vienna' and hung up. It took me a little while to cool off, but then I was delighted, and when I had finished what I was doing I rang him back. We had a very stimulating conversation, happy and completely relaxed. He congratulated me on the prize, and said how much he would like to see me. He would be looking in at the Conservatoire at two o'clock today, but I suggested that he try and make it at five o'clock, as that was the time when I would be there for the playthrough of *Red Mask*. This evening he would be going to Terioki, but would be returning on Monday and would telephone me then. He was planning to learn Tcherepnin's concerto to perform it in Moscow, and asked me to prepare the ground with Tcherepnin. He had an invitation to play in Pavlovsk in July. He would be remaining in Russia until October or November, but would then be going to Berlin, apparently for a concert in Leipzig.

With that we said goodbye, and I went in as arranged to the Conservatoire, but Zakharov did not show up. Tcherepnin and I played through *Red Mask* and had a talk about the Moscow invitation, which I told him I had declined. Tcherepnin replied that of course it was interesting that I should be asked to go, so to speak, straight from school to the concert platform, but he agreed that it could also be very useful to go to London. Diederichs had said he would speak again to the organizers to see whether I could appear in the second half of the summer. Ziloti then appeared and Tcherepnin with my assistance played him *Red Mask*. It sounded very effective in the composer's performance. Ziloti said to me that he would like to have my manuscript[1] as soon as possible in order to have the orchestral parts made from it, but he could not say when the concert would take place, as an important consideration would be his foreign touring commitments. Tcherepnin thanked me very much for my help and asked me to remember that in him I would always have a friend ready to help me anywhere and in any way. 'You dedicated to me your Scherzo for four bassoons, so in revenge I may dedicate to you a piece for solo bassoon!' Laughing over this, we parted.

In the evening I stayed at home writing my diary and practising one or two pieces for London.

25 May

Since my relations with the Ruzsky girls cooled I have almost stopped visiting their household. I rang up Nikolay Pavlovich in advance of both the competition for the piano and the Graduation Concert; he was very friendly and promised to come backstage afterwards, but on both occasions something happened to prevent this. He had invited me to come to their house, and I promised to do so, but seeing in my mind's eye the desiccated physiognomies of 'Herodias'[2] and Tatyana, I was not rushing to fulfil my obligation. This morning I telephoned Nikolay Pavlovich and he invited me to lunch; I was delighted to accept, and went. The girls made themselves almost completely agreeable and the parents could not have been more charming. After lunch, when the womenfolk withdrew, Nikolay Pavlovich sent for champagne and opened one bottle after another, the first glass being to celebrate my winning of the prize. At six o'clock I made my escape. Outside, the weather was wonderful, the streets were full of people dressed in their best, Kamennoóstrovsky was green and the sun was shining. My head was spinning, something I detest; I love champagne as a drink but getting drunk gives me no pleasure at all. I walked home to try to dispel at least some of the tipsiness from my head. No one was at home so I did nothing in particular and slept for two hours. After that I worked out chess moves, wrote my diary and practised the piano.

26 May

Slept wonderfully. After lunch massacred Mlle Roblin at chess with seven mates in a row. Caught up on my diary and read up on Sweden, Denmark

---

1 Of the Sinfonietta.
2 Ira Ruzskaya. The Russian spelling of the name makes the sardonic play on words clear.

and Hanover. In the evening played vint. Telephoned Zakharov, but he has not yet returned from Terioki.

27 May

Zakharov is back and telephoned. Another very nice conversation; he suggested meeting today at Shreder's shop, but I said that I had still not organized myself to choose a piano and therefore felt embarrassed to show my face there. Instead I suggested going to visit Myaskovsky tomorrow, and we agreed on that. Yesipova is in Luga and is said to be not at all well. We might go to see her together. It's not a journey I would make on my own, four weary hours there and four back, but with Zakharov it would be a pleasure.

After my English lesson I went to see Jurgenson to hear his decision on the *Ballade*. I really did not know what he was going to say; I expected him to pull a face and haggle about the price, but he did nothing of the sort and agreed on 150 roubles, merely asking that over the winter I let him have an opus made up of piano pieces or songs to compensate for the relatively uncommercial cello piece. I was delighted to receive 150 roubles. Hurrah, I was once again a wealthy man, and no longer would have to put up with the misery of having no more than 42 kopecks in my pocket.

And so, pleased with life, I set off down Nevsky Prospect and went into the 'Northern Journeys' office, where I asked all kinds of questions about my proposed itinerary and bought myself a fascinating train timetable covering the whole of Europe, guidebooks to the principal European cities. I put in an application to the Town Hall for a passport to travel abroad and then went back home, where my flourishing of a thick wad of notes from my wallet produced a most satisfying effect. When I telephoned Kolechka about Zakharov's and my proposed visit tomorrow, he was thrilled to hear about the *Ballade* and congratulated me on getting such a good price for it. I continued studying my guidebooks. Eleonora rang up from Pavlovsk and invited me to come and see them there; I should like to very much, provided I can find the time before my departure: today I am going to the Sokol and tomorrow to N.M. If I can I shall also go to see the Meshcherskys, whom I love dearly. Nina is still away staying with her friend, but comes back at the end of this week.

1 June

I love getting an early-morning train: going somewhere in the early morning is somehow invigorating. I asked to be woken at seven although in fact I was already awake by then. It was earlier than it need have been; the suitcases (I still had to take two) were already packed, and there was nothing else that had to be done. I set off in high spirits and with none of my former forebodings. The only sad thing was that Mama would be on her own for two weeks in St Petersburg. The concierge took a long time to get me a cab (I had to conserve funds on this trip and so did not want to spend money on a motor taxi). Eventually a cab appeared and I set off. All I had by way of hand luggage was a small bag; the two yellow suitcases were destined for the luggage van. An unexpected pleasure at Five Corners: a new music shop with my Sonata in the window. I arrived at the station uncharacteristically early, but this was a good thing: as it was a Sunday the crowds were terrible and I only just managed to give in my luggage in time, checking it only as far as Stockholm because Zakharov had confused me and I still was not certain whether to proceed further along my route or his. The train was already standing at the platform: I found a seat in a carriage, put my bag on it and went back on to the platform.

Mlle Roblin, who had still been asleep when I left the house, had managed to dash to the station to see me off, which was kind of her. A further apparition was the 'famous prizewinner' Hansen[1] accompanied by her sister, both of them dressed in brilliant white from head to toe, and Georges Zakharov, who was taking them to stay at the Zakharov dacha in Terioki. They cast sidelong glances at Mlle Roblin, and once the train had started and I went to sit with them in their third-class carriage(!), could not forbear to enquire how I had bidden farewell to my girlfriend? I confounded them with my unexpected response to their questions: 'She is so pretty, isn't she?'

The journey as far as Terioki slipped by imperceptibly, so engaged were we in our lively chatter, in which the sisters were full of charming attentions to me. They admired my musical letter to Boris, which it seems is now successfully going the rounds. 'Even Zoryusya liked it.' Hm. This provoked an unambiguously meaning laugh. We arrived at Terioki, where the Hanseatics were expecting Boris to meet them, and I was also hoping that he would take the opportunity of coming to say goodbye to me, but either he felt like digging his toes in today or he forgot what time the train was due. In any case, it's not important. I went in to the restaurant car to have lunch, and found a very international clientele there: Swedes, Germans and Finns. After stuffing myself I went back to my compartment; just before Vyborg I pressed myself to the window on the left-hand side and looked at the cemetery where Max's grave is – that is, I did not see precisely the cross on his particular grave, but I could see clearly the group of crosses among which I knew his to be. And once again the sun, the green of the countryside, and the sense of life thrusting through the ground consoled me for the fate of my friend. But the train puffed on speeding me towards my destination.

1 Cecilia Hansen, her sister being Elfrieda.

It grew warm and stuffy, and the soot covering everything began to be irritating. There was a foreign kind of feeling inside the compartment, which contained six of us plus, as a punishment from God, a small child. But as the train forged ahead, so did the hour, and the air grew gradually cooler. The soot also decided to leave us alone, and by the time we neared Åbo[1] everything was marvellous. Anyone claiming that Åbo is a Russian town would have a hard time defending his position: the people, the houses, the signboards, everything looked foreign. The train stopped briefly at the station and then took us straight on to the pier, coming to rest immediately by a white steamer already crammed full of passengers. Between us and the boat was a small shed through which we were required to pass in order to board. Inside the shed we were confronted by two helmeted policemen, demanding our passports, which they undertook to return during the voyage.

I made haste to get on board, in the somewhat naive hope of getting a better cabin, and was instantly struck by a feeling of being abroad: it was a Swedish vessel and I was unable to communicate in a single word of any relevant language. By the staircase leading down to the cabins I saw a Swedish woman with a large sheet of paper, evidently in charge of cabin allocation, surrounded by a cluster of passengers. At this point I remembered that the 'Northern Journeys' bureau had offered me a reservation on the boat, so I went boldly up to the Swede announcing '*Bestellung*'[2] and my name in a firm tone of voice. Sure enough, my name was on the list and I was allocated an excellent cabin with two berths, but unlike our Black Sea steamers or our trains there was no upper berth, both were on the lower level. I hurried back on deck and started scribbling a postcard to Mama, but had no time to write more than the address. The hooter hooted, the passengers waved their handkerchiefs, a group of country schoolmistresses on an excursion sang a psalm, and we slowly got under way. I put on my overcoat and settled myself on the upper deck, towards the bows.

The ship glided over the flat calm, mirror-like water and we emerged from the bay, only to find another, larger one beyond it, and then a succession of islands and creeks that seemed to go on for ever. Only then did I understand the meaning of the note I had read in the guidebook: 'Only an hour and a half on the open sea.' Nearly the whole voyage lay between these islands, so that only for about an hour and a half during the night were we clear of them. The islands were small or medium-sized, stony and for the most part covered in spindly trees. Scattered around without rhyme or reason they stretched as far as the eye could see. I felt marvellously well and enjoyed the voyage tremendously.

1 Åbo is the Swedish name, used by Russians when Finland was part of the Russian Empire, for the Baltic port of Turku.
2 'Reservation' (German).

It began to grow cold and the deck gradually emptied of passengers. I went below and saw that supper was being served. In the Swedish manner, there was a large table in the centre covered with a mass of different *hors d'oeuvre*, some of them not very sophisticated but in huge quantities. Everyone goes to the table and helps himself, and there then follow one or two supper dishes. I did not know the procedure, and since everyone had already served himself and was sitting down by the time I arrived, I did not know what to do and felt uncomfortable. Eventually I did manage to get my supper, however, and then went back on deck to face the cold and the wind. Recalling that we would be arriving in Stockholm early in the morning, and that the approach would be interesting to see, I went below to sleep.

2 June

I slept a whole hour longer than I had intended, but in fact this made no difference because as we were travelling westwards the clocks had been put back an hour during the voyage, and we were already in the Central European time zone. I went on deck, where it was extremely cool and, sadly, overcast. We were threading our way through skerries, quite pleasant to look at, but the beauty of Stockholm's situation has been so talked up that one's expectations are very high. The entry into Stockholm's harbour produced no great impression on me, possibly because of the weather. Once the steamer had docked at the pier, I had to wait a considerable time for my luggage to be hauled out. In the customs shed, which was identical to the one at Åbo, transit labels were stuck on the cases, to be taken off again on leaving the country. Not knowing the language and being encumbered by the luggage, I hailed the first hotel representative I happened across; he put my cases in a car, said something or other to the driver and I sped off through the town, which is certainly very beautiful. We stopped outside a hotel of modest appearance, which I entered boldly stating my requirements in German. They understood me perfectly, gave me a room and paid my taxi fare, which incidentally they forgot to add to my bill, something I realized only after I had left the city. Leaving my bags in the room I went out to explore the town, first of all to the travel agency where I had arranged to pick up some Swedish money (most unattractive, rather like Finnish money). As well as being given a small map of the town I found out without difficulty about steamers to England, and booked a through ticket for the whole of the remainder of my journey.

I then went for a walk through the streets of Stockholm, looking about with interest to observe Swedish men and women. We are used to the Germans, the French and the English, but we know little about the Swedes. On the whole they presented an agreeable appearance: the men tall and strapping and the women, while not especially beautiful, mostly well formed. I went into a small restaurant by the bridge next to the Palace and ran into a clean-shaven Russian, an actor or something of the sort, whose acquaintance I had made on the steamer. He was not alone, but in the company of two other Russians. They were all young, not particularly intellectual, pretty wild in their behaviour, but good-humoured and anxious to see and experience as much as possible. I joined them and we set off along the meandering embankments. These quays are most ingenious, since Stockholm consists of a series of peninsulas, linked by a small number of bridges. The buildings on the quaysides are magnificent, and whenever the sun did appear from behind the clouds the city looked splendid.

We came to the Northern Museum, an imposing edifice facing on to gracious boulevards. The museum's collection, however, I found less attractive: a series of rather cramped rooms full of domestic utensils, innumerable wooden artefacts of northern peoples, all contributing to a depressing sense of monotony, poverty and ugliness. The most interesting exhibits were in the large room to the left of the entrance, containing relics of former days of Sweden's grandeur: knightly suits of mail, various objects of booty and plunder. I thought of those savage times when a knight, encased from head to foot, could with one massive blow from his sword smash to pieces another's coat of mail. I was moved by the sight of Gustavus Adolphus's holed and bloody shirt. I do not remember much history, but the tragic death of the short-sighted monarch has somehow lodged in my memory.[1] My companions did not accompany me into the museum, but when I emerged I joined up with them, and they dragged me off to the Skandsen. Precisely what this was nobody knew, but they assured me that it was very interesting, so we went. It turned out to be a large, hilly park with a number of historical antiquities and other miserable objects dotted about in it. It was tedious and very time-consuming. The sun was now shining on us mercilessly. Two of our group decided they wanted to go swimming, while the third member and I waded across the creek and went to look at the Palace. The interior was much like any palace: long galleries of rooms furnished in different styles with paintings on the walls, decorated floors and vases in alcoves. To the tourist without much time to spend on it, the outside of the Palace is in its grave northern symmetry more interesting.

It was now half past three in the afternoon. I was so tired I hardly made it back to the hotel and collapsed into bed. When I awoke I found it hard to bestir myself. A disappointment awaited me: when I went to my friends'

---

1 The legendary Swedish King, 'the Lion of the North', was killed at the Battle of Lützen in 1632 in what amounted to a Pyrrhic victory for the Protestant Swedish forces over the Catholic forces of the Holy Roman Empire. He was notoriously short-sighted and carried a specially made hand glass.

hotel, where they had also gone to rest, it was half an hour later than the time we had agreed to meet, and they had already left without me. Then I lost my street plan of the town. The final straw was that at the travel agency they had obtained my ticket, but it proved to be very expensive: 135 crowns, that is 75 roubles, to Newcastle. Mama's shares had not been doing well and she had not been able to give me much money, and the more I had to spend at this stage the less I would have for London.

Reconciling myself to my misfortunes I ascended the Katerina-Hissen, a local Eiffel Tower in miniature, from the top of which I had a marvellous view of the city. I then went for an enjoyable ride in one of the open-topped omnibuses that dash round the streets with inimitable velocity and skill; I observed the courage and agility with which Swedish girls negotiate the steep cliffs and in the evening strolled along the boulevards, wandered about the parks and sat in cafés to watch Stockholmers *en famille* taking the air in the parks and cafés. I had the same impression as in the morning: the men strong and vigorous, the women shapely, their faces alert and by no means ill-favoured, but no beauties to be seen.

3 June

At half past nine in the morning my suitcases and I left for the jetty to go by steamer through the Göta Canal to the Trollhetten Falls, that is to say almost the whole way across Sweden. This was a trip I had been looking forward to: I wanted to see the Swedish countryside, the trip along the canal, through the locks and the lakes, was in itself interesting, and finally it was pleasant to be able to rest for two days, so to speak in Nature's bosom, which I felt I had been missing. In any case I was tired to the depths of my being after the exam, after Petersburg and after seeing the sights of Stockholm.

The boat was small and cramped but had been made as comfortable as circumstances could allow: a larger vessel would not be able get through the locks. On the other hand, canal sailing avoids the pitching and rolling of the open sea and the consequent need to ensure the boat's stability, so it was quite high out of the water and had several decks.

There were two passenger decks, a saloon and a fair number of two-berth cabins, on the small side but quite tolerable. We cast off to the accompaniment of much waving of handkerchiefs from those seeing off their friends, in the Swedish manner just from the wrist, the rest of the arm being held out horizontally, until we disappeared from view round the bend. Apparently until evening we would be sailing along the coast between the skerries and only after that would we enter the canal itself and penetrate into the country. This part was not terribly interesting, as I had already had more than my fill of reefs and skerries at Åbo and again at Stockholm. The wind had got up, and the sun that had beaten down on us so mercilessly yesterday while we were walking round Stockholm was today hidden behind the clouds. It was grey and, most disagreeable of all, cold.

The passengers on board were not a very elegant company, and consisted of all different nationalities. I heard mostly Swedish and English spoken, and occasionally German. My cabin companion proved to be a pleasant gentleman of German extraction who directed many compliments at Russia and was generally a pleasant conversation companion during the voyage. I did not see any attractive women, with the possible exception of a young Swedish girl of about fifteen, who was not in herself very attractive but possessed such an inexhaustible repertoire of simpering coquettishness that one would think she had not a single natural gesture at her disposal. She was at least entertaining to watch. She spoke nothing but Swedish and was travelling with very severe-looking parents.

I slept deeply in the afternoon and then went up to freeze on deck – the Réamur thermometer showed 8 degrees. We crossed a small segment of 'real' sea where the boat did roll and some people were sick (I was not among them, and this is important because I have been afraid of getting seasick between Norway and England), and towards evening entered the canal. The wind dropped, nature smiled and all was well. The canal is narrow, too narrow for two boats to pass one another, and all around is the beautiful, peaceful, serene, green scenery. The steamer glides slowly over the surface of the motionless waters of the canal. There is a curiously seductive fascination in watching the agitated surface of the wake churned up by the propeller slip away behind the stern of the boat. We go into the first of the locks. The heavy gates close behind us, our way forward blocked by similar gates in front of us. Cables tie the steamer up to bollards to stop her rocking while small sluice gates at the bottom of the forward gates open to allow water to gush in and boil around the boat. Imperceptibly we rise up to the same level of the canal stretching out before us, upon which the gates open and we sail on.

I went below to sleep, because the German guidebook indicates that there will be interesting things to see early tomorrow morning.

4 June

My cabin companion is a charming man, but he got up at five o'clock and took an age to put on his clothes, preventing me from going back to sleep until he went out. I dozed for another hour but then went to sleep until half past eight so that by the time I went out we had passed through a whole series of locks. My neighbour declared that it had been a splendid sight, and also told me that while the boat was going through a lock one could stroll about in the delightfully lush Swedish countryside. It was most annoying.

However it was some consolation that the sun was shining brightly and promised fine weather all day. I went down to drink coffee in the restaurant, which was empty except for one lone young woman, an American by the look of her. I bowed, sat down and buried my face in my coffee cup, at which she opened the conversation by saying something in English. I answered by indicating that I could not understand a word she was saying. She then tried in French, and we had a pleasant conversation for about ten minutes.

I went back on deck. The boat was making gentle progress along the canal amid picturesque scenery redolent of peace, contentment and good husbandry. At times the canal was raised above the level of the land, restrained by dykes. In the afternoon we arrived at Motala, the point at which the canal joins Lake Vattern. Here the steamer waited an hour, and we passengers were free to stroll about. Not far away, by the side of the canal, stood a memorial marking the grave of the engineer who had constructed the canal. I looked at it with awe and respect. Accompanied by the young lady I had met at breakfast, who turned out to be not an American but a German (a 'suffragette', according to my neighbour, because her reason for being in Stockholm was to attend a conference on equal rights for women), I looked round the sleepy little provincial town. Hardly any of its inhabitants were venturing forth from the palisades and fences of their gardens, so all was quiet, welcoming and somnolent. No doubt they could only regard with a kind of pitying curiosity these strange beings who go by the name of 'tourist' and for some reason feel it necessary to wander all over the globe looking at everything, poking their noses into everything.

After thirty-six hours of sitting about on the boat it was very pleasant to run about on shore, but we returned 'home' to continue our voyage. The boat was sailing across a wide lake, the smiling landscape disappeared, so I went below for a nap in my bunk and when I returned to the deck, the sun was beginning to set. The steamer glided along the canal, which by this time had become a chain of little lakes, evidently on land that had been flooded, since the boat's passage was marked with buoys. Then another stretch of the canal proper, with trees drooping into its smooth waters, followed, just to provide entertainment, by two more locks, and then more flooded land marked with buoys, all of this illuminated and gilded by the slanting rays of the setting sun. I found a superb vantage point right in the bows of the ship where, concealed from the rest of the vessel by a wooden parapet, I sat on a coil of rope daydreaming and taking pleasure in my voyage.

We had passed through the highest point of the canal, and after supper began the slow descent through the locks. This began with a series of eight, which took more than hour to traverse. I suggested another walk to the young suffragette. She agreed readily and, chattering away merrily in German, we enjoyed our stroll, returning to our ship, a fine sight, so tall and so white, as she passed through the last of the locks. It was quiet on deck, most of the passengers were asleep, except for a few taking the air stretched out on chaises-longues and casting knowing smiles – entirely misplaced, needless to say – in the direction of the returning couple. I went to my cabin, where I found my cabin companion already happily snuffling in his sleep.

5 June

Waking up in the morning and looking through the porthole I thought we must be crossing a lake whose shores were so far away as to be barely visible. I knew that it was a long stretch of water and there would not be anything interesting to see, so did not hurry to get out of bed. By the time I went out on deck we had re-entered the canal, reaching Trolhetten around midday, the town whose most famous attribute is the great waterfall and where I would be transferring from ship to train in order to continue my journey to Christiania. Because the steamer had to negotiate a string of locks in Trolhetten itself, all the passengers disembarked in a rush to view the falls. My neighbour and I were among the first to get ourselves into a carriage and be taken to the waterfall, which was not far away. The falls are beautiful and impetuous, although smaller than those on the Rhine. We began by scrambling among the rocks at the foot of the falls, and looking up at them I tried to allow myself to be overwhelmed by the sense of the enormous mass of water being borne down on me. Then we climbed up to look down at the falls from high up on the bridge that had been thrown across the gorge: this was a powerful spectacle.

My companion, who was continuing the voyage further on, then left me, anxious lest she miss the boat's departure, but I went on along the bank because the water's precipitous descent continued for some way. The water now turbulently gushed between the rocks, now sinuously wound its way round deep hollows in the riverbed. The passengers straggled picturesquely among the rocks surrounding the waterfall. I soon found my suffragette again who, to my surprise, was arm in arm with the youthful Swedish *poseuse*. When I joined them, the latter was very happy to stop and talk, but alas she knew no word of any other language but Swedish. This was a matter of regret. We walked down to the lowest of the locks to which the steamer would eventually have to descend. While waiting we walked through the field and lay down under a tree. I allowed myself to tickle the cheek of the *poseuse* with a straw, eliciting in response a skittish inclination of the head and a stern reproof from the suffragette: 'Nicht ergern'.[1]

When the boat arrived the suffragette and I shook hands in parting in a

---

1   *Sic*. Presumably 'Nicht ärgern': German for 'Don't annoy her'.

very friendly manner, and I should have liked to do the same with the Swedish girl, but she, anticipating my gesture, said that her hands were not clean and would not extend her hand to me. At first I was rather shocked by this, but later discovered that abroad it is not the invariable custom to shake hands when bidding farewell; indeed it is practically unknown among the young.

I had an hour and a half before my train left, so I climbed up in a leisurely fashion to the top of the bank. The silence of the forest combined with the turbulence of the waterfall; the rocks and the pines brought back memories of Finland. I thought of Max, and wanted to dedicate to his memory the symphony I was composing in my mind. I sat on a rock and watched the water flowing past.

But now it was time to look for the railway station. My suitcases were already there. Still absorbed in my thoughts of Max, under the ineffaceable and often overwhelmingly powerful spell of his personality, I made my way to the station, tracked down my luggage, had something to eat and boarded the train to Christiania which had just pulled in.

It was three o'clock, the sun was shining, I found a place and stretched out along the seat. The railway carriages here are magnificent, far superior to those in any other country: wide, spacious and comfortable. Of course it was not quite so good when there were six people to a compartment, but that is everywhere the way of it when one travels second class. I went into the restaurant wanting some beer, but found that the rule here is no alcohol, even beer one can only get with a meal. So there was no help for it but to order a sandwich with the beer; I drank the beer and left the sandwich to the flies, of which incidentally there cannot have been more than a couple on the whole train.

At last the sun went down and it grew pleasantly cool. We crossed the Norwegian border and entered the land of Grieg. Customs officials poked their nose into my travelling bag and went on their way. I went outside on to the open step of the carriage and spent there almost all the remainder of the journey, several hours. Norway was a feast for the eyes: green, fresh, a mixture of mountainous and open country, forests and fields, all beautiful and interesting to look at. I was delighted to find myself in Norway, a foreign country but an attractive and welcoming one. I thought of Peer Gynt and regretted not having read more of Hamsun, Ibsen and other northern writers. We passed rocky hillsides and dived into tunnels and on one occasion near a large town crossed over a magnificent waterfall.

As the evening drew on it became quite cold. I put on my overcoat, but eventually had to withdraw inside the carriage itself. On the left side of the train there appeared a wide bay beside which Christiania was situated. It took a long time for us to wind our way round the bay, but eventually we pulled in below the roof of a grand station. Carrying my small bag in my hand I left the station and went on to the street, having prepared myself by reading in my Russian all-Europe guidebook that 'the main street Karlyohansgade, on which most of the hotels are to be found, starts directly from the railway station'. However, as far as I could see there was no main street starting from the station. I struck off to the left, along some kind of boulevard, but it did not appear to offer anything very promising, so I retraced my steps to the station and read more carefully the name of the small street that did indeed start directly in front of it. Making out with some difficulty that the name of the street was Karl Johans Gade and that it must therefore be the important Karlyonhansgade of my guidebook, I cursed Christiania as a hole no better than Kharkov and, travel bag in hand, set out along the 'main street'. Quite soon it broadened out, shops and fine buildings began appearing and the street became one appropriate to grace a civilized city. I was feeling tired and wanted to find a comfortable billet for the night. Although my financial situation hardly permitted luxury I went into the best hotel I could find, the Grand Hotel, and was extremely happy to be given an inexpensive room there.

After settling myself in and dining in the hotel's comfortable restaurant, I sallied forth on to the street and found Christiania to be a very attractive place. The liveliest part of Karl Johans Gade was just by the entrance to the hotel, a beautifully laid out grass- and tree-lined boulevard, thronged with well-dressed crowds out to enjoy themselves. The people pleased me much more than the Swedes had done: the fresh-faced, often pretty and always shapely Norwegian women were a welcome and attractive sight. The men were also better looking than the Swedes. They are a fresh, wholesome and well preserved people immediately inviting trust, one instinctively feels a liking and a generally favourable disposition towards them. I thoroughly enjoyed my saunter along the boulevard amid this gay, nicely turned-out crowd. I did not stay out for long though; I was soon overcome by fatigue, returned to my hotel, and slept.

6 June

After a wonderful sleep I went out with joyful anticipation, acquired a street map in a travel bureau, and sat on a shady bench on the boulevard to acquaint myself with the disposition of the various monuments and sights of the city. The map had a suggested tour for those wishing to get to know the town, and this I made thorough use of. The town does not make a particularly strong impression; its best feature is the park laid out on a hillside on its northern extremity. This is a beautiful and interesting space with an attractive square-shaped ornamental lake on the summit of a knoll and a tower, from the top of which one has a good view of the bay, the town and its surroundings. But strange as it may seem I liked the town, it was a friendly sort of place and I was glad that I had come there. I went at random into a little restaurant on the Kongens Gade where I had an excellent lunch. The speciality was the enormous crabs and lobsters displayed to advantage in the window, but I had to watch my expenditure and I decided not to order any of these animals.

After lunch I retired from the heat back to the Grand Hotel, where in the spacious, cool reading room I wrote postcards to all my friends. These amounted to more than a score and I expended on them a quantity of ink, postcards, time and splendid Norwegian stamps, which were larger than usual and colourfully illustrated by reason of the Jubilee. It transpires that Christiania has been in existence for a hundred years and there is an exhibition to commemorate this to which Norwegians from the length and breadth of the country have flocked, hence the animated and finely garbed crowds on the street. So I had been fortunate to come at a time when Norwegians were more on display and in greater numbers than usual. And so, having written a pile of cards, I went down to the pier and boarded a small steamer that sailed round the bay on which Christiania is situated. It was not the most fascinating excursion and it lasted more than two hours, but there were nice views and I spent most of the time dozing on a deckchair. On my return I dined again in the excellent Kongens Gade restaurant, wrote some pages of my 'travel impressions' in the hotel, and then made my way to the station to continue my journey to Bergen. I had at my disposal a most comfortable berth in the sleeping car, and went to bed early as I wanted to be up betimes in the morning.

7 June

The line between Christiania and Bergen crosses the spine of Scandinavia so the train went up as high as the permanent snow line. Although I very much wanted more sleep, I forced myself to get up at five in the morning because it was so interesting to see the winter landscape. When the train stopped I got out for a walk. The snow crunched beneath my feet but although the day was crisp and fresh it was not too cold to go out just wearing a jacket. The train moved on and soon we found ourselves plagued by long corridor walls rising above the permanent way to protect it from snowstorms and avalanches. The outline of the mountains is less elaborate than in Switzerland or the Caucasus, but the endless wastes of snow on snow – they are magnificent! At last we began to lose height and it grew warmer, we heard the babbling of brooks and there were signs of spring. The mountains became more jagged and interesting, and we came to a region of lakes, thundering waterfalls and green-clad precipices. Although less magnificent than the views afforded by Switzerland, they were wilder and more untouched by man. Our train wound its way past deep, intricately formed lakes, along shores sliced through by cliffs tumbling right into the water.

A couple of hours later we were in Bergen, which proved to be a dirty, dusty town. Leaving my things at the station I went down to the pier to find out if the boat for Newcastle would be docking any time soon. I made my enquiries in English, the first phrases I had essayed in this language. People found it hard to understand what I was saying, and I in turn could make out only with difficulty that the boat was delayed by several hours. There was no help for it, I just had to waste the best part of a day in this ugly town. In front of me lay thirty-six hours on the open sea. Knowing that the German Sea[1] was notorious I worried about the boat pitching and rolling and was afraid that I would be seasick for the whole voyage. I even had moments of neurasthenic alarm that we would go the bottom of the ocean, but the sight of such a number of vessels docked at the pier calmed me and banished these thoughts.

The jetty was crowded with people bustling about their business and the thought occurred to me, what if Max had not really shot himself but the body found had been that of someone else, and he had fled abroad to find happiness elsewhere? Suppose I were to meet him again, here on the jetty? The fantasy took hold and obligingly produced image after image in my mind as I wandered round the town, sunk in my daydreams. Eventually I roused myself to go into a café with a little garden attached, drink some beer and scribble out some of my travel notes. I should have liked to find Grieg's grave, but it was some way out of the town, a train journey away.

At last the steamer put in an appearance, a large, spacious and comfortable ship. I took my luggage on board and occupied a cabin. My neighbour, an elderly Englishman, was wonderfully gracious but my lessons proved unavailing and I could understand practically nothing of what he said, so for the most part our communication was carried on in the manner of two deaf mutes. He introduced me to several of his acquaintances, but here again matters could progress no further than amiable smiles. The passenger list seemed to consist exclusively of English people.

A misfortune then befell me: during the morning, while we were coming through the Scandinavian mountains and I had spent the whole time leaning out of the open window, I got a draught in my eye and now it started to water from time to time. It was horribly uncomfortable, especially at dinner, when I looked like someone in the grip of an uncontrollable fit of weeping.

The sea was quite calm and the ship did not roll at all.

---

1 The North Sea.

8 June

It seems to be my fate to have cabin companions who, delightful though they are, nevertheless get up at five o'clock in the morning! This happened this morning when, it being Sunday, my Englishman as a faithful son of his church wished to say his prayers at daybreak. The trouble in my eye came and went, but its continual weeping spoilt the voyage. When we were far out of sight of land the boat did begin to roll a little, but not enough to make one sick. The wind had considerable dampness in it, and not wishing to leave the deck I drank some whisky in order to warm up. I played chess against some commercial travellers on the boat, and won every game. By evening the ship was rolling quite strongly, but by this time I was used to it and hoped there would be a real blow. For a long time when all the other passengers had retired to their cabins I strolled on the deck, which had enough length to be pleasant to walk on. By midnight I was tired enough to want to go to bed myself, so went in search of my cabin.

9 June

We docked at Newcastle at seven o'clock in the morning. I bade farewell to my Englishman, who introduced me to his nieces: these were somewhat reserved English girls, not unattractive, slightly reminiscent of Umnenkaya. He invited me to come and stay as his guest. Customs opened my luggage and gave it a cursory examination, after which I took some kind of antediluvian phaeton through the grim streets of the town to the railway station. Here I was astonished by two things: (1) there is no second class in England, you travel either first or third class, but third is comfortable, well upholstered and clean and everyone goes third class, first being the preserve of the seriously rich or the incurably snobbish; (2) nobody took care of my luggage and when it was put in the guard's van I was not given any receipt for it, so on arrival in London I simply went to collect it without saying anything to anybody.

And so the train pulled out of Newcastle on its four-hour journey to London. We rushed along at incredible speed; I enjoyed looking out of the window swaying about on my softly upholstered third-class seat. The prospects seen from the window were green and pleasant, more beautiful than Germany, somewhere in between Switzerland and France. My companions in the carriage were well educated and clean, superior to what one would expect to find in a second-class carriage in rural Russia. We were summoned to lunch in the restaurant car, and the journey to London sped by in no time.

Arriving in London I made do without a porter: remembering that I was after all a 'Sokol', I hoisted up my two suitcases and the travel case and hailed a taxi. Carefully enunciating the address, I was driven to Clifton Gardens where I was greeted first of all by Maria Ivanovna and then my dear Andreyevs. My London life had begun.

9 June – 7 July
London

The Andreyevs had installed themselves in Clifton Gardens with their old friend Maria Ivanovna, an old maid obsessed with the niceties of fashionable behaviour but rather abrupt in manner – not to put too fine a point on it, lacking in courtesy. Russian in origin, she has lived in England for twenty years without leaving the country, but she still worships everything Russian, including the Andreyevs. I was found a room in a nearby house, but we all lunched, dined and spent our time together. At first Maria Ivanovna's liking for the Andreyevs extended also to me, but this was largely by inertia, and as I responded in kind to all her rudenesses we not infrequently fell out and quarrelled. The Andreyevs however were always kindness itself to me.

I had brought with me a letter from Tcherepnin to Otto Kling,[1] a Director of the Breitkopf und Härtel music shop and a great admirer of Russian music. Armed with Tcherepnin's letter and dressed in top hat and morning coat, I presented myself to Kling, who proved to be a delightful gentleman and placed at my disposal an excellent room in his establishment where I could practise. The room had several grand pianos, an armchair, a table and marvellous caricatures of musicians on the walls. In it had worked at different times Tcherepnin, Scriabin, Rachmaninov and other Russian musicians.

Since my most immediate musical plan was the complete revision from scratch of the Sinfonietta for Ziloti's concert, I set to work with a will, spurred on by the amenities offered by the room. I went there about ten o'clock every morning and worked until one, returning home for lunch.

The Diaghilev season was at its height; Nikolay Vasilievich[2] was due to sing in the opera the day after tomorrow. I knew Nouvel was in London, and recalling his predilection for hanging about productions of Russian music, asked Nikolay Vasilievich to find out if anyone in the theatre knew his address. Nikolay Vasilievich asked Diaghilev and he, on hearing my name mentioned, said that he would like to meet me as he had things to discuss with me. This was like a revelation to me: I had come to London knowing

---

1   The Swiss publisher Otto Kling was at this time Director of the London branch of Breitkopf und Härtel, but at the outbreak of the First World War he acquired the English firm of J. & W. Chester, which he rapidly made into a powerful publishing house, entering into a contract with Stravinsky among other leading composers.
2   Andreyev.

that Russian music was all the rage now, and of course I was hoping to make some connections in that field. I had for a long time had the greatest interest in Diaghilev and his activities and had no hesitation whatsoever in wanting to enter into a relationship with this brilliant entrepreneur; now suddenly to find that the entrepreneur himself was anxious to make contact with me was like unexpectedly hitting the bull's eye.

Diaghilev asked Andreyev to bring me backstage, so in two days' time we went to do this. I was nervous about the forthcoming encounter with someone I knew to be a fascinating personality and one, moreover, of legendary charm. On this first occasion Diaghilev did not appear, but a couple of days later at *The Nightingale*[1] we finally met. He was a supremely elegant figure in top hat and tails, and extended a white-gloved hand to me saying that he was very glad to meet me having long wanted to do so. He invited me to come to any of the performances he was presenting, said he would be interested to have my opinion of *The Nightingale*, and wished to meet me in the next few days to have a serious talk and to listen to my compositions. We would arrange this meeting through Nouvel. With that we parted; soon after I saw Nouvel, who told me that Diaghilev wanted to commission a ballet from me.

In the meantime Kling had introduced me to Bantock,[2] the Director of the Birmingham Music Conservatoire, a most charming gentleman who invited me to stay with him for a couple of days. It was very nice in Birmingham; I enjoyed being there and defeated everyone at chess. On my return to London I received a letter from Nouvel to the effect that Diaghilev was inviting us to lunch. On the appointed day I called for Nouvel and we went together to the restaurant. Diaghilev was late as usual, and we waited for twenty minutes in the sitting room outside the restaurant. Nouvel chaffed me about being at heart a thoroughgoing careerist and speculated to what lengths I would go to further my affairs with Diaghilev. The great man now appeared accompanied by Massine, his latest love. Massine was still just a youth; he danced wonderfully in Strauss's *Joseph*.[3]

The lunch was excellent. It began with melon, which I liked. We started talking about ballet. I advanced my decidedly independent views on the subject, but Diaghilev paid little attention and talked continually about all kinds of nuances and subtleties in recent tendencies in ballet that held little interest for me. For example, some choreographers invent movements to mirror the music as closely as possible, whereas others are more interested in

---

1 Stravinsky's *Le Rossignol*, in the original three-act opera version to Stepan Mitusov's libretto based on Hans Christian Andersen's fairy tale. The first performance had taken place in Paris a month earlier. Acts II and III were later arranged by the composer as a one-act ballet, *Le chant du rossignol*.
2 Granville Bantock (1868–1946), composer, at the time Principal of the Midland School of Music in Birmingham.
3 The ballet *Josephslegende* (*The Legend of Joseph*), Op. 63 (1914).

using the choreography to form a counterpoint to the music. At the first convenient opportunity I attempted to turn the conversation away from ballet towards opera. We talked for a while about *The Gambler*, which I proposed as an ideal subject for an opera, but Diaghilev showed no interest at all in this and immediately reverted to the ballet.

After lunch we repaired to the Breitkopf shop so that he could listen to my compositions. I played: (1) Sonata No. 2; (2) *Maddalena*; (3) Piano Concerto No. 2. He liked *Maddalena* least of all; he was pleased by the last two movements of the Sonata; and the Second Piano Concerto sent him into ecstasies.

'Now we should begin our lunch all over again!' he exclaimed, meaning that he now understood how we should be talking, and what about.

I was offered seats for all the performances, and a few days later he invited me to the *salon* of the Cecil Hotel for further discussions. Everything was as it should be: the *salon* a room of devastating elegance. Diaghilev was extremely unpunctual but when he arrived tea was served and we began to talk. Diaghilev's idea was no more and no less than to present my Piano Concerto as a stage production, that is to say with me playing while the dancers dance on the stage. He even had a subject in mind, or rather not so much an actual subject as the sort of territory where one might be found, such as for example Lel and the Snow Maiden, only Lel should not be a little pastoral shepherd boy, more of a grotesque, comic figure.

My immediate reaction was that this was a stupid idea, but thinking that it would hardly be politic to say so outright, I attempted to steer him towards the idea that it would be better and more successful to commission an entirely new ballet score.

'But I most definitely want my next season to have something by you in it, and I suppose that you will not have time to compose a completely new ballet by then.'

There was one other project: to create a ballet from my pianoforte pieces, to be orchestrated by me. In any case all this would be subject to further discussion with Nijinsky, who was due to arrive in London in a few days' time. The mention of Nijinsky's name provoked an unnatural gleam in Diaghilev's eyes. However, Nijinsky did not come, but instead Diaghilev came again to listen to the Second Piano Concerto in the company of the Spanish painter Sert.[1] After the first-movement cadenza Sert, who did not realize that I understood French, cried, 'Mais c'est une bête féroce', and then, seeing that I did understand, was most apologetic.

They were both rapturous over the Concerto, Diaghilev to my mind

---

1 José Maria Sert (1876–1945) was the first non-Russian artist to be invited by Diaghilev to design a production for the Ballets Russes. The first of these was the Strauss ballet *The Legend of Joseph*.

rather incautiously so, since to be so enthusiastic before any agreement had been signed was not very prudent. He considered that among my more attractive characteristics was a tendency towards a nationalist style, glimpses of which could be seen from time to time. In his opinion this augured well for the future but for the present it was overlaid by an international musical language.

In the time elapsing between these evenings I went often to the theatre where I could always make use of one of the four seats in row 7 that were reserved for Diaghilev. On this occasion *Petrushka* afforded me greater pleasure than last year in Paris, and I could state without any qualification that I liked it. Unfortunately *The Rite of Spring* was not in the repertoire for this season.

The next time I saw him, Diaghilev introduced me to his principal ballet conductor Monteux,[1] a very nice man, and we were supposed to be lunching with Beecham,[2] a London millionaire with whom Diaghilev worked in association and who exerted a huge influence on music in London. But Beecham had gone off somewhere, and so the three of us lunched together at the Savoy Hotel. After lunch, at Breitkopf's, I played the First Piano Concerto to Diaghilev and Monteux; they liked it not so much for the music as for its tempo and *élan*. Monteux invited me to play in Paris next winter; he has a high-quality symphony orchestra concert series there. I then played them some small pieces from Op. 12 and the first of the *Sarcasms*. As the time for my departure was approaching, Diaghilev said to me, 'Do not leave without talking to me.'

I had hoped to be able to leave taking a signed contract with me, but this was not to be the case. When, the day before my departure, I went backstage, Diaghilev was in a state of great agitation over something or other – somebody was not able to sing or dance – and our conversation was hopelessly distracted. All I could get from him was that on my return to St Petersburg I should contact Nouvel and Karatygin, and they would put me in touch with a proper Russian writer, Gorodetsky[3] for example, who would provide

1 Pierre Monteux (1875–1964), conductor responsible for the premieres of *Petrushka*, *The Rite of Spring* and *Daphnis et Chloé*. Among the orchestras with which he later became most closely associated were the Boston Symphony, the Concertgebouworkest and the London Symphony Orchestra.
2 Sir Thomas Beecham (1879–1961), the subsequent founder both of the London Philharmonic Orchestra and the Royal Philharmonic Orchestra, was at this time devoting most of his considerable financial resources and creative energy to the Royal Opera at Covent Garden.
3 Sergey Gorodetsky (1884–1967) had founded with Nikolay Gumilyov the movement in poetry known as Acmeism as a reaction to the Symbolism of Bryusov, Sologub, Balmont and Blok. The most brilliantly gifted of the Acmeists were Anna Akhmatova (for a time Gumilyov's wife) and Osip Mandelstam. After the Revolution, Gorodetsky irretrievably damaged his reputation by his slavish recasting of the libretto of *A Life for the Tsar* into *Ivan Susanin*, and above all by denying any connection to the Acmeists and posthumously denouncing Gumilyov, who was arrested and executed in 1921.

me with a ballet libretto. He, Diaghilev, would be in Moscow and St Petersburg in August, and should I be in Kislovodsk he would write to me there for final negotiations and to sign a contract. With that we parted.

All in all, therefore, I had managed to make a very good career opening for myself in London. There is no doubt that, bypassing all our Russian institutions, I had triumphantly launched myself on the broad European highway of the Diaghilev company. It had always seemed to me that this enterprise was made for me, and I for it. The whole trip to London, undertaken as it was with no definite objective in view, had nevertheless appealed to me as an idea that had the potential to bring me much good. I definitely have a nose for such things; I had felt for a long time that something was bound to succeed in my relations with Diaghilev. When I was preparing for the Competition I was quite sure, in the face of opposition from all my friends, relations and teachers, that I was right to decide to play my Concerto, because I sensed that only with this piece would I be able to overwhelm the judges in such a way that, electrified rather than sitting in sober judgement, they would award me the prize.

Now a few words about how I spent the rest of my time in London.

I would rise at nine o'clock, drink coffee with a roll and butter, honey or jam in the English manner. I then sat on the top deck of an open-topped omnibus and went to Breitkopf where I applied myself diligently to the revision of the Sinfonietta. Even so, in the month I was there I only managed to complete the first movement. At one o'clock I had to gather up my score and take the bus back to have lunch, because heaven forfend I should be late. In the afternoon I often played bridge with Nikolay Vasilievich and Maria Ivanovna, or went on an excursion with the Andreyevs, or sat and wrote letters. I also went frequently to the Russian theatre, and sometimes went walking in Hyde Park, where loving couples billed and cooed on the grass with endearing abandon. Once we went to a music-hall, which was most entertaining except that, sadly, without a good grasp of English a lot of it passed me by (and a month's stay was not enough to get me speaking the language). Nikolay Vasilievich and I went to a boxing match together: I loved this, finding in it something entirely new: at critical moments the crowd would literally howl.

On Sundays we, like all properly brought-up residents of London, went out of town, not taking Maria Ivanovna with us, which upset her greatly. An especially good trip was the one to Windsor, which at my instigation we undertook on top of a bus. This was quite a lengthy journey on a highway smooth as parquet, followed by a tour of the castle, then lunch, despatch of some postcards and then return to town by train. Another excursion was to the delightful Kew Gardens with its stunning Orangery for tropical plants, where one goes up staircases and across bridges through such dense thickets of strange, exotic giant vegetation one might think oneself deep in the jungles of Brazil. The gardens themselves are beautiful, and this was altogether a wonderful excursion. It was rare, however, for Anna Grigorievna and me to avoid squabbling over something or other, indeed by the end of the month we were quarrelling so frequently that a coolness grew up between us. Nikolay Vasilievich's character is so exceptional that he and I had cross words only once, and that was on the subject of Maria Ivanovna. Anna Grigorievna left London before the main party, and the best expedition of all was the last one, without her: Andreyev, his friend Roksikov who happened to be in London at the time, and I. Andreyev said, 'Come on, lads, today I'll treat you to lunch in an Italian restaurant.'

We were delighted. We drank Chianti, grew merry, went to Richmond Park and then took a boat along the river Thames to an old castle. It was altogether a wonderful time.

In my last days I chased all over London with Roksikov buying things: shirts, an overcoat, a suit (a marvellous white and black one), a racquet for Katya Schmidthof, and so on. I ran out of money so Nikolay Vasilievich lent me three guineas. On the morning of the 7th I set off with Roksikov back to Russia. Andreyev was to follow a week later. I carried away with me a glowing impression of London, as well as having taken a great step forward here, above all I liked the place, and I liked English people as well even though their tendency to self-glorification and self-satisfaction irritated me and I took every chance I could to praise Russia in every way: Russian music is today without a shadow of a doubt the best, indeed the only music, and when in Birmingham people said to me triumphantly, 'See how marvellous everything is here!' I would be quick to reply, 'Splendid! Almost as good as what we have in Russia.'

And so Roksikov and I set off for Ostend, where we spent the late afternoon and evening walking on the beach looking at the people and feeling awkward at still being in our travelling clothes. We looked at the Kursaal, and I should have liked to go into the casino but was told that after a whole series of procedural formalities it would be the next day before I could get an entry card, so I gave up the idea. We bought bathing costumes to disport ourselves in the sea, and in the evening travelled on through Brussels to Cologne. The next morning, after a cursory look at the overwhelming Cathedral, we transferred to a D-Zug[1] for Berlin.

Arriving in Berlin at four o'clock, the first thing we did was lose sight of one another. Not over-concerned about this I took a car and went to my beloved Tiergarten where I wandered about for some time and drank beer. I did not see a single good-looking German woman. I dined at the Kempinsky

---

1 *Direct-Zug* – express through train.

and then went on the Underground to a randomly picked destination, purely to compare the Berlin Underground with London's. London's is indisputably superior, but I did end up in a part of town called Schöneberg with streets of a reassuring solidity and well-being the like of which I had never seen elsewhere: broad, long, peaceful, tree-lined avenues with wide pavements and a road surface like glass. The houses were imposing and had large, well-spaced windows that bore witness to the spaciousness of the apartments within. It was a wonderful part of town.

The air was warm and still. I took an open-topped car and went to the station, where I found the long-suffering Roksikov. We got on our way to Russia, stopping at Alexandrov for Customs checks. However, we stayed in our carriage because the line from Alexandrov to Warsaw is narrow gauge, as it is in Europe, so the same train continues as far as Warsaw. It was a curious sensation to be travelling through Mother Russia[1] in a foreign train. In Warsaw we were obliged to traverse the dusty streets going from one station to the other. Although it is true I did not go through the centre of the city I did not much like what I saw, but I was struck by the Jews in their fine long-skirted coats, beards and side whiskers. In no other city would you find examples like this! Warsaw was where Roksikov and I parted company, but not before I was obliged to borrow five roubles from him, as I had completely run out of money!

Although I was on my way back to St Petersburg, I wanted to go via Moscow so that I could hear a performance of *Dreams* conducted by Yurasovsky. After an exhausting twenty-four hours in a sultry, suffocatingly dusty train, I arrived in Moscow as evening was falling, to be met by Katyusha Schmidthof. My information about the concert was not quite accurate: it was not taking place until the following day, so as I really did not want to wait I left the same night for Petersburg after spending a couple of hours with Katyusha. Her mother is now seriously ill with a recurrence of her cancer. I felt deeply sorry for the poor girl, and as the train bore me at headlong speed towards Petersburg while I sat by the open window revelling in the glorious fresh air, I thought of what would become of her when her mother dies, and whether it might be possible to arrange for her and my mother to be together.

11 July

At half past eight in the morning I disembarked on to the platform of the Nikolayevsky station. From the heat in Petersburg I might as well have been in Africa, the wind was not so much dusty as a veritable simoom. There was

---

1 Poland formed part of the Russian Empire until it was surrendered to the German Powers by the Treaty of Brest-Litovsk that ended Russia's participation in the First World War.

a strike of tram workers in the suburbs as a result of which the trams could not be turned round: the usual sort of horrible trick Petersburg residents have to put up with in the summer.

Mama was overjoyed to see me and we talked for hours, I about London and Diaghilev, she about the strike and the boredom of her life in Petersburg. Certainly it cannot have been easy or pleasant to spend a month alone in such sultry heat. Mama was anxious to get out of Petersburg as soon as possible, but I wanted to stay for at least a week. Apart from anything else I could not think of going away until I had resolved the question of the libretto. The first thing I did, therefore, was telephone Nouvel. He complained shrilly that he was up to his ears in work and it would be at least Tuesday before he would be able to think of anything else. In any case, matters concerning a libretto must be pursued through Karatygin, so would it not be better for me to contact him directly? It was true that it would be simpler and more pleasant not to have to deal with the bumptious Nouvel. I twice telephoned Karatygin, but the only response was silence.

I spent the day with Mama, sorting out my things and showing her my various purchases.

12 July

Failing once again to get Karatygin on the telephone I went myself to his apartment. It was locked up tight, and the concierge downstairs informed me that Karatygin was staying with Gessen on Kamenny Island. Since I was acquainted with Gessen I wasted no time in going there and happened on the whole family at lunch, with Karatygin. When I told him that Diaghilev was commissioning a ballet from me, he said, 'I'm delighted; I have been telling him for some time he should work with you, but he was afraid you would not produce anything very substantial, and would not orchestrate it well. I must admit I had not particularly recommended you to him for your powers of orchestration.

I broached the question of the libretto and suggested a collaboration with him. He replied that the best person to produce a libretto would be the elderly[1] Sergey Gorodetsky, and since he lived in Petersburg, or at any rate near by, it would be best to make contact with him. Gessen kindly undertook to find out from his office where Gorodetsky lives, and will invite both of us to his house the day after tomorrow to talk about the ballet.

After this the conversation turned to the world war, which was everywhere in the air and seemed to my hosts to be unavoidable. This was a

---

1 Gorodetsky was at this time thirty years of age, to Prokofiev's twenty-three and Karatygin's thirty-nine.

notion to me as unwelcome as it was completely unexpected, and I returned home cast down by fears of the impending catastrophe. The evening papers increased the sense of alarm. At home there was talk of nothing else but the war in Europe.

13 June

Following the desperate heat, the rain fell in sheets just as I was planning to go to Terioki to the Zakharovs. I decided to ignore the rain and went all the same, jettisoning none the less my desire to show off my new suit. I put on a waterproof coat and the despised galoshes, and set off. As I had hoped it would, the rain eased off by the time I got to Terioki. When with eager anticipation I entered the spacious Zakharov dacha I found the whole family at the table. Exclamations of surprise and joy all round, with an especially friendly welcome from Boris. A place was quickly found for me, but I had almost no chance to eat, so much did I have to tell them about London, about Diaghilev and my plans. Relations with Boris were affectionate and easy; all the old shadows have vanished.

After the meal he pressed me to play the Second Sonata, which he had not heard from my hands and which evidently he had not fully worked out himself. I played the Sonata, and he liked it very much. Present were also the Hansen sisters, who are frequent guests at the dacha. We walked, drank afternoon tea; Borya asked me many questions about London and spoke at length about the war. Lyova Karneyev came; Lida and Zoya had gone away today to stay with friends at Yukki, which prompted Boris to say that they would be sorry to be absent on such a day.

We played croquet; I groaned to think of my former prowess as champion. Against Lyova I won one game and lost two; against Borya won two, lost one. Strange: in the past I usually lost to Boris. Lyova listed his favourite girls, so the conversation would go something like this: 'And what is No. 20 doing these days?' Before, he used to imitate my croquet championships, now it's my approach to classifying girls. In the evening we went with the Hansens to a local theatre, and I went straight from there to the train. Zakharov invited me to come and stay with him, which was very kind of him, but I doubt that I shall be able to take up the invitation this summer.

Very happy, I returned to St Petersburg.

14 July

Apparently Russia's robustly warlike threats have had an effect on Austria and Germany, where there the talk is of conciliation, so perhaps there will not be a war in Europe.

I telephoned Gessen in Kamenny Island, as he had promised to try to arrange for me to meet Gorodetsky today, but the news was that although Gorodetsky was somewhere in Petersburg there seemed to be no way of getting in touch with him. We would have to wait. I wrote my diary. I missed not having a piano: my old one has been taken away to sell and I am not getting the new one just yet. N. V. Andreyev forwarded to me a letter from Nina Meshcherskaya, which I was delighted to receive; I should love to see her. She complains that she is sometimes so bored she wants to hang herself. In reply I sent her a comic verse on the subject of her realizing this plan.

Went to the Nikolayevsky station to post this letter and incidentally to buy the Moscow papers. In one of them there was a review by Derzhanovsky of Yurasovsky's concert, featuring long and laudatory but rather pointless reflections on N.M.'s First Symphony and a passing reference to the 'wonderful' *Dreams*. In fact it is a pity that I did not wait another day in Moscow to hear it: if it had sounded good I could have offered it to Jurgenson in the autumn, but as it is it will have to go back on the shelf once again.

15 July

In the morning Zakharov rang up asking me to accompany him in Rachmaninov's Second Concerto, which he is to play in Pavlovsk on the 25th. I was amazed to find that he had not managed to learn another concerto but five years on was still playing the same old Rachmaninov. All the same, the work itself is enchanting. I agreed readily and at three o'clock was at Shreders. To my astonishment Zakharov's playing has improved out of all recognition: in place of its former artificiality and affectation it now has a genuine softness and intimacy. I congratulated him on the successful transformation and this seemed to give him real pleasure. At any rate he has become an exceptionally dear person. We went together to Jurgenson, where I wanted to find out what had happened to the proof of the *Ballade*. The elderly and supremely ineffectual manager of the shop, one of the Jurgenson family, had laboriously noted down on a scrap of paper in May where and when I was going to be during the summer, but had mixed everything up and sent the proof to Kislovodsk, where it was presumably gathering dust in the post office. In Petersburg I had little else to do and could have happily got on with it, but once I got to Kislovodsk I wanted to occupy myself with the Sinfonietta, which would take up all my time.

I said goodbye to Zakharov and went to see the concierge in Gorodetsky's building to see what might have become of the gentleman, since neither Karatygin nor the recently returned Nurok had been able to get any answer from him on the telephone. The doorman said that they had just come back to the city, which gladdened my heart and, since I was not personally acquainted with him, I asked Karatygin to make another attempt to ring him up.

Dressed in my new suit, which gave me a uniquely elegant 'English' air, I went to Pavlovsk in the company of the Zakharovs, Boris and Vasily. At Pavlovsk I was met by Damskaya, but not wishing to fall immediately into her embraces I stayed close to the brothers. The conductor was Glazunov, and my God how boring, how featureless and amateurishly contrived his Third Symphony appeared after the new things I had been listening to in London. Basically Diaghilev's tastes and the outrageous liberties Stravinsky had taken in his *Nightingale* had already left their mark on me, and I no longer had patience with the bland and predictable flavour of Glazunov's neatly logical progressions. By comparison with my earlier compositions I intend my ballet to be a great modernistic leap forward; I have begun to cool towards the lyricism of my Violin Concerto, which I loved so tenderly before my departure for London. What I need to do now is create a ballet that will make people gasp and stretch their eyes, and after that I can settle back to the benign peace of my Violin Concerto.

Needless to say I did not stay to listen to the second half of the Glazunov concert, preferring to talk to my friends. I glimpsed Bushen fleetingly, while Volodya Deshevov came rushing up to me: 'Seryozha, what do you think! I've got married!' Pfui! You could have knocked me down with a feather. 'Have you completely lost your mind? What a dreadful misfortune!' It seemed a strange and irrational thing to have done, although in fact he is twenty-five years old, but his enthusiasm and lively energy make him appear no more than fifteen. I was struck dumb.

A lot of my friends were there, and when I ran into the Damskaya sisters I went for a walk with them. Eleonora's comment on the tales I had to tell was that I had become disgustingly famous. When we got back to the station we had tea just as the concert finished, disgorging hordes of people on to the street. Boris passed by, but did not say anything. Tea over, we exchanged handshakes and I went back to St Petersburg.

At the station in Petersburg I encountered Glazunov, so I stopped and greeted him. He smiled pleasantly, but as I had really nothing to say to him I continued on my way. Glazunov looked pale and slightly under the influence; I turned round to see him disappearing into the buffet.

Mama and our servant had gone to a demonstration, during which a massive crowd surged through the streets of Petersburg until it was broken up by the police. Mama had almost been knocked off her feet, and had been quite frightened. The political horizon is darkening and growing more threatening. Austria has declared war on Serbia.

16 July

Began writing out a revised version of the Sinfonietta. When I write in ink, I never scratch out errors as I go along, I mark them with a cross and then correct them later all at the one time. This correcting procedure is what I was doing today. It is rather exhausting work, one's eyes get tired focusing on the point where the knife is doing its work, and one's hand tires also.

In the afternoon I went with Mama along Nevsky to see what was happening with demonstrations and expressions of patriotism, but nothing particular seemed to be going on. Karatygin told me that a meeting with Gorodetsky had at last been arranged, for seven o'clock tomorrow at Gessen's apartment on Kamenny Island. Thank God for that.

Met Shura Frolov at the Tsarskoselsky station[1] and talked with him of the war.

17 July

Wrote a detailed account for my diary of my piano competition. This day is so vividly engraved in my memory I was not afraid of forgetting any of the details: on the contrary, I had put it aside at the time partly with a view to being able to describe it later with greater clarity. Today, while I was writing, the events were just as powerful emotionally as they had been on that day, and I lived once again the heat of battle.

Nadya Rayevskaya came round in the afternoon, and talked of the war. Andryusha Rayevsky[2] has been drafted into a regiment. Kolechka Myaskovsky, as a former officer, will presumably also have to go. A less likely warrior would be hard to imagine!

At five o'clock I set off for the Islands, had a bit of a walk and then at seven presented myself at Gessen's. There again the talk was of nothing but war and, understandably for a European family, more inclined to pessimism and less to patriotism.

Gorodetsky arrived. What I had been told about him may be summed up as follows: he is not much read today, but there are those who do read him; he is considered one of today's most talented poets; as for his appearance he is mainly famous for the length of his nose. When he appeared I realized it was not only his nose that was long but his whole body: my own stature is not small but even I had to look up at him.

More importantly, behind the unprepossessing exterior there lurked a gentleness of feature, voice and manner that altogether produced a beguiling

---

1 The station for Tsarskoye Selo.
2 Prokofiev's cousin Andrey. Nadezhda (Nadya) was his wife.

impression. He was quite extravagantly dressed. All in all, rather an attractive individual.

After dinner, during which the conversation focused on the war, Karatygin proposed that he, Gorodetsky and I should take our coffee out on the terrace and there begin to discuss our business. I started by setting out the position from the outside, so to speak: what the ballet was intended for and when it had to be ready. I then moved to the inner mainsprings of the sort of ballet we should aim to create: (1) drawn from Russian life; (2) either dramatic or comic but not just neutral, that is to say water that is either boiling or freezing but not tepid; (3) dense and complex with rapid development of the action; (4) there should not be any moments without action on stage; (5) it should consist of five or six short scenes and last in total about half an hour. Gorodetsky was evidently taken with the concept and said that this was very much how he himself had envisaged it: a piece in one continuous action. I then played him my compositions, which delighted him, and he declared with enthusiasm that he understood me, could see what was needed, and would be happy to get to work on the ballet.

I added that I envisaged the ballet beginning with its most important piece of action 'so that a latecomer missing the rise of the curtain would not be able work out what was going on'. Gorodetsky: 'Splendid idea!!' The ballet could end with a wild dance, not in such a way as to give the impression of having been dragged in on purpose, but forming the culminating point of the entire production to which everything previous would have led up and with which the performance would end. Gorodetsky also liked this plan, and said that as soon as he had made some rough sketches of the scenario he would send them to Kislovodsk.

Bidding farewell to our hosts we went out together on to Kamennoóstrovsky Prospect and there parted, very pleased with one another. When I got home I told Mama that my business with Sergey Gorodetsky had been successfully concluded for the time being, and we could leave as early as tomorrow. The earlier the better, as we seemed to be heading for war, and if such was indeed the case then there would be tremendous demand for travel on the railways and we would have trouble getting tickets. If troop movements start, it could even be that all passenger traffic on the railway would be stopped. We discussed our plans and decided that we would leave tomorrow if we could.

18 July

I kept waking up during the night for fear of oversleeping, and as soon as I got up in the morning went to the town station to see about tickets. We put off our departure for two more days and I obtained tickets to Kislovodsk for

Sunday. We would break the journey in Moscow in order to deposit a strongbox in the bank containing all our share certificates, as we had heard that St Petersburg was strategically too vulnerable to defend if anything happened. I shall also get myself a strongbox in Petersburg and put in it all my manuscripts, diaries and letters. At the town station I saw the former Miss Nikolskaya. She was now evidently married to the tall, strapping officer who was getting a ticket at the next window. Everyone was looking at her, but her face seemed different; she must have done something to it. She saw me and looked closely at me, but I pretended not to have seen her.

In the afternoon I rooted through all the drawers in my desk and the cupboards selecting what I planned to put in the fire-proof box: diaries, bound volumes of letters and letters that were still loose, music manuscripts, the 'Yellow Book' and other such documents. The result was a huge pile, enough to fill a whole trunk.

In the evening I went to Pavlovsk, where Tilya Hansen was playing. I walked with the Damskaya sisters and went backstage to the artists' room to see Hansen. Both Hansen sisters were very nice. In spite of the war preparations they had gone to Vilnius to give a concert there but had barely managed to get back at all, so crowded were the trains: there was a huge exodus from western Russia. I shall not be able to get to Terioki either: all troop detachments in Finland are being brought fully up to strength and there are only a couple of trains a day for dacha residents. I can just imagine the hordes of people.

Cecilia played very well and had a great success. But the second half of the concert was never completed: it was interrupted by a fellow in a state of frenzied excitement reading out loud a telegram about the rupture of diplomatic relations with Germany. The audience became agitated, there were loud cries of 'Hurrah!', flags were unfurled, and the concert was transformed into a demonstration. One poor music-lover complained that his enjoyment was being spoiled, but the crowd turned on him and he barely managed to make his escape from the belligerence of the mob. Someone else was weeping, on the street there were shouts of 'Down with Austria', and a violinist I knew clutched me anxiously by the sleeve. I went through the crowd with the Damskayas, and as I parted from them urged them to come to Kislovodsk.

I boarded the train back to Petersburg, where a bath was waiting for me, and could not avoid noticing the number of serious, worried faces all around: war with Germany is now certain. There are two ways of looking at it: the conventional point of view is that it is such an appalling catastrophe that one's hair stands on end with the horror of it, but from the historical perspective it is terribly interesting!

19 July

In the morning papers yesterday's news about war with Germany was not confirmed. I lugged the strongbox containing my manuscripts as far as a cab and went to the Volzhko-Kamsky Bank, which I had chosen partly because I knew the bank's director, Konshin, who had recently transferred from the State Bank. The dimensions of my box were 6 by 6½ by 11 vershoks[1] and I filled it cram full to the brim. After that there were all kinds of pre-departure chores to accomplish: get back my watch from the menders, find my Russian–English text book, and so on. The streets were constantly crowded with recruits, groups bound for the war on their way to join their units. Those accompanied by their wailing womenfolk were downcast; those on their own marched cheerfully and sang songs. When one detachment met another one they would shout 'Hurrah', in fact on every side one heard 'Hurrahs' and 'God Bless the Tsar'. Even when there was in reality nothing to be heard, the ears still rang with 'Hurrah'. It was, it must be admitted, a nerve-racking experience.

This evening I went to the Nikolayevsky station to find out if there had been any alterations to the train timetable and if it would still be possible to travel tomorrow. The timetable had indeed been amended, but apparently we could still go; the Nikolayevsky line was the only one still accepting civilian passengers, all the others had only one train a day on which, needless to say, it would be quite impossible to find a place.

St Petersburg is on a war footing.

20 July

The newspapers were very late in coming out. Eventually something calling itself the *Petersburg Gazette* was brought in, which at the conclusion of a long official statement declared that at ten minutes past seven yesterday evening Count Purtales,[2] the German Ambassador, handed to a declaration of war to Sazonov,[3] the Minister of Foreign Affairs. We greeted this news calmly as we had been expecting it every day for some time past. The declaration of war had occurred just as I was peacefully going to the Nikolayevsky station to find out about the trains.

Spent the morning packing. Telephoned Alexey Pavlovich Meshchersky to ask if he had any messages or commissions for his family. We had a very nice

---

1 A vershok was a unit of length a little less than 2 inches, so the box was approximately 12 inches × 13 inches × 22 inches.
2 Count Friedrich Purtales (1853–1925), German Ambassador to the Imperial Court of St Petersburg from 1907 until 1914.
3 Sergey Sazonov (1860–1927), Tsarist Minister of Foreign Affairs from 1910 until 1916.

talk, and he said he very much wanted me to stay with the family. His view of the war was serious, but on the whole optimistic. At noon I went again to the station to check on the trains, but everything seemed still to be in order. At the Kazan Cathedral there were public prayers before an icon that had been carried out of the cathedral; the crowd was enormous. It was a wonderful, bright day with beautiful white clouds sailing across a clear blue sky. I met N. P. Ruzsky: Tanya and Ira, who had both completed Red Cross courses, had been called up and were going to the front. For this I could forgive them much. Nikolay Pavlovich himself has plans to organize a field hospital and is going to the battle zone. Shurik and Andryusha Rayevsky came to lunch with us at home: Andryusha has received his call-up papers and will be going to join his brigade at Luga.

I telephoned all the Zakharovs to try to find out where Boris is, but could get no answer from any of the numbers. I called the Hansens and learned that he had come back from Terioki and was staying with them, but at that moment had gone out with Tilya to see what was happening on the streets. If the flames of war spread they will probably go to somewhere on the Don at the end of the summer, well away from the threat of war. Before leaving to catch the train I had a wonderful conversation with Boris. He said he would come to see me off, but as is his wont, did not turn up. Our train was due to leave at eight o'clock in the evening, but owing to wartime conditions we were ready to get going at two o'clock, our taxi loaded to the gunwales with all the goods and chattels we were taking with us. There was quite a crush at the station, but thanks to our having arrived in good time we managed to check in our luggage without undue haste and find our places in the carriage as soon as we could get access to them.

At this point the 'hardships of war' began to manifest themselves: whether by accident or design I do not know, but the seats in our carriage had been sold twice over and there were therefore eight claimants for the four places in each compartment. There was just about room for everyone to get somewhere to sit, at the cost of forgoing any hope of a night's sleep, but as well as themselves everyone had a vast amount of baggage with them, far too much to be accommodated in the overhead racks or under the seats, so all the corridors were filled with luggage. The double complement of ticket-holders pushed and shoved themselves into the carriage, creating hideous bottlenecks, the passengers began to panic in the crush, while the stationmaster added to the confusion by screeching that no more people would be allowed into the carriage. Altogether it was mayhem. In the end the stationmaster gave it up as a bad job and went off, saying that he would try to have another carriage added to the train. Not having much faith in this, people stayed put in our overcrowded carriage, but eventually another carriage was put on and we moved to it. There we were comfortably installed, or rather we would have been comfortable had it not been for our fellow traveller, a German who spoiled our enjoyment in spite of all his efforts to keep quiet and make himself inconspicuous. Patriotism obliged us to hate him.

21 July

In Moscow the rain fell in sheets, slush was everywhere, there were no porters and all the cabs (anyone, indeed, who possessed a horse) had been drafted to the war effort. Staggering under our innumerable belongings, some carried by ourselves and some by a peasant and a little boy doing a bit of private trade on the side as porters, we trudged through the puddles and threaded our way through crowds of marching reservists to the nearby Ryazan station. There we learned that although there were no express trains we would be able to get on a train that left in two hours, and so leaving the luggage in the left-luggage room we hurried into the town to complete our business there.

What we had to do was rent a strongbox in the Kupechesky Bank[1] and deposit in it all the share certificates I had advised Mama to take away from Petersburg and bring to Moscow. As a result of a particularly repellent cab-driver (they were in extremely short supply anyhow), the equally repulsive state of the roads and the appalling weather, we barely had time to manage this task, and when we got back to the station the porter we engaged informed us that the train was in and already full to overflowing, although we had seats reserved on it. But this train was only going as far as Ryazan.

Fortunately, the stationmaster had been inspired to order up another one, going to Kozlov, so we made a dash for it. My God, what a frenzy! It was like being on the German border. Dragging all our things out of one train into another, fighting for seats, shoving cardboard boxes through windows, and so on and so on. In the end we disposed ourselves as follows: four people sitting side by side on one seat opposite four on the other side, two sitting on suitcases in the gangway and two more on separate seats by the other window – in all, twelve people in one compartment. The upper bunks were pulled out and filled with baggage. Half the passengers were officers who had been recalled to their units in the Don region, the Caucasus, etc. A quarter were their wives and families, and the remainder were civilian travellers.

Even before the train pulled out of the station, everyone started talking about the war, and this went on without a moment's pause from noon until eleven o'clock at night, when we arrived at Kozlov. Outside it poured with rain, inside it was stuffy and there was no possibility of opening the windows.

---

1   Merchant Bank.

The first telegrams to arrive from the battlefield caused general rejoicing: 'The Cossacks have routed a German regiment of dragoons.' How delicious! Even the crack German cavalry with its iron discipline falters before the charge of our ferocious Cossack horde with its whooping war-cries and lances at the level. The whole carriage joined in the mood of exaltation, everyone talked to his neighbour, arguing and absorbed in the discussion. All the same, eleven hours of this sort of thing is pretty tiring. As soon as the rain eased off I went outside on to the outer step to breathe some fresh air.

The name of one station, 'Diaghilevo', cheered me up and made me think of London and my beloved ballet. At eleven o'clock at night we got to Kozlov, where we faced once again the total absence of porters, the mounds of luggage, the dense crowds milling about in confusion and the universal ignorance of whether, whither and when there might be any trains. On top of all this the rain poured down incessantly and we were crushed by fatigue. With truly heroic efforts I secured a porter and, grabbing hold of his arm not to let him go, uncovered the existence of a first-class carriage on a train going to Rostov. Dodging between locomotives and a shunting train we made our way to it, then collected Mama and, taking possession of a half-compartment, locked all the doors. The guard got a very large tip of a rouble, people tried to force open the door and shouted at us, but we remained obstinately deaf and mute. Eventually the carriage began to move and we were coupled to the Rostov train. Happy at last to be settled in comfort, we fell asleep.

22 July

Our train was following a military timetable, and there was only one locomotive for a train of eighteen carriages, so our progress was at a snail's pace. It took us all that night, all the next day and all the next night to get to Rostov. The crowds of passengers began to thin out and although we could only proceed slowly, we did so peacefully. On two occasions the engine was unable to negotiate the gradient, and we stopped in a field. Because we were not passing through any major centres we could not get any fresh newspapers. I tried to read some Gorodetsky, but the book I had was of verses from 'Russian Mythology and Legends' and was written in too esoteric a style for me.

23 July

We arrived in Rostov at eleven o'clock in the morning and once again found ourselves plunged into a seething cauldron of humanity. A monstrously long train carrying reservists to the front was now disgorging, now swallowing thousands of people, some being seen off by wailing womenfolk. Someone was playing a squeezebox, others were singing. A train pulled in from Kislovodsk with seventy people to each carriage instead of the usual twenty-four. We discovered that more people were coming away from there than were going there, for among those taking the waters had been many officers with their families. My God, what frenzied commotion, agitation, dashing hither and yon, the storming of carriages followed by the despairing cries of those who failed to get in! My head was spinning from the six hours we had to wait at Rostov station, until at length at six o'clock we boarded a train that would take us further, and I was overcome with relief that at least for the time being we could forget about the war. Outside the carriage was the warm summer night.

At all the little stations we went through we were besieged by officials asking us whether we had any news about the war: 'We're living in the middle of the steppe, no one ever tells us anything.'

I was glad to relate the victory of the Cossacks and Japan's agreement to join the Triple Alliance, but that being all the information I had, could tell them no more.

24 July

We drew near to Mineralnye Vody at seven o'clock in the morning. Old friends began to appear on the name boards of the stations we passed: Beshtau, Zmeika, Zheleznaya Gora. Mount Elbrus reared up on the horizon with startling clarity. On cue came memories of Max: I had been afraid that when I returned to these places I would be overwhelmed by them, but the war and the millions of sacrifices it would bring in its train somehow reconciled me to what had happened to Max, and made me view human life more philosophically. Here was Mineralnye Vody, here was the table at which Max and I hurriedly downed a bottle of champagne before my departure for Moscow when I went to play my First Concerto for the first time. In a way it eased my heart and made me feel glad to see again the places where two years ago I had been so happy.

We changed trains to a little branch line for summer visitors and set off once more. Here was the station at Beshtau where Max and I fired revolvers; here was Karrs – a small German settlement, now no doubt an accursed place; here the lush green field hard by the track where Max and I planned to walk with our girls; here, finally, Pyatigorsk. But what was this meeting our eyes on the platform?! The station was crowded with people waiting for a train to carry them north, to the war, weighed down by luggage and anxiety and the fear of not being able to get on the train. I hardly recognized the platform at Pyatigorsk.

We carried on further, to the little wayside halt at Skachek, then

Yessentuki. Here Mama disembarked, as she would spend three weeks with the Smetskoys taking the waters at the spa. We fussed about handing innumerable boxes and cases through the window, then made our parting embraces and I continued to Kislovodsk.

At long last, therefore, the train reached Kislovodsk. I put my bags in the left-luggage room and walked across the park to find the Tsvetkov dacha where the Meshcherskys were staying. The weather was ravishingly beautiful: it was pleasantly warm from the sun shining in a sky more indigo than blue, the clouds brilliantly white, the grass lush and full of life. I had been told that nearly all the population had fled the moment war began, but this did not seem to be the case. Many people had left, but many had stayed, and this was so far away from the 'war zone' that the peace and quiet of the spa town was an astonishing contrast with the seething hubbub of Petersburg and the bustling crowds on the railway.

I was incredibly happy to be in Kislovodsk. I found myself translated from a curdled, stifling atmosphere into fresh air and sunshine. Dear Kislovodsk, you were like an old friend! Happily I went through the Narzan Gallery and across the park. The very first thing that attracted me, of course, were the little tables set out for chess, with a score or two of bent backs enticingly signifying play. Suddenly I heard someone hailing me – Nina, Talya, their cousin Serge Bazavov, the law student Tomkeyev – in short all the Meshchersky family young. Exclamations, questionings, explanations, and we set off in a group for the dacha.

24–31 July
Kislovodsk

At Vera Nikolayevna's invitation I stayed with them, sharing a room with Serge Bazavov, the student whose exceptional good nature I had already encountered with so much pleasure at Gurzuf. The Meshcherskys had taken the upper floor of the Tsvetkov dacha, which had spacious, high-ceilinged rooms and was about fifteen minutes' walk from the Narzan Gallery.

This year life was quieter than last. Oleg was not there, having been called up. Bobrovsky, Nadya Planson and others were also absent. However an elegant Englishwoman made it clear she was attaching herself to all our walks and excursions. I felt wonderful in Kislovodsk. The war did not worry us: there did not seem to be any major battles while the minor skirmishes ended to our advantage. Liège had held out; we believed in victory, and rubbing our hands with glee talked of the 7 million strong Russian army.

I had decided to take a break from work for my first week in Kislovodsk, and revelled in my freedom to do nothing. My principal activity was playing chess in the park, where I happened on the start of a tournament. Eleven people were taking part, playing two games each, and the level was medium strength, category 3 to 4. But to play the necessary twenty games for the tournament would obviously take some time. I began with four wins, continuing the glorious run of victories that had begun with my game against Capablanca. But eventually I had to suffer a defeat. Nevertheless my result at the end of the first part of the tournament was good: 7½ points. I got very absorbed in the play and spent whole mornings sitting there. At home we played bridge: Talya, Serge, his sister and the traditional bridge marital partnership of Nina and me playing together.

Nina and I did not spend too much time together, but when we did it was friendly: sometimes we quarrelled and sometimes were very affectionate, but on the whole we were less interested in one another than we had been in Gurzuf. After such a long time apart, little Nina had lost her special attraction for me. I felt thoroughly content and at ease, I was in good spirits and was content for my horizons to be bounded by the trivialities of everyday life. I was sure of my future and felt I lacked nothing. Talya and I became the best of friends.

After I had been there a week, however, my relations with Nina entered a period of extreme tenderness. This took place after a very long conversation during which Nina recalled with unconcealed emotion her former love affair with 'America', by whom she meant Zaitsev. The romance had blossomed before my arrival in Gurzuf and ended in September when Nina, in bitter despair following a final break, went to Berne. There, until her feelings began to subside, she had been very unhappy, and even now the old wounds can still make themselves felt. Her story, lightly sketched with glancing allusions and hints, produced on me an unexpected rush of tenderness for its heroine. Generally there is nothing particularly remarkable about Nina, but sometimes such a charge of electricity builds up within her that contact with it produces sparks.

Turning again to life in the dacha, its placid surface was soon ruffled by the absence of news from the head of the family. Because of the war and the chaos on the railways it was hard enough to get urgent telegrams through, and for ordinary people there was no chance at all. Vera Nikolayevna, however, paid no attention to this and deluged Petersburg daily with telegrams. Getting no response to any of them, she went almost out of her mind with worry. To crown it all, she discovered that 25,000 had been transferred to her account from Petersburg, at which she decided that Alexey Pavlovich must be near death. Bridge was forbidden, and Vera Nikolayevna appeared red-eyed and dishevelled until a whole sheaf of telegrams was received all at once, containing the information that Alexey Pavlovich was alive and well, and the 25,000 had been transferred purely as a safety net. Everyone cheered up at once, and set to with a will preparing for a grand charity concert in the Kursaal for families of the reservists who had been called up.

This concert was being organized by a group of worthy charitable ladies with whom Vera Nikolayevna had only the most tenuous connection, having done no more than pass on to them the information that she knew of two ballerinas staying in Pyatigorsk, and that in Kislovodsk there was the winner of the St Petersburg Conservatoire Piano Competition, none other than myself. Taking part in the concert would be Safonov,[1] who spent every summer in Kislovodsk, Tartakov[2] and various other local and non-local celebrities. The Meshcherskys knew Safonov quite well because he was married to Vyshnegradskaya,[3] to whose family the Meshcherskys were close.

I was taken to meet Safonov at the time when the programme for the concert was being thought about. They knew a little about me, I suppose, as a talented musician, but more importantly as one on whom praise was being lavished. For my part I was interested to meet this family, since I regarded Safonov as, along with Rachmaninov, the best conductor in Russia. He proved to have an enormous quantity of children, several overgrown sons and *n* daughters. The eldest was a lovely girl, already married; the second – a seventeen-year-old called Varya – was quite a curious individual, and after her was an entire staircase of younger ones. I talked a whole lot of nonsense, but nothing about music to their Papa: in their eyes I am a revolutionary while he is a conservative.

1–10 August
Kislovodsk

The charity concert took place on 1 August, but the lackadaisical ladies who were organizing it did not get around to putting up any posters until ten hours before the start of the event. As a result nobody knew anything about it, and in spite of the local popularity and renown of Safonov there were only about seventy people in the hall. On the day of the concert chaos reigned in the Meshchersky household: a couple of very silly girls (the ballerinas) arrived from Pyatigorsk, I tried on evening dress, having left my tails in St Petersburg; the Meshchersky girls fretted that there would not be

---

1 Vasily Safonov (1852–1918), pianist, conductor and teacher. Famously combative as a pedagogue, he had been Rector of the Moscow Conservatoire from 1889 to 1905 (spectacularly falling out with Ziloti), after which he moved to New York for a spell as Chief Conductor of the New York Philharmonic from 1906 to 1909).
2 Joachim Tartakov (1860–1923), singer (baritone, a celebrated Onegin) and director of productions at the Mariinsky Theatre.
3 Alexander Vyshnegradsky, Mme Safonova's brother, was as head of the International Bank one of Tsarist Russia's richest and most powerful bankers. Alexey Meshchersky became a director of the International Bank, incurring thereby – according to his daughter's memoirs – the aristocratic disdain of his formidable wife, who regarded the commercialization of the banking and stock-exchange world as the unacceptable face of captalism (N. A. Krivosheina (Meshcherskaya), *Chetyre treti nashey zhizni*, YMCA Press, Paris, 1984).

anyone in the audience. My own attitude to performing was one of total indifference: no one here knew me, nor would anyone understand anything of the works I was going to play. It might have helped slightly if they had put 'Conservatoire Prizewinner' on the poster, but they did not have the wit to do that. The whole thing was a comedy of errors. Mama, making her first visit to the Meshcherskys, came over from Yessentuki; she arrived at dinner time and there was so much noise going on it would have driven anyone out of their mind. Nina came into my room to see if I was acceptably dressed, straightened my tie and said that I looked so nice 'I could just kiss you'. I bowed in acknowledgement and kissed her. Nina giggled and ran off.

Since no one ever wants to be the first one on at a charity concert, and I could not have cared less about any of it, I said I would begin the proceedings with my Sonata No. 1 and play some smaller pieces in the second half. We set off for the Kursaal in a great gaggle. I permitted myself the luxury of arriving in the wings fifteen minutes late, but even then there was still no audience to be seen, nor any of the artists, nor the lady organizers. We went for a walk. An hour later we were all assembled: fifty members of the audience, the artists, and two lady organizers. Mme Vasilieva, the only musically qualified organizer (by virtue of having once been a student of Safonov) appeared backstage (all her colleagues were selling flowers and sweet cakes) and anxiously enquired of the assembled artists whether the concert should go ahead before as few as fifty listeners, or not.

We decided it should, and I stepped out to play my Sonata on a Steinway specially imported for the occasion from Mineralnye Vody. But, oh horrors, it kept emitting a sort of ringing noise, caused by something metallic lying on the strings which bounced merrily from one end of the piano to the other, jangling frenetically in the process. Only my awareness that this would be sounding less annoying to the audience than it did to me allowed me to get to the end of the Sonata. The experience of playing it against the background of the bouncing nail was so horrible that it was all I could do to force myself not to get up and leave the stage. At the end I rose from the piano in a furious temper, and after angrily going through the perfunctory motions of bowing to the public, expressed my feelings backstage in no uncertain terms. I then left the Kursaal. At first I was resolved not to play in the second half, but then I calmed down and remembered the attitude I had adopted towards the whole idea of the concert, which was not in any way to take it seriously. I returned to the wings.

Mme Vasilieva: 'I hear you have expressed dissatisfaction with the piano?'

I replied that I considered it unforgivable negligence on the part of the organizers to provide a piano into which nails had been tipped.

'Am I to understand that you are accusing me?' asked Mme Vasilieva.

'If you regard yourself as one of the organizers, then the answer is yes,' I replied.

Mme Vasilieva grew extremely agitated and said that I was not so famous as to have any right to protest about nails having been tipped into the piano, and that a civilized gentleman would withdraw the remarks I had just made.

Following this one of the Kursaal staff extracted from the piano an actual screw (which gave me the opportunity to remark that this was probably the very one that had come loose from Mme Vasilieva's head) and I went out to play the 'Gavotte', the Scherzo from the Second Sonata, the 'Harp' Prelude and Etude No. 4. I bowed twice to acknowledge the applause and then sat in the artists' room having a pleasant conversation with Tartakov and Valitskaya, singers from the Mariinsky Theatre. It turned out that Kislovodsk did boast one admirer of my music, who knew all my compositions and came backstage to express his pleasure at meeting me. After the concert I took Mama back to Yessentuki and then came home to the Meshcherskys' dacha. In the programme, apparently, they had got my name wrong and put Pokrovsky instead of Prokofiev.

After this excitement life resumed its usual uneventful tenor. I decided that I had taken enough time off and it was time to get back to work. My chess tournament, incidentally, had collapsed: too many of the participants had dispersed and the organizers were unable to bring it to a conclusion. I had succeeded in playing sixteen of my twenty matches, winning thirteen of them, and was lying in second place, a civil servant called Melnikov having gained nine points out of a possible nine. The tournament was abandoned and the prize money donated to the Red Cross.

I therefore turned my attention to: (1) the Sinfonietta; (2) studying English with the Meshcherskys' English governess Miss Isaacs, the same lady who never moved a step away from the girls and interfered in all their escapades. However she proved to be an excellent teacher, and I even began to speak a little. The girls snorted with derision on hearing my pronunciation, but I said, 'Just you wait; in a year's time I shall be able to laugh at yours.'

I concentrated on the second and third movements of the Sinfonietta, subjecting them to a radical revision. The middle section of the second movement is completely new, although the material has been taken from another piece I was working on contemporaneously with the Sinfonietta and intended for an orchestral work, *Landscape*, that I never completed. For the third movement I composed an entirely new main theme, and altered the rest beyond recognition. So far it is turning out very nicely, and well put together.

The Safonovs, Mr and Mrs, came to tea with the Meshcherskys. I was quite sure that Mme Vasilieva would have dropped all sorts of poison into their ears about me and accordingly adopted a reserved demeanour. Even so, I was on the point of telling them about the screw that had fallen out of her head into the piano, when Vera Nikolayevna successfully changed the subject. We had our photograph taken, and Nina and I quarrelled.

The following day at six o'clock in the morning we set off to walk in the hills. All the young ones came: Nina, Talya, myself, Serge Bazavov, the law student Tomkeyev, a pleasant but rather adolescent youth, and Miss Isaacs. I promised to be nice to Nina, and since she is not much good at going up hills, towed her along on the end of my walking stick. She was grateful for this, and when we at last got to the top of Saddle Mountain[1] and sprawled exhausted on the hay, Nina and I found ourselves side by side. Taking advantage of a bulge in the hayrick that concealed us from the prying eyes of Miss Isaacs, we lay together in the most affectionate position, enhancing the enjoyment of our repose with kisses. On the way back Nina and I again found ourselves on our own, having chosen a shorter way than the others. We were enjoying ourselves along the way until we were caught up by a puffing and panting Tomkeyev, begging us to pause and wait for Miss Isaacs who, he said, was dragging herself along as if about to give birth to a tortoise. This last image gave rise to such general hilarity that it served as a topic of conversation until we got home.

Because I had been walking without a hat (very fashionable) the sun had burned my face mercilessly and for the next five days the skin peeled off. A curious, and not particularly pleasant effect. There were no more amorous interludes with Nina but, in contrast with the first week I was there, I did flirt with her a little. Our romantic relationships were interrupted by numerous quarrels, never a day passing without one. Twice a week I went to Yessentuki to see Mama. I left at 3.15, spent two hours there and came back by the six o'clock train. I was very glad to see my beloved Yessentuki again.

I received a letter from Katyusha: her mother has died of cancer. I am deeply sorry for poor Katyusha: at sixteen she is left alone to face a life of hardship. This is a heavy burden and I feel for her most sincerely.

I am very interested, even a little concerned, to know what has become of Myaskovsky. There has been no news of him for two months now, and it is obvious that as a former officer he has been taken for active service. How could this happen to Kolechka, helpless as he is! I wrote to ask his sisters and also to Zakharov, and am now waiting for letters back from them. In the meantime there was a telegram to the Meshcherskys from the front informing them that Colonel Komarov, their uncle, has been killed. There were tears, and a Requiem Mass said for him. And indeed it is a hard blow when war comes directly into the home. Confused messages are coming from the battleground: the Germans have overrun Belgium, Queen Wilhelmina has retreated to Aachen amid fears that the Germans will strike there in full strength, the French and English forces did not succeed in securing their defences and are being destroyed. We have begun to attack on the border

---

1 Bolshaya Sedlo-Gora and Malaya Sedlo-Gora (Big and Little Saddle Mountain) are two peaks just outside Kislovodsk from which spectacular view of Elbrus and the Caucasus range are had.

with Germany, but it is not clear how seriously, and the death of Colonel Komarov has made us feel that we must have lost many men. Even so, we all still believe we shall be victorious; the walls are hung with maps cut from the newspapers, and on the big map of Europe, defeated Germany is shown divided among the Allies.

11–20 August
Kislovodsk

This period is distinguished by the exceptionally affectionate relations that subsisted between Nina and me. This state of affairs came about in the following way. On the night of the 11th Nina had a pain in her heart; she suffered all night and came to coffee the following morning pale, weak and downcast. I felt sorry for her and tried all I could to divert and console her. The next day her ailment passed away and we managed to quarrel as usual. Just before going out, I was gripped for some reason by a depression – probably remorse at having done so little work when I needed to be getting on with the Sinfonietta: whatever the cause it was several months since I had been in such a bad mood and it lasted all day right through dinner, during which I sat hunched over my plate not speaking to anyone. After dinner I sat down at the piano and started to play right through my repertoire without stopping, full of expression and affording myself great satisfaction.

When I had finished playing Grieg's *Ballade*, Nina, remembering the sympathy I had shown her the day before, came up with the obvious intention of being kind to me. But still feeling cross, I chased her away and continued playing. Afterwards I went out for a walk, only to find that two hours in the fresh air were enough to dispel my mood, and I came back for tea in the most excellent frame of mind. Now, however, I encountered nothing but disdain from Nina, and when we were saying good night she stuck out her hand with a contemptuous jerk in a gesture she had informed me earlier she had employed with 'America' after they had broken off their relations. Next morning she repeated the same greeting, and heaped utter scorn on me all through lunch. But since Nina is in reality so very nice, I would not let her alone after lunch but bombarded her with jokes, facetious remarks and demonstrative affection, to which after a time her resistance crumbled and she began to laugh.

That day Nina and Talya were planning to visit the Safonovs, where they quite often went to sketch with the daughters, who were also artists. Safonov himself had several times expressed an interest in hearing my sonatas, and therefore I thought that on one of these occasions I would go along too and play them to him. I asked Nina if she would permit me to accompany them this afternoon to the Safonovs. Nina, who had by no means yet forgiven me, shrugged her shoulders, and snorting contemptuously said, 'All the same to me!'

Nevertheless, just as she was leaving to go to Safonovs she came to the table where I was sitting at the chessboard and asked, 'Well, are you coming to the Safonovs?'

With that she went out, and I played bridge with the Bazavovs, brother and sister. About an hour and a half later the game had finished, and I thought I would go, but on the way I bumped into a returning Nina, who had been overtaken by such a crippling migraine that she had had to come home. All her bantam-cock aggression had vanished, she was quiet and yielding. She told me I would be a delightful young man if only it were not for my stupid outbursts and rudeness. I still meant to go to the Safonovs, and everyone else was going out for a walk, leaving Nina alone with her migraine. She said, 'If you were really a nice boy you would stay and look after a poor little sick girl.'

I really did want to go, because it was extremely interesting to me to play my sonatas to Safonov, but I immediately changed my mind and stayed with Nina. We sat for an hour and half talking in the most amicable way imaginable, and from then on our relations were of the friendliest, never clouded by a single quarrel. The next day, on the pretext that the samovar in the dining room was emitting clouds of smoke, we retired to my room where we sat and read an article by Mikhailovsky about the war in *Russian Word*. Then we played some duets: a Beethoven symphony and even some Tchaikovsky. Nina played lots of wrong notes and got lost a few times, but she did play.

Getting back to my visit to the Safonovs, this took place a few days later. I played both sonatas to an audience consisting of the whole Safonov family. The First Sonata was received without much enthusiasm, but the Second was warmly applauded, especially the descending chord progression in the third movement. My pianism drew praise, and there was a request to borrow the score, which was very flattering. Mulya, daughter number 3, aged seventeen, told Talya that she would learn my Second Sonata.

I did not bow to Mme Vasilieva, saw my Kislovodsk admirer occasionally in the park, and played hardly any chess. On the other hand at home bridge flourished, much to Vera Nikolayevna's chagrin. The 'married bridge couple', Nina and I, now formed a peaceful and harmonious partnership, and success attended its union. But bridge playing came to an end on the 17th with the departure of Serge Bazavov for the capital, for Tomkeyev was running after a girl somewhere or other and was rarely to be seen and so we were lacking a fourth. I was very sorry to see Serge go: going to bed at night there was no one to talk to about the war and military strategy, and in the mornings no one with whom to debate whether or not it was time to get up.

I went to Yessentuki three times. The place was definitely emptying.

Mama finished her course of treatment and prepared to come over to Kislovodsk, whither the Smetskoys had already moved. Myaskovsky's whereabouts were discovered: he was in Borovichi as an instructor in some kind of Home Guard training company, but the only topic he wrote about was music. I was infinitely pleased to get his letter: it is excellent news that he is in a Home Guard regiment, at least in the near future there is no risk of his coming under fire.

The progress of the war continued to inspire confidence: fears that the French and English forces would be annihilated in Belgium seemed to have been unfounded and the conflict had resulted for the time being in a stalemate; this relieved much of our apprehension. On the other hand our own forces were advancing step by step into East Prussia, and every day seemed to bring news of the capture of yet another town, so that in time we came to regard this as a normal development. In these circumstances, when on the 19th I cheerfully went to the station to see off N. N. Smetskoy, who was leaving, and to greet my mother, who was coming from Yessentuki, the news that two of our corps had been defeated and three generals killed came like a thunderclap. Some people immediately began to lose heart, others criticized our leaders, yet others said this was only to be expected from the Germans! I was very upset, but said that after all one could hardly expect to take Berlin without casualties. There were some who agreed with this, but others considered me a silly little boy.

I carried on with my English studies, satisfied as before with the instruction I was getting from Miss Isaacs. In the evenings, after ten o'clock when Vera Nikolayevna (whom I had nicknamed Wilhelm on account of her despotic nature) sent Nina and Talya off to bed, I stayed behind with Tomkeyev. Reluctant to go home to where he was staying, he stayed dozing in his chair with the newspaper, while I wrote out my English translation. Eventually we would eat a piece of watermelon and say good night. I had lessons twice a week and learned sixty new words.

I was very happy during my stay in Kislovodsk.

20–31 August[1]

A marvellous time. But to begin with, the general pattern: my morning walks, four hours of English in the evenings.

22 August

Departure of Tomkeyev.

---

1 These entries are in note form and almost illegible (note by the editor of the Russian edition).

23 August

Talya's birthday. The present. Caviare.

25 August

Arrival of Alexey Pavlovich.

26 August

Talya's name-day. A glorious morning.

    I accompanied Alexey Pavlovich to the bath house, abandoning my usual morning work. He is clearly fond of me. The rain stopped after lunch. Vera Nikolayevna asked me to invite Mama for afternoon tea. Guests, photographs, Mama deafened by the noise. In the evening Safonov's concert. Before dinner I am sitting in the chaise-longue. Nina comes out towards the end, dressed and with a red flower in her belt, looking entrancing. I gazed at her in rapture. Her smile and her eyes. Suddenly Nina comes up behind me and kisses me passionately. After dinner the young people go in advance. I sit between Nina and Talya and flirt shamelessly with Nina. We walk off to one side together.

    'After all, you do love me, don't you, Seryozha, a lot?'

    'Of course I do, a lot.'

30 August

I come back from seeing Mama in high spirits. Play the piano. The Manifesto.[1] Nina shivers as if from the cold. Everyone goes to see Safonov off. I walk with Nina and talk all the time about the Manifesto. I protest, calling it a stupid idea. Safonov gone, I walk home in silence. At dinner, however, relations are restored.

    After dinner I sit down at the piano; Nina immediately comes up. A moment of embarrassment; Nina comes closer and I propose some duets, which I know she loves doing. We play Beethoven's Symphony No. 3. Alexey Pavlovich wants to hear an act from *Kitezh*. All night dreaming and thoughts about our impending 'divorce'.

---

1 One can only speculate on the precise nature of the 'Manifesto' or 'Decree', but the later references make it clear that Nina Meshcherskaya had instigated some kind of summing up of the present state of the relationship along with a prescription for its further conduct.

31 August

Came to a decision in the morning and began to feel good about it. While I was working Nina came into my room and sat on the balcony. I told her I had decided to accept the Manifesto ...

11 September

At noon precisely I left the Nikolayevsky station and took a taxi across the newly renamed capital Petrograd. The war and the new name have left no mark on the city's external appearance. Petrograd had a welcoming air to it.

At home it was lovely to see Mama again, and to get a pile of letters (including one from Lyolya Zviagintseva, with touching expressions of half-childish infatuation), one from the Studio requesting some information about myself, which I hastened to provide by means of the telephone. My call was courteously received and I was invited to call in tomorrow, and I was also informed that I already had two students. In fact I did not expect any more than that, being pretty sure that this institution, while having the best of intentions, has very few students. I had a talk with Zakharov, who is being considered for a teaching position at the Conservatoire (that's nice!) and we agreed to meet in a few days' time. I then went to Shreder to see about the piano I had won. I amused myself imagining the scene as I enter the shop: an assistant asks to speak to the manager and says, 'Sir, the winner of the prize has come about his piano. He's in the front lobby now.'

'Oh, to hell with him, these people are always hanging about. Give him the worst one you can find and let him take that.'

In reality it went like this. I was received by the manager and we had a chat about this and that. He then showed me three pianos, all good although at first glance they seemed terribly small. But they were all priced at 1,050 roubles, which is quite a sum. If I did not like any of these instruments, there would be another consignment from the factory in a week's time. I played them for a while, then thanked them and went away, promising to come back with a friend. Then I went to see the other Shreder, a tuner and piano dealer, who had taken my old Ratke to sell it for me. But he was complaining that business was very bad because of the war. My piano was standing forlornly in a corner, unsold, and meanwhile I have no money, but at least I have the hopeful prospect of getting 600 roubles whenever someone buys my piano.

Instead of going home I walked along Nevsky and Morskaya and met an extraordinary number of friends: Ruzsky, the Andreyevs, Yershov and others, about fifteen of them altogether. Ruzsky was affable, but rather obviously preening himself on the military successes of his cousin. He dropped a hint that one composer had already written a cantata on the capture of Lvov.[1] Tanya and Ira have become nurses and are in Lvov. Not bad! The Andreyevs, both husband and wife, were extremely nice: we are very close friends. All the carping that went on between Anna Grigorievna and me in London is forgiven and forgotten. Yershov was unshaven and had a sour expression on his face; I hear that because of his efforts on behalf of Wagner he is now being ostracized.

Returning home, I had a long telephone conversation with Damskaya in which, choking with laughter, I recounted my time in Kislovodsk. She told me that the Conservatoire was, as usual, heaving with people. All sorts of people were talking about me. She had seen Struve, Lipinskaya, Tcherepnin, Nikolayev and many others of my friends. She spotted Belokurova outside a music shop looking in the window and laughing. When Damskaya went to see what was the matter, she saw that there was a large poster in the window bearing the legend 'Novelties', and below it my Piano Concerto. Very pleasing.

12 September

In the morning I wrote my diary entries for Kislovodsk. Went to the Volzhko-Kamsky Bank to collect my music and all the documents and letters I had deposited there. In the afternoon Kokochka Shtember came with me to Shreders to give me his opinion about the pianos. He began to play on them, very well. He was enthralled by the account of my successes in London. I then went to the Studio, which occupies a fine-looking apartment on the corner of Liteiny Prospect and Simeonovskaya Street. The proprietor of the Studio, Mme Levenstern, is a very nice woman with an air of mild anxiety. It does not look as though things are going too well there. I have two students, both girls, one from Moscow and the other coming to me from the Conservatoire where her teacher was Kimont.[2] It doesn't embarrass me at all to be associated with such a modest establishment, in fact I rather like it. I shall be getting 7 roubles a month in my hand, which is excellent. The same as a retired soldier's pension.

I walked back along Nevsky but this time did not meet anyone I knew, and merely succeeded in making myself tired. At home I read my diary for my stay in Gurzuf last year and the month of September that followed it. Callously I was rejoicing in my victory over Zaitsev at the very time that Nina was dying of unrequited love for him. Now at this distance I could find this drama of Nina's, at the time glimpsed only fleetingly between the lines, very touching.

At eight o'clock Nadya Shtember rang up and started jabbering away:

---

1 See p. 743 n. 1.
2 Marzellina Kimont-Yatsyna (1884–?), pianist and teacher at the St Petersburg Conservatoire.

'Kokochka has been saying you've become such a darling person, and if you'll only come over to us this evening you'll be a darling person squared! Please say you'll come!'

I went. Nadya and Sonya have grown into such giantesses that it is positively alarming to look at them, especially after Nina. They are both pretty in a slightly coarse way. We all call each other 'thou'. Kokochka played the Liszt Concerto with great brilliance, a little hard but very well. I played them my Piano Concerto No. 1, which all the young ones liked very much.

13 September

At ten o'clock I went to the Alexander Nevsky Monastery to attend the Requiem Mass for Anna Nikolayevna Yesipova on the ritually prescribed forty days after her death. About thirty of us were present, many of her entourage to whom I am indifferent or actively hostile. The choir sang with refined artistry, but the music was very bad. An idea came to me of writing a Mass that would be severe, sad and passionate. I went to see Tchaikovsky's grave. Anna Nikolayevna's was completely covered in flowers. Gabel spoke very kindly to me.

After the Mass Zakharov and I went to Shreders, where he approved the same piano as Shtember, and I requested that it be delivered to me. It will come on Tuesday, and within a week they will make the little silver plaque bearing witness to the fact that this is the prize piano. I am thrilled by the little silver plaque.

Lunched at home, and afterwards, delighted to have a reason to go in there again, at two o'clock went to the Conservatoire for Anna Nikolayevna's second Requiem Mass. Meeting Tcherepnin I embraced him; he had not shaved and it was like kissing a hedgehog. Even so he was very nice, and we had a good talk. Struve has acquired a tan and grown more beautiful, she is lovely to look at and I much enjoyed talking to her. There was a great mass of people and noise – I may be dead and gone as far as the Conservatoire is concerned, but life goes on after me.

At home the proofs of Op. 12 awaited me, and working on them gave me the most tremendous joy. How I loved seeing again my dear, variegated little pieces! Not only that, but it is good that the war has not affected Jurgenson's operations. I must send him the Second Piano Concerto, because I simply have to scratch up some money from somewhere or other.

In the evening I carried on enjoyably correcting the proofs and had a telephone conversation with Damskaya. All of a sudden, who should ring up but Nina. It was lovely to speak to her, I was delighted to hear from her and we talked cheerfully about all manner of things. I had expected that our 'divorce' would result in a complete freeze, but this was splendid. I rejoiced to hear the several endearments she interpolated into her conversation.

14 September

Corrected proofs until noon, after which I went to have lunch with Zakharov. I was late, and they were all sitting at table by the time I got there. After lunch Boris and I talked in his room, and I played him some of the pieces from Op. 12. He particularly enjoyed 'Rigaudon' but was unhappy with some parts of the 'March' where my technique failed me. Returned home at three and continued tidying up the Sinfonietta, and at five went to pay a call on the Meshcherskys.

I felt a slight flutter of nerves as I neared their house, but I was looking forward to seeing Nina. As I came in she was sitting alone at the piano. Our conversation was easy and relaxed, which gladdened my heart. Outwardly I preserved the form of the 'Manifesto' on which we had agreed.

While I sat at home in the evening revising the Sinfonietta and finishing the proofs I felt the warm glow of Nina in my heart. Bashkirov telephoned and invited me: I said I would be pleased to visit him on Thursday.

15 September

Scratched out and pasted in corrections to the Sinfonietta. I did not work well this morning. All the same, by two o'clock I had learned a hundred new words in English, and went to Mokhovaya Street for my lesson with Miss Isaacs. The lesson went with a swing, and afterwards I went to Gostiny Dvor[1] where I had arranged to meet Damskaya. We went for a walk that lasted two hours.

In the evening I attempted to write my diary entries for my stay in London, and spent a long time on the telephone ringing all over the place to try to find Gorodetsky. Karatygin says that: (1) he is not involved in the war; (2) he has made a start on the ballet. Diaghilev has contrived to do extremely well out of the war: having secured huge advances for a tour of German cities, he has pocketed the money and is going off to tour America. There's talent for you!

Made a start on the proofs of the *Ballade*. In the Petrograd branch of Jurgenson they told me that the Moscow Jurgenson, Boris Petrovich, has been called up as a former officer and is now somewhere in Tula. Imagine that, elderly and grey as he looks! Where am I going to get any money now? I have no one to send my Second Piano Concerto to!

Finished the proofs of Op. 12 and started on the proofs of the *Ballade*, which has been lying untouched since Kislovodsk. I worked on them until lunchtime and then went to the Studio for my 'entrance exam'.

---

1 The big department store on Nevsky Prospect.

I did not know whether to laugh or cry: I had only one student, and she spent all the time staring at her feet and speaking in a deep bass voice. Mme Levenstern introduced us and then left the room. I made her play whatever she could. She drummed her way quite efficiently through 'Gradus ad Parnassum', stumbling occasionally from fright, and then played some scales and arpeggios. I strolled about the room revelling in my professorial status. I asked her what Beethoven she had learned, and finding out that she was learning his Second Sonata, asked her to bring it to the next lesson. With that I released her and sent her on her way.

Leaving the Studio I walked along Nevsky, where I met Shteiman. He has composed some kind of symphonic work and wants me to come and see him. Shteiman is a very nice fellow but a terrific politician, and one cannot trust him.

In the evening I went with Mama to the Andreyevs, where we were supposed to be playing vint, but this was not possible as one player did not turn up. There were rumours that Vera Nikolayevna might come, and suddenly there was a ring at the door and there they all were: she, Nina and Talya. Nina settled herself near me, and went straight into her former attention-seeking mode. In Kislovodsk I had promised Nina I would write a song that would reflect her personality and, perhaps, our relationship. Nina had been treasuring this promise, and now I announced that the song I was going to write would be to an abbreviated text from Hans Andersen's *The Ugly Duckling* – would that not exactly fit her personality? At first Nina thought I was just teasing her, but when she saw that I was in earnest about wanting to write something on the theme of *The Ugly Duckling*, she said she would think about it.

We spent the whole evening together, and once more there were sweet nothings and innuendos, clearly showing that not all her Kislovodsk feelings had died within her.

17 September

In the morning I finished the proofs of the *Ballade*, and at three o'clock accompanied Mama to the Meshcherskys to greet Vera Nikolayevna on her name-day. These days it is the fashion instead of giving chocolates and flowers to make a donation of money to the wounded, and indeed Vera Nikolayevna had asked me to do this. I declined, on the grounds that I had no money at all, but yesterday evening sent her by post a greetings card and a receipt for 2½ roubles with a note saying this represented 'a pound and a quarter of good-quality chocolates'. It was the first time Mama had been to visit them in Petersburg, and when we arrived Vera Nikolayevna did not appear for quite some time, so we were entertained by the daughters. Nina and I discussed *The Ugly Duckling*, and then Nina wanted me to play *Meistersinger* in the four-hand version, but I put her off by avoiding the issue and then making a joke of it, at which Nina declared she was offended.

On the way home called at Shtembers and also bought two copies of *The Ugly Duckling* (in two different translations). At home I telephoned Golubovskaya, but although she is Nadezhda[1] she is Jewish and therefore declined my congratulations. I did the same to Damskaya, on behalf of her sister, and Zakharov. He is disappointed not to have been appointed to the Conservatoire faculty, but they are not taking on any new staff this year. He was nice, and suggested arranging a session of bridge.

At eight o'clock they finally delivered my prize piano. As may be imagined, I was thrilled with it, pleased and proud in every way. Not only that, but I have been very much missing an instrument these last days.

I played through everything I know on the new piano, but began to be troubled by a headache. Telephoned Nina, ostensibly to talk about *The Ugly Duckling*. She promised to make a shortened version of it and send it to me by post, but as we were saying goodbye, let me know that she was very distressed by my behaviour.

18 September

I had a bit of a headache in the morning, as a result of which I did not do much serious work on the Sinfonietta as I had been wanting to do since acquiring the piano. I did, however, come up with an invention for the second subject of the Finale. I played through the proofs I had corrected, then played some more on the piano generally, and read some English. At three o'clock I went to see Shteiman, who had asked me to look through his symphonic piece. It was an excessively involved score, and not very clearly written in pencil. I did eventually make it out, but got very tired doing so. We spoke of Diaghilev and the various ways in which he makes agreements. I decided that I must definitely compose a ballet irrespective of the war and of the lack of a contract, and then we would see. Diaghilev had shown such enthusiasm for my music that as long as his company continued to exist I was sure my ballet would be put on. What I now had to do was find Gorodetsky.

In the evening I went to Kalashnikov Quay, right out in the sticks, to Bashkirov. He was as welcoming as ever, we related our respective summers and then discussed the war endlessly. He spoke passionately and in detail about it and was obviously deeply immersed in the progress of events. I listened to him with great interest. His sister, whom I think I had met before, then rang up and invited both of us to her house. We set off to Frantsuzsky

---

1 Vera (Faith), Nadezhda (Hope) and Lyubov (Love, Charity) all have the same saint's day.

Quay, where his sister, a very nice woman and a Princess, which one I don't know, occupies a magnificent apartment. About ten guests were there, playing bridge. We played chess. In spite of innumerable protests on my side I was obliged to play some of my compositions and *Tannhäuser*. Bashkirov, as usual, was overcome with emotion by *Tannhaüser* and, accompanying me down the staircase to see me out so smothered me with attention that I was quite stupefied. He even asked me if I would give him lessons. I walked home through the damp but pleasant weather, annoyed with myself to be going to bed so late that although I had planned to work in the morning I would now probably lose half the day again.

19 September

So it proved; I slept until half past eleven and managed to do no more than study some English.

It has been announced in the newspapers that the Ziloti concert has been postponed until the following season as the Court Hall has been given over to the care of the wounded. Strangely enough I am not very upset by this: (1) I no longer have to rush to complete the fifth movement of the Sinfonietta; (2) this year the audience will be so preoccupied with other matters that my appearance would not create much of a stir.

At two o'clock I had a lesson with Miss Isaacs then went to the Studio. My new student, the second of the two, the one who studied with Kimont at the Conservatoire two years ago, is dark-haired and inclined to be podgy, and turned in quite a decent performance albeit with a superficial technique. The other one, by contrast, who was at the last lesson, has a more robust technique with some fire in it. As for interpretation, I went through with her in detail the Second Sonata of Beethoven, spending three-quarters of an hour on her lesson. Afterwards I walked along Nevsky and Morskaya and returned home.

In the evening I had meant to work, but thought better of it and decided to go to the Sokol. I telephoned Kokochka Shtember, he came to call for me and we went together. I wondered whether the Sokol, whose motto is 'Unity for the Slav Peoples', might be taking an active part in the great struggle and feared lest its regular gymnastic sessions might suffer.[1] But it was not so: the sessions were carrying on as usual, that is to say the Slavs do not appear to be concerned about uniting. I am very pleased by this, since the only reason I go to the Sokol is for the gymnastics.

After our session Shtember came back to my house and listened to Op. 12, at which he went into ecstasies and gave me his verdict on them, giving the preference to 'Legenda', 'Allemande' and the Bassoon Scherzo.[2]

1 See p. 187 n. 1.
2 'Scherzo humoresque', Op. 12 No. 9.

20 September

In the morning I wrote out the Scherzo of the Nietta.[1] After lunch I went for a walk, partly to take the proof of the *Ballade* to Jurgenson. He apologized for having held up the second proof: this was because the engraver, a German, had been taken off to Vologda[2] and the plates appeared to have gone with him; they were now trying to get them back.

I walked home along Nevsky Prospect. Was delighted to receive a letter from Nina with *The Ugly Duckling* condensed into six pages, along with some brief thoughts about the treatment and an invitation to come to see her to revive her 'flagging spirits'. Nina also enclosed a group photograph from the summer in which she was staring straight at me. Her *Ugly Duckling* outline was not at all bad and I immediately set to work composing music for it, spending the whole of the evening thus happily employed. This is the style I want to make my own, and it will come to flower in my opera, when I write one.

21 September

All morning on the *Duckling*. It may represent the birth of a new style in my compositions, but it is one that has been maturing for more than a year now. The concept came to me eighteen months ago while I was listening to the Inn Scene from *Boris Godunov*, and it found its first expression in the *Musical Letter to Zakharov* that I wrote last autumn.

At one o'clock Yurasovsky visited me. He has come to Piter on military business as he is being sent on active service as a medical orderly. As usual he talked a great deal, but he was nice, and had very complimentary things to say about *Sarcasms*. We went for a walk along Nevsky. Nina rang at six about *Duckling*: we talked, and laughed a lot. I told her that immediately below the title *The Ugly Duckling* the score would say: 'to whom it is dedicated'. This sent Nina into a rage: 'No more of your horrid jokes, I want a serious dedication, and I ask you please not to do this', and more in the same vein.

I laughed heartily, and was invited to dine the following evening. I shall go of course, and with pleasure. In the evening I composed some more successful episodes of the *Duckling* and enjoyed working on the piece. Bashkirov, still in thrall to my performance of *Tannhäuser*, insisted on inviting me again to his sister's. When I arrived he was sitting in the window waiting

---

1   The Sinfonietta, Op. 5, later revised as Op. 48.
2   Vologda, three hundred miles to the east of Moscow, was traditionally a place of exile (Stalin was exiled there in 1911), and a holding area for prisoners of war and nationals of hostile combatant countries in wartime.

for me to come. While we talked he told me many interesting things, among them about a certain Mme Strakhovich, to whom he had introduced Capablanca who had fallen in love with her; it was due to her that he had failed to capture the first prize. I played him Schumann's *Fantasiestücke*, which he loved, and then he brought me home in his car.

22 September

Composed *Duckling* until one o'clock and finished the first scene, representing the fence the duckling jumps over by a massive C major chord. Shtember came to bring back my Op. 12 which he had borrowed to play, and once again enthused over 'Legenda', 'Allemande' (the first time it has had a real success, which delighted me), the Bassoon Scherzo and 'Capriccio'. In the last named I crossed out the dedication 'to Vera Nikolayevna Meshcherskaya' since I considered it an outrage that a piece I love should have been so roundly condemned by her as rubbish. It now proudly states 'to Talya Meshcherskaya': for some time I have wanted to dedicate a work to Talya, and she loves the 'Capriccio'. I am sure this rededication will cause a furore in the family. But for the time being I said nothing and went to dine with them.

Nina looked green and nervous. She sat me down at the piano and made me play the *Meistersinger* duet with her. She was behaving rather oddly, sometimes jumpy, at other times criticizing me and telling me I was upsetting her. She was most displeased at my project of dedicating *The Ugly Ducking* 'to him' and insisted that it bear a serious dedication. After dinner she took me downstairs to show me some verses for songs, and then we stayed in one another's company sitting lovingly side by side in the billiard room. The 'Decree' has been in force for twelve days now.

When I was bidding everyone farewell and preparing to leave with Tomkeyev, Nina came downstairs with me, when Vera Nikolayevna, suddenly coming out of the drawing room, almost discovered our *tête-à-tête*. I went home on foot and several times caught myself with a smile that would not leave my face.

23 September

Duckling in the morning, then a lesson with Miss Isaacs, then off to the Studio. My first student, the redheaded Kozlova, played Beethoven's Second Sonata really rather well. She says she is practising four hours a day. It was pleasant to work with her, showing her a mass of things, correcting her rhythm, her touch, her phrasing. The other student had not learned anything; all she did was look at me with pleading eyes. I suggested that next time she should come to her lesson with something prepared. Walked back home along

Nevsky. Had a long telephone conversation with Damskaya: somehow or other Eleonora had contrived to find out Gorodetsky's address for me and I wrote him a letter today. In the evening was at the Sokol and did gymnastics to the point of exhaustion.

24 September

Probably because of my exertions with last night's gymnastics I woke up with a headache. I find that my headaches are of the kind that will pass off if I get deeply involved in some activity and forget that my head hurts – then the pain actually goes. For this reason I settled down to *The Ugly Duckling*. True, I managed only a few disconnected passages of new material, but I did make a fair copy of all that I have composed so far. This, the pleasure of turning a series of rough, random jottings into the beginnings of an orderly whole, is an activity I so much enjoy that my headache all but disappeared. Taking advantage of the magnificent weather I strolled along Nevsky and the Embankment, feasted my eyes on the sun dancing on the waters of the Neva, and then went back home. I telephoned Nina, who alternated between being very nice and not very nice. When the call had finished I felt upset by her attitude and went for the evening to Bashkirov's, as he had been pressing me to do. He was as welcoming as usual, and excited by my playing, especially of 'Aufschwung'.[1] He said that his sister, the Princess Magalova, was equally enthusiastic, and he read me his article about the war (good) and some of his poetry (not so good). He asked me if I would give him lessons, and I agreed, because I need money. He walked me home, and on the way said that when the war was over he was going to buy himself a big Peugeot car; he proposed that we should go together in it to Constantinople via Kiev, Odessa and Romania. That would be simply wonderful. I adore long car journeys; Max and I had often made plans to do just that. This is a proposition that really thrills me.

25 September

My name-day. Yesterday, when I got home, Mama told me that Nina had telephoned, and the Meshcherskys were planning to come here to congratulate me on my saint's day. I loved the idea of Nina coming to my place. In the morning I looked at one or two places in the *Duckling*, but was not really in the mood for work. Mama presented me with 25 roubles – riches indeed, bearing in mind that on the one hand there is a war on and on the other I am completely out of funds. Went into the Conservatoire at two o'clock and spent a happy hour there seeing a lot of my friends. Struve looks even

---

1 The second piece in Schumann's collection *Fantiasiestücke*, Op. 12.

prettier and no longer seems to want to avoid me; it is a real pleasure to look at her. Alpers beckoned me over and in the course of a conventional exchange shyly contrived to let me know of her partiality to me. I returned home and tidied up my room somewhat for the arrival of the Meshcherskys: Nina, Talya and Vera Nikolayevna. The girls were very nice, wandered all over the house but mostly in my room where they wanted to look at everything. I played them what I had composed of *The Ugly Duckling*, they obviously had not expected it to be 'so good' and at times were in ecstasies over it. We drank chocolate.

The Meshcherskys were in a hurry and left soon afterwards. In the evening Mama had a visitor, Mme Pavskaya; I replied to my name-day greetings and wrote a letter to Morolyov.

26 September

I jumped out of bed early in the morning so as to be able to get on with *Duckling*, then learned my English vocabulary and went to see the Ruzskys. Yesterday I had remembered to congratulate Nikolay Pavlovich on Ira's birthday and he had been so touched by this that he invited me to lunch today, saying that in a few days' time he would be going to the battle zone. He had managed to get himself comfortably installed in the carriage of one or other of the generals in charge of the action, and thus accompanied will go round Verzhbolovo and Lvov. I was very envious of this. Monsieur and Madame were extremely hospitable and talked with justifiable pride about their cousin, justifiable because he is at the present the hope of all Russia, and indeed of me.[1] Nikolay Pavlovich's brother, Dmitry Pavlovich, was very keen that I write a patriotic *oeuvre*, but I declined.

From the Ruzskys I barely got to Miss Isaacs in time for my lesson, and from there went on to the Studio, where I had a new student, a fidgety young woman in an unusually transparent blouse who giggled all the time from nervousness and dropped me a curtsy on leaving. The curtsy was something of which I subsequently boasted right and left, to general incredulity that anyone would curtsy to me.

---

1 General Nikolay Vladimirovovich Ruzsky (1854–1918) had just been given command of the North Western Front, at that time in retreat from East Prussia. He had earned this promotion from the success – which made him a household name – of his previous command, of the Third Army, in recapturing the city of Lvov from the Austro-Hungarian army in August. Ruzsky ultimately assumed command of the entire Northern Front, including Petrograd, and became the prime mover of the military commanders' determination to achieve the abdication of the Tsar as representing the only hope for future successful prosecution of the war. It was Ruzsky who received from the Tsar's hands the signed abdication document in the Imperial train on 2 March 1917 (old style). His patriotically inspired actions earned him no favour with the Bolsheviks: in October 1918 in Pyatigorsk General Ruzsky was taken hostage and summarily executed with characteristically callous brutality by the Cheka, along with fifty-eight other distinguished military and aristocratic leaders of the ancien régime.

Went for a walk, then home, read some English, went to the Sokol and talked for ages on the telephone to Damskaya.

27 September

I wanted to complete the *Duckling*, because I had been invited to the Meshcherskys in the evening and they wanted me to bring it. But it was not to be: the Duckling's 'wanderings' proved to be altogether too weighty and serious, and instead of finishing the piece I had to go back and completely redo this section. It came out very well, however. I particularly like the passage 'sometimes he sat for a long time in the rushes'.

Vera Nikolayevna asked that Mama call her, because Talya is now working as a nurse in the Alexandrovsky Hospital just near us, and would like to come in to us for a cup of tea and a rest (a pity it is Talya, not Nina, but Nina could never be a nurse). Talya came today with her friend Mlle Khrenova, but I had to leave soon after they arrived. At five o'clock I came back to find Seryozha Sebryakov, and then after him Bashkirov appeared for his lesson. He has good hands, but the level of his abilities is still no more than rudimentary. He is a particularly weak sight-reader: the most he could do was haltingly stumble through an easy Mozart sonata! I had imagined he would be a much better player then he is, and would never have taken him if I had not liked him. After the lesson he said to me, 'Sergey Sergeyevich, I take it the fee for the lessons is as I understood it from our last discussion.'

'I don't recall giving you to understand anything in this connection.'

'No, but you did mention ten roubles being a normal fee for prizewinners.'

'Boris Nikolayevich, I've no intention of overcharging. I've never given lessons before. Why should I rob you . . .'

'Oh please, what is this talk of robbing me? I think it's absolutely the right fee.'

'As you wish, Boris Nikolayevich.'

Needless to say, I have not the least objection to the ten roubles, and my hint to him had been very cautiously expressed. Just at the moment, when my pockets are empty, the ten roubles are extremely welcome, and I am actually quite proud that my services are valued at ten roubles.

Some time after eight Mama and I went to the Meshcherskys, where Nina appeared with her neck somewhat coquettishly wrapped up, as she had a sore throat and a cold and was running a slight temperature that she attempted to conceal but that added a mild blush to her cheeks. *The Ugly Duckling* received an intimate play-through on the piano, both Talya and Nina going into raptures over it. Anna Grigorievna did not come to listen, but Nikolay Vasilievich gave it his seal of approval. At tea Nina seated me beside her and told me that 'America' had now sunk halfway below the waves, to be replaced by a large but unpopulated (?!) land mass. After that we went into the study to write a letter to Oleg. Nina announced to me that on reflection she had decided the 'Decree' must be restored to its full force.

We parted friends. I put Mama in a tramcar and walked home considerably upset and convinced that Nina has a unique talent for pulling in several directions at once. It also runs like a red thread through everything she says about other people. But at the present time I feel as though there is a sixteen-inch cannon pointing straight at me, just like at the city of Antwerp.

28 September

For a whole week I faithfully spent every morning composing more of the *Duckling*. Today I think I am entitled to take a break. I played Scriabin's Sonata No. 6 and found in it much to interest me. Last year I was not able to understand it fully. After that I still got around to a bit more of the *Duckling*. Mama and I went together to visit Papa's grave. I wanted to find the grave of the recently deceased Lyadov, but in this was not successful. The Scythian-style memorial to Rimsky-Korsakov pleased me greatly. Returned home, to find that Gorodetsky had not telephoned. Yesterday, in response to my letter, he called and said that he had thought of a subject for the ballet. He needed to have my opinion on the proposal and also to hear more of my music, and then he would be primed and ready to go. He asked me to call on him yesterday evening, but I was going to the Meshcherskys and could not. He then promised to let me know today when we could meet, but did not get in touch. I telephoned Eleonora and went for a walk with her in the sunshine, and then to call on the Rayevskys, who had returned from the country.

As for Nina and her intention to revive the 'Decree', I gave this some thought and decided that if she were determined to carry it into effect I must mount a counter-attack. My answer would be: all right, then either we quarrel terminally or there is an end to all 'decrees'.

In the evening I stayed at home, read some English, played the piano and wrote my diary.

29 September

At night I dreamed of Nina, and she was also in my thoughts during the morning. Took the corrected proofs of Op. 12 to the post and mailed them. Wrote some of the *Duckling*, but not a lot. I am very happy with my life.

Talya and Mlle Khrenova lunched with us, both in white nurses' uniforms. I did not have anything very urgent to do, so after lunch I played the piano for them, among other things Myaskovsky's Sonata, which Talya liked, and then ran through for them my game against Capablanca. Talya rang home, and realizing that she was speaking to Nina, I took over the phone. After Nina asked some questions about the *Duckling* and I enquired about her health today, she said, 'After you went the other evening I spent a whole hour thinking long and hard.'

'Well, I did say to you, please don't think!'

'But I did, and I have come up with rather a subtle manoeuvre.'

'It's bound to be some nasty trick or other.'

'No, not nasty at all, something that will be beneficial to me and to you.'

'Thank you for your consideration.'

Then she invited me to come and play duets, and I said I would come on Wednesday.

We talked for quite a long time and then said goodbye. As I saw Talya and her friend to the door I was cudgelling my brains as to what Nina's subtle manoeuvre could be. Obviously it must be in some way replace the 'Decree', and presumably would involve calling a halt to over-amorous relations. I resolved to mount a counter-attack: to drop completely out of sight so that she would hear and see nothing whatsoever of me for at least a week. Let her repine in the company of her ingenious plan, and then we shall see what we shall see.

I made a fair copy of what I had written of the *Duckling*, read some English and at eight o'clock went out to see Bashkirov, who had invited me. On the tram I bought a newspaper with the latest news and read that a German submarine had sunk the cruiser *Pallada* with loss of the whole crew. The whole crew, how dreadful! When I arrived at Bashkirov's I was still in shock from the catastrophe. At eleven o'clock his parents and brother (the one who had gone out to dinner in his nightshirt) came back from the theatre, where they had been to see the patriotic play *The Disgrace of Germany* and had all, especially the brother, been profoundly stirred by it. The brother asked me, as a personal favour to him, to go and see this play. Boris Nikolayevich undertook to get tickets, and I agreed to go on Wednesday, thinking that it would give me an excuse not to play duets with Nina.

Today I rang up Zakharov and we had a good conversation. He apologized for forgetting my name-day. On Saturday I am arranging a 'bridge cripples foursome' with besides myself Zakharov, Bashkirov and Nikolayev – all of us stumblers at the game.

30 September

The pace of composition of the *Duckling* has slowed and it is generally not going so well. At the beginning the tale had a comic character, but as it gets towards the end it grows more serious and is somehow less well suited to the music. I therefore studied my English vocabulary and read some English writing as well. At half past two I had another lesson in the language, during which I managed with great difficulty to converse in English on the subject of the war. Miss Isaacs was delighted that I am beginning to be able to speak the language. I then went to the Studio, where my new student did not turn up and there were just the two: the red-haired girl and the dark-haired girl. The dark-haired one played badly, as usual, but the redhead was good and I enjoyed working with her. My manner is like Yesipova squared: I impose very precise demands and know exactly what it is I want to achieve. In my opinion I am an excellent teacher and my students should do very well. After the lesson the Director of the Studio asked me how my students were getting on; I praised the redhead and criticized the brunette.

I walked home along Nevsky and then read (with enjoyment) some English. Nina rang up before I left to go to the Sokol to tell me that Talya and her friend would be coming to lunch with us tomorrow. She asked whether I was coming to her tomorrow evening and I said that I would more likely be going to *The Disgrace of Germany*. At this she became angry: 'Well, you'd better make up your mind whether you are definitely coming or not!'

'Probably tomorrow I shall be able to inform Talya one way or the other.'

The conversation took a somewhat acid tone, just what is needed. All the same, at the Sokol I was a bit melancholy. I should like to find true love.

1 October

Today I began to see the end of the *Duckling*, although there is some of it with which I am not happy. There was one point that caused Talya to splutter; I think I see what she means and will revise it. Nina telephoned to tell Talya what time she should come home.

'Are you coming this evening?'

'Bashkirov hasn't called me yet. When you rang I thought it would be him. I probably won't come.'

'As you wish, in that case you needn't bother. You needn't bother ever coming, for that matter.'

'All right.'

With that the conversation came to an end. When Talya left I went for a walk along Nevsky and Morskaya and when I returned it was time for Bashkirov to come for his lesson. To my surprise I did not feel too out of sorts or upset during the lesson. Then we had something quick to eat and went to the theatre. The play penetrates so near the heart of any patriot that it quite takes the breath away to see it. It is often crude and will lose much of its effect as soon as the war is over, but there are very good things in it. One marvellous moment is a raid by the German patrol on a Russian country estate, and there was another moment that sparked a vivid memory of Kislovodsk: when the two lovers took advantage of the momentary absence of all the other characters to embrace tenderly behind a curtain . . .

Someone took my hat in place of his own. I was afraid that its original wearer might be bald, so I stuffed a handkerchief into it so that it should not come into contact with my head.

2 October

Today things clarified themselves for me and I finished the *Duckling* in great style. There was a letter from Myaskunchik[1] from which I learned that he was twenty versts away from Petrograd. Although he was not allowed to say where his unit was stationed, the letter was postmarked in the village of Kapitolovo; I got out the map and found it. I wrote back to ask if it is possible to visit him, and if it is then Boryusya and I will go to see him. In the afternoon I made a fair copy of the *Duckling*, contentedly read some English, and then went to Schmidt's music shop on behalf of the Sokol, because it was Schmidt who was printing my Sokol 'March'. I would have been able to get it except that Schmidt, being a German citizen, has been deported and no one in his establishment seems to know anything. In the evening I stayed at home and played the piano – it is a good time to start learning the Second Piano Concerto so as to avoid a great rush at the last moment. I am so glad to have finished the *Duckling*. While I am waiting for Gorodetsky – who has again vanished from sight – to come up with his ideas for the ballet, it would be good to finish two of the *Sarcasms* and at least the fourth movement of the Sinfonietta. After the ballet I must get on with composing the opera I plan, on a light, fast-moving theme with plenty of action on the stage. If the subject Gorodetsky comes up with is not suitable for the ballet I shall concentrate on my beloved Violin Concerto.

Mama came home late in the evening from the Alexandrovsky Hospital where she has been helping to dress the injuries of the war wounded, who started to arrive in the capital in huge numbers today. Listening to her stories I began to tremble and felt ashamed that I was concerning myself with the *Duckling*, but . . . of course there is a sense in which it is unpardonable egotism to sit idly by while people are perishing. But still during peace-time there are masses of unfortunate folk and people who are ill, and at such times one is still allowed to laugh; the only thing is that at the present time there are a thousand times more of them. How diabolically crass this war is, and with what grave countenances is the idiocy being pursued!

3 October

Since the *Duckling* is finished I slept a little later than usual and did not do any composing but played the Second Concerto, the *Toccata* and Deshevov's Scherzo,[2] and studied the subtle nuances of the English language. Lunched with Yurasovsky, now encased in a soldier's greatcoat as tomorrow he goes to

---

1   Myaskovsky.
2   The last of the ten pieces in Op. 12, the 'Scherzo', is dedicated to Vladimir Deshevov.

the front as a medical orderly – his task will be to bear the wounded away from the battlefield. Had he not volunteered as a medical orderly, by Christmas he would have been drafted as a private soldier. Although we were joking about it, I did not find it altogether an easy thing to be seeing off a person who was in line to be shot at.

Had my English lesson and afterwards went to Jurgenson to find out if Myaskovsky's Sonata No. 2 had been published yet (it had not), and as my hat had been substituted for another at the theatre and I did not want to strut around in another's, I was wearing a cycling cap. I did my best to avoid Nevsky in order to have less chance of meeting people who know me, but almost the first people I met were Eleonora and her mother, to whom she introduced me. Her Mama is quite nice, much better than I remember from before.

Dined at Anna Grigorievna's, who was excited by the idea of *The Ugly Duckling* and when she heard the music became even more so. She took the score in the first instance to learn it, and plans to sing it 'in every city'. Left her and went to the Sokol; Kolya Ruzsky has taken to going there as well.

When I got back home I was telephoned by Hartmann,[1] a composer I know by sight at concerts. Once he had introduced himself he extended an invitation to me from the I.R.M.S.[2] to appear in their series in December or January in my Piano Concerto No. 1. The I.R.M.S.! This is the concert series that was once upon a time so influential but has now run to seed owing to hopeless management and boring programmes. Between them Glazunov and Artsybushev have ruined the concerts. And all of a sudden this archconservative institution invites me, and with my Concerto to boot – Mahomet invited into a Christian monastery! I was completely dumbfounded and even asked the question, 'Which I.R.M.S. series, exactly?'

'The Petrograd branch, which puts on a series every winter,' replied Hartmann unhurriedly.

Thanking him for the honour he did me and signifying my agreement, I expressed my surprise that they would issue such an invitation to me. What seems to have happened is this: the concert committee consists of Artsybushev, Hartmann and one other person. Hartmann is interested in my music, while I had invited Artsybushev to the Graduation Concert in the spring at which, after hearing my Concerto performance, he appeared backstage,

---

1   Foma (Thomas de) Hartmann (1885–1956), composer, pianist and conductor. A student of Yesipova, Taneyev and Arensky, his compositions in Russia tended towards the Nationalist style and were much influenced by Musorgsky, but he seems to have privately harboured more radical ambitions, because in 1919 he emigrated, first to Paris and then to New York, where he fundamentally changed his style to embrace polytonal and polyrhythmic techniques. Not to be confused with the German composer Karl Amadeus Hartmann.
2   Imperial Russian Musical Society – Imperial'noye Russkoye Muzikal'noye Obshchestvo.

introduced himself and paid me a compliment. I remember telling Myaskovsky and Karatygin about this at the time, and both of them snorted derisively: 'Oh yes, you're so likely to be invited to the I.R.M.S. now!' They regarded the idea as inconceivable, even ludicrous as, to be fair, so did I.

Hartmann kept me quite a long time on the telephone talking about all manner of things, and was extremely friendly, asking me to visit him. He asked me what my fee would be, to which I replied that I did not know, but presumably they had a tariff and it would be easier for them to make me an offer. I am delighted at this turn of events.

4 October

I have taken to getting up late; still in bed at a quartet past ten. Today I tried to do something with [orchestrating] the two *Sarcasms* I had identified, but nothing would come of it. I did some revision of the Sinfonietta, but on the whole achieved little. After one o'clock I went to the Conservatoire to see friends, but could find almost no one there, the place seemed deserted today. Tcherepnin has an abscess in his throat. He's been going about muffled up in a beaver collar since August, and now, see, he's got a cold. I finally exchanged my foreign travel passport for a Russian one, bought a French newspaper, a notebook and a coloured shirt, because all mine are from London and have short sleeves. In the evening Zakharov and Nikolayev came to play bridge; Bashkirov was ill and cried off. Andreyev had also promised to come but in the end could not make it. Zakharov is quite a reasonable player, and Nikolayev can also play a decent hand. Both were very stylishly dressed, in morning coats. Zakharov muttered into his beard that I issue invitations to play bridge but when you come there's no one to play with. I replied, 'Just you wait, your job is to play well at your concert, and mine is to arrange a good bridge session.' He behaved very nicely and politely, and really made an effort with the cards. The *Duckling* went down very well and he said it should definitely be orchestrated.

5 October

I thought out the conclusion of the Sinfonietta's Scherzo and buried myself in Rimsky-Korsakov's course on orchestration, thinking about the conclusion both from the musical and the instrumentation points of view, but did not write a single note. After lunch Kobylyansky wormed his way in to show me his syrupy trill-bedizened Etudes. Although he graduated in theory of composition, he is hopeless.

I then took myself off in the sunshine on foot to the Islands, calling on the way for Bashkirov to come with me, but he was still not well enough. What a marvellous woman his sister is though, our Princess.¹ She is a year older than him, but looks like a young girl. So I went on, quite happy to be by myself, to Aptekarsky Island, walked out to the Strelka and then back again. The mixture of sunshine and mist seemed to lay a milky covering over everything as I walked home again to dinner. The walk had tired me, but I still wanted to do some work. A wild idea: to compose a quartet. This is exactly what I should not do just at the moment, think up new projects when I have so many old ones still unfinished: the *Sarcasms*, the Sinfonietta, the songs (up to six), the ballet, piano variations, the Violin Concerto! Yet another wild idea: to make the quartet diatonic, using only the white notes of the keyboard, and for the main theme of the first movement to be built out of sevenths.² Even so, the composition of the themes and the music came very easily today.

Who should telephone, but Nina. She asked whether I was ever going to visit them or ring up, and had she not telephoned herself today, would I have stayed silent until 1915? I replied that my silence was pure coincidence; I had been very busy for the last three days. She demanded insistently that I go to see them today. My response was couched in the urbane tones proper to a friendly but distant young man of her acquaintance, which roused her to fury. I attempted to turn the conversation to other matters, but she said that previously I had upset her in one way and was now doing so in another, and that if I did not go to see her today there would be an end to our relationship altogether (?!). This was the last invitation she would ever extend to me and as far as she was concerned if I did not accept it I would cease to exist. I said that I would do my best to be sure and call on them sometime soon, but was unable to do so today. She said that as I did not wish to come today she was not interested in future visits, so goodbye, and put the phone down. I lay for a while on the sofa, my temples throbbing. I then settled down to the quartet. One theme followed another and I even began to think I might complete the first movement this very day. But in fact this was a long way off.

6 October

Wrote out the conclusion of the Sinfonietta's Scherzo, and played my Second Piano Concerto. Then I went for a walk, read the newspaper and some English. In the evening I went to Bashkirov's, and was introduced to his friend Mlle Gruzenberg, the daughter of a well-known barrister. The three of us visited the field hospital for the wounded that he and his sister had established and equipped most comfortably. It was the first time I had had

---

1   Princess Varvara Magalova, sister of Boris Bashkirov and wife of Prince Magalov. The pianist Nikita Magalov (1912–1992) was their son.
2   The opening of the Fifth Act of *The Fiery Angel*. [Subsequent note by author.]

direct experience of wounded people. When we arrived they were studying a map of Europe. They seemed very cheerful, but we realized that the more seriously injured among them were confined to their beds and were suffering greatly.

From the hospital we went on to Bashkirov's brother. He has taken a detached house rather than an apartment; from the outside it did not look very impressive, but inside it had been gilded and embellished like a jewel-box. Some of the rooms had been 'styled' by a designer but others were simply beautiful, although there were some lapses of judgement: artificial palm trees on the staircase, carpets of too deep a red in the brown/blue study.

7 October

Completed the Scherzo of the Sinfonietta. Had my English lesson. Went to the Studio, where my only student was the ever-reliable Kozlova. I received my fee: 14 roubles . . . I had not expected to get the money today and was quite delighted to do so, as I had not a cent in my pocket. Went for a walk, returned home, continued work on the Sinfonietta, and before going to the Sokol called in at the Andreyevs to give them *The Ugly Duckling*. Anna Grigorievna was quite overcome with pleasure and excitement. She said that the previous evening she had been at the Meshcherskys and had told them how much she liked the piece. Wonderful timing! I said, 'The girls are very upset with me, are they not?'

'You mean Nina,' conceded Anna Grigorievna. 'But I told her that you fall out with everyone; you and I have had our quarrels in the past – but we are still friends.'

8 October

Nouvel telephoned: 'Diaghilev has cabled from Florence asking for your address and also to know if you are getting on with composing the ballet.'

My answer was to curse and swear and explain that as I had not been able to get anything out of Gorodetsky I had not yet made a start on the ballet. I added, 'In any case I had been imagining that this spring there would not be much call for ballet in London and Paris because of the war.'

'I have heard,' said Nouvel, 'that Diaghilev has changed his plans and is going to tour America.'

I begged him to wait a couple of days before replying to the telegram, and in the meantime promised to do my best to clarify matters with Gorodetsky. That would be wonderful! To be in America in May . . . would be perfect. A shame about the war. It would be strange to leave everything and go to America at a time when people are killing one another in Warsaw, but there is nothing I can do to help, and Diaghilev's company will be going in any case. So my way is clear to seek out Gorodetsky and extract from him precisely what he has done!

I went to his house on Malaya Posadskaya, which proved to be a charming little tree-lined street, and found my way to Gorodetsky's door, on which instead of ringing a bell you had to bang with a wooden knocker. But he was not at home. I left a trenchantly worded note and returned home. Studied English assiduously because, my friends, America! I then gave Bashkirov his lesson, who today was green about the gills and in pain from his operation two years ago for appendicitis. He was as nice as always, although while waiting for his taxi he bored me to death talking about philosophy. He invited me to visit him this evening but I was going to the Damskaya sisters. It was the first time I had visited them at home, and I enjoyed myself very much. Vera and even Eleonora looked very pretty. I spent the whole evening there and did not notice the time going by.

Managed to speak to Sergey Gorodetsky on the telephone. He has come up with a subject for the ballet and tomorrow I shall go to his house to discuss it with him.

9 October

Worked on correcting the proofs of the score of the First Piano Concerto, which have been with me for two months now. In the afternoon I went for a walk and then continued working on the proofs. Ziloti telephoned. I thought his concerts were still taking place, and was worried that the fifth movement of the Nietta was still not ready, but he told me that the Sinfonietta would be included in the following season, and as soon as I do finish it, it would be good to send it to the copyist. Ziloti spoke in an exceedingly friendly tone of voice, which surprised me greatly.

At half past seven I was applying the wooden doorknocker to Gorodetsky's door. The apartment he occupies is nice, but he received me in a room illuminated by a single candle and furnished with a low couch. Odd. He was dressed in a white flannel shirt. Generally speaking, he is a nice fellow. The scenario had been merely sketched out, not finished, and was quite insubstantial as regards content. The subject revolves round Russian idols of the ninth century, a theme whose aroma I found to my surprise very attractive, and the concept of bulls appearing in the sky to herald the sunrise sent me into raptures. We got down to serious discussion of the subject, inventing, creating, cutting and trimming, I discovered in myself a great store of creative talents, debated hotly, cudgelled my brains, and can say with some pride that I was responsible for devising half the scenario. The result of all this was that in the space of an hour a five-scene ballet was created.

Scene 1. The god Veles (the sun god) has a daughter Ala, a carefree young goddess. Tar, god of the dark regions, wishes to abduct her, but is powerless against the light of the sun (i.e. Veles). When the sun sets, Ala is carried off by Tar. She is pursued by a simple mortal, a singer, who wishes to rescue the goddess because he has fallen in love with her.

Scene 2. Evening. The chase. The singer succeeds in snatching Ala, but the god of darkness takes her back again.

Scene 3. A fjord in the far north. Tar has put Ala in chains. Night. Tar wishes to possess Ala but each time he attempts to do so the clouds part, allowing the moon to shine through. The moon maidens appear in the moonbeams; Tar is powerless against the light and the moon maidens protect Ala.

Scene 4. Dawn. The singer again pursues Ala and catches up with her. A struggle ensues and the mortal is killed. Bulls pass across the sky, all kinds of devilry occur and the sun rises: Veles has come in search of his daughter. He defeats Tar and at that moment Ala's chains fall away. She has fallen in love with the singer and is grief-stricken at his death.

Scene 5. Day. The same setting as Scene 1. Through immolation, Veles transforms his daughter's brave rescuer into a god. Ala, however, throws herself into the flames consuming the body of her lover and the opposite process befalls her – she becomes mortal. Alas, once again they inhabit different spheres.

Gorodetsky is wedded to this conclusion. I have nothing against it provided only the audience is able to make out what is going on. I joke that it reminds me of the story of the two friends, the lift and the staircase. One goes up in the lift to the sixth floor while the other runs down the staircase, and then the other way round, so they never succeed in meeting. We telephoned Nouvel to ask him to send a telegram to Diaghilev saying that 'Prokofieff travaille avec Gorodetsky.' We had tea. Gorodetsky's wife, Nympha Gorodetskaya,[1] whom I had seen occasionally at concerts, insisted that I play for them. I cannot make her out at all, but she treated me very kindly. When an engineer friend arrived to read some poetry I sat sprawled out on the low sofa with a mound of cushions between the Nymph and her sister, while we talked of mutual acquaintances: Tcherepnin, Lyadov, Karatygin. Gorodetsky promised that tomorrow he would put in order and complete the writing of everything we discussed today, and the day after I would come to him again.

---

1 Nympha Belle-Kohl-Lyubomirskaya was the somewhat highly scented *nom de plume* chosen by Anna Gorodetskaya, *née* Koselskaya, for her writings. The literary *salon* over which she presided, attended by Symbolist and Acmeist poets, could be equally exotic: the *pièce de résistance* would be a block of ice encasing roses which, when the ice was smashed with an axe, were presented to the assembled poetesses.

10 October

In the morning I again applied myself to the proofs of the Concerto and finished them; alas only one-third of the work, as Jurgenson engraves large scores movement by movement, hence the rest of it is still to follow. At my English lesson I received praise from Miss Isaacs for the progress I have made. At seven o'clock I got a telephone call from Nina, who five days ago had said that everything was over between us. I explained that I was about to go out to a concert: they also apparently had planned to go, Nina being anxious to see and hear Zakharov, but Vera Nikolayevna then changed her mind. Later on Nina reproached me with being heartless and said that she was spending her evenings knitting scarves for the wounded and cursing me. I took pleasure in replying to her with the polite indifference of a not very close acquaintance, and attempting to change the subject, which drove her into a frenzy. I mentioned to her that I was working with Gorodetsky on a ballet, in which one of the scenes took place in a fjord. In the summer she and I had fantasized about her having left her husband and meeting me in a Norwegian fjord, and how passionate our embraces would be. Ever since 'fjord' had symbolized for us the expression of passionate conjugal feelings. The conversation ended like this:

I: 'If you like, I will telephone you and tell you about the concert.'
Nina was delighted. 'Wonderful! When will you call?'
'Today, at half past one.'
Silence. Then angrily, having realized I was teasing, 'Go to the devil!'
Pause. Then, agreeably, 'Fine, I'll just go there now.'
Then the receiver snapped down.

I went to the concert with a degree of anticipation, not having been to any concerts for some time, and I also hoped to see many of my friends. Quite a few of them were there although not, as a matter of fact, as many as I had been expecting. I sat with Nadya and Sonya Shtember, who invited me to call on them. Kokochka had gone to Moscow and they were lonely. Zakharov stumped noisily on to the platform and played the Bach–Busoni Fugue averagely well but never reaching the heights. On the other hand, after the interval he accompanied Hansen magnificently in Nikolayev's Violin Sonata, which was not at all a bad piece, although derivative. For an encore he played my 'Gavotte', which was warmly applauded and even elicited a call for the composer. The Andreyevs, husband and wife, sang indifferently. Hansen had a huge success. I had been expecting that there would be supper at the Zakharovs afterwards, but in fact this was not appropriate as it was really Hansen's concert, not his. I had hoped to see the Karneyev sisters, but only Lyova came. At night I dreamed of Zakharov, Hansen, the concert and Nina.

11 October

Did not get up until eleven. Then went to post the corrected proofs of the Concerto movement to Jurgenson. When I returned home I found it impossible to work. Clothes and linen are being collected all over Petrograd for the relief of war-ravaged Poland, and Mama has agreed to form a collecting point. Flags hang from the entrance to our building and there is a big poster on the door, so the telephone and the doorbell go continually and people bring in great bales of old clothes. Mama and a couple of students, one male and one female, are writing down everything they receive, sorting the material, issuing receipts – so there is nowhere to get to the piano and work. I am very disgruntled and mentally consign them all to the devil, even though in principle I support the relief effort. I sat in my room and diligently studied English so as not to waste time.

Went for a stroll, hoping to meet Vegman. I find it very touching that this beautiful girl with her classically Greek nose should be in love with me. I made a point of passing along the street she takes to go to the Conservatoire. The Court Orchestra has announced a series of fourteen (!) concerts with works by Petrograd composers, beginning with some who are scarcely still breathing: Napravnik and Cui, interspersed with some of quite scandalous ineptitude such as Ivanov, Shenk,[1] Kalafati and others. Towards the end of the series there are some rather livelier names: Tcherepnin, Myaskusha, and finally the cheeky young chappies Stravinsky and me. Not only that but each concert is to be repeated three times in aid of the wounded, making a total of forty-two concerts!

Talya telephoned Mama to invite her and me to dinner tomorrow. Mama declined on her own account because of the collection, and said that I would telephone. I did so, and Nina answered. I started off by saying that I would not be able to come tomorrow, but Nina cut me off and, deliberately ignoring this question, asked me about yesterday's concert. But when I started to tell her about it, she said that her kissel[2] was getting cold.

'If you can't come tomorrow, come some time during the week, on Tuesday or whenever you can. That is, if you would like to,' she added.

'But Talya is with her patients in the evenings, Vera Nikolayevna will probably be busy, so it's not a very attractive prospect for me to spend time in the company of the furniture and your sour-looking physiognomy!'

'On the contrary, today my physiognomy is very cheerful.'

'Well, anyway, your blancmange is getting cold. Goodbye!' and I put down the receiver.

---

1 Pyotr Shenk (1870–1915), composer and pianist, responsible for the foundation of the Society of Russian Composers.
2 A kind of blancmange.

I was less pleased with today's conflict than previous ones.

At nine o'clock I was at Gorodetsky's, and his first words convinced me that he was completely lacking in any sense of dramatic imagination. He conceives of ballet as a series of *tableaux* rather than action. My first requirement, that the action should start immediately the curtain rises, had been entirely forgotten. Scene 2 had been eliminated altogether.

I said I was not happy with any of this, and lay down in dismay on the sofa. The thought of having to find a new librettist, to explain my ideas all over again, to wait while a new scenario was prepared, my God how infinitely depressing. Out of consideration for his feelings I tried to think of some way of making something of his subject, and little by little we both became absorbed, began thinking of effects and movements, and the ballet took wing once more. I was responsible for the following inventions: the people lying face downwards as the curtain rises; a new scenario for Scene 2; the alternation of moonbeams and clouds in Scene 3; also the monstrous vision and the *coup de théâtre* at the final curtain when the singer is transformed into an idol. By the end the ballet had genuinely caught fire in our imagination; we were both in a state of pleasurable excitement. I asked Nouvel to send a telegram to Diaghilev as from me, asking whether Romanov[1] would definitely produce the ballet, because we were now in need of a choreographer to settle the details.

12 October

I decided to ignore the crowds of students and closeted myself in the drawing room to get on with composing the ballet. I worked with great absorption although some of the music came out a trifle crudely. However, the continual phone calls and people coming in and out of the next room prevented me from concentrating, and I soon substituted reading English for trying to compose. At two o'clock I went out to pay some calls, which had been mounting up for some time. I went to the Damskys; to the Safonovs, who had invited me when they left Kislovodsk but who were not at home when I called; to Korsak; to Kotova. Having an hour to spare and finding myself on Kirochnaya Street I decided on impulse to drop in on the Meshcherskys as I was feeling slightly guilty at not having shown my nose there for two weeks.

In the evening we had a very nice bridge party at home with Zakharov, Andreyev and Serge Bazavov. Zakharov is not a terribly good player but he

1 The young Mariinsky balletmaster, Boris Romanov (1891–1957) had choreographed three productions for Diaghilev, in 1913 (Florent Schmitt's *La tragédie de Salomé*) and 1914 (Strauss's *Josephlegende* and Stravinsky's *Le Rossignol* – the opera; the later ballet *Le Chant du rossignol* was staged by Massine).

is lucky, and always seems to win. I outlined the plot of the ballet to Nikolay Vasilievich, and he gave it his blessing.

As Jurgenson had sent the proofs of Op. 12 I settled down to work on them, while all the other rooms were stacked from floor to ceiling with clothes and articles for Poland. Every minute another donor would come loaded down with parcels, so that we gave up keeping the door closed. There were now five students of both sexes taking care of the contributions, and the work went on until midnight. A large lorry arrived, but it was not big enough to take away everything that had been collected. I was sure they were bringing infection into our apartment, but I could not avoid being interested in this collection of stuff, and I was touched by the efforts of the students; I was solicitous in seeing they had enough to eat at dinner, and in the evening, when work was done and they asked me to play the piano to them, I played Chopin's Scherzo No. 2.

When they had left I played through Scriabin's Sonata No. 6, the second time I had done so. Its harmonic language has a subtly aristocratic, *recherché* flavour, and this is something quite new to me because up until now I have had a sceptical attitude to Scriabin's later sonatas.

14 October

Slept late again today, then applied myself to the ballet. A telegram from Diaghilev: could I come to Rome via Salonika and bring the piano score of the ballet with me, and would I like to perform the Second Piano Concerto there? I called Nouvel for advice. Not that I had anything against going to Italy, but having to get there across Bulgaria and through the mines in the Adriatic was not such an attractive proposition. In any case, the project could not happen in the immediate future, for the ballet was not yet started and I had not learned the Concerto. In a month's time the situation would be clearer, but until then I shall wait for another telegram from Diaghilev telling me who the choreographer is to be. All the same, to go to the sun just now, to wear a light suit, to be able to stroll on the beach and look at Italian women – that would be marvellous!

I set to work feverishly on the ballet.

Talya Meshcherskaya came; it was a long time since she had been to us owing to the amount of work she has to do. I showed her the telegram from Italy, and also the proof of the 'Capriccio', telling her that it was now dedicated to her. 'But I shall dedicate a march of some kind to Vera Nikolayevna,' I added, 'something rather more tasteful, since this piece is considered to be such "rubbish".'

I was at the Studio and then at half past seven at the Sokol, which has moved to a Finnish building on Konyushennaya Street, our own premises having been requisitioned for the wounded. The new place is more cramped. Many of the Sokolites cannot stand me because I never bow to them. This amuses me, and I adopt an especially arrogant air. Kolya Ruzsky told me that Nikolay Pavlovich has been appointed Deputy Head of the Red Cross and is departing for Lvov.

15 October

I asked to be woken at half past eight and pressed on with the ballet. I decided to compose it in five to six weeks and then to notate it at record speed. The work is going extremely well, although my English is suffering in consequence and I did not learn all my vocabulary for Miss Isaacs today. I spent the evening with Bashkirov, who has been trying to telephone me for three days without success and had come to the conclusion that I was angry with him. He was very taken with the subject of the ballet, and promised to think about it himself, letting his imagination run over the details. He took me home afterwards.

16 October

The ballet is going marvellously. I have begun the first, second and third scenes simultaneously. The actual composition is flowing better than yesterday, when in places I found I was piling up all kinds of contrivances that did not ring true: today everything is growing of itself. I deployed all manner of musical ideas and snatches of themes that I had conceived in the spring and noted down on scraps of paper, but sometimes it was a terrible job to track down these pieces of paper, so scattered about had they been. Went for a walk in the afternoon. Telephoned Zakharov. With reckless extravagance we plan to get a car next Wednesday and go to see Myaskuna.[1]

In the evening visited the Damskaya sisters and once again the time passed so pleasantly I did not notice it. Eleonora has a pain in her heart, and her nerves are on edge because of the saga with her suitor, whom she has turned down twice and who today left to go to the front, the very hottest part of it. He is on her conscience. I had to help her compose several letters, which task I fulfilled with great artistry.

17 October

Today I concentrated on the third scene and thought it all out to the end; the orchestration is also more or less planned out. I gave the moon maidens

1 Myaskovsky.

a theme (very nature-descriptive) that I had originally envisaged as a second subject for some other work, but it is an ideal one to illustrate the moon maidens: cold, gentle, other-worldly and enigmatic.

Went to my English lesson at half past one. I had not learned so many words for today, nevertheless was praised and told there was every hope I would soon be able to speak really well. I then went to the Conservatoire to listen to the Quinquennial Competition, in which female students who have graduated during the past five years are eligible to compete. I got there near the end to hear Poznyakovskaya play Liszt's *Mephisto* with staggeringly pearly brilliance. If only there were a modicum of brains to occupy the vacuum inside her skull she would be a marvellous pianist. Unfortunately I missed hearing Golubovskaya and Katyusha Borshch. I sat with Borovsky, who wants to come and see me, but I put him off because of the ballet. Afterwards I mixed with the hopefuls awaiting the awarding of the prize, my old flame Katya Borshch among them. She has regained her former beauty, flirted very amiably with me (and I with her) and asked me to give her my Concerto. Most willingly. She is married now and lives in Helsingfors.

18 October

Progress on the ballet was much stickier today and I did not achieve much. Read some English. Nyamochka[1] telephoned; he has returned to Petrograd for a couple of days and is expecting me this evening. Gave Bashkirov a lesson and declined his invitation so as to hurry to Nyamochka, whom I found to be looking wonderful, tanned and vigorous. The evening slipped by pleasantly with Asafyev also in the company. I enjoyed playing through Nyam's Second Symphony with him. Borisulya[2] had called in during the afternoon and, according to Myaskovsky, was boasting about how acclaimed his performances had been and how he had been engaged to appear in the I.R.M.S. and elsewhere. Nyamochka will either have to return to his unit to strengthen the defences of the capital, or else he may actually be sent to the front. In the latter case he will stay another five days or so in Petrograd and we shall have another chance to meet. If he does go to the battle zone he is not likely to be in the thick of the fighting since his sapper company is in effect a semi-militia unit and will be mostly deployed in the rear.

19 October

Oh, how sweetly Nina and I were kissing in my dreams! I thought how nice it would be to go to the Meshcherskys this evening for dalliance with Nina. As

---

1 N. Ya. Myaskovsky.
2 Boris Zakharov.

it happened she telephoned at midday, but I was in the middle of composing the ballet and when I went to the telephone I was cross at being interrupted. She alerted me to the fact that Talya and her friend would be coming to lunch today, and told me with pride that on Friday they had all been to hear *Kitezh* and how wonderful it had been. Reading between the lines: I had not been invited, although it was I who had played them the score, one act every other day, in the summer. 'Goodbye for now, Seryozha,' she caressingly ended the conversation.

I said goodbye hastily, wanting to get back to the ballet. But then I began to regret it: after all, on the one hand I had been wanting to go to see them this evening, and on the other hand I adopted this abrupt way of speaking. When Talya arrived and rang Nina to say when she would be coming home, I took over the conversation and said, 'By the way, please will you find out from your concierge if the books you gave me to read are all right ...'

I had been given the books a month ago, and Nina was sure that I was still reading them. I savoured in advance the effect of my question, and was not disappointed. Nina was appalled, and I laughed heartily. However, seeing that I was joking and presumably in a good mood, she said, 'All the same, Seryozha, if you have a moment some time, do remember that I have still not heard the *Duckling*, and you must come and play it to me ...'

'You are asking the wrong person. The *Duckling* is with Anna Grigorievna and she is learning it. She can sing it to you, I don't have the music here and I don't remember it by heart. Anyway, I don't know why you should be so interested in it ...'

'What do you mean: why I should be so interested?'

'Well, after all, there is hardly any of your text in it now, I changed it all; and your name doesn't appear on the dedication ...'

Nina seemed rather taken aback and the conversation soon ended. Obviously she was so offended by the removal of the dedication (although I did not actually remove it, I only said I had not written her name: there is no doubt that the *Duckling* is dedicated to Nina) that she did not want to speak to me at all.

Anna Grigorievna came to pay a call on Mama, and asked me if I would give a joint recital with her in the Small Hall, when half of the programme would consist of me performing my compositions, and she would sing the other half including some of my songs. I fear, however, that we would not attract a full house, and to give a concert to a half-full hall is beneath my dignity. My response was therefore vague, and I did not endorse her plans.

We dined with the Rayevskys. I spoke English to Katya Ignatieva.

Shurik is going to the front today. We gave him our blessing and sat for a moment in the drawing room.[1] We bade him farewell and, choking back the

---

1 It is a tradition in Russian households to sit together in silence before taking leave of a house or undertaking an important journey.

tears, Uncle Sasha said, 'Be of good cheer!' I then went off to Bashkirov, to talk to him about the ballet. He is extremely interested in it and is busy dreaming up all sorts of little extra touches in it, although in essence he is not capable of any useful invention. His cousin also came in, who has served some time at the front and had all manner of hideous tales to relate, for example about an Austrian, both of whose eyes had been shot out, the sockets swarming with worms. For two days he crawled about over the shattered arms and legs of his comrades until he had to be tethered to a rope. A drama of unimaginable horror!

Later on my playing qualified for some complimentary remarks from this same cousin and we exchanged some caustic remarks on the subject of attitudes to new music.

20 October

For the last two days the ballet has not been progressing very well and this has upset me greatly. Today I did manage to get some of it done, not very much, but some. At two o'clock I had my session with the Englishwoman and then went to the Studio, where they rearranged my future teaching timetable to Mondays. After all, I only have two students; the third, she of the famous curtsy to me, has not appeared since.

In the evening I went to Gorodetsky. It is difficult to ring him up, since he lives on the fifth floor while the telephone is down by the concierge who is never there, but yesterday I caught him, so to speak, on the wing by telephoning at the precise moment he was descending the stairs past the telephone. He was very interested to learn that I had already composed much of the music, and asked me to come to him. There has been no telegram from Diaghilev with news of who the choreographer will be, but we decided that for the time being we would not worry about this.

Our most immediate task was to clarify the opening scene, since at present all we have is a crowd of people lying face downwards as the curtain rises, and at the end Chuzhbog's[1] abduction of Ala. The middle of the scene is missing, and we must use it to arouse the audience's interest in Ala and the Poet. Also, I need the plot of the ballet to generate dramatic action immediately; I regard all rites and ceremonies as basically descriptive and do not want to start with them.

Today both Gorodetsky and I came up with new ideas for the opening, but both had to be discarded. Gorodetsky's was that the Poet, having successfully infiltrated a company of priests making a sacrifice, would attempt to abduct Ala, only to be attacked by the priests. In the ensuing fracas Chuzhbog would himself carry off Ala. I objected that an attempt by the

---

1 The 'Alien God', the God of Darkness.

Poet on Ala would constitute an offence to the gods, and that would contradict his ultimate transmogrification into an idol in the fifth scene.

My idea was that at the rise of the curtain there would be a magnificent funeral procession passing through the prostrate figures on the ground bearing the body, not of the slain Poet but of a fallen hero. The priests make an appeal on his behalf, to which Ala responds by resurrecting him. General rejoicing. Chuzhbog abducts Ala and the hero, grateful to have been resurrected, sets off in pursuit to rescue her. This would definitely be an effective beginning to the ballet, but Gorodetsky objected that the resurrection of the dead finds no place in the Ancient Church Slavonic texts. He went into raptures over the juicy extracts I played him; they evidently inspired him and he said he would think more about the opening.

21 October

Influenced by Gorodetsky I set to with renewed ardour on the ballet, working all morning until three o'clock in the afternoon, and got on well with the third scene. I think continually about the orchestration and am accumulating a whole series of questions; I plan to go in sometimes to the orchestration class, to try out various instruments and consult with Tcherepnin.

Went for a walk in the afternoon, read some English, wrote my diary and talked on the telephone to Damskaya. I composed a letter for her to send to her young man, who has now proposed to her for the third time and whom she likes, although not enough to marry him. We set a new record for telephone calls: an hour and a half in the afternoon and another hour and a half in the evening, altogether three hours in a single day.

22 October

This morning I did not get down to the ballet until eleven o'clock since I overslept and suffered the punishment of a heavy head. But once I started, the work went well. After two hours I read some English and played through the Second Concerto because I had dreamt that I was going out on stage to perform it at the Imperial Russian Musical Society without knowing it. After that, Bashkirov came for his lesson (he is getting on well), we dined together and then he took me back to his house, at which I did not protest too strongly since I had a headache coming on. Bashkirov was, as ever, extremely nice, he read me some Balmont and presented me with a photograph of himself which I had been looking at during the evening and which had struck me with its marvellously relaxed pose, and wrote on it an inscription: 'You have perfected your mastery of the language of the Gods.' He took me halfway home in his car, and on the way told me that he planned to buy a new Peugeot in Paris.

23 October

The ballet moved a few steps nearer completion. Some time after noon I was in the Conservatoire to look in on the orchestration class and discuss the possibilities of the small trumpet,[1] low horns, etc., but two different classes were going on with Lyapunov in the hall and Glazunov in the foyer, and Tcherepnin running between the two. So I waited until the end of the class, at which Tcherepnin hailed me cheerily and we had a good talk. He said he was glad I was paying attention to orchestral colour and was sure the results would be fruitful. After saying goodbye to him I hurried to my English lesson. I hardly saw anyone in the Conservatoire, but Steinberg asked me, 'I hear you are writing a ballet on an Indian theme?'

'Worse than that,' I said. 'Scythian.'

Steinberg pretended to fall down in a swoon.

Walking back along Nevsky and Morskaya Street, I returned home and caught up on my diary. I had intended to see Gorodetsky, but a girl telephoned from his home to say that he was ill and in bed. My suspicion is that he has not managed to think of a new concept. His indolence is such that you couldn't even make porridge with him. I am exasperated by him.

In the evening I stayed at home and entertained Katya Ignatieva, who looked at our summer photographs, wanted to know all about the Meshcherskys, read my reviews and generally took up half the evening. I was not bored, however. After she left I read a story in English by Conan Doyle.

24 October

Did not compose much, but planned out in detail most of the fourth scene. But it is a great misfortune to have a collaborator so lacking in imagination as Gorodetsky. Instead of my task being simply to write the music, I am having to invent the whole scenario! Had a most satisfying telephone conversation with Zakharov.

On Sundays he, Andreyev, Nikolayev and I make up a bridge four at my house. Bashkirov, who is not a bridge player, says, 'When people with not much to think about get together, they communicate by means of cards.'

The I.R.M.S. had the good sense to send me tickets for all their concerts, the first of which is tomorrow. I went to the Sokol, then talked on the telephone to Damskaya, and practised the Second Piano Concerto.

---

1 Presumably the little F trumpet, also known as the Bach trumpet, a modern version of which is used for Bach's Second Brandenburg Concerto.

25 October

Continued work on the fourth scene today, not so much composing as planning it. I had the idea of Chuzhbog striking the Poet with a hundred-pood[1] stone. I then continued work on Scene 3: Chuzhbog's attempts to violate Ala.

In the afternoon I read Conan Doyle in English. Bashkirov came for a lesson. We have been working now for a month, and I think he is making progress. He wanted me to go to dinner with him and was very insistent, but I went to the first I.R.M.S. concert, an all-Tchaikovsky programme. Although I love Tchaikusha, I was less interested in his music, especially in the limp performance it received from Malko, than I was in the palette of its orchestral sounds, since this is what I am mostly thinking about at the moment with reference to my ballet. Alas, the first movement of the Second Symphony is dreadfully badly constructed, and in places sounds simply bad. Things are better in the Third Orchestral Suite, but even there most of it is extremely modest.

I was pleasantly surprised to see in the audience a good number of musicians and general public. A lot of people asked me about my forthcoming appearance with the Second Piano Concerto, and others praised my Second Sonata.

26 October

I slept very late indeed, but still managed to work a little on the ballet. Wrote to Jurgenson asking him to advance me 100 roubles 'on future fees'. I remembered Tcherepnin saying that Jurgenson can be very accommodating on that score and is prepared to help starving composers in their hour of need. Nina rang up this morning to ask if her sister was lunching with us. I was polite and aloof with her. I was planning to visit them this afternoon, but after the telephone call was on the point of deciding not to go, however, when I reflected that I had not been there for two weeks, I changed my clothes and went.

The whole family was sitting at the tea table, and the atmosphere was very lively. I was lending half an ear to Nina when the bell rang and everyone exclaimed, 'It's the young people on their first visit!' On enquiring which young people I learned that it was Erdely bringing his new wife. This was most interesting. The handsome young law student Erdely, now a Second Lieutenant in an infantry regiment and wearing a crimson tunic, had been the passionate love of Nina's life until he had been supplanted by Zaitsev. Erdely, who had served at the front and been wounded, was now married to a woman of strikingly beautiful appearance but dubious reputation. He

---

1 A pood is 16.38 kilograms, so this stone would weigh over one and a half tonnes.

appeared in the dining room with his elegantly made-up wife, limping and with his arm in a sling. I was fascinated to see how he and Nina would greet one another, but fortunately for Nina the telephone rang at the critical moment and she chattered animatedly into it for several minutes. Later we all sat down at the table. Erdely has lost some of his good looks and seemed uneasy.

To begin with, the conversation turned on his experiences and the war. It then moved on to music and me. I was asked to play some excerpts from the Second Piano Concerto, so we went into the drawing room and I sat at the piano. Talya joined me, while Nina sat to one side with Erdely and the others all in a group. Vera Nikolayevna related the story of the transferred dedication of the 'Capriccio' from herself to Talya as if it were an amusing anecdote (I always said that she was a clever woman; there was no sense in getting angry about it, and to turn it into a joke was much more intelligent). We then sat in a circle talking. Erdely and his wife left. I talked to Alexey Pavlovich. Declining the host's invitation to dine or simply visit during the coming week, but promising to come to dinner the following Sunday, I quickly left to return home.

Had dinner at home with Andreyev, Zakharov and Nikolayev and then played bridge, which was most enjoyable, Andryunchik finding himself relieved of 7 roubles. I won 3½ roubles, which in my present state of poverty is manna from heaven. I played some passages from Scenes 2 and 3 of the ballet, and was astonished at how well they were received. Zakharov was very excited by them, and I said that praise from him was a very bad sign, it meant that I would have to start all over again from the beginning.

27 October

After last night's bridge I worked successfully on Ala's dance before Veles. I particularly like the form I have given it: (1) an outpouring of joy at her liberation; (2) a kind of mystical rite; (3) a slightly affected gratitude; and (4) a joyful dance.

Went to the Englishwoman for my lesson and then to the Studio. My redheaded Kozlova is working hard aiming for a 5, and is coming on promisingly. Went to the Sokol and got very tired.

Romanov came at half past nine in the evening. Nouvel received a telegram yesterday from Diaghilev asking him to get me together with Romanov, who has been invited to stage my ballet.

He proved to be a quite young man, nervous but pleasant in manner. I gave him a detailed account of the origins of the ballet, and its content. He listened with evident interest and said he found it very interesting. He asked for a couple of days to think about the era in which it is set, and the narrative, and then he would come again to acquaint himself with the music and to talk further.

I wrote to Gorodetsky asking him to be present as well. The stuffed shirt has become ill, with what I do not know, sloth perhaps. I tried to go and see him yesterday, despite his indisposition, but he replied that it was out of the question.

28 October

I was so worn out and worried yesterday that this morning I woke up with the beginnings of a bad headache. Nevertheless I managed to compose a little and to work out in my mind the conclusion of Scene 4. Ala is still not sufficiently a being of this world to abandon herself completely to grief and despair at the corpse of the Poet. Puzzlement, distraction, questioning of fate, tenderness – these are her feelings.

My headache had become so bad by two o'clock that I went out for a walk in the wet weather.

In the evening, in the best of spirits, I went to see Zakharov. He had nothing of particular interest to tell me. Female company consisted of the Hansen sisters; the Karneyev girls were not there. Nothing has been seen or heard of them for some time. In the Zakharov household the 'Two Cecilias' reign unchallenged. Incidentally, the last named conjures the most wonderful sounds from the violin by using the side of the bow hairs, a unique effect! Somehow I must incorporate it into the ballet. We had some music, and left to go home at half past one.

I walked home, my head full of ideas for an opera on *The Gambler*. This is terribly interesting. The *Duckling* gave me an opportunity to experiment a little with my new operatic style, and the ballet has taught me how to compose dramatic scenes. I shall develop the scenario for *The Gambler* myself and write the libretto. It will be better like that, because I shall be able to imagine the music along with the text. It will be a revolution in the art of opera and demonstrate the pomposity of Wagner (the 'antimusic' principle).

29 October

Did not start work on the ballet until eleven o'clock. Planned the sunrise in Scene 4. In this case I am conceiving it not as a manifestation of nature but as a procession of the forces of heaven, culminating in the appearance of the Sun God himself.

An unexpected discovery: my ballet threatens to be very long. Certainly there is no need for it to be ultra laconic, but plain laconic it should certainly be.

In the afternoon I strolled over to the Conservatoire to get a ticket for this evening's concert. Did not see anyone I especially wanted to.

Received a charming letter from Grigory Jurgenson (Boris Petrovich is now a Warrant Officer(!) in Tula, so my dealings are with Grigory) sympathizing with my poverty-stricken plight. I had written to him joking that I was starving; he seems to have taken me seriously, which is a little disconcerting. Be that as it may, the letter was quickly followed by 100 roubles, and my indigent state is at an end.

Bashkirov came for a lesson, stayed to dinner, and we went together to the chamber music concert in aid of the field hospital the Conservatoire has established. The programme, consisting of performances by teachers at the Conservatoire, was deadly dull; Bashkirov yawned from boredom, I slightly less so. Quite a lot of people I knew, not many students. NB: a flame-haired, black-browed female student. Very attractive.

On my return home I found a letter from Gorodetsky naming a time for the meeting with Romanov, and a little postscript that he had not appreciated the tone of my letters, which had included phrases such as 'rather lazy' and 'you don't seem to give a damn'. At first this PS astonished and upset me, then it made me angry that such a lazybones should be offended at having this pointed out to him. I was going to reply that I had not intended the tone of my letters to please him, but then decided that it was not worth feuding over something so unimportant. Once the ballet is finished I need never have anything to do with him again.

30 October

I did not feel very well today and felt disinclined to compose. I made use of the time to finish proofreading Op. 12, which has been gathering dust for three weeks now, and I really do look forward to my charming Op. 12 being published as soon as possible.

Had an English lesson, went for a walk, and then to the Sokol.

Romanov telephoned to say that he had a meeting today and would I please tell Gorodetsky that we could meet at four o'clock tomorrow. I gladly did so, the more so as after Sokol I am usually tired, as indeed I was today.

31 October

I wanted to finish Scene 3 today, but did not quite succeed although there is not much left to do: the end of Chuzhbog's final attempt on Ala and a brief conclusion. At this point I encountered a minor difficulty: on the one hand each successive assault by Chuzhbog should be stronger than its predecessor, but on the other hand I did not want to orchestrate the last one too massively and bring the brass into play, otherwise the offstage trumpet will not be able to cut through the chaos on stage.

I did not go out at all in the afternoon but stayed in reading some English, correcting proofs and writing my diary, so I was very pleased when evening came and it was time to go out to the first student concert of the season. I always enjoy these occasions, and today was no exception. The Conservatoire is like an old friend. Since Damskaya had bought my ticket for me I sat with her all evening. We chattered non-stop from start to finish, and during the interval I composed for her another letter to her 'Sergusya'. He is still determined to marry her, knowing that she likes him, but she is 'playing a game of chess' with him, a game to which for love of the art I am interested in contributing. Had a joyful reunion and a lively conversation with Dranishnikov.

1 November

Weariness from such intensive compositional activity on the ballet made it rather an effort to get back to work today. Also it is not very inspiring to be working with such uncommitted collaborators – they both telephoned today to say that they would not be able to come at four o'clock. But I pulled myself together and soon became absorbed in the final section of Ala's dance before the Sun. In general, and this has been a pleasant surprise, the fourth scene seems almost to have composed itself and is almost finished. It will be short, and that is no bad thing. In the second scene I did get bogged down in the fight dance, but this is a very difficult thing to compose in the kind of shattering style I envisage.

A letter from Myaskunchik: he is being sent to Peremyshl.[1] How about that?! I am extremely concerned.

Bashkirov asked me to dine with him, give him a lesson and spend the evening there. I went, and was agreeably surprised to find his sister there. As I have had the honour to mention before in this diary, she is someone I have liked ever since my impromptu visit to her house on Frantsuszkaya Embankment. Today she was even more interesting than the first impression I had of her. A slight figure, her hands in her suit pockets, a cigarette clamped between her teeth (rather than her lips), with eyes like her brother's but even more beautiful, and a lively personality – that is my pen portrait of the twenty-four-year-old Princess. To begin with I adopted a rather truculent tone, but soon melted. After dinner I played them the whole of Schumann's *Carnaval*. The Princess had taken music as a major subject at the Institute,[2] but had then dropped it for five years. She now wants to take it up again under my supervision, knowing that with other teachers, such as her former

---

1 Peremyshl (Polish Przemyśl), an Austro-Hungarian-held garrison town on the border between Poland and Ukraine, was the scene of heavy fighting between Austrian and Russian forces in the early months of the First World War. Captured by the Russians in 1915, it was retaken a few months later by the Central Powers.
2 Probably the Bestuzhev Institute.

Institute professors Lavrov and Miklashevskaya, she would not achieve anything. In short, she wants me to work with her.

Personally I would welcome having her as a student, and so agreed without undue protestations, but for only one lesson a week. Then I added, 'The trouble is that with ladies I do my teaching at my home...'

'That would not be convenient, but if it is a matter of time then I can send a car for you on each occasion.'

I made an appointment for the first lesson to be on Thursday, after my English lesson, and declined the offer of the car, saying that instead of going for a walk that day I would come from Mokhovaya to Frantsuszkaya Embankment on foot. She, by the way, teaches English to wounded soldiers in the field hospital she has set up jointly with her brother, and today professed herself delighted with their excellent pronunciation.

Wrapping herself in an elegant fur coat, she made her *adieux*, while I stayed a little longer with Bashkirov.

2 November

Finished off Ala's dance to the Sun. In the afternoon studied English and read. Was proud of myself for being able to read a short story that I had been told in the autumn I would be able to understand only by the spring, and then only provided I applied myself diligently to my studies. At four o'clock I went to Gorodetsky, who had recovered from his illness, and together we finally sorted out Scene 4. He still finds Scene 1 unconvincing, and we did not succeed in settling on a final version. We are to meet with Romanov next week. My epistolary attacks had genuinely offended him, but harmony appeared to be restored after I explained to him in a friendly manner that he was not playing his full part in our joint work.

From Gorodetsky's I went to the Meshcherskys and dined with them before they went to the theatre to see *Woe from Wit*.[1] Talya wanted me to go with them, but I declined. There was literally no interaction between me and Nina, although we sat next to each other at dinner and she talked animatedly. She was coughing and did not look well. By all appearances the 'chess game' has ended in a draw. I left in a disgruntled frame of mind.

Went in to the Chess Club, but there were only about seven people there, talking about the call-up of the Second Militia.[2]

---

1   See p. 12, note 2.
2   The terms First Militia and Second Militia derive from the 'Time of Troubles' (1604–13) when civilian armies were raised to defend the Motherland and to counter the occupation of Moscow by Polish interventionists and their Boyar allies. It was the Second Militia, raised in Nizhny Novgorod in 1612 by Kozma Minin and led by Prince Dmitry Pozharsky, that succeeded in ejecting the Poles from the Kremlin, thus symbolizing the determination of the Russian

3 November

At ten o'clock in the morning I went to the general rehearsal for the Conservatoire concert. For how many years have these rehearsals been close to my heart! Today I went with the keenest anticipation. The conducting class had clearly not settled down enough to perform, and the conductors were Glazunov, Tcherepnin and 'new student' Lyapunov. As always when Tcherepnin himself conducts, he was in an excellent mood, and greeted me affectionately: 'Ah, Seryozhenka, I am delighted to see you. You are your customary cheerful and contented self!'

Notwithstanding this, the news about the call-up of second-category militiamen was far from bringing joy to my heart. Dranishnikov, Gauk and I talked earnestly on the subject. They said that if we were called up it would be only to guard prisoners and bridges, and there was no question of our being sent to the front. I joked that, on the contrary, the Second Militia was such a rabble that in any assault on a fortified stronghold we would be sent in the van to fill up the trenches, so that the real assault soldiers would be able to walk over us.

When all's said and done, however, it would certainly be interesting if we were eventually to be put under arms.

4 November

I dreamed that I was carrying a rifle and seemed to be defending a bridge, possibly the Potselúy Bridge across the Moika. Altogether this stupid Militia business is spoiling my mood. Rumour has it that the 1915 call-up will be in January, and the 1916 call-up in May, with the militia (the first five to ten years) in one of the gaps in between.

Today I did not compose any of the ballet; I did not feel any inclination, and in any case it is time for a break as I have been working intensively for three weeks. I practised the Second Piano Concerto a little, and worked on my English. Congratulated Aunt Katya on her birthday.

In the evening I went to the Conservatoire concert. Eleonora had asked me to bring Bashkirov along, and I telephoned him, but he said that a carbuncle had erupted on his neck and also he was suffering from toothache, which annoyed me a good deal. Saw many friends at the concert. Nearonova told me that my First Piano Concerto is exciting admiration all round, and

---

people to fight to the death for their country. The obligation to do so in time of need lay upon all Russian citizens, so Prokofiev, although exempt from conventional military service as the only son of a widow, could not expect to be relieved from conscription in the Second Militia should the Tsar decide to call upon it.

one student is going so far as to submit it as his graduation performance. The Concerto seems, indeed, to be turning into a textbook.

Glazunov's performance called forth an ovation, and I was pleased that Tcherepnin was greeted in the same way. After the concert I saw the Damskaya sisters home because Eleonora wanted another consultation with me: it seems her suitor has made a *démarche* by appealing directly to her guardian, and tomorrow her guardian has asked to see her.

5 November

Did no composing in the morning, but practised the piano.

Could I not be excused conscription on the grounds that I would be much more use to Russia in the field of art than I would be in a barracks?

In the afternoon I went for a walk and then taught Bashkirov, who did in truth arrive with his neck all bandaged up.

In the evening I called at the invitation of Karatygin on a certain Mme Piankova. Karatygin wanted the celebrated *diseuse* Ozarovskaya to outline for me a subject for a ballet that had occurred to her while touring the Archangelsk province. The subject (in ten scenes!) did have some connection with primitivism, but was not very balletic; in any case, since I already have the best part of three scenes completed I am not likely to want to abandon them in favour of another idea, however good.

6 November

A letter from Jurgenson, very reproachful at my pretended starvation in order to extract 100 roubles from him while all the time I am in reality quite well off. I suppose I could have expected such a letter, although in fact I did not. In reply I sent off a circumstantial, and in its final phrases venomous, letter, that took me several hours to compose. Went to my English lesson. Prince Magalov, on behalf of his wife, begged my indulgence in requesting the inaugural lesson with his wife to be at any time on any day except today, since today was their daughter's name-day. I rearranged it for tomorrow at half past two. Went to the Sokol.

7 November

As has become my disgraceful habit of late, rose at eleven and read the papers. I then practised the Second Concerto and some of the piano pieces. At two o'clock went with some pleasurable anticipation to my new pupil on Frantsuzskaya Quay. She was looking less attractive today. I was greeted by the Prince, a most courteous gentleman, who conducted us to the piano and then left us. My new pupil was evidently very nervous, and indeed her playing was full of horrible solecisms: uneven chords, a grasp of rhythm amounting to $2 \times 2 = 5$, the weak accents in the bar played more strongly than the strong ones, and so on. I worked with her for an hour, which I enjoyed, and then we talked for about three minutes and I left, having satisfied myself that the following Thursday would not be the name-day of anyone else in the household.

Walked home and studied English, my mood, however, darkened by the thought that here I was learning English but in two months' time I might be learning how to shoot at a moving target.

At eight o'clock went to the student concert, a trifle embarrassed by the fact that at all such events I would invariably be seen sitting with Damskaya. But I ignored this. It was not a particularly attractive programme, although the time passed pleasantly enough not to notice. On the way home Damskaya and I discussed tactics: her guardian was summoning her to talk about the wedding. This was serious: we plotted our strategy for the counterattack.

8 November

Practised the piano. At two o'clock Zakharov called for me and we went together to Rimsky-Korsakov, the son of the composer,[1] who is starting a new musical magazine in collaboration with the wealthy Suvchinsky.[2] Because wartime is not a very propitious time to start up such a journal, he has organized a series of concerts of contemporary Russian music this winter. I shall perform my Sonata and some other pieces on 29 November. Zakharov has also been invited as a soloist (Myaskovsky Sonata, Medtner, etc.). He has been singing the praises of the *Duckling* to them and brought me along to play it through to them. Zakharov is convinced this is going to be an excellent organization and is a great supporter of it. I very much liked Andrey Rimsky-Korsakov. Although Suvchinsky was formerly very critical of my compositions, he is now very complimentary about them and even sings themes from them. They tried their best to come up with original opinions about the *Duckling*, but could not in the end find anything very intelligent, and decided that it should be sung by Zherebtsova-Andreyeva in their January concert.

---

1 Andrey Rimsky-Korsakov (1878–1940), musicologist and critic, was the son of Nikolay Rimsky-Korsakov. The magazine he was establishing, with funds largely supplied by Suvchinsky, was the *Musical Contemporary* (*Muzykalny Sovremennik*).

2 Pierre (Pyotr) Suvchinsky (1892–1985), a wealthy man of impressively wide culture, wrote on musical and general cultural matters. As well as backing the *Musical Contemporary* journal financially he was its editor for several years. After emigrating in 1920 he became a close and trusted friend of Prokofiev. Emigrating in 1921, first to Berlin and thence to Paris, his interests in new music and range of correspondents embraced Prokofiev and Stravinsky in particular and extended as far as Pierre Boulez's *Domaine Musical* and Karlheinz Stockhausen.

9 November

Got up with a headache. Practised. Called on Ossovsky.

After dinner went with Mama to see Korsak, where I stayed about an hour and then went to see Bashkirov. As I left I asked Korsak, who is close to the War Minister, if the Second Militia was likely to be called up in the near future. He said that this step was still some way off: there was no shortage of personnel; any deficiencies lay in equipping the soldiers with uniforms. The autumn conscription and the one that would be implemented in January would yield 1,600,000 men. Training and equipping that number would present such a huge task that there would be no time to think about calling up the Second Militia. Even the First Militia was by no means exhausted.

I therefore felt completely reassured on this count. I later learned that the decision to call up the Second Militia would not be made by the War Minister but would occur, if at all, by the Tsar's fiat, and that people so conscripted would not serve in uniform but in civilian clothes. So I could be going to war in a frock-coat.

Bashkirov was terribly apologetic but he would have to ask me to wait on my own for ten minutes. For this purpose I occupied his study, sank deep into an armchair, put my feet up on the table and buried myself in the newspaper.

When we finished tea and were talking, his cousin Zhenechka arrived. He is a passionate chess player whom I have defeated on several occasions and who now wanted his revenge. Bashkirov implored me to beat him once again so that he could enjoy watching his face as I did so. It was a serious game, but I was twice interrupted by phone calls from Damskaya, whom I had asked to ring me with news of her visit to her uncle and guardian at which her suitor, freshly arrived back from the war, was also going to be present. The situation would thus amount more or less to a betrothal, and poor Eleonora was being subjected at once to the pressure being exerted by her relations and to the passionate pleadings of her suitor, of whom she is in fact quite fond. She drew strength from our telephone conversations to gird up for the forthcoming fray. After the second call (at around midnight) I came to the conclusion that the situation was grim: they were going to marry her off, and I began to be worried about her. Back in the game, I lost a pawn and then, I honestly do not know quite how it happened, six moves later I had comprehensively destroyed my opponent, to the enormous delight of Bashkirov.

10 November

After a week's break from the ballet, today I took it up again with renewed vigour. Not that I produced much, I spent more time playing through the existing material and looking at Tcherepnin's *Narcissus*. I like this music very much, it is so elegant and descriptive, even if every note in it has been lifted from somewhere else.

I was due to ring Eleonora to find out the result of yesterday's battle, and had many forebodings about it since I was sure the battle would have been lost. But my 'minister' had robustly beaten off all the attacks, and although her suitor was 'very handsome' and they had kissed most agreeably, she had not given her consent.

After my English lesson and the Studio I hurried home to teach Bashkirov, the second time he had changed the time of his lesson. As he left he pressed me to come to him this evening: they were giving a concert for the benefit of the wounded, with all kinds of popular singers, clowns, invited guests and so on. Despite all Bashkirov's blandishments and arguments that an evening without me was no evening at all, I was committed to the Sokol and firmly resisted.

So to the Sokol, and then a telephone call to Fyaka to atone for the abrupt termination of our telephone conversation three days ago. The poor girl has flu and is confined to the house, is terribly bored, and of course there can be no question of our planned trip on Saturday. I enquired whether she was more or less pretty than she had been, and if she thought of me often. Her reply was, 'Every day.' I promised to visit her.

11 November

Today I settled down more seriously to the ballet and even the Sunrise came out well. At three o'clock I went to Koussevitzky's rehearsal to hear Myaskovsky's *Alastor*. Because the Court Hall has been given over to house the wounded, Koussevitzky has to present his concerts in the Maly Theatre, with the orchestra on the stage where the sound is very dull. *Forte* passages simply disappear; when the flutes play *piano* or the double-basses *pianissimo*, they can be heard only by straining the ears. In *Alastor*, at the best of times a piece with its longueurs, Koussevitzky dragged out the tempi, thereby doing serious damage to the work. Much of it afforded me great pleasure, however, even though as a whole the work is, if I may put it so, lacking in compactness. But its sound-world is wonderful, in places truly remarkable. At the moment I am preoccupied with orchestral timbres and therefore place particular value on this aspect.

Practised the piano, and in the evening went to the student concert. There were not many people there, and it was a short programme. Once again I sat with Eleonora, and afterwards we talked about the saga of her young man. He is the Adjutant to someone or other, and has had to return to the army, but is coming back again on Saturday for a final attempt to extract a decision.

This ordinarily would not matter very much, but now Eleonora's mother has begun putting pressure on her.

12 November

I have got into the bad habit of not starting work until eleven o'clock. The ballet did not progress much today, as I spent most of the time thinking about it. At three o'clock I went to visit Nina. She has lost a lot of weight and has shrunk. I felt sorry for her and experienced feelings of great tenderness towards her. We spent the whole time at the piano, because at her request I had brought with me *Narcissus* and Myaskovsky's Sonata, and played them to her. Only when I was leaving did I embrace and kiss her, and felt a twinge of embarrassment. We said goodbye until Saturday and I departed with a rush of affection for Nina.

Bashkirov was an hour late, no more and no less, for his lesson today. I was angry about this and kept him waiting for another quarter of an hour before going in to him. After the lesson we dined and then went to the Maly Theatre for the Koussevitzky concert. Eleonora came with us; Bashkirov interests her and I was glad to introduce them to one another in the hope of drawing her away from her 'handsome' suitor. But I was peeved with Bashkirov today because of the lesson and was extremely severe with him, which upset him very much. *Alastor* was even better at this second hearing than it had been at the first, but it is still a long work with some tedious passages. I saw Eleonora home after the concert. She took to Bashkirov, but he did not take to the Scriabin, which again put him in my bad books.

13 November

Today I succeeded in completing my long-contemplated music for the defeat of Chuzhbog by physical force and by the rays of light. On the piano it does not sound especially remarkable, but in its orchestral colours it promises to be absolutely overwhelming.

Revised my English homework and went to my lesson.

Later on, the Sokol, and in the evening a telephone conversation with Nina, who has asked me to orchestrate some Belgian song or other for a charity concert.

14 November

Rose early today, at nine, and went to the symphony orchestra rehearsal. They were performing Lyadov – and very dull it was. Jejune ideas, cramped harmonies and counterpoint so academic as to be positively sickening made a sorry impression. Tcherepnin was as charming as ever. Putting on a sly expression, he sat down and said, 'I've started on a ballet as well – and on a Russian theme, too!'

Back at home I worked on the fourth scene, and when I had composed the music for the horrid creatures who were dragging Ala with them, and the chains falling from her, I realized to my surprise that the third scene was finished. That was nice!

At four o'clock I went over to Frantsuzskaya Embankment to my Princess, who was looking incredibly pretty today but whose playing was so dreadful that it drove me to distraction. She is evidently in such awe of me that she is terrified. Came home and read aloud a long novel in English. I'm already reading full-length novels.

In the evening I went to play bridge at Danilov's, where in the company of Zakharov, Danilov's father and two brothers Taube, I played a seriously concentrated evening of ten rubbers lasting until three o'clock in the morning.

15 November

Practised the Sonata and some pieces for the 'Contemporaries' evening. I don't know if I ought to play the Deshevov 'Scherzo', somehow I cannot seem to learn it thoroughly. At three o'clock I went to see Nina. Her duet playing is now pretty good, and we romped through Tchaikovsky's *Francesca*.[1]

After a hurried dinner I dashed to the 'Contemporaries'[2] concert, in fact such was my haste that I left my folder containing *Narcissus*, my Concerto and the Scriabin sonata that I meant to give to Zakharov in the cab. But I need not have been in such a rush: the concert started not at eight but at half past nine, and there was as yet no one in the hall. So I went into the Great Hall to hear Korsakov's *Triglav*,[3] mainly to listen to the orchestration, which indeed sounded marvellous. Gorodetsky enquired tenderly what had happened to me and why I was not ringing him up. I replied, 'Because whenever I see you I lose all desire to compose for a week.' But Gorodetsky decided to be nice and not take offence, and said that he had had some splendid ideas for the first scene, so I took his arm and promised to come and see him on Tuesday.

Svetlov, Diaghilev's assistant, said that there was no news from Diaghilev, who is now in Rome. Vasily Zakharov congratulated me on a laudatory

1 *Francesca da Rimini*, Symphonic Fantasia after Dante, Op. 32.
2 The original 'Evenings of Contemporary Music' had lapsed but a new incarnation had begun with the active involvement of Suvchinsky and Andrey Rimsky-Korsakov; no longer in the dimly lit room of the Becker piano factory, they would now take place in the Small Hall of the Conservatoire.
3 *Night on Mount Triglav*, symphonic sketch (arrangement for orchestra of Act III of the opera *Mlada*).

article that had appeared today in the *Russian Musical Gazette*. The Alpers family was there in a body, exuding friendliness. After *Triglav* and the interval, I returned to the 'Contemporaries' concert, where despite the fact that this was the inaugural event by a new organization there was a good crowd, the critics were out and a reasonable sprinkling of musicians as well. I am to play at the next concert.

16 November

In the morning the opening of the Scherzo of the Violin Concerto got composed, after which I did some piano practice on the Sonata No. 2. I must be sure to play it really well, and the short pieces as well. Not only that, but on Friday I have to perform at the Studio in a concert intended to demonstrate exemplary playing (!) to the students.

Went to see Eleonora, who played very well my 'Gavotte' in an arrangement for harp. She is starting to complain that life is boring without her 'Seryozha', and should she not perhaps get married after all? I was glad that she had at least had a look at Bashkirov, and gave her his portrait, while I myself went off to dine with the man himself. After dinner he and I strolled about their enormous hall and chatted, then went to sit in the comfortable drawing room where he regaled me with interesting insights into the philosophical and religious views of Tolstoy. In came the chess-playing cousin, the 'child of the sun' as Bashkirov calls him, and I played a difficult two-hour game with him which I eventually won in a convincing manner. Then his sister arrived, looking very beautiful, wearing just a touch of make-up. 'I've been practising all day for my lesson,' she said to me. 'My husband thinks I am already improving.'

I played Schumann, which enchanted her, and at supper afterwards she was very attentive that I had enough to eat. But I was tired and wanted to go home.

17 November

Having gone to bed at three I got up late. I spend half my life oversleeping. Probably the ballet would get on faster if I worked regularly in the mornings, but even so it is moving, thus for the time being there is no urgency; it can drift happily along.

At two o'clock I was with Miss Isaacs, then to the Studio, where the feebler of my two students took advantage of our *tête-à-tête* to grumble that I did not seem to be pleased with her, I was not very interested in working with her, and she really did not know what to do. I made little attempt to disabuse her of these perceptions, but set out clearly the areas in which she was inadequate and what she must do in order to improve in them.

At home an idea for the conclusion of the third scene came to me, but I did not succeed in finishing it. The Sokol at seven o'clock, and later on Nina telephoned. They were having guests the next day, the Andryushes[1] were promising to attend, bringing the *Duckling* with them, which Anna Grigorievna would hum through. My Mama is occupying herself with one of the Ministry of Justice's field hospitals, of which Vera Nikolayevna happens to be in charge. Both of them have discovered a penchant for organization and are delighted with one another.

18 November

I meant to work on the ballet, but instead had more ideas for the opening of the Violin Concerto Scherzo. I can see that it is not going to be particularly profound, but it is attractive and will 'come off'. At one o'clock I went into the Conservatoire to collect the score of *Triglav* as I wanted to look at some details of the orchestration. Friebus kindly let me have it until tomorrow. I hardly saw anyone else I knew. From the Conservatoire I went to Gorodetsky and played him Scene 4, which delighted him and put him in a sunny mood: 'graphic, fresh, savage', and so on. He then went through his new concept for the first scene, which this time was ideal. The only thing I suggested was to keep the people lying face downwards as the curtain rises. We then made a few changes and corrections. I am now happy with the first scene and am greatly looking forward to composing it, all the more so as the very beginning already exists and I have made a start on the music for the priests (it is startlingly new). Gorodetsky says that he has finally understood what I need for a libretto.

In the evening I accepted the invitation to the Meshcherskys. Mama came straight from the hospital to dine, so was already there when I arrived. Anna Grigorievna, however, could not come because her son (from her first husband), newly commissioned as an officer, had been drafted to the front, and she was in a state of great distress. Universal acute disappointment at the postponement of the *Duckling*, for which everyone had been waiting. We all sat around with nothing to do waiting for the bridge to start. When the guests started to arrive, Zaitsev with exquisite courtesy bowed to everyone, but was rather distant with me. Nina chose a discreet moment to tell me that she hoped I would behave myself, and I sat next to her at dinner; we sparred a bit, not for any particular reason, just for love of the art.

In response to importunate pleading I agreed to play the *Duckling* without any singing, just humming the words. This sent the host into ecstasies and he rushed skipping about the room urging the assembled company to

---

[1] The Andreyevs, husband and wife.

come and listen to it. Everyone huddled round the piano, but Nina went off with Zaitsev and one other person into a corner and talked throughout. I was not so much angry as astonished and could not understand this particular chess move of Nina's at all. When the *Duckling* was over everyone (except the above-mentioned group) applauded loudly and surged round me. Mama said goodbye and we left, paying no attention to the trio sitting at the far end of the hall. When I was already on the staircase Nina came running out: 'Serge, aren't you going to shake hands with me to say goodbye?!'

At night I was pursued by visions of bridge, kings, queens, Nina, Zaitsev, and so on. At last, at seven o'clock, although it was still dark, I awoke fully, unable to sleep any more, and wondered if there was not some early rehearsal to which I could go? But there was no rehearsal, and at nine o'clock I went back to sleep until eleven.

19 November

When I got up I had absolutely no desire to compose, so practised the Sonata and at one went into the Conservatoire. (1) I had to return *Triglav*; (2) I had promised to talk to Eleonora about her ever more complicated affairs. We did so for a whole hour. Then I walked her home, and in answer to her questions about how I was doing, related the events of the previous evening. Eleonora considers that I am indecently jealous.

In the afternoon I taught Bashkirov and in the evening went to Zakharov. The business with Nina was filling all my thoughts and naturally upsetting me. I expected her to ring today, and indeed she did so during Bashkirov's lesson. I said that I could not talk at the moment but would ring myself this evening. While at Zakharov's I did so and we had a pleasant conversation as though nothing had occurred, and she invited me to come to see her and play Tchaikusha's Sixth Symphony with her. 'I've already gone through it with Talya, but I expect poor old Tchaikusha was turning in his grave . . .'

'So that when I play it with you, half of Tchaikovsky will be lying peacefully and the other half will be revolving.'

20 November

Although I got up late, I still managed to do something with the first act. The outline we have now I like very much, and I am happy conceiving the music for it. But as it happened I did not get much done; Myaskovsky's brother-in-law telephoned to say that Nyamchik is in Lvov, and a lady was going today to see him and take all kinds of warm things to him. If I cared to write him a letter she would be able to carry it to him. I had been meaning for some time to set out my impressions of *Alastor*, and hastened to get down to a letter. I had still not done so when I had to go to my lesson with Miss Isaacs, so I finished it off in a post office somewhere, took it round to the lady and then went with a headache to the Sokol to clear it away.

All Petrograd is now talking of the call-up of the Second Militia. Although many authoritative sources (Korsak, Pavskaya) do not believe it is going to happen, others are convinced that conscription will start in December or, at best, in February. Of course this will be for defence purposes, not for active service. But one never knows: if it should happen that five or ten corps are lost somewhere then the Second Militia will be sent under fire. Occasionally I worry that I shall be wrenched away from my normal life, shall lose my freedom and perhaps have to spend a year in activities that are utterly alien to me; then again I am sometimes frightened; but other times I am not worried at all and even find the prospect interesting. After all it would be a pity for such a great event as this conflict not to touch me and pass me by with no experience of it in any way.

21 November

Today the composition of the scene with the priests and Lolly and Ala went wonderfully well and I completed nearly all of it. At three o'clock I went to see Nina.

In the evening I played at the Studio and was much put out, sitting in the dining room, that there was a delay in my turn to perform, because I was in a hurry to get to the Conservatoire to listen to the student concert. Zoya Lodi gave an interminable performance of Yulia Weisberg's tedious song-cycle *Songs from the Japanese*. Finally I got to play my Sonata, which I think went very well: soft and tender in the right places (this is a new quality I have been cultivating in my playing) and the Finale technically excellent. With the final chord still sounding I rapidly made my exit from the Studio and as I descended the stairs I could hear the audience applauding and calling for me to return to the stage. I arrived at the student concert in time for the last work in the programme, talked to Dranishnikov, and afterwards escorted the Damskaya sisters home.

22 November

The first scene is shaping up very well and I am pleased with it. Ala's eyes radiate fire, and later passages show signs of being interesting as well. Altogether life would be good if it were not for this stupid business of the Second Militia. I telephoned Nina, who wanted to know how it had gone yesterday at the Studio. It was a delicious conversation, at the end of which she announced that while I had formerly been in the habit of visiting them once a month, I had been three times during the past week; this was suspicious and for this reason I should not appear again before another two weeks have passed.

Bashkirov came for a lesson and extended an invitation to one of his *soirées*, but I said I would come tomorrow as this evening I wanted to go to the I.R.M.S. concert. The programme was of Franck, Elgar and Chausson and provoked terminal gloom.

23 November

Although I overslept, I did achieve a little with the ballet. 'Today we advanced three metres' as the French state in their *communiqués* from the front. I am deeply interested in the battle for Łódź; I ask for the morning papers to be brought to me in bed and then in the evening buy all the latest dispatches. It is a desperate struggle with the Germans throwing hundreds of thousands of men into the attack, but it is one we must win: the soldiers on both sides are of equivalent calibre but we have better leaders.[1] Wrote my diary and had a phone conversation with Eleonora. Her lover has rejoined his unit for two weeks; she is missing him and would like to write him a nice letter. I feel this constitutes a reverse in the chess game and take her roundly to task for her weakness.

Dined at Bashkirov's and spent the whole evening very happily with him. We are becoming ever closer friends: (1) we plan to travel the world together; (2) he wants to become my concert impresario. We played a splendid game of chess which I won.

24 November

Did no composing today but I studied the works I am going to play at the 'Contemporaries' concert (not to be confused with the 'Evenings of Contemporary Music' which have now gone off into the sunset but to the memory of which I am dedicating my ballet, a step into a new future and an acknowledgement of my regard for my former friends). Went to my English lady, for whom I am attempting to learn more vocabulary.

Taught at the Studio and then, tired, returned home. Telephone conversation with Eleonora. The girl has done bravely: yesterday's talk has borne fruit. Today she sent her man a letter breaking off relations for a year.

At seven o'clock to the Sokol, where there is talk of the Second Militia call-up, and afterwards I went to the Rayevskys for the name-day of the two Yekaterinas, where I also heard that this policy had been decided upon. I am

---

1 The Russian army, under the command of Nikolay Ruzsky's cousin General Ruzsky, was engaged in a desperate and ultimately successful struggle to halt the German advance through Poland.

hardly ever at the Rayevskys these days, but they had a lot of guests today and there were three tables of vint.

25 November

The newspapers have extensive coverage of the battle for Łódź, from which it can be deduced that it has ended in a victory for our forces. On the other hand, private sources told us on the telephone that the city has been lost. It is hard to understand what is going on but it seems unlikely that we have suffered a serious defeat if the General Staff is announcing a victory. I did not compose today but wrote many entries still outstanding in my diary, practised for Saturday and talked for almost an hour with Nina on the telephone. She may be going for a time to Tsarskoye, asked me to visit her there saying that we would walk together to Pavlovsk, and on that day we would, in the course of conversation, change our pronominal status.[1]

Nouvel telephoned that Diaghilev was showing signs of life, that he was still in Rome whence he had telegraphed to enquire about my ballet. I asked Nouvel to reply that the music was ready for four of the five scenes and that I needed to be informed who the designer would be. I was not, of course, telling the whole truth about four of the five scenes being finished: the only one that is completely finished is the fourth, the third all but, Scenes 1 and 2 half done. Nurok and Nouvel will come tomorrow to listen to the ballet.

26 November

Some very successful composition for the Scherzo of the Violin Concerto. Practised the 'Scherzo' from Op. 12, which obstinately refuses to lie under the fingers.

At six o'clock Bashkirov came for his lesson with the reliable information that we are to be called up on 22 December. I reacted bravely to this news, and we spent a good deal of time discussing how best to arrange matters so that we could remain in the city. Everyone now seems to be talking about the call-up, but the date on which the Tsar will publish a proclamation about our conscription is said to be 6 December, his name-day.

Following Bashkirov, the critic Walter came to audition the repertoire I shall be playing on Saturday. He did the same thing when I played my Concerto at the Graduation Concert and now wants to acquaint himself thoroughly with my works before he writes about them.

---

1 The Russian language retains the use of the second person singular for intimate friends, family and servants, and the second person plural for formal and polite discourse. The distinction is crucial, and a move from one to the other (normally from the latter to the former, of course) is accompanied by symbolic acknowledgement of intimacy, such as the *Bruderschaft* ritual of drinking a ceremonial toast. See also p. 167 n. 2.

27 November

Concluding that from next week I am likely to have to get up at six o'clock in the morning, I allowed myself to sleep until noon. Went to the Conservatoire with the object of sounding out the ground with Tcherepnin about how to exploit the privileges of my musical eminence in the event of being conscripted. Tcherepnin was very alarmed and did his best to persuade me that I must at all costs arrange to stay in Petrograd.

This made me too late for the Sokol and I did not go. Nouvel and Nurok came in the evening, listened to the ballet, but I fear they understood nothing of it. They spoke of it very enthusiastically, however, and generally we had a nice time of it. They very much liked the 'March'[1] I wrote for Morolyov, and also the Deshevov 'Scherzo'.

28 November

Practised the programme for tomorrow's concert and studied English. Thought about Nina.

At three o'clock saw my English woman for a lesson. Gorodetsky has still not telephoned to say whether he is coming today with Romanov. There is no end to the problems with this man. It is not clear how the sun is to set in the first scene, and I cannot compose any more of it until I know this.

Stayed at home in the evening; Katya Ignatieva came round.

29 November

Rose at half past eleven. It is now rumoured that the December conscription of the Second Militia will not happen after all. Rang up Shreder to ask if I could look at the piano on which I am going to play this evening, but it has already been despatched to the Conservatoire. In return for his prize I am doing Shreder the honour of playing one of his pianos.

Went to the Conservatoire where I met Nikolay Nikolayevich with all the conductors, among them Kreisler, whom I have not seen for half a year. I am nervous about the 'Scherzo' but overall am confident I will be all right. Handschin[2] played the organ for me to demonstrate what the instrument is capable of: he is very keen that I should write a piece for piano and organ. There is nothing for this combination in the literature, but it seems to me it could be very interesting.

---

1 Ten Pieces for Piano, Op. 12 No. 1, 'March', dedicated to Vasily Morolyov.
2 Jacques Handschin (1886–1955), organist and musicologist, professor at the St Petersburg Conservatoire.

After this I stayed at home practising, thinking about Nina, writing my diary and talking to all those solicitous souls, who emulating the procedure when someone is ill, telephone to enquire how I am feeling before a concert. Andrey Rimsky-Korsakov telephoned to say that he had taken my hint and written to Jurgenson suggesting that it would be desirable to have Op. 12 published by today's date, that is to say the day of its performance. I was keen that this should happen because I was afraid that I might have so incensed Grigory that he would delay publication for half a year, besides the fact that the publishing house is in any case terribly overloaded with work. But reply had been received that although Op. 12 would not be ready in time for the concert it would be in the next few days.

I was not nervous before the concert even though I was well aware that there was evidently a great deal of interest in my appearance and it was important for me to play well. When all is said and done, this was the first appearance by the new prizewinner even if the prizewinner did not himself attach any very great significance to it. I arrived at the start of the concert and took much pleasure in listening to the whole programme. My nerves were steady, perhaps a flutter of anxiety while I was actually playing, but really not very much at all. In the interval I was visited by Zakharov, Bashkirov and the Meshcherskys, three of whom came (not their mother) and sat with my mother (Nina between her father and my mother!). Bashkirov sat in the front row of seats applauding frenziedly. Zakharov brought the score and displayed much interest throughout. I started with the Sonata No. 2, which I much enjoyed performing, and which was greeted with wild acclaim. I was called back to take a bow three times and saw the whole of our dear Maly Zal applauding me. Most satisfying. The secret of a good performance lies in paying no attention whatsoever to the hall or the audience, in a word to the environment, before or during the performance, and simply to concentrate on the music. As soon as it is over, one can bow as much as one wants.

Having taken my three bows I took a short rest and then came out again to play the six pieces from Op. 12. 'Legenda' I took quite slowly, but it was well received. 'Prelude' was of course a favourite. In the middle of 'Rigaudon' I thought of Fyaka; she was, incidentally, sitting in the third row and by turning my head slightly I could see her. I played it in a different manner from previously, a bit slower and very passionately. It was a huge success, almost enough to make me encore it. After Nina's piece came Talya's 'Capriccio'. I played it with great affection, but it had no success whatsoever. Without quite meaning to I played the 'March' rather fast but it came out very fleet and was the most liked of all. I smudged some of the 'Scherzo' and left out some notes in the passages in thirds, but nobody except the dedicatee would notice. That was all. A very great success. Several times I came out to bow, while the audience stood to applaud. At one end I could see the Meshcherskys and at the other Bashkirov clapping like a machine-gun. Backstage I racked my brains to think what to play for an encore, and eventually remembered the 'Gavotte', which I played to great public satisfaction.

Zakharov and Hansen came backstage, Zakharov and everyone else outdoing themselves in praise of the advances in my pianism since the spring. Andrey Rimsky-Korsakov said, 'Listen to that furore! An impresario could make a lot of money out of you!'

Golubovskaya was of the same opinion as Zakharov. Verochka Alpers came to offer her congratulations. Bashkirov did not leave my side for a second. Damskaya did not come because today is the anniversary of the death of her father. She was very interested in the concert and very much wanted to have a look at Nina (she was the first person Nina asked about, as well) but had to stay at home on this day.

When the audience had dispersed and I had cooled down, I walked with Bashkirov along Morskaya and Nevsky and then took a tram home along Zagorodny. Mama was delighted and congratulated me.

Went contentedly, even if my nerves were still somewhat strung up, to bed, regretting that there was no kindly shoulder of Nina's against which to snuggle up and go to sleep. Just her shoulder, nothing else, it somehow fits me perfectly and is so comforting. But as I made my way to the concert I was thinking: how terrible it would be if I had a wife!

30 November

Was woken by Romanov ringing me up to find out how the ballet was progressing, and promising to come and see me tomorrow. I was very glad to hear this and told him that I was tired of Gorodetsky's prevarications and general indifference to the project, to such an extent that I felt inclined to drop it altogether. Romanov promised to bring Gorodetsky along with him. I then lay down again to catch up on my 'ten hours of sleep'.

In the afternoon I did nothing very much, having little inclination to compose. Mostly I spoke on the telephone to people wanting to congratulate me on the success of yesterday's concert. One of them was Nina, who tried her best to find something to criticize, but ended up against her will by praising me. Before my performance she had been 'desperately anxious' all through the interval. She confessed to having felt rather strange sitting between her father Alexey Pavlovich and my Mama. Her parting shot was to add that she had liked me very much yesterday evening. Not without a touch of humour she described 'how Zakharov had hung around her and then bowed deferentially', to which she responded coldly because she does not like him – vulgar and self-satisfied. Incidentally, I also introduced Zakharov to Bashkirov, who did not take to him either.

Borovsky complimented me on having turned into an absolutely excellent pianist: my touch, gradation of attack, refinement of detail, and so on. Surely I must have been practising a great deal? I replied that I hardly practised at all, but the human organism has the ability to develop on its own after the initial impetus: I had practised seriously in the spring to provide that impetus, but the fruits had come not then, in the spring, but now, after the passage of time. I dined at Bashkirov's and we talked after dinner: he regretted that I am not a mystic and bored me to death with his talk about mysticism. At half past ten Demchinsky came accompanied by his wife and by Alekhine. Demchinsky, a great talker and conversationalist, a man of huge but highly paradoxical intellect, had come determined to do verbal battle with Alekhine. But suddenly there was a new target in the shape of me and my new ballet, and to Bashkirov's enormous pleasure the whole evening was spent in a battle of words with me: 'You have a fine story for your ballet all but five minutes, but the whole essence of the story is contained within those missing five minutes.'

1 December

Managed to puzzle out some of my English, my concert having dampened much of my zeal to acquire elegant powers of expression in that language. After the lesson I went to the Studio, where my lazy student is at last beginning to make some progress. When I made a glancing reference to her idleness she expostulated that there could now be no question of this. Kozlova is going to play the Grieg sonata at the student's concert, and indeed can now give quite a decent account of it. For even greater stimulus I said that if I had time I would come to the concert to listen to her, at which she began to plead with me to come, saying that if I did not she would not play.

2 December

Got up late, but this will be the last time. Since there seems no prospect of getting any sense out of Romanov or lazybones Gorodetsky, I have decided to get on with the orchestration of Scene 4: tomorrow I shall get up early and set to.

Today I went in to the Conservatoire to have a look at how they were progressing with the production of *Rusalka*. Dranishnikov told me how thrilled he had been with my performance on Saturday.

On the way home Max's stick fell out of the cab. I realized this within two minutes, jumped out of the cab and went back to look for it, but although I twice went over the distance I thought we must have travelled, there was no sign of it. Then I remembered that the cab had been followed by a militia detachment, which must have picked up the stick. By now the detachment had disappeared, and I had no idea which way it would have turned. In any case it would have been impossible to see which of them was carrying my stick. So it was lost. Deeply depressed I returned home, and even three laudatory reviews failed to lift my mood. Mama said that Nina had telephoned and asked me to return her call. But I was not in the mood and did not ring; when she herself rang I could not muster any affectionate phrases with which to console her. Yet the poor girl was really in need of consolation: she was still confined to the house and was chafing under the restrictions, and on top of that a close family friend, Mme Littauer, had died suddenly so all the talk in the household was concerned with the subject of death, there was the Requiem Mass to arrange, and so on. The result of our telephone conversation was that Nina became extremely distressed. In the end I said that I would come to see her tomorrow on a visit of sympathy, and asked her to ring at noon to say whether I could or not. Afterwards I was sorry that I had upset Nina, but was glad at the prospect of seeing her tomorrow.

At eight o'clock I went to the student concert where I sat next to Eleonora and we discussed our 'chess strategy'. She also has her problems! She had sent her wounded young man a loving letter of sympathy and had received such a moving reply that her heart was melting with tenderness for her suitor. At the start of the evening she really put me off by going on about how the campaign I was myself involved in was being fought with great intelligence and skill, how I was completely in thrall to it, and how it would undoubtedly end in marriage. This interpretation I resisted strongly, regarding it as a fearful imprecation at a time when life was just about to spread its wings and such interesting developments were on the horizon ... how could I go to Rome, or America, with a wife in tow?! But then again, how nice it would have been to go to sleep on her shoulder yesterday evening, and what sweet dreams I had had of her in the morning! This final remark produced a great effect on Eleonora. It appeared that I was voicing almost word for word what she herself felt about her lover, believing that she was alone in her stupidity. But now it seemed that everyone is just the same.

Eleonora was terribly upset by this discovery, and it suddenly became clear to me that marriage for me would be equivalent to captivity, and I rejoiced at the deliverance this knowledge brought me. No, no, not for the world! I left her to go and play the four-hand version of *Petrushka* in a brilliant performance with Nikolayev that brought the house down. The audience split into those who groaned, those who clutched their heads in disbelief and those who cheered in ecstasy. I have a new and ardent supporter in Suvchinsky. From a position of invariable criticism he cannot now praise me enough. And he is personally charming. I played some of my own compositions. Zakharov enthusiastically praised *Petrushka*. Inevitably the Hansen sisters (both of them, 'Cecilia' and 'Sardinia') were present. Can it really be that Cecilia is betrothed to Boris?!

3 December

Rose at ten and, God be praised, settled down to the score of Scene 4. At the moment it is going swiftly and easily, as a result of my having given so much thought to it. I am notating it on large manuscript paper, not taking too much care to make it look beautiful, indicating repeated bars and passages with the ✗ sign and frequently marking passages *col such-and-such* instead of writing everything out in full.

The time passed in a flash and I realized that it was already half past twelve, while Nina had promised to telephone me at twelve. Assuming that she had gone to the funeral, I carried on working. By two o'clock she still had not telephoned. Wanting very much to see her, I grew concerned and could not understand what could have happened. At three o'clock I rang up myself, but Nina was cold, still put out by yesterday's conversation. She had not felt inclined to call me at twelve, and as everyone was resting today after the funeral it would not be convenient for me to call. This evening I would receive a letter from her, containing the fulfilment of a request I had made, followed by ten words that I would understand if I had sufficient powers of imagination and perception. For my part I could make nothing of this, and said that the last thing I wanted was to upset her, that I very much regretted her tears yesterday, and that if she would permit it I would come to see her tomorrow.

After this telephone call, on my way to the printers, Ull, about the publication of my Sokol 'March', I racked my brains to think what she could be planning now. A final break? That would be an unexpected end to it all! And I felt a great sadness that it might all be coming to an end.

During Bashkirov's lesson I was handed a letter smelling deliciously of her scent. Inside was a review from *Muzyka* that I had indeed asked for (as I now remembered) and a note which I was expecting to reveal Nina's decision. But all it said was: 'I am sending you this review from *Muzyka* that you asked for.' What could this mean? Whatever it was, it could not be as bad as I had feared.

In the evening I continued orchestrating the ballet.

4 December

Rose at nine. The orchestration is proceeding apace, and I have reached the Sunrise. I had promised to ask Nina precisely at noon if I might visit her today, but in the event I was late and at ten minutes past she rang me herself to ask when I would be coming.

At a quarter past three I was by her side. She was sitting alone under the lamp, looking wonderful, and knitting a scarf, the same one as before. I could see that she was pleased I had come, and that made me feel good. Talya arrived from paying calls. Together all three of us went upstairs to have tea, and then to the piano for Nina and me to play a duet version of Glazunov's Fifth Symphony I had brought with me. After that we talked downstairs, still the three of us, for another quarter of an hour, and Nina professed herself shocked that I had not read *Anna Karenina*, to which I objected that nowadays I only read books in English, so if I were to read *Anna* it would have to be in an English translation.

5 December

The pace of writing out the score slackened today: I got stuck in the Sunrise. The counterpoint, part-writing and passagework has all been worked out but none of it has been committed to paper, and this proved to be work of such great complexity that it could not be hurried. Even so, it is turning out very well. The orchestration of this scene is also, by all appearances, very successful and shows every sign of being one of the more splendid aspects of the ballet. But I am finding it very difficult to think what should be added to the three string parts to make the rising of the sun more of a 'sunburst'.

At three o'clock I went for my English lesson, and in the evening attended the student concert. Nina called: the doctor had been to see her yesterday evening. He found the upper part of her lungs collapsed; the Petrograd air was bad for her and tomorrow she must go away for two weeks to stay with her cousin in Tsarskoye. She begged me to write to her there and to visit her, to which I gladly agreed; I feel very sorry for the poor girl.

6 December

The Sunrise has turned out to be extraordinarily complex: passages for the flutes, oboe lines – all this needs to be done. I talked again to Nina and as before it was a very pleasant conversation. I will go and see her tomorrow. After lunch I called on Olga Ruzskaya to congratulate her on Nikolay Pavlovich's name-day; he is in Lvov. To my surprise I met Tanya there, who was back from Lvov to spend two weeks at home. She has filled out and her complexion is paler than it was; also she has taken to making extravagant sheep's eyes at people. She says she has quite got out of the way of conducting herself in polite society, and Petrograd strikes her as disagreeably remote from the war. She greeted me with great reserve, but I was interested to hear about Lvov so questioned her closely and soon we were conversing very freely.

I hurried home for Bashkirov's lesson but he did not turn up, following which I told him that I would not be coming to dinner tomorrow. For the first time in our acquaintance he was angry with me. In the evening I went to the third of the 'Contemporaries' concerts and heard some deeply uninteresting songs by Shvedov.[1] Made haste to get home in time to write to Nina and drop the letter in the post before eleven o'clock.

7 December

A letter from Nina, four pages liberally sprinkled with flashes of wit and humour, but I hardly had time to read it when there was a telephone call from Katya Schmidthof, who has come with her aunt to Petrograd for thirty-six hours. It was a difficult telephone connection to her in the Northern Hotel, and we were cut off several times. I had to hurry to make the twelve o'clock train to Tsarskoye, the one by which Nina was expecting me to arrive, and caught it only by the skin of my teeth. It was a gloriously bright, sunny day, a dusting of snow, later this year than usual, lay on the fields, and I stood for the whole journey on the outside platform with the window open revelling in nature. But what a sour note was sounded by the Warsaw train on the track parallel to ours, carrying troops to the battle front. One group of people with no desire whatever to fight, will come face to face with another group thinking only of the homes they have left behind, for the purpose of disembowelling one another. What stupidity!

On the station at Tsarskoye Selo I ran slap into Kokochka Shtember who it appears is now living and working here, and who had come to meet Tyulin.[2] Our paths lay in the same direction, and we made a merry gang as we set off, throwing snowballs and gambolling like lambs, on the way towards the 'Colony'. I stopped for a minute at Kokochka's and then went on to Nina, who was installed in a tiny dacha with her cousin and her cousin's husband, whom I knew only slightly. Nina was looking small and cheerful. We soon decided the weather was so marvellous we should go out, so we put on outdoor clothes, went outside and picked up two cabs with the husband and wife in one and Nina and I in the other, to go over to Pavlovsk.

Home again we lingered for a while and then went to meet Talya and Alexey Pavlovich. Talya did not come, but Alexey Pavlovich brought with him some Austrian war trophies: a knapsack and a bayonet, which we examined with great curiosity. I soon left to return home, despite Alexey Pavlovich's pressing invitation to stay.

On my return to Petrograd Bashkirov failed to come for his lesson, pleading illness, which annoyed me very much. At seven o'clock I was at the Rayevskys to see Shurik, who had a few days' leave from the war. He had not

---

1 Dmitri Shvedov (1899–1981), teacher and composer, mainly of vocal and choral works (one of them on a Scythian subject) and three operas.
2 Yuri Tyulin (1893–1978), musicologist and composer, later a distinguished writer on various aspects of music theory and biography, professor at the St Petersburg Conservatoire and later at the Moscow Conservatoire and Gnessin Russian Academy of Music.

been thought to be in any great danger as he had been appointed Adjutant to the Brigade General, but in fact he and the General had been subjected to such withering fire that only half their company had survived. Shurik had been carrying a two-pound bar of chocolate in his belt bag, and a splinter of shrapnel had lodged in this chocolate. A fraction to the left or to the right and the shrapnel would have been in Shurik's stomach.

Leaving the Rayevskys I crossed the whole city and came to Vasilievsky Island for Vasily Zakharov's birthday. He had invited me for vint, but by the time I arrived the tables were all made up. We played 'Ninth Wave' and I had three roubles taken off me. I took Cecilia Hansen into supper; she had arrived with Boris Zakharov, they are now an inseparable couple. Can they really be planning to get married? Why not, after all: she is a good match – famous, young and in her own way decorative.

8 December

As soon as I got up I went to the Northern Hotel to see Katya Schmidthof, taking her a box of chocolates. Katya has put on weight and was looking pink and fresh. We had a lovely talk about old friends, then I took her to the Petersburg Gymnasium, where she wanted to meet friends. Then I returned home.

I practised the Second Piano Concerto a little (it is high time I buckled down to it) and went to the Conservatoire to see the rehearsal of *Rusalka*,[1] which is now well under way; performances start in a week's time. Dranishnikov, to whom Tcherepnin allotted barely one rehearsal, conducted so well that he has now been given all four performances. This is a great achievement – in my day such gluttony would have been unimaginable. I am happy for Dranishnikov: he is a fine musician and a talented person. It is very good that he in particular should be singled out for advancement in this way. I love him very much, and he repays me in kind.

Tcherepnin took me by the hand and made me tell him the content of my ballet. When I obeyed, he was clearly very pleased by the story. I was glad to see Mlle Shapiro,[2] nevertheless I got tired listening to the rehearsal and came home in a bad mood, which was, however, completely blown away by the Sokol.

9 December

Settled down to finish off the Sunrise, but however energetically I worked it crawled along and I simply could not bring it to a conclusion. It is so contra-

---

1 Opera (1856) by Dargomyzhsky.
2 Klara Shapiro, student at the Conservatoire.

puntal. All the same, it is going to sound magnificent. In the afternoon I went out to buy Nina a present. Tomorrow is her birthday, and for a month and a half now, every time we meet or have a telephone conversation, she has mentioned that I must give her something for her birthday. I have been racking my brains to think what. In the end I promised to give her some of my perfume, which always arouses great admiration but the name of which I have always refused to divulge in spite of her most importunate appeals. Nina particularly wanted it, and on several occasions pleaded with me to tell her what it is called, but I would not. Accordingly, today I bought a little metal box measuring about 3½ × 1½ × 1½ vershoks[1] with thick sides and a beautiful lock. At Harrach[2] I bought a small crystal bottle, then I filled the chest with cottonwool in various colours supplied by Eleonora, poured some of the famous perfume into the bottle and wrapped the whole thing up. The chest fastened in such a clever fashion that you could not tell it was a box: it looked more like a paperweight made of solid metal. In its outer paper wrapping, it might have been an iron.

Went to my lesson with the English lady, who continues to regard me as her best student although latterly I have not been as conscientious as before. I took my Sokol 'March' to the military censor, since it needs his approval to be printed. In the evening I continued writing out the score, wrote my diary and talked on the telephone to Eleonora. She has invited her young man, who is now recuperating in hospital on the Dvina, to come with her on a pleasure trip to Yukki. This is certainly an original notion, but I reproached her for taking unnecessary risks.

10 December

Today is Nina's birthday, she is nineteen. I took my far-from-lightweight present and, by agreement with Talya, met her at two o'clock at Tsarskoye station. Along with me came Lieutenant Littauer (whose mother had recently died) and another officer friend of the family. Her parents had been out earlier in the day, and by the time we arrived were already preparing to leave for home. I handed Nina her present, which obviously intrigued her greatly. In answer to her enquiry as to what it was, I said it was an iron.

At this point a large box of chocolates was opened, and we all fell upon it. The conversation turned to other topics, but Nina kept returning to the subject of the present. Each time it raised a laugh: some said it was a box containing perfume, others that it was a paperweight, but I maintained that

---

1 Approximately 6 inches × 2½ inches × 2½ inches.
2 Harrach crystal, from the glassworks established by Count František Arnošt von Harrach in Hradec Králové in Bohemia, had been highly prized since winning medals at the Great Exhibitions in London and Paris.

it was an iron of a new and improved design, but I declined to explain how to use it. Eventually Nina lost her temper and the 'iron' flew under the table. This was not such a good idea, since the bottle inside might break. I said that if Nina would give me some solemn undertakings I would reveal the secret. We went into another room, where I told her that it was indeed 'my' perfume (but of course I did not give the name), and that if Nina would give me her solemn oath that she would not give it to anyone else nor attempt to find out herself what it was called but keep it exclusively for herself, just as I had done, then I would give her the key. Nina hastened to give me her word, we kissed tenderly, and Nina, the key in her hand, rushed to open the box. But here was another curious thing: Cadine in the bottle does not smell anything like itself. Only when it has been rubbed on the hands or sprinkled on a handkerchief for a few minutes does the scent ripen to its full strength.

More hilarity, until eventually everything calmed down. Nina was satisfied as to the authenticity of the precious liquid and was very happy with her present. We ordered a troika to take us for a drive. The officer left to go to Peterhof, which meant that Littauer, Talya, Nina and I squashed into the troika. We were very jolly, uncorked a bottle of Marsala we had grabbed to take with us, and drained it to the dregs. Before we finished it we all drank to our *Bruderschaft*, Nina with Littauer, he with Talya, I with him, Nina with me and I with Talya, all teasing and squabbling and kissing one another in the highest of spirits.

On the way back we sang songs, and although we were all still calling each other 'you' from time to time we slipped imperceptibly into 'thou'. Kuchinsky,[1] our host, came in and the din increased to impossible proportions. By this time everyone was on 'thou' terms; another bottle was drunk, we cried 'bitter!'[2] to the Kuchinskys, banging the table and rattling the crockery so much that they had to capitulate and kiss. The fun was fast and furious until finally Talya and Littauer left, but even then Nina did not want me to go. I stayed another hour, and then left.

I got back to town at ten o'clock. Bashkirov telephoned, but I was curt with him and declined his invitation to go to a spiritualist *séance*.

11 December

Caught up today with my diary. Studied English. Proposed a lesson to Bashkirov at two o'clock, five o'clock and ten o'clock, but he was not free for any of those times. This is disaster, I'm losing a second lesson and am badly in need of money. In the evening I was at the Sokol and much enjoyed my gymnastics.

---

[1] The husband of Nina Meshcherskaya's cousin.
[2] See p. 203 n. 1.

12 December

Left the 'Sun' not quite finished and started orchestrating the pursuing demons. I think they will be very entertaining. Around one o'clock went to the general rehearsal of *Rusalka*. The whole Conservatoire population goes to these general rehearsals and they are always interesting. Gabel was as usual charming to me, accompanying me right through the Conservatoire building into the rehearsal. Dranishnikov conducted the opera with skill and authority, delighting both Tcherepnin and his friends. Tcherepnin sat me down next to him in the front row and we exchanged opinions of the opera. There is no doubt that Dargomyzhsky possesses dramatic instincts, but as a whole the opera is diffuse both musically and dramatically, and in its power to attract. But there are beautiful things in it.

Needless to say, I saw a lot of friends at the rehearsal.

Back at home I wrote Nina a short letter addressing her as 'thou' and then went back to the Conservatoire for the debut performance of the small orchestra, in which Gauk, Kreisler and once again Dranishnikov displayed themselves on the podium. For better or worse I feel at home here, these are my people. Kreisler's conducting was a trifle awkward. Gauk, who incidentally has got married, gave a very committed and not half bad performance; Dranishnikov was assured, but nothing like as good as he had been in the opera. His sister kept asking me my opinion of her brother, and while I was warming to this theme revealed her great admiration for my music – apparently she could not stop trembling when she first heard my Piano Concerto No. 1 – but she did not know me at all as a person although she had heard much about my pugnaciousness, self-confidence and other such characteristics. I said to her, 'On the other hand you will find some people who think I am a very nice, amiable chap, but that what I compose is incomprehensible rubbish.'

13 December

Friebus enquired whether orchestra parts needed to be made for my Second Concerto or whether they already existed. I told him that although there were parts they had been so badly written out it would be better to make new ones, otherwise there could be a disaster with the orchestra. This was partly true but it also partly had an ulterior motive: if there were to be new orchestral parts it would give me an opportunity to make some changes in the score, because in the meantime I had developed greater powers as an orchestrator and there were several places where I could improve what I had previously written. I therefore agreed with Friebus that I would bring the score to him in a week's time and he would make new copies of the parts from it. For this reason I sat down today with the Concerto and pasted in the appropriate passages in the score. I think that in the concluding bars there could be a new passage for the piano, as otherwise the piece ends rather modestly for the soloist.

Bashkirov came at five o'clock. I greeted him somewhat coldly, but he was so affable and had such interesting things to say that by the time he left we had quite restored our good relations. I had a letter from Nina, using the 'you' form, but with a good many endearments slipped in. She is being nice to me again.

In the evening I went to the Imperial Russian Musical Society concert, devoted to the works of Glazunov. The first piece I heard was *The King of the Jews*,[1] a feeble work but with one or two very good numbers in it and wonderful effects, you could not tell how they were achieved, such as far-off echoes from Pilate's feasting as Christ was being led to his execution.[2] Tcherepnin, a smell of vodka on his breath, sat with me and was very amiable. Vasily Zakharov, apprehensive about the call-up of the Second Militia, has enrolled in the Red Cross and is going to Tiflis where he will be put in charge of the stores. He appeared today in uniform, tremendously smart and delighted that he is going to Tiflis.

14 December

Went to the matinee performance of *Rusalka*, but it is definitely an uninteresting opera to hear twice. There were not many people I knew there and even fewer I found attractive, so I was rather bored. It lasted until six o'clock, and although I had been invited to Bashkirov's and afterwards to his brother's (the same who had gone out to dinner in his nightshirt) I declined both in favour of working at home: catching up on my diary, studying English vocabulary and writing to Nina, a task in which I took great pleasure.

15 December

Mlle Roblin arrived at eight o'clock in the morning: she is staying with us for a week. I continued looking through the Concerto and made changes to the things that dissatisfied me, mostly very minor ones. Studied English, then to my English lady for a lesson, then to the Sokol, and in the evening Zakharov

---

1 Incidental music composed in 1914 for a mystery play written by the Grand Duke Konstantin Konstantinovich ('K.R.') and performed in the Hermitage Theatre by a large cast of amateur actors (including the Grand Duke in the role of Joseph of Arimathea) with professional musicians and dancers choreographed by Mikhail Fokine.
2 'NB: clarinets doubling trumpets – keep in mind for the Sunrise in the ballet.' [Subsequent note by author.]

came in to play to me Tcherepnin's *Tale of the Fish and the Fisherman*,[1] which he is due to play at the 'Contemporaries' concert. A marvellous piece, and I think Zakharov will make a good job of it. I find it very touching that Zakharov seeks my opinion; in general relations between us could not be better.

1   Transcription for piano of the ballet *The Tale of the Fisherman and the Fish*, based on Pushkin's fairy tale.

Index

Aachen, Belgium 728
Abashidze, cello student 252
Abkhazia 54n
Åbo 692, 695
Abramychev, Dmitry (Dima) 54
Abramycheva, Olga, student 17, 20, 23, 67, 115, 184
Abutkov, composition student 28
Adriatic Sea 758
Africa 710
Akafyev, Nikolay (Kolya) 11
Akhmatova (Gorenko), Anna Andreyevna, poet xxii
Akhron, Iosif Yulievich, violinist and composer 4n, 5
Akhron, Isidor Yulievich, pianist 4, 89, 115, 116, 118, 141, 161, 215, 349
Akimenko, composition student 53, 90
Akimenko, Fyodor Stepanovich, composer 53n, 588n
Akimenko, Yakov Stepanovich, composer and writer 588
Akopera, *see* Mariinsky Theatre
Aktseri, professor of singing 354, 348, 355, 563
Alapin, Semyon Zinovievich, chess player 20, 584
Albania 379
Alekhine, Alexander Alexandrovich, chess grandmaster 584, 640–42, 644, 646, 649, 652–4, 657, 665, 670–71, 675, 787
Alexander Building, St Petersburg 179–80, 498
Alexander Nevsky Monastery 735
Alexandrinsky Theatre 202
Alexandrov, border town between East Prussia and Poland 710
Alexandrovsk, Ukraine 471
Alexandrovsky Garden 159, 160, 466n
Alexandrovsky Hospital 744, 748
Alexeyev, mature student 92
Alfyorov, bank official 260, 278, 297, 313, 321, 335, 348, 363, 379, 411, 418, 541
Alpers, Boris Vladimirovich (Borya), brother of Vera 72, 81, 94, 201, 270, 273, 278, 465
Alpers family 69, 87, 138, 183, 190, 255, 517, 546, 564, 620, 778
Alpers, Lyudmila Vasilievna, mother of Vera 69, 81, 92, 133, 314, 340

Alpers, Sergey Vladimirovich (Seryozha), brother of Vera 81, 270, 274, 314, 465, 510, 608–9
Alpers, Vera Vladimirovna (Verochka) 19, 20, 39–40, 61–2, 66, 72, 81, 87, 96, 114, 115, 148, 157, 162, 165, 204, 255, 786; Easter card with Kitezh quotation, 48–9, 51, 51n; compared with Esche, 67; ancestry 69; SP plays duets with 77; not in love with despite saintly personality 88, 113; mutual friendship with Max Schmidthof, 92–3, 108–9, 111, 113; father composer, 94; summer correspondence agreed, 97–8, 104; attachment to SP, 119–20; SP visits home, 121–2; SP meets Ossovsky there, 122–3; ranked as No. 3 female friend, 142; decent playing in student concert, 145, 255; accompanies SP to Ossovsky's house, 145; disparaged by Elfrieda Hansen, 158; SP's romantic walk with, 166; becomes disenchanted with, 183; explanation for coldness demanded, 263, 270, 274; SP's rudeness, 278-9; poor playing at student concert, 314; sues for peace, 366; accidentally shakes hands, 404; requests meeting, 574; new encounter, 608; friendship restored, 629; acknowledges love for SP, 743
Alpers, Vladimir Mikhailovich, father of Vera 69, 94, 121–2, 314, 340
Alpnachstadt 457
Alupka 303, 339, 471, 475, 478
Alushta 312, 339, 351
America, United States of xiii, xiv, xv, 345; desire to travel to, 433, 442, 454, 478, 593, 616; 436, 449; Zakharov practises English for, 545; SP reads about, 579; Karatygin's review opens door to, 616–17; Struve's knowledge of, 617; Diaghilev planning tour to, 736; SP hopes to join, 752–3; unhelpfulness of married state, 788
Andersen, Hans Christian 705n; 'The Ugly Duckling', 737, 738, 740
Andreyev, baritone 433, 547
Andreyev pâtisserie 287
Andreyev family (the Andreyevs) 432–4, 442, 511, 516, 522, 535, 541, 570, 572, 598, 624, 632, 704, 733, 799; New Year party at, 279; their

interest in 2nd Piano Concerto, 370, 488;
kindness to M. G. Prokofieva in Paris, 428, 431;
SP visits at home, 487, 497, 499–501, 526, 541,
572, 624, 632, 737; accompany SP to Astoria
Hotel, 496; see off Meshcherskys at station,
525, 527; 535; accompany SP to art exhibition,
539; congratulate SP on winning prize, 664;
expeditions to Windsor and Kew, 708–9; SP
presents with *The Ugly Duckling*, 752
Andreyev, Nikolay Vasilievich, tenor 279n,
487–8, 508, 510, 523, 526, 528, 535, 561, 572, 574,
579, 713, 734, 744, 757–8, 764, 766; suggests
opera librettist, 218; professional career, 218n;
SP searches for and finds in Paris, 426–9;
SP accompanies to London, 432–8, 441–2;
invites SP to London again, 580, 704–9; sings
indifferently, 755
Andrienko, singing student 266
Animisova, piano student 8, 9, 9n, 11, 20, 33–4,
54, 67, 115
Annenkov, Conservatoire official 339
Antique Theatre, St Petersburg 514, 514n
Antwerp 745
Apollon magazine 85n, 155–6, 263, 523–4, 549,
552–3
Aptekarsky Island, St Petersburg 751
Apukhtov, Alexey Nikolayevich, poet 30n, 562n
Aquarium restaurant 216, 228, 646
Arakina, singing student 266
Arensky, Anton Stepanovich 432; opera *Nal
and Damayanti*, 39
Armashevskaya, student 440
Artistic Opera Company 276–7, 280, 295, 329
Artsybashev, Mikhail Petrovich, writer 371n;
On the Brink, 371, 512
Artsybushev, Nikolay Vasilievich, composer and
music administrator 57n, 122–3, 208, 295, 410,
419, 512, 527, 677, 749–50; opera *Jealousy* 540
Asafyev, Boris Vladimirovich (pseudonym Igor
Glebov), composer and critic xii, xiii, xvii,
5–7, 5n, 15, 39, 53, 61n, 163, 489, 760; ballets
The Fountains of Bakhchisarai, 5n; *The
Flames of Paris*, 5n; *The Stone Guest*, 5n;
children's opera *The Snow Queen*, 6
As It Happened, play 345
Aslanov, Alexander Petrovich, conductor 598,
599n; career, 234n; not on top of tempos for
1st Piano Concerto, 234; enquires about
works for children, 316; discusses *Dreams*
and 2nd Piano Concerto for Pavlovsk (summer 1913), 351–2; SP and composer play
Myaskovsky's 2nd Symphony 4-hand version, 364, 398–9; 404; invites SP to conduct
Dreams, 410–11, 417; 463; reschedules 2nd
Piano Concerto performance, 466–7; SP
plays through 2nd Piano Concerto, 484–5;
gives advice at rehearsal, 486; praises after
performance, 488–9; AA reports good review,
494–5; SP attempts to persuade inclusion
of Myaskovsky's *Alastor*, 637; plays 4-hand
version of Myaskovsky's 1st Symphony, 648,
680; AA's enviable domestic circumstances,
680; drags tempo of Symphony, 681, 685; asks
SP not to interfere at rehearsal, 684
Astoria Hotel, St Petersburg 498, 501–3, 508–9,
512, 515–16, 521, 666; room identified as chic
by Max Schmidthof, 344; same room occupied by Meshcherskys, 496; SP addresses
humorous card to Nina Meshcherskaya, 506;
SP visits Meshcherskys there, 508, 523; SP
attends performance by Isadora Duncan, 523;
Capablanca stays there, 683
Astrakhan 339,
Astruc, Gabriel, *see* Paris, Théâtre des Champs
Elysées
Auer, Leopold Semyonovich, violinist and
teacher 148, 347, 380, 391, 531; as teacher of
Iosif Akhron, 4n; performs at Russian
Musical Society Jubilee Concert, 132; distin-
guished pupils, 132n; performs Tchaikovsky's
Violin Concerto, 134; SP plays for class,
157–9; success impresses Elfrieda Hansen,
159; fails to nominate student for proposed
Tolstoy Memorial Concert, 188; and for
November 1913 concert, 531; disagrees with
colleagues over student strikes, 188n; leads
orchestra for Jubilee Concert, 259; concert
tour with Yesipova, 527; recitals with
Yesipova, 547; as teacher of Nalbandyan, 592
Austrian Archduchess 585

Bach, Johann Sebastian 502, 609, 679; Fugue in
G minor, 5, 15; Fugue in C minor (Well-
Tempered Clavier Book II), 50; Fugue in C
sharp major, 338; *The Art of Fugue*, 367, 535,
574, 581, 595, 614–15, 617–21; *Passacaglia* in C
minor, 516–17, 523, 535, 538; *Chaconne* arr.
Busoni, 755
Bai, piano student 338, 376, 378, 392, 397, 405
Baidar Pass 303
Baidar Gates 471
Baidari 339
Bakhchisarai 339
Bakst, Léon (Lev Rosenberg), painter and
designer 598, 632n, 639
Baku, Azerbaidjan 547
Balaclava 339
Balakirev, Mily Alexeyevich 70n; *Islamey*, 621
Balayev, Nikolay Vasilievich, teacher of Russian
12, 16, 40, 48, 369

INDEX 801

Balin, bank official 260
Ballets Russes 10n, 426n, 428–30, 585, 598n, 632n, 752–3, 757n
Balmont, Konstantin Dmitrievich, poet xiii, 90n, 144n, 154n, 763
Bantock, Granville, composer 705
Barber, Samuel, composer 103n
Barinova, Maria Nikolayevna, pianist and teacher 26, 332, 335, 376–7
Barkov, Captain V. N. 409, 510
Bashkirov, Boris Nikolayevich (pseudonym Boris Verin), wealthy amateur poet 679, 686, 736, 747, 750, 764, 770–2, 774, 785–6, 796; meets and invites SP, 671–2; SP meets brother Vladimir and cousin Yevgeny (Zhenechka) 671, 674; BB invites SP to meet Capablanca 682–3; introduces SP to sister, 738–42; claims responsibility for Capablanca's affair with Mme Strakhovich, 741; requests piano lessons from SP, 742; agrees fee, 744; SP meets BB's parents, 746; BB with sister establishes field hospital for war wounded, 751–2; SP visits brother's house, 752; BB takes lessons with SP, 753, 760, 765, 768, 775–6, 780, 783, 789; cousin relates war atrocities, 762; BB reads Balmont, 763; SP introduces BB to Eleonora Damskaya, 776; BB discusses religious and philosophical views of Tolstoy, 778; plans to travel together, 782; and to become SP's impresario, 782; SP meets Demchinsky at BB's, 787; is bored by BB's talk of mysticism, 787; BB fails to come to lessons, 790–91; invites SP to spiritualist seance, 794;
Bastian, Mlle, attachment of Boris Zakharov 229
Batareyny Road, St Petersburg 526
Batum 296, 339, 476, 483
Bazavov, Sergey (Serge) 473, 479–83, 487–8, 495, 517, 523–5, 527, 610, 669, 723–5, 757; SP meets sister, 724, 730
Bechstein pianos 327
Becker, Yakov Davydovich, piano manufacturer 614, 656–7; Becker Piano No. 28002 660
Bedrinskaya, actor 279
Beecham, Sir Thomas 707
Beethoven, Ludwig van 129, 158, 194, 217, 272, 466n, 502, 564, 730; WORKS: String Trio (unidentified), 108–9; 3rd Piano Concerto, 5; 9th Symphony, 38, 482; 'Appassionata' Sonata, 113; Thirty-Two Variations in C minor, 118; Sonata No. 31 in A flat, 180; 'Waldstein' Sonata, 184; 'Pathétique' Sonata, 236; 7th Symphony, 297, 305–6, 528, 531, 536, 539–42; Violin Concerto, 297, 528, 532–3, 535–6; 4th Symphony, 314, 343–4, 350, 353;

Sonata No. 32 in C minor, 338, 368, 550, 574, 595–6, 601, 608, 614–15, 617–20; 'Kreutzer' Sonata, 354; 'Hammerklavier' Sonata, 368; Sonata No. 2 in A, 737, 739, 741; Coriolan Overture, 372; Symphonies 1–9, 474; 8th Symphony, 422; Symphony (unidentified) 4–hand version, 730; 3rd Symphony 4–hand version, 732
Belanovsky, Arseny Stepanovich, priest 24,
Belanovsky, Stefan Stepanovich, priest 24,
Belgium 424, 731; Queen Wilhelmina of, 728
Belokurova, Serafima, singing student 380, 382, 390, 531, 538, 550, 553, 556, 560, 567, 569–70, 575, 608, 623, 631, 734
Belling, Erast, conductor 207, 606
Beloóstrov, border station between Russia and Finland 165n, 179, 179n
Beloúsov, Yevsey Yakovlevich, cellist 470, 516, 544–5, 546, 586, 582, 589, 593
Belsky, Vladimir Ivanovich, librettist 122
Belyayev Circle xxii, 57n, 61n, 596n
Belyayev Concerts 57–8, 79, 99, 122–4, 361, 371–2, 402, 410, 418–19, 508, 511–12, 514, 526–7, 548, 586, 606, 614, 632
Belyayev, Mitrofan Petrovich, industrialist and philanthropist 57n, 70n
Belyayev, Viktor Mikhailovich, critic 607
Benditsky, piano student 547
Benois, Alexander Nikolayevich, painter and designer xiii, 357n, 425, 514n, 598n, 639
Benois, Maria, see Tcherepnin, Maria Albertovna
Benois, Mme, piano student, second wife of Alexander Benois 216, 224, 267, 425, 425n
Berdyansk 408
Berezovskaya, Nyura, Conservatoire student 89, 114–15, 131, 143, 147, 154, 158; car trip to the Islands with, 139–141
Berg, Alban: Wozzeck 272n
Bergen, Norway 701–2
Berlin, Friedrichstrasse 419, 420–21, 422–3, 448, 460, 461–2, 567, 615, 688, 709–10; Tiergarten, 423, 461, 709; Charlottenburg, 423; Kempinsky Hotel, 423, 461, 709; Zoo, 423; Wertheim, 423; Hotel Metropole, 461; Schöneberg, 731;
Berlin, A. M., piano student 121, 161, 216, 224, 267, 367, 620, 658, 664, 674
Berlioz, Hector: Benvenuto Cellini 297, 528
Berne, Switzerland 454–5; Kornhaus Bridge, 545, 665, 724
Bernhardt, August Rudolfovich, former Conservatoire Director 10, 10n, 188n
Bernstein, Leonard 102n
Bernstein, Nikolay Davydovich, critic 599, 599n

Bernstein, Osip, chess master 640–41, 644, 646–7, 649, 652–4, 657
Beshtau 105–7, 722
Bessel, Vasily Vasilievich, music publisher 655, 667, 679–80, 685
Bessonova, Yevgenia Nikolayevna (Zhenya), piano student 8, 20, 22, 29–30, 45, 46, 49, 78, 81, 115, 121, 159
Bessonova, Mme, Yevgenia's mother 35
Bestuzhev Institutes 69n, 549, 769
Bezrodny, cello student 592, 606–7, 626, 631–4, 641, 642–3
Bikhter, Mikhail Alexeyevich, conductor 525, 545, 667
Birmingham, England 705; Music Conservatory, 705; 709
Biryulin, Conservatoire student 139–141
Bizet, Georges: *Carmen* 281, 476, 535, 540, 545
Black Hundreds 18n
Blackburne, Joseph (The Black Death), chess master 640–42, 644, 646, 649, 657
Black Sea xii, 368, 384, 454, 692
Black Sea Express 296, 307–8, 310
Bloody Sunday Massacre 188n
Blumenfeld, Felix Mikhailovich, composer, conductor and teacher 368, 399, 406, 510, 592, 600, 634, 644, 677
Bluvshtein, Luiza, piano student 557, 631
Bobrovich, singing student (tenor) 245, 251, 269, 320, 337, 340, 475, 477, 483
Bobrovsky, Grigory (Grisha), painter 473, 477–9, 482, 517, 523, 525, 723
Boccaccio, Giovanni: *The Decameron* 218
Bogdanov-Berezovsky, Dr Mikhail 515
Bogdanov-Berezovsky, Valerian Mikhailovich 515n
Bolshevik regime xvii
Borislavsky, Sokol member 402, 541, 678–9, 681, 683
Borkovsky family 11
Borodin, Alexander Porfirievich 467, 494
Borodin family (friends of Deshevov) 494
Borovichi 731
Borovsky, Alexander Kirillovich, pianist xiii, 121, 134, 151, 161, 165, 183, 190, 216, 224, 230, 311, 336, 425, 470n, 529, 677, 760, 787
Borovsky family 654
Mme Borovskaya, mother of Alexander 336, 464
Borshch, Yekaterina Samoilovna (Henrietta, Katya, Katyusha), piano student 132–3, 142, 152, 157, 165, 187, 190, 291, 335, 376, 381, 760
Borzhom 339
Boulogne 433, 442
Boyars Court Hotel, Moscow 324–5, 327

Boyle, Robert, scientist 506; Boyle and Mariotte, 506–7, 506n
Brahms, Johannes 57, 258; *Rhapsody*, 71; *Paganini Variations*, 161; Violin Concerto, 397, 399, 401, 404
Brandl, Varvara Nikolayevna 105–7
Braudo, Yevgeny Maximovich, musicologist and writer 498
Brauer, conducting student 36
Brazil 709
Breitkopf and Härtel, music publishers 704, 706–8
Brest-Litovsk, Treaty of 710n
Briand, Maria Isaakevna 429
Bridge, card game 281, 500, 525–8, 533, 572, 580, 591, 599, 610, 614, 628, 635–6, 653, 708, 724, 730, 739, 746, 757, 764, 766, 777, 779
Brienz, Lake 456–7
Bronnitskaya Street, St Petersburg 112, 115, 151, 507
Bruderschaft ritual 167, 190, 225, 262, 287, 621, 783, 794
Brudno, singing student 330
Brussels 709
Bryusov, Valery Yakovlevich, poet 38n
Bryskin, Arkady Borisovich, conductor 325
Budarina, Conservatoire student and chess enthusiast 644, 654, 663, 675, 678, 681–2
Budberg, chess player 60
Bulgaria 758
Burakinskaya, piano student 47
Bushen, Alexandra Dmitrievna, piano student 514, 516, 527, 530, 532, 538, 540–42, 551–2, 559, 566, 573, 575, 593, 595, 597–8, 600, 602, 604, 608, 613, 714; as unknown admirer, 504, 508, 510; accompanies on walks to the Islands, 525–6; good walking companion, 526, 533; knowledge of French and German, 533; discusses Wagner, 535; enthusiastic about *The Gambler*, 537; accompanies to Moscow premiere, 557, 600, 602, 604, 608; passionate defence of SP as composer, 564; learns to skate, 567, 571–2; buys and learns SP's works, 582; advice on coping with hand fatigue, 661
Busoni, Ferrucio 26n; arrangement of Bach *Chaconne*, 795
Buxtehude, Dietrich 161; Prelude and Fugue in D minor, 160
Byron, Lord: *Childe Harold* 36n

Calvocoressi, Michel 236, 271, 278, 432, 665, 666
Canada 617, 631
Capablanca, José Raul, chess grandmaster: demonstrates mastery, 582; SP declines simultaneous match, 636; JC's clear expecta-

tion of victory in tournament, 640, 647, 657; has late night at Aquarium with woman friend, 646; matches against Lasker, 650, 652–3, 669–72; defeated by Tarrasch, 673; takes 2nd place to Lasker, 675; SP challenges in simultaneous matches, 678–9, 681–2, 724, 745; meets JC at Bashkirov's, 682–3
Caspian Sea 339, 368
Catherine The Great, Empress 301n
Caucasus 105, 110, 165n, 182, 185, 296, 344, 347, 368, 384, 532, 602, 701, 720
Caucasus Range 728n
Chabrov, actor 555
Chagall, Marc 657n
Chaliapin, Fyodor Ivanovich 68, 429, 437–8
Chamonix 450
Chausson, Ernest 782
Chekhov, Anton Pavlovich 18n, 19n, 309, 435n, 464n, 476; 'Ward No. 6', 228; 'A Dreary Story', 416; Collected Letters, 475–7; 'Gloomy People', 476n; *The Cherry Orchard*, 639n, *Three Sisters*, 639n
Chernov, Mikhail Mikhailovich, composer and musicologist 38, 41, 45
Chester, J. & W., music publishers 704n
Chévillard, Camille 432
Chigorin, Mikhail Ivanovich, chess master 5, 37–8, 52
Chopin, Fryderyk: Etude (unidentified) 63; Etude in C Op. 10 No. 1, 71; *Ballade* (unidentified), 187, 332; *Ballade* No. 3, 251; Sonata No. 2 in B flat minor, 292, 308, 315, 368, 558, 564, 567, 571, 574, 579, 595, 601, 608, 614, 617–19; Scherzo No. 2, 758
Chornaya Rechka 409
Christiania, Norway 698, 699–701; Karl Johans Gade, 700; Grand Hotel, 700; Kongensgade, 701
Christian Science xiv
Christ Saviour Cathedral, St Petersburg 603
Chudovsky, Valerian Adolfovich 60, 60n, 63, 524, 539, 550, 552, 553
Chuprynnikov, Mitrofan Mikhailovich, tenor 408, 560
Chuvash folk music 306
Civil War, Russian xiii
Clarens, Switzerland 453
Clementi, Muzio: Study in Octaves 47
Coates, Albert, conductor 655–6, 655n, 677
Codina, Carolina, *see* Prokofieva, Lina Ivanovna
Cologne 424, 709
Conan Doyle, Sir Arthur 764, 765
Conius, Georgy Eduardovich 151
Constantinople 742
Contemporary Concerts 773, 777, 778, 785–6, 790–91, 797

Cooper, Emil Albertovich, conductor 181, 193, 209, 211, 435
Coppée, François, playwright 218, 218n
Court Orchestra 70, 80, 81–5, 207, 241, 280n, 324, 606, 756
Court Theatre 204
Craig, Gordon 464n
Crédit Lyonnais 418
Crimea 111, 296–7, 299, 307–10, 313, 348, 363, 370, 384, 392, 398, 407, 483, 581, 587, 668, 686
Crooked Mirror theatre 313, 516, 517–18, 522
croquet 170, 172, 177, 229, 409, 491, 712
Cuba restaurant 266–7, 388
Cui, César Antonovich 190, 402; *The Snow Prince*, 36, 42, 45, 756
Curtis Institute, Philadelphia 103n
Czerny, Carl: Study in A flat, 47

Damskaya, Eleonora Alexandrovna 344, 346, 572: long-running friendship with SP, 330n; requests work for harp, 330; Prelude in C written, 330; transcribed for piano, 330; SP has long telephone conversations with, 527, 532, 571, 581, 597, 599, 607, 611–12, 642, 654, 680, 690, 735, 742; record for length set, 585; sits with SP at concerts, 551, 595, 608–9, 627, 674, 685, 773; enemy of Bushen, 576; SP thinks of at New Year, 575; SP accompanies to Conservatoire Ball, 579–80; ED's interest in Capablanca, 582, 642, 644–5; practical joke with exam scores, 609; predicts SP's success in exam, 617; congratulates SP on prize, 620, 663; SP sends white roses for confirmation, 628; ED appointed to 'cabinet', 608, 618, 629; accompanies SP to Palm Sunday Festival, 630–31; excursions with SP and Struve, 635, 637–8, 668–70, 736; SP shows 1st Piano Concerto to, 644–5; characteristics shared with Max Schmidthof, 684; meets SP at Pavlovsk, 714, 717; problems with suitor (the 'chess game'), 759, 763, 768, 772, 774–6, 778, 780, 788; SP introduces to Bashkirov, 776, 778; plays 'Gavotte' in arrangement for harp, 778
Dancer, The, play 380
Danilov, A. 224, 777
Danilov, Nikolay 226n, 777
D'Anthès, Georges, *see* Heeckeren, Georges-Charles d'Anthès
Dargomyzhsky, Alexander Sergeyevich 306–8, 328, 405; *Rusalka*, 306n, 328, 332, 341, 787, 792, 795, 796; *Malorossiisky Kazachok*, 306–7, 315, 328, 332, 337, 340; *Chukhonskaya (Finnish) Fantasia*, 306, 308, 310, 312, 315, 328, 332, 337–8, 340; *The Stone Guest*, 307, 328–9, 337–8, 345; 'The Little Golden Cloud Passed

The Night', 328, 337; *The Wedding*, 332, 334, 337–8, 340
Daudet, Alphonse: *Sappho, moeurs parisiennes* 175
Davydov, Karl Yulievich, cellist and teacher 589n
Debussy Claude 126, 549, 551–2, 552–3, 573; *Le Martyre de Saint Sébastien*, 411; *Jeux*, 544; *L'Après-midi d'un faune*, 598n
Deisha-Sionitskaya, Maria Adrianovna, exhibition and concert organizer 129–30, 149–50, 153, 199, 208, 545
Dekabristy Street, *see* Offitserskaya Street
Demchinsky, Boris Nikolayevich 60–61, 787
Demchinskaya, V. F. (wife of Boris Demchinsky) 707
Demidov, Prokofy 419n
Den' (*The Day*) newspaper 496, 543, 676, 679
Denmark 689
Derzhanovsky, Vladimir Vladimirovich 713, as publisher of *Muzyka*, 212, 492, 592; helps to arrange performance of *Dreams* in Sokolniki Park, 217; involvement in Free Theatre, 464; helps to arrange audition of *Maddalena*, 469–70, 533–4; declines to print SP's article about Sabaneyev, 516, 522; dismisses Sabaneyev, 604; arranges Moscow recital, 522; changes date, 536, 544, 546–7; Moscow recital takes place, 587–90; has SP to stay for Koussevitzky Orchestra performance of 1st Piano Concerto, 602–4; attempts to get *Maddalena* produced in Moscow, 670
Deshevov, Vladimir Mikhailovich (Volodya) 63, 94, 183, 190, 192, 287, 375, 446–7, 463, 468, 486–9, 493–4, 551, 598, 714
Deshevov, Sergey Mikhailovich (Seryozha) 494
Devil's Bridge, The, Switzerland 458–9, 458n
Diaghilev, Sergey Pavlovich (Serge) xiii; describes programme of Tchaikovsky's 6th Symphony, 349n; SP enquires for Tcherepnin and Andreyev in Paris, 429; wishes to meet SP, 585; fails to meet in St Petersburg, 591; quarrels with Nijinsky, 684n; initial meetings and discussions with SP in London, 704–8; suggests Gorodetsky as librettist, 711; influence of Diaghilev's taste on SP, 714; plans US tour for Ballets Russes during war, 736, 752–3; cables SP from Italy, 752, 783; invites SP to Rome, 758; nominates Romanov to choreograph *Ala and Lolli*, 766
Diederichs, Andrey, piano manufacturer and concert promoter 687, 688
Diederichs Gebrüder 687n
Diederichs, Leonid 687n
Disgrace of Germany, The, play 746–7

Dmitrieva, Olga 54
Dmitrieva, Olga Petrovna 55
Dnieper river 420
Dobryshin family 33
Dobrzhenets, violin student 8, 14, 22n, 23, 46
Dobychina, Nadezhda Yevseyevna, gallery owner 656
Dohnányi, Ernst von 464n, 555
Donon restaurant 269
Dostoyevsky, Fyodor Mikhailovich: *The Idiot*, 525; *The Gambler*, 535–7, 706, 767
Dranishnikov, Vladimir Alexandrovich, conductor 291, 304n, 307, 316, 320, 340n, 344, 353, 356, 378, 390, 515, 565, 598, 631, 677, 769, 771, 781, 787; assistant conductor to SP, 272, 290; composer of Piano Variations, 360; senior member of conducting class, 502; SP praises accomplishments, 530, 539, 600, 792; SP invites to accompany concerto graduation performance, 591, 596, 627, 636, 647, 661; pleased by success of SP's recital exam, 620; accompanies play-through of 1st Piano Concerto for professors, 650–51; and for Tcherepnin, 656–8, 668; SP meets sister, 656, 795; supports SP in simultaneous chess matches against Capablanca, 678–9, 681–2; achievements in conducting *Rusalka*, 792, 795; less assured with orchestra in concert 795
Dresden 436
Driesen von Osten, Baron 514n, 571, 631
Drozdov, pianist 67, 95
Drozdov, Anatoly Nikolayevich, pianist and musicologist 67, 77–8, 162, 338, 354, 356, 376–7, 379, 619, 664
Dubasov, piano professor 161, 337, 349, 643, 664
Dubyago, piano student 50
Dubyansky, Alexander Markovich, piano student 216, 307
Dudal, piano student 530–31
Dulov, pianist 623–4
Duncan, Isadora 666
Durdina, Kira and Nina, cousins of Zakharov 224, 414–16
Dutch Step (skating) 285, 285n, 573
Duvidzon, Conservatoire student 563
Dvina river 793
Dvinsk 287, 318, 420, 514
Dzhiarguli, Conservatoire official 95, 125, 188

East Prussia 420n
Elbrus, Mount 722, 728n
Elgar, Sir Edward 782
Elkan, Yevgeny Venyaminovich, pianist 4, 15, 53, 90
Engineers Palace 37, 223

INDEX

An Ensign of the Regiment, play 357
Erasmus, friend of Sergey Sebryakov 545
Erdely, former suitor of Nina Meshcherskaya 765–6; wife, 765
Esche, Sofia Nikolayevna 8n, 45, 48, 63–4, 66–8, 95, 146, 156–9, 161, 233, 413, 417, 419, 507, 509, 549, 562, 569, 573
Esche, Yelizaveta Nikolayevna 8, 16, 17, 20, 35, 65–5, 69, 94–5, 97, 118, 142, 146, 162
Essipoff, Annette, *see* Yesipova, Anna Nikolayevna
Evenings of Contemporary Music xxii, 38, 41–2, 48, 63, 65–6, 72, 86, 91, 130, 155–6, 193, 213–15, 218, 227, 591, 593, 595–6, 599, 601, 607, 634, 654, 782; 'Contemporaries', 489
Evening Times, St Petersburg newspaper 585, 665, 673
Eydkuhnen, border town 462

Fayet St Germain, France 450
Feinberg, singing student 251, 266
Feinberg, Samuel Yevgenievich, pianist 343n
Feona, Alexey Nikolayevich, actor and director 22–4
Ferni-Giraldoni, Carolina, singer and violinist 259, 259n
Field of Mars, St Petersburg 347
Figner, Nikolay Nikolayevich, tenor, Director of People's House 281, 281n, 287, 569
Filippieva, Natalya Nikolayevna, friend of Nina Meshcherskaya 647, 690
Fillipov's pâtisserie 98, 98n, 310, 326, 330
Finland 312, 699, 717
Finland Station, St Petersburg 256, 311, 383, 385, 386, 406, 468, 490, 637
Firsova, Lyubov Yakovlevna, sister of Olga Smetskaya 333
Fliege, Conservatoire student 8, 14, 33, 46, 67, 115
Florence, Italy 752
Flüelen, Switzerland 459
Flyamb, chess player 583–4
Fohström, Alma von Rodé, singer and teacher 382, 550
Fokine, Mikhail Mikhailovich, dancer and choreographer 357n, 632n, 796n
Folkestone, England 433, 442
Fonbrune, Pierre de, son of Mme Guyonnet 443
Fontanka river, St Petersburg 223, 254, 658–9, 683
Fouqué, Friedrich de la Motte, poet and playwright 58n
Four Cantons Lake, *see* Vierwaldstatter See
Franck, César 782; Sonata for violin and piano, 360
Franstsis, Nelli, piano student 262, 309, 314, 322, 381, 677
Franstsuzskaya Embankment, St Petersburg 738–9, 769–70, 777
Free Theatre, Moscow 464, 468–9, 492, 553, 554–6, 590
Frehlich, tailor 369, 373, 375, 378, 381
Freyman, chess player 20
Friebus, Alexander Ivanovich ('Diminished Fifth'), Conservatoire librarian 339, 339n, 571–2, 615, 631, 779, 795
Friedrich, piano student 151
Frolov, Alexander (Shura), acquaintance 715
Frolov, Yury, acquaintance 25, 39, 40, 49, 69, 546
Frolova sisters 21, 39, 40, 49
Furman, conducting student 26, 132

Gabel, Stanislav Ivanovich, bass singer and Opera Class director 95, 96, 243, 251, 266, 294, 319, 329, 338–9, 345, 403, 560, 568, 624, 626, 647, 650, 663, 677; history, 95n; nominates singer for Tolstoy concert, 188; declares choristers unavailable to sing SP's choral works, 203–4; demonstrates affection for SP, 244, 272, 562, 735, 795; appreciates SP's accompaniments for opera class, 247; nervous about performances, 256; agrees Lidia Umnova best candidate for Lel in *Snow Maiden*, 259; cancels opera performances without revealing true reason, 295; gives SP leave of absence to go to Crimea ,298; intervenes in rehearsal of *The Queen of Spades*, 314; dissatisfied with preparation of *The Wedding*, 332, 337; satisfied, 340; absorbed in *Falstaff* rehearsal ,515; pleased with makeshift stage in Small Hall, 530; teased by SP about squeaking shoes, 532–3; conducts at Lyadov Jubilee Concert, 546; approves SP's conducting of *Rigoletto* and *Aida*, 557; jury member for SP's graduation recital exam, 619; praises performance of *Tannhäuser*, 620; hints at, SP's good exam result, 621; searches for pianist before start of *Figaro* performance, 629; blames SP for poor performance by chorus, 630; SP presents with copy of 1st Piano Concerto, 644; considers SP's chances of winning competition damaged by choice of 1st Piano Concerto, 654; jokes about Glazunov autographing photographs, 678;
Gabel, Mme 265
Galkovsky, composition student: opera *The Gypsies* 36, 43, 45, 58, 80, 217
Galperin, piano student 621, 627, 636, 659
Gauk, Alexander Vasilievich, conductor 269,

307–8, 320, 340, 344, 515, 539, 548, 598, 600, 632, 679, 771, 795
Gelbak, chess player 502
Gelever, P., piano professor 265, 396, 557, 645, 664
Geneva, Switzerland 448–50, 453, 635
Geneva, Lake 449, 453–4, 455, 457, 631
George V, King 437
Georgian Military Highway 292, 339
German and Grossman piano 38
Gessen, Iosif Vladimirovich, editor of *Rech* (*Speech*) newspaper 612, 616, 634, 711, 713, 715
Ginger Whiskers, *see* Petrovich, Alexey Stepanovich
Gladkaya, Sofia Nikolayevna, singing professor 263
Glagoleva, Leonida Mikhailovna, piano student 16, 17, 19–20, 22, 26, 33, 44–5, 49, 51, 67, 115, 119, 123, 126, 131, 134, 157, 161, 165, 191; ill-advisedly decides to play in Conservatoire Ball programme, 34–5; plans to study with Drozdov, 77; asks SP to supply Assyrian music for dance, 78–9, 80–81, 86–7; enters into summer correspondence with SP, 98, 104, 118, 124; attends Conservatoire Ball together with SP, 138–9, 141–2, 144; decision to go skating together, 142, 144; ranked as No. 2 female friend, 142, 158; partiality to SP reported, 156; abortive expedition to Sestroretsk 162–3; engagement and marriage to Vladimirsky, 192, 201–3
Glagoleva, Mme, mother 35, 138
Glagoleva, Sofia Mikhailovna (Sonya), sister 123–4
Glazunov, Alexander Konstantinovich xxi, xxii, 42, 46, 50, 53, 59, 113, 128, 132, 157, 159, 161, 192, 216, 235n, 249, 251, 252, 257, 267, 295, 320, 372, 377, 378–9, 382–3, 393, 395–6, 401–4, 410, 417–19, 430, 497, 508, 512, 514n, 531, 538, 542, 564, 566, 568, 570–71, 584, 609–11, 619–21, 629–30, 633–4, 636, 644, 647–8, 650, 663, 666, 668, 672, 674, 676–8, 714, 749, 764, 771, 796; resignation from Conservatoire and reappointment as Director, 10n, 188n, 368n; subsidizes student party, 14; distributes complimentary tickets, 125, 134; disciplines Saminsky, 15; courtesy in listening to student requests 656; inscription of Glinka score to youthful SP, 357; SP bids farewell, 678; SP's opinion of compositions, 26, 77, 158, 194, 248, 253, 259, 261, 263, 332, 361, 417; AG's support for SP's Symphony in E minor, 56, 62–3, 65–71, 77, 80–85; approval of SP's 'White Swan', 144; support for inclusion of SP's works in Conservatoire concert, 188–9; rejection of further works by SP in Conservatoire concert, 205–6; criticism of *Dreams*, 191; and of Sinfonietta, 203; neutral stance in SP's altercation with Lyadov, 90–91; involvement in SP's change from Winkler to Yesipova, 101–2; hostility to SP's Piano Concerto No. 1, 235, 663–4, 666; presented with score by SP, 644; agrees play-through to professors, 648, 650–51; member of Belyayev Circle, 57n, 70n; member of RME Editorial Board, 208; as conductor, 245, 256; Tcherepnin's negative opinion of conducting skills, 261; alcoholism, 73, 79, 146, 150, 297
Glebov, Igor, *see* Asafyev, Boris Vladimirovich
Glebova, Tamara Andreyevna (Tamochka) 325, 498, 551, 637; mother 553
Glen, Alfred Edmundovich von, cellist and teacher 589, 589n
Glière, Reinhold Moritsovich, composer 59, 62, 129–30, 133, 151, 152–3, 182, 208–9, 212, 325, 366; Symphony No. 2, 153; Symphony (unidentified), 604
Glière, Mme (wife) 208–9, 211, 325
Glinka, Mikhail Ivanovich: 'Somnenie' ('Doubt'), 33, 34; opera *Ruslan and Lyudmila*, 131, 145–6, 293, 382n; *Reminiscences of a Night in Madrid*, 243; opera *A Life For The Tsar*, 318–9, 382n; *Kamarinskaya*, 352, 357
Glinka Museum 95
Gluck, Christoph Willibald 502
Gnessin, Mikhail Fabianovich 498
Gnessina, Yelena Fabianovna 498n
Godlevsky, family friend 262
Godowsky, Leopold, pianist 544–5
Goethe, Johann Wolfgang von: *Faust* 318n
Gogol, Nikolay Vasilievich xx; *Evenings on a Farm Near Dikanka*, 507
Goldenblum, Moritz Arnoldovich, conductor 145, 207
Goldevkskys, acquaintances 579
Golubovskaya (Khaslavskaya-Golubovskaya), Nadezhda Iosifovna, pianist 148, 148n, 162, 165, 190, 192, 216, 265, 504, 508, 525–6, 537, 566, 598, 601, 607–8, 610, 618, 660, 674, 677, 679, 760, 786 : SP enjoys company, 155; chess partner, 185, 516, 575, 607–8; intelligence as musician, 307, 559, 641, 738; walk to The Islands, 514; asks SP to accompany exam concerto performance, 584; rivals for Rubinstein Prize, 584, 627, 636, 641, 648, 659, 663; SP does not hear recital exam, 615; joint selection of Becker piano for concerto exam, 656–7; visits Chess Club with SP, 657; 'historic' chess match waiting for results of

concerto competition, 658, 661–2; graduation concert, 675; mother, 661

Goncharova, Natalya (Natasha), singing student 248, 257, 324, 361, 366, 390, 394, 417, 447, 503; SP uses intimate form of address, 247; carries on flirtation, 249, 254, 281, 290, 306, 308, 323, 341, 382; sings and also resembles Kupava in *Snow Maiden*, 256; asks for myrtle from Crimea, 297; SP thinks of her at Pushkin's Grotto in Crimea, 303; works with her on Countess scene in *The Queen of Spades*, 313–14; her snobbishness, 360; pre-performance panic, 408; expedition to The Islands, 408–9; SP receives letters from, 431, 502

Goncharova, Natalya Sergeyevna, painter 303n

Goncharova, Natalya Nikolayevna, wife of Alexander Pushkin 293n, 303n

Gorky, Maxim (Alexander Maximovich Peshkov), writer 464n

Gorodetsky, Sergey Mitrofanovich, poet 707, 707n, 708, 711, 713–14, 715–16, 721, 736, 738, 742, 745, 748, 752, 753–4, 757, 762–3, 764, 767–70, 777, 779, 784, 786–7

Gorsky, singing student 107–8

Gorsky, Alexander Alexeyevich, balletmaster and choreographer 684n

Göschinen, Switzerland 458–9

Gostiny Dvor, Petersburg department store 736

Goulard water 364, 364n

Gounod, Charles: *La Reine de Saba*, 78, 78n; *Faust*, 131, 145–6, 294, 298, 316, 318n, 340, 341–2, 344–5, 530, 532, 537, 539; *Roméo et Juliette*, 185, 195

Gradus ad Parnassum 737

Grevs, Zora 277, 285, 400, 404–5, 506

Grevs, Yelena Isaakevna 150n

Griboyedov, Alexander Sergeyevich, *Woe from Wit*, play in verse 12, 281n, 770

Grieg, Edvard 699; 'Promenade of the Gnomes', 34; Humoresque in D major, 51; two-piano arrangement of Mozart sonatas, 121–2; Piano Concerto in A minor, 213, 530; Piano Sonata, 282, 787; *Ballade* for piano, 729

Grotrian-Steinweg piano 306n

Gruzenberg, Mlle, friend of Bashkirov 751

Gurzuf, Crimea 302, 339, 407, 431, 447, 467–70, 472–83, 484, 486–8, 492, 494–5, 497–9, 510, 523, 526, 636, 723–4, 734

Gumilyov, Nikolay Stepanovich, poet 38n

Gungerburg 167–8

Gunpowder Works 312

Gunsberg, Isidor, chess master 640–42, 644, 646–7, 649, 657

Gurko, friend of Alexandra Schmidthof 397–8

Gurland, Ilya, novelist and playwright 18n; *A Local Shakespeare*, 18

Gustavus Adolphus, King of Sweden 694, 694n

Guyonnet, M. and Mme 443–4

Gvirtsman, Ilya Iosifovich, violin student 8, 17–18, 20, 22n, 23, 33–4, 46

Handschin, Jacques, organist and teacher 784

Hall of the Nobility (Court Hall, now Great Hall of the Philharmonia), St Petersburg 226, 538, 603, 603n 739, 775

Hall of the Nobility (now Kolonny Zal), Moscow 603, 603n

Hamsun, Knut 699

Handel, Georg Frideric 437, 502; *Judas Maccabaeus*, 243, 245, 266, 289, 291, 306; Organ Concerto (unidentified), 523

Hanover 690

Hansen, Cecilia Genrikhovna (Tilya), violinist 4n, 147n, 157, 265, 318, 413, 487, 489, 493, 501, 513, 533, 535, 536, 539–41, 580, 676, 691, 712, 717, 719, 755, 767, 786, 788, 792

Hansen, Elfrieda Genrikhovna (Frieda), pianist 147–9, 152–5, 157–60, 161–2, 163–5, 184, 187, 191, 216, 255, 265, 305, 487, 489, 501, 513, 535, 571, 618, 623, 658, 691, 712, 717, 719, 767, 788

Harrach, crystal dealers 793, 793n

Hartmann, Thomas de (Foma Alexandrovich), composer 749, 750

Hawaii xiii

Haydn, Josef 315, 502, 521; WORKS: Symphony No. 94 in G, Hob. 1:94 ('Surprise'), 285, 291, 308, 320; Symphony (unidentified), 521

Heeckeren, Georges Charles d'Anthès 293

Heeckeren, Baron 293n

Heifetz, Jascha 4n, 541, 584

Helsingfors 521, 529, 760

Helsingfors Philharmonic Orchestra 463n

Helsinki, *see* Helsingfors

Henselt, Adolf: Variations for piano, 361; transcription of Beethoven's *Coriolan*, 372

Hofman, Nadezhda Ludwigovna, pianist 544

Hofmann, Josef, pianist 146

Hofmann, Yelena, piano student 121, 134, 161, 191, 213

Hotel Luxe, Moscow 587

Ibsen, Henryk 699

Ignatiev, Pavel (Palya) 37, 112

Ignatieva, Katya, *see* Rayevskaya, Yekaterina Alexandrovna

Igumnov, Konstantin Nikolayevich 325n

Ilyin, son of Anna Yesipova 132, 151–2, 161, 162, 216

Imatra 256–7

Imperial Russian Musical Society 131, 295, 536, 749–50, 760, 763–5, 782, 796
Interlaken, Switzerland 455–6
Ippolitov-Ivanov, Mikhail Mikhailovich: *Asia*, 251; *Ruth*, 251, 256–7, 265
Iretskaya, Natalya Alexandrovna, singing professor 407, 563, 679
Iron-Cement, SP's shares in 260, 344
Isaacs, Miss, English teacher 482, 723, 727–8, 731, 736, 739, 741, 743, 746, 755, 759–60, 762, 764, 766, 768, 772, 776, 778, 781–2, 784, 790, 793, 796
Islands, The, St Petersburg 93, 140–41, 298, 330, 365, 399, 406, 408–9, 514–15, 516, 518, 533, 665, 750
Ivanov, Missing Persons Bureau official 392
Ivanov, Mikhail Mikhailovich, composer 756
Ivanov-Smolensky, singing professor 220
Ivanova, piano student 61
Ivanovskoye 222

Japan xiii
Jardin des Anglais, Geneva 449
Joachim, Joseph, violinist 592n
Joanne, Adolphe: *Itinéraire de la Suisse*, 447–8, 453, 455, 459, 460
Joyce, Archibald 531n; *Songe d'automne*, 531
Jungfrau mountain, Switzerland 455
Johansen, music shop in St Petersburg 120
Juilliard School of Music, New York 470n
Jurgenson, Boris Petrovich, music publisher 70n, 252, 255, 327, 548, 588, 655: rejects works submitted by SP, 93; Ossovsky's letter of recommendation to, 208–9; Glière's publisher, 209; agrees to publish Opp. 1, 2, 3, 4, 209–10; SP offers 2nd Sonata, 242; BJ accepts, 249; comments on SP's youth, 258; discusses blamelessness of Taneyev, 264; SP offers 1st Piano Concerto, 285, 291–2, 296; BJ agrees to publish, 325–6; unwilling to publish *Dreams* and *Ballade*, 333; SP receives proofs of Opp. 4 and 11, 391, 405; SP proposes fee of 1000 roubles for Op. 12, 381; agrees 500 roubles 554–5; sends 1st Piano Concerto to be engraved, 529–30; BJ queries principle of transposing instruments all written in C, 544; SP proposes to offer *Maddalena*, 547; full score of 1st Piano Concerto not yet engraved for Moscow premiere, 602; printed and available, 639; SP offers *Ballade*, 645; rejected, 654; SP regrets not re-offering *Dreams*, 713; proposes offering 2nd Piano Concerto, 735; BJ called up as former officer and posted to Tula, 736; promoted to Warrant Officer, 767–8

Jurgenson, Grigory Borisovich, son of Boris Jurgenson 767–8, 772, 785
Jurgenson Music Publishers (Moscow) 70, 70n, 182, 189, 198, 208–9, 334, 464, 735, 756, 758, 765
Jurgensons Music Publishers (St Petersburg) 120, 525, 568, 573, 582–3, 594, 615, 639, 655, 687, 690, 713, 736, 740, 749
Jurgenson, Pyotr Ivanovich, founder of music publishing firm 70n

Kachalov, Vasily Ivanovich, actor 639
Kachenovsky, G. P., friend of Morolyov 366
Kachenovskaya, wife of G. P. Kachenovsky 637
Kajanus, Robert, Finnish conductor 463
Kal, Professor Alexey Fyodorovich 553, 624, 685
Kalafati, Vasily Pavlovich, composer 61, 756
Kalantarova, Olga Kalantarovna, pianist 102, 213, 292, 329, 612–13, 616–19, 663–4, 666
Kalashnikov Quay 671, 682, 738
Kale 205
Kaliningrad, *see* Königsberg
Kalinkin Bridge 659
Kalinovsky, acquaintance of Alpers family 87, 94, 121
Kamennoóstrovsky Prospect 93, 140, 222, 465, 370, 373, 503, 514, 689, 716
Kamenny Island 93n, 365, 370, 519, 533, 711, 713, 715
Kamenska 165
Kamyshanskaya, V. M., student 92–4, 96, 108–9, 125, 131, 148
Kankarovich, Anatoly Isaakovich, conductor 5, 6n, 14, 18, 36, 52, 62, 86, 90, 131–2, 134, 142, 159; drafts complaint about Tcherepnin, 26–7; plays percussion with SP in student orchestra, 53–4; appointed summer conductor in Voronezh, 99–10; proposes programming SP's Sinfonietta and E minor Symphony there, 100, 104–5; instructs SP in conducting technique, 127–8; appointed Director of Simferopol Institute of Music, 201, 208; proposes including *Dreams* in Pavlovsk Summer Concerts, 208; experiences disappointment in career, 436
Kant, Immanuel xiv
Kapitolovo 748
Kapustina, Sofia (Sofochka) 224, 227
Karagichev, Boris Vasilievich 492
Karatygin, Vyacheslav Gavrilovich, composer and critic 494, 507, 572, 750, 754; history, 72n; considers Myaskovsky already dated, 72; hosts Yovanovich playing SP's works, 85; offers opinion that SP is talented but lacks restraint, 86; plays own compositions at *Apollon* concert, 155; and at Bestuzhev

INDEX   809

Institute, 549; writes glowing review of 1st Piano Concerto in *Apollon*, 263; is authorized to propose repertoire for Free Theatre, 468; SP reveals he has become conservative and likes Tchaikovsky, 485; congratulates SP on 2nd Piano Concerto, 489; writes favourable review in *Rech*, 491, 524, 592; hosts private play-through of 2nd Piano Concerto, 498; approves 'Legenda', 553; brackets SP with Scriabin, Stravinsky and Myaskovsky as modern classics, 593; effect resonates, 594–5, 606; praises SP's recital for Contemporary Concerts, 598; invites SP to illustrate lecture, 598, 606–7; and at Bestuzhev Institute, 631; brokers invitation for SP to meet Gessen, 612, 616; proposes SP's participation in revived Evenings of Contemporary Music, 634; suggests Bessel as publisher for Ballade, 655, 679–80; congratulates on Concerto exam performance, 661, 664; adds weight to pressure on Ziloti to programme Sinfonietta, 665, 667; Diaghilev nominates to act as go-between with Gorodetsky, 707, 711, 715–16, 736; proposes Ozarovskaya as alternative provider of ballet subject, 772
Karelia 165n
Karelian Isthmus xxvii
Karneyev, Lev (Lyova, Simpoponchik) 170–71, 409, 414–15, 494, 504, 519–21, 712, 755
Karneyev family 170–71, 226–7, 350–51, 519–21
Karneyeva, Lidia 170–71, 177, 190, 192, 224–7, 229–30, 239–40, 277, 285, 304, 310, 312, 314, 323, 327, 350–51, 358, 360, 366, 370, 377, 386, 391–4, 399–400, 412, 407, 409, 413–16, 419, 431, 442, 459, 465, 487–91, 493–4, 501, 504, 506–7, 510, 513, 516–17, 528, 535, 571, 579, 658, 712, 755, 767
Karneyeva, Zoya 170–71, 177, 190, 192, 224, 227, 229–30, 239–40, 277, 285, 291, 304, 310, 312, 323, 337, 350, 358, 360, 366, 370, 377, 386, 391–4, 399–400, 402, 409, 413–16, 419, 431, 442, 459, 465, 487, 488–91, 493–4, 504, 505–7, 510, 513, 516–19, 521, 522, 528, 535, 658, 712, 755, 767
Karnovich, composition student 362, 387, 394, 404; Variations for Orchestra, 362, 378, 380, 387, 390, 392, 394, 396–7, 403–4
Karrs 722
Karsky, Alyosha 301, 309
Kaspari, photographer 270, 296, 299, 336, 346, 354, 363, 498
Kavos sisters 311, 571
Kazachenko, Grigory Alexeyevich, composer 485, 487
Kazan 340, 341

Keck, copyist 82
Kedrov, Nikolay Nikolayevich, singer and teacher 263
Keller, piano student 664, 673
Kellomyaki 165n, 222–3
Kerch 347
Kerensky, Alexander Fyodorovich, Prime Minister of Provisional Government xiii
Kerzin, A. M. 211n
Kerzina, Maria 211, 211n
Kessel, friend of Meshchersky family 517
Kessler, Joseph, Etude in F minor 50
Khaikin, Dr 172
Khantsin, Isabella, student 330, 347, 358
Khariton, piano student 627, 660
Kharkov, Ukraine 298, 305, 470, 484, 700
Kherson, piano student 659
Khessin, Alexander Borisovich, conductor 204, 206–8, 264, 404
Khodanskaya, Princess 69
Khrenova, Mlle, friend of Natalya Meshcherskaya 744–5, 761
Kiev 65, 165n, 272n, 297, 360, 507, 527, 641, 683, 742
Kilshtedt, Maria Grigorievna, poet 58n
Kimont-Yatsyna, Marzellina Ivanovna, piano professor 734
Kind, Anna Karlovna 267n
Kind, Serafima, piano student 636, 644, 656, 659, 662
Kirlian, Conservatoire student 139, 143, 152, 153, 162, 201
Kirochnaya Street (home of Meshchersky family) 757
Kirov Theatre, Leningrad 24n, 272n, 539n
Kirsch, Nina, acquantaince 274
Kishinskaya, Varvara (Varya) 375
Kishinsky family, friends of Meshchersky and Ruzsky families 375
Kislovodsk 106, 108, 223–4, 237, 241–2, 306, 445, 623, 650, 653, 669, 708, 713, 716–17, 723–33, 736–7, 747, 757; chess tournament, 723–4, 727; war families charity concert in Kursaal, 725–7, 734
Kislovodsk Express 470, 505
Kleinmichel, Countess Maria: dacha, 519; *Memories of a Shipwrecked World*, 519n
Klimov, Mikhail Georgevich, conductor 27, 42, 294, 309, 313–14, 316
Kling, Otto 704, 704n, 705
Klingman, Yelena Maximovna (16A) 249, 251, 273, 281, 285–90, 309, 318, 320, 382, 390, 514, 539, 552–3, 631, 637
Knipper-Chekhova, Olga 435n
Kobylyansky, Alexander Nikolayevich, piano

and conducting student 94, 185, 206, 598, 750; Etudes, 750
Kokovtsov, Count Vladimir Nikolayevich, Prime Minister 318
Kolakovsky, violin professor 199
Kolomiitsev, conducting student 26, 131, 132, 159, 185
Kolomyagi 491
Komarov, Colonel, relation of Meshchersky family 728–9
Komarovo, see Kellomyaki
Kommissarzhevsky Theatre 22
Kommissarzhevskaya, Vera Fyodorovna, actor 22n
Königsberg 421
Konshin family 370, 509, 532, 536, 568, 579, 639
Konshin, Alexey Vladimirovich, banker 199, 246, 272, 286, 318, 356, 598, 718
Konshina, Lilia Alexeyevna 230, 536
Konshina, Tata 311, 536
kopecks on railway lines 638
Koposova-Derzhanovskaya, Yekaterina Vasilievna, wife of Vladimir Derzhanovsky, singer 470, 544, 546, 589
Korguyev, violin professor 401
Korsak, Maria Pavlovna 77, 79, 85, 114, 262, 276, 281, 298, 370, 375, 410, 524, 569, 575, 639, 757, 774
Korsak, Vladimir Yevstatievich, St Petersburg Chief Public Prosecutor 77n, 138, 774, 781
Kotova, acquaintance 757
Kotte, E., woodwind professor 289, 316
Koussevitzkaya, Natalya Konstantinovna 553
Koussevitzky, Sergey Alexandrovich xii, xiii, xvii, 150, 153n, 190, 192, 206–8, 310, 319, 321–2, 324–5, 326–7, 329, 333, 527, 547, 549, 551–3, 566, 590, 595, 601, 775–6
Koussevitzky Concert Bureau 491
Kozlov 720–21
Kozlova, Music Studio pupil 741, 747, 752, 766, 787
Kozlova, M.G., musicologist and editor xixn, xxiin
KR, see Romanov, Grand Duke Konstantin Konstantinovich
Krasavitsa, Lake 229
Krasnoye Selo 707
Krasny Bridge 288
Krasovksaya, singing student 320
Kreisler, conducting student 515, 548, 568, 570, 581, 586, 600, 605–6, 613–14, 662–3, 668, 784, 795
Kremlin, The 770n
Krestovsky Island 93n, 277, 365, 526, 533
Kreutzer, conducting student 619–21, 623–4, 631–2, 638, 642

Kreutzer, Leonid Davydovich, pianist and conductor 50
Krivosheina, Nina, see Meshcherskaya, Nina Alexeyevna
Kronstadt 184, 221–2, 262
Kruglovsky, singing student 245, 249, 260, 265–6, 269, 306, 335
Kryukov Canal 329, 355
Kryzhanovsky, Ivan Ivanovich composer, critic and doctor 42, 42n, 155, 211, 598, 607, 685, 687
Kuchinskaya, cousin of Nina Meshcherskaya 791, 794
Kuchinsky (Kuchinskaya's newly-wed husband) 791, 794
Kudrin, chess player 102
Kuklin, singing student 330–31
Kupechesky Bank, Moscow 720
Kuokkale xxvii, 165n, 393, 406–7, 413, 416, 468–9, 485–6, 497, 517
Kuprin, Alexander Ivanovich, writer: The Duel, 357
Kursk 420
Kursk Station, Moscow 469
Kuskova, piano professor 621, 645, 662–3
Kuznetsova, piano student 161, 216
Kuzovkova, Conservatoire student 89, 94, 110, 114, 139–41, 143
Kvisisano restaurants 334, 334n, 417

Ladoga, Lake 222n, 256n
Lamm, Olga Petrovna, writer xv
Lamm, Pavel Alexandrovich, pianist, musicologist and writer 589
Landsman (Terioki) 392–3, 397
Large (Bolshoy) All–Union Symphony Orchestra 602n
Lasker, Emanuel, chess grandmaster 5, 37–8, 506, 628, 640–42, 644, 646–7, 649–50, 652–4, 657, 665, 669, 670–72, 675, 678, 679
Lasker, Mme 647, 675
Lapina, piano student 377
Lausanne, Switzerland 450, 453–4
Lavrov, Nikolay Stepanovich, piano professor 329, 336, 353–5, 596, 643, 664, 673, 770
Lazerson, violin student 248
Lebedev, chess player 20
Lebedintseva, friend of SP's mother 355, 443, 445–6
Ledink, violin student 148
Leiner's restaurant 308, 323, 328, 338, 341, 369, 372
Leipzig 688
Lemba, Artur Gustavovich, pianist and composer 24, 50, 53–4, 58, 67, 619, 663–4; Piano Concerto, 53–4; Symphony, 80

Leningrad, siege of 5n
Leningrad Conservatoire 148n
Lenkina, Zinaida (Zina), singing student 290, 308–9
Leonov, chance train travelling companion 323
Lermontov, Mikhail Yurevich: "'Tis dreary and gloomy' 411
Leschetitskaya, Mme, singing professor 286, 408
Leschetitsky, Theodor (Fyodor) Osipovich, pianist and teacher 4n, 5n, 408n
Leskov, Nikolay Semyonovich, writer: *At Daggers Drawn*, 7, 7n; 'Lady Macbeth of the Mtsensk District', 7n; *Cathedral Folk*, 8, 8n
Lesnoy 505
Levashovo 312, 506
Levenfisch, Grigory Yakovlevich, chess player 583, 584
Levitskaya, Yelena, Conservatoire student 201, 204, 220
Liège, Belgium 424, 723
Lieven, Baron, *see* Lieven-Orlova, Magda Gustavovna
Lieven-Orlova, Magda Gustavovna, writer 218n, 289, 573–4; *Maddalena*, 218–9, 289n
Ligovo 357–8
Lind, Jenny 382n
Lintvaryova, Voida Alexandrovna, piano student 263, 290, 305, 537
Lipinskaya, Conservatoire student, friend of Lidia Struve 593, 600, 611, 620, 625, 631, 638, 734
Lipyansky, violin student 399
Lisi Nos, seaside resort 222
Liszt, Franz 4n, 315; WORKS: *Mephisto Waltz*, 152, 164, 187, 338, 760; 'Feux Follets', 186; *Les Préludes*, 191, 566; Sonata in B minor, 212–13, 216, 227; Piano Concerto No. 1 in E flat, 363, 377, 378; Piano Concerto No. 2 in A, 373, 528–9, 532, 536–8, 542, 566, 648; *Mazeppa*, 368; transcription of Overture to Wagner's *Tannhäuser*, 368, 574–5, 579, 581, 596–8, 605, 608, 610, 612, 617–18, 620, 627, 648, 651, 653–6, 658–61, 666, 668, 674, 683, 739–40
Littauer, Mme, friend of Meshchersky family 788–9
Littauer, Lt Vladimir (Mme Littauer's son) 793–4
Litvak, piano student 255
Livshitz, Raissa Mikhelovna (Raya), piano student 216, 251, 305, 371
Lodi, Zoya Petrovna, singing professor 781
Łódź, Poland 782–3
Lokhvitskaya, Mirra, poet 90n
Lomanovskaya, singing student 95
London 433–42, 497, 504, 580, 664, 668, 673, 679, 683, 686–9, 703–9, 711–2, 721, 734, 752: Charing Cross Station, 433, 437; River Thames, 433, 437, 709; Clifton Gardens, 434, 704; Oxford Street, 435; Regent Street, 435; Drury Lane Theatre, 435, 437–8; Piccadilly, 436; Hyde Park, 436–7, 708; Westminster Abbey, 437; St. James's Park, 437; Houses of Parliament, 437; London Zoo, 438; Morton Hotel, 439; Paddington Station, 439–40; Cecil Hotel, 706; Savoy Hotel, 707; Kew Gardens, 708–9; Richmond Park, 709; boxing match, 708
Lotto 338, 575
Louis XIV of France 222n, 443
Lourié, Artur Sergeyevich, composer, futurist xxii
Lucerne, Switzerland 449, 458–9
Luga 221, 690, 719
Lukich, Esper 224
Luna Park, St Petersburg 419, 419n 466
Lunacharsky, Anatoly Vasilievich, writer, critic, politician, Bolshevik cultural commissar xiii
Lungernsee, Switzerland 457
Lützen, battle of 694n
Lvov, student composer 203, 206
Lvov (town) 734, 743, 759, 790
Lyadov, Anatoly Konstantinovich, composer and teacher xxi, xxii, 5, 7, 10, 14–16, 51, 57n, 61, 117, 149, 168, 189, 191, 193, 208, 248, 368n, 754, 776–7; SP composes Sonata in C minor (Sonata No. 5 of juvenilia) for AL, 47, 117; conversations about chess, 52–3, 53n, 193; AL's anger over SP's productions for Form exam, 90–91; SP remains as Practical Composition pupil, 96; SP revises Sonata No. 2 (juvenilia) for AL, 119, 119n, 189; SP's student quartet provokes fury, 126; successor more acceptable, 126; further lessons with AL abandoned, 130, 137; resignation of AL with other professors in 1905, 188n, 368n; member of Belyayev Concerts board, 410, 419; is given jubilee concert, 546, 550, 552, 558; SP visits grave, 745; WORKS: *Apocalypsis*, 362; *The Bride of Messina*, 550; *Polonaise*, 552, songs, 550, 552
Lyapunov, Sergey Mikhailovich, composer, pianist, teacher xxii, 148n, 343, 532, 534, 536, 552, 582, 596, 619, 620–21, 643, 662–4, 764, 771
Lyashchenko, Yekaterina Ippokratovna, friend of SP's parents 87, 94, 102
Lyuban 323
Lyuts, chess player 61
Lyutseradsky, G. I., architect 466n
Lyutz, Kira 301

Lyutz, Klara 301
Lyutz, Maria (Marusya) 287, 301, 304, 307–8, 313
Lyutz family 301, 304, 366

Magalov, Nikita, pianist 751n
Magalov, Prince 772–3
Magalova, Princess Varvara Nikolayevna, sister of Boris Bashkirov 738–42, 751, 769–70, 772–3, 777, 778
Makovsky, Sergey Konstantinovich, poet, art critic and gallery owner 85, 85n, 552, 553n
Maksutov, Admiral Prince Pavel 275n
Maksutov, Prince Dmitry Pavlovich (Mitya) 23
Maksutova, Princess Alexandra 275, 275n
Malinskaya, piano student 103, 114–15, 121, 161, 618, 659, 661
Malko, Nikolay Andreyevich, conductor 24, 27, 54, 70, 765
Malmgren, Yevgraf, cellist 26
Maly Theatre, St Petersburg 40, 156, 345, 357, 379–80, 535, 775–6
Malyutin, Boris Yevgenievich, chess player, President of the St Petersburg Chess Society 15, 18, 35–6, 59, 574
Mandelbaum, singing student 293–4, 320, 419, 625, 627–8, 630
Mandelshtam, Osip Emilievich, poet xxii
Mardzhanov (Mardzhanishvili), Konstantin, actor and director 464n, 540n, 554–5, 590
Maria Ivanovna, London friend of Andreyev family 434, 704, 708–9
Mariinsky Theatre, St Petersburg 41, 68, 204, 218, 226n, 298, 316, 339n, 342, 344, 357, 368n, 466, 569–70, 585, 655, 677, 727
Mariotte, Edmé, scientist 506
Markus, Nadezhda Eduardovna, sister-in-law of Boris Zakharov 224
Markus, Vladimir Eduardovich (Volodya), brother-in-law of Boris Zakharov 224
Marly, Château de 222n
Marshall, Frank, chess grandmaster 640, 642–4, 646, 649, 652, 654, 657, 675, 679
Maslova, Tatyana, Conservatoire student 566
Massine, Leonid Fyodorovich, dancer and choreographer 705, 757n
Maupassant, Guy de: 'Pierre et Jean' 337
Mauvais Pas, path across glacier, Switzerland 451–2
Medem, Alexander Davydovich, composer and pianist 41, 50, 67, 86, 155, 214, 510, 619, 655, 664
Medtner, Alexander Karlovich, conductor and pianist 212n
Medtner, Nikolay Karlovich, composer and pianist 149, 333, 367, 535, 585, 591, 593, 595, 631, 773; WORKS: 'Fairy Tale' (unidentified),

7, 93, 117, *Sonaten-Triade*, 149, 'Fairy Tale' Op. 6, 160
Merhwolf, Rudolf, composition student 203, 203n, 206, 372
Meingard, Conservatoire student 16
Melik-Pashayev, Alexander Shamilievich, conductor 269n
Melnikov, winner of Kislovodsk chess tournament 727
Mendelssohn (Mendelssohn-Bartholdy), Felix: *Meeresstille und glückliche Fahrt*, 27; Piano Trio in D minor, 341; Prelude and Fugue in E minor, 113–14, 118; *Etude* in B minor, 365
Mengelberg, Willem, conductor 295, 572
Menuhin, Yehudi 157n
Merezhkovsky, Dmitry Sergeyevich 524
Meriin, Vera, Conservatoire student 244, 308
Merimanova, piano student 133–4, 158
Meshcherskaya, Natalya Alexeyevna (Talya) 375, 478, 480, 495, 498, 500, 503, 510–12, 517, 522, 610, 614, 628, 632, 665, 723, 725, 727–9, 731, 737, 752, 770, 780, 789–91, 793–4; more attractive than her sister, 279; good musician and artist, 472–3; nocturnal excursion to Tartar village near Gurzuf, 474–5; sketches SP's portrait, 479; close relations with SP based on music, 636, 724; birthday and name-day, 732; 'Capriccio' dedicated to, 741, 758, 766, 785; visits SP's home, 743; works as nurse, 744–5, 747, 756, 758, 761
Meshcherskaya, Nina Alexeyevna 417, 431, 436, 447, 478, 482, 490, 495–6, 501, 503, 510, 512, 516, 522, 574, 632, 795–6; father leaving home, 150n, SP's initial attraction to, 363, 375, 407, 472, 499; SP's stay in Gurzuf, 472–83, 499; NM's previous attachment to Zaitsev, 473, 477, 481, 487, 494–5, 497, 500, 508, 517, 527, 724, 734, 744; SP dedicates 'Rigaudon' to, 473–4, 498, 500, 785; hot and cold relations, 475, 477, 480, 481, 483, 486, 491, 502, 504, 508–9, 517–18, 540, 575, 592, 606, 628, 665, 713, 724, 726, 728–30, 732, 736, 737, 742, 744, 745, 747, 751, 755–6, 761, 770, 775, 779, 784–5, 787–90; 'decree', 732–3, 735, 736, 741, 744–6; paints portrait of SP, 476; NM's wrong notes in Rachmaninov song, 479; drinks whisky, 481; SP sends postcard addressed to 'Fyaka', 506, 508; NM as card player, 508–9, 523, 610, 628, 653, 669, 724, 730; SP as elephant and NM as pug, 613; NM's absence abroad, 521; SP sees off at station, 524; NM returns, 606; SP's stay in Kislovodsk, 650, 669, 690, 723–33; NM's absence in Berne, 665, 713, 724; SP plays duets with, 730, 732, 741, 745, 776–7, 780, 791; *The Ugly Duckling*, 737–8; NM pro-

vides libretto for, 740–41; visits SP's home, 742–3; Anna Zherebtsova assesses SP's relationship with, 752; SP dreams of, 745, 760–61; NM's former attachment to Erdely, 765–6; inability to be a nurse, 774; asks SP to reduce frequency of visits, 781–2; discusses change of pronominal status, 783, 794–6; sits between her father and SP's mother at concert, 785; SP dismisses thoughts of marriage 786; death of Mme Littauer, 788, 793; lung illness diagnosed, 790; SP buys birthday present, 793–4

Meshcherskaya, Vera Nikolayevna 495, 508, 512, 524, 572, 613, 636, 665, 723, 725, 727, 732, 755–6; unhappy marriage, 150n; SP plays duets with, 350, 474, 482; SP does not care for, 375; SP's pen portrait of, 472; ill health, 472, 545; dictatorial tendencies, 473, 476–7, 480–82, 517, 669, 730–31; sister, 473; niece Vera, 473; nephew Sasha (cadet), 479–80, 481, 483–4, 669; snobbishness, 480, 725n; request to play 'Rigaudon', 500; SP dedicates 'Capriccio', 507, 509, 510–11, 545, 557, 622, 628; removes dedication and rededicates to Natalya Meshcherskaya, 741, 758, 766; VM gives advice on *Tannhäuser*, 610; comments on composer as pianist, 610; praises SP's conducting of *Figaro*, 632; concern for husband's safety, 724; SP makes name-day donation to charity, 737; VM visits SP's home, 743; asks for daughter to lunch with Prokofievs, 744; works with M. G. Prokofieva in field hospital, 779

Meshchersky, Alexey Pavlovich 375, 495, 500, 502, 515, 523–4, 766; leaves wife, 150n; industrialist, 472; the 'Russian Ford', 477n; suffers migraine attacks, 475; amused by 'Fyaka' nickname, 508; affection for SP, 512, 732; asks SP to play from *Kitezh*, 639, 732; invites to lunch and excursion, 665; views on conduct of war, 718–19; death feared by wife, 724; becomes director of International Bank, 725n; sits with SP's mother at concert, 786–5; brings back war trophies, 791

Meshchersky family 246, 289, 294, 311, 347–8, 350, 363, 370, 374, 407, 409, 410, 467, 508, 510, 523, 524, 526, 569, 606, 613–14, 623–6, 628, 635–6, 639, 646–7, 654, 690, 723, 727, 736, 741, 742, 752, 757, 760, 764–5, 770, 779; dislike of Ruzsky family, 374, 613; invites SP to dacha in Gurzuf, 472–83; apartment in Astoria Hotel, 496, 501, 502, 503, 512; visit to Pivato restaurant and cinema, 512; visit to Crooked Mirror, 516, 522; family's affection for SP, 610; death of relation Col. Komarov, 728–9; Mushka (pet dog), 723

Metelyova, Mme, violinist 55

Meyerhold, Vsevolod Emilievich, theatre director xiii, 539n

Meyerovich, Alfred Berngardovich, pianist 77, 87, 95

Mikhailovsky, war correspondent 730

Mikhailovsky Palace 37n; *see also* Engineers Palace

Mikhelson, Irina Sergeyevna, pianist and teacher 95, 619, 663–4, 677, 770

Mikhelson, pianist 677

Miklashevskaya, Irina, *see* Mikhelson, Irina Sergeyevna

Miklashevsky, piano professor 50, 147, 373

Miliant, Mme, friend of M. P. Korsak 281

Mindlin, piano student 367

Mineralnye Vody 107–8, 392, 722

Minin, Kozma 770n

Mir Isskustva (World of Art) 85n, 598n

Mirolyubov, P. I., former resident of Terioki 170n

Missing Persons Bureau 382, 387, 392

Mitusov, Stepan, librettist 705n

Mizinova, Lika, wife of Alexander Sanin 435n

Moika Canal, St Petersburg 331, 347, 771

Molchanov, singing student 539

Monte Carlo 205, 218, 247, 322, 647, 654

Montenvers, Switzerland 450–51

Monteux, Pierre, conductor 707

Montreux, Switzerland 453

Morenschild, singing student 543, 556, 563, 679

Morolyov, Vasily Mitrofanovich 366, 397, 492, 637, 743; approves of SP's Sonatina, 6; Sonata No. 1 Op. 1 dedicated to, 6n, 181; intimate form of address used in correspondence, 15; chess-playing and piano-playing sessions at Sontsovka, 180–81; visits St Petersburg, 194; nicknames SP's early piano pieces 'doggies', 235n; invests in SP's stock exchange venture, 273, 278; wants to withdraw investment, 334; SP visits Nikopol with Max Schmidthof, 299–300; SP wants to send VM 2nd Sonata, 568

Morskaya Street, St Petersburg 141, 160, 276, 289, 298, 322, 330–31, 334, 344, 347, 354, 496, 502, 505, 541–2, 548, 594, 615, 628, 670, 679, 733, 739, 747, 764, 786

Moscow Arts Theatre 435n, 464n, 634, 639

Moscow Conservatoire 70n; Maly Zal, 587

Moscow Gazette 525

Moscow Philharmonia 396, 399, 406

Moscow recital by SP 470, 522, 530, 532, 536–7, 544, 547–8, 581, 583, 586, 587–90, 597

Motseikevich, piano student 331, 377–8, 393–5, 404

Mozart, Wolfgang Amadeus 272, 315, 319, 367, 502, 585, 605, 679; WORKS: *Don Giovanni*, 217,

459; *The Magic Flute*, 294, 298, 308, 320; *The Marriage of Figaro*, 583, 592–3, 595, 596–7, 621–30, 632–3, 636; Symphony No. 40 in G minor, 243; Sonata in C major, 328, 331, 334; Variations for Piano, 328, 335, 339, 348, 574, 574n, 596, 608, 611, 613–14, 618–19; Fantasia in C minor, 367–8, 574n, Sonata (unidentified), 744

Mravinsky, Yevgeny Alexandrovich 269n

Muftel, amateur composer 332–3

Muir & Merrilees, department store 423, 423n

Muizhel, Viktor Vasilievich, writer 374–5

Mukhin Hotel, St Petersburg 150

Müllers, piano shop in Moscow 587

Munich International Exhibition 473n

Music Drama Theatre, St Petersburg 525, 535, 545

Music Hall, St Petersburg, *see* People's House

Music Studio 650, 667, 733–4, 736–7, 739, 741, 743, 746, 752, 758, 762, 766, 778, 781–2, 787

Musical Contemporary, journal 773n

Musorgsky, Modest Petrovich 429; WORKS: *Boris Godunov*, 40n, 272n, 437–8, 521, 525, 589n, 740; *Khovanshchina*, xxvii, 428–9, 589n; *Pictures from an Exhibition*, 553

Muzyka (*Music*), Moscow music magazine 212, 371–2, 410, 492, 516, 536, 548, 581, 586, 607, 648, 687, 789

Myaskovsky, Nikolay Yakovlevich (Kolya, Kolechka, Myaskusha, Nyamochka) xii, xv, xvii, 61, 94, 102, 114, 115, 126, 130, 161, 163, 165, 181, 192, 216, 377, 395, 411, 431, 475, 484, 485, 491, 493, 500, 527, 529, 541, 543, 547, 554, 586, 601, 621, 628, 643, 690, 759; critical of SP's Sonatina, 6; approves 3rd Sonata (juvenilia), 9; criticizes SP's 4th Sonata (juvenilia), 25; hears SP's exam, 50; advises SP to change to Yesipova, 72, 72n; attends Court Orchestra play-through of SP's E minor Symphony, 82–5; discouraging about SP's plan to unify his Sinfonietta, 99; is SP's main musical correspondent over summer, 104; praises SP's Winkler Etudes, 119; advises SP not to publish F minor Sonata as Op. 1, 156; praises SP's pianism, 189, 590; helps with rehearsals and proof-reading of *Dreams*, 190, 207; proclaims SP's merits in Moscow leading to acceptance of *Dreams* and *Autumnal*, 212; transcribes *Dreams* for 4 hands, 322, 339, 345; approves play-through of Bassoon Scherzo, 275; finds SP's use of parallel ninths superior to Scriabin's, 275; approves SP's embryonic 2nd Piano Concerto, 275–6; rejects SP's idea for 3rd Piano Concerto, 297; criticism of SP's conducting ability, 320, 345, 404, 542, 590; praise for conducting, 630, 677; proof-reads SP's Opp. 4 and 11, 405; approves 'Rigaudon' and 'Legenda', 464; gives good advice on SP's 2nd Piano Concerto, 486, 488; makes corrections to score, 487, 494, 625; help requested in orchestrating *Maddalena*, 466–8, 502–5, 513, 681; invites SP to meet Saradzhev to discuss *Maddalena*, 492, 495, 681; pursues Derzhanovsky about *Maddalena*, 670; consulted by SP on *Maddalena*, 499; and on his review of Sabaneyev's compositions, 499, 501; approves revised Andante of SP's 1st Piano Concerto and Deshevov Scherzo, 513; proof-reads SP's 2nd Sonata, 522; approves 'March' from Op. 12 and 'The Boat Cast Off', 522; suggests *The Idiot* as opera subject, 525; defends SP's system of scoring transposing instruments to Jurgenson, 544; SP plays 'Capriccio' to NM, 546; opinion of SP's *Sarcasms*, 580–81; praises SP's *Ballade*, 587; takes SP to meet Yavorsky, 587–8; argues against SP's changes to *Ballade*, 645; discouraging on SP's decision to play 1st Piano Concerto in graduation exam, 654–5; congratulates SP on performance, 661, 664; incredulity at SP's invitation to appear at IRMS concert, 750; opinion of Strauss's *Salome*, 22; offended by Lyadov's criticism 90–91; admires Rimsky Korsakov's Sinfonietta, 99; writes article as 'Misanthrope' in *Muzyka* lambasting conservatism of Belyayev Concerts, 371–2, 410, 648; Ziloti's anger at article, 665, 667; admiration for Shaposhnikov, 378; receives letter from SP about *Petrushka*, xxii, 429, 436; considers *Sacre du printemps* innovative, 464; disagrees with SP's assessment of *The Bells*, 557; views on Debussy, 573; finds Tcherepnin's *Red Mask* thin on material, 687; SP criticizes NM's 7th Sonata, 48; exam results, 52–3; composes symphony in parallel with SP, 56–7, 59, 65; accompanies SP to Evenings of Contemporary Music, 63; SP regards NM as supremely literate musician but not great composer, 65; close friendship with SP inhibited by age difference, 111; but SP extremely attached to, 112; forms musical triumvirate with SP and Zakharov, 169; sketches for 2nd Symphony found acceptable by SP, 184; SP plays duet version of *Alastor*, 322; NM accepts SP's suggestions, 340; SP advocates Pavlovsk performance of *Alastor*, 352; SP plays 4-hand version of NM's 1st Symphony to Aslanov, 364, 398; not willing to play NM's Cello Sonata in Moscow, 470; praises NM's

Cello Sonata, 587; and songs, 589–90; SP and NM play 4-hand version of NM's 1st Symphony to Aslanov, 648, 680–1; SP writes impressions of *Alastor*, 780–81; SP's 'Carnaval' (juvenilia) dedicated to NM, 235; 1907 early piano piece dedicated to NM used for revised 'Despair', 310; NM presents SP with Rimsky-Korsakov's *Orchestration*, 366; SP dedicates 'Mazurka' from Op. 12 to NM, 447–8, 504; performance of 1st Symphony in Pavlovsk, 683–5; NM studied harmony with Kryzhanovsky, 41n; appeals to Glazunov for recommendation to publish songs, 70; works performed at Evenings of Contemporary Music, 72, 193, 597, 634; Karatygin's view that NM's music already dated, 72–3; regarded by SP as particular expert on symphonic music, 110; is first St Petersburg composer to be accepted in Moscow ,182–4; regarded there as oracle, 212; has songs accepted by RME, 182; letter-writing style similar to Tchaikovsky's 245; dedicates *Alastor* to SP, 276; revised version of *Maddalena* dedicated to NM, 521, 522; described as modern classic by Karatygin, 593; 2nd Symphony rejected by RME, 637; included with SP in Court Orchestra's series of Petrograd composers, 756; *Alastor* performed by Koussevitzky, 775; ill health, 11, 14, 16; lack of interest in women, 133, 133n; no other interests except music, 175; plays vint, 138, 246, 262, 607, 610, 622; plays bridge 528, 580; visits Zakharov in Terioki, 174–5; SP tries to interest NM in Sokol, 186; NM acquires new piano, 274; introduced to Max Schmidthof, 274; likely to be conscripted as former officer, 715; SP's concern for his safety, 728; reassured, 731, 748; NM posted to Peremyshl, 769; then to Lvov, 780; NM's sisters, 728; WORKS: Piano Sonata No. 1 in D minor, 3n, 4, 544, 745, 773, 776; Piano Sonata No. 2 in F sharp minor, 749; Piano Sonata in one movement (1907), 3n, 6; Piano Sonata No. 3 in A flat, 48; Piano Sonata in E minor (1905), 3, 4; 'Flofion' (12 Miniatures for piano), 3n; Seven Songs on texts by Baratynsky (Meditations), 3n; String Quartet in F, 3n; *Sonata Pittoresque*, 6, 7; Symphony No. 1 in C minor, 56, 62, 65, 352, 637, 648, 680, 681–2, 684–5, 687–8, 713; Symphony No. 2 in F sharp minor, 184, 364, 398–9, 637, 760; Symphony No. 3, 548, 687; Symphony No. 4, 548; Symphony No. 5, 548; Songs 'Circles', 65, 517; 'Blood', 65, 72; Fairy Tale ('Silence'), 211–12; *Alastor*, 276, 297; 322, 352, 637, 775–6, 780–81; piano transcription of *Dreams*, 345; Cello Sonata No. 1, 470, 470n, 522, 544, 587, 589, 654; *Premonitions: Six Sketches to Words by Z. N. Gippius*, 589n; *Two Sketches to Words by Balmont*: 'The Valley Shrine', 'Pan and Psyche', 589n

Nadson, Semyon Yakovlevich, poet: 'Life' 34
Nalbandyan, Ovanes, violin professor 102, 380, 592
Naples, Italy: Menagerie 475
Napravnik, Eduard, composer and conductor 756
Narva-Yiesun, *see* Gungerburg
Narvi 167
Narvsky Gate 357
Narzan Gallery, Kislovodsk 723
Natasha, friend of Lidia Umnova 408
Navy Ball 379, 536
Nearonova, singing student 650, 679, 685, 771
Nemirovich-Danchenko, Vladimir Ivanovich 639n
Nevsky Prospect, St Petersburg 15, 18, 20, 179, 256, 270, 272, 274, 276, 287, 289, 296, 310, 322, 328, 330, 336, 344, 370, 398, 417, 502, 505, 541, 542, 548, 620, 628, 679, 683, 690, 715, 733–4, 736–7, 739–40, 742, 747, 749, 764, 786
Neuchâtel, Lake, Switzerland 454–5, 457
Neuhausen, Switzerland 460
Newcastle, England 695, 702, 703
New Athos, *see* Novy Afon
New Times newspaper 496, 649
Nezlobin, Konstantin Nikolayevich, theatre impresario 540, 540n
Nice, France 530
Nicolai, Otto, composer: *The Merry Wives of Windsor* 36
Niessen, Mount, Switzerland 455–7
Nijinsky, Vaclav, dancer and choreographer 684n, 706
Nikisch, Artur, conductor 47, 655n
Nikolay I, Tsar 293n
Nikolay II, Tsar 263, 771n, 774, 783
Nikolayev, Leonid Vladimirovich, pianist and teacher 129–30, 152, 155, 161, 183, 191, 209, 214, 237, 257, 264, 341, 353–4, 355–6, 366, 373–4, 510, 553, 593, 598, 608–9, 618, 627, 638, 662–3, 676, 734, 746, 750, 764, 766, 788; Violin Sonata, 755
Nikolayevsky Bridge 221, 412, 526
Nikolayevsky Station, Moscow 327, 556
Nikolayevsky Station, St Petersburg 182, 287, 296, 298, 308, 310, 322, 328, 347, 398, 469, 501, 626, 710, 718, 733
Nikolskaya, Ariadna (Radochka), piano student 251–2, 255, 273, 307, 315, 326, 328, 332, 336, 341, 353–4, 355–6, 359–60, 362, 398, 552, 623, 651, 717

Nikolsky Garden 97, 130, 132, 160, 204
Nikolsky Lane 293
Nikolsky Market 93, 109
Nikolsky Square 204
Nikopol 180–81, 296, 299–300, 399
Nikopol-Mariupolsky, shares held by SP 286, 344
Nimzowitsch, Aron, chess master 574, 583–5, 591, 640–42, 644, 646, 649, 652–3
Ninth Wave, card game 172, 792
Nizhny Novgorod 339, 770n
Nodelman, Ira, piano student 14, 16, 20, 23, 67, 113
Nord-Express 424–5
North Donetsk Railway, shares held by M. G. Prokofieva 210
Northern Hotel, St Petersburg 791–2
Northern Journeys, travel agency 690, 692
Norway 668, 696, 698–702
Norwegian fjord 755
Nouvel, Walter Fyodorovich, writer, music critic of *Mir Isskustva* magazine xxii, 40, 156, 190, 489, 494, 498, 704–5, 707, 711, 752, 754, 757–8, 766, 783–4
Novaya Derevnya 93, 109, 163, 222, 413, 519, 533
Novich, Nikolay Ivanovich, Conservatoire General Subjects teacher 46
Novikova, Lyudmila, Conservatoire student 358, 362, 363–4, 366
Novodevichi Monastery and Cemetery, St Petersburg 466, 515, 616
Novorossiisk 54, 55, 220
Novy Afon 55
Nuremberg, Germany 460–61
Nurok, Alfred Pavlovich, critic and concert organizer xxii, 41, 85–6, 155, 190, 214, 489, 494, 498, 585, 591, 593, 598, 713, 783–4

Obolenskaya, Princess 23
Obolonsky High School 375
Obukhovo 376
Odessa, Ukraine 525, 527, 532, 742
Oddolary Cliffs, Crimea 303
Offitserskaya Street, St Petersburg 298, 329, 334, 342, 344, 352–3, 405, 419n
Ogonyok, satirical magazine 514, 514n
Okhta river, St Petersburg 412
Oktyabrsky Station, *see* Nikolayevsky Station
Old Believers, religious sect 7n
Olga Borisovna, Class Inspector 217, 647–8, 650–51, 678
Olshansky, Boris Konstantinovich, Conservatoire student 348
Operetta Theatre, St Petersburg 549
Old Orthography 594n

Orchestra Lamoureux, Paris 432n
Orlov, Alexander Ivanovich, conductor 602–4
Orlov family (Magda Lieven-Orlova) 370, 573–4, 579
Orlov, Nikolay Andreyevich, pianist 325
Orlov, S., conducting student 12, 26, 112, 132, 263
Osipov, Conservatoire mature student 92
Osipova, Conservatoire student 20, 46
Ospovat, piano student 33–4, 78
Ossovskaya, Varvara Alexandrovna, piano professor 115, 117, 122–3, 131, 145, 162, 193, 250, 331–2, 349, 370, 392, 530, 559, 625, 665
Ossovsky, Alexander Vyacheslavovich, music critic and administrator 87, 145, 370, 774; SP introduced by Ruzsky, 79; AO suggests Sinfonietta for Belyayev Concerts, 122–4; offers SP pass to Ziloti concerts, 123; arranges inclusion of Sinfonietta in Sheremetyev Concerts series, 145; SP seeks help with introduction to RME, 153, 157; AO pressed by Nurok to help get 1st Piano Sonata published, 155; offers to introduce SP to Koussevitzky, 207–8, 321; writes letter of recommendation to Jurgenson, 209; advises on submission of *Dreams* and *Ballade* to RME, 333; enlisted to advise board of Belyayev Concerts, 410; praises 2nd Piano Sonata, 547; helps persuade Ziloti to programme SP's Sinfonietta, 665, 667
Ostend, Belgium 709; Kursaal, 709
Ostrovsky, Alexander Nikolayevich, playwright 571
Ouchy, Switzerland 453–4
Ozarovskaya, diseuse, 270, 772
Ozarovsky family, friends of Karatygin 193, 270n
Ozerov, Conservatoire student 593–4
Ozerki, resort town 11, 506, 533

Palachek, Osip Osipovich, singer and opera producer 46, 250, 256, 266, 309, 319, 328, 344, 515, 519, 521–2, 543, 546, 558–9, 561, 565, 593, 599, 629, 630
Palasova, Nyura, Conservatoire student 155, 158, 162, 164–5, 191
Palen, Count Konstantin Ivanovich, chess player 582
Paletik, piano professor 9
Pallada, Russian Navy cruiser 746
Palmer, Christopher, writer xiv, xivn, xviiin
Panayev Theatre, St Petersburg 540n
Pargolovo 312; Pervoye, Vtoroye and Tretye Pargolovo, 506, 506n
Paris, France 416, 419, 421, 425–32, 434–7,

442–5, 448–9, 460, 497, 566, 585, 591, 598, 615, 683, 707, 752; Eiffel Tower, 425, 427, 430–31, 463; Gare du Nord, 425; Champs Elysées, 426; Théâtre des Champs Elysées, xxvii, 426–9, 426n; Boulevard des Italiens, 426; Café de la paix, 427; Louvre, 430; Salon, 430; Bois de Boulogne, 428, 431, 444; St Germain, 444; Gare de Lyon, 445
Parviainen, shares held by SP 286, 286n, 290, 381
Patience, card game 494
Paul I, Emperor of Russia 37
Pavlinov, acquaintance 366
Pavlovnina, Maria, singing student 276, 281, 287, 569, 570
Pavlova, Maria Nikolayevna (Marusya), singing student 200–201, 204, 220–21, 260–61, 267, 377, 404–5, 562, 590
Pavlova, Marina (Marinochka) 545
Pavlovsk 69, 165, 187, 405, 413, 465, 468, 663, 690, 783, 791; 2nd Piano Concerto premiere, 72n; proposed, 351–2, 368, 417; performance preparation, 447, 473, 477; rehearsals, 485–6; general rehearsal and premiere, 487–9, 495–6; reaction compared to graduation concerto performance of 1st Piano Concerto, 661; concerto admired by Bushen, 504, 508, 510; Yesipova does not mention, 513; reviewed by Karatygin, 491, 524, 592; and by N. Bernstein, 599n; Bezrodny cellist in orchestra, 592; *Dreams* proposed by Kankarovich, 208, 220, 233; proposed to Aslanov, 351–2, 368; Aslanov proposes SP as conductor of *Dreams*, 410–11, 417; 1st Piano Concerto performed under Aslanov, 234, 367; reviewed by N. Bernstein, 599, 599n; excursions to Pavlovsk, 363–4, 394–5, 399–400, 412, 635; Myaskovsky 2nd Symphony proposed, 364; SP persuades Myaskovsky to offer *Alastor* to Aslanov, 637; SP plays Myaskovsky's 1st Symphony to Aslanov, 648, 680; rehearsal, 681–2, 683–4; performance, 685; Zakharov engaged for Pavlovsk, 688; SP hears Glazunov 6th Symphony, 417; 3rd Symphony, 714; Robert Kajanus, 463; Tchaikovsky 6th Symphony, 485; Cecilia Hansen, 717; patriotic demonstration disrupts concert, 717
Pavskaya, Nadezhda Vladimirovna 403, 743, 781
Pavsky family 7, 21n, 25, 33, 546
Pavsky, Ivan (Vanya) 7n, 21
Peace of Paris xxvii,
Peer Gynt 699
People's House, St Petersburg 281, 292–3, 466, 569
Peremyshl 769, 769n

Peretz restaurant 276, 289, 292, 295, 306, 319, 328, 335, 347, 360
Persiani, diplomat 354
Pervaya Rota Street, St Petersburg, home of the Prokofiev family 81n, 114, 305, 328, 351, 412, 463–4, 466–7, 485–6, 489–91, 493–4, 496–7, 499, 501–4, 683
Peterhof 222
Peterhof Prospect 659
Petersburg Gazette newspaper 312, 491, 543, 599n, 718
Petersburg Listok newspaper 490, 543
Peterschule 491
Peter The Great (Tsar Pyotr I) 222n
Petrenko, Yelizaveta Fyodorovna, singer 435
Petri, B. E., dancer friend of Glagoleva 80–81, 86
Petrograd 733
Petrodvorets, *see* Peterhof
Petrokokina, Vera Dmitrievna, Class Inspector 286–7, 308, 310, 418, 562
Petronius, Gaius 222n; *Satyricon*, 222
Petrov, oboe student 152, 162
Petrov, Alexey Alexeyevich, music theorist 91, 374, 374n
Petrov brothers, priests and ecclesiastical history teachers 4
Petrova, E. M., acquaintance 9
Petrova, Nadezhda (Nadya), acquaintance 29
Petrovich, Alexey Stepanovich ('Ginger Whiskers'), Conservatoire history teacher 6–7, 43–4, 45–6
Petrovsk 339
Petrovsky Island 526, 533
Petz, singing student 279
Piankova, Mme, friend of Karatygin 772
Piastro, Mikhail (Misha), violin student 8, 17, 20, 23, 55–6, 95, 148, 162
Piastro, Tosya 152, 158, 162
Piastro *père* 55–6, 94
Pigs, dice game 416
Pivato restaurant, St Petersburg 512, 614
Planson, Nadezhda (Nadya) 474–7, 723
Platonov, singing student 43, 62
Poe, Edgar Allan 684n
Pogozhev, Vladimir Petrovich, amateur composer, Director of Imperial Theatres 410, 547
Poincaré, President 437
Poklonnaya Gora 505
Pokrov Church, St Petersburg 92
Poland 756, 758
Polotskaya-Yemtsova, Sofia (Sara) Semyonovna, pianist 553, 598
Polyakov, Miron Borisovich, violin student 259
Ponofidin, Sergey Ivanovich 11

Popova, Antonida (Tonechka), singing student 335–6, 408
Popova, Marina (Marinochka) 460
Popova, Nadezhda (Nadya), Conservatoire student 77, 132, 173
Popova, Yelena, singing student 286, 318, 592
PortoRiche, Georges de, French poet and playwright 218; *L'Amoureuse*, 218n
Pototsky family 138, 585
Pototsky, Stepan Alexandrovich, surgeon 21, 21n, 138
Potseluyev Bridge, St Petersburg 363, 771
Potyomkin, chess player 61
Pouishnoff, Leff, *see* Pyshnov, Lev
Pozharsky, Prince Dmitry 770n
Poznyakovskaya, Natalya, pianist 343, 343n, 377–89, 394, 399, 401, 551, 617, 620, 659, 760
Pravda newspaper 664n
Presnyakov, Valentin Ivanovich, movement teacher and opera director 279, 560
Princes Islands, Turkey xii
Prokofiev, Oleg Sergeyevich, SP's son xiv, xivn, xv, xxn
Prokofiev, Pyotr Alexeyevich, SP's uncle and godfather 9, 12, 16, 21, 23
Prokofiev, Serge Jr, SP's grandson xvi, xvii, xxiv
Prokofiev, Sergey Alexeyevich, SP's father 29, 34, 36, 88; burdened by duties, 9, 12; meets Taneyev with SP, 23; advises SP to postpone public concert activities until after Fugue course, 42; persuades SP to cram academic syllabus, 48; opposes move from Winkler to Yesipova, 71–2, 72n; ill with influenza, 77; insists on SP taking diploma in 1909, 96; gives SP drawing instruction, 103; becomes seriously ill, 154, 157, 172–3; hopes for recovery fade, 164; SP visits hospital, 163; father dies, 167–8, 176–7; SP settles affairs in Sontsovka, 180; Vera Alpers delays writing condolences, 183; father would have been proud of SP's achievements, 190, 613; SP visits grave, 271, 366, 418, 466, 515, 616, 638, 745; SP reads geography books presented by father, 564

PROKOFIEV, SERGEY SERGEYEVICH
Music, general thoughts on, 99; score writing and correcting, xiv, 372, 715, 789; views on transposing instruments, 528, 544; move from Alexander Winkler to Anna Yesipova as piano teachers, 47, 71–2, 71n, 100–103, 169; Yesipova, lessons with, 112–15, 124, 128–9, 137, 143, 154, 160–61, 183–4, 194–5, 212–17, 227–8, 230, 240, 244, 250, 255, 260, 292, 308, 314–15, 328–9, 332, 343–5, 348–9, 354, 360, 365, 367–8, 377–9, 493, 507, 510, 513–14, 524, 530, 532, 535, 540, 550–51, 558, 564, 574–5, 574n, 581, 600–601, 605, 613, 616–17, 621, 658–9, 663, 666; Anatoly Lyadov, dispute with, 89–92; Wagner, 21, 47, 342, 356; Scriabin, meeting with, 150–51; approaches to conductors, 205–8; Schoenberg, 214–15; dreams of Tchaikovsky, 275; meets Koussevitzky, 326–7; breakthrough in conducting technique, 127–8, 186; fired by idea of writing opera and possible subjects, 217–8; plan for series of instrumental concertos, 290; problem of staleness from overstudy, 338; first thoughts on graduation recital programme, 338; respect for traditional forms, 346–7; balance of work between pianist and conductor, 319; composer-pianist, 129, 610–11; improvisation, 444–5; technique of memorizing, 534, 571–2, 574; concentration during performance, 594, 785, 787; contemplates writing comic opera, 585

As conductor 9, 10, 13, 26–8, 36, 39, 51, 125–8, 130, 132, 146, 154–5, 158–9, 184–91, 195, 243–5, 251, 253, 256–7, 259, 261, 262, 264, 266, 271–2, 289–95, 306–8, 310, 312–16, 318–20, 328–30, 332, 334, 337–40, 343–5, 352–3, 357, 362, 378–82, 390, 392–3, 394–7, 399, 401, 403–5, 668, 676–7; complimented by Ziloti and Aslanov, 404; 509, 511–12, 515, 518, 521–2, 523, 528–30, 531–2, 535–43, 550–51, 557–63, 567–71, 582, 585–6, 591–3, 596–7, 599–601, 605, 607–8, 612–18, 622–3, 624–30; potential engagements as conductor, 492, 665, 667, 687–8, 689, 739, 753

Religion and philosophy, feelings on, xiv; morale and general state of mind, 23, 118–19, 124, 143, 187, 205; ambition to excel, 71, 499; father's death, reflections on, 168; fortune-telling, 278; mortality, reflections on, 616; eyesight, fears of losing, 573; militia, fear of being conscripted into, 770–72, 770n, 774, 781–2, 784, 796

Travel, desire to, 528; round the world, 564, 566–7, 579, 616, 782; to America, 433, 442, 454, 478, 593, 616; 436, 449; round Europe, 623, 624, visits to Caucasus, 54–6, 105–8, 181; with Max Schmidthof, 299–305; projected trip with Max Schmidthof, 339, 351, 379; visits to Moscow, 149–51, 152–3, 208–12, 324–8, 469–70, 554–6, 586–90, 602–4; visits to Terioki, 170–76, 177–8, 224–6; visit to Imatra, 256–7; visits to Paris, London, Switzerland, 419–63; to London via Scandinavia, 690–710

Romantic attachments: approach to and need for friendship, 16, 24, 26, 65, 67, 69, 127, 130, 143–4, 389; girls, ranking of, 142–3, 154–5, 158; Morolyov, Vasily, friendship with, 180–81, 194, 299–300; Boris Zakharov, friendship formed with, 168–70, 182, 223; estrangement from, 227–30, 237–40, 250, 267–9; reconciliation with, 387–9, 405–6, 414–16, 431, 446, 465, 469, 487; Musical Letter to, 529, 529n, 532; friendship fully restored, 489–91, 493, 499–500, 502, 504, 507, 510, 513, 546, 559, 568, 638, 666, 688, 690–91, 712–13, 719, 728, 733, 735–6, 738, 746, 750, 757–9, 764, 766–7, 773, 780, 785, 788, 792, 796–7; Maximilian Schmidthof, friendship formed with, 92–3, 108–10; disrupted by hostile letter, 110–12, 123; MS's hostility to Zakharov, 240, 386; reconciliation with SP, 116–18; friendship deepens, 287–8, 294, 296; hostility of Irina Ruzskaya, 297; visit to Caucasus, 299–305, 581; projected longer trips, 339, 351, 379, 742; visit recalled, 471, 722; discussion of Schopenhauer, 366; reasons underlying suicide, 383–6; recognition of true situation, 387; SP dreams of Max, 518; Max described as ruthless, 398; 2nd Piano Concerto dedicated to Max's memory, 401, 559; link with family retained, 402; Max's ring worn in memory, 402; last word of suicide letter, 408; early promise as composer not fulfilled, 411–12; memories of fireside evenings, 597; possible impetus to suicide of reading novel *At the Brink*, 512; Max's grave, 528, 611–12, 691; characteristics shared with Eleonora Damskaya, 684; desire to dedicate symphony to Max, 699

Pastimes: chess 5, 15–16, 18, 20–21, 22, 24–5, 29, 35–8, 52–3, 59–61, 63, 79, 81, 97, 104, 124, 156–7, 164–5, 176, 180, 185, 193, 234, 317, 328, 331, 390, 406, 481–2, 502, 506–7, 516, 526, 540, 559, 574–5, 582–4, 585, 597, 602, 607–9, 615, 618, 622, 628, 630, 634, 637–9; 1914 St Petersburg International Tournament, 640–47, 649n, 652–4, 661–2, 668–9, 655, 657–8, 670–72, 675; article for *Den'*, 676, 679; 689, 705, 723–4, 727, 730, 739, 770, 774, 782; simultaneous matches with José Capablanca, 678–9, 681, 682–3; skating, 142, 252, 254, 260, 270, 273, 275, 278–80, 285, 285n, 288, 291, 298, 311, 366, 562, 567, 571–3, 575, 579, 581–2, 595, 597, 600; croquet, 170, 172, 177, 229, 409, 491, 712; bridge, 199, 281, 500, 525–8, 533, 572, 580, 591, 599, 610, 614, 628, 635–6, 653, 708, 724, 730, 739, 746, 757, 764, 766, 777, 779; vint 112, 138, 151–2, 167, 200, 246, 262, 281, 356, 382, 395, 479–80, 530, 533, 541, 549, 561, 575, 591, 594, 607, 610, 622, 632, 669, 737, 783, 792; lotto, 338; ninth wave, 172, 792; pigs, 416; *Sechsundsechzig*, 441, 478, 481, 500, 572, 579, 581; walks, *passim*; walking sticks, 365, 379, 394, 498, 501, 787;

English, study of, 668–9, 673–4, 679, 681–4, 690, 727, 731, 736, 738–9, 741, 744–6, 748–9, 752, 755, 757, 760, 762–4, 766, 768, 773, 776–8, 781–2, 784, 787, 790, 793–4, 796

WORKS

JUVENILIA

'Doggies' (piano pieces), 28n, 235n; Sonatina in C minor, 6, 7, 9, 280; Piano Sonata No. 2, 6, 119, 181; Piano Sonata No. 3 in A minor, 9, 280; Piano Sonata No. 4, 6, 16, 22, 25, 41; Piano Sonata No. 5, 47; 'Reproach', 28, 30; 'Eastern Song', 28, 30; 'Tragedy', 28; 'Humoresque démoniaque', 28, 30, 30n, 65; 'Carnaval', 235, 310; Violin Sonata in C minor (1903) theme used for cello *Ballade* Op. 15, 242; 'Fête sacrée', 30; 'Processional', 30; 'Entreaties', 41 ; 'Snow', 42, 62, 72, 275, parallel ninths in, 275; 'Scherzo', 62; 'Thou wast meek but dangerous', 90, 94–5; 'Blacksmith, forge chains for my heart', 65; *Undina*, opera, 42, 58; Symphony in E minor, 56–7, 58–9, 62–3, 65, 124, 241, 280, 522, 666, 687; assessment by Glazunov, 67–71; play-through by Court Orchestra, 79–85; proposed Voronezh performance, 100

MATURE WORKS

Op. 1 Sonata No. 1 in F minor, 1909, 6n, genesis, 119, 181; 120, 122; approved by Yesipova and pedalling inserted, 129, 367; 130, 132, 149; first performed in Moscow, 153; 155, 156, 157; dedicated to Morolyov, 181–2; 188; performed at Conservatoire concert, 189–90, 192; 193, 194; accepted by Jurgenson, 208–10; 217, 244; orchestration contemplated, 280; 314, 321, 345, 367, 381, 547, 563, 575, 582; hostile review by Viktor Belyayev, 607; 613, 615, 673, 686, 691, 726, 730

Op. 2 *Four Etudes*, 1909, 117, 119, 120, 122, 129, 130, 149, 153, 155, 156, 193, 209, 211, 213, 215, 279, 325, 485, 488; No. 1 in D minor, 193, 325; No. 2 in E minor, 193; No. 3 in C minor, 211, 213, 215, 522, 525, 553, 589, 598, 603, 613, 617, 618, 620–21; No. 4 in C minor, 122, 129, 193, 279, 485, 488, 549, 575, 604, 727

Op. 3 *Four Pieces for Piano*, 1911, 217, 504, 575; No. 1 'Fairy Tale', 28, 30, 62, 72, 85, 156, 209, 279, 516, 522, 525, 549, 589, 656; No. 2 'Shutka' ('Jest'), 209, 213, 215; No. 3 'March', 209, 213, 215, 504, 522, 589; No. 4 'Phantom', 28, 209, 213, 215

Op. 4 *Four Pieces for Piano*, 1910–12, 217, 291, 310n, 321, 369, 391, 405, 464; No. 1 'Reminiscences', 42, 209, 369; No. 2 'Elan', 42, 209, 323; No. 3 'Despair', 85, 86, 209, 291, 310, 316, 321,

322, 508, 514, 522, 575, 589; No. 4 'Suggestion diabolique', 65, 66, 85, 130, 209, 246, 323, 369, 522, 523, 536, 575, 589, 607; parallel ninths in, 275; choosing title for, 321

Op. 5 Sinfonietta, 1909, revised 1914, 99–100, 103, 117, 122–3, 124, 130, 137, 145, 149, 155, 156, 157, 199, 203, 205, 206–8, 212, 217, 289, 713, 715, 727, 729, 736, 738, 740, 748, 750, 751, 752; proposed Voronezh performance, 104–5; proposed Ziloti performance, 665, 667, 689, 704, 668, 708, 739, 753

Op. 6 *Dreams*, symphonic tableau for orchestra, 1910, 164, 181, 188, 189, 190, 191, 199, 206–7, 208, 210–12, 219–20, 235, 326, 327, 333, 339, 345, 351, 352, 363, 394, 411, 417, 467, 485, 687, 710, 713; chronology, 233; Myaskovsky's 4-hand piano transcription, 322

Op. 7 *Two Poems for female chorus and orchestra*, 1909–10, No. 1 'The White Swan', 137, 144, 145–6, 147, 149, 155, 156, 203–4, 206–7; No. 2 'The Wave', 154, 155, 156, 203–4, 206–7, 217

Op. 8 *Autumnal* for small orchestra 1910, 206–7, 209, 211–12, 219–20, 235, 622, 623, 624, 630

Op. 9 *Two Poems for voice and piano*, 1910–11, No. 1 'There Are Other Planets', 516–7, 545, 623; No. 2 'The Boat Cast Off', 30, 307, 522, 526, 545, 562, 610

Op. 10 Piano Concerto No. 1 in D flat major, 1911–12, xii, 212, 217, 241, 246, 258, 263, 271, 273, 278, 285, 286, 288, 290, 291–2, 295, 296, 300, 310, 312, 319, 321, 323, 324, 325, 326–7, 367, 373, 378, 399, 402, 403, 417, 418, 432, 448, 468, 511, 512, 513, 514, 527, 528, 529, 530, 544, 548, 586, 588, 590, 591, 592, 594, 595–7, 600–606, 613–15, 616, 621–3, 625–8, 632, 636–9, 641, 643, 644–5, 647–51, 653–61, 664, 666, 668–9, 672–4, 676–7, 685–6, 722, 734–5, 749–50, 753, 755–6, 760, 771–2, 783, 795, 796; genesis and first performances, 234–5; analysis of structure, 236–7; piano-orchestra balance, 280; first metropolitan performance, 491, 600, 602–4; submitted to and rejected by Belyayev Concerts Committee, 508–14, 526; dismissed as musical mud, 599; opinion revised, 599n; played to Diaghilev and Monteux, 707; 2-piano reduction, 529

Op. 11 *Toccata* for Piano, 1912, 249, 326, 338, 363, 369, 391, 405, 464, 468, 522, 622, 624, 664, 666, 673, 748

Sans op. Etude contemplated for Op. 12, 464–5, 492

Sans op. March for the Sokol Club, 492, 509, 511, 515, 531, 547–8, 634, 748, 789, 793

Op. 12 *Ten Pieces for Piano*, 1906–13, 330, 374, 381, 446, 447, 492, 555, 707, 735, 736, 738, 739, 741, 745, 758, 768, 785; No. 1 'March', 492, 493, 522, 736, 784–5; No. 2 'Gavotte', 241, 279, 314, 334, 348, 350, 356, 370, 374, 524, 549, 727; dedicated to Boris Zakharov, 194, 315, 448, 755, 786; arr. for harp, 778; No. 3 'Rigaudon', 374, 381, 394, 395, 405, 410, 411, 464, 473–4, 485, 498, 500, 522, 547, 549, 589, 604, 736, 785; No. 4 'Mazurka', 447–8, 503, 504; No. 5 'Capriccio', original dedication to Vera Meshcherskaya, 507, 509, 545, 546, 557; SP tries to convince VM, 622; re-dedication to Natalya Meshcherskaya, 741, 758, 766; unsuccessful at Contemporaries Concert, 785; No. 6 'Legenda', 447, 464, 486, 522, 547, 553, 589, 727, 739, 741, 785; No. 7 'Harp' Prelude in C: as work for harp dedicated to Eleonora Damskaya, 330, 334, 344, 346, 511, 514, 572; as piano piece, 330, 334, 485, 488, 498, 522, 547, 549, 572, 589, 598, 604, 655, 785; ; played to Capablanca, 683; No. 8 'Allemande', 381, 739, 741; No. 9 'Humoresque Scherzo', 505, 548, 739, 741; No. 10 ' Deshevov Scherzo', 447, 505, 507, 513, 748, 777, 783, 784, 785

Op. 12a 'Humoresque Scherzo' for four bassoons, 253, 274, 275, 281, 288, 289, 292, 316, 399, 505, 689

Op. 13 *Maddalena*, opera, 230, 235, 241, 464, 466–8, 469–70, 492, 495, 496, 501, 573–4, 589, 601, 654, 656, 670, 706; impulse to compose, 217; source of libretto, 218–19; scenario, 219; Myaskovky's offer to orchestrate, 502–5; 513, 515, 516–17, 518, 519, 521, 522, 547, 548, 553; considered for production by Free Theatre, 554–6

Op. 14 Sonata No. 2 in D minor, 1912, 242, 279, 295, 315, 324, 326, 334, 350, 374, 470, 501, 502–3, 522–3, 529, 547, 549, 561, 568, 573, 575, 581, 582–3, 590, 594, 605–7, 614, 631–3, 666, 686, 712, 727, 730, 765, 773, 777–8, 780, 781, 785; composition, 234; completion, 241; Jurgenson purchases, 249; SP's particular affection for, 307, 501; dedication to Max Schmidthof, 518; publication, 559; first Moscow performance, 588; performed for 'Contemporaries', 598, 600; performed for Diaghilev, 706

Op. 15 *Ballade* for cello and piano, 1912, composed for N. P. Ruzsky, 241–2, 252, 272, 306, 309, 323, 325, 326, 333–4, 335, 339, 536, 543, 631–4, 637, 647, 674, 713, 736, 737–8, 740; submitted to RME, 363; chosen as chamber music graduation work, 368, 583, 606–7; Moscow recital with Beloúsov 470, 516, 522,

543, 587, 589, 626, 634, 641–3; offered to Jurgenson Moscow, 555, 645; rejected, 654–5; analysis for *Muzyka*, 581; performances for 'Contemporaries', 593, 598, 634; offered to Bessel, 680; withdrawn, 685; offered to Jurgenson Petersburg, 687, 690

Sans op. *A Musical Letter to Boris Zakharov* 529, 530, 532, 691, 740

Op. 16 Piano Concerto No. 2 in G minor, 1913, xii, 72n, 242, 245, 247, 249, 254, 259, 270–72, 275–8, 281, 288, 297, 307, 309, 313, 317, 322, 329, 330, 333, 336, 341, 343, 346–7, 349–52, 355, 357, 360–62, 365–6, 370, 372, 374–5, 378, 380–81, 401, 412, 413, 417, 446–7, 463–4, 466–8, 473, 475–6, 484, 494, 492, 497–9, 507n, 508–14, 524, 526, 529, 547, 566, 591, 599n, 601, 604, 614, 645, 648–9, 661, 677, 680, 735–6, 748, 751, 763–6, 771–2, 777, 792, 795–6; disliked by Maria Grigorievna, 252; SP's fears of never finishing, 257; cadenza, 275–6, 349–50, 355, 362; piano–orchestra balance, 279–80; dominant role of soloist, 359; transparency of orchestration, 359, 361, 370; proposed as work for graduation performance, 368; scale of Intermezzo, 373; premiere at Pavlovsk, 485–9, 491, 600n; reviews, 495–6; cadenzas described as capricious emptying of inkwell, 599n; Diaghilev's vision as a ballet, 706–7; Diaghilev's invitation to perform in Rome, 758; 2-piano reduction, 388, 396, 446, 447, 468, 485, 585, 591

Op. 17 *Sarcasms*, Five Pieces for Piano, 1912–14, 507n, 509, 572, 580–81, 601, 740, 748; orchestral version contemplated, 613, 750; No. 1, 580, 580n, 581, 707; No. 2, 566; No. 3, 509, 581; No. 4, 581

Op. 18 *The Ugly Duckling*, fairy tale for voice and piano, xii, 740–42, 744–50, 761, 767, 773; conception, 737–8; Nina Meshcherskaya's draft libretto received, 740; dedication, 740, 741, 761; interest of A. G. Zherebtsova-Andreyeva, 749, 752; private hummed-through performance, 779–80

Op. 19 Violin Concerto No. 1 in D major (derived from Concertino), xii, 486, 545, 558, 592, 634, 664, 680, 683, 714, 748, 778–9, 783

Sans op. abandoned *Ala and Lolli*, ballet: Diaghilev commission, 707–8, 711, 738; difficulties contacting Gorodetsky, 713–14, 736, 742, 745, 748, 752; initial conception of ballet, 715–16; Diaghilev's telegrams, 752, 758, 766, 783; initial scenario, 753–4; Boris Romanov as choreographer, 757, 766, 768; SP's irritation at collaborators, 764, 767–70, 777; 758–60, 762–71, 774–84, 787, 790, 792–3, 795

Op. 20 *Scythian Suite*, 1914–15, xii, 248n

Op. 22 *Visions Fugitives* for piano 1915–17: 90n

Op. 23 *Five Poems for voice and piano* No. 3 'Trust Me' (Boris Verin), 671n

Op. 24 *The Gambler*, opera, 1915–16, xii, 60n, 539n

Op. 25 Symphony No. 1 ('Classical') 1916–17, xii

Op. 26 Piano Concerto No. 3 in C, 1917–21, 235n, 280n, 343n; first thoughts later shelved, 280–81

Op. 28 Piano Sonata No. 3 in A minor, 1917, 280n

Op. 29 Piano Sonata No. 4 in C minor, 1917, 280n

Op. 29a Andante of Sonata No. 4 transcribed for orchestra, 1934, 280n

Op. 33 *The Love for Three Oranges*, opera, 1919, 272n, 539n

Op. 37 *The Fiery Angel*, opera, 1919–27, 60n

Op. 81 *Semyon Kotko*, opera, 1939, 589n

Op. 82 Piano Sonata No. 6 in A, 1939–40, 589n

Op. 87 *Cinderella*, ballet, 1940–44, 589n

Op. 91 *War and Peace*, opera, 1941–52, 589n

Sans op. uncompleted *Landscape* 727, String Quartet, 751

Autobiography xix–xi, xx, 6n, 13n, 53n, 60n, 72n, 78n, 155n, 281n, 537; *Soviet Journal*, 1927, xiv, xx; other writings (short stories), xiv, xx

Prokofiev, Svyatoslav Sergeyevich, son xi–xvi, xvii, xxiv

Prokofieva (née Codina), Lina Ivanovna, SP's first wife xiii, xiv, xv

Prokofieva (née Mendelson), Mira Alexandrovna, SP's second wife xv, xvn

Prokofieva, Maria Grigorievna, mother of Sergey Prokofiev xii, xvii, 4, 9, 23, 29–30, 36, 48, 52, 55, 82, 87, 88, 180, 274, 291, 299, 321–2, 335, 342, 352, 355, 365, 366, 370, 395, 421, 442, 443, 453, 459–60, 499, 501, 518–19, 521, 539, 556, 585, 602, 614, 621, 664, 685, 688, 691–2, 711, 733, 786; relations, 16, 21, 37, 370, 443, 513, 533; maternal advice, 62, 142; exchange of birthday and name-day presents, 305, 510, 591, 645; loans to SP, 296, 623; sympathy at Max's disappearance, 383; passes on news of Max, 397; pleasure at SP's competition result, 663; expresses gratitude to Winkler, 102; to Yesipova and hears compliments, 216; attends Conservatoire events, 132–33, 263–5, 546; Easter services, 369, 637–8; attends performances by SP and of his music, 33–4, 50,

53–4, 190, 262, 320, 339, 470, 542, 562, 597, 613, 623, 630, 643, 658, 780; baffled by 2nd Piano Concerto, 252; friendships with Pavsky family, 7, 33, 403, 546; with Smetskoy family, 181, 234, 296, 333, 467, 731; with Andreyev family, 508, 541, 561, 632, 737, 761; with Korsak family, 276, 639, 774; with Louise Roblin, 10, 317, 320, 322, 685; with Meshchersky family, 726, 732, 737, 742, 744, 756, 785, 787; assists at field hospital, 748, 779; organizes collection point at home for relief of Poland, 756–7, 758; hospitality at home, 338, 516, 527–8, 594, 610; husband's final illness, 164; grief at his death, 177, 185; visits grave, 271, 418, 466, 515, 638, 745; investments, 210, 278, 286, 412, 607, 695, 720; visits to Mineralnye Vody, 108; to Sukhum, 182, 230, 239, 242, 507; to Kislovodsk, 234, 505, 716, 731; to Yessentuki, 105–107, 467, 726, 727–8; journey to Caucasus at outset of First World War, 719–23; desire to visit Paris, 419; plans travel to Paris, 355, 390; undertakes journey, 421–5; stays in Paris, 425–31; in Royat, 445–8; returns via Berlin, 462; attends war demonstrations in St Petersburg, 714–15
Prokopovich, *see* Metelyova, Mme
Pshibyshevsky, Boleslav Stanislavovich, composer 605n; *Dreams*, 605
Pskov 331
Purtales, Count Friedrich, German Ambassador to the Imperial Court 718
Pushkin (town) 165
Pushkin, Alexander Sergeyevich 293, 302; WORKS: *Yevgeny Onegin*, 36, 42; *Boris Godunov*, 40, 58, 58n; 'The Miserly Knight', 40; 'The Tale of the Fish and the Fisherman', 796n
Putilov Works 357–8, 357n
Puzyrevsky, undistinguished Conservatoire professor 659
Pyatigorsk 105n, 107, 233–4, 241, 292, 296, 383, 411, 602, 722, 725
Pyshnov, Lev, pianist 85, 134, 151

Raab, Wilhelmina Ivanovna, singer and teacher 599, 599n
Rabinovich, M. A., piano student 332, 360, 377–8, 404
Rachmaninov, Sergey Vasilievich xiii, 211n, 333, 377, 704, 725; WORKS: *The Miserly Knight*, 40n; Liturgy of St. John Chrysostom, 226; Piano Concerto No. 1, 228, 374; Piano Concerto No. 2, 325, 556, 713; Piano Concerto (unidentified), 300, 648; Serenade (unidentified), 300–301; *Isle of the Dead*, 325, 556; 'How Fair This Spot', Op.21/7, 479; *The Bells*, 556–7

Radlov, Nikolay Ernestovich 539n
Radlov, Sergey Ernestovich 539, 539n
Radlova, Anna 539n
Ranushevich, Yekaterina Mikhailovna, composer 28; 'Two Little Clouds', 28
Rapperswill, Switzerland 459
Rapp-Kleze, singing student 266
Rastropovich, composition student 30
Ratke, piano manufacturer 38, 581, 666, 733
Rausch, *see* Traubenberg, Baron Rausch von
Ravel, Maurice: *Daphnis et Chloé* 429–30
Rayevskaya (née Meyendorf), Nadezhda (Nadya), Andrey Rayevsky's wife 262, 275, 715
Rayevskaya, Yekaterina Alexandrovna (cousin Katya) 9n, 37, 106, 112, 275, 277–8, 498, 505, 525, 549, 637, 761, 764, 782, 784
Rayevskaya (née Zhitkova), Yekaterina Grigorievna (Aunt Katya) 9, 112, 177, 275, 287, 369, 505, 515, 525, 542, 549, 771, 782
Rayevsky, Alexander Alexandrovich (cousin Shurik) 9n, 37, 202, 262, 275, 281, 579, 719, 761, 791–2
Rayevsky, Alexander Dmitrievich (Uncle Sasha) 9n, 23n, 112, 138, 281, 287, 395, 420, 673, 761–2
Rayevsky, Andrey Alexandrovich (cousin Andryusha) 9n, 29, 83, 155n, 275, 281, 579, 715, 719, 782
Rayevsky family 7, 9, 33, 77, 112, 138, 157, 182, 199, 246, 254, 262, 281, 281n, 318, 370, 373, 382, 395, 463, 484, 497–8, 513, 533, 549, 575, 583, 606, 639, 646, 661, 664, 668, 673, 745, 761, 782–3, 791–2; funeral of Liza (servant), 530
Réamur scale 305, 305n, 696
Reberg, Dr Alfred Ernestovich, Sontsovka family doctor 7n
Reberg family 88, 298
Reberg, Nina Alfredovna 7n, 304, 366, 484, 637
Reberg, Vera Alfredovna 7, 304
Reberg, Zinaida Alfredovna 7n, 304, 484
Rech (*Speech*) newspaper 491, 496, 612, 616, 685
Red Cross 719, 727, 759, 796
Reger, Max 169; Sonata, 616
Réjane, Gabrielle, French actor 218n
Repino, *see* Kuokkale
Revel, Estonia 580
RGALI (Russian State Archive of Literary Art) xv n, xvi, xxvi
Rhine river 460, 698
Rhône river 448
Richter, Nikolay Ivanovich, pianist 214
Richter, Svyatoslav Teofilovich, pianist 214n, 589n
Ridal, opera class teacher 17, 19
Riemann's Dictionary 341, 341n

Rimsky-Korsakov, Nikolay Andreyevich xxii, 69, 307; delays starting course, 5; protest resignation at Government handling of 1905 student strike, 10n, 188n; new concept for Theory of Composition course, 21; admires Glazunov's 7th Symphony, 26; admires Galkovsky's *The Gypsies*, 42; teacher of Kryzhanovsky, 42n; Steinberg marries daughter, 44; report on SP's work in Theory of Composition and Orchestration, 51–2; death and SP's last memories of him, 57–8; Belyayev's support, 57n; R–K teacher of Wihtol, 61n; SP attends memorial concert, 67; R-K passes reins of Belyayev Concerts to Artsybushev, 122; negative impression created by R–K's *Chronicle of my Musical Life*, 350; SP critical of conclusion of R-K's version of *Khovanshchina*, 429; SP visits R-K's grave, 616, 745; WORKS: *The Legend of the Invisible City of Kitezh and the Maiden Fevronia*, 6, 25, 48, 51, 67, 122, 368n, 628, 636, 732, 761; *Battle for Kerzhenets (Kitezh)*, 639; *Mlada*, 46n, 777n; *Servilia*, 46n; *The Snow Maiden*, 57, 243, 247, 253, 259, 260–1, 262–3, 266, 279, 279n, 281, 286, 292, 331, 348; *The Golden Cockerel*, 58, 122, 130, 677; *The Maid of Pskov (Pskovityanka, Ivan The Terrible)*, 67, 243–4, 246, 251, 257; *May Night*, 87, 99; *The Tale of Tsar Saltan*, 122n; *The Tsar's Bride*, 131–2, 185, 195, 203, 584; *Sadko*, 310, 410, 535; *Kashchey The Immortal*, 554, 679; *Sheherezade*, 430, 489, 571, 582–3, 585–6, 591–2, 598n; Piano Concerto, 24–5, 50, 57, 67, 98, 102, 307, 596n; *Spanish Caprice*, 243, 261, 265; Symphony No. 2 ('Antar'), 355, 366, 366n; *Serbian Fantasy*, 608; *Night on Mount Triglav*, 777–80; edition of *Khovanshchina*, 429; orchestration of numbers from Schumann's *Carnaval*, 430; *Chronicle of My Musical Life*, 244–5, 350; *Orchestration*, 366, 750

Risler, Edouard, pianist 566

Roblin, Mlle Louise, SP's former governess 9–11, 317, 320–22, 328, 331, 366, 685, 689, 691, 796

Roerich, Nicholas, painter 514n

Roksikov, friend of Nikolay Andreyev 709–10

Romania 742

Romanov, Boris Georgievich, choreographer 757, 766–70, 784, 786–7

Romanov dynasty 318, 321

Romanov, Grand Duke Konstantin Konstantinovich 441, 441n, 465, 469, 796n; son Konstantin Konstantinovich, 441, 441n, 465, 469

Romanovsky, Gavriil Ivanovich, pianist 265, 294–5, 299, 370, 465, 508, 512, 523–4, 547, 613–4, 673

Rome 758, 777, 783, 788

Rosebery, Lord 466n

Rosenkrantz, Karl Wilhelmovich, chess player 20

Rosenstein, Yakov, cellist 593, 596–8, 677

Rostopchin, Count, lawyer, friend of Meshchersky family 523

Rostov-on-Don 55, 165n, 207–8, 547, 721–2; Don Region, 720

Roulette 446

Rowanberry liqueur 686

Royat, France 443, 445–8, 470

Rozanova, piano professor 97, 155, 164

Rozhanovich sisters (Ala, Olga) 285, 306, 538–9

Rozovsky, Solomon, composition student 26, 53, 90, 404

Rubinstein, Akiba Kivelevich, chess master 5, 37–8, 628, 640, 642–3, 645, 647, 649, 652–3, 657, 671, 679

Rubinstein, Anton Grigorievich, composer and pianist, first Director of the St Petersburg Conservatoire 132, 279n, 497n, 537; WORKS: Etude, 63; Etude in C, 71; Piano Concerto (unidentified), 134; Piano Concerto No. 4, 248; Piano Concerto No. 2, 251, 257, 366

Rubinstein, Nikolay Grigorievich 70n

Rudavskaya, Antonida Alexandrovna (Tonya, Tonechka, Antosha), Conservatoire student 161–2, 181, 216, 366, 468; SP meets and is attracted to, 131, 133, 146–7, 163–4; SP pursues in Teriioki, 165–7, 172–80; ranked No. 5 girl friend, 142–3; higher, 155; No. 3, 158; disappears from view, 153; reappears, 154; lack of intellect, 154, 204–5; ungrammatical letter-writer, 181; benefits of maintaining correspondence, 182; AR meets train on SP's return to St Petersburg ,182; relationship continues, 183–5, 191–2, 195, 223; mutual recognition that not a serious love affair, 194; frequency of quarrels, 187, 204, 222; sweetness of reconciliation, 187; terms of endearment, 190; straightforwardness of AR's character, 194–5; father's anti-Semitism, 200; trip to Kronstadt, 221–2; other excursions, 222–3, 351; also pursued by Zakharov, 239, 262; SP dreams of, 273; relationship cools, 239, 261; reveals lung illness, 377; visit to theatre, 379–80; SP meets AR again, 595; AR retired as 'cabinet minister', 623

Rubin, mature Conservatoire student 92

Rusinov, Head of Conservatoire Academic Studies 3, 46, 580; wife, 580

Russian Music Editions 153, 157, 181–4, 208, 274,

307, 327, 333, 352, 591, 637, 645, 648–9
Russian Musical Gazette 777–8
Russian National Anthem 319–20, 322
Russian Orthodox Church xxvii, 37n, 188n, 201n, 202, 637
Russian Symphony Concerts xxii
Russian Word (*Russkoye Slovo*) newspaper 730
Russische Musikverlag, *see* Russian Music Editions
Ruzskaya, Irina Nikolayevna (Ira) 199, 272, 297, 311–12, 363, 403, 499, 507, 532, 536, 547–8, 598, 689, 719, 734, 743
Ruzskaya, Tatyana Nikolayevna (Tanya) 272, 287, 297, 306, 311, 348, 356–7, 403, 499, 507, 532, 536, 547–8, 598, 689, 719, 734, 790
Ruzskaya, Olga Petrovna 333, 375, 561, 579, 689, 743, 790
Ruzsky family 226, 312, 358, 494, 495, 536; SP visits, 138, 157, 193, 297, 305–6, 333, 363, 375, 499, 531–2, 547, 561, 639, 743; stays in their Kislovodsk dacha, 237, 242; invited to stay in Volga dacha, 407; family's reported debt problems, 348; apparently resolved, 356–7; SP prefers parents to children, 375, 598; family said to have become wealthy, 531, 579; dislike of Meshchersky family, 613
Ruzsky, Nikolay Nikolayevich (Kolya) 311, 507, 598, 749, 759
Ruzsky, Nikolay Pavlovich 53n, 266, 297, 499, 507, 598, 613; SP introduced by M. P. Korsak ,77, 79, 85; mutual affection, 199; SP pressurizes to intervene with Glazunov, 203; writes *Ballade* for NR, 241–2, 306; NR's limitations as cellist, 252, 272, 323; name-day celebrations, 253, 561; SP invited to NR's table at post-concert dinner, 265, 267; NR recommends *Ballade* to other cellist, 333–4, 339n; advises on travel to Volga, 370, 379; sympathy on death of Max Schmidthof, 403; ambivalent reaction to 2nd Piano Concerto, 403; lavishness of hospitality, 547, 689; plans to organize hospital and visit front, 719; appointed Deputy Head of Red Cross, 759; posted to Lvov, 790; proud of war-hero cousin, 733–4, 743
Ruszky, General Nikolay Vladimirovich 743, 743n
Ryazan 551, 720
Ryazan Station, Moscow 720
Ryazhsk 323

Sabaneyev, Leonid Leonidovich 234, 324, 492, 493, 499, 501, 516, 525, 590, 604
Saburov, Pyotr Petrovich, music–loving chess acquaintance 165, 345, 354, 361, 370, 372, 377, 406, 524, 539–40, 542, 579, 582, 639, 642, 657, 678–9
Sacchetti, Livery, Conservatoire professor 78, 78n, 87, 339, 514n, 553
Saddle Mountain, Caucasus 728
Sadovskaya, Yevgenia, Conservatoire student 19–20, 33–4, 42–3, 48–9, 54, 154–5, 552
Safonov family 729–30, 757
Safonov, Vasily Ilyich, conductor 538, 725–6, 725n, 729–30, 732
Safonova, Mme, née Vyshnegradskaya 725, 725n, 727
Safonova, Mulya Vasilievna 730
Safonova, Varvara Vasilievna (Varya) 725
St Isaac's Cathedral, St Petersburg 496
Saint Petersburg Chess Club xxi, 15, 18, 20–22, 35–6, 38–9, 53, 59–61, 63, 155, 185, 390, 502, 526, 574, 582–3, 622, 628, 630, 640–41, 643–5, 647, 649, 652–6, 669–70, 673, 675, 678, 681, 770; Higher Education Establishment Chess Tournament, 526; Jubilee All-Russia Tournament, 574, 582–4; 1909 International Tournament, 124, 640; 1914 International Tournament, xxi, 628, 639–41, 643, 645, 649, 652–3, 654–6, 665, 669, 670–73, 675–6, 679
St Petersburg Conservatoire xii, xx, xxi; SP's affection for, xxi, 112, 279; canteen established, 25–6; Winter Balls, 33–5, 138–41, 200, 579–80, 630–31; orchestra, 70, 80; Easter Prime Service, 637, 638; Jubilee Concerts, 128, 131–4, 243–5, 248, 251–2, 254–5, 257, 261–5, 345, 376, 404; Graduation Concerts, 94, 96, 110, 162–3, 349, 355, 362, 365, 378–80, 387, 390, 392, 394–7, 400–405, 411, 621, 656, 664, 666, 668–70, 672–4, 676–9, 685, 689, 749–50, 783; Rubinstein Prize, xii, xiii, xxi, 183, 332–3, 338, 367–8, 546, 548, 574, 583–4, 591, 594–7, 607, 608, 612, 614–23, 627–8, 632, 636, 641, 648–51, 654–64, 666, 674, 689, 708, 715, 725, 735, 738, 785
Saint–Saëns, Camille 435n; WORKS: *Suite algérienne*, 25; Piano Concerto (unidentified), 164, 584, 673; Piano Concerto No. 4 in C minor, 377–9, 401–4; *Samson et Dalila*, 435n
Sakhovsky, Conservatoire student 264
Salonika 758
Salwe, George, chess master 37
Saminsky, Lazar Semyonovich, composer and conductor 4, 13, 15, 26, 28, 36, 52–3, 63, 66, 132, 159, 398, 529, 677, 685
Samolyot Travel Agency 379
Sanb, Mlle, English teacher 668–9, 673–4, 679, 681–4, 690
Sanin (Sanin-Schoenberg), Alexander Akimovich, opera and theatre director 435, 514n

Sankt Peterburge Zeitung 6\n, 491
Saradzhev (Saradzhian), Konstantin Solomonovich, conductor 327, 493; SP meets in Moscow, 211; KS first rejects scores of *Dreams* and *Autumnal* then changes mind, 212; SP performs 1st Piano Concerto with KS, 234, 326; KS programmes Shaposhnikov's ballet suite, 378; involvement with establishment of Free Theatre, 464; principal conductor, 470; SP plays *Maddalena* to KS, 469; KS considers production possible, 495; approves at Free Theatre audition, 554–6; offers SP position of Assistant Conductor at Free Theatre, 492; SP stays with KS for Moscow recital, 586–8, 590; and for Koussevitzky Concerts performance of 1st Piano Concerto, 602–4; plays vint at SP's home, 607, 610, 622
Saradzheva, Mme 592, 602, 604
Saratov 389
Sarnersee, Switzerland 457
Sasha, 'toady' student of Yesipova 510
Savenko, friend of Zakharov family 465
Saviour of the Blood Church, St Petersburg 93
Sazonov, Sergey, Tsarist Foreign Minister 718
Scarlatti, Domenico 537
Schaffhausen, Switzerland 460
Schböschen Worth, Switzerland 460
Schiffers, Emanuel Stepanovich, chess master 52
Schiller, Gottfried von: *Die Braut von Messina* 550n
Schindler, Kurt, American composer and publisher 685–7
Schirmer, G., music publishers 686n
Schlotburg 222n
Schlüsselburg 222, 222n, 312n, 330, 668–70
Schmidt, horn player 8
Schmidt, publisher of SP's *Sokol March* 748
Schmidthof, Maximilian Anatolievich 133, 134, 165, 192, 245, 252, 259, 263–5, 294, 318, 369, 438; interest in philosophy, xiv; meets SP and friendship develops, 92, 108–9; knowledge of music, 93, 110, 381, 411; intelligence, 93, 333; wit and verbal dexterity, 109; ill health, 96–7, 110, 292; relationship with Maria Lyutz, 287, 301, 304, 307–8, 313; relations with mother, sister and aunt, 251, 305, 366, 370, 385, 397–8, 411; rift with SP occasioned by angry correspondence, 110–12, 113; reconciliation, 116–18; strength of attachment, 246, 287, 299, 308, 401–2, 500; hostility of and towards SP's other friends, 240, 291, 297, 350, 378, 388–9, 403; financial irresponsibility and love of extravagance, 246, 289, 302, 321, 335, 348, 363–4, 365, 366–7, 371, 373, 379, 381–2, 383–5; managing aunt's theatrical business in Yessentuki, 383; fantasy life, 384, 386, 387; insecurity, 411–12; character compared with Damskaya's, 684; Yellow Book, 247, 249, 278; caricatures and practical jokes, 307, 336, 341, 353–5, 359–60; trip to Nikopol and Crimea, 297–8, 299–304, 308, 309, 478, 484, 581, 587; other planned trips, 234, 292, 296, 339, 344, 355, 365, 368, 371, 379; attends SP's performances, 102, 190, 320, 338, 339, 341; other concerts, opera and theatre performances attended with SP, 251, 255, 258, 261–2, 266, 276–7, 280, 332, 334, 336, 338, 345, 353, 355, 357, 374, 377, 380; correspondence with SP, 104, 164, 286, 307, 312, 313–4, 324, 326, 366; meals and conversations with SP, 119, 131, 243, 261, 293, 315, 328, 338, 341; walks with SP, 92, 93, 270, 272, 274, 278, 310, 319, 322, 323, 330, 334, 344, 347, 351, 357, 359–60, 362, 363, 365, 366, 370–71, 373; walking sticks exchanged with SP, 379; preserved, 394, 443, 498, 501; lost 787–8; suicide, 382–7, 391–2, 396, 397–8, 400–2, 403, 413, 512, 529; SP searches for grave, 528, 611–12, 691; MS reads Artsybashev's *On the Brink* 512; SP's memories of MS, 383, 387, 391–2, 394, 398, 405, 408–9, 411, 413, 416, 424–5, 431, 457, 463, 471, 484, 496, 500, 507, 517, 552, 587, 602–3, 628, 650, 699, 722, 742; dreams of, 518; SP dedicates works to MS's memory, 241, 401, 559, 699; as student of Ossovskaya, 145, 250, 331, 370; as pianist, 123, 164, 295, 349, as composer, 116–17, 411
Schmidthov-Lavrova, Alexandra Nikolayevna 308, 366, 382, 385–6, 391, 397–8, 401–2, 588, 602–3, 710, 728
Schmidthof-Lavrova, Yekaterina Alexandrovna (Katya) 251, 309, 381, 386, 392, 410–12, 407, 411, 431, 447, 547, 555, 568, 588, 602–3, 637, 710, 728, 791–2
Schmitt, Florent: *La Tragédie de Salomé* 757n
Schmitz, Elie Robert 432, 432n
Schoenberg, Arnold 72n, 214–5, 667; *Drei Klavierstücke*, Op. 11 (1909), 214–15, 218
Schnitzler, Artur: *The Veil of Pierrette* 464n, 555
Schopenhauer, Artur xiv, 366
Schubert, Franz 315; Symphony No. 4 ('Tragic') 40, 125; Symphony No. 8 ('Unfinished') 128
Schumann, Robert 194, 315, 778; WORKS: 'Traumeswirren', 50; *Toccata*, 98, 100, 121, 530–31; Sonata No. 1 in F sharp minor, 338, 368, 507, 510, 525, 527, 530, 534, 574, 595, 614, 617–20; Sonata No. 2 in G minor, 345, 348–9, 360; Sonata No. 3 in F minor, 572; *Carnaval*, 357, 430, 627, 769; *Fantasiestücke*, 741;

'Aufschwung', 742; Piano Concerto, 362–3, 369, 372; Piano Trio (unidentified), 532
Schweiger, piano student 167, 213, 224
Scriabin, Alexander Nikolayevich xiii, 90, 93, 98, 149–51, 153, 155, 188, 258, 326, 367, 535, 585, 593, 704, 776; WORKS: Symphony No. 1, 258; Symphony No. 3 ('Divine Poem'), 42, 57n, 143, 149–51, 361, 411; Symphony No. 5, 181; *Poème d'extase*, 80, 99, 124, 131, 325; *Poème satanique*, 180, 258; Sonata No. 5, 122, 124, 258; Sonata No. 6, 516, 745, 758, 777; Sonata No. 7, 258, 274; Sonata No. 9, 516; Sonata No. 10, 516; 24 Preludes Op. 11, 258; Etudes, 275, 343; Piano Concerto, 327; *Prometheus, Poème du feu*, 538, 540; *Poème* (unidentified), 609–10
Scutari 379
Sebryakov family 370
Sebryakov, Sergey Alexeyevich (Seryozha) 192, 545, 640, 665, 744
Sebryakova, Nadezhda (Nadya) 192
Sebryakova-Zhitkova, Dr Tatyana 192n, 288, 545n
Sechsundsechzig (Sixty-Six), card game 441, 478, 481, 500, 572, 579, 581
Second Militia Reserve 770–74, 781–4, 796
Seleznova, singing student 556
Senilov, Vladimir Alexeyevich, composer 41, 498
Serbia 714
Sergievskaya Pustynya 165
Sergievskaya Street, St Petersburg 112, 114, 182, 463–8, 485–6, 493, 499–502, 533
Sert, José Maria 706
Serov, Alexander Nikolayevich, composer: *Judith* 68
Sestroretsk 163, 165, 370, 396, 676
Sebastopol, *see* Sevastopol
Sevastopol 55, 111, 180, 296, 298, 303–4, 307, 339, 351, 470–71, 477, 483–4
Severyanin, Igor (pen-name of Igor Lotarev) 549, 549n
Sezhenskaya, Maria Mikhailovna, distant relative 366
Shakespeare, William 437; *Romeo and Juliet*, 539n
Shalyt, Conservatoire student 332, 347, 363–4
Shandarovsky, Conservatoire student 117
Shandarovskaya, Conservatoire student 661
Shapiro, Klara, Conservatoire student 792
Shaposhnikov, Adrian, composer 378, 685; Introduction and Dance of the Maidens (*The King's Feast*), 380–81, 391–2, 394, 396–8, 404, 529
Sharoyev, piano student 288, 305
Shaw, George Bernard 71n
Shchepkina-Kupernik, Tatyana Lvovna, playwright and translator 19, 19n; *Portrait of a Summer*, 19–20, 29
Shcherbachov, Vladimir Vladimirovich, composer 664, 664n; *Procession*, 665, 668–9, 676–7
Shenk, Pyotr Petrovich, composer 756
Sheintsvit, Clavdia ('The Pillow') 411, 468, 485, 487; sister 468, 485, 487, 619
Shenshin, Alexander Alexeyevich 324, 400, 589
Sheremetyev Concerts 46–7, 145, 155, 157
Sheremetyev, Count Alexander Dmitrievich 46n; Sheremetyev dacha, 358
Sheremetyev Orchestra 70, 204, 207, 331
Sherry cobbler 167
Shevchenko Theatre, Kiev 272n
Shifrin, flautist 292
Shkarovskaya, piano student 532, 534, 536–7, 539, 541–2, 566
Shlifsteyn, Samuel, musicologist and editor 30n
Shmargoner, Maria, *see* Briand, Maria Isaakevna
Shmayevsky, piano student 186, 215
Shneye, piano student 367
Shostakovich, Dmitry Dmitrievich 129n, 165n, 588n, 664n; Symphony No. 1, 24n
Shreder, Ivan Karlovich, piano manufacturer 14, 468, 485, 690, 713, 733–5, 738, 784
Shteiman, Mikhail Osipovich, conductor 128n, 132, 159, 192, 426, 504, 538, 542, 564, 568; conductor of Conservatoire female chorus, 128; SP admires as conductor, 185; but determined to equal, 186; MS proposes Tolstoy memorial concert, 188; suggests SP writes opera, 217; has contract with Diaghilev Company, 429, 435–6; excursion to Windsor, 438–41; visit to Music Hall in London, 441–2; accompanies SP to *Carmen*, 545; approves SP's conducting of *Aida*, 569; SP likes but regards as untrustworthy, 737; looks at score of MS's orchestral composition, 738
Shtember family 247, 361, 372, 509
Shtember, Nikolay Viktorovich, pianist 305, 308, 537, 542, 616, 621, 755, 791; qualities as pianist, 186–7, 215–6, 546; enrols as Sokol member, 186, 558, 583, 586, 592–3, 595, 608, 739; visits Terioki with SP, 224–5; SDP visits Shtember home, 361, 372; dedicates *Toccata* to NS, 468; M.G. Prokofieva wants to hear NS play, 546; NS approves of 2nd Sonata, 583; approves SP's Beethoven, 608; praises exam recital performance, 620; and final concerto performance, 660; SP quotes NS's maxim on opera performances, 628; NS

advises SP on choice of prize piano, 734–5; expresses enthusiasm for Op. 12, 741; moves to Tsarskoye Selo, 791
Shtember sisters (Nadya and Sonya) 372, 595, 626, 734–5, 755
Shtember, Viktor 509
Shtrimmer, Alexander Yakovlevich, conducting student 502, 515
Shubert, Pavel Khristoforovich, piano student 113, 151–2, 157, 162, 186, 224
Shverubovich, Vasily, see Kachelov, Vasily Ivanovich
Shurtsman, horn player 8
Shuvalov, Count 506n
Shvarts, piano student 33–5, 148
Shvedov, Dmitry Nikolayevich, composer 791
Sibelius, Jan 463n; *En Saga*, 463
Sig (fish) 686
Simbirsk 679
Simferopol 201, 208, 286–7, 301, 302n, 304, 308–9, 313, 339, 341, 383, 484
Siverskaya 165
Skachek, Caucasus 722
Skalon, Konstantin (Kostya) 21, 33, 138, 167
Skalon, Yelena (Lyolya) 21, 33, 138, 167
Skhefals, bootmaker 313
Skomorokhs 260n
Skorunsky, piano and conducting student 272, 309, 313–14
Sladkopevtsov, Vladimir, actor 571
Smetskaya, Olga Yurievna 54–5
Smetskoy, Nikolay Nikolayevich 43, 105, 731
Smetskoy family 54, 181, 234, 296, 467, 731
Smirnova, Vera Yakovlevna, piano student 134
Smith, Mme, London friend of Andreyev family 436; son Petrushka, 436
Smolensky Cemetery 413, 502
Sobinov, Leonid Viktorovich, singer 26, 125–6, 128n
Sofia Ivanovna, Max Schmidthof's aunt 370, 382–7, 397–8, 400–401
Sokol Gymnastic Club 187, 187n, 402, 470, 505, 509, 511, 515, 521, 524, 429–32, 534, 540, 543, 546–7, 550, 558, 560; gala evening, 563; 564, 567, 572–3, 575, 581, 583, 586, 592–3, 595–7, 599, 605, 608, 611–13, 615, 617, 624, 628, 635, 653, 666, 669, 673, 676, 680, 683, 688, 690, 704, 739; desire for Slav unity, 739; 742, 744, 747, 749, 752, 758–9, 764, 766, 768, 772, 775–6, 778, 781–2, 784, 792, 794, 796; Dobrotina (acquaintance), 563, 653; SP's *Sokol March*, 402, 509, 511, 515, 531, 547–8, 634, 748, 789, 793
Sokolniki Park, Moscow 211–12, 219, 233–4, 687–8

Sokolov, Nikolay Alexandrovich, composer 90, 125, 676
Solomon, Conservatoire student 586
Solovyov, Nikolay Feopemptovich, composer and teacher 28, 92
Solovyov, S., conducting student 269, 272, 298, 308
Sologub, Fyodor (pen-name of Fyodor Teternikov) 571
Sontsov, Dmitry Dmitrievich, estate owner 11, 186
Sontsovka 56, 62n, 96, 110, 112, 115, 142, 167, 180, 186, 220, 237, 305, 585, 676
Sosnitsky, Vice-President of St Petersburg Chess Society 646, 675
Souvchinsky, Pierre, see Suvchinsky, Pyotr Petrovich
Sovetskaya Muzyka (*Soviet Music*) magazine xx
Spendiarov (Spendiaryan), Alexander Afanasievich, composer and conductor 598, 602, 604; symphonic study *Three Palms*, 602
Spit, The, see Strelka
Spitz, Switzerland 455
Spivak, singing student 584–5
Spivakovsky, composition student 206
Stackelberg, Baron Konstantin Karlovich 84–5, 84n
Stanchinsky, Alexey Vladimirovich, composer 493, 501, 516, 525
Standard, The, royal yacht 483, 572
Staraya Derevnya 370
Staraya Russa 226
Steinberg, Maximilian Oseyevich, composer and teacher 44, 120, 156, 263, 362, 366, 644, 663–4, 764
Steinitz, Wilhelm, chess master 37
Steinway piano 327, 726
Stieglitz School 414, 416
Stockholm 691, 693–5, 696; Palace, 694; Northern Museum, 694; Skandsen, 694; Katerina-Hissen, 695
Strauss, Richard 126; WORKS: *Salome*, 22, 126, 169; *Der Rosenkavalier*, 272n, *Ariadne auf Naxos*, 289, 332; *Elektra*, 316–7; *Don Quixote*, 572; *Josephslegende*, 705, 757n
Stravinsky, Igor Fyodorovich xiii, xxii–xxiii, 61n, 72n, 155, 262, 279n, 429, 464, 593, 597, 667, 670, 704n, 756
Stray Dog Café, St Petersburg xxii, 352
Strelka, The 141, 373, 514, 519, 533, 751
Strindberg, August 466n
Stroganov Bridge 533
Struve, Lidia N., Conservatoire student 598, 612, 614, 620, 625, 627, 650, 734; SP attracted to, 593–4, 609, 624; appointed 'cabinet mini-

ster', 595; 'Prime Minister', 608, 629; demoted, 675; international background, 617, 631, 638; shyness, 606, 609, 622; lisp, 631; SP teases about exam with Glazunov, 609–11; excursions with SP and Damskaya to Palm Sunday Festival, 631; to Pavlovsk, 635; to Terioki, 637–8; to Schlüsselburg, 668–70; helps write inscription in French to Calvocoressi, 665; rebuffs SP's proposal to go to Sestroretsk, 674–5; makes perceptive character sketch of SP, 680; matures in style and beauty, 643, 735, 742–3

Struve, Nikolay Gustavovich, director of RME 333

Struve, Vasily Vasilievich, chess partner 20–22, 24, 25, 29, 36, 39, 609

Subbotin, Oleg Mikhailovich 473, 477–82, 525, 528, 530, 594, 599, 607, 610, 612, 614, 622, 628, 635, 653, 669, 676, 723, 745

Sukhodolsky, Vladimir, financial backer of Moscow Free Theatre 590, 590n

Sukhum 54–5, 180–82, 205, 208, 219–20, 223, 230, 239, 242, 335, 505, 507

Summer Garden, St Petersburg 93, 182, 223, 347, 370, 630–31, 669

Superfluous Man 36

Suuk-Su, Crimea 474, 482

Suvchinsky, Pyotr Petrovich, music critic, editor, philanthropist xiii, 773, 787

Suvorov, Marshal Alexander 458–9, 458n

Svetlanov, Yevgeny Fyodorovich, conductor 269n

Svetlov, Valerian Yakovlevich, ballet critic, assistant to Diaghilev 777

Sweden 679, 683, 689, 693–9; Motala, 697; Lake Vattern, 697; Trollhetten Falls, 695, 698–9; Göta Canal, 695–7

Switzerland 447, 448–61, 474, 504, 585, 594, 701–2

Sviridenko, S, see Sviridova, Sofia Alexandrovna

Sviridova, Sofia Alexandrovna, poet and writer on music 44

Syapne, railway station 397

Sydney Symphony Orchestra 24n

Syropyatova, piano student 106

Tallin, see Revel
Tamerlaine The Great 55
Taneyev, Sergey Ivanovich: SP meets ST with father at concert of ST's music, 23; travels together on train to Moscow, 149; ST writes letter of introduction to Scriabin, 150; praises SP's Deisha-Sionitskaya recital, 153; suggests transcribing Buxtehude fugue, 160; seen as providing access to Jurgenson, 182; writes letter recommending 1st Sonata, 189; rejected 193; SP visits and plays *Dreams*, 210–11; Etude No. 3 and 'Reminiscence', 211; SP attributes predilection for dissonances to ST, 233; ST described as saintly figure by Jurgenson, 264; ST's songs criticized and attributed by Tcherepnin to ST's cloistered and isolated life, 289; SP dreams about playing fugue by ST in exam, 542; invites ST to Moscow recital, 587; ST responds, 588; approves SP's 2nd Sonata and makes helpful comments but teases about modernism, 590; WORKS: Piano Trio, 149; songs, 289

Tarrasch, Siegbert, chess master 506, 640, 644, 646, 649, 652–3, 657, 670–73, 675

Tarsky, playwright and actor 357

Tartakov, Joachim Viktorovich, singer and director 725, 725n, 77

Tartu, see Yurev

Taube brothers, friends of Zakharov 777

Tauride Gardens, St Petersburg 463, 490

Taushan-Bazar 302

Tbilisi, see Tiflis

Tchaikovsky, Modest Ilyich: *Life of P. I. Tchaikovsky*, biography in 3 volumes, 244–5, 247, 273, 275, 291, 307–8, 312, 345, 349, 636

Tchaikovsky, Pyotr Ilyich 4n, 19n, 36, 70n, 244–5, 274–5, 291, 307, 313, 317, 345, 476, 485; Requiem Mass held on 20th anniversary of death, 529; 538, 564, 735, 765; WORKS: Piano Concerto No. 1, 95, 244, 253–5, 259–60, 376, 378, 382, 391, 392, 394, 396–7, 401, 404, 595, 648; Symphony No. 2, 765; Symphony No. 5, 125; Symphony No. 6, 349, 485, 508, 780; Suite No. 3, 765; Violin Concerto, 134; *The Oprichnik*, 128; *The Maid of Orleans*, 245, 249, 263, 266, 209, 543; *The Queen of Spades*, 271–3, 275, 286–8, 290–91, 293–4, 296, 307, 309, 316, 323, 330–31, 335, 338, 345; *Yevgeny Onegin*, 276–7, 530, 532, 537, 539; *Scherzo à la Russe*, 160; *Italian Caprice*, 186; *Romeo and Juliet*, 248; *Serenade for Strings*, 313; *The Tempest*, 571; *Francesca da Rimini*, 777; Piano Trio, 301, 350, 536; String Quartet No. 1, 301; 'On the Golden Cornfields', 309; Letters, 350

Tcherepnin, Maria Albertovna, wife of Nikolay Tcherepnin 253, 256, 539

Tcherepnin, Nikolay Nikolayevich 10n, 25, 42, 191, 244, 259, 262, 264, 266, 269, 292, 299, 305, 331, 341, 344, 347, 366, 372, 392–3, 403, 405, 475, 531, 534, 546–9, 572, 633, 637, 647, 654, 656, 669, 734–5, 750, 754, 765, 772, 795; as conducting teacher, 119, 124, 137, 143, 185, 285, 290–91, 294, 306–7, 310, 313–16, 318–19, 330, 334, 352, 357, 359, 382, 502, 504, 509–13, 515,

517, 521, 523, 535, 548, 551, 557, 562, 582, 585, 591, 592–3, 595–7, 610, 617–18, 624–5, 665, 668; SP as NT's conducting student, 9, 10,13, 15, 26–8; NT recommends joining opera class, 36; gives SP first conducting assignment, 51; highly critical, 127; surprised and delighted, 128; rejects SP as conductor in RMS Jubilee concert, 132; again critical, 146; assigns *Ivan The Terrible* to SP for Jubilee Concert, 243, 251; NT approves, 257; 246; wife regards SP as more *sculpté*, 253; SP denied opera rehearsals, 256; NT allocates opera and concert repertoire, 271–2; critical of SP's conducting, 288; enthusiastic about Dranishnikov, 308, 792; considers it possible to talk to SP conductor to conductor, 320; dispute over tempi for *The Wedding*, 337–8; claims credit for seeing SP's potential as conductor, 340; appoints SP deputy in NT's absence, 340, 343; expresses high hopes for SP as conductor, 356; SP declines offer to conduct *Onegin* and *Faust* with piano, 530; SP's progress praised by Glazunov, 538, 542; personal relationship: fails to allocate passes for Ziloti concert, 12–13; SP does not respect NT, 13; NT provides passes, 18; for Shreder concert, 14; relationship improved, 156; SP plans to dedicate Sinfonietta to NT, 199; post-concert dinner, 267; NT permits leave of absence, 297–8; supports SP's plan to go to Paris, 397; SP seeks NT out in Paris, 426–7, 430, 432; NT seeks SP out in Gurzuf, 498; SP regards NT as no more than fair-weather friend over Belyayev Concerts proposal, 586; SP dedicates 1st Piano Concerto to NT, 626, 657; professional relationship: NT begins to believe in SP as composer, 156; disbands orchestra for *White Swan*, 146, 155; supports *Dreams* for inclusion in Tolstoy concert, 188, 192; becomes avid supporter, 193; supports inclusion of *White Swan* and *The Wave* for student orchestra concert but finds Sinfonietta too difficult, 203; urges Sinfonietta on Sheremetyev Concerts, 203, 207, 289; suggests opera subjects, 217–18; conflicts with Palechek lead to disagreement with SP, 543, 558–60, 560–61, 563–4, 565–6, 570; effect of this on *Sarcasms*, 566; relationship settles down again, 583; SP does not apologize, 593; effect on SP's conducting opportunities, 593; praises SP's Contemporary Concerts recital, 598–9; promises to conduct 1st Piano Concerto, 606; advises ignoring hostile criticism, 607; praises exam recital, 620; gives opinion of SP as talented but over-confident, 636; urges Sinfonietta on Ziloti, 665, 667; tells Ziloti SP one of only three composers taking music forward, 667; backs inclusion of 1st Piano Concerto in Graduation Concert, 666, 668–9; NT as composition mentor: 15, 26–8; specific advice, advocacy and coaching on early E minor Symphony, 80; on *White Swan*, 137, 144; on 1st Piano Concerto, 235–6; on bassoon quartet, 274, 281, 288; considers Countess scene in *The Queen of Spades* one of greatest scenes in all opera, 287; explains true reason for cancellation of opera performance, 295; discusses principles of orchestration, 360; Karnovich *Variations*, 362, 390; Graduation Concert (1913), 378, 380, 394–5, 399; supports SP over fitness to conduct, 401, 404; tells Nurok 'God in your old age has sent you Prokofiev', 498; coaches conducting of orchestral concert (November 1913), 528–9, 532, 536–8, 542; proposes to conduct SP's 1st Piano Concerto in Belyayev Concerts, 527, 548, 586, 606, 614; NT's general praise for SP, 538, 542; shares delight in Mozart, 595; coaches SP in *Figaro* 608, 612–3, 614, 622, 624–5, 629–30; asks for Tsybin to conduct 2nd performance of *Figaro*, 622–3; advises SP on final recital programme, 614; suggests providing professors with score of 1st Piano Concerto for final exam, 632, 643; coaches, 657–8; praises *Tannhäuser* performance, 660; letter to Otto Kling, 704; advises on orchestration of *Ala and Lolli*, 763–4; on libretto of *Ala and Lolli*, 792; NT as conductor, 27, 185; dismissive of Glazunov as conductor, 261; 248–9, 252, 328–9, 332, 338, 378; possibility of appointment as Director of Moscow Philharmonia, 396, 406; 599, 771; opts to conduct first performance of *Figaro* himself, 599, 600–601, 608, 610, 614–15, 622–3; NT as composer Piano Concerto, 270; opinion of Taneyev, 289; admiration for French composers, 544; included in Court Orchestra concert series, 756; WORKS: songs, 289; orchestration of piece from *Carnaval*, 430; *Narcisse*, 632, 636, 777; *Le Pavillon d'Armide*, 10n, 357; *Narcisse et Echo*, 10n, 548, 632, 636, 775–7; *The Enchanted Kingdom*, 10n; Piano Concerto, 270, 688; *Le Masque de la mort rouge*, 684, 687, 688–9; *Le Destin*, 684n; *Tale of the Fish and the Fisherman*, 797

Telyakovsky, Vladimir Arkadievich, Director of Imperial Theatres 568–9

Tereshchenko, N. S., chess acquaintance 345, 582–4

Terioki xxvii, 165, 167–78, 221, 224–6, 228–9,

237, 239, 240, 256, 277n, 386, 391–3, 407–9, 411, 413–6, 446, 465, 476, 487, 490–1, 493–4, 505, 517, 637–8, 688, 690–91, 712, 717, 719
Terpelevskaya, piano student 121
Théâtre Astruc, *see* Paris, Théâtre des Champs Elysées
Theatre and Art magazine 495
Thomas Cook and Sons 460
Thousand and One Nights 218
Thun, Lake, Switzerland 455–7
Tietz, piano student 134, 367, 618, 658
Tiflis 55, 292, 296, 339, 344, 529, 796
'Tigress, The', singing student 685
Tines, France 452
Timofeyev, Grigory Nikolayevich, critic 156
Timofeyeva, singing student 592, 610–11, 668, 667–8
Titanic, The 457, 531n
Tobizen, Governor of Kharkov 37, 138
Tolstoy, Lev Nikolayevich 188, 188n, 778; *Anna Karenina*, 790
Tolstyakov, conducting student 131, 132, 159
Tomkeyev, law student, friend of Meshchersky family 723, 728, 730, 731, 741
Torletskaya, Maria, *see* Yershova, Maria Ivanovna
Torletsky, Conservatoire student 581, 639
Traubenberg, Baron Konstantin Rausch von, sculptor and chess player 39, 39n, 61, 185, 633, 638–9
Treskin, M. I., Director of Vilnius I.R.M.S. 536–7
Trient river, Switzerland 452–3
Troitskaya, piano student 47
Troitsky Bridge 93, 109, 192
Tsarskoye Selo 199, 218, 224, 399, 400, 463, 468, 486, 494, 635, 783, 790, 791, 793–4
Tsarskoye Selo station 410, 487, 497, 499, 715, 791, 793
Tseitlin, piano student 367, 658
TSGALI (Central State Archive of Literary Art, *see* RGALI
Tsintinator, chemist in Kislovodsk 234
Tsvetayeva, Marina, poet 571n
Tsybin, Vladimir Nikolayevich, conductor 266, 285, 294, 316, 340, 344, 353, 356, 378, 543, 547, 548, 565, 567, 605, 607, 629, 678; background and subsequent career, 251n; given appearance in Jubilee Concert, 251; conducts Ippolitov-Ivanov's *Ruth*, 256; comes to grief in rehearsal, 257; but gives decent performance, 265; moved by Countess's scene in *The Queen of Spades*, 287; allocated *Rigoletto*, 271–2, 515, 557; problems with inexperienced orchestra, 558; nicknamed 'Tsypin' by SP's mother, 291, 291n; conducts Dances from *Rusalka*, 332, 341; deficiencies as conductor, 337–8, 349; these agreed by Tcherepnin, 674; Rosenstein however praises, 677; appointed No. 2 to SP on conducting course, 502; allocated *Flying Dutchman* and *Euryanthe* Overtures, 528, 538; success at Graduation Concert, 540–42; female chorus singers rude to VT, 543; causes rift with Tcherepnin, 559, 561, 566; reconciled, 568; summer season in Baku or Rostov, 547–8; presented backstage to Telyakovskyt, 568–9; joins post-performance supper party, 570; hopes of Mariinsky appointment dashed, 585–6; poor account of *The Marriage of Figaro*, 593; SP's practical joke in telephone booth, 596; VT allocated 3rd performance of *Figaro*, 599, 615, 617–18; asks to swap with SP, 622–3; SP strenuously objects, 623; schedule problem resolved, 624; performance scheduled at unsatisfactorily short notice, 633; VT's Symphony described as modest and insignificant, 676
Tuchkov Bridge 413
Tula 466, 736, 768
Turku, *see* Åbo
Tvordovsky, conducting student 567, 570, 600, 631
Tyulin, Yury Nikolayevich, musicologist and composer 791
Tyursevo 494
Tyurisyavi 638

Udelny Park 413, 533
Udelnaya 505
Ufa 405
Ukraine xvii
Ulanovsky, Dr. dentist 408
Ull, printer of *Sokol March* 789
Umnov family 271, 334, 340, 350, 410, 412, 417
Umnov, Ivan Ivanovich, Lidia's father 247, 271, 410, 412–13, 551
Umnova, Mme (Matrona) 413
Umnova, Lidia Ivanovna (Umnenkaya, Glupenkaya, 17A), singing student 245, 247, 255, 264, 265, 272, 273, 281, 285, 305, 307, 316, 319, 329, 339, 340, 344, 351, 355, 358, 368, 400, 401, 408, 410, 411, 424, 425, 468, 485; SP meets and is attracted to, 242–3, 246, 248; pursues relationship, 310, 313–15, 317, 320–21, 335, 337–8, 340, 345, 412; LU disappears from view, 274, 285, 288, 291, 295; reappears, 309; SP suspects LU is indifferent to him, 292, 308, 310; fails to meet at rehearsal, 293–4; devises successful strategy to meet, 298; persuades to go walking, 331, 347–8; LU declines walk to The Islands, 399; agrees to go by boat

to Yelagin Island, 406; declines another walk, 495; SP writes teasing card from train, 323–4; and from Kuokkale, 416; writes from Paris, 427; and from London, 436; receives replies, 431; but ungrammatical, 447–8; SP takes to *The Valkyrie*, 342–3; and *Siegfried*, 352–3; family background, 247; SP invited to family home, 271, 333–4, 350, 370; visits dacha in Kuokkale, 407, 469, 485; parents' lack of sophistication, 412–13; SP dreams about LU, 273; suppresses thoughts of marrying, 342–3; realizes this is longest-running relationship to date, 346; first quarrel and thoughts of relationship cooling, 353, 407; SP cuts out and sends uncomplimentary article from *Ogonyok*, 374–5; strongly objected to, 375; SP teases about cholera infection, 376; harmony restored, 376, 390; LU summers at Kuokkale, 393; excursion to Pavlovsk, 394–5; SP invites to Sestroretsk, 396; contact continues but on more neutral basis, 486–7; irregular meetings, 497; SP invites to his Graduation Concert, 403; final quarrel and end of relationship, 503, 517; LU sings Lel in *Snow Maiden*; 243, 249–50, 256, 259, 262–3, 266; Glazunov compliments, 252; extremely self-critical, 254; SP regrets not going to see LU to give support, 254; selected to appear in Jubilee Concert, 250, 256–7, 262–3; pre-concert panic, 258–62; well reviewed, 271, 312, 348; not allowed by family to attend post-performance dinner, 271; cast as Polina in *The Queen of Spades*, 272, 313–14; does not sing Siébel in *Faust*, 539; sings indifferently in student concert, 551

Ust–Tosna 222

Valitskaya, Mariinsky Theatre singer 727
Vanscheidt, Konstantin, horn player 7, 8
Varunts, Viktor, musicologist and editor xixn
Vasilieva, singing student 89, 337–8
Vasilieva, Mme, organizer of charity concert in Kislovodsk 726–7, 730
Vasilievsky Island 141n, 160, 165, 199, 204, 223, 489–90, 687, 792
Vegman, Yekaterina Ernestovna (Katya), Conservatoire student 575, 580, 595, 605, 612, 620, 629, 631, 656
Vengerova, Isabella Afanasievna, pianist and teacher 103, 349, 600, 614, 619, 627, 663–4
Verdi, Guiseppe: *Rigoletto*, 271–2, 290, 294, 330, 340, 345, 509, 515, 543, 557–61, 563, 566–70, 599; *Falstaff*, 509–12, 515, 518–19, 522; *Aida*, 531, 543, 546–8, 550–52, 556–64, 566–7, 569–71, 585, 599, 626, 629, 665

Vernayaz, Switzerland 452–3
Versailles 443
Verzhbilovich, Alexander Valerianovich, cellist 132, 188n
Verzhbolovo 420, 462, 743
Vienna 490, 513, 523, 545, 641, 688
Vienna restaurant, St Petersburg 338, 388–9, 485, 571, 621, 642
Viardot, Pauline 407n
Vierwaldstatter See, Switzerland 457–8, 459
Vikinsky, singing student 556
Viktorov, Nikolay Viktorovich, baritone 11
Villik, violin student 22n, 33, 34
Vilnius 309, 323, 420, 536–7, 717
Vingt-et-un 481
Vinogradov, Mstislav Vsevolodovich, piano student 116, 119, 120, 126, 215
Vint, card game 112, 138, 151–2, 167, 200, 246, 262, 281, 356, 382, 395, 479, 480, 530, 533, 541, 549, 561, 575, 591, 594, 607, 610, 622, 632, 669, 737, 783, 792
Vladikavkaz 339
Vladimirsky, engineer, fiancé of Glagoleva 192–3, 201–3
Volga river 5, 97, 363, 365, 368, 370, 384, 387, 389, 405–7, 420, 509
Volhynia 364
Volkonsky, Prince Sergey Mikhailovich 571, 571n
Volkov Cemetery 375–6
Vologda 339, 740, 740n
Volzhko-Kamsky Bank 718, 734
Von Glazenup, Horse Guards officer 360
Voronezh 100, 104–5
Vvedensky 533
Vyborg 165n, 256, 391, 393, 397, 400, 506, 518, 528, 611, 691
Vyborg District (St Petersburg) 505
Vyshnegradsky, Alexander, dancer 725n
Vyshnegradsky, Ivan Alexandrovich 306, 306n, 318, 329; Andante from Symphony, 306, 329, 340

Wagner, Richard 47, 258, 311, 315, 458–9, 472, 535, 624, 734, 767; WORKS: *The Ring of the Nibelungen*, 40–41, 44, 47, 342, 458, 674; *Rheingold*, 531; *The Valkyrie*, 45, 311, 342, 353, 459; *Siegfried*, 351, 353; *The Twilight of the Gods*, 4, 188; *The Flying Dutchman*, 21; Overture to *The Flying Dutchman*, 528, 542; *Tannhäuser*, 18, 21, 279; *Lohengrin*, 21; *The Mastersingers of Nuremberg*, 280–81, 461, 476, 625–6, 628, 738, 741; *Parsifal*, 331, 570; *Siegfried Idyll*, 23
Wahrlich, Hugo, conductor 82–5, 206–7, 241, 280n, 316

Walking sticks 365, 379, 394, 498, 501, 787
Walsh, Stephen, writer and biographer xxii
Walter, Viktor Grigorievich, violinst and critic 674, 783
Walter-Kühne, Yekaterina Adolfovna, harp professor 511
Warsaw 710, 752
Warsaw Station, St Petersburg 513, 586
Weber, Carl Maria von: *Konzertstück* for piano and orchestra, 243, 308, 313, 316, 319–20; Overture to *Euryanthe*, 528, 538, 542
Weininger, Otto, pathologist and philosopher: *Geschlecht und Charakter (Sex and Character)* 466, 466n
Wertheim, Berlin department store 423
Weisberg, Yulia Lazarevna 362, 549; song-cycle *Songs from the Japanese*, 781
Wenzel, Vladimir, piano professor 281, 292, 306, 362–3, 365–6, 369, 372, 381, 537
Wihtol, Iosif Ivanovich (Jazeps Vitol), composer and teacher xxii, 61, 61n, 66, 88, 91, 149, 241; *Latvian Fantasy*, 592n
Wilson, Edward O., biologist and philosopher: *Consilience, The Unity of Knowledge* xxiii
Windsor, England 438–41, 708
Winkler, Alexander Adolfovich, pianist and teacher 19, 57, 61, 68, 77, 117, 161, 191, 530; background, 4n, 5n; SP studies privately with AW during Conservatoire closure, 188n; AW's punctuality, 5; praises SP, 15; nervousness before his students' exams, 47; allows SP to study Rimsky-Korsakov Concerto for end-of-year exam, 50; promoted to full professorship, 61; praise for Deshevov, 63; and Golubovskaya, 641; asks to see SP's compositions, 66–7; SP's growing determination to change from Winkler to Yesipova, 47, 71–2; Winkler's fair-minded attitude, 100–103; AW reveals to SP his criticism of Yovanovich's performance at Evenings of Contemporay Music, 86; SP writes Etudes Op. 2 and dedicates to AW, 117–18; SP's respect for Winkler, 119; presents copy of 2nd Sonata, 381; AW supervises SP's transposition and sight-reading exam, 609–10; congratulates SP on winning Rubinstein Prize, 663; votes for SP, 664; Mme Winkler, 655
Winter's store, St Petersburg 274, 276
Winter War of 1939 xxvii
Wirballen, *see* Verzhbolovo
Wittgenstein, Ludwig 466n
World of Art, *see Mir Isskustva*
World War I 711–2, 714–8; declaration of, 718; 719, 723, 729–31, 733, 736, 738, 742, 748, 752, 762, 766, 791; patriotic demonstrations, 714–15, 717, 719–20, 746; war despatches, 721–2, 728–9, 782–3

Yablonskaya, Mme V. O. 246, 262, 273, 562
Yablonskaya, Wanda 133, 138, 190, 420
Yablonsky family 138, 278, 373
Yakhontov, brother-in-law of Boris Bashkirov 674, 682
Yalta, Crimea 106, 303, 305, 339, 471–2, 478, 481–2
Yanovsky, David, chess master 5, 640, 641–2, 644, 646, 649, 653–4, 675
Yaroslavl 339
Yasin (Yasensky), composition student 591; *Monastère mystérieuse*, 591; *Magdal*, 668, 676
Yastrebov, B. N., friend of Konshins 311, 370
Yatsenko, N. R. xxiin
Yatsyna, piano student 362–3, 365, 369, 372
Yavorsky, Boleslav Leopoldovich, music critic and writer 324, 588, 601
Yekaterina Mikhailovna, Class Inspector 643
Yekaterina Nikiforovna, housekeeper to the Meshchersky family 482
Yekaterinhof, St Petersburg 223, 351, 408
Yekaterinodar 24, 165, 333–5, 339
Yekaterinoslav 480, 383
Yelagin Island 93n, 365, 370, 406–7, 519, 533
Yelena Georgievna, Princess of Sachsen-Altenberg, the Conservatoire's Patron 264, 297
Yelizavetgrad 165
Yellow Book 244, 247, 249, 278, 507, 717
Yemilyanovka 351, 357
Yershov, Ivan Vasilievich, tenor 132, 157, 281n, 318, 350, 524, 613, 733–4
Yershova, Maria Ivanovna (Marusya) 157, 561, 613
Yesipova, Anna Nikolayevna 77, 117–18, 123–4, 131, 133, 137, 183, 195, 201, 220, 250, 254, 288n, 292, 302n, 306, 314, 328, 334, 338, 344–5, 348–9, 360, 363, 366, 408n, 493, 507, 514, 524, 532, 548, 574n, 581, 583, 605, 618–9, 640, 659; history and career: 4n; SP's desire to join class, 47; hears SP perform, 50, 71; AY performs in London, 71n; Zakharov instrumental in securing AY's agreement, 100, 169; move from Winkler's class agreed, 100–103; SP joins class, 112–15; SP's pleasure at higher standards and new classmates, 119–21, 124; AY asks to hear SP's compositions, 128–9, 132–3; describes 1st Piano Sonata as interesting and supplies pedal markings, 129; performs in Jubilee Concert, 132, 134; introduces son Ilyin, 132; SP's pattern of work for AY, 143; hears *The White Swan*, 146; invites SP socially, 151–2, 224, 305, 595; ill health, 154, 550–51, 558,

564, 601, 613, 690; recovery enough to go skating, 600; class exam performances, 160–61, 190, 343, 377–8, 658; SP visits with Zakharov in Gungerburg, 167, 170; and Tsarskoye Selo, 199–200; AY criticizes SP's performance of 'Waldstein' Sonata, 184; recommends more Beethoven to acquire serenity, 217; praises SP's account of Tchaikovsky Concerto, 244; gives lesson on Chopin 2nd Sonata, 308; criticizes Chopin Polonaises, 354; approves approach to Bach fugue, 535; does not comment on *Tannhäuser* performance, 613; does not attend rehearsal for graduation recital, 616; SP plays entire programme to AY at home, 617; Golubovskaya joins class, 185; AY resigns with other professors over student strikes, 188n; dismisses SP's 1st Piano Sonata as unmusical, 194, 367; dismisses Glazunov 2nd Sonata, 194; resistant to SP's proposal of Liszt Sonata for exam recital programme, 212–13; unwilling to give permission for SP to appear at Evenings of Contemporary Music, 213–14, 227; supportive of SP's 1913 exam recital performance, 215–16; confirms high mark, 216; compliments M G. Prokofieva on SP's progress, 216; SP enjoys good standing, 255; loses confidence in AY's presence, 260; SP concludes AY's teaching doing more harm than good, 315; AY angered by SP's criticism of Zakharov's choice of Rachmaninov Concerto, 228; SP's praise of AY regarded as significant, 230; SP joins forces with Zakharov to buy name-day present, 240; daughter hears SP conduct, 286; AY unimpressed by SP's developing relationship with Koussevitzky, 329; refers to SP as 'puppy', 332; SP fears AY will not allow his own works to be included in graduation recital programme, 367; recital programme agreed, 367–8; SP sees AY off at station, 379; SP makes present of fruit, 505; concerned to have done no practising for 6 months, 505; malicious report of 2nd Piano Concerto performance at Pavlovsk defended by Zakharov, 510, 513; SP fears AY has excluded him from her class for performing at Pavlovsk without permission, 513; choice of concerto for graduation performance left open, 513; AY resists inclusion of complete Schumann sonata in graduation recital programme, 527, 530; approves contemporary work for this programme, 535; recital tour with Auer, 527; returns, 530; gives recital in Petersburg with Auer, 547; Lyapunov awards high mark because SP does not play like AY

student, 621; SP visits AY after Rubinstein Prize victory, 663; requests AY's support for inclusion of 1st Piano Concerto in Graduation Concert, 666; attends Requiem Masses for AY, 735; SP's teaching method 'like Yesipova squared', 747

Yessentuki 105–8, 234, 347, 383, 411, 445, 467, 602, 644, 723, 726–8, 730–31

Yevdokia Silvestrovna, friend of Vera Meshcherskaya 473, 476, 495

Yevpatoria 113

Yovanovich, Mladlen, pianist 85–6, 279

Ysaÿe, Eugène, violinist and composer 29

Yukki, spa resort xxvii, 294, 311–12, 315, 505–8, 712, 793

Yurasovsky, Alexander Ivanovich, composer and conductor 319, 319n, 324–7, 366, 536, 555, 587–9, 602, 604, 710, 713, 740, 748–9; WORKS: *In The Moonlight*, 324; *Phantom*, 324; Piano Concerto, 325; Piano Trio, 346

Yurev, Finland 29

Yusupov Garden, St Petersburg 252, 254, 260, 273, 276, 285, 288, 562, 567, 571–4, 579, 597

Yuzhin, David, tenor 281n

Yverdon, Switzerland 454

Zagorodny Chapel, St Petersburg 401, 489

Zagorodny Prospect, St Petersburg 618, 786

Zaitsev, Kirill 407, 473, 477, 483, 487, 495–7, 500–501, 504–5, 508, 517, 523–8, 606, 685–6, 724, 729, 734, 744, 779–80; mother, 496–7, 523

Zakharov, Boris Stepanovich 4, 43, 53, 81, 94, 102, 112, 115–16, 119, 130, 134, 151, 181, 186, 189, 191, 201, 207, 216, 244, 260–62, 270, 279, 285, 287, 290, 305, 310–11, 332, 338, 351–2, 367, 393, 404, 409–11, 431, 433, 457, 471, 497, 499–501, 504, 506–7, 528, 568, 638, 659, 666, 690–91, 714, 728, 748–9, 777, 780, 788, 792; shows SP song composed, 6; invites to play chess, 14, 18; exchanges visits, 38; plays 4-hand version of Scriabin *Divine Poem*, 42; misunderstanding over *Kitezh* Easter card, 48; undertakes to approach Yesipova, 71, 100–101; attends Court Orchestra play-through of SP's Symphony, 82–3, 85; listens to SP's repertoire for Yesipova, 113–14, 122, 129, 137; plays in Yesipova's class 118; with SP visits Yesipova in Gungerburg, 167; and Tsarskoye Selo, 199–200, 212; 181; plays 'Gavotte' in Yesipova's class, 194; cites SP as authority on merits of Yesipova as teacher, 230; invites SP to Terioki, 165, 167, 168–76, 177–8, 224–5, 228–9; nature and strength of friendship with SP, 182–3, 223–6; emphasis on self-discipline, 200; relationship begins to cool over BZ's indifference to SP's problems with Yesipova, 227–8; SP taxes with callousness, 229–30; sends caustic letter, 230; serious rift develops, 237–40; SP critical of BZ's playing of Glazunov Concerto at rehearsal, 245, 259; but concedes good performance at concert, 261; successfully opposes choice of BZ as soloist, 248; returns BZ's handkerchief with spiteful comment, 250; flaunts close friendship with Max Schmidthof, 250–51, 291; has interval drink with BZ, 265; has frank talk about estrangement, 267–9; casts doubt on dedication of 'Gavotte' to BZ, 315; 320; BZ much disliked by Max, 369; SP fears Max might have tried to murder BZ, 386; BZ withdraws from recital, 328; graduation recital, 343; chamber music performance, 360; concerto performance, 377–8; SP considers decision not to award BZ prize correct, 405; with SP's assistance gives successful performance of Rachmaninov's 1st Piano Concerto, 228; Derzhanovsky rejects BZ for Moscow recital, 470; BZ's pianism praised by Godowsky, 544–5; plays to Austrian Archduchess, 584; SP wishes to re-establish friendship with BZ, 387–9, 405–6; contact renewed in Terioki, 414, 465; BZ's strange attitude to SP, 415–16; BZ on Grand Dukes' guest list, 441, 465, 469; SP writes from France and receives quick reply, 446; BZ attends premiere of SP's 2nd Piano Concerto, 487, 489; friendly but cautious relations restored, 490, 491, 493–4; BZ defends 2nd Piano Concerto to Yesipova, 510, 513; SP writes *Musical Letter to Zakharov*, 529; acknowledged, 532, 559; *Letter* admired by Hansen sisters, 691; SP dreams of BZ before graduation performance and regards as bad omen, 656; BZ telephones SP unexpectedly on return from Vienna, 688; 690–91; SP revisits Terioki and plays 2nd Sonata, 712; previous close relations restored, 712, 797; SP accompanies BZ in Rachmaninov 2nd Piano Concerto and notes great improvement in playing, 713; BZ considered for teaching position at Conservatoire, 733; does not obtain, 738; approves SP's choice of prize piano, 735; approves 'Rigaudon' but not 'March', 736; and scenes from *Ala and Lolli*, 766; plays bridge, 746, 750, 757–8; performs Bach–Busoni *Chaconne* and Nikolayev Violin Sonata with Cecilia Hansen, 755; engaged for I.R.M.S. concert, 760; accompanies SP to meet Andrey Rimsky-Korsakov, 773; and attends SP's performance at Contemporary Concerts, 785–6; plays programme for Contemporary Concerts to SP, 796–7; courts and eventually marries Cecilia Hansen, 157n, 767, 788, 792

Zakharov family 170–76, 177–8, 230, 239, 261, 377, 389, 393, 413, 465, 491, 493–4, 637–8, 712, 719

Zakharov, Georges Stepanovich 224, 350–51, 393, 414–15, 494, 691

Zakharov, Nikolay Stepanovich 172

Zakharov, Stepan Stepanovich 224–5,

Zakharov, Vasily Stepanovich (Vasya) 190, 224–6, 228, 240, 369, 410, 571, 714, 792, 796

Zakharova, Luiza Alexeyevna 491, 494, 544–5, 571, 579

Zakharova, Vera Stepanovna 224, 738

Zakharova, Zinaida Eduardovna 175–8, 224–5

Zakharchenko, chance travelling companion 422

Zeberg, piano student 201

Zeiliger, Alexander Vladimirovich, pianist 161, 201, 216, 305, 328, 332, 343, 352, 360, 378–9, 404–5, 425

Zelenogorsk, *see* Terioki

Zelikman, A.V., piano student, SP's rival for the Rubinstein Prize 251, 255, 257, 259, 261, 595, 597, 627–8, 636, 644, 648, 656, 659–63, 666, 676–7

Zheleznaya Gora 722

Zheleznovodsk 106

Zherebtsova-Andreyeva, Anna Grigorievna, singer 332, 373–4, 390, 428, 434, 436, 497, 523, 525, 550, 562, 569, 570, 594, 683, 744, 752, 755; SP attends New Year party, 279; AZ-A's background, 279n; recitals always interesting because of intelligence and taste, 288–9, 355; conversation about going to America 433; AZ-A accidentally reveals identity of Zaitsev, 487; appointed to full professorship at Conservatoire, 508; likes SP's song 'There Are Other Planets', 517; sings this song in recital, 623; and 'The Boat Cast Off', 526; SP plans to write set of 6 songs for AZ-A, 545; AZ-A sings Lyadov songs at his Jubilee Concert, 552; and Debussy songs at reception for Debussy, 553; engagements in London, 572, 666; asks SP to listen to her class exam and report, 685–6; SP and AZ-A quarrel in London, 709; conflicts resolved, 734; AZ-A likes *The Ugly Duckling* and plans to sing it 'in every city in the world', 749; suggested for revised Contemporary Concerts in January 1915, 773; SP does not endorse AZ-A's proposal for a joint recital in Small Hall, 761; AZ-A does not sing in private play-through of *Ugly Duckling* because of worries about her son being drafted to front, 779

Zhitkova, Tatyana Grigorievna (Aunt Tanya) 4, 9, 11, 20–21, 29, 33–4, 50, 54, 55, 87, 112, 177, 181, 185, 190, 502

Zhukovsky, Vasily Andreyevich, poet 58n; 'The Sea', 56, 56n; 'Svetlana', 65n

Ziloti, Alexander Ilyich, pianist and conductor 12, 18, 79, 85, 94, 123, 162, 207, 226n, 318, 404, 494, 498, 529, 544, 556, 616, 644, 648, 665, 667, 684, 688–90, 704, 739, 753

Zimbalist, Efrem Alexandrovich, violinist 33n

Zimbalist, Solomon Venyaminovich, cellist 33, 34

Zimmermann, August and Julius, music publishers 212, 347, 685, 687

Zinoviev family 354, 540

Zinoviev, A. D. 534n

Zmeika 722

Znosko-Borovsky, Yevgeny Alexandrovich 155–6, 155n, 176, 583–4, 654, 672–3, 675

Zuckertort, Johann Hermann, chess master 37

Zurich 459–61

Zurich, Lake 459

Zurmüllen, piano professor 331, 395

Zvyagintseva, Yelena (Lyolya), Mme Derzahnovskaya's half-sister 589–90, 603, 637, 733

1 The author's mother, Maria Grigorievna Prokofieva, née Zhitkova
2 The author's father, Sergey Alexeyevich Prokofiev
3 Alexander Glazunov and Anna Yesipova at the Glazunov dacha in Ozerki
4 Sergey Prokofiev in 1910, photograph by Vasily Morolyov

5 Lyadov's Theory of Composition class at the St. Petersburg Conservatoire, 1905. Prokofiev is sitting at the extreme right, Lyadov is at the keyboard. Also pictured are (l – r) standing: Kobylyansky, Asafyev, Grossman, Kankarovich; sitting: Fiveysky, Shpis
6 Rimsky-Korsakov and Glazunov in Rimsky's room at the Conservatoire.

7 The 1907 general studies class at the Conservatoire. Front row l – r: Bessonova, Shulzinger, Nodelman, Ospovat, Anisimova, Alpers. Second row l – r: Glagoleva, Popova, Petrovich (history teacher), Balayev (Russian literature teacher), Petrov (priest, ecclesiastical law teacher), Glazunov, Abramycheva, Abramychev (assistant head of academic studies), Fliege, Kadovskaya, Shvarts, Samaryatinova. Third row l – r: M. Piastro, Gvirtsman, Vanscheidt, Schmidt, Villik, Prokofiev, Dobrzhenets

8 The Great Hall of the St. Petersburg Conservatoire during a performance
9 The Small Hall of the St. Petersburg Conservatoire

10 The St. Petersburg Conservatoire at the beginning of the 20th century
11 Nevsky Prospect, St. Petersburg, *c.* 1910
12 Terioki Railway Station before 1917, when it was demolished and replaced

Saharoffin komea pitsikoristeinen huvila.

13 Anna Yesipova, 1903 portrait by an unknown artist
14 Portrait of the author in 1913. The inscription reads: *I hereby certify: 1) this is definitely my physiognomy; 2) it was definitely presented to Lidusya; 3) Lidurochka is definitely not a durochka* but a very nice girlochka. Sergusya in 1913.* *silly little girl
15 The Zakharov dacha in Terioki

16 Sergey Diaghilev

17 Boris Bashkirov (the poet Boris Verin)

18 Nikolay Tcherepnin

19 Nikolay Myaskovsky

20 The author at the Conservatoire Ball, January 1908

21 The author's son, Sviatoslav Prokofiev

22 With Boris Zakharov, Lidia and Zoya Karneyeva, after the first performance of the Second Piano Concerto, Terioki, August 1913

23 Playing a piano reduction of Wagner's *Die Walküre* to Vasily Morolyov at Nikopol, 1910

24 With Boris Zakharov at Terioki, 1913
25 Vasily Morolyov's photo of the author arriving at the Morolyov house in Nikopol, 1913, with Max Schmidthof sitting on Prokofiev's left
26 Contestants (in italics) and organisers of the 1914 St. Petersburg International Chess Tournament. Seated (l – r): *Gunsberg*, *Blackburne*, *Lasker*, *Tarrasch*, *A. Burn*, R. Gebhardt, *Rubinstein*, *Bernstein*, *Capablanca*, *Yanovsky*. Standing (l – r): S. Weinstein, *Marshall*, *Alekhine*, N. Maximov, *Nimzowitsch*, B. Malyutin, P. Saburov, E. Talvik, J. Sosnitsky, N. Znosko-Borovsky, V. Rubinov, D. Korolyov, N. Lokhvitsky, Ye. Znosko-Borovsky